THE OXFORD HANDBOOK OF

AFRICA AND ECONOMICS

VOLUME 2
POLICIES AND PRACTICES

THE OXFORD HANDBOOK OF

AFRICA AND ECONOMICS

VOLUME 2
POLICIES AND PRACTICES

Edited by
CÉLESTIN MONGA
and
JUSTIN YIFU LIN

OXFORD
UNIVERSITY PRESS

OXFORD

UNIVERSITY PRESS

Great Clarendon Street, Oxford, OX2 6DP,
United Kingdom

Oxford University Press is a department of the University of Oxford.
It furthers the University's objective of excellence in research, scholarship,
and education by publishing worldwide. Oxford is a registered trade mark of
Oxford University Press in the UK and in certain other countries

Published in the United States of America by Oxford University Press
198 Madison Avenue, New York, NY 10016, United States of America

British Library Cataloguing in Publication Data

Data available

Library of Congress Control Number: 2015936455

ISBN 978-0-19-968710-7

Acknowledgments

WHEN asked by a journalist why he writes books and even manages to get other things done along the way, Wole Soyinka, Africa's first Nobel Prize in literature simply replied: "the masochist in me, I suppose." The editors of this two-volume *Oxford Handbook of Africa and Economics* have not done nearly as much writing as Soyinka. Still, they can relate to his rationale for spending many long hours and sleepless nights among papers and books, trying to bring a complex but exciting task such as this one to fruition.

No book of any scope gets done without deep involvement of a very large number of people, most of whom remain anonymous. By definition, a handbook of (nearly) encyclopedic ambitions and size such as this one necessarily required a lot of help from our friends. While we cannot recognize all of those who gave much-needed support, we wish to acknowledge the advice, encouragements, and guidance of a number of very special people and institutions.

The idea for this book arose out of a couple of firm convictions. The first was that despite being one of the most intellectually challenging regions in the world it was still under-researched—or some of the cutting-edge work done about Africa was not sufficiently featured in the most prestigious reference books at major university presses. The second was that, despite all the media coverage of the continent (perhaps because of it), Africa's contribution to economic knowledge had not been told. What was missing and might be of enduring value, we thought, was a kaleidoscopic presentation of some of the various ways in which economic science has tried to explain the African condition, and how the continent's peculiarities had shaped the field of economics.

Strangely, our friends Alexie Tcheuyap, Cilas Kemedjio, and Ambroise Kom, who are professors of comparative literature and philosophy—not economics—were the first to enthusiastically embrace the idea of a handbook, and to suggest the kind of intellectual strategy that could underline it and make it unique. We are grateful to their wonderful intuition and pertinent advice, which gave us the energy and confidence to develop the initial ideas into a proposal.

Hippolyte Fofack, Jean-Claude Tchatchouang, Eugène Ebodé, Hervé Assah, Rémi Kini, and Geremie Sawadogo were cheerleaders from day one, and constantly reminded us why it was intellectually and symbolically important that the first handbook on Africa and economics ever produced by Oxford University Press in its 600 years of history be comprehensive and diverse, and reflect perspectives that are not always given the visibility they deserve.

Paul Collier's searching criticisms of the initial proposal forced us to clarify our argument and approach. His generous advice and marginalia at each step of the process provided a great sense of direction that helped us avoid many pitfalls.

Managing top-notch researchers to deliver on a complex project in a very short period of time is a bit like herding cats. Fortunately, we had a blueprint on how to proceed with minimum risks of slippage on the timetable and budget. David Malone, with whom we worked on a previous Oxford University Press project, offered strategic and tactical advice from the very beginning of the process. We were fortunate to tap into his wisdom and expertise.

Elizabeth Asiedu and Mustapha Nabli could easily have been co-editors of this *Handbook*. Their extraordinary generosity and commitment make it difficult to express adequately the critical role these friends have played in the development and completion of this project. With her well-known toughness and brilliance, Asiedu single-handedly brought to the team many high-flying researchers who rarely have time for such intellectual endeavors. Among other things, she convinced several of her colleagues from the Association for the Advancement of African Women Economists (AAAWE) to lend support to the *Handbook*, bringing unique perspectives to economic topics where their voices are not often heard.

Despite a schedule as busy as that of heads of state, Nabli provided detailed and sharp comments on various drafts of the main chapters of the *Handbook* and generously opened his rich Rolodex to help us recruit contributors. Thanks to his stellar reputation across the entire Arab world, we were able to attract many of the top researchers in his network of friends, former colleagues, and students to this task. One of them is Hakim Ben Hammouda, who co-wrote two chapters with Nabli while working as Finance Minister in the transition government of Tunisia at the most difficult period of his country's history. We thank him for that.

Fabien Eboussi Boulaga's and Valentin-Yves Mudimbe's amazing analytical abilities, and their sustaining goodwill and humor, made the preparation of this *Handbook* an exciting task carried out with some of the most fertile minds in the world. Prior to their intellectual work in the realm of philosophy, Africa has suffered from the lack of sophisticated scholarly attention. This *Handbook*, in many ways, was produced out of our profound regard for their pioneering work on the epistemology and ontology of the continent.

Joseph Stiglitz and Roger Myerson not only contributed chapters to the *Handbook* but provided excellent advice and suggestions on its main themes. Stiglitz, whose theoretical work on a wide range of issues addressed in this *Handbook*, deserves a special expression of gratitude for his friendship and mentorship. Olivier Blanchard, Jeffrey Sachs, Richard Joseph, Xiaobo Zhang, and Akbar Noman, colleagues and kindred spirits with whom we have interacted about various economic topics, also helped shape this book by recommending potential contributors and convincing them to be part of the journey.

A team of 137 contributors from dozens of countries in all continents worked hard to complete this two-volume *Handbook* in record time. Many of them command great attention because of their reputation, and normally would only be contacted through highly paid agents. Yet, they all agreed to work on this project without requesting honorarium or fees, with the humility which is the other side of true greatness. Our debt to all the colleagues and friends who accompanied us on this project is impossible to repay, or even to acknowledge appropriately.

One of the many advantages of being an economist in the World Bank research department was the bountiful advice that one's colleagues provide, even unwittingly. In addition to Kaushik Basu's early and strong endorsement of the *Handbook* project (and his stunning humility to contribute a chapter himself, with Alaka Basu), we benefitted from thoughtful discussions of various topics studied in this *Handbook* with Shanta Devarajan, Marcelo Giugale, Asli Demirgüç-Kunt, Luis Serven, Aart Kraay, and Bertrand Badre.

The positive response received from Jim Yong Kim, the World Bank Group President, eliminated the bureaucratic impulses, processes, and red tape that almost always surround such a high-visibility project. A true intellectual himself, Kim shielded the *Handbook* project from the politically correct: in just one cryptic email message to his senior staff, he saluted the initiative for the *Handbook* and also gave all the intellectual freedom and latitude to explore issues and policies without ever wondering whether the contributors to the project shared "official" World Bank views on any topic under study.

As President of the African Development Bank, Donald Kaberuka was not simply a gorgeous mind with genuine commitment to the economic development of the African continent and an uncanny ability to seize new ideas, he was the first to spontaneously offer intellectual and financial support for the preparation of this *Handbook*. It did not occur to him that he might have been subsidizing a "World Bank" initiative, He simply asked what kind of help was needed and made it available, never expecting anything in return except a compelling volume. A true gentleman. We hope he will not be disappointed with the final outcome.

Finn Tarp, Director of UNU-WIDER, whose intellectual engagement with Africa dates back decades, had a similar attitude, providing funding for the project and contributing himself (with Tony Addison and Saurabh Singhal) a seminal piece on the economics of development aid. Mthuli Ncube and Ernest Aryeetey, two of the most prominent and busiest African economists, also strongly supported this project and always found the time to meet the deadlines—even when fighting jet lag and multiple other requests. We are grateful for their help.

Jean-Claude Bastos de Morais, an entrepreneur and investor who promised his Angolan grandmother to make a difference for the African continent, has been an unusual philanthropist in supporting young African economists and cutting-edge research and innovation. This project benefited from his many ideas and help.

Jiayi Zou and Yingming Yang of the ministry of Finance in China, together with the leadership and the students of the National School of Development at Peking University, offered substantial financial and logistical help to organize an authors' workshop in Beijing for the discussion of draft chapters. Xiaobo Zhang organized an unforgettable field visit that allowed many participants to have a first-hand look at concrete examples of entrepreneurship and industrialization in a dynamically growing economy. Xi Chen, Irene Jing Lu, Hongchun Zhao, and Premi Rathan Raj devoted time and energy to coordinate all events at every single phase of the project. We thank them for their generosity and abnegation.

Madeleine Velguth and Gertrud G. Champe, who are not economists, heroically translated a few chapters, overcoming the obstacles of technical jargon to produce what we hope are polished and highly readable texts. Wei Guo was a creative and energetic research assistant, always coming up with several possible solutions to each problem. Togolese artist Akué Adoboé graciously offered pictures of his paintings for the covers of the two volumes. We are deeply appreciative of such help.

The team at Oxford University Press, especially Adam Swallow, Michael Dela Cruz, Aimee Wright, Sarah Kain, and Sophie Song, patiently and effectively guided us through the process. Long after our own work was done, they were (and are) still spending time and energy to the *Handbook* project.

Last but not least, our families tolerated our often long absences—including when we were physically at home but locked in libraries. We would like to thank Chen Yunying, Kephren and Maélys, for being our inspiration.

CONTENTS

PART II MICROECONOMIC AND SECTORAL ISSUES

PART III INSTITUTIONAL/SOCIAL ECONOMICS

PART IV OLD AND NEW DEVELOPMENT PLAYERS

PART V LOOKING FORWARD

LIST OF FIGURES

List of Tables

LIST OF CONTRIBUTORS

Tony Addison is Chief Economist/Deputy Director of the United Nations University's World Institute for Development Economics Research (UNU-WIDER) in Helsinki, Finland. Professor of Development, University of Manchester; Executive Director of the Brooks World Poverty Institute (BWPI) University of Manchester (from 2006 to 2009); Associate Director of the Chronic Poverty Research Centre (CPRC). Books include *From Conflict to Recovery in Africa* (Oxford University Press), *Making Peace Work: The Challenges of Economic and Social Reconstruction* (Palgrave Macmillan), and *Poverty Dynamics: A Cross-Disciplinary Perspective* (Oxford University Press). He also published articles in the following journals: *Journal of Development Economics, World Development, Journal of International Development, and Journal of Development Studies.*

Gloria Afful-Mensah holds an MPhil degree in Economics from University of Ghana and is currently a PhD student at Milan University. She worked as a Research Associate at the Department of Economics, University of Ghana. Her areas of interest includes Development Finance and Private Sector Development.

Jenny C. Aker is Assistant Professor of Development Economics at the Fletcher School Department at Tufts University. She is also a Non-Resident Fellow at the Center for Global Development, a member of the Advisory Board for CDA and the Boston Network for International Development (BNID). Jenny completed her PhD in agricultural economics at the University of California, Berkeley, and works on economic development in Africa, with a primary focus on the impact of information (and information technology) on development outcomes, particularly in the areas of agricultural markets, education, financial inclusion, and social protection programs.

Emmanuel Akyeampong is Professor of History and of African and African American Studies at Harvard University. He is a former editor of the *Journal of African History* and of *African Diaspora* and the author or editor of several books including *Drink, Power and Cultural Change: A Social History of Alcohol in Ghana* (1996); *Between the Sea and the Lagoon: An Eco-Social History of the Anlo of Southeastern Ghana* (2001); *Themes in West Africa's History* (2006); and *Dictionary of African Biography* (six volumes) (2013).

John C. Anyanwu is Lead Research Economist in the Development Research Department of the African Development Bank. Prior to joining the AfDB, he was full Professor of Economics, Department of Economics & Statistics, University of Benin, Nigeria, and Economic Adviser to Resident Representative, WHO, Lagos, Nigeria. John holds a PhD and MSc in Economics from the University of Ibadan and a master's degree in Entrepreneurship and Economic Development from the University of Houston, Victoria. He is the editor of the *African Development Review*, a quarterly journal of the AfDB. John has authored over 100 journal articles, and a number of books and book chapters.

Ernest Aryeetey is the Vice Chancellor of University of Ghana and a Professor of Economics. He was previously the Director of the Africa Growth Initiative at Brookings Institution, Washington, DC, and also the Director of Institute of Statistical, Social and Economic Research at the University of Ghana. His research work has focused largely on African institutions, both formal and informal, and their role in economic development. He is currently Board Chair of the United Nations University World Institute for Development Economics Research.

Ragui Assaad is Professor of Planning and Public Affairs at the University of Minnesota's Humphrey School of Public Affairs and director of graduate studies for its Master of Development Practice program. He is a Research Fellow of the Economic Research Forum in Cairo, Egypt, and serves as its thematic director for Labor and Human Resource Development. His current research focuses on labor markets in the Arab world, with a focus on youth and gender issues as they relate to education, transition from school-to-work, employment and unemployment, informality, responses to economic shocks, migration, and family formation.

Ousmane Badiane is Africa Director for the International Food Policy Research Institute (IFPRI). He oversees IFPRI's regional offices for West and Central Africa in Senegal and Eastern and Southern Africa in Ethiopia. Dr. Badiane coordinates IFPRI's food policy research, capacity strengthening activities, policy communications, and partnerships across Africa. Since 2004, he has been instrumental in leading IFPRI's research and technical support to guide the implementation of the Comprehensive Africa Agriculture Development Programme (CAADP). Dr. Badiane is a Fellow of the African Association of Agricultural Economics and recipient of an honorary doctoral degree from the University of KwaZulu, Natal, South Africa.

Mina Baliamoune-Lutz is Professor of Economics at the Coggin College of Business and Distinguished Professor (2012) at the University of North Florida, and Research Fellow at the Economic Research Forum (ERF). She has recently served as President of the African Finance and Economics Association (AFEA), and was a research fellow at the International Center for Economic Research (ICER) in Turin, Italy (2005–2012). Professor Baliamoune-Lutz's research focuses primarily on the effects of formal and informal institutions, trade, financial flows, and financial reforms on economic transformation and human well-being in Arab and African countries. She co-edited the book *Women in African Development—The Challenge of Globalization and Liberalization in the 21st Century* (Africa World Press, 2005), and has published numerous journal articles and book chapters. Her empirical work on the effects of policy and institutional reforms in Africa has received significant recognition. She has been a regular contributor to research themes debated at the United Nations World Institute for Development Economics in Helsinki (UNU-WIDER), and has contributed to the United Nations Commission for Africa/African Development Bank/UNDP Annual Economic Conference on Africa, and the European Report on Development. Professor Baliamoune-Lutz holds a PhD in Economics from Northeastern University.

Alaka M. Basu is on leave from her position as professor in the Department of Developmental Sociology. For six years she was also the Director of the South Asia Program at Cornell University. She has taught at Jawaharlal Nehru University (JNU) in Delhi and at the Harvard

School of Public Health. She is a social demographer with strong interests in public health. Alaka Basu has published widely in the areas of reproductive health and family planning, gender and development, child health and mortality, and the context and politics of population policy. She served on the governing boards of the Population Association of America (PAA), the International Union for the Scientific Study of Population (IUSSP) and the Population Council in New York. She was also the chair of the IUSSP Scientific Committee on Anthropological Demography and a member of the Committees on Reproductive Health and on Population Projections of the National Research Council at the US National Academy of Sciences. She is currently on the Editorial Boards of *Population and Development Review* and *Asian Population Studies*.

Kaushik Basu is Senior Vice President and Chief Economist of the World Bank and C. Marks Professor at Cornell University. He was previously Chief Economic Adviser to the Indian Government. He did his undergraduate studies at St. Stephen's College, Delhi, and PhD at the London School of Economics. Professor Basu has published in development economics, industrial organization, and game theory. He is the author of *Beyond the Invisible Hand* (Princeton University Press) and *Analytical Development Economics* (MIT Press). Professor Basu has received honorary doctorates from Fordham University, New York, and the Indian Institute of Technology, Bombay. In 2008 he was conferred one of India's highest civilian awards, the Padma Bhushan by the President of India.

Andrew Berg is Assistant Director and chief of the Development Macroeconomics Division in the IMF's Research Department. Previously, he was in the Fund's African Department and mission chief to Malawi. He has also worked at the US Treasury and as an associate of Jeffrey Sachs. He has a PhD in Economics from MIT and an undergraduate degree from Harvard. He has published articles on sustained growth accelerations, the macroeconomics of aid, and prediction of currency crises. His current research agenda includes inequality and growth, debt sustainability, the management of natural resource wealth, and monetary policy in low-income countries.

Jean-Claude Berthélemy is Professor and Dean of the School of Economics at Paris 1 Pantheon Sorbonne University. He is also a corresponding member of the French Academy of Social Science (Académie des sciences morales et politiques). He has been earlier in his carrier Director of research division at the OECD Development Centre, Director of the CEPII (Centre d'études prospectives et d'informations internationales), and Vice President of EUDN (European Development research Network). He has published extensively on development economics and has been a consultant for various international organizations, including the African Development Bank, World Bank, UNDP, UNIDO, UN-WIDER, European Commission.

Sophie Bessis is Franco-Tunisian. She graduated in history (agrégée d'histoire) from Paris-Sorbonne University. She has worked for years in the fields of economic policies of development, north–south relationships, the condition of women in the sub-Saharan Africa and the Arabic world. Currently, she is associate researcher at IRIS (Institut des relations internationales et stratégiques, Paris). She has published many books. The latest ones being *Western Supremacy, The Triumph of an Idea?* (Zed Books,2002); *Les Arabes, les femmes, la liberté* (Albin Michel, 2007); *La Double Impasse, l'universel à l'épreuve des fondamentalismes religieux et marchand* (La Découverte, 2014).

Haroon Bhorat is Professor of Economics and Director of the Development Policy Research Unit at the University of Cape Town, South Africa. He has co-authored two books and published over 150 academic journal articles, book chapters, and working papers, covering labor economics, poverty, and income distribution. He is a Non-resident Senior Fellow at the Brookings Institution and a Research Fellow at the Institute for the Study of Labour. Professor Bhorat holds a highly prestigious National Research Chair, is a Director on the Western Cape Tourism, Trade and Investment Promotion Agency Board, and has served as economic advisor to former Ministers of Finance.

Joshua E. Blumenstock is Assistant Professor at the Information School and an Adjunct Assistant Professor of Computer Science and Engineering at the University of Washington. His research develops methods and theory for the analysis of large-scale behavioral datasets, with a focus on how such data can be used to understand processes of human and economic development in poor and marginalized regions of the world. Joshua has a PhD in Information Management and an MA in Economics from the University of California, Berkeley, and Bachelor's degrees in Computer Science and Physics from Wesleyan University.

Julia Cagé received her Economics PhD from Harvard University in 2014. She joined Sciences Po, Paris, as an Assistant Professor in Economics in July 2014. She is a former student of the Ecole Normale Supérieure (Paris) and received her MA in Economics from the Paris School of Economics in 2008. She specializes in Political Economy, Economic History, and International Economics. She is particularly interested in the media, especially the question of how media competition affects the provision of information and political attitudes. She is also working on international trade, studying the impact of trade liberalization on developing countries.

Stephen O'Connell is Chief Economist of USAID and Gil and Frank Mustin Professor of Economics at Swarthmore College. His research focuses on macroeconomic policy in sub-Saharan Africa, and most recently on monetary policy and monetary union in East Africa. He spent 2013 as a Visiting Scholar at the IMF, where he worked on monetary policy frameworks in low-income economies. He is a former member of the Programme Committee of the African Economic Research Consortium, and co-edited the AERC's two-volume *Political Economic of Economic Growth in Africa, 1960–2000*.

Xavier Debrun is Deputy Division Chief in the IMF Fiscal Affairs Department. After obtaining a PhD in International Economics from the Graduate Institute of International Studies in Geneva, he joined the IMF in 2000, working mainly in the Fiscal Affairs and Research Departments. In 2006–2007, he was a Visiting Fellow at Bruegel—Brussels' leading think tank on European economic issues—and a Visiting Associate Professor at the Graduate Institute in Geneva. His research interests include monetary integration, political economics and macro-fiscal issues. He published widely on these issues in professional journals, IMF series, and books.

Asli Demirgüç-Kunt is the Director of Research in the World Bank. After joining the Bank in 1989 as a Young Economist, she has held different positions, including Director of Development Policy, Chief Economist of Financial and Private Sector Development Network, and Senior Research Manager, doing research and advising on financial sector and private sector development issues. She is the lead author of World Bank Policy Research Report 2007, Finance for All? Policies and Pitfalls in Expanding Access. She has also created the World Bank's Global Financial Development Report and directed the issues on Rethinking the Role of the State in Finance (2013), and Financial Inclusion (2014). The author of over 100 publications, she has published widely in academic journals. Her research has focused on the links between financial development and firm performance and economic development. Banking crises, financial regulation, access to financial services including SME finance are among her areas of research. Prior to coming to the Bank, she was an Economist at the Federal Reserve Bank of Cleveland. She holds a PhD and an MA in economics from the Ohio State University.

Jean-Jacques Dethier is Adjunct Professor at Georgetown University, where he teaches graduate courses on development, and a Senior Fellow at the Centre for Development Research, University of Bonn. He worked at the World Bank from 1985 to 2014, as Research Manager, Country Economist, and other positions. He also worked for ILO and was a consultant for USAID, FAO, IFAD, the Arab Monetary Fund, and IOC. He has worked on all continents and has published extensively on development policy, macroeconomics and public finance. He holds a PhD in Economics from the University of California, Berkeley (1984), an ABD PhD from the Free University in Berlin, Germany (1976), and a Law Degree from the University of Liège, Belgium (1975).

Hamed El-Said (PhD) is Chair and Professor of International Business and Political Economy at the Manchester Metropolitan University Business School (UK). He acted as an advisor to the United Nations al-Qaeda and Taliban Monitoring Team (2008–2013). From 1990 to 1992, he served as a member of the Centre for Strategic Studies, then the research arm of HRH Prince Hassan ben Talal (Crown Prince of Jordan between 1965 and 1999). In 2008, he headed the research team of the United Nations Counter Implementation Task Force's Working Group on Addressing Radicalisation and Extremism that Lead to Terrorism. He has published extensively on the Arab World. His latest publications include *New Approaches in Fighting Terrorism: Designing and Evaluating Counter Radicalisation and Deradicalisation Programs.*

Ibrahim Ahmed Elbadawi is currently Director of Economic Policy & Research Center at the Dubai Economic Council, and before that was a Lead Economist at the Research Department of the World Bank. He has published widely on macroeconomic and development policy, democratic transitions and the economics of civil wars and post-conflict transitions. He is a Research Fellow at the Center for Global Development; Associate Editor of the *Middle East Development Journal*; Thematic Research Leader for "Natural Resource Management and Economic Diversification" at the Economic Research Forum for the Middle East and member of the Advisory Board of the Arab Planning Institute.

Chris Elbers studied econometrics and mathematical economics at the University of Amsterdam and now is the Desmond Tutu Chair Holder of the Faculty of Economics and Business Administration at the VU University Amsterdam. He is a fellow of the European Union Development Research Network (EUDN), the Tinbergen Institute and the Amsterdam Institute for International Development (AIID). His main research activities are in the fields of poverty measurement and impact evaluation.

Bichaka Fayissa is Professor of Economics, Jones College of Business at Middle Tennessee State University. His research focuses on the Economic Growth and Development Policies of African Economies.

Augustin Kwasi Fosu is Professor, Institute of Statistical, Social and Economic Research (ISSER), University of Ghana. He is also Extraordinary Professor, Faculty of Economic and Management Sciences, University of Pretoria; and Research Associate, CSAE, University of Oxford. Previously he was Deputy Director, UNU-WIDER; Senior Policy Advisor (Chief Economist), UN Economic Commission for Africa; and Director of Research, African Economic Research Consortium (AERC). He holds a PhD in economics from Northwestern University, USA. Among his many editorial responsibilities are co-editor of the *Journal of African Economies* (Oxford) and member of the editorial boards of such journals as the *Journal of Development Studies, Oxford Development Studies, World Bank Economic Review*, and *World Development*.

Marcelo M. Giugale is the Senior Director of the World Bank Group's Global Practice on Macroeconomics and Fiscal Management, the professional home of the Group's 300-plus macroeconomists. An international development leader, his 25 years of experience span the Middle East, Eastern Europe, Central Asia, Latin-America, and Africa, where he led senior-level policy dialogue and over 30 billion dollars in lending operations across the development spectrum. A Fellow of the US National Academy of Public Administration, he has published on macroeconomic policy, finance, subnational fiscal rules, development economics, and applied econometrics. He holds a PhD from the London School of Economics.

Wafik Grais has long experience in international development and finance, notably as former Director at the World Bank and Founder and Chairman of a Cairo-based Financial Advisors company. Wafik Grais brings global financial experience on the topics of financial systems assessments, corporate governance, Islamic finance, and public policy. He is currently an independent international advisor with expertise in Islamic finance, private equity, corporate governance, and real estate. Wafik Grais holds a PhD in economics from the University of Geneva and a BSc in economics and another in Political science from the same university. He is fluent in Arabic, French, and English.

Jan Willem Gunning is Emeritus Professor of Development Economics at the VU University Amsterdam. He is a former staff member of the World Bank, has been a professor in Oxford, where he directed the Centre for the Study of African Economies and is the General Secretary of the Royal Netherlands Academy of Arts and Sciences. With Chris Elbers he has worked on the effects of risk on growth in Africa and on the limitations of randomized controlled trials in impact evaluation.

Kenneth Harttgen is an economist who works at the center for development and cooperation (Nadel) at ETH Zurich, Switzerland. He holds a PhD in economics from Göttingen University. Since 2007, he has worked for several international organizations as a consultant, including FAO, UNDP, UNIFEM, UNESCO, and the World Bank. His main research interest is in empirical microeconomics, poverty, inequality, and population dynamics in developing countries.

Calestous Juma is an internationally recognized authority on the role of science, technology, engineering, and innovation in sustainable development. He is Professor of the Practice of International Development at Harvard Kennedy School. In 2014–2015, he was MLK Visiting Professor in the Department of Urban Studies and Planning at the Massachusetts Institute of Technology. He is Director of HKS Science, Technology, and Globalization Project and Agricultural Innovation in Africa Project. He is Faculty Chair of the HKS **Edward S. Mason** Fellows Program and Faculty Chair of the Innovation for Economic Development Executive Program and the Mason Fellows Program. He has been elected to several scientific and engineering academies.

Ioannis N. Kessides's areas of specialization are energy policy, competition, regulatory, and privatization policies in network utilities, market structure and firm conduct, determinants of entry and exit, and contestability analysis. Until July 2013, he was Lead Economist, Development Research Group at the World Bank. Prior to joining the World Bank in 1990, he taught industrial organization and microeconomics at the University of Maryland. More recently, he taught a course on public policy towards business at the Woodrow Wilson School (Princeton University). He received a BSc degree (with honors) in physics from Caltech, an MA in plasma physics (nuclear fusion), and a PhD in economics from Princeton University.

Michael Kevane is Associate Professor of the Economics Department at Santa Clara University. He is past President of the Sudan Studies Association, and co-director of Friends of African Village Libraries. Recent research focuses on how libraries promote reading, with articles published in *Libri, World Libraries*, and *Bulletin des Bibliothèques de France*. He is co-editor of *Kordofan Invaded: Peripheral Incorporation and Social Transformation in Islamic Africa* (Brill, 1998) and author of *Women and Development in Africa: How Gender Works* (Lynne Rienner, 2014, 2nd edition).

Leora Klapper is a Lead Economist in the Finance and Private Sector Research Team of the Development Research Group at the World Bank. Her publications focus on corporate and consumer finance, entrepreneurship, corporate governance, and risk management. She is a founder of the Global Financial Inclusion (Findex) database, which measures how adults around the world save, borrow, make payments, and manage risk. Prior to coming to the Bank she worked at the Board of Governors of the Federal Reserve System, the Bank of Israel, and Salomon Smith Barney. She holds a PhD in Financial Economics from New York University Stern School of Business.

Odongo Kodongo is Senior Lecturer of Finance and Director of PhD Programs at Wits Business School. He researches on asset pricing, foreign exchange rates, and cross-border capital flows and financial markets, with publications in top international journals.

Caroline Krafft received her master's degree in public policy from the University of Minnesota's Humphrey School of Public Affairs and is now a PhD Candidate in the Department of Applied Economics at the University of Minnesota. Her research examines issues in development economics, primarily labor, education, health, and inequality in the Middle East and North Africa. Current projects include work on early childhood development, labor market dynamics, life course transitions, human capital accumulation, and fertility.

Frannie A. Léautier is Founding Partner and CEO of Mkoba Private Equity Fund. She was Vice President and Chief of Staff at the World Bank; Executive Secretary of the African Capacity Building Foundation; Founder and Managing Partner of the Fezembat Group. She is also a Director of the PTA Bank; Director at Large AERC; founding Board Member of the Nelson Mandela Institute for Science & Technology; founding member of the *Journal of Infrastructure Systems*; member of the editorial board of the *Journal of African Trade* (JAT); Board Member UONGOZI Institute; and Visiting Committees at MIT Corporation. She holds a master's and PhD from MIT, was distinguished professor at Sciences Po.

Keun Lee is Professor of Economics at the Seoul National University, and the director of the Center for Economic Catch-up. He has been awarded the 2014 Schumpeter Prize for his monograph on *Schumpeterian Analysis of Economic Catch-up: Knowledge, Path-creation and the Middle Income Trap* (2013, Cambridge University Press) by the International Schumpeter Society. He is also the President-Elect of this Society. He is a member of the Committee for Development Policy of UN, a co-editor of Research Policy, and a member of the governing board of Globelics. He obtained a PhD degree from the University of California, Berkeley, and has worked at the World Bank, the University of Aberdeen, and the East West Center.

Willi Leibfritz has a PhD in Economics and worked until 2001 with the IFO economic research institute in Munich as Head of Department for Macroeconomic Analysis and until 2007 with the OECD in Paris as Head of Division in the Economics Department. Since then he has worked as a consultant for the OECD, the World Bank and the African Development Bank. In recent years he has worked as Co-ordinator of the African Economic Outlook (AEO). The AEO is an annual product of collaborative work by three international partners: the African Development Bank, the OECD Development Centre and the United Nations Development Programme.

Justin Yifu Lin is Professor and Honorary Dean, National School of Development at Peking University. He was the Senior Vice President and Chief Economist of the World Bank, 2008–2012. Prior to this, Mr. Lin served for 15 years as Founding Director of the China Centre for Economic Research at Peking University. He is the author of 23 books including *Against the Consensus: Reflections on the Great Recession, the Quest for Prosperity: How Developing Economies Can Take Off, Demystifying the Chinese Economy,* and *New Structural Economics: A Framework for Rethinking Development and Policy*. He is a Corresponding Fellow of the British Academy and a Fellow of the Academy of Sciences for Developing World.

Tsitsi Makombe is Senior Program Manager at the International Food Policy Research Institute (IFPRI). Tsitsi manages research activities of IFPRI's Africa regional offices for West and Central Africa and East and Southern Africa. She also provides programmatic support to various projects and notably the Regional Strategic Analysis and Knowledge Support System (ReSAKSS), an initiative in support of the Comprehensive Africa Agriculture Development Programme (CAADP).

Joseph Leina Masawe is currently the Director of Economic Research and Policy at the Bank of Tanzania, a position he has held since 2007. Prior to this Dr. Masawe was a senior advisor to the executive director for Africa group one constituency at the International Monetary Fund. He has published widely on monetary policy and general economic policy.

Paul R. Masson, until his retirement in 2011, taught international economics at the University of Toronto. Starting at the Bank of Canada after a PhD in 1973 from the London School of Economics, he then worked at the OECD and the IMF, from which he retired in 2002. In 2007–2008, he was Special Adviser to the Governor of the Bank of Canada. He has published several books, including *The Monetary Geography of Africa*, with Catherine Pattillo, which examines the history of the use of currencies in Africa and prospects for further monetary integration. He has also published a number of articles on policy credibility, financial crises, contagion, and exchange rate regimes.

Margaret McMillan is Professor of Economics at Tufts University and a Research Associate in the NBER's program on International Trade and Investment. In 2009, she was appointed the Director of the Development Strategies and Governance Division of the International Food Policy Research Institute. McMillan holds a PhD in economics (with distinction) from Columbia University an MPA from Princeton University and a BA in mathematics and economics (*summa cum laude*) from Boston University. Before coming to academia, she taught math in the Republic of Mali, managed a project for the World Bank in the United Republic of Tanzania and worked as a financial analyst at Lehman Brothers. McMillan's research interests lie in the areas of international trade, investment, and development. She is the recipient of numerous awards for her research. In 2005, she was named the William and Flora Hewlett Foundation Fellow at the Radcliffe Institute for Advanced Study. She is also a recipient of research grants from the National Science Foundation, the Center for Aids Research and the NBER Africa Project. She is currently the principal investigator on a multi-million dollar project funded by the Economic and Social Research Council of the UK designed to enhance the understanding of economic growth and structural change in sub-Saharan Africa. Her work has been featured in *The New York Times* and the NBER Digest and has been published in a wide range of leading economics journals.

John Mathews is Professor of Strategy at Macquarie Graduate School of Management, Macquarie University, Sydney. He has taught at MGSM for the past 15 years, and was from 2009 to 2012 concurrently the Eni Chair of Competitive Dynamics and Global Strategy at LUISS Gardi Carli University in Rome. He has specialized in the catch-up strategies of firms and countries in East Asia, publishing widely in this field. In 2014 his new book, *Greening of Capitalism: How Asia is Driving the Next Great Transformation*, was published by Stanford University Press.

Jaime de Melo is Emeritus Professor at the University of Geneva, is Scientific director at FERDI an invited professor at the Johns Hopkins University Bologna Center. He is a CEPR fellow, a member of EU-GDN, and a non-resident scholar at Brookings. He worked at USAID from 1972 to 1976, taught at Georgetown University from 1976 to 1980, and at the University of Geneva from 1993 to 2012. From 1980 to 1993, he held various positions in the research Department at the World Bank. He serves on several editorial boards and was editor-in-chief of the *World Bank Economic Review*, 2005–2010.

Nadir Abdellatif Mohammed is the Country Director for the Gulf Countries, Middle East and North African region, of the World Bank. He obtained MPhil, PhD (Cantab) and post-doctoral qualifications in economics from the University of Cambridge. He also worked as researcher/lecturer in Universities of Cambridge, Oxford, and Addis Ababa. He publishes widely on issues of defense economics, economic development, and fiscal policy. He worked in the African Development Bank and the Islamic Development Bank before joining the World Bank Group in 1998.

Célestin Monga is Managing Director at the United Nations Industrial Development Organization (UNIDO). He previously worked as Senior Advisor and Director at the World Bank and has held various board and senior positions in academia and financial services. A graduate of MIT, Harvard, and the universities of Paris 1 Panthéon-Sorbonne, Bordeaux, and Pau, Dr. Monga was the Economics editor for the five-volume *New Encyclopedia of Africa* (Charles Scribner's, 2007). His published works have been translated into multiple languages.

Germano Mwabu is Professor of Economics at the University of Nairobi and a resource person at the African Economic Research Consortium. His primary research interests are in the fields of health economics and poverty analysis.

Karmen Naidoo obtained both an honors degree and a master's degree in Economics from the University of Cape Town. She also holds a Master's Degree in Development Economics from the School of Oriental and African Studies, University of London. Karmen has previously worked in the areas of financial system development and financial inclusion in a variety of African economies. Since joining the DPRU, Karmen has worked extensively on assessing skills gaps and the impact of the training of firm employees in South Africa. Furthermore, she has been involved in profiling, through the use of micro-datasets, poverty, inequality, and labor markets in selected African economies.

Malokele Nanivazo is a visiting scholar at the University of Kansas in the Department of Economics. In this capacity, she conducts research on various topics related to gender economics such as family planning, education, entrepreneurship and poverty. Her expertise in gender economics enhances her research in economic development and international economics. Specifically, her economic development research centers on poverty, growth, rural transformation, trade, and foreign aid. Malokele Nanivazo also has teaching experience in graduate and undergraduate classes in macroeconomics, development economics, and international economics. Prior to joining the University of Kansas, she worked as a research fellow at the United Nations University–World Institute for Development Economics Research (UNU-WIDER). As a research fellow at UNU-WIDER, she was involved in the Research and Communication on Foreign Aid Project (ReCom) as the focal point for the "Gender and Foreign Aid" theme. In addition, she was the lead author for the Democratic Republic of Congo case study in UNU-WIDER's Reconciling Africa's Growth, Poverty and Inequality Trends: Growth and Poverty Project (GAPP). Malokele Nanivazo holds a PhD in Economics from Southern Illinois University Carbondale in 2011, which concentrated on economic development and international trade. She is a member of the African Finance and Economics Association, American Economic Association and the International Association for Feminist Economics.

Léonce Ndikumana is Professor of Economics, Department of Economics and Director of the African Development Policy Program at the Political Economy Research Institute, University of Massachusetts, Amherst. His research is on capital flight, domestic investment and financial intermediation, macroeconomic frameworks for growth and employment, and the politics and economics of conflict in Africa. He is a Honorary Professor of Economics at the University of Stellenbosch and a member of the United Nations Committee for Development Policy. He holds a doctorate in economics from Washington University in St. Louis, Missouri, and is a graduate of the University of Burundi.

Benno Ndulu is Governor of the Bank of Tanzania. Having served as Professor of Economics at the University of Dar-es-Salaam, he joined the founder team of the highly acclaimed research network the African Economic Research Consortium and served as its Executive Director. He later joined the World Bank and served in various managerial capacities including as Research Manager. He has published widely on growth, governance and financial sector development in Africa.

Mwanza Nkusu is Senior Economist at the International Monetary Fund where she has worked since 1998. She received her BSc in Applied Economics (Distinction) from the University of Kinshasa, MSc in Policy Economics from the University of Illinois at Urbana–Champaign (UIUC), and PhD in Economics from the UIUC. Dr. Nkusu's research interests include monetary and exchange rate policies, international economics, and economic development.

Akbar Noman is at Columbia University where he combines being a Senior Fellow at the Initiative for Policy Dialogue (IPD) with teaching as an adjunct at the School of International and Public Affairs. Professor Noman's numerous publications include Strategies for African Development (jointly with Joseph Stiglitz) in Akbar Noman et al. (eds) *Good Growth and Governance in Africa: Rethinking Development Strategies*. He has wide-ranging experience of policy analysis and formulation in a variety of developing and transition economies, having worked extensively for the World Bank as well as other international organizations and at senior levels of government. His other academic appointments have been at the University of Oxford (where he was also a student) and the Institute of Development Studies at the University of Sussex.

Christian Nsiah is Associate Professor of Economics and Finance at Baldwin Wallace University in Berea, Ohio. His research interest include international finance, international trade, economic growth, technical change, and development (especially in the developing world). His current research projects focus on the determinants and impact for foreign capital inflows (e.g. remittance, foreign, tourism receipts) on economic growth and development, spatial issues in relation to trade and development, and financial efficiency of publicly traded companies and the impact of the financial crisis.

Yaw Nyarko is Professor of Economics at New York University and the Director of the Center for Technology and Economic Development. He is also the Co-Director of the Development Research Institute, winner of the 2009 BBVA Frontiers in Knowledge Award on Economic Development Cooperation, and Founding Director of NYU Africa House. A theoretical economist, his current work focuses on models where the economic actors engage in active learning about their environments and human capital models of economic growth and development. He is the author of many published research papers and the recipient of numerous awards and grants, including many from the National Science Foundation. He has been a consultant to many organizations including the World Bank, the United Nations, and the Social Science Research Council.

Eric Kehinde Ogunleye is currently affiliated with the African Development Bank Nigeria Country Office as Country Macroeconomist. Until very recently, he was a Special Adviser to the Chief Economic Adviser to the President of Nigeria, responsible for policy research and advisory assignments on diverse socioeconomic issues. He also served as Special Assistant to the President of Nigeria, focusing on international trade and finance. Earlier, he worked with the African Center for Economic Transformation where he engaged in providing policy research and advisory services for African governments, especially on economic transformation issues. Other previous experiences spanned UNU-WIDER, UNCTAD and WTO in addition to teaching and research experience as a Lecturer in the University of Calabar, Nigeria.

Kalu Ojah is Professor of Finance and Director of the Master in Finance & Investment at Wits Business School, University of Witwatersrand, Johannesburg. He is an active researcher with over fifty refereed articles and is co-editor of the *African Finance Journal*.

Keijiro Otsuka is Professor at the National Graduate Institute for Policy Studies in Tokyo. He received his PhD in Economics at the University of Chicago in 1979, was formerly chairman of board of trustees of International Rice Research Institute (2004–2007) and President of International Association of Agricultural Economists (2009–2012). He received the Purple Ribbon Medal from the Japanese government in 2010 and is the Fellow of International, American, and African Associations of Agricultural Economists. He is co-author or co-editor of 21 books. Currently he is an editorial board member of *Economic Development and Cultural Change* and *Agricultural Economics*

Peter van Oudheusden is an economist and works at the Finance and Private Sector Development Research Group at the World Bank. He has a PhD and MSc from Tilburg University.

Ruth Uwaifo Oyelere is currently Visiting Faculty in the Department of Economics at Emory University. She is also currently a Research Fellow for the Institute for the Study of Labor, Bonn Germany and a Research Affiliate for the Households in Conflict Network. Uwaifo Oyelere's research interests are in development economics, the economics of education, labor and demographic economics, and health economics. She has published widely in general and specialty academic journals, including the *American Economic Review, Economics of Education Review, Journal of Development Economics,* and *Journal of African Economies.* She is also a recipient of a university teaching award.

John Page is Senior Fellow in the Global Economy and Development Program at the Brookings Institution and a Non-resident Senior Fellow of the World Institute for Development Economics Research (UNU-WIDER). He is visiting professor at the National Graduate Institute for Policy Studies, Tokyo, Japan and a Research Associate of the Centre for the Study of African Economies at Oxford University and the Oxford Centre for the Study of Resource Rich Economies. From 1980 to 2008 Dr. Page was at the World Bank, where his senior positions included Director, Poverty Reduction, Director, Economic Policy, and Chief Economist, Africa.

Catherine Pattillo is Chief of the Low-Income Countries Strategy Unit in the Strategy, Policy and Review Department at the International Monetary Fund. Prior to that, she was a mission chief in the Western Hemisphere Department, and worked in the African and Research Departments. She earned a BA from Harvard University and a PhD in economics from Yale University. Before joining the IMF, she was a fellow at Oxford University, Centre for the Study of African Economies, and St. Antony's College. Her research interests and published articles are in the areas of growth, investment, debt, monetary and exchange rate policies, aid, currency crises, macroeconomic policies and firm performance in Africa, and monetary unions in Africa.

Frank Place is Senior Research Fellow at the International Food Policy Research Institute, working in the Policies, Institutions and Markets CGIAR Research Program. Previously he worked for nearly 20 years at the World Agroforestry Centre in Nairobi and before that at the Land Tenure Center, University of Wisconsin and the World Bank. He has a PhD in Economics from the University of Wisconsin, Madison.

Rafael Portillo is Senior Economist in the Research department of the International Monetary Fund. Mr. Portillo holds a PhD from the University of Michigan. His research interests are in the area of monetary and fiscal policy in developing countries, with a focus on the development of macroeconomic models. He joined the IMF in 2005.

Peter Quartey holds a PhD in Development Economics from the University of Manchester (UK), MSc in Quantitative Development Economics (University of Warwick, UK), BA and MPhil Economics (Ghana). He is an Associate Professor in Development Economics and currently the Head, Department of Economics, University of Ghana and Director EPM Programme. He is also an Economist with the Institute of Statistical, Social and Economic Research, University of Ghana. He was formerly the Deputy Director, Centre for Migration Studies (University of Ghana). His areas of specialization includes development finance, private sector development, poverty analysis and impact evaluation.

Jeffrey D. Sachs is a world-renowned economics professor and leader in sustainable development. He serves as the Director of The Earth Institute, Quetelet Professor of Sustainable Development, and Professor of Health Policy and Management at Columbia University. He is Special Advisor to United Nations Secretary-General Ban Ki-moon on the Millennium Development Goals. Professor Sachs is Director of the UN Sustainable Development Solutions Network, as well as co-founder and director of the Millennium Villages Project. He has authored three *New York Times* bestsellers in the past 7 years: *The End of Poverty, Common Wealth*, and *The Price of Civilization*. His most recent book is *To Move the World: JFK's Quest for Peace*.

Stephanie Seguino is Professor of Economics at the University of Vermont, USA; Professorial Research Associate at the School of Oriental and African Studies (SOAS), University of London. Prior to obtaining a PhD from the American University, she served as an economist in Haiti in the pre- and post-Baby Doc era. Her current research explores the relationship between inequality, growth, and development. A major focus of that work explores the effect of gender equality on macroeconomic outcomes. She is an instructor in the African Program for Rethinking Development Economics (APORDE) and Associate Editor of *Feminist Economics* and *Journal of Human Development and Capabilities*.

Saurabh Singhal is a Research Fellow at the World Institute for Development Economics Research. His research interests include the political economy of development, applied econometrics, and experimental economics. Some of his current projects analyze issues related to health, education, and conflict. He holds a PhD in economics from the University of Southern California and an MA in economics from the Delhi School of Economics.

Joseph Stiglitz is University Professor at Columbia University, the winner of the 2001 Nobel Memorial Prize in Economics, and a lead author of the 1995 IPCC report, which shared the 2007 Nobel Peace Prize. He was chairman of the US Council of Economic Advisors under

President Clinton and chief economist and senior vice president of the World Bank for 1997–2000. Stiglitz received the John Bates Clark Medal, awarded annually to the American economist under 40 who has made the most significant contribution to the subject. He is a member of the National Academy of Sciences and a corresponding Fellow of the British Academy and the Royal Society.

Finn Tarp is Professor of Development Economics at the University of Copenhagen; and since 2009 Director of the UNU World Institute for Development Economics Research (UNU-WIDER). He has more than 35 years of experience in academic and applied development economics, including 20 years of work in some 35 developing countries. Finn Tarp is a leading international expert on issues of development strategy and foreign aid; and he was appointed to the Council of Eminent Persons (CEP) advising the Chief Economist of the World Bank in 2013. For further information (including a detailed CV with publications) see www.econ.ku.dk/ftarp.

Jean-Claude Tchatchouang is Senior Advisor to the World Bank Executive Director for 24 African countries. He previously served as economist at the International Monetary Fund and at the Banque des Etats de l'Afrique central, the central bank that serves six the countries which form the Economic and Monetary Community of Central Africa.

Mark R. Thomas is a manager at the World Bank, where he leads that institution's global engagements on debt relief, debt sustainability, and public debt management. In over 20 years of working in development he has worked on Africa, Latin America, and Asia, including periods living in Brazil and Turkey. He has served as adjunct faculty at the Woodrow Wilson School (Princeton University), Georgetown Public Policy Institute, and McGill University. He is a Freeman of Llantrisant, Wales.

Josselin Thuilliez is a tenured CNRS researcher (Centre National de la Recherche Scientifique) at the Centre d'économie de la Sorbonne. He received his doctorate in economics from Paris 1 University and has worked with the Malaria Research and Training Center, Bamako, Mali on several studies since 2007. His research currently focuses on development and health economics in Africa and Europe, understanding the impact that health policies have on economic outcomes such as income, education, and productivity. He also has expertise in conducting longitudinal studies in Africa, comparative evaluations using experimental or quasi-experimental designs, and analysis of large-scale microeconomic census data such as Demographic and Health Surveys in Africa.

Yvonne Tsikata is the World Bank President's Chief of Staff. Prior to this, Ms. Tsikata was the Sector Director for the Poverty Reduction and Economic Management Department of the Europe and Central Asia Region. Ms. Tsikata joined the World Bank in 1991 as a Young Professional. Since then she has held various positions, including being the World Bank's Country Director for the Caribbean Region (2007–2011). Prior to that, she was Sector Manager for the Poverty Reduction and Economic Management Unit in the Africa Region. She also held positions in the World Bank's International Trade Department and Independent Evaluation Group. Between 1998 and 2001, while on leave from the World Bank, she served as a senior research fellow at the Economic and Social Research Foundation in Dar-es-Salaam, Tanzania, as a consultant to the Organisation for Economic Co-operation and Development in Paris and to the United Nations University's World Institute for

Development Economics Research in Helsinki. Before joining the World Bank, Ms. Tsikata taught monetary theory and macroeconomic policy at New York University, where she earned her graduate degrees. Her research interests have focused on international trade and aid effectiveness.

Filiz Unsal is an economist at the Strategy, Policy and Review (SPR) Department of the International Monetary Fund. Before joining the SPR Department, she worked in the Research Department and Asia and Pacific Department. She received her PhD in Economics in 2009, and MSc in Economics and Finance in 2006 from University of York. Her research interests include monetary and macro-prudential policies for developing countries. She has published in several academic journals, including the *International Journal of Central Banking, the IMF Economic Review, Journal of Asian Economics*, among others, and has written several policy papers

Yan Wang is Visiting Professor at School of Business, George Washington University and Senior Fellow, National School of Development, Peking University. Previously she worked as Senior Economist and Team Leader in the World Bank for 20 years. She also served as Coordinator of the OECD-DAC and China Study Group for two years (2009–2011). She has authored and coauthors several books and journal publications and received twice the SUN Yefang Award in Economics. She received her PhD from Cornell University, and taught economics before joining the World Bank.

Maureen Were is Research Manager at the Research Centre, Kenya School of Monetary Studies, Central Bank of Kenya. She has written and published a number of research papers on various topics including monetary policy in Kenya, trade, macroeconomic issues and gender. In 2013, she won the Mo Ibrahim Leadership Fellowship award aimed at preparing upcoming African leaders and was attached at the World Trade Organization in Geneva for a period of one year, during which most of the contribution to the book chapter was undertaken. She holds a PhD in Economics.

Liang Xu is a PhD candidate in African history at Harvard University. He holds a PhD in International Relations from Peking University (2010). His current research examines Asian investment and South Africa's industrial policies in black homelands under apartheid and the long-term impact on small towns in South Africa.

Derek Yu is Senior Lecturer in Economics at the University of the Western Cape and part time researcher at the Development Research Unit of the University of Cape Town. His main research areas are labor economics and development economics.

INTRODUCTION

....

AFRICA'S EVOLVING ECONOMIC POLICY FRAMEWORKS

....

CÉLESTIN MONGA AND JUSTIN YIFU LIN

1 DISAPPOINTING THE QUEEN AND THE AFRICAN POLICYMAKERS

....

IT sometimes takes a royalty to bring a major economic issue to the global agenda and spark the kind of conversation that helps reassess public policies and practices. During a mostly ceremonial visit to the London School of Economics in November 2008, at a time when the global crisis—subsequently known as the Great Recession—was in full swing, Queen Elizabeth of the UK asked the faculty there a simple and falsely naïve question: "Why had nobody noticed that the credit crunch was on its way?"[1] Her Majesty's inquiry prompted the British Academy to convene a forum on 17 June 2009 to debate that question, with experts from academia, business, the City, its regulators, and government, invited to offer thoughts and recommendations. Contributors from a wide range of backgrounds shared opinions, which were then summarized in a letter sent to the Queen in July 2009.

The letter, a three-page missive, blamed the crisis on "a failure of the collective imagination of many bright people." It also noted that some people actually did foresee the crisis, even though the exact form that it would take and the timing of its onset and ferocity were predicted by nobody.

> But against those who warned, most were convinced that banks knew what they were doing. They believed that the financial wizards had found new and clever ways of managing risks.

---

[1] According to media reports, the Queen asked Luis Garicano of the economics management department at the London School of Economics, about the origins of the credit crisis, saying: "Why did nobody notice it?" Garicano responded: "At every stage, someone was relying on somebody else and everyone thought they were doing the right thing." The Queen described it as "awful." See *The Telegraph*, July 26, 2009.

Indeed, some claimed to have so dispersed them through an array of novel financial instruments that they had virtually removed them. It is difficult to recall a greater example of wishful thinking combined with hubris. There was a firm belief, too, that financial markets had changed. And politicians of all types were charmed by the market. These views were abetted by financial and economic models that were good at predicting the short-term and small risks, but few were equipped to say what would happen when things went wrong as they have.

(Besley and Hennessy 2009)

Many economists had indeed warned about imbalances in financial markets and in the global economy[2] and the "psychology of denial" and complacency that gripped the financial and political world and eventually led to the global recession (Lin 2013). As noted by Krugman,

Of course, there were exceptions to these trends: a few economists challenged the assumption of rational behavior, questioned the belief that financial markets can be trusted and pointed to the long history of financial crises that had devastating economic consequences. But they were swimming against the tide, unable to make much headway against a pervasive and, in retrospect, foolish complacency.

(Krugman 2009)

Many African researchers and policymakers too had long warned about the profoundly unbalanced structure of the world's global trading and financial system, and the negative dynamics of the uniformly designed policy frameworks that had dominated much of development thinking and practices since the 1980s. They often pointed out the inconsistencies of the macroeconomic, structural, and institutional policies implemented across Africa, generally under the strong guidance of international development institutions (Galbraith and Monga 1994), the lack of ownership of those who were supposed to implement them, the consistently poor results of these policies (Mkandawire and Soludo 2003), and the pervasive failures of governance that often made these policy prescriptions worse than the economic and social diseases they were supposed to cure (Olukoshi 1998, 2003).

But it was Queen Elizabeth's seemingly innocent questioning of the economics discipline that gave most of publicity to the need for accountability from the engineers of failed economic policies. Perhaps inadvertently, she brought some of the obscure technical debates that had always existed among academic economists to the forefront of policymaking and policy discussions. Newspapers columns and popular magazines devoted pages and special issues to the re-examination of the validation criteria of economic knowledge, and to the assessment of policies that led to the 2007–2009 crisis. Prominent economists were regularly given the opportunity to intervene in the debates, with many Nobel laureates taking different sides.

In these heated and often angry exchanges the most unexpected *mea culpa* and plea for rethinking came from the International Monetary Fund (IMF), the global institution long perceived at the sacred temple of orthodoxy. In a series of landmark papers published under the leadership of none other than its economic counselor and director of research, the IMF conceded that some if its earlier policy recommendations were off the mark. "It

---

[2] See for instance Roubini (2008), Galbraith (2009), or Stiglitz (2010a, b).

was tempting for macroeconomists and policymakers alike to take much of the credit for the steady decrease in cyclical fluctuations from the early 1980s on and to conclude that we knew how to conduct macroeconomic policy. We did not resist temptation. The crisis clearly forces us to question our earlier assessment." (Blanchard et al. 2010: 199). This humble statement, followed by a more "granular" rethinking of macroeconomic policies (2013), was all the more remarkable that it came from one of the most distinguished macroeconomists of our time, the former chair of the MIT Economics department, and the author of a paper released only a few months earlier asserting that "the state of macro is good" (Blanchard 2009).

Blanchard was right to do the unthinkable and lead not only the IMF but also the broader community of "mainstream economists" to question the pertinence of the policy advice given to poor and rich countries for decades. That advice often led to the adoption and implementation of misguided economic policies, with heavy financial, economic, social, and human costs in advanced economies and in developing countries as well. The intellectual impact of the "Blanchard revolution" was such that the IMF also decided to subsequently revisit many important economic issues that had traditionally been kept outside of the realm of macroeconomics: inequality, structural transformation, gender economics, etc.

It is now widely acknowledged that the Great Recession was not just a balance sheet crisis. It had deeper underlying causes, and highlighted most notably the need for the economies of the United States and Europe to upgrade their policy frameworks and comply with the requirements of a structural transformation associated with the move from manufacturing to a service sector economy (Stiglitz 2013, 2011). Developing countries too face the same challenge because sustained economic growth is both the result and the cause of structural changes (Kuznets 1966; Monga 2012; Lin and Monga 2014). Most countries that remain poor have failed to achieve structural transformation, that is, they have been unable to diversify away from agriculture and the production of traditional goods into manufacturing and other modern activities.

In Africa, the world's region with the most difficult development challenges, low-productivity and subsistence agriculture and informal activities continue to play a dominant role, accounting for about 80 percent of the labor force. Recent empirical work confirms that the bulk of the difference in growth between Asia and developing countries in Latin America and Africa can be explained by the contribution of structural change to overall labor productivity (McMillan and Rodrik 2011). African policymakers long understood the importance of structural change and did their best to transform their economies right from the late 1950s and early 1960s. Unfortunately, they followed economic development strategies that were inconsistent with the comparative advantage of their economies—just like many of their developing country counterparts. They promoted inward-looking strategies that relied on nonviable industries and firms, and built non-performing and unsustainable economic systems. Intellectual adjustment had to be made to such failed strategies. But the dismantling of the distortions too abruptly and the adoption of policies preventing governments from facilitating the emergence of new industries consistent with the country's comparative advantages (those were recommendations by the proponents of the second wave of development thinking under the neo-classical framework known as the Washington Consensus) also created new problems and led to disappointments. Since then, development economists working on Africa have struggled to come up with new ideas, few of which have really integrated the intellectual benefits and the policy lessons from the first two waves (early structuralism and neo-classical economics).

This introductory chapter of Volume 2 of the *Oxford Handbook of Africa and Economics* discusses Africa's changing economic policy and institutional frameworks, and presents the ways forward. Section 2 chronicles the rise and fall of the main economic strategies adopted by most African countries after independence, and highlights their rationale and shortcomings. Section 3 draws the lessons to be learned from failures and successes, and stresses the inappropriate tendency of African policymakers to take as reference models the most advanced economies, and try to replicate their strategies and policies mimetically. Section 4 suggests that economic policy in developing countries be primarily conceived as an exercise of strategic selection. Section 5 concludes by presenting the objectives of this volume while insisting on the need for humility in the quest for relevant knowledge.

2 A Bottle of Beer versus a Bottle of Water: Economic Policy Disappointments in Africa

Despite some persistently grim headlines—about terrorism in the Sahel and in East Africa, the outbreaks of violence, the lingering civil wars in localized places, or the threat of the Ebola virus—Africa's economic reputation has improved markedly in recent years where it counts the most, that is, with local entrepreneurs and global investors. Africa, a continent of 54 countries, has had many success stories, which have not, unfortunately, received as much attention as they deserve—mainly because in some places there are undeniable serious problems. Few people know that nine of the world's 20 fastest-growing economies of the past 20 years are in Africa. And it is not just the resource-rich countries that are growing strongly: 20 sub-Saharan countries that do not produce oil averaged gross domestic product (GDP) growth rates of 4% or higher during the 2000s. Private capital to Africa is higher than foreign aid, averaging more than US$50 billion a year. Sub-Saharan Africa is projected to grow well above 5% a year in the medium and long term. Poverty levels are declining while education and health indicators—especially secondary school enrollment rates and life expectancy—are showing real improvements.

But the sustainability of progress in the long run is far from certain, and skeptics point to some of the fundamental remaining challenges: Africa's recent growth has largely mirrored rising commodity prices, and commodities still constitute the largest share of its exports. Moreover, in sub-Saharan Africa, the manufacturing sector, which is the main driver for sustainable, broad-based growth and employment creation, still accounts for the same small share of overall GDP that it did in the 1970s. Not surprisingly, some of the rapidly growing countries, such as Burkina Faso, Mozambique, and Tanzania, have not managed to substantially reduce their poverty rates despite the overall decline in poverty on the continent. And while most of Africa's civil wars have ended, political instability remains widespread in both North and sub-Saharan Africa.[3] In addition, most African countries suffer from state capture and corruption, their infrastructure is in poor condition, and their human capital levels are low—with most of the well-trained engineers, nurses, and medical doctors migrating

---

[3] See Devarajan and Fengler (2013) for a critical analysis of the optimistic and pessimistic narratives of Africa's economic prospects.

after graduation.[4] "In much of Africa, it is easier to find a bottle of beer than a glass of clean water," once observed the famous Kenyan scholar Ali Mazrui.

It is impossible to predict whether the general improvement of the economic outlook observed in recent years is a firm trend for the decades ahead and a sign of even better things to come for the entire region. But one can go beyond the headlines and the concerns about current events to review the deeper causes of Africa's still unsatisfactory economic performance. The examination of the conditions under which economic policies have often been designed and implemented in Africa reveals some similarities with the situation observed by analysts of the Great Recession: it shows the prevalence of dominant modes of thinking that generally promote a uniform set of macroeconomic and structural policies across countries, regardless of their levels of economic development and economic structure. These so-called conventional-wisdom policies have come in several big waves, and too often been geared towards unrealistic objectives (drive for "modernization"). For most of the past several decades, they have been carried out with a level of self-confidence and feel-good attitude among policymakers, which ultimately led to disappointing results.

In fact, post-independence economic policies in much of Africa followed the broad patterns observed elsewhere in the developing world after World War II. They all started with the intellectual and emotional legacies of the painful experience of slavery and colonialism, which led many African political leaders to set as their main goal the fastest possible modernization of their economies. It has been reported that Kwame Nkrumah wanted the Ghanaian economy to surpass that of England almost the day after independence. A noble political goal perhaps, but a foolish predicament for economic policy, for reasons discussed below.

First-generation development economists and policymakers emphasized the importance of structural change and saw structural differences as a result of market failures.[5] Not surprisingly, they proposed to use government interventions to facilitate structural change through import substitution and gave priority to modern advanced industries. It was a period when protective devices such as quantitative restrictions on imports and exchange controls to manage the balance of payments were first used on a large scale by most countries. Using Keynesianism as the main intellectual foundation for their analyses, early development economists advocated a "dirigiste dogma" (Lal 1983), positing as the central tenant of their theories that developing countries were irremediably different from industrial countries. Most developing countries and multilateral development institutions followed these policy recommendations.

Starting in the early sixties, the newly independent Sub-Saharan countries benefited from a rapid rise in the value of their exports. This led to an increase in their foreign exchange revenues and government revenues. This surge in income was stimulated by ambitious public policies aiming at increasing both investment and consumption. While often justified by the

---

[4] Some researchers have noted the potential long-term economic benefits of brain drain for African countries, most notably in terms of future remittances that contribute to growth. But these analyses typically neglect or underestimate the large negative costs for African societies, not only in terms of public finance (the cost of training students in public academic institutions) but also in terms of lost positive externalities (the migration of well-educated young people always amount to important social losses). Moreover, while remittance flows are positive resources for the balance of payments, empirical studies highlight the fact that they tend to finance mainly consumption and housing.

[5] See the Introduction (*Handbook*, Volume 1).

poor state of infrastructure and the dominating social needs of the population (especially in the areas of education and health) who had suffered centuries of slavery and colonization, a lot of these investments were oversized and ill-designed. Fueled by the nationalistic dream of the new political leaders, large projects and programs dominated government plans—often conceived on the model of Soviet Gosplan, regardless of the ideological background of the ruling elites. These projects and programs also generated large current expenditures, as they required a large number of civil servants with salary levels often equivalent to ten times the average income per capita, or high levels of operation and maintenance spending. Across the continent of Africa, they led to the kind of "macroeconomic of populism" analyzed by Dornbusch and Edwards (1991) in Latin America. Furthermore, for ideological, political, and sometimes economic reasons, and also for reasons of pure greed, some leaders opted for the nationalization of large fraction of the production apparatus. As noted by Guillaumont and Guillaumont Jeanneney, "they were encouraged along this direction by the ease with which they could obtain foreign loans owing to abundant international liquidity" (1994: 18).

In the 1970s, many private American, European, and Japanese banks had at their disposal important deposits from members of the Organization of Petroleum Exporting Countries (OPEC) cartel—the so-called petrodollars. Acting under the assumption that even poor developing countries cannot go bankrupt, these banks started lending money to African countries with little rigorous analysis of their justification. Countries like Zaire (under the iron fist of President Mobutu Sese Seko), Kenya (Jomo Kenyatta) or Ivory Coast (Félix Houphouet-Boigny's) were provided large loans that, under normal circumstances, would have been considered unwise. They were considered financially viable, as the prices of commodities (coffee, cocoa, copper, diamonds) through which they obtained foreign exchange were relatively high.

These loans were used to finance large investment projects with little or no economic rationale, imports of luxury consumption goods, and personal bank accounts in European banks.[6] Yet, by the early 1980s, the situation had changed considerably. OPEC had become less effective as a cartel, which drove down oil prices and substantially reduced petrodollars held as deposits in western banks. Also, the United States had elected Ronald Reagan as President, whose fiscal policy consisted mainly of large tax cuts and big buildup in military spending. The combination of these two factors (the limited availability of petrodollars on the international lending market and the need for funds to finance the large US fiscal deficit) drove interest rates upward. To make matters worse, the world economy plunged into recession in the early 1980s and commodity prices on which African countries relied for foreign exchange decreased to historic lows. Confronted with the rapid increase of interest rates on their variable-rate loan repayments, these countries were on the verge of default on their external debt. Since the loans they obtained in the 1970s were used to pay for politically motivated projects or expansive luxury goods—not productive investments—only one

---

[6] For several decades, Cameroon was the highest consumer of French Champaign in the world on a per capita basis. See Monga (2006). There was also a rationalization of personal enrichment by some of the strong men who ruled African countries during the first decades of independence. When he was once asked by a journalist during a press conference if it was true that he had a personal bank account in Switzerland, former Ivorian President Félix Houphouet-Boigny responded angrily: "Is there a serious man on earth today who does not own a Swiss bank account?"

option was left to them: turn to multilateral financial institutions like the World Bank and the IMF for help.

Across Africa, the results of the first major wave of post-independence economic policy were disappointing, and the gap with the industrialized countries widened. From a macro-economic perspective, the evolution of Africa in the sixties and seventies can be described as follows: after independence, most African countries quickly experienced a persisting imbalance between aggregate domestic demand and aggregate supply, and this was reflected in a worsening of their external payments and an increase in inflation. In some countries, the main explanation was the importance of external factors such as the rise in foreign interest rates or an exogenous deterioration in terms of trade.[7] But in most cases, the demand–supply imbalance could be traced to the inappropriate government policies that expanded domestic demand (consumption and investment) too rapidly relative to the productive capacity of the national economy. For over a decade, foreign financing was available and allowed these countries to sustain the large expansion of demand, albeit at the cost of a widening deficit of the current account of the balance of payments, a loss in international reserves, worsening of external competitiveness, and heavier foreign debt. This was eventually accompanied by declining growth rates, the aggravation of poverty, and the loss of creditworthiness. Indeed, as foreign investors and creditors who had been too lax in their willingness to put money in Africa suddenly became reluctant to do so, these countries had no other choice but to undergo a macroeconomic or structural adjustment.

From the perspective of economic development strategy, the main problem with that first wave of development policy was not government interventions per se, but the initial choice of goals, too ambitious, and inconsistent with African countries' endowment structure at their low levels of economic development. In the 1960s and 1970s it was indeed impossible to successfully develop competitive capital-intensive industries in countries whose comparative advantage was in labor-intensive sectors. Critics of these early industrial policies implemented in many African countries just after independence argued that they introduced profound distortions: limited public resources were used to pursue unsustainable import-substitution policies. To reduce the burden of public subsidies, governments sometimes resorted to administrative measures—granting the non-viable enterprises in prioritized industries a market monopoly, suppressing interest rates, overvaluing domestic currency, and controlling prices for raw materials. Such interventions themselves introduced further distortions, sometimes even causing shortages in foreign exchange and raw materials. Preferential access to credit deprived others of resources. There was a high opportunity cost. While industrial policies were often blamed for these disappointing outcomes, failures in the selection of development strategies were the real source of the problem, as they often led to inconsistent macroeconomic policies and unsustainable governance practices. Yet the focus of many analysts was on these macroeconomic policies and governance issues, which are endogenous to the development strategy (Lin 2009).

---

[7] The deterioration of the terms of trade identified by Barro (1997) as a major impediment to growth clearly affected some countries where post-colonial economies relied heavily on a few major commodities like cocoa (Ivory Coast, Ghana), groundnuts (Senegal), cotton (Mali, Upper Volta-Burkina Faso), coffee, timber (Cameroon), etc.

The failure of the government interventions inspired by the first-wave of development thinking generated a new wave, which highlighted government failures and adopted a radically different to economic policy, one that focused on the essential function of markets in allocating resources, ignored the structural differences among countries at different levels of development in their policy recommendations, and expected the structural change to happen spontaneously in the process. There again, multilateral institutions and development agencies were the main advocates for this second wave of economic policies in Africa through their programs. They based much of their policy advice and conditionality on stabilization and structural adjustment programs that reflected the new dominant paradigm and promoted economic liberalization, privatization, and the implementation of rigorous stabilization programs. That second development policy framework known as the Washington Consensus and implemented through structural adjustment programs (SAPs) also quickly became dominant. It emphasized getting prices right, creating a stable market environment, strengthening the institutions necessary for markets to function well (property rights, good governance, business environment, and the like), and building human capital (education and health) to supply the increasingly skilled labor required by advances in technology.

Unfortunately, the results of these policies for growth and employment generation were also disappointing and often highly controversial. Many analysts who later assessed their results observed that they led to "lost decades" in Africa's economic development. They pointed to drastic cuts in government spending and public sector wages, which caused the collapse of non-viable firms in the old priority sectors and often generated poor public service delivery—especially in the education and health sectors—low morale for civil servants, and low productivity. Not surprisingly, African researchers were often the harshest critics of Washington Consensus policies: listing the causes of what they called "Africa's endemic poverty and pervasive underdevelopment," Mkandawire and Soludo, for instance, pointed to "several acts of omission and commission" by the African people and their leaders, the very weak initial conditions, the short but peculiar history of post-independence colonial heritage, the "hostile external environment," and the role of the international community, namely "multilateral development institutions (especially the Bretton Woods institutions) and bilateral agencies (former colonial masters) ... Throughout the adjustment years, the Bretton Wood institutions seized much of the initiative, and foreclosed the debate by literally insisting that it was either their way or nothing, with African scholars and policymakers largely relegated to reactive protest." (2003: 1–2). Lipumba noted that the policy framework underlying SAPs "did not explicitly analyze the link between adjustment policies and the long-term development objectives of building effective institutional capacity to design and implement development policies, investing in human resources, and improving infrastructure to promote poverty-eradicating economic growth." (1994: 2).

Assessments of SAPs by Bretton-Woods institutions themselves have evolved over time. The 1989 World Bank report attempted to address some of the development issues that were left out by SAPs (institutional weaknesses and insufficient technical and administrative capacity, the role of external factors in African economic crises, the legacy of colonial history, etc.). The report also identified investments in infrastructure and in human capital (education and development) as prerequisites to long-term success. A few years later, a study that reviewed the experiences of highly successful East Asian economies (World Bank 1993) noted that they "adopted policies at variance with the notion of the 'level playing field' of open-market free enterprise." Governments there targeted specific industries for rapid development. In key areas, resource allocation was strictly managed. Trade in manufactured exports was promoted by government-established marketing institutions.

However, another World Bank report (1994), entitled *Adjustment in Africa*, adopted the narrow focus of short-term financial crises and concluded that adjustment policies were working well. The 1994 report insisted that African countries that reduced their deficits through real exchange rate depreciation, liberalization of their trade and foreign exchange allocation system, liberalization of marketing of inputs and outputs in the agricultural sector, and reduction of agricultural taxation, achieved a turnaround in their macroeconomic performance. The Report also acknowledged that "adjustment alone is inadequate for long-term sustainable development" but did not elaborate much on the findings of the 1989 report. The World Bank subsequently released several other performance evaluation with more or less the same key finding: countries that implement SAPs consistently eventually experience improvements in their economic performance. Over recent years, the Bank has emphasized in its evaluation the fact that foreign aid and SAPs are most effective in countries with "good" policy and institutional environments. Cross-country analyses carried out by the IMF on the experience of their programs also conclude that they are, by and large successful—whatever success means....In a report, Hadjimichael et al. note that "on the whole, African countries that have effectively implemented comprehensive adjustment and reform programs have shown better results." (1996: 1).

In recent years, reports from both the Bretton-Woods institutions have been more nuanced in their assessments of SAP-based policy frameworks. In a multi-volume evaluation the World Bank undertook to learn from the experience of the 1990s, a member of the senior leadership team wrote that the findings "confirm the importance for growth of macro-stability, of market forces governing the allocation of resources, and openness. But they also emphasize that these general principles translate into diverse policy and institutional paths, implying that economic policies and policy advice must be country-specific and institution-sensitive if they are to be effective. The central message of this volume is then that there is no unique universal set of rules." (Nankani 2005: xii–xiii).

The subsequent Growth Report (Commission on Growth and Development 2008) funded by the World Bank identified distinctive characteristics of successful growth, using 13 high-growth economies since 1950 as examples, and explored how developing countries can emulate them. The report proposed ingredients for a growth strategy but concluded that there are no "silver bullets" to solve poverty in developing countries, and no single recipe, as the policy mix will depend on the specific situation in each country. In the words of his main author, Nobel laureate Michael Spence, they identified the ingredients for growth, but not a recipe.

The editors of the *Handbook*—whose views are not necessarily shared by other contributors—are much more confident than Professor Spence on the possibility of identifying a general recipe for effective economic policies—they are also quite optimistic about the future of development policy in Africa and in the developing world. We believe that all low- and middle-income countries can achieve sustained and inclusive growth, provided that they draw the right lessons from past experiences, and make the best use of the key ideas in economic thinking and policies over the past decades. In a nutshell, the recipe called New Structural Economics (NSE) is to design and implement an economic policy based on the economic structure of the economy, which is endogenous to its factor endowment structure. Sustained economic development is driven by changes in factor endowments and continuous technological innovation. The factor endowments in a country are given at any specific time and changeable over time. A country's comparative advantages and thus its optimal industrial structure at any specific time are determined by its factor endowments at that time. Upgrading the industrial structure in a given country requires the upgrading of the factor endowment structure from one that is relatively abundant in labor and natural resources to one that is relatively abundant in capital, and the corresponding introduction of new technologies, as well as improvement in hard (tangible) and soft (intangible) infrastructure to reduce the transaction costs and risk of economic operations.

It follows that the best way to upgrade a country's endowment structure is to develop its industries at any specific time according to the comparative advantages determined by its given endowment structure at that time (Lin and Monga 2013). The economy will then be most competitive and successful in today's world of global trade, the economic surplus will be the largest, and the capital accumulation and the upgrading of factor endowment structure will be the fastest possible. For private firms in a country to enter industries according to the country's comparative advantages, relative factor prices must fully reflect the relative abundance of those factors, and those prices can be determined only through competition in a well-functioning market. Therefore, the market should be the basic institution of the economy.

Technological development should be an important driver of any economic policy framework. While advanced economies must produce at the global technology frontier and have to invest continuously in new research and development to achieve technological innovation, developing countries have the potential to achieve a rate of technological innovation several times higher than that of advanced countries. For the introduction of new technologies, African countries can turn their backwardness into an advantage by borrowing or adapting technologies that have already matured in richer economies to reduce the costs and risks of technological innovation.

Upgrading the industrial structure as well as the corresponding improvement in hard and soft infrastructure, however, entails coordination of investments and compensation for externalities generated by first movers that cannot be internalized by private enterprises. Without this coordination and compensation, the process of economic development will be slow. African governments should therefore play an active role in facilitating structural change through mitigating the coordination and externality problem. Following that general policy framework would help Africa achieve its unlimited growth potential, and quickly overcome Ali Mazrui's paradox of economies that can generate a few vibrant private capital-intensive industries to produce beer, but seem unable to provide basic public services such as clean water for the population.

3 SHERLOCK HOLMES SYNDROME AND WHOLESALE IMPORTATION OF ECONOMIC POLICIES

It is necessary to identify the biggest mistakes of the past and draw from the painful experiences the truly relevant policy principles for African countries to confidently move forward. Having argued in the previous section that comparative advantage is the silver bullet for success, one can point to two strategic mistakes, which in turn have invalidated much of the economic policies implemented in Africa since the end of the colonial period: first, in thinking about convergence with industrialized countries and the task of transforming low-income countries into industrialized economies, African policymakers have too often selected the wrong comparators and benchmarks, and set the wrong objectives for themselves. Second, these compounding mistakes have generated a false economics of preconditions, and the wrong policy prescriptions.

3.1 The wrong model economy and reference

It is absolutely legitimate for political leaders in low-income countries to try to emulate the success of others in advanced economies. It is obviously legitimate, for instance, for the Democratic Republic of Congo (DRC), a country with $300 in GDP per capita, to try to be like Canada and there is indeed no reason for the many hardworking citizens of Kinshasa not to expect living the supposedly good life of the not so hardworking people of Montreal. However, the current endowment structures of two economies are so different that it would not make much analytical sense to study them with the same tools and to derive policy recommendations from similar econometric models. Both countries are resource-rich but it would be inappropriate for economists to rigidly and mechanically apply analytical tools and policy prescriptions designed for capital-intensive and technologically advanced Canada to the capital-poor, labor-abundant DRC. The model economy that the DRC may want to "emulate" in 2014 should not be the resource-rich advanced economies of Canada or the United Kingdom in 2014 but, perhaps, Brazil or Malaysia when their GDP per capita were only about $1000. There is a viable path to prosperity and an optimal sequencing of development strategies that low-income economies ignore only at their own perils (Lin and Monga 2011).

These observations do not reflect some kind of teleological view of economic development: a country can move faster from one step to the other and Walt Rostow was incorrect in suggesting an almost linear process with a rigid timing in the various "stages of economic development." The evidence that his theory was erroneous is the acceleration of economic history: prior to the eighteenth century, it took 1400 years to double income in the Western world. In the nineteenth century, it only took about 70 years. In the twentieth century, it only required about 35 years. The changing pace of performance among individual countries is even more encouraging: it took 150 years for Great Britain to initially double its income. The United States needed 50 years to do the same. Without the natural resources, excellent infrastructure, or the kind of human capital that Britain, the United States, or the Scandinavian countries had, China did it in just 8.5 years in the nineties. By cleverly exploiting the benefits of backwardness in a world where trade opportunities and global value chains are powerful engines for sustainable growth, African countries can succeed even faster.

It should be noted, however, that some economists and policymakers may draw the wrong inference from these stylized facts of modern growth: looking at the speed of China's or South Korea's success and their industrial structures today, they mistakenly conclude that low-income economies can achieve prosperity without developing manufacturing, by just launching high-value-added industries or encouraging the emergence of tradable services. Such strategies, which violate comparative advantage, would not be sustainable. Trying to

develop sophisticated, capital-intensive industries and services in a $500 per capita econ-
omy whose comparative advantage is still in labor-intensive industries is the problem: with
a labor force of some 600 million people, most of them low-skilled workers, Africa put less
than 20% of its labor force in the formal sector.

The lesson here is not that poor economies should try to circumvent the steps of industrialization and jump from low-productivity agriculture to high-tech industries and
services when they are capital-scarce and have poor infrastructure and business environments; rather, they should try to put the largest possible fractions of their labor force to
work by developing industries that are consistent with their existing (and changeable) comparative advantage. The dynamics of more people working in the formal sector, earning
gradually decent incomes and developing soft skills and their human capital, eventually
moves the economy into more sophisticated, high-value-added industries and sectors.
Of course, good public policies can help speed up the evolution of an economy's endowment structure and compress the timing of structural transformation. Unfortunately, the
most dominant modes of thinking among development economists and African policymakers continue to neglect the need for industrial upgrading in low-income countries. It
still advocates the benchmarking of poor economies with high-income economies chosen
as the model to be emulated. That has been a recipe for disappointment for much of the
post-independence era.

3.2 The wrong assumptions/preconditions

Choosing the wrong model- or reference economy to be copied carries some heavy implications and leads to risky optical errors: instead of seeing the resources that are already in place
in each poor country and focusing the intellectual and policy resources to *maximizing the
existing assets and building on successes to accelerate reforms*, one only focuses on the *missing
ingredients* for growth and prosperity, and quickly becomes obsessed with the long list of
preconditions to be fulfilled—before the growth process can be ignited. This is a disturbing
trend, and a counter-productive intellectual attitude.

That mindset of "missing elements" and that obsession with "gaps" have translated
into a particular intellectual posture: economists have confined themselves to the role of
detectives—if not prosecutors. Without fully realizing it, many development practitioners
behave like characters in Arthur Conan Doyle and Agatha Christie novels. They have converted themselves into Sherlock Holmes or Hercule Poirots, whose divine mission is to find
what is wrong with low-income countries, not *what may be right* and sufficient there to start
something good. The "gap" mentality among researchers has therefore stimulated the emergence of a dominant brand of development policy that is basically an obsessive (if not compulsive) quest for the "deficiencies" to be corrected.

Of course, the search has produced long lists of true or false deficiencies, real or imaginary
gaps, and truly missing or illusory ingredients for development recipes, which are presented
as necessary elements to consider for economic progress. But the whole exercise has not paid
off. In fact, the search has created more problems for economists and policymakers than it
has brought solutions. Instead of focusing on what each country—even the poorest—already
has and upon which a viable development strategy could be built, the compulsive search
for the missing gap has validated and legitimized the notion that little can be done in poor

countries unless a long list of preconditions are met. Instead of adopting the mindset of how to maximize whatever little production factors are in place, development economists have too often devoted their energy and creativity on what must be done as preconditions for growth and prosperity. Instead of looking at the glass as half full, they have consistently seen it as almost completely empty.

Yet, we know from the history of development that no single successful economy in the world started out with ideal country conditions. Successful development processes always emerge from average if not very poor infrastructure, institutional and policy environments. Neither the United States, nor did Great Britain had "excellent" infrastructure stocks prior to the Industrial Revolution or even in the years and decades after that. China did not have "adequate" market institution, infrastructure and levels of human capital when Deng Xiaoping launched the shocking economic journey of growing the economy by nearly 10% a year for three decades and lifting out of poverty some 600 million people.

By succumbing to a sort of Sherlock Holmes syndrome, development experts miss what should be the main focus of economic policy in low-income countries, which is structural transformation—the transfer of human resources and capital to the most productive activities. Economic policy then becomes a sort of random exercise of expectations: governments are advised to simply achieve macroeconomic stabilization—that is, to meet some quantitative targets of monetary and fiscal policies—and engage in a very large number of reforms to liberalize the economy, with the hope that all this will eventually free up the magic of the market and provide the appropriate incentives to the private sector to invest in the "right" industries and create decent employment for the largest possible share of the labor force. In some ways, economic policy becomes a prayer (Monga 2014).

The fact that such contemplative approach to economic policy is still widely spread in African countries reflects the lingering effects of SAPs, and the hysteresis of a development agenda limited to the Washington Consensus policies. Yet, these policies were mainly designed to address macroeconomic imbalances experienced by developing countries in the 1980s. Macroeconomic stabilization and structural reforms were then necessary but certainly not sufficient conditions for prosperity. They were never really necessarily recipes for creating employment. Those African countries that have restricted their economic policy framework and their entire development strategy to such a laissez-faire approach may have achieved good general macroeconomic indicators—usually at a high social and political cost—but they often find themselves stranded in low-equilibrium situations when it comes to employment creation and inclusive growth. A case in point is that of Rwanda, which scores consistently among the top performers in almost all categories of the World Bank Doing Business Indicators while its economy does not seem to generate enough employment in the formal sector. The country has indeed made remarkable progress on structural reforms and improved its business environment. However, it has not devoted its limited resources to the kind of good labor-intensive industries that are consistent with its current endowment structure. As a result, broad-based prosperity has not reached large segments of its population. Fortunately, Rwanda is now implementing a more proactive employment-generation strategy.

Rwanda's case is not anecdotal. Several other countries, around the world have made good progress in improving their business environments without attracting the kind of private investment and foreign capital that they would need in industries and sectors that are employment-creating and consistent with their comparative advantage.

4 Economic Policy as Strategic Selection

What then needs to be done? The simple and generic answer to that difficult question is for African policymakers to learn from the past and the present, and rethink their economic strategies and policy frameworks in light of the large body of knowledge available. But learning is a challenging exercise. "Learning is not child's play, Aristotle said; we cannot learn without pain." (*Politics* V.v.). His wisdom was echoed by that of Ancient Rome's leading intellectual Seneca, who observed that "a day of the learned is longer than the life of the ignorant." (*Ad Lucilium* LXXVIII). African policymakers have been through a difficult decades-long journey trying to get the economic policy framework right. Their cumulative experiences through early structuralism, Washington Consensus policies, and lessons from both failed and successful development strategies observed elsewhere in the developing world, provide a wide knowledge basis for making better decisions in the future. While the specifics of the appropriate country policy framework would obviously vary across places and time to reflect the economy's particular endowment structure at any given moment and the country's revealed or latent comparative advantages, a few useful principles may be derived from experiences and practices.

It may be useful to start by drawing some basic but often ignored lessons from economic history. The long-run statistics put together by Angus Maddison indicate that for some 1400 years prior to the Industrial Revolution all countries in all regions of the world were low-income. There were no "industrialized" or "developing" economies since all nations were poor. Income per capita in any African country equaled that of the United States or Sweden. The divergence that started taking place in the late eighteenth century did not happen by chance: good ideas generated prosperity in some places while bad ideas took hold in others. Modern economic growth is a process of industrial, technological, and institutional upgrading that reflects the changing dynamics of comparative advantage and endowment structure. Ignoring it leads to policy prescriptions that defy the laws of economics and disappointments—most notably to what Ernest Aryeetey calls "negative diversification" (moving labor from low-productivity, subsistence agriculture, to low-productivity, informal services).

The standard argument underlying policymaking in Africa in recent decades was that markets were efficient, so there was no need for government to intervene either in the sector allocation of resources or in the choices of technique. And even if markets were not efficient, governments were not likely to improve matters. But as noted by Stiglitz et al. (2013), the 2008–2009 global crisis has shown that markets were not necessarily efficient and, indeed, there was a broad consensus that without strong government intervention—which included providing lifelines to certain firms and certain industries—the market economies of the United States and Europe may have collapsed. It is a mistake to blindly trust markets: some of the most important national and global policy objectives (equality of opportunity for all citizens, pollution control, climate change, etc.) are simply often not reflected in market prices.

The main challenge to development experts is to provide policymakers clearer road maps that are consistent with the key principle of economics: the allocation of scarce resources to industries, sectors, and geographical areas with the highest possible payoffs. This requires being rigorous selection of the industries, sectors, and places where to invest the country's limited resources, and careful targeting of the reform efforts. As Hausmann et al. (2008) show, not all binding constraints are equal—and nor do they deserve the same amount of efforts by policymakers. Development policy should aim at identifying actionable sets of actions and measures with a high probability of success. It should avoid offering laundry lists of reforms that are politically difficult to implement and may not immediately yield the intended results. Leaving economic policy to the imaginary wisdom of the market is taking a bet on the painful economics of chance, and approaching economics as a prayer. Prayers may or may not be answered. And different industries require different types of infrastructure. And since low-income country governments do not have the financial resources to accommodate all industries at once, it is best to work with the private sector to identify the industries where the economy has comparative advantage, and focus on providing specific infrastructure and transparent, limited, incentives that would allow these industries to grow.

One simply has to look at the list of recent success stories in African countries to understand the role that industrial policies have already been playing: textiles in Mauritius, apparel in Lesotho, cotton in Burkina Faso, cut flowers in Ethiopia, mango in Mali, and gorilla tourism in Rwanda all required that governments provide *different* types of infrastructure. The refrigeration facilities needed at the airport and regular flights to ship Ethiopia's cut flowers to the auctions in Europe are obviously quite different from the improvements required at the port facilities for textile exports in Mauritius. Similarly, the type of infrastructure needed for the garment industry in Lesotho is distinct from the one needed for mango production and export in Mali or for attracting gorilla tourism in Rwanda. Because fiscal resources and implementation capacity are limited, the government in each of those countries had to prioritize and decide which particular infrastructure they should improve or where to optimally locate the public services to make those success stories happen.

It should be acknowledged that the very words "selection" and "targeting" tend to immediately raise concerns about "industrial policies" by activist governments. Yet governments are "activist" in one sense or the other. The question is whether their "activism" is devoted to creating the optimal conditions for agents to strive and to addressing coordination and externalities that prevent the private sector to flourish and generate jobs, or to try to supporting firms and industries that are nonviable because they are inconsistent with the economy's comparative advantage. All governments in the world are constantly engaged in various forms of industrial policies—they take actions that favor certain industries more than others and therefore shape the sector allocation of the economy. In all countries, some industries, sectors, and even firms are favored within the legal framework and often heavily subsidized, in non-transparent ways. Everything governments do or choose not to do benefits or can be captured by vested interests.

It follows that the popular distinction between the so-called broad, neutral, "horizontal" industrial policy (one that does not target specific industries) and "vertical" policies (to support specific industries) is a myth: the line between the two is bound to be blurry. Even the most innocuous macroeconomic policy such as a particular exchange rate policy, which is presented not as "industrial policy" but as "neutral" and "broad-based," favors directly and indirectly some sectors, industries, social groups, and even regions to the detriment of others. Even when there is no change in exchange rate policy, some private agent groups benefit while others lose (Stiglitz et al. 2013). Likewise, infrastructure development is often presented as a suitable tool of economic policy because of its perceived "neutrality" vis-à-vis particular households or firms. Yet there is nothing neutral about the choice of infrastructure that a country needs at any given time, or where and when it should be built. These decisions always involve some political judgment about priorities, and therefore constitute industrial policies. The same is true for education, which is often mistakenly presented as "neutral." Therefore, the question is not *whether* any government should engage in industrial policy but *how* to do it right and in a transparent fashion.

In sum, all governments in the world, regardless of their politics, engage in industrial policies every single day. In fact, the entire budget exercise, which consists of submitting to Parliament a law that grants different tax rates and different expenditure levels, programs, and projects, to different industries, sectors, and regions, is itself industrial policy. Therefore, the policy challenge for Africa is not to engage in semantics debates about what industrial policy is but to come up with better guiding principles on how the economies of the continent could perform better in moving human, capital and financial resources out of subsistence sectors into higher-productivity sectors. For the process to be efficient, coordination issues and externalities issues must be addressed. Markets typically do not manage such structural transformations on their own well. And governments must play no more but no less of their facilitating role in the process.

5 Objectives of this Handbook: Tackling the Spence Paradox

The contributions assembled in this second volume of the *Oxford Handbook of Africa and Economics* present various narratives of the past, present, and future of economic policy in Africa. They focus on policies and practices, and try to offer critical analyses that make new and original arguments about a diverse set of topics. In conformity with the long tradition of the *Oxford Handbook* series, they survey essential questions and issues, weigh in on crucial debates, and advocate specific opinions. As evident in the clear stance taken by the editors themselves both in this introductory chapter and in their own contributions in this volume, the various chapters explore areas of controversy and offer new perspectives of interpretation. The general aim is to highlight and evaluate the most fruitful areas of current research and outline approaches and issues that seem most likely to define the field for subsequent generations.

One of the anonymous reviewers who evaluated the project for this book raised the important issue of intellectual independence and balance in coverage. She/he wrote: "While a balanced analysis of approaches without developing the defense of any particular paradigm would be very welcome this is not likely to be the outcome of a volume edited by a current World Bank employee and the former chief economist of the Bank. If I was to propose the volume, I would reduce the number of topics and get two essays on each one from an orthodox economist and one from a critic of orthodoxy. I realize this is not how handbooks are typically written ... " The reviewer also warned about the risk of giving too much prominence to mainstream economists, to the detriment of those who challenge the orthodoxy.

We hope that the collection of chapters and viewpoints expressed in this *Handbook* shows that it was perhaps a legitimate concern but the presupposition was unjustified. The mere affiliation with the World Bank or any other organization says very little about one's intellectual or ideological views. The broader point about mainstream-versus-unorthodox is probably more difficult to address satisfactorily. This volume was not conceived to settle political and ideological differences among economists working on Africa but to selectively highlight interesting and/or new knowledge. Moreover, the potential benefits of inviting contributors according to the binary categorization mainstream-versus-unorthodox were likely to be marginal since neither the so-called "orthodoxy" nor the "critique of orthodoxy" are monolithic intellectual entities.

It should also be noted that despite its scope the objective of this project was not to produce an encyclopedia of all scholars that have done important work on Africa. While many notable economists are part of the team, the main criteria for consideration of topics and contributors, similar to the one stated in the Introduction of Volume 1,[8] was whether they could highlight the various ways in which economic policies have been understood, designed, and implemented in Africa, and how Africa has influenced and enriched the global economic practices. These are obviously matters of judgment but we expect the reader of this volume to find included several major trends and different schools of thought about economic policy—including those seen as of the policy frameworks derived from mainstream economics.

The very broad theme of a project titled "Handbook of Africa and Economics" made it challenging to come up with an organizational structure that would do justice to its breadth and scope. There are infinite ways of categorizing subjects in a theme as large and complex. One could choose from JEL codes, to typical breakdowns of economic developments to popular categories of the discipline, to a series of thematic titles which reflect the specificity of African development, to something reflecting one's own interest. We finally chose to use categories that may reflect the some of the specificity of African development. We opted for a simple classification of topics that minimizes the risk of redundancy, though we also believe that no particular categorization would avoid some level of overlap, as this is more art than science.

This volume devoted to economic policies and practices is organized under five main headings and includes 49 chapters by economists who hold different perspectives on the various topics studied. The book begins with a collection of chapters on the macroeconomics of growth and structural transformation. Africa's growth experience and strategies are reassessed by some of the best experts in the field, and complemented by discussions of fiscal and monetary issues. Issues of natural resource management, debt and debt relief, savings and capital flight, and trade and regional integration are also addressed. The second section focuses on microeconomic and sectoral issues. It includes papers on the economics of land tenure; agricultural development; capacity building; gold mining and social change; new technologies; infrastructure; financial inclusion, financial market developments, and Islamic finance; and regulatory reform. The third section deals with some important institutional and social questions whose relevance to economic development is crucial: school enrollment, attainment, and returns

[8]   Volume 1 is devoted to "Concepts and Context."

to education; brain drain; health—with a focus on the economics of malaria; marriage; gender; and the media. The fourth section surveys the development players, focusing on the changing roles of non-governmental organizations, trade unions, development banks, international financial institutions, foreign investors, China (the most dominant bilateral lender on the African economic scene), and migrated workers who provide remittances to their home countries. The final section takes a look at the future. It surveys lessons in economic policy from Africa's experience, and sheds light on the long-term economic opportunities that the continent may derive from its unique demographic structure.

Africa is widely thought to be on the verge of take-off. The various perspectives in this volume might be useful in guiding Africa's new phase of development. The ultimate ambition of this *Handbook* is to contribute to solving what may be termed the Spence Paradox—the notion, discussed above, that despite many decades of progress in economic thinking and experiences in various development models, there is still not a clear roadmap ("recipe") that policymakers from low- and middle-income countries could follow to overcome the curse of poverty. We certainly hope that despite the often diverging approaches to economic policy adopted by the various contributors to this compendium, there is enough useful and relevant knowledge in the following pages to provide clear guidance to policymakers in Africa and elsewhere.

References

Barro, R.J. (1997). *Determinants of Economic Growth: A Cross-Country Empirical Study.* Cambridge, MA, MIT Press.

Besley, T., and P. Hennessy (2009). Letter to the Queen. London, British Academy, July 22.

Blanchard, O., Dell'Ariccia, G., and Mauro, P. (2013). Rethinking Macroeconomic Policy II: Getting Granular. IMF Staff Discussion Note 13/03.

Blanchard, O., Dell'Ariccia, G., and Mauro, P. (2010). Rethinking macroeconomic policy. *Journal of Money, Credit, and Banking,* 42(Suppl):199–215.

Blanchard, O.J. (2009). The state of macro. *Annual Review of Economics,* 1(1):209–228.

Commission on Growth and Development (2008). *The Growth Report: Strategies for Sustained Growth and Inclusive Development.* Washington, DC: World Bank.

Devarajan, S., and Fengler, W. (2013). Africa's economic boom: why the pessimists and the optimists are both right. *Foreign Affairs,* May–June:68–81.

Dornbusch, R., and Edwards, S, (eds) (1991). *The Macroeconomics of Populism in Latin America.* Chicago, University of Chicago Press.

Galbraith, J.K. (2009). Who are these economists, anyway? *Thought and Action,* Fall:87–97.

Galbraith, J.K., and Monga, C. (1994). Où en est l'économie du développement aujourd'hui? *Afrique 2000,* 18:67–75.

Guillaumont, P., and Guillaumont, S. (eds) (1994). *Adjustment and Development.* Paris: Economica.

Hadjimichael, M.T. et al. (1996). *Adjustment for Growth: The African Experience,* Occasional Paper 143, Washington, DC: IMF.

Hausmann, R., Rodrik, D., and Velasco, A. (2008). Growth diagnostics, in N. Serra and J.E. Stiglitz (eds), *The Washington Consensus Reconsidered: Towards a New Global Governance.* New York: Oxford University Press, pp. 324–354.

Kuznets, S. (1966). *Modern Economic Growth*. New Haven, CT: Yale University Press.

Lal, D. (1983). *The Poverty of Development Economics*. London, Institute of Economic Affairs.

Lin, J.Y. (2009). *Economic Development and Transition: Thought, Strategy and Viability*. New York: Cambridge University Press.

Lin, J.Y. (2013). *Against the Consensus: Reflections on the Great Recession*. New York: Cambridge University Press.

Lin, J.Y., and Monga, C. (2014). The evolving paradigms of structural change, in B. Currie-Adler, R. Kanbur, D. Malone, and R. Medhora (eds), *International Development: Ideas, Experience, and Prospects*. New York: Oxford University Press, pp. 277–294.

Lin, J.Y., and Monga, C. (2013). Comparative advantage: the silver bullet of industrial policy, in J.E. Stiglitz and J.Y. Lin (eds), *The Industrial Policy Revolution: the Role of Government Beyond Ideology*. New York: Palgrave Macmillan, pp. 19–38.

Lin, J.Y., and Monga, C. (2011). "Growth Identification and Facilitation: The Role of the State in the Dynamics of Structural Change". *Development Policy Review*, 29(3):259–310.

Lipumba, N.H.I. (1994). *Africa Beyond Adjustment*. Policy Essay no. 15. Washington, DC: Overseas Development Corporation.

McMillan, M., and Rodrik, D. (2011). *Globalization, Structural Change and Productivity Growth*. Cambridge, MA: Kennedy School of Government, Harvard University.

Mkandawire, T., and Soludo, C. (eds) (2003). *African Voices on Structural Adjustment*. Dakar: Codesria.

Monga, C. (2014). Truth is the Safest Lie: A Reassessment of Development Economics, Keynote Address at the Global Development Network Annual Conference, Accra, Ghana.

Monga, C. (2012). Shifting gears: igniting structural transformation in Africa. *Journal of African Economies*, 21(Suppl 2):ii19–ii54.

Monga, C. (2006). Commodities, Mercedes-Benz, and adjustment: an episode in west African history, in E.K. Akyeampong (ed.), *Themes in West Africa's History*. Oxford: James Currey, pp. 227–264.

Nankani, G. (2005). Foreword. *Economic Growth in the 1990s: Learning from a Decade of Reform*. Washington, DC: World Bank, pp. xi–xiii.

Olukoshi, A.O. (2003). The Elusive Prince of Denmark: Structural Adjustment and the Crisis of Governance in Africa, in T. Mkandawire and C. Soludo (eds), *African Voices on Structural Adjustment*. Dakar: Codesria, pp. 229–273.

Olukoshi, A.O. (1998). Extending the frontiers of structural adjustment research in Africa: some notes on the objectives of Phase II of the NAI Research Programme, in P. Gibbon and A.O. Olukoshi (eds), *Structural Adjustment and Socio-Economic Change in Sub-Saharan Africa: Some Conceptual, Methodological, and Research Issues*. Research report no. 102. Uppsala: Nordiska Afrikainstitutet, pp. 49–99.

Roubini, N. (2008). Rising Risk of a Systemic Financial Meltdown: The 12 Steps to Financial Disaster. *Marketoracle.co.uk*, February 12.

Stiglitz, J. (2013). The Lessons of the North Atlantic Crisis for Economic Theory and Policy. *Voxeu.org*, May 9.

Stiglitz, J. (2011). Rethinking macroeconomics: what failed and how to repair it. *Journal of the European Economic Association*, 9(4):591–645.

Stiglitz, J. (2010a). Contagion, liberalization, and the optimal structure of globalization. *Journal of Globalization and Development*, Volume 1, Issue 2, ISSN (Online), doi: 10.2202/1948-1837.1149.

Stiglitz, J. (2010b). Risk and global economic architecture: why full financial integration may be undesirable. *American Economic Review*, 100(2), May, pp. 388–392.

Stiglitz, J., Lin, J.Y., Monga, C., and Patel, E. (2013). *Industrial Policy in the African Context*, in J. Stiglitz, J.Y. Lin, and E. Patel (eds), *The Industrial Policy Revolution II: Africa in the 21st Century*. New York: Palgrave Macmillan, pp. 1–24.

World Bank (1994). *Adjustment in Africa: Reforms, Results, and the Road Ahead.* New York: Oxford University Press.

World Bank (1993). *The East Asian Miracle: Economic Growth and Public Policy.* New York: Oxford University Press.

World Bank (1989). *Sub-Saharan Africa: From Crisis to Sustainable Growth.* Washington, DC: World Bank.

PART I

THE MACROECONOMICS OF GROWTH AND STRUCTURAL TRANSFORMATION

CHAPTER 1

AFRICAN GROWTH STRATEGIES

The Past, Present, and Future

AUGUSTIN KWASI FOSU AND
ERIC KEHINDE OGUNLEYE

1.1 INTRODUCTION

FOLLOWING independence, African countries were determined to attain sustained economic growth and development. Ever since, several growth strategies have been conceived, developed, experimented with, and implemented. While many of these strategies bear country-specific attributes, there are common threads across countries; indeed several strategies are continental in focus. The changing growth strategies over the years have influenced the growth dynamics and trajectories of most countries on the continent. As in Rodrik (2007: 15), by "growth strategies" we mean "economic policies and institutional arrangements aimed at achieving economic convergence with the living standards in advanced countries."

During the pre-independence period, the growth strategy across Africa was dominated by colonial thinking. Growth initiatives focused on the production of agricultural produce in the African colonies for exporting to the Northern/Western markets. Infrastructure development policies were structured around this thinking. Thus, the construction of roads and railways focused on transporting agricultural products from the hinterland to the seashore for exporting. Shortly after independence, however, African countries had a new-found opportunity to develop their own growth strategies, especially beginning in the late 1950s. Most of the countries embraced Import Substitution Industrialization (ISI), with industrialization then perceived as the strongest catalyst for economic growth. Efforts were geared toward modernizing agriculture with a view, à la Arthur Lewis, to releasing surplus labor for gainful engagements in industrial activities.

Beginning in the late 1970s, the African economies generally began showing visible signs of inherent structural imbalances that demanded a change in growth strategy. Given these structural challenges, the Washington Consensus emerged, driven largely by the Bretton Woods Institutions (BWIs). A main feature of this strategy was the Structural Adjustment Program (SAP), involving macroeconomic stabilization with fundamental structural rebalancing. The policy instruments comprised mainly currency devaluation in the foreign exchange market and price liberalization in other markets, privatization of government-owned enterprises, and fiscal revenue cuts in non-productive and social activities such as subsidies in consumer goods and services. Overall, the strategy was designed to accord more prominent roles to market forces and to private enterprises.

Today, growth strategies are dictated by the emerging challenges and economic realities facing countries on the continent, prominent among which is global competitiveness for trade and investment. As globalization has tended to contribute to deindustrialization in many African countries, however, SAP seems to be losing favor on the continent. There now appears to be increasing interest in revisiting issues of industrial policy, especially in light of the phenomenal success of China and other East Asian and Pacific countries in the use of such policies. In addition, other emerging issues are expected to further shape the growth strategies on the continent over the medium to the longer term. These issues include: discoveries of crude oil in many African countries, changing global energy policy, development of alternatives to crude oil and gas, and concern for the environment.

This chapter provides a chronicle of African economic growth strategies. Following this introduction, section 2 examines the strategies during the pre-independence era, while section 3 provides an account of the strategies in early post-independence period. Section 4 focuses on the Washington Consensus. Section 5 then assesses the post-Washington Consensus growth strategies developed in reaction to the perceived failure of the Consensus to deliver the expected economic growth and development outcomes. Section 6 discusses the present growth strategies across African countries, dictated by current economic realities and the need for improved competitiveness in trade and investment. The concluding section then projects an outlook for optimal economic growth strategies in Africa for the medium-to-long term.

1.2 PRE-INDEPENDENCE GROWTH STRATEGIES

African countries had limited say in the conceptualization, development, or implementation of the growth strategies during pre-independence. The colonial governments were in charge, as in Ghana for instance, where they initiated four ten-year consecutive development plans and a five-year development plan shortly before independence (Green 1965): the First Ten-Year Plan (1920–1930), Second Ten-Year Plan (1930–1940), Third Ten-Year Plan (1946–1956), Fourth Ten-Year Plan (1951–1961), and Five-Year Plan (1951–1956).

In Nigeria, the first attempt at crafting a growth strategy began in 1946. As in Ghana, there was the Ten-year Plan of Development and Welfare for Nigeria. The primary aim of the strategy was to guide the use of financial resources made available to the colony by Britain for development and welfare of the colony (Adamolekun 1983).

In the 1950s, when most African countries were colonies of Great Britain and France, Arthur Lewis's two-sector growth model informed the economic development paradigm.

The model was developed originally for Latin America and Caribbean countries, and later adapted for African countries, with the view that developing countries should follow the path taken by the industrialized economies after the Second World War. As these colonies were believed to have very small domestic markets, insufficient capital, and shortage of skilled labor, it was thought that the best growth strategy would be infusion of physical and human capital as well as technology from the capital-rich industrialized countries. The intent was to produce for exporting to meet the industrialized countries' demand.

An alternative development strategy was being conceived at the Bandung Conference of 1955, held in Bandung, Indonesia. As the first large-scale meeting of Asian and African states, the conference was aimed at promoting Afro-Asian economic and cultural cooperation, contrary to the colonial strategy.

An important consensus from the above conference was the need for African and Asian developing countries to loosen their economic dependence on the leading industrialized nations. This goal was to be achieved through the exchange of experts and technical assistance among these countries, including the establishment of regional training and research institutes. Thus, this conference helped lay the foundation for the subsequent South–South economic relations and growth strategies that have become much more prominent in recent times.

1.3 EARLY POST-INDEPENDENCE GROWTH STRATEGIES

The leaders of African countries emerging from colonization saw an opportunity to chart a new course intended to improve the welfare of the people and expand economic opportunities (Sutton 1961). As more and more countries gained independence, efforts at finding self-designed policy options intensified. A two-pronged approach to growth was often adopted: continental and country-specific strategies.

1.3.1 Continental strategies

The Yaounde Convention was one of the earliest post-colonial North–South growth frameworks adopted in Africa. Signed in Yaounde in 1963 between 18 African countries, on the one hand, and six European Economic Community (EEC) States, on the other, the Convention made provision for cooperation in four core areas: trade; financial and technical cooperation; freedom of establishment, services, payments, and capital movements; and institutions. The subsequent Yaounde Convention that came into effect in 1971 affirmed the preferential trade relationship between the two parties and added development assistance and loan support for growth initiatives in African countries through the European Development Fund (EDF). However, most of the goals contained in these agreements were hardly realized. Furthermore, the Organization of African Unity (OAU), now the African Union (AU), was established in 1963, with the overriding purpose of promoting the unity and solidarity of African countries and act as a collective voice for the African continent on its quest for continental growth strategy. However, the preoccupation of the OAU became political rather than economic.

With the start of economic growth deterioration in the latter part of the 1970s, precipitated in great part by the oil supply shocks of the 1970s, Africans and African institutions began recognizing the inherent structural problems associated with the region's growth. Hence, several initiatives were put forth by African institutions intended to tackle the perceived growth challenges. The initiatives were based on the conviction that Africa faced acute socioeconomic problems that needed to be addressed urgently. Some of these self-developed continental growth strategies include the Monrovia Declaration of Commitments (MDC); Lagos Plan of Action (LPA); and Final Act of Lagos (FAL).

The MDC, adopted in July 1979, was aimed at reversing the adverse economic growth trend, with African leaders adopting a far-reaching regional approach based on collective self-reliance.[1] The LPA was adopted at the Second Extraordinary Session of the Heads of States and Governments of the OAU convened in July 1980 in Lagos, Nigeria. A highly comprehensive action that touched on virtually all areas of African economic life, the LPA clarified the MDC and proffered specific strategies for achieving the objectives set out in the Declaration (Onwuka and Seasy 1985), with the state as the primary agent for growth and development. Laudable as the Plan was, however, it suffered a major defect: blaming only the foreign colonial powers for Africa's economic crisis while exonerating the post-colonial African elites. The one-sided nature of the Plan led some observers to dub it as "economically illiterate" (Clapham 1996: 176).

The FAL was a resolution among African heads of state and government on the required action to achieve successful implementation of the previous strategies for the economic, social and cultural development of Africa (OAU 1980). The motivating factor behind this strategy was the belief that collectivity was the key to rapid, self-sustaining and self-reliant development of African member countries and Africa as a whole. In this instance, as in the case of the LPA, the state would be the engine of growth, and its role should thus be expanded. This strategy has its own inherent weaknesses and would soon result in structural imbalances that became obvious later on.

1.3.2 Country-specific strategies

While these continental growth strategies were ongoing, there were also country-specific growth initiatives that generally followed the colonial legacy in which economic planning was seen as the main route to sustained growth. Centralized planning initiatives, most of which were medium and long term in nature, became the main feature of immediate country-specific post-independence growth strategies in Africa, from the early 1960s until the 1980s. The main feature was that the government, especially at the national level, was responsible for the conceptualization, resource allocation and implementation of development planning. Ghana and Nigeria, for instance, initiated several successive national

---

[1] http://www.au.int/en/sites/default/files/assembly_en_17_20_july_1979_assembly_heads_state_government_sixteenth_ordinary_session.pdf (accessed Oct 15, 2013).

development plans during this period. However, limited resources and poor planning limited successes achieved from these strategies.

The growth philosophy during this period was dominated by the economic thinking that government should be responsible, not just for public policy, but also for the provision of goods and services. This school of economic thought was based on the belief that developing countries suffered from considerable market failure, necessitating an active role of government to overcome such an impediment. In pursuance of this thinking, most African governments created a number of state-owned enterprises to manage critical sectors, such as agriculture, water, electricity, and telecommunications. Indeed by the mid-80s, there were no less than 39 marketing boards in 18 African countries (van der Laan and van Haaren 1990). These institutions were meant to overcome market-failure problems due to, for instance, weak market infrastructure, poor market information leading to information asymmetry, and a weak regulatory framework.

Moreover, as African countries began to emerge from colonial rule, there was the general belief among the leaders, and consistent with the school of thought at the time, that industrialization was the key to economic growth and development. Thus Ghana, one of the first African countries to attain independence, engaged Arthur Lewis to fashion an industrial policy for the country at independence. Lewis' (1954) solution was rather straightforward: structurally transform the subsistence-based agricultural economy into a modern industrial economy and growth would naturally follow. This growth paradigm, consistent with the Prebisch (1950) and Singer (1950) hypothesis, that primary products would be subject to declining terms of trade, provided the guidance for many African countries to vigorously pursue the ISI strategy. Government, therefore, decided to be directly involved in production by establishing state-owned enterprises (SOEs).

Unfortunately, emphasis on industrialization led to a major neglect of agriculture and food production, leading to increasing net food imports. While the Lewis model assumed rising agricultural productivity over time, the reverse actually occurred in African countries generally. In the meantime, industrialization depended critically on foreign capital, whose price rose, necessitating the imposition of foreign exchange controls. This policy resulted in substantial overvaluation of the domestic currencies and, in turn, in both consumption and production inefficiencies. In particular, the implied urban-bias nature of the policies were detrimental to agricultural development and to the economy generally (Bates 1981). Meanwhile, governments found it necessary to protect the highly inefficient domestic industries, lest they wither and die under foreign competition. The policies entailed both high tariffs on imported items and substantial government subsidies.

Beginning in the mid-1970s, especially following the first oil supply shock in 1973 and again in 1979, most African economies began to experience serious macroeconomic imbalances. These experiences led many of the governments to borrow to finance their current account deficits, resulting eventually in external debt problems by the 1980s, especially when the commodity booms of the 1970s gave way to busts in the early 1980s (Greene 1989). In short, many African governments were simply broke and required external assistance. In 1981, the World Bank commissioned a study to provide a comprehensive analysis of the African economies, the "Berg Report," which would become the basis for the Washington-Consensus growth strategies for Africa.

1.4 THE WASHINGTON CONSENSUS

The *Accelerated Development in Sub-Saharan Africa: An Agenda for Action*, otherwise known as the Berg Report, published by the World Bank in 1981 laid the foundation for the Washington Consensus and provided an intellectual basis for the World Bank's growth strategy for Africa. The Report underscored the depth of the African economic crisis, discussed the underlying factors, and set forth new priorities and program orientations required to promote and sustain faster growth. The Report's policy prescriptions have been described by some critics as an antithesis of the LPA in every respect (Soludo 2003). It categorized the broad range of factors militating against growth in Africa into internal, external, and domestic policy inadequacies. The most critical policy shortcomings identified by the Report included inappropriate exchange rate and trade policies; overextension of public sector due to weaknesses in planning, decision-making and in management capacities; and tax, exchange rate, and pricing policies that were biased against agriculture.

The purpose of this growth strategy was to liberalize markets and restructure African economies, lessen the level of dominance of unproductive public sector investment, induce sustained growth with price stability, attain fiscal stability, and achieve sustainable balance of payments. Economic restructuring and limited government economic interventions constituted the key for attaining growth. In exchange, the BWIs would provide loans conditional on countries' adoption and implementation of the SAP policy prescriptions.

To improve economic growth, three policy prescriptions were put forward: (i) liberalize trade and exchange rate policies; (ii) increase efficiency of resource use in the public sector; and (iii) improve agricultural policies. Markets were to provide the main guidance for growth, contrary to the LPA. Emphasis was also placed on the need to improve agricultural development, through enhanced incentives and infrastructure services to farmers, while the liberalized foreign-exchange regime was intended to eventually eliminate the urban-bias policies under the control regime (e.g. Fosu 2008a; Fosu and O'Connell 2006). Also prescribed was the need to downsize the public sector, for the purpose of promoting sustainable budget deficits and improving efficiency.

There has been much criticism of the Washington Consensus, including a key charge that it lacked appropriate sequencing. It is argued, for instance, that while improved productivity and openness were prescribed, it might have been better to ensure that productivity, especially in agriculture, was first given maximum attention. Underdeveloped institutions should have also been improved, requiring appropriate strategies for a satisfactory measure of success, before opening up, so that sectors could withstand the pressures of international competition. This criticism seems particularly germane to the financial sector. Indeed, the World Bank has acknowledged this perverse sequencing as one of the major factors that constrained performance of Africa's financial sector following the reforms (Elbadawi 1992; World Bank 1994). While there were varying reactions to the Consensus, ranging from partial acceptance to full acceptance, most African governments generally accepted the Washington Consensus growth strategy, though the degree of implementation varied markedly across countries (Green 1998).

The literature is replete with the socioeconomic effects of implementation of the Washington Consensus growth strategy on African countries (Ali 2003; Bhattacharya and Titumir 2001; Bazaara 2001; Corbo and Rojas 1992; Centre for Development Research 1995; Elbadawi 1992; Green 1998). Adjustments in the reforms were necessitated by the dire economic situations faced by many people in the region. For example, there were widespread job losses resulting from the required downsizing of public spending, rationalization of public institutions, and large-scale privatization of public enterprises (Hettige et al. 1991; Mosley 1994; Mutasa 2000). In addition, it has been argued that the reductions in government expenditures affected the social sector disproportionately (Hussain et al. 2004; McGregor 2005). The Consensus has, furthermore, been blamed for deindustrialization (Lall 1995; Mytelka 1989; Mkandawire and Soludo 1999). Finally, oft-criticized is the "strait-jacket" nature of the Washington Consensus that forced governments to adopt reforms without adapting them to local conditions. Many of these criticisms were perceived to be valid and have, indeed, led to some modifications of the concept of the Consensus such as the "second-generation" reforms. For instance, Rodrik (2006, table 1) proposed the "augmented Washington Consensus," which includes institutional measures.

There are redeeming features of the Consensus, nonetheless. First, the deplorable states of the budgets for many African governments were usually such that both deindustrialization and diminution of social sector spending had already begun *prior* to the implementation of the reforms (Fosu 2012a, b). Second, institutional reforms take time, and many of these economies required immediate attention in terms of changing course. Third, the overall African evidence does not seem supportive of the hypothesis that public spending on education or health fell, at least disproportionately, in the 1980s or early 1990s from the pre-SAP levels (Fosu 2007, 2008b; Sahn 1992). Fourth, though a number of the African economies undergoing reforms did not appear to have recovered, many of those resilient to the global recession of the early 1990s had undertaken the reforms (Fosu 2012b).[2] Finally, the implementation of the Consensus did not necessarily entail complete rigidity. For example, when it became apparent that the SAP was generating significant social costs in Ghana, the Programme of Action to Mitigate the Social Costs of Adjustment (PAMSCAD) was initiated to soften such adverse impacts and to facilitate the reforms (Fosu 2013a).

1.5 THE POST-WASHINGTON CONSENSUS

Nevertheless, the perceived failure of the Washington Consensus strategy in achieving the desired growth and socioeconomic benefits in Africa led to the development of several growth strategies that served either as complements or alternatives. First, improving institutions became an important focus as an extension of the Consensus, as discussed above. Second, alternatives to the Consensus were championed primarily by the ECA and the OAU. Some of these are ECA's Priority Program for Economic Recovery (APPER)

---

[2] Fosu (2012b) identifies 12 countries as having bucked the dismal SSA growth in the early 1990s. Furthermore, most of these countries had undergone structural adjustment. Indeed, this feature appeared to dominate terms of trade improvements as a key contributor to the growth success.

covering 1986–1990; United Nations Program of Action for Africa's Economic Recovery and Development (UN-PAAERD) in 1986; African Alternative Framework to Structural Adjustment Programs for Socio-Economic Recovery and Transformation (AAF-SAP), launched in 1989; The African Charter for Popular Participation in Development and Transformation in 1990; Conference on Security, Stability, Development and Co-operation in Africa (CSSDCA) in 1990; New Agenda for Development of Africa (UN-NADAF) in 1991; African Economic Community in 1991; Millennium Partnership for the African Recovery Programme MAP in 1997; Compact for African Recovery in 2000; The Omega Plan in 2001; New Partnership for Africa's Development (NEPAD) and African Peer Review Mechanism (APRM) in 2001.

A look at these proposed strategies reveals that the immediate efforts at finding alternatives or modifications to the Washington Consensus was made by African institutions and Africans, complemented by the international partners. It is also noteworthy that all these proposed programs were redirecting policy actions toward the pillars of pre-SAP African policy initiatives, namely, the ownership of proposed reforms and polices. It became clear, therefore, that Africans would resume the primary role of crafting growth strategies and reforms for the continent, with the international community playing a supportive and complementary role. In this regard, the strategy was a reversal of the philosophy and methodology of the Washington Consensus, which is generally believed to have been crafted in Washington. Nonetheless, in all fairness, subsequent reform policies emanating from Washington seem to have responded, at least partially, to criticisms that greeted the initial version of the Washington Consensus. Indeed, it is quite likely that the above "home-grown" strategies may have influenced that transformation.

In fact, in response to the several criticisms that trailed it, the Washington Consensus growth strategy was adjusted (World Bank 1989). While the macroeconomic stabilization and liberalization goals remained unchanged, the policy was gradually refocused from short term to medium term and finally to long term. The timeframe for achieving the macroeconomic goals was extended, first, from three to five years and later to 15 years. Another milestone change involved giving SAP—the policy thrust of the strategy—a "human face," by mitigating its negative social consequences. More emphasis was placed on poverty reduction, thereby making absolute poverty reduction a goal for both macro and sectoral policies. The strategy moved from the "stabilization" phase between early 1980s to the mid-1980s, to the "adjustment with growth" phase that lasted throughout the rest of the 1980s, and later to the "adjustment with poverty alleviation" phase that started in the early 1990s.

Furthermore, the country-specific World Bank-assisted Poverty Reduction Strategy Papers (PRSP) was started in 1999, with poverty reduction as a major objective of the growth strategy. Championed by the BWIs, the core pillars of this strategy are macro- and structural policies, improved governance, prioritization of appropriate sectoral policies and programs, and realistic costing of proposed projects. The strategy was designed to ensure country-driven, participatory, broad-based, result-oriented, comprehensive, multidimensional, and development partner-coordinated process. One major challenge of this growth strategy, however, was the limited capacity of the African countries to draft the required reports to the specification of the BWIs. Circumventing the capacity constraint has required the BWIs' assistance, resulting in limited ownership of the contents of these reports and, hence, of the implied growth strategies by the respective countries.

Among the post-Washington Consensus strategies initiated in the African region, NEPAD is probably the most prominent. It acknowledged democracy and good governance as conditions for sustainable development and made provisions for setting up the APRM as a complementary part of the strategy.

NEPAD was a merger in July 2001 of the MAP, Compact, and Omega Plan. This initiative aims to extricate Africans and the continent from the malaise of underdevelopment and exclusion in the globalizing world. It further identified several priority sectors requiring special attention: physical infrastructure, especially roads, railways, and power systems linking neighboring countries; information and communications technology; human development, focusing on health and education, including skills development; agriculture; and promoting diversification of production and exports, with a focus on market access for African exports to industrialized countries. This initiative appears to have certain features of the Washington Consensus of fiscal expenditures rationalization and reliance on foreign countries as the major source of finance through foreign aid and debt relief.

Complementary to NEPAD, APRM is a voluntary review process that focuses on four thematic areas: democracy and political governance; economic governance and management; corporate governance; and socioeconomic development. By the end of 2013, 33 countries had signed up to the APRM,[3] with 17 having undertaken their first review and a few have started the second review process.[4] The process has contributed to improving investor confidence and promoting good governance among African countries. One key limitation of the APRM is its voluntary nature, leading to limited sign-up by countries, especially those with relatively poor governance, and weak political commitment to policy recommendations, especially of issues that are considered not to be politically expedient. Countries also lack capacity to implement the rigorous and highly demanding requirements of the APRM process.

1.6 CURRENT GROWTH STRATEGIES

Economic growth strategies in Africa are currently highly country-specific and mainly multidimensional, with a focus on not just growth but inclusive growth. The strategies are based on the political, social, economic, demographic, and environmental realities on the continent. The Washington Consensus and post-Washington Consensus growth strategies appear not to have succeeded in creating sufficient private-enterprise jobs to at least compensate for the job losses resulting from downsizing the public sector. They also appear not to have sufficiently reduced poverty as well as revamped and restructured the economies of African countries.

---

[3] Algeria, Angola, Benin, Burkina Faso, Cameroon, Chad, Congo (Brazzaville), Djibouti, Egypt, Ethiopia, Gabon, Ghana, Kenya, Lesotho, Liberia, Malawi, Mali, Mauritania, Mauritius, Mozambique, Niger, Nigeria, Rwanda, Sao Tome & Principe, Senegal, Sierra Leone, South Africa, Sudan, Tanzania, Togo, Tunisia, Uganda, and Zambia.

[4] Ghana, Rwanda, Kenya, South Africa, Algeria, Benin, Uganda, Nigeria, Burkina Faso, Mali, Mozambique, Lesotho, Mauritius, Ethiopia, Sierra Leone, Tanzania, and Zambia.

The need to improve on the weaknesses of these earlier growth strategies called for a change in course. In addition, economic realities facing Africa generally have undergone transformation. Today, most countries in the continent are globally integrated than ever before. The current growth strategies in many African countries are generally focused on structural and macroeconomic reforms, trade and investment promotion, and incentivizing the private sector to enable it play its role as the main driver of economic activities. In this regard, the present growth strategies may be viewed as modified and more pragmatic versions of the Washington Consensus, but which likely take into account certain country-specific realities. Current strategies put much emphasis on intra-continental trade, with special attention to the various regional trade groupings. Also important is the external trade relationship, with increasing importance of South–South trade, especially with China, but also with India and Brazil (Ogunleye 2012).

African governments are pursuing different growth strategies in the form of programs, projects and policies structured toward accelerating growth and development. Usually, these strategies are packaged as long-term visions. Beginning in the 1990s, many African countries began developing long-term economic blueprint intended for achieving middle income-country status, globally competitive economies with vibrant industrial and manufacturing sectors, and diversified economic base with improved job creation and poverty reduction. Generally, these strategies often propose sector-specific and macroeconomic targets, identify the pillars and enablers that would contribute to achieving the targets, outline the programs and projects and their costs, assign tasks to relevant government agencies, and identify the method for monitoring progress. These long-term visions are usually distilled into medium- to short-term interventions.

Prominent among the current long-term strategies is improving the business environment generally through institutional, legal and regulatory reforms. At continental and regional levels, initiatives targeted at reducing infrastructure deficiency include: Program for Infrastructure Development in Africa (PIDA),[5] covering the areas of ICT, energy, transport and water resources; Infrastructure Consortium for Africa (ICA), which focuses on scaling up infrastructure financing through private sector and donor participation; Africa Infrastructure Country Diagnostic; EU-Africa Infrastructure Trust Fund; G20 Infrastructure Action Plan; Trans-Sahara Gas Pipeline Project; and West African Gas Pipeline Project.

Many African countries have also developed growth strategies that mainstream the private sector as the main driver of growth, focusing on reforms aimed at cutting the cost of red tape. Several African countries have indeed made significant progress in this respect and have been listed among the top reformers on the World Bank Doing Business Indices.[6] A number of countries in the region are developing competitiveness, anti-trust and consumer protection policies aimed at strengthening private sector competition.[7] To ensure

---

[5] This strategy is jointly coordinated by the African Union (AU), New Partnership for Africa's Development (NEPAD), and African Development Bank (ADB).

[6] See World Bank Doing Business Reports of various years.

[7] There are both country-specific and regional examples in this respect. Some of the country-specific examples are Gambia, Ghana, Nigeria, and South Africa, while regional examples are COMESA, ECOWAS, SADC, and UEMOA.

an effective growth strategy that promotes inter-generational equity in the exploitation and utilization of natural resources, several resource-rich African countries such as Angola, Botswana and Nigeria have established Sovereign Wealth Funds.

Given the global environmental challenge and specific vulnerabilities of African countries to climate change and other environmental concerns, "green" growth is fast becoming an emerging trend in the African growth strategy. It involves addressing issues of pollution, environmental degradation and climate change challenges. Many countries have embraced this growth strategy by incorporating environmental considerations into their wider growth strategies.

Another prominent feature of the current growth strategy is the increased regional, South-South and North–South integration through trade, investment and aid. With high recognition of the need for increased intra-regional trade and investment and active economic cooperation, almost all African countries are members of at least one regional economic community. The desire to enhance the contribution of trade to development, while also making trade arrangements WTO compatible, many African countries have lowered trade barriers among each other, culminating in the comprehensive and interim EU–ACP economic partnership arrangements (EPA), beginning January 2008 and designed to cover a period of 20 years.[8] A similar arrangement with a continent-wide focus is the African Growth and Opportunities Act (AGOA) and the New Partnership for Africa's Development (NEPAD). While the AGOA provides an opportunity for African countries to further open their economies and build stronger market integration with the US markets, NEPAD provides an "integrated strategic framework" within which member countries of the AU collectively and individually bring about a holistic socioeconomic development of the continent through partnership with the North.

Increased economic ties with other Southern countries outside the continent have also taken center stage in the current African growth strategies. Brazil, China, and India have been very active in this respect. China especially has been acting as both a development and business partner in these strategies (Ogunleye 2011). Through loans, financial assistance and direct investment, African countries have generally integrated China into their growth strategies. It is not uncommon for such countries to receive substantial project-specific and infrastructure development support from China in pursuance of implementing their annual budgets. China has initiated the Forum for China–Africa Cooperation (FOCAC) as a platform for strengthening its cooperation and partnership with Africa. In addition, there is the African–Asian Business Forum that provides a more general framework for the developing Asian countries' partnership with African countries, intended to promote growth through business cooperation.

---

[8] As of November 2013, In West Africa, Cote d'Ivoire and Ghana had initialed the interim EPA with EU in 2007. While the former signed in 2008, the latter has not signed and none has been ratified. The regional agreement is currently being negotiated. In Central Africa, Cameroon is the only country that has signed the interim EPA, in 2009. The Agreement is yet to be ratified. Regional negotiations are focusing, among other things, on market access, services and investment, rules of origin, cultural cooperation, and fiscal impact. In Eastern Africa, Burundi, Rwanda, Tanzania, Kenya, and Uganda initialed an EPA framework that focuses on trade in goods but has not signed the Agreement. In Southern Africa, Botswana, Lesotho, Swaziland and Mozambique have signed the interim EPA while Namibia initialed but has not signed. Negotiations are still ongoing in all the regions.

1.7 OUTLOOK AND PROSPECTS FOR FUTURE AFRICAN GROWTH STRATEGIES

Several issues are expected to shape the future of growth strategies in Africa. First is the concern for the environment that demands shifting focus toward green growth. The second involves discoveries and development of alternatives to crude oil and natural gas such as shale gas in the USA, Australia, Canada, and China. Third is the heavy investment in developing electric automobiles by advanced economies, with the potential for significant reductions in global demand for crude oil. Fourth, increased global competition for trade and investment might imply alternative growth strategies by African countries, in order to ensure greater competitiveness. Finally, there are the issues concerning the implications of the nature of the external environment for crafting optimal trade strategies, including external assistance, trade partnerships, and WTO rules.

African countries have generally been incorporating global concerns for the environment into their respective growth strategies. In the medium to the long term, it is expected that an increasing number will actually mainstream green growth in these strategies. The leadership and direction being provided by leading African institutions such as the African Development Bank and UN agencies are expected to further deepen this process.

Recent discoveries of shale oil and gas in large quantities in the USA, Canada, and China, as well as heavy investment in developing hybrid and electric automobiles by technologically advanced economies, would redefine the global energy market demand for crude oil and natural gas. These developments will likely have serious implications for the outlook of growth strategies in Africa, especially for the growing number of net oil exporters on the continent. Hence, African countries will do well to rethink their crude oil-reliant strategies. One future direction would be to craft growth policies that encourage development of industrial and manufacturing value chains involving crude oil and petroleum products. In addition, growth strategies need to define clear policies for preventing Dutch disease and other associated challenges, such as the resource curse,[9] and the suboptimal inter-temporal resource allocation usually associated with natural resources.

The increased global competition for trade and investment and limited global competitiveness of African countries in this process are reshaping growth toward regional inward-looking strategies. More than ever before, African countries are emphasizing intra-regional trade and investment and increased regional economic integration. The prospect of this strategy is very high given the significant progress over the recent past. In the Central African Economic and Monetary Community (CEMAC), West African Economic and Monetary Union (WAEMU), ECOWAS, COMESA, EAC, and SADC, significant progress has been recorded in harmonizing markets, as well as achieving single currency unions and macroeconomic convergence (IMF 2013a, b; AfDB 2011; ECA/AU 2013; Davoodi 2012; and Belle 2010).

While external aid has played an important role in support of especially post-conflict and fragile countries, and of reforms in many countries on the continent, it cannot be relied

---

[9] For a fascinating paper on the Nigeria case, see Sala-i-Martin and Subramanian (2013).

upon for long-term development (Fosu 2013c). Thus, African countries should provide a clear strategy for improving domestic resource mobilization and utilization. Of course, this does not imply that external aid ought to be discounted. Development partners indeed have the commitment under the Monterrey Consensus to provide support at the target level of 0.7% of their respective GNIs as aid to developing countries. In addition, given their own historical experiences in development practices, it would be unfair for developed countries to now restrict the policy space for lagging developing countries through TRIPs and TRIMs under WTO (Fosu 2013d).

The current trend suggests that African countries will be more regionally inward look-ing and self-reliant in their conceptualization, development, and implementation of growth strategies in the continent. Furthermore, while regional integration will facilitate trade among African countries, policy harmonization may be required for increasing the bargain-ing power of these countries in dealing with external agents by minimizing especially the supply elasticity of investment and other services to the continent (Fosu 2004). Concern for the environment is also expected to become more prominent in the continental growth strategies, and so will be South–South economic relations.

Going forward, growth strategies in Africa should focus more on the sustainability and inclusivity of growth. Unfortunately, growth resurgence over the last decade or so has not sufficiently translated into job creation, especially for youth, who have become increasingly dominant in the population distribution. Nor has the growth been sufficiently translated to human development including poverty reduction, despite significant progress on growth in many African countries. This outcome suggests that the level of inequality requires greater attention in Africa than has been accorded so far (Fosu 2009, 2010a, b). Thus, African coun-tries must at least stay on course with structural reforms and macroeconomic stability, while ensuring the necessary quality of human capital development, complemented with physi-cal infrastructure development. Such a strategy would enhance the role of the private sector as the main agent of growth, with the public sector guiding the economic outcome toward greater equity. To achieve such an outcome would require not only appropriate regulatory policies but an optimal fiscal allocation, which would in turn call for the quality of governance that ensures that economic efficiency does not give way to political expediency (Fosu 2013b).

References

Adamolekun, L. (1983). *Public Administration: A Nigerian and Comparative Perspective*. London: Longman.

AfDB (2011). *Regional Integration Strategy Paper 2011—2015*. Tunis: African Development Bank.

Ali, A.G. (2003). Structural adjustment programs and poverty in sub-Saharan Africa: 1985–1999, in T. Mkandawire and C.C. Soludo (eds), *African Voices on Structural Adjustment*. Dakar: CODESRIA/IDRC.

Bates, R.H. (1981). *Markets and States in Tropical Africa*. Berkeley: University of California Press.

Bazaara, N. (2001). Impact of Liberalisation on Agriculture and Food Security in Uganda. Final Report for the National Steering Committee.

Belle, M. (2010). Regional Economic Integration in SADC: Progress, Prospects and Statistical Issues for Monetary Union. IFC Bulletin No. 32, Basel: Bank for International Settlements, pp. 85–95.

Bhattacharya, D., and Titumir, R. (2001). *Bangladesh's Experience with Structural Adjustment: Learning from a Participatory Exercise*. Dhaka, Bangladesh: SAPRI, pp. 94–115.

Centre for Development Research (1995). *Structural Adjustment in Africa: A Survey of the Experience*. Copenhagen: Centre for Development Research.

Clapham, C. (1996). *Africa and the International System*. Cambridge: Cambridge University Press.

Corbo, V., and Rojas, P. (1992). World Bank-supported adjustment programs: country performance and effectiveness, in V. Corbo, V.S. Fischer, and S. Webb (eds), *Adjustment Lending Revisited: Policies to Restore Growth*. Washington, DC: The World Bank.

Davoodi, H.R. (2012). *The East African Community After Ten Years Deepening Integration*. Washington, DC: International Monetary Fund.

ECA/AU (2013). Assessment of progress on regional integration in Africa. Meeting of the Committee of Experts of the Sixth Joint Annual Meetings of the ECA Conference of African Ministers of Finance, Planning and Economic Development and AU Conference of Ministers of Economy and Finance, Abidjan, Côte d'Ivoire, 21–24 March.

Elbadawi, I. (1992). World Bank Adjustment Lending and Economic Performance in Sub-Saharan Africa in the 1980s: A Comparison of Early Adjusters, Late Adjusters, and Non-adjusters. Policy Research Working Papers WPS 1001. Washington, DC: The World Bank.

Fosu, A.K. (2004). The social impact of globalization: the scope for national policies, in M. Vivarelli and E. Lee (eds), *Understanding Globalization, Employment and Poverty Reduction*, ILO Volume. New York: Palgrave/Macmillan, pp. 327–348.

Fosu, A.K. (2007). Fiscal allocation for education in sub-Saharan Africa: implications of the external debt service constraint. *World Development*, 35(4):702–713.

Fosu, A.K. (2008a). Anti-growth syndromes in Africa: a synthesis of the case studies, in B. Ndulu, S. O'Connell, R. Bates, P. Collier, and C. Soludo (eds), *The Political Economy of Economic Growth in Africa 1960–2000*. Cambridge: Cambridge University Press, pp. 137–172.

Fosu, A.K. (2008b). Implications of external debt-servicing constraint for public health expenditure in sub-Saharan Africa. *Oxford Development Studies*, 36(4):363–377.

Fosu, A.K. (2009). Inequality and the impact of growth on poverty: comparative evidence for sub-Saharan Africa. *Journal of Development Studies*, 45(5):726–745.

Fosu, A.K. (2010a). The effect of income distribution on the ability of growth to reduce poverty: evidence from rural and urban African economies. *American Journal of Economics and Sociology*, 69(3):1034–1053.

Fosu, A.K. (2010b). Does inequality constrain poverty programs? Evidence from Africa. *Journal of Policy Modeling*, 32(6):818–827.

Fosu, A.K. (2012a). Ghana: the development record and the Washington Consensus, in E. Aryeetey, S. Devarajan, R. Kanbur, and L. Kasekende (eds), *Oxford Companion to the Economics of Africa*. Oxford: Oxford University Press.

Fosu, A.K. (2012b). The African economic growth record, and the roles of policy syndromes and governance, in A. Noman, K. Botchwey, H. Stein, and J. Stiglitz (eds), *Good Growth and Governance in Africa: Rethinking Development Strategies*. Oxford: Oxford University Press, pp. 175–218.

Fosu, A.K. (2013a). Country role models for development success: the case of Ghana, in A.K. Fosu (ed.), *Achieving Development Success: Strategies and Lessons from the Developing World*. Oxford: Oxford University Press, pp. 265–283.

Fosu, A.K. (2013b). Growth of African economies: productivity, policy syndromes and the importance of institutions. *Journal of African Economies*, 22(4):523–551.

Fosu, A.K. (2013c). Impact of the global financial and economic crisis on development: whither Africa? *Journal of International Development*, 25(8):1085–1104.

Fosu, A.K. (2013d). Development success: historical accounts from the more advanced countries, in A.K. Fosu (ed.), *Development Success: Historical Accounts from More Advanced Countries*. Oxford: Oxford University Press, pp. 1–19.

Fosu, A.K., and O'Connell S.A. (2006). Explaining African economic growth: the role of anti-growth syndromes, in F. Bourguignon and B. Pleskovic (eds), *Annual Bank Conference on Development Economics (ABCDE)*. Washington, DC: World Bank, pp. 31–66.

Green, R. H. (1965). "Four African development plans: Ghana, Kenya, Nigeria and Tanzania". *The Journal of Modern African Studies*, 3(2): 249–279.

Green, R.H. (1998). A cloth untrue: the evolution of structural adjustment in sub-Saharan Africa. *Journal of International Affairs*, 52(1):207–232.

Greene, J. (1989). The external debt problem of sub-Saharan Africa. *IMF Staff Papers*, 36(4):836–874.

Hettige, H., Steel, W.F., and Wayem, J.A. (1991). The impact of adjustment lending on industry in African countries. Industry Series Paper No. 45, Washington, DC: World Bank.

Hussain, M.N., Mohammed, N., and Kameir, E.M. (2004) Resource mobilization, financial liberalization, and investment: the case of some African countries, in T. Mkandawire and C.C. Soludo (eds), *African Voices on Structural Adjustment*. Dakar: CODESRIA/IDRC.

IMF (2013a). Central African Economic and Monetary Community: Staff Report on Common Policies for Member Countries. IMF Country Report No. 13/322.

IMF (2013b). West African Economic and Monetary Union: Staff Report on Common Policies for Member Countries. IMF Country Report No. 13/92.

Lall, S. (1995). Structural adjustment and African industries. *World Development*, 23(12):2019–2031.

Lewis, W.A. (1954). Economic development with unlimited supplies of labor. *Manchester School of Economic and Social Studies*, 22(2):139–191.

McGregor, S. (2005). Structural adjustment programmes and human well-being. *International Journal of Consumer Studies*, 29(3):170–180.

Mkandawire, T., and Soludo, C. (1999). *Our Continent Our Future: African perspectives on Structural Adjustment*. Dakar: CODESRIA; Trenton, NJ: Africa World Press.

Mosley, P. (1994). Decomposing the effects of structural adjustment: the case of sub-Saharan Africa, in R. Van Der Hoeven and F. Van Der Kraaij (eds), *Structural Adjustment and Beyond in Sub-Saharan Africa*. The Hague: Ministry of Foreign Affairs.

Mutasa, C. (2000). *A Critical Appraisal of the World Bank Policies in Developing Countries*. Zimbabwe: Poverty Reduction Forum and Institute of Development Studies.

Mytelka, L. (1989). The unfulfilled promise of African industrialization. *African Studies Review*, 32(3):77–137.

OAU (1980). *The Lagos Plan of Action for the Economic Development of Africa, 1980–2000*. Addis Ababa: Organization of African Unity.

Ogunleye, E.K. (2011). The EU and China: friends or foes for sustainable regional infrastructure development and resource extraction in Africa? in J. Men and B. Barton (eds), *China and the European Union in Africa: Partners or Competitors?* Farnham: Ashgate.

Ogunleye, E.K. (2012). Trade and regional integration in Africa: trends, patterns and longer-range future prospects, in R.D. Thrasher and A. Najam (eds), *The Future of South-South Economic Relations*. London: Zed Books.

Onwuka, R., and Seasy, A. (1985). *The Future of Regionalism in Africa*. Basingstoke: Macmillan.

Prebisch, R. (1950). *The Economic Development of Latin America and Its Principal Problems.* New York: United Nations.

Rodrik, D. (2006). Goodbye Washington Consensus, hello Washington confusion? A review of the World Bank's economic growth in the 1990s: learning from a decade of reform. *Journal of Economic Literature,* XLIV(December):973–987.

Rodrik, D. (2007). *One Economics, Many Recipes: Globalization, Institutions, and Economic Growth.* Princeton: Princeton University Press.

Sahn, D.E. (1992). Public expenditures in sub-Saharan Africa during a period of economic reform. *World Development,* 20(5):673–693.

Sala-I-Martin, X., and Subramanian, A. (2013). Addressing the natural resource curse: an illustration from Nigeria. *Journal of African Economies,* 22(4):570–615.

Singer, H.W. (1950). U.S. foreign investment in underdeveloped areas: the distribution of gains between investing and borrowing countries. *American Economic Review, Papers and Proceedings,* 40:473–485.

Soludo, C.C. (2003). In search of alternative analytical and methodological frameworks for an African economic development model, in T. Mkandawire and C.C. Soludo (eds), *African Voices on Structural Adjustment.* Dakar: CODESRIA/IDRC.

Sutton, F. X. (1961). Planning and rationality in the newly independent states in Africa. *Economic Development and Cultural Change,* 10:42–50.

Van der Laan, H.L., and van Haaren, W.T.M. (1990). African Marketing Boards Under Structural Adjustment: The Experience of Sub-Saharan Africa During the 1980s. Working Papers No 13. Leiden: African Studies Centre.

World Bank (1981). *Accelerated Development in Sub-Saharan Africa: An Agenda for Action.* Washington, DC: World Bank.

World Bank (1989). *Special Program of Assistance: Proposal for the Second Phase.* Washington, DC: World Bank.

World Bank (1994). *Adjustment in Africa: Reforms, Results, and the Road Ahead,* Washington, DC: The World Bank.

CHAPTER 2

···

AFRICA'S QUIET REVOLUTION

···

MARGARET MCMILLAN AND
KENNETH HARTTGEN

2.1 INTRODUCTION

···

IT has been well documented that structural change—that is, the reallocation of economic activity away from the least productive sectors of the economy to more productive ones—is a fundamental driver of economic development (Herrendorf and Rogerson 2012; Duarte and Restuccia 2010). In particular, the movement of labor out of less productive semi-subsistence agriculture and into the more productive sectors of manufacturing or services in both urban and rural areas is needed to sustain increases in overall productivity and living standards and drive poverty reduction, both from a theoretical standpoint and from actual experiences of countries throughout stages of their development.[1] In other words, countries that pull themselves out of poverty also exhibit positive structural change.[2]

Until very recently, African countries have been largely absent from empirical analyses in this literature, and thus there is little evidence on how structural change has played out in African countries since achieving independence half a century ago. A major reason for this absence is data, as economic data to undertake such analysis has been largely unreliable or non-existent for most African countries. Importantly, data issues still constrain the analysis of structural change in Africa. Recent attempts to shed new light on growth using alternative sources of data (cite Alwyn Young 2012 and de Vries, Timmer, and de Vries 2013). are welcome but much more could be done. These issues are important enough to warrant a separate section in this chapter called "The Data Problem."

---

[1] See Herrendorf and Rogerson (2011) for an overview of and many references on this subject.

[2] The converse is not true, however: all countries with structural change do *not* also achieve poverty reduction. Structural change into protected or subsidized sectors comes at the expense of other activities, and is therefore not associated with sustained growth out of poverty for the population as a whole. Structural change is effective at reducing poverty only when people move from lower into higher productivity activities.

A deeper reason for the lack of research on structural change in Africa is poverty itself. Until recently, few African countries have enjoyed the sustained economic growth needed to trace out the patterns of structural transformation achieved in earlier decades elsewhere. The start of the twenty-first century saw the dawn of a new era in which African economies grew as fast or faster than the rest of the world. Examining the recent process of structural change in Africa, and how it has interacted with economic growth, could yield enormous benefits. For one, the theory and stylized facts of structural change offer several predictions about the allocation of the factors of production for countries at different stages of development and, as sub-Saharan Africa is now by far the poorest region of the world, including African countries could enrich the current understanding of the mechanisms that drive structural change. Perhaps more importantly, and most pertinent to this paper, is that such an analysis could offer insight regarding the continent's recent economic performance—both its prolonged period of weak economic growth since the 1970s, as well as the period of stronger growth over the past decade.

We begin our analysis by asking whether it is reasonable to compare structural change in Africa to other regions during the same time period. Average incomes in Africa are significantly lower than in East Asia, Latin America, and all other regions and, if countries at different stages of development tend to exhibit different patterns of structural change, the differences between Africa and other developing regions may be a result of their different stages of development. Motivated by this possibility, we explore how the *level* of employment shares across sectors in African countries compare to those in other countries, controlling for levels of income. We find that African countries appear to fit seamlessly into the pattern observed in other countries. In other words, given current levels of income per capita in Africa, the share of the labor force in agriculture, manufacturing and industry is roughly what we would expect.

Our analysis also reveals that African countries stand to benefit the most from structural transformation, and have begun to reap those gains. Indeed, McMillan and Rodrik (2011) (hereafter, M&R) find a significantly positive correlation between a country's level of development and its' sectoral variation in productivity levels; in other words, the poorer a country is, the wider is the gap between the most productive and least productive sectors in that country. There is thus a potential for enormous economic gain in African countries from reallocating activity from low to high productivity sectors. For reasons not well understood, this potential was not realized over much of the period between 1960 and 2010. However, more recent work demonstrates that structural change in Africa has begun to contribute to Africa's growth (MR&V 2013; De Vries et al. 2013).

The reasons for the turnaround are not well understood but there are a number of recent events that could have made this possible. For example, several African countries were still consolidating structural adjustment well into the late 1990s (Thurlow and Wobst 2004). And by 2000, a number of countries were well positioned to take advantage of the commodity price boom that began in 2000 and that persists to this day. Indicators of governance for many countries in Africa began to pick up in the early 1990s and continued to rise between 2000 and 2010. And the incidence of civil conflict has fallen over this same period. African countries have witnessed commodity booms before but it may be that the combination of improved governance and the improvement in external factors have come together in a way that benefits more people than it has in the past.

To explore this possibility, we use information on occupation, gender, age, employment status and location from the Demographic and Health Surveys (DHS). The DHS are nationally representative surveys designed to collect detailed information on child mortality, health, and fertility, as well as on household's durables and quality of the dwelling. However, these surveys are also designed to collect information on education, employment status and occupation of women and men between the ages of 15 and 49. Importantly, the design and coding of variables (especially on the type of occupation, educational achievements, households assets, dwelling characteristics) are generally comparable across countries and over time. Finally, the sample includes considerable regional variation. Ninety surveys are available for 31 African countries and 92 surveys for 37 non-African countries and for most countries multiple surveys (up to six) have been conducted between 1990 and 2011.

Using the DHS and focusing exclusively on Sub-Saharan Africa, we find that for the period 1992–2012: (i) labor force participation of both men and women increased; (ii) there was a shift in male occupations away from agriculture and services to manufacturing and; (iii) there was a shift in female occupations away from services toward agriculture and manufacturing. By contrast, we find that in the earlier period which covers 1990–1999: (i) labor force participation of both men and women fell and; (ii) there was a shift in male occupations into services and agriculture. Given that many fewer women report working, these trends are broadly consistent with our previous findings: the majority of workers in the African countries for which we have data are reporting that they are earning more of their income from manufacturing and services and less from agriculture. We also find that a much larger share of men report working in manufacturing than is currently reported in national statistics.

The rest of this paper is organized as follows. In section 2 we place our discussion of structural change in historical context and characterize the nature of structural change in Africa over the period 1960–2010. We show that countries in Africa are where we would expect them to be given their current levels of income. We also present evidence that structural change contributed positively to economic growth in Africa between 1960 and 1975, negatively to economic growth between 1975 and 2000 and then positively to economic growth between 2000 and 2010. In section 3 we discuss the "data problem" and describe our empirical approach to understanding structural change in Africa. Section 4 explores potential explanations for the patterns we observe in Africa from 1992–2012. Section 5 concludes by interpreting the results in a broader context and highlighting directions for future research.

2.2 BACKGROUND: STRUCTURAL CHANGE IN AFRICA AND ELSEWHERE

Traditionally, the concept of structural change has been framed in terms of reallocation of economic activity between three broad sectors—agriculture, manufacturing and services—which accompanies and facilitates the process of economic growth. In early stages of economic development, people devote a disproportionate share of their abundant labor and scarce capital to agriculture and other "traditional" activity, since they have no other way to feed themselves and meet basic needs. As these resource-poor rural people accumulate capital, diminishing returns on the limited agricultural land lead them to invest an increasing share of their capital and labor in other activities. Increases in national income and purchasing power also help to pull workers and their savings out of agriculture into more "modern" skill- and capital-intensive sectors like manufacturing and services. These more dynamic sectors—particularly manufacturing, but also services such as financial interme-diation, wholesale and retail distribution, education, and healthcare—can grow much more rapidly than agriculture because they are not constrained by the available farmland, and also because they face more elastic demand.

The process of structural change is integral to the ability of developing countries to pull themselves out of poverty, and was recognized as such by early development econo-mists such as Lewis (1955). Lewis and others observed the historical reallocation of work-ers from traditional agriculture to "modern" industry in Europe, North America, and East Asia, and predicted that other regions would follow the same development process. Duarte and Restuccia (2010) find that structural change has indeed played a substantial role in the productivity catch-up of developing countries in their sample—relative to the USA—over the period 1950–2006. As predicted, the gains are particularly dramatic in the sectors with international trade. They find that productivity differences in agriculture and industry between the rich and developing countries have narrowed substantially, while productivity in services has remained significantly lower in the developing coun-tries relative to rich countries. Thus, developing countries with the most rapid growth rates have typically reallocated the most labor into high-productivity manufacturing, allowing aggregate productivity to catch up.[3] Duarte and Restuccia (2010) conclude that rising productivity in industry, combined with structural change out of agriculture and into industry, explains 50% of the catch-up in aggregate productivities among developing countries over their sample period of 1950–2006. Notably, this sample does not include any African countries.

More recent work by Rodrik (2012) underscores the importance of this type of structural change. Using a large panel of countries, he finds that since 1960 formal sector manufac-turing has exhibited *unconditional* convergence in labor productivity regardless of country- or regional-level factors. This finding is important because it suggests that the destination sector in which less developed countries eventually catch up with the productivity levels of developed countries is manufacturing.

Some stylized facts of the pattern of structural change over the course of development have emerged from this literature. As countries grow, the share of economic activity in agriculture monotonically decreases and the share in services monotonically increases. The share of activity in manufacturing follows an inverted U-shape: increasing during low stages of development as capital is accumulated, then decreasing for high stages of development where higher incomes drive demand for services and labor costs make manufacturing difficult. Herrendorf et al. (2011) document this pattern for a panel of mostly developed countries over the past two centuries, and Duarte and Restuccia (2010) document a similar process of structural change among 29 countries over the period 1956–2004.

---

[3] Conversely, where the manufacturing sector stagnates and structural transformation involves primarily reallocation of workers into lower productivity sectors, aggregate productivity is slower, especially among developing countries whose productivity in services remains low—both relative to agriculture in other countries and to other sectors within the country.

With this insight in mind, we turn to an exploration of the evolution of the distribution of employment between sectors across levels of income experienced in Africa and how it compares to the patterns seen historically in other regions over the course of development. Using the patterns seen in other regions historically as a baseline, we will be able to gauge the extent to which structural change in Africa compares to what we would "expect" based on its income levels. To this end, we started by aggregating the nine sectors in the database used by McMillan and Rodrik (2011) into Agriculture, Industry and Services by adding manufacturing, mining, construction, and public utilities to make "Industry," adding wholesale and retail trade, transport and communication, finance and business services, and finally community, social, personal, and government services to create "Services" and leaving "Agriculture" as-is.[4] To this sample, we add an additional ten countries for which we were able to obtain data on employment shares for these three sectors[5]. Our measure of "development" is log GDP per capita in international dollars from Maddison (2010).

Figure 2.1 plots employment shares in agriculture, industry and services, respectively, on the y-axis and log GDP per capita on the x-axis for the 19 African countries in our sample for the years 1990 and 2005. The share of employment in agriculture decreases, and that in services increases, monotonically with income, and the share in manufacturing also monotonically increases. In other words, recent patterns of structural change in Africa fit into the stylized facts of other regions' historical development. Note that Industry does not follow the inverted-U shape documented in Herrendorf et al. (2011) and Duarte and Restuccia (2010), but this is because each country's GDP per capita is below the threshold at which the rate of change of Industry's employment share changes from positive to negative.[6]

Though Figure 2.1 suggests the patterns of reallocation between agriculture, industry and services are qualitatively similar to the stylized facts based on the experience of other regions, it may be that they differ quantitatively. For instance, though Figure 2.1 confirms that the agricultural employment share and services employment share in Africa decrease and increase, respectively, with level of income, it could be that the *level* of agricultural or services employment in Africa is higher than in other regions (the latter being argued in Badiane 2011), perhaps because of resource endowments or productivity levels. To investigate this question, we obtained data used in Duarte and Restuccia (2010), which contains shares of hours worked in the three broad sectors for a panel of 29 countries (none of which is in Africa) from 1950–2006.[7][8] Again we obtained GDP per capita for these countries from Maddison (2010). By directly comparing the relationship between income levels and the

---

[4] This aggregation is consistent with that used in Duarte and Restuccia (2010), who also use the GGDC database (along with other sources) to construct their dataset.

[5] Data for this exercise are based on household and labor force surveys and were obtained from Alun Thomas at the IMF.

[6] Herrendorf et al. (2011) note that this peak in Industry's employment share occurs at a log GDP per capita of about 9. Mauritius, whose GDP per capita is the highest in our sample and was about 9 in 1990, fits into this peak: its log GDP per capita increased to roughly 9.5 in 2005 and its share of employment in Industry decreased.

[7] Data were downloaded from Margarida Duarte's website on 7/24/2012.

[8] Note that the Duarte and Restuccia (2010) data measure share of hours worked, whereas our data measure share of total employment.

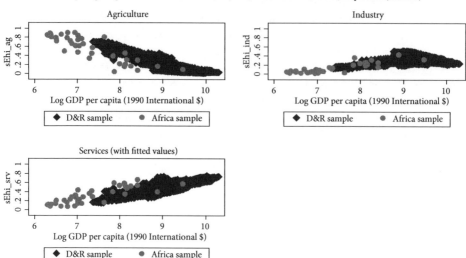

FIGURE 2.1 Employment shares of three broad economic sectors.

Notes: Note that Africa data measure sectoral share of total employment whereas D&R data measure share of total hours. Hours shares from Duarte and Restuccia (2010) cover 29 countries from 1950–2006. Their data were accessed 07/24/2012 from Duarte's website. GDP from Madison (2010).

distribution of employment in Africa in recent years with other regions over the last several decades, we can get an idea of whether the process of structural change in Africa is playing out differently than we would expect given current levels of income.

Figure 2.1B again plots employment shares in agriculture, industry and services, respectively, on the y-axis and log GDP per capita on the x-axis simultaneously for our sample of African countries and for those in Duarte and Restuccia (2010). Each country in our sample again has two data points (1990 and 2005) and each country in the Duarte and Restuccia (2010) sample has all available data points. Two things are immediately evident from Figure 2.1B. First, per capita incomes in recent years in most African countries in our sample are lower than those seen in most of the world since 1950. Second, the distributions of employment among the African countries fit almost seamlessly into those seen over the past six decades in other regions. In other words, controlling for income, the quantitative patterns of structural change in Africa are roughly what we would expect based on what has transpired elsewhere.

Thus, our preliminary analysis reveals that when we compare the *levels* of employment in Africa alongside other regions across levels of development, the pattern among our sample of African countries appears to fit seamlessly into that experienced by other regions. It also reveals that (i) the countries in Africa remain the poorest countries in the world and (ii) the scope for growth enhancing structural change in Africa is significant. With this in mind, we turn now to a description of the patterns of structural change across Africa.

The contribution of structural change to Africa's growth is presented in Figure 2.2 for the period 1960 to 2010 and is based on de Vries, Timmer, and de Vries (2013). Figure 2.2 is based on a new dataset compiled by the Groningen Growth and Development Center (GGDC) for Africa that includes data on value added and employment for 12 African countries for nine sectors and broken out by gender. The results for the period 2000 to 2010 are similar to those presented in McMillan, Rodrik, and Verduzco (2013) (MR&V). The main difference between the two sets of results is that de Vries et al. (2013) decompose the structural change term into two components: static and dynamic. Thus, overall growth is decomposed into three terms: within sector productivity growth, a static reallocation effect and a dynamic reallocation effect. Within sector productivity growth is a familiar term that measure changes in value added per worker for a given sector and time period. The static reallocation effect measures the change in overall value added per worker that arises as workers move from sectors with below (above) average productivity levels to sectors with above (below) average productivity levels. It is positive when workers move from relatively low productivity sectors to relatively high productivity sectors and negative when the reverse occurs. It does not take into account the possibility that worker flows will have an impact on sectoral productivity growth rates. The dynamic reallocation effect also known as the cross term or interaction term (van Ark 1996; Timmer 2000) represents the joint effect of changes in employment shares and sectoral productivity. It is positive (negative) if workers are moving to sectors that are experiencing positive (negative) productivity growth. Hence, de Vries et al. have decomposed the structural change term used by McMillan and Rodrik (2011) and McMillan, Rodrik, and Verduzco (2013) into two terms: whether workers move to above-average productivity *level* sectors (static reallocation effect) and whether productivity *growth* is higher in sectors that expand in terms of employment shares (dynamic reallocation effect).

Figure 2.2 makes it clear that the period 1975–1990 was a period of economic decline for most African countries; within sector productivity growth was negative and the combined static and dynamic reallocation effects contributed slightly positively to economic growth.

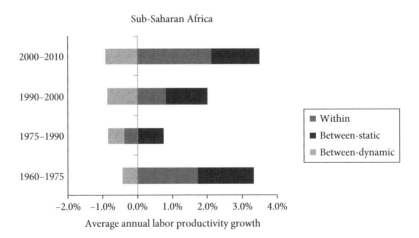

FIGURE 2.2 Sub-Saharan Africa: Average annual labor productivity growth.

Source: de Vries, G. J., Timmer, M.P., and de Vries, K. (2013). "Structural Transformation in Africa: Static Gains, Dynamic Losses", GGDC Research Memorandum #136.

Table 2.1 Sectoral contribution to within–sector component and changes in employment shares

	Contribution to within-component		Change in employment share	
	1990 to 2000	2000 to 2010	1990 to 2000	2000 to 2010
Agriculture (agr)	0.49	0.72	−2.19	−9.82
Mining (min)	0.19	0.18	−0.53	−0.19
Manufacturing (man)	0.11	0.13	−1.46	0.60
Utilities (pu)	0.11	0.11	−0.06	0.08
Construction (con)	−0.06	0.32	0.27	0.98
Trade services (wrt)	−0.22	−0.05	0.93	5.46
Transport services (tsc)	0.10	0.23	0.29	0.83
Business services (fire)	−0.03	0.05	0.61	0.77
Government and Personal services (cspsgs)	−0.05	0.38	2.13	1.31
Total Economy (sum)	0.63	2.10		

Notes: 1. Contributions to within-component of productivity growth are based on unweighted average of productivity decomposition for all African countries in the GGDC's Africa Sector Database. 2. Numbers in table represent percentage points. 3. Changes in employment shares based on average (weighted) Africa-wide changes.

The net result is that growth in economy wide value added per worked was negative during the period 1975–1990. This is in stark contrast to the period 1960–1975 and the period 2000–2010. Like MR&V (2013), de Vries et al. (2013) find that *overall*, structural change contributed positively to Africa's growth during the period 2000 to 2010. Figure 2.2 also shows that within sector productivity growth during Africa's most recent decade in history was greater than within sector productivity growth during the period 1960–1975. This is good news for Africa given recent concerns over developing countries' ability to follow the path of Asia where structural change was a key driver of economic growth.

Also encouraging is the fact that within sector productivity growth has been steadily increasing since 1975 and the fact that its contribution to overall growth doubled between 1990–2000 and 2000–2010. Moreover, Table 2.1 shows that the bulk of the within sector productivity growth has come from increases in output per worker in agriculture. Overall, the combined static and dynamic effects of structural change remain muted indicating an as yet unexploited source of potential growth for the countries of Africa.

However, it is worth emphasizing that the static reallocation effects of structural change are likely to have had a significant positive effect on the wellbeing of individuals across Africa. As noted by both M&R (2011) and de Vries et al. (2013), the majority of labor reallocation in recent years has been characterized by a movement of labor out of agriculture and into services. On average, output per worker in services is more than double output per worker in agriculture. The implication is that as workers move from agriculture to services, consumption levels also rise. Indeed, in a background paper for the World Development Report 2013, McMillan and Verduzco (2012) show that for a handful of countries the correlation between value added per worker and consumption per worker across sectors is 0.85.

To better understand the implications and sustainability of Africa's recent growth epi-sode, we take a two-pronged approach. We start by digging into the robustness of the changes in employment shares using data from the Demographic and Health Surveys. Using the DHS, we are able to examine changes in occupational shares by country and dis-aggregated by age, gender and location. This is preceded by a brief discussion of some of the issues surrounding data quality in Africa. In section 4, we follow up with an examina-tion of plausible explanations for observed changes in employment shares.

2.3 The Data Problem

Sectoral employment shares for Africa are difficult to come by even at the most aggregate of levels. For example, the World Bank's World Development Indicators reports employment shares for only six African countries for the period 2000–2010. This is one of the things that prompted researchers at the Groningen Growth and Development Center to construct a new database for 12 African countries that includes value added and employment shares for 12 African countries, nine sectors and by gender for the period 1960–2010.

The fact that data quality is an issue is not new and in fact, the quality of statistics in Africa varies widely across countries. Indeed, two of the countries not examined by Jerven (2013), Ethiopia and Botswana have very well staffed and highly competent statistical agencies. More recently, the *Review of Income and Wealth* dedicated a special issue to the quality of African socioeconomic data (volume 2013:59(2)). With any luck, this renewed attention to data quality in Africa will prompt an increase in resources devoted to the staffing and mod-ernization of statistical offices in Africa. Because so much activity in Africa takes place in the informal sector, it will be especially important to devote resources to finding creative ways to account for informal sector activity in the national accounts.

Both to circumvent some of the issues surrounding data quality and also to obtain a larger more representative sample, we focus in this paper on changes in employment shares using information from the Demographic and Health Surveys to study changes in employment shares. The Demographic and Health Surveys (DHS), are conducted by *Macro International Inc., Calverton, Maryland* (usually in cooperation with local authorities and funded by USAID). Established in 1984, more than 200 standard DHS from around 70 countries have been conducted between 1985 and 2012. For most countries more than one survey (up to seven) is available. The average sample size is about 5000 to 30 000 house-holds. The DHS provide detailed information on population, health, nutrition, and edu-cation as well as on household's durables and quality of the dwelling. Although the DHS are not naturally designed as Labor Force Surveys, the DHS provide comprehensive infor-mation on employment status and occupation characteristics of women and men aged between 15 and 49 (sometimes between 15 and 59). Because the DHS samples are nationally representative, they include employment in both the formal and informal sectors. In this paper, we make no attempt to distinguish between the two and only note that they are both included.

An distinct advantage of using the DHS to analyze determinants and trends of occupa-tion types across countries and over time is that the design and coding of variables (espe-cially on the type of occupation, educational achievements, households assets, dwelling characteristics) are generally comparable across countries and survey rounds. A clear disadvantage of the DHS data is that household income and expenditures are not reported.

We restrict our sample to African countries for which at least two DHS are available allowing us to analyze trends over time. The large coverage of countries and survey years provides us with a sample size of 24 African countries capturing a period between 1990 and 2011. In a separate paper we compare the countries in our sample to the excluded countries to assess whether our sample is somehow biased toward for example countries not in conflict. We find that our sample of African countries is representative of sub-Saharan Africa.

To assign individuals to occupational categories, we rely on the question on occupation for women and men. The DHS provide a grouped occupation variable that relies on the question that asks what the respondent mainly does for work.[9] The respondent's response is grouped into one of eight categories: not working, professional/technical/managerial, clerical, sales, agricultural—self employed, agricultural—employee, household and domestic, services, skilled manual, and unskilled manual. We further combine the groups of clerical, sales and services into one group. As an additional category we combine women and men from agricultural self-employment and agricultural employees into an overall group of agricultural occupation. Finally, we include a category "in school" to account both for difference between the young and old and also to establish trends in schooling over time. Thus, we are left with six "occupational" categories for adults: agriculture, services, skilled manual labor, unskilled manual labor, professional and not working. For youth—those aged 16–24—we add the category "in school" to make it seven "occupational" categories in total.

The first thing we note is the enormous cross-country heterogeneity in employment shares. For example, in the year 2000, the share of the working population engaged in agriculture in Rwanda was 84% while in that same year, the share of the population engaged in agriculture in Namibia was only 11%. Reporting a continent wide average is problematic because not all countries are surveyed in the same year. Similarly, there is quite a bit of heterogeneity in changes in employment shares over time across countries. For example, although *on average* the share of the population working in agriculture fell by around 6 percentage points over the decade 2000 to 2010, in Madagascar it increased by 12 percentage points between 1997 and 2009 while in Mozambique it fell by almost 16 percentage points between 1997 and 2011.

Likewise, there is significant heterogeneity across gender, age groups and location. For example, in Ethiopia in 2000, the share of all working women who report that they work in agriculture is 54% while the share of all working men who report that they work in agriculture is 72%. Additionally, between 2000 and 2011, the share of women in Ethiopia who report that they work in agriculture fell by 17 percentage points while the share of men reporting that they work in agriculture fell by only 7 percentage points. Not surprisingly, rural inhabitants are much more likely to report that they work in agriculture and youth are less likely to report that they work in agriculture. These last two facts are true for all countries in the sample and for all years.

In Figure 2.3, we report an unweighted average of changes in sample means for all countries in our sample across all occupations broken out by gender. Since gaps between survey years vary, we first annualize changes in means and then multiply this number by ten to get an idea of

---

[9] Variable v717. What is your occupation, that is, what kind of work do you mainly do?

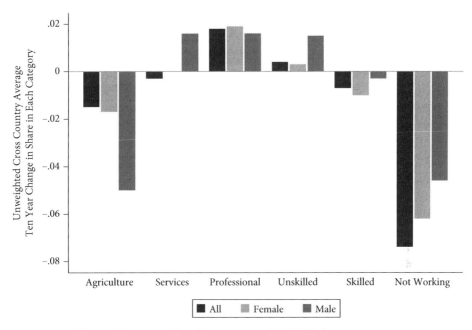

FIGURE 2.3 Change in occupational structure using DHS data.

Source: Author's calculation using DHS data.

Notes: 1. Average ten-year changes are computed as a simple unweighted mean of country specific ten-year changes. Country-specific ten-year changes correspond to the coefficient on the final year dummy of a country-specific regression of occupation on time dummies with the first year excluded; these changes were then annualized and multiplied times ten to get the predicted ten-year change.

2. Countries in sample include: Benin, Burkina Faso, Chad, Cote d'Ivoire, Cameroon, Ethiopia, Gabon, Ghana, Guinea, Kenya, Lesotho, Madagascar, Mali, Mozambique, Malawi, Namibia, Niger, Nigeria, Rwanda, Senegal, Tanzania, Uganda, Zambia, Zimbabwe.

the changes that took place during the decade 2000 to 2010. The red bars indicate changes for females and the blue bars indicate changes for males; grey bars are for the entire population and are skewed toward the results for females since overall there are many more females than males in the sample. The results for males are more or less consistent with what others have written about changes in employment shares in Africa. The share of the male labor force reporting that they work in agriculture fell by an average of 6 percentage points while the share of the male labor force working in services, professional jobs and unskilled manual jobs each rose by almost 2 percentage points. For women, the occupational shifts are less pronounced and entail a 2 percentage point decline in the share of the population reporting that they work in agriculture and an equivalent increase in the share of the population reporting that they work in professional jobs. We also learn something new from Figure 2.3: labor force participation has increased by a little over 6 percentage points for women and 4 percentage points for men.

Figure 2.4 shows the striking changes that are taking place among rural youth. Over a ten-year period, males are almost ten percentage points less likely to report that they work in agriculture and 12 percentage points more likely to report that they are in school. The results for females are similar although not as large. These results are noteworthy because the rise in commodity prices increases could have just as well lead to a reduction in the share of the young remaining in school due to the increased opportunity cost of schooling.

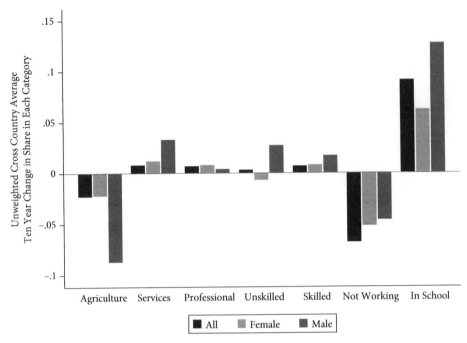

FIGURE 2.4 Occupational changes among rural youth, 2000 to 2010.

In summary, using an alternative source of information—the DHS—we have shown for a much larger sample of countries, that continent wide shifts in occupational structures broadly mimic results found using household surveys, census data and labor force surveys. We have also shown substantial increases in labor force participation and rural schooling not previously documented. Finally, we have documented a substantial degree of heterogeneity in changes in employment shares across countries, gender, location and age group. In the next section, we exploit this heterogeneity to better understand the relationship between commodity prices, governance and changes in employment shares across Africa.

2.4   EXPLAINING CHANGES IN EMPLOYMENT SHARES: 1993–2012

All of the previous results point to a decline in the share of the population engaged in agriculture across Africa over the past two decades. This decline has on average been matched by an increase in the share of the population working in services, professional jobs, and unskilled manual labor. It has also been accompanied by a significant increase in the share of rural youth staying in school and an increase in labor force participation. It has not been accompanied by an increase in the share of employment in formal sector manufacturing. Nevertheless, as noted previously, these structural changes have brought about significant increases in living standards for those able to move out of agriculture.

Figure 2.2 summarizes the changes by decade and naturally leads one to ask the following distinct but related questions: why do things seem to be turning around and how sustainable is this recent growth episode in Africa? Put differently, how might one go about explaining the stark differences between Africa's economic performance from 1975 to 1990 and its more recent performance from 2000 to 2010? Without a better understanding of what is driving Africa's recent performance, it is impossible to know whether or not the recent growth is sustainable.

The most obvious reason for the turnaround is the spike in agricultural commodity prices. Figure 2.5 shows the trend between 1960 and 2010 in country-specific indicators of agricultural commodity price shocks. To obtain these indices, we follow Henderson, Roberts, and Storeygard (2013). These indices summarize the individual commodity price environment each country faces by appropriately weighting the different prices of commodities exported by each country. Clearly, the commodity price increases between 2000 and 2010 are the largest and most prolonged in Africa's recent history.

There is a second plausible explanation for the turnaround. There are strong indications that governments in Africa are becoming more "developmental." One good example of this is the Comprehensive Agriculture Development Programme (CAADP). CAADP is an Africa led and owned agenda that serves to provide a common framework for policy and partnership renewal in the agricultural sector. CAADP's primary objectives are to increase investment in agriculture and improve agriculture policy and strategy design and implementation. Through these outcomes, CAADP is supposed to help meet the goals of higher growth, poverty reduction, and food and nutrition security. Specific benchmarks for participating countries are to allocate at least 10% of the national budget to the agricultural sector and achieve an annual agricultural growth rate of 6%.

Using the Polity IV database, we confirm a general trend towards improved governance across Africa. Figure 2.6, plots the population weighted average Polity IV score for countries in sub-Saharan Africa between 1960 and 2011.[10] To determine whether the particular Polity IV is driven by changes in the composition of the sample—depending on which countries have data for a particular year—we note that the scores for most countries appear in the dataset around the 1960s and 1970s and as soon as a country shows up in the data, all observations for subsequent years are non-missing. Hence, the sample of countries for a particular year can only change if a new country is added to the dataset, possibly because that country gained independence in that year. Of the 46 sub-Saharan Africa countries in the Polity IV dataset, 23 countries have data starting in 1960. Nine more countries have data starting between 1961 and 1965; eleven additional countries have data starting between 1966 and 1975; and, three more countries start having data from 1990 on.

To account for these changes in the composition of the sample as new countries appear in the sample, we divided the countries into four main cohorts. The first cohort includes only those countries with data starting in 1960; the second includes all countries with data from 1965 on; the third includes countries with data from 1975; and, the last cohort includes all countries with data from 1990 on. We show the trends of the weighted average for each

---

[10] The Polity IV has a particular coding for certain variables. These special codes can take values such as −66, −77, or −88. In order to get scores that were not affected by these coding issues, we ignored these values when calculating the average scores.

(A)

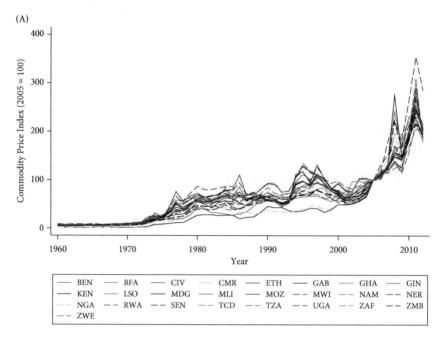

—— BEN	······ BFA	—— CIV	——— CMR	—— ETH	—— GAB	······· GHA	—— GIN
—— KEN	—— LSO	—— MDG	········ MLI	—— MOZ	– – MWI	····· NAM	– – NER
····· NGA	– – RWA	–· SEN	··· TCD	·· TZA	·· UGA	··· ZAF	– – ZMB
·· ZWE							

(B)

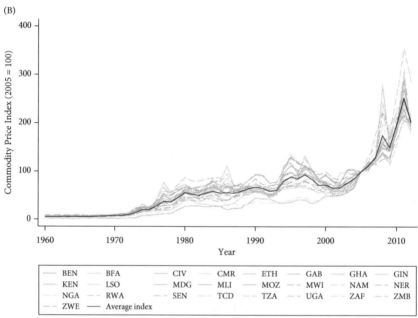

····· BEN	—— BFA	—— CIV	——— CMR	—— ETH	—— GAB	······· GHA	—— GIN
········ KEN	—— LSO	—— MDG	—— MLI	—— MOZ	– – MWI	····· NAM	– – NER
····· NGA	– · RWA	– – SEN	··· TCD	·· TZA	·· UGA	··· ZAF	– – ZMB
·· ZWE	—— Average index						

FIGURE 2.5 (A) Commodity price indices by country.

Source: Authors' calculations following Henderson, Roberts, and Storeygard (2013), using data from several sources. Commodity prices come from UNCTAD except for maize, natural gas, rubber, silver, tea, tobacco, logs, and sawn wood, which come from The World Bank's Pink Sheet dataset (Sept. 2013 update). Export shares were calculated from Freenstra (2005) data. Consumer price index for the US comes from US Bureau of Labor Statistics and GDP data in current dollars comes from the Penn World Tables version 7.

Notes: Included commodities are aluminum, bananas, beef, cattle hides, coconut oil, cocoa beans, coffee, copper, copra, cotton, crude petroleum, cottonseed oil, groundnut oil, iron ore, jute, lead, linseed oil, manganese ore, pepper, palm oil, rice, sisal, sunflower, soybeans, sugar, soybean oil, tin, wheat, zinc, maize, natural gas, rubber, silver, tea, tobacco, logs, sawn wood.

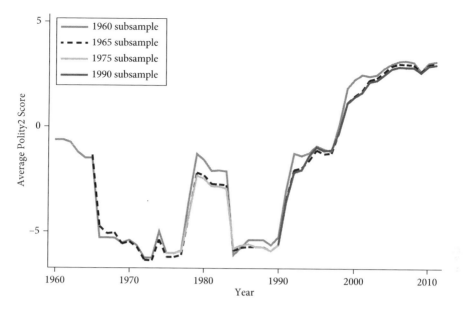

FIGURE 2.5 (B) Average commodity price index.

Source: Authors' calculations following Henderson, Roberts, and Storeygard (2013), using data from several sources. Commodity prices come from UNCTAD except for maize, natural gas, rubber, silver, tea, tobacco, logs, and sawn wood, which come from The World Bank's Pink Sheet dataset (Sept. 2013 update). Export shares were calculated from Freenstra (2005) data. Consumer price index for the US comes from US Bureau of Labor Statistics and GDP data in current dollars comes from the Penn World Tables version 7.

Notes: Included commodities are: Aluminum, bananas, beef, cattle hides, coconut oil, cocoa beans, coffee, copper, copra, cotton, crude petroleum, cottonseed oil, groundnut oil, iron ore, jute, lead, linseed oil, manganese ore, pepper, palm oil, rice, sisal, sunflower, soybeans, sugar, soybean oil, tin, wheat, zinc, maize, natural gas, rubber, silver, tea, tobacco, logs, sawn wood.

Average index refers to the yearly simple average across countries.

cohort in solid, bright lines. Red corresponds to the 1960 cohort, yellow to the 1965 cohort, green to the 1975 cohort, and blue to the 1990 cohort. As can be seen, the lines for each cohort follow each other very closely; hence, the addition of new countries to the sample has virtually no effect in the trends of the average scores.[11]

Finally, the poor performance of Africa during the period 1975–1990 is not all that surprising as it coincides with the period of structural adjustment in many African countries. Post-independence, many countries in Africa maintained and expanded the large parastatal sector that had its roots in the colonial period. Most of these large firms proved to be economically and socially unsustainable, leading to more than a decade-long process of structural adjustment that started in the early 1980s and lasted well into the 1990s. The

---

[11] These trends could also be influenced by a single or a few large countries. To check this, we took subsamples of each cohort and included the average scores for these subsamples in the graphs. For each cohort, we took subsamples at random: ten random draws of 50% of the cohort sample and another ten random draws of 25% of the cohort samples. If a single country is driving the trends then, the trends of the random subsamples should differ considerably from that of the cohort's full sample. Again, the full sample and the subsamples across cohorts broadly follow the same trends.

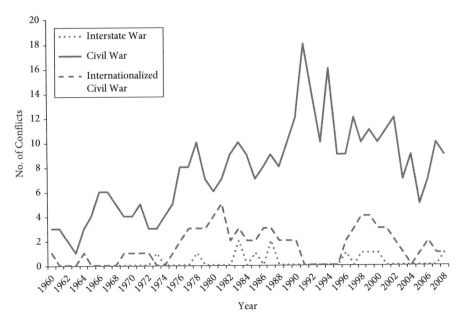

FIGURE 2.6 Average Polity 2 score for sub-Saharan Africa.

Source: Authors' calculations using data from the Polity IV Project and
The World Bank's WDI dataset.

Notes: 1. Graph shows a weighted average of the Polity 2 score (weighted by population) in the Polity
IV dataset. The Polity 2 score is the revised combined polity score which is the result of substracting
the "autoc" score from the "democ" score. It scores how democratic or autocratic a regime is and ranges from −10
(strongly autocratic) to +10 (strongly democratic).

2. Solid bright lines are population-weighted averages of the individual country scores for each cohort: the 1960
cohort (red), 1965 cohort (yellow), 1975 cohort (green), and the 1990 cohort (blue).

3. Countries included are: Benin, Burkina Faso, Cameroon, Central African Republic, Chad, Congo Brazzaville,
Congo Kinshasa, Ethiopia, Gabon, Ghana, Guinea, Ivory Coast, Liberia, Madagascar, Mali, Mauritania, Niger,
Nigeria, Senegal, Somalia, South Africa, Sudan, Togo, Rwanda, Sierra Leone, Tanzania, Burundi, Uganda, Kenya,
Malawi, Zambia, Gambia, Botswana, Lesotho, Equatorial Guinea, Mauritius, Swaziland, Zimbabwe, Guinea-Bissau,
Angola, Cape Verde, Comoros, Mozambique, Namibia, Eritrea, and South Sudan.

consequences of these structural adjustment programs included large layoffs that in some
countries resulted in an anomalous urban to rural migration. Thurlow and Wobst (2004)
provide a vivid account of this sort of thing in Zambia. They show that the period of structural adjustment in Zambia was marked by a significant decline in the share of the labor force
employed in the formal sector and a movement of labor out of industry and back to agriculture. They show that much of this was precipitated by the privatization of state owned factories. Finally, they show that between 1999 and 2001 things were beginning to turn around
in Zambia. They attribute the turnaround to a more stable macro and political environment
in which the government was able to mitigate the effects of Zambia's copper exports on the
exchange rate and domestic prices.

The story in Mozambique is not so different. After a prolonged period of civil war,
Mozambique entered into its first structural adjustment program with the World Bank in
1987 (McMillan et al. 2003). The first period of reform lasted until 1990. A second more
aggressive period of reform began in the early 1990s. One of the casualties of this reform was

state-owned enterprises. For example, by the end of 1994, all of the formerly state-owned cashew-processing factories had been privatized releasing thousands of workers who typically returned to agriculture because little else was available. It is only in recent years that the cashew-processing sector in Mozambique is beginning to hire new workers. However, the scale of the sector is still much smaller than it was under state ownership.

To assess the possibility that changes in commodity prices and governance could be driving recent changes in occupational shares across Africa, we combine our country specific measures of commodity prices and governance with DHS data on occupational shares. The purpose of this exercise is not to draw causal inference but rather to describe patterns in the data that can help us to think more carefully about structural change in Africa. For example, if we find a correlation between our measures of governance and changes in employment shares, then it may be worth thinking more carefully about how to identify this relationship in a more convincing way and in a way that gets at the underlying mechanisms at work.

In Table 2.2, we report the results of running a regression of an individual's occupational choice on education levels, gender, location, country specific agricultural commodity prices, a country specific measure of governance, and a country specific measure of the incidence of conflict. All specifications include a common time trend and country fixed effects to control for international business sector fluctuations and time invariant country characteristics such as geographical characteristics and colonial history. The results in Table 2.2 reveal a number of stylized facts. First, education levels and occupational status are highly correlated and seemingly linear. That is—higher levels of education are more strongly associated with a decreased likelihood of working in agriculture. Second, women are less likely than men to report that they are working. Third, urban youth are more likely to report that they are not working than rural youth. And finally, young females are less likely than their male counterparts to be in school. Although not shown on a country-by-country basis, these results hold when the regressions are run on a country by country basis.

Turning now to the correlations between commodity prices, governance and employment shares some suggestive patterns emerge. First, the rise in commodity prices is associated with an increase in labor force participation, a reduction in the share of youth in agriculture and an increase in the share of youth in school. For youth, the rise in commodity prices is associated with a significant reduction in the likelihood of working in agriculture. The rise in commodity prices is also associated with an increased likelihood of working in services. Similarly, improvements in governance are associated with an increase in labor force participation and an increase in the likelihood that youth are in school. A direct comparison of the magnitudes of the coefficients is not possible because commodity prices and governance are measured in different units.

To compare the relative importance of governance and commodity prices, we can multiply the estimated coefficient by the actual average change in the explanatory variable across the sample period. For example, the magnitude of the actual impact of commodity prices on the likelihood of labor force participation for the older population is equal to the estimated coefficient of -0.043 times the average change in commodity prices over the sample period of 0.661 or around 3 percentage points. One of the most striking results (not reported in Table 2.2) is our finding that together the increase in the quality of governance and the rise in commodity prices are associated with a 10 percentage point increase in the likelihood that

Table 2.2 Occupational regressions, full sample

| | Panel A: Old population (age 25+) | | | | | | Panel B: Young population (age 16 to 24) | | | | | | |
| | All agricultural workers | Professional workers | Clerical, sales, and services workers | Unskilled workers | Skilled workers | Not working | All agricultural workers | Professional workers | Clerical, sales, and services workers | Unskilled workers | Skilled workers | Not working | In school |
	(1)	(2)	(3)	(4)	(5)	(6)	(7)	(8)	(9)	(10)	(11)	(12)	(13)
Female	-0.0889*** [0.00130]	-0.0120*** [0.000720]	0.178*** [0.00124]	-0.0177*** [0.000678]	-0.0613*** [0.00101]	0.207*** [0.000928]	-0.0890*** [0.00228]	-0.00567*** [0.000870]	0.168*** [0.00208]	-0.0401*** [0.00139]	-0.0514*** [0.00174]	0.209*** [0.00196]	-0.0778*** [0.00157]
Urban	-0.444*** [0.00140]	0.0182*** [0.000793]	0.282*** [0.00152]	0.0457*** [0.000799]	0.0773*** [0.00109]	0.0299*** [0.00117]	-0.486*** [0.00223]	0.0105*** [0.000925]	0.276*** [0.00250]	0.0610*** [0.00148]	0.0798*** [0.00182]	0.103*** [0.00201]	0.00765*** [0.00139]
Incomplete primary	-0.0581*** [0.00164]	0.00216*** [0.000569]	0.0315*** [0.00153]	0.00406*** [0.000779]	0.0168*** [0.00108]	-0.0315*** [0.00138]	-0.0621*** [0.00264]	0.000857 [0.000650]	0.0293*** [0.00254]	0.00441*** [0.00131]	0.0254*** [0.00179]	-0.0259*** [0.00241]	0.294*** [0.00161]
Complete primary	-0.130*** [0.00219]	0.0193*** [0.000880]	0.0614*** [0.00207]	0.00785*** [0.00117]	0.0366*** [0.00155]	-0.0352*** [0.00177]	-0.118*** [0.00345]	0.00682*** [0.000976]	0.0474*** [0.00327]	0.0119*** [0.00200]	0.0507*** [0.00247]	-0.0241*** [0.00312]	0.225*** [0.00213]
Incomplete secondary	-0.251*** [0.00206]	0.0938*** [0.00135]	0.0980*** [0.00217]	0.00620*** [0.00109]	0.0511*** [0.00161]	-0.0377*** [0.00172]	-0.209*** [0.00358]	0.0404*** [0.00161]	0.0949*** [0.00373]	0.0185*** [0.00207]	0.0712*** [0.00283]	0.0110*** [0.00320]	0.606*** [0.00191]
Complete secondary	-0.316*** [0.00286]	0.233*** [0.00306]	0.106*** [0.00363]	-0.0270*** [0.00148]	0.0122*** [0.00252]	-0.0756*** [0.00264]	-0.254*** [0.00548]	0.169*** [0.00492]	0.132*** [0.00658]	-0.0257*** [0.00303]	0.0181*** [0.00460]	0.0359*** [0.00525]	0.236*** [0.00369]
Higher	-0.367*** [0.00254]	0.555*** [0.00354]	-0.0717*** [0.00350]	-0.0415*** [0.00131]	-0.0613*** [0.00204]	-0.0740*** [0.00269]	-0.307*** [0.00750]	0.417*** [0.0113]	-0.0157 [0.0112]	-0.0386*** [0.00470]	-0.0190*** [0.00663]	-0.0456*** [0.00922]	0.596*** [0.00607]
Log of Agric. Commodity price index	0.00348 [0.00586]	-0.00942*** [0.00300]	0.0207*** [0.00561]	0.00934*** [0.00308]	-0.00791* [0.00414]	-0.0428*** [0.00510]	-0.0257*** [0.00970]	-0.00900** [0.00355]	0.0889*** [0.00909]	-0.000974 [0.00527]	-0.0317*** [0.00677]	-0.0780*** [0.00877]	0.0160** [0.00658]
Revised Combined Polity Score	0.000735* [0.000335]	0.00202*** [0.000167]	0.00148*** [0.000330]	-0.00379*** [0.000209]	-0.000718*** [0.000249]	-0.00442*** [0.000278]	0.000166 [0.000552]	0.00109*** [0.000194]	0.00371*** [0.000531]	-0.00369*** [0.000354]	-0.000705*** [0.000399]	-0.00101** [0.000445]	0.00591*** [0.000306]

	(1)	(2)	(3)	(4)	(5)	(6)	(7)	(8)	(9)	(10)	(11)	(12)	(13)
Country experienced any kind of conflict	0.0289***	0.0122***	0.00731***	-0.0179***	-0.0238***	0.0228***	0.0537***	0.00865***	-0.00190	-0.0293***	-0.0457***	0.0550***	0.0408***
	(0.00251)	(0.00137)	(0.00260)	(0.00131)	(0.00178)	(0.00215)	(0.00403)	(0.00151)	(0.00414)	(0.00235)	(0.00306)	(0.00371)	(0.00261)
Constant	0.637***	0.112***	-0.127***	0.0921***	0.113***	0.145***	0.864***	-0.00532	-0.227***	0.000365	0.236***	0.370***	-0.0964***
	(0.0468)	(0.0250)	(0.0449)	(0.0254)	(0.0332)	(0.0185)	(0.0359)	(0.0135)	(0.0336)	(0.0193)	(0.0265)	(0.0603)	(0.0242)
Observations	488,206	488,206	488,206	488,206	488,206	613,781	183,584	183,584	183,584	183,584	183,584	284,198	380,486
R-squared	0.352	0.265	0.202	0.061	0.051	0.126	0.336	0.139	0.201	0.065	0.062	0.122	0.281

*** $p<0.01$, ** $p<0.05$, * $p<0.1$.

Notes: 1. Robust standard errors in parentheses.

2. Female = 1 if person is a woman; Urban = 1 if person lives in an urban environment.

3. Sample for regressions in columns (1) to (5) and (7) to (11) includes all working individuals not currently attending school. Sample for regression in columns (6) and (12) include only individuals not currently working and not currently attending school. Sample for regression in column (13) includes only young individuals (age 16 to 24).

4. All regressions include country and year fixed effects.

rural youth are enrolled in school. Of the 10 percentage point increase, 6 percentage points are attributable to the rise in commodity prices and 4 percentage points are attributable to the increase in the quality of governance. Both the magnitude and significance of this latter results warrant further investigation given the importance of human capital in the process of structural change.

2.5 Moving Forward: Africa's Quiet Revolution

Africa's current growth has sparked a heated debate over its sources and sustainability. Some argue that growth across the continent is fundamentally a result of rising commodity prices and that if these prices were to collapse, so too would Africa's growth rates. Others lament the so-called de-industrialization of Africa. They worry that without a vibrant manufacturing sector, unemployment will remain high and the economies of Africa will not catch up to the more advanced countries of the world. Finally, some warn that youth unemployment could lead to an "Arab Spring." Taken together, one could conclude that recent success will be short lived.

In this chapter, I have argued that these observations miss some important changes across the continent—what I will refer to as Africa's quiet revolution—that lead us to be cautiously optimistic about the sustainability of Africa's economic progress. This quiet revolution includes a substantial decline in the share of the labor force engaged in agriculture, an unprecedented increase in the numbers of rural children in secondary school, significant improvements in governance and a rise in agriculture. For now, the revolution remains quiet, because the synergies between these various developments are only just starting to be realized.

Moving out of agriculture has been associated with increased living standards for millions of people (M&R 2011, 2012). This is because agriculture in Africa has been dominated by subsistence farmers and very low labor productivity. We have shown in this paper, that moving out of agriculture has also been accompanied by a 10 percentage point increase in the likelihood that the rural young stay in school. While education does not guarantee structural change, no country has been able to sustain economic growth without investments in human capital. Finally, although not traditionally accounted for in the structural change literature, the increase in labor force participation is a kind of structural change that is growth enhancing.

We have also shown that the decline in the share of the labor force engaged in agriculture has coincided with an increase in value added per worker in agriculture in several African countries. Our results are consistent with work by Keith Fuglie (2012) at the US Department of Agriculture who reports that for the first time in decades, total factor productivity growth in Africa is rising. Progress is slow at roughly 1% per year, but for the previous decades, total factor productivity growth in agriculture was negative in most African countries.

It is probably no accident that these structural changes have coincided with an overall increase in the quality of governance in Africa. A number of political scientists have found that rural people in Africa vote more often than their urban counterparts and overwhelmingly vote for the incumbent, whereas urban residents tend to be much more supportive of the opposition. As education and living standards in rural areas improves, it will become increasingly difficult for incumbents to buy these votes. In an empirical investigation into this issue, Bates and Block (2013) found that increased political competition across Africa is a strong empirical predictor of the rise in total factor productivity growth in agriculture. According to them, the emergence of electoral competition has altered political incentives, resulting in both sectoral and macroeconomic policy reforms that benefit farmers.

The reason this is so important is that, paradoxically, it is very likely that hope for the "modernization" of Africa that will bring formal sector jobs needed to sustain productivity growth lies in the agricultural sector. Consider some of the recent investments in labor-intensive manufacturing. The Chinese, Indians, and Europeans are all investing in Ethiopia's leather sector. The Indians and Europeans are investing in fruit processing in Ghana. The Americans and the Swiss are investing in cashew processing in Mozambique. While access to relatively cheap labor is an attraction, it is not the primary reason for these investments. Rather it is access to high quality raw materials.

For example, a recent survey of foreign investors in leather processing and manufacturing, finds that the single most important reason for investment in Ethiopia's leather sector is the country's potential to produce some of the highest quality leather in the world. This potential has not yet been realized because of the disorganized nature of the livestock industry and traditional practices that make much of the hides unsuitable raw materials. The result is that many firms now import up to two thirds of the hides they then turn into shoes, gloves and bags for export.

The lesson is clear: additional investments in the livestock sector have the potential to create more formal jobs in the leather industry while at the same time bettering the lives of the rural poor. And the good news is that these sorts of investments could happen relatively quickly leading to more of the kind of structural change that we would like to see take place in Africa.

As we have discussed, changes are taking place that could lead to faster agricultural productivity growth in the future. But there is a lot more that could be done to transform the agricultural sector more quickly. With a little bit of luck and more pressure from an increasingly educated population, policies that promote faster productivity growth in agriculture could be the key to the modernization of Africa leading to more rapid structural changes that brings better jobs and higher labor productivity growth.

Acknowledgments

This research was funded by the Economic and Social Research Council (ESRC) and the UK government's Department for International Development (DFID) as part of the DFID/ESRC Growth Program, grant agreement ES/J00960/1 and by the African Development Bank. The authors wish to thank Inigo Verduzco for excellent research assistance. The authors would also like to thank Thomas Alun, Louise Fox, Doug Gollin, Remi Jedwab, Will Masters, Dani Rodrik, Jan Rielander, and Abebe Shimeles for helpful comments.

REFERENCES

Badiane, O. (2011). "Agriculture and Structural Transformation in Africa." Stanford Symposium Series on Global Food Policy and Food Security in the 21st Century. Center on Food Security and the Environment. Stanford, California: Stanford University.

Bates, R.H., and Block, S.A. (2013). "Revisiting African Agriculture: Institutional Change and Productivity Growth." *Journal of Politics*, 75(2), April: 372–384.

Blades, D. (1980) "What Do We Know About Levels and Growth of Output in Developing Countries? A Critical Analysis With Special Reference to Africa". Economic Growth and Resources: Proceedings of the Fifth World Congress, International Economic Association, Tokyo, Vol. 2, pp. 68–75.

Bondestam, L. (1973). "Some notes on African statistics: collection, reliability and interpretation." Research report Nordiska Afrikainstitutet, Uppsala.

Brautigam, D., McMillan, M.S., and Tang X. (2013). "The Role of Foreign Investment in Ethiopia's Leather Value Chain." PEDL Research Note - ERG project 106. Available at http://pedl.cepr.org/sites/default/files/Research%20Note_Brautigam_McMillan_Tang.pdf.

Devarajan, S. (2013). "Africa's Statistical Tragedy". *Review of Income and Wealth*, 59(2):1–7.

Egerö, B., and Henin, R.A. (1973). The Population of Tanzania. An Analysis of the 1967 Population Census. Dar es Salaam: Bralup.

de Vries, G.J., Timmer, M.P., and de Vries, K. (2013). "Structural Transformation in Africa: Static gains, dynamic losses." *GGDC research memorandum*, 136:696–739.

Duarte, M., and Restuccia, D. (2010). "The role of the structural transformation in aggregate productivity." *The Quarterly Journal of Economics*, MIT Press, 125(1):129–173, February.

Edmonds, E., and Pavcnik, N., "The Effect of Trade Liberalization on Child Labor," *Journal of International Economics*, 65(2), March 2005: 401–441.

Ellis, S. (2002). "Writing Histories of Contemporary Africa". *Journal of African history*, 43 (1):1–26.

Fuglie, K.O., and Rada, N.E. (2013). "Resources, Policies, and Agricultural Productivity in Sub-Saharan Africa." ERR-145, U.S. Department of Agriculture, Economic Research Service, February 2013.

Henderson, V. J., Roberts M., and Storeygard A. (2013). "Is Urbanization in Sub-Saharan Africa Different?" Policy Research Working Paper (No. 6481). The World Bank, Washington D.C. June.

Herrendorf, B., Rogerson, R., and Valentinyi, A. (2014). "Growth and Structural Transformation", in P. Aghion and S.N. Durlauf (eds), *Handbook of Economic Growth*, vol.2, chapter 6.

Jerven, M. (2013). "Poor Numbers: How We are Misled by African Development Statistics and what to Do about it." Cornell University Press.

Lehohla, P. (2008). "Statistical Development in Africa in the Context of the Global Statistical System". *Statistical Journal of the IAOS: Journal of the International Association for Official Statistics*, 25(1):27–45.

Lewis, W. (1955). "The Theory of Economic Growth." Irwin.

Maddison, A. (2010). "Statistics on World Population, GDP and Per Capita GDP, 1-2008 AD." Groningen: University of Groningen.

McMillan, M.S., and Rodrik, D. (2011). "Globalization, structural change and productivity growth" NBER WP No. 17143.

McMillan, M.S., and Verduzco I. (2012). "Measuring the Impact of Structural Change on Labor's Share of Income." Background Paper for the World Development Report 2013. World Bank.

McMillan, M.S., Rodrik, D., and Welch, K.H. (2003). "When Economic Reform Goes Wrong: Cashew in Mozambique," Brookings Trade Forum 2003, Washington, DC.

McMillan M.S., Rodrik, D., and Verduzco, I. (2013). "Globalization, Structural Change, and Productivity Growth, with an Update on Africa." World Development. In press. Available online: November 2013.

Rodrik, D. (2012). "Unconditional Convergence in Manufacturing." Working Paper, July 2012, http://www.hks.harvard.edu/fs/drodrik/Research%20papers/Unconditional%20convergence%20rev%205.pdf.

Rogers, E.M. (1962). Diffusion of Innovations. Free Press.

Thurlow, J., and Wobst, P. (2004). "The road to pro-poor growth in Zambia" DSGD discussion papers 16, International Food Policy Research Institute (IFPRI).

Timmer, M.P. (2000). "The Dynamics of Asian Manufacturing. A Comparison in the late Twentieth Century." Cheltenham: Edward Elgar Publishers.

van Ark, B. (1996). "Sectoral Growth Accounting and Structural Change in Post-war Europe." Chapter 3 in B. van Ark and N. Crafts "Quantitative Aspects of Post-war European Economic Growth." Cambridge: Cambridge University Press.

Young, A. (2012). "The African Growth Miracle". Journal of Political Economy, 120(4), August: 696–739.

CHAPTER 3

MONETARY POLICY ISSUES IN SUB-SAHARAN AFRICA

ANDREW BERG, STEPHEN O'CONNELL,
CATHERINE PATTILLO, RAFAEL PORTILLO,
AND FILIZ UNSAL

3.1 INTRODUCTION

THE environment for monetary policy in sub-Saharan Africa (SSA) underwent a funda-mental transformation over the period from 1985 to 2005. Central banks, largely freed from fiscal dominance, became capable of pursuing inflation and stabilization objec-tives through market-based policies. Among countries operating independent cur-rencies, median inflation peaked in the first half of the 1990s. Foreign exchange black markets, which had been pervasive in 1990, were virtually absent by 2000. Starting in the mid-1990s, the institutional independence of many central banks was buttressed through new legal charters that increased the prominence of price stability among the central bank's objectives.[1]

The central banks that have emerged from two decades of economic reform pursue conventional objectives in unconventional environments. Like their counterparts in the emerging-market and industrial countries, they favor market-based instruments and are obliged to reconcile any real-side objectives with medium-term price stability. They operate managed floats and are committed to transparency in the conduct of policy. But the econo-mies within which they operate differ sharply from those in richer countries. Domestic sup-ply shocks play a prominent role in macroeconomic fluctuations, as do global food and export prices, remittances, and foreign aid. Unlike their richer counterparts, moreover, these central banks have until recently mainly targeted inflation at one remove, via the use of monetary aggregates as intermediate targets; and have used balance sheet items rather than short-term interest rates as operational targets. These choices reflect in part the legacy of money-based

---

[1] This chapter focuses on countries with independent currencies and exchange rates, thus excluding the 15 countries of the CFA Franc zone. On this topic, see Masson and Pattillo (2005) and Gulde and Tsangarides (2008).

stabilization policies and the persistent influence of the IMF's "financial programming" approach to monetary policy, but also concerns about the rudimentary nature of domestic financial markets and the lack of reliable empirical evidence on how short-term interest rates feed through to output and inflation.

Monetary policy frameworks in SSA are still evolving. Ghana adopted an inflation-targeting (IT) regime in 2007, and Uganda has announced its intention to adopt IT in the near future. Other countries are interested in adopting modern, forward-looking, policy regimes, even if they do not formally adopt inflation targeting. As in other regions that went through similar transitions, the role of money targets going forward has been the source of much discussion.

Following a brief historical overview, sections 3–7 address a set of ongoing issues in the conduct of monetary policy among central banks operating independent currencies in SSA.[2] Section 3 reviews the peculiar challenges of characterizing the monetary transmission mechanism in a rapidly changing environment. We next study the role of monetary aggregates (section 4) and of the exchange rate (section 5) and consider fiscal/monetary interactions (section 6). Section 7 examines the monetary policy response to food price shocks. In Section 8 we discuss modern analytic frameworks that can help integrate many of the foregoing issues and serve as a platform for forecasting and policy analysis. Section 9 concludes by considering the operational and research agenda.

3.2 THE MONETARY POLICY LANDSCAPE

The monetary policy landscape in SSA has changed profoundly during the last three decades. In the 1980s, monetary policy was subordinated to the objective of financing large government deficits. This led to high inflation and, in combination with fixed exchange rates, overvalued real exchange rates. Countries reacted to balance of payments difficulties by tightening exchange and trade controls, leading to rampant smuggling and large foreign exchange premiums in parallel markets. Under financial repression, with high taxation and controlled low interest rates, demand for parallel market foreign exchange surged. At some point, the authorities began to lose control of a vicious circle (Masson and Pattillo 2005).[3]

From the mid-1980s to the late 1990s countries began reform programs, often with exchange rate unifications and movement toward more market-determined, flexible exchange rates, and dismantling of exchange and trade controls (Figure 3.1).[4] As in other developing regions, the number of countries with de facto managed or floating exchange rates in SSA increased by about 50% between 1980 and 1990 (Figure 3.2). This

---

[2] We omit South Africa, an emerging-market country whose monetary policy issues differ enough from those of low-income Africa to require separate treatment.

[3] There was, however, a wide variety in the degree of (de facto and de jure) exchange rate flexibility, trade controls, and institutional arrangements for monetary policy among SSA countries. See Honohan and O'Connell (1997) for a detailed summary.

[4] In some cases, the reforms were brought by conditionalities from the IMF/World Bank accompanying new adjustment loan programs.

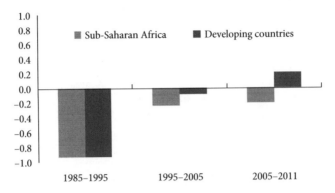

FIGURE 3.1 Capital account openness (Chinn–Ito) index[1] (period averages, in percent).

[1] Excluding countries with fixed exchange rate regimes. A higher number indicates a more open capital account.

Source: http://web.pdx.edu/~ito/Chinn-Ito_website.htm.

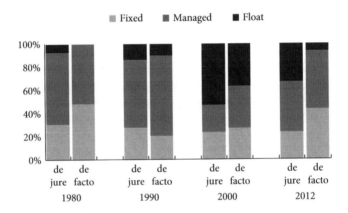

FIGURE 3.2 Exchange rate classification (sub-Saharan Africa).[1]

Source: AREAER Database IMF.

[1] Excludes CFA Zone countries.

transformation was accompanied by a shift to some form of money targeting in more than half of SSA.

Other key elements of the two-decade transition were sharp reductions in central bank financing of government and financial liberalizations that eliminated interest-rate controls and introduced competition into the banking sector. With assistance of IMF-supported programs, substantial debt relief, and a favorable external environment, domestic credit to government declined from an average of 13% in 1985–1995 to 8% in 1995–2005 and has remained broadly at that level to date. The re-establishment of fiscal control provided support for money-based disinflation programs to bring down inflation to single digits (or near single) in the context of higher economic growth and higher international reserves by the late 1990s, in line with the experience in other developing countries (Table 3.1).

Table 3.1 Inflation, growth, and international reserves in SSA:[1] 1985–1995, 1995–2005, 2005–2012

	1985–1995			1995–2005			2005–2012		
	Inflation	Growth	International reserves	Inflation	Growth	International reserves	Inflation	Growth	International reserves
Mean	28.7	2.5	6.8	14.9	4.4	9.0	10.1	5.8	14.0
Median	16.5	3.5	4.6	13.3	4.2	8.8	9.2	5.5	12.7
Standard Deviation	18.8	4.5	3.0	10.6	4.3	3.1	5.1	2.6	2.8
Developing countries—Mean	27.9	1.3	7.3	17.1	4.4	12.4	8.0	5.5	15.8

[1] Excluding countries with exchange rate pegs according to 2012 AREAER.

Source: World Economic Outlook Database. Annual data (y/y growth) is used to calculate inflation and GDP growth. International reserve are in percentages of GDP.

Table 3.2 Bank deposits, private credit, and spreads: SSA[1]

	(Mean, in percent)			Developing countries
	1985–1995	1995–2005	2005–2010	2005–2010
Bank deposits to GDP	16.8	23.2	29.3	37.5
Private credit to GDP	11.7	14.8	20.5	28.9
Interest rate spreads	11.8	14.0	11.3	9.9

[1] Excluding countries with exchange rate pegs.
Source: International Monetary Fund.

Liberalization of direct controls over the commercial banking system helped alleviate the prolonged financial repression (Adam and O'Connell 2005).[5] Real interest rates turned positive in 1995–2005, averaging 5% as compared with about −11% in the previous decade. Interest rate spreads, around 11%, have remained high but are comparable to other developing countries (Table 3.2). Bank deposits and private credit as a share of GDP steadily increased during the last three decades (Table 3.2). Deeper financial markets in SSA in turn increased the role of market signals and the importance of managing expectations in the implementation of monetary policy.

Many policy changes have been institutionalized in SSA through reforms cementing central bank independence and the adoption of new central bank charters. The majority of the central banks in the region have *de jure* (legislated) independence,[6] and their *de facto* independence has been on average (0.26) very close to the developing countries' average (0.25), using the measure in Lucotte (2009).[7] Moreover, 70% of SSA countries had accepted Article VIII of the IMF's Articles of Agreement by the late 1990s (more than 90% as of 2012), committing to refrain from imposing restrictions on payments and transfers for current account transactions and to refrain from discriminatory currency arrangements or multiple currency practices.

The *de jure* policy regime in place in most countries is best characterized as a hybrid regime (IMF 2008). An overview of the objectives and targets of monetary policy in the region reveals a set of managed floaters with a variety of conventional-looking objectives (price and exchange rate stability), but with money aggregates still present as both operational and intermediate targets (Table 3.3).

De facto monetary policy regimes are also classified as money targeting in about 80% of SSA countries with scope for independent monetary policy, but flexibility is the norm and target misses are common (section 4).[8] Monetary policy lets bygones be bygones: when there is a miss, targets catch up with the new level of money balances, rather than attempting to undo the miss and preserve the previously targeted levels. Moreover, such flexibility in

[5] For countries in SSA with available data (and excluding pegs), the financial reform index reported by Giuliano et al. (2010) more than doubled on average in the decade between 1985–1990 and 1995–2000 (the countries are Ghana, Kenya, Madagascar, Mozambique, Nigeria, South Africa, Tanzania, and Uganda).

[6] Central Bank Legislation Database, International Monetary Fund, 2012.

[7] These calculations are based on the methodology outlined in Cukierman (1992) for de facto independence and Cukierman et al. (1992) for de jure independence.

[8] Based on AREAER 2011 data, International Monetary Fund. Among 18 countries with managed/floating exchange rates, 14 countries have money targeting, two countries have IT, and two countries have mixed regimes.

Table 3.3 De jure monetary policy framework in sub–Saharan Africa

Regimes	Policy objectives	Intermediate target	Operational target 1	Main instruments
Pegs (23)	Stability of the exchange rate regime (23) Price stability (23) Economic growth (12)	Private sector credit (1)	Exchange rate (23)	Open market operations Foreign exchange sale
Money targeting (18)	Price stability (all countries) External competitiveness (5) Exchange rate smoothing (12) Economic growth (9)	Monetary aggregates (16)	Reserve money (18)	Open market operations (17) Foreign exchange sales (18)
Inflation targeting (3)	Price stability (all countries) External competitiveness (1) Exchange rate smoothing (1)		Interest rate (3)	Open market operations (3) Foreign exchange sales (3)

Source: IMF (2008).

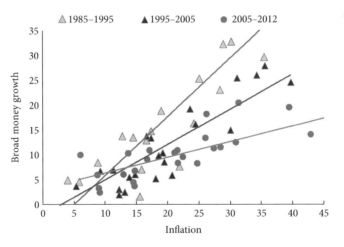

FIGURE 3.3 Broad money growth and inflation: SSA.[1]

[1] Excluding countries with exchange rate pegs.
Source: World Economic Outlook Database.

the implementation of monetary policy is not associated with increases in inflation, except in high inflation countries (IMF 2008). Indeed, the empirical relationship between money growth and inflation seems to be weakening in the last decade, making monetary aggregates less useful as intermediate objectives, at least in countries with low to moderate inflation (Figure 3.3). In this case, the monetary aggregates do not—and presumably should not—dictate monetary policy. Rather, even within the framework of monetary aggregate targeting the key questions involve when to miss the targets and by how much, and how to reset them for the next period.

Many countries in the region are in the process of modernizing their monetary policy frameworks. A few countries, such as South Africa and Ghana, have adopted a formal IT regime. Under IT, (i) the inflation forecast serves as the intermediate target, (ii) the interest rate typically serves as the operational target, and (iii) communication of the current inflation assessment and likely future policy decisions becomes a key component of central bank policy. Uganda has announced its intention to adopt IT in the next few years.

While other countries may not be planning to formally adopt IT, many are interested in adopting elements of modern policymaking. By "modern monetary policy framework" we have in mind a framework for countries with a floating or managed floating exchange rate regime in which: (i) monetary policy is forward-looking; (ii) stabilizing inflation is the guiding objective for monetary policy, along with other possible goals; and (iii) the central bank emphasizes communication strategies centered on the inflation outlook. Achieving these objectives typically involves improved liquidity management, greater reliance on the price (interest rate) channel of transmission, and the development of in-house forecasting and policy analysis capacity. Of course this sounds a lot like IT or perhaps inflation forecast targeting (IFT) or "IT-lite".[9] Indeed, IT and variants are the dominant form of monetary policy regime for countries with floating and managed floating exchange rates.[10] However, we avoid this terminology for several reasons. First, IT and IFT are loaded terms that carry very specific if controversial meanings; we mean to be as general as possible. Second, and more specifically, there is a wide range of flexible operational frameworks that would fit our definition of "modern" but might not be considered IT, or even "IT-lite", such as regimes with a role for macro-prudential policies, money as an intermediate target or substantial role for exchange rate intervention, as we will see below.

As countries transition toward modern regimes, the role of money targets, which remains the *de jure* regime, within the broader framework, has been a topic of much discussion in the policy and research agenda. There is a broad range of experiences, from countries in which money targets no longer play a systematic role in monetary policy (such as Kenya) to countries in which money targets occupy center stage (such as Tanzania). Even in the latter countries, however, the implementation of money targeting is becoming increasingly flexible, with target ranges defined instead of discrete targets and increasing attention paid to the use of open market operations and standing facilities to steer short-term interest rates. In this context, modernizing monetary policy frameworks becomes a priority.

While monetary aggregates may play a fundamentally transitional role in monetary policy in SSA, and indeed this transition is well underway, the exchange rate is likely to continue to play an important role. Essentially no countries conduct pure floats; all use sterilized interventions at least from time to time, for various purposes. This aspect of hybrid policymaking is unlikely to go away in the near term, making further research in this area a priority.

---

[9] See Stone (2003).   [10] See Rose (2007).

Most central banks in SSA lack a comprehensive analytic framework for thinking about the impact of shocks on inflation and the role of policy in offsetting them. While there is great benefit in applying insights and analytical frameworks developed elsewhere to SSA, it is also important to adapt these frameworks to reflect both the specific structural characteristics and policy issues. We review some of these efforts in this chapter.

3.3 THE MONETARY TRANSMISSION MECHANISM

The nature of the monetary transmission mechanism (MTM), defined as the link between monetary policy instruments and macroeconomic outcomes, is an active and unsettled area of research in SSA. Mishra and Montiel and Spilimbergo (2012) argue on a priori grounds that the main channels of monetary policy are likely to be weak and unreliable in countries with underdeveloped financial markets and limited *de facto* exchange-rate flexibility. Empirically, these authors found that the correlation between short-term interest rates and bank lending rates is weaker in SSA than in higher-income regions, while Mishra and Montiel (2012) concluded from a survey of the vector autoregression (VAR) evidence that the impulse responses to monetary policy shocks are typically too weak and statistically unreliable in low-income countries to support the successful use of countercyclical monetary policy.

Another line of research recognizes a further difference between SSA and advanced countries: the vastly greater amount of research effort that has gone into specifying VARs that yield the "right" signs. Arguably, the strongest evidence that monetary policy "works" in developed countries comes not from VARs but from the history of the Volker disinflation and the Great Depression. Even in the USA, with its uniquely long, stable data series and policy regimes, economists experimented for many years before arriving at acceptable results, for example, solving the "price puzzle" that inflation seemed to rise after a monetary policy shock and the "liquidity puzzle" that interest rates tended to rise in response to an increase in the money supply.

This second line of research emphasizes recognizes that transmission is surely different in SSA, but that that empirical work depends on careful, tailored attention to low-income country (LIC)-specific complications, including the nature of the regime and the shocks and methodological issues such as short time series and the endogeneity of transmission to (the frequent) changes in the policy regime.

Berg et al. (2013), for example, conducted an event study of the coordinated, large, and somewhat unexpected tightening of monetary policy by four members of the East African Community (Kenya, Rwanda, Tanzania, and Uganda) in late 2011 as they struggled with volatile commodity prices. They find clear evidence of a working transmission mechanism: after a large policy-induced increase in the short-term interest rate, lending and other interest rates rise, the exchange rate tends to appreciate, output growth tends to fall, and inflation declines (see Figure 3.4 and Figure 3.5). A further lesson from these cases is that the nature of transmission depends on the nature of the regime perhaps even more than on more structural parameters such as the

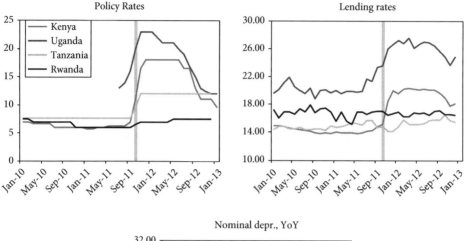

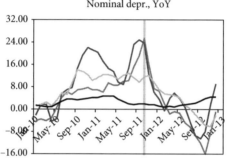

FIGURE 3.4 East Africa: selected macro-variables, Jan. 2010–Dec. 2013.

Source: Berg, Charry, Portillo, and VIcek (2013).

depth of the financial system, and therefore that transmission (e.g. from short rates to long rates) can change rapidly as the regime changes (e.g. from the use of money as an instrument, where short rates contain little information about policy, to interest rate instruments).[11]

Li et al. (2013) attempted to reconcile elements of these two lines of research by focusing on the question of whether data-intensive VAR-based methods may be poorly suited to the data conditions typical of low-income countries. They show that short data samples, measurement error, and high-frequency supply shocks that are characteristic of LIC applications substantially reduce the power of VAR-based inference on the MTM. They also highlight the endogeneity of transmission to the policy regime, noting that as simple a change as a move towards substantial smoothing of interest rates can dramatically strengthen the transmission mechanism.

This brief review of the evidence leaves many questions unanswered. But it serves to highlight some of the themes of this chapter, including the need to focus on the nature of the policy regime, to which we now turn.

---

[11] On the endogeneity of transmission to the regime, see O'Connell, Pattillo, Portillo, and Unsal (forthcoming). See also Mbowe (2012a, b) who finds using bank-level data that lending volumes respond more than lending rates to short-term interest rates, consistent with a credit-rationing equilibrium as in Stiglitz and Weiss (1981).

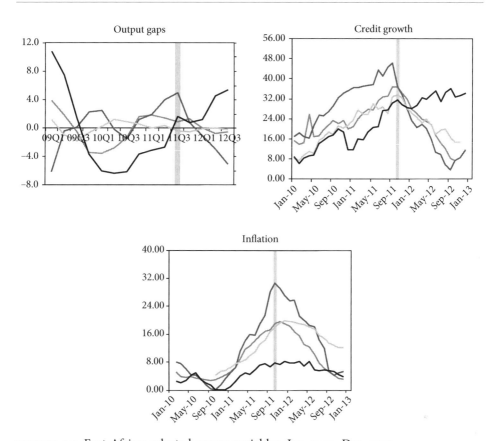

FIGURE 3.5 East Africa: selected macro-variables, Jan. 2010–Dec. 2013.

Source: Berg, Charry, Portillo, and Vlcek (2013).

3.4 FLEXIBLE MONEY TARGETING

The operational frameworks in use in many African central banks are a legacy of IMF stabilization programs that employed Financial Programming (Polak 1957, 2005) to derive limits on the growth of net domestic assets of the central bank. These frameworks employ monetary aggregates as intermediate targets. As interbank markets and markets for short-term government securities have deepened, African central banks have begun to pay greater attention to short-term interest rates as operational targets, following long-established practice in emerging-market and industrial-country economies. In this section we focus on the role of flexibility in systems that use monetary aggregates as intermediate targets.

The monetary block of a Financial Programming exercise consists of the equilibrium condition: $Z_t H_t = P_t Y_t / V_t$, where the left-hand side is the supply of a broad money aggregate (H_t is the monetary base and Z_t is the appropriate money multiplier) and the right-hand side uses a simple quantity theory to express the demand for that aggregate as the ratio of nominal GDP to velocity (P_t is the price level, Y_t is real GDP, and V_t is velocity). Assuming that this equation holds continuously, inflation over the coming program year can be expressed as

$$\pi_{t+1} = \Delta h_{t+1} + \left[\Delta z_{t+1} + \Delta v_{t+1} - \Delta y_{t+1} \right]$$

where lower-case letters denote logs and π_{t+1} denotes the inflation rate $\left(\pi_{t+1} \equiv \Delta p_{t+1} = p_{t+1} - p_t \right)$. Given a projection for the term in square brackets, monetary equilibrium implies that an inflation objective of the form $\pi_t \leq \pi^*$ requires a ceiling on the growth rate of reserve money.

In practice, IMF programs tend to treat the two components of reserve money asymmetrically, combining a floor on net international reserve accumulation with a ceiling on the growth of net domestic assets (and, in many cases, a separate ceiling on domestic credit to the government). If the floor on reserve accumulation is binding, of course, this combination of performance criteria is equivalent to a ceiling on reserve money growth.

In practice, target misses are the norm rather than the exception. IMF (2008) found that among countries with recent trend inflation below 10%, there was no correlation between violations of explicit or implicit program targets for reserve-money growth and deviations of inflation from the program ceiling. The same was not true for high-inflation countries, however: among countries with pre-existing inflation above 10%, reserve-money misses were positively correlated with inflation misses.

This result, and more generally the novelty of money aggregate targeting in the global context, begs the question: why have money targets at all? There are several not mutually exclusive answers to this question.

Most fundamentally, the targets are a legacy from a time when weak credibility, time inconsistency, and conflicting goals between the IMF and central banks necessitated clear and observable intermediate targets. In this view, the target misses observed in low-inflation SSA countries in recent years reflect a tension between the potential credibility benefits of clearly observable intermediate targets and the costs in terms of the optimality of monetary policy.[12]

Absent credibility or time consistency problems, central banks can set money targets in advance but will want to deviate as new information comes in.

- *Supply shocks* would call for partial accommodation. The inflation/money-target misses would be positive, but this does not reflect bad monetary policy; on the contrary avoiding this positive correlation would induce excessive monetary policy response to the supply shock.
- *Money demand* shocks would call for full accommodation, inducing a (fully optimal) zero inflation-miss/money-target-miss correlation.
- Only a *monetary policy shock*—a spontaneous loosening of monetary policy—would induce a suboptimal positive correlation between inflation misses and money target misses.

---

[12] An on-line appendix presents a simple model in the Barro-Gordon (1983) tradition that fully articulates this analysis.

One way to rationalize the monetary policy shock is that it represents a conflict of interest between the authorities and the IMF, where the authorities have a higher inflation target or are pursuing a higher level of output than that consistent with macroeconomic stability.

This suggests that low correlations between money-target misses and inflation misses among low-inflation countries are consistent with the pursuit of stabilization objectives in the absence of severe forms of inflation bias or conflicts of interest with the IMF. Program sanctions are unlikely to be triggered in such situations, because an ex post consultation will typically support a benign interpretation of the central bank's actions. Expectations are anchored not by the credible prospect of program penalties, but by a domestic institutional configuration that supports a credible commitment to low inflation (and a zero money-target miss on average). With credibility secured by other means, the countries in this category can be described as operating a system of *flexible money targeting*.[13]

In view of this analysis, is there any reason to continue to pay any attention to intermediate money targets in such countries? Of course, one reason is the residual concern about the credibility of the monetary authorities. But there are other possibilities. Berg, Portillo, and Unsal (2010) formalize flexible money targeting and analyze the optimal weight on money aggregates as intermediate targets. There are no credibility or time-commitment problems, but the central bank only observes key variables such as output and inflation with a lag. Money market variables such as interest rates and money aggregates—which reflect all these other shocks—are observed in real time. In addition, reflecting highly underdeveloped financial markets, the central bank observes "the" interest rate imperfectly. In this framework, there is a case for giving some weight to the achievement of previously-set intermediate money targets: they allow better responses to unobserved demand shocks, at a cost of inappropriate tightening in the face of positive money demand shocks.

Continued financial development and capital account liberalization will presumably create ongoing instability in money demand. At the same time, institutional development in central banks, sustained progress with overall macroeconomic management, and further experience with flexible money targeting, will likely encourage SSA central banks to follow the lead of others around the world and move away from intermediate money targets over time.

A further factor pushing in this direction involves the ability of the public to understand the policy stance in the context of flexible money targeting (Bindseil 2004). The problem is simple: the private sector cannot cleanly separate deviations from announced money targets into changes in the central bank's policy stance and changes that constitute responses to fluctuations in money demand. O'Connell, Pattillo, Portillo, and Unsal (in progress) will show that in a money-targeting regime, the private sector's signaling problem undermines the transmission of monetary policy shocks to aggregate demand. Lack of clarity is one reason why the central bank of Uganda abandoned its experimentation with an explicitly flexible money-targeting regime in 2009, and adopted inflation targeting "lite" with a short-term interest rate as its main policy instrument.

---

[13] The IMF has recently introduced a new modality for monetary policy conditionality with these countries in mind. It explicitly acknowledges flexibility vis-à-vis money targets, and analyzes monetary policy along a number of dimensions. See IMF (2014).

3.5 ROLE OF THE EXCHANGE RATE

The role of the exchange rate in the monetary policy frameworks in SSA, and developing countries more generally, has been the subject of much research and debate since the 1980s.[14] Here we focus on the conduct of managed floating regimes.

3.5.1 Exchange rate stability from a monetary policy perspective

In a survey of de jure monetary policy frameworks in SSA, IMF (2008) finds that most central banks in the countries with independent monetary policy cite exchange-related issues as one of their policy objectives. Adam and O'Connell (2005) find that substantial foreign exchange intervention is the norm, and that very few countries approximate a clean float. Some of these regimes may be indistinguishable from a pegged exchange rate, at least for some time, and the de facto commitment to the peg may dominate other policy concern, including inflation. In other cases, however, the nominal exchange rate may be serving as an operating target, alongside other instruments such as reserve money or interest rates. In these countries, the exchange rate may be used in direct support of certain objectives, such as inflation or external competitiveness; there may not be a strong commitment to a particular level and the exchange rate may be adjusted as needed.

3.5.2 Exchange rate interventions as a separate instrument of monetary policy

Recent work has re-emphasized the importance of the multiplicity of targets and instruments in monetary (or central bank) policy. In addition to the short-term interest rate or reserve money instrument, central banks in developing countries have often made use of foreign-exchange (FX) interventions as a separate instrument.

Two recent papers have analyzed the role of interventions as a separate policy tool (Ostry et al. 2012; Benes et al. 2015) and support several points. First, for interventions to serve as a separate instrument, they must operate through different channels than the monetary policy channel. This narrows the focus to sterilized interventions, that is, interventions that do not affect the stance of monetary policy (as measured, for example, by the interest rate). Sterilized interventions generate changes in the gross holdings of assets by the public. The resulting changes in risk premia, through a portfolio balance effect, move the exchange rate.

There is no consensus in the macro-literature on whether sterilized interventions actually work. However, central banks in developing countries believe that FX interventions are

---

[14] Masson and Pattillo (2005) provide a comprehensive and historical overview of exchange rate regimes in SSA up to the early 2000s.

effective (see Neely 2008; BIS 2005). This is more likely to be the case in low-income countries such as in Africa, where domestic and foreign assets are imperfect substitutes and markets are relatively thin.

These authors analyzed hybrid regimes, where both interest rates and sterilized intervention are used, and find that there can be some advantages to managing the exchange rate via interventions in the presence of certain shocks. By offsetting the impact of a temporary shock to foreigners' risk premia on the domestic interest rate, the central bank can stabilize the exchange rate and thereby insulate the economy. This insulation allows the use of the interest rate for domestic stabilization policy.

However, there are also important limits to intervention policy. Successful intervention policy requires that the authorities distinguish between temporary and permanent changes in equilibrium real exchange rates. While the former can be successfully offset by interventions, the latter can force the central bank to run out of reserves or accumulate reserves indefinitely. Benes et al. (2015) distinguished between policies that "lean against the wind" and policies that target an exchange rate level: the former limit the amount of reserve accumulation or draw-down that can result from persistent changes in the exchange rate, and are therefore more robust to uncertainty about the nature of the shocks.

An additional complication is that, in an environment of incomplete information and imperfect credibility, exchange rate management may send confusing signals about the commitment of the authorities to their inflation objectives. Such confusion by private agents is not unwarranted, as central banks may themselves feel conflicted. One implication is that the communication strategy of central bank may have to include a clear and well understood hierarchy of objectives.

3.6 FISCAL AND MONETARY INTERACTIONS

The interaction between fiscal and monetary policy is a time-honored topic in macroeconomics.[15] Here we provide a review of several fiscal-monetary interaction issues in SSA. It is helpful to think of these interactions as falling along a range from pure fiscal dominance to some constraints on monetary policy stemming from concerns with fiscal solvency, to pressures stemming from the real effects of fiscal policy.

3.6.1 A range of fiscal and monetary policy interactions

The most extreme form of fiscal/monetary interaction is fiscal dominance, defined as a situation in which monetary financing is necessary to close the government funding gap and the

---

[15] The modern strand emphasizes the fiscal theory of the price level (FTPL) (Leeper 1991; Woodford 1995; and many others). One insight is that fiscal policy, and specifically the need for inter-temporal solvency, can influence the price level even when there is no direct monetary financing of the deficit. Another is that active monetary policy, i.e. policies in which real interest rates increase aggressively in response to inflation, may destabilize inflation if fiscal policy is not geared toward stabilizing government debt. See Baldini and Poplawski-Ribeiro (2011) for a discussion of the evidence on FTPL in SSA.

inflation rate becomes endogenous to fiscal policy.[16] This was a chronic problem in SSA, as documented in Adam and O'Connell (2005), but it has largely been resolved starting in the 1990s. The improvement continued in the 2000s, to the point where many governments had become net creditors to the central bank.[17]

An intermediate type of fiscal and monetary interaction exists in which the central bank can control inflation, but in which its policy conduct may be influenced by fiscal pressures. One such example is when the central bank does not tighten policy as aggressively as it would like to out of concern for the effect of that policy on fiscal solvency. Pressures of this type are likely to materialize in regimes, such as IT, in which the central bank takes direct responsibility for short-term interest rates.[18] Similarly, tighter monetary policy may hurt the bottom line of the central bank. If transfers from the Treasury are necessary to cover central bank operating costs, and the negotiations over these transfers pose a challenge to central bank independence, the bank may hesitate to act as aggressively as it otherwise would. If they are so severe that the Taylor principle is not satisfied—that is, real interest rates do not rise in the face of rising inflation—fiscal dominance would result. But even when the pressures are not that severe, such concerns can still result in higher and more volatile inflation.

The third type of fiscal interaction results from the effects of fiscal expansions and financing operations on the equilibrium (or natural or neutral) real interest rate. One of the insights from the new-Keynesian literature is the importance of the natural rate of interest for the conduct of monetary policy: in order to avoid the buildup of inflationary or deflationary pressures, monetary policy must steer interest rates toward the natural rate. By its very nature, fiscal policy has implications for the natural rate of interest rate, for example, expansions in government spending that are financed domestically require an increase in real interest rates. If interest-rate setting falls behind such increases, aggregate demand and inflationary pressures will follow. As argued in Agenor and Montiel (1999) for the case of emerging markets, and Berg et al. (2010) for the case of SSA, several features in developing countries may amplify the effects of fiscal shocks on equilibrium real interest rates. These features complicate the environment in which monetary policy operates.

3.6.2 Management of aid and other external flows

A related topic is the management of external resource flows, such as aid. Berg et al. (2007) document how, during aid surge episodes in several African countries with managed floats

---

[16] In the absence of fiscal adjustment, efforts to tighten monetary policy may result in further increases in inflation, under the expectation that the fiscal costs of tight policies will have to be monetized in the future. This is the so-called "tight-money" paradox. Buffie (2003) argues that several episodes of inflation acceleration in SSA during the late 1980s to early 1990s can be explained by this mechanism.

[17] The curtailing of fiscal dominance does not imply that monetary financing has been eliminated altogether. Provided the financing is small enough, central banks can (and often do) retain control of their operational targets, either a short-term interest rate or reserve money, simply by sterilizing the initial credit to the government.

[18] This type of concern may have implications for the choice of policy regime. For example, it has often been argued that the main objective behind the Fed's adoption of broad money targeting under Chairman Volcker was to help implement a substantial increase in real interest rates without having to take direct responsibility for the level of the interest rate.

(Ghana, Mozambique, Tanzania, Uganda), concerns about real appreciation resulted in large accumulations of reserves. This policy response may have helped contain the appreciation pressures. But it also resulted in a peculiar situation in which the authorities tried to use the aid twice: once to increase government spending, and once to increase the stock of reserves. The private sector was crowded out as a result, mainly through higher interest rates (when the accumulation was sterilized) and in some cases also through the inflation tax (when otherwise).[19]

Models used to analyze this policy choice (Berg et al. 2010a, b) contain specific versions of the two-instrument/two-target mechanisms discussed in more generality in section 5. There is also a fiscal dimension—the interaction with the spending of the aid. They also underscore the "real," as opposed to purely monetary, nature of reserve accumulation and raise the issue of whether greater coordination of reserve policy with fiscal policy could help improve macroeconomic outcomes. Explicit coordination may require refining the concept of central bank independence, however.

Having discussed some of the key issues with respect to policy regimes in SSA, we now turn to what is perhaps the salient structural feature of SSA countries with respect to monetary policy: the large role of commodity and in particular food price shocks.[20]

3.7 Food Price Shocks: Implications for Monetary Policy

Understanding domestic food price dynamics, including their possible spillovers to non-food prices, and their link with both international food prices and domestic policy decisions, is one of the most crucial questions in monetary policy in Africa.

3.7.1 Food prices and the structure of inflation in African countries

Developing countries allocate a larger share of their factors of production to the agricultural sector to cover food consumption needs. As a result, the average food share in the CPI in sub-Saharan Africa is close to 50%, compared with 16% in the OECD. Inflation in African countries is therefore heavily influenced by food prices.

The importance of food prices has a number of implications. Unlike the generalized increase in prices observed in most countries, inflation in African countries may be driven by changes in food prices relative to other prices in the economy. One simple way to gauge the above influence is to decompose inflation (π_t) into two parts:

---

[19] See Berg et al. (2010a,b), Adam et al. (2009), and Buffie et al. (2008, 2010) on the pros on cons of various policy responses in this context.

[20] Another salient structural feature, the underdevelopment of the financial system and its implication for monetary policy, is discussed for example in Agenor and Montiel (2008) and Baldini et al. (2015).

$$\pi_t = \left(1 - \gamma_F\right)\tilde{\pi}_t + \gamma_F \pi_{F,t} = \underbrace{\tilde{\pi}_t}_{A} + \underbrace{\gamma_F \Delta p_{F,t}}_{B}$$

$\tilde{\pi}_t \left(\pi_{F,t}\right)$ denotes non-food (food) inflation, $\Delta P_{F,t}$ denotes changes in the relative price of food, that is, food inflation minus non-food inflation, and γ_F is the weight of food in the CPI. Interpreted this way, inflation in every country is the sum of (i) a generalized increase in prices $\tilde{\pi}_t$ (assumed for simplicity to be captured by non-food inflation), and (ii) changes in the relative price of food. Portillo et al. (2013) made use of the above equation to study the properties of inflation in Africa (at business cycle frequency). These authors find that in the median African country in their sample, headline inflation is four times more volatile in Africa than in the US, with term B contributing to about 50% of the volatility of headline in the former, compared with only 1% in the latter. This is not just due to the higher food share: relative food prices are three times more volatile in African countries than in the USA. But what drives changes in the relative price of food?

3.7.2 Domestic shocks to food production

Much of the intra-annual volatility in inflation in SSA is due to weather shocks. Food inflation can oscillate from double digit to deflation in a matter of months.[21] In addition, unlike in developed countries, the absence of capital deepening in the agricultural sector leaves food production increasingly exposed to weather shocks.

Because shocks to domestic food production raise inflation and lower output, their prevalence has implications for the correlation between output and inflation in low-income countries. Portillo et al. (2013) show that this correlation is negative, unlike in developed countries where the correlation is positive. The negative correlation reflects the relative importance of supply (mainly food) as opposed to demand shocks in inflation dynamics in Africa, not an indictment of the Phillips curve.

These food supply shocks do not typically spill over to non-food prices, suggesting that some of the food price volatility is understood to be transitory and therefore does not have major implications for the design of monetary policy, as we will see below.

3.7.3 International food price shocks

Much of the debate on food inflation in Africa in recent years has focused on the role of international food prices. The world economy has recently experienced two episodes of rapid increase in commodities prices, including food; first in 2006–2008 (often referred to as the food and fuel crisis) and more recently in 2010–2011. To give a sense of the magnitude, during the 12 months between June 2007 and June 2008, the index of international food commodity prices compiled by the IMF increased by 39.2%, relative to the US CPI.

---

[21] See Portillo et al. (2013).

Table 3.4 Month inflation dynamics 2007–2008, sub-Saharan Africa. Median country

	Non-food inflation	Changes in the relative price of food	Headline inflation
September-07	4.9	1.5	6.2
September-08	7.8	8.0	12.1

Source: IMF Staff Calculation.

Not surprisingly, the episode coincides with a significant increase in the relative price of food, and inflation, in SSA, as documented in Table 3.4.[22]

One of the issues extensively discussed in this episode was the impact of the international food price spike on domestic food prices. A simple way of assessing this relation is to assume that the food basket is a Cobb–Douglass function of imported food and a domestic (non-traded) component, where a is weight of imports and the measure of pass-through. After some algebra, the following relation emerges:

$$\Delta p_{F,t} = \frac{a}{1-a\gamma_F}\left(\Delta p_t^* + \Delta s_t\right) + domestic\ shocks$$

Δp_t^* is the change in the international price of food relative to the US CPI and ΔS_t measures the rate of depreciation of the real exchange rate relative to the USA. For a given degree of tradability of the food basket, a real appreciation will reduce the inflationary pressures stemming from higher international food prices. Understanding what drives the real exchange rate response to an international food price shock is therefore an important area of research.

As Table 3.5 indicates, there is a considerable difference between the international spike and the relatively modest increase in relative food prices in the median African country

Table 3.5 Relative food prices 2007–2008, sub-Saharan Africa. Median country

	Changes in the international relative price of food	Changes in the real exchange rate	Changes in the domestic relative price of food
September-07	5.1 (a)	−5.3 (c)	1.5 (e)
September-08	39.2 (b)	−16 (d)	8 (f)
Passthrough=(f–e)/ (b–a+d–c+(f–e)*γF)		0.24	

Source: IMF Staff Calculation. Changes in the international relatives price and the real exchange are calculated for June 2008 and June 2007, respectively, to allow for full extent of pass-through.

[22] This table and the results presented here draw on IMF World Economic Outlook (2011).

during this period. The difference is accounted for by two factors: a substantial real appreciation and relatively low pass through, with the latter accounted for by differences in food baskets and imperfect tradability of some items. Many countries also implemented several trade and fiscal measures that may have weakened the relationship.

3.7.4   Food prices also reflect domestic demand pressures

Although the previous discussion has emphasized the supply side drivers of food price inflation, it is important to stress that these prices also reflect domestic demand pressures, including the stance of monetary policy, both through their effects on generalized price pressures and the relative price of food. Food prices tend to be more flexible than non-food prices, implying that they may well reflect aggregate demand pressures first or more than the rest of the economy. In other words, food prices increases may precede non-food prices in time, but one must be careful in interpreting such causality as implying that food price developments spill over to the non-food sector.

3.7.5   How should policy respond to an increase in food prices?

To the extent increases in food prices reflect supply shocks, the policy response to such an increase has been the subject of much debate in macroeconomics. A common adage is that the central bank should accommodate "first-round" effects of supply shocks but respond (i.e. tighten policy) to "second-round" effects. What is meant by first-round effects is not always explicit but is usually assumed to depend on the weight of the commodity in the CPI. This direct effect is usually contrasted with possible spillovers from commodity prices to non-food (or core or sticky-price) inflation and wages—second round effects.

Implicit in the policy advice is the notion that a supply shock requires an adjustment in relative prices. Holding core inflation constant, an increase in headline inflation helps implement these necessary relative-price changes; this reasoning supports the first part of the adage. Core inflation embodies the distortions resulting from nominal rigidities. Stabilizing core—rather than headline inflation—is desirable from a welfare perspective, and therefore justifies the second part of the adage.[23]

Much of the literature focuses on whether second round effects can be avoided. Blanchard and Gali (2007) argue that, in the presence of real wage rigidities, some spillovers from supply shocks to core inflation are inevitable. In this case a trade-off emerges between (core) inflation stabilization and output stabilization. Central banks with imperfect credibility may also experience spillovers if inflation expectations become de-anchored, and again a policy tightening may be needed to regain credibility.[24]

---

[23] See Aoki (2001). In practice, part of this policy challenge is bypassed insofar as central banks target a forecast of inflation and therefore accommodate temporary changes in inflation, regardless of which inflation index they target.

[24] See Alichi et al. (2010). Other recent contributions on this topic include Anand and Prasad (2010) and Catao and Chang (2010).

It remains an open question whether second round effects are more or less severe in LICs. Policy credibility is lower so spillovers should be more likely (IMF 2011). In addition, real income may need to fall by more, given the structure of the economy. These larger pressures may translate into large spillovers (Blanchard and Gali 2007; Adam 2011). Little is known, however, about the relative importance of these rigidities in SSA. As discussed above, the region is regularly subject to (domestic) food price shocks, which do not usually spill over to non-food.[25]

An aspect of the policy response that is often overlooked is that first-round effects are difficult to define, especially regarding shocks to international food prices. This is because, as discussed above, equilibrium changes in the domestic relative food price depend on equilibrium changes in the real exchange rate. Portillo and Zanna (2015) show a wide range of first round effects, depending on the country's access to international capital markets, the trade balance in food and the size of trade and other elasticities.

We now turn to analytic frameworks that can help assess the sources of volatility and the appropriate stance of policy, including in the face of food price shocks.

3.8 Analytic Frameworks for Monetary Policy

The move to more flexible and forward-looking policy regimes creates practical and analytic challenges for financial programming. This framework provides few clues as to how flexibility should be deployed. In particular, it does not help disentangle the various shocks (supply, aggregate, demand, money demand) or suggest implications for monetary policy. This shortcoming was displayed prominently both during the food and fuel crisis of 2007–2008 and the global financial crisis. In the case of food price shocks, it was very difficult, if not impossible, to map the discussion about first and second-round effects into clear implications for money targets, as a target miss may be consistent with either a policy tightening or a loosening. In practice, the assessment of policy has typically shifted to the inflation outlook and the level of interest rates, but in some cases the emphasis on money targets has also resulted in erratic policies.

As this example illustrates, there is great need for models to undertake policy analysis in LICs, as these countries modernize their monetary policy regimes. In our view, these models must meet two criteria. First, they must reflect modern thinking on monetary policy, drawing on both state-of-the-art macro-theory and current practice in central banks in advanced and emerging markets. Second, they must be tailored to address key low-income-country specific issues.

3.8.1 Recent analytical contributions

Despite the importance of the topic, there has been very little work in the academic and policy literature tailored to low-income countries. As a result, central banks in these countries

---

[25] This limited spillover is reflected in the relatively smaller inflation inertia in LICs, which is often interpreted as a proxy for the importance of second round effects.

have lacked guidance when deciding how to respond to shocks, especially since the food and fuel crisis of 2007–2008, and policy has at times been erratic, that is, policy has been tighter or looser than what was warranted by the state of the economy. We briefly review some recent work in this area here.

Andrle et al. (2013, forthcoming) develop an analytical framework for low income countries, with two applications to Kenya, a country that is representative of the policy challenges in recent years. They build on similar frameworks used in central banks in advanced and emerging markets, which are based on new-Keynesian open economy models but with an emphasis on data filtering (with the use of the Kalman filter) and forecasting.[26] One key feature is the emphasis on gaps in output and the real exchange rate as drivers of inflation, and considerable effort therefore goes toward disentangling gaps and trends empirically.

In Andrle et al. (forthcoming), the authors extend the standard framework to study food and non-food inflation. The model is used to filter macroeconomic data from Kenya and decompose most series into gaps and trends, including for relative food prices, as well as identify the relevant macroeconomic shocks. They find that imported food price shocks account for part of the recent inflation spikes, but more importantly, that accommodative monetary policy also played an important role. Their analysis indicated that short-term interest rates needed to increase substantially to offset the latest inflationary pressure, which is what the central bank of Kenya (CBK) implemented by the end of 2011.

Andrle et al. (2013) focused on the implementation of flexible money targeting: target design, potential link with interest rate policy, and interpretation of target misses, that is, deviations of realized reserve money from its target. The latter point acknowledges that hitting targets is in itself a policy decision, and the authors provide a model-based interpretation of target misses, for example, whether they reflect policy or money demand shocks.

Alichi et al. (2010) developed a model of endogenous policy credibility to study the optimal path of disinflation and the attainment of an inflation target, and apply it to Ghana. They find that the output inflation trade-off is more severe at earlier stages of credibility, and policy needs to be geared toward achieving its target, at the expense of output. As the central bank builds credibility, the trade-off improves, which allows for much more flexibility in responding to supply shocks.

Baldini et al. (2015) developed a dynamic stochastic general equilibrium (DSGE) model with a banking sector to analyze the impact of the financial crisis on Zambia, and the role of the monetary policy response. These authors view the crisis as a combination of three related shocks: a worsening in the terms of the trade, an increase in the country's risk premium, and a decrease in the risk appetite of local banks. They characterize monetary policy as "stop and go": initially tight, subsequently loose, for reasons related to the money-targeting framework in place in Zambia. One important lesson from this analysis is cautionary: monetary policy can add unnecessarily to macroeconomic volatility, but even well-designed and implemented policies may not be able to do much to resist the volatility associated with the sorts of shocks encountered by Zambia during the crisis.

Central banks in the region are gradually making use of these types of models. The model themselves do not produce the forecasts or determine policy, as these are based mostly on

---

[26]   See Berg, Karam, and Laxton (2006) for an exposition of a simple operational model along these lines. An influential paper on new-Keynesian open economy models is by Gali and Monacelli (2005).

judgment. However, the models can help discipline policy analysis, interpret the data and facilitate the production of coherent forecasts and alternative scenarios, and provide systematic input for policy formulation. This is part of a broader effort to develop in-house forecasting and policy analysis systems (FPAS), drawing on best practices that have emerged from the experience of central banks in other regions.[27]

It is not straightforward to compare these newer models to financial programming. On the one hand, financial programming contains no behavioral, structural, or causal relationships among the variables, normally the core elements of a macroeconomic model. On the other hand, the continued attraction of financial programming lies in the fact that its main identities focus attention on the interaction of reserves, monetary policy, fiscal policy, and macroeconomic outcomes. Such interactions are highly complex and indeed beyond the scope of most current macroeconomic models, from the simple practical models presented in Andrle et al. (2013, forthcoming) to the large DSGEs such as the IMF's Global Integrated Monetary and Fiscal Model (GIMF) (Kumhof et al. 2010).

We have seen that progress can be made by using relatively simple modern macroeconomic models that focus on only a few of these mechanisms. However, where the nexus of monetary policy, sterilized intervention, fiscal policy, and exchange rates and reserves cannot readily be disentangled in the policy regime, the analytic situation is also more complicated. Models such as those discussed in section 5 on exchange rates and section 6 on aid can be useful. But they have yet to be proven operationally useful, and the challenges are daunting.

3.9 Conclusion

The coming decade will be marked by rapid institutional modernization and continued learning-by-doing by central banks in SSA. Financial development will continue apace, bringing the management of financial vulnerability and the capital account to the fore alongside traditional policy concerns. Mobile money and other aspects of financial sector development and increased integration with world capital markets will mean that instability in demand for monetary aggregates will continue, the interest rate channel of monetary policy may strengthen, and the costs of policy failures may rise. Meanwhile access to world capital markets and a proliferation of natural resource discoveries imply that fiscal and capital account volatility may also be increasing in some countries.[28]

But with what policy regime? Looking beyond SSA, now is an unsettled time for monetary policy theory and practice. A few years ago, it might have been straightforward to predict that those SSA countries would look to inflation targeting as a model. It still remains the case that the main challenge for SSA countries is to get from here to there in good form, given the many specific difficulties discussed in this chapter. But what "there" will look like also remains an open question. Even now, with all the innovation in monetary

---

[27] See Laxton, Rose, and Scott (2009) for a thorough description of FPAS.

[28] On mobile money, see Davovan (2011) and Weil et al. (2011). Capital account developments are discussed in IMF (2011, 2013). Natural resource discoveries and monetary policy implications are discussed in IMF (2012a, b), Dagher et al. (2012), and Wills (2013).

policy instruments in advanced countries, some version of inflation targeting seems to be the main benchmark.[29] But important questions remain. As advanced and emerging market countries experiment with a number of alternative instruments, and as sterilized intervention remains as popular as ever, how this instrument should be integrated into policy regimes in SSA is perhaps the most interesting open policy and research question on the table.

One byproduct of modernizing monetary policy frameworks may be a new appreciation of the limits of monetary policy. As frameworks become more transparent and well grounded analytically, central banks will have to face some tough choices about the extent to which they can seriously aim directly at faster medium-term growth of output or employment, or at competitive or stable real exchange rates. And when shocks are to the financial sector or to the relative price of food, monetary policy can readily make things worse, but even well-executed policy cannot smooth things out entirely. The canonical inflation-targeting framework and its relatives are in a sense especially unambitious: they do not even promise to anchor inflation itself, just long-run inflation expectations.

This lack of ambition is probably appropriate. Given the prevalence of supply shocks, uncertainties about transmission, and the generally high degree of underlying macroeconomic volatility in many SSA countries, the firm anchoring of inflation expectations will be a great achievement. It eliminates one important potential source of volatility and thereby serves indirectly to stabilize the rest of the economy, promote financial sector deepening, and longer-term growth. This is surely ambitious enough.

Acknowledgments

We thank Michael Atingi-Ego, Salim Darbar, Célestin Monga, R. Armando Morales, Bozena Radzewicz-Bak, Finn Tarp, Peter Van Oudheusden, and seminar participants at the Author's Meeting of the Oxford Handbook of Africa and Economics. The views expressed herein are those of the authors and should not be attributed to the IMF, its Executive Board, its management, or to USAID.

References

Adam, C. (2011). On the macroeconomic management of food price shocks in low-income countries. *Journal of African Economies*, 20:63–9.

Adam, C.S., and O'Connell, S.A. (2005). *Monetary Policy and Aid Management in Sub Saharan Africa, mimeo.* Oxford: University of Oxford; Swarthmore: PA: Swarthmore College.

Adam, C., Connell, O., Buffie, S., and Pattillo, C. (2009). Monetary policy rules for managing aid surges in Africa. *Review of Development Economics*, 13(3):464–490.

---

[29] On the (relatively positive) experience of emerging market economies with inflation targeting during the global financial crisis, see de Carvalho Filho (2011). More generally, see the contributions in Reichlin and Baldwin (2013).

Agenor, P.-R., and Montiel, P. (1999). *Development Macroeconomics*. Princeton: Princeton University Press.

Agenor, P., and Montiel, P. (2008). Monetary policy analysis in a small open credit-based economy. *Open Economies Review*, 19(4):423–455.

Alichi, A., Clinton, K., Dagher, J. et al. (2010). A Model for Full-Fledged Inflation Targeting and Application to Ghana, IMF Working Paper 10/25.

Anand, R., and Prasad, E. (2010). Optimal Price Indices for Targeting Inflation under Incomplete Markets, IMF Working Paper 10/200.

Andrle, M., Berg, A., Morales, R. et al. (forthcoming). On the Sources of Inflation in Kenya: A Model-Based Approach. *South African Journal of Economics*.

Andrle, M., Berg, A., Berkes, E. et al. (2013). Money Targeting in a Modern Forecasting and Policy Analysis System: an Application to Kenya, IMF Working Paper 13/239.

Baldini, A., Benes, J., Berg, A. et al. (2015). Monetary Policy in Low-Income Countries in the Face of the Global Financial Crisis: A Structural Analysis. *Pacific Economic Review*, 20(1):149–192.

Baldini, A., and Poplawski-Ribeiro, M. (2011). Fiscal and monetary determinants of inflation in low-income countries: theory and evidence from sub-Saharan Africa. *Journal of African Economies*, 20(3):419–462.

Barro, R.J., and Gordon, D.B. (1983). A positive theory of monetary policy in a natural-rate model. *Journal of Political Economy*, 91(4):589–610.

Benes, J., Berg, A., Portillo, R., and Vavra, D. (2015). Modeling Sterilized Interventions and Balance-Sheet Effects of Monetary Policy in a new-Keynesian Framework. *Open Economies Review*, 26:81–108.

Berg, A., Aiyar, S., Hussain, M. et al. (2007). The Macroeconomics of Scaling Up Aid: Lessons from Recent Experience. IMF Occasional Paper 253.

Berg, A., Charry, L., Portillo, R., and Vlcek, J. (2013). The Monetary Transmission Mechanism in the Tropics: A Narrative Approach. IMF Working Paper 13/197.

Berg, A., Mirzoev, T., Portillo, R., and Zanna, L.F. (2010a). The Short-Run Macroeconomics of Aid Inflows: Understanding the Interaction of Fiscal and Reserve Policy. IMF Working Paper 10/65.

Berg, A., Gottschalk, J., Portillo, R., and Zanna, L.F. (2010b). The Macroeconomics of Medium-Term Aid Scaling-up Scenarios. IMF Working Paper 10/160.

Berg, A., Portillo, R., and Unsal, D.F. (2010). On the Optimal Adherence to Money Targets in a New-Keynesian Framework: An application to low-income countries. IMF Working Paper 10/134.

Blanchard, O., and Gali, J. (2007). Real wage rigidities and the New-Keynesian Model. *Journal of Money, Credit and Banking*, 39:35–66.

Bindseil, U. (2004). *Monetary Policy Implementation: Theory, Past, and Present*. Oxford: Oxford University Press.

Buffie, E. (2003) Tight money, real interest rates, and inflation in sub-Saharan Africa. *IMF Staff Papers*, 50(1):115–35.

Buffie, E., Adam, C., O'Connell, S., and Pattillo, C. (2008). Riding the wave: monetary responses to aid surges in low-income countries. *European Economic Review*, 52(8):1378–1395.

Buffie, E., O'Connell, S., and Adam, C. (2010). Fiscal inertia, donor credibility, and the monetary management of aid surges. *Journal of Development Economics*, 93(2):287–298.

Catão, L., and Chang, R. (2010). World Food Prices and Monetary Policy. IMF Working Paper 10/161.

Cukierman, A. (1992). *Central Bank Strategy, Credibility and Independence—Theory and Evidence*. Cambridge, MA: MIT Press.

Cukierman, A., Webb S., and Neyapti, B. (1992). Measuring the independence of central banks and its effect on policy outcomes. *World Bank Economic Review*, 6:353–398.

de Carvalho Filho, I. (2011). 28 months later: how inflation targeters outperformed their peers in the great recession. *B.E. Journal of Macroeconomics*, 11(1):1–46.

Gali, J., and Monacelli, T. (2005). Monetary policy and exchange rate volatility in a small open economy model. *Review of Economic Studies*, 72:707–734.

Giuliano, P., Mishra, P., and Spilinbergo, A. (2010). Democracy and reforms: evidence from a new dataset. *American Economic Journal*, 5(4):179–204.

Gulde, A.M., and Tsangarides, C. (2008) *The CFA Franc Zone: Common Currency, Uncommon Challenges*. Washington, DC: IMF.

Honohan, P., and O'Connell, S.A. (1997). Contrasting Monetary Regimes in Africa. IMF Working Paper 97/64.

International Monetary Fund (2008). Monetary and exchange rate policies in sub-Saharan Africa, in *Regional Economic Outlook, Sub-Saharan Africa*. Washington, DC: IMF, Chapter 2.

International Monetary Fund (2011). Target what you can hit: commodity price swings and monetary policy, in *World Economic Outlook*. Washington, DC: IMF, Chapter 3.

Kumhof, M., Laxton, D., Muir, D., and Mursula, S. (2010). The Global Integrated Monetary and Fiscal Model (GIMF)—Theoretical Structure. IMF Working Paper 10/34.

Laxton, D., Rose, D., and Scott, A. (2009). Developing a Structured Forecasting and Policy Analysis System to Support Inflation-Forecast Targeting (IFT). IMF Working Paper 09/65.

Li, B., O'Connell, S., Adam, C. et al. (2013). VAR meets DSGE: Uncovering the Monetary Transmission Mechanism in Sub-Saharan Africa. Swarthmore, PA: Swarthmore College.

Lucotte, Y. (2009). *The Influence of Central Bank Independence on Budget Deficits in Developing Countries: New Evidence from Panel Data Analysis*. New Orleans: Laboratory of Economics in Orleans, University of Orleans.

Masson, P.R., and Pattillo, C. (2005). *The Monetary Geography of Africa*. Washington: The Brookings Institution.

Mbowe, W. (2012a). *Interest-Rate Pass-Through: An Empirical Investigation on Tanzania*. Research Department, Bank of Tanzania.

Mbowe, W. (2012b). *The Bank Lending Channel of Monetary Policy Transmission: Dynamic Bank-Level Panel Data Analysis on Tanzania*. Research Department, Bank of Tanzania.

Mishra, P., and Montiel, P. (2012). How Effective is Monetary Transmission in Low-Income Countries? A Survey of the Empirical Evidence, IMF Working Paper 12/143.

Mishra, P, Montiel, P., and Spilimbergo, A. (2012). Monetary transmission in low-income countries: effectiveness and policy implications. *IMF Economic Review*, 60:270–302.

Neely, C.J. (2008). Central Bank Authorities' Beliefs about Foreign Exchange Intervention. *Journal of International Money and Finance*, 27(1):1–25.

Ostry, J.D., Ghosh, A.R., and Chamon, M. (2012). Two Targets, Two Instruments: Monetary and Exchange Rate Policies in Emerging Market Economies. IMF Staff Discussion Note SDN/12/01.

Polak, J.J. (1957). Monetary analysis of income formation and payments problems. *IMF Staff Papers*, 6(1):1–50.

Polak, J.J. (2005). The IMF monetary model at forty, in J. Boughton (ed.), *Selected Essays of Jacques J. Polak, 1994-2004*. New York and London: Sharpe, pp. 209–226.

Portillo, R., and Zanna, L.F. (2015). On the First-Round Effects of Food Price Shocks: the Role of the International Asset Market Structure. IMF Working Paper 15/33.

Portillo, R., Zanna, L.F., O'Connell, S., and Peck, R. (2013). Implications of Structural Transformation for Monetary Policy and Inflation, Manuscript, IMF.

Reichlin, L., and Baldwin, R. (eds) (2013). *Is Inflation Targeting Dead? Central Banking After the Crisis.* London: CEPR.

Rose, A. (2007). A Stable International Monetary System Emerges: Inflation Targeting is Bretton Woods, Reversed. *Journal of International Money and Finance,* 26(7):663–681.

Stiglitz, J., and Weiss, A. (1981). Credit rationing in markets with imperfect information. *American Economic Review,* 71(3):393–410.

Stone, M. (2003). Inflation Targeting Lite. IMF Working Paper 03/12.

Woodford, M. (1995). Price level determinacy without control of a monetary aggregate. *Carnegie-Rochester Conference Series on Public Policy,* 43:1–46.

CHAPTER 4

....

THE FUTURE OF AFRICAN MONETARY GEOGRAPHY

....

PAUL R. MASSON, CATHERINE PATTILLO,
AND XAVIER DEBRUN

4.1 INTRODUCTION

....

AFRICA has a long and interesting history of currency use, ranging from the circulation of cowrie shells, supply of silver for English "guineas", and the use of Maria-Theresa thalers in East Africa well after they ceased to circulate in Europe (see Masson and Pattillo 2005, for a survey of some of this history). More recently, Africa has provided insights into the operation of currency unions, since there are two longstanding monetary unions based on the CFA franc (CFA stands for Communauté Financière Africaine in West Africa and Communauté Financière d'Afrique in Central Africa) plus an exchange rate union based on the South African rand that has operated for almost a century in one form or another.

The "monetary geography" of the continent, that is, its pattern of currency use (a term due to Cohen 1998), is also slated to change in the future if the planned and proposed monetary unions for Africa eventually come about. Not only does Africa provide the most examples of any continent of extant currency unions extending beyond national borders, but African countries also have plans to continue along that path. The main reasons for the interest in new monetary unions are twofold: first, regional integration is seen as a way to achieve greater prosperity and better governance, given generally small and low-income countries with relatively weak institutions; and, second, the example of European monetary integration, culminating in the creation of the euro zone, kindled enthusiasm in other regions of the world, and especially in Africa.

In what follows, the economic performance of monetary-union countries is briefly discussed in section 2 and compared with that of countries with independent currencies. Economic policy making in many African countries has evolved over recent decades toward greater exchange rate flexibility, lessening of fiscal dominance and some strengthening of central bank independence. Macroeconomic policy reforms have been widely adopted, and fiscal policies, though still under stress, are generally more sustainable. These changes have improved the viability of independent currencies.

Moreover, there are reasons to be skeptical that some of the African monetary union projects will actually come about. Section 3 surveys the various proposed monetary union, highlighting that target dates have often been missed in the past. Treaties have sometimes been signed by heads of state with little appreciation of their implications, in order to make a gesture of support for regional integration. When the time comes to take costly measures that are required to achieve it, the political will is often not there. It is therefore important to consider the economic costs and benefits of participating in a monetary union, and section 4 provides a comprehensive economic model that quantifies both the advantages of monetary unification and the costs, which are related to fiscal asymmetries and the resulting pressures on monetary policy, and to the traditional optimum currency area concerns about different shocks hitting the various economies. This model is used to address two questions: (i) are the existing monetary/exchange rate unions (CFA franc zones and the Common Monetary Area of Southern Africa) desirable on economic terms, and (ii) should they be expanded or new monetary zones be created? These two issues are addressed in sections 5 and 6, respectively. The quantitative analysis gives a qualified yes in some cases, but not in others—especially those with little trade, large differences in fiscal discipline, and low or negative correlations in their terms of trade shocks. The model does not, however, consider political factors, which are often the prime motivating factor for monetary union projects.

An additional element has lessened the enthusiasm for monetary unions, and that is the crisis in the euro zone that has threatened to destroy it. The main lesson that should be drawn from this crisis is that other regional institutions and regional flexibility need to be strengthened to make a monetary union work, and these require regional solidarity and political will. Time will tell whether this lesson will get traction in Africa, and whether the potential members of monetary unions are willing to sacrifice national sovereignty in favor of fiscal federation and supra-nationality. This is discussed in section 7, which also sketches some conclusions.

4.2 Comparative Performance of Monetary Union Countries

As noted, there are three monetary/exchange rate unions in Africa. There is an extensive literature on the advantages and disadvantages of "hard" currency pegs and monetary unions. It will not be surveyed here, but the advantages of greater stability and lower transactions costs resulting from commitment to a credible peg or sharing a common currency are set against the loss of the use of monetary policy and exchange rate adjustment to achieve macroeconomic objectives.[1] Cutting across this dichotomy is the issue of whether

---

[1] Recent applications to Africa include Tsangarides and Qureshi (2008), Tavlas (2009), and Khamfula and Tesfayohannes (2004).

countries—especially those in Africa—benefit from the policy flexibility when they have it, or rather take it as a license to run over-expansionary monetary policies and finance wasteful government spending. A related issue is the size of other gains that might result from sharing a common currency: while controversial, the literature suggests an important boost in intraregional trade and investment from monetary union membership, with induced favorable effects on growth.

A comparison of the data on the performance of African countries that are members of a monetary union with those that are not can provide some limited insights into these issues. The limits to the exercise relate to the fact that there are relatively few monetary unions, and each has its particularities. The West and Central African CFA franc zones are longstanding monetary unions, but their impact is strongly affected by additional features: a peg to the French franc (since 1999, to the euro), and a guarantee of convertibility financed by the French Treasury. Formal econometric analysis has been done, especially comparing the CFA franc zones with other sub-Saharan African (SSA) countries, with inconclusive results. Early literature concluded that the two CFA zones provided better real economic performance that the rest of SSA (Guillaumont and Guillaumont 1984; Devarajan and de Melo 1987), but the overvaluation of the currency deteriorated economic growth, requiring a large devaluation in 1994. Monga (1997) argues that the CFA franc zone is not an optimum currency area. In what follows, a comparison of several broad macroeconomic aggregates will be presented, as well as a discussion of the extent of intra-regional trade within monetary unions compared to the rest of SSA.

Table 4.1 suggests that the three monetary exchange rate unions—WAEMU (West African Economic and Monetary Union), CEMAC (Communauté Econonomique et Monetaire de l'Afrique Centrale), and the CMA (Common Monetary Area)—have consistently fared better in terms of inflation than the rest of SSA, but output performance has not shown a clear pattern relative to the other countries. Low inflation for the CFA franc zones has reflected that of its exchange rate anchor, the French franc and the euro—except following the CFA franc devaluation in 1994. CEMAC's good output performance has been dominated by the increase in oil output, which also largely affects its fiscal position; but oil exploitation has little or nothing to do with the exchange rate regime (since oil is priced in dollars and the costs of extraction depend on physical characteristics rather than domestic wages). As for the CMA, since monetary policy is decided by South Africa, and its partners are only 10% of total GDP, the monetary union is largely irrelevant for the zone's aggregate performance. So it is difficult to draw strong conclusions concerning the net advantages of being a member of a monetary union. Another important development that is evident in Table 4.1 is that non-monetary union countries have markedly improved their performance over the roughly 30 years summarized there. This improvement is evident in stronger economic growth, lower inflation, and better fiscal positions.

African countries trade relatively little among themselves, so that the trade creation effects of monetary union membership are difficult to discern from the raw data (Coe and Hoffmaister 1998). A reason for this is provided by the Gravity Model: African countries have low levels of gross domestic product (GDP), hence provide limited export markets compared to advanced countries in Europe, North America, or Asia. In addition, exports of primary commodities typically are processed elsewhere; since African countries produce few manufactures, this also reduces African bilateral trade.

Table 4.1 Real GDP growth, inflation, and general government balance, 1980–2012.

	Real GDP growth (%)			Inflation (%)			Fiscal balance (% of GDP)			Net credit to government[1] (% of GDP)		
	1980–95	1995–05	2005–12	1980–95	1995–05	2005–12	1980–95	1995–05	2005–12	1980–95	1995–05	2005–12
Average												
Sub-Saharan Africa	2.9	4.6	4.9	75.5	30.7	8.4	−4.4	−2.6	−0.8	7.6	6.7	3.3
WAEMU	2.2	3.6	4.1	12.0	4.9	3.3	−4.3	−3.1	−1.5	3.0	2.4	0.3
CEMAC	3.5	9.7	4.1	7.9	4.0	3.5	−6.6	1.3	5.4	7.5	4.8	−6.1
CMA	4.0	3.4	3.6	13.2	7.2	6.4	−0.9	−0.8	−0.3	2.2	−4.2	−9.6
Non-MU fixed exch. rate countries	3.9	2.1	4.1	30.1	8.9	9.2	−4.7	−5.9	−3.9	9.7	17.9	21.5
Non-MU other countries	2.3	4.8	6.4	162.6	69.5	12.5	−4.2	−2.4	−1.2	10.4	8.0	4.7
Median												
Sub-Saharan Africa	2.5	3.8	4.6	11.9	6.8	7.6	−4.2	−2.9	−1.9	6.2	4.1	−0.2
WAEMU	2.5	4.0	3.7	6.1	3.6	3.3	−5.3	−3.0	−2.1	1.7	3.5	0.4
CEMAC	2.9	3.7	4.0	6.4	3.7	3.8	−4.2	1.5	5.4	5.5	5.5	−2.9
CMA	4.2	3.3	3.9	13.6	7.4	6.2	−1.4	−1.3	−1.0	2.8	0.4	−7.7
Non-MU fixed exch. rate countries	3.6	2.3	2.9	12.0	5.3	10.3	−4.9	−5.5	−2.8	9.9	4.4	7.3
Non-MU other countries	2.1	4.4	6.2	24.0	13.5	11.3	−4.3	−3.5	−2.5	11.6	5.1	4.8
Standard deviation												
Sub-Saharan Africa	2.6	6.3	2.3	321.0	115.1	5.1	3.3	4.6	5.0	10.7	20.5	20.9
WAEMU	1.1	1.8	1.4	17.4	4.2	0.5	2.7	1.6	2.7	3.9	3.3	3.9
CEMAC	2.1	15.3	1.1	5.1	1.6	0.9	4.3	4.0	5.2	7.7	2.6	12.3
CMA	1.8	0.6	1.2	0.9	0.7	0.3	1.1	2.0	2.4	3.8	11.3	9.7
Non-MU fixed exch. rate countries	4.0	5.7	2.4	31.1	5.2	4.4	4.0	6.9	4.9	6.6	28.3	38.9
Non-MU other countries	2.6	2.8	2.3	499.9	181.6	4.5	2.7	3.6	4.4	14.8	26.1	18.4

Sources: World Economic Outlook.
[1] Excludes Liberia, Zambia, and Zimbabwe.

While WAEMU has reasonably high intraregional trade, CEMAC does not—no doubt reflecting in large part the commodity composition of its exports of crude petroleum. Again, the CMA's trade is dominated by South Africa, for which, given its size, trade with its CMA partners constitutes only a small fraction of its total trade. However, disentangling the various factors using the Gravity Model for Africa suggests that African countries sharing a common currency do trade more among themselves by roughly a factor of two (Masson and Pattillo 2005), tending to confirm the findings of Rose (2000) that membership in a monetary union can increase trade substantially.

4.3 Status of Monetary Union Projects in Africa

4.3.1 East African Community

While monetary union was seen in the early years of the East African Community (EAC) as a rather distant goal, a number of successful steps in the economic integration process, and a November 2013 EAC Monetary Union Protocol signing have put monetary union higher on the agenda. The EAC was established in 2000 with founding members Kenya, Tanzania, and Uganda; Rwanda and Burundi joined later in 2007. A customs union protocol, established in 2005 with the introduction of a common external tariff and gradual elimination of internal tariffs, and a common market protocol signed in 2010, envisaging free movement of goods, persons, labor, services, and capital were previous milestones in the regional integration process. While important progress has been achieved, implementation of these initiatives has been slow. Some of the main challenges to the customs union have been the slow pace of eliminating non-tariff barriers, which can partly offset the effects of internal tariff reduction, and the trade problems of overlapping memberships in other regional economic communities; on the common market side, difficulties have been inadequate dispute settlement mechanisms and incomplete harmonization of procedures. To expedite the implementation process, a new structure of national implementation committees and a regional committee have been set up.

EAC policymakers are modeling several features of the planned process of convergence and gradual building of common monetary institutions on the experience that led to the European monetary union, including the realization that the road to monetary union is a long one. While in 2007 the heads of state had decided to fast-track implementation of the monetary union, advancing the targeted launch date from 2015 to 2012, the monetary union protocol signed by the heads of state in November 2013 and was ratified by all five countries by early 2015, establishes a more realistic timetable: a plan to introduce the EAC single currency by 2024 in member states that comply with the convergence criteria. An East African Monetary Institute (EAMI) will be set up as a precursor to the eventual establishment of a common central bank with a system of national central banks as its operational arms. The single exchange rate will be floating. The details of the legal and institutional framework that would govern surveillance and enforcement of the convergence process have not yet been specified.

To qualify, countries are expected to meet the convergence criteria and comply with them for at least three years. The common currency will be established if at least three countries meet the criteria. The primary convergence criteria are ceilings on headline inflation (8%), fiscal deficit including grants (3% of GDP), and gross public debt (50% of GDP in net present value terms); and a floor on reserve coverage (4.5 months of imports). In addition, there are three indicative criteria on core inflation, the fiscal deficit excluding grants, and the tax-to-GDP ratio. These objectives are ambitious, but not infeasible given the strong macroeconomic performance in the region in recent years.

In addition to EAC protocols, several other forces are pushing forward economic and financial integration in the EAC. The November 2013 launch of the East African Cross Border Payment System, an integrated payment and settlement system, is a concrete operational step. Some harmonization of improved monetary policy instruments, cross-border financial sector supervision in the face of increasing financial integration, and the potential for several ambitious regional infrastructure projects are also important developments. Political momentum for further regional integration in the EAC, including monetary union, is clearly on the upswing. Translating this into the political will to work toward an effective common market, macroeconomic convergence, harmonized policy frameworks, and the complex institutional process of adopting a common currency is the next challenge, and the signs are encouraging.

4.3.2 Economic Community of West African States/West African Monetary Zone

The plan for monetary union in West Africa is a proposed common currency among the members of Economic Community of West African States (ECOWAS) that are not presently part of WAEMU. The non-WAEMU countries, that is, Nigeria, Ghana, the Gambia, Guinea, and Sierra Leone, intend to create a common currency area (West African Monetary Zone, WAMZ) and eventually to merge it with the WAEMU to form a single-currency area for the whole of ECOWAS.[2] The launch date for the WAMZ's common currency, the eco, initially set for 2003, was postponed to July 2005, then until December 2009, and subsequently further postponed until 2015 (and the ECOWAS currency to 2020).

The zone has set four primary convergence criteria that are prerequisites for entry into the monetary union: single digit inflation; a fiscal deficit to GDP ratio (excluding grants) of 4% or less; central bank financing of the fiscal deficit as a percent of the previous year's tax revenue of 10% or less, and gross international reserves equal to three months of imports or more. Six secondary criteria (which do not have to be met for the launch to take place) include a positive real interest rate, a stable real exchange rate, the settlement of all public domestic arrears, targets for public investment and tax collection, and a ceiling on public wage expenditure.

A "Roadmap for the ECOWAS Single Currency Programme" was approved by a council of WAMZ ministers and governors. A range of institutions are responsible for particular

---

[2] Liberia has declined to participate, while the remaining member of ECOWAS, Cape Verde, is pegged to the euro.

activities under the roadmap, including the ECOWAS commission, central banks in the region, WAEMU commission, the West African Monetary Institute (WAMI—precursor to the planned West African Central Bank—which monitors convergence criteria) and the West African Monetary Authority (WAMA, with some responsibility of monitoring, coordinating and implementing the ECOWAS Monetary Cooperation Programme, as well as a serving as a multilateral payment facility to promote trade).

WAMI has made some progress toward developing the institutional framework necessary to underpin a monetary union. Some draft legal statutes have been prepared, and a joint payments system in the Gambia, Guinea and Sierra Leone is under development. WAMA is at earlier stages on activities related to the ECOWAS monetary union, commissioning studies on harmonization of statistics, bank accounting and reporting frameworks, and financial regulatory and supervisory frameworks.

While leaders continue to endorse the monetary union plans, some observers have noted that there is limited real forward movement on the needed institutional steps, that repeated postponements and the still unrealistic timetable have undermined momentum for the project, and, most importantly, that political commitment appears limited.

4.3.3 Southern African Development Community

The Southern African Development Community (SADC), the largest regional economic community in SSA, adopted a Regional Indicative Strategic Development Plan (RISDP) in 2003. The plan sets out a timetable for deepening regional integration, calling for the creation of a free trade area (FTA) by 2008, a customs union by 2010, a monetary union by 2016, and a single currency by 2018. The FTA, comprising 12 of the 15 SADC member states, was launched in August 2008 when a phased program of tariff reductions that was specified to occur in the previous eight years resulted in 85% of the intraregional trade attaining zero duty. Phasing down of tariffs on sensitive products continued after the launch. The customs union, however, was not established as planned in 2010, mainly due to the problem of overlapping memberships: almost all SADC countries (with the exception of Angola and Mozambique) already belong to other customs unions.

Following the stall in the process at the customs union stage, the way forward on regional economic and financial integration in SADC is somewhat murky. A 2010 assessment of the RISDP found that much more effort was needed on the agenda, and that implementation had been limited. A broader independent review of the plan has been undertaken.

Where does this leave the idea of monetary union in the region?[3] SADC's Committee of Central Bank Governors, chaired by South Africa, made a few steps that are useful groundwork, including establishment of a real time gross settlement system; implementation of a best banking practice, norms and standards initiative; and development of a model central bank law. SADC governments agreed on a set of macroeconomic

---

[3] In 2009, the former governor of the Reserve Bank of South Africa noted that proposals were being considered for a common central bank for the Common Monetary Area (currency area comprised of South Africa, Lesotho, Namibia, and Swaziland), where the smaller countries would participate in formation of monetary policy, and this could serve as a springboard for a SADC central bank (BBC Monitoring Africa, 2009). Proposals do not seem to have moved forward, however.

convergence indicators (inflation, fiscal balance, public debt, current account balance, and real GDP growth) that continue to be monitored. However, the path toward monetary union has been confronted by the reality of the very wide disparities in per capita incomes and economic structures across SADC's 15 economies—including middle income, low-income, and fragile countries, and an oil exporter. Serious consideration of monetary union does not seem to be a real issue on the economic or political agenda at this time.

4.4 A Model for Evaluating the Desirability and Feasibility of African Monetary Unions

The traditional optimum currency area model pioneered by Mundell (1961) associates the costs of joining a monetary union with the likelihood that different countries or regions will face asymmetric output shocks. The benefits of membership in a monetary union are typically not modeled, but are implicit: namely the greater usability of a currency that circulates over a wider domain. Since the benefits are not modeled, it is difficult to assess the seriousness of the costs; moreover, these costs are moderated by other factors, namely factor mobility and fiscal transfers, but a metric is not provided for their effect in reducing the costs. Therefore, any empirical application of optimum currency area (OCA) criteria is necessarily inconclusive, and often relies on comparison of the asymmetry of shocks with existing (and therefore by assumption viable) monetary unions.

A different approach is taken here, namely to provide an explicit model of the economic costs and benefits, and use as criterion for the feasibility of a monetary union that it must increase the welfare of member countries. The model includes the costs identified by the OCA literature—asymmetric output shocks—but in addition includes a dimension that is of crucial importance for the policies of a central bank that is not independent of the fiscal authorities—the extent of fiscal discipline, or, conversely, the size of the government's financing needs. As for the benefits of membership in a monetary union, they are related to the reduced temptation to engineer monetary surprises as in Barro and Gordon (1983), because the regional central bank cannot exploit the exchange rate with other members of the monetary union to stimulate output.

The model is a variant of Debrun, Masson, and Pattillo (2005), where it was applied to the ECOWAS monetary union. It has been used to assess other monetary union proposals in Masson and Pattillo (2005), Debrun, Masson, and Pattillo (2011), and Debrun and Masson (2013); more details of the model can be found in any of these publications.

A key feature is that the central bank (national or regional) is assumed not to be independent; instead, it maximizes the same objective function as the government. In addition to keeping inflation low, its objectives include financing a target for government spending, minimizing taxes, and maximizing output. Output is affected by exogenous terms of trade shocks and by inflation surprises.

4.4.1 Basic equations and equilibria

Economic activity in each country i responds to macroeconomic policies through an open-economy Phillips curve with traditional new-classical features:

$$y_i = y_N + c\left(\pi_i - \pi_i^e - \tau_i\right) - \sum_{k \neq i, k=1}^{n} \theta_{i,k} c\left(\pi_k - \pi_k^e\right) + \varepsilon_i \tag{1}$$

for $i = 1, \ldots, n$, and where y_i is the logarithm of output of country i, y_N is the natural rate of output, π_i denotes its inflation rate, τ_i represents a tax rate on firms' turnover (and also tax revenues in proportion of output), $\theta_{i,k}$ captures the intensity of monetary policy spillovers from country k to country i, and ε_i is a transitory terms-of-trade disturbance with zero mean and finite variance. A superscript "e" designates a rationally expected value. The interpretation of equation (1) is straightforward. The central bank's policy instrument is assumed to be inflation. Unexpected inflation raises output, while distortive taxation reduces it (Alesina and Tabellini 1987). Spillovers from monetary policies elsewhere in the region are negative, in line with the presumption that depreciations boost competitiveness at the expense of regional trade partners, and are assumed proportional to the size of trade between pairs of countries.

In addition to their joint impact on output, monetary and fiscal policies are linked through an instantaneous budget constraint forcing government expenditure to match revenue, including seigniorage:

$$g_i = \mu \pi_i + \tau_i - \delta_i \tag{2}$$

where g_i is the level of socially beneficial government expenditure in percent of output and δ_i symbolizes inefficiencies in budget execution, funds allocated to "white elephants" and other wasteful projects, or resources lost through corruption or theft.

Under monetary autonomy, each country has three policy instruments: the tax rate, the level of expenditure and the rate of inflation. Equilibrium policies are those maximizing a quasi-linear utility function:

$$U_i^G = \frac{1}{2}\left\{-a\left(\pi_i - \tilde{\pi}_i\right)^2 - b\tau_i^2 - \gamma\left(g_i - \tilde{g}_i\right)^2\right\} + y_i \tag{3}$$

where a tilde denotes socially optimal levels and positive parameters capture trade-offs among objectives. The authorities dislike deviations of public expenditure and inflation from specific targets ($\tilde{g}_i$ and $\tilde{\pi}_i$, respectively), as well as variability in distortive tax rates—over and above the induced output loss. In contrast to more conventional (fully quadratic) utility functions, output enters linearly—as in Barro and Gordon (1983)—indicating that the authorities welcome increases in output with a constant marginal utility. To restore the trade-off between inflation and output variability (which reflects government's concern for macroeconomic stability), the inflation target is assumed to depend on terms-of-trade shocks as follows:

$$\tilde{\pi}_i = -\eta \varepsilon_i \tag{4}$$

with $\eta > 0$.

Under monetary union with membership M, a common central bank (CCB) chooses monetary policy to maximize an output-weighted sum of members' utilities. Critically, the CCB also faces different constraints than does a national central bank. First, it is effectively taking into account M national fiscal targets and budget identities. Second, the CCB internalizes the fact that its policy decisions cannot affect national outputs through bilateral exchange rate changes vis-à-vis other members of the union. Formally, the CCB perceives steeper *national* Phillips curves (equation (1′)) than a national central bank.

$$y_i = y_N + c\left(1 - \theta_i^M\right)\left(\pi_M - \pi_M^e\right) - c\tau_i - \sum_{k \in M} \theta_{i,k} c\left(\pi_k - \pi_k^e\right) + \varepsilon_i \quad \text{for all } i \in M \tag{1′}$$

With $\theta_i^M = \sum_{k \in M} \theta_{i,k}$.

Not only can the CCB not stabilize country-specific shocks, but its policy is also less effective at stabilizing common shocks (by a factor $\left(1 - \theta_i^M\right)$ in each country i).

The benchmark case for welfare evaluations is a regime of complete monetary policy autonomy (flexible exchange rates) with politically dependent central banks that cannot pre-commit to first-best policies. Monetary and fiscal policies are determined jointly by minimizing deviations of the effective tax rate, public expenditure and inflation from their respective targets.

Since policymakers cannot pre-commit, they are limited to time-consistent policies that systematically deviate from the first best, reflecting the government's penchant for using monetary policy to boost activity beyond potential—instead of raising the potential through politically costly structural reforms—and the willingness to raise revenues to offset the waste of public resources. The time-consistent inflation rate is given by

$$\pi_i^* = \frac{\gamma\mu b}{\Lambda}\left(FN_i\right) + \frac{(b+\gamma) + \gamma\mu}{\Lambda}c - \frac{a(b+\gamma)\eta}{\Lambda}\varepsilon_i, \tag{5}$$

with $\Lambda = a(b+\gamma) + \gamma\mu^2 b > 0$ and $FN_i = g_i + \delta_i$, the *financing need*. Because the utility function is quadratic in all its arguments except output, the policy biases are spread across all instruments. Hence, while inflation is too high, productive public spending is too low and distortionary taxation, too high, when compared to the first best outcome. In a monetary union, the central bank will pick an inflation rate that reflects the weighted average of public sector financing needs and it will internalize the lesser effectiveness of the union-wide policy in affecting national output levels (equation (6)).

$$\pi_i^{M*} = \frac{\gamma\mu b}{\Lambda}\left(FN_A^M\right) + \frac{\left(1 - \theta_A^M\right)(b+\gamma) + \gamma\mu}{\Lambda}c - \frac{a(b+\gamma)\eta}{\Lambda}\varepsilon_A^M, \tag{6}$$

for all $i \in M$, with $x_A^M = \sum_{i \in M} \omega_i^M x_i$, for $x \in \{FN, \theta, \varepsilon\}$ (cross-country, output-weighted averages within M). It is then straightforward to show that the average inflation rate in a monetary union is lower than the (weighted) average of national inflation rates under monetary autonomy:

$$\pi_A^{M*} = \underbrace{\pi_A^*}_{\substack{\text{Average inflation} \\ \text{under national} \\ \text{policies}}} - \underbrace{\frac{\theta_A^M (b+\gamma)}{\Lambda} c}_{\substack{\text{Average reduction in the} \\ \text{Barro-Gordon bias.}}} . \tag{7}$$

Thus monetary unification yields benefits similar to the delegation of monetary policy to a (somewhat) independent central bank: the inflationary bias is reduced because all the national Phillips curves faced by the CCB are steeper by a factor that increases with the intensity of regional trade links. In line with OCA literature, the costs of unification arise from the inadequacy of the regional monetary policy in the face of country-specific shocks because the CCB can only respond to the union-wide shock. In addition, there is another cost here related to fiscal asymmetries: the common monetary policy depends on the average of financing needs of member countries, FN_A^M, and to the extent that it is higher than financing needs for country i, FN_i, it may reduce country i's welfare. Conversely, a country may import fiscal discipline and low inflation if $FN_A^M < FN_i$. Thus, whether the ratio FN_A^M / FN_i is greater or less than one is crucial for whether a country i loses or gains from fiscal asymmetries with respect to its partners in a monetary union.

4.4.2 Calibration

The calibration of the model's parameters and some sensitivity tests are described in Debrun, Masson, and Pattillo (2011). The utility function values a, b, and γ are taken from that study, where parameters were chosen to fit cross-country fiscal and inflation data for 29 SSA countries over 1994–2005. The cross-country average money–income ratio over that period provided the estimate for μ

The key *financing need* variable *FN* consists of two components: society's target for government spending and a diversion wedge due to inefficient tax collection and wasteful spending that adds to the amount that needs to be financed, without increasing welfare. Aggregate government spending and revenues for the African countries where data were available were regressed on governance indicators to gauge directly what amounts of excess spending and tax losses were due to poor governance. The governance indicators were then set to their "ideal" levels: the resulting figures for ideal government spending give the estimate for $\tilde{g}$, and the difference between the ideal and actual figures for the deficit provides the estimate for δ. In the model simulations reported below, financing needs and the variance–covariance matrix of percent changes in the terms of trade (TOT) were updated to 2000–2011.

Variances of TOT shocks and of output and inflation are used to calibrate two other key parameters that capture the stabilization role of monetary policy (η) and the effect of the latter on output (c). These estimates were redone using more recent data, and taking account of the fact that output variance in the model depends both on the variance of output shocks and the extent of stabilization policy, while the variance of inflation (from equations (5) and (6)) depends on the variance of output shocks and of financing needs. Solving these two equations together for a subsample of countries—those classified as having floating exchange rates—and averaging them across countries give our estimates of η and c.

The estimated parameter values are as follows: $a = 1.20359$, $b = 2.33295$, $\gamma = 2.35337$, $\mu = 0.37657$, $\eta = 1.252962$, and $c = 0.720843$. Relative to the earlier calibration (Debrun, Masson, and Pattillo 2011), the value of η is considerably lower (lowering the costs of asymmetric shocks) and that of c is somewhat higher (raising the gain from a monetary union's reduction of the Barro–Gordon inflation bias). A more complete description of the calibration is available from the authors.

4.5 EXISTING MONETARY UNIONS IN AFRICA: ARE THEY ECONOMICALLY VIABLE?

The model described in the previous section can be used to assess the net economic benefits of the existing African monetary/exchange rate unions, namely the CFA franc zones and the Common Monetary Area in Southern Africa. In each case, the common currency area can be compared to the counterfactual of separate currencies issued by each of the member countries, which would be independently floating. The model calculates the net welfare gain or loss from the choice of exchange rate regime, taking into account the desire to use monetary policy to pursue stabilization policy by resisting output shocks, as well as the aims of keeping inflation low and financing the government. Because the measure of welfare gives a unit weight to the linear term in the log of output, the metric for welfare gains or losses is percentage points of GDP: that is, an increase in welfare of 0.01 is equivalent to the welfare gain from a one percent increase in the permanent level of output.

It is important to recognize that the model, though more comprehensive than the usual OCA analysis since it quantifies both costs and benefits, and introduces fiscal asymmetries as an additional element, does not capture all relevant aspects. Among those things left out, it does not explicitly quantify the costs of absence of intraregional mobility and flexibility—particularly of labor—nor does it assess the regional infrastructure (payments mechanisms, banking supervision, lender-of-last resort, fiscal federalism) needed to make a monetary union work. On the benefit side, the model emphasizes the gains from reducing the bias towards excessive inflation; it does not attempt to measure the network externalities (lowering transactions costs) of using a currency over a wider domain. However, the extent of trade internalized within the monetary union—a key variable in the model—may proxy those externalities.

The assessment also excludes political factors, which as discussed can be of great importance: they are often the motivating factor in monetary union projects, and conversely lack of political will and regional solidarity may doom an otherwise attractive project. However, the model may shed light on the political durability of monetary unions nevertheless: those monetary unions that do not yield economic benefits can be expected to lose political support. It seems likely that even strong political will in favor of a common currency may not be enough to ensure its survival in the face of evident economic costs.

4.5.1 CFA franc zone

Turning first to WAEMU, model simulations suggest that membership in the monetary union is beneficial to each of the member countries (Table 4.2). The net gains reflect

Table 4.2 Net welfare gain[1] of WAEMU membership, and selected indicators

	Net gain	Due to: Monetary externality	Fiscal asymmetry	Shock asymmetry	Regional GDP share (%)	Correlation with average shock (%)	Financing need FNa/FN
Benin	0.87	1.44	−0.45	−0.13	8.9	55.6	1.052
Burkina Faso	1.28	1.44	−0.09	−0.07	10.4	75.2	1.011
Cote d'Ivoire	1.28	1.44	−0.06	−0.10	39.7	91.2	1.007
Mali	1.93	1.44	0.56	−0.05	10.9	92.2	0.941
Niger	0.77	1.44	−0.06	−0.61	6.8	21.7	1.007
Senegal	1.48	1.44	0.18	−0.14	18.2	37.6	0.980
Togo	0.93	1.44	−0.37	−0.15	5.0	86.8	1.043

[1] Percentage points of GDP.

a combination of factors. In particular, the net welfare gain can be decomposed into three parts: (i) the monetary externality which is offset when the common central bank internalizes monetary spillovers, hence increasing welfare; (ii) fiscal asymmetries, which can produce a gain if the average fiscal discipline across the member countries is stricter than for the given country, and conversely; and (iii) shock asymmetries, which produce a loss for the country concerned except in the unlikely event that its output shocks are perfectly correlated with those of its partners.

Table 4.2 shows that for the calibration of parameters described in section 4, most of the gains result from the monetary externality, while there is little cost to shock asymmetries, except for Niger. Fiscal asymmetries produce some moderately large gains and losses, but not so large as to offset the gains from having a central bank that faces reduced incentives to provide excessive monetary stimulus. The table shows why this is the case: shock correlations are relatively high (except for Niger), and the financing needs of WAEMU member countries are relatively uniform, making them good candidates for joint membership in a monetary union.

The other CFA franc zone, CEMAC, is also relatively homogeneous in that most of its members are oil exporters, and thus have correlated shocks to their terms of trade. Their governments are not, however, as stable as those in WAEMU (which, with the notable exceptions of Côte d'Ivoire and Mali, have generally avoided civil unrest and have made progress towards democratic accountability), and several of them—including Chad and Central African Republic—have experienced persistent civil wars. They are also subject to the effects of the "curse of oil"—namely corruption and poor governance. Because of this and data problems, the net welfare gain of membership in CEMAC is not evaluated here. One can note, however, that the cohesion and policy coordination among the countries of CEMAC is notably less than among those of WAEMU.

4.5.2 The Common Monetary Area

The CMA has a long history, dating back to 1916. Known for a long time as the Rand Zone, it still is an arrangement dominated by South Africa—not surprisingly, given its size relative to the smaller members—Lesotho, Namibia, and Swaziland. South Africa sets monetary policy for the area, which is more properly described as an exchange rate union since, in fact, each of the countries issues its own currency. However, the smaller countries are required to ensure the convertibility of their currencies into rand (which also serves as legal tender in those countries, as well as in South Africa) at parity, and this means that monetary policy is determined by the South African Reserve Bank (SARB).

The CMA's durability would seem to be proved by its continued existence for almost a century, but as with other monetary unions the CMA has been accompanied by other elements of mutual advantage that help to make it attractive. However, it is possible that these other encouraging factors may diminish over time. One of these is the existence of the Southern African Customs Union (SACU)—including the members of the CMA plus Botswana—which has in the past provided a generous sharing of the tariff revenues to its poorer members. A renegotiation of the SACU agreement has limited some of those benefits, and it is possible that other changes may occur in the future. So the model's evaluation of the benefits of the monetary union alone may well be relevant.

Table 4.3 CMA: welfare comparison of asymmetric union with autonomy

	Net gain 1/	Due to:	Monetary externality	Fiscal asymmetry	Shock asymmetry	memo:	GDP share (%)	Correlation with average shock (%)	Financing need FNa/FN	Net gain vs. symmetric monetary union 1/
Lesotho	6.98		0.59	7.30	−0.79		0.6	22.4	0.470	0.06
Namibia	1.06		0.59	0.80	−0.32		2.9	20.4	0.899	0.08
South Africa	0.59		0.59	0.00	0.00		95.5	100.0	1.000	0.11
Swaziland	1.59		0.59	3.69	−2.63		1.0	27.8	0.651	0.01

1/ Percentage points of GDP..

Table 4.3 indicates that the CMA indeed seems beneficial for each of its members. This is accounted for by the large amount of trade the smaller members (two of which are land-locked) do with South Africa, and the fact that South Africa, which sets monetary policy, has a relatively lower financing need (as ratio to GDP) than its smaller partners. The gain to South Africa from membership is solely accounted for by the elimination of the temptation to use monetary stimulus at the expense of its partners; this reduction of the Barro–Gordon bias toward inflationary policies is welfare enhancing. In contrast, neither fiscal nor shock asymmetries matter for it, since the SARB sets monetary policies purely on the basis of those variables for South Africa, not for an average of all the countries as would be the case in a symmetric monetary union. A welfare comparison with such a fully symmetric mon-etary union (last column) suggests that the existing asymmetric CMA is better—essentially because the anchor country, South Africa, has more disciplined fiscal policies.

4.6 Should Existing Monetary Unions Be Expanded, or New Ones Created?

As described in section 3 above, Africa has seen a number of proposals to create new mone-tary unions; there have also been a few new members of the CFA franc zones as well as nego-tiations with other potential members—in particular, Guinea-Bissau joined WAEMU in 1997, while Mali rejoined after earlier withdrawing from it, and Equatorial Guinea joined the customs union that was the precursor to CEMAC in 1983. Regional integration is an impor-tant objective of the African Union (AU)—indeed, its reason for being—and the treaty creat-ing it envisions a single currency for Africa. Regional economic communities are mandated by the African Union, and many of them have plans for the creation of regional currencies, in some cases already embodied in treaties endorsed by member countries. However, in most cases monetary unions are distant goals, rather than objectives that guide current policy. The most actively pursued monetary project is the proposed creation of a common currency for the EAC.

4.6.1 The East African Community

In December 2013, heads of state of the five member countries signed a monetary union protocol, which establishes a ten-year timetable for proceeding to an East African Monetary Union (EAMU). While some details have yet to be decided, the plan would create a regional central bank, and establish close coordination of fiscal policies and tight limits on govern-ment deficits, as well as the creation of other new community institutions before introducing the single currency.

While the countries have close economic links, the breakdown of the earlier mon-etary union comprised of the original members of the EAC—Kenya, Tanzania, and Uganda—raises questions about the size of potential benefits. Model simulations based on data for 2000–2011 suggest that those benefits are relatively modest (Table 4.4), and even negative for Uganda, which because of its more disciplined fiscal policy might

Table 4.4 Net welfare gain[1] of EAMU membership and correlations, 2000–2011

		Due to:			Correlations:				
	Net Gain	Monetary Externality	Fiscal Asymmetry	Shock Asymmetry	Burundi	Kenya	Rwanda	Tanzania	Uganda
Burundi	3.37	1.03	2.43	−0.02	1.00	0.80	0.94	0.91	0.98
Kenya	1.91	1.03	0.91	−0.01	0.80	1.00	0.77	0.89	0.84
Rwanda	1.16	1.03	0.14	−0.02	0.94	0.77	1.00	0.85	0.95
Tanzania	0.36	1.03	−0.68	−0.01	0.91	0.89	0.85	1.00	0.89
Uganda	−0.14	1.03	−1.19	−0.01	0.98	0.84	0.95	0.89	1.00
Memo: Net Energy Exports/GDP (%)					−2.74	−3.99	−1.96	−4.63	−2.99

[1] Percentage points of GDP.

suffer from pressures on the common central bank to provide monetary financing. Nevertheless, these countries are quite favorably placed at the moment to share the same monetary policy because of high correlations between their terms of trade shocks. Other evidence (Rusuhuzwa and Masson 2013) also confirms that their economies are relatively synchronized.

The picture changes, however, when consideration is given to the structural shifts that their economies are forecast to face in coming decades. In particular, Uganda has commercially exploitable quantities of oil; large quantities of gas have been found offshore of Tanzania; and oil has recently been discovered in Kenya. Plans are being made to construct a refinery in Kenya, oil pipelines in the region, and a liquified natural gas (LNG) plant in Tanzania. Though the impact of the discoveries cannot be accurately gauged at this point, it seems likely that substantial amounts of oil and gas will be exported by the EAC in the future. Should Kenya, Tanzania, and Uganda become net oil and gas exporters, while Burundi and Rwanda do not, the correlation of output shocks would radically change. In particular, a rise in world energy prices would be favorable for the first three countries, but unfavorable for Burundi and Rwanda, tending to make their terms of trade move in opposite directions.

Rather than making a forecast of the amounts of oil and gas to be exported, different scenarios for oil and gas exports and their importance relative to the GDPs of Kenya, Tanzania, and Uganda were constructed, and their effects on macroeconomic variables simulated. In particular a low export scenario and a high export scenario were considered. Net energy exports as ratios to GDP for other African net energy exporters range from 2–5% (Côte d'Ivoire and Cameroon) to 30–40% (Nigeria and Gabon). Non-African countries' figures go as high as 45–50% (Saudi Arabia, Kuwait, and Qatar) and 58% (Brunei).

Two fairly conservative scenarios were envisioned for the three future EAC energy producers. In the low export scenario, Kenya, Tanzania, and Uganda would move from their current net energy import positions to net export positions equal to 3% of GDP, while in the high export scenario, the three countries were assumed to become net energy exporters equal to 20% of GDP. In each case, this would imply a larger increase for Tanzania than for Kenya and Uganda, as ratios to their respective GDPs, as a result of Tanzania's initially larger net import position as a ratio to GDP. But given the different sizes of their economies, the scenario implies a larger actual increase in energy exports in Kenya than in the two others, when measured in barrels per day of oil equivalents. Only the high export scenario is reported here; it would put the three EAC countries in the middle ranks of world energy exporters.

Effects on the calculated correlations of the high export scenario are presented in Table 4.5, along with model simulations of the effect on welfare of forming a monetary union. Decomposing the commodity terms of trade into two components, energy and non-energy, helps one to understand the nature of the effects. In these terms, the change in the log of the commodity terms of trade (TT) as defined in Spatafora and Tytell (2009) can be written

$$dLog(TT) = (X_e - M_e)dLogP_e + (X_n - M_n)dLogP_n \qquad (8)$$

where P_e, P_n, X_e, X_n, M_e, M_n are the prices, export volumes, and import volumes of energy and non-energy commodities, respectively. In the initial situation, all five EAC countries are net importers of energy and net exporters of non-energy commodities. The scenarios for the future have Burundi and Rwanda remaining net energy importers, but Kenya, Tanzania,

Table 4.5 Net welfare gain[1] of EAMU membership and correlations, high energy exports scenario

	Net gain	Due to: Monetary externality	Fiscal asymmetry	Shock asymmetry	Correlations: Burundi	Kenya	Rwanda	Tanzania	Uganda
Burundi	1.56	1.03	2.43	−1.83	1.00	−0.66	0.94	−0.65	−0.64
Kenya	1.91	1.03	0.91	−0.01	−0.66	1.00	−0.56	0.99	0.99
Rwanda	−0.43	1.03	0.14	−1.6	0.94	−0.56	1.00	−0.56	−0.55
Tanzania	0.36	1.03	−0.68	−0.01	−0.65	0.99	−0.56	1.00	1.00
Uganda	−0.49	1.03	−1.19	−0.36	−0.64	0.99	−0.55	1.00	1.00
Memo: net energy Exports/GDP (%)					−2.74	20.00	−1.96	20.00	20.00

[1] Percentage points of GDP.

and Uganda becoming net energy exporters (the non-energy positions of all five remain the same). Thus if we ignored their non-energy positions, the positive correlations of Table 4.5 would become negative correlations for Burundi and Rwanda with respect to each of the other countries.

Table 4.5 shows that this scenario substantially changes the matrix of correlations. Now, all the pairwise correlations between Burundi and Rwanda on the one hand, and Kenya, Tanzania, and Uganda, on the other, are strongly negative. In addition, the correlations between pairs of oil exporting countries increase, as could be expected since the first term in equation (8) becomes more dominant; the correlations are now all above 0.99. So the creation of significant net energy exporters in effect divides the EAC into two blocs, each of which may well constitute an optimum currency area, but together they are unlikely to do so. The low export scenario gives qualitatively similar, but less dramatic, results.

The welfare consequences of forming a monetary union among all the five countries, assuming that net energy exports of Kenya, Tanzania, and Uganda equal 20% of their GDP, are considerably less favorable than when evaluated using the current export structure. The net gain for Rwanda has now turned into a net loss, while that of Burundi is more than cut in half. Despite the fact that Uganda's correlations with the other two energy producers are now very high, this is not enough to counteract the unfavorable effects of the fiscal asymmetry. Two of the five countries are now estimated to lose out from a monetary union relative to keeping their own currencies and the ability to use monetary policy to offset their country-specific shocks.

Does this mean that EAMU is doomed from the start, if one believes the high-energy-export scenario? No, but these simulations highlight the need for other policies to palliate potentially unfavorable effects—for instance, some element of redistribution of oil revenues within a federation of East African states. Necessarily, this would involve some community-wide control over fiscal policies, which could also make monetary union membership more palatable for Uganda since it could enforce fiscal discipline on other national governments. These changes would make the EAC into a true federation of countries, which is indeed an objective that is embodied in the EAC treaty. The lessons from Europe have reinforced the recognition within East Africa that closer integration in a number of dimensions is needed to make a monetary union work. If these lessons are taken to heart and the investment in institution-building is made, then EAMU may well improve welfare in the countries of the EAC.

4.6.2 Expanding the West African Economic and Monetary Union to include Economic Community of West African States

As described, the ECOWAS treaty calls for the replacement of national currencies in the region by a single currency. Since eight of the 15 ECOWAS countries—those members of WAEMU—already share the CFA franc and a common central bank, it is natural first to consider whether adding other countries to WAEMU would be mutually beneficial to the potential new member and to existing members. In what follows, countries are hypothetically

Table 4.6 Welfare implications of adding countries one by one to WAEMU (in % of GDP)

Net welfare gain/loss for new member 1/		Net welfare gain/loss for existing WAEMU members 2/:						
		Benin	Burkina Faso	Cote d'Ivoire	Mali	Niger	Senegal	Togo
Gambia	−0.15	0.06	0.06	0.05	0.05	0.06	0.06	0.06
Ghana	1.29	0.37	0.38	0.43	0.40	0.38	0.37	0.40
Guinea	0.24	0.09	0.08	0.05	0.07	0.10	0.09	0.06
Nigeria	2.29	−1.28	−1.34	−1.75	−1.60	−1.33	−1.14	−1.70

1/ Relative to independent currencies in percent of GDP.
2/ Relative to existing WAEMU monetary union in percent of GDP.

added one by one to WAEMU, then a monetary union including all ECOWAS countries is evaluated. Data problems have prevented including Cape Verde, Liberia, and Sierra Leone in the exercise (as well as Guinea-Bissau in WAEMU), so the larger monetary union considered here would be comprised of eleven countries (out of the fifteen ECOWAS members).

Table 4.6 adds the Gambia, Ghana, Guinea, and Nigeria individually to the existing WAEMU. Two results stand out. First, adding the first three of the non-WAEMU countries is beneficial to existing members, though gains are modest except in the case of Ghana. Second, adding Nigeria to the existing monetary union would not be in the interest of existing members, though it would be welfare enhancing for Nigeria itself, which would gain from a more stable currency.

The reasons for these two results are revealed by Table 4.7, which considers a monetary union that would include all the countries and gives some background data. Nigeria would constitute over half of the GDP of the group, and hence would tend to dominate its monetary policy. However, being a large oil exporter its terms of trade move very differently from those of its potential partners, and this explains why most of them would face a negative correlation with the average shock for the ECOWAS. In addition, Nigeria is estimated to have a greater financing need than the average for the union (as indicated by a value for FNa/FN in the last column that is less than unity). This adds to the welfare losses faced by Nigeria's partners in a potential ECOWAS monetary union since it would imply a higher average inflation rate.

In sum, a full ECOWAS monetary union faces severe shortcomings, with the problem constituted by Nigeria being difficult to solve. Unlike the EAC, where one can imagine that welfare costs caused by potential terms of trade asymmetries could be mitigated by greater political integration, this is much more challenging where there is one large county

Table 4.7 Net gain from ECOWAS monetary union (11 countries) and selected indicators

	Net welfare gain/loss (%) 1/	Regional GDP share in percent	Correlation with average shock (%)	Financing need FNa/FN
WAEMU				
Benin	−0.31	2.9	19.0	1.185
Burkina Faso	−0.37	3.4	−0.1	1.138
Cote d'Ivoire	−0.71	13.0	−44.4	1.133
Mali	−0.60	3.6	−38.8	1.059
Niger	−0.35	2.2	−20.1	1.134
Senegal	−0.19	6.0	44.4	1.103
Togo	−0.67	1.6	−22.6	1.175
others				
Gambia	−0.52	0.4	17.5	1.365
Ghana	0.14	7.5	−51.7	1.196
Guinea	−0.17	3.6	−2.7	1.298
Nigeria	3.10	54.8	83.8	0.901

1/ In percent of GDP; relative to existing monetary union for WAEMU members, relative to independent currencies for others.

that already has fiscal problems (including conflicts between the federal government and the states). While some further expansion of WAEMU may be possible, the aim of a single ECOWAS currency seems likely to remain a distant objective.

4.6.3   Expanding the Common Monetary Area to include Southern African Development Community

The Southern African Development Community aims to promote monetary integration in the region and to create a monetary union. Previous analyses have suggested that the countries are too dissimilar to be an effective union, though Debrun and Masson (2013) give a somewhat more nuanced view. Model simulations using data for 2000–2011 compare the welfare for existing members and potential new entrants. One can envision two scenarios for expansion. In one scenario, the current CMA keeps its asymmetry in which South Africa sets monetary policy. In a second scenario, the CMA is replaced by a symmetric monetary union in which a regional central bank determines monetary conditions in response to developments in the whole region. The first scenario seems conceivable for a limited expansion to include at most a few neighboring countries; however, a wider grouping would necessarily call into question the dominance of South Africa, and a symmetric monetary union with a regional central bank that took over control of monetary policy would seem the likeliest outcome should a SADC monetary union come to pass. Therefore, we consider only the second scenario, first with the addition one by one of the remaining SADC countries, and finally a monetary union that included all of SADC—though data problems force ignoring Angola, Democratic Republic of the Congo, Mauritius, and Seychelles.

The results of adding individual countries to a symmetric monetary union are presented in Table 4.8, in which countries are added one by one. Welfare of new members is calculated relative to a regime with an independent monetary policy, while welfare of CMA members is calculated relative to that prevailing in the (asymmetric) CMA. It is notable that admitting some members with important trade links, in particular, Botswana and Zimbabwe, would

Table 4.8 Welfare implications of adding countries one by one to a symmetric CMA

Net welfare gain/loss for new member 1/		for existing CMA members 2/:			
		Lesotho	Namibia	South Africa	Swaziland
Botswana	2.41	0.20	0.26	0.25	0.23
Malawi	3.94	−0.06	−0.07	−0.08	−0.05
Mozambique	3.30	−0.02	−0.03	−0.04	−0.03
Tanzania	1.05	−0.08	−0.11	−0.13	−0.06
Zambia	2.10	−0.03	−0.02	−0.04	−0.02
Zimbabwe	1.82	0.14	0.16	0.17	0.17

1/ Relative to autonomy, in percent of GDP.
2/ Relative to existing asymmetric CMA, in percent of GDP.

Table 4.9 Welfare implications of a SADC monetary union (10 countries)

	Net Welfare Gain/Loss 1/	Regional GDP Share (%)	Correlation with Average Shock (%)	Financing Need FNa/FN
CMA				
Lesotho	0.54	0.47	32.90	0.496
Namibia	0.71	2.43	51.01	0.949
South Africa	0.65	79.10	93.64	1.055
Swaziland	0.69	0.82	49.71	0.687
Others				
Botswana	2.83	3.17	54.35	0.823
Malawi	4.64	1.13	48.08	0.681
Mozambique	3.97	2.39	37.35	0.742
Tanzania	1.84	5.24	51.38	0.960
Zambia	2.80	3.11	52.25	0.836
Zimbabwe	2.33	2.16	53.74	0.895

1/ Relative to the existing asymmetric CMA for CMA members, relative to autonomy for others, in percent of GDP.

increase welfare of existing CMA members—including South Africa, despite its giving up control over monetary policy. However, the other potential new members would not be viewed favorably, essentially because they are too dissimilar with respect to their fiscal policies and the shocks they face.

A more favorable evaluation emerges from a scenario in which all the countries of SADC join a monetary union together (Table 4.9). In this case, because the trade internalized in the monetary union is large enough, the monetary externality dominates the fiscal and shock asymmetries and produces gains both for existing CMA members and the other countries. This illustrates the scale economies for larger monetary unions of reducing the Barro–Gordon bias by eliminating negative spillovers of monetary policy operating through exchange rate movements.

Of course, these simulations ignore other real-world aspects of monetary integration—for instance, the need to create the infrastructure of integrated payments systems, harmonized financial regulation, etc.—and the regional institutions that would discipline fiscal policies and cushion asymmetric shocks. While work on infrastructure is underway, piloted by committees of central banks, the deeper political integration of SADC still has a long way to go.

4.7 Lessons from the Euro Zone and Concluding Remarks

The criteria for membership in the lead-up to the creation of monetary union in Europe emphasized the need for fiscal discipline, and the Stability and Growth Pact (SGP) aimed to ensure that fiscal deficits did not interfere with monetary policy once the euro zone was created. These efforts are widely seen to have failed, as the sanctions in the case of excessive deficits needed to be imposed by other euro zone members who themselves were likely also to face sanctions. Revisions to the SGP have not been more successful, and the global economic crisis produced massive overshoots of the 3% deficit ceiling.

What was less well recognized were the other elements of institution building that needed to accompany a monetary union. These include, but are not limited to, close coordination of banking supervision—in the limit, a supra-national agency to carry it out—and a lender-of-last-resort facility at the euro zone level. They also include the willingness of member countries to bail out others in extreme circumstances. And political federation seems necessary to coordinate fiscal policies and limit excessive deficits effectively, where there are dangers both of financial markets underestimating the risks of unsustainable policies and of shutting borrowers out of financial markets when things go wrong.

The travails of the euro zone seem to have been taken to heart by the East African Community. The EAC Monetary Union Protocol (2013) calls for countries—as preconditions to joining the monetary union—to harmonize and coordinate their fiscal policies, integrate their payments and financial systems, formulate common rules for regulation and supervision of financial systems, and adhere to strict macroeconomic convergence criteria. The monetary union, once formed, is to establish an EAC central bank, mechanisms to build resilience and manage macroeconomic shocks, an enforcement mechanism, and an institution responsible for financial services.

Of course, the devil is in the details, and those details have yet to be worked out. The deadline for EAMU creation is a decade away, which should allow sufficient time to establish new institutions and to test the political will of the signatories. It is notable that the EAC Treaty itself includes the goal of political union, which has thus—at least in principle—already been agreed.

More generally, African regional economic communities will have to decide whether they are willing to abandon some of the elements of national sovereignty to achieve the deeper integration that a monetary union requires to operate successfully. In a number of cases, the weaker requirements of free trade areas and customs unions have not yet been fully complied with by member countries, despite commitments to do so. It seems likely that the further constraints on national policies and the needed delegations of powers to regional institutions will limit the scope for possible expansions of African monetary unions in coming decades.

ACKNOWLEDGMENTS

We are grateful to Célestin Monga for comments, and to Sibabrata Das for research assistance. This chapter should not be reported as representing the views of the IMF. The views expressed in this chapter are those of the authors and do not necessarily represent those of the IMF or IMF policy.

REFERENCES

Alesina, A., and Tabellini, G. (1987). Rules And Discretion With Noncoordinated Monetary And Fiscal Policies. *Economic Inquiry*, 25: 619–30.

Barro, R., and Gordon, D. (1983). A positive theory of monetary policy in a natural rate model. *Journal of Political Economy*, 91:589–610.

Coe, D., and Hoffmaister, A.W. (1998). North-South Trade-Is Africa Unusual? Working Paper No. 98/94, June.

Cohen, B. (1998). *The Geography of Money*. Ithaca: Cornell University Press.

Debrun, X., and Masson, P.R. (2013). Modelling monetary union in Southern Africa: welfare evaluation for the CMA And SADC. *South African Journal of Economics*, 81(2):275–291.

Debrun, X., Masson, P.R., and Pattillo, C. (2005). Monetary union in West Africa: who might gain, who might lose and why? *Canadian Journal of Economics*, 38(May):454–481.

Debrun, X., Masson, P.R., and Pattillo, C. (2008). Modeling policy options for Nigeria: fiscal responsibility, monetary credibility, and regional integration, in P. Collier, C. Pattillo, and C. Soludo (eds), *Economic Policy Options for a Prosperous Nigeria*. London: Palgrave-McMillan, pp. 93–120.

Debrun, X., Masson, P.R., and Pattillo, C. (2011). Should African monetary unions be expanded? An empirical investigation of the scope for monetary integration in sub-Saharan Africa. *Journal of African Economies*, 20(AERC Suppl 2):ii104–ii144.

Devarajan, S., and de Melo, J. (1987). Evaluating participation in African monetary unions: a statistical analysis of the CFA zones. *World Development*, 15(4):483–496.

EAC Monetary Union Protocol (2013). Protocol on the Establishment of the East African Monetary Union. East African Community, Arusha, Tanzania. http://www.eac.int/legal/index.php?option=com_docman&task=doc_download&gid=204&Itemid=47.

Guillaumont, P., and Guillaumont, S. (1984). *Zone franc et développement africain*. Paris: Economica.

Khamfula, Y., and Tesfayohannes, M. (2004). South Africa and Southern African monetary union: a critical review of sources of costs and benefits. *South African Journal of Economics*, 72(1):37–49.

Masson, P.R., and Pattillo, C. (2005). *The Monetary Geography of Africa*. Washington, DC: Brookings Institution Press.

Monga, C. (1997). A Currency Reform Index for Western and Central Africa. *The World Economy*, 20(1): 103–125.

Mundell, R. (1961). A theory of optimum currency areas. *American Economic Review* 51(4):657–665.

Rose, A. (2000). One money, one market: estimating the effect of common currencies on trade. *Economic Policy*, 30:9–45.

Rusuhuzwa, T.K., and Masson, P.R. (2013). Design and implementation of a common currency area in the East African Community. *African Journal of Business Management*, DOI: 10.5897/AJBM2013.7006.

Spatafora, N., and Tytell, I. (2009). Commodity Terms of Trade: The History of Booms and Busts. IMF Working Paper WP/09/205, September.

Tavlas, G. (2009). The benefits and costs of monetary union in Southern Africa: a critical survey of the literature. *Journal of Economic Surveys*, 23(1):1–43.

Tsangarides, C., and Qureshi, M. (2008). Monetary union membership in West Africa: a cluster analysis. *World Development*, 36 (7):1261–1279.

CHAPTER 5

THE CFA FRANC ZONE
A Biography

JEAN-CLAUDE TCHATCHOUANG

5.1 INTRODUCTION

THE monetary regime and banking institutions of a large majority of African countries reflect in many ways an extension of what exists in their respective metropolitan centers. In fact, most of the present-day African monetary systems institutions were initiated by the colonial powers. While many African states have taken some steps to achieve some relative autonomy on matters of monetary policy, strong political and economic linkages with their former ruling entities remain. This is certainly the case of the CFA franc zone, subject of this chapter.

The CFA franc zone today encompasses 14 Western and Central African countries grouped in two monetary unions, of which the currency, the CFA franc, has been tied since its inception in 1945[1] to the French franc and to the euro (with the disappearance of the French in 2000) via a fixed exchange rate arrangement. The four central features of the zone are the convertibility of the CFA franc (the common currency of zone members), the pooled reserves system each union operates through the French Treasury, the fixed parity rate between the CFA franc and the French franc (and the euro after 1999), and the free capital mobility within the countries of the Zone and France.

Prior to the 1980s, it was widely believed that the membership in the zone would support economic growth and reduce the need for economic adjustment. The guaranteed convertibility of the CFA franc combined with its fixed parity to the French franc would provide a stable investment climate for both foreign and domestic investors, which in turn would

---

[1] The CFA franc was created on 26 December 1945, along with the CFP franc. The reason for their creation was the weakness of the French franc immediately after World War II. When France ratified the Bretton Woods Agreement in December 1945, the French franc was devalued in order to set a fixed exchange rate with the US dollar. New currencies were created in the French colonies to spare them the strong devaluation, thereby facilitating exports to France. French officials presented the decision as an act of generosity.

contribute to economic growth and development (Devarajan and de Melo 1987; Elbadawi and Majd 1996).

In the 1980s, however, poor economic performance of the CFA zone countries relative to non-CFA zone countries in Africa led many to question the benefits of participating in the zone (Allechi and Niamkey 1994; Monga and Tchatchouang 1996). By the 1990s, it was widely held that the CFA franc had become overvalued, contributing to poor economic performance. Because the rules of the zone precluded use of the nominal exchange rate as a policy instrument, governments were forced to rely on other policies to counter the impact of the overvaluation. Many believed that the CFA zone countries were sufficiently equipped with policy instruments to achieve real exchange rate depreciation, but the use of these policies resulted in expenditure reduction in general, and decline in investment in particular (Devarajan and de Melo 1991). Though the countries of the zone elected to devaluate the CFA franc in early 1994, the fixed parity with the French franc, and later with the euro was maintained and as long as it prevails, the nominal exchange rate remains unavailable as a tool for policymakers should the CFA franc again become overvalued. Continued poor performance of the zone economies compared to non-CFA countries in Africa indicate that the arrangements between the CFA zone and France are not viable and call for a change.[2]

This chapter discusses alternatives to the fixed parity rate between the CFA franc and the euro. In the CFA zone, proponents of the fixed rate points to its ability to provide stability by linking inflation levels of the African countries to the inflation level in France and Europe, while opponents of fixed parity argue that, because it fails to change in response to shocks, the exchange rate sends incorrect signals to the domestic economies. There are a number of exchange rate arrangements that differ from the fixed parity rate by degrees of flexibility, and the appropriateness of each depends upon the economic setting in which it is used. This chapter will evaluate these alternatives in the setting of the CFA franc zone.

The remainder of this chapter is organized as follows. Section two will review the history, organization, and objectives of the CFA franc zone. The principles which govern the franc zone are the result of the peculiar relationship between France and her former colonies. This relationship has important consequences on the way the exchange rate arrangements play out in the zone. Section three discusses whether the CFA franc zone is an optimal currency area.[3] Section four focuses on the exchange rate, briefly defining exchange rate concepts to provide a framework for a discussion of the performance of the CFA franc zone. It also presents a typology of exchange rates and how and why they are chosen. Section five discusses whether a fixed parity rate is an appropriate exchange arrangement for the CFA franc zone based on the economic performance of the CFA zone countries. Section six surveys alternatives to a fixed parity rate and briefly assesses their advantages and disadvantages in the setting of the CFA franc zone. It will also discuss practical considerations for changing the exchange rate arrangement in West and Central Africa.

[2] See Ibrahim Edbadawi and Nader Madj (1992), *Fixed parity of the Exchange rate and economic performance: a comparative study*, World bank Policy research working Papers, 1992; Aloysius Ajab Amin (2000), *Long term Growth in the CFA countries*, World Institute for Development Economic Research, August 2000; Issiaka coulibaly and Junior Davis (2013), *Exchange rate regimes and economic performance: Does the CFA zone membership benefit their economies?* MPRA Paper No 54075.
[3] There are several criticisms of the theory of optimum currency areas, which are not discussed in this chapter. For references to these limits, see Célestin Monga (1997).

5.2 THE BIRTH OF A MONETARY UNION

The CFA franc zone finds its origin in the political and economic relations between France and her former African colonies. During the 1930s and the 1940s, France established currencies in each of its colonies that were pegged to the French franc. By the end of the Second World War, the currencies of the French colonies in Africa were consolidated into "le franc des Colonies Françaises d'Afrique" (CFA franc). Its parity was set in October 1948 at 0.5 CFA per French franc. The CFA was issued initially by the central bank of France's overseas territories (Caisse Centrale de la France d'Outre Mer). However, following the independence of France's former African colonies in the early 1960s, responsibility for issuing currency and overseeing the functioning of the zone was shifted to two regional central banks. These central banks were originally dominated by France, but by the early 1970s their control shifted to the member countries.

The membership of the CFA franc zone has changed over time with the departure (and subsequent reentry in the case of Mali) of some former French colonies and the entry in recent years of two sub-Saharan African countries that had no colonial relations with France and are not French speaking (Equatorial Guinea in 1985 and Guinea Bissau in 1997). The zone currently comprises eight West African countries (Benin, Burkina Faso, Cote d'Ivoire, Guinea Bissau, Mali, Niger, Senegal, and Togo) that are members of the West African Economic and Monetary Union (WAEMU). Their common currency was rebaptized from "franc des Colonies Françaises d'Afrique" to "franc de la Communauté Financière de l'Afrique" (CFA franc), which is issued by the "Banque Centrale des Etats de l'Afrique de l'Ouest" (BCEAO). The zone also comprises the six countries (Cameroon, Central African Republic, Chad, Congo Republic, Equatorial Guinea, and Gabon) that are members of the Central Africa Economic Monetary Cooperation (CAEMC) and of the "Banque des Etats de l'Afrique Centrale" (BEAC), which issued the "franc de la Communauté Financière de l'Afrique Centrale" (CFA).

The two CFA currencies are legal tenders only in their respective region. However, because of the guaranteed convertibility into the euro, the free capital mobility between each region and France, and the fact that the two CFA francs have the same parity against the euro, the CFA franc zone has traditionally been considered as one currency area with a single currency. France is represented in the executive boards of the two regional central banks and has traditionally been the main trading partner and provider of extensive technical and financial assistance to all member countries of the CFA franc zone.

The CFA franc zone functions under a number of key operating principles: (i) a fixed parity against the euro, adjustable if required by economic conditions after consultations with the French government and unanimous decision of all member countries within each monetary area; (ii) convertibility of the CFA franc into the euro; (iii) guarantee of convertibility by France through the establishment by each regional central bank of an operating account with the French Treasury; (iv) free capital mobility between the two regions and France; and (v) the pooling of foreign exchange reserves of each regional monetary area.

Thus the CFA franc zone effectively operates as a credit mechanism organized by France which, while serving to maintain the guaranteed convertibility of the CFA franc, simultaneously grants all holders of CFA franc access to the international capital markets. So the characteristics of a currency-board type of monetary system are in place. However, the Banque de France is not involved in formal terms, and the fixed CFA franc exchange rate is guaranteed instead by the French Ministry of Finance and administered by the exchequer (Treasury). The credit creation mechanism is in turn derived from the system in which the French Treasury traditionally also functioned as the bank of the state and local prefectures.

To preserve the principles referred to above, and as a means of encouraging financial discipline, a number of operating rules are stipulated in the statutes of the central banks. These rules require that each central bank: (i) maintains at least 50% of its foreign assets in its operating account with the French Treasury; (ii) maintains a foreign exchange cover of at least 20% for its sight liabilities; and (iii) limits credit to each government of member countries to a ceiling equivalent to 20% of that country's government revenue in the previous year. Taken together, observance of these operating rules limits in practice the potential drawings by the two central banks from their overdraft facility with the French Treasury.

With the accession of France to EMU on January 1, 1999, the only change was the recalculation of the CFA franc peg so that the exchange rate was quoted in euros instead of French francs, while the CFA franc zone system, its instruments and its *modus operandi* all remained unchanged.[4]

5.3 Is the CFA Franc Zone an Optimum Currency Area?

One way of evaluating the economic performance of the CFA franc zone is in terms of a currency area, a concept introduced by Mundell (1961). An optimum currency area (OCA) is defined as a region characterized by high degrees of the following criteria: factor mobility, economic interdependence, sectoral diversification, and wage and price flexibility (Mason 1994). The basic idea behind an OCA is that these four criteria are able to act as substitutes for, or simply reduce the need of, exchange rate adjustment. For example, a terms-of-trade shift might increase demand for a good in one country of a currency area, leading to inflation in that country, while decreasing demand for the same good in another country of the area, increasing unemployment there. If factor mobility exists, adjustment through a movement in the supply of labor could replace exchange rate adjustment.

Regarding the CFA zone's ability to meet these criteria, Boughton (1992) stated that "there are positive aspects on each front, but on none of these economic grounds would the zone appear to be a natural candidate for a common currency area."

Notwithstanding some economic progress achieved since the devaluation in 1994, the CFA franc zone remains confronted with sizable domestic and external imbalances and continue to be subject to structural rigidities and vulnerable to exogenous shocks. Additional reform efforts are required by all individual CFA franc countries to achieve a sustainable expansion of output as well as to promote regional integration and preserve the exchange

---

[4] The legal basis for the changeover was provided by Article 109(5) of the Treaty of Maastricht. This documents the sovereign right of EMU participant states to negotiate in international bodies with non-EMU counties on economic and monetary matters and to enter into treaties with them.

arrangement. In this context, it is generally recognized that the CFA franc zone does not meet the conventional criteria for the formation of optimum currency areas, even after 60 years of existence.

With a total population of about 136 million in 2010, the CFA franc zone roughly compares to the Russian Federation (the ninth most populous nation in the world) while its combined GDP of $142 billion compares to that of Kazakhstan. The annual average per capita income reached US$1044.0 in 2010, far below the per capita income in sub-Saharan Africa of USD1202.0[5]. The zone is dominated by Cameroon and Cote d'Ivoire, which account for 30% and 40% of their regional output respectively. The per capita income of the richest country, Equatorial Guinea, at USD16,000.0 in 2010, is 32 times larger than that of the poorest country, Central African Republic (CAR).

The CFA franc zone remains a fairly heterogeneous entity, with very limited intra-regional trade, and highly dependent on the production and export of limited number of primary commodities, with a narrow industrial base, making them highly vulnerable to external shocks. Intra-regional trade has traditionally remained modest, because of limited size of domestic markets, poor regional transportation and communication facilities, and high protection of domestic producers. Estimates indicate that intra-regional trade amounted to about 11% of total external trade of the WAEMU countries, 6% of the CAEMC countries, and 9% of all the CFA countries.[6] By comparison, intra-regional trade in European Union exceeds 60% of EU total international trade.

The key macroeconomic convergence criteria used in gauging progress towards monetary union include: annual inflation rates below 3%, a positive fiscal balance (excluding grants and foreign-financed investments), and an annual level of public debt to GDP of less than 70%. According to the IMF, after a sharp increase from 17 to 27 from 2004 to 2008, the annual number of violations has declined to its 2004 level, which, however, is still very high.

The requirement of business cycle synchronization is important of an OCA in that it guarantees symmetric responses to both real domestic and foreign nominal shocks affecting member states economies. The evidence however suggests that the production structures and structural characteristics of WAEMU and CAEMC zone economies differ significantly. For instance, all CAEMC states (with the exception of the diamond-exporting Central Africa Republic) are mainly oil exporters, with oil accounting over 90% of exports and 40% of GDP. WAEMU states, on the other hand, are mainly non-oil agricultural commodity exporters. The implications of these divergent production structures is that CAEMC states tend to respond differently from WAEMU states (with exception of Cote d'Ivoire) when faced by external shocks.

The spillover effects of the underlying differences in economic structures between WAEMU and CAEMC is a worrisome policy issue. For instance, the evidence suggests that, while liquidity has systematically been declining in the WAEMU zone since 2004, CAEMC states have been characterized by high excess liquidity in commercial banks. The high excess liquidity in CAEMC is the result of higher oil revenues that have improved the fiscal space for CAEMC governments. These elements explain why the stance of monetary policy in the

---

[5] Data from the Africa Development Indicators 2012/2013.
[6] Data from WAEMU and CAEMC annual reports.

WAEMU has been markedly different from that in the CAEMC and why the feasibility of a common monetary policy for both regions is limited.

Recent work on economic integration among a set of countries in a monetary union has shown that to be optimal it is important to also coordinate fiscal policies of member countries. Given the structural differences among the members of the union, fiscal policies are used as stabilizers. In the case of the United States for instance, Sala-i-Martin and Sachs (1992) showed how the federal fiscal system is used to offset economic shocks in different regions of the union. No comparable scheme of this nature exists in the CFA franc zone. Thus, the "fiscal federalism" that helps the US, Germany, and many other federal regions succeed despite economic structural divergence, is totally absent in the CFA franc zone.

5.4 FLEXIBLE VERSUS FIXED RATE: A CONCEPTUAL FRAMEWORK

The exchange rate plays two main roles in an economy: (i) it can help achieve and maintain international competitiveness; and (ii) it can act as stable anchor for domestic prices. The choice of an exchange rate regime, then, reflects a government's preferences for domestic economic stability and for independence in determining the appropriate mix of macroeconomic targets (inflation versus employment) (Salinger and Stryker 1994).

There are basically two exchange rate concepts: the nominal exchange rate and the real exchange rate. The nominal exchange rate is simply the value of one country's currency in terms of another, in order words, the price of foreign exchange. The exchange rate can be determined by market forces or it can be set by a government, in which case the government would be required to defend an increase in the currency's value. If the price of foreign exchange were to decrease (an appreciation of the exchange rate), demand for foreign exchange might exceed supply and the government could be required to meet that excess demand with foreign exchange reserves.

The nominal exchange rate measures the relative prices of currencies. The real effective exchange rate (REER), on the other hand, measures the relative price of two goods (Edwards 1994). The REER, then, can be seen as the measure of country's competitiveness in producing tradable goods[7].

For countries that cannot change the value of the nominal exchange rate, (which is the case for those in the CFA zone), the REER is influenced primarily by controlling domestic inflation. This can be done with policies that either restrict aggregate demand or expand aggregate supply. Countries that can change the nominal exchange rate may devalue a currency to compensate for increases in inflation. However, this increase in the nominal exchange rate often causes domestic price levels to increase, negating the intended effect of the devaluation.

---

[7] It should be noted here, even in just a footnote, that one can find at least five definitions of the REER in the literature. See Célestin Monga's chapter on the economics of African monetary unions in this *Handbook*.

At the equilibrium level, the REER clears the foreign exchange market (the supply of and demand for foreign exchange are equal, and the current account is balanced). If the REER is below its equilibrium level, the demand for foreign exchange currency exceeds its supply, and the currency is said to be overvalued. The result is that tradable goods become relatively cheap compared to non-tradable goods. To correct for overvaluation, a country can devalue the currency. The basic goal of any devaluation is to increase the price of tradable goods relative to non-tradable goods. The desired result is twofold: first, to shift domestic consumption toward domestically produced goods by making imports more expensive and second, to increase domestic production of tradable goods, as their price is now higher in domestic currency terms. All else equal, the REER will increase in value (depreciate), demand for foreign exchange in the home country will decrease, the supply of foreign exchange will increase, and the REER will move toward the equilibrium level.

Alternatively, a government can try to stimulate the effects of a devaluation, either with expenditure reducing policies (fiscal and monetary policies), expenditure switching policies (trade and exchange rate policies), or some combination of the two. The goal of expenditure reducing policies is to lessen domestic consumption and investment, thereby restoring balance to the current account. Expenditure switching policies attempt to reduce the demand for foreign exchange by shifting economic activity between the tradable and non-tradable sectors.

The type of exchange rate employed by a country will have a bearing on which policies will be more effective in achieving a country's economic objectives. In choosing an exchange rate arrangement, a country must weigh up two different sets of concerns. First, the choice of an exchange rate arrangement depends on three things: (i) policymakers' objectives, (ii) the source of shocks to the economy, and (iii) the structural characteristics of the economy in question. Second, with both a fixed parity rate and a clean float, a government cannot use the nominal exchange rate as a policy instrument to achieve either internal or external balance. The options that lie between theses extremes, for instance a crawling peg or a managed float, allow a government to alter the nominal exchange rate to appreciate or depreciate the value of the REER.

Exchange rate arrangements are typically divided into two categories, fixed and flexible. Fixed exchange rate arrangements generally involve pegging the value of the exchange rate either to one other currency or to a basket of currencies. Flexible exchange rates allow the nominal exchange rate to either adjust to a predetermined indicator or to be determined by market forces.

Between 1945 and 1973 (the Bretton Woods period), fixed exchange rates were standard practice worldwide, with most currencies fixed to the US dollar by an adjustable peg. However, fixed rates became increasingly difficult to maintain as world capital markets developed in the 1960s. Exchange rate adjustments became more frequent to account for inflation differences, and as devaluations appeared imminent, capital flight would ensue. After 1973, most major currencies were floating while developing countries maintained fixed rates. This changed in the 1980s with the introduction of structural adjustment programs, when many developing countries began to add flexibility to their exchange rate regimes.[8]

---

[8] See World Bank (The Berg Report) (1981), Accelerated Development in Sub-Saharan Africa, Washington, DC.

In the post-Bretton Woods period, the focus of the debate concerning exchange rate choice in the developing world was whether these countries should peg their currencies to a basket or the currency of a major trading partner (Devarajan and de Melo 1987). In 1976, 63% of developing countries pegged their exchange rate to the currency of an industrial country. But, by 1989, only 38% of developing country currencies were pegged to a single currency. For the same two years, the number of countries fixing their exchange rate with a currency basket increased from 13% to 23%.

The increase in the number of basket and floating arrangements was partly in response to a desire to minimize the adverse effects caused by fluctuations between the major currencies since the implementation of the floating exchange rates in 1973. Examples of adverse effects include uncertainty about the profitability of investment in the traded goods sector, and problems in managing foreign exchange reserves, public finances, and external debt. In addition, high domestic inflation rates were an important factor in the increase in the number of flexible arrangements in developing countries. Flexibility allows the nominal exchange rate to adjust for inflation differentials, which can help maintain a constant REER. Furthermore, flexibility relaxes the political burden of devaluation, as a government is not forced to take full responsibility for changing the value of a currency, as is usually the case with a fixed peg arrangement.

Corden (1993) presented two approaches for determining exchange rate policy: *the real targets approach* and *the nominal anchor approach*. The nominal anchor approach advocates fixing a country's exchange rate to the currency of a low-inflation country. This is the approach that has been followed in the CFA franc zone. Corden warned, however, that a commitment to a fixed exchange rate arrangement can be risky without both discipline and credibility. The discipline to maintain a fixed rate requires strong monetary and fiscal policies to ensure that real adjustment is not prevented, and a government's commitment to such policies plays a large role in determining the credibility of the arrangement. As Williamson (1993) noted, should discipline falter, a devaluation may be needed to realign the REER, which in turn can lead to a loss of credibility of the exchange rate regime.

In the CFA franc zone, the commitment to the French government to support the institutional arrangements of the zone has maintained the credibility of the CFA franc. Yet the inability of the CFA countries to change the nominal exchange rate appears to have contributed to the economic downturn in the late 1980s. Nevertheless, the CFA countries and France have elected to keep the fixed parity arrangement between the CFA franc and the euro, even while the majority of developing countries have added varying degrees of flexibility to their exchange rate regimes.

What has been the impact of the fixed rate on the economies of the CFA franc zone members? This question is discussed in the nest section.

5.5 THE CFA FRANC: CHRONICLE OF A DEATH FORETOLD?

The two principal benefits of pegging the exchange rate to a single currency are (i) the facilitation of trade among the countries whose currencies are linked by reducing uncertainty in the value of the currency; and (ii) the promotion of domestic price stability in the country pegging its currency, as the fixed nominal exchange rate acts as an anchor for domestic price levels. The latter depends on the willingness of a government (or the governments of the CFA countries and France in the case of the franc zone) to support the exchange rate through appropriate fiscal and monetary policies.

There are also some potentially bad consequences to an exchange rate peg. The primary drawback is for a developing economy to be caught by the strengthening of a developed country's currency (Dornbush 1988), which is what occurred in the CFA franc zone in the 1980s. Additional drawbacks include (i) a loss of flexibility in defining domestic monetary and fiscal policy (Salinger and Stryker 1994); and (ii) a possible barrier to regional trade efforts, as different countries in a region may peg their currencies to different developed country currencies, increasing exchange rate variation between the developing countries (Crockett and Nsouli 1977). This section shows that in the late 1980s and the early 2000s, even though the CFA zone had achieved price stability, external conditions changed so that the drawbacks increased relative to the benefits.

During the period from the early 1950s to the mid-1980s, the economic performance of the CFA franc countries compared favorably with that of other sub-Saharan African countries, the former achieved stronger real GDP growth and lower inflation. However, during 1986–1993, the economic and financial situation of the CFA franc zone seriously deteriorated, initially driven by external shocks and inadequate policy adjustments by member countries (Clément 1994). By the late 1980s, the CFA franc had become seriously overvalued, and both operations accounts were rapidly accumulating deficits, putting heavy pressure on the French Treasury. Additionally, internal structural problems (e.g. demographic pressures, rapid urbanization, and poor economic management) constrained productivity growth in the zone (relative to France), further contributing to overvaluation (Dioné et al. 1996).

The overvalued CFA franc particularly hurt the countries of the zone in two areas, production and investment. Van de Walle (1991) noted that during the late 1980s overvaluation was "in the process of demolishing the production apparatus in these countries, resulting in deep economic recession." Local products were unable to compete with imported goods, and agricultural production shifted away from tradable goods. In addition, the overvaluation encouraged the use of imported inputs as factors of production, further hurting domestic production incentives. The strong currency also discouraged foreign investment, as investors began to doubt the ability of the zone to maintain convertibility of the CFA franc in the face of overvaluation. Furthermore, capital flight became a problem as the overvaluation endured.

The worsening of the terms of trade led to a substantial depreciation of the equilibrium real effective exchange rate of the zone. However, in the absence of nominal exchange rate flexibility, and in the context of a sizable strengthening of the French franc against the US dollar following the Plaza Accord among the G5 countries, the CFA franc appreciated markedly in nominal effective terms. The internal adjustment efforts pursed by most CFA franc countries gave rise to only a modest depreciation of the real effective exchange rate of the CFA franc countries as a group that was not sufficient to offset the impact of the terms of trade loss, thereby leading to competitiveness problems.

The operating rules, and in particular the statutory limit on government borrowing from the central banks, did not prove adequate to instill fiscal discipline. Against the background of narrowing government revenue base, these statutory ceilings were exceeded significantly by several CFA franc countries, particularly during the early 1990s. Moreover, the fiscal imbalances and the external public debt of the CFA franc countries increased substantially in relation to their GDP during 1986-1993. The large fiscal imbalances also contributed to the emergence of sizable domestic and external payment arrears, as well as to a major weakening of the soundness and financial position of the banking systems in the CFA franc zone. In addition, the two regional central banks sustained large declines in their net foreign assets, necessitating a rundown of their deposits in the operations accounts with the French Treasury and a limited use of their overdraft facilities.

Because changing the parity rate of the CFA franc was considered a last resort, the zone member countries were forced to rely on other policies to change the REER and simulate the effects of devaluation (e.g. export subsidies and import taxes). Van de Walle (1991) argued that these policies created "incredible incentives for fraud and rent seeking, particularly when the high level of overvaluation necessitates greater distortion of the market prices." He also argues that the failure to reduce overvaluation of the CFA franc was political in nature, as governments lacked the financial discipline to achieve a depreciation of the REER. The social groups that benefitted from cheap imports were primarily urban workers, whose support was important to the government, and the overvaluation also provided revenue to the state via financial policies implemented to mimic the effects of devaluation (e.g. import taxes in rice).

Faced with economic conditions that continued to deteriorate, the members of the franc zone eventually devalued the CFA franc on January 12, 1994, doubling the parity rate of 50CFA francs per French franc to 100CFA francs per French franc.[9] The devaluation was accompanied by extensive fiscal, wage, monetary, and structural measures, and it received substantial financial support from the International Monetary Fund (IMF) and the World Bank (Clément 1994).

The new policy package, with devaluation as its central piece, contributed to a resumption of growth in real per capita income in the CFA franc zone at a rate of 0.8% a year during 1994–1996, after annual decline of 2.6% during 1986–1993. After a sharp initial increase following the devaluation, the zone's inflation rate was brought down to single-digit levels by end of 1996. Fiscal imbalances were reduced, with primary balance shifting to a modest surplus after sizable deficits during 1986–1993. The overall balance of payments deficits were also contained, while the external public debt burden was eased significantly for most CFA franc countries through concessional debt relief. By May 1997, about half of the gains in external competitiveness—as measured by changes in the consumer price-based real effective exchange rates—brought about by the devaluation were preserved.

As an integral part of the adjustment efforts, the two regional central banks shifted away from direct instruments of monetary control toward indirect market-based instruments, and established interbank money markets and new central bank financial instruments through auctions.

---

[9] After France joined the Euro Zone at a fixed rate of 6.65957 French francs to one euro, the CFA rate to the euro was fixed at CFA 665.957 to each euro, maintaining the 100 to 1 ratio.

The 1994 devaluation was successful in achieving its stated aims, as growth rates recovered and inflation controlled. Yet, adherence to the fixed parity rate continues to hinder the ability of the CFA countries to adjust to changing external conditions in a timely manner. As long as the fixed parity remains in place, external shocks and slow productivity growth can again cause an overvaluation of the CFA franc.

This is exactly what happened over the 2000–2005 period. In their 2006 study of the equilibrium real exchange rate of the CFA franc, Yasser Abdih and Charalambos Tsangarides found out that, after 1994 and a few years of "correction," both CAEMC and WAEMU REERs remained above their equilibrium levels for the rest of the period of analysis as a result of changes in the underlying fundamentals, which differed for the two regions. The CAEMC REER temporarily exceeded its equilibrium level in 1999, and again during the period 2001–2004, with statistically significant misalignments during those episodes. In the case of WAEMU, there were no statistically significant misalignments after the devaluation until a short period in 2003–2004 (Abdih and Tsangarides 2006).

In the case of CAEMC, the REER appreciated by about 13% in the 2001–2005 period as a result of 23% increases in terms-of-trade, and a depreciation caused by government consumption and productivity decreases (2% and 7%, respectively) and openness increase (about 1%). For WAEMU, in the period 2001–2005, the REER appreciated by about 12% as a result of increases in the term-of-trade and government consumption (accounting for an appreciation of the equilibrium real exchange rate in the order of about 9% each), while the increases in investment and openness and decreases in the productivity index contributed to REER depreciations of 2, 1, and 3%, respectively. Abdih and Tsangarides also observed very different speeds of adjustment for the two regions. For the CAEMC region, on average, about 0.12% of the overvaluation is eliminated every year, which implies that, in the absence of further shocks, about half of the gap would be closed within 5.6 years. However, for the WAEMU region, the adjustment is faster, with 0.24% of the gap is eliminated every year implying that, in the absence of further shocks about half of the gap would be closed within 2.9 years, almost half the time estimated for the CAEMC.

Williamson (1991) has developed a set of four qualifications that, if all are met, would identify a country as a good candidate for a fixed exchange rate regime. First, a country's economy must be small and open, and thus meet the requirements of membership in a larger currency area. The economies of the CFA zone are small and open, and they are members of a larger currency area, so this qualification is satisfied. Second, at least 50% of a country's trade must be with the country to whose currency it is pegging. Williamson deems 60% more than adequate, but 40% not enough. While the CFA countries certainly met this qualification when the CFA franc was established, they do not meet it now.

Third, the country must pursue macroeconomic policies that will result in a domestic rate of inflation that matches the rate of inflation in the country to whose currency it is pegging. This qualification is met by the CFA franc countries; its average inflation rate for all zone countries is 3%, compared with also the same level for France and for the EU. Fourth, the country must have institutional arrangements in place that can guarantee the credibility of the fixed rate arrangement. The CFA franc countries meet this requirement via the convertibility guaranteed by the French Treasury, though the 1990s changes regarding the convertibility of the CFA franc have lessened the currency's credibility.

Thus, the CFA franc zone countries meet three out of Williamson's four qualifications for use of a fixed exchange rate, when applying these qualifications to arrangement between the CFA franc and the euro. The primary reason why the fixed rate no longer appears to be appropriate for CFA countries is that their trade has become more diversified, and the fixed rate no longer provides as much benefit as in the past of facilitating international trade. External conditions have also changed significantly since the establishment of the CFA franc zone, and as African countries' trade has diversified, movements in the euro have, at times, hurt their competitiveness in world export markets.

5.6 EXCHANGE RATE OPTIONS FOR THE CFA FRANC ZONE

Williamson (1991) also stated that "the objective of exchange rate management is to keep the actual exchange rate reasonably close to the target, in order to give the correct price signals to a market economy." He added that the choice of the exchange rate management strategy should depend on the economic conditions, and that the way the target rate is determined and adjusted over time is always very important. The objective should be to determine the REER that allows a country to achieve its goals, and then manage the nominal exchange rate to maintain the target REER. The target rate should satisfy the following criteria: (i) it should not cause economic incentives to change erratically over time; and (ii) it should adjust to account for persistent real shocks and to ensure external equilibrium can be achieved.

We have already discussed the *nominal anchor* approach to exchange rate management. The alternative approach is the *real targets* approach. The real targets approach advocates the use of the nominal exchange rate as a policy tool to attain economic objectives, especially when the current account is in deficit. This approach depends on three assumptions: (i) nominal wages and the price of non-tradable goods must not adjust fully to account for a nominal devaluation, meaning that the economy must experience a real devaluation; (ii) real devaluations must lead to substantive changes in the long run, for example increased exports; and (iii) shocks faced by a country, whether external or internal, must be different from shocks faced by the anchor country, should the currency be pegged (Corden 1993).

When assessed only against these assumptions, it appears that the CFA countries are well suited for the real targets approach. We indicated previously that the 1994 devaluation did lead to a real devaluation (as wage and price increases did not match the magnitude of the devaluation), and the devaluation also induced a supply response, especially in the agriculture sector. Therefore, the first two qualifications for the real targets approach are met. Finally, the economic shocks facing the CFA countries are much different from those facing their trading partners, mainly industrial countries. The CFA countries mainly export primary products, and a decline in world prices decrease would not hurt industrial countries as it would for the CFA countries. In addition, with the coming into force of the fiscal compact in the Eurozone, France is increasingly subjected to limits on its deficits and, thus, cannot be counted upon to continue proving unlimited lines of credit to buffer the CFA franc, even if it wanted to do so. The fact that the French treasury would not be able to inject unlimited amounts of liquidity without further consequences casts doubts on the credibility of the CFA franc fixed regime going forward. Future constraints on the guarantee of convertibility by France imply that the CFA franc countries would need to maintain increasingly higher levels of foreign reserves by themselves. The main problems with the requirement of increasingly higher future reserve levels are that reserve accumulation continues to be largely supported by oil exports, and oil bases are fast depleting. Higher reserves cover also has an opportunity cost in terms of lost investment and growth. An empirical study by Gulde and Tsangarides suggests that during 1999–2004, the total cost of holding reserves amounts, on average, to 0.5% and 1.6% of annual GDP in CAEMC and WAEMU respectively. Thus, without the French convertibility guarantee, overall CAEMC GDP growth would fall by 0.5% annually due to higher level of required reserves (Gulde and Tsangarides 2008). This would raise the question of how to manage the exchange rate in the current institutional arrangements of the CFA franc zone.

Four options, listed below would be available to the CFA countries should they choose to exit from the current monetary arrangements.

5.6.1 Pursuing the goal of an OCA for each sub-region

Considering that the WAEMU and the CAEMC have each a common central bank, and each sub region has already established its own customs union with a common external tariff, its own common market allowing for free mobility of goods and factors of productions and its own economic union allowing for the integration of monetary and fiscal policies, these sub-region groupings-WAEMU and CAEMC- could independently pursue the goal of becoming an OCA by setting up the "CEMAC Franc" and the "WAEMU Franc" within the framework of a system of stable exchange rates with fluctuation margins. Choosing this type of regime would likely be prompted by considerations relating to the revamping of regional integration, on one hand, and to the existence of a dominant State on both sides (Cameroon and Côte d'Ivoire), that should be able to impose rules on members and support the related costs. Some of the new issues to be addressed by this new monetary strategy include the question as to whether the new CFA franc should be disconnected to the euro with the suppression of the "Operation Account," and the consequential loss of the French guarantee of convertibility of the CFA franc. The solutions will depend on the capacity of member states to undertake, jointly and equally, the necessary measures for convergence of economic, financial and social policies in the new monetary territory. Anyway, such a move calls for more boldness from the CFA member countries in order to avoid the Malian and Malagasy experiences.

5.6.2 Pegging to a basket

This exchange rate arrangement has the same advantages as a single currency peg, and it attempts to minimize the disadvantages by accounting for the fact that few countries trade exclusively with one other country. By not pegging to a single currency, a country can minimize adverse effects resulting from movements in the exchange rate of any one of its trading partners. Thus, a basket peg provides macroeconomic stability by minimizing changes in the REER. Crokett and Nsouli (1977) identified four alternatives for use as basket pegs: an export-weighted index, an import-weighted index, a bilateral trade index, and an index based on the SDR. They argue that a basket peg based on an import-weighted index is the most useful for developing countries. An export-weighted index would not be as effective because most developing countries export primary commodities, and world prices for these goods are independent of trade partners. As imports are more diversified, an import-weighted index will be more representative of the patters of trade. They also argue that pegging to the SDR can be practical as its value is well known and may reduce exchange rate variability between developing countries.

How might this exchange rate be applied to the CFA zone? The first step would be to decide on a trade index of the main economic partners for the zone. Based on the preceding argument, the appropriate choice would be an import-weighted index. The fact that imports to the WAEMU are more diversified than imports to the CAEMC countries suggests that different peg rates for the two unions should be considered.

5.6.3   Crawling pegs

Under a crawling peg arrangement, a currency is adjusted at frequent intervals by relatively small amounts, though the actual size and timing of the adjustments are random, in the sense that they are unannounced (Dornbusch 1988). The goal of a crawling peg over the long run is to fix the REER by adjusting the nominal exchange rate for inflations differentials, whether against a single currency or a basket of currencies. The frequency with which these adjustments occur provides some certainty to the value of the exchange rate. In other words, even though traders may not know exactly when the exchange rate will move, they know that it will not get too far out of line with an indicator such as the consumer price index.

The primary benefits of a crawling peg are (i) it limits speculative activity surrounding the exchange rate; and (ii) it depoliticizes the process of exchange rate management by eliminating the temptation to delay adjustment. However, though a crawling peg prevents a rise in the general price level from affecting a country's international competitiveness, external shocks can still cause appreciation of the REER. Thus, a crawling peg arrangement may still require additional policies to maintain its effectiveness.

One of the fears of ending the fixed arrangement between the CFA and the euro has been that the anchor for inflation provided by the arrangement would be lost. The anticipated result is higher rates of inflation in the African economies, leading to frequent adjustments of a crawling peg. However, Corden (1993) found that, for a sample of ten countries that switched from a fixed rate to a flexible rate, seven were able to maintain inflation rates reasonably close to the rate before the switch through conservative monetary and fiscal policies. Therefore, a crawling peg can be an appropriate rate for the CFA zone, provided monetary and fiscal discipline is maintained.

5.6.4   Currency floating

Floating exchange rates can either be dirty (managed by the government) or clean (wholly determined by market forces). With a dirty float, a government frequently adjusts its exchange rate based upon developments in its current account balance or payments position (Guitian 1994). Generally, a stable floating exchange rate regime can be maintained if the foreign exchange market allows capital to shift easily between domestic and foreign assets, via sufficient depth, forward exchange facilities, and markets for stocks and securities (Salinger and Stryker 1994). Yet because such capital markets do not exist in most developing countries, floating rates have generally not been regarded as viable alternatives for them. However, the number of developing countries implementing floating exchange rates has increased, primarily in response to severe balance of payments problems. Many developing countries simply do not have the reserves needed to defend a fixed exchange rate. Indeed, one of the main benefits of a floating exchange rate "is that it minimizes the need for foreign exchange reserves" (IMF 1993). Additional reasons countries have chosen the floating exchange rate include: lack of information necessary to determine a basket or crawling peg; macroeconomic stability; and political considerations.

In a practical sense, the debate over the introduction of floating exchange rates in developing countries has focused on the degree of centralization of the system for determining the nominal exchange rate. For example, one of the key questions to be addressed is whether auctions or private sector (interbank) markets should be used, and will non-bank foreign exchange dealers be allowed to participate in the latter?

There are at least three conditions for successful management of a flexible exchange rate, in terms of delivering low and stable inflation at the same time as the exchange rate works as a real shock absorber (Mar Gudmundsson 2006). First, the existence of a foreign exchange market with some minimum depth and efficiency; second, a domestic anchor for monetary policy; third, minimum independence and capacity of the central bank in order to be able to deliver an effective monetary policy.

The importance of floating exchange rates of the CFA is perhaps most relevant in the scenario where each of the member countries is faced with the decision of which exchange rate arrangement to use, should the franc zone cease to exist.

5.7 CONCLUSION

The majority of the studies on the OCA in Africa are centered on the CFA countries, perhaps because they are part of a more highly integrated monetary system than the rest of Africa and the relatively good quality of relevant data. Most of the studies suggest that increased monetary integration leading to monetary union would *not* be beneficial. Several reasons are suggested from the literature. Primarily, the heterogeneity of external and internal shocks that increase the cost of abandoning exchange rate controls, and the heterogeneity of fiscal demands (as highlighted by the work of Debrun, Masson, and Patillo 2003) which would require strict, possibly asymmetric central bank arrangements to make monetary union beneficial.

There are a number of scenarios that can play out in the CFA zone in the near future, one of which is to end the fixed parity with the euro. When this occurs, will France be willing or able to guarantee the convertibility of the CFA franc without fixed parity? And will the CFA zone continue to exist, or will monetary integration and cooperation end.

Given that many regions in Africa are contemplating to create their monetary unions, the OCA studies in Africa should focus on designing an OCA index along the lines of Celestin

Monga (1997) to evaluate the economic outcome of entering a monetary zone. Such a framework would enable a systematic analysis of the suitability of Africa and its regions to enter into a currency union.

References

Abdih, Y., and Tsangarides, C.G. (2006). FEER for the CFA Franc. IMF Working Paper WP/06/236.

Allechi, M., and Niamkey, M.A. (1994). Evaluating the net gains from the CFA franc zone membership: A different perspective. *World Development*, 22(8):1147–1160.

Boughton, J.M. (1992). The CFA Franc: Zone of fragile Stability in Africa. *Finance and Development*, 29(4):34–36.

Clément, Jean A. P. (1994) Striving for stability: CFA franc realignment. *Finance and Development*, 31(2):10–13.

Crockett, A.D., and Nsouli, S.M. (1977). Exchange rate policies for developing countries. *Journal of Development Studies*, 13(2):125–143.

Corden, W.M. (1993). Exchange rate policies for developing countries. *Economic Journal*, 103(416):198–207.

Devarajan, S., and de Melo, J. (1987). Evaluating Participation in African Monetary Union: A Statistical Analysis of the CFA Zones. *World Development*, 15(4):483–496.

Dornbusch, R. (1988). Overvaluation and trade balance, in D. Rudiger, F. Leslie, and C.H. Helmers (eds), *The Open Economy: Tools for Policymakers in Developing Countries*. New York: Oxford University Press for the World Bank.

Edwards, S. (1994). Exchange rate Misalignment in Developing Countries, in R.C. Barth and W. Chorng-Huey Wong (eds), *Approaches to Exchange Rate Policy: Choices for Developing and Transition Economies*. Washington, DC: International Monetary Fund.

Elbadawi, I., and Majd, N. (1996). Adjustment and economic performance under a fixed exchange rate: a comparative analysis of the CFA zone. *World Development*, 24(5):939–951.

Gulde, A.M., and Tsangarides, C. (2008) *The CFA Franc Zone: Common Currency, Uncommon Challenges*. Washington, DC: IMF.

Masson, P., and Pattillo, C. (2003). *The Monetary Geography of Africa*. Washington, DC: Brookings Institution.

Monga, C. (1997). Currency reform for Western and Central Africa. *World Economy* 20(1):103–126.

Monga, C., and Tchatchouang, J.C. (1996). *Sortir du Piège Monétaire*. Paris: Economica.

Mundell, R.A. (1961). A theory of optimum currency areas. *American Economic Review*, 51(2):657–665.

Sala-i-Martin, X., and Sachs, J. (1992). "Fiscal federalism and optimum currency areas: Evidence for Europe from the United States, in: M. Canzoneri, V. Grilli, and P. Masson (eds) *Establishing a Central Bank: Issues in Europe and Lessons from the U.S.* Cambridge: Cambridge University Press.

Van de Walle, N. (1991). The decline of the franc zone: monetary policies in francophone Africa. *African Affairs*, 90:383–405.

Williamson, J. (1991). Advice on the choice of an exchange rate policy, in E. M. Classen (ed.), "Exchange rate policies in developing and post socialist countries". San Francisco: International Centre for Economic Growth and ICS Press.

Williamson, J. (1993). Exchange rate management. *Economic Journal*, 103(416):188–197.

CHAPTER 6

....

AFRICAN MONETARY UNIONS
An Obituary

....

CÉLESTIN MONGA

6.1 INTRODUCTION

RUDI Giuliani, the New York mayor who galvanized his city in the days following the September 11, 2001, terrorist attacks, often talks about the most puzzling scene he witnessed that day. As he walked towards the World Trade Center where the tragic events had occurred, one of his aides told him: "Mayor, it's terrible. People are jumping out of the buildings. It's a disaster up there." He looked up, and saw debris coming off the buildings that had just been struck by the hijacked airplanes, but did not see people. He discounted the comments by his aide, thinking that it was an exaggeration. Or that his colleague might have just seen the same debris but somehow he saw them as human beings. Because the thought of human beings throwing themselves out 100 floors was so foreign to anything he had ever seen before. Yet he quickly realized that the situation was beyond worrisome and truly desperate:

> And as we are walking toward the scene, which was only two blocks away, looking up, all of a sudden I see a man throwing himself out of the 101st, 102nd floor ... that scene, of the man throwing himself off the building, I probably relive more than any other. When I go back to September 11th and think about it—lots of memories, but the one persistent and most difficult one is watching that man throw himself from the 101st, 102nd floor. Because it probably shocked me, and I just watched the whole thing. I just stopped and watched the whole thing. And then I saw other people doing it ...
>
> (quoted by Forbes 2011)

The fact that many fully conscious citizens who founded themselves trapped in the highest floors of the two World Center towers chose to escape the burning and melting skylines by throwing themselves to certain death must indeed have been daunting event to witness. It is also an extreme illustration of the mysterious ways in which the human mind makes rational or irrational decisions, optimizing under constraints and doing benefit–cost calculations in ways that are difficult to understand for agents who are not put in the same situation....

Looking at the economic challenges facing African policymakers today—at a time when 1 billion people still live below a very low income poverty rate (arbitrarily) set at US$1.25 a day—it is hard not to wonder about their decision-making process on crucial issues such as the choice of an exchange rate, and their increasing willingness to join or create monetary unions which they hope will help their economies escape from perpetual misery. While the political leaders in Dakar or Kinshasa are obviously not in the type of life-or-death situation in which innocent people found themselves in the burning and melting skylines of New York on 9/11, their assessments of the options available to them certainly appears to reflect the same urgency; and their tendency to adopt monetary policy decisions that guaranteed low growth and pervasive poverty to their countries is equally puzzling.

Given the strategic importance of monetary and exchange rate choices for small open economies in today's global economy, decisions being made by African policymakers also translate into life opportunities or death sentences for millions of ordinary African citizens whose daily existences are directly impacted by such choices. Perhaps a hundred years from now when future economic historians use the tools of behavioral economics to analyze the policy decisions made by the African policymakers—especially their either passive, uninformed, or stubborn willingness to join, remain in, or create monetary unions that clearly hampered their already difficult quest for prosperity—the rationality underlying the choices made will seem clearer than they are today.

The theoretical and empirical literature on the various ways of selecting an exchange rate regime and designing the appropriate monetary strategies broadly distinguishes three main approaches: the first is based on the theory of optimal currency areas, which aims at maintaining external balance and price stability (Tavlas 1993). Small open economies are typically advised to choose a fixed exchange rate, unless they have a diversified production and export structure, low factor mobility, high inflation differential with their main trading partners, and a not too geographically concentrated trade.

The second approach focuses on the typology of shocks faced by the economy, suggesting that exchange rate flexibility should be the default option for countries that tend to face real shocks causing shifts in the demand for domestic goods. The third approach emphasizes the importance of credibility and suggests that flexible regimes are generally needed to allow for fluctuations in the nominal exchange rate that are not automatically associated by private agents as changes in government policy—by contrast to fixed exchange rates that are politically more difficult to adjust. Of course, each country situation is unique and requires consideration of specific factors.

There is no other way to assess them: African monetary unions have underperformed—and African economies have been very slow to undergo structural transformation (Monga 2012a). The existing monetary unions failed to bring about economic prosperity and poverty reduction. Growth and employment creation rates in their member countries have been abysmal. Yet, the African political leaders have consistently chosen to forge ahead with these unions whose primary goal appears to fulfill the Kwame Nkrumah dream of a politically united Africa. Just like their European counterparts who decided to move towards the construction of a politically united Europe after World War II, African leaders have attempted since the wave of independences in the 1950s and 1960s to build the United States of Africa, but without taking the bold institutional and economic coordination decisions that would make the dream become reality. As a result, they have only gained the worse of both worlds: a politically divided continent with fragmented national economies that trade little with each other and often use currencies pegged at a fixed exchange rate to a very strong French franc or Euro. By giving up the crucially important tool for macroeconomic adjustment to shocks that a national currency is, these African leaders who joined or remained in politically-motivated monetary unions acted in almost "suicidal" way for their national economies: unlike the 9/11 victims who had no choice but to throw themselves into the abyss of certain death, the African leaders made the already bad economic situation of their poor countries even worse.

This chapter discusses the experience of African countries with monetary unions, focusing on the CFA Zone where that experience has been the longest and the deepest history of integration. The remainder of this chapter is organized as follows: section 2 briefly discusses how the intellectual legacy of colonialism led to distorted expectations and the neglect of the exchange rate—a crucial tool for improving the standards of living in open economies. Section 3 provides the analytical framework for understanding why trade reforms did not yield positive results in the fixed exchange rate environment. Section 4 draws some lessons from that macroeconomics of masochism, which consists in pegging the exchange rate of small, poor economies to a strong currency. Section 5 reexamines the criteria for assessing the validity of monetary unions regardless of whether they peg their currency or not. Section 6 offers concluding thoughts.

6.2 Monetary Unions: Simply Underperforming or Structurally Flawed?

6.2.1 High and low expectations

Once upon a time, African economies were the hope of the world. In the early 1960s for instance, most of these newly independent countries benefited from a rapid rise in the value of their exports. This led to an increase in their foreign exchange revenues and government revenues. The surge in income was stimulated by ambitious public policies aiming at increasing both investment and consumption. While often justified by the infrastructure and social needs (especially in education and health) who had suffered centuries of slavery and colonization, a lot of these investments were oversized, ill-designed, and poorly targeted. Igniting structural change through strong interventionist policies was the dominant intellectual framework at that time (Lin and Monga 2014). Fueled by the nationalistic dream of the new political leaders, large projects and programs dominated government plans in capital-intensive industries—often conceived on the model of Soviet Gosplan, regardless of the ideological background of the ruling elites. These projects and programs also generated large current expenditures, as they required a large number of civil servants with salary levels often equivalent to ten times the average income per capita, or high levels of operation and maintenance spending. Furthermore, for ideological, political, and sometimes economic reasons, and also for reasons of pure greed, many countries opted for the nationalization of large fraction of the production apparatus. As noted by Guillaumont and Guillaumont

Jeanneney, "they were encouraged along this direction by the ease with which they could obtain foreign loans owing to abundant international liquidity." (1994: 18).

In the 1970s, many private American, European, and Japanese banks had at their disposal important deposits from members of the Organization of Petroleum Exporting Countries (OPEC) cartel—the so-called petrodollars. Acting under the assumption that even poor developing countries cannot go bankrupt, these banks started lending money to African countries with little rigorous analysis of their justification. Countries were provided large loans which, under normal circumstances, would have been considered unwise. They were considered financially viable, as the prices of commodities (coffee, cocoa, copper, diamonds) through which they obtained foreign exchange were relatively high.

These loans were used to finance big investment projects with little or no economic rationale, imports of luxury goods, and personal bank accounts in European banks (Monga 2006). Yet, by the early 1980s, the situation had changed considerably. OPEC had become less effective as a cartel, which drove down oil prices and substantially reduced petrodollars held as deposits in western banks. Also, the United States had elected Ronald Reagan as President, whose fiscal policy consisted mainly of large tax cuts and big buildup in military spending. The combination of these two factors (the limited availability of petrodollars on the international lending market and the need for funds to finance the large US fiscal deficit) drove interest rates upward. To make matters worse, the world economy faced a major recession in the early 1980s and commodity prices on which African countries relied for foreign exchange decreased to historic lows. Confronted with the rapid increase of interest rates on their variable-rate loan repayments, these countries were on the verge of default on their external debt. Since the loans they obtained in the 1970s were used to pay for politically motivated projects or expansive luxury goods—not productive investments—only one realistic option was left to them: turn to multilateral financial institutions like the World Bank and the IMF for help.

In macroeconomic terms, the evolution of sub-Saharan Africa in the 1960s and 1970s can be described as follows: after independence, most African countries quickly experienced a persisting imbalance between aggregate domestic demand and aggregate supply, and this was reflected in a worsening of their external payments and an increase in inflation. In certain cases, the main explanation was the importance of external factors such as an increase in foreign interest rates or an exogenous deterioration in terms of trade. But in most cases, the so-called demand-supply imbalance could be traced to the inappropriate Government policies that expanded domestic demand (consumption, investment) too rapidly relative to the productive capacity of the national economy.

For a while, additional foreign financing was available and allowed these countries to sustain the large expansion of demand, albeit at the cost of a widening deficit of the current account of the balance of payments, a loss in international reserves, worsening of external competitiveness, and heavier foreign debt. This was eventually accompanied by declining growth rates, the aggravation of poverty, and the loss of creditworthiness. Indeed, as foreign investors and creditors who had been too lax in their willingness to put money in sub-Saharan Africa suddenly became irrationally reluctant to do so, these countries had no other choice but to undergo a macroeconomic or structural adjustment.

Despite Africa's economic misery, there was always great optimism about countries in a monetary union, most notably those in the CFA Zone. Such optimism stemmed from the notion that participation in the monetary union would foster economic growth, attract foreign investment, and reduce the need for adjustment. Conventionally associated with economic stability attributed to the fixed exchange rate with France and guaranteed convertibility of their currency, the CFA Zone economies have experienced economic declines similar if not worse to that of non-CFA countries, and had to adopt structural adjustment programs. In fact, until the early 1980s, CFA Zone economic performance by many measures was superior to other African countries. To "put it in its most prudent form" as Berg and Berlin did, the general conclusion from the literature was that "membership in the CFA zone did not hurt economic growth performance between the early 1960s and the early 1980s, though growth was slower than in non-African countries" (1993: 6). However, the Zone started showing signs of difficulties in the mid-1980s as the accumulated effects of changes in the world environment, persistent current account deficits, laxity and mismanagement in the implementation of fiscal and monetary policies, and delays in adjustment. An empirical comparison of the performance of CFA members with that of countries shows that "[the CFA countries] did not adjust by as much as they needed to. Furthermore, their growth performance was disappointing. Under every estimate, Zone members' GDP growth rates fell behind those of their counterparts, including the other African states" (Devarajan and De Melo 1990, 24.)

CFA countries generally fared quite well on inflation. However, for reasons explained in section 3, their union did not promote intra-regional trade (de Melo and Tsikata, *Handbook*, this volume, Chapter 11. Because of the very negligible part of each member's share of external trade with the others, the CFA Zone countries did not benefit from one of the major advantages of a single currency, which is resource savings on transaction costs among themselves. Some authors explain the small amount of intra-regional trade in large part by the limited internal market for the type of tradable goods which are commercialized by the CFA Zone members; indeed, by choosing a development strategy based on the export of cocoa, crude oil, coffee, phosphates, and other commodities, those countries ended up with an export structure which is a function of the demand for raw material in the industrialized world. Despite the so-called free transferability of capital within the Zone, very limited operations actually take place among countries. Banking networks were not conceived to stimulate economic activity and free market, but rather as recycling circuits and framework of economic domination of France on its former colonies (Honohan 1990). Financial intermediation did not really occur within the monetary union: from Dakar to Brazzaville, there are several thousand kilometers, but not really any "institutional infrastructure" to efficiently organize modern business. The main reason for this is the absence of incentives for banking and financial institutions to integrate when they operate in low-growth, low income countries that have little trade among themselves.

6.2.2 Analytics of the standards of living: the pre-eminent role of the real exchange rate

The question of low economic growth in African monetary unions is therefore a central one for economic analysis and policy. What happened? Did they underperform because of poor management or bad luck? Were they fundamentally flawed given Africa's post-independence economic context? In order to answer those questions, it is useful to briefly discuss the analytics of the standards of living, and how it applies to the broad macroeconomic strategy adopted by the African countries—all small open economies. This helps understand the importance of the real effective exchange rates (REER), especially when countries decide to give up their monetary sovereignty in order to join a monetary union.

Given their current structure, their fragmented nature, and their need to boost external trade for foreign exchange, the ability of African countries to improve their standard of living will ultimately depend on two key elements: higher productivity growth (output per worker) and better terms of trade (the price of exports relative to the price of imports, or put another way, the quantity of imported goods a country receives per unit of export).

Why is productivity important? In principle, any given country that would not trade with others could raise its consumption per capita in only three ways:

1. by putting aside as investment for the future only a smaller fraction of current output, and by devoting more of its productive capacity to manufacturing goods for current consumption;
2. by putting a larger fraction of its population to work; and
3. by increasing its productivity so that each worker produces more.

Clearly, option (i) would not be sustainable, as lower levels of investments will eventually cut into the country's ability to produce and to consume. Option (ii) could work for a while in countries where a substantial fraction of the population is unemployed, or if the social dynamics of the country brings new groups into the work force—this would clearly be the case in most African countries where a very large segment of the work force is unemployed or underemployed. But option (iii), that is, raising productivity, would really be the only important way to achieve sustained long-term growth in living standards. Empirical studies show that in most countries, the evolution of real consumption per capita is usually very closely correlated with that of productivity.

Because African economies are mostly small "open economies" in the sense defined by Dornbusch (1988) and rely heavily on trade, an important part of their output is sold abroad as exports so that they can earn foreign exchange and pay for their imports, which they consume. Therefore, these countries can also increase their per capita consumption in two ways:

1. by importing more without selling more abroad—which implies that they have to find the money to pay for the extra imports (borrowing or sale of their assets); or
2. by managing to obtain better prices for their exports so that they do not need to pay the extra cost of their additional imports.

Option (1) is possible only for countries with sufficient reserves and excellent creditworthiness to pay the extra cost but cannot be sustained for a long period of time—as borrowing needs to be repaid at some point.

Option (2) is the most realistic but it implies that African countries are able to convince foreigners to pay more for their exports. This can only be done through higher productivity, that is, producing better goods and services. This helps understand the importance of terms of trade, which in turn highlights the pre-eminence of the real exchange rate.

The analytics of the story is straightforward: The standard of living (*SL*) is defined as the purchasing power of the income produced by an hour of work. Labor productivity is defined as the amount of output per hour worked (*α*). With the price of domestic output denoted *P* and the consumer price index denoted *Q*, the purchasing power of an hour of work is

$$SL = \alpha P / Q \tag{1}$$

The consumer price index is a function of domestic prices and import prices. Assuming that it is an exponentially weighted average,

$$Q = P^{l-b} x (P^*)^b \tag{2}$$

where 1 – b is the share of domestic goods in spending. Substituting in the previous equation yields

$$SL = \alpha (P / P^*)^b \tag{3}$$

This formula shows there are two ways of increasing the standard of living (*SL*): the first is to improve labor productivity (a higher output per hour increases consumption, regardless of whether the increase is traded abroad or consumed domestically). The second is to through better terms of trade, as an increase in the prices at which any country sells its products, relative to those it buys imports (*P/P**), raises its real income. The importance of the terms of trade channel also highlights the preeminent role of the real exchange rate.

6.2.3 The tragic burden of overvalued exchange rates

The economic literature on real exchange rates uses numerous and often contradictory definitions. One can identify at least five of them (Edwards 1988: 47):

- the purchasing power parity definition, *ePPP = EP*/P*, where the real exchange rate is equal to the nominal exchange rate (*E*) multiplied by the ratio of the foreign price level (*P**) to the domestic price level (*P*);
- the dependent economy definition of relative prices of tradables to non-tradables, excluding taxes on trade, *e = EP*T/PN*, where (*P*T*) is the world price of tradables, and (*PN*) the domestic price of non-tradables;
- the domestic relative price of tradables to non-tradables, *e = PT/PN*;
- the domestic relative price of importables to non-tradables, *e = PM/PN*, where (*PM*) is the domestic price of imports;
- the domestic relative price of exportables to non-tradables, *e = PX/PN*, where (*PX*) is the domestic price of exports.

Using anyone of such definitions, empirical studies or REER evolution in African monetary unions, most notably the CFA Franc Zone, have consistently shown appreciation and even overvaluation. These trends are not easy to measure in the African context, because data are often not available, and one of the key indicators, which is the gap between the official rate of exchange and that prevailing in parallel markets, is often nonexistent—because of free convertibility. Moreover, the quest for an "equilibrium exchange rate" raises several issues: whether it is defined as one that brings about internal and external balance (a good rate of growth and a sustainable medium-term balance of payments)[1], or as a rate sustainable without special policy measures, that will permit a reasonable rate of growth, the equilibrium exchange rate implies the choice of a base period, the "equilibrium year(s)."

Notwithstanding these methodological issues, researchers at the Bretton Woods institutions computed a series of indexes to measure by how much the CFA franc for instance had become overvalued in the 1980s (Devarajan and Hinkle 1994). By weighting each partner country price change by its relative importance in the trade of the reference country using 1985 as base year, they examined the following evolution of the real effective exchange rate (i.e. the trade weighted and inflation adjusted). They observed that the 1980s witnessed the worsening of the Zone's competitiveness REER indicators appreciated by nearly 40 percent while the terms of trade collapsed, falling by exactly the same proportion between 1985 and 1992, as the prices of the major commodities (coffee, cocoa, oil) dropped sharply. Declining terms of trade reduced real income levels and exacerbated poverty. In countries pursuing a flexible exchange rate policy, a decline in the terms of trade would normally be compensated for by depreciating the real effective exchange rate to restore the profitability of domestic export industries.[2] Yet, exactly the opposite happened in the CFA Zone. Other unpublished studies carried out for the 2000 years came to similar conclusions.

There are three main causes of exchange rate overvaluation: expansion in domestic demand, loss of export revenue, and deficits in the external balance. In the past decades, most African countries experienced all three, though at different degrees. With the post-independence euphoria and optimism, the general government consumption and the gross public investment increased rapidly in the 1960s and 1970s when the main public policy goal was to achieve economic modernization. Monetary union member countries were expected to gain macroeconomic stability and be immune from profligate fiscal policies because they generally had stringent limits on how much fiscal deficit could be financed by central banks. In the CFA Zone, one important rule has always limited members' recourse to central bank credit to 20 percent of the previous years' government revenue.

However, the architects of these institutional arrangements neglected one of the most important equations in macroeconomic stabilization, which is the following:

$$\varphi \equiv \delta + \varepsilon + \gamma, \tag{4}$$

where φ is the fiscal deficit, δ is money creation, ε is domestic borrowing (credit from the private sector), and γ is foreign borrowing.

---

[1] See section 6 below for strategies to address external imbalances.

[2] A World Bank study devoted to 28 devaluation episodes in 21 developing countries between 1962 and 1980 concluded that "in the vast majority of cases the devaluation were preceded by a severe loss of international liquidity and by a worsening of the different accounts of the balance of payments. In most cases the devaluation was triggered by an acute loss of reserves, which made impossible for the authorities to continue to defend the peg. The ultimate causes, however, were expansive macro-policies that became inconsistent with the maintenance of a fixed nominal rate". See Edwards (1985). These observations are consistent with theoretical models by Krugman (1979) and Obstfeld (1984).

While there has always been a formal rule on δ there was no limitation on ε and γ. Not surprisingly, some countries took advantage of that gap in the rules to borrow extensively on commercial terms to finance government expenditures. The debt service obligations incurred by most African governments grew very rapidly in the 1960s and 1970s and complicated the difficulties of fiscal reforms engaged in the 1980s and 990s. The fact that monetary policy in the CFA Zone has always been conducted at the regional level under surveillance of the French monetary authorities enhanced discipline and limited somewhat the use of monetary financing of fiscal deficits; however, over several decades, many countries were able to circumvent the rules, using three sets of tactics: accumulating government arrears (large amounts of unpaid bills from public procurement); favoring substantial commercial bank crop credits to intermediaries and to national marketing agencies; and obtaining central bank rescheduling for arrears on loans given to public enterprises).

The fiscal deficit problems in African monetary unions were compounded by the fact that public spending was too often allocated to consumption (mainly public sector wages and benefits) and to unproductive investment. This raised the important issue of sustainability of government finances.

Fiscal sustainability does not simply entail the government's ability to finance itself, but it requires government's fiscal and monetary policies to be consistent with the expected growth, inflation and interest rates. Sustainability does not necessarily require government to pay off its debt in the long run, but it needs real debt to accumulate at a rate lower than the real interest rate paid on it. In other words, the government is accountable for the net real interest rate (real interest rate, r, minus the real growth rate, μ) paid on the debt to GDP ratio, b_o. This can be financed either with a primary surplus $g-\tau$, or with seigniorage revenue, represented by the inflation tax paid on the money demand to GDP ratio, $C_i(r + \pi)$ (a decreasing function of nominal interest rate, $r + \pi$). This sustainability condition is represented as:

$$(g - \tau) + (\pi + \mu) \cdot L(r + \pi) = (r - \mu) \cdot b_0$$

(5)

This can be used to assess whether the primary fiscal balance in any given monetary union member country (C_i) was in line with the long-run sustainability condition. Despite their consistently lower expected average inflation rate, the CFA countries for instance also had lower (or even negative) growth rates. As a result, it always appears that they need relatively high primary deficits to project fiscal sustainability in the long run. The concern that low growth rates and the possibility of unexpected high interest rates (especially on external debt) may pose serious macroeconomic threats have led institutions such as the International Monetary Fund to recommend that these countries reduce their fiscal deficits and drastically limit any non-concessional borrowing. While such recommendations make sense from a purely accounting viewpoint, they assume that new debt would only finance unproductive investment, and therefore are inconsistent with the needs of low-income countries with large infrastructure gaps and low domestic savings base.

African countries have also suffered from a substantial decline in their terms of trade for long periods of time. The relatively high rate of export expansion, which had been the engine of growth in the 1960s and 1970s, dropped substantially in the 1980s. Furthermore, as import prices rose after 1985 while export prices fell considerably, export revenues often dropped, which caused a decline in the purchasing power of exports. The total exports of goods and nonfactor services decreased in real terms by large margins. Deficits in the external balance were also observed in most countries.

The consequences of the REER overvaluation were painful in the CFA countries: first, there was the loss of competitiveness. Empirical studies show that manufacturing costs for instance exceeded those in comparator countries (Barbier 1989). There was also a loss of domestic production, employment, and fiscal revenues. The economic depression exacerbated the accumulation of arrears in the public sector. This caused serious liquidity problems for the banking system and encouraged speculation, which led to capital flight.

Faced with such difficulties, the CFA countries were forced to adopt structural adjustment programs aiming at stabilizing their economies. They did so in the late 1980s and early 1990s but without seriously tackling overvaluation of exchange rate, the very issue at the heart of their macroeconomic imbalances. The failure of trade reforms implemented for some two decades highlights the burden of their misaligned exchange rate—and the cost of the monetary union under difficult economic constraints.

6.3 How Monetary Unions Prevented Potential Trade Dividends

Before global value chains became the dominant feature of international trade, small open economies had to rely mainly on trade reforms to change the patterns of their interactions with international markets and stimulate their exports. Because many developing countries were constrained by distortions from their misguided import-substitution policies of the 1960s and 1970s, trade liberalization policies (reduction of tariffs, relaxation or suppression of quotas, simplification of export and import procedures) were thus designed to avoid economic inefficiencies and to restore market equilibrium.

Depending on the structure and the initial position of each country (in terms of balance of payment equilibrium), there are various ways to implement such liberalization. Although evidence on the link between trade reform and economic recovery has been inconclusive (Pack 1988; Havrylyshn 1990), conventional wisdom from empirical studies is that developing countries can improve economic performance through trade policy changes, providing that issues of macro-compatibility and time-inconsistency are addressed.

- *The compatibility issue.* Trade reforms should be among a set of macroeconomic policies which are compatible. That is, "trade restrictions, the exchange rate, and budgetary-cum-monetary policy must be coordinated in such a way as to avoid depletion of foreign exchange reserves" (Collier and Gunning, 1992: 1). The compatibility problem arises when trade liberalization is undertaken and no other policies are changed. The reduction of tariffs and the removal of quotas lower the domestic price of imported goods and thereby reduce the demand for money. This important "stock effect" creates an excess supply of money, and a payments deficit.

There are three possibilities for achieving compatibility.

The first option is to offset the reduction in the prices of imports with exchange rate devaluation. Since we have the relation:

$$PM = P^* W \cdot x \cdot e \cdot x \times (1+t),$$

(6)

where (PM) is the domestic price of imports, (P^*W) the international price in dollars, (e) the exchange rate in units of domestic currency per dollar, and (t) the nominal rate of protection; hence, increasing (e)—through a devaluation of the national currency—will cancel the effects of reducing (t), and (PM) will remain at the same level (Figure 6.1).

The second method is to use external aid to finance a deficit until the money supply is sufficiently depleted. The excess money supply resulting from the price level reduction is purchased by the Government with finanacial aid. This causes temporary Dutch disease (provisional increase in the output of the non-tradable sector), but finally, if the Government does not use the money to increase its expenditure, compatibility can be achieved. This is shown on the Neary and Purvis (1982) diagram (Figure 6.2).

The third possibility is to combine devaluation and aid. The impact effect of liberalization shifts the economy from the monetary equilibrium locus to the left. Thereafter there is a gradual realignment which is achieved by devaluation and by the money supply reduction effect (Figure 6.3).

- *The consistency issue.* Christiansen et al. observed that "the most important factor in determining the ability of a country to adopt and implement any major policy revision is the support of domestic interests. In other words, economic policy formulation does not occur in a political vacuum" (1988: 103). The time-inconsistency issue arises when trade reform is adopted in an environment where private agents believe that it will be unsustainable, for political or economic reasons. Therefore, they do not react as the government expects; instead of investing in the export-import sectors, they try to benefit from speculation (i.e. buying imports when they are temporarily cheap), or they postpone their investments. Even if they decide to import assets, they will not fully behave as if the context was normal.

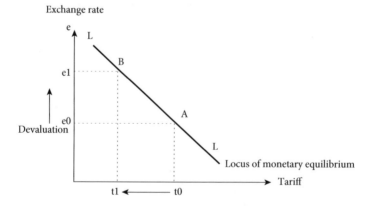

Given the equation PM = P*W x e (1+t), moving the economy from
point A to point B would not change the price of imports.

FIGURE 6.1 Equilibrium through devaluation.

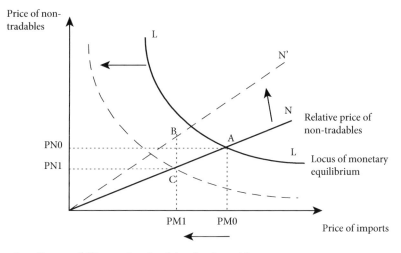

FIGURE 6.2 Compatibility maintained by foreign aid.

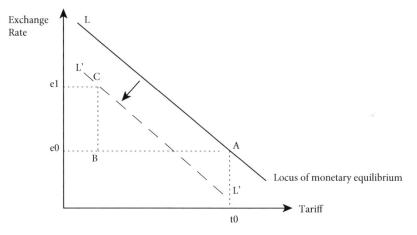

Because of aid, the reduction of the money supply shifts the monetary locus from LL to L'L'. The impact effect of liberalization moves the economy from A to B. Thereafter, there is a gradual adjustment to C, partly due to devaluation.

FIGURE 6.3 Combining devaluation and foreign aid.

6.4 MACROECONOMIC MASOCHISM: SOME PAINFUL LESSONS

The economic experience of African countries that are members of a fully functioning monetary union such as the CFA Zone sheds new light on the issues discussed above. It also highlights some painful lessons of ineffective macroeconomic management. This section briefly discusses these lessons, and explains why the various strategies to address external deficits (from difficult deflationary policies to an unwelcomed devaluation) failed to ignite the process of structural transformation—even if they eventually led to moderate growth in the late 1990s and 2000s.

Trade and financial sector reforms and other measures of internal adjustment fail for many reasons. First, exchange rate misalignment typically leads to credibility problems, with private agents doubting about the ability of government officials to effectively address competitiveness issues. The lack of trust between officials and the business community, and the macroeconomic situation of the country (balance of payment deficits in some countries, high fiscal deficits and high public debt in others, capital flight, shortage of reserves), often aggravated by political instability or uncertainty, make the implementation of any serious adjustment reforms particularly difficult. In such situations, the monetary authorities are forced to recognize the failure of strategies based internal adjustment as means to correct exchange rate misalignment. Their only recourse is devaluation, or the exit from the monetary union.

6.4.1 An illusory strategy for tackling the balance of payments deficit

There are various ways of dealing with a balance of payments deficit.[3] When policymakers assume that misalignment is not a structural problem but simply induced by macroeconomic inconsistencies in previous periods, they act as if the problem is temporary. A good illustration is the strategy adopted by CFA countries of the Franc Zone in the eighties and early nineties. In order to address their increasingly unsustainable balance of payment imbalances, most of the countries of the Zone used a variety of options in the period 1984–1993, except the devaluation. Some changed the policies governing their international transactions. Other financed external deficit through accumulation of external debt and arrears, or altered domestic monetary and fiscal policies to increase net exports and capital inflows—with mixed results. In fact, most of them selected a combination of these options.

Some of these policies aimed at affecting the current account. Trade taxes and subsidies, quantitative restrictions and other non-tariff barriers intended to directly changing the relative prices were thus adopted, often with perverse results: in contradiction with official goals of reducing the government's role in agricultural production and marketing activities for instance, including the liberalization of input markets and the gradual elimination of subsidies on fertilizers as well as the transfer of functions from state agencies to private ones or agricultural producers themselves, such policies generally ended up creating even more state intervention in the market, with the purchasing prices of agricultural products raised by official decrees as governments tried to protect the purchasing power of farmers. Even when farmer fertilizer subsidies were gradually removed, pressures from the rural elites who benefited from the old policies resulted in slippage in the implementation of reform policies. It is indeed often the case that after the enactment of various measures of trade liberalization, internal politics, and social pressures from the local media and the domestic producers leads to a reversal of the policy: the removal of import controls, painfully felt by the local

---

[3] See Monga (2012b).

manufacturers, is strongly opposed and governments find ways of reapplying reference prices and quantitative restrictions to a large number of products.

Other policies focus on the capital account. When the external accounts of the Franc Zone deteriorated in the 1980s, the two central banks of the monetary union decided to put severe restrictions on capital flows. These measures generally achieved their desired effect, and prevented further capital flight from African countries of the Franc Zone. However, they also cast doubt on the strength of one of the main pillars of the Franc Zone—free convertibility and unlimited transfers (Monga 1993) External debt management techniques also served to postpone the balance of payment problem by accumulating arrears, and by obtaining rescheduling in the framework of structural adjustment programs, many African countries were able to maintain a relatively high level of external deficit.

From a theoretical standpoint, the obvious way for addressing the balance of payment disequilibrium is "to eliminate the source of the macroeconomic disequilibrium—that is, the inconsistency between macroeconomic policy and the nominal exchange rate" (Edwards 1988: 23). This is the use of disinflation with automatic adjustment. The government can then either wait for the economy to adjust on its own, or accompany this internal adjustment strategy with a set of complementary measures aiming at restoring competitiveness. In their desperate attempt to avoid a nominal devaluation of their currency—seen as detrimental to the most powerful social groups (urban dwellers, civil servants and other elites and politically risky, the leaders of the CFA countries adopted such internal adjustment strategies for as long as possible in the late 1980s.

The argument was essentially made by a group of scholars who strongly argued that bringing about realignment through the use of devaluation would lead to very high inflation in the CFA countries, and very heavy social costs (Guillaumont and Guillaumont 1991; Cocquet and Daniel 1992). Instead, they recommended that real depreciation of exchange rate be achieved through expenditure reduction, which normally lowers the price of non-tradables relative to tradables. The rationale behind such an option was that deflationary fiscal and monetary policies would bring aggregate demand and supply into balance, and depress the relative prices of non-tradables in order to liberate resources for increasing production of tradables. According to this framework, some structural reforms would facilitate the adjustment: liberalization of markets; restoration of price flexibility; improvement of the resources allocation process; reduction of the size of the public sector, which is a burden on public finance; subsidies to private sector production, etc.

Under the supervision of the French technostructure for cooperation (which includes institutions like the ministry of Cooperation, *Caisse Française de Développement, Direction du Trésor* of the ministry of Finance, *Banque de France*) and the World Bank, these measures were adopted in the CFA countries: in Senegal for instance, the government decided to increase import duties and subsidize exports; they proved difficult to implement because the policy was costly and seemed to favor existing exporters. Then, it was decided that the basis of subsidy determination would be value added, instead of total value of exports. But this also proved impossible to calculate in a consistent manner because very few firms had accounting procedures allowing a clear computation of their value added. Furthermore, the budgetary impact of the subsidy scheme became very rapidly a matter of concern for the government. Eventually the program was not implemented. A similar attempt was made by the government of the Ivory Coast in the mid-1980s (Lavy et al. 1991). But again, because of budget pressures, the policy was abandoned in 1988.

Other CFA countries chose to focus on raising import duties. In Benin for instance, the government had to face the economic consequences of strong nominal devaluations in neighboring Nigeria, with a sharp deterioration in terms of trade and an overvalued currency; they imposed high tariffs, quotas, and other forms of informal taxation (i.e. patrol controls at the Nigerian border, trying to raise the transportation costs of foreign goods, and to discourage importers). However, because of Benin's weak administrative capacity, the government could not implement its own policy. As a result, the fraudulent import of Nigerian goods was organized in Benin by the very businessmen who were benefiting from export subsidies.

Cameroon also adopted similar measures (high level of import duties, and some export subsidies) but actually did not focus much on trade policies. Instead, the government attempted to restore competitiveness by reducing the budget deficit and factor costs. Wages were cut by 70 percent in 1993. Yet, because of the collapse of domestic demand and economic activity, the public sector wage bill as a percentage of government revenue generally remained high, which (mis)led many experts, including those working with the Bretton Woods institutions, to believe that the general level of public wages was abnormally high.

All these policies yielded little results. The magnitude of macroeconomic imbalances across the monetary union was such that disinflationist policies were not sufficient for the automatic adjustment to occur. Yet, by sticking to that interval adjustment strategy, these countries paid a heady economic and social price. Eventually, the CFA nominal devaluation finally appeared to be the only possible way for achieving realignment.

6.4.2 From deflationary policies to devaluation

It is always difficult to precisely measure the impact of any particular policy on the economy, since the results generally depend on "the other elements of the policy package," and "the structure and characteristics of the individual economy" (Collins 1988). However, there is wide consensus on the diagnostic that the decision to implement disinflation strategies led to heavy social and financial costs in all the CFA countries. This happened for several reasons: first, the real exchange rate became misaligned as a consequence of terms of trade shocks, and not because of internal inflationary policies, which could not occur anyway, since the Franc Zone rules do not allow any large budgetary deficits. For long periods of time, revenues from exports[4] and import substitutes declined while domestic prices and wages remained unchanged; worsened the appreciation of the CFA franc, and diminished incentives for producing tradable goods. Given the large number of people living in the agricultural sector, the poverty situation deteriorated in those countries.

Second, contradictions in trade policies, that governments could not implement anyhow, raised the credibility issue—public revenues were often inadequate to actually fund export subsidies, and high tariffs on imports led to massive and almost institutionalized fraud on

---

[4] Between 1989 and 1992, cocoa exports decreased by 6.2 percent in the Ivory Coast, and by 14 percent in Cameroon; groundnut exports in Senegal fell by 37.6 percent during the same period; coffee exports in Cameroon also decreased by 27.6 percent. Source: World Bank African Development Indicators, January 1995.

custom duties. Furthermore, capital restrictions did not work either. Strategies were often developed by private agents with excess savings to circumvent the restrictive rules (Herrera 1994).

Third, internal adjustment did not bring about a supply response because of many structural problems facing the private sector in the CFA countries. The underdeveloped "modern" financial sector in those countries—by opposition to a vibrant informal financial sector—needed to be restructured. But among other difficulties (poor management, lack of confidence, decreasing volume of deposits, high real interest rates causing adverse selection and moral hazard, portfolios dominated by non-performing loans, important arrears on loans to public enterprises, predominant role of the state), the CFA franc overvaluation stimulated capital flight and illiquidity. Thus, the financial sector could not provide funds for private investment. The credit market imperfections led to negative output response (Monga 1997a).

Fourth, internal adjustment had some perverse effects on public finance. In countries with narrow tax bases, the rigidity of a fixed exchange rate is always likely to cause fiscal problems. In most African countries, tax bases are often highly dependent on external trade because it is far easier to collect customs duties and sales taxes than to collect income taxes. Since the exchange rate determines the prices at which imports are sold, a country whose exchange rate is overvalued is likely to experience a drop in revenues as its ability to finance imports by exporting diminishes. The country's rate of growth subsequently decreases, with demand for imports reduced accordingly.

In theory, countries with a fixed exchange rate can achieve competitiveness by adopting deflationary policies bringing government spending in line with revenue; however, in the case of CFA countries, the overvaluation persisted for nearly a decade in the eighties and early nineties, and the fiscal imbalances were compounded by the fall off in revenues derived from both import tariffs and taxes levied on the sales of import substitutes. Faced with such realities, the monetary authorities of the CFA Zone eventually realized that a deepening of internal adjustment strategy would have pushed the zone further into a deflationary spiral with high social and economic costs. They agreed to use the devaluation as the ultimate strategic tool for dealing with unsustainable balance of payments deficits. They announced a devaluation of 50 percent of the CFA franc vis-à-vis the French franc on January 12, 1994—a uniform rate of devaluation across all the 13 countries of the CFA Zone at the time, countries with different levels of overvaluation and different economic structures.

The realignment, accompanied by measures to control demand and foster a recovery in supply, was expected to improve productivity, and to restore the zone's competitiveness. It was supposed to lead to a shift in resources from the less growth-oriented sectors to the more dynamic sectors—the agricultural sector being the first to benefit from such an operation. In terms of prices and volumes of exports and imports, these expectations can be shown on the graphs below which begin with the initial situation presented in Figures 6.4 and 6.5.

The theoretical assumptions and expectations underlying the CFA parity change were as follows: the demand curves for imports would remain unchanged, since they reflect the evolution of demand as a function of price. By contrast, the supply of imports would change, because the same products coming from abroad at the same price as expressed in foreign currencies would become more expensive when converted into local currency.

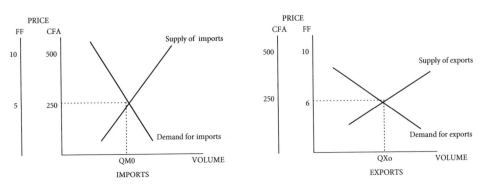

FIGURE 6.4 Situation before the CFA devaluation.

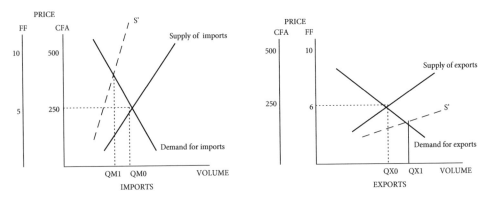

FIGURE 6.5 Expected results after the devaluation.

Thus, the quantity of imports would decrease. This was expressed by the 100 percent shift on the y-axis (rate of devaluation from the suppliers' perspective), relatively to each point on the x-axis. The same rationale held for exports. The change in exports was to be determined by the new exchange rate, from the perspective of the local producers. African commodities would become 50 percent cheaper (roughly speaking) on external markets. Assuming that the demand for exports remained unchanged, the price in CFA converted into foreign currencies would be lower than before, providing incentives for supply response.

Did that actually happen? For sure, these countries achieved higher rates of growth after 1994, though few convincing empirical studies have systematically assessed the impact of the parity change. The average growth of output for the CFA Zone was estimated at 1.2 percent in 1994 after being negative for many years, and the trade balances improved notably. However, growth rates in the Zone in 1993–2013 were much lower than in any sample of African countries with comparable endowment structure. Throughout the Zone, nominal wages were generally kept under control in the public sector and in the private sector as well. In most CFA countries, as a result of the shift in relative prices, output in the tradable goods sector responded rapidly, and the patterns of private consumption seemed to be changing, shifting from imported goods to locally produced goods such as livestock, vegetables and food crops.

There were some additional economic benefits to the 1994 devaluation. All countries reached comprehensive agreements with the Paris Club to secure debt relief on CFA concessional terms and with multilateral development banks for debt reduction. However, some skepticism has remained about the capacity of these countries to restore their long-term competitiveness even after using the exchange rate tool. The positive but still modest growth rates recorded in the period 1995–2014 in the context of pervasive poverty, limited opportunities for employment creation in the formal sector, and high unemployment and underemployment levels, gave credence to critics of monetary unions. More importantly, the strengthening of the Euro in the 1990s and early 2000s automatically translated to real appreciation of the CFA franc, and wiped off much of the competitiveness gains from the 1994 devaluation.

These developments raise the broader question of the effectiveness of traditional monetary unions in the context of small economies with low income, low domestic demand, dissimilar industry structures, and little intra-regional trade—especially in a world where the integration of poor economies to global value chains appears to be a viable avenue for sustained growth and employment creation (Monga 2014).

6.5 BACK TO BASICS: ON THE VALIDITY OF AFRICAN MONETARY UNIONS

The general reluctance to question the very purpose of the existence of the Franc Zone, and to assess the viability of all the available options for CFA countries today, including issuing separate national currencies, reveals the de facto ideological distortions and political considerations which dominates the design of economic policies for Africa. This is somewhat surprising, especially after more than seven decades of a monetary experiment that has clearly yielded little economic growth for these small open economies, and given the lessons of the Eurozone crisis, which highlighted the difficulty of achieving real convergence for backward economies that are part of a monetary zone. In fact, the reluctance of CFA countries to assess the costs and benefits of their membership to the Eurozone, and the willingness of more African countries to even launch new monetary unions—with the goal of establishing a single currency for the continent as soon as possible (Masson and Pattillo 2004)—point to the extent to which politics and other externalities intervene in shaping the monetary future of those countries. Drawing lessons from the theory of optimum currency areas and public finance analysis, this section briefly discusses the options available to African countries that are currently part of monetary unions.

6.5.1 Validity of the optimum currency areas argument

In the absence of foundations for economic integration, at least in the short run, there is no economic justification for the existence of a unique currency used in any grouping of African countries, which bears the costs of a single currency without yielding the corresponding benefits. In considering how an individual country, Cameroon, for example, might approach the decision of whether to leave the CFA Zone of fixed exchange rates, it might be helpful to use the check list provided by the theory of optimal currency areas—a blueprint primarily developed by Mundell (1961).[5] From a theoretical standpoint, it turns out that since the CFA Zone is not an optimum currency area, most of its members would not benefit from staying in the union.

For a small open economy whose primary strategic goal should be to ensure external competitiveness connect its industries to global value chain, and take advantage of the infinite benefits of world trade, the cost of relinquishing a major adjustment tool such as the exchange rate is just too large. The first disadvantage for a country with an open economy like Cameroon joining a monetary union is the fact that it gives up the right to elaborate and implement a national monetary policy. Staying in the CFA Zone therefore implies relinquishing monetary sovereignty forever, and giving up indefinitely one of the most powerful public policy tools available. The inability to quickly change the money supply deprives the government of an adjustment mechanism which is particularly useful when the country faces brutal changes in output.

Let's suppose that two countries of the BEAC Zone, Cameroon and Gabon, offer the same type of products for a given period of time. If, for any reason, African consumers shift their preferences away from Cameroonian goods to Gabonese goods, the result will be a decline in output in Cameroon (downward movement of the demand curve) and a higher level of unemployment, and an increase in output in Gabon (upward movement), with a higher savings rate in Gabon (Figure 6.6).[6] Assuming that the current account is defined in monetary terms as the difference between domestic output and domestic spending, both countries will face an adjustment problem: a current account deficit in Cameroon, due to the shift in spending from national goods to foreign goods, and a current account surplus in Gabon, due to the increase of value of output and the saving of extra disposable income.

According to economic theory, two economic mechanisms normally help to address such issues: wage flexibility and labor mobility.

- If wages are flexible in the two countries, Cameroonian workers will diminish their expectations, in order to offset the unemployment pressure created by the decrease in total output. Conversely, Gabonese workers will increase their wage claims, because of the excess demand. The combined effects of wages adjustments (downward in Cameroon, upward in Gabon) will eventually stabilize the aggregate demand and supply at levels which maintain total output at their initial levels (Y_0 on the graphs below):

---

[5] Several subsequent studies have expanded Mundell's basic arguments; a good overview is found in Tower and Willett (1976). For subsequent reassessments, see Wihlborg and Willett (1991); de Grauwe (1992); and Tavlas (1993).

[6] This follows the standard aggregate demand analysis, which assumes a negatively sloped demand curve, implying that when the domestic price level increases the domestic output declines (this is the substitution effect of a price increase); we do not take into account the monetary effect according to which there is always an increase in the domestic real interest rate when the domestic price level goes up, eventually leading to the reduction of aggregate demand. Likewise, our analysis of the supply curves indicates competition in the output markets: firms are willing and capable of supplying more goods as prices increase.

- If there is mobility of labor, Cameroonian workers who lose their jobs because of the decrease in aggregate demand will migrate to Gabon, in order to seize the new employment opportunities—since there is excess demand for labor over there. Such movements of the working population would limit the need for wage reductions in Cameroon and wage increases in Gabon, and offset the inflationary pressures. Likewise, the current account deficit in the former would be automatically offset by the fact that there is a de facto cut in private spending due to migration.
- If none of the above conditions exists, then the need for adjustment will be high in both countries. The only way they could solve the problem would be to use the exchange rate (re-evaluation of the Gabonese currency, and devaluation of the Cameroonian currency). That an option does not exist within the monetary union.

Another major inconsistency in the African monetary union arrangements is the difference in industrial structure among the members, and the reluctance of policymakers to address this issue across country borders. Again, the reasoning here is based on the optimum currency area argument: the greater the trade within the zone, the larger the gains from a single currency and the smaller the incentive for members to seek adjustments through individual monetary strategies and flexible exchange rates. Yes, as seen above, the union did not stimulate intra-zone trade. Furthermore, in spite of the fact that they are small open economies specialized in the production of raw materials, the CFA Zone members have divergent economic structures (oil producers versus non-oil producers), and would tend to perceive and to react differently to adverse external shocks.

The picture is complicated by one of the insights that Krugman (1992) brought to the debate over optimum currency areas. According to his analysis based on economic geography, the lack of similarity in industry structure is actually the final outcome of an efficient monetary integration. His argument runs as follows: the interaction of increasing returns and transportation costs leads to uneven regional development, facilitating clustering in some places, and thus creating core regions, and periphery. However, reducing transportation costs would have two effects: it would facilitate the location of production where it is cheapest, but it would also facilitate concentration of production in one location, so as to realize economies of scale. This new economics of space tends to lead to the localization of industries in areas where the returns are higher, and eventually to the "specialization" of regions

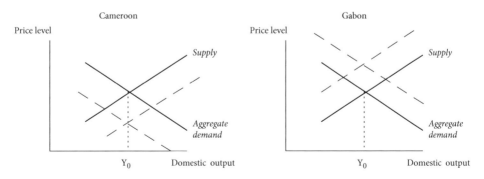

FIGURE 6.6 Shifting consumer preferences and adjustment.

and/or countries within a union—therefore, members of a monetary union end up with different economic structures.

There are obviously some limits to the use of Mundell's framework in the assessment of the viability of monetary unions, especially in the African context. Four types of criticism have been leveled against the theory of optimum currency areas: the first one is ascribable to authors who simply reject the theory, because it is empirically difficult (almost "impossible") to test it in many African countries since in the absence of any reliable data and time series, it raises many methodological issues (Tchundjang 1980).

A second type of criticism is related to the extent to which differences between country economic structures are important enough to become a matter for concern. Questions have been raised: how important are differences in economic performance between countries? Is a demand shock concentrated in one country a likely event? Is this not offset by the importance and the structure of trade, as suggested by de Grauwe? "Trade between the industrial European nations is to a large degree intra-industry trade. This trade is based on the existence of economies of scale and imperfect competition (product differentiation). It leads to a structure of trade in which countries buy and sell to each other the same categories of products. Thus, France sells cars to and buy cars from Germany. And so does Germany. The structure of trade leads to a situation where most demand shocks will affect these countries in a similar way. For example, when consumers reduce their demand for cars, they will buy fewer French and German cars. Thus, both countries' aggregate demand will be affected in similar ways" (1992: 31). This is clearly not the case in African countries where intra-trade is negligible, especially within industries, and shocks are asymmetric (de Melo and Tsikata 2015).

There is also a critique of Mundell's assumption that differences in labor markets (institutional arrangements, behavior of unions) will disappear over time, as monetary union takes place. This point was made convincingly by McDonald and Solow (1981), showing in their model that unions are different across countries because of different degrees of centralization. In such situations, it is uncertain that monetary integration can erase these differences. This point is even more salient in the African context where empirical work on trade unions has consistently shown their deep historical differences and peculiarities (Bhorat 2012). Moreover, in African countries where the employment rate within the formal sector of the economy (public and private) rarely reaches 10 percent of the labor force, differences in labor markets go well beyond the trade-off between the real wage level and the level of employment (Monga 2014).

6.5.2 Validity of the public finance argument

Even those who would challenge the relevance of the theory of optimum currency areas in Africa would nonetheless acknowledge the importance of the public finance argument in the evaluation of the monetary union. There are two main issues here: the lack of fiscal coordination among countries that already belong to a monetary union (i.e. the CFA countries), and the creation and distribution of seigniorage.

6.5.2.1 Lack of coordination

Long before the European Union crisis of the late 2000s, economic research on economic integration had shown that monetary union, with its explicit coordination of monetary and exchange rate policies, also implies some form of cooperation in the fiscal policies of member countries. Given the structural differences among the various areas of a union, fiscal policies are used as stabilizers. In the case of the United States for instance, Sala-i-Martin and Sachs (1992) studied how this insurance mechanism has worked for nine regions: they estimated that from 1970–1988, a US$1 decline in a region's income led to a 33–37 cent fall in tax payments to Washington and to a 1–8 cent increase in transfer revenues; thus, at least a third of a region's economic difficulties was offset by the federal fiscal system. On the other hand, unduly divergent fiscal policies can lead to unbearable strains within the union, especially if they create to conflicting balance of payments movements—unless the financial consequences are offset by external assistance (Bhatia 1985).

Despite some broad and often very general and non-binding policy statements, African countries that have joined monetary integration processes have not committed to fiscal coordination of such strength. Thus, the type of fiscal federalism that helps the USA, Germany, or other federal country function as an effective currency area (beyond the economic diversity of regions) is absent in Africa. This issue has been recognized within the CFA Franc zone and some institutional mechanisms are gradually introduced to achieve that goal. But in the absence of strong, supranational regulatory bodies, enforcement is likely to remain a major issue. An illustration of the problem is the statutory limit on credit from the banking system to central governments (20 percent of the previous year's tax revenue), adopted as an effective way of inducing fiscal coordination: in practice, governments circumvent the rule by turning to other means of financing budgetary deficits, such as external borrowing, payment arrears, or the use of various deposits with the treasuries.

6.5.2.2 *The seigniorage issue*

The relationship between money growth and inflation, well analyzed in the quantity theory of money, implies that any increase in the nominal supply of high-powered money, unless concurrently fueling an increase in aggregate demand, will lead to a proportional increase in the price level. Defined as government revenue from money creation, seigniorage can sometimes amount to relatively high proportions of GDP. As noted by Fischer, "there are governments for which seigniorage constitutes over 10 percent of total revenue on average. [It] is thus not a minor factor for these governments." (1982: 301). It is a source of revenue because simply by printing money to pay for its expenditures, a government generates inflation, thus lowering the real value of payments; it taxes existing holders of money balances.[7]

---

[7] Gaudio (1991) explains the analogy between seigniorage (the inflation tax) and the exercise tax on a commodity. The tax-payers are the holders of the nominal assets (cash); the tax-base is the money stock; the tax rate is the rate of inflation (or rate of money growth, as the two rates are assumed to be equal). As with other forms of taxation, government revenue is represented by the product of the tax rate and tax base: *seigniorage = money growth × real money supply*. This result can also be obtained from a simpler expression of real government revenue from money creation: seigniorage revenue = $(M_t - M_{t-1})$/Price level (a), where M is the nominal money supply. If we set μ as the rate of money growth, then we have a second equation: $M_t = (1+\mu) M_{t-1}$. Substituting equation (b) into (a), we obtain: seigniorage = $\mu(M/P)$, which is the initial expression.

Is seigniorage large enough in the CFA Zone and in other African countries considering forming a monetary union to justify the emphasis placed on it in the analysis? While it is likely to be an important consideration in case of a currency reform, there will be differences, across countries, in the degree to which it is relied upon by individual governments. Reliance on seigniorage seems to be positively correlated with the share of agricultural output in an economy (it is more difficult to implement a direct taxation system targeting the peasants), with the degree of urbanization (the larger the informal sector in big cities, the weaker the ability of the administration to collect taxes), and with observed political polarization and instability (Cukierman et al., 1992). Those are indeed the characteristics of many of the CFA countries. But empirical estimates show that seigniorage use has been relatively low in the CFA Zone (Monga 1995). In the absence of high inflation, it was not "active" (deliberate); it was rather "passive," since it was obtained by providing high-powered money to meet the growing demand, without creating inflation. In assessing of the ability of CFA countries to use seigniorage as a financial tool, one should also take into account the potential losses in transfers from France, which would no longer exist in the case of the dismantling of the current monetary union. But given the relatively small amount of financial flows that African countries are currently receiving from Paris, and given the limited perspectives they can expect in that domain (notably because of the economic and political changes which are taking place in Europe), one can conclude that the opportunity cost of giving up the use of seigniorage is already too high for CFA countries.

6.6 Conclusion

This chapter has reviewed the outcomes of monetary integration in Africa, focusing on countries of the CFA Zone. While economic integration among nations of the world has increased sharply in the past half century, leading to significantly improved standards of living for most countries, the failure of such coordination processes is obvious in sub-Saharan Africa where average gross national income was US$1200 in 2012 (World Development Indicators).

The collapse of the terms of trade of many African countries in the mid-1980s, followed by rising interest rates and a steady appreciation of the French Franc to which the currencies of 14 countries were pegged at the time, (all these events taking place in unstable political environments, with weak institutions and lack of what Collier (1991) calls "the agencies of restraints,"), led to overvaluation of national currencies, budget deficits, and unsustainable current account deficits. Although several Western countries reacted by providing enough liquidity to support most of the African leaders, at least up to the early 1990s, the structural adjustment programs adopted across the continent did not lead to any positive change in the fundamentals.

Still, African leaders have reiterated the goals of fostering economic and monetary integration stated already in 1963 at the birth of the Organization of the African Union (the current African Union). And three sets of factors are leading African nations to become more intertwined in spite of government policies aiming at preserving micro-nationalism: technological changes, which have reduced distances and fostered information flows (telecommunications); social changes, which are causing the reorganization of traditional structures and creating heavy pressure for low skill workers to migrate across borders; and the emergence of a strong civil society (business groups, non-governmental organizations, traditional associations, churches, etc.). But informal economic integration is still a marginal phenomenon, and has not stimulated the strong institutional and policy basis is required for monetary integration and a single currency to be effective in a continent constituted of highly different economies.

In the absence of fiscal and economic coordination, and the given the high likelihood that the Euro will remain a strong currency, and the disengagement strategy adopted by France in Africa (because of the increasing cost of supporting undemocratic African governments, the growing responsibilities imposed by its membership in the European Union, and the increasing attractiveness of markets and partners in Eastern Europe and elsewhere in the developing world), the opportunity cost of maintaining a single currency is too high for the CFA countries (Monga 1997b). The same challenges apply to other African countries that are considering joining or creating a monetary union. In that context, the decision to adopt a single currency pegged to the Euro or any other strong currency by a group of small open economies whose only way out of poverty is external trade in world markets is a political statement rather than an economic necessity. It will continue to determine the economic fate of African economies in an era when integration into global value chains requires maintaining competitiveness. Unfortunately, the monetary history of these countries over the past several decades has been primarily one of misguided policy choices, as they tried to contain crises and panic through even worse policy mistakes. Just like some of the 9/11 victims observed by Rudi Giuliani—those people who felt compelled to jump to their death in order to escape the flames in the crumbling buildings. African policymakers have often made difficult monetary situations worse. Yet, contrary to the 9/11 victims, they did not have to.

References

Barbier, J.-P. (1989). *Réflexions sur la compétitivité, comparaison Afrique-Asie*. Paris: Caisse Centrale de Coopération.

Bhatia, R.J. (1985). *The West African Monetary Union, An Analytical Review*. IMF Occasional Paper No. 35, Washington, DC, May.

Berg, E., and Berlin, P. (1993). *Exchange Rate Issues in the Franc Zone*. Background Note Prepared for Seminar on the CFA Franc, USAID, Bethesda, MD, DAI, January.

Bhorat, H., Goga, S., and van der Westhuizen, C. (2012). Institutional wage effects: revisiting union and bargaining council wage premia in South Africa. *South African Journal of Economics*, 80(3):400–414.

Christiansen, R., Christensen, C., and Edwards, B. (1988). Issues of political economy in formulating donor policy toward sub-Saharan Africa, in S.K. Commins (ed.), *Africa's Development Challenges and the World Bank, Hard Questions, Costly Choices*. London: Lynne Rienner Publishers, pp. 91–114.

Cocquet, B., and Daniel, J.-M. (1992). "Quel avenir pour la Zone Franc?" *Observations et diagnostics économiques, Revue de l'OFCE*, Paris, OFCE no. 41, July, pp. 241–291.

Collier, P. (1991). Africa's External Economic Relations: 1960-1990. *African Affairs*, 90(360):339–356.

Collier, P., and Gunning J.W. (1992). *Aid and Exchange Rate Adjustment in Trade Liberalization*. Oxford: CSAE, p. 1.

Collins, S.M. (1988). Multiple Exchange Rates, Capital Controls, and Commercial Policy, in R. Dornbusch and F.L.C.H. Helmers (eds), *The Open Economy, Tools for Policymakers in Developing Countries*. The World Bank EDI Series. New York: Oxford University Press, pp. 128–164.

Cocquet B., and Daniel, J.-M. (1992). *Quel avenir pour la Zone Franc?* Observations et diagnostics économiques. Revue de l'OFCE, Paris, OFCE No. 41, July.

Cukierman. A., Edwards, S., and Tabellini, G. (1992). Seigniorage and political instability. *American Economic Review*, 82(3):537–555.

De Grawe, P. (1992). *The Economics of Monetary Integration*. New York: Oxford University Press.

de Melo, J. and Tsikata, Y. (this volume). Regional Integration in Africa: Challenges and Prospects. *The Oxford Handbook of Africa and Economics*. Oxford: Oxford University Press.

Devarajan, S., and de Melo, J. (1990). Membership in the CFA Zone: Odyssean Journey of Trojan Horse? Working papers, Washington, DC: World Bank, August.

Devarajan, S, and Hinkle, L.E. (1994). The CFA franc parity change: an opportunity to restore growth and reduce poverty. *Afrika Spectrum*, 29(2):131–151.

Dornbusch, R. (1988). Balance of payment issues, in R. Dornbusch and F. Leslie C.H. Helmers (eds), *Open Economy: Tools for Policymakers in Developing Countries*. New York: Oxford University Press, pp. 37–53.

Edwards, S. (1985). Exchange Rate Misalignment in Developing Countries: Analytical Issues and Empirical Evidence. CPD Working Papers, Washington, DC: World Bank.

Fischer, S. (1982). Seigniorage and the case for a national money. *Journal of Political Economy*, 90(2):295–313.

Forbes, S. (2011). Remembering 9-11: The Rudi Giuliani Interview. *Forbes Magazine*, September 9. Retrieved from http://www.forbes.com/sites/steveforbes/2011/09/09/remembering-911-the-rudy-giuliani-intrview/print.

Gaudio, J. (1991). An inquiry into the nature of seigniorage. *Harvard College Economist*, 13(2):37.

Guillaumont P., and Guillaumont Jeanneney, S. (1991). *Exchange Rate Policies and the Social Consequences of Adjustment in Africa*, in A. Chhibber and S. Fischer (eds), *Economic Reform in Sub-Saharan Africa*. Washington, DC: World Bank, pp. 12–24.

Havrylyshn, O. (1990). Trade policy and productivity gains in developing countries. *The World Bank Research Observer*, 5(1):1–25.

Herrera, J. (1994). *Les effets des mesures relatives à la convertibilité du Franc CFA BEAC*. Etude No. 94075, Paris, GIS DIAL ORSTOM, 6 January 1994, mimeo.

Honohan, P. (1990). Monetary Cooperation in the CFA Zone. PRE Working Papers, N° WPS 389, Washington, DC: World Bank.

Krugman, P. (1992). *Geography and Trade*. Cambridge, MA: MIT Press.

Krugman, P. (1979). A model of balance of payments crisis. *Journal of Money, Credit and Banking*, 11(3):311–325.

Lavy, V., Newman, J.L., Salomon, R., and de Vreyer, P. (1991). *Response to Relative Price Changes in Côte d'Ivoire, The Implications for Export Subsidies and Devaluations*, in A. Chhibber and S. Fischer (eds), *Economic Reform in Sub-Saharan Africa*. Washington, DC: World Bank, pp. 251–273.

Lin, J.Y., and Monga, C. (2014). The evolving paradigms of structural change, in B. Currie-Adler, R. Kanbur, D. Malone, and R. Medhora (eds), *International Development: Ideas, Experience, and Prospects*. New York: Oxford University Press, pp. 277–294.

McDonald, I., and Solow, R. (1981). Wage bargaining and employment. *American Economic Review*, 71: 896–908.

Monga, C. (2014). Winning the jackpot: job dividends in a multipolar world, in J. Stiglitz, J.Y. Lin, and E. Patel (eds), *The Industrial Policy Revolution II: Africa in the 21st Century*. New York: Palgrave Macmillan, pp. 135–172.

Monga, C. (2012a). Shifting gears: igniting structural transformation in Africa. *Journal of African Economies*, 21(Suppl 2):ii19–ii54.

Monga, C. (2012b). The Hegelian dialectics of global imbalances. *Journal of Philosophical Economics*, 6(1):1–52.

Monga, C. (2006). Commodities, Mercedes-Benz, and adjustment: an episode in West African history, in E.K. Akyeampong (ed.), *Themes in West Africa's History*. Oxford: James Currey, pp. 227–264.

Monga, C. (1997a). *L'argent des autres—Banques et petites entreprises en Afrique: le cas du Cameroun*. Paris: LDGJ-Montchretien.

Monga, C. (1997b). A currency reform index for Western and Central Africa. *World Economy*, 20(1):103–125.

Monga, C. (1995). *The Case for Currency Reform in Western and Central Africa: Elements for a Political Economy of Utopia*. Cambridge, MA: MIT Dewey Library.

Monga, C. (1993). Monnaie et politique en Zone Franc. *Afrique 2000*, 15(October):65–74.

Mundell, R.A. (1961). The theory of optimum currency areas. *American Economic Review*, 51(September):717–725.

Neary, J.P., and Purvis, D.D. (1982). Sectoral shocks in a dependent economy: long-run adjustment and short-run accommodation. *Scandinavian Journal of Economics*, 84:229–253.

Obstfeld, M. (1984). Balance of payment crisis and devaluation. *Journal of Money, Credit and Banking*, 16:208–217.

Pack, H. (1988). Industrialization and trade, in H. Chenery and T. Srinivasan (eds), *Handbook of Development Economics*. Amsterdam: North Holland.

Sala-i-Martin, X., and Sachs, J. (1992). Fiscal federalism and optimum currency areas: evidence for Europe from the United States, in M. Canzoneri, V. Grilli, and P. Masson (eds), *Establishing a Central Bank: Issues in Europe and Lessons from the U.S.* Cambridge: Cambridge University Press.

Tavlas, G.S. (1993). The new theory of optimum currency areas. *World Economy*, 16:663–686.

Tchundjang Pouémi, J. (1980). *Monnaie, servitude et liberté, La répression monétaire de l'Afrique*. Paris: Editions Jeune Afrique Conseil.

Tower, E., and Willett, T.D. (1976). The Theory of Optimal Currency Areas and Exchange Rate Flexibility. Princeton Special Papers in International Economics, No. 11, Princeton University, May.

Wihlborg, C.G., and Willett, T.D. (1991). Optimal currency areas revisited, in C.G. Wihlborg, M. Fratianni, and T.D. Willett (eds), *Financial Regulation and Monetary Arrangements After 1992*. Amsterdam: North-Holland.

CHAPTER 7

....

CHALLENGES OF CENTRAL BANKING IN AFRICA

....

BENNO NDULU AND JOSEPH LEINA MASAWE

7.1 INTRODUCTION

....

THE role and contribution of central banks to African development has undergone very significant metamorphosis, but central banks in Africa still face considerable challenges. From a broader developmental role, which included the provision of development finance for the period between 1960 and 1995, the goals of central banking in the majority of African central banks sharply narrowed to focus on price stability since mid-1990s. More recently, however, following the global financial crisis, the central banks in the region are paying attention to ensuring that the monetary policy stances are not inimical to growth, particularly when economies are faced with significant instabilities from contagion or exogenous shocks. Hence, while ensuring the preservation of the primary goal of price stability, central banks are now designing frameworks for supporting growth in a countercyclical framework and giving greater attention to financial stability and central bank independence.

7.2 THE CHALLENGE OF LINKING INFLATION CONTROL AND GROWTH

....

7.2.1 Growth and inflation dynamics in Africa

High inflation in the advanced economies in the 1970s and in emerging economies in the 1980s and 1990s was instrumental in shaping modern thinking about the practice of central banking. In 1980s and early 1990s economies in Africa were subjected to intensive adverse external and internal shocks leading to the continent to perform badly. However, African economies have on the whole performed well and maintained a high growth momentum since the mid-1990s after engagement in various adjustment programs, and also partly due to a prolonged upswing of the global economy. In the past ten years, average growth in Africa has surpassed that of East Asia. Data suggest that parts of the continent are now experiencing fast growth. According to World Bank reports the economies of African countries grew at rates that match or surpass global average rates. Before the global financial crisis, the top nations in 2007 included Angola with a growth at 23.2%, Equatorial Guinea at 21.4%, Sudan at 12.2%, Ethiopia at 11.5%, Seychelles at 10.1%, Uganda at 8.1%, Rwanda at 7.6%, Mozambique at 7.3%, and Tanzania at 7.1%. The catching-up of African economies has been widespread with the exception of only a few countries.

On the other hand, adverse external shocks, such as the global financial crisis in 2008, and political events such as the "Arab Spring" in 2011, adversely affected the continent's average growth. Growth momentum eased to an average of 4.2% between 2008 and 2011 due to poor performance in exports. However, the crisis of 2008–2009 has led to a marked but only temporary slowdown in growth as the African economies recovered their growth to an average of 6.6% in 2012, which is more than double the rate of growth of the global economy. This also compares favorably with a growth rate of 3.5% recorded in 2011.

Excluding South Africa, which was hit by the recession, the sub-Saharan economy actually grew by 5.8% between 2001 and 2012. Some individual countries had even higher growth rates. Several countries, such as Democratic Republic of Congo, Ethiopia, Ghana, Nigeria, Rwanda, Tanzania, and Zambia, have been growing at a strong pace of an average of 6.5% or more in each of the past three years, that is, 2010, 2011, and 2012.

However, high inflation recorded in the early 1980s and mid-1990s undermined the role of the African currencies as a medium of exchange. African countries have however, undertaken efforts to reduce the rate of inflation, with results being positive. Sub-Saharan Africa (SSA) recorded a decrease in inflation from an average of 21.1% between 1995 and 2000, to 10.1% between 2001 and 2005, before dropping to a single digit of 8.8% between 2006 and 2012.

7.2.2 Optimal level of inflation in Africa

One of the most fundamental objectives of macroeconomic policies in Africa is to sustain high economic growth together with low inflation. However, there has been considerable debate on the appropriate level of inflation for economic growth. Until recently, many economists believed that moderate inflation makes the economy perform better.

A number of theoretical studies argued that depending on its level inflation can either promote or harm economic growth. For instance, Lucas (1973) explained that low inflation allows overcoming rigidity of nominal prices and wages. In addition, inflation can realign relative prices in response to structural changes in production during fast modernization periods. In this case inflation is quite important for economic growth. On the other hand, high inflation discourages long-term investments and distorts the tax system (Romer 2001). Empirical research has showed that it is only when inflation exceeds some critical level when it impedes economic growth. Otherwise inflation has a favorable impact on growth.

Therefore, there are theoretical arguments for a positive inflation-growth relationship for low levels of inflation and a negative one for high levels. For that reason, an inflation–growth relationship is non-linear and there exists some inflection point which changes impact from favorable to undesirable. Given this argument, we employed the threshold model used by Khan and Senhadji (2001) to explore the non-linear relationship between growth and inflation in Africa. The model takes on the following conditional form:

$$g = \beta_0 + \beta_1 \pi_t + \beta_2 D(\pi_t - k) + \varepsilon_t \tag{1}$$

where g is economic growth rates, π_t is the rate of inflation at time t, k is the threshold level of inflation (i.e. the rate of inflation at which structural break occurs), and ε_t is the random error term. The dummy variable D is defined in the following way:

$$D = \begin{cases} 1 \, if \, \pi_t > k \\ 0 \, if \, \pi_t \le k \end{cases} \tag{2}$$

The coefficient of the dummy variable (β_2) measures the effect of inflation rate on the economic growth when it is greater than the assumed structural break level (i.e. inflation is high) and the opposite for the coefficient of inflation rate (β_1). By estimating regressions for different values of k, which is chosen in an ascending order (i.e. 1, 2, and so on), the optimal value k is obtained by finding the value that maximizes the R^2 from the respective regressions. This also implies that the optimal threshold level is that which minimizes the residual sum of squares (RSS).

Our analysis indicates that the optimal level of inflation for Africa is 8.0%; thus inflation rates exceeding 8% are associated with lower economic growth. Below this threshold, the correlations are positive and significant for some levels and insignificant to other levels. The estimated optimal level of inflation in Africa does not deviate far away from 11–12% estimated by Khan and Senhadji (2001) for developing countries. Adam C.J Ndulu, B.J, and Sowa, N.K. estimated the seigniorage-maximizing inflation rate for Ghana, Kenya, and Tanzania using a quadratic equation and found the inflection point to be around 11–15%. It can be concluded therefore that the average level of inflation of 7.1% recorded for the past three years, 2009 and 2012, which is below 8.0%, promotes growth in Africa.

7.2.3 Rethinking the practice of central banking

Most central banks have a firm commitment of maintaining price stability in order to promote economic growth. More recently, however, a great deal of attention has been drawn to the question of how central banks contribute to promoting economic development. It has been argued that in order for the central bank to play its role of development as economic agent, it should not content itself with the simple role of price stability. It should play a much wider role in ensuring macroeconomic stability. It is clear that while the most important function of the central bank is to promote price stability, the end to this objective is to stimulate the national economy through the growth process. Some scholars therefore argue that central banks should aim at promoting the process of economic growth to jump-start a long-term reeling economy.

After the recent global financial crisis and the events in the Euro zone, the question in Africa has been whether to preserve the narrow definition of central banking goal of price stability or to take a broader developmental role, which would imply measures to promote growth and contain contagion. Many central banks in Africa are now putting more emphasis on financial stability in their objectives, given the susceptibility of African economies and banking systems in particular, to global shocks. However, despite this new emphasis, it is important to ensure that price stability clearly remains the primary objective. Financial instability affects economic activities through creating uncertainties that heighten risk aversion, increasing the cost of borrowing and thus reducing financial resources available for investment. The impact on activity is compounded by weak demand that is transmitted to more reduction in demand as unemployment increases and consumer confidence weakens. Weak cash flows and reduced asset values among firms and households put them in an even harder position to access credit. We need to put up frameworks for preventing financial instabilities and devise mechanisms for mitigation of their impact when they occur, as this may even affect the price stability objective and growth.

7.3 CHALLENGE OF EXOGENEITY OF INFLATION DRIVERS

The challenge for the conduct of monetary policy in African countries is exacerbated by the fact that food and energy prices constitute the bulk of the consumer price index (CPI) weights. The average share of food in national consumption baskets in developing countries range between 20% and 50% compared with 12% and 15% in advanced countries (Luis and Roberto 2011). For example, in Tanzania, food prices account for close to 48% of the CPI basket—by far the largest single component, with energy and transport costs accounting for a further 9% each. Likewise, in Kenya the share of food in the CPI is around 40% and fuel accounts for a further 18%.

Against this background, the key question is how should monetary authorities in developing countries react when their economies are hit by these exogenous shocks? In terms of its impact on inflation, monetary policy works through its effects on aggregate demand and in particular the private sector components of aggregate demand: private consumption, investment, and net exports. If monetary policy can influence the level or growth rate of aggregate demand, ensuring that it does not outstrip the growth of aggregate supply, a central bank can exert control over inflation over the medium term. However, supply side shocks which hike the rate of inflation pose a dilemma for monetary policy. Monetary policy cannot bring down the prices of food or fuel, because these prices are not determined by the level of aggregate demand in the economy, rather they are determined mainly by supply and demand in the individual markets for food and fuel. Food prices are by and large determined by weather conditions. In many developing countries, food crop agriculture, particularly the production of staple foods of maize, beans, and rice, is overwhelmingly rain fed. Food price variation is therefore high and dependent on rainfall variation. On the other hand, fuel prices are determined by supply conditions in the world market. Both of these factors are outside the control of central banks.

This environment makes a central bank's policy decisions both more difficult and more constrained. If central banks were to be too aggressive in attempting to pull down inflation by tightening monetary policy, the main impact of the tightening would be felt in the non-food sectors, especially the service industries, which would face a reduction in demand for their output and hence would run the risk of recession. So the question is how far should central banks ignore supply side induced inflationary pressures? The conventional argument for handling supply side shocks is to distinguish between core (excluding food and energy prices) and non-core components of inflation and employ monetary policy instruments to stabilize core inflation, reacting to non-core prices only to the extent that they have second round feedback to core inflation (Kollmann 2002; Gali and Monacelli 2005). While this prescription would make perfect sense for industrialized countries where non-core components accounts for a relatively small share of the headline inflation, this approach will be more challenging for developing countries, because, as mentioned before, non-core items account for a significantly large share of the headline inflation. In addition distinguishing between the first and second round inflationary effects of a supply side shock may be quite challenging not least because the two can occur simultaneously, but also because the pervasive data problems such as the lack of updated input–output tables in most African countries would make it even harder to disentangle first- and second-round effects. So the dilemma is how to manage the impact of supply shocks on inflation without either allowing inflationary expectations to rise or pushing the economy into recession through an overly aggressive response.

So, with supply side shocks dominating inflation dynamics, monetary authorities in developing countries confront the trade-off between competing objectives: inflation and output stabilization. Advanced countries which are exposed predominantly to demand side shocks do not face this trade-off because demand shocks move output and inflation in the same direction. In this case, a central bank reaction to a positive demand shock, for example, an interest rate hike to bring down inflation, will simultaneously serve to eliminate the excess aggregate demand. On the contrary, supply side shocks move inflation and output in the opposite directions. For example, an adverse shock in the world oil price which results in domestic inflationary pressures will simultaneously drive up production costs thereby reducing output. In this case, leaning aggressively against inflationary pressures of supply shocks, for example, by hiking interest rates in order to bring down inflation, will simultaneously serve to reduce the output growth—exacerbating the adverse effects of the shock on the economy and therefore running the risk of pushing the economy into a recession.

7.4 THE CHALLENGE OF FISCAL DOMINANCE

Fiscal dominance in Africa dates back to 1960s following a greater role that governments assumed in directing economic activities in newly independent countries. The 1960s was generally regarded as the decade of African political independence or liberation as most African countries (initially colonies) had matured into nationhoods. Leaders of the independent countries realized that political decolonization will remain meaningless unless it results into a corresponding breakthrough in economic independence. The priority task for the newly independent African countries was therefore to steer economic growth through national economic plans.

The first phase of development planning in Africa spanned the 1960s and was characterized by centralized planning with three to five year planning phases. During this period, at least 32 African countries had national development plan (UNECA 2013). These plans promoted state-engineered economies with resources allocated through central government budgets.

Successful implementation of the economic plans was, however, an uphill task as immediately after independence, most African economies encountered a stoppage in the inflow of private capital coupled with a sizable overall capital outflows. Further, internal sources of revenue to finance the economic plans were limited as domestic tax sources that were considered to be a "nuisance" were abolished as the countries gained independence. As government liabilities increased, tax revenues declined, and financing of fiscal imbalances from foreign sources were expensive or unavailable, the immediate source of finance for a number of governments was the central banks. In SSA, the period before economic crisis from 1960 to 1971 was marked by a modest central bank lending to government, averaging 4.3% of GDP. In the same period for North Africa, government borrowing from the central bank averaged 4.6% of GDP. The crisis and recovery period for SSA was marked by relatively higher dependency on central bank borrowing than the countries in North Africa. The North African oil-rich countries were not as affected by the increase in the world oil prices as the counterpart SSA countries. However, the seven-year cycle of drought in Africa from 1974 to 1982 was felt by the entire continent. Dependence on central bank financing of government in the crisis increased for the entire continent, although higher for SSA than North Africa.

Notwithstanding the economic reforms, dependency on central bank financing has remained high. According to the World Bank (2013), fiscal deficit in Africa averaged 2.1% of GDP for the period from 1990 to 2011, with only Algeria and Botswana recording fiscal surpluses of 2.2% of GDP and 3.7% of GDP, respectively, over the period. During the 1990s, many African countries reformed their central bank legislation. One of the key reforms was restricting central bank financing of the government. The restriction on deficit financing was necessary as it was considered as major cause of inflation. Although these reforms have brought in some positive changes, monetary policies in many African countries continue to, more or less, respond to fiscal policies through expansion in central bank balance sheets to purchase government debt. This relationship could later, lead to macroeconomic instability in the region.

7.5 Challenges of the Depth of Markets and Weak Monetary Policy Transmission

The benefits of well-functioning and deep financial markets in an economy have been extensively documented. Such markets are important not only because they support economic development by providing a mechanism for mobilization and allocation of financial resources, but because they also enhance the effectiveness of monetary policy. Financial systems of most African countries have undergone substantial changes over the last few decades. The median ratio of liquid liabilities to GDP in Africa rose from 20% in 2000 to 31% in 2011, whereas that of deposits to GDP increased to 22% from 12% in the same period.

Likewise, the median ratio of banks credit to the private sector to GDP went up to 18% in 2011 from 11% recorded in 2000 (Cull and Beck 2013). The financial improvement has been broad based, mainly contributed by financial reforms undertaken across the region in more than two decades ago.

Despite the achievements, financial markets in most African countries are still not well developed, weakening the effectiveness of the monetary policy. Africa's financial sector underdevelopment reveals itself when compared with similar economies outside the region. By using data for 2011 and a sample of low- and lower-middle income countries in SSA and by comparing the median for this group to that of low- and lower-middle income countries outside Africa, Cull and Beck (2013) concluded that Africa's banking systems are small, costly, and focused on the short-term end of the yield curve. Cull and Beck's results indicate that the median ratio of liquid liabilities to GDP for the non-African developing countries was 47%, being much higher than the median of 32% for African countries, while the median ratio of deposits to GDP was 38% for the non-African countries compared with 25% in Africa. During the period, the median private credit to GDP ratio was 34% in non-African countries, nearly twice of the 18% level for the African countries.

Although African banks are more profitable, they are, on average, less efficient and operate in a less competitive environment. Cull and Beck (2013) noted that, in 2011, the median net interest margin for the low- and lower-middle income African countries was 5.9% compared with 4.7% for a similar group outside Africa. Similarly, the interest rate spread between the lending and deposit rates was 10.3% in Africa higher than 8.2% outside Africa, partly due to higher operating costs. The high interest rate spreads, which also reflect the level of concentration and competitiveness in the banking sector, contribute to the crowding out of credit to the private sector in favor of holding more reserves than required. It is estimated that, in Africa, the market share of the three largest banks is about 73% (World Bank 2006). Also, using data for 2011, Cull and Beck (2013) suggested that the share of the five largest banks was 81% in low- and lower-middle income African countries, much higher than 64% in similar countries outside Africa.

The literature is rich of factors that may have contributed to the underdevelopment of financial markets in Africa. The factors are related to limited macroeconomic stability, inadequate financial products diversification, ineffective enforcement of laws and regulations, and inadequate transparency and availability of information, which are important for reducing screening costs and preventing adverse selection. The institutional framework is also central to the smooth functioning of financial systems because well-established property rights, together with an efficient judicial system, foster investors' confidence while lowering screening and monitoring costs. The literature in this area tends to support the view that institutional capacity is low or lacking in most African countries particularly with respect to property rights and contract enforcement. As an illustration, a World Bank study Making Finance Work for Africa, 2006, cites an inefficient registration system for moveable assets and the lack of adequate documentation for ownership claims as the number one reason why individuals do not apply for or are denied loans. Collateral requirements in Africa are the second highest in the world, at 137% of the value of the loan (The Africa Competitiveness Report 2009). Therefore, in order to minimize risks banks tend to favor large enterprises and government assets, dwarfing intermediation. Likewise, because of the lack of information on creditors and the perceived default risk, financial system in most of these countries is fragmented with a large part of the population lacking access to formal financial institutions.

Cull and Beck (2013) assessed access to and use of financial services basing on bank accounts per 10 000 adults and bank branches per 100 000 adults in low- and lower-middle income African countries compared with similar group in non-African countries using data for 2011. They found that there were only 15 bank accounts for every 100 adults in African countries compared with 42 for non-African countries, whereas there were only 3.1 branches per 100 000 adults in Africa, just one third of 9.6 branches in similar countries outside Africa.

The weakness in the financial sector is not limited to the banking sector alone, but also cuts across the African capital markets. Mishra and Montiel's (2013) survey of different studies on the key indicators of financial environment across SSA tends to support this view. The findings in these studies suggest that the ratio of stock market capitalization to GDP in low-income countries in SSA is relatively small at 0.19 compared with 2.12 for advanced countries. While the stock market turnover ratio is 0.04 for low-income SSA countries below 0.35 for developed countries, the stock market total value traded per GDP is 0.01 for SSA compared with 0.83 for advanced countries. This situation is partly attributed to relatively low efforts by African countries in developing the stock markets as measured by securities market index. In their review Mishra and Montiel (2013) indicated that the securities market index for low-income countries in SSA is 0.51 below 0.67 for developed countries implying that SSA countries lag developed countries in terms of policies to develop domestic bond and equity markets including the creation of basic framework such as the auctioning of Treasury bills or establishment of a security commission; policies to further establish securities markets such as tax exemptions, introduction of medium and long-term government bonds to establish a benchmark for the yield curve or the introduction of a primary dealer system; policies to develop derivative markets or to create and institutional investor's base; and policies to permit access to the domestic stock market by non-residents. Dahou et al. (2009) attributed the under development of stock markets in Africa to a combination of factors including low income levels, ineffective collateral registration systems, weak judicial institutions, exposure to external shocks, and a scarcity of human capital and financial infrastructure. Also, contributing to this are the dearth of domestic investment opportunities, and the small number of portfolio options such as property, deposits, equities, and bonds.

The underdevelopment of the financial system in Africa weakens the transmission of monetary policy actions to the macroeconomic variables namely inflation and output. Generally, the fragile banking system makes it difficult for a central bank to aggressively use policy interest rates to achieve domestic objectives as large changes in interest rates may have potentially devastating consequences on the balance sheets of weak banks. The lack of well-developed financial markets implies that the interest rate channel of monetary policy transmission may be less effective and that feedback from the market about monetary policy may be limited. Mishra and Montiel (2013) noted that presence of poorly developed domestic bonds and stock markets reduce the scope of operation of the conventional interest rate channel and the asset channel respectively. Also, contributing to this is the existence of relatively small formal financial sectors, less competitive banking systems characterized by large interest margins and high concentration ratios. The transmission from policy instruments to market interest rates in Africa is also hindered by shallow or dormant interbank markets (Laurens 2005). Less favorable institutional environment may also constrain the effectiveness of monetary policy through the bank-lending channel, which is said to be more appropriate for developing countries. Also, contributing to the ineffectiveness of the bank-lending channel in Africa are the small size of and imperfections in the financial sector.

Sacerdoti (2005), for example, observes that banks in Africa tend to extend limited amounts of credit to the private sector, as the result of underdeveloped institutional means to cope with credit market frictions that increase the cost of financial intermediation. Instead, these banks have tended to hold 30–50% of their deposits as reserves at the central bank and in the form of short-term foreign assets. Saxegaad (2006) estimates that, in 2004, excess reserves amounted to 13% of deposits on average in SSA, a reflection of banks' unwillingness or inability to lend, which limits the impact of monetary policy on bank credit. To the extent that credit market frictions make deposits at the central bank, government bonds, and foreign securities much closer substitutes among themselves than these alternative assets are with private sector credit, this situation would tend to weaken the transmission mechanism through the bank-lending channel.

7.6 Changing Approaches to Monetary Policy Implementation

With the low level of financial market development, data scarcity, and other structural rigidities, most sub-Saharan countries adopted monetary targeting as their operational framework, mainly to preserve monetary policy independence, including the ability to respond to domestic shocks. The framework provided a relatively successful anchor against inflation especially in the decade to 2009. Real gross domestic product (GDP) grew by an average of 5.6% between 2002 and 2008, making Africa the second-fastest growing continent in the world after Asia (UNECA and AUC 2012). Also, during the period, inflation trended in single digits. This development was made possible by the fact that there was less need to use monetary policy for the active management of aggregate demand due to the benign external economic environment (characterized by booming commodity prices and inflows of external finance) that facilitated robust real output growth.

The achievements notwithstanding, the experience from the post-2008/09 global financial crisis, tends to suggest that using the monetary targeting framework could be more challenging due to a number of reasons. First, the external environment facing SSA economies is becoming less giving and more volatile. Second, because of money demand instability, the framework is becoming less useful in controlling inflation when it is at low levels.[1] Also, the lack of a stable relationship between monetary aggregates and inflation makes the framework a poor choice for intermediate target. O'Connell (2008) argued that control of monetary aggregates in the face of shifts in the velocity of circulation of money—or mistakes in forecasting velocity—could exacerbate instability in interest rates, exchange rates and output, if prices are sticky in the short run. Third, the monetary targeting framework assumes that actual output does not deviate from potential output, but this could be less important as the SSA economies develop, become more urbanized and more integrated into the global economy. With increased integration, aggregate demand shocks emanating from the global

---

[1] Thornton's (2008) study covering 36 African countries indicates that the relationship between money growth and inflation is weak at low rates of inflation (below 10%) but strong at inflation rates above 10%.

economic fluctuations will have major impact on real growth requiring a more active stabilization role of monetary policy.

With the shortcomings of the monetary targeting framework, macroeconomic management in SSA going forward will presumably require a broader view of policy objectives, with greater priority accorded to, among others, output stabilization alongside the control of inflation. Already, some African countries have shifted to using inflation targeting. The countries include South Africa, Ghana, and Mauritius. Here, inflation forecast is used as the key guide to monetary policy decisions. Presently, Kenya has adopted a hybrid monetary policy framework involving elements of both inflation targeting and monetary targets (Adam et al. 2010). Other countries using monetary targeting frameworks have also allowed for more flexible approach to monetary targets to accommodate volatility in the world economy and the velocity of money. Faced with strong inflows of foreign exchange—from aid and capital flows—in the 2000s, some central banks, such as Uganda, responded by accumulating international reserves by more than planned, to stem an appreciation of their exchange rates, and by allowing monetary growth to rise above targeted levels in order to avoid having to fully sterilize the inflows of foreign exchange by issuing domestic securities, which could crowd out bank lending to the private sector (Kasekende and Brownbridge 2010). Also, with the rapidly expanding economy, Tanzania is gradually migrating from reserve money targeting to interest rate targeting.

7.7 THE CHALLENGE OF CENTRAL BANK INDEPENDENCE

The initial impetus for changes in central bank governance was the wide spread inflation in the 1970s. Research pointed to the time inconsistent problem whereby a central bank with a high degree of discretion in conducting monetary policy would find itself under constant political pressure to boost the economy and reduce unemployment, but since the economy cannot exceed its potential GDP or its natural rate of unemployment over time, this policy will instead lead to higher inflation in the long run (Barro and Gordon 1983). One solution to this problem was to delegate monetary policy to individuals who are highly averse to inflation and insulate them from the rest of government (Rogoff 1985). Another solution was to give stronger incentives to a central bank's management for controlling inflation (Walsh 1995). In either case, greater independence for the central bank could help to provide the policies necessary to achieve lower inflation.

Measurement of central bank independence has generally focused on a set of legal characteristics that can be obtained from the institutions statutes. Broadly speaking, these legal characteristics relates to four aspects of a central bank's independence from government. First, independence is greater when the central bank management is insulated from political pressure by secure tenure, and independent appointment. Second, the central bank enjoys greater freedom when the government cannot participate in or over run its policy decisions. Third, independence is greater when central bank's legal mandate specifies a clearly defined objective for monetary policy. Finally, financial independence of the central bank relies upon restrictions that limit lending to the government.

Over time central bank independence has increased significantly from the 1980s levels to the present both from the developed to the developing countries. More central banks are enjoying independence than ever before. In Africa, central bank independence is a welcome development. Many countries in the continent are calling for greater central bank independence, which has varied from constitutional provisions as provided for in Kenya, Uganda, and others to operational provisions in central bank laws in many other counties including Tanzania. However, central bank independence in Africa is faced with many challenges including the ones that will be discussed now.

First, the degree of independence varies greatly among different central banks. Political and government interferences also vary with those with limited independence being unable to act independently. Pressure to support government lending sometimes go above the set limits, affecting the monetary policy implementation function of the respective central banks.

Second, is the public's general understanding of the central bank's actions. Even central banks that have been granted a high degree of independence under the central bank law (e.g. by having clear objectives and the powers necessary to achieve them, a board with security of tenure, as well as financial and budgetary autonomy) must still work hard to ensure a public understanding of the benefits of price stability and the central bank's role in achieving this objective.

Third, literature has shown that banks with central bank independence are more successful in reaching the goal of low inflation rate in the developed world. In Africa, studies have shown that independence contributes to reducing inflation but is not a sufficient condition to resolve the problem. Other accompanying measures such as the commitment of governments to hold a responsible balanced budget are required. This requirement may be difficult to meet in many African countries, because of the general lack of consensus between economic and political authorities on how to fight inflation.

Central bank independence is one of the key requirements for countries that are implementing an inflation-targeting regime. However, weak monetary, financial institutions and fiscal dominance in those countries sometimes render them unable to establish or maintain this prerequisite, making it difficult to implement their monetary policies.

The high cost of liquidity sterilization in African countries is common. In extreme cases some central banks may have to be accommodated in the government budget in order to implement monetary policy. In such situations central banks' independence is threatened.

The post-financial crisis era and its demands for a more expanded central banking role from the traditional price stability will also cause challenges to central banking independence over time as the arguments for independence to pursue the goal of price stability may not hold for the expanded role of central banking. Accountability and transparence are other challenges that will face central banks in this new expanded role.

To many countries that have granted their central banks more independence, the idea that central banks should be completely independent has come under criticism. This criticism focuses on the danger that a central bank that is independent will not be accountable. Although maintaining low and stable inflation is an important societal goal, it is not the only macroeconomic goal; monetary policy may have no long-run effect on real economic variables, but it can affect the real economy in the short run. In a democracy, delegating policy to an independent agency requires some mechanism to ensure accountability. For this reason, reforms have often granted central banks instrument independence while preserving a role for the elected government in establishing the goals of policy and in monitoring the central bank's performance in achieving these goals.

7.8 ARE AFRICAN CENTRAL BANKS OVEREXTENDED IN THEIR REGULATORY MANDATE?

There has been some debate on the role of central banks in prudential supervision of financial institutions. In most of developed countries the practice has been to create a single agency that is responsible for supervision of the banking, securities and insurance sector with minimal involvement of central banks. In African countries this has not been the case. The practice has been towards, central banks regulating banking institutions while other regulators regulate each financial sector independently.

In developing economies, involvement of the Central banks in supervising financial institutions is considered important taking into consideration the low level of development in the financial sector. In most African countries, Securities Markets, Insurance and Pension Funds are not well developed and this has resulted into the banking sector being the most significant part of financial system. In Tanzania for example the banking industry accounts for 75% of all assets of the financial system.

Despite this similarity in structure, there is considerable variability the regulatory mandates of African central banks. In Rwanda and Malawi for example, the central banks regulate the full range of financial institutions. In other countries, like Tanzania, Kenya, Uganda, Ghana, and Nigeria, in addition to regulating the banking system, the central banks have been given the mandates for ensuring financial stability.

Involvement of central banks in supervising financial institutions has its advantages. Firstly, most SSA financial systems (excluding South Africa) are neither complex nor sophisticated. Most institutions are restricted to core commercial banking thus blurring of the boundaries between financial intermediaries. This makes it reasonable to bring all financial intermediaries under the supervision of central banks. Secondly, it is clear that involvement in financial regulation can harness central banks' expertise in macro-financial analysis that can in turn inform the design of macro-prudential tools. This role in macro-prudential policy can also be viewed as completing the central bank's tool set when both monetary policies and macro-prudential policies are used in complementary ways. It has also been widely argued that because prudential regulation is closely related to macroeconomic stability, both operations should reside in a unified agency. This will ensure that data from the banking sector, which is a critical input in ensuring macroeconomic stability, are easily available to central banks. Third is the question of solvency assessment. Central banks, as lenders of last resort, will only be called upon to lend to commercial banks after a full assessment of the status of the respective commercial bank to ensure that the problem is a liquidity rather than a solvency problem. In this instance, supervisory information on individual commercial banks becomes a key input in arriving at a decision. Therefore, the involvement of central banks in supervising these institutions is considered important in terms of enhancing the ability of central banks to make quick assessments and arrive at a decision in times of crisis.

Fourth, given that central banks have the responsibility of preventing systemic risk in the financial system, hence preserve the integrity of financial markets, it becomes more practical when the banking supervision function is within the mandate of central banks. The central banks focus on systemic stability allows them better perspective of the likelihood and potential impact of macro-shocks in both domestic and international markets.

Fifth is the ability of central banks in gauging systemic impact. Access to supervisory information helps the central bank gauge the systemic impact of a crisis on other institutions and the broader economy hence the ability to form a quick judgment on whether or not to intervene. With very vivid demonstration from the global financial crisis of the spillover effects from one segment of the financial system, micro–macro prudential coordination has become a requirement of financial stability framework. Lastly is the issue of technical capacity. In most African countries, technical capacity on financial systems in concentrated at central banks, which makes central banks more effective in supervising financial institutions. These explanations present a case for the unified approach to regulation adopted in African countries and the rationale for the central bank to play a dominant role in the framework.

The benefits mentioned notwithstanding, an enhanced regulatory role of the central bank does not go without potential costs. A comparison of benefits and costs of an expanded role of central banks in financial regulation needs to take full account of these potential costs. A number of arguments have been advanced and each therefore merits careful consideration.

The conflict of interest argument is based on the possibility that supervisory concern about the fragility of the banking system might influence the central bank to allow a more accommodative monetary policy stance at the expense of price stability. It is reasoned that with sole discretion of monetizing financial distress, a central bank can even fuel a systemic risk because bailing out a financial institution can ultimately derail monetary policy and aggravate financial instability. Expanding on the conflict of interest argument, Goodhart and Schoemaker (1995) further argued that the cyclical effects of both regulatory and monetary policy tend to conflict. They opined that monetary policy tend to be countercyclical whilst regulation is pro-cyclical stating further that it is harder to increase capital during a recession when bank costs are high and profits are very low.

The central bank will face important tradeoffs when insolvent financial institutions need to be closed down, and, at the same time, those institutions have previously borrowed from the central bank against collateral whose value has fallen. How likely is it that the central bank will take action and incur potentially large losses on its balance sheet? It seems more likely that the central bank will practice forbearance to avoid those losses. That, however, will keep insolvent institutions alive and ultimately hamper the necessary reallocation of scarce capital.

This has culminated in the argument that to ensure an effective enforcement of banking regulation free of conflict of interests, monetary policy and banking supervision must be assigned to separate institutions. However, firewalls between monetary and supervisory departments of the central bank would always remain artificial as the crucial decisions would always have to be taken by the central bank's top management. Similarly, as earlier stated, currently market developments such as the increase in the number of financial conglomerates and the blurring of the boundaries between financial products make sector-based regulation increasingly less viable. This is from the fact that the trend has been that more institutions are now offering more than one financial products, such as bancassurance; hence, a different regulatory authority to regulate the same institution does not seem to be economical and efficient. Therefore there are economies of scale and scope available to an integrated regulator, and there is value in being able to allocate scarce regulatory resources efficiently and effectively.

From all these discussions and arguments, it can be clearly seen that there is no direct answer as to which regulatory model will maximize the intended outcome of supervising financial institutions. While giving central banks more powers to supervise financial institutions will assist central banks to perform its other functions, such as implementation of monetary policy and lender of last resort function, there is risk of inefficiency in performing some supervisory functions due to concentration of powers in the same individuals who at times must make conflicting decisions. It is therefore important to strike a balance between the perspectives in order to ensure safe, sound, and stable financial systems in developing countries. However, considering the current level of development of financial sectors in Africa, it can be argued that central banks could concentrate on regulating banking institutions, while other regulators regulate other financial institutions, such as insurance and security markets, but ensure that a mechanism for coordinating the different regulators is in place. This will facilitate the sharing of information which will enable both sides make appropriate decisions regarding the stability of the institutions they regulate.

7.9 Conclusion

The role and functions of central banks in Africa has undergone very significant changes. Although history shows that central banks in Africa have contributed quite significantly to growth, they still face considerable challenges, including the inflation challenge, which caused a large proportion of factors accounting for inflation originating from the supply side.

Fiscal dominance has been and is also still a challenge to monetary policy, as governments' resorting to central banks to finance their deficits continues to be a problem.

The depth of markets and weak monetary policy transmission is still a major challenge in Africa, although financial systems in these countries have undergone substantial changes over the last few decades. This puts greater importance on the deepening of financial market agenda in Africa. Finally, the debate against and in favor of separation of central banking and prudential supervision is ongoing, with the shift in Africa being towards consolidating the supervisory mandate of financial institutions with central banks.

References

Adam, C., Maturu, B., Ndung'u, N., and O'Connell, S. (2010). Building a Kenya Monetary Regime for the 21st Century. Mimeo.

Adam, C.J., Ndulu, B.J., and Sowa N.K. (1996). Liberalization and seigniorage revenue in Ghana, Kenya and Tanzania. *Journal of Development Studies,* 32(4):531–553.

Barro, R. J., and D. B. Gordon. (1983). A Positive Theory of Monetary Policy in a Natural-Rate Model. *Journal of Political Economy,* 91:589–610.

Cull, R., and Beck, T. (2013). Banking in Africa. Policy Research Working Paper 6684, World Bank.

Dahou, K., Omar, H.I., and Pfister, M. (2009). Deepening African Financial Markets for Growth and Investment. *Ministerial Meeting and Expert Roundtable of the NEPAD-OECD Africa Investment Initiative*, 11–12 November 2009.

Gali, J., and Monacelli, T. (2005). Optimal Monetary and Fiscal Policy in a Currency Union, NBER Working Papers 11815, National Bureau of Economic Research, Inc.

Goodhart, C., and Schoenmaker, D. (1995). Should the functions of monetary policy and banking supervision be separated? *Oxford Economic Papers*, New Series, 47(3):539–560.

Kasekende, L., and Brownbridge, M. (2010). Post Crisis Monetary Policy Frameworks in Sub-Saharan Africa. http://onlinelibrary.wiley.com/doi/10.1111/j.1467-8268.2011.00280.x/abstract.

Khan, M.S., and Senhadji, A.S. (2001). Threshold effects in the relationship between inflation and growth. *IMF Staff Papers*, 48(1):1–21.

Kollmann, R. (2002). Monetary policy rules in the open economy: effects on welfare and business cycles. *Journal of Monetary Economics*, 49(5):989–1015.

Lucas, R.E. Jr. (1973). Some International Evidence on Output-Inflation Tradeoffs. *The American Economic Review*, 63:411–425.

Luis, A., and Roberto, C. (2011). Global food prices and inflation targeting. http://www.voxeu.org/article/threat-rising-food-prices.

Mishra, P., and Montiel, P. (2013). How effective is monetary transmission in low-income countries? A survey of the empirical evidence. *Economic Systems*, 37(2):187–216.

O'Connell, S. (2008). *Inflation Targeting as a Monetary Policy Framework: Issues and Concerns, revised version of a paper prepared for the Seminar on Monetary Policy and Inflation Targeting*. Abuja: Central bank of Nigeria.

Romer, D. (2001). *Advanced Macroeconomics*, second edition. McGraw-Hill.

Rogoff, K. (1985). The Optimal Commitment to an Intermediate Monetary Target. *Quarterly Journal of Economics*, 100:1169–1189.

Sacerdoti, E. (2005). Access to Bank Credit in Sub-Saharan Africa: Key Issues and Reform Strategies. IMF Working Paper 05/166. Washington, DC: International Monetary Fund.

Saxegaard, M. (2006). Excess Liquidity and Effectiveness of Monetary Policy: Evidence from Sub-Saharan Africa, Working Paper WP/06/115, Washington D.C., IMF.

The Africa Competitiveness Report (2009). http://www.afdb.org.

Thornton, J. (2008). Money, output and inflation in African economies. *South African Journal of Economics*, 76(3):356–366.

UNECA (2013). 50 years of Development Planning in Africa—lessons and challenges, http://www.uneca.org/, accessed 21 October, 2013.

United Nations Economic Commission for Africa and African Union Commission (2012). Unleashing Africa's Potential as a Pole of Growth: Issues Paper, A Paper Presented at the Meeting of the Committee of Experts of the 5rd Joint Annual Meetings of the AU Conference of Ministers of Economy and Finance and ECA Conference of African Ministers of Finance, Planning and Economic Development, Addis Ababa, Ethiopia, 22–25 March 2012.

Walsh, Carl E. (1995). "Optimal Contracts For Central Bankers". *The American Economic Review*, 85:150–167.

World Bank (2006). Making Finance Work for Africa. Africa Region, International Bank for Reconstruction and Development. http://siteresources.worldbank.org/INTAFRSUMAFTPS/Resources/MFWfAFinalNov2.pdf.

World Bank (2013). World Development Indicators (2013). Washington, DC: World Bank. doi: 10.1596/978-0-8213-9824-1.

CHAPTER 8

··

FISCAL POLICY IN AFRICA

··

WILLI LEIBFRITZ

8.1 INTRODUCTION

AFRICA'S economic performance has significantly improved during the past decades and the continent has become more resilient to external shocks. Better macroeconomic conditions are going together with more solid public finances, which illustrates the positive inter-relationship between economic and fiscal developments. This chapter examines the main areas of fiscal policies in Africa, notably fiscal developments over the longer term and during business cycles, the size and allocation of government spending, the tax design and the quality of fiscal institutions. It also discusses the main challenges that Africa's fiscal authorities are facing.

Stronger budgetary positions together with an appropriate composition of spending are generally associated with higher economic growth (Gupta et al. 2005). In Africa, over the past three decades there has been a clear improvement in budgetary positions, which has helped to boost economic growth through higher national savings and improved macroeconomic stability. Africa's average fiscal deficit, which had amounted to around 7% in the 1980s declined steadily during the 1990s and the 2000s, and during 2006–2010 it was close to zero. This latter period included some years with surpluses during the economic boom before the global economic recession 2009 but also a large deficit of above 5% during this recession. Since then Africa's average fiscal position has again improved but remains weaker than before the recession. Fiscal consolidation was widespread in Africa but it was more pronounced in oil-exporting countries than in oil-importing countries. The reason was that in resource-rich countries revenues increased more (benefiting from higher commodity prices) and spending was more contained than in the other countries.

Africa's successful fiscal consolidation was largely achieved by increasing revenues. While public expenditures declined (as % of gross domestic product (GDP)) during the 1990s, spending shares later increased again and are now back to the levels of the early 1980s. Improved political and macroeconomic conditions, more fiscal discipline, and debt relief have all contributed to fiscal consolidation in Africa. According to the joint World Bank-IMF Low Income Countries Debt Sustainability Analysis, of the African countries that have been examined in recent years, almost two-fifths were at low or moderate risk of debt distress while around one-fifth were at high risk. Reasons for debt distress in the latter countries were often high accumulation of foreign debt relative to export earnings but also prospects of little improvements under base case assumptions. The main reasons for the favorable develop-ment in the low-risk countries were relatively low external debt due to debt relief, prudent fiscal policies in the past and relatively favorable economic and fiscal prospects (see also the chapter by Marcelo M. Guigale and Mark R. Thomas (Chapter 12, *Handbook*, this volume).

8.2 FISCAL POLICIES DURING BUSINESS CYCLES

While Africa's fiscal positions have improved over time, budgetary developments remain volatile in many countries notably due to boom and bust cycles of commodity prices. They are also vulnerable to volatile export volumes and capital flows caused by volatility of the world economy and turbulences in international financial markets. While this would call for macroeconomic stabilization through appropriate fiscal policies there are differ-ent views about their effectiveness. Indeed, many economists downplayed the stabiliza-tion task of fiscal policy, one of the three famous objectives of fiscal policy as described by Richard Musgrave (Musgrave 1959). Their arguments were based on theoretical con-siderations (neo-classical rational expectations theory with the Ricardian equivalence hypothesis) and practical problems (forecasting risks, implementation lags, etc.). Given these problems and risks with fiscal demand management, these economists concluded that short-term economic stabilization should be left to monetary policy while fiscal pol-icy should focus only on an appropriate allocation of resources and income distribution, that is, the other two areas of Musgrave's fiscal policy objectives. With the Great Recession of 2009 the view that fiscal policy should help to mitigate output volatility gained again in importance. It has also been suggested that as part of a new structural economics frame-work investing in productivity-enhancing bottleneck-releasing infrastructure would have positive effects on the economy both in the short term and the longer term, thus reconcil-ing the Keynesian view about the usefulness of active fiscal policy with the neo-classical view (Lin 2012).

Developing countries have often to cope with highly volatile tax revenues and revenue volatility is aggravated if aid flows are also procyclical (Bulir and Hamann 2003). If the higher revenues during boom periods are used to increase government spending, rather than building buffer stocks, there is no fiscal space for increasing spending during cyclical downturns. As a result spending has to be cut when tax revenues decline. Several empiri-cal studies found that fiscal policies in developing countries including in Africa tend to be mostly procyclical thus aggravating boom–bust cycles (Ilzetski and Vegh 2008; Carmignani 2010; Montiel and Servén 2006, and the literature mentioned there). Another study finds for African countries that government spending has from 1980 to 2000 indeed been procyclical in almost two-thirds of the 46 countries in the sample. However, this share declined to less than 40% after 2000 and in the majority of countries spending was acyclical or countercycli-cal. As according to this study more countries escaped from procyclicality, Africa's resilience against external shocks improved, which also helped to better cope with the Great Recession of 2009 (Leibfritz and Rottmann 2013). It is also noticeable that during this global recession aid flows to Africa did not decline as had been feared but continued to increase, which also supported Africa's resilience to this external shock.[1] But despite past improvements, finding an appropriate fiscal response to economic shocks remains an important challenge for African countries. Creating fiscal space during economic upturns and ensuring debt sustainability over the medium and longer term helps countries to follow countercyclical or at least acyclical spending policies during economic downturns.

8.3 PUBLIC FINANCE MANAGEMENT

An effective public finance management is needed to implement government policies. It must provide adequate financial resources, allocate them efficiently to priority areas and respond to policy changes. This enables governments to effectively and cost-efficiently deliver basic public services and to obtain their economic and social goals while at the same time being able to respond to unforeseen events and ensuring fiscal sustainability. Elements of a high-quality public finance management are an efficient and transparent process of preparing and implementing the budget; effective spending controls and auditing; a high degree of discipline, accountability, and transparency at all levels of government and administration. Many countries around the world have supplemented their traditional annual budgets by medium-term budget frameworks and have also adopted fiscal rules to ensure fiscal sustainability. While such budget tools can help to improve policies, they are no magic bullet and depend on the quality of the existing public institutions. Medium-term budget frameworks require an appropriate costing of expenditure plans and have also to cope with the limited predictability of government resources (Lienert and Sarraf 2001).

African countries are making efforts to improve basic services and infrastructure but there is still much room to further improve the quality of spending and to target spending better to fostering growth and reducing poverty. To this end African countries have also modernized their public finance management systems, often with the help of development partners including African Development Bank, World Bank, International Monetary Fund, the European Union, and national donors. But progress has been uneven and reforms to laws and procedures have not always led to better performance. In the 24 countries where the African Development Bank (AfDB) has supported public financial management reforms, the average Country Policy and Institutional Assessment (CPIA) score for quality of budgetary and financial management increased from 3.22 out of 6 in 2005 to 3.78 in 2011 (African Development Bank 2012).

More and more African countries have adopted Medium Term Budget Frameworks (MTBF) with medium term budget estimates for spending agencies over three to five years. Several countries (such as Burkina Faso, Cameroon, Malawi, Rwanda, South Africa, Tanzania, and Uganda) have gone further by introducing Medium-Term Expenditure Frameworks (MTEF), sometimes including performance-based budgeting (PBB). In South Africa, reforms appear to be most advanced. Starting after the end of apartheid in 1994, a series of reforms has been implemented since then to bring budgetary frameworks

---

[1] Total ODA net flows to Africa increased from US$ 39.5 billion in 2007 to US$ 45.2 billion in 2008 and to US$ 47.8 billion in 2009 (AfDB et al. 2013).

to best international practices. From December 1997 onwards, South Africa adopted a medium-term budget framework with the publication of the Medium-Term Budget Policy Statement (MTBPS) and the Medium-Term Expenditure Framework (MTEF) (du Plessis and Boshoff 2007). In 2009, a new Ministry of Performance, Monitoring and Evaluation (PME) was created within the presidency. Its main tasks are to facilitate the development of plans for cross-cutting priorities or outcomes of government, monitoring and evaluating the outcomes of these plans, and monitoring the performance of individual national and provincial government departments and municipalities (Engela and Ajam 2010).

Fiscal rules aim to strengthen fiscal discipline. More than a third of African countries are currently committed to such rules. As sound fiscal policies facilitate the task of monetary policy, fiscal rules were adopted in all countries that participate in monetary unions: the eight member countries of the West African Economic and Monetary Union (WAEMU)[2] and the six member countries of the Central African Economic and Monetary Community (CEMAC)[3] have introduced supranational fiscal rules in 2000 and 2002 respectively. Several other countries have adopted national fiscal rules, such as Botswana (since 2003), Cape Verde (since 1998), Kenya (since 1997), Mauritius (since 2008), Namibia (since 2010), and Nigeria (since 2007). These rules refer generally to central governments but differ to some extent between countries (Budina et al. 2012).[4] Bova et al. (2013) found for advanced countries that the fiscal stance tends to be more acyclical with a fiscal rule, while in developing countries including Africa it remains on average procyclical. This study even suggests that procyclicality has tended to increase in emerging market and developing economies following the adoption of a fiscal rule. This view is, however, not confirmed by Leibfritz and Rottmann (2013), who found that among the previously mentioned African countries with fiscal rules in three countries spending was on average counter-cyclical after 2000 (Botswana, Cabo Verde,

---

[2] The WAEMU members are Benin, Burkina Faso, Côte d'Ivoire, Guinea-Bissau, Mali, Niger, Senegal, and Togo.

[3] The CEMAC members are Cameroon, Central African Republic, Chad, Republic of Congo, Equatorial Guinea, and Gabon.

[4] In *WAEMU member countries*, the fiscal balance of central governments (excluding foreign-financed capital expenditures) should be balanced or in surplus and the stock of total public debt should not exceed 70% of GDP. The rules exclude public investment or other priority items from the ceiling. There is an escape clause for temporary large fall of GDP and government revenue. In *CEMAC member countries*, the basic structural fiscal balance of the central government should be in balance or surplus. The structural balance is calculated by replacing actual oil revenue by its three-year moving average. In addition, the non-oil basic fiscal balance should be in balance or in surplus. The rules exclude public investment or other priority items from the ceiling. In addition, the stock of total public debt must be kept below 70% of GDP. In *Botswana*, the central government expenditure should not exceed 40% of GDP, and 30% of total expenditure should be directed toward development spending, which includes all capital spending and the recurrent spending for health and education. In *Cabo Verde*, domestic borrowing should not exceed 3% of GDP and the stock of public dent should not exceed 60% of GDP (although this latter ceiling is not binding and does not require action). *Kenya* has policy goals for debt ratios although these are not binding and subject to change. Recently the stock of public debt should be below 45% of GDP. In addition, the government overdraft at the central bank is limited to 5% of revenue of the previous year. Furthermore, total revenue should be 21–22% of GDP. In *Mauritius*, the legally mandated debt ceiling is currently 60% of GDP and up from 2018 it is 50% of GDP. There is an escape clause for emergencies and large public investment projects. In *Namibia*, government expenditure should be below 30% of GDP. In addition, the stock of public debt should not exceed 25–30% of GDP. In *Nigeria*, the central government deficit should not exceed 3% of GDP.

Nigeria), while in 12 countries it was acyclical (Burkina Faso, Cameroon, Chad, Republic of Congo, Côte d'Ivoire, Equatorial Guinea, Gabon, Kenya, Mauritius, Namibia, Niger, Senegal) and only in four countries spending was procyclical (Benin, Central African Republic, Mali, Togo). This finding suggests that having a fiscal rule may help to improve spending policies but it does not shield a country from procyclical fiscal behavior. Using cyclically adjusted fiscal targets and/or well-defined escape clauses in recessions, together with appropriate enforcement arrangements during boom periods, could help to escape procyclicality.

The Open Budget Survey of the International Budget Partnership (IBP), a group of independent researchers, provides information about *budget transparency and accountability*. The 2012 edition (Open Budget Survey 2012) covers 100 countries, of which 30 are in Africa. It shows that budget transparency and accountability differs widely across the continent. According to this survey South Africa ranks second in the world after New Zealand and with an OBI score of 90, it belongs to the group, which is classified as providing "extensive information" (OBI scores 81–100). Uganda also scores highly (rank 18) and belongs to the country group, which is classified as providing "significant information" (OBI scores 61–80). The next group, classified as providing "some information" (OBI scores 41–60) includes Namibia, Malawi, Ghana, Botswana, Kenya, Mozambique, Tanzania, Liberia, and Mali. The following group, which provides only "minimal information" (OBI scores 21–40), includes Sierra Leone, Morocco, Sao Tomé and Principe, Angola, and Burkina Faso. And the group with the poorest performance, which is classified as providing only "scant or no information" (OBI scores 0–20), includes Zimbabwe, Democratic Republic of Congo, Nigeria, Egypt, Algeria, Tunisia, Cameroon, Senegal Rwanda, Zambia, Chad, Benin, and Equatorial Guinea. In recent years several African countries have improved their scoring such as Uganda, Angola, and Morocco, while the performance of others, including Egypt, worsened. In Egypt, the political turbulences, which led to the overthrow of the political regime in 2011 adversely affected budget transparency as the most important budget document, the Executive's Budget Proposal was not published during the assessment of this survey.

8.4 Public Spending

The size of public sectors, as measured by *spending levels*, differs a lot between African countries. Africa's average government spending ratio (% of GDP) has recently been slightly above 30%. But in a few countries spending ratios were around 40% or higher, such as in Lesotho, Sao Tomé and Principe, Algeria, Angola, Republic of Congo, Cabo Verde, and Namibia. At the same time, in several countries spending ratios were only around 20% or lower, such as in Ethiopia, Madagascar, Sudan, Central African Republic, Uganda, Sierra Leone, and Guinea-Bissau. The differences in spending levels reflect not only different abilities or efforts to mobilize public resources but also different political priorities. In Africa there is no clear relationship between spending and income levels. Both among the poorest countries and among the richer countries there are some with relatively large and others with relatively small public sectors. As a result, the regression line between spending ratios and per capita GDP is rather flat (Figure 8.1).

One must be aware, however, that the size of public sector as measured by government spending as percentage of GDP does not fully capture the role of governments on the

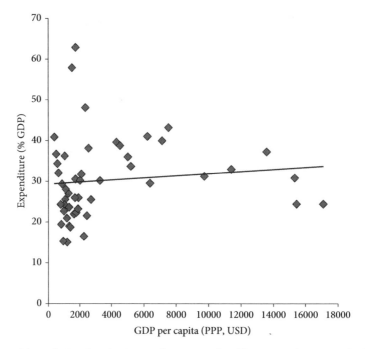

FIGURE 8.1 The relationship between the ratio of public expenditure to GDP and per capita incomes in Africa Data for 2012.

economy. Besides the traditional fiscal instruments, which affect government spending and revenues, there are also other tools with similar economic impact but without direct effects on the government budget. For example, controlling prices and rents subsidizes consumers at the cost of producers and has similar effects as granting consumer subsidies and financing them through taxes, which increases the size of the public sector. While the traditional fiscal instruments appear to be more efficient and are more transparent, there is some evidence that developing countries with less efficient public administrations resort more to these quasi-fiscal instruments than more advanced countries (Tanzi 1995).

Among African countries there is also only a weak positive relationship between the size of government spending (as % of GDP) and the level of human development (as measured by the human development index (HDI)), and the relationship between the size of government spending, and the inequality adjusted human development index (IHDI) is even weaker (Figure 8.2)[5]. This suggests that higher spending does little to improve human development and income distribution. Indeed there are several African countries with relatively low government spending levels and relatively high HDIs and IHDIs, such as Mauritius and Gabon,

---

[5] The IHDI equals the HDI when there is no inequality across the population but falls below the HDI as inequality rises. With inequality in life expectancy, education and income across the population IHDI falls below HDI. In most of Africa, this loss in HDI due to inequality was in 2012 about 35% and higher than in South Asia (29%), Latin America (26%), East Asia (21%), and Europe and Central Asia (13%). In Africa the two countries with the highest losses of HDI due to inequality were Angola (44%) and Namibia (43%) while Mauritius suffered the lowest loss (13%) (AfDB et al. 2013).

while in some other countries government spending levels are much higher while HDIs and IHDIs are much lower, such as in Lesotho, Angola, and Djibouti.

Where public spending is used productively it helps to boost growth. But high public spending together with high deficits or taxes can also be a drag on the economy and threaten macroeconomic stability. The poor relationship between government spending and human development suggests that the quality of spending matters as much or even more than its quantity. Indeed, the impact of government spending on economic growth and human development depends on the *composition of spending* and on spending efficiency (i.e. maximizing results for a given level of spending) and spending effectiveness (i.e. achieving a certain level of results with a minimum level of spending). Public expenditure that increases the stock of human and physical infrastructure and/or enhances their productivity can be labeled as "productive" as it boosts growth potential (Devarajan et al. 1996). Spending on economic and social infrastructure, such as for public transport facilities, energy supply, education, and healthcare belong to this category as such spending tends to enhance growth potential and human development. As redistributing income through the tax system is limited (see below) the allocation of spending to basic services and transfers to the poor is also of key importance for improving equity. When examining the size of infrastructure spending it must be considered that governments are more and more procuring public services through partnerships with the private sector (PPPs). Where this is the case the amount of public spending on investment and infrastructure services understates the full size of such spending and its positive effect on growth and human development. But the positive effects of public spending may not materialize in countries with weak governance or few checks and balances as government officials may use spending as vehicles for rent-seeking (Keefer and Knack 2007).

In Africa, despite some progress, there are large infrastructure bottlenecks, which impede growth. As regards to the *quality of transport and trade-related infrastructure*, the latest

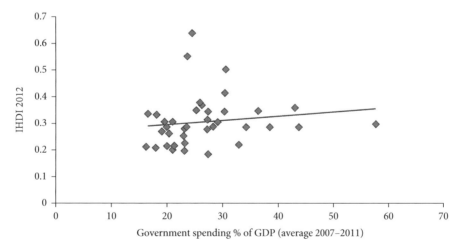

FIGURE 8.2 Relationship between levels of government spending and levels of inequality-adjusted human development.

Note: The Inequality-adjusted Human Development Index (IHDI) equals the Human Development Index (HDI) when there is no inequality across the population but falls below HDI when inequality rises.

performance index as collected from international surveys by the World Bank for the years 2008–2012 includes 41 African countries. According to this survey the average scale for Africa was only 2.34 on a scale from 1 (worst) to 5 (best). For comparison: the scales were 3.61 in China, 3.07 in Brazil, 2.87 in India and around 4 in most industrial countries. But there are large differences between African countries with the best transport infrastructure performance in South Africa (3.79), followed by Morocco (3.14), Egypt (3.07), Tunisia (2.88), Mauritius (2.83), Botswana (2.82), Malawi (2.78), and Namibia (2.72). The poorest transport infrastructure performances among the African countries included in this survey (with scales around or below 2) were recorded in Djibouti, Burundi, Libya, Eritrea, Rwanda, Gambia, Comoros, and Democratic Republic of Congo. This survey also shows that many African countries improved their transport infrastructure during the past decade (notably Guinea-Bissau, Namibia, Sierra Leone, Egypt, Angola, and Botswana) while in several countries the assessment of transport infrastructure worsened (such as Djibouti, Ghana, Libya, Senegal, Democratic Republic of Congo, Gambia, Madagascar, and Nigeria).

As regards to education, *public spending on education* has been in Africa on average in recent years between 4.5% and 5% of GDP. This was higher than in India (3–3.5%) and similar as in South Korea. In several countries public spending on education was 6% of GDP or higher (Botswana, Burundi, Republic of Congo, Ghana, Kenya, Lesotho, Namibia, South Africa, Swaziland, Tanzania, Tunisia), while in other countries it was 3% of GDP or lower (Central African Republic, Chad, Democratic Republic of Congo, Equatorial Guinea, Eritrea, Gambia, Guinea, Liberia, Madagascar, Zambia, Zimbabwe).

Given the poor status of health in many African countries there is a high demand for quality health care. Governments and private institutions including donors have responded by increasing *health spending*. During 2008–2011 total spending on health amounted on average in Africa to 6.3% of GDP of which less than half (2.9% of GDP) was spent by the public sector and the other part (3.4% of GDP) by the private sector. Total health spending in Africa was higher as a percentage of GDP than in China (5% of GDP) and in India (3.9% of GDP). Public health spending was slightly higher than in China (2.7% of GDP) and significantly higher than in India (1.1% of GDP). In a few African countries total health spending (as % of GDP) was higher or close to the levels in developed countries (Sierra Leone, Liberia, Lesotho, Burundi, Malawi, Swaziland, and the Democratic Republic of Congo). In these countries public spending on health amounted to between 7.6% of GDP in Lesotho and around 3% of GDP in Burundi, Democratic Republic of Congo, and Sierra Leone. However, in a number of African countries, total health spending was only around 3% of GDP or lower (Republic of Congo, Gabon, and Seychelles) and in several countries public spending on health was only between around 1% and 2% of GDP (such as in Cameroon, Central African Republic, Chad, Republic of Congo, Côte d'Ivoire, Egypt, Eritrea, Gabon, Guinea, Guinea-Bissau, Kenya, Morocco, Nigeria, and Uganda). Despite relatively high average public and private spending on health, the status of health in Africa has not significantly improved during this period, which shows the deep-rooted health problems in many countries but also suggests that there is a high potential for increasing the cost-efficiency and effectiveness of health spending.

The economic implications of *military spending* depends on the circumstances in the country, in particular how it is financed and how it affects other spending and, most importantly, if it prevents or facilitates conflicts. In a growth model study of Africa, d'Agostino et al. (2012) found a negative effect of military spending on economic growth. With the end of the Cold War and of the worst conflicts in Africa, there was hope that military spending in Africa could decline, thus freeing resources for economic and social development. However, according to SIPRI, the Stockholm International Peace Research Institute, military spending in Africa increased sharply after the 1990s. This was fuelled by new security concerns such of terrorist activities of al-Qaeda activities in North Africa and Boko Haram in Nigeria but also regional ambitions of individual countries. According to World Bank data, military expenditure in African countries has recently been on average between 1.5% and 2% of GDP although in several countries (Algeria, Angola, Djibouti, Mauritania, Morocco, Namibia, Sudan, and Swaziland) it was between 3% and above 4%.

8.5 SOURCES OF GOVERNMENT REVENUES

When designing a tax system a balance must be struck between different objectives, in particular the fiscal objective (creating enough revenues), the efficiency objective (keeping adverse effects on economic performance to a minimum) and the equity objective (that people consider it as fair). But with their lower income levels, the larger informal sectors (including large agricultural sectors and many small firms) and less efficient tax administration, meeting these objectives for collecting taxes is more difficult than in more developed countries.

Tax policy in developing countries is therefore "often the art of the possible rather than the pursuit of the optimal" (Tanzi and Zee 2001). With large parts of economic activity remaining undeclared, it not only raises equity and efficiency problems but could also create a vicious circle of low government revenues, poor public services, a high tax burden on the formal sector causing unfair competition between firms and individuals, and reinforcing incentives to shift activities to the informal sector. Addressing these problems requires not only appropriate tax policies and tax administration but also favorable general framework conditions for formal sector activities and government institutions more generally, including better control of corruption. (See also Chapter 11, *Handbook*, Volume 1.) However, the informal sector cannot fully escape taxes. If money, which is earned in the informal sector is spent on purchases from the formal sector these sales are taxed. Furthermore, firms in the informal sector cannot claim VAT tax receipts on their inputs and also bear VAT on these inputs. Given the large size of the informal sector and poor tax administrations it is not surprising that low-income African countries obtain most of their tax revenues through indirect taxes. While the VAT revenues also suffer from relatively low compliance in many countries, tax collection is eased by the fact that a sizeable portion of it is usually collected at the border in a similar way as trade taxes (Keen and Simone 2004).

In addition to ordinary taxes, governments can also absorb real resources from the private sector by running fiscal deficits and financing these by printing money and causing inflation. This leads to an "*inflation tax*" due to higher seigniorage revenue for the government. The inflation tax has to borne by the private sector as its real money stock is reduced by rising prices. As informal transactions are generally financed through cash, the informal sector holds more cash and thus has to bear a relatively large part of the inflation tax. This could, perhaps also explain why inflation is often higher in countries with large informal sectors and poor tax administration. Between 1990 and 2004 in low-income countries seigniorage revenues amounted to some 9% of overall government revenues (exclusive of seigniorage) (Montiel and Servèn 2006). Many African countries have in the past also resorted to the "inflation tax" to finance government spending. But inflation and seigniorage revenues have significantly declined in recent years in most countries and there is now a general recognition that macroeconomic stability and sound fiscal and monetary policies are preconditions for high and sustained economic growth. This also means, however, that it has become even more important to improve the collection of ordinary taxes.

In African countries excluding the major oil exporters the *tax level* as measured by the tax-to-GDP ratio was on average 18 % in 2011. This is much lower than in OECD countries (around 34%) but slightly higher than in India (15.5%). Considering the differences in GDP per capita levels African countries are not significantly different from non-African countries with respect to tax collection (AfDB et al. 2010). African countries also increased tax ratios over time even though challenges remain to further improve tax collection. Africa's major oil-exporting countries have much lower tax-to-GDP ratios (excluding oil revenues), ranging from less than 2% in Equatorial Guinea and Libya, around 5% and 6% in Nigeria and Angola to around 10% in Algeria and Gabon. The low non-resource revenues in resource-rich countries could be the result of less need to collect such revenue given the abundance of resource rents and a political choice to grant higher tax exemptions/tax holidays but may also point to less efficient tax collection due to higher corruption in some of these countries (Thomas et al. 2013).

Because of the low tax base many African countries continue to depend heavily on *foreign aid* (ODA). In 2008, Africa collected on average US$ 441 of taxes per capita and received US$ 41 of aid per person, so that aid represented less than 10% of tax revenues. However, of the 48 countries for which data was available, aid exceeded tax revenues in 12 countries and was larger or equal to half of tax revenues in 24 countries, and exceeded 10% of tax revenues in 34 countries. But in nearly one-third of the countries aid represented less than 10% of tax revenues. Those countries, which became least dependent on ODA, are often resource-rich countries, which benefited from rising commodity prices (AfDB et al. 2010).

The inter-relationship between aid and tax revenues is complex and depends on the circumstances. If ODA helps countries reaching higher levels of income and reducing poverty their tax base increases and they can "graduate from aid." Tax revenues then substitute aid. This positive substitution effect will be supported if ODA also helps to improve tax collection. However, if the availability of ODA reduces incentives for government to raise domestic resources there is a negative substitution effect between taxes and aid and countries are caught in an aid dependency trap. Various authors have pointed to the negative effects of aid on incentives for good governance, tax efforts, and budgetary planning (Ross 2004; Moss et al. 2006; Heller and Gupta 2002). But the effectiveness of aid on governance and on the economies in general depends on how it is provided, its timing and if it is accompanied by measures, which create pressures for accountability (Collier 2008). Indeed, comparing ODA receipts with a measure of tax effort of 33 African countries does not reveal a clear relationship (Figure 8.3).

In Africa there are large differences in the *tax mix* between countries. These reflect the differences in income levels and economic structures, notably the availability of resource wealth. The most balanced tax mix is found in more developed and more diversified economies such as South Africa. International trends in tax policies and trade liberalization are

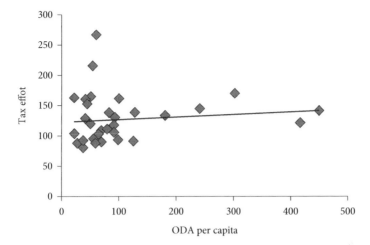

FIGURE 8.3 Tax efforts and aid in African countries.

Note: The tax effort indicator is calculated by dividing actual tax share by an estimate of how much the country should be able to collect given the structural characteristics of its economy. A value of 100 implies that actual tax revenue equals potential tax revenue. The numbers refer to 2006/2007. The tax effort measure in the graph excludes resource rents and Africa's major oil exporting countries are also not included. These countries typically have high resource rents and very low non-resource tax efforts.

Source: AfDB et al., 2010 and author's calculations.

also affecting the tax mix. As in most African countries trade- and growth-increasing effects of lower tariffs are not strong enough to compensate for reduced trade tax rates, trade liberalization must be accompanied by other policies to maintain fiscal stability, such as increasing other taxes, improving tax administration and/or limiting spending (United Nations Economic Commission for Africa 2004).

Indirect taxes amounted in 2006/2007 in Africa on average to below 6% of GDP. They are highest in "upper-middle income" countries (around 7% of GDP), which is close to the respective share of OECD countries. In "lower income" countries this share has been 6% of GDP while in "lower middle income" countries it has been just above 4% of GDP. Owing to trade liberalization trade taxes declined in Africa, but not everywhere. In lower income countries they remained on average at around 3.5% of GDP. Among indirect taxes the value added tax (VAT) has become more and more important. Many countries have replaced their excises, sales taxes or turnover taxes by VAT and most of African countries now have such tax. Most countries have standard VAT rates between 14% and 18%. Standard VAT rates are lower in Nigeria, Djibouti Angola, Comoros, and Ghana. While many countries apply single rates some have one or more reduced rates for specific items such as food and energy.

The shares of *personal income taxes and non-resource corporate income taxes* remain small in most countries. On average and as a percentage of GDP, direct (non-resource) taxes increased slightly during the past decade from around 4% to around 5%. The international trend of reducing statutory income tax rates also affected tax policies in many African countries. Most countries now apply progressive personal income taxes with top marginal rates of between 30% and 40%. In a few countries top marginal tax rates are lower, such as in Botswana (25%) and Egypt (20%). But in several countries top marginal rates are higher, such as in Senegal, Central African Republic, Republic of Congo, Democratic Republic of Congo (50%), and in Chad (60%). But Mauritius and Madagascar followed some other countries and introduced a flat personal income tax with rates of 15% and 23% respectively.

Statutory corporate income tax rates have also been gradually reduced, following international trends. An important motive has been to attract foreign direct investment (FDI). FDI can indeed be an important source for economic growth and policymakers in many countries use tax measures to attract FDI. But according to empirical studies taxes are not the main determinant for FDI but play only a marginal role compared with other determinants. Only when other investment conditions are similar taxes may be decisive for the location (Tavares-Lehman et al. 2012). In many African countries statutory rates have been lowered to between 25% and 35%. The average corporate tax rate in Africa was in 2013 around 29%, similar as the Latin America average (28%) and somewhat higher than in the OECD (25%) and in Asia (22%). In Mauritius the statutory corporate tax rate is only 15% while in some other countries corporate tax rates are much higher, such as in Comoros (50%), Chad and Democratic Republic of Congo (40%). However, in contrast to many industrial countries where the lowering of tax rates has been accompanied by a broadening of the tax base, in many African countries tax preferences and exemptions even increased and continue to narrow the tax base. As a result, many African countries have foregone to fully utilize the revenue potential, which was created by the rising share of (non-resource) profits in GDP (AfDB et al. 2010).

Africa's resource-rich countries, notably oil exporters, rely mainly on *taxes from extractive industries.* These resource taxes include royalties and corporate income taxes on resource extraction activities. With the commodity price boom during the last decade the share of resource taxes in total tax revenues of African countries has increased. In the oil-exporting countries Equatorial Guinea, Republic of Congo, Angola, Gabon, Nigeria, and Chad, resource taxes amount to between around 70% and 90% of tax revenues. There is a risk that multinational firms evade taxes by shifting before-tax profits to their affiliations in lower tax jurisdictions abroad through understating export prices, overstating input prices or other transactions (transfer pricing). In order to reduce such tax evasion through transfer pricing OECD countries and many non-OECD countries including South Africa have adopted the "Arm's Length Principle." It states that cross-border transactions between different parts of a multinational firm should not be different from those that would be agreed between independent firms. While the principle is clear its practical implementation is sometimes complex and there are ongoing discussion and sometimes disputes between governments and multinationals about the appropriate and fair taxation of extractive industries. See also the chapter by Ibrahim Elbadawi and Nadir Mohammed Natural Resources: Precious Boon or Precious Ban?

An effective *tax administration* requires a highly qualified, highly motivated, and well-equipped staff in sufficient quantity that is efficiently allocated among the various administrative functions including auditing. It should also be able to work independently from political interference and be supported by efficient international cooperation. All this increases the efficiency of tax collection and the likelihood to catch tax evaders. But taxpayers should also be able to meet their obligations without undue costs. The task of the tax collectors is eased if the tax burden is relatively low, if the number of taxes is relatively small and if the tax law is clear, relatively simple and give tax collectors relatively little discretionary power for determining tax liability. An educated public, where corruption is not a serious problem and which perceives taxes as essential for financing public goods and services also facilitates tax collection. In many countries, notably in developing countries including in Africa, several of these preconditions for an efficient tax administration are not fulfilled

The World Bank Paying Taxes report compares the tax burden and costs of tax compliance worldwide (World Bank and PwC 2013). It covers the period 2004–2011 and the latest edition includes 185 countries including 51 African countries. It calculates for a case study firm the total tax rate (tax costs as a percentage of profits) and two compliance indicators: the number of tax payments (frequency with which the company has to file and pay different types of taxes), which is a proxy for the administrative burden and the length of compliance (hours spent to comply), which is a proxy for the complexity of the tax system. According to this study, the overall tax burden of firms (tax rate and administrative costs) is in Africa (on average) the highest in the world while the complexity of tax systems is (on average) the second highest after South America. This illustrates the large potential for improving tax policies and tax administration in Africa. The African Tax Administration Forum (ATAF) as well as international organizations (World Bank, IMF, and OECD) and national donors try to improve tax administration through sharing best practices in tax policies and revenue governance.

Africa has made some progress in easing the burden of paying taxes. The total tax rates declined significantly due to lower corporate income tax rates and the replacement of turnover or sales taxes by VAT systems in many countries. As VAT allows the deduction of input taxes it avoids the cascading effect of the turnover tax so that the tax burden of firms declines. Since 2011 more countries have replaced the cascading turnover tax by VAT so that Africa's average tax rate on firms has further declined. If the few other African countries, which still have a turnover tax (such as Eritrea), would also introduce a VAT system, Africa's total tax rate of the case study firm would come close to the world average. But the burden of tax compliance has only slightly declined from 2004 to 2011 and remains high. Further improvements in this area would significantly improve conditions for private sector activity in these countries. Within Africa several countries stand out with respect to the ease of paying taxes and belong to the 50 best-practice countries of the 185 covered worldwide (Mauritius, Seychelles, Rwanda, South Africa, Botswana, Liberia, and Zambia). But a large number of African countries rank very poorly in this international comparison, which is largely due to their high administrative burden on firms and the complexity of their tax systems.

References

AfDB, OECD, ECA (2010). *African Economic Outlook 2010.* Special Theme: Public Resource Mobilisation and Aid. Tunis: AfDB, OECD, ECA.

AfDB, OECD, ECA (2013). African Economic Outlook 2013. Tunis: AfDB, OECD, ECA.

African Development Bank (2012). *Development Effectiveness Review 2012 Governance.* Tunis: AfDB, OECD, ECA.

Bova E., Carcenac, N., and Guerguil, M. (2013). Fiscal Rules and Procyclicality of Fiscal Policy in the Developing World, Paper presented at the IMF-World Bank Conference on Fiscal

Policy, Equity and Long-term Growth in Developing Countries. Washington, DC, April 21-22, 2013.

Budina N., Kinda, T., Schaechter, A., and Weber, A. (2012). Fiscal Rules at a Glance: Country Details from a New Dataset, IMF Working Paper 12/2012.

Carmignani, F. (2010). Cyclical fiscal policy in Africa. *Journal of Policy Modeling*, 32(2):254–267.

Collier, P. (2008). *The Bottom Billion*. Oxford: Oxford University Press.

d'Agostino G., Dunne, J.P., and Pieroni, L. (2012). Assessing the Effects of Military Expenditures on Growth, in *The Oxford Handbook of the Economics of Peace and Conflict*. Oxford: Oxford University Press.

Devarajan, S., Swaroop, V., and Zou, H. (1996). The composition of public expenditures and economic growth. *Journal of Monetary Economics*, 37:313–344.

du Plessis, S., and Boshoff, W. (2007). A fiscal rule to produce counter-cyclical fiscal policy in South Africa, Stellenbosch Economic Working Papers: 13/07.

Engela, R., and Ajam, T. (2010). Implementing a Government-wide Monitoring and Evaluation System in South Africa, ECD Working Paper Series, No. 21, World Bank.

Gupta, S., Clements, B., Baldacci, E., and Mulas-Granados, C. (2005). Fiscal policy, expenditure composition, and growth in low-income countries. *Journal of International Money and Finance*, 24(3):441–463.

Heller, P.S., and Gupta, S. (2002). Challenges in Expanding Development Assistance, IMF Policy Discussion Paper 02/5. Washington DC: IMF.

Ilzetski, E., and Vegh, C. (2008). Procyclical Fiscal Policy in Developing Countries: Truth or Fiction? NBER Working Paper 14191.

Keefer, P., and Kanck, S. (2007). Boondoggles, rent-seeking and political checks and balances: Public investment under unaccountable governments. *Review of Economics and Statistics*, 89:566–572.

Keen, M., and Simone, A. (2004). Tax policy in developing countries: some lessons from the 1990s and some challenges ahead, in S. Gupta, B. Clements, and G. Inchauste (eds), *Helping Countries Develop: The Role of Fiscal Policy*. Washington, DC: International Monetary Fund.

Leibfritz, W., and Rottmann, H. (2013). Fiscal Policies During Business Cycles in Developing Countries: The Case of Africa, CESifo Working Paper 4484, November 2013.

Lienert, I., and Sarraf, F. (2001). Systemic Weaknesses of Budget Management in Anglophone Africa, IMF Working Paper, December.

Lin, J.Y. (2012). *The Quest for Prosperity*. Princeton: Princeton University Press.

Montiel, P., and Servén, L. (2006). Public Finance and Growth in low-income countries: A selective overview, unpublished manuscript.

Moss, T., Peterson, G., and van de Walle, N. (2006). An Aid-Institutions Paradox? A Review Essay on Aid Dependency and State Building in Africa, CGD Working Papers 74. Washington, DC: Center for Global Development.

Musgrave, R.A. (1959). *The Theory of Public Finance*. New York: McGraw-Hill Book Company.

Open Budget Survey (2012). International Budget Partnership (IBP).

Ross, M. (2004). Does Taxation Lead to Representation? *British Journal of Political Science*, 34.

Tanzi, V. (1995). Government Role and the Efficiency of Policy Instruments. IMF Working Paper October 1995.

Tanzi, V., and Zee, H. (2001). Tax policy for developing countries. *IMF Economic Issues* No. 27.

Tavares-Lehmann, A.T., Coelho, A., and Lehmann, F. (2012). Taxes and foreign direct investment attraction: a literature review, in R. Tulder, A. Verbeke, and L. Voinea (eds), *New policy Challenges for European Multinationals*. Bingley: Emerald Group Publishing Limited.

Thomas, A., and Trevino, J.P. (2013). Resource Dependence and Fiscal Effort in Sub-Saharan Africa, IMF Working Paper August 2013.

United Nations Economic Commission for Africa (2004). Fiscal Implications of Trade Liberalization on African Countries, African Trade Policy Centre, No. 5, September 2004.

CHAPTER 9

AFRICAN DEBT AND DEBT RELIEF

MARK R. THOMAS AND MARCELO M. GIUGALE

9.1 INTRODUCTION

AFRICA's foreign debt is an emotive topic. For decades, it has generated a mountain of debate. Debt relief has single-issue non-governmental organizations (NGOs) dedicated entirely to its promotion. Yet misconceptions and a dearth of accurate information persist.

Now is an enlightening moment to revisit Africa's debt and its forgiveness. The Heavily Indebted Poor Countries (HIPC) debt relief initiative has mostly run its course. Of the 39 eligible HIPCs, only four have yet to access irrevocable debt relief.[1] For many beneficiaries, several years have elapsed since comprehensive debt relief, allowing some perspective. Moreover, partly owing to the reconciliation work involved in debt relief and follow-up efforts to support public debt management, data have become better, allowing a stock-taking based on facts.

This chapter takes a chronological approach, with the aim of a broad review of the narrative of debt accumulation, debt relief, and surrounding debates, from post-colonial independence to the present. There is no claim to be exhaustive. We aim to give historical perspective. Many official and academic publications on African debt and debt relief are narrowly focused on the issues of the moment: the case for or against, or details of design and implementation. We take the opportunity to step back. Moreover, the global economic climate has now changed, with exploration and discovery of natural resources in Africa combining with the fiscal space created by debt relief, to warrant a new look at the policy challenges of the next decade.

Remembering the past seems no guarantee against being condemned to repeat it. Some emerging patterns in African borrowing contain echoes of recent history that suggest greater caution is still needed.

---

[1] The remaining "unforgiven" HIPCs are Chad, Eritrea, Somalia, and Sudan.

9.2 THE GREAT AFRICAN DEBT ACCUMULATION, 1970–2000

9.2.1 Initial conditions

As African economies gained independence at the end of the colonial era, they carried light debt burdens. The earliest standardized data start in 1970 and were compiled by Abbas and Christensen (2010). In 1970 the ratio of gross debt to GDP in Ethiopia was 8%, Senegal 18%, and Tanzania 17%. These examples are representative. Of 23 countries for which we have continuous data since 1970, only two (Mali and Zambia) entered the 1970s with gross public debt above 50% of GDP.

Consequently, throughout the early 1970s, debt service was not an issue of great concern in most African economies, as it represented easily manageable fractions of government revenues. Debt service recorded from the early 1970s is rarely greater than 2% of gross national income (GNI). World Bank figures show Cameroon's debt service in 1971–1975 at between 1.1% and 1.6% of GNI. Ghana's ranged between 0.7% and 2.0%, Kenya's from 1.3% to 1.7%. In 1970, debt service for low-income sub-Saharan Africa (SSA) averaged 1.3% of GDP and 5.2% of exports.[2]

Low debt service may even have encouraged neglect. Mali, where gross public debt already exceeded 50% of GDP in the early 1970s, recorded debt service payments of less than 1% of GNI. Much of the debt taken on by African governments had not yet created large budgetary costs, coming as it did from concessional sources with low interest, long maturities, and grace periods. Zambia is the only country in our sample where debt service was already posing problems in the 1970s, averaging more than 5% of GNI.[3]

9.2.2 Lost decades

The pace of subsequent debt accumulation was uneven across countries and time. In 1980, seven of the 23 countries for which we have continuous data had debt to GNI above 50%; only five years later, this number had doubled. By 1995, when the pressure for debt relief was coming to a head, all bar Swaziland had debt-to-GDP ratios above 50%, and half were above 100%.

The 1980s saw an unprecedented accumulation of public debt in Africa, as governments increased borrowing from a mix of rich-world export credit agencies and development banks. Outside Africa, most notably in Latin America, the debt crises of the 1980s have created the perception that the 1973 oil shock drove generalized debt accumulation in the developing world. In Africa the evidence does not support this view. In the 1970s African debt ratios remained under control; sudden increases were rare. After 1980, jumps in debt burdens became commonplace. Between 1981 and 1987, each year a third or more of our

---

[2] World Bank, Development Data Platform, downloaded September 19, 2013.
[3] Abbas and Christensen (2010).

sample increased debt-to-GDP by 10 percentage points or more. By 1987, these economies had added 45 percentage points to debt-to-GDP on average relative to the beginning of the decade, a rate of accumulation that was four times faster than in the 1970s.[4] By 1984, external public debt in low-income SSA had risen to 54% of GDP, compared to only 17% in 1970.[5]

The early 1990s saw even more steeply rising debt. African governments addressed increasing debt service needs, as older borrowing finally generated repayment streams, by turning increasingly to the multilaterals. In 1991–1994, our sample added a further 46 percentage points to debt-to-GDP on average. The rise of debt ratios from the mid-1970s to the mid-1990s was exponential: each sub-period saw rates of debt accumulation more rapid than that preceding.

Growth in debt was not always predictable from budget figures. Because debt burdens are expressed as ratios with ability to pay as the denominator, these indicators rise when national income, exports, or government revenues fall in recessions, crises, or war. Furthermore, many quasi-fiscal liabilities, such as bail-outs of banks or state-owned companies, are recorded "below the line," excluded from fiscal deficits. Third, as many debt obligations are in "hard currency," real exchange rates have strong effects on debt burdens. In a simple regression analysis using African data, the real effective exchange rate and an indicator variable for armed conflict explain nearly one-quarter of within-country variation in the external government debt variables compiled by Abbas and Christensen (2010).[6]

Ethiopia serves to illustrate. After more than a decade of armed conflict in Eritrea, Ethiopia's public debt burden rose to about 80% of GDP by the mid-1980s. Yet despite war and famine, the authorities restricted inflation to an average of less than 5% throughout the decade and maintained the currency peg of about two birr to the US dollar that had survived since the 1970s. In 1987–1992, public debt-to-GDP remained in check, rising slightly from 85% to 92%. But in 1991 inflation spiked to 35% and the following year the currency peg slipped for the first time since the 1960s, reaching five birr to the dollar by 1993. Public debt, mostly denominated in hard currency, then shot up to 150% by 1994. The episode is a portrait in miniature of African debt dynamics of the period. The causation from fiscal to debt performance is complex, non-linear, and hard to trace through immediate effects.

9.2.3 Early debt relief: the Paris club

The debt build-up of the 1980s and 1990s occurred alongside incipient debt relief efforts from bilateral creditors. In 1979, the United Nations Commission for Trade and Development (UNCTAD) meetings agreed on a write-off of US$6 billion of the debt of 45 countries.[7] G7 summits through the 1980s created a series of agreements, first to give relief on interest payments, later to write down principal. The Toronto terms put forward by Canada in 1987 (33%

---

[4] Figures up to this point in this section come from Abbas and Christensen (2010).

[5] World Development Report, 1986. Svendsen (1987) reports that arrears and IMF purchases increase this ratio to about 74% of GDP.

[6] The statement is based on a fixed-effects regression, using a balanced panel of ten African countries across 25 years. The conflict variable is that defined by the University of Uppsala Conflict Data Program and the Peace Research Institute, Oslo. See Gleditsch et al. (2002). Regression results are available from the authors on request.

[7] UNCTAD 1983, reported in Easterly (2002).

debt relief in present value terms) were the start of a series of ever kinder Paris Club treatments with names reminiscent of Cold War spy novels, culminating in Cologne terms (90% relief) in 1999.[8] Yet, as Easterly (2002) notes, these initiatives did too little too late to arrest the upward tendency in African debt ratios.

Early debt relief initiatives also reflected the shifting composition of African debt burdens. These burdens, in stark contrast to most of Latin America during the same decades, were mostly owed to official creditors. According to the OECD, in 1975 African long-term external debt stood at US$16 billion, of which a quarter (US$4 billion) was owed to OECD export credit agencies. By 1980, the total had increased to US$44 billion, with the largest part of the increase (40%) due to OECD export credit agencies. Little wonder, then, that 1970s debt relief efforts came from this quarter. The 1980s then saw a shift away from export credit to multilaterals. This would be crucial in the design of the later debt relief efforts. By 1985, African long-term external debt stood at US$74 billion; a third of the increase from 1980–1985 came from multilaterals, twice the increment from export credit agencies.[9]

In conclusion, if African debt ratios were alarming in the 1980s, by the 1990s they were suffocating. Although underlying fiscal forces contributed, debt accelerations were driven by episodes of civil strife, recessions, and sudden depreciations that drove up the relative value of external debt. The 1980s also saw a shift in the composition of borrowing, towards multilaterals and bank lending, away from the export credit dominated composition of the 1970s, which in the 1990s started to be written off. Yet these early efforts by creditors to curtail African debt were not enough; debt ratios continued to rise.

9.3 COMPREHENSIVE DEBT RELIEF: HIPC AND MDRI

9.3.1 The debate

In August 1982 Mexico defaulted on its external debt. Argentina followed in late 1982 and Brazil the following year. Latin America's three largest economies ceased paying interest on the debts they had run up in the wake of oil price increases and the resulting capital flows, as petrodollars were absorbed by western hemisphere current account deficits.

These events set the tone of the early debt relief debate. Although official bilateral debt relief efforts had included a raft of African countries, the dominant tone of discussions until the 1990s remained one of restoring *private* capital flows and enabling economic growth to render borrowers' debts sustainable.

Under the headline "World Bank Criticizes Lag in Third World Aid," *The New York Times* reported in May 1988 that the "international strategy" for resolving the debt crisis was being jeopardized by the refusal of *private* banks to "increase their new lending" to 17 low-income countries. At the same time Canada was putting forward new "Toronto" terms of debt rescheduling at the G7 summit hosted by that city. But the World Bank report that had taken the private

---

[8] See the comprehensive account in Gamarra, Pollock, and Braga (2009).
[9] See Svendsen (1987).

sector to task was, in the words of *The New York Times*, "strongly against any generalized plan of debt forgiveness, arguing that debtor countries must reach mutually acceptable agreements with their creditors that will enable them to continue borrowing for their development in the future." The Bank's (and others') approach to African debt was at this point still subsumed under the market-based approach pursued to date for Latin America.

A year later, a 1989 press briefing from the IMF used similar distinctions to put the main emphasis on new lending rather than debt forgiveness. Arguing that debt service reduction was "a new idea," the IMF suggested more time was needed to study it. IMF Managing Director Michel Camdessus, talking about possible relief on interest payments, went on record: "There are several ways of obtaining what we want, namely debt reduction. We can reduce the principal of the debt. We can [provide] collateral to reduce the flow of interest payments. We can also assist the country with new money. And what finally matters is the relief we are able to provide on the balance of payments of the country." The emphasis was still squarely on *liquidity* rather than *solvency*.[10]

The corresponding theoretical economic concept was debt *overhang*. Although the word was already in figurative use, conceptual precision was brought by Paul Krugman in a seminal 1988 paper, "Financing versus Forgiving a Debt Overhang." Like many theoretical contributions of the time, the model hinged on incentive effects, in this case those arising from the returns from investment in an indebted economy accruing to creditors rather than to the borrower.[11] Under some circumstances, forgiveness by creditors worked better than new finance, even for the creditors. The paper gave a theoretical underpinning to the observed success of market driven initiatives such as the Brady Plan.

Yet the concept of debt overhang in this theoretical sense was not really relevant in Africa.[12] The debtor of Krugman's world was genuinely financially constrained: apart from the incentive problems described, there was no technical constraint on turning a dollar of finance into a dollar of productive investment. A parallel economic literature was at the same time questioning the effectiveness of aid at generating growth in African (and other low-income) countries, suggesting that growth was not constrained by the availability of finance in these economies, but by something else (usually coming under the general rubric of governance).[13]

As the Baker Plan of the 1980s and the Brady Plan of the 1990s negotiated with market lenders the requisite "haircuts" to reignite borrowing countries' economic growth, and as official lenders upped their lending to African economies, many of which found themselves in increasing debt distress, attention refocused from Latin America to Africa. The tenor of discussions duly took a turn away from market-based debt "reduction" towards a more aid-based, and at times moralistic (even religious), rationale for "forgiving" debt.[14]

This coincided with the onset of the first true debt relief. Paris Club treatments prior to 1987 had rescheduled payments without any debt cancellation: the present value of

---

[10] *Washington Post*, April 5, 1989.

[11] The paper was an extension to international economics of the moral hazard of limited liability earlier explored by Sappington (1983).

[12] See Chauvin and Kraay (2005). See also Gil Sander, Hjört, and Thomas (2007) and references therein.

[13] For an up-to-date and detailed discussion of African growth, see Young (2012).

[14] The term "Jubilee" is biblical in origin, referring to a practice of periodical atonement, emancipation, and laying land fallow (*Leviticus* 25: 9–11).

repayments remained unchanged. For the first time, in 1987, the Paris Club agreed to lengthen grace periods and maturities, in effect reducing the present value of repayments, creating "Venice Terms" for African borrowers, the first in a series of softer terms.

In the ensuing debate, as Paris Club debt relief treatments incrementally wrote down bilateral debts incurred by Africa from export credit agencies dating back to the 1960s, the issue of the "seniority" of the Bretton Woods institutions injected an insistent streak of conservatism into their positions.[15] Debt relief posed a technical challenge to the legal foundations of both the Bank and the Fund. Their Articles of Agreement imposed seemingly thorny restrictions on the ability of these institutions to renegotiate the terms of their lending.[16]

The arrival at the World Bank Presidency of James D. Wolfensohn in 1995 seems, with hindsight, to have been a turning point. In September 1995, press reports circulated of a Bank staff proposal for a "multilateral debt facility" to help a group of borrowers labeled for the first time as the Heavily Indebted Poor Countries. The US Treasury was reportedly "cautiously positive." Yet the World Bank still steered clear of any direct reference to "writing off" or "forgiving" debt, for fear of the implications for its credit rating.[17]

In the summer of 1996, HIPC debt relief topped the agenda of the G7 summit in Lyons. Opposition from some governments (notably Germany) to the sale of IMF gold was to stall progress for a few weeks. But earlier fretting over credit ratings had given way to a newfound confidence on the part of Mr. Wolfensohn. He and his management now said that the Bank's US$120 billion of callable capital created room for the institution to act unilaterally.[18]

The HIPC initiative was first presented for approval to the boards of IDA and the IMF in August 1996 and announced to the world in September.[19] The original cost estimate now looks almost comically low: US$8.2 billion, assuming a write-down of about 20% of the debt stock of an estimated 20 qualifying countries.[20] Moreover, in this original form, it did not envisage actual delivery of debt relief until three years of agreed performance by beneficiary countries. The world would have to wait for the turn of the century to see debt relief for Africa of any size or scope.

9.3.2 The early years of HIPC, 1996–1999

The HIPC Initiative was different from previous debt relief for two reasons. First, it attempted to tie *all* creditors into a framework of *comparable treatment*. All calculations of debt relief

---

[15] Bulow and Rogoff (2005) argue that the seniority of the Bretton Woods institutions has no basis in international law. This absence of documentary underpinnings does not imply, however, that their management's concerns about *perceived* seniority were entirely misplaced. One of the tenets of international law is that precedent may be established as *customary international law* if this is based on a belief of a legal foundation (*opinio juris*).

[16] An in depth "legal reconstruction" of the HIPC Initiative from this perspective can be found in Guder (2009).

[17] *Washington Post,* September 15, 1995.

[18] *The Guardian*, July 2, 1996.

[19] IDA Board document M96-927, "The HIPC Debt Initiative—Elaboration of Key Features and Possible Procedural Steps," August 16, 1996.

[20] Birdsall and Williamson (2002).

and expected burden sharing by creditors were to be based on the assumption that all of a country's external creditors would forgive an equal proportion (the "common reduction factor") of the debt they were owed, calculated in present value terms.[21] This was an approach to bringing discipline to debt rescheduling that had been developed by the Paris Club of bilateral creditors, an organization at which both IMF and World Bank held observer status and to which they routinely reported their views on borrowers' economies. (Several of the details of HIPC debt calculations and relief provision had their roots in the technical approach taken by the Paris Club.)

The second innovation was that HIPC debt relief aimed to bring countries to predetermined debt sustainability thresholds. These were defined as ratios of exports or government revenues, whichever was most binding.[22] In the 1996 version, these ratios were debt-to-exports of between 200% and 250% (depending on the volatility of the country's exports, under the "export window") and debt-to-revenue of 280% (under the "fiscal window"). These ratios would be reduced in 1999 to 150% and 250%, respectively.

A third element of HIPC was the conditioning of debt relief on policy performance (initially only IMF macroeconomic conditionality, later extended to tailored triggers in sectors important for poverty reduction, with the World Bank in the lead). The aim was to ensure that the resources channeled to countries by the new debt relief initiative would be used for poverty reduction. However, although a difference of degree, such contingency was not strictly new, since debt relief from the Paris Club had been similarly linked to performance under IMF programs.

Almost as soon as the new initiative was announced, it was attacked on all three of these fronts. On comparable treatment, the objection came from donor governments that the approach did not recognize their efforts to date as bilaterals. In 1996, the view of UK Chancellor of the Exchequer Kenneth Clarke was that bilateral creditors had "done their bit." The objection held some merit. Assessment of eligibility for HIPC debt relief was against debt ratios after "traditional debt relief," which meant the Paris Club's "Naples Terms," under which two-thirds of bilateral debts were cancelled. However, this aspect of HIPC design (which was the only formal recognition in the debt relief architecture of the Bretton Woods institutions' senior creditor status), was to survive these early objections as pragmatism prevailed.

The criticisms of the debt sustainability criteria would prove more persistent and came in two flavors. First, that the thresholds were too high. On this, the critics would eventually win, as by 2005 the main multilateral creditors committed to greater debt relief in the form of the Multilateral Debt Relief Initiative (MDRI).

---

[21] Present value terms control for the fact that equal nominal debts can imply widely differing repayment streams based on interest rates, maturity, grace period, currency, etc. PV calculations bring all loans into a common currency (e.g. "2005 US dollars") to control for this. The percentage difference between the PV of repayments on a loan and a transaction at commercial terms is the loan's "concessionality" or "grant element."

[22] In addition to the notion of "most binding" (i.e. the criterion that gave the most relief), the revenue threshold was only proposed for countries with exports above 40% of GDP (later reduced to 30%). Furthermore, to address the "moral hazard" of countries qualifying through this fiscal window by not raising enough taxes, a revenue threshold of 20% of GDP was applied (later reduced to 15%).

Second, some NGOs made the link between debt sustainability and the future availability of aid.[23] This argument received short shrift from donor governments, who were politically unable to make long-term financial commitments, and by extension it was not entertained by the management of the World Bank and the IMF. However, from the borrowers' perspective, as well as from the balance-sheet perspective of the development banks, this concern was prescient and remains relevant.

The third criticism of HIPC, which persists to this day, concerned the embedded IDA and IMF "conditionality." From the donors' perspective this was important to avoid wasting scarce ODA resources; for many NGOs with long histories campaigning against structural adjustment and, later, rebranded versions of policy-based lending, this was a bitter pill. One strand of criticism was to prove influential: that the original HIPC requirement of three years' performance under an IMF program caused excessive delay in relief.

In April 1998, Uganda was the first nation to reach HIPC completion point and receive irrevocable debt relief from most creditors. Uganda qualified for a debt reduction of US$347 million, 20% of the present value of its external debt. From the creation of HIPC to June 1999, only four HIPCs actually received any financial assistance under the program. Of these, only Mozambique received a major debt reduction (63%).[24]

In response to this inertia the HIPC Initiative was "enhanced" in September 1999. From today's perspective, this is when the contours of HIPC as it has been put into practice came into being and the vision of comprehensive debt relief for Africa started to be realized. Not only were the target debt ratios reduced and eligibility criteria eased (doubling the estimated cost at the time from US$31 billion to US$63 billion),[25] but the link with country-owned Poverty Reduction Strategy Papers (PRSPs) was created.[26] This link has had a profound influence on the aid architecture of the new millennium, with lasting effects on donor coordination and client relationships.

9.3.3 Delivery: the new millennium

From 2000 onwards the HIPC machinery rolled into action. The number of qualifying countries has hovered around forty, mostly African. Individual nations have flitted in and out of this set according to the vagaries of GDP accounts, natural resource discoveries, uncertainties over debt levels, traditional bilateral debt relief, and, in certain cases, a refusal to participate based on concerns about reputation or financial access. From today's vantage point it may seem surprising that in the original 41 eligible countries in 1996 appeared Equatorial Guinea (2012 per capita GDP estimated at about US$24,000), Angola (US$5,500), Vietnam (2011

---

[23] This line was pursued most avidly by Oxfam and religious groups such as the UK Catholic Agency for Overseas Development (CAFOD). For some organizations, *any* lending to poor countries was viewed as immoral.

[24] The other three were Uganda, Bolivia, and Guyana, which received debt reductions under the original initiative of 20%, 13%, and 24%, totaling only about $1 billion in PV terms (IMF-World Bank Development Committee Report, September 23, 1999).

[25] These costing figures include Liberia, Somalia, and Sudan, which were treated as special cases in early HIPC documents due to their arrears to multilaterals.

[26] There were further technical changes to the initiative not reported here.

external debt at only about 40% of exports), Myanmar, and Laos (whose government early on stated they wanted nothing to do with the initiative).[27] Conversely, countries not originally included that have since participated include Afghanistan, Comoros, and The Gambia.

By 2005 HIPC had committed US$38 billion to 28 countries.[28] In loose terms, HIPC had reached its financial half-way point. Yet, if anything, the international debate around debt relief had heated up. The millennial religious overtones of Jubilee 2000, with its endorsement from Pope John Paul II, was superseded by the star-appeal of "Drop the Debt," Bono and Bob Geldof. Twenty years earlier Geldof had helped orchestrate "Live Aid" and in 2005 reprised the effort with "Live 8," to create pressure for further debt relief at the G8 Summit in Scotland in July 2005. Bono had created DATA (Debt, Aid, Trade, Africa) in 2002, with funds from the Gates and Soros foundations, among others,[29] and was an articulate advocate for the idea that debt relief efforts to date had been ineffectual.[30]

In the first half of 2005 a variety of plans for additional debt relief swirled around. At stake were several concerns. Primary was the desire to extend debt relief beyond existing mechanisms, in response to public opinion and the stated aims of several donor governments. Two doubts nagged. One was the financial sustainability of the international aid architecture: how would development banks be able to lend if they had no repayment streams? A second was fairness: as *The Economist* asked in a 2004 article, why should Uganda get a clean slate and Bangladesh nothing? Donor views differed. The US administration, under George W. Bush, had little time for the multilaterals at the best of times, and was eager to forgive debt and move towards a system of grants in place of loans. The British Government was warmer towards the multilaterals as vehicles of donor harmonization and willing to commit greater sums. Other nations such as France, Germany, and Japan, at various points put forward proposals reflecting concerns for equity across countries and less willingness to provide sweeping debt relief (in certain cases because of domestic legal constraints).

The result was inevitably a compromise. Concerns about the "financial integrity" of multilateral lenders were met with promises from donors to "make whole" these institutions. Most notable of these balance sheet concerns were the World Bank and the African Development Bank; the new commitments being asked of the IMF were smaller in relation to its finances and other institutions were initially excluded from the new mechanism, dubbed the Multilateral Debt Relief Initiative (MDRI). Concerns of fairness across countries were ultimately ignored in favor of expediency: it was simpler to restrict attention to the existing set of HIPCs. Simplicity prevailed and the new initiative lent itself admirably to communication: the multilaterals would wipe the slate clean of all debts owed by the HIPCs the previous December.

---

[27] There has been an interesting regional bias in countries' willingness to contemplate participation in HIPC. African governments have in general participated, even after initial doubts (Ghana), or debated their exclusion (Kenya). Asian governments have shown extreme reluctance to be considered (e.g. Bangladesh, Laos, Nepal, Sri Lanka), even when some may have qualified for considerable assistance.

[28] This headline figure includes ten countries that had only reached decision point and were therefore receiving only a part of their full HIPC debt relief as interim debt relief. HIPC Status of Implementation, August 19, 2005.

[29] DATA merged in 2008 with the ONE Campaign.

[30] Roodman (2010) states that the 1999 enhanced initiative "offered to roughly halve the debts of the HIPCs—far short of what Jubilee 2000 and realism demanded."

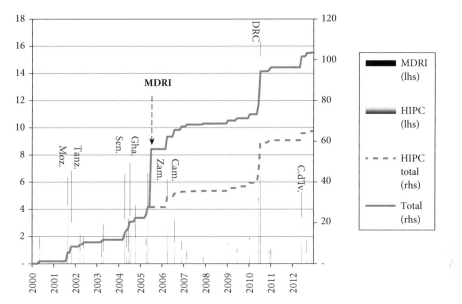

FIGURE 9.1 Africa's debt relief timeline (USD, billion).

Source: IMF/World Bank, HIPC Initiative and MDRI Statistical Update, December 2013.

Debt relief is imputed to the completion point date. For simplicity, the limited early commitments under the original HIPC initiative are imputed to completion point under the enhanced HIPC initiative.

MDRI (including the subsequent matching promise from the Inter-American Development Bank) increased millennial debt forgiveness by approximately one-half again over the HIPC Initiative. At the time of writing, HIPC has cost about US$59 billion, MDRI about US$35 billion (both in 2011 present value). Of this total of US$94 billion (rising to about US$113 billion when the remaining four countries qualify), more than two thirds, about US$64 billion, has come from the multilaterals. Of the US$30 billion from other sources, bilaterals contributed US$27 billion (US$22 billion from the Paris Club).

The vast majority of these flows have gone to Africa (Figure 9.1). Of the 39 HIPCs, 33 are African. Of the US$126 billion nominal cash flows committed to the countries that have so far reached decision point or completion point, US$106 billion (84%) have gone to Africa. The whole millennial debt relief effort has been five-sixths African. By the closure of the initiative, in today's dollars, Africa expects to have received a financial injection of the order of US$100 billion.

To these numbers should be added the cost of Paris Club debt relief to Nigeria in 2005, which reduced an initial stock of about US$30 billion by US$18 billion.[31] (Kenya's Paris Club deals in 2000 and 2004 treated only US$300 and US$350 million respectively.)

Looked at from the perspective of the multilaterals, despite the soothing words of donors, HIPC and MDRI have undoubtedly knocked holes in the agencies' balance sheets. The World Bank has been particularly affected. IDA commitments under HIPC are projected to

---

[31] Federal Republic of Nigeria, Debt Management Office (2005). The main creditors were the UK ($8.0 billion), France ($6.2 billion), Germany ($5.3 billion), and Japan ($4.4 billion). Nigeria's deal equated approximately to Naples terms.

reach about US$15 billion if all candidate countries qualify. MDRI has added a further US$24 billion, for a total of US$39 billion. To compare, IDA replenishments between MDRI and 2012 totaled only US$91 billion.

9.4 THE EFFECTS OF DEBT RELIEF

The efficacy of these transfers can be judged in at least three ways: in terms of financial transfers, effects on anti-poverty spending, and long-run debt sustainability.

In purely financial terms, especially set against international concerns in the 1990s about slow delivery, debt relief looks like quite a success. HIPC and MDRI have orchestrated a net transfer to African economies of the order of US$100 billion. The reduction in liabilities of the 30 African economies that have so far benefited has been significant. On average (unweighted mean), African debt ratios decreased from 112% of GDP before debt relief to 30% after. In GDP-weighted terms the decrease was from 45% of GDP to 20%, a reduction of more than a half.[32]

A related question is the immediate effect on countries' budgets through reductions in the burden of debt service (through both interest charges and repayments of principal). Measuring this effect is complicated by the fact that some countries, prior to relief, were running arrears and in some cases not servicing external debt at all. Indeed, assessing the effect on economies of "returning to the fold," including not only receiving debt relief but also reinitiating debt repayments, has been a source of controversy and confusion in the dialogue with debt campaigners almost from the start.

Looking at the raw numbers, the 36 HIPC graduates paid external debt service of US$5.1 billion in 2004. By 2010 this figure had fallen to US$2.7 billion.[33] Not all of this decrease is necessarily owing to debt relief, but it may also nonetheless understate its effect, given that some of these countries had already started to receive debt service relief by 2004 and some had still not received such relief by 2010.

Reduction in debt service is the lowest bar against which the success of debt relief could be judged. In this sense, HIPC has done what it set out to do in the simplest terms. What about deeper development effects and long-term debt sustainability?

From its inception the HIPC Initiative has attempted to define and monitor "poverty-reducing" expenditures. This exercise is inevitably fraught with technical caveats: countries define such categories differently and may change their own definitions over time. Many spending categories are infuriatingly broad: can *all* education spending be viewed as anti-poverty? Still, what evidence we have suggests that anti-poverty spending in HIPCs has increased substantially.[34]

Based on countries' own definitions of poverty-reducing spending, in the thirty-six HIPCs that have to date received debt relief, such spending rose from about US$10.8 billion

---

[32] Stucka, Merotto, and Thomas (2014).

[33] IMF and World Bank (2013a).

[34] Ideally one would wish to treat debt relief as an experiment and compare the evolution of poverty reducing spending in African HIPCs with that in non-HIPCs. Unfortunately the data are not available with the same focus on anti-poverty spending in non-HIPCs.

in 2004 to about US$32.6 billion by 2010, an increase in the share of government revenue from about 44% to about 51%, and in the share of GDP from 6.9% to 9.1%.[35]

These rough and ready numbers receive some support from academic studies. One study of twenty-four African HIPCs over 1991–2006 found that "debt relief affects public finance behavior in a [desirable] way [$1...] effects being similar to those of [$1...] program grants."[36] This assessment is more optimistic than an earlier assessment covering 1989-2003, which found positive effects of debt relief on social spending only in countries that had improved their institutions in parallel.[37] The difference between these assessments, beyond estimation strategy and country coverage, is likely due to the later period covered by the former study, because the volume of debt relief is greater. Other studies have tried to trace an effect from debt relief to outcomes, through expenditures, for example on education and health. There is some evidence of these effects particularly in education, where one study found "significant changes in the size of educational expenditures, dropout rates in primary schooling, repetition rates in secondary schooling, and student-teacher ratios."[38]

A further effect of debt relief may be to reduce the need for future taxation to repay debt. Consistent with this, one study finds evidence that stock prices of multinationals with subsidiaries in HIPCs rise on news of debt relief to each country, possibly indicative of "debt overhang or similar effects."[39]

Debt relief efforts have all along articulated debt sustainability as their main goal. The Paris Club states its role as "to find coordinated and *sustainable* solutions to the payment difficulties experienced by debtor countries." Early IMF and World Bank communications referred to the objective of the HIPC Initiative, "to *bring a country's debt burden to sustainable levels*, subject to satisfactory policy performance."

Yet, despite these affirmations, debt sustainability is an elusive concept. The Paris Club's "five key principles" contain no such definition.[40] The original design of the HIPC Initiative included the determination of country specific targets for debt ratios based on assessments of "vulnerability" based on the variability of countries' exports, but this approach was swiftly abandoned in favor of a more transparent and mechanical method.

The definition of debt sustainability now used by the Bretton Woods institutions (and accepted by several other bodies) is complex and based on the statistical analysis of episodes of debt default and correlates in developing countries. Based on the empirical finding that the likelihood of default depends not only on debt burden but also on countries' institutional strengths, the framework uses tailored debt burden thresholds for borrowing countries and assesses whether countries breach these thresholds over twenty years, summarizing the findings in a risk rating.[41]

---

[35] IMF and World Bank (2013b).

[36] Cassimon and van Campenhout (2008).

[37] Dessy and Vencatachellum (2007).

[38] Crespo Cuaresma and Andronova Vincelette (2009).

[39] Raddatz (2009).

[40] The five Paris Club principles are "Case-by-Case," "Consensus," "Conditionality," "Solidarity," and "Comparability of Treatment."

[41] The original framework is based on Kraay and Nehru (2006). It has since been modified based on updated empirical analysis. See IMF and World Bank (2012).

The results are superficially comforting; deeper analysis reveals cause for concern.[42] In 2006, of the 36 African low-income countries assessed, 18 were either in debt distress or at high risk, thirteen were at moderate risk, and only five were at low risk. By 2012, only nine countries were in debt distress or at high risk, 14 were at moderate risk, and 13 were at low risk. Clearly things have improved, and debt relief is a big part of this story. Still, the category of countries at moderate risk contains several countries where post-HIPC borrowing patterns have driven up debt ratios quite rapidly, in ways that suggest the gains from debt relief could be undone in a few years (e.g. Ghana, Uganda, Senegal, and Mozambique).

A final measure of success is the effect of debt relief on countries' policies. Under its principle of "conditionality," the Paris Club states that in addition to "need," it negotiates treatments with countries that "have implemented and are committed to implementing reforms to restore their economic and financial situation, and have a demonstrated track record of implementing reforms." HIPC contains a more extensive approach embodied in "floating completion point triggers," laid out in each country's HIPC decision point document.

Anecdotally, there is no doubt that HIPC completion point focused minds. In many cases, debt relief followed not long after the establishment of peace after bouts of war or civil unrest (e.g. Republic of Congo, Liberia, Sierra Leone, and Côte d'Ivoire). In almost all, comprehensive debt relief received understandable prominence in local media, with an effect on governments' determination to secure decision point and completion point under HIPC.

The World Bank Country Policy and Institutional Assessment (CPIA) rates IDA borrowers' performance in four areas: economic management, public sector management, social inclusion, and structural policies.[43] On economic management, the twenty-nine graduated African HIPCs improved their average rating from 3.33 in 2005 to 3.53 in 2012; the remaining African countries declined from 3.11 in 2005 to 3.06 in 2012 (overall, low- and middle-income countries went from 3.55 to 3.45). On social inclusion, the 29 improved their average from 3.16 in 2005 to 3.28 in 2012; other African countries had flatter performance, at 2.97 in 2005 and 3.02 in 2012 (low- and middle-income countries went from 3.29 to 3.32). On both dimensions, graduating African HIPCs significantly outperformed both other African countries and developing countries overall, suggesting that the conditional approach to debt relief may have played a role strengthening policies and institutions.[44]

To summarize, until 2000, debt relief to African countries, mainly under the auspices of the Paris Club with some participation from the London Club (of commercial banks), had failed to get most countries' debt ratios under control. The original HIPC Initiative, created in 1996, got off to a slow start, frustrating African governments, donors, and debt campaigners. When the HIPC Initiative was enhanced in 1999, more than half of Africa's economies qualified. Since then, we have seen a balance sheet transfer of unprecedented magnitude to Africa, which is now being reinforced by natural resource discoveries and an increase in private capital flows to many African economies.

---

[42] Stucka, Merotto, and Thomas (2014).

[43] The CPIA rates countries from one (worst) to six (best) on 16 indicators; historical data are only published as cluster averages.

[44] Nine countries comprised the "control group": Angola, Cape Verde, Eritrea, Kenya, Lesotho, Nigeria, Sudan, Chad, and Zimbabwe. On the other two dimensions (public sector management and structural policies), average progress was weaker overall and there were no discernible differences between graduating HIPCs and other African countries.

9.5 NEVER AGAIN?

Jubilee 2000 has been described as "one of the most successful international, non-governmental movements in history."[45] Yet to those who campaigned throughout the 1990s and saw their efforts culminate in the cancellation of most African debt, the battle is not yet won. In response to a recent Internet post on African debt, a representative of Jubilee called for debt relief for Jamaica, the Philippines, and El Salvador, as well as the monitoring of borrowing by the private sector in low-income countries.[46] How realistic is this? How likely?

Further official debt relief is unlikely for three reasons. The first can be traced to the 2008 financial crisis. Donor governments throughout the West are tightening belts, and overseas development assistance is under as much scrutiny as any other spending.

Related is a waning public appetite for debt relief. Jubilee and others may in this sense be the victims of their own success. With debt relief having wiped the slate nearly clean for more than half of Africa's governments, it is harder to make the case that further relief is a priority.

Debt campaigns have to some extent switched tactic from the pragmatism of the late 1990s to moral arguments. A common concept, adapted from legal origins, is that much developing country external debt is "odious." According to one recent discussion, "in its initial use, the expression 'odious debts' identified those debts that a state or a government had contracted with a view to attaining objectives that were prejudicial to the major interests of the successor state or government or of the local population."[47] This narrow definition covers debts such as those used to finance war or subjugation, which may be repudiated by a successor regime (e.g. the treatment of South Africa's war debts when Great Britain annexed the Transvaal in 1900, after the Boer War). Debt campaigners have expanded the concept, ascribing the epithet to lenders, regimes, and countries and suggesting that odiousness may be inferred when debts finance projects that are "criminal," "unfair," or "ineffective." Some campaigners have applied these concepts in "debt audits" of borrowers (such as Ecuador, which defaulted on two Eurobonds in 2009 citing "illegalities").[48]

Yet despite occasional statements from borrowers justifying defaults, the concept of odious debt has had little traction among African countries. Apart from the legal complexities, African growth strategies rely too much on capital inflows for arguments of odiousness to seem attractive.[49]

The third reason a new round of debt relief is an unlikely prospect—the composition of new debt flows to Africa and the increasing role of the private sector—is the subject of the next section.

---

[45] Roodman (2010).

[46] World Bank website, *Nasikiliza*, October 2012.

[47] Nehru and Thomas (2009).

[48] See Wong (2012).

[49] Nehru and Thomas (2009) emphasize "the likely effects of a legalistic approach to odious debts on development finance… Lenders would be obliged to 'price in' the future possibility that their loans would… be declared odious. The likely effects on the flows of finance to developing countries are not hard to discern."

9.6 THE CHANGING FACE OF
INTERNATIONAL LENDING

Since the 2008 financial crisis, the international economy has interacted powerfully with lightened African balance sheets. The key features have been the "search for yield," created by near zero bond yields in the main industrialized economies, combined with natural resource discoveries across Africa.

Low yields in the OECD have driven global financial flows towards the higher returns of emerging markets. Africa is still considered at the frontier, but some of the larger African economies, such as Nigeria, Angola, Kenya, and Ghana, have seen significant growth in foreign participation in sovereign bond markets, local and Eurobond (Figure 9.2).

At the same time, African mineral finds have multiplied. This fact is not unrelated to debt relief, which was both a cause and a consequence of the economic stability of the past decade in Africa. Stability is a prerequisite of much mineral exploration, which has boomed in post-debt relief Africa. The resulting mineral discoveries in turn attract new investments, many of them debt creating, and an increased appetite in optimistic African borrowers for much-needed transformational projects.

Rising public debt in the presence of rising public revenues from natural resources is a likely sign that a boom is not being well managed. There are other telltale signs to look for to evaluate resource-led expansions. Are contracts published? Are there cautious and counter-cyclical budgetary or fiscal rules in place that effectively govern spending (e.g. using an independently recommended, long-term equilibrium price, as Chile does for copper)? Are any savings set aside in a sovereign wealth fund? Is there a disciplined approach to public investment appraisal, execution, and maintenance? Are audits timely and public? In many of Africa's natural resource-rich economies, the answers to these questions are still in the negative.[50]

Ghana is a powerful example. After comprehensive debt relief under HIPC in 2004 and MDRI in 2006, Ghana's public and publicly guaranteed external debt fell from more than 100% of GDP prior to decision point in 2002 to below 15% after MDRI in 2006. Oil discoveries in the Gulf of Guinea came on line in 2011, boosting GDP growth to above 11% that year, with the promise of greater government revenues to come. By 2013, Ghana's public debt had risen back to 50% of its GDP. But Ghana's new creditors are a very different mix from those that forgave its millennial debt. HIPC reduced Ghana's debt by US$2.2 billion, of which half (US$1.1 billion) came from multilaterals and a further US$830 million from the Paris Club; MDRI lifted another US$3.9 billion. By 2012, nearly half of Ghana's external debt was to Eurobond holders and the Chinese government. In 2013, Ghana issued a new US$1 billion Eurobond.

Given the low likelihood of further official debt relief, attention naturally turns to these new flows. Will the current commercial expansion lead to an "African Brady Plan," thirty plus years after the Latin American original?

---

[50] Giugale (2014).

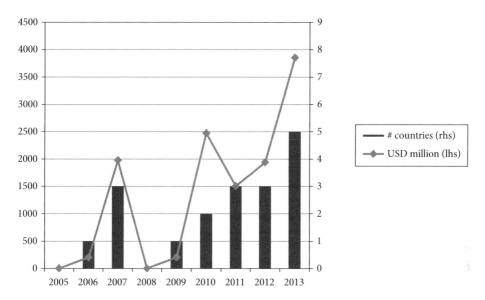

FIGURE 9.2 International sovereign bond issuance by sub-Saharan countries (excluding South Africa).

Source: Dealogic, Bloomberg and Moody's (2013).

9.7 CONCLUSION

The story of Africa's post-colonial debt accumulation, the debate surrounding its inevitable forgiveness, and the transition to the post-HIPC world we are now witnessing is a long and winding road. It is a hundred billion dollar story, the bill paid both by donor governments and—less often acknowledged—by African governments themselves, as likely reduced access to official finance in future.

Beyond this unquantifiable effect on aid flows, which was a concern of early naysayers, other concerns were mostly proven unfounded. In particular, worries that debt relief would discourage private investment into Africa have quickly been left behind. Indeed, the opposite worry, that commercial lenders may "free-ride" on debt relief, now seems more relevant.

Africa's debt build-up was the product of the persistent over-optimism of the official sector, spiked in the 1970s with the self-interest of rich-world export credits and in the 1980s with the well-intentioned lending compulsion of the major multilaterals.

When relief finally arrived, it came as the product of pressure from NGOs from the industrialized nations. Appropriately, it manifested itself as a coordinated effort between the same donor creditors that had driven the original build-up, who leaned on the technical attributes of the Bretton Woods institutions to orchestrate the lenders.

This effort has largely been a success, both as resource transfer and as increased spending on anti-poverty programs in Africa. Success can also be seen in policy terms, as an era of African macroeconomic stability has been reinforced.

Today, Africa's financial challenges are of a different, threefold, nature. Manage expectations from the surge in mineral activities across the continent. Use the money wisely, through effective public investment and stewardship of the macroeconomic effects. Finally, strengthen public debt management, which, despite much attention, remains a complex and largely unmet challenge. The multilaterals' Debt Sustainability Framework funnels grants to the most vulnerable countries. But this leaves unaddressed the financial flows from many bilateral and commercial sources. Every other modern episode of major international capital flows into developing economies has culminated in defaults. There is no obvious reason why Africa should be exempt from this historical regularity.

Twenty-first-century Africa may thus have more to learn from Latin America than from its own recent past. Brazil, Mexico, and others have moved on from past defaults and learned to manage their way in international markets. The increasingly private-sector capital flows to Africa now offer greater freedom from the strictures of multilaterals and the whims of donors, allowing Africa's governments to chart their own course. For any governments that may misjudge the new and unfamiliar financial currents, the solution, years hence, is unlikely to come from donors.

ACKNOWLEDGMENTS

The authors would like to thank Reza Yousefi and Biya Albert for research assistance and H. Marie Werner for able editing.

REFERENCES

Abbas, S.M.A., and Christensen, J.E. (2010). The Role of Domestic Debt Markets in Economic Growth: An Empirical Investigation for Low-Income Countries and Emerging Markets. IMF Staff Paper.

Birdsall, N., and Williamson, J. (2002). Delivering on Debt Relief: From IMF Gold to a New Aid Architecture. Washington, DC: Petersen Institute for International Economics, Chapter 2, p. 13.

Bulow, J., and Rogoff, K. (2005). Grants versus loans for development banks. *American Economic Review*, 95:393–397.

Cassimon, D., and van Campenhout, B. (2008). Comparative fiscal response effects of debt relief. *South African Journal of Economics*, 76(3):427–442.

Chauvin, N.D., and Kraay, A. (2005). What has 100 billion dollars' worth of debt relief done for low-income countries? *International Finance*, EconWPA. http://ssrn.com/abstract=818504.

Crespo Cuaresma, J., and Andronova Vincelette, G. (2009). Debt Relief and Education in Heavily Indebted Poor Countries, in C. Primo Braga and D. Dömeland (eds), *Debt Relief and Beyond*. Washington, DC: World Bank.

Dessy, S.E., and Vencatachellum, D. (2007). Debt relief and social services expenditure: the African experience, 1989-2003. *African Development Review*, 19(1):200.

Easterly, W. (2002). How did heavily indebted poor countries become heavily indebted? Reviewing two decades of debt relief. *World Development*, 30(10):1677–1696.

Gamarra, B., Pollock, M., and Braga, C. (2009). Debt relief to low income countries: a retrospective, in C. Primo Braga and D. Dömeland (eds), *Debt Relief and Beyond*. Washington, DC: World Bank.

Gil Sander, F., Hjört, J., and Thomas, M.R. (2007). When Does Debt Hinder Growth in Low-Income Countries? World Bank Knowledge Brief, February 2007.

Giugale, M.M. (2014). *Development Economics: What Everyone Needs to Know.* New York: Oxford University Press, pp. 24–26.

Gleditsch, N.P., Wallensteen, P., Eriksson, M., Sollenberg, M., and Strand, H. (2002). Armed conflict 1946–2001: a new dataset. *Journal of Peace Research*, 39(5):615–637.

Guder, L.F. (2009). *The Administration of Debt Relief by the International Financial Institutions.* Vol. Bd. 202. New York: Springer.

IMF and World Bank (1999). *Development Committee Report.* Washington, DC: IMF and World Bank.

IMF and World Bank (2005). *HIPC Status of Implementation.* Washington, DC: IMF and World Bank.

IMF and World Bank (2012). *Revisiting the Debt Sustainability Framework for Low-Income Countries.* Washington, DC: IMF and World Bank.

IMF and World Bank (2013a). *Heavily Indebted Poor Countries Initiative and Multilateral Debt Relief Initiative Statistical Update.* Washington, DC: IMF and World Bank.

IMF and World Bank (2013b). *HIPC Initiative and MDRI Statistical Update.* Washington, DC: IMF and World Bank.

Kraay, A., and Nehru, V. (2006). When is external debt sustainable? *World Bank Economic Review*, 20(3):341–365.

Nehru, V., and Thomas, M.R. (2009). The concept of odious debt: some considerations, in C. Primo Braga and D. Dömeland (eds), *Debt Relief and Beyond.* Washington, DC: World Bank.

Nigeria, Federal Republic of Nigeria (2005). *Nigeria's Debt Relief Deal with the Paris Club.* Abuja: Debt Management Office.

Raddatz, C. (2009). Multilateral Debt Relief through the Eyes of Financial Markets, World Bank Policy Research Paper 4872.

Roodman, D. (2010). *The Arc of the Jubilee.* Washington, DC: Center for Global Development.

Sappington, D. (1983). Limited liability contracts between principal and agent. *Journal of Economic Theory*, 29(1):1–21.

Stucka, T., Merotto, D., and Thomas, M.R. (2014). *African Debt: How Clean is the Slate?* Washington, DC: World Bank.

Svendsen, K.E. (1987). *The Failure of the International Debt Strategy*, Vol. 13. Copenhagen: Centre for Development Research.

Wong, Y. (2012). *Sovereign Finance and the Poverty of Nations: Odious Debt in International Law.* Cheltenham: Edward Elgar, pp. 93–97.

World Bank (1986). *World Development Report, 1986.* Washington, DC: World Bank.

World Bank, IDA Board document M96-927, The HIPC Debt Initiative—Elaboration of Key Features and Possible Procedural Steps, August 16, 1996.

Young, A. (2012). The African growth miracle. *Journal of Political Economy*, 120(4):696–739.

CHAPTER 10

··

SAVINGS, CAPITAL FLIGHT, AND AFRICAN DEVELOPMENT

··

LÉONCE NDIKUMANA

10.1 INTRODUCTION

AT the turn of the century Africa's story had changed, from that of hopelessness to exuberance in the face of yet another African renaissance. Growth surged in the continent, even weathering the storm of the Great Recession of 2008–2009, with Africa emerging as the second fastest growing region in the world after Asia. Despite this growth resurgence, however, concerns remain. The most fundamental concern is that growth has not been accompanied by commensurate reduction in poverty. Moreover, it has been characterized by high inequality, and generally it has not been broad based. From a long-term perspective the question is whether this recent growth resurgence is sustainable. In particular, the issue is whether the saving rates are sufficient to support high and sustained growth and development.

Historically, countries that have achieved and sustained high growth rates are those that were able to maintain high domestic saving rates, enabling strong and sustained domestic investment and employment creation. In the case of African countries, domestic saving has remained low, leading to high investment-saving gaps and increased dependence on external capital. A key reason is the inadequate performance in domestic saving mobilization in the public sector and in the private sector. But a factor that has been often overlooked is the leakage of resources through capital flight. The financial hemorrhage of the continent is both a chronic problem and a looming crisis. The levels of capital flight have exploded over the past decade. Thus, efforts to build a solid base for long-term growth and development in Africa must involve strategies to improve efficiency in public and private domestic resource mobilization as well as policies to curb and prevent further capital flight from the continent. This chapter aims to explore these issues with both a look in the rear-view mirror and a forward-looking examination of the saving-capital flight-development nexus.

The chapter discusses the record of domestic saving in Africa from a historical and comparative perspective, and it identifies the causes of low performance in saving mobilization. This is followed by an analysis of the linkages between capital flight and domestic saving. Here the nature, magnitude and trends of capital flight are presented with illustrative statistics. Next the chapter reviews the drivers of capital flight so as to inform the discussion of strategies to stem capital flight as a means to increase domestic saving. The chapter offers some policy recommendations for raising saving and preventing capital flight which revolve around two sets of strategies—incentives-based and institutions-based strategies. It concludes that emphasis should primarily be on the latter.

10.2 Saving and Development in Africa

10.2.1 Why care about saving?

10.2.1.1 Saving as a condition for growth

There is a long tradition in the economics literature that views saving as an indispensable condition and driver of economic prosperity. Sir Arthur Lewis believed that the main challenge to the analysis of economic development was to understand how an initially low-saving economy can transform into an economy with high voluntary saving rates (Lewis 1954). In the same tradition, economic growth models have been developed on the premise that saving is the main source of capital accumulation, which in turn is the main driver of long run growth. This is the basis of the standard growth model developed by Robert Solow and subsequently expanded by his successors.

Modern literature on African economic development has embraced this view that saving is necessary for long-run economic growth. A study on savings in South Africa opens with the statement that "low domestic saving rates in South Africa may perpetuate a low-growth trap" (Aron and Muellbauer 2000, abstract). Reform policies aimed at stimulating growth such as the structural adjustment programs (SAPs) of the 1980s and 1990s were also founded on the premise that raising domestic saving would ignite growth. Thus financial market liberalization, and especially the removal of interest rate repression, was expected to raise real interest rates, which in turn would raise domestic saving and therefore growth.

The empirical evidence on the link between growth and saving is mixed at best. The evidence clearly supports a positive relationship running from saving to growth in the short run. In both cross-country settings as well as country-level analyses, higher levels of saving appear to lead to higher rates of economic growth (Elbadawi and Mwega 2000). In addition, the evidence shows that, in the spirit of Sir Arthur Lewis, episodes of transition to higher saving precede short-run spurs in gross domestic product (GDP) growth (Rodrik 2000). Studies that confirm this relationship in the case of African countries include Elbadawi and Mwega (2000). Further evidence on Africa and other regions can be found in Loayza, Schmidt-Hebbel, and Servén (2000). The relationship between saving and growth is, however, less robust in the long run. While studies find a positive relationship between the level of saving and long-run GDP growth, there appears to be no evidence that transitions to higher saving rates lead to permanently higher growth rates. A spur in saving leads to an initial increase in growth, but the growth rates return to pre-transition levels after a short period (Rodrik 2000). This finding is consistent with the classical Solow growth model, where increases in savings rates raise growth only during a transitory period but have no effects on the growth rate in the steady state in the absence of an increase in productivity or growth of the labor force.

The reverse causal relationship seems to be more robust: a spurt in growth permanently raises saving to higher rates. This may be due to consumption and saving habit formation, which tend to be persistent over time. The evidence on a positive long-run impact of growth on saving and a short-term positive relationship running from saving to growth has important policy implications. On the one hand, the evidence suggests the possibility of a virtuous cycle of high growth–high saving as well as a low saving–low growth trap. On the other hand, the evidence suggests that policies that directly target to raise the growth rate are also good for raising the saving rate. Thus, countries that invest in infrastructure to raise productive capacity and alleviate production constraints, allocate resources to technology and innovation, invest in human capital development, and make deliberate interventions to raise agricultural productivity will achieve higher growth rates accompanied by higher saving rates. Higher growth rates and higher saving rates are mutually perpetuating over time; thus while saving appears as a key to economic prosperity, in fact it is the latter that enables the saving-growth relationship to materialize in the first place and to be sustained over time.

10.2.1.2 *Saving as a condition for investment*

Investment is a critical condition for economic growth. In fact empirical evidence has established that investment is the most robust driver of long-run growth (Levine and Renelt 1992). It is for this reason that investment is at the centre of all growth policies and development strategies in general. It is also for this reason that it is important to understand the relationship between saving and investment.

Conventional wisdom regards saving as the main means of financing investment. From a purely national accounting perspective, the relationship between saving and investment is obvious. Saving is determined as income not consumed, which therefore is allocated to investment. But from a theoretical perspective, the key justification of the relationship between saving and investment is based on market imperfections. At the microeconomic level, imperfections in the credit markets—such as those arising from information asymmetries—force firms to rely on their internal funds (saving) to finance investment. At the aggregate level, the link between saving and investment arises from imperfections in capital mobility (Feldstein and Horioka 1980). If capital is freely mobile across countries, then there would be no relationship between domestic investment and domestic saving. Any good investment at home would be funded by either domestic saving or foreign capital. A tight relationship between saving and investment is an indication of restrictions in international capital flows. In light of these theoretical predictions, the link between domestic saving and investment should be strong in the case of African countries, especially in sub-Saharan Africa given underdeveloped financial markets and high perceived country risk, which makes it difficult for African firms to access international capital markets.

It is difficult to find systematic empirical evidence of a strong positive relationship between saving and investment in the case of African countries especially at the aggregate level. Elbadawi and Mwega (2000) examined whether saving leads investment in sub-Saharan Africa. They find no supporting evidence either in the short run or in the long run. However, the evidence from this and similar aggregate data-based studies is not sufficient to dismiss a link between saving and investment in Africa. Studies based on firm level data find that firms finance their investment primarily with internal funds, suggesting the existence of binding constraints to access to credit markets. In addition, empirical studies find that there is a strong positive effect of financial development on domestic investment (Ndikumana 2000).[1] This constitutes indirect evidence of the importance of domestic saving for investment. Indeed, the role of financial intermediaries is to collect savings from surplus agents (savers) and channel it to deficit agents (investors). Hence, the relationship between saving and investment relies critically on sufficient amount of savings on the one hand, and on the efficacy of financial intermediation.

There may be other reasons why studies searching for a direct relationship between saving and investment fail to find supportive evidence in the case of African countries. The first is that, as indicated above, financial intermediation may not be effectively and efficiently channeling saving into investment.[2] This is consistent with Keynes' view that investment is not constrained by saving but by credit supply: "The investment market can be congested through shortage of cash. It can never be congested through shortage of saving" (Keynes 1973: 222). This would be consistent with the positive links between investment and financial development.[3]

The second is that there are non-financial factors that constitute binding constraints to domestic investment in African countries. These include physical constraints such as low supply and poor quality of infrastructure especially power and transportation, long distance to input and output markets especially for landlocked countries, soft infrastructure (regulation), governance, and political instability. From an analytical perspective, this implies that empirical tests that focus on the direct link between domestic saving and domestic investment may be inconclusive without overruling the existence of a positive relationship between the two variables. From a policy perspective, it implies that strategies for promoting domestic investment should not be limited to stimulating domestic savings; the other non-financial factors of investment must be addressed simultaneously through appropriate interventions and reforms.

10.2.1.3 *Saving as hedge against shocks*

Saving plays an important role as a hedge against shocks both at the microeconomic and aggregate level. At the household level, savings enable households to smooth consumption over time and shield expenditures against shocks to income. This is especially important for rural and agriculture dependent households whose income is subject to the vagaries of the weather and other natural disasters. Uncertainty over income is also due to the unpredictability of market prices for agricultural products. This affects both the consumption and borrowing capacity of farming households (see Karlan, Kutsoati, McMillan, and Udry 2011).

---

[1] A substantial number of studies on other regions document robust evidence of a positive link between saving and domestic investment. See Ndikumana (2005) and Ndikumana (2000) for a survey and useful references on this subject.

[2] For an illustration with the case study on the financial sector in Burundi, see Nkurunziza, Ndikumana, and Nyamoya (2012).

[3] Also see Pollin (1997) and Berthélémy and Varoudakis (1994).

At the aggregate level, domestic saving serves as a buffer against shocks to international capital inflows. It is important for preventing financial crises or minimizing their impact on the domestic economy. However, high domestic saving does not constitute full proof protection against financial crises. This was demonstrated in the case of East Asian countries which suffered severe financial crisis in 1997–1998 despite high levels of domestic savings. The high saving rates did not protect them from the consequences of high exposure to excessive foreign currency denominated borrowing by banks.

In the case of African countries, low domestic saving expose them to risks associated with high dependence on foreign resources, especially official development assistance. Following sudden declines in official aid and private capital inflows, African economies may experience difficulties in sustaining their levels of investment, especially public investment.

10.2.2 The record on domestic saving in Africa

10.2.2.1 Aggregate trends and patterns

As in other developing countries, domestic saving rates are generally low in African countries, resulting in chronic investment–saving gaps (Table 10.1). For sub-Saharan Africa, the average gross domestic saving ratio to GDP declined from 22.8% in the 1970s to 20% in the 1980s and plummeted to 15.5% in the 1990s before recovering thereafter. There are important cross-country variations in domestic saving. The most pronounced differences are between oil and mineral resource rich and resource-scarce countries. The former generally exhibit higher levels of saving thanks commodity booms.

In the majority of African countries, domestic saving rates steadily declined starting from the mid-1970s. This declining trend was mostly driven by a decline in public sector saving, which was not compensated by private saving. The case of South Africa is illustrated in Figure. 10.1. In fact, public saving and corporate sector saving moved in opposite direction systematically since the early 1980s. A recent spur in corporate saving in the second half of the 2000s corresponds with a plunge of government saving in the same period. Household savings have systematically declined since the mid-1980s.

The low values of recorded saving rates in Africa do not adequately represent the true levels of saving especially in the informal sector. The majority of households hold their saving in the form of non-financial assets such as land and cattle, which are not recorded in the national accounts. The low banking penetration in the rural areas and the generally low access to formal financial services is also another contributor to both low saving mobilization and high informality of saving. On average, less than 20% of the population has access to formal banking services. Moreover, African banking systems offer only a limited range of saving instruments. For example, pension systems and other long-term saving mechanisms are non-existent or underdeveloped. This is one of the reasons why financial resources in African systems are concentrated on the short end, exhibiting ineffective maturity transformation and hindering the financing of long-term investment. Furthermore, banking services are costly and use cumbersome practices; this discourages potential depositors, especially among the non-financially literate population. So, to a large extent, statements about low levels of saving in African economies are in fact statements of low mobilization of potential saving and inadequate reporting of non-financial forms of saving.

Table 10.1 Saving and investment: Africa and other developing countries

	Africa			Sub-Saharan Africa (SSA)			Oil-rich Africa			Mineral-rich Africa			Non-African developing countries		
	1980–89	1990–99	2000–12	1980–89	1990–99	2000–12	1980–89	1990–99	2000–12	1980–89	1990–99	2000–12	1980–89	1990–99	2000–12
Gross domestic investment (% GDP)*	24.3	19.7	21.5	20.8	17.6	19.4	22.5	22.1	24.2	18.2	17.9	20.6	25.2	24.2	24.3
Gross domestic savings (% GDP)	20.1	17.2	21.0	20.0	15.5	16.3	20.5	19.8	33.4	10.2	10.7	11.8	15.6	15.3	15.4
Investment–saving gap (% of GDP)	4.2	2.5	0.5	0.8	2.1	3.1	2.0	2.3	-9.2	8.1	7.2	8.9	9.6	8.9	8.9
GDP Growth (%)	2.9	2.5	4.5	2.1	2.1	4.6	3.3	3.1	5.6	2.7	2.6	4.1	3.0	3.1	4.5
GDP per capita growth (%)	0.1	0.01	2.2	-0.7	-0.6	2.1	0.3	0.4	3.1	-0.2	-0.2	1.7	1.0	1.5	3.2

* gross domestic investment = gross capital formation.
Source: World Bank, World Development Indicators; African Development Indicators (for SSA and Africa averages).

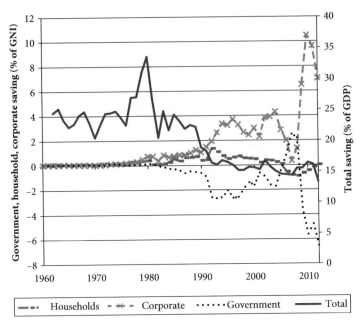

FIGURE 10.1 Trend in saving rates in South Africa, 1960–2012.

10.2.2.2 *Evaluation of economic policies for promoting domestic saving*

African countries have adopted a number of initiatives and policy reforms to stimulate domestic saving with mitigated results. As indicated earlier, one of the key objectives of the market-based reforms of the 1980s and 1990s under the SAPs was to stimulate domestic investment. This was meant to be achieved by financial sector reforms aimed at raising real interest rates to encourage domestic saving and attract foreign capital. Fiscal austerity measures under the SAP were also expected to raise public sector saving or at least to reduce the deficits. Moreover, to the extent that these policies were to create a stable macroeconomic environment, this was supposed to increase growth, which would raise domestic saving. The results of these market-based reforms were less than satisfactory. First reforms failed to raise real interest rates substantially. And even when interest rates rose, the saving response was small.

Many African countries also adopted government-sponsored saving programs to stimulate domestic savings. These included mandatory saving in the civil service as well as the creation of public saving and loan institutions targeting a wide penetration in both the urban and rural areas. The record of these initiatives has been mixed, but largely disappointing. Many of the public or publicly sponsored institutions were victim of mismanagement and political patronage that undermined their financial viability. Bad experiences with these institutions has left a sour taste about government-owned or sponsored financial institutions. This negative perception has extended to development banks. This is a rather unfortunate outcome arising from the conflation of the concept of development banking with negative experiences in poorly managed national development banks. Yet, development banks can run efficiently and have a major positive impact on domestic investment and growth. An example is the Industrial Development

Corporation, a government owned development bank in South Africa, which has been a major player in financing both public and private investment (Ndikumana 2009). A successful strategy for financial system development must aim at improving the functioning of both commercial financial institutions and development financing oriented public institutions.

10.2.2.3 *Saving and sustainable growth*

The low saving record in African countries raises a critical question about prospects for sustainable growth and development in the continent. As discussed and documented in the literature, history shows that countries that have achieved high growth rates on a consistent basis have done so by maintaining high levels of savings for extended periods. The question then is whether African countries can achieve and sustain high growth rates without achieving and maintaining high saving rates. A growth model without saving is difficult to conceptualize. To the extent that growth is substantially driven by capital accumulation, expansion of production capacity, increased competitiveness, and access to markets, it is difficult to imagine how that can be achieved without a strong domestic resources base. High growth without a strong saving base is likely to be ephemeral. And more fundamentally, a development agenda that is not founded on a country's own domestic resources is a compromised agenda. Therefore, we conclude that there is no viable option for Africa to achieve sustainable growth and development without strong domestic saving.

10.3 SAVING AND CAPITAL FLIGHT IN AFRICA

10.3.1 What is capital flight and why do we care?

10.3.1.1 *Defining capital flight*

The term capital flight has been given many interpretations in the economic literature and in the press, leading to confusion and misinterpretations. In the popular press, capital flight is presented as illegal or illicit financial flows. It is housed in the same domain as money laundering, tax evasion, transfer pricing, underground trafficking. Yet, while these activities are illicit, not all of them amount to capital flight. At the same time, while most capital flight may be deemed illicit,[4] it is not possible to make this determination a priori from the data that are used to calculate capital flight, which involves a reconciliation of recorded capital inflows (mainly external borrowing and foreign direct investment) and the use of these resources (to cover the current account deficit and accumulation of reserves).

---

[4] Capital flight may be illicit in one of three ways: when it consists of money acquired illegally and transferred abroad; when funds are transferred abroad illicitly by violating capital account regulations; when capital is hidden abroad and therefore not being subject to taxation and other government regulations.

The term capital flight means capital flows from a country that are not recorded in the country's Balance of Payments (BoP). If all the transactions were correctly and systematically recorded, inflows would balance out with outflows, except for small and random statistical errors as recorded in the "net errors and omissions" line of the BoP. Where large discrepancies are observed, in other words, where there is substantial "missing money" in the BoP, this is taken as an indication of the presence of capital flight. The methodology for the estimation of capital flight is detailed in Ndikumana and Boyce (2010) and Ndikumana, Boyce, and Ndiaye (2015). This methodology is summarized in the flowing equation:

$$ADJKF_{it} = \Delta DEBTADJ_{it} + DFI_{it} - \left(CA_{it} + CRES_{it}\right) + MISINV_{it} + RID_{it} \tag{1}$$

where ADJKF is adjusted capital flight,[5] $\Delta DEBTADJ$ is the change in the stock of external debt outstanding adjusted for exchange rate fluctuations, DFI is net direct foreign investment, CA is the current account deficit, $CRES$ is net additions to the stock of foreign reserves, $MISINV$ is total trade misinvoicing, and RID is the adjustment for underreported remittances.

Measuring illicit financial flows is an even more daunting task than estimating capital flight. While capital flight involves outflows that are not recorded and therefore can be estimated by comparing recorded foreign exchange inflows and their uses, some illicit financial flows are actually within the recorded outflows, except that it is not possible to distinguish them from licit flows. Thus money that is acquired illicitly, for example, through trade of illegal goods such as narcotics, can enter into the domestic banking system and from there be transferred abroad for safe keeping. On its way out of the country, such money looks like any other money, and is duly recorded in the BoP. It is therefore not capital flight, but it is nonetheless illicit.

Capital flight and other illicit financial flows from Africa and other developing countries are facilitated by the services offered by the so-called secrecy jurisdictions, safe havens, tax havens, and offshore financial centers. These territories offer a combination of low or no tax on corporate profit and interest income, high banking secrecy, as well as easy and opaque company incorporation laws that are attractive to owners of both honest and illicit wealth. For owners of legally acquired wealth, these territories offer opportunities to minimize their tax liabilities and are therefore sought for what can be justified on the ground of portfolio management. But these centers are also sought for illicit purposes. They help owners of illicitly acquired wealth to conceal it and therefore avoid prosecution.

10.3.1.2 *Magnitude and trends of capital flight*

The evidence in the literature clearly shows that capital flight is a major development issue facing the majority of African countries. The problem is not new, and it is getting worse over time. The existing estimates suggest that over the past decades since 1970, the continent has

---

[5] The qualifier "adjusted" comes from the fact that this formula is an extension of the basic definition of capital flight as a Balance of Payments "residual" proposed by the World Bank (1985), which is calculated as $KF_{it} = \Delta DEBT_{it} + DFI_{it} - \left(CA_{it} + CRES_{it}\right)$., where $\Delta DEBT$ is the change in debt stock without adjustment for exchange rate fluctuations

lost over one trillion dollars due to capital flight (African Development Bank and Global Financial Integrity 2013; Boyce and Ndikumana 2012; Ndikumana and Boyce 2011a, 2012; Ndikumana et al. 2015). In addition to leakages of resources in the Balance of payments, including embezzlement of public external debt, a major channel of capital flight is trade misinvoicing, both underinvoicing of exports and overinvoicing of imports. Resource-rich countries, especially oil exporters feature prominently on the top of the list in terms of volume of capital flight: Nigeria, Angola, Gabon, Congo, the Democratic Republic of Congo and Sudan. In addition to high resource endowment, these high capital flight countries also happen to have a poor governance record. It therefore appears that capital flight is not driven by resource endowment per se, but by a combination of natural resource wealth and poor governance.

Capital flight from African countries is large both in absolute terms as well as in relation to the size of the economies and compared to other financial flows. For the continent as a whole and for most of the countries, the accumulated stock of capital flight exceeds the stock of debt, ironically making the continent a "net creditor" to the rest of the world. While the absolute value of capital flight from Africa may be smaller than that from other regions (Henry 2012), capital flight represents a heavier drain on the economy in the case of African countries. African countries exhibit higher ratios of capital flight in relation to GDP, domestic capital accumulation, foreign direct investment and official development. The annual flows of capital flight also represents a large share of the investment gap faced by African countries, suggesting that these countries could partly bridge this gap if they could retain these funds on the continent.

10.3.1.3 Causes of capital flight

So what drives capital flight from African countries? Some have argued that capital flight is not different than other financial flows and that it can be explained by the same factors that drive portfolio allocation decisions by economic agents (Collier, Hoeffler, and Pattillo 2001; Collier, Hoeffler, and Pattillo 2004). Under this view, capital flight from Africa is motivated by the search for higher risk-adjusted returns to investment.

A simple conceptual framework for that view can be sketched as follows. Consider that private operators maximize returns to savings by choosing between domestic investment and foreign assets. In a simple two-period model, individuals maximize their well-being or utility subject to the following constraints (Fofack and Ndikumana 2009):

$$C_t + I_t + F_t = W_t \tag{2}$$

$$C_{t+1} = I_t(1 + r(1 - \tau)) + F_t(1 + \rho) \tag{3}$$

C is consumption, I domestic investment, F foreign assets (or capital flight), W wealth, r the rate of return on domestic capital, ρ the rate of return on foreign capital, and τ the tax rate. The two equations can be consolidated as:

$$c_t + \frac{1}{1+r}c_{t+1} = W_t + \frac{\rho - r}{1+r}F_t - \frac{r\tau}{1+r}I_t \tag{4}$$

Equation (4) suggests that return differentials in favor of foreign assets as well as distortionary taxation of domestic assets induce capital flight. In addition, capital flight induces more capital flight due to the returns it generates through interest earnings.

The portfolio choice view of capital flight contends that poor economic conditions, high political instability, and poor governance in African countries raise the risk of investment and therefore reduce the expected returns to investment in Africa relative to investment abroad. In particular, it is argued that domestic assets may face higher risk arising from currency depreciation, devaluation, inflation, and financial instability (Dornbusch 1985), risk of expropriation (Kant 2002; Khan and Haque 1985), expectations of higher taxation, and lower public guarantees on private debts (Eaton 1987). In that sense, capital flight would be just about savvy African wealth holders seeking higher returns to their investments abroad. It would also be about African wealth holders voting with their feet to somehow penalize governments for bad governance that threatens their wealth.

The view of capital flight as portfolio choice is questionable on conceptual and empirical grounds. First the argument about the portfolio management motive can only hold for honestly acquired capital. But capital flight includes funds that were illicitly acquired which the owners seek to conceal abroad. In such case asset holders are more interested in the protection of the assets than in the returns to investments. In that perspective, safe havens offer a perfect venue to pack these funds. In these jurisdictions, asset holders often receive negative interest rates on their deposits, "a premium for security" they are happily willing to accept (Australian banker Erhard Fürst quoted in Lessard and Williamson 1987: 83). As Walter (1987: 107) pointed out "If confidentiality has value, then asset holders engaging in capital flight should be willing to pay for it." Confidentiality is the primary motive for holding stolen assets in secrecy jurisdictions.

Empirical evidence also has little to offer in support of the portfolio theory view of capital flight. Actual risk-adjusted returns to investment tend to be higher in African countries than in the rest of the world. This has been more so in the recent years as the developed world plunged in a recession while African countries weathered the storm surprisingly well. Yet, capital flight has continued to increase during the economic expansion over the past two decades. Moreover, capital flight has not abated during and following financial liberalization. In fact, the era of financial liberalization since mid-1995 has seen an escalation of capital flight.

Furthermore, if risk and returns calculations were the main drivers of capital flight from Africa, how then can we explain movement of capital in both directions? If savvy African investors are unwilling to invest in Africa, why would equally savvy foreign investors find it worthy investing in the continent? There must be something that the African wealth holders know that foreign investors don't. But most likely, the reverse home bias is an indication that African wealth holders have something to hide.

The empirical literature has documented a number of factors that consistently appear to be robust determinants of capital flight. First, capital flight tends to persist and exhibit hysteresis. In other words, countries seem to be caught in a capital flight trap (Ndikumana and Boyce 2003, 2011b; Ndikumana et al. 2015). The evidence suggests that these countries must undertake robust and systematic measures to "shock" the system out of its proneness to capital flight. The second key result from empirical analysis is a tight positive relationship between capital flight and external borrowing, suggesting that part of capital flight from

Africa is funded by embezzlement of public debt. This implies that some of the external debt is in fact odious in that it did not benefit the African people (Ndikumana and Boyce 2011a). Third, as mentioned above, the evidence shows that African countries that are both rich in natural resources and have poor governance exhibit higher levels of capital flight. This suggests that capital flight may be fuelled by embezzlement of the proceeds of resource exports and corrupt management of natural resource exploitation as well as illicit behavior by multinational corporations operating in the sector. Fourth, conventional measures of risk and returns to investment do not correlate systematically with capital flight. This implies that high real interest rates are not a deterrent to capital flight. Thus policies aimed at raising interest rates notably as a means of controlling inflation, which is the prominent policy orientation in most African countries, have little chance of preventing capital flight. In contrast, by keeping interests high, such a policy orientation discourages domestic investment (Fofack and Ndikumana 2015). Thus addressing capital flight requires a strategy that goes beyond market-based policies.

10.3.1.4 Impact of capital flight

Capital flight is a serious development problem in Africa for several reasons. First, capital flight has negative effects on the economy by reducing government revenue directly through embezzlement of public resources and indirectly through the reduction of the tax base. This can be illustrated by formulating the government budget constraint as follows:

$$G_t + (1+r)B_{t-1} = \tau(Y_t - F_t) + R_t + \Delta B_t + \Delta M_t \tag{5}$$

where G is government expenditure, B government borrowing, Y is gross income, R government revenue from sources other than taxes on domestic assets, and ΔM seigniorage or money creation. Capital flight (F) affects the government's budget by directly reducing the tax base. Each dollar of capital flight implies a revenue loss to the government of τF. As a result the government must borrow more (domestically and from abroad, ΔB, or resort more to money creation (ΔM). These pressures on the government budget erode the government's capacity to finance social services and public investment. By draining domestic resources, capital flight perpetuates dependence on external aid even as it undermines aid effectiveness.

Second, by draining government resources, capital flight retards progress in poverty reduction. Further negative effects on poverty reduction arise through the negative effects of capital flight on growth. In addition, by widening inequality, capital flight further reduces the gains from growth in poverty reduction. Moreover, as a result of these perverse effects on government revenue, domestic investment, and growth, capital flight constrains employment creation and undermines public service delivery including education, health and sanitation, which in turn increases poverty. While the literature on the quantitative impact of capital flight on African economies is still thin, the evidence in the few existing studies is quite powerful. It shows that if African countries had been able to invest flight capital domestically, all of them would have accelerated their progress to reaching the objective of halving poverty by 2015 (MDG goal 1), and the goal would be reached in a good number of countries which otherwise would not have been able to do so (AfDB, OECD, UNECA, and UNDP 2012; Nkurunziza 2012, 2015). There are also indirect effects of capital flight arising from the payment of external debt that fuelled it. These effects especially materialize through reduced provision of public services such as health, resulting in increased infant mortality (Ndikumana and Boyce 2011a) and other negative health effects.

Third, even as capital flight is partly caused by bad governance, there are also important negative effects in the reverse direction. Capital flight weakens governance as the perpetrators of capital flight manipulate the regulatory and judiciary systems to shield their illicit transactions and facilitate further capital flight. Governance breakdown is perpetuated and exacerbated by contagion and habit formation effects of capital flight; this partly explains the persistence of capital flight over time (Ndikumana and Boyce 2003).

Finally, capital flight has important distributional and equity implications. The holders of capital flight who are also guilty of tax evasion incur a relatively smaller tax burden than the poor who do not have the opportunity to conceal their wealth in safe havens. As a result, the middle class and the poor effectively subsidize consumption of public services by the rich. As the rich accumulate wealth that is tax shielded, the middle class and the poor incur the full burden of taxation and at the same time are deprived of public services due to lower tax collection. This increases income inequality. Inequality is also increased through exchange rate effects. This is because capital flight holders are shielded against losses due currency depreciation while the poor and middle class who hold all their wealth domestically bear the full cost of depreciation.

10.3.2 How does capital flight affect domestic saving?

Capital flight may be one of the causes of low domestic saving in African countries for a number of reasons. The first is a direct effect through allocation of private wealth in foreign assets as opposed to holding domestic assets. This can be illustrated by using equation (2) where saving is substituted for investment and rearranging as follows:

$$S_t = W_t - C_t - F_t \qquad (6)$$

where S is saving and all other variables are defined as earlier. As can be seen in this equation, capital flight directly drains private saving. In a similar fashion equation (5) can be rearranged to show that capital flight reduces government saving by reducing tax revenue as a result of the reduction of the tax base (private wealth held domestically).

Capital flight also affects saving indirectly through its effects on domestic investment and growth. By depressing capital accumulation, growth is retarded as capital flight increases. As a result, lower growth leads to lower investment as discussed earlier.

10.3.3 Preventing capital flight as a saving strategy

The foregoing discussion provides some insights on ways to stimulate saving. In particular, this chapter posits that fighting capital flight is an essential element of the strategy to stimulate domestic saving in Africa. In this regard, the discussion in this section is organized around two sets of strategies: incentive-based strategies, and institutions-based strategies for both fighting capital flight and stimulating domestic saving.

10.3.3.1 Incentive-based strategies

Following the discussion on the motivation and drivers of capital flight, strategies to reduce capital flight as a way of raising domestic savings incorporate two important premises. First, to some extent, capital flight may be induced or influenced by risk and returns to investment, broadly defined to include considerations for security of assets with regard to extortion, expropriation, or any other politically motivated risks. In this case, wealth holders prefer foreign assets over domestic assets if the risk-adjusted returns on domestic investment are lower than exchange rate adjusted interest rates abroad. Second, capital flight is also motivated by either taxation evasion or tax avoidance, or fear of prosecution of financial crime in the case of stolen money, fraud, money laundering, illicit trafficking, and other crimes that generate dirty capital.

These two considerations can be summarized in the following simple set-up. Consider that wealth holders choose between domestic and foreign assets so as to maximize their expected returns. Leaving aside normal recorded outward investment flows to focus on capital flight, the decision can be formally represented as follow (Fofack and Ndikumana 2015):

$$\max_F R = i_f F + i_d \left(W - F \right) - h(F) \tag{7}$$

where F is capital flight, i_f is foreign interest rate (adjusted for expected exchange rate appreciation/depreciation), i_d domestic interest rate, W is total wealth, and $h(F)$ represents the cost of transferring capital abroad, which here we assume to depend on the volume of capital flight; that is, $h(F) = \rho(F).F$ where $\rho(F)$ the unit cost function.

The first-order condition is:

$$\frac{\delta R}{\delta F} = \left(i_f - i_d \right) - \left(\rho + F.\rho_F \right) = 0 \tag{8}$$

which is solved to yield the following

$$i_f - i_d = \rho + F.\rho_F \tag{9}$$

This result implies that the "optimal" allocation of wealth between domestic and foreign assets is reached when the interest rate differential is equal to the marginal cost of capital smuggling. The nature of the cost function is such that the unit cost varies with the volume of capital flight. Capital flight operators "learn by doing" in the practice of smuggling capital abroad. Over time, they acquire skills and establish networks which help them circumvent regulations with impunity. In other words, there is "habit formation" in capital flight (Ndikumana and Boyce 2003). For these reasons, the unit cost of transferring funds abroad declines as capital flight increases; that is $\rho_F < 0$.

In addition to the volume of capital flight, other factors that affect the marginal cost of transferring funds abroad are elements associated with the regulatory environment and the legal system. In particular, financial liberalization, capital account liberalization, and full currency convertibility can make it easier to move money across borders. In contrast, an efficient legal system makes capital flight more costly.

From this analysis, it follows that strategies aimed at discouraging capital flight as a means of stimulating domestic saving should take into consideration agents' incentives regarding the allocation of wealth between domestic and foreign assets. Traditionally, policies have focused on raising the real interest rates and removing market distortions to reduce the difference between the foreign return and the domestic return to investment in favor of the latter. But these policies have not been successful as saving does not respond strongly to market interest rates. It is nevertheless important to pay attention to non-interest rate factors that may encourage saving. In this context expanding the range of saving instruments through the deepening of financial markets and especially the creation of long-term instruments such as pension funds and other retirement instruments are an important avenue to explore.

10.3.3.2 *Institutions-based strategies*

The model in equations (7–9) implies that capital flight may be reduced, and thus saving increased by raising the cost of smuggling capital out of the country. This is where institutions-based strategies come into play. Capital flight is perpetuated when predicate crimes that generate illicit wealth and illicit international transfer of funds are not properly prosecuted and penalized. Therefore, the first area of focus in an institutions-based strategy aimed at preventing capital flight and raising domestic saving is to end impunity of financial crime. Such strategy involves reforms and strengthening of the regulatory framework and the legal system. This requires reforms that are accompanied by adequate investments in human capacity building in regulatory authorities and the legal systems in the areas of financial and economic intelligence, investigation, prosecution, and deterrence of financial crime. In addition to strengthening regulatory and legal systems, it is also important to ensure their political independence to enable them to properly investigate and prosecute financial crime. This is especially important because the perpetrators of capital flight often include government officials as well as politically connected domestic and foreign private actors. Thus there is a high risk of obstruction of financial crime investigation by politically influential actors that have something to hide.

Given that capital flight involves a shared responsibility between agents in African countries and their counterparts in destination territories including safe havens, successfully combating capital flight requires close cooperation between African countries and international community. African countries can also leverage legislations and conventions in developed countries and international institutions that are aimed at combatting financial crime and corporate sector corruption (see Ndikumana 2013). African countries will also need financial support from their development partners to invest in capacity building and acquire the necessary infrastructure to establish strong anti-financial crime institutions. Making progress in preventing capital flight will naturally yield positive benefits in terms of increased domestic saving.

10.4 CONCLUSION

There is no doubt that the landscape of African economies has changed since the turn of the century, especially marked by improved macroeconomic performance in terms of growth and macroeconomic stability. In that sense, Africa is indeed a changed continent from three decades ago. In this regard, African economies offer a fertile ground for economic analysis in the coming years. In the context of the analysis of the linkages between saving, capital flight and development undertaken in this chapter three interesting questions emerge. The first is whether the growth resurgence in Africa is evidence of saving-led growth and whether it is sustainable. Evidence shows that the rise in saving rates during the growth acceleration is concentrated among oil-rich countries. These countries have also grown faster than resource-poor countries. However, while oil-rich countries recorded rising saving rates, their investment rates did not rise proportionately. This raises concerns about the sustainability of the growth momentum in the medium term.

The second question then is what does it take to translate rising domestic savings into rising domestic investment. The issue is not solely a matter of efficiency of financial intermediation. It also has to do with the nature and source of the rise in domestic saving. In the case of resource-rich countries, the rise in domestic savings accrues primarily in the public sector through tax revenue and resource rents. The question is why rising public savings do not systematically translate into rising domestic investment. One possibility is that governments have not used these savings to increase public investment. Another is that these savings have little spillover effects on domestic financial intermediation, in the sense that they do not stimulate domestic bank credit and the development of long-term lending instruments. The question of composition of domestic saving has not received much attention in the literature, which has focused on aggregate savings. Yet, understanding the drivers of private and public domestic saving, and the linkages between the two and domestic investment is essential for designing appropriate policies for stimulating sustainable growth. Research aimed at shedding light on these issues would add much value to the policy debate.

The third question arising from the analysis in this chapter is more of a paradox, whereby the period of growth and saving acceleration exhibits explosion of capital flight from the continent. Growth acceleration and improvement of macroeconomic stability implies a reduction in sovereign risk, which should raise the appetite for domestic assets compared to foreign assets. This would reduce capital flight. This theoretical prediction does not seem to apply to African countries. The evidence implies that capital flight from Africa is not, at least not to a significant extent, the result of actions by private asset holders seeking higher returns abroad or protection of their savings against policy-induced risk or political risk. Therefore, standard economic analysis of portfolio decisions needs to be coupled with institutional analysis to uncover deep fundamental factors that drive capital flight from Africa. The evidence has clear implications for strategies aimed at both raising domestic saving and addressing the problem of capital flight. We propose two sets of strategies. One is an incentives-based strategy aimed at increasing the attractiveness of domestic investment relative to foreign assets. This would address the part of capital flight that may be motivated by portfolio diversification. The second is an institutions-based approach aimed at strengthening the regulatory and legal systems to enable adequate investigation, prosecution, and prevention of financial crime. We argue that African countries should focus mostly on the latter. This will help deter illicit acquisition of wealth, embezzlement of public assets, and illegal transfer of private funds into safe havens. Given that capital flight involves shared responsibility between African actors and agents in the international financial system particularly in safe havens, combatting capital flight from Africa requires a global compact between African governments and their counterparts in advanced economies to improve transparency and accountability in the global financial system.

References

AfDB, OECD, UNECA, and UNDP (2012). *African Economic Outlook 2012*. Paris and Tunis: OECD Publications.

African Development Bank, and Global Financial Integrity (2013). *Illicit Financial Flows and the Problem of Net Resource Transfers from Africa: 1980-2009*. Washington, DC and Tunis.

Aron, J., and Muellbauer, J. (2000). Personal and corporate saving in South Africa. *World Bank Economic Review*, 14(3):509–544.

Berthélémy, J.C., and Varoudakis, A. (1994). Intermédiation Financière et Croissance Endogène. *Revue Economique*, 3:737–750.

Boyce, J.K., and Ndikumana, L. (2012). *Capital flight from Sub-Saharan African countries: Updates 1970-2010*. PERI Research Report. Amherst, MA: Political Economy Research Institute.

Collier, P., Hoeffler, A., and Pattillo, C. (2001). Flight capital as a portfolio choice. *World Bank Economic Review*, 15:55–80.

Collier, P., Hoeffler, A., and Pattillo, C. (2004). Africa's exodus: Capital flight and the brain drain as portfolio decisions. *Journal of African Economies*, 13(2):15–54.

Dornbusch, R. (1985). External debt, budget deficits, and disequilibrium exchange rates, in G.W. Smith and J.T. Cuddington (eds), *International Debt and the Developing Countries*. Washington, DC: World Bank.

Eaton, J. (1987). Public debt guarantees and private capital flight. *The World Bank Economic Review*, 1(3):377–395.

Elbadawi, I.A., and Mwega, F.M. (2000). Can Africa's saving collapse be reversed? *World Bank Economic Review*, 14(2):415–443.

Feldstein, M., and Horioka, C. (1980). Domestic saving and international capital flows. *Economic Journal*, 90(358):314–329.

Fofack, H., and Ndikumana, L. (2009). Capital Flight Repatriation: Investigation of its Potential Gains for Sub-Saharan African Countries. World Bank Policy Research Working Paper (Vol. 5024). Washington DC: World Bank.

Fofack, H., and Ndikumana, L. (2015). Capital flight and macroeconomic policy, in I. Ajayi and L. Ndikumana (eds), *Capital Flight from Africa: Causes, Effects and Policy Issues*. Oxford: Oxford University Press, pp. 130–164.

Henry, J.S. (2012). *The Price of Offshore Revisited*. London: Tax Justice Network.

Kant, C. (2002). What is capital flight? *World Economy*, 25(3):341–358.

Karlan, D., Kutsoati, E., McMillan, M., and Udry, C. (2011). Crop Price Indemnified Loans for Farmers: A Pilot Experiment in Rural Ghana. *Journal of Risk and Insurance*, 78(1):37–55.

Keynes, J.M. (1973). *The Collected Writings of John Maynard Keynes*. London: Macmillan.

Khan, M.S., and Haque, N.U. (1985). Foreign borrowing and capital flight: A formal analysis. *International Monetary Fund Staff Papers*, 32:606–628.

Lessard, D.R., and Williamson, J. (1987). *Capital Flight and Third World Debt*. Washington, DC: Institute for International Economics.

Levine, R., and Renelt, D. (1992). A sensitivity analysis of cross-country growth regressions. *American Economic Review*, 82(4):942–963.

Lewis, A.W. (1954). Economic development with unlimited supplies of labor. *Manchester School*, 22:141–145.

Loayza, N., Schmidt-Hebbel, K., and Servén, L. (2000). Saving in developing countries: an overview. *World Bank Economic Review*, 14(3):393–414.

Ndikumana, L. (2000). Financial determinants of domestic investment in sub-Saharan Africa: evidence from Panel Data. *World Development*, 28(2):381–400.

Ndikumana, L. (2005). Financial development, financial structure, and domestic investment: international evidence. *Journal of International Money and Finance*, 24(4):651–673.

Ndikumana, L. (2009). Revisiting development finance institutions for the purpose of accelerating African economic development, in UNECA (ed.), *Proceedings of the 2006 African Economic Conference*. Nairobi, Kenya: AERC for AfDB.

Ndikumana, L. (2013). The Private Sector as Culprit and Victim of Corruption in Africa. PERI Working Paper (Vol. 330). Amherst, MA: PERI.

Ndikumana, L., and Boyce, J.K. (2003). Public debts and private assets: Explaining capital flight from Sub-Saharan African countries. *World Development*, 31(1):107–130.

Ndikumana, L., and Boyce, J.K. (2010). Measurement of capital flight: methodology and results for sub-Saharan African countries. *African Development Review*, 22(4):471–481.

Ndikumana, L., and Boyce, J.K. (2011a). *Africa's Odious Debts: How Foreign Loans and Capital Flight Bled a Continent*. London: Zed Books.

Ndikumana, L., and Boyce, J.K. (2011b). Capital flight from sub-Saharan African countries: linkages with external borrowing and policy options. *International Review of Applied Economics*, 25(2):149–170.

Ndikumana, L., and Boyce, J.K. (2012). Capital flight from North African countries. PERI Research Report. Amherst, MA: Political Economy Research Institute.

Ndikumana, L., Boyce, J.K., and Ndiaye, A.S. (2015). Capital flight: measurement and drivers, in I. Ajayi and L. Ndikumana (eds), *Capital Flight from Africa: Causes, Effects and Policy Issues*. Oxford: Oxford University Press, pp. 15–54.

Nkurunziza, J.D. (2012). Illicit financial flows: a constraint on poverty reduction in Africa. *ACAS Bulletin*, 87.

Nkurunziza, J.D. (2015). The potential effect of capital flight on the rate of poverty reduction in Africa, in I. Ajayi and L. Ndikumana (eds), *Capital Flight from Africa: Causes, Effects and Policy Issues*. Oxford: Oxford University Press, pp. 81–110.

Nkurunziza, J.D., Ndikumana, L., and Nyamoya, P. (2012). The Financial Sector in Burundi. NBER Working Paper (Vol. 18289). Cambridge, MA: NBER.

Pollin, R. (1997). Financial intermediation and the variability of the saving constraint, in R. Pollin (ed.), *The Macroeconomics of Saving, Finance and Investment*. Ann Arbor, MI: University of Michigan Press.

Rodrik, D. (2000). Saving transitions. *World Bank Economic Review*, 14(3):481–507.

Walter, I. (1987). The mechanisms of capital flight, in D.R. Lessard and J. Williamson (eds), *Capital Flight and Third World Debt*. Washington, DC: Institute for International Economics, pp. 103–128.

World Bank (1985). *World Development Report 1985*. Washington, DC: World Bank.

CHAPTER 11

REGIONAL INTEGRATION IN AFRICA
Challenges and Prospects

JAIME DE MELO AND YVONNE TSIKATA

11.1 INTRODUCTION AND OVERVIEW

OVER the last 30 years, Regional Integration Agreements (also referred to as Regional Trade Agreements (RTAs) or Preferential Trade Agreements (PTAs) to underline that these agreements almost always involve preferential access) have been spreading everywhere including across Africa (see Figure 11.1), where they have also been called Regional Economic Communities (RECs). During the period, the landscape of PTAs has changed drastically. In the late 1970s, North–South PTAs represented almost 60% of all PTAs while South–South PTAs represented only 20%. By 2010, two-thirds of PTAs were South–South and North–North only one-quarter. In 2010, the 58 African countries were involved in 55 PTAs, of which 43 were South–South and 12 were North–South. PTAs have also increasingly become cross-regional. Of the 55 African PTAs, 31 are cross-regional.[1]

These changes in the landscape reflect an increasing participation of developing countries in world trade. In Africa especially—where 49 of the 50 least developed countries (LDCs) are located—the changes also reflect a shift of interest away from unilateral preferential trade provided by the generalized system of preferences (GSP), the Lomé and Cotonou agreements for Africa, Caribbean and Pacific (ACP) countries, and more recently the Everything but

---

[1] The regional classification follows the World Trade Organization (WTO) nomenclature. The WTO counts include notified and non-notified PTAs. The numbers are high because a PTA that includes goods and services is notified twice, and accessions to existing PTAs are counted as a new PTA. Thus, the steeply rising number of PTAs over the past 30 years reflects both a growing number of countries involved in PTAs and a growing number of memberships of each country. Figures are from WTO (2011, Table B1). This paper focuses on the economic effects of South-South African RTAs. It does not cover the North-South PTAs (e.g. the European Partnership Agreements or Euro-Med Agreements) viewed as less controversial, as northern partners are relatively close to the frontier in terms of cost efficiency, see Melo et al. (1992); Oyejide et al. (1999); Schiff and Winters (2003); and WTO (2011).

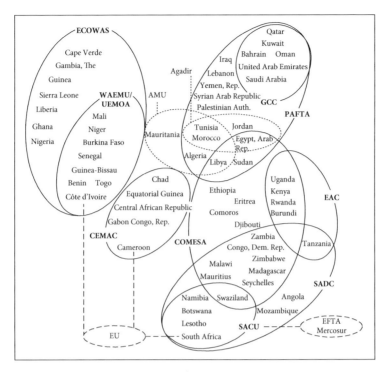

FIGURE 11.1 Regional arrangements in Africa.

Source: Acharya et al. (2011, Figure 2.18).

Arms (EBA) as well as Africa Growth Opportunity Act (AGOA). The lowering of trade barriers in Organisation for Economic Co-operation and Development (OECD) markets and the increasing number of beneficiaries of preferential access has eroded the value of these preferences.[2] This shift towards South–South integration also reflects a desire to include the LDCs into regional production networks. Further, it is a means to strengthen developing countries' bargaining power in multilateral trade negotiations. Notwithstanding the growing importance of trade in natural resources, African countries have remained bystanders in the stalling of the current multilateral negotiations. One way to acquire influence in the future is through successful regional integration.

PTAs are good politics, but to survive they must extend beyond unfilled good intentions and have a sufficiently sound economic basis, the focus of this chapter. Our assessment of the literature is that regional integration is the way ahead as there are many regional externalities that can only be addressed through regional cooperation. However, the linear model of integration from goods markets to monetary and fiscal integration has slowed the progress

---

[2] The gains from receiving duty-free status are greatly reduced by the fact that most-favored-nation (MFN) rates on traded goods are zero or close to zero. WTO (2011) estimates that, if preferences were fully utilized, all preferences together would reduce the global trade-weighted tariff from three to 2% with a drop of only 0.1 due to the non-reciprocal preferences mentioned here. This is why the Introduction to a recent handbook on preferential trade agreements for developing countries is justly entitled "Beyond Market Access" (Chauffour and Maur 2011).

towards integration in the world economy. In addition to political benefits, reductions in trade barriers have helped to integrate markets, although this integration has been disappointing because of high trade costs documented here. Moving beyond removal of barriers at borders to the next stage of deeper integration has been even slower as African RTAs continue to be negotiated as an exchange of market access at the expense of non-partners rather than as an exchange of domestic reforms for attracting the foreign direct investment (FDI), which would provide the backbone services necessary to participate in the growing fragmentation of production worldwide.

Section 2 describes African RECs, their membership, main characteristics, and some of their objectives. Section 3 discusses the interplay of geography, politics, and efficiency; all strong arguments in favor of integration on a regional basis in Africa. Evidence is reviewed in section 4. Challenges ahead are covered in section 5.

11.2 THE LANDSCAPE OF AFRICA'S LINEAR INTEGRATION MODEL

At a deep level, regional integration in Africa has its roots in the political forces determined by the colonial legacy that resulted in a configuration of geographically artificial states where arbitrary borders coupled with great ethno-linguistic diversity contributed to the continent's high number of conflicts and to its high trade and communication costs (Alesina et al. 2003; Alesina et al. 2011; Portugal-Perez and Wilson 2009). In Africa as a whole, but in sub-Saharan Africa (SSA) in particular, the RECs were to be the "building blocs" of the hoped-for African union in the immediate post-colonial era. Now, they are central for implementing the New Partnership for Africa's Development (NEPAD). In short, the RECs were and continue to be the glue that will cement African unity.

An early phase of integration started during the first decades of independence, and was enshrined in the Lagos Plan of Action, an initiative of the Organization for African Unity, adopted by the heads of states in 1980. The proposed framework was for African integration into pan-African unity and continental industrialization by the division of the continent into RECs that would constitute a united economy, the African Economic Community. Three regional integration arrangements were supported by the Economic Commission for Africa: Economic Community of West African States (ECOWAS); Common Market for Eastern and Southern Africa (COMESA), and the Economic Community for Central African States (ECCAS), and later, the Arab Maghreb Union (AMU).

This first phase corresponded to the heyday of central planning when faster industrialization would take place if carried out at the regional level under free trade among members with high tariff barriers applied to non-members, and during which an inward-looking integration also reflected a desire to develop independently from the former colonial masters. Economic unification would be the solution to Africa's development dilemma and, for many, to work it would require a political union. However, the leaders of these young post-independence African states were reluctant to encourage the erosion of national sovereignty and the emergence of a supra-national authority, which would have been necessary to coordinate and manage the affairs of the hoped-for African union. (Even in Europe, it took

30 years to accept the principle of subsidiarity.)[3] In addition, as discussed below, the great diversity across Africa (resource-rich and resource-poor, coastal and landlocked, artificial borders, many ethnic groups and languages) translated into different interests that strengthened countries' insistence on the "respect for the sovereignty and territorial integrity of each State and the inalienable right to independent existence" as written in the Organisation of African Unity (OAU) charter of 1963. Commitment to pan-Africanism was weakened, leading to a vagueness and multitude of objectives (see some examples, Table 11.1), which helped states gloss over the issues that divided them.

The outcomes of the first phase of African PTAs were insightfully reviewed by Foroutan (1992). After observing that the gross national product (GNP) of SSA was about the same as Belgium's, she noted it would be hard to imagine Belgium divided into "forty-something independent countries, each with its own isolated goods and factor markets" (234). She also pointed out that the skewed distribution of benefits resulting from the great disparity among members required large compensation from the gainers to the losers, large partly because regional trade was mostly inter- rather than intra-industry: absent central funding raised by less distortionary means, funds were either obtained by distortionary taxes negating any efficiency gains from eliminating protection among partners, or trade barriers were not removed.[4] So, with the exception of integration of the franc zone in Economic and Monetary Community of Central African States (CEMAC) and West African Economic and Monetary Union (UEMOA) (see Table 11.1), implementation never reached the Free Trade Area (FTA) status, let alone deeper integration.

Starting in the 1980s, and later, following the end of the cold war, initiatives entered a second, more outward-looking, phase. Most were a revival of previous efforts that had either been abandoned, such as the East African Community (EAC), or not implemented, such as the Common Market for Eastern and Southern Africa COMESA, while others were new with significant membership overlap (Figure 11.1) reflecting countries "hedging their bets." To this day, this overlap complicates the task of policy coordination and slows down attempts at "deep integration" as large membership makes it difficult to reach consensus to delegate authority to regional bodies. For example, Zambia, is both a member of the COMESA Customs Union (CU)—which requires applying Common External Tariff (CET) to non-members—and of the Southern African Development Community (SADC) FTA, putting the country in a conflicting position.

Table 11.1 lists ten major PTAs along with some characteristics and objectives. Objectives are wide-ranging and ambitious, reflecting the desire to dissimulate the heterogeneity of

---

[3] Subsidiarity indicates that decision-making jurisdiction should coincide with a public good's spillovers (multilateral institutions for transnational public goods, regional institutions for regional public goods, such as infrastructure, especially for landlocked countries, and national institutions for national public goods.

[4] For example, in West Africa, preferential customs duties (e.g. the "Taxe de coopération régionale" applicable to partners" industrial products were tailored to the "protection needs" of the least advantaged partners. In Europe, France delayed progress towards deeper integration when it opposed the planned move in the Treaty of Rome from unanimity to majority voting in the European Council fearing that it would have to adopt policies it would oppose. The conflict over sovereignty was also apparent when several countries opted out of the Lisbon Treaty 2007, which further strengthens EU institutions and inches towards qualified majority voting.

Table 11.1 Main (WTO recognized) plurilateral preferential trade agreements in Africa

Abbreviation	Name of RTA	Type of agreement	Members	Year originated	Year agreement signed	Objective
AMU (11.56)	Arab Maghreb Union	Free Trade Area	Algeria, Libya, Mauritania, Morocco, Tunisia	1988	1989	- Economic and political unity among Maghreb countries.
Agadir (21.66)	Agadir Agreement	Free Trade Area	Egypt, Jordan, Morocco, Tunisia	2001	2004	- Establish an FTA among members prior to a Euro-Mediterranean FTA as envisaged in The Barcelona Process. - Boost competitiveness of their products into European Union (EU) markets; expand co-operation, commercial exchange and free trade between members. - Agadir Agreement spectrum includes customs, services, certificates of origin, government purchases, financial dealings, preventive measures, intellectual property, standards and specifications, dumping and mechanisms to resolve conflicts.
EMCC/CEMAC (6.24)	Economic and Monetary Community of Central Africa	Customs & Monetary Union	Cameroon, Central African Republic (L), Chad (L), Congo, Equatorial Guinea, Gabon	1959[1]	1994	- Create a common market based on the free movement of people, goods, capital and services. - Ensure a stable management of the common currency. - Secure environment for economic activities and business in general. - Harmonize regulations of national sectoral policies.
COMESA (8.04)	Common Market for Eastern and Southern Africa	Customs Union	Burundi (L), Comoros, DR Congo, Djibouti, Egypt, Eritrea, Ethiopia (L), Kenya, Libya, Madagascar, Malawi (L), Mauritius, Rwanda (L), Seychelles, Sudan, Swaziland (L), Uganda (L), Zambia (L), Zimbabwe (L)	1965[2]	1993	- Achieve sustainable economic and social progress in all Member States through increased co-operation and integration in all fields of development particularly in trade, customs and monetary affairs, transport, communication and information, technology, industry and energy, gender, agriculture, environment and natural resources.

(continued)

Abbreviation	Name of RTA	Type of agreement	Members	Year originated	Year agreement signed	Objective
EAC (12.07)	East Africa Community	Customs Union	Burundi (L), Kenya, Rwanda (L), Tanzania, Uganda (L)		1999	- Widen and deepen cooperation among Partner States in, among others, political, economic and social fields for their mutual benefit. To this extent the EAC countries established a Customs Union in 2005 and a Common Market in 2010. Enter into a Monetary Union and ultimately become a Political Federation of the East African States.
ECOWAS (7.23)	Economic Community of West African States	Trade, Currency, Political Union	Benin, Burkina Faso (L), Cape Verde, Cote d'Ivoire, Gambia, Ghana, Guinea, Guinea-Bissau, Liberia, Mali (L), Niger (L), Nigeria, Senegal, Sierra Leone, Togo	1 965[3]	1975/1993	- Achieve a common market and a single currency. Provide for a West African parliament, an economic and social council and an ECOWAS court of justice to replace the existing Tribunal and enforce Community decisions. The treaty also formally assigned the Community with the responsibility of preventing and settling regional conflicts.
PAFTA (9.45)	Pan-Arab Free Trade Area	Free Trade Area	Bahrain, Egypt, Iraq, Jordan, Kuwait, Lebanon, Libya, Morocco, Oman, Palestine, Qatar, Saudi Arabia, Sudan, Syria, Tunisia, United Arab Emirates, Yemen		1997	- Elimination of customs duties and other fees and duties having similar effects. - Eliminate all non-tariff barriers, including administrative, monetary, financial and technical barriers. - Preferential treatment for least developed member states.
SACU (21.07)	Southern African Customs Union	Customs & Monetary Union	Botswana (L), Lesotho (L), Namibia, South Africa, Swaziland (L)	1910[3]	2002	- Facilitate the cross-border movement of goods between the territories of the Member States. - Create effective, transparent and democratic institutions to ensure equitable trade benefits to Member States. - Promote conditions of fair competition in the Common Customs Area and investment opportunities.

Table 11.1 Continued

Abbreviation	Name of RTA	Type of agreement	Members	Year originated	Year agreement signed	Objective
SADC (11.45)	Southern African Development Community	Free Trade Area	Angola, Botswana (L), Lesotho (L), Malawi (L), Mauritius, Mozambique, Namibia, South Africa, Swaziland (L), Tanzania, Zambia (L), Zimbabwe (L)	1980[4]	1996	- Enhance growth and poverty alleviation; support the socially disadvantaged through Regional Integration. - Evolve common political values, systems and institutions; Promote and defend peace and security. - Promote self-sustaining development on the basis of collective self-reliance and the inter-dependence of Member States. - Achieve complementarity between national and regional strategies and programmes. - Achieve sustainable utilisation of natural resources and effective protection of the environment. - Strengthen and consolidate historical, social and cultural affinities.
WAEMU / UEMOA (10.33)	West African Economic and Monetary Union	Customs & Monetary Union	Benin, Burkina Faso (L), Côte d'Ivoire, Guinea-Bissau, Mali (L), Niger (L), Senegal, Togo		1994	- Increase competitiveness through open markets; rationalize and harmonize the legal environment. - Convergence of macro-economic policies and coordination of sectoral policies; create a Common Market. - The coordination of sectoral policies.
GCC (8.92)	Gulf Cooperation Council	Political & Economic Union	Bahrain, Kuwait, Oman, Qatar, Saudi Arabia, United Arab Emirates		1981	- Formulate similar regulations in religious, finance, trade, customs, tourism, legislation and administration. Establish a common currency.

Source: WTO (2013) RTA database http://rtais.wto.org/UI/PublicMaintainRTAHome.aspx

Note: 1. Creation of Equatorial Customs Union;

2. Creation of Preferential Trade Area for Eastern and Southern Africa;

3. First agreement signed;

4. Creation of Southern African Development Community; (L) for landlocked members.

Figures in parentheses are the Trade Complementarity Index (TCI) of the respective RTAs at the year of agreement signed. $TCI_{ij} = 100 \left[1 - \sum_k \left[\frac{|m_i^j - x_i^j|}{2} \right] \right]$ where m_i^k is product k's share in country i's total imports, x_j^k is product k's share in country j's export to the world. A maximum score of 100 indicates that the two countries are ideal trading partners. A lower score indicates that the two countries export similar products and there may not be much scope in expanding one's exports to the other. In comparison, European Common Market has a TCI of 41.71 in 1962; Mercosur at 24.21 in 1994; NAFTA at 58.02 in 1994.

interests. In addition to promoting industrialization, the objectives include harmonization of regulations and policies—Agadir Agreement; monetary unions—COMESA, EAC, Gulf Cooperation Council (GCC); promoting democracy (SACU) and expanding the development of the least-developed members—Pan Arab Free Trade Area (PAFTA) and Southern African Customs Union (SACU). The ECOWAS treaty calls for the establishment of a West African parliament, an economic and social council, and an ECOWAS court of justice to enforce community decisions. The community is also formally assigned with the responsibility of preventing and settling regional conflicts, which clearly indicates the importance of political objectives.

Of the ten PTAs listed in Table 11.1, only three have aimed for FTA status, all others aiming for deeper integration, with integration moving along the linear model of integration following a stepwise integration of goods, labor and capital markets, and eventually monetary and fiscal integration. Goods market integration would start with an FTA, then move on to a CU with a CET. Along this sequence, excluding SACU, none of the PTAs in Africa has yet reached full CU status as many goods are excluded from the CET; the COMESA CU launched in 2009 only requires countries to give a list of goods they wish to submit to the CET for a five-year transition period. In the next phase, countries would move to a common market with integration of labor and capital markets culminating in a monetary union. For example, the EAC, the most advanced regional agreement among the six retained for further scrutiny, moved to a customs union in 2005, then to a common market in 2010, with the next planned step being a monetary union for 2015.

In Table 11.1, three agreements stand apart. SACU, the oldest customs union in the world, is the only full customs union with revenue sharing among African RTAs, so there is no need for costly-to-meet rules of origin (RoO). Established by a colonial power, it is not replicable and hence, not considered further. With a high dependence on oil revenues and exports of services and shared religious beliefs, the GCC is also deeply integrated even though progress towards a monetary union is stalled—because of its low applicability elsewhere, it is not covered here. Owing to membership in the franc zone, UEMOA and ECOWAS members share a common currency, and have achieved deeper integration. Since monetary unions figure prominently among African PTA objectives, UEMOA is kept for discussion, but in all statistics, ECOWAS will only include non-UEMOA members. This leaves us with a focus the following six agreements: COMESA, EAC, ECOWAS (minus UEMOA members), UEMOA, PAFTA, and SADC.[5]

Table 11.1 also gives two indicators that capture characteristics important in explaining the dilemma facing African RECs. First it indicates when a country is landlocked to reflect that landlocked and coastal countries have opposite interests as coastal members wish to control (and hence raise costs) of goods crossing their territories. Next is the Trade Complementarity Index (TCI), a measure of the gains from trade (a high/low) value for the index indicates that the two countries have great (low) gains from trading with each other as the two countries exhibit (do not exhibit) complementarity. The low values of these indices, compared to those of other RTAs mentioned in Table 11.1, point to negligible efficiency gains

---

[5]   Five of the six CEMAC members are petroleum exporters while none are among UEMOA members. In its tally of 14 African RECs, WTO (2011: 152) states that nine have a full economic union as the specified objective, one aims for a Common Market (COMESA), while the remaining ones aim for FTA status. The optimism in reaching these objectives is exemplified by SADC's timetable: reach FTA status by 2008, a CU by 2010, a common market by 2015, a monetary union by 2016, and a single currency by 2018.

from specialization-induced gains through inter-industry trade. On a worldwide basis, measures of intra-industry trade are also the lowest for African RTAs (Brulhart 2009).

11.3 EFFICIENCY, GEOGRAPHY, AND POLITICS IN AFRICAN REGIONAL AGREEMENTS

The literature on regionalism has shifted from early emphasis on efficiency, to the political economy of preferential versus multilateral trade liberalization and more recently to the possibility that regionalism could undermine multilateralism (Freund and Ornelas 2010). In Africa, however, political motives, geography, and the distribution of gains across FTAs trump the traditional efficiency effects first discussed by Viner (1950). We review them here.

11.3.1 The political dimension

The prevalence of conflicts in Africa's recent history points to the importance of political motives in the region's recent PTA history. As put by the government of Rwanda, its trade strategy is to promote "regional integration *and* cooperation" (italics added) and in the case of ECOWAS, the Community of States has the "…. the responsibility of preventing and settling regional conflicts" (cited in Melo and Collison 2011). Establishing a regional trade bloc can provide security and confidence to build supra-national institutions that will deliver regional public goods as was done in the European Community over a half-century starting with the European Steel and Coal Community (ESCC) in 1953.[6] Oates (1972) tells about the costs and benefits of common policies: a trade-off between the benefits of common policies which depend on the extent of cross-border policy spillovers and their costs, which depends on the extent of policy preference differences across member countries. Common decision-making internalizes the spillovers but it moves the common policy away from its preferred national policy (i.e. a loss of national sovereignty). In Africa, spillovers are important as transport and communications infrastructure are under-provided, but the ethno-linguistic diversity across "artificial" borders suggests strong differences in policy preferences hindering the supply of public goods through the adoption of common regional policies.

The experience of RTAs around the world supports the view that economics and politics are complements (rather than substitutes as argued by the defenders of multilateralism). RTAs reduce the probability of war through two channels. First, trade-creating exchange takes place, increasing the opportunity cost of war. Second, as political scientists have argued, sufficiently deep RTAs reduce information asymmetries as partners know each other better. Then incentives for countries not to report their true options in an attempt to extract concessions are reduced. Discussions among members spill over to political issues

---

6. Shortly before signing of the ESCC, Robert Schuman, then French Minister of Foreign Affairs said in a speech on May 9, 1950 that: "…. Through the consolidation of basic production and the institution of a new High Authority, whose decisions will bind France, Germany and the other countries that join, this proposal represents the first concrete step towards a European federation, imperative for the preservation of peace."

diffusing political disputes that could escalate into political conflicts. These two channels reduce the probability of costly conflicts. By the same token, globalization which involves a shift of trade towards distant partners reduces this opportunity cost increasing the likelihood of conflicts. Martin et al. (2012) built these insights into a bargaining model where rational states will enter into an RTA if the expected economic gains from trade creation and the security gains resulting from decrease in the probability of disputes degenerating into war exceed the political costs of entering the RTA.

Martin et al. (2008) found that increased bilateral trade deters bilateral war because it increases the opportunity cost of war while multilateral openness has the opposite effect. In subsequent work, Martin et al. (2012) found support for their theory of PTA formation: country-pairs with large economic gains from RTAs and high probability of conflict are more likely to sign an RTA. Although their dataset does not include African countries, the findings should apply to the predominantly intraregional African PTAs (that is why they are often called RECs) even though the opportunity cost of war would be small for countries that trade little. Viewed in this light, the costs associated with negotiating the deep African RTAs (SACU, CEMAC, and UEMOA) have been borne by colonizers. Increased trade among members then raised the opportunity cost of future wars among members by increasing their interdependence. Guillaumont (2013) reports that franc zone members have had about half as many yearly conflicts as other SSA countries.

11.3.2 Geography

Country size, remoteness, uneven distribution of natural resources, and associated rents were not considered in the evaluations of the first wave of African RTAs.[7] Meanwhile the diagnosis of Africa's lagging performance was shifting from a discussion of external versus internal constraints (Collier and Gunning 1999) towards the role of physical and economic geography (Gallup et al. 1999; Collier and Venables 2009; and Venables 2011). Regional integration implications of this emphasis on geography are stark.

Consider first size and scale effects. African economies are usually small, resulting in monopoly power. Price–cost margins will be higher for many growth-related activities. Transport cartels will raise further already high transport costs (Teravaninthorn and Raballand 2008). Credit will be more expensive because of a monopolized banking sector. Savings will generate small increases in the capital stock because of the high relative price of investment goods in gross

---

[7] Limão and Venables (2001) were the first to provide orders of magnitude of the importance of infrastructure and geography on trade in Africa when they showed that 50% of the difference in shipping costs for a standard 40-foot container across destinations was accounted for by differences in the quality of infrastructure. In addition to confirming the high costs of being landlocked, they detected additional costs to overland distance (1000 kilometers of overland distance added on average US$1380 to container freight costs, against only US$190 by sea) for landlocked countries compounded by border delays, uncertainty, higher insurance costs, and charges by transit countries. Their key finding was that "hard" infrastructure accounted for nearly half of the transport cost penalty borne by intra-SSA trade. This change of diagnosis from the under-trading found by Foroutan and Pritchett (1993) was also confirmed by Coulibaly and Fontagné (2006) for aggregate and disaggregated trade flows in West Africa, predicting that if all roads were paved in the region, trade would almost treble.

domestic product (GDP) resulting from market power.[8] Larger cities are also known to result in higher productivity through a variety of channels (lower transport and communication costs, greater competition, etc.). Taking into account that country population and country area determine city size, citing evidence that a doubling of city size in developed countries is estimated to raise productivity by three to 8%, Collier and Venables (2009) estimated that combining ten countries in which the largest city has three million people would lead to a country with the largest city having a population of 19 million, over six times more than the largest city in the fragmented countries. Emphasizing the benefits from a larger population and less instability, Guillaumont (2013: 280) estimated that if each of the CEMAC and UEMOA CUs had been integrated into a single economy over the period 1976–2011, average annual per capita income growth in CEMAC (UEMOA) would have been higher by 1.7 (1.9) percentage points, respectively.

Diminishing returns to resource extraction and remoteness also point out to large gains from integration as, more than elsewhere, African PTAs involve countries with very different characteristics in terms of access to resources. Take PAFTA, a mix of resource-poor (Djibouti, Egypt, Morocco, Sudan, Tunisia) and resource-rich (Bahrain, Kuwait, Oman, Qatar, and United Arab Republic) countries. Take also the EAC, a mix of coastal (Kenya and Tanzania) and remote landlocked members (Burundi, Uganda, and Rwanda). As shown in Table 11.1, Africa has 15 landlocked countries largely specialized in natural-resource-based production patterns that, unlike footloose manufactures, face diminishing returns. Remoteness coupled with sharply diminishing returns for resource-based exports results in a low-supply response to regional integration initiatives explaining the small response of trade shares to reduction in trade barriers in Table 11.2.

As pointed out by Collier and Venables (2009), these are the circumstances when regional integration has the highest payoff. Consider the implications of diminishing returns and the lack of foreign exchange. Take two identical isolated economies with a fixed labor supply and a foreign exchange constraint—their isolation preventing them from entering footloose activities. Were they to integrate, their size would double and their output would increase and the brake of diminishing returns would be pushed back. Next consider isolation where one partner is landlocked and the other is a coastal partner having access to an activity for the world market that is not subject to diminishing returns. The coastal partner's wage will be set by the world price for the footloose activity while the wage for the landlocked partner will be lower, determined by labor supply and diminishing returns. Migration from the landlocked to the coastal economy would close the wage gap and bring efficiency gains. Large migratory movements have indeed taken place in Africa but, in the absence of deep integration, the non-citizen status acts like a border for trade in goods, giving rise to a political backlash all the stronger in Africa's ethnically fragmented environment.

11.3.3 Efficiency and distributional effects

Evaluations of the first phase of African RTAs reviewed by Foroutan (1992) were largely concerned with Viner's (1950) trade creation (TC) and trade diversion (TD) effects resulting from the second-best nature of discriminatory trade liberalization. In the African context, the consensus was that TD was likely to dominate TC for several reasons. First, preferences

[8] Collier and Venables (2009) report results by Caselli (2007) that after controlling for GDP per capita, increasing labor force by a factor of ten reduces the relative price of investment by 10%.

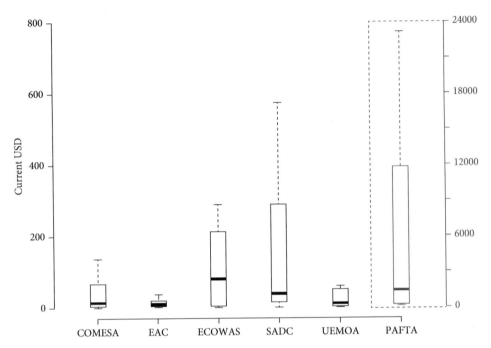

FIGURE 11.2 Fuel, ores, and metals exports per capita by RTA groups (2012 US$).

Source: Authors' calculations from World Development Indicators (World Bank, 2013).

were granted among partners with very limited supply capabilities so that the partner receiv-ing preferences would not be able to displace entirely third-country exports, a prerequisite for a welfare-improving change since price in the partner granting preferential access would remain unchanged. Second, there were large cost differences between the most efficient members in the group and the lowest-cost external producers resulting either in no effect from granting preferential access—or negligible effects on intra-regional trade (see Figure 11.2 and Table 11.2). And in the case of discernible trade effects, these large cost differences would all but guarantee that the net effect would be welfare-reducing as the TD effects result-ing from subsidizing the inefficient partner would dominate any TC effect via a lower price on domestic markets. As discussed in Melo et al. (1992), recognizing the benefits from the possibility of exploiting economies of scale would still not be enough for preferential trade liberalization to trump non-discriminatory liberalization, uni- or multilateral.

Viner's (1950) analysis was most relevant for "similar" economies where cost differences were not too pronounced so the choice of a partner did not matter much as there was scope for the pro-competitive, scale, rationalization, and increased variety gains associated with an increase in intra-industry trade to take hold. These are the large gains that were only recognized in the "new trade theory" of the 1980s inspired by the success of European integration that resulted in intra-industry rather than inter-industry specialization. In the African context, none of these gains materialized as inter-industry trade remained low and intra-industry trade continued to be non-existent (Brulhart 2009). Moreover, whatever limited increase in trade between mem-bers, distributional effects were likely to be large which explains why, in the absence of compen-satory funds, integration efforts were abandoned. Two channels were at play.

Table 11.2 Trade effects of RTAs in Africa, two years before and five years after implementation dates.

	(1)	(2)	(3)	(4)	(5)	(6)	(7)	(8)	(9)	(10)
	Import/GDP (%)			Trade Intensity		Trade Propensity		Average distance of trade		
RTA	Extra-bloc Imports	Total Imports	Imports (Max, Min)	Intra-bloc	Extra-bloc	Intra-bloc	Extra-bloc	ADOT	ADOTP	ADR
COMESA										
1991–2	18.0	18.6	(69.6, 6.8)	9.9	191.8	1.1	21.6	6037.7	9553.7	0.61
1997–8	18.5	19.4	(82.4, 5.9)	7.5	164.1	1.4	31.1	6142.8	9617.9	0.63
EAC										
1997–8	18.0	20.0	(24.8, 12.9)	199.9	655.8	20.3	66.5	5972.5	9562.0	0.63
2003–4	20.4	23.9	(30.4, 19.4)	279.4	615.0	31.1	68.4	4850.6	9189.5	0.53
ECOWAS										
1991–2	36.5	37.0	(47.4, 7.7)	5.3	226.2	1.6	67.5	5116.1	8207.7	0.62
1997–8	34.5	35.7	(45.7, 17.3)	10.3	315.4	3.7	113.3	5928.5	8303.6	0.71
PAFTA										
1995–6	22.5	25.0	(63.5, 9.1)	3.9	39.7	1.2	11.9	4428.8	7052.0	0.61
2001–2	19.9	22.6	(53.0, 14.2)	3.9	41.5	1.2	13.2	5030.7	7339.6	0.67
SADC										
1994–5	18.1	19.7	(76.1, 13.6)	11.4	107.7	2.4	22.3	7144.5	10574.7	0.68
2000–1	19.6	21.5	(58.9, 12.5)	15.3	147.8	3.9	37.8	7530.3	10316.3	0.73
UEMOA										
1992–3	19.5	20.6	(56.5, 7.6)	74.9	604.6	12.1	97.6	5096.2	8199.1	0.62
1998–9	22.9	24.6	(50.3, 9.8)	96.9	701.6	21.3	154.3	5239.4	8072.4	0.65

Source: Authors' calculations from IMF (2013) Direction of Trade Statistics (DOTS).

Notes: UEMOA countries are excluded from ECOWAS. Except for ADOT measures, all figures are average of t-1 and t-2, and average of t+4 and t+5, i.e. two years before and five years after implementation, respectively. For average distance of trade (ADOT) ratios, averages of t+9 and t+10 (10 years after implementation) are used; average distance ratio (ADR).

First was a likely divergence in incomes across partners rather than a convergence as was observed during the successive waves of European integration. Even though many factors contribute to the world's ranking by per capita income, there is a tight fit between a per capita ranking of countries and one according to their physical or human capital per worker. Consider then an FTA between two Northern countries, France and Portugal, both above the world's average per capita income (and hence capital–labor endowment) and two Southern countries, Kenya and Uganda, both below the world average capital–labor endowment. As shown by Venables (2003), an FTA between Kenya and Uganda will be trade-diverting as Uganda will substitute low-cost Northern manufactures by high-cost Kenyan manufactures while Kenya will benefit from the low-cost imports of agricultural products from Uganda. By contrast, by the same reasoning, an FTA between the two Northern partners will close their income gap as Portugal benefits from France's low-cost manufactures while France shifts towards Portugal's relatively costly agricultural products.[9] So if the members of an RTA cluster have economies performing above average, the forces of agglomeration will prevail and convergence will occur as resources flow to the weaker members as has happened with European Union (EU) integration. But in a cluster with no strong economies, perhaps in part because of weak institutions, resources will flow to the strongest member in the group, resulting in divergence.

Take now an FTA between a landlocked country, with very limited access to world markets so it can only hope to sell to its geographically close neighbor, and a partner that is less isolated with relatively more natural resources. These two countries are price-takers on world markets but, because of its lesser neighborhood isolation, under preferential access the landlocked country could trade a range of products with its neighbor. Then, as shown by Venables (2011), an FTA between the two will lead to trade creation for the relatively resource-poor landlocked country whose terms of trade will improve while the resource-rich partner will experience trade diversion. Estimates by Carrère et al. (2012) for PAFTA support these predictions: once controlled for other determinants of trade in a panel gravity model, they show TC effects for the resource-poor members and TD effects for the resource-rich members.

Figure 11.2 displays a boxplot of per capita values of exports of fuels, ores, and metals for the six REC groups. It shows a very large disparity in per capita US$ values of fuel and ores across countries in different groupings (raising difficulties regarding integration within the different RECs, and even more so across the different RECs as intended in the Tripartite Agreement discussed later on) and also among members in any group. As discussed later, this is a situation when the gains from economic integration would be greatest, but at the same time the most difficult to achieve because of opposing interests between members.

11.4 AFRICAN REGIONAL INTEGRATION: ANY EFFECTS ON TRADE?

Many studies (e.g. Wacziarg and Welch 2008) have shown that trade, investment, and growth have increased following reductions in protection. However, with great volatility in growth

---

[9] The collapse of the EAC (Kenya, Uganda, and Tanzania) in 1977 has often been attributed to Uganda and Tanzania perceiving they were not getting a fair share from the customs union. Schiff and Winters (2003) discuss other factors impinging on the efficiency implications of partner choice.

coupled with external and internal shocks, detecting any growth effects of African RTAs has so far proved elusive. Even in the case of the deep integration in UEMOA, when compared with other non-oil exporting SSA countries, Guillaumont (2013) failed to find lasting differences in growth rates over the last 30 years.[10]

The first expected effect of a PTA is an increase in trade among members via three channels. The first is a reduction in tariffs between members; the second is a reduction in non-tariff barriers (NTBs); the third, and hardest to apprehend, is via the two components of trade facilitation: a "hard" component related to tangible infrastructure such as ports, roads, highways and telecommunications; and a "soft" component related to transparency, customs management, the business environment and other intangible institutional aspects that affect the ease of trading. The first two are the outcome of measures taken under "shallow" integration and are easier to capture than the third, which is associated with "deep" integration. Because the data on trade patterns only reveals the outcome of all measures taken (and other intervening factors), it is difficult to disentangle effects due to regional trade policies from those due to trade facilitation that could be undertaken on a regional or unilateral basis. Together, these three channels make-up trade costs whose outcome is revealed in trade data. Evidence on these three channels is now reviewed moving from descriptive patterns to model-based estimates.

11.4.1   Reduction in trade barriers: trade creation and trade diversion effects

Figure 11.3 traces the evolution of intraregional trade shares in GDP around the time of the implementation of the RTA. These intraregional trade shares are volatile (hence two-year averages for the figures reported in Table 11.2) and usually low (below 10% or about one-tenth of the trade of extra-bloc trade) with only PAFTA and SADC showing rising trends. As a comparison, excluding the EU, the share of intra-RTA trade worldwide rose from 18% in 1990 to 34% in 2008 (from 28% to 51% if EU included) (WTO 2011, Figure B6). Moreover, compared with other gravity-based estimates of the increase in bilateral trade upon entry into an FTA—between 37% for Martin et al. (2012) and 68% for Baier and Bergstrand (2007)—these increases in trade are small.

Disentangling between TC, that is increasing the volume of trade with a partner that is already a low-cost supplier, and TD, that is increasing the volume of trade with a partner that is not the low-cost supplier, requires looking at the numbers more closely since any increase in intra-bloc shares in Figure 11.2 could come from either (or both) TC and TD. A substitution of extra-bloc imports by intra-bloc imports following the removal of internal barriers to trade would result in an increase in intra-bloc trade shares and this could be the result of TD.

---

[10]   We restrict discussion to ex post studies. Examples of results from ex-ante computable general equilibrium (CGE) simulation models are discussed in Schiff and Winters (2003). Tarr and Rutherford (2010) estimate that gains from liberalization of the services sector in Tanzania would be large with the largest gains coming from unilateral trade liberalization.

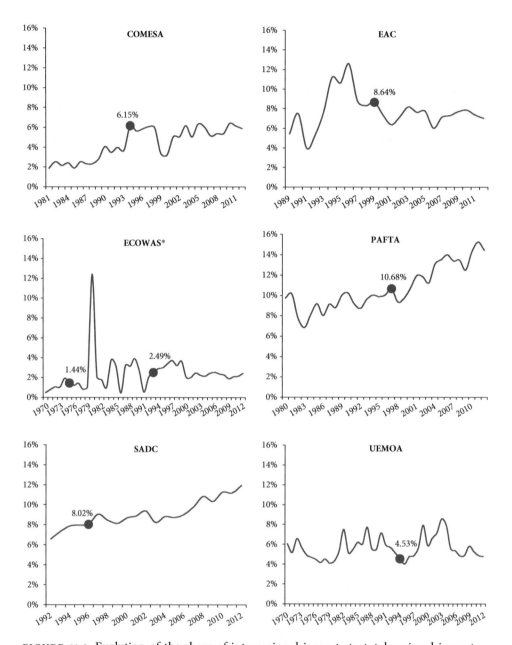

FIGURE 11.3 Evolution of the share of intraregional imports to total regional imports.

Source: DOTS, IMF (2013).

Notes: The red dot on the plot line in each panel indicates the agreement's implementation date (and when the organization becomes active for ECOWAS); UEMOA countries are excluded from ECOWAS. Spike in ECOWAS import share in 1980 was due to zero import activity in Nigeria that year.

Table 11.2 reports the evolution of several trade indices. No clear pattern emerges across the RECs. Reflecting the low share of intra-bloc imports, the extra-bloc shares in GDP are low, increasing marginally in only a few cases (by comparison, the elasticity of world trade to world GDP rose from around 2% in the 1960s to 3.4% in the 2000s). Each group was also characterized by large differences in import shares in GDP (column 3) around the time of implementation. Columns 4 and 5 report trade intensity indices, a first counterfactual at attempting to capture what might have happened in the "anti-monde". As they are the ratio of trade shares, in the absence of preferential agreements, they should not change much. In Table 11.2, intra-bloc and extra-bloc trade intensities rise sharply for ECOWAS, SADC, and UEMOA. So, over the seven-year period around the agreement, the increase in the share of GDP spent on imports from members (intra-bloc) and on non-members (extra-bloc) rose more than the increase in non-member shares in world trade. The EAC is the only bloc where extra-bloc trade intensity fell suggesting the possibility of trade diversion. Finally, the trade propensity indices in columns 6 and 7 capture the joint effect of any bias in trade patterns and the effects of RTAs over trade volumes since they are the product of the trade intensity indices and the openness ratio. Sharp increases are observed for all groups except PAFTA, suggesting an overall increase in openness, but not directly attributable to RTA implementation.

Each RTA group g has n members indexed over i and j and k is an index over the whole sample, $\left(i, j = 1, \cdots, g, k = 1, \cdots n; X_i = \sum_k x_{ik}; X_w = \sum_i \sum_k x_{ik}\right)$

$$\text{Trade Intensity Index is } TII_g = \frac{1}{n}\sum_i TII_i \,; TII_i = \frac{\sum_j x_{ij} / X_i}{\sum_{k \notin g} \sum_j x_{kj} / X_w}.$$

$$\text{Trade propensity (TP): is } TP_g = \frac{1}{n}\sum_i TP_i \,; TP_i = TII_i * \frac{X_i}{Y_i}.$$

Average distance of trade in year t (ADOT$_t$) for RTA group g is given by the un-weighted average across n members, $ADOT_g^t = \frac{1}{n}\sum_{i \in g}\sum_j \frac{x_{ijt}}{X_{wt}}D_{ij}$ where X_{ijt} are exports belonging to an RTA and j all partners t, X_{wt} are world exports in t, and D_{ij} is distance (in kilometers) between i and j, where i and j are each country within the respective RTAs. The potential average distance of trade $\left(ADOT_g^{p,t}\right)$ is given by the volume of trade predicted by GDPs and distance between partners

$$ADOT_g^{p,t} = \sum_{i \in g}\sum_j \frac{X_{ijt}^p}{X_{wt}^p}D_{ij}; \quad X_{wt}^p = \sum_i \sum_j X_{ijt}^p; \quad X_{ijt}^p = \sum_i \sum_j \frac{Y_{it}Y_{jt}}{Y_{wt}}.$$

$$ADR_g^t = \frac{ADOT_g^t}{\left(ADOT_g^{p,t}\right)}$$

The average distance ratio for group g is given by

The outcomes observed in Table 11.2 reflect changes in internal versus external-trade costs and in external-trade costs across partners. So when countries enter into an RTA, other changes may be taking place, including a reduction in their external- and internal-trade costs and also in their trade costs with non-RTA partners. Most of these changes can be captured by estimates from the gravity model estimates reported later, but a preliminary look at the data is also useful. Since countries choose their trade partners so as to minimize trade costs, if trade costs with non-RTA partners fall more rapidly than with partners, (and this could be due to a fall in trade costs in the foreign country), then, on the plausible presumption that RECs are regional (the case for most African RTAs), the ADOT for RECs will rise rather than fall while the opposite will happen if it is trade costs among members that fall the most. Taking two-year averages, column 8 reports the evolution of the simple ADOT two years before signature and ten years after; the long time-period used is to give enough time for other trade facilitation measures to show up in the data. All RECs except the EAC show an increase of the ADOT (column 8), suggesting a "death of distance" biased towards far-away partners.

In a further step towards a model-based prediction assume, along the lines of the well-accepted gravity model that, in a frictionless world, potential trade would be proportional to the trading partners' GDP. Then, multiplying GDPs by the distance between the partners and summing over all partners gives the frictionless gravity-predicted average distance of trade for country (or REC) i, denoted here as the potential distance of trade ($ADOT^P_i$). Averaging over members in a REC, gives a measure of the potential distance of trade. This measure (which takes a maximum value when all countries are of the same size) will increase when there is less dispersion in the group and over a long period when there is convergence in incomes. The evolution of this measure in column 9 indicates a slight convergence in only half of the RECs (COMESA, ECOWAS, and PAFTA).

If the gravity model is an adequate description of bi-lateral trade, and if integration fosters convergence in incomes among members, then the ratio of actual trade ($ADOT_i$) to potential ($ADOT^P_i$)—here called the average distance ratio (ADR_i)—is an indirect measure of trade costs: falling values of the ratio (i.e. a regionalization of trade and convergence) then reflects a decrease in relative trade costs and/or convergence in incomes. These ADRs displayed in column 10 are around 0.6, suggesting that, on average, these RECs trade 40 % less than predicted by gravity-related variables in a frictionless world. Figure 11.4 shows that the EAC is the only grouping displaying a regionalization of trade. For the others, the ratio increases (points above the 45° line). This could be due to a combination of factors including relatively fewer reductions in trade barriers regionally and/or a combination of reduction in trade barriers in extraregional countries, or trade facilitation measures with greater cost reductions for extraregional trade.[11]

---

[11]   Rising ADRs do not inform on whether changes reflect larger volumes with existing partners (the intensive margin) or with new far-away partners (extensive margin). Carrère et al. (2013) discuss the so-called 'distance puzzle' revealed by gravity-model estimates suggesting that trade costs have been falling less rapidly in low-income countries, an observation corroborated by Arvis et al. (2013).

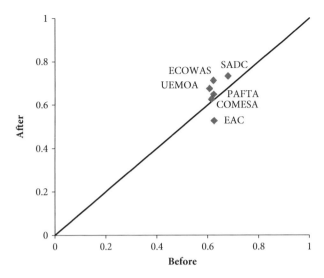

FIGURE 11.4 ADR (simple averages), two years before and ten years after implementation.

Source: Authors' calculations from IMF (2013).

11.4.2 Gains from deep integration and trade facilitation: gravity-based estimates

The gravity model is the workhorse of the great majority of work on the effects of trade policies on trade flows. It is remarkably consistent with two strong stylized facts in the data: (i) exports rise proportionally with the size of the destination market and imports rise proportionately with the size of the origin country (both captured in the average distance of trade ratios ADOT defined and reported in Table 11.2); (ii) there is a strong negative relation between physical distance and trade (captured in the ADOP measure in Table 11.2). It also turns out that "structural" gravity (i.e. theory-consistent gravity; see Head and Mayer 2013) comes out of a large family of trade models. Three features make it very relevant to assess the trade effects of African RTAs. First, gravity underlines that a country's per capita income is closely related to the country's "real market potential": Being close to Nigeria, Liberia should have a high market potential. Second, it lends itself to the incorporation of trade costs indicators beyond bilateral distance so that it can capture the bilateral trade effects of any reduction in trade costs. So Liberia, a close neighbor to Nigeria, will have a smaller market potential than Belgium, another small country because of high trade impediments in Nigeria. Liberia's market potential will also be low if Liberia's capabilities are low, perhaps because of deficient hard and soft infrastructure. Third, dummy variables can control for other important determinants of bilateral trade: common border, common language, landlocked, etc... Importantly for any appraisal of RTAs, dummy variables that capture membership in an RTA or in a monetary union have routinely been incorporated in many applications of the gravity model that have been assembled in several meta-analyses.

Head and Mayer (2013) report two robust results from their compilation of estimates from a large number of gravity models. First, dummy variables for FTA membership are always statistically significant (median coefficient of 0.28 implying an FTA-induced increase in trade of 32% after controlling for other intervening factors). The trade effects of common currencies have larger positive coefficients. In general, high standard errors indicate that these coefficients are not estimated precisely due to problems of endogeneity, missing variables and the choice of econometric techniques to handle the large number of zeroes in the data. As an example, these estimates are confronted with the possibility of endogeneity as countries could be brought to sign a currency union because they trade a lot in the first place.[12] In another recent study of UEMOA, Carrère (2013) estimates that intraregional trade for members is four times above gravity-predicted trade (trade creation) while extraregional trade is 20% less (trade diversion). She also establishes that the greater intraregional trade associated with sharing a common currency comes from less volatility in bilateral exchange rates which accounts for 50% of the increase in intraregional trade. Finally, using a composite index for "hard" infrastructure along the lines proposed by Limão and Venables (2001), she simulates the effects of a harmonization of the value of the infrastructure index at the regional level to the mean across partners, obtaining large increases in exports from harmonization of infrastructure.

As with all effects captured by dummy variables or composite indices like those drawn from the many indicators in the World Bank's DB data base, one is not sure of the underlining links between the policy levers and the outcomes of interest captured in these results: having controlled for gravity covariates, is it better roads, rail, telecommunications, or a better-functioning regulatory environment that contribute most to the attributed increase in intraregional trade? In another approach, taking inspiration from Engel and Rogers (1996), drawing on time series of prices of three agricultural commodities (millet, sorghum, manioc) across 142 markets in 15 national and regional markets in West Africa, Araujo-Bonjean and Brunelin (2013) found (i) that a reduction in relative price differences through time across UEMOA members; (ii) a larger variance in relative prices when markets are separated by a border; (iii) controlling for distance, a much stronger "border effect" for country-pairs involving one UEMOA and one non-UEMOA country than for country-pairs involving two UEMOA countries.

The importance of logistics and delays in reducing trade of African countries also comes out from Freund and Rocha's (2011) study of African exports based on the shipping of a standard 40- foot container for a large sample of countries. They estimate that Africa's export volumes are 16% below what is expected but that once the time-to-export is entered as a proxy for trade facilitation in a standard gravity trade model, the significance of the African dummy disappears in accounting for bilateral trade volume. A one-day reduction in inland travel time translates into a 2 percentage point decrease in all importing country tariffs. Of the three components of domestic delay (documentation, transit time, and port handling and customs clearance), they find that inland transit is the most important. Moreover, including global positioning system (GPS) travel time, which accounts for the quality of the road, does not affect the coefficient of the Doing-business inland transit-time, suggesting that the problem for inland transit is soft (border delays and/or efficiency of security checkpoints) rather than hard (quality of the road network) infrastructure. Institutions and soft

---

[12] Estimates are from Head and Mayer (2013, Table 4).

infrastructure would then be more important than geography in accounting for Africa's low trade volumes.

These results reveal the shortcomings of the linear model of integration where behind-the-border measures aiming to reduce trade costs were largely ignored across African RECs (Hartzenberg 2011). While this is probably due to the difficulty in gaining the confidence necessary to get collection action on the move discussed earlier, many behind-the-border measures could still have been undertaken unilaterally. In complementary (also based on shipping costs of a standard container in a large cross-section of 110 countries including 22 African countries) cross-section estimates to those of Freund and Rocha (2011), and after having dealt with the high collinearity across the World Bank's Doing Business (DB) indicators by principal component methods, Portugal-Perez and Wilson (2012) estimated that cutting trade costs half-way to the level in Mauritius would be equivalent to a 7.6% cut in tariffs faced by Ethiopian exporters across all importers. They also find that the marginal effect of their transport efficiency and business indicators on exports decreases with income. While potentially informative, these cross-country estimates still suffer from the "lack of internal validity" as they cannot really identify the effects of improvements in infrastructure net of confounding influences (Cadot et al. 2014).

11.5 CHALLENGES AHEAD

Small fragmented and isolated economies with resources distributed very unequally among them make a compelling case for African countries to integrate regionally to reap efficiency gains, exploit scale economies, and reduce the thickness of borders. At the same time, as emphasized in this survey, in the absence of compensation mechanisms, the unequal distribution of gains has hampered progress. Moreover, until recently at least, regional integration in Africa was founded on a twentieth-century exchange of market access at the expense of outsiders and on the "linear model of integration" that neglected the importance of tackling behind-the-border impediments to trade. With the reduction in trade costs and the subsequent fragmentation of production, twenty-first-century regionalism is about a new bargain: an exchange of domestic market reforms for FDI which brings home the service activities necessary to participate in the global value chain. In this new environment, where trade is trade in tasks and involves increasingly an exchange of intermediate goods, protection (or exchange of market access) amounts to depriving oneself from participating in global outsourcing. It is against this changing background that Africa's "old regionalism" building on exchange of market access has to be evaluated. Indeed, Asian regionalism has been characterized by "race to the bottom" tariff-cutting to bring about the services needed to diversify and participate in international production networks (Baldwin 2011). This is why Africa's linear model of integration focusing on barriers to goods trade at the expense of trade in services, which has been growing far more rapidly than trade in goods, has been criticized (UNECA 2010).

Looking ahead, two developments are on the horizon. First are the pan-African hard infrastructure projects that finally tackle regional spillovers. Buys et al. (2006) carried out a cost–benefit analysis to explore the returns on a pan-African program of road infrastructure development, estimating a pay-back of one year on the investment with US$254 billion of additional trade generated over the project's estimated lifetime at a cost of about US$32 billion. Successful large infrastructure projects will contribute to defragmenting Africa by reducing transport costs directly (Portugal-Perez and Wilson 2012; Brenton and Isisk 2012). Another channel emphasized here is the building of social capita through spreading of information, which should enhance trade and, hopefully, reduce the probability of conflicts.

Second is the African free trade zone or tripartite FTA among COMESA, EAC, and SADC that should help solve the overlapping membership dilemma by bringing free trade among the 26 members by (i) removing tariffs and NTBs and implementing trade facilitation which will include a harmonization of RoO;[13] (ii) applying the subsidiarity principle to infrastructure to improve the transport network; (iii) foster industrial development. Signed in 2008, it is ambitious but not yet operational. However, as pointed out by Erasmus (2012), what was going to be a "single undertaking" to establish a proper FTA is at risk by the setting up negotiating principles around a variable geometry that would allow the co-existence of different trading arrangements with small integrating effects.

ACKNOWLEDGMENTS

An earlier version of this chapter was presented at a workshop on the "Oxford Handbook of Africa and Economics" in Beijing 8–10 December 2013. Special thanks to Phoebe Wong for help and Céline Carrère, Julie Regolo, and the editors for comments. Melo thanks FERDI for support.

REFERENCES

Acharya, R., Crawford, J., Maliszewska, M., and Renard, C. (2011). Landscape, in J.P. Chauffour and J.C. Maur (eds), *Preferential Trade Agreement Policies for Development: A Handbook.* Washington, DC: World Bank, pp. 37–68.

Alesina, A., Devleeschauwer, A., Easterly, W. et al. (2003). Fractionalization. *Journal of Economic Growth*, 8(2):155–194.

Alesina, A., Easterly, W., and Matuszeski, J. (2011). Artificial states. *Journal of the European Economic Association*, 9(2):246–277.

Araujo-Bonjean, C., and Brunelin, S. (2013). Le Commerce Agricole en Afrique de l'Ouest et du Centre: Les frontières sont-elles abolies? *Revue d'économie du développement*, 27(1):5–31.

Arvis, J.F., Duval, Y., Sheperd, B., and Utokham, C. (2013). Trade Costs in the Developing World: 1995–2010. WPS 6309. Washington, DC: World Bank.

Baldwin, R.E. (2011). 21st Century Regionalism: Filling the Gap between 21st Century Trade and 20th Century Trade Rules. CEPR Policy Insight 56. Washington, DC: CEPR.

---

[13] RoO are necessary to prevent "trade deflection" in FTAs, i.e. importing from the low-tariff partner and selling in the high-tariff partner. Everywhere, RoO have been unnecessarily complex and have benefited the strong lobbyists of inefficient industries of the strongest partners in the FTA, see Erasmus et al. (2006) for an appraisal of RoO in SADC largely imposed by South African protectionist lobbies. SADC RoO are more restrictive than COMESA's.

Baier, S., and Bergstrand, J. (2007). Do free trade agreements actually increase members' international trade. *Journal of International Economics*, (71):72–95.

Brenton, P., and Isisk, G. (eds) (2012). *De-Fragmenting Africa: Deepening Regional Trade Integration in Goods and Services*. Washington, DC: World Bank.

Brulhart, M. (2009). An account of global intra-industry trade 1962–2006. *World Economy*, 32(3):401–459.

Buys, P., Deichmann, U., and Wheeler, D. (2006). Road Network Upgrading and Overland Trade Expansion in Sub-Saharan Africa. Policy Research Working Paper 4097. Washington, DC: World Bank.

Cadot, O., Fernandes, A., Gourdon, J. et al. (2014). Evaluating aid for trade: a survey of recent studies. *World Economy*, 37(4), 516–529.

Carrère, C. (2013). UEMOA et CEMAC: Quelle performance en matière de commerce? *Revue d'économie du développement*, 27(1):33–60.

Carrère, C., Gourdon, J., and Olarreaga, M. (2012). Natural resource heterogeneity and the incentives for and impact of regional integration, in N. Diop, D. Marotta, and J. de Melo (eds), *Natural Resource Abundance, Growth, and Diversification in MENA*. Washington, DC: World Bank, pp. 175–197.

Carrère, C., de Melo, J., and Wilson, J. (2013). The distance puzzle and low income countries: an update. *Journal of Economic Surveys*, 27(4):717–746.

Caselli, F. (2007). The marginal product of capital. *Quarterly Journal of Economics*, 122(2):535–568.

Chauffour, J.P., and Maur, J.C. (eds) (2011). *Preferential Trade Agreement Policies for Development: A Handbook*. Washington, DC: World Bank.

Collier, P., and Gunning, J. (1999). Explaining African economic performance. *Journal of Economic Literature*, 37(1):3–22.

Collier, P., and Venables, A.J. (2009). Commerce et performance économique: la fragmentation de l'Afrique importe-t-elle? *Revue d'économie du développement*, 23(4):5–39.

Coulibaly, S., and Fontagné, L. (2006). South-south trade: geography matters. *Journal of African Economies*, 15(2):313–341.

Engel, C., and Rogers, J. (1996). How wide is the border? *American Economic Review*, 86(5):112–125.

Erasmus, G. (2012). Redirecting the Tri-partite FTA Negotiations. TRALAC Trade Brief S13TB02/2013. Stellenbosch: TRALAC.

Erasmus, H., Flatters, F., and Kirk, R. (2006). Rules of origin as tools for development: some lessons from SADC, in O. Cadot, A. Estevadeordal, A. Suwa-Eisenman, and T. Verdier (eds), *The Origin of Goods: Rules of Origin in Preferential Trade Agreements*. Oxford: Oxford University Press, pp. 259–295.

Freund, C., and Ornelas, E. (2010). Regional trade agreements. *Annual Review of Economics*, 2(1):139–166, 09.

Freund, C. and N. Rocha (2011). What constrains Africa's exports? *World Bank Economic Review*, 25(3):361–386.

Foroutan, F. (1992). Regional integration in sub-Saharan Africa: past experience and future prospects, in J. de Melo and A. Panagariya (eds), *New Dimensions in Regional Integration*. Cambridge: Cambridge University Press, pp. 234–271.

Foroutan, F., and Pritchett, L. (1993). Intra-sub-Saharan African trade: is it too little? *Journal of African Economies*, 2(1):74–105.

Gallup, J., Sachs, J., and Mellinger, A. (1999). Geography and economic development, in B. Pleskovic and J. Stiglitz (eds), *Annual World Bank Conference on Development Economics 1998*. Washington, DC: World Bank, pp. 127–178.

Guillaumont, P. (2013). Impact de l'intégration sur la croissance. In A.-M. Geourjon, S. Guérineau, P. Guillaumont, and S. Guillaumont-Jeanneney (eds), *Intégration Régionale pour le développement de la Zone Franc*. Paris: Economica, pp. 250–284.

Hartzenberg, T. (2011). Regional integration in Africa. Staff Working Paper ERS-2011-14. Geneva: WTO.

Head, K., and Mayer, T. (2013). Gravity Equations: Workhorse, Toolkit, and Cookbook. CEPR Discussion Paper 9322. Washington, DC: CEPR.

IMF (2013). Direction of trade statistics. Washington, DC: IMF.

Limão, N., and Venables, A.J. (2001). Infrastructure, geographical disadvantage, transport costs and trade. *World Bank Economic Review*, 15:451–479.

Martin, P., Mayer, T., and Thoenig, M. (2012). The geography of conflicts and regional trade agreements. *American Journal: Macroeconomics*, 4(4):1–35.

Martin, P., Mayer, T., and Thoenig, M. (2008). Make trade, not war. *Review of Economic Studies*, 75(3):865–900.

Melo, J. de, Panagariya, A., and Rodrik, D. (1992). The new regionalism: a country perspective, in J. de Melo and A. Panagariya (eds), *New Dimensions in Regional Integration*. Cambridge: Cambridge University Press, pp. 159–193.

Melo, J., and Collinson, L. (2011). Getting the best out regionalism: some thoughts for Rwanda, IGC WP#0886.

Oates, W. (1972). *Fiscal Federalism*. New York: Harcourt Brace.

Oyejide, A., Ndulu, B., and Greenaway, D. (eds) (1999). *Regional Integration and Trade Liberalization in sub-Saharan Africa. Volume 4. Synthesis and Review*. New York: Macmillan.

Portugal-Perez, A., and Wilson, J. (2012). Export performance and trade facilitation reform: hard and soft infrastructure. *World Development*, 40(7):1295–1307.

Portugal-Perez, A., and Wilson, J. (2009). Why trade facilitation matters to Africa. *World Trade Review*, 8(3):379–416.

Schiff, M., and Winters, A. (2003). *Regional Integration and Development*. Washington, DC: Oxford University Press and the World Bank.

Tarr, D., and Rutherford, T.F. (2010). Modeling services liberalization: the case of Tanzania. *Journal of Economic Integration*, 25:644–675.

Teravaninthorn, S., and Raballand, G. (2008). *Transport Prices and Costs in Africa: A Review of the Main International Corridors*. Washington, DC: World Bank.

UNECA (2010). Assessing Regional Integration in Africa IV. ECA Policy Research Report. Addis Ababa: UNECA.

Venables, A.J. (2011.) Economic integration in remote resource-rich regions, in R. Barro and J.W. Lee (eds), *Costs and Benefits of Economic Integration in Asia*. New York: Oxford University Press, pp. 187–207.

Venables, A.J. (2003). Winners and losers from regional trade agreements. *Economic Journal*, 112(490):747–761.

Viner, J. (1950). *The Customs Union Issue*. New York: Carnegie Endowment for International Peace.

Wacziarg, R., and Welch, K. (2008). Trade liberalization and growth: new evidence. *World Bank Economic Review*, 22(2):187–231.

World Bank (2013). *World Development Indicators*. Washington, DC: World Bank.

WTO (2011). *World Trade Report 2011. The WTO and preferential trade agreements: From co-existence to coherence*. Geneva: WTO.

CHAPTER 12

NATURAL RESOURCES IN AFRICA

Utilizing the Precious Boon

IBRAHIM AHMED ELBADAWI AND NADIR ABDELLATIF MOHAMMED

12.1 INTRODUCTION

SAVE for a few notable successes, the overwhelming evidence suggests that the development experiences of resource-rich developing countries (RRDCs) have, at best, been mediocre and, indeed, disastrous for most. The record in Africa confirms this international experience. Despite the recent sustained average growth in African oil economies since 1999, natural resources in most African RRDCs were, by and large, not well managed and the continent remains poor and conflictive. Indeed, save for a few countries, most notably Botswana, the oil and mineral riches have so far been "precious bane" for Africa's development. The experience of countries such as Nigeria, Gabon, and Angola with resource extraction and economic development and economic growth demonstrated that the windfall from natural resources do not always result in better outcomes in terms of economic growth (income per capita for the population at large) and poverty reduction in these countries (e.g. Elbadawi and Kaltani 2008).

There are various sources of information and lessons of best practices on ways to accelerate economic growth and development in RRDCs. The Africa Mining Vision, which was jointly developed by the African Union (AU) and the United Nations Economic Commission for Africa (UNECA) provides a road map for RRDCs to accelerate economic growth and poverty reduction efforts and to avoid the "resource curse." The Natural Resource Charter also provides useful tools that help Africa's RRDCs to frame their policies. The insight from these initiatives as well as lessons from other RRDCs that are relevant to the African context could be grouped into three major pillars:

1. get the best deal and the prices for the resources;
2. adopt appropriate fiscal policies to utilize the resources effectively; and
3. distribute equitably and build appropriate institutions.

These three pillars are premised on the presence of accountable polity and effective economic governance, an issue that is extensively discussed in a companion chapter in this volume (Elbadawi and Mohammed 2014a). This chapter offers a roadmap for African RRDCs to promote good economic and political governance and to effectively utilize the natural resources for the benefit of its citizens based on international experiences and the experience of African countries with natural resources in the past five decades.

12.2 THE ROADMAP FOR EFFECTIVE UTILIZATION OF AFRICA'S NATURAL RESOURCES

12.2.1. Get the best deal and prices for the resources

12.2.1.1 Assess the available resources

There is a need for global partnership involving African countries with developed countries which host most of the big multilateral extractive companies to agree on common parameters to ensure that the continent is receiving full benefits from its resources and the private sector is engaged in profitable activities that are fair, legal and transparent. One important element of this partnership should focus on the assessment of natural exhaustible resources.

African countries should redouble their efforts, individually and collectively, to assess and survey the sub-soil exhaustible natural resources. There is considerable asymmetry of information between African RRDCs and major multinational companies specializing in resource extraction about the availability of resources. These companies have the needed human and financial resources, skills and technology to survey sub-soil resources. A major initiative to undertake geological surveys, with the support of multilateral financial institutions, will assist RRDCs in engaging with multinational companies with adequate knowledge of the resources that can be utilized. The acquired knowledge will strengthen negotiating position of these governments with private companies and will ensure that they avoid sub-optimal deals. The knowledge will also help the authorities to decide on the most appropriate exploitation strategies given the exhaustibility of the resources.

12.2.1.2 Seek transparent and competitive processes for exploration and extraction

Once African countries have a good assessment of the available natural resources, they should solicit interest from multinational companies to extract the resources through open and transparent processes, including invitations for competitive bidding in exploration and extraction. Many other developing countries confirmed that such processes will lead to better outcomes (e.g. Iraq) in comparison with the unsolicited bids or deals that take place behind closed doors. Competition will ensure that Africa can also reap some benefits at the exploration stage including some benefits to localities where exploration take place (e.g. road infrastructure) that can be negotiated with winning companies.

On view of the rising role of major emerging economies in Africa, the ruling elites in the continent should address this challenge adequately. Going forward the balancing act that these elites have to achieve would probably present an important lesson for the development literature. The Africa Progress Panel (2013: 5) stressed that African countries "should institute transparent systems of auctions and competitive bidding for concessions and licenses, as well as tax regimes that reflect both the real value of their countries' natural resource assets and the need to attract high quality investment."

12.2.1.3 Get it right from the beginning and negotiate good contracts

Weak capacity to negotiate extractive industry agreements remains one of the key challenges that many developing countries face as they seek to translate their countries' natural resources wealth into sustainable economic development. Contracts for exploration and subsequently production of exhaustible natural resources are of long-term nature. The contracts are also highly complex and governments may be less informed about technical details and geological endowments than the private multinational companies which have access to sophistical geological, financial and sectoral expertise as well as experienced legal teams during the negotiations process. If the initial contract does not accord to the country a fair deal for its extracted natural resources, the country will not be able to correct for this initial mistakes for decades to come and the losses will be huge. Therefore, it is pivotal that African countries negotiate good contracts with potential investors from the beginning.

African countries should seek assistance from multilateral financial institutions, main bilateral donors, and international NGOs in this process (e.g. the World Bank, Africa Legal Support Facility, the Extractive Industries Technical Advisory Facility, and the Extractive Industries Trust Fund). They should also start building capacity in Pan-African institutions (e.g. AfDB, AU) and regional centers of excellence as well as national universities. In these contracts, it is important that African RRDCs diversify the tax instruments (combining royalty, explicit tax on profit, corporate income taxes) as well as considerations for taking equity in the joint ventures for the extraction enterprises. This combination will also ensure revenue collection throughout the extraction process (starting from exploration and early production phases).

12.2.1.4 Beware of tax avoidance and transfer pricing

Fiscal loses due to tax avoidance is a global issue impacting both developed and developing countries. It became among the global priorities for G8 and G20 in the post-financial crisis period with increased efforts of developed countries to supplement their fiscal revenues. The scale of the problem is even larger in developing countries, particularly those RRDCs. One clear indication of the severity of the problem is the large number of resource companies that are incorporated in low tax jurisdictions and their use of profit shifting techniques to minimize taxes paid to developing countries (transfer pricing).[1] Abusive transfer pricing and thin capitalization practices in the extractive industries are believed to be common particularly in Africa where governments' capacity to address the issue is weak or lacking.

---

[1] About two million companies and ten thousand banks are domiciled in tax heavens.

The Africa Report Panel (2013: 19) urged African resource rich countries to revise the design of their tax regimes which were designed to attract FDI during periods of low commodity prices and involved extensive tax concessions, tax holidays, low royalty payments and exemptions from corporate taxes. It stated that the "Hemorrhaging of resource revenues that occurs through secretive deals and the operations of offshore companies is an unconscionable plight on the lives and hopes of their citizens. Full disclosure is the most effective tourniquet."[2] In addition, it estimated the cost to Africa from trade mispricing[3] at about US$ 38 billion annually between 2008 and 2010. It added "Put Differently, Africa could double aid by eliminating unfair pricing practices." While African countries resisted out-right asset nationalization as the case in many other regions as well as revision to the mineral development agreements (MDAs) or stability pacts, it is important that African countries are fully aware of profiting shifting and tax avoidance practices in new contracts. Countries could also amend exiting tax and royalty agreements if conditions warrant as was recently done by Zambia, Tanzania, Ghana, Cote d'Ivoire, Mali, South Arica, Democratic Republic of Congo, and Namibia. Finally, measure to encourage equity participation by African countries in new extractive ventures will ensure receiving appropriate benefits from extractive activities.

12.2.1.5 *Avoid bundling deals particularly those uncompetitive*

Resources for infrastructure (RfI) arrangements that provide companies and governments of other countries with the right to utilize precious mineral resources in return of infrastructure projects deprive Africa from ensuring maximum returns for its natural resources as well as losing when non-priority poorly-identified infrastructure projects are implemented. RfI usually entails extraction rights to a mine (or an oil field) in exchange for turnkey infrastructure not related to the extractive activities. The proponents of such deals emphasize the issue of speed in building infrastructure. However, while these bundles may be quicker, they tend to deprive the country of the true value for its resources and with infrastructure projects executed without adequate social and environmental safeguards. The deals takes place behind closed doors and are prone to corruption and bribes and the selected projects tend to be of political nature. As such, African countries lose twice in such deals. Practical experiences also demonstrated that such deals do not get implemented or suffer from significant delays as both parties to the deal tend to re-negotiate its terms. A better alternative is to solicit competitive deals and auctions for the natural resources and then follow internationally recognized systems to build the needed infrastructure also through open and competitive prices to ensure the best technology and best prices for well identified and appraised projects. The international community has a responsibility in preventing sub-optimal non-transparent deals in the extractive sector through building coalitions that promote increased transparency in extractive activities.

---

[2] Africa Progress Panel (2013: 8).
[3] High levels of intra-company trade which create scope for trade "mispricing" and enabling companies to report profits to low tax jurisdictions.

12.2.2 Adopt appropriate fiscal policies to utilize the resources effectively

12.2.2.1 Adopt fiscal rules to prevent negative impact of volatility

Many RRDCs have in the past suffered from volatility of revenues and boom-bust cycles and saved relatively little of the natural resource income.[4] Because of the exhaustibility of non-renewable natural resources and the volatility in their prices, RRDCs should aim to transform their natural resource wealth into (human, domestic capital and foreign financial) assets with the objective of generating future income while shielding their national economies from volatility that have been detrimental for sustained and fast rates of economic growth.[5] Today, most of the RRDCs adopt fiscal rules—some are more successful than others—to smooth spending from volatile revenues as well as ensuring inter-generational justice by saving some of the income into wealth funds (sovereign wealth funds, stabilization funds, future generation funds, etc.) for use by future generations.

Fiscal rules in RRDCs are important and effective to mitigate government profligacy and confer credibility to the conduct of macroeconomic policy by removing discretionary interventions by successive governments in power. In addition, fiscal rules are necessary to stabilize government expenditure at levels consistent with long-term fiscal sustainability targets. For resource-rich developing countries, fiscal rules are pertinent in promoting budgetary savings and countercyclical macroeconomic stabilization policy by decoupling government expenditures from revenue volatility.[6]

There is more scope to design better fiscal rules to curb spending to sustainable levels and save the rest of the extractive proceeds for rainy days when revenue inflows fall short (in stabilization funds or other similar funds). The fiscal rules should be compatible with the resource horizons for exhaustibility considerations. Elbadawi and Nandwa (2012) summarized the best practices in setting such fiscal rules: the rules should be simple and easy to understand; are clearly defined relative to indicators; be enforceable (require parliamentary enactment); be consistent with other macroeconomic policies (particularly exchange rate and monetary policy); and their implementation should be transparent (in terms of budget accounting and forecasting) and verifiable (independent audits). Most countries prefer price rules with long backward-looking formulas to have smoother expenditures paths -though they may systematically overshoot or undershoot actual revenues- such as Mongolia (16 years) and Mexico (10 years).[7]

12.2.2.2 Ensure inter-generational transfers and set SWFs

For countries with shorter resource extraction horizons, it is important to save part of the revenues for periods when the revenues started to fall and for future generations. Most

---

[4] After adjusting for deletion of these natural resources.

[5] See Geiregat and Yang (2013: 9).

[6] Elbadawi and Nandwa (2012).

[7] Daniel et al. (2013) reviews various experiences with fiscal rules that rely price formulas to smooth expenditures.

RRDCs have now set up Sovereign Wealth Funds (SWFs) or future generation funds to spread resource wealth over longer horizons. Resources revenues which are higher than those budgeted for are saved in these funds and invested mostly in foreign financial assets. For macroeconomic stability and coherence of the fiscal policy domestic investments by these funds should not be encouraged and RRDCs should rely on the budget for the identification and execution of its investment projects.

12.2.2.3 *Increase domestic investment and build domestic assets*

The traditional approach of saving and investing the bulk of the proceeds from extraction of natural resources into foreign asserts and consuming only a constant portion equal to the returns on the resource wealth (known as the Permanent Income Hypothesis (PIH)) may be more restrictive for the RRDCs which have enormous needs to domestic capital and building human resources in comparison with developed countries. African RRDCs should be encouraged to adopt fiscal rules that will ensure adequate level of domestic investments that are also compatible with their domestic capacity as well as preserving macroeconomic stability. Collier et al. (2010) defined this as "investing in investing" by gradually removing existing bottlenecks and improving capacity to select, appraise and implement investment projects.[8]

Save for South Africa and Botswana, Africa being home for several resource-rich but capital-poor countries should provide an opportunity for testing the efficacy of the new approaches to investing the resource surplus in building domestic capital rather than externalizing it abroad, as would be prescribed by a permanent income hypothesis. According to this view, there is scope for current utilization of the resources in building needed infrastructure and upgrading human capital which are essential for long-term growth and for the benefit of current and future generations. And, should the investment be properly managed the social returns of "investing in domestic capital" would be much higher than under the alternative PIH approach. Therefore, the massive infrastructure and human capital needs in many African RRDCs may imply higher returns than return on financial assets if appropriate domestic investments have been undertaken. Such investments will spur economic growth and are likely to increase non-resource revenues as well.[9]

12.2.2.4 *Increase efficiency of public spending*

While there is considerable scope for increasing domestic investments in African RRDCs, it is crucial that government capacity to undertake such investments is enhanced and the efficiency of public spending is increased. First, resources are wasted by spending on untargeted subsidies that benefit the rich and distort the economy, and on consumption and investments not essential for long-term development. In most RRDCs energy subsidies are high and benefit mostly middle and high income families. Second, public investment

---

[8] According to the authors, "investing in investing" hinges on three pillars: the capacity to manage the process of public investment; the environment for private investment; and the unit cost of public goods for public and private investment.

[9] Daniel et al. (2013: 21).

management (PIM) systems needs to be upgraded and the ability to select, appraise, implement and monitor public investments is enhanced. Third, improvements in public procurement and public financial management systems are crucial to improve their effectiveness, efficiency and transparency.

12.2.3 Distribute equitably and build appropriate institutions

12.2.3.1 Distribute geographically with larger share to producing regions to prevent future conflicts

Several studies have shown that RRDCs are more likely to be ruled by autocrats and are more likely to experience civil wars.[10] Rather than fueling conflicts, proceeds from natural resources could be utilized well to cement peace and stability in the continent. Arrangements for wealth sharing and inter-fiscal transfers can be designed to provide disincentive for regions with rich resources to seek secession.[11] Allocation of a small fixed share of the proceeds from extractive activities to the region/state within which the resources are being utilized proved useful in conflict prevention. Special interventions by governments and companies active in resource utilization in the community in which activities take place, safeguarding local environment, improving infrastructure and promoting human resource development in these communities is also essential.

12.2.3.2 Build state institutions to prevent conflict and secessionist movements

African countries should strive to strengthen political institutions and transition to democracy to strengthen the momentum for rapid economic development and growth. This is important in particular for countries with abundant natural resources. It has been argued in the literature that democratic societies that strikes natural resource finds are likely to make them work for development, while those that discover oil and mineral under autocratic polity are likely to experience the curse, due to the corrosive effect of the newly discovered resource on governance.[12] Strengthening political accountability and oversight on the executive branch of the government are particularly important in RRDCs.[13] The recent oil and gas discoveries in nascent but steadily strengthening democracies in Mozambique, Ghana and to a lesser extent Tanzania, Uganda and Libya would provide a natural experiment of sort for assessing this hypothesis.

---

[10] See Mohammed (1994) and Ross (2012).
[11] Mohammed (2010).
[12] Elbadawi and Kaltani (2008) and Elbadawi and Soto (2014).
[13] See Elbadawi and Nandwa (2012).

12.2.3.3 *Allocate a smaller portion as transfers or dividend to citizens*

Unfortunately, in most resource rich countries such institutional requirements for successful investment-driven approach do not exist, including for the case of most African resource-dependent countries, which tend to be ruled by unstable and understandably myopic regimes. Therefore, arguably, under such volatile economic and political institutions distribution of the rents through direct cash transfers (conditional or unconditional) and/or dividend payments could be an effective way to mitigate the resource curse that afflicts these countries. In addition to reducing poverty through augmenting consumption and enhancing welfare at the household level, there is strong evidence that the cash could also be effectively used by households to build their physical and human capital and, hence, increase growth and better manage risk. Also, very importantly, cash transfers out of resource rents open up possibilities of building up a tax system that can produce a more accountable delivery of public services (including the much needed infrastructure). Again, Africa is likely to be the region that most likely to consider such options and, hence, provide useful lessons for the development community. Technology and accumulated experiences from other developing countries would allow the application of such transfers and the identification and targeting of households and individuals.

African RRDCs could also set a small portion of the proceeds from extractive industries (e.g. 10%) for direct dividend payments to citizens as is the case with Alaska State in the United States. Such payments will have various benefits. First, it will cement national feelings, stimulate public interest in the sector, and raise demands for more information and disclosure given their direct interest in the proceeds. Second, it will help alleviate extreme poverty given the weakness of the formal social safety nets in the continent (assuming the dividend is entirely consumed by these families), raising effective demand and stimulating economic growth. Third, if part of the dividend payments is used for social services (e.g. education), it will also stimulate future growth and development. Fourth, if only part of the dividend is saved or invested by some families, it will enhance levels of domestic savings and investments which are essential for long-term economic growth.

12.2.3.4 *Promote diversification of production and exports*

RRDCs require increased levels of diversification in their production and exports in comparison with all other countries because of the exhaustibility of the natural resources, their labor market characteristics (the capital intensive nature of the extractive industries) and the impact of the Dutch disease on tradable sectors. Diversification is crucial for sustaining income growth in these countries and therefore for inclusive growth to be sustained backward and forward linkages need to be developed between the resource sector and the wider economy. Experience of successful RRDCs (e.g. Mexico, Chile, Indonesia) suggest the importance of macroeconomic stability, avoiding wild swings in the real exchange rates, financial deepening, building infrastructure, enhancing human capital, building state institutions as well as undertaking various vertical and horizontal government interventions. For examples, Mexico managed to address risks by hedging its export proceeds on option markets. Chile had successful experience with fiscal rules. It also widened its base of resource exports by diversifying into more sophisticated products rather than exporting of ores and by aggressive horizontal and vertical policies focusing on the business climate and support to the agricultural and fishery sectors. Malaysia and Indonesia were successful in macroeconomic policy and prevention of exchange rate appreciation.

12.3 THE WAY AHEAD

This chapter proposes a three-pronged strategy for managing Africa's rising natural resource riches.

First, getting the best deal and prices for the resource. Efforts to assess sub-soil exhaustible resources, soliciting competitive and transparent process for their exploitation; negotiating good contracts that maximize fiscal revenues and limit tax avoidance and transfer pricing; and avoiding bundling of deals involving extraction and infrastructure building are crucial for Africa to maximize benefits from its exhaustible resources.

Second, efficiently utilizing the resource by adopting the "right" fiscal institutions. African RRDCs should adopt appropriate fiscal policies and build effective institutions to effectively utilize the resource. This can be achieved by designing good fiscal rules that reduce impact of volatility and ensure intergenerational equity; setting of Sovereign Wealth Funds that invest the resources externally; strengthening institutions that prevent future conflicts; allowing for high levels of domestic investments through the budget; and raising the efficiency of public spending.

Third, equitably distributing the resource to maximize the society's welfare. African RRDCs should ensure equitable distribution of natural resources proceeds by proving for a reasonable share to the regions and communities within which the extractive activities take place; increase the size of transfers and building social safety nets; and provide for a small share of the revenues to all citizens in the form of a divined are key policies to achieve this objective.

It is a no-brainer that the proposed roadmap for turning Africa's precious resources into a boon for the Continent's development requires a minimum threshold of good economic and political governance. Though this remains a major challenge, Africa's stable democratic transition has steadily contributed to improving both economic and political governance, especially in the new entrants to the natural resource club. Moreover, as we argue in Chapter 5 (*Handbook,* this volume), the two global programs of the Extractive Industries Transparency Initiative (EITI) and Natural Resource Charter (NRC) should improve policymakers' knowledge about how to manage resource-based economies as well as promote the transparency and accountability of the processes.

REFERENCES

Africa Progress Panel (2013). Equity in Extractives: Stewarding Africa's Natural Resources for All, Summary Report of the Panel, 10 May 2013, Cape Town, South Africa.

Collier, P., van der Ploeg, F., Spence, M., and Venables, A. (2010). Managing resource revenues in developing economies. *IMF Staff Papers*, 57(1):84–118.

Daniel, P., Gupta, S., Mattina, T., and Segura-Ubiergo, A. (2013). Extracting Resource Revenue, *Finance & Development*, 50(3):19–22.

Elbadawi, I., and Kaltani, L. (2008). The macroeconomics of oil booms: lessons for sub-Saharan Africa, in M. Martin (ed.), *Managing Commodity Booms in Sub-Saharan Africa*. Nairobi, Kenya: African Economic Research Consortium, Chapter 3.

Elbadawi, I., and Nandwa, B. (2012). Saving and Investment Strategy and Economic Convergence for Oil Rich Uganda paper presented at the African Economic Research Consortium, Kampala, Uganda, 27 February 2012.

Elbadawi, I., and Soto, R. (2014). Resource rents, institutions and violent civil conflict. *Defence and Peace Economics*, pp. 1–25, April. http://dx.doi.org/10.1080/10242694.2013.848579.

Geiregat, C., and Yang, S. (2013). Too much of a good thing? *Finance & Development*, 50(3):8–11.

Mohammed, N. (1994). The development trap: militarism, environmental degradation and poverty in the south, in G. Tansey, K. Tansey, and P. Rogers (eds), *A World Divided: Militarism and Development After the Cold War*. London: Earthscan, pp. 44–66.

Mohammed, N. (2010). Wealth Sharing Arrangements for Conflict Prevention/Resolution and Economic Growth in Developing Countries Paper Prepared for the World Development Report on Conflict and Fragility Washington, DC: World Bank, April 2010.

Ross, M. (2012). The *Oil Curse: How Petroleum Wealth Shapes the Development of Nations*. Princeton: Princeton University Press.

CHAPTER 13

....

REDISCOVERING STRUCTURAL CHANGE
Manufacturing, Natural Resources, and Industrialization

....

JOHN PAGE

13.1 INTRODUCTION

....

ONE of the early insights of development economics was that because poor countries typically have large differences in output per worker across sectors, the movement of resources from low productivity to high productivity uses can be a major engine of growth (Lewis 1954; Kuznets 1955; Chenery 1986). The variation in productivity across sectors in Africa is particularly large: the average ratio of highest to lowest productivity sectors is 7.5 to 1, double that for Latin America and Asia (McMillan and Rodrik 2011). Such large productivity differences show the scope that exists in Africa for growth enhancing structural change.

There is little evidence, however, that significant structural change has accompanied Africa's post-1995 growth turnaround. The region's growth has been driven primarily by new energy and mineral discoveries, rising commodity prices, and substantially improved economic management (Arbache and Page 2009). Recent research suggests that until quite recently structural change may have reduced, rather than increased, economic growth in Africa (McMillan and Rodrik 2011; AfDB 2013). These are warning signs that Africa's economic success may be fragile: economies that have made the transition from low- to high-income status typically have experienced significant changes in their economic structure.

Not surprisingly, a growing number of academics, policymakers, and development practitioners interested in Africa are rediscovering structural change.[1] This chapter focuses on the role of industrialization—including economic activities that have firm characteristics similar to manufacturing, such as tradable services and agro-industry—in structural

---

[1] See for example AfDB (2013), Center for African Transformation (2013), and World Bank (2013a).

transformation. It presents a view of why there is so little industry in Africa and outlines the changes in public policy that are needed to accelerate structural change.

13.2 STRUCTURAL CHANGE AND MANUFACTURING

One measure of the structural transformation needed to sustain Africa's growth is given by comparing the output and employment structure of a "typical" low-income African economy with the structure of a "benchmark" middle-income country (MIC) at the time it achieved middle income status.[2] The biggest structural deficit is in manufacturing where the value added share and the labor share are about half of the benchmark value (Table 13.1). Despite nearly 20 years of growth, agriculture still represents a large share of the typical African economy, especially in terms of employment, reflecting the dualism that continues to mark the region's economies.

Historically, manufacturing has driven structural change. Growth in income at early stages of development is associated with very rapid increases of the share of manufacturing in total output (Dinh et al. 2013). Manufacturing is a high value-added sector into which labor can flow. The average ratio of labor productivity in manufacturing to agriculture in low-income Africa is 3.8 to 1. Given the very large difference in output per worker and the potential of manufacturing to absorb labor, industrialization presents a significant opportunity for growth-enhancing structural change.

Africa's share of manufacturing in gross domestic product (GDP) has remained the same for more than 40 years. In 2010 it was 10%, slightly lower than in 1970s. The region's share of manufacturing in GDP is less than one-half of the average for all developing countries, and, in contrast with developing countries as a whole, it is declining. Manufacturing output per capita is about one-third of the global developing country average (Page 2013a). Only four African countries—Madagascar, Mozambique, Lesotho, and the Ivory Coast—have a share of manufacturing in total output that exceeds the predicted value for their level of income. Many of the region's recent growth success stories—Ethiopia Ghana, Kenya, Tanzania, and Uganda—have manufacturing value added shares that are well below their predicted values (Dinh et al. 2013).

That Africa has experienced so little structural change through growth of manufacturing is worrying in itself, but recent research points to two further structural threats to the region's long-run growth, lack of diversity and sophistication in production and exports. Globally, more diversified production and export structures are associated with higher incomes per capita (Imbs and Wacziarg 2003; Cadot, Carrere, and Strauss-Kahn 2011), and countries that produce and export more sophisticated products—those that are primarily produced

---

[2] The following benchmark countries and years were identified: China (2000), India (2007), Indonesia (2004), Korea (1968), Malaysia (1968), Philippines (1976), and Thailand (1987). The simple averages of the sectoral shares of value added and employment for these seven countries in the benchmark year appear in Table 13.1 as the structural characteristics of the benchmark MIC. Additional description of the assumptions and method may be found in Page (2012a).

Table 13.1 Africa's structural deficit, 2005

	Share of sector in GDP				Share of sector in labor force				Relative labor productivity			
	AGR	IND	MFG	SER	AGR	IND	MFG	SER	AGR	IND	MFG	SER
Benchmark middle-income country	21.7	12.2	21.9	44.2	45.2	6.6	11.6	36.6	0.48	1.85	1.89	1.21
Africa low-income average	27.8	11.8	11.1	49.3	63.1	5.1	6.6	25.2	0.44	2.31	1.68	1.96
Africa middle-income average	4.8	10.9	17.1	67.2	8.6	11.9	16.8	62.7	0.56	0.92	1.02	1.07
Africa resource-rich average	17.8	29.6	8.3	44.3	45.4	4.8	6.5	43.4	0.39	6.17	1.28	1.02

Notes: Africa low-income sample ETH, MWI, GHA, KEN, MAD, MOZ, SEN, TZA.
Africa middle income sample MUS, ZAF.
Africa resource-rich economies BOT, LES, NGA, NMB, ZAF.
Sources: McMillan and Rodrik (2011) database, World Bank WDI database, author's calculations.

by countries at higher income levels—tend to grow faster (Hausmann, Hwang, and Rodrik 2007; UNIDO 2009). These stylized facts suggest that what Africa makes matters.

Since the middle of the 1970s, Africa has been making too few of the kinds of products that matter for its growth. Exports are highly concentrated in primary commodities and minerals. Per capita manufactured exports are less than 10% of the developing country average. The region has low levels of manufactured exports in total exports and of medium- and high-technology products in manufactured exports (UNIDO 2009). Between 1975 and 2005, the sophistication of the manufacturing sector in 16 of the 18 African economies for which data are available declined.[3] The decline in manufacturing sophistication was especially sharp in the region's early industrializers—Kenya, Ghana, Tanzania, and Zambia (Page 2012a).

13.3 INDUSTRIES WITHOUT SMOKESTACKS

Major technological changes in transport and communications have broadened the range of options for growth-enhancing structural change. Industry no longer needs smokestacks: tradable services and some agricultural value chains increasingly share firm characteristics with manufacturing. Information and communications technology have made many high value-added per worker "modern impersonal" services tradable. Like manufacturing, these tradable services benefit from technological change and productivity growth (Triplett and Bosworth 2004). The global agricultural value chain in horticulture—fresh fruit, vegetables, and flowers—is increasingly dominated by lead firms that coordinate vertical supply chains similar to modern manufacturing (Humphrey and Memedovic 2006).

The range of business processes that can be traded—processing insurance claims, desktop publishing, the remote management and maintenance of IT networks, compiling audits, completing tax returns, transcribing medical records, and financial research and analysis—is constantly expanding. Global trade in services has grown faster than trade in goods since the 1980s (Ghani and Kharas 2010). From 2000 to 2011 services exports from Africa grew six times faster than goods exports and are now about 20% of the total exports of the average non-resource-rich sub-Saharan African country. Africa has a strong natural resource based comparative advantage in tourism, and tourist arrivals over the next ten years are forecast to grow faster than the world average (World Bank 2010b).

The transport of fresh produce over long distances became possible with the development of refrigeration and "cold chains" linking production and consumption points. Keeping products fresh (maintaining the cold chain) and transferring them quickly from farm to shelf adds value. Value is also added through packaging, preparation, and innovation. In spite of high transport costs, such items as washed and trimmed mange-tout, prepared fruit salads, trays of prepared mixed vegetables, and flower bouquets in retail packs can be produced more cheaply in low-income countries due to lower labor costs (Tyler 2005). Led by Kenya, a number of African producers have succeeded in establishing niche markets in the production of cut flowers and out of season crops.

---

[3] For a detailed description of how production sophistication is calculated, see UNIDO (2009).

13.4 Why Has Industry Bypassed Africa?

Over the last 20 years developing countries as a whole increased their share of global manufacturing production from less than 20% to more than 35%. But, while Asia became the "world's factory," Africa's share of global manufacturing remained at 1.2%, half of which was produced by South Africa (UNIDO 2009). Tradable services and horticulture represent a very small share of the global market (World Bank 2010b). Three major forces have shaped the explosion of trade in manufacturing, modern impersonal services, and horticulture: falling long-run transport and communications costs, the capability to compete on quality and price, and economies of agglomeration. Together, these three drivers of industrial location help to explain why industry—with and without smokestacks—has failed to grow robustly in Africa.

13.4.1 Transport, communications, and trade in tasks

There has been a spectacular reduction in transport and communications costs in the global economy over the past 20 years. Freight costs have halved since the mid-1970s, driven by investments in transport infrastructure, better use of capacity, and technological progress. The major cost declines have been in road and air transport; ocean freight rates have declined relatively little since the 1980s. Transportation cost differences affect the competitive position of regional markets—generally they are higher in Africa than in Asia—and high volumes reduce costs further, reinforcing the competitive advantage of existing industrial locations (Hummels 2007). International variations in communication costs have a significant influence on trade patterns and have a greater impact on trade in differentiated products than on trade in homogenous goods (Fink, Mattoo, and Neagu 2002).

The significance of the changes in transport and communications costs is perhaps nowhere more apparent than in the explosive growth of trade in tasks. As transport and coordination costs have fallen, it has become efficient for different steps of production—or "tasks"—to be located in different countries (Grossman and Rossi-Hansberg 2006). Services, like back office operations and accounting, which were previously integrated components of enterprises can now be spun off and subcontracted. With fresh fruit and vegetables there is a trend towards growing to order, under contract to major European supermarkets. Task-based production has expanded dramatically in the past 20 years. In 1986–1990 imported intermediates were 26% of total intermediate inputs. By 1996–2000 they had risen to 44% (UNIDO 2009). A recent estimate by the OECD places intra firm trade by multinational companies based in its members at 8–15% of total trade (OECD 2010).

Trade in tasks has greatly increased the impact of "beyond the border" constraints to trade. Because new entrants to task-based production tend to specialize in the final stages of the value chain, "trade friction costs"—the implicit tax imposed by poor trade logistics—are amplified. Poor trade logistics constrain Africa's ability to compete. The region has an average ranking of 121 out of 155 countries in the World Bank (2010a) Trade Logistics Index. It performs especially badly in terms of trade related infrastructure, but poorly functioning institutions and logistics markets also increase trade friction costs. Port transit times are long, and customs delays on both imported inputs and exports are significantly longer for African economies than for Asian competitors. A plethora of small and uneconomic national airlines limits the region's ability to compete in horticulture and tourism (World Bank 2013b).

13.4.2 Firm capabilities

In most industries technology can be purchased, but the skills needed to use it effectively are tied up in people.[4] Productivity and quality depend primarily on the know-how and working practices possessed by the individuals making up a firm. These "firm capabilities" are used in the course of production and in developing new products (Sutton 2012). Globally, firms are competing in capabilities, constantly trying to adjust productivity and product quality to changing market conditions. Part of the answer to why African has failed to industrialize is that too few of its firms have the capabilities needed to enter what Sutton (2012) terms the international price-quality "window" in low wage goods.[5]

Building capabilities first involves introducing a higher level of capability to a firm or group of firms. This is often a result of foreign direct investment (FDI). Beyond FDI three other mechanisms play an important role in capability building (Sutton 2012): (i) interaction between firms and equipment suppliers, (ii) exchanges of information between suppliers and buyers with a reputation for high quality, and (iii) close and continuing contractual relationships between buyers and sellers involving two-way movements of technical and engineering personnel. The spillover of capabilities comes mainly through supply chain relationships (Harrison and Rodriguez-Clare 2009).

Africa lacks two key sources of firm capabilities, manufacturing FDI and non-traditional exports. Since the 1990s FDI in manufacturing has been concentrated in Asia. While Africa has attracted about the same share of FDI in GDP as Asia over the past ten years, it has been in mining and minerals. Less than 2% of global FDI has gone into African manufacturing (World Bank 2011). Lack of export dynamism has also constrained the ability of the region to build more capable firms. Demanding buyers and repeated relationships are characteristic of global markets in manufactures and horticulture. There is evidence that African manufacturing firms increase their productivity by exporting, but too few African firms export.[6]

13.4.3 Agglomeration

Manufacturing industries tend to concentrate in geographical areas driven by common needs for inputs, access to markets, knowledge flows, and specialized skills (UNIDO 2009).

---

[4] Recent research on the role of management in developing country industry documents the large variations in productivity and management practices across firms even within narrowly defined industrial sectors. See, for example, Bloom and Van Reenen (2010).

[5] In a series of *Enterprise Maps* sponsored by the International Growth Centre, John Sutton has documented the nature and extent of firm capabilities in Ethiopia, Ghana, Mozambique, Tanzania, and Zambia. Of the 50 leading firms in each economy, only about 25% are owned and managed by domestic investors. See, for example, Sutton and Kellow (2010).

[6] See, for example, Soderbom and Teal (2003) and Bigsten et al. (2004).

Modern services exhibit scale and agglomeration economies similar to manufacturing. They are particularly responsive to "thick" labor markets where an abundance of highly skilled workers are found (Ghani and Kharas 2010). A growing empirical literature documents the significant productivity gains to firms from industrial agglomeration.[7] Because of the productivity boost that agglomerations provide, starting a new industrial location is a form of collective action problem. If a critical mass of firms locates in a new area, they will realize productivity gains, but no single firm has the incentive to move to a Greenfield site in the absence of others. Because Africa has few large-scale, modern industrial agglomerations, it is more difficult for existing firms to compete and more difficult to attract new industry.

Governments in Asia and Latin America have fostered industrial agglomerations by concentrating high quality institutions, social services, and infrastructure in special economic zones (SEZs) (UNIDO 2009; Farole 2011, Dinh et al. 2013). Africa's experience with SEZs has been largely unsuccessful. African SEZs have a much lower density of enterprises within their geographical boundaries than the zones in Asia or Latin America. Infrastructure and institutions within the zones have not been sufficiently good to attract global investors. In Asia SEZs have acted as a tool for capability building through the development of vertical supply chains between the zones and the domestic economy. In Africa SEZ-based firms have few links with firms outside the zone (Farole 2011).

13.5 A Complicating Factor: Natural Resources

Africa is highly dependent on natural resources, and new discoveries in previously non resource-dependent economies such as Ghana, Kenya, Mozambique, Tanzania, and Uganda raise the prospect that an increasing number of African economies will become more resource dependent. This poses an additional challenge for structural transformation. Natural resource abundance makes it more difficult to compete in industries unrelated to the natural resource. During a commodity boom the income from resource extraction increases the demand for all goods. In the case of traded goods the increased demand can be met by imports, but the production of non-tradable goods is usually characterized by rising marginal costs and their price rises relative to traded goods. The foreign exchange market reflects this in a real exchange rate appreciation. This is the Dutch disease.

Exchange rate appreciation reduces tradable goods production and the ability to enter new, more sophisticated production and export lines. Not surprisingly, Africa's resource-rich economies trail the non-resource-rich on every indicator, of industrial development, sometimes by wide margins. The share of manufacturing in GDP in resource-rich African countries is about 8%, lower than non-resource-rich economies in Africa by about a third and trailing even the least developed countries (Table 13.1). The share of manufactured exports in total exports is 15 percentage points lower in resource-rich economies. All of the region's

---

[7] See UNIDO (2009) for a survey of the relevant literature.

resource exporters have production and export structures that are less sophisticated than would be expected on the basis of their level of per capita income (Page 2011).

13.6 CONVENTIONAL WISDOM: FIX THE INVESTMENT CLIMATE

Conventional wisdom has been that Africa's lack of industry is primarily due to its poor "investment climate"—the regulatory, institutional and physical environment within which firms operate. This is partly true. Indirect costs attributable to the investment climate are higher in Africa than in Asian competitors (Eifert, Gelb, and Ramachandran 2005; Dinh et al. 2013). But, efforts to fix the investment climate have been misdirected. Since the mid-1990s African governments have been pressed by their international development partners to focus on reforms in trade, regulatory and labor market policies designed to reduce the role of government in economic management.[8] This approach is misguided in two respects. First, it fails to use economy- and industry-specific information to identify the binding constraints to faster industrial development, and, second, it has distracted attention from two important physical constraints to industrial development: infrastructure and skills.[9]

Firm level surveys highlight infrastructure deficiencies as a significant barrier to industrial development in Africa. Sub-Saharan Africa lags at least 20 percentage points behind the average for low-income countries on almost all major infrastructure measures (World Bank 2007b).[10] In addition the quality of service is low, supplies are unreliable, and disruptions are frequent and unpredictable. Road infrastructure has received scant attention. There has been little strategic orientation of Africa's infrastructure investments to support industrialization and until quite recently little willingness on the part of Africa's development partners to finance infrastructure (Page 2012b).

Africa's skills gap with the rest of the world constrains its ability to compete. Secondary and tertiary access and quality lag other regions significantly. Employer surveys report that African tertiary graduates are weak in problem solving, business understanding, computer use, and communication skills (World Bank 2007a). Education and training for tourism, both in language skills and in industry specific skills, are also deficient (World Bank 2013b). In manufacturing there is a strong link between export sophistication and the percentage of the labor force that has completed post-primary schooling (World Bank 2007a). There is also evidence that manufacturing enterprises managed by university graduates in Africa have a higher propensity to export and that firms owned by university educated indigenous

---

[8] The most widely used benchmark of regulatory burden is the World Bank *Doing Business* ranking. Seven of the ten *Doing Business* indicators "presume that lessening regulation is always desirable whether a country starts with a little or a lot of regulation" (World Bank 2008: xv).

[9] This is partly due to the way in which the annual *Doing Business* reports are written and used by the World Bank and other donors. The reports strongly convey the message that lack of progress in reforming the institutions and regulations covered by the survey constrains private investment and growth. See Page (2012b) for a critical review of the *Doing Business* program in Africa.

[10] The largest gaps are for rural roads (29 percentage points) and electricity (21 percentage points).

entrepreneurs have higher growth rates (Page 2012a). Trade in services requires high level cognitive and language skills, and the fastest growing services sectors are the most education intensive (Ghani and Kharas 2010).

13.7 New Thinking: A Strategy for Industrial Development

Investment climate reforms, even broadly defined to include greater investment in infrastructure and skills, are unlikely to prove sufficient to meet Africa's industrialization challenge. One of the striking aspects of the three drivers of industrial location is the extent to which they are interdependent and mutually reinforcing. Exports improve capabilities but depend on having a critical mass of capable firms. Firm capabilities are a source of agglomeration economies, which in turn improve productivity and competitiveness. FDI is a means of attracting more capable firms but is unlikely to be attracted to sparse industrial landscapes. Put in orthodox terms the industrialization process is characterized by a set of externalities and coordination failures that are specific to industry.

Coordinated public actions are essential to overcome the constraints to industrial development imposed by Africa's current deficits in industrial exports, firm capabilities and agglomerations. There is substantial convergence of views on the desirable characteristics of policy interventions designed to promote industrialization—limiting incentives to "new" activities, enforcing automatic sunset provisions, setting clear benchmarks for performance. There is also a strong consensus that agencies with demonstrated competence and a high degree of autonomy are needed to manage the policy process (Harrison and Rodriguez-Claire 2009). Ownership by the top political leadership and a high degree of coordination across various ministries and agencies is critical (World Bank 1993).

A strategic approach to industrialization is particularly important to the Region's natural resource exporters. Tradable goods production outside the natural resources sector depends not only on the exchange rate, but also on the investments and institutional innovations that governments make to enhance competitiveness. Natural resources exporters can mitigate the worst effects of the Dutch disease through appropriately designed strategies for diversification of the economy (Page 2011).[11]

The suggestion that governments can successfully develop and implement strategies for industrial development is at the center of the decades-long controversy over industrial policy. What is often overlooked in the debate over "picking winners" is that governments make industrial policy every day via the public expenditure program, institutional and regulatory changes, and international economic policy.[12] These choices tend—sometimes inadvertently—to favor some enterprises or sectors at the expense of others, and in Africa they often lack a coherent strategic focus. Rather than piecemeal efforts at improving the

---

[11] The ability of natural resource exporters such as Chile, Indonesia, and Malaysia to diversify their economies illustrates the diversity of strategic approaches available. See Page (2011).

[12] Rodrik (2009) makes a similar point.

investment climate, Africa needs a strategy for industrial development focused on boosting exports, building firm capabilities, and creating industrial clusters.

13.7.1 Creating an "export push"

Given its late start, Africa will need an "export push"—a coordinated set of public actions to address the critical constraints to industrial exports—to break into global markets.[13] Here, there is an important role for regulatory reforms. Export procedures—including certificates of origin, quality, and sanitary certification, and permits—can be burdensome. Duty drawback, tariff exemption, and VAT reimbursement schemes are often complex and poorly administered (Farole 2011). Given the region's twin deficits in trade logistics and firm capabilities, investments in trade-related infrastructure and skills development are keys to success. Public actions should be focused on and judged by of non-traditional export performance.

A simple, time-bound system of preferences for non-traditional African exports to high-income countries can provide temporary support for new export activities. At present different OECD countries have different trade preference schemes, and most of them are not well designed or effective (Collier and Venables 2007). One option is for the United Nations to designate a separate class of Least Developed Manufacturing Countries for countries that are not strictly "LDCs" but are low-income and have little manufacturing. This category could then be used by WTO members in devising a common preferential trading scheme that would apply to the vast majority of African countries.[14] To recognize the reality of task-based trade, preferences should feature liberal and simple rules of origin.

Exchange rate protection—deliberately maintaining an undervalued real exchange—can act as a second-best policy to offset the costs of the distortions that constrain industrial exports (World Bank 1993; Rodrik 2008). Sustaining a depreciated real exchange rate, however, requires higher saving relative to investment or lower expenditures relative to income. Postponing consumption in a poor economy has a welfare cost, and the payoff to export growth while likely to be positive is uncertain. This argues for starting out with modest exchange rate protection and using non-traditional export performance as a gauge of success. Overvaluation—particularly in the case of natural resource exporters—should be strenuously resisted.

13.7.2 Acquiring and building capabilities

Policies and institutions for attracting foreign direct investment (FDI) are a key tool in capability building. Ireland has provided an institutional model for attracting and keeping FDI that has become international best practice over the past 20 years. Four features of this model play a crucial role: high-level political ownership, independence, high quality

---

[13] Export push strategies were a feature of development policy among the Asian tigers. See World Bank (1993).

[14] See Collier and Venables (2007) and UNIDO (2009) for such proposals.

personnel, and focus (Barry 2004). Although Africa has FDI agencies, frequently the top political leadership lacks interest, personnel practices, and compensation policies are not sufficiently attractive to make it possible to recruit the high-caliber staff needed, and the agencies are frequently burdened with multiple objectives, diluting focus. African governments who are serious about attracting more capable firms will need to move toward best practice.

The transfer of capabilities to other firms depends largely on firm-to-firm interactions. Removing obstacles to the formation of these relationships is important. Some of these obstacles are as simple as immigration policies that inhibit the temporary entry of engineering and managerial personnel. Others operate through tariff and non-tariff barriers to the import of capital equipment or procurement rules. Foreign investors are often disconnected from domestic value chains by regulations governing Special Economic Zones (SEZs), limiting the potential for transfer of capabilities (Farole 2011). These regulations should be revised to permit the movement of goods and people into and out of the zones. A promising new area in capability building is the development of public–private partnerships to provide management training (Page 2012b).

Especially in resource-rich economies, there may also be a role for public action to promote the formation of value chains linked to the natural resource. This is an area where governments will need to exercise great care. The world is littered with the results of unsuccessful "domestic content programs" based on quantitative targets imposed on foreign investors or "offset" investments required as part of resource extraction agreements. A more fruitful approach is for the public sector to develop programs—ideally in partnership with the foreign investor—to improve the technology and skills of potential supplying firms and to certify quality.

13.7.3 Supporting industrial agglomerations

SEZs are an important tool of spatial industrial policy. In East Asia and Latin America spatial policies have supported an export push through the creation of export processing zones (EPZs) (Farole 2011; Dinh et al. 2013). In countries with unreliable public infrastructure, services export companies look for customized facilities such as IT parks (World Bank 2010c). Most African governments have failed to recognize the potential of SEZs to promote industrial clusters. Often, SEZ programs are put in place and then left to operate on their own with little effort to link the zones to the broader industrial development effort.

Making Africa's SEZs world class will be a challenge. It will require profound changes in management—including the recruitment of high quality business-oriented staff. Surveys of Africa's SEZs document widespread failure by free zone authorities to engage constructively in a dialogue with their private sector clients (Farole 2011). Zone-specific changes in the regulatory regime affecting exports can be introduced to reduce the administrative burdens on exporters. Significant upgrading of infrastructure both within and outside the zones is needed. Business support services, training, and skills upgrading programs focused on the needs of zone-based investors can be introduced. To address the collective action problem FDI policy should be designed to encourage a critical mass of investors to locate in the SEZ within a short period of time. FDI agencies will need to sell the zone in addition to selling the country.[15]

13.7.4 The challenge of close coordination

Because understanding the binding constraints to industrialization requires very detailed information on the industry and the environment within which firms are operating, close coordination between the public and private sectors is central to the success of an industrialization strategy. Meaningful public–private exchange of information can aid in the design of appropriate public actions and provide feedback on implementation (Rodrik 2009; Harrison and Rodriguez-Claire 2009). The massive literature on rent seeking, however, suggests that there is a significant risk of capture of the coordination process by private interests.[16] Developing institutions that can encourage the two-way flow of information between the public and private sectors while reducing the risk of capture will be a major challenge for African governments.

One donor-driven institutional initiative—high level "President's Investors Advisory Councils"—has with few exceptions failed to generate much enthusiasm in the business community or many concrete results.[17] In general the Councils have been better at focusing attention and provoking action on an agenda of previously identified regulatory reforms than they have been at setting their own agenda. Outside of regulatory reform, rather than focusing on a limited number of specific constraints to firm performance and attempting to resolve them, Councils have tended to become fora for very general public–private dialogue. This has led to multiple recommendations for action–often unsupported by analyses–that for the most part have failed to be taken up (Page 2013b).

13.8 CONCLUSIONS

Africa faces a significant structural deficit—the result of two and a half decades of deindustrialization and increasing dependence on natural resources. Today Africa's manufacturing sector is smaller, less diversified and less sophisticated that it was in the decade following independence. Agro-based industry and tradable services, while promising, are still in their

---

[15] China has launched a recent initiative that may provide a model for spatial policies in Africa. It has sponsored the development of five "official" SEZs aimed at supplying the Chinese market. The Chinese government has not involved itself in the design or direct operation of the SEZs, but it has organized marketing events in China to promote investment in the zones (Brautigam and Tang 2011).

[16] See, for example, Krueger (1974). A balanced review of the relevance of this literature is contained in the report of the Spence Commission on Growth and Development (World Bank 2008).

[17] The Councils were one product of the joint tour of Africa by Horst Koehler, then Managing Director of the IMF, and James Wolfensohn, then President of the World Bank. Councils were created by the Presidents of Benin, Ghana, Mali, Mauritania, Senegal, Tanzania and Uganda. International Finance Corporation sponsored public-private dialogue (PPD) mechanisms, which are strikingly similar in their design, are present in ten additional African countries.

infancy. Without structural change the region runs the risk of not sustaining its growth momentum.

While the global industrial economy is a harder place in which to succeed that it was when the East Asian Tigers and China entered the market, there are reasons to believe that breaking into global industry is still possible. Rising real wages and domestic demand in Asia may provide incentives for task-based production to seek alternative locations. Agro-based industry and tradable services, including tourism, offer the prospect of developing complements to mass manufacturing.

Investment climate reforms are still important, but they must be reprioritized and refocused. Urgent action is needed to address Africa's growing infrastructure and skills gaps with the rest of the world. For most African countries conventional wisdom will not be enough. Trade in tasks, firm capabilities, and agglomeration economies tend to favor existing industrial locations. A coordinated strategy for industrial development focusing on an export push, policies and institutions to attract and transfer firm capabilities and spatial industrial policies is needed. So too are institutional innovations that promote coordinated action within the public sector and that manage the tension between close coordination with the private sector and capture.

References

AfDB (2013) *African Economic Outlook 2013: Structural Transformation and Natural Resources* Tunis: African Development Bank.

Arbache, J.S., and J. Page (2009) "How Fragile Is Africa's Recent Growth?" *Journal of African Economies* 19: 1-24.

Barry, F. (2004). Export Platform FDI: the Irish Experience. *EIB Papers,* 9(2):8–37.

Bloom, N., and Van Reenen, J. (2010). Why do management practices differ across firms and countries? *Journal of Economic Perspectives,* 24(1):203–224.

Brautigam, D., and Xioyang, T. (2011). African Shenzhen: China's special economic zones in Africa. *Journal of Modern African Studies,* 49(1):27–54.

Cadot, O., Carrere, C., and Strauss-Kahn, V. (2011). Export diversification: what's behind the hump? *Review of Economics and Statistics,* 93(2):590–605.

Center for African Transformation (2013). *Africa Transformation Report, 2013.* Accra: Center for African Transformation.

Chenery, H. (1986). Growth and transformation, in H. Chenery, S. Robinson, and M. Syrquin (eds), *Industrialization and Growth: A Comparative Study.* New York: OUP.

Collier, P., and Venables, A.J. (2007). Rethinking trade preferences: how Africa can diversify its exports. *World Economy,* 30(8):1326–1345.

Dinh, H.T., Palmade, V., Chandra, V., and Cossar, F. (2013). *Light Manufacturing in Africa: Targeted Policies to Enhance Private Investment and Create Jobs.* Washington, DC: World Bank.

Eifert, B., Gelb, A., and Ramachandran, V. (2005). Business Environment and Comparative Advantage in Africa: Evidence from the Investment Climate Data. Working Paper 56. Washington, DC: Center for Global Development.

Farole, T. (2011). *Special Economic Zones in Africa: Comparing Performance and Learning from Experience.* Washington, DC: World Bank.

Fink, C., Mattoo, A., and Neagu, I. (2002). Assessing the Impact of Communication Costs on International Trade. World Bank Policy Research Working Paper 2929 Washington, DC: World Bank.

Ghani, E., and Kharas, H. (2010). The service revolution in South Asia: an overview, in E. Ghani (ed.), *The Service Revolution in South Asia*. New York: Oxford University Press, pp. 1–32.

Grossman, G., and Rossi-Hansberg, E. (2006). The rise of offshoring: it's not wine for cloth anymore. *Federal Reserve Bank of Kansas City Proceedings*, 59–102.

Harrison, A., and Rodriguez-Clare, A. (2009). Foreign investment, and industrial policy for developing countries, in D. Rodrik and M. Rosenzweig (eds), *Handbook of Development Economics*, vol. 5. The Netherlands: North Holland.

Hausmann, R., Hwang, J., and Rodrik, D. (2007). What you export matters. *Journal of Economic Growth*, 12(1):1–25.

Hummels, D. (2007). Transportation costs and international trade in the second era of globalization. *Journal of Economic Perspectives*, 21(3):131–154.

Humphrey, J., and Memedovic, O. (2006). *Global Value Chain in the Agri-food Sector*. Vienna: UNIDO.

Imbs, J., and Wacziarg, R. (2003). Stages of diversification. *American Economic Review*, 93(1):63–86.

Krueger, A. (1974). The political economy of the rent seeking society. *American Economic Review*, 64(3):291–303.

Kuznets, S. (1955). Economic growth and income inequality. *American Economic Review*, 45(1):1–28.

Lewis, W.A. (1954). Economic development with unlimited supplies of labour. *Manchester School*, 22(2):139–191.

McMillan, M., and Rodrik, D. (2011). Globalization, Structural Change and Productivity Growth NBER Working Paper 17/143. Cambridge: National Bureau of Economic Research.

OECD (2010) "Intra-industry and Intra-firm Trade and the Internationalization of Production", *OECD Economic Outlook 71*. Paris: OECD.

Page, J. (2011). The Diversification Challenge in Africa's Resource Rich Economies. *Africa Economic Research Forum Senior Policy Seminar XIII, Maputo, Mozambique Proceedings*. Nairobi: AERC.

Page, J. (2012a). Can Africa industrialize? *Journal of African Economies* 21(Special Issue 2): ii86–ii124.

Page, J. (2012b). Aid, the Private Sector and Structural Transformation in Africa UNU-WIDER Working Paper 2012/21. Helsinki: UNU-WIDER.

Page, J. (2013a). Should Africa industrialize? in L. Alcorta, W. Naude, and E. Szrmai (eds), *Prospects for Industrialization in the 21st Century*. Oxford: Oxford University Press.

Page, J. (2013b). Industrial Policy in Practice: Africa's Presidential Investor's Advisory Councils WIDER Working Paper Helsinki: UNU-WIDER (forthcoming).

Rodrik, D. (2008) "The real Exchange Rate and Economic Growth", *Brookings Papers on Economic Activity, Fall 2008*. Washington, DC: The Brookings Institution.

Rodrik, D. (2009). Industrial policy don't ask why? Ask how? *Middle East Development Journal*, 1(1):1–29.

Soderbom, M., and Teal, F. (2003) "Are Manufacturing Exports the Key to Economic Success in Africa?" *Journal of African Economies*, 12(1):1-29.

Sutton, J. (2012). *Competing in Capabilities: Globalization and Development, Clarendon Lectures in Economics*. Oxford: Oxford University Press.

Sutton, J., and Kellow, N. (2010). *An Enterprise Map of Ethiopia*. London: International Growth Centre.

Triplett, J.E., and Bosworth, B. (2004). *Productivity in the US Services Sector: New Sources of Economic Growth*. Washington, DC: Brookings Institution Press.

Tyler, G. (2005). Critical Success Factors in the African High Value Horticulture Sector. Background paper for the Competitive Commercial Agriculture in Sub-Saharan Africa Study. Washington, DC: World Bank.

UNIDO (2009). *Industrial Development Report, 2009*. Vienna: United Nations Industrial Development Organization.

World Bank (1993). *The East Asian Miracle: Economic Growth and Public Policy*. New York: Oxford University Press.

World Bank (2007a). *Expanding the Possible in Sub-Saharan Africa: How Tertiary Institutions Can Increase Growth and Competitiveness*. Washington, DC: The World Bank.

World Bank (2007b). *Accelerating Development Outcomes in Africa: Progress and Change in the Africa Action Plan*. Development Committee Paper Washington, DC: The World Bank.

World Bank (2008). *Doing Business: An Independent Evaluation*. Washington, DC: Independent Evaluation Group, World Bank.

World Bank (2010a). *Connecting to Compete: Trade Logistics in the Global Economy*. Washington, DC: World Bank.

World Bank (2010b). *Africa's Trade in Services and Economic Partnership Agreements*. Washington, DC: World Bank.

World Bank (2010c). *The Global Opportunity in IT Based Services*. Washington, DC: World Bank.

World Bank (2011). *Global Development Indicators*. Washington, DC: World Bank.

World Bank (2013a). *Africa's Pulse*. Washington, DC: World Bank.

World Bank (2013b). *Tourism in Africa: Harnessing Tourism for Growth and Improved Livelihoods*. Washington, DC: World Bank.

CHAPTER 14

....

INNOVATION CAPABILITIES FOR SUSTAINABLE DEVELOPMENT IN AFRICA

....

KEUN LEE, CALESTOUS JUMA, AND JOHN MATHEWS

14.1 INTRODUCTION

As stated in the UN Conference on Sustainable Development, the concept of sustainable development involves three dimensions, namely economic, social, and environmental dimensions. Among the three dimensions of sustainable development, economic sustainability is concerned with spreading prosperity and as a result reducing poverty. The second or social aspect concerns equity and has recently been formulated into emphasis on inclusive development. The third or environmental aspect is about the ecological and resource crises faced today and which threaten the development prospects of countries around the world.

While these dimensions are all related to each other, we take science, technology and innovation as holding a key to link them and having a potential of addressing effectively the problems in three areas together (Lee and Mathews 2013).[1] This chapter outlines ways by which Africa can build innovation capabilities needed to address sustainability. It focuses on the role of learning mechanisms and channels of access to foreign knowledge to augment domestic capabilities as part of innovation systems. The chapter is divided into four sections. The first section reviews the potential of innovation in enabling sustainable development in its three dimensions. The second section examines Africa's latecomer advantages and the feasibility and necessity of switching to an alternative growth paradigm. Section three discusses and compares three different types of failures, market failure, system failure and capability failures, to note that the last failure is more unique to Africa and developing countries and prevents them from realizing their full innovation potential. The last section examines specific policy strategies in building up innovation capabilities of African countries.

....

[1] The term "innovation" will be used in the rest of the chapter to mean "science, technology and innovation."

14.2 ROLE OF INNOVATION IN FOSTERING SUSTAINABLE DEVELOPMENT

Innovation plays several roles in development in general and in the sustainability transition in particular (Juma and Lee 2005). First, innovation can be a way to sustain economic growth in developing countries and Africa where people tend to experience short-lived growth only. Growth in developing countries tended to be short-lived because the global competitiveness of its products relies on cheap labor. Developing countries compete with each other by trying to offer low-priced goods, leading to declining prices. Second, innovation can reduce hunger and poverty by helping to increase agricultural productivity thereby lowering food prices (Juma 2011). Third, innovation can promote sustainability by offering new environmentally friendly modes of economic production and consumption. The inability of the conventional fossil-fuelled industrial model to scale up and spread prosperity demands an alternative model of sustainable development driven by innovation. Advancing a nation's capacity in innovation and its effective application in economic activities are therefore essential factors for expanding peoples' capabilities and achieving sustainable development. However, most African countries are lacking in innovation capabilities, which leads to "capability failure" (Lee 2013b), a more serious problem than market failure (Cimoli et al. 2009) or system failure (Nelson 1993; Lundvall 1992; Metcalfe 2005).

While some latecomer economies have been remarkably successful in catching up, many others have not been able to join the catch-up club (Lee 2013a). While short-lived growth must be one of the causes of the poverty trap in low- or middle-income countries, it is also linked to the so-called "adding-up problem." The adding-up problem refers to the situation in which many developing countries flood the market with similar goods that they tend to be better at producing, thus relative prices of these kinds of goods decrease, making these sectors less profitable (Spence 2011). For example, seeing some success of the flower industry in Kenya, several neighboring countries are also jumping into the same industries, which are to a certain extent induced by the flower-purchasing businesses from the high-income countries.

Adding-up problems are also serious in the case of labor-intensive low-end goods production and exports in Africa countries. They compete with each other by trying to offer lower wage rates for assembly sites to attract foreign direct investment (FDI) businesses. However, some success with exporting industries with the OEM (original equipment manufacturing) arrangement tends to raise wages accordingly and eventually their price competitiveness declines. Such businesses have to compete with next tier African countries, which are able to offer cheaper labor to foreign investors (Lee and Mathews 2012). Given such structure, processing industries in Africa cannot be certain about their long-term positions in global value-chains. One way out should be to move up to higher value-added activities in the same industries, which could support higher wages in activities the next-tier countries are not yet capable of executing. Otherwise, a country would experience growth slow-down and fall into the so-called "middle-income trap." It is a situation of being caught between low-wage manufacturers and high-wage innovators because its wage rates are too high to compete with low-wage exporters and their level of technological capability is too low to allow them to compete with the advanced countries.[2]

We can reason that only when more successful African countries such as Mauritius move on from selling these low-end goods to the next stage of making and selling higher-value-added or high-end goods, will they leave room for the followers to continue to sell low-end goods and maintain their footing on the development ladder. From this view, it is important for a country to quickly move beyond specialization in low-end or labor-intensive goods to higher end goods so that other followers may avoid unnecessary competition. This will also help to reduce tension among countries seeking to integrate their economies while producing the same classes of products. Such succession has happened in Asia, with the Korean and Taiwanese taking over the room left by the Japanese, and in turn, as these two advanced, the next tier countries moved in the former places left by Korea and Taiwan.

Similarly, innovation can help increase agricultural productivity, which can then reduce hunger and malnutrition. One-third of sub-Saharan Africa's population is chronically hungry. High food prices force people to purchase less food and less nutritious food. Growth in agriculture is at least two to four times more effective in reducing poverty and hunger than in other sectors because agriculture contributes 34% of GDP and 64% of employment (Juma 2011). A World Bank study has shown that caloric availability has a positive impact on agricultural productivity (World Bank 2008: p. 53). Innovation can help solve this problem by raising agricultural productivity.

Sustaining economic growth is important because growth is essential for creating jobs, spreading prosperity and reducing poverty. Then, given the incidence of adding-up problem and the related middle-income trap, we can see the need for innovation in both differentiating African products from each other and adding value to them. However, innovation has been limited in Africa despite its importance in sustaining economic growth. Furthermore, Africa is expected to find new or different modes of utilizing innovation for development because of the rising environmental costs of conventional growth models.

14.3 LATECOMER ADVANTAGES AND AFRICA

Much of the research on technological development focuses on catching up in the mature industries. It is Freeman and Soete (1985) and Perez and Soete (1988) that suggested the idea of leapfrogging with a focus on the role of the new technological paradigm, which stimulates the clustering of new industries. Emerging technological paradigms serve as windows of opportunity for the country that is catching up. Because they are not locked into old technological systems, these countries can seize new opportunities in emerging or new industries. The area of information and communications technologies, especially in mobile telephones, has demonstrated the power of such windows of opportunity. Other emerging platforms such as genomics, biopolymers and new materials offer similar windows of opportunity. In fact, the phenomenon of exponential scientific advancement and technological abundance provides Africa with more windows of opportunity than its Asian predecessors had (Diamandis and Kotler 2012). Futhermore, Africa's heterogeneous market characteristics

[2] For similar definitions and more discussions, see Lin (2012) and World Bank (2010, 2012).

allow it to customize catch-up models to market size. The rise of regional integration and promotion of intra-Africa trade allows the continent to adopt diverse catch-up strategies that are suited to the different market sizes (Juma 2011).

Perez and Soete emphasize the advantages of early entry into new industries when barriers such as intellectual property rights are low. This is because knowledge tends to reside in the public domain in the early days of new technology. Moreover, under such conditions there are no firmly established market leaders. In the initial stages of a new technological paradigm, the performance of technology is not stable and not dominated by a single firm. If there is adequate human capacity to access the knowledge and create new additional knowledge, entry into emerging technologies can be easier than during the later stage of technological evolution. The strategy of leapfrogging makes more sense during paradigm shifts because the incumbent tends to ignore new technologies and stays with existing dominant technologies (Lee 2013a).

African countries can capture latecomer advantages by adopting green technologies, thereby leapfrogging the stage of "carbon lock-in" that is holding back the developed world (Mathews 2013). Almost all the technologies involved in renewable power generation, energy efficiency, heat and power cogeneration, development of alternative fuels, and transport systems emanate from the advanced world. However, possibilities for applying them are found for the most part in Africa, where carbon lock-in does not act as a constraint. There is an historic opportunity for African countries to build new industrial systems based on renewable energies and resource efficiency that will generate advantages for the countries concerned (and serve as export platforms for their future development) as well as provide a pathway of sustainable development for the rest of the world.

It is a period of opportunity for the entry of African firms, especially when they have government R&D support and financing. Newly emerging or short-cycle technology sectors do not automatically mean that there are no entry barriers. It takes sustained technological effort to harness such emerging opportunities. For example, the wind turbine industry in China and India used to be dominated by European firms. With local technological effort and government support including local content requirements on FDI firms, local firms have made significant and successful entry into the sector (Lema et al. 2012).

Market-based approaches are often inadequate to bring in the new technologies needed to replace unsustainable old ones in time to avert irreversible environmental damage (Altenburg and Engelmeier 2012). Policy intervention may therefore be justified to correct market failures and make green technologies more profitable than less sustainable ones. One way to make them profitable is to create artificial rents (e.g. through smart subsidies) to lure capital into socially desirable green investments. In other words, temporary rents can induce deployment of green technologies, thereby spurring technological learning and allowing producers to reap economies of scale. Now, an emerging literature indicates a revival of industrial policy, such as Lin and Stiglitz (2013) and Aghion et al. (2011).

However, using rents as incentives also risks misallocation and political capture. Such instruments need to be managed carefully with a clear timetable for future withdrawal (as was done with rents flowing from government subsidies in East Asian countries).

14.4 CAPABILITY FAILURE AS A BARRIER TO INNOVATION

Development is more about capability building than it is about optimizing given resources (Lee and Mathews 2010). Then, we can reason that neo-classical economics is not fully relevant for development because it is all about optimization of existing resources. It also implicitly assumes that all resources are accessible and we only have to consider how to utilize them most efficiently (Nelson 2008). In reality for most African countries, what matter more is not to use resources in an optimal way but how to build up various capabilities, especially in the private sector (Lee and Mathews 2010).

Typical market failure justification of R&D subsidy arises from the perceived positive externality of R&D and its resulting undersupply (Greenwald and Stiglitz 2013). In this view, firms are assumed to be capable of conducting R&D. The problem is considered to be simply that they are unable to produce the optimal amount. The reasons for this are sought outside the firm, such as in the capital market or risk market, where government's corrective action is recommended.

However, in most developing countries private firms are unable to pursue and conduct in-house R&D. They consider it an uncertain endeavor with uncertain returns. Thus, the problem is not less or more R&D but "zero" R&D. In fact, R&D-to-GDP ratio becomes flat among the middle-income countries, which means that they are not paying enough for R&D (Lee 2013a). This is serious because middle-income countries are the ones that should start paying more attention to innovation. This suggests that the failure to innovate is the root of the middle-income trap, as verified by Lee and Kim (2009).

In contrast to the typical argument for government activism based on market failure or system failure, "capability failure" is a stronger justification for government activism. In African countries where firms have a low R&D capability, a safer way of doing business is to buy or borrow external technologies or production facilities and specialize in less technical methods or assembly manufacturing. To move beyond this stage, effective forms of government activism is needed, not simply by providing R&D funds but by using various ways to cultivate R&D capability itself.

As shown in the case of Thailand, government policy tends to be limited to providing tax incentives without implementing explicit measures to encourage firms to take on greater risks to innovate (Chaminade et al. 2012). More effective and alternative forms of intervention include transfer of R&D results from universities, public research institutes and public-private R&D consortia to enterprises. This has been used widely and successfully in Korea and Taiwan.[3] Such direct intervention is important because knowledge is a public good and because in many cases there is an absence of opportunity for effective learning. This is often due to inherited conditions or policy failure. Higher technical training is also essential for building the capacity needed to make the sustainability transition (Juma 2007).

In this respect, industrial policy is not about choosing winners but about choosing good students and matching them with good teachers or bringing them to good schools. Good

---

[3] For details, see Mathews (2002), Lee and Lim (2001), and Lee et al. (2005).

schools may be in the form of licensing-based learning (of tacit knowledge) or public–private joint R&D projects, in which direct and cooperative learning can take place. By contrast, institutions that merely supply R&D funding might not serve as good schools. Expanding this analogy, market failure can be expressed as: "I will pay for your school so that you may take more classes." System failure (Metcalfe 2005; Bergek et al. 2008; Dodgson et al. 2011) on the other hand may be expressed as: "Go to school and make more friends." Both views do not pay enough attention to key factors such as the initial aptitude of students, what is taught to them in schools, who the teachers are, and how they teach their students. In the capability view, these aspects are crucial to a successful industrial policy. Thus, the capability failure view is essentially about the importance of raising the level of capabilities of the firms (students) and the various learning methods to be provided during the dynamic course of learning. In sum, both tuition fees (R&D funds) and good friends (linkages to other components in the system) in schools are needed, but the critical factors are the students themselves, a good curriculum, a knowledgeable teacher, and effective teaching methods or pedagogy. Table 14.1 summarizes the aforementioned arguments.

14.5 BUILDING INNOVATION CAPABILITIES

14.5.1 Stages of learning and capability building

There are several stages of learning and capability building that eventually involve the final stage of leapfrogging. In the initial stage latecomer countries tend to specialize in mature industries. An example is textile products where latecomers produce for export markets via an original equipment manufacturer (OEM) arrangement with firms from advanced countries. OEM is a specific form of subcontracting under which a finished product is made to the buyer's exact specifications. Examples of the OEM or FDI-based assembly-type products

Table 14.1 Market failure, system failure, and capability failure

	Market failure	System failure	Capability failure
Focus	Market institutions	Interaction among actors	Actors (firms)
Source	Knowledge as public good	Cognition failure from tacitness of knowledge	historically given No learning opportunity
Example problem	Sub-optimal R&D	Lower R&D effects	No R&D
Solutions	R&D subsidies	Reducing cognitive distance	Access to knowledge and help in learning
School analogy	Tuition support	Making more friends	Targeting student learning
Relevance	Africa and advanced countries	Africa and advanced countries	More unique to Africa countries

Source: Lee (2013b).

include consumer electronics, automobiles, and telecommunication equipment. These arrangements are typical of low-income or middle-income countries. From the 1970s to the early 1990s, OEM accounted for a significant share of the electronic exports of Taiwan and Korea, and served to facilitate technological learning (Hobday 2000).

In this mode of learning-by-doing or exporting, the by products are job creation and foreign exchange earnings, and the policy tools often include tariffs and undervaluation of currencies that are less sector-specific or horizontal. A desirable structure of tariff may be asymmetric, such as higher tariffs for sectors that are being promoted and lower tariffs for imported capital goods. Such asymmetric tariffs increased the world market share of Korean products (Shin and Lee 2012). Other forms of horizontal interventions are needed to build physical infrastructure. While the OEM is an effective way of catching up at the early stage of economic growth, it is somewhat uncertain as a long-term strategy because foreign vendor firms may move their production orders to other lower-wage production sites (Lee 2005). Currently, a similar trend is underway among flower producers in East Africa as foreign vendor firms buy flowers not only from Kenya but also from neighboring countries catching up with Kenya.

In this respect, OEM firms should prepare longer-term plans to transition to original design manufacturing (ODM) and finally to original brand manufacturing (OBM). ODM firms carry out most of the detailed product design, and the customer firms of ODM companies continue with marketing functions. Meanwhile OBM undertakes manufacturing, design of new products, R&D for materials, processing of products, as well as sales and distribution for their own brand. The path from OEM to ODM to OBM has become the standard upgrading process for the latecomer firms. Modified examples of such upgrading in flower firms in Africa would be producing flowers that can last longer, have specific smells and use fewer pesticides. All these require innovation. A transition to OBM in the flower industry would require African firms to enter into marketing and set up their own outlets with their own brands in Europe. Such a transition to ODM or OBM is not easy but serves as a narrow path to the middle or even higher income status. Another model available for African countries endowed with rich resources is a combination of "black" and "green" development, where cash from exports of natural resources can be used to finance entry into green industries (Lee and Mathews 2013).

In general, transition to the middle-income stage and beyond calls for more sector-specific or vertical intervention policies. This is because the country must identify its niche between low-income countries with cost advantages in low-end goods and high-income countries with quality advantages in high-end goods. At this stage, public policy should focus on two kinds of upgrading: entry into new industries; and upgrading to higher-value segment in existing industries, which is to upgrade the overall industrial structure (Lee and Mathews 2012). Short-cycle technology-based sectors are candidate niches for latecomers (Lee 2013a). The main issue is how to break into medium short-cycle technology-based products or into the higher-valued segment of the existing sectors. Good targets for such an (import substitution) entry are those products that latecomers have to import at higher prices due to oligopolistic market structure dominated by incumbent countries or firms. A best existing example is China's telephone switch development in the 1980s and 1990s (Lee, Mani, and Mu 2012). The lessons have implications for African countries that produce oil but export it as crude oil without refining it. They can build more oil refineries based on mature or medium short-cycle technologies. The task is possible since the technology needed to build oil refineries is old, mature and easily available at cost. The process would be similar to the Korean entry into steelmaking through a state-owned enterprise in the early 1970s.

The final stage of leapfrogging involves public–private R&D efforts that target emerging rather than existing technologies. In this case, the role of the government, research-oriented universities and public labs share the risks of the choice of technologies and promote initial market creation. Specifically, coordinated initiatives on exclusive standards and incentives for early adopters are essential in reducing the risks associated with weak initial markets. Examples of this strategy can be found in the renewable energy markets of China, Brazil, and India, which involve the transition toward low-carbon economies. Options for Africa in low-carbon technologies include wind, solar, biogas, and geothermal energy sources.

An example is the use of solar power in the desert grasslands rural area in Jigawa State of Nigeria. Given that there was no water supply in this semi-desert area, a traditional option was open wells with rope and bucket, hand pumps, or government-supplied diesel-powered pumps that work only until they break down or until villagers run out of money to buy the expensive diesel. Now, solar-powered pumps solved the problem as they are designed to run maintenance-free for eight-to-ten years or more.

Another example is the O&L Groups in Namibia. Established by Mr. Shilongo, this company started from retail and brewery, and then diversified into dairy and even solar energy. Owing to government support (against a South African company's price dumping to kill this company), they survived, and grew quickly with their sales reaching about 4% of GDP of that country. In this sense, this conglomerate can be a called a "Samsung" of Namibia. Given that Namibia imports electricity from South Africa and Angola, this company plans to enter more into energy business, including wind power, although they have first to solve the hurdle imposed by grid monopoly by the government.

Some examples in Africa are really about the adoption of new technologies rather than local innovations. But adoption is a stepping stone for learning and eventual innovation. Manufacturing companies in East Asia, such as Samsung and Hyundai Motors in Korea, all started from adoption of foreign technology for production, learned from using them, found a way to enhance productivity by mastering production technologies, and finally even acquired design technology (R&D capability) to be able to conduct their own machineries and equipment (Lee 2005, 2013).

14.5.2 From the GPG model to FLG model of learning

The three stages in the above scheme can be further elaborated with a focus on the changing roles of government research institutes (GRIs) or public research organizations (PROs). The essence of such a latecomer model of technological development is the tripartite cooperation involving government research institutes, private firms and government ministries (GPGs). Under this model the actors have different roles depending on the stage of development. Every technological development should involve R&D, production and marketing. This implies that government research labs are in charge of R&D; private firms undertake production; and government ministries handle marketing in the form of direct procurement or protection by tariffs and exclusive standards.

The case of the telephone switch in Korea and China would be the most typical representation of this model. Under this model (let us call it GPG1) R&D is mainly done by GRIs or public research organs (Table 14.2). Private firms are in charge of manufacturing and the government helps marketing through procurement of the domestically made products. There are other variations on the model depending on the level of capabilities in private firms and the public agents involved. The case of the digital TV and CDMA mobile phone in Korea is another variation that can be called a GPG2 (Lee et al. 2005). In the GPG2 model, the costs and risks of R&D are shared between government research institutes and private firms, and the GRIs watch technology trends and coordinate to bring diverse actors into the consortium. The GPG2 model is a more advanced form of the GPG arrangement. It is only possible when the capabilities of private firms are advanced enough to undertake more R&D.

Another variation of the GPG model is the case of government agents doing both R&D and production. This is possible when capabilities of private firms are low or the projects involve more production and less R&D with some start-up costs. This variation can be called GPG0, though it is actually not GPG but GG without P (without involvement of private firms). Steel development in Korea by the government-owned enterprise POSCO is an example.

The opposite case to this GPG0 mode is that of GPG3 or PG, where government research institute is missing. An example is the case of the development of the automobile industry spearheaded by Hyundai Motors. In this case, the government or a government research institute was not involved in R&D but its role was limited to providing protection of the infant industry by tariffs (Lee and Lim 2001). Since R&D was done by a private firm or

Table 14.2 From GPG model to FLG (foreign actor to local firm government) model

First stage	GPG0	FLG0
Tech transfer/R&D	PRO/Foreign actor	Foreign cooperation partner
Production	SOEs/Private firms	Local firm (private, SOEs)
Market promotion/protection	Gov't	Gov't
Second stage	**GPG1**	**FL–P–G (FLG1)**
R&D	PROs	Joint R&D by foreign and local PROs/firms
Production	Private firms	Local private firms
Market promotion/protection	Gov't	Gov't
Third stage	**GPG2**	**G–P–G2 (FLG2)**
R&D	Public and private joint R&D	Local public and private joint R&D
Production	Private firms	Local private firms
Market promotion/protection	Gov't	Gov't
Fourth stage	**GPG3 (PG)**	**G–P–G3 (FLG3)**
R&D	Private firms	Local private firms
Production	Private firms	Local private firms
Market promotion/protection	None	None

Source: Lee and Mathews (2013).

Hyundai Motors, this is a GP rather than GGP model, where private firms do both R&D and production.

Based on the Korean experience, there are four modes of state activism for technological development with increasing private sector participation. First, there is the GPG0 (or GG) mode where the government does market provision and state-owned enterprises undertake both R&D and production. Second, in the GPG1 model R&D is done by GRIs and production is undertaken by private firms. Third under the GPG2 model more R&D is shifted to private firms that cooperate with GRIs. Finally, the GPG3 (or PG) model has private firms doing both R&D and production. In all of these variations, the role of the government (or ministries involved) tends to focus on guaranteeing initial market creation in the form of procurement policies, and local market protection by tariffs or exclusive setting of standards.

In the above discussion, the focus has been on the roles of government ministries or research labs. However, one common element across the four modes of technological development is that they are all involved in accessing foreign knowledge in diverse channels. In this regard, foreign knowledge is critical, without which the latecomers' catching-up effort is often at risk and is too time consuming and costly (Lee 2005). In general, the diverse channels of knowledge access and learning include such modes as training in foreign firms and institutes, OEM, licensing, joint ventures, co-development with foreign specialized R&D firms, transfers of individual scientists or engineers, reverse brain drain, overseas R&D centers, strategic alliances, and international mergers and acquisitions (Lee 2005). Successful technological development by latecomers tends to involve government support, access to foreign knowledge, and private firms' efforts. The weight and specific role of the three elements differ by sector and level (or stage) of economic development.

The above GPG model can be modified as the model of international technology assistance for African countries. This can involve cooperation between foreign actors, local firms, and government (FLG). A simple idea is to put foreign actors (foreign research organization invited by the donor government or the United Nations) in the place of the GRI/PRO in the GPG model so that foreign actors (cooperating partner) conduct R&D to transfer the results to local (private or state-owned) firms in African countries (stage FLG0). Then, in the next stage or FLPG, foreign partners conduct joint R&D with local R&D organization or firms. Then, in the third stage, the aid-receiving African country is able to conduct R&D locally through private-public partnerships, which is equivalent to GPG2. The final stage is, of course, where all functions are performed by private actors.

The Green Revolution of the 1960s and 1970s and the System of Rice Intensification (SRI) are examples of the FLG model. The Green Revolution involved the introduction of packages of high-yielding varieties (of rice, wheat, rice and maize), fertilizers, pesticides, new management practices and irrigation. The packages brought about a dramatic increase in productivity and production. The Green Revolution, initiated with support from the Ford and Rockefeller Foundations and led by Norman Borlaug, is regarded as having saved over a billion people from starvation. Much of the initial research on rice and wheat had already been done in American universities but needed to be adapted to local conditions. This required the creation of new international research institutes, initially the International Maize and Wheat Improvement Center (CIMMYT) in Mexico and the International Rice Research Institute (IRRI) in the Philippines (Juma 2011). These institutions were later brought under the auspices of the Consultative Group on International Agricultural Research (CGIAR).

Today the CGIAR is a consortium of 15 research institutes working on agroforestry, biodiversity, dry areas, food policy, fish, forestry, livestock, maize and wheat, potato, rice, semi-arid tropics, tropical agriculture, and water. As part of this international initiative, local governments expanded roads, improved irrigation systems, and provided electrical power to support farmers to adopt the new technology. International lending was also made available to promote the package. Research collaboration at the international level also led to the birth and expansion of national agricultural research institutes. These centers were able to adapt the internationally developed varieties of rice and wheat to local conditions.

In the Indian case, the government played a key role in the diffusion of new seed varieties. The government, with the financial support from the World Bank and technical assistance from the Rockefeller Foundation, established state seed corporations in most major states in the 1960s, which led to the creation of the seed industry in India (Juma 2011). SRI was started in the early 1980s after participating groups from 40 countries first assembled in Madagascar in 1983. Then, it rapidly spread to more countries with the assistance of Cornell University. India is regarded as one of the biggest beneficiaries of this initiative.

14.6 CONCLUSIONS AND IMPLICATIONS

This chapter has argued that innovation can play a critical role in expediting the transition to a sustainable mode of development, especially through industrial restructuring and fostering of green growth. A critical concept in this transition is leapfrogging including stage skipping, whereby African countries can jump into a new ecofriendly techno-economic paradigm. The concept of green growth has an intuitive appeal because it is the developed countries that have the most infrastructural inertia in terms of "carbon lock-in," whereas African countries have the opportunity to leap to new green innovation systems that are unconstrained by such lock-in. They also have powerful competitive advantages based on their abundance of resources (sun, land, water), which can be utilized as sources of energy, both to power the industrial development of the latecomer itself but also to provide an export platform.

The revival of agriculture also offers new opportunities to leapfrog into green technologies. For example, Burkina Faso adopted insect-resistant genetically modified (GM) cotton that has significantly reduced the amount of insecticides that would have been used if it had pursued older production methods (Vitale et al. 2010). In fact, the country was able to skip the first generation of GM cotton and go straight to the second generation that used stacked genes. Such leapfrogging cannot be done without the existence of the local research capabilities needed in the various stages of the cotton production value chain.

Indeed, if African countries want to undertake such leapfrogging in areas of green innovation, they need to build up technological capabilities and access the vast fund of knowledge available in other countries around the world (Juma 2012). It is not enough to simply focus on technology acquisition and foreign direct investment. Efforts must be made to promote indigenous innovation, utilizing public research institutions as well as universities. The next step is to promote the diffusion of new clean and green technologies through incentives that stimulate their uptake by new local sectors. Brazil's biofuels program, with its empha-sis on providing rural employment and its building of national domestic value chains for bioethanol and biodiesel production, is an example of the social inclusiveness that can be generated by green growth strategies. Africa can pursue such strategies in areas such as solar photovoltaics and wind power.

To sustain economic growth, the rebalancing of the development agenda should empha-size not only infrastructure or business climate improvement but also cultivation of private firms and their innovation capabilities. Thus, African countries should be allowed policy space to nurture their local firms. Local firms are unlikely to emerge and flourish if they are exposed from the beginning to competition with foreign goods. Having elementary school players competing in the same soccer tournament with professional players is not a fair game. To further facilitate the cultivation of firm-level technological capabilities, inter-national organizations such as the World Bank and the United Nations may consider start-ing new initiatives to promote local–foreign partnerships (LFPs). This can be regarded as a modification of private–public partnerships (PPPs) involving R&D consortia. While the lat-ter involves private firms and public research facilities as was successfully practiced in East Asia, LFP involves private firms in less developed countries cooperating with public R&D units from industrialized countries to solve production problems. The approach can also be used to implement new business ventures for import-substitution or export-generation in mature or emerging technology sectors.

An international assistance program that might be called "Innovation Corps" can be launched to help firms in Africa. The innovation members would be a team of foreign experts from public R&D units, retired engineers from private sector, and policy practition-ers from foreign governments. Such teams can help solve technical bottlenecks in African country firms in the area of innovation and management consulting and know-how. The Korean government has promoted such programs to help the small and medium-sized enterprises (SMEs). The United Nations Industrial Development Organization (UNIDO) has a similar program that can be expanded.

There are many examples of technological leapfrogging that have been practiced around the world including in Africa and have had tangible impacts on patterns of production and consumption. However, a greater policy intervention is called for to expedite the diffu-sion of new technologies needed to maintain the upgrading momentum. Various forms of incentives are needed to correct market failures and coordination failures and to achieve economies of scale. The international community may consider setting up a global fund to support R&D into new environmentally friendly technologies and to promote their diffusion.

In sum, this chapter has argued that green growth is a feasible goal for Africa countries, enabling them to create a sustainability path, with a part of the revenue from exporting raw materials, from "Black to Green" development. Green growth offers the best chances for social inclusiveness, given that many sources of renewable energy will have to be developed in rural areas and can offer employment and social infrastructure for rural communities. This is a promising way forward for Africa countries. But to achieve it Africa will have to focus its long-term attention on building innovation capabilities.

ACKNOWLEDGMENTS

An earlier version of this was presented at the Conference for this volume held in Beijing, December 2013, and the authors thank Jean-Jacques Dethier, Alan Gelb, Akbar Noman, and Bichaka Fayissa for useful comments. Section 5 draws heavily on Lee and Mathews (2013).

REFERENCES

Aghion, P., Dewatripont, M., Du, L. et al. (2011). Industrial Policy and Competition. CEPR Discussion Papers 8619, C.E.P.R. Discussion Papers.

Altenburg, T., and Engelmeier, T. (2012). Rent management and policy learning in green technology development: The case of solar energy in India. Paper presented at the 2012 Globelics Conference, Hangzhou, China.

Bergek, A., Jacobsson, S., Carlsson, B. et al. (2008). Analyzing the functional dynamics of technological innovation systems: a scheme of analysis. *Research Policy*, 37(3):407–429.

Chaminade, C., Intarakumnerd, P., and Sapprasert, K. (2012). Measuring systemic problems in national innovation systems: an application to Thailand. *Research Policy*, 41(8):1476–1488.

Cimoli, M., Dosi, G., and Stiglitz, J.E. (2009). *Industrial Policy and Development: The Political Economy of Capabilities Accumulation*. New York: Oxford University Press.

Diamandis, P., and Kotler, S. (2012). *Abundance: The Future is Better than You Think*. New York, Free Press.

Dodgson, M., Hughes, A., Foster, J., and Metcalfe, J.S. (2011). Systems thinking, market failure, and the development of innovation policy: the case of Australia. *Research Policy*, 40(9):1145–1156.

Freeman, C., and Soete, L. (1985). *Information technology and employment: An assessment*. Science Policy Research Unit, University of Sussex.

Greenwald, B., and Stiglitz, J. (2013). Industrial policy, creation of a learning society and economic development, in J. Stiglitz and J. Lin (eds), *Industrial Policy Revolution*. New York: Palgrave MacMillan.

Hobday, M. (2000). East versus Southeast Asian Innovation systems: comparing OEM- and TNC-led growth in electronics, in L. Kim and R. Nelson (eds), *Technology, Learning and Innovation: Experiences of Newly Industrializing Economies*. Cambridge: Cambridge University Press, pp. 129–169.

Juma, C., and Yee-Cheong, L. (2005). *Innovation: Applying Knowledge in Development*. London: Earthscan.

Juma, C. (2007). Technological learning and sustainability transition: the role of institutions of higher learning in Africa, in OECD/Department of Science and Technology, South Africa, in *Integrating Science & Technology into Development Policies: An International Perspective*. Paris: OECD Publishing.

Juma, C. (2011). *The New Harvest: Agriculture Innovation in Africa*. New York: Oxford University Press.

Juma, C. (2012). *Technological Abundance for Global Agriculture: The Role of Biotechnology*. HKS Working Paper No. RWP12-008. Cambridge, US: Harvard Kennedy School, Harvard University.

Lee, K. (2005). Making a technological catch-up: barriers and opportunities. *Asian Journal of Technology Innovation*, 13(2):97–131.

Lee, K. (2013a). *Schumpeterian Analysis of Economic Catch-up: Knowledge, Path-creation and Middle Income Trap*. Cambridge: Cambridge University Press.

Lee, K. (2013b). Capability failure and industrial policy to move beyond the middle-income trap: from trade-based to technology based specialization, in J. Lin and J. Stiglitz (eds), *New Thinking in Industrial Policy*. Basingstoke: Palgrave.

Lee, K., and Kim, B.Y. (2009). Both institutions and policies matter but differently at different income groups of countries: determinants of long run economic growth Revisited. *World Development*, 37(3):533–549.

Lee, K., and Lim, C. (2001). Technological regimes, catching-up and leapfrogging: findings from the Korean industries. *Research Policy*, 30(3):459–483.

Lee, K., and Mathews, J. (2010). From the Washington Consensus to the BeST Consensus for world development. *Asian-Pacific Economic Literature*, 24(1):86–103.

Lee, K., and Mathews, J. (2012). Firms in Korea and Taiwan: Upgrading in the Same Industry and Entries into New Industries for Sustained Catch-up, in J. Cantwell and E. Amann (eds), *The Innovative firms in the Emerging Market Economies*. New York: Oxford University Press, pp. 223–248.

Lee, K., and Mathews, J. (2013). STI for Sustainable Development, UN: committee for development policy. Background paper No. 16.

Lee, K., Lim, C., and Song, W. (2005). Emerging digital technology as a window of opportunity and technological leapfrogging: catch-up in digital TV by the Korean firms. *International Journal of Technology Management*, 29(1–2):40–63.

Lee, K., Mani, S., and Mu, Q. (2012). Divergent stories of catchup in telecom: China, India, Brazil, and Korea, in F. Malerba and R. Nelson (eds), *Economic Development as a Learning Process*. Cheltenham, UK: Edward Elgar, pp. 21–71.

Lema, R., Berger, A., and Schmitz, H. (2012). China's Impact on the Global Wind Power Industry. Discussion Paper 16/2012, German Development Institute.

Lin, J., and Stiglitz, J. (eds) (2013). *New Thinking in Industrial Policy*. Palgrave.

Lin, J.Y. (2012). *The Quest for Prosperity: How Developing Economies can take off*. Princeton, NJ: Princeton University Press.

Lundvall, B.-A. (1992). *National System of Innovation: Toward a Theory of Innovation and Interactive Learning*. London: Pinter Publishers.

Mathews, J.A. (2002). The origins and dynamics of Taiwan's R&D consortia. *Research Policy*, 31(4):633–651.

Mathews, J.A. (2013). The renewable energies technology surge: A new techno-economic paradigm in the making? *Futures*, 46:10-22.

Metcalfe, J.S. (2005). Systems failure and the case for innovation policy, in P. Llerena, M. Matt, A. Avadikyan (eds), *Innovation Policy in a Knowledge-based Economy: Theory and Practice*. Germany: Springer, pp. 47–74.

Nelson, R. (2008). Economic Development from the perspective of evolutionary economic theory. *Oxford Development Studies*, 36(1):9–21.

Nelson, R. (1993). *National Innovation Systems: A Comparative Analysis*. New York: Oxford University Press.

Perez, C., and Soete, L. (1988). Catching-up in technology: entry barriers and windows of opportunity, in Dosi et al. (eds), *Technical Change and Economic Theory*. London: Pinter Publishers, pp. 458–479.

Shin, H., and Lee, K. (2012). Asymmetric protection leading not to productivity but export share changes: the case of Korean industries, 1967–1993. *Economics of Transition*, 20(4):745–785.

Spence, M. (2011). *The Next Convergence: The Future of Economic Growth in a Multispeed World*. New York: FSG Books.

Vitale, J. et al. (2010). The commercial application of GMO crops in Africa: Burkina Faso's decade of experience with Bt Cotton. *AgBioForum*, 13(4):320–332.

World Bank (2008). World Development Report. Washington, DC: World Bank, p. 53.

World Bank (2010). *Exploring the Middle-Income-Trap: World Bank East Asia Pacific Economic Update: Robust Recovery, Rising Risks*, Vol. II. Washington, DC: World Bank.

World Bank (2012). *China 2030: Building a Modern, Harmonious, and Creative High-Income Society*. Washington, DC: World Bank.

PART II

MICROECONOMIC AND SECTORAL ISSUES

CHAPTER 15

LAND TENURE AND AGRICULTURAL INTENSIFICATION IN SUB-SAHARAN AFRICA

KEIJIRO OTSUKA AND FRANK PLACE

15.1 INTRODUCTION

NATURAL resources in sub-Saharan Africa (SSA) continue to deteriorate due to increasing population pressure on limited land. Natural forests and communal grazing areas have been declining and converted to crop fields (Meybeck and Place 2014). Deforestation is a major concern, as it is known to be a major cause for greenhouse gas emission in developing countries (IPCC 2011). Soil fertility continues to be degraded in many places due to the intensification of farming systems without replenishment of sufficient amounts of nutrients, which threatens the sustainable development of agriculture in SSA (Meybeck and Place 2014). On the other hand, there are signs of natural resource restoration. First, more trees are naturally regenerated or planted by farmers. In Niger, as much as five million hectares have been regenerated by farmers on their own farmland (Reij et al. 2009). In more humid areas, farmers are planting trees as woodlots (Bamwerinde et al. 2006), mixed with crops in their fields (Garrity et al. 2010), and on the edges of crop fields (Holden et al. 2013). Second, some forests are managed by communities, which have contributed to the restoration of some degraded forests (Jumbe and Angelson 2006). Third, in forest margins, crop fields under shifting cultivation are replaced by fields growing commercial tree crops such as rubber, coffee, oil palm, and cocoa (Otsuka and Place 2001). Although commercial tree fields are much inferior to virgin forests in terms of the biomass and biodiversity, they are very productive and provide livelihood for poor smallholders. Fourth, in highly populated areas, intensive farming systems are widely practiced, in which manure is applied to crop fields and crop rotation with leguminous crops or intercropping of cereals and beans is practiced (e.g. Yamano et al. 2011). Nitrogen-fixing trees are also more widely planted on crop fields now so that there is much greater use of organic nutrients to enhance soil fertility. Such farming practices contribute to maintaining and improving soil fertility and, hence, to the yield growth of maize and other upland crops in SSA (Otsuka and Larson 2015).

Land ownership rights and land tenure security are known to be major determinants of land use, investments in the land improvement, and intensification of farming (Otsuka and Place 2001). Where individualized rights are established on agricultural land, farmers invest in longer-term improvements, including tree planting, crop rotations, manuring, and soil conservation (Holden et al. 2009, 2013; Deininger and Jin 2006 for Ethiopia; Deininger and Ali 2007 for Uganda). For example, tree cover as percent of land area increased on farms and decreased off farms over a 30-year period in Uganda (Place and Otsuka 2000) and farmers now grow trees on the edge of crop fields in East Africa, because they have acquired secure individualized land use rights (Holden et al. 2013). Despite its importance, however, land tenure insecurity is still a major problem in many countries in SSA (Namubiru-Mwaura and Place 2013). Therefore, in order to restore natural resource environments, increase crop yields sustainably, and improve livelihoods of the poor rural population in SSA, how to strengthen land tenure security is a major policy issue.

This chapter reviews the literature on the role of evolutionary changes in land tenure in the intensification of farming systems in SSA. Section 2 provides a conceptual framework to understand the link between population growth, changes in land tenure, and agricultural intensification. In order to test the relevance of the conceptual framework, section 3 examines the data on population pressure and land use changes and reviews the relevant literature, whereas section 4 undertakes a review of the literature on agricultural intensification. Finally, section 5 provides implications of this study for land tenure and agricultural development policies in SSA.

15.2 CONCEPTUAL FRAMEWORK

Traditionally, land was owned collectively by the community, clan, lineage, or extended family under customary land tenure systems in SSA, but they have been evolving toward individualized tenure (Bruce and Migot-Adholla 1994). As early as the 1960s Boserup (1965) argued that increasing population density affects the evolution of farming system from an extensive, land-using system to an intensive, land-saving system. Her arguments were later elaborated by Ruthenberg (1980), Binswanger and McIntire (1987), and Pingali, Bigot, and Binswanger (1987), among others. The essence of the Boserupian theory is no different from more formal analysis of induced innovations by Hayami and Ruttan (1985). However, while Boserup discusses only changes in the farming system or technological change, Hayami and Ruttan analyze not only induced technological change but also the induced institutional innovations that support the technological change. Indeed, whether intensified farming system can emerge without institutional changes is questionable because transition to intensified farming systems requires investment in land improvement and, hence, the institution to strengthen and protect property rights on land.

In our view, neither the Boserupian theory nor the Hayami and Ruttan framework is sufficient for fully explaining evolutionary changes in land tenure institutions in SSA. Boserup did not discuss how agricultural intensification takes place, whereas the inducement mechanism envisaged by Hayami and Ruttan is not strong enough to realize major gains in agricultural productivity. In our conceptual framework portrayed in Figure 15.1, we provide integrated links among population growth, evolutionary changes in land tenure institutions, and the intensification of farming systems.

When land is abundant, land-using, extensive farming systems, such as slash and burn farming, are practiced. As population grows, uncultivated land, for example, forest land and woodland, is brought into cultivation. Typically land is held in under a customary system, in which uncultivated land is controlled by the chief on behalf of the community and cultivated land including fallow land is "owned" by a group of kin-related people (e.g. lineage, clan, and extended family). Land use rights are secure under this system so long as the land is cultivated (Sjaastad and Bromley 1997; Bruce and Adholla 1994; Otsuka and Place 2001; Place 2009); otherwise, cultivators who have converted uncultivated land cannot reap the benefit of long-term land investments with assurance. After one to two seasons of cultivation, the

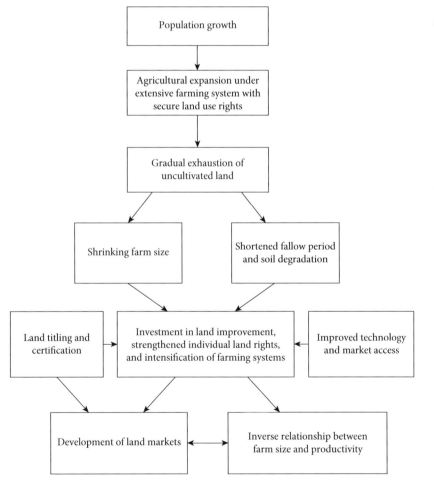

FIGURE 15.1 Conceptual framework of the evolution of land tenure, land management, and land markets.

soil quality declines and land is put into fallow for a few decades for complete restoration of soil quality. Since it is not clear whether the present cultivator is interested in cultivation of the same plot decades later, the leader of the family group controls this piece of land for temporary allocation and inheritance among family members.

If population growth continues, uncultivated land is gradually exhausted. This leads to shortened fallow periods, which, in turn, tends to lead to soil degradation until secure individualized land rights institutions are established to induce investment in land improvement. Also observed at this stage is increasing labor-farmland ratio and shrinking farm size. These are the signs of increasing scarcity of land, which is expected to lead to an intensified, land-saving farming system according to the theories of Boserup (1965) and Hayami and Ruttan (1985).

As Otsuka and Place (2001) point out, in order to shift from an extensive farming system to an intensive farming system, for example, sedentary farming with little or no fallowing, investments in land improvement are usually required. Examples are planting of commercial trees, the construction of irrigation facilities, drainage canals, terraces, and fences, and the application of manure and compost. In order to assure that investment benefits accrue to investors, not only land use rights but also transfer rights must be strengthened (Besley 1995). Transfer rights are important to provide proper investment incentives because the rights to rent out and sell land confer benefits of land investments under a variety of occasions when investors need cash. Our hypothesis is that investments in land improvement can also strengthen individual land rights, which lead to intensification of farming system (Otsuka and Place 2001; Holden and Otsuka 2014).

Western Ghana provides an example of individualization of land rights. In locations where uterine matrilineal inheritance system prevailed, men traditionally owned land and were expected to transfer it to his sisters' sons. Now inter vivos transfer of land is made from a man to his wife and children in the name of "gift," including daughters, provided that the wife and daughters helped the husband establish cocoa fields by engaging in weeding (Quisumbing et al. 2001). Gift land is characterized by strong individual land rights and accounted for roughly one-third of cocoa area in this region around 2000. In matrilineal and matrilocal society in Central Malawi, trees naturally grown on the crop field belong to the wife's family but trees planted by husband are owned by him, so that upon divorce or death of his wife, he can cut down his trees and sell them before going back to his home village (Place and Otsuka 2001). Similarly, wet land reclaimed by men by their hard work for vegetable production using traditional irrigation is owned by them with rights to sell in this matrilineal society. These examples demonstrate that investment in land improvement and farming intensification strengthens individual land rights. Brasselle et al. (2002), Place and Otsuka (2002), and Baland et al. (1999), among others, also found in Burkina Faso and Uganda, respectively, that investments in trees led to strengthened individual land rights.

In his review of the literature on land tenure and investment incentives in West Africa, Fenske (2011), found that while secure tenure is significantly associated with fallow and tree planting, the link between land tenure security and other investments is generally weak. One of the possible reasons for this weak link is attributed to the tendency that individual land rights are strengthened by investment. In other words, the expected returns to investment are high, even if land rights are weak ex anté, if investment enhances land rights ex post. Thus, weak tenure security may not discourage investment in land, if the latter strengthens tenure security. In our view, the simultaneous determination of land rights and investment is likely to blur the empirical link between land rights and investments.[1]

Place and Hazell (1993) found that tenure security did positively affect the adoption of some land investments, but did not find evidence that inputs are used more intensively on parcels of higher tenure security in Ghana, Kenya, and Rwanda. Benefits from inputs are often not long term and so tenure security is less important. It may also be that inputs are more or less equally intensively used on parcels of lower and higher tenure security, to the extent that higher input intensity, land investment, and ex post tenure security are positively correlated.

Population pressure has unambiguously reduced farm sizes in Africa and led to greater individualization of land rights on these farms. The implications for tenure security are several. Individualization itself has generated greater tenure security for the farmers who increasingly acquire land through inheritance or purchase from farmers, rather than the conversion of uncultivated land, and can use and transfer the land as they wish.[2] On the other hand, because of the pressure on land and reduction in farm size, land rental markets have developed where tenants may not have long-term use rights. Moreover, land shortage creates heightened conflict over land resources among family members over inheritance and between neighbors disputing over boundaries. These causes for insecurity need to be managed and will be discussed in section 5. It is also important to point out that the general trend towards increasing security of tenure is not equally shared by women or some migrant communities in SSA (Place 2009).

Land titling, certification, or registration may or may not strengthen individual land rights (Bruce and Migot-Adholla 1994). Place and Migot-Adholla (1998) found no effect of land title on investment and productivity in Kenya. We support the observation of Deininger (2003) that moves toward establishing formal tenure systems have also resulted in increased tenure insecurity in many countries, because of the conflicts between traditional rights and newly created legal land rights. That is to say, if land titling was implemented before land rights are individualized spontaneously, titling is likely to create conflicts among family members, who collectively "own" the same piece of land. Once the individualization of land rights has been achieved endogenously, land registration is likely to strengthen land rights because of the absence of overlapping land rights among family members. Indeed, many studies in Ethiopia, where individual cultivation rights have been established, for example, Holden et al. (2009) found that land registration and certification has resulted in more investment and higher land productivity.

We hypothesize that the availability of improved technology and improved market access will stimulate investment in land by enhancing its rate of return. This, in turn, will enhance individual land rights and facilitate intensification of farming systems. Hayami and Ruttan (1985) argued that in the case of Asia, the Green Revolution was induced to take place precisely when land had become scarce relative to labor in the late 1960s. The inducement process, however, is not simple because public-sector research and extension systems had to be greatly improved to realize a Green Revolution. In our view, lack of development of appropriate

[1] What matters is land rights after investment, not necessarily change in land right. Thus, if land rights are secure from the beginning and unchanged, it provides strong investment incentives.

[2] Similarly, the conversion of uncultivated land into cultivated land confers strong use right.

technologies (e.g. as in the case of maize) or an effective extension system (e.g. for lowland rice) is often observed to impede investment and intensification in SSA (Otsuka and Larson, 2015). On the other hand, improved market access leads to the production of such high value and profitable crops as flowers, vegetables, and fruits in some parts of SSA, possibly because improved technologies are often imported and less dependent on domestic research systems.

The intensification of farming systems confers an advantage to smallholder farmers over large farmers. As Hayami and Otsuka (1993) argued, the monitoring cost of hired labor is quite high in spatially diverse farm environments, so that labor-abundant smallholders relying on family labor is more efficient than large land-abundant farmers relying on hired labor. Consequently, an inverse relationship between farm size and productivity, particularly crop yield, has been widely observed in South Asia (Otsuka 2007). To our knowledge, however, such an inverse relationship had seldom been reported in SSA until recently, at least partly because the farming system was relatively extensive, requiring little hired labor. If an extensive farming system, such as slash and burn farming, is practiced, we can hardly expect to observe any correlation between *cultivated* farm size and productivity. Recently, however, the inverse relationship is found by numerous studies in SSA (e.g. Holden et al. 2009; Carletto et al. 2013; Larson et al. 2014; Holden and Fisher 2013). Unless the farming system is sufficiently intensified and demand for labor is significantly increased, we hardly expect to observe such an inverse relationship.

The intensification of farming system increases the value of land, so that allocation of land from less productive to more productive producers becomes important for efficient agricultural production. Since land transfer rights are relatively well established and the inverse relationship between farm size and productivity has emerged, land markets tend to develop. According to the latest surveys of the literature by Holden et al. (2013) and Holden and Otsuka (2014), land markets, both land rental and land sales, have become active in many African countries where population density is high. Furthermore, they find that both land rental and sales transactions are pro-poor, meaning that land-abundant farm households tend to rent out or sell land to land-poor households, who are generally poor. This is consistent with the observed inverse relationship. However, the fact that the inverse relationship is observed implies that land markets are not working fully efficiently so as to wipe out any productivity gap. In Ethiopia where land rights have been strengthened by the land certification program, land renting has become more common, suggesting that successful policy intervention can also potentially stimulate land market transactions.

Based on the conceptual framework on the evolutionary changes in land rights and intensification of farming systems shown in Figure 15.1 we review the empirical literature and statistical data on population growth, changing land use, and agricultural intensification in the following two sections, before discussing the policy options in the final section.

15.3 POPULATION PRESSURE AND CHANGING LAND USE

The majority of countries in SSA are agriculture-based despite several decades of significant net migration to urban areas. The proportion of rural population ranges from 70% to

80% in most countries in the first decade of this century (see Table 15.1). The annual growth rate of rural population is generally high, exceeding 2.0% per year in many countries, which has led to an expansion of crop land, pastures and rangeland ("arable" land). In the case of the Sahelian countries of Mali, Burkina Faso, and Niger, arable land has expanded by about 20% between 1990 and 2009. Yet, arable land per person has declined in many countries, with major exceptions being Burkina Faso, Mali, and Sierra Leone among countries listed in Table 15.1. In SSA as a whole, arable land per person has been continuously declining over the last 50 years, and by 2010 it had become nearly a half of the level in 1960 (Figure 15.2). Although arable land per person in SSA is still much higher than in Southeast and South Asia, cultivated area per person would not be substantially different between densely populated countries in SSA and most countries in Asia, because of the vast rangeland area in SSA, as shown in Table 15.2. According to Headey and Jayne (2014), the average density of population relative to cultivated farmland in 12 high population-density countries in SSA (172 persons per km^2), including the three largest countries of Nigeria, Ethiopia, and Democratic Republic of Congo, is comparable to that in East Asia (199 persons per km^2) in 2010.

Cultivated land area expanded partly because of the expansion of arable land area and partly because of the conversion of pastures and rangeland into cultivated land. The rate of expansion of cultivated land was particularly high in Mali and Sierra Leone, where arable land per person was also high, indicating that cultivated area expanded mainly because of

Table 15.1 Rural population, its growth rate, and arable land per person in rural areas in selected countries in SSA

	Proportion of rural population (%)		Annual growth rate of rural population (%)	Arable land per person in rural areas (ha)[a]	
	2000	2011	2000-11	2000	2011
Burkina Faso	82	73	1.7	0.32	0.36
Ethiopia	85	83	2.3	0.15	0.16
Ghana	56	48	0.9	0.21	0.19
Kenya	80	76	2.2	0.16	0.13
Liberia	56	52	2.3	0.13	0.11
Malawi	85	84	2.7	0.24	0.23
Mali	72	65	2.0	0.45	0.48
Mozambique	71	69	2.2	0.21	0.21
Niger	84	82	3.5	1.27	0.90
Nigeria	58	50	1.6	0.24	0.22
Rwanda	86	81	2.4	0.11	0.11
Sierra Leone	64	61	1.3	0.12	0.19
South Sudan	83	82	4.1	n.a.[b]	n.a.[b]
Tanzania	78	73	2.4	0.25	0.25
Uganda	88	84	2.9	0.22	0.19
Zambia	65	61	2.4	0.28	0.25

[a] Arable land includes all land for annual and perennial cultivation and pastures.
[b] Not available.
Source: FAOSTAT.

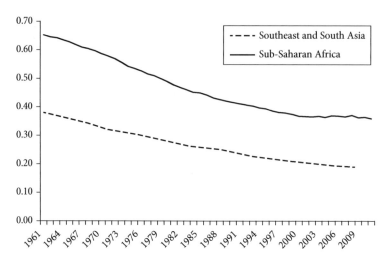

FIGURE 15.2 Changes in arable land per person in rural areas in Southeast and South Asia and sub-Saharan Africa.

the conversion of pasture and rangeland in these countries (Table 15.2). In countries where cultivation area increased only modestly from 1990 to 2011 (e.g. Kenya, Liberia, Nigeria, Rwanda, Tanzania, Uganda, and Zambia), arable area per person in rural area declined or at best remained constant.

Arable land area has expanded importantly because of the conversion of forest land and woodland. Table 15.3 shows that forest area accounts for roughly 30% of total land area in SSA in 2010 but it has been decreasing rapidly over the last two decades. Meybeck and Place (2014) point out that "the increasing competition for land use, including agricultural expansion, is a major driver of deforestation." Hertel (2011) argued that productivity growth on existing farmland is needed to ease the demand for new farmland being brought into cultivation and to help conserve the world's remaining forest from being destroyed to meet rising food demand. Under customary land tenure systems, uncultivated land, including forests, woodland, and communal grazing land, has historically been "available" for cultivation, in view of the fact that village chiefs tend to approve the request of village people to convert them to cultivated fields (Otsuka and Place 2001). Therefore, increasing population growth, food demand, food insecurity, or rising food prices would accelerate the pace of deforestation, even though the remaining forest areas have shrunk.

Reflecting increasing scarcity of land, small farmers account for a sizable share of agricultural production and in many instances their contribution is growing. For example, over 75% of the total agricultural outputs in Kenya, Tanzania, Ethiopia, and Uganda are produced by smallholder farmers with average farm sizes of about 2.5 ha (Salami et al. 2010). In countries in West Africa, e.g., Burkina Faso, Mali, and Niger, the farm sizes are relatively large with average size of three hectares and above. Differences in agro-ecological conditions, rural population density, and farming systems explain why some countries have larger farm sizes than others (Nyambiru-Mwaura and Place 2013). Comparable time series data on farm size is available only for a few countries, and even in those cases, the data

Table 15.2 Arable and cultivated land areas in selected countries in SSA

Country	Arable land in 2011 (million ha)[a]	Proportion of cultivated land (annual and perennial) in 2011	Percentage change in cultivated area in 1990–2011
Burkina Faso	11.8	49.0	61.2
Ethiopia	35.7	44.0	48.8
Ghana	15.9	47.8	58.3
Kenya	27.5	22.4	12.4
Liberia	2.6	24.0	26.0
Malawi	5.6	66.8	56.9
Mali	41.6	16.8	228.8
Mozambique	49.4	10.9	46.7
Niger	43.8	34.3	53.3
Nigeria	76.2	51.4	22.2
Rwanda	1.9	76.6	24.1
Sierra Leone	3.4	36.0	98.9
South Sudan	28.5	9.7	n.a.[b]
Tanzania	37.3	35.7	33.0
Uganda	14.1	63.6	30.7
Zambia	23.4	14.7	18.0

[a] Includes all land for annual and perennial cultivation and pastures.
[b] Not available.
Source: FAOSTAT.

Table 15.3 Forest area in 2010 and its changes by sub-region in SSA

	Forest in 2010		Annual rate of change (%)	
	Area (1000 ha)	% of land area	1990–2000	2000–2010
Eastern and Southern Africa	267 517	27	−0.62	−0.66
Western and Central Africa	328 088	32	−0.46	−0.46
Total	595 605	30	−0.53	−0.55

Source: FAO (2010).

are unreliable due to inconsistency of measurement. According to Jayne et al. (2012), who used nationally representative survey data, the average farm size declined from 2.28 hectares in 1997 to 1.86 hectares in 2010 in Kenya, and from 1.20 hectares in 1984 to 0.71 hectare in Rwanda. They also point out that "roughly 40% of Kenya's rural population resides on five percent of its arable land." Thus, at least in relatively high population density countries in SSA, farm size has been declining and rural population tends to be concentrated in agro-ecologically favorable areas.

Yet, according to the FAO (2012), Africa has still significant areas of suitable land for agriculture which is uncultivated, that is, about 70% of total land area. Currently, 183 million hectares of land is under cultivation, while there is approximately 452 million hectares of additional suitable land which is not cultivated. Indeed, in the case of Mali, Burkina Faso, and Niger, the change in cultivated area has exceeded 50% between 1990 and 2009 (Table 15.2). Similarly high expansion rates are also found in Ghana, Sierra Leone, and Malawi. FAO (2012), however, predicts a slowing of cultivated area expansion in SSA due to a variety of factors such as the low fertility of the uncultivated land. While there remains a significant amount of suitable but uncultivated land, the FAO baseline scenario to 2050 predicts an expansion of a modest 50 million hectares under cultivation.

The question is whether overall, land is still abundant in SSA. There may be scope for more land expansion in the larger countries of Sudan, Democratic Republic of Congo, Angola, and Mozambique, but in many other countries such as Kenya, Nigeria, and Rwanda the land frontier has already largely been closed. Thus, it must be understood that various countries in SSA are at different stages of the evolution of land tenure institutions and land management. It must be also recognized that much of the remaining land suffers from various constraints such as ecological fragility, low fertility, and lack of infrastructure (Meybeck and Place 2014). Moreover, to date in many African countries, the state continues to own a large portion of valuable land, even though evidence has shown that this is conducive to mismanagement, underutilization, and corruption (Nyambiru-Mwaura and Place 2013). Jayne et al. (2012) add that "since the rise of world food prices after the mid-2000s, many African governments have made concerted efforts to transfer land out of customary tenure systems (where the majority of rural people reside) to the state or to private individuals who, it is argued, can more effectively exploit the productive potential of the land." Such state land policies are bound to worsen both access to land and the security of tenure on the land of smallholders, particularly in land scarce countries.

Consistent with our conceptual framework, Dreschel et al. (2001) confirmed a significant relationship between population density, reduced fallow periods, and soil nutrient depletion in sub-Saharan Africa farming system. Although there are relatively few studies which identify the impact of population pressure on soil fertility, there are a large number of studies reporting soil degradation. The degradation can occur in several ways; it can be soil erosion, physical degradation, or loss of organic matter. Then, nutrient depletion and chemical degradation of the soil may occur. A recent study based on trends in net primary productivity suggests that 24% of areas were degrading between 1981 and 2003, including many areas that were not previously classified as degraded (Oldeman, Hakkeling, and Sombroak 1991). Of the degrading area, about 20% is cropland, which occupies about 12% of surface area (Bai et al. 2008). The FAO (2011) has developed a land degradation assessment methodology (LADA), which found 25% of land being classified as highly degraded or affected by a high degradation trend.

Globally, only half the nutrients which crops take from the soil are replaced, with particularly significant nutrient depletion in many African countries. Henao and Banaante (2006) estimated that 85% of African farmland had nutrient-mining rates of more than 30 kg/ha of nutrients annually. In some Eastern and Southern African countries, annual depletion is estimated at 47 kg/ha of nitrogen, 6 kg/ha of phosphorus, and 37 kg/ha of potassium (FAO 2011). When farming systems do not include fertilization or nitrogen fixation, losses from nutrient mining and related erosion are even higher (Sheldrick, Syers, and Lingard 2002). FAO data suggest that by 1996, 550 million hectares of land were degraded through agricultural mismanagement.

The productivity loss due to soil degradation is pronounced in SSA (Meybeck and Place 2014). As much as 25% of land productivity has been lost due to degradation in the second half of the twentieth century in Africa (Oldeman 1998). Because of the importance of agriculture to African economies, this has cost between 1% and 9% of GDP, depending on the country (Dregne, Kassas, and Rozanof 1991; Dreschel et al. 2001). When soils become highly degraded, the use of conventional inputs such as mineral fertilizer can become ineffective as demonstrated on maize in western Kenya (Marenya 2008). Globally, Tan, Lal, and Wiebe (2005) note that the ratio of crop yield to NPK fertilizer application has fallen dramatically between 1961 to 2000, from 494 to 71, which, in part, reflects the negative effects of reduction in soil fertility.

Although many of the studies cited above did not assess the impact of population pressure directly, they attribute the recent soil degradation to reduction in the fallow period and inadequate vegetative cover coupled with lack of nutrient inputs. In all likelihood, the continued population pressure has resulted in the exhaustion of uncultivated land in many customary land areas in SSA, which has led to shrinking farm size, shortened fallow periods, and soil degradation.

15.4 LAND TENURE AND AGRICULTURAL INTENSIFICATION

It is a logical consequence of the induced innovation theory formalized by Hayami and Ruttan (1985) that the tension caused by increasing scarcity of resources stimulates technological change to save those resources as well as new institutions that support such technological change. It is difficult to think of situation that fits this scenario better than the contemporary situation of African farming, particularly in densely populated areas. The incentives for induced innovation have been created by population pressure on limited land resources and are clearly reflected in soil degradation. In order to escape from such adverse conditions, what is needed is investment in land improvement, for example, the construction of terraces, irrigation and drainage systems, application of manure and compost, and planting of nitrogen fixing legumes and trees. Such investment leads to the intensification of the farming system, which brings about larger amount of outputs from a given area of land. In order to support such investments, secure land tenure institutions or strong individualized land rights must be induced to be established so as to ensure that investor reaps the future benefits accrued from current investment. If the theory of induced innovation works in the African context, we should be able to observe *simultaneously* (i) investments in land improvement, (ii) strengthened individual land rights, and (iii) intensification of farming system.

While we admit that the direct evidence is weak, we would like to point out that numerous new changes are observed in the landscape of African farming, which is unlikely to be understood without considering the simultaneous changes in investment, land rights, and farm intensification. They include (i) fairly active investments in land improvement, (ii) intensification of farming system, (iii) inverse relationship between farm size and productivity, and (iv) the development of land markets.

According to the cross-country study by Headey and Jayne (2014), changes in capital per hectare, which includes land structures, irrigation, plantation crops, livestock and livestock structures, machinery and other farm equipment, is significantly boosted by increase in population density. According to their analysis, this holds in SSA as in other regions. A positive association between population density and tree planting and a negative association between population density and fallow period were also found by Otsuka and Place (2001). Place et al. (2006) found a significant number of investments made by Kenyan farmers in densely populated highland areas, including terracing, water management, and tree planting, especially by those in areas with better market access. A number of important land investments are found to have been made in Ethiopia and Uganda (Deininger and Jin 2006; Deininger and Ali 2007) and investment in tree crops remains high among hundreds of thousands of farmers in many countries (e.g. coffee in Ethiopia, Kenya and Uganda; cocoa in Cote d'Ivoire and Ghana; rubber in Liberia and Nigeria).

Headey and Jayne (2014) also found that changes in a large number of indicators of agricultural intensification, including nitrogen application per hectare, cropping intensity, and total value of crop output per hectare, are positively associated with changes in population density. There are also numerous examples of the use of woody and herbaceous legumes, which fix atmospheric nitrogen, and the use of soil and water conservation practices and crop residues in densely populated areas in SSA (Reij et al. 2009). Such practices tend to improve soil fertility and intensify crop production (Place and Binam 2013). There are noted cases of intensified soil fertility management throughout SSA, with higher fertilizer use especially in Kenya (Jayne et al. 2003) and through use of integrated soil management practices (Place et al. 2003) and some of this intensification has been found to be facilitated by improved tenure security afforded by permanent land acquisition (e.g. Manyong and Houndekon 2000).

In densely populated highlands in Kenya, Yamano et al. (2011) observed that traditional zebu cows have been gradually replaced by cross-bred cows between traditional and European cows. These cows are several times as productive as traditional cows in terms of not only milk production but also production of manure. Cross-bred cows are stall-fed by cultivated feed grasses and other supplements, and cow manure or compost is applied to crop fields. This observation is important, because stall-feeding of cows, production of feed crops, and application of manure/compost are the essence of the agricultural revolution, which took place prior to the industrial revolution in England (Timmer 1969).

According to our own observations based on the RePEAT data collected by the National Graduate Institute for Policy Studies from 2004 to 2012 (Table 15.4), hybrid maize and intercropping of maize with beans with the capacity to fix nitrogen were increasingly adopted, as were crops of commercial value in the highlands of Kenya. While the number of both traditional and improved cross-bred cows decreased, the former decreased more sharply. As a result, the application of organic manure increased, even though the application of mineral fertilizer decreased during a time of rising fertilizer prices. Interestingly, because of the intercropping, maize yield did not increase appreciably with the intensification of farming system, but total crop yield did increase significantly from 2004 to 2012. This is consistent with the finding of Headey and Jayne (2014) that although population density positively affects many indicators of intensified farming systems including total value of production per unit of land, it does not affect cereal yield.

Table 15.4 The emerging new farming system in the highlands of Kenya

	2004	2012
No of sample farms	699	692
Application of inorganic fertilize (sum of N, P, and K, kg/ha)	57.10	47.11
Application of organic fertilizer (kg/ha)	2,285	2786
Adoption of hybrid maize (%)	58.13	82.25
Intercropping with beans (%)	86.09	79.30
Proportion of nepiah grass area (%)	13.29	11.91
No. of traditional cows(no. per household)	1.85	1.17
No. of cross-bred cows (no. per household)	2.95	1.93
Maize yield (kg/ha)	1907	2125
Real value of maize production per ha (ksh/ha)[a]	30,975	37,156
Real total value of crop production per ha (ksh/ha)[a]	52,645	67,063

a. ksh means Kenyan shilling, which is expressed in 2009 real prices.

The adoption of cross-bred cows and the application of manure to banana fields are common in Western Uganda, where population density is relatively high. We would also like to point out that this intensified farming system is seldom practiced in maize growing areas of Uganda, where land is more abundant relative to labor than in Kenya. How generalizable this observation is remains a major empirical question to be explored. Apart from intensification of cereal production, there is also intensification through diversification into more profitable but costly crops such as fruits and vegetables. According to Tschirley (2011) this shift is taking place most rapidly in Kenya due to land pressure and is just emerging in other countries such as Zambia and Mozambique.

The inverse relationship between farm size and productivity is likely to appear only if farmland is cultivated intensively based primarily on family labor. Indeed, to our knowledge, the inverse relationship between farm size and crop yield per hectare was reported only recently in SSA. Holden et al. (2009) is one of the first studies to report this phenomenon in SSA. By now there are a large number of other studies that report the inverse relationship in SSA. It is difficult to explain such observations without considering the increased intensification of farming systems in recent years.

When land becomes scarce and farming system is intensified, the value of land increases. In order to use and allocate valuable land efficiently, incentives must be created to reallocate land from less productive to more productive producers. Land transaction, be it renting or selling, can occur only if rights to transfer land, including rights to rent out or sell, have been established. Both Holden et al. (2009) and Holden et al. (2013) report active transactions of land from land-abundant, large farms to labor-abundant, small farms, which is consistent with the widely observed inverse relationship between farm size and productivity in SSA. In particular, land rental markets contribute to both efficiency and equity by transferring land rights from large farmers to small farmers, for example, in Kenya as reported by Jin and Jayne (2013). In his literature review, Place (2009) pointed out that formal or informal land sales have occurred in areas of increased land pressure, arising from both population growth and commercial opportunities.

15.5 POLICY OPTIONS

In many parts of SSA, population pressure has exhausted uncultivated land and reduced farm size. The increasing scarcity of farmland has increased pressure to intensify farming systems, which require investments in land improvement. For farmers to undertake long-term investments, their future land rights must be secure. Individualization of land rights is often accelerated by population pressure which has transformed land acquisition processes from clearing and allocation towards intra-familial inheritance. Commercialization of agriculture also induces behaviors to establish individual claims to land. In addition, according to our literature review, such investments in land tend to strengthen individual land rights spontaneously, which contribute to higher productivity of land not only directly but also indirectly through facilitating informal land transactions. In order to accelerate such changes, government should implement policies to strengthen land rights and to improve profitability of intensified farming systems by means of investing in agricultural research and extension systems and infrastructures. Conferring land titles or certificates will improve farmers' access to formal credit, which, in turn, will stimulate the use of purchased inputs, such as inorganic fertilizer, and further investments in land improvement.

In land-abundant regions where vast tracts of uncultivated land still exist, the appropriate policy options are different. In such regions, the customary land tenure system prevails and individualization of property rights is low. A problem is that the state often directly infringes on rights or sanctions outsiders to make claims on land in such areas under the guise of available land. Since land rights are insecure, farmland tends to be infrequently fallowed, which leads to soil degradation. Since farmland is owned collectively by a group of kin-related people, granting land title to a particularly member or a group of members would create tenure conflict, rather than tenure security. One possible solution is to grant collective entitlement of the family land. Or if the village community is tightly structured with trust among community members, conferring land title to the community as a whole is another possible option. To the extent that transaction cost of settling conflicts over land among family members and boundary disputes between neighbors is lower than the cost of litigation, the land policies that respect the traditional communal land rights are expected to improve land tenure security.

In densely populated areas, government should support the spontaneously emerging intensification of farming systems for productive use of land and poverty reduction. As is predicted by Hayami and Ruttan (1985), induced innovations are taking place which lead to the intensification of agriculture in SSA. However, they are not significant enough to realize major productivity gains. We fully support the argument of Meybeck and Place (2014) that intensive integrated soil management practices will need to become standard practice, with complementary investment in soil conservation, crop rotations and intercropping, inorganic fertilizer, and organic nutrient management with animal manure, green manures and agroforestry, and crop residues. A major constraint on the dissemination of such intensive farming system is the lack of research on the development of highly productive "integrated farming systems," and the complementary dissemination activities that would support them. It must be clearly recognized that development of such improved farming system, which accompanies the effort to invest in soil improvement, will not only intensify the farming system but also strengthen the individual land rights. Improved access to markets brought about by investment in roads and telecommunication networks will have the similar effects, as it will increase the rates of return to investment in land improvement and the advantage of intensive farming systems.

Once land becomes scarce and, hence, valuable, land competition and conflict becomes prevalent between individuals. Thus, it makes sense to strengthen tenure security by granting land titles or certificates to individual farmers. A major issue is to develop a system of formal private land rights documentation that is affordable and accessible in rural areas. Recent programs by the Government of Ethiopia (certificates) and the Government of Rwanda (titles) have been very cost-effective in allocation of initial documents of tenure to millions of smallholder farmers. Land whose transfer rights are officially recognized can be used as collateral for formal credit and, hence, its ownership stimulates investment and purchase of inorganic fertilizer and other inputs. In all likelihood, concerted efforts to strengthen land rights, stimulate investment in land, and promote intensified farming system will lead to sustainable management of land, higher productivity of farming, and poverty reduction in SSA.

REFERENCES

Bai, Z., Dent, D., Olsson, L., and Schaepman, M. (2008). *Global Assessment of Land Degradation and Improvement: 1. Identification by Remote Sensing.* Wageningen: World Soil Information.

Baland, J.-M., Gaspart, F., Place, F., and Platteau, J.P. (1999). *Poverty, Tenure Security and Access to Land in Central Uganda: The Role of Market and Non-market Processes.* CRED, Department of Economics, University of Namur, Belgium.

Bamwerinde, W., Bashaasha, B., Ssembajjwe, W., and Place, F. (2006). The Puzzle of Idle Land in the Densely Populated Kigezi Highlands of Southwestern Uganda. *International Journal for Environment and Development,* 3(1):1–13.

Besley, T. (1995), Property rights and investment incentives: theory and evidence from Ghana. *Journal of Political Economy,* 9(3):903–937.

Binswanger, H.P., and McIntire, J. (1987). Behavioral and material determinants of production relations in land-abundant tropical agriculture. *Economic Development and Cultural Change,* 36(1):73–99.

Boserup, E. (1965). *The Conditions of Agricultural Growth.* Chicago: Aldine.

Brasselle, A.-S., Gaspart, F., and Platteau, J.-P. (2002). Land tenure security and investment incentives. *Journal of Development Economics,* 67(2):373–418.

Bruce, J. W., and Migot-Adholla, S.E. (eds) (1994). *Searching for Land Tenure Security in Africa.* Hunt/Kendall.

Carletto, C., Savastano, S., and Zezza, A. (2013). Fact or artefact: the impact of measurement errors on the farm size-productivity relationship. *Journal of Development Economics,* 103:254–261.

Deininger, K. (2003). *Land Policies for Growth and Poverty Reduction.* Oxford: World Bank and Oxford University Press.

Deininger, K. and Ali, D. (2007). Do Overlapping Land Rights Reduce Agricultural Investment? Evidence from Uganda. World Bank Policy Research Working Paper 4310. Washington, DC: World Bank.

Deininger, K., and Jin, S. (2006). Tenure security and land related investment: evidence from Ethiopia. *European Economic Review*, 50(5):1245–1277.

Dregne, H., Kassas, M., and Rozanof, B. (1991). A new assessment of the world status of desertification. *Desertification Control Bulletin*, 20(1): 7–18.

Dreschel, P.L., Gyuele, D., Kunze, O., and Cofie, O. (2001). Population density, soil nutrient depletion and economic growth in sub-Saharan Africa. *Ecological Economics*, 38(2):251–258.

FAO (2010). Global Forest Resources Assessment 2010, FAO Forestry Paper 163.

FAO (2011). *The State of World's Land and Water Resources for Food and Agriculture* (SOLAW)— Managing systems at risk. Rome: FAO, London: Earthscan.

FAO (2012). *Agriculture Towards 2030/2050: The 2012 Revision*. Rome: FAO.

Fenske, J. (2011). Land tenure and investment incentives: evidence from West Africa. *Journal of Development Economics*, 95(2):137–156.

Garrity, D., Akinnfesi, F., Ajayi, O. et al. (2010). Evergreen agriculture: a robust approach to sustainable food security in Africa. *Food Security*, 2(3):197–214.

Hayami, Y., and Otsuka, K. (1993). *The Economics of Contract Choice: An Agrarian Perspective*. Oxford: Clarendon Press.

Hayami, Y., and Ruttan, V.W. (1985). *Agricultural Development: An International Perspective*. Baltimore: Johns Hopkins University Press.

Headey, D., and Jayne, T.S. (2014). Adaptation to land constraints: is Africa different? *Food Policy*, 48:18–33.

Henao, J., and Banaante, C. (2006). *Agricultural Production and Soil Nutrient Mining in Africa: Implications for Resource Conservation and Policy Development: Summary*. Muscle Shoals, USA, International Fertilizer Development Centre.

Hertel, T. (2011). The global supply and demand for agricultural land in 2050: a perfect storm in the making? *American Journal of Agricultural Economics*, 93(2):259–275.

Holden, S.T., Deininger, K., and Ghebru, H. (2009). Impact of low-cost land certification on investment and productivity. *American Journal of Agricultural Economics*, 91(2):359–373.

Holden, S. T., and Fisher, M. (2013). Can Area Measurement Error Explain the Inverse Farm Size Productivity Relationship? CLTS Working Paper No. 12. Centre for Land Tenure Studies. Ås, Norway: Norwegian University of Life Sciences.

Holden, S. T., and Otsuka, K. (2014). The role of land tenure reforms and land markets in the context of population growth and land use intensification in Africa. *Food Policy*, 48:88–97.

Holden, S. T., Otsuka, K., and Deininger, K. (eds) (2013). *Land Tenure Reforms in Asia and Africa: Assessing Impacts on Poverty and Natural Resource Management*. Hampshire: Palgrave Macmillan.

Holden, S.T., Otsuka, K., and Place, F. (eds) (2009). *The Emergence of Land Markets in Africa: Assessing the Impacts on Poverty, Equity, and Efficiency*. Baltimore: Resources for the Future.

IPCC (2011). *IPCC Special Report on Renewable Energy Sources and Climate Change Mitigation*. Prepared by Working Group III of the Intergovernmental Panel on Climate Change. O. Edenhofer, R. Pichs-Madruga, Y. Sokona, K. Seyboth, P. Matschoss, S. Kadner, T. Zwickel, P. Eickemeier, G. Hansen, S. Schlömer, C. von Stechow (eds). Cambridge University Press, Cambridge, United Kingdom and New York, NY, USA, 1075 pp.

Jayne, T.S., Chamberlin, J., and Muyanga, M. (2012). *Emerging Land Issues in African Agriculture: Implication for Food Security and Poverty Reduction Strategies*. Stanford: Center on Food Security and the Environment, Stanford University.

Jayne, T.S., Govereh, J., Wanzala, M., and Demeke, M. (2003). Fertilizer market development: a comparative of Ethiopia, Kenya and Zambia. *Food Policy* 28:293–316.

Jin, S., and Jayne, T.S. (2013). Land rental markets in Kenya: implications for efficiency, equity, household income, and poverty. *Land Economics*, 89(2):246–271.

Jumbe, C.B.L., and Angelson, A. (2006). Do the poor benefit from devolution policies: evidence from Malawi's forest co-management program. *Land Economics*, 82(4):562–581.

Larson, D., Otsuka, K., Matsumoto, T., and Kilic, T. (2014). Should African rural development strategies depend on smallholder farms? An exploration of the inverse productivity hypothesis. *Agricultural Economics*, 45(3):355–367.

Manyong, V., and Houndekon, V. (2000). Land Tenurial Systems and the Adoption of Mucuna Planted Fallows in the Derived Savannas of West Africa. CAPRi Working Paper Number 4. Washington, DC: International Food Policy Research Institute.

Marenya, P. (2008). *Three Essays on The Effect of* Ex-ante *Soil Fertility on Smallholder Fertilizer Use Behavior*. Ph.D. Dissertation, Department of Natural Resources, Cornell University, Ithaca, New York.

Meybeck, A., and Place, F. (2014). *Food security and sustainable resource use—what are the resource challenges to food security paper presented at the conference on* Food Security Futures: Research Priorities for the 21st Century, Dublin, Ireland, 11–12 April 2013.

Namubiru-Mwaura, E., and Place, F. (2013). Securing land for agricultural production, in AGRA *Africa Agriculture Status Report: Focus on Staple Crops*. Nairobi, Kenya: Alliance for a Green Revolution in Africa.

Oldeman, L.R. (1998). Soil Degradation: A Threat to Food Security? Report 98/01, Wageningen, Netherlands, ISRIC.

Oldeman, L.R., Hakkeling, R.T., and Sombroak, W.A. (1991). *World Map of The Status of Human-Induced Soil Degradation: An Explanatory Note,* 2nd revised edition. Wageningen, Netherlands, ISRIC, and Nairobi, UNEP.

Otsuka, K. (2007). Efficiency and equity effects of land markets, in R.E. Evenson and P. Pingali (eds), *Handbook of Agricultural Economics,* Volume III. Amsterdam: Elsevier, pp. 2671–2703.

Otsuka, K., and Larson, D. (eds) (2013). *An African Green Revolution: Finding Ways to Boost Productivity on Small Farms.* Dordrecht: Springer.

Otsuka, K., and Larson, D. (eds) (2015). *In Pursuit of an African Green Revolution: Views from Rice and Maize Farmers' Fields.* Dordrecht: Springer.

Otsuka, K., and Place, F. (eds) (2001). *Land Tenure and Natural Resource Management: A Comparative Study of Agrarian Communities in Asia and Africa.* Baltimore: Johns Hopkins University Press.

Pingali, P., Bigot, Y., and Binswanger, H.P. (1987). *Agricultural Mechanization and the Evolution of Farming Systems in Sub-Saharan Africa.* Baltimore: Johns Hopkins University Press.

Place, F. (2009). Land tenure and agricultural productivity in Africa: a comparative analysis of the economics literature and recent policy strategies and reforms. *World Development*, 37(8):1326–1336.

Place, F., Barrett, C., Freeman, H. et al. (2003). Prospects for integrated soil fertility management using organic and inorganic inputs: evidence from smallholder African agricultural systems. *Food Policy*, 28:365–378.

Place, F., and Binam, J. (2013). Economic Impacts of Farmer-Managed Natural Regeneration in the Sahel: End-of-Project Technical Report for Free University Amsterdam and IFAD, mimeo. World Agroforestry Center, Nairobi, Kenya.

Place, F., and Hazell, P. (1993). Productivity effects of indigenous land tenure systems in sub-Saharan Africa. *American Journal of Agricultural Economics*, 75(1):10–19.

Place, F., and Migot-Adholla, S. (1988). Land registration and smallholder farms in Kenya. *Land Economic*, 74(3):360–373.

Place, F., Njuki, J., Murithi, F., and Mugo, F. (2006). Agricultural enterprise and land management in the highlands of Kenya, in J. Pender, F. Place, and S. Ehui (eds), *Strategies for Sustainable Land Management in the East African Highlands*. Washington, DC: World Bank and International Food Policy Research Institute, pp. 191–216.

Place, F., and Otsuka, K. (2000). Population pressure, land tenure, and tree resource management in Uganda. *Land Economics*, 76(2):233–251.

Place, F., and Otsuka, K. (2001). Tenure, agricultural investment, and productivity in the customary tenure sector of Malawi. *Economic Development and Cultural Change*, 50(1):77–99.

Place, F., and Otsuka, K. (2002). Land tenure systems and their impacts on agricultural investments and productivity in Uganda. *Journal of Development Studies*, 38(6):105–128.

Quisumbing, A.R., Payongayong, E., Aidoo, J.B., and Otsuka, K. (2001). Women's land rights in the transition to individualized ownership: implications for tree-resource management in Western Ghana. *Economic Development and Cultural Change*, 50(1):157–182.

Reij, C., Tappan, G., and Smale, M. (2009). Agroenvironmental transformation in the Sahel: another kind of green revolution, IFPRI Discussion Paper 00914. Washington, DC: International Food Policy Research Institute.

Ruthenberg, H. (1980). *Farming Systems in the Tropics*. Oxford: Clarendon Press.

Salami, A., Kamara, A.B., and Brixiova, Z. (2010). Smallholder agriculture in East Africa: Trends, constraints and opportunities, Working Papers Series No. 105. Tunis, Tunisia: African Development Bank.

Sheldrick, W.F., Syers, J.K., and Lingard, J. (2002). A conceptual model for conducting nutrient audits at national, regional, and global scales. *Nutrient Cycling in Agroecosystems*, 62(1):61–72.

Sjaastad, E., and Bromley, D. (1997). Indigenous land rights in sub-Saharan Africa: appropriation, security, and investment demand. *World Development*, 25(4):549–562.

Tan, Z., Lal, R., and Wiebe, K. (2005). Global soil nutrient depletion and yield reduction. *Journal of Sustainable Agriculture*, 26(1):123–146.

Timmer, C.P. (1969). The turnip, the new husbandry, the English agricultural revolution. *Quarterly Journal of Economics*, 3(3):375–395.

Tschirley, D. (2011). What is the Scope for Horticulture to Drive Smallholder Poverty Reduction in Africa? Policy Synthesis Number 88, Department of Agricultural, Food and Resource Economics, Michigan State University, East Lansing, Michigan.

Yamano, T., Otsuka, K., and Place, F. (eds) (2011). *Emerging Development of Agriculture in East Africa: Markets, Soil, and Innovations*. Amsterdam: Springer.

CHAPTER 16

....

AGRICULTURE, GROWTH, AND DEVELOPMENT IN AFRICA
Theory and Practice

....

OUSMANE BADIANE AND TSITSI MAKOMBE

16.1 INTRODUCTION

....

AFRICA has achieved a much-improved agricultural and economic growth performance over the last 15 years. The growth was particularly strong during 2003–2010, when the agricultural sector grew at an average annual rate of almost 4%.[1] Meanwhile, gross domestic product (GDP) and GDP per capita grew at a remarkable 5.4% and 2.6% over the same period, respectively. The improved growth performance comes after decades of ebbing growth that started in the late 1970s, reaching crisis proportions in the 1980s, and only began to show signs of recovery in the mid-1990s. The improved growth is more akin to that achieved by the continent at the dawn of independence, when growth performance was stronger than that of South Asia. The recovery has been mirrored in development indicators, including declining rates of poverty and hunger following improvements in economic and agricultural growth.

With about two-thirds of Africa's population residing in rural areas where it largely relies on agriculture for subsistence and incomes, performance of the agricultural sector continues to have important implications for food security, growth, and development of the continent. Thus, scholars and development practitioners have questioned whether the recent growth recovery will last or fizzle out. For example, while as much as two-thirds of recent agricultural growth has been found to be due to favorable domestic prices, there is strong evidence that some of the growth is the result of productivity gains through greater efficiency of factor

---

[1] Unless noted otherwise, data figures refer to those of Africa, south of the Sahara while growth rates are calculated using data from the World Bank, WDI, 2012 and 2013.

use (Nin-Pratt, Johnson, and Yu 2012). Technical change so far has played a rather limited role. More importantly, however, the recent growth recovery proves that Africa's agricultural sector has become more responsive to higher investment in the sector and improvements in the policy and institutional environment, following reforms of the 1980s and 1990s.

A key strategic question facing African economies in the coming decades is how to transit from recovery to structural transformation, in order to deepen the ongoing growth process and broaden its impact on livelihoods. While Africa's unstable development performance over the last five decades has been due to a myriad of factors, it is also symptomatic of the effectiveness, or lack thereof, of the continent's policy choices concerning agriculture, growth, and development. Charting a future course, thus, requires a critical review of the theory and practice of agriculture, growth, and development in Africa. In particular, it is important that future growth policies and strategies reflect advances in the theory of economic development, lessons from successfully transformed economies, and adjustments imposed by prevailing and emerging changes to the global economic environment. Therefore, the chapter examines how Africa can accelerate its recent growth recovery and spur a structural transformation. Specifically, section 16.2 reviews how development theory and practice in Africa have evolved and the role agriculture has played therein. Section 16.3 discusses challenges and opportunities to an agriculture-led growth strategy. The pace and pattern of structural transformation in Africa is assessed in section 16.4 while section 16.5 derives policy implications for advancing a successful structural transformation. The concluding section 16.6 summarizes key findings of the chapter.

16.2 EVOLUTION OF DEVELOPMENT THEORY AND PRACTICE IN AFRICA AND THE ROLE OF AGRICULTURE THEREIN

The theory and practice of economic growth and development, and in particular the role played by the agricultural sector therein, have evolved over the years. Africa's development trajectory has often involved the coexistence of conflicting themes running in parallel and often constantly changing development objectives, in particular as they relate to the roles of (i) industry versus agriculture in spurring growth and development and (ii) government and the public sector versus markets and the private sector in regulating economic activity and aiding growth and development (Figure 16.1).

16.2.1 Industry-led growth, 1950s to 1970s

Early development theorists viewed the agricultural sector as a source of "surplus labor" whose share in the economy declined during the course of development, thus, playing only a passive role in economic development and transformation. Dominant paradigms of this time include dual economy theories (Lewis 1954; Ranis and Fei 1961). In Lewis's dual economy, surplus labor is transferred from a traditional (rural) agricultural sector, where it is

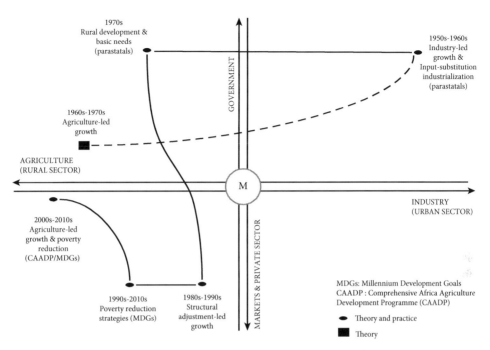

FIGURE 16.1 Evolution of development theory and practice in Africa.

"M" denotes the imaginary point where growth and development exhibit no bias between (i) agriculture and industry, and (ii) government, markets, and the private sector.

assumed to have a marginal product that is negligible, zero, or even negative, to a modern (urban), non-agricultural/ industrial ("capitalist") sector. Greater output in the capitalist sector creates more jobs and higher incomes, while profits are reinvested in the modern sector to enable capital formation. Generated income trickles down to the rest of the economy and stimulates overall economic growth. Ranis and Fei (1961) extended the Lewis model by highlighting the importance of agriculture in the expansion of the modern industrial sector. In particular, according to them, if growth in the agricultural sector is negligible and does not produce sufficient food supplies to support the whole economy, then agriculture can constrain growth in the modern sector.

In line with the predominant economic thinking, governments across Africa embraced import substituting industrialization (ISI) strategies, especially in the 1960s and 1970s. The ISI thesis advocated for priority to be accorded to import substitution of manufactured goods rather than production of agricultural exports (Eicher and Staatz 1990), as a means to counter the secular decline in the terms of trade of primary commodities and reduce foreign dependency, particularly on capital. With ISI strategies, countries would be able to allow infant industries to grow with the production of simple manufactured goods for imports, under the protection of tariffs and quotas on imports and an overvalued exchange rate to allow importers to more easily import capital goods such as the machinery needed to make the manufactured goods. Countries were to begin with making light consumer goods before moving onto intermediate and capital goods. The state intervention required to support industrialization policies was in line with the prevailing economic thinking—that government had a large role to play in curbing market failure and aiding rapid industrialization and economic growth.

The ISI strategy was, however, not implemented as intended by its proponents. For instance, the level of protection on infant industries was higher than recommended, and some countries adopted the paradigm under the auspices of socialism, which often called for greater state intervention in economic activity. On balance, the paradigm did not help improve Africa's economic performance; in fact, following the adoption of ISI strategies, Africa as a whole witnessed low and negative per capita growth during the 1970s.

As a corollary of ISI, agricultural strategies during this period were designed to generate fiscal resources to finance the nascent industrial sector, ensure self-sufficiency, and reduce dependency on the West. Starting in the colonial era, the expansion of cash crops primarily for export was part of a growth strategy followed by governments. Agriculture was targeted because it was the principal economic activity that often generated the most foreign exchange through its exports. And although smallholder farmers for the first time had the opportunity to farm cash crops, colonial governments with the support of donors largely supported large-scale farms, plantations, and ranches (Eicher 1992).

Collection of revenues from export crops was done through government agencies (parastatals) and in particular marketing boards. Pan-seasonal and pan-territorial pricing were introduced to guarantee a single price across seasons and regions, respectively. However, such a measure discouraged private investment in storage and transportation (Barrett and Mutambatsere 2005). Government intervention became more pronounced in post-independence Africa, as newly independent governments maintained marketing boards because they provided a means of controlling the marketing of strategic food and export cash crops and subsidizing food prices for urban consumers and producers. Furthermore, government intervention often increased during times of economic crisis. For example, following the 1974 oil price shock, governments responded to declines in real prices for Africa's agricultural exports and shortages in commodity markets with input subsidies to incentivize producers of agricultural exports and smallholder farmers who grew the bulk of food crops for local consumption. Yet, marketing boards incurred very high costs due to the high cost of covering remote areas under pan-territorial pricing and high storage costs under pan-seasonal pricing (Kherallah et al. 2002).

Overall, the agricultural sector was thus not seen as a source of growth per se, but as playing an important supporting role in the ISI strategy. Just as in the case of industry, strategies in the agricultural sector saw little room for the private sector. Governments took the lead through the use of public enterprises, which not only competed with private sector operators but often banned them outright. The first two decades of post-independence Africa were, thus, characterized by strong biases in favor of industry as a source of growth and of government as the main economic player. Additionally, with industrial-led growth policies, Africa missed an opportunity to industrialize agriculture by developing its agribusiness and agro-processing sectors and thus help raise incomes. Moreover, only limited investments were made in rural infrastructure, market development, agricultural research and development (R&D), and extension, which in turn slowed down the spread of technology needed to promote agricultural productivity growth. While efforts were made to develop education and training facilities for infant industries' labor force, little or no effort was made to develop agricultural training facilities (Degefe 1994). Thus, ISI policies buttressed the neglect of agriculture in government strategies while overvalued exchange rates effectively discouraged agricultural production. Yet, agriculture was the only viable source of resources, especially labor and capital, to support industrialization.

16.2.2   Agriculture-led growth, 1960s to 1970s

In the early 1960s, signs of the first "paradigm shift" were becoming apparent (Ellis and Biggs 2001). Smallholder farmers were now seen as vital for growth and development. The notion of an agriculture-led growth strategy was influenced by the works of Johnston and Mellor (1961), Shultz (1964), and others, who placed emphasis on the role of smallholder farming in spurring overall economic growth and development. Johnston and Mellor (1961) showcased important linkages between agriculture and non-agriculture and the importance of agricultural growth in raising incomes and foreign exchange earnings and generating capital and labor to benefit the industrial sector. Increased agricultural productivity growth is expected to stimulate overall economic growth and development through linkages in production and consumption. Empirical studies have provided evidence of substantial multiplier effects from agricultural growth, with consumption linkages shown to account for over 80% of the agricultural growth linkages in Africa and Asia (Delgado et al. 1998; Haggblade and Hazell 1989).

The important and active role played by agriculture in development was reinforced by the small farm "efficient but poor" thinking. Schultz (1964) demonstrated that poor farmers were efficient given their factor endowments and that when given the right incentives, they could make rational choices to invest in agriculture and adopt modern technologies to help transform agriculture. Schultz's ideas were demonstrated by the Green Revolution in Asia and Latin America that began in the mid-1960s. The Green Revolution consisted of modern inputs supported by public investments and policies favorable to agriculture that drastically increased crop production. Investments included those in agricultural R&D, irrigation, rural roads, and providing credit to farmers. The Green Revolution increased food supplies and was able to effectively deal with rising hunger levels in Asia particularly; it lifted many out of poverty and contributed to economic growth in the two regions. It was an important precursor to the regions' economic transformation. It therefore buttressed the importance of science-based technology in transforming traditional agriculture and spurring growth, development, and transformation. It also highlighted the important role government has to play in creating an enabling environment through policies and investments that stimulate agricultural productivity growth.

Although an agriculture-led strategy and small farmer focus dominated development thinking in the 1960s and 1970s, it was largely disconnected from development practice in Africa. In particular, while in theory, industry-led and agriculture-led growth themes ran in parallel (especially in the 1960s and 1970s), the notion of an agriculture carried by the smallholder farmer as an autonomous economic agent and linked to the broader economy through a private sector-driven agribusiness industry did not find its way into development practice in Africa. The government was still seen as the key player and parastatals continued to displace private sector actors from actively participating in development. Nonetheless, Africa has had agricultural successes, albeit outside this period, which included increased yields of improved maize in East and Southern Africa and rapid growth of cotton production in West Africa (see Spielman and Pandya-Lorch 2009).

16.2.3   Rural development and basic needs, 1970s

During the 1970s, growing poverty, particularly in rural areas, and inequality shifted the focus of policy debates and research to the interactions between economic growth and equity. By the early 1970s, it had become clear that previous development paradigms of industrialization were not working. The rural–urban divide had grown as income inequality rose sharply between rural and urban areas. The urban biased nature of industrialization policies had resulted in sprawling cities as large numbers of rural workers migrated to urban industrial centers in search of employment despite the industrial sector's inability to rapidly absorb the influx of workers. Compared to urban areas, rural areas were characterized by less road infrastructure and fewer hospitals, schools, and other basic services (Yudelman 1976).

To address growth and equity issues, donors and international development agencies shifted their support to *integrated rural development (IRD) projects* which sought to increase agricultural productivity together with access to social services such as health and education in rural areas (Yudelman 1976; Staatz and Eicher 1990). The World Bank substantially increased its investment in these projects and broadened its lending to include small farmers. With the goal of aiding the rural poor, its projects included financing of agricultural research, extension services, marketing, provision of credit, and small-scale irrigation, and went beyond agriculture to include clean water, rural roads, education, and health services (Binswanger 1998). African leaders strongly endorsed rural development projects, as illustrated by Tanzania's Ujamaa villagization program, modeled after the Chinese commune system (Yudelman 1976). Development practitioners also experimented, during the same period, with the *basic human needs (BHN) approach*. This paradigm became prominent during the mid-1970s and had three key objectives: ensuring adequate real incomes, increasing access to public social services, and promoting the participation of affected people in the formulation and implementation of development programs and policies (Streeten et al. 1981). The call to directly address poverty and inequality through IRD and BHN projects implicitly dealt with the agricultural and rural sectors. African governments made increased agricultural production, particularly food production, their priority for achieving food self-sufficiency and alleviating poverty. In particular, agricultural policies and programs pursued by governments, as part of IRD and BHN projects, largely benefited from substantial micro-level research that looked into understanding the agricultural and rural sectors and their possible contribution to reducing poverty and increasing overall economic growth (Yudelman 1976; Eicher and Staatz 1990). To ensure the success of policies that favored food production and small farmers, the establishment of local governments and cooperatives was seen as indispensable and was advocated during this period (Streeten et al 1981; Yudelman 1976). Moreover, meeting basic human needs called for significant government intervention, which was in step with development practice of the time (Hayami 2003). Yet, despite these efforts, agricultural policies related to BHN and IRD projects were largely unsuccessful due to high costs of design, administration, and implementation. Moreover, most low-income countries' efforts to meet basic needs were largely unsuccessful as indicators such as literacy rates, life expectancy, and infant mortality did not improve.

16.2.4 Structural adjustment-led growth, 1980s to 1990s

By the end of the 1970s, Africa was faced with reduced global demand for its commodities, declining terms of trade, declining per capita incomes, overvalued real exchange rates, growing and unsustainable budgets, foreign exchange deficits, stagnating official development assistance (ODA), and a serious debt crisis (Cornia 1987). The increasingly difficult economic situation left African leaders disillusioned by global development strategies that they felt had failed to deliver on their promises. With a sense that early development strategies had been largely determined by foreign actors, African leaders and technocrats under the aegis of the Organization of African Unity (OAU) decided it was time for Africa to take matters into its own hands, come up with a strategy to reverse the growth malaise, and place Africa on a trajectory toward sustained economic growth and self-sufficiency. Several consultations among Africa's leadership resulted in the "Lagos Plan of Action for the Economic Development of Africa, 1980-2000" (LPA) and the "Final Act of Lagos" (FAL) in 1980. This was unprecedented, as for the first time African leaders had developed an Africa-wide effort for transforming the continent's economic development. Needless to say, the LPA and FAL were not implemented as planned, as another competing strategy burst onto the scene and dominated all others.

In 1981, the World Bank introduced its own action plan for Africa, commonly known as the "Berg Report" (see World Bank 1981). Recommendations of the Berg Report were to be implemented through structural adjustment programs (SAPs). SAPs were comprised of short-term macro-economic stabilization policies spearheaded by the International Monetary Fund (IMF) and structural policies led by the World Bank. Essentially, SAPs sought to roll back three decades of development practices that were significantly biased in favor of industry as the lead growth sector and government as the lead development actor, thus marginalizing agriculture and the private sector. The Berg Report called for several agricultural policy reforms meant to remove what it considered a longstanding bias against agriculture. The economic crisis of the 1980s helped to reveal the inefficiencies and costliness of the marketing boards, and their removal or reduced role was seen as a means of opening up participation by the private sector and bringing about market-determined prices. Thus, the agricultural reforms included liberalization of agricultural input and output prices by reducing or removing subsidies on inputs such as fertilizers; doing away with pan-seasonal and pan-territorial prices; reducing overvalued exchange rates; removing government regulatory controls in input and output markets; and privatization by withdrawing marketing boards from pricing and marketing activities and restructuring public enterprises (Kherallah et al. 2002; Jayne et al. 2002). The Berg Report's emphasis on export agriculture was strikingly different from the LPA, which called for food self-sufficiency and reduced dependence on exports.

Like the broader SAP paradigm, the subject of agricultural policy reforms and their impact has not been without controversy. First, the expected agricultural supply response was muted because reforms focused on macro-level and sectoral interventions without addressing important microeconomic policies targeted at, inter alia, improvements in agricultural technologies, infrastructure, and market institutions that are essential for an effective supply response (Barrett and Carter 1999). However, according to Kherallah et al. 2002, cotton in Benin and Mali, coffee in Uganda, and cashew nuts in Mozambique experienced some positive supply responses as liberalization moved price incentives in favor of tradables rather than food crops. Meanwhile, the removal or reduction of input and output subsidies and pricing regulations resulted in reduced fertilizer use for key staple crops and in higher food prices, which were detrimental to the food security of low income households particularly net food buyers. Yet, liberalizing markets helped to reduce marketing margins and thus resulted in lower retail prices of key staple crops (Badiane and Shively 1997; Badiane and Kherallah 1999; Kherallah et al. 2002). However, the extent of implementation of agricultural policy reforms varied from country to country. Jayne et al. (2002) explored the notion that market policy reforms and liberalization had been a "false premise" since in many Eastern and Southern African countries reforms were not fully implemented while in others they were reversed and only in a few countries were reforms consistently implemented.

While the impact of policy reforms may have been mixed at least during the reform period, recent improvements in macroeconomic indicators, economic and agricultural growth, and poverty reduction have been ascribed to macroeconomic and agricultural sector policy changes that were implemented during the 1980s and 1990s (Badiane 2008). This suggests that the benefits of structural adjustment may have come much later than was anticipated. Nonetheless, SAPs attempted with some success to move the center of gravity of development thinking and practice away from government toward the private sector, leaving market forces to determine prices, and closer to a neutral position between agriculture and industry.

16.2.5   Poverty reduction strategies, 1990s and 2010s

A decade into SAPs, measures of social and economic progress in Africa had shown no marked improvement. Concerns over the lack of meaningful progress in the developing world and in Africa in particular resulted in international summits at which various targets for promoting sustainable human development were set and later compiled in 2000 as the Millennium Development Goals (MDGs).

Meanwhile, apprehensions over limited poverty reduction, the ineffective policy conditionality of SAPs, and the non-participatory nature of development programs resulted in a 'shift' in the World Bank's thinking on how best to carry out development work (World Bank 2009). Thus, in 1999 the World Bank and the IMF came up with the Poverty Reduction Strategy Paper (PRSP) approach which lays out macroeconomic and social programs and policies to be pursued by a country over a three- to five-year period in order to promote growth and reduce poverty in line with the MGDs. The World Bank and IMF sought to have low-income countries lead strategy priority setting and preparation of country PRSPs through a participatory process.

Assessments of PRSPs suggest that while countries acknowledge the important role of agriculture in accelerating "pro-poor" growth, agricultural policies of the SAP era have largely been maintained. In addition, the PRSP rhetoric on the importance of agriculture was not matched initially by increased investments in the sector by either governments or donors. Countries have continued to espouse the need to liberalize agricultural input and output markets and trade as well as foster privatization of parastatals. In most PRSPs, a distinction is made between the role of government and that of the private sector and areas in which the two can partner. For instance, governments are choosing to focus on the provision of public goods that are needed for the agricultural sector to operate efficiently such as rural and agricultural infrastructure, research, extension, storage facilities, and pest and disease control. Meanwhile the private sector is encouraged to actively participate in agricultural service delivery through input supply, marketing of output, agro-processing, and providing and ensuring access to agricultural services such as extension, marketing information, and micro-finance. Given increased attention to environmental sustainability, PRSPs have also promoted this in agriculture through, for example, integrated pest management techniques and conservation tillage.

While the PRSP approach has tried to move away from the strong private sector emphasis and sectoral neutrality of SAPs, it is debatable whether it has indeed been a sea-change shift in development thinking and practice. Some have argued that it has been mere "window-dressing," as core tenets of SAPs have been maintained and not reevaluated while ownership and participation under the PRSP approach have been severely limited in some countries.

16.2.6 Agriculture-led growth and poverty reduction, 2000s to 2010s

Up until the 1990s, major changes in Africa's development agenda had originated from outside the continent. Two of the main criticisms leveled against SAPs and PRSPs relate to their externally driven nature and lack of effective, broad-based participation of African stakeholders. Thus, starting in the late 1990s there were strong calls for inclusive, country-led and owned development strategies.

Consequently, the early 2000s, saw resolute efforts by African leaders to claim the driver's seat and lead Africa's development agenda under the New Partnership for Africa's Development (NEPAD), an Africa-wide initiative adopted by the African Union in 2002. NEPAD emphasizes peer review and mutual accountability at the highest political level to drastically improve political and economic governance across the continent. NEPAD has put agriculture at the forefront of Africa's development agenda. And in 2003, African leaders endorsed the Comprehensive Africa Agriculture Development Programme (CAADP) as the main framework for guiding country actions in achieving the poverty and hunger MDG and stimulating broad-based economic growth through agriculture-led growth. The embrace of an agriculture-led growth strategy by NEPAD was less a consequence of greater attention to theory than a simple conclusion drawn from observing one development agenda after the other fail to generate meaningful progress despite agriculture's enormous potential.

While recognizing the central role of the private sector, CAADP calls for bold action by governments to boost investments and create the conditions for accelerated growth. It commits African governments to invest at least 10% of country budgets in the agricultural sector to help deliver a 6% annual agricultural growth rate. In their agricultural strategies and investment plans, governments have committed to work with the private sector to increase investment for the sector and create an enabling environment for the private sector to participate in input supply, marketing of outputs, and agro-processing. CAADP promotes country leadership and ownership, participatory and inclusive policy dialogue and review, and mutual accountability across different stakeholders. In countries where the agricultural sector has witnessed remarkable performance such as Ghana, Mozambique, and Rwanda, the CAADP process has had strong political commitment and support, often at the highest levels of government. The government, donors, farmers' groups, private sector, and civil society all play important roles in the CAADP roundtable process which includes agreeing to a common vision for agriculture, planning investments, and monitoring performance and commitments. One of CAADP's main innovations has been the use of high-quality, locally based analysis to support priority setting, planning, and implementation. This embrace of evidence-based policy planning and implementation has linked CAADP more strongly to the theory of economic development than past development agendas. This has also raised the credibility of the agricultural agenda within governments and with various development partners and has thus created a stronger consensus and partnerships around the agenda. The case for agriculture-led growth has been bolstered by growing empirical literature to support the poverty-reducing effect of agricultural growth. The evidence shows a significant and direct relationship between agricultural productivity growth and poverty reduction (Irz, Lin, Thirtle, and Wiggins 2001; Thirtle, Lin, and Piesse 2003). It also shows accelerated agriculture-led growth to have greater opportunities for broad-based poverty reduction than non-agriculture led-growth (Diao et al. 2012). According to these studies, growth in the non-agricultural sector *alone* does not have the same broad impact on poverty reduction as that of the agricultural sector.

Many African countries have launched the CAADP process and developed agriculture strategies and investment plans. While the degree of implementation has varied from country to country, CAADP implementation has been occurring at a time of improved growth and increasing investments in the agricultural sector. CAADP has thus swung the pendulum toward agriculture in contrast to past ISI strategies and has brought about more balanced roles of the government and private sector within the agricultural sector.

16.3 Challenges and Opportunities to Agriculture-led Growth

Globalization and trade liberalization have created both opportunities and challenges for agricultural development and for the vast number of smallholder farmers across Africa. While they have created new market avenues for farmers and the potential to lower food prices for consumers, farmers face greater competition in local and international markets. Increased globalization means that Africa finds itself under increasingly different circumstances from those faced by Asia in the 1960s. Falling transportation costs, growth in international finance, higher levels of trade exchange with the rest of the world, and greater degrees of openness of domestic economies have together gradually reduced the dominant role of domestic demand in stimulating growth and economic transformation. The greater role of domestic demand combined with lower levels of external competition in domestic markets meant that supply-raising agricultural technology advances could go a long way toward addressing the growth challenge in Asia in the 1960s. African countries find themselves today in a different situation as advances on the supply side are more intricately linked to factors on the demand side. African countries do not only have to produce more, they also have to "sell" better, in far more competitive domestic as well as external markets. In addition, globalization provides opportunities for African countries to access and apply information and communication technologies and other technical know-how to overcome physical, institutional, and infrastructural obstacles, which several decades ago were major constraints to growth and development.

Emerging markets and growing demand for biofuels in developed nations and land acquisitions in African nations have created additional opportunities and challenges for Africa. Biofuels will likely play a greater role in the future of the global economy and, thus, should be integrated in development strategies of African countries. Foreign direct investments (FDI) in agriculture and land acquisitions present opportunities to bring in much needed capital and know-how to spur agricultural growth, but also create risks of undermining food production and displacing locals from their land. The fact that the bulk of the poor and vulnerable live in rural areas and have access to land, which can be made more productive, provides African nations with an effective lever in the fight against poverty. It is, therefore, important for African countries to find additional modalities to attract FDI without jeopardizing access to land by the poor and vulnerable.

Over the last century, the world, has witnessed an increased frequency of climate variability and incidence of climatic shocks. Most climate change projections show that Africa is likely to have disproportionately more frequent climate shocks (droughts and floods) in the future. Projections also predict reductions in major staple crop yields in Africa and increases in real crop prices which will compromise food security. But unlike the developed world, Africa will be least able to cope with the ramifications of climate change, particularly in the context of an agriculture that is predominately rain-fed and whose small farmers use traditional technologies that are not well adapted to climatic disasters. Thus, there are growing efforts to make development efforts more resilient to climatic risks, and increasingly African countries are incorporating issues of building resilience and risk management into their agricultural strategies. Also, Africa has the largest remaining potential for agricultural production of any region, and should benefit from price increases in the long run, if it manages to mitigate the impact of climate change on the competitiveness of its agricultural sector.

Political pluralism and rent-seeking behavior may undo the benefits of the SAP era reforms, largely associated with macroeconomic stabilization. The risk of policy reversal, that is, a return to the failed policies of the 1960s and 1970s, is real in the absence of institutional memory and in the presence of a new generation of African leaders who have not experienced the consequences of these policies. The risk of policy reversal became evident during the 2007–2008 global food price crisis which put pressure on African governments to respond swiftly to minimize any harmful impact on the poor and avert food protests. As a result, price controls, export prohibitions, and other distortionary interventions in input and output markets were put in place. It is, therefore, critical that even in times of crisis countries maintain a favorable policy environment for agriculture that keeps the sector competitive and creates incentives for farmers to produce more and access markets for their products.

16.4 STRUCTURAL TRANSFORMATION IN AFRICA

Africa needs to accelerate its recent improved growth and transit to structural transformation. All successfully industrialized economies have gone through a transformation that involves a shift in the relative importance of economic sectors during the course of economic development. This is generally characterized by having a decreasing share of agriculture in national output and employment, an increasing share of industry and services in national output, and a high degree of urbanization. An important part of structural transformation is that as economies mature, they acquire greater capabilities to produce more sophisticated, higher valued goods. The basket of goods a country ends up producing competitively determines its level of economic performance and income. Goods for which demand expands globally as incomes rise around the world can be exported in larger quantities and at high prices for a long time. Such goods are associated with higher levels of productivity and incomes. The more a country succeeds in producing such goods, the more wealth it will build, and the richer it will get.

Therefore, managing a successful structural transformation poses two key challenges: sustainably raising labor productivity in the agricultural and rural sectors and gradually diversifying into higher valued goods outside agriculture in higher productivity, urban-based manufacturing and service sectors. When countries adopt strategies to meet these challenges, the economy grows and the levels of output and productivity per worker in the agricultural sector rise, while the shares of agriculture in national employment and output decline, due to faster growth in the rest of the economy. The result is a rise in overall per capita incomes while incomes in the rural and agricultural sectors converge toward those in the non-agricultural sector. Moreover, in countries that have successfully transformed, the difference in labor productivity in agricultural and non-agricultural sectors approaches zero given better integration of the labor and capital markets (Timmer 2009). Despite its relative decline, the agricultural sector plays an active role in the structural transformation and income convergence processes.

The failure of ISI strategies of the 1960s left most African countries without bold and credible strategies to promote a successful transformation. Thus, during most of the five decades since independence, African countries have experienced productivity-reducing structural transformation reflected in labor migrating from an underperforming agricultural sector with rising productivity into a non-agricultural sector characterized by falling productivity and an oversized, lower-productivity service sector (Badiane 2011).[2] Until the early 2000s, agricultural labor productivity had stagnated despite a rapid decline in the sector's employment and GDP shares in most African countries. Concurrently, productivity has been falling in the non-agricultural sector while employment has risen in the sector. In that process, labor migration out of agriculture has outpaced labor growth in the non-agricultural sector, thus, further undermining productivity growth. As a consequence, the agricultural sector is now significantly smaller while the service sector is significantly larger than has been observed historically in other countries at a similar level of development. Estimations of the relationship between per capita income levels and the relative sizes of the agricultural and

---

[2] In national accounts, for much of Africa, the service sector includes a high degree of informal and low productivity activities in which a large segment of the underemployed are engaged.

service sectors using a sample of 210 countries over the period from 1960 to 2008, invariably show that, for most African countries, the actual share of agricultural GDP is distinctly lower than the size that would have been expected based on the level of per capita incomes (Badiane 2011). The opposite is observed for the service sector, whereby observed shares are higher than expected. This sectoral growth imbalance has, thus, delayed structural transformation and slowed productivity and income growth across Africa.

16.5 Rethinking Future Growth and Development Strategies in Africa

16.5.1 Modernizing the informal service sector and developing agribusiness

The current structure of African economies is characterized by the dominance of an informal service sector, which in most countries now constitutes the largest reservoir of low-productivity labor. Therefore, the theory based on the dual-economy model may not work as expected anymore in what has become a *de facto* three-dimensional economy—agriculture, industry, and informal services. The strategic tension or trade-off is no longer just between industry-led and agriculture-led growth. The possible contribution of a service-led strategy to the broader growth and development agenda in the context of economies in early stages of development may now deserve equal consideration. The heavy concentration of pre-industrial activities (e.g. handicrafts) and low productivity labor in the large informal service sector offers additional options to the traditional model of industrialization based on manufacturing, agribusiness, and agro-processing industries. Future strategies of industrial growth that also emphasize enterprise creation and growth in order to modernize the informal sector may do more, in the short to medium run, to raise labor productivity and reduce poverty than strategies that only target traditional manufacturing.

According to Sonobe and Otsuka (2011), growth and modernization of the informal sector will need to address transaction costs related to information asymmetries, contract enforcement, innovative knowledge spillovers, and insufficient managerial capital. To deal with these transaction costs in Africa, they propose a cluster based industrialization (CBI) approach that has been successful in Asia. CBI strategies can help facilitate migration of informal enterprises in the service sector into the more productive, formal segment of the economy. In Africa, CBI strategies will need to target the agribusiness sector while focusing on areas with high productivity and technology spillover potential, such as peri-urban processing industries, high agro-climatic potential areas, and regional transport corridors.

16.5.2 Renewed industrialization strategies

During the process of structural transformation industrial enterprises need to leverage existing assets into new and/or related businesses and learn how to combine and recombine assets to establish new businesses and address new markets (Teece 2000). To foster industrial growth, African countries need renewed industrialization strategies that build on the current growth recovery with the goal of raising the number of successful entrepreneurs while addressing information and coordination externalities that can deter entrepreneurship growth. These externalities, including those related to knowledge generation and diffusion, will have to be addressed through technology, infrastructure, regulatory, and macroeconomic policies. Industrialization policies should aim to expand the stock of technology capabilities and their applications to create new, higher valued goods (Lall 2000). Such policies should not target the manufacturing sector exclusively but also the informal sector with its large concentration of pre-industrial handicraft activities. Product innovation and upgrading in this sector is required to tap into the rapidly growing middle class demand in urban areas for more sophisticated household goods. African countries will have to (re)discover ways of stimulating industrial growth and learn from emerging Asian countries, where public action in support of industrial growth by effectively tackling these complex externalities has been a central element of their economic development (Mathews 1996). The industrialization strategies proposed by Lin (this volume) based on China's experience need to be explored in more African countries. They include first identifying sectors of comparative advantage and then establishing industrial parks and economic zones to reduce transaction costs due to poor infrastructure and institutions while the government plays a facilitating role. In turn, this enables industrial upgrading and further improvements in infrastructure and institutions.

16.5.3   Promoting agricultural productivity growth

Asia and Latin America's Green Revolution demonstrated the significant role of agricultural productivity growth in achieving broad-based economic growth and accelerating structural transformation. The revolution highlighted the important role smallholder farmers can play in raising production when given access to improved technologies, inputs, credit, and marketing systems. Increasing investments in agricultural R&D is, therefore, essential for not only sustaining Africa's recent growth recovery but accelerating its transformation. Empirical evidence has shown investment in agricultural R&D to have the highest returns in productivity and poverty reduction (Fan and White 2008). Complementary investments are needed to build or improve irrigation, road, and storage infrastructure, and to develop higher value chains and markets. Furthermore, the public sector will have to play an important role in developing, adapting, and spreading agricultural technologies while creating an enabling environment for public–private partnerships and the private sector to invest in the sector and support agricultural technology development, diffusion, extension, and marketing. African countries, therefore, need to broaden partnerships and alliances under the CAADP agenda to leverage public and private sector investments in agriculture including R&D.

16.5.4   Greater convergence of social and growth policies

The existence of large-scale poverty in Africa together with increasing democratization and global activism have raised the demand for social services in a historically unprecedented manner. African countries are under growing pressure to find sufficient resources to meet the rising demand for social services while investing enough to accelerate agricultural productivity growth under tight budget constraints. The challenge, therefore, faced by African countries is one of allocating public resources efficiently and effectively such as to realize, in a sustainable way, economic, social, and environmental goals.

Future growth strategies need to find ways to maximize the impact of the significantly larger social service investments on labor productivity in the agricultural and rural sectors. For instance, the analysis of the effects of health service expenditures among farm households in Uganda by Badiane and Ulimwengu (2013) shows that expenditures on health consultation services have the largest impact on reducing morbidity related agricultural inefficiency compared to expenditures on drugs and hospitalization. The results suggest that health programs can contribute more to raising agricultural labor productivity by emphasizing access to consultation services through primary care. Analysis of other programs in the health, education, and social protection sectors may yield similar results.

16.6 Conclusion

Africa's improved growth performance over the last 15 years has been remarkable. It is in sharp contrast to the poor performance witnessed following independence up until the mid-1990s. After independence, countries subscribed to development paradigms with continuously shifting objectives and in particular a strong bias in favor of industry at the expense of agriculture and government and public sector at the expense of markets and the private sector. While countries embraced the theory associated with ISI strategies of the 1960s and 1970s, the competing theory in favor of an agriculture-led growth strategy was largely ignored during this period. The stance resulted in government failures that prevented industry from taking off while it distorted market forces in the agricultural sector. It contributed to delaying Africa's structural transformation and thus resulted in a productivity reducing structural change—characterized by labor migrating from an agricultural sector with rising productivity to a non-agricultural sector consisting of a large service sector and falling productivity. Addressing the large pool of low productivity and low skilled labor may now require moving away from the traditional dual-economy model toward a three-dimensional model that emphasizes the role of the informal service sector in development strategies.

The continent also needs renewed industrialization policies to develop comparative advantages in higher value goods and target the manufacturing sector and support agro-processing and infant industries by addressing information and coordination externalities. The experience of cluster based industrialization strategies that have proved to be successful in Asia could provide useful lessons for modernizing not just the manufacturing but also the large informal segment of Africa's service sector.

The CAADP agenda has highlighted the importance of country-led and owned strategies and bold commitment led by governments to increase investments and embrace evidence-based policies and inclusive review and dialogue mechanisms for an improved agricultural sector governance and performance. Country ownership and leadership ensure consistency and continuity in policies and strategies which are critical for long term success. A CAADP like approach for the industrial sector may be in order. As theoretical and empirical evidence and Asia and Latin America's Green Revolution demonstrate, agricultural productivity growth is essential for not only broad-based economic growth and poverty reduction but also for bringing about a structural transformation. Investments in agricultural R&D, transportation and storage infrastructure, and market development are an imperative. Allocating growing social service investments to maximize their impact on agricultural productivity growth will contribute to meeting both social goals and growth objectives. Moreover, policies in agriculture, industry, and the informal service sector will need to be supported by more balanced roles of the government and the public sector with that of markets and the private sector.

References

Badiane, O. (2008). "Sustaining and Accelerating Africa's Growth Recovery in the Context of Changing Global Food Prices." Policy Brief No. 9. Washington, DC: International Food Policy Research Institute.

Badiane, O., and Shively, G. (1997). "The Response of Local Maize Prices to the 1983 Currency Devaluation in Ghana." Discussion Paper 12. Market and Structural Studies Division. Washington, DC: International Food Policy Research Institute.

Badiane, O., and Kherallah, M. (1999). Market liberalization and the poor. *Quarterly Journal of International Agriculture*, 38(4):341–358.

Badiane, O. (2011). *Agriculture and Structural Transformation in Africa*. Stanford Symposium Series on Global Food Policy and Food Security in the 21st Century. Stanford: Center on Food Security and the Environment. Stanford University.

Badiane, O., and Ulimwengu, J. (2013). Malaria incidence and agricultural efficiency in Uganda. *Agricultural Economics*, 43(1):15–23.

Barrett, C.B., and Mutambatsere, E. (2005). Marketing boards, in L.E. Blume and S.N. Durlauf (eds), *The New Palgrave Dictionary of Economics*, 2nd edn., London: Palgrave Macmillan, pp. 1–12.

Barrett, C.B., and Carter, M.R. (1999). Microeconomically coherent agricultural policy reform in Africa, in J. Paulson (ed.), *African Economies in Transition. Vol. 2: The Reform Experience*. London: MacMillan, New York: St. Martins, Chapter 6, pp. 288–347.

Binswanger, H.P. (1998). Agricultural and rural development: painful lessons, in C.K. Eicher, and J.M. Staatz (eds), *International Agricultural Development*, 3rd edn. Baltimore: The Johns Hopkins University Press, Chapter 17, pp. 287–299.

Cornia, G.A. (1987). Economic decline and human welfare in the first half of the 1980s, in G.A. Cornia, R. Jolly, and F. Stewart (eds), *Adjustment with a Human Face. Volume 1. Protecting the Vulnerable and Promoting Growth*. Oxford: Oxford University Press, Chapter 1, pp. 11–47.

Degefe, B. (1994). An African perspective on long-term development in sub-Saharan Africa, in G.A. Cornia and G.K. Helleiner (eds), *From Adjustment to Development in Africa: Conflict, Controversy, Convergence, Consensus?* New York: St. Martins Press, Inc, Chapter 3, pp. 49–68.

Delgado C., Hopkins, J., Kelly, V. et al. (1998). *Agricultural growth linkages in Sub-Saharan Africa*. IFPRI Research Report No. 107. Washington, DC: International Food Policy Research Institute.

Diao, X., Thurlow, J., Benin, S., and Fan, S. (eds) (2012). *Strategies and Priorities for African Agriculture: Economywide Perspectives from Country Studies*. Washington, DC: International Food Policy Research Institute.

Eicher, C.K., and Staatz, J.M (eds) (1990). *Agricultural Development in the Third World*, 2nd edn. Baltimore: The Johns Hopkins University Press.

Eicher, C.K. (1992). African agricultural development strategies, in F. Stewart, S. Lall, and S. Wangwe, (eds), *Alternative Development Strategies in Sub-Saharan Africa*. New York: St Martins Press, Chapter 3, pp. 79–102.

Ellis, F., and Biggs, S. (2001). Evolving themes in rural development 1950s–2000s. *Development Policy Review*, 19(4):437–448.

Fan, S., and White, A. (2008). Lessons learned: major findings and policy implications, in S. Fan (ed.), *Public Expenditures, Growth, and Poverty: Lessons from Developing Countries*. International Food Policy Research Institute. Baltimore: Johns Hopkins University Press, Chapter 7, pp. 225–239.

Spielman, D., and Pandya-Lorch, R. (eds) (2009). *Millions Fed: Proven Successes in Agricultural Development*. Washington DC: International Food Policy Research Institute.

Haggblade, S., and Hazell, P. (1989). Agricultural technology and farm-nonfarm growth linkages. *Agricultural Economics*, 3(4):345–364.

Hayami, Y. (2003). From the Washington consensus to the post-Washington consensus: retrospect and prospect. *Asian Development Review*, 20(2):40–65.

Irz, X., Lin, L., Thirtle, C., and Wiggins, S. (2001). Agricultural Productivity Growth and Poverty Alleviation. *Development Policy Review*, 19(4):449–466.

Jayne, T.S. Govereh, J., Mwanaumo, A. et al. (2002). False promise or false premise? The experience of food and input market reform in Eastern and Southern Africa. *World Development*, 30(11):1967–1985.

Johnston, D.G., and Mellor, J.W. (1961). The role of agriculture in economic development. *American Economic Review*, 51(4):566–593.

Kherallah, M., Delgado, C.L., Gabre-Madhin, E. et al. (2002). *Reforming Agricultural Market Reforms in Sub-Saharan Africa*. Baltimore: Johns Hopkins University Press.

Lall, S. (2000). Technological change and industrialization in the Asian newly industrializing economies: achievements and challenges, in Kim, L. and R. Nelson (eds), *Technology Learning and Innovation: The Experience of Newly Industrializing Economies*. Cambridge: Cambridge University Press, Chapter 2, pp. 13–68.

Lewis, W.A. (1954). Economic development with unlimited supplies of labor. *The Manchester School*, 22(2):139–191.

Lin, J.Y. (this volume). China's rise and structural transformation in Africa: ideas and opportunities. *The Oxford Handbook of Africa and Economics*. Oxford: Oxford University Press.

Mathews, J. (1996). High technology industrialization in East Asia. *Journal of Industry Studies*, 3(2):1–77.

Nin-Pratt, A., Johnson, M., and Yu, B. (2012). Improved Performance of Agriculture in Africa South of the Sahara. International Food Policy Research Institute (IFPRI) Discussion Paper 01224. Washington DC: IFPRI.

Ranis, G., and Fei, J.C.H. (1961). A theory of economic development. *American Economic Review*, 51(4):533–565.

Schultz T.W. (1964). *Transforming Traditional Agriculture*. New Haven: Yale University Press.

Sonobe, T., and Otsuka, K. (2011). *Cluster-Based Industrial Development: A Comparative Study of Asia and Africa*. New York: Palgrave Macmillan.

Streeten. P, Burki, S.J., ul Haq, M. et al. (eds) (1981). *Things First: Meeting Basic Human Needs in the Developing Countries.* Oxford: Oxford University Press.

Teece, D.J. (2000). Firm capabilities and economic development: implications for newly industrializing economies, in L. Kim, and R. Nelson (eds), *Technology Learning and Innovation: The Experience of Newly Industrializing Economies.* Cambridge: Cambridge University Press, Chapter 4, pp. 105–128.

Thirtle, C., Lin, L., and Piesse, J. (2003). The impact of research-led agricultural productivity growth on poverty reduction in Africa, Asia and Latin America. *World Development,* 31(12):1959–1975.

Timmer, P.C. (2009). *A World Without Agriculture: The Structural Transformation in Historical Perspective.* The American Enterprise Institute for Public Policy Research. Washington, DC: The American Enterprise Institute Press.

World Bank (1981). *Accelerated Development in Sub-Saharan Africa: An Agenda for Action.* Published for the World Bank by Oxford University Press.

World Bank (2009). *Comprehensive Development Framework (CDF).* Washington, DC: World Bank.

World Bank (2012). *World Development Indicators.* Washington, DC: World Bank.

World Bank (2013). *World Development Indicators.* Washington, DC: World Bank.

Yudelman, M. (1976). Agriculture in integrated rural development: the experience of the World Bank. *Food Policy,* 1(5): 367–381.

CHAPTER 17

....

CAPACITY DEVELOPMENT FOR TRANSFORMATION

....

FRANNIE A. LÉAUTIER

17.1 WHY DOES AFRICA NEED CAPACITY?

To sustain high economic growth and ensure growth generates jobs and poverty reduction, Africa needs to develop capabilities to transform its economies. For effective investing using domestic resources or external aid, Africa requires capacity to develop successful strategies, implement development plans, negotiate aid, as well as collect and manage taxes and other domestic revenues. To achieve sustainable development results, reduce poverty, and guarantee food security, Africa is compelled to continue to transform agriculture, develop human capital, build institutions that can ensure the continent benefits from its vast natural resources, secure fair trade deals, and manage under uncertainty.

A lot of effort has been expended to build capacity in Africa with mixed results. This chapter considers a working definition of capacity development and uncovers the characteristics of capacity that are linked to stages of development and to Africa's unique combination of a vast geographical territory with high potential for regional integration; a rich endowment of natural resources; a youthful and growing population; and a wide variety of states of achieved stability and economic growth over the years. The opportunity to use these unique characteristics and transform them into human and institutional capacity is tremendous. Thus developing a successful approach to capacity development in Africa is highly strategic. Given that capacity development is both a science and an art, and not all approaches succeed at the same level, lessons need to be extracted from within a variety of sources of economic theory and Africa's own achievement.

The concept of capacity has various definitions depending on practice. In this handbook we develop a definition from an analytical and theoretical perspective. Using a concept of a capacity system with different levels including individual, organizational, societal, and sectoral, we add context by looking at geographical and spatial perspectives. We also bring in the question of building capacity in crisis. This analytic approach allows a broad definition of capacity to be developed, yet allows it to be specific enough to encompass the variety of contexts in Africa.

326 MICROECONOMIC AND SECTORAL ISSUES

Because of the tremendous challenges Africa is facing in implementation, we shed light on the issue of capability. We advance capability based theories, using concepts from the theory of the firm and organizational performance, with specific reference to ability to create value; seize opportunities and learn from them; understand learning patterns, and learn from existing organizations and practices; static and dynamic capabilities and the concept of search and learning; and capability to build organizations from personal experience. The potential for Africa to transform its unique combination of endowments by focusing on the best approach to implementation of its policies and programs is the key highlight in this section.

In this chapter we also bring out the issue of accumulation of knowledge and capabilities at both individual and organizational level, building on the concepts of investment in human capital. Such an approach can help explain controversies like the educated unemployed, performing economies at low human capital levels, and states dependent on natural resources but not capable of managing their transformation. We touch briefly on the role of education in building human capital and acquiring formal skills, but also in research and innovation. The chapter also covers problem solving knowledge embedded in organizations and brings in ideas from "animal spirits" as applied to capacity development. Africa's rich cultural assets and historical tradition of learning and sharing, positions it well to tap into knowledge and ideas as a source of growth and development.

The chapter includes a brief exposition on the notions of "capabilities" in the sense of "feasibility to achieve." The chapter ends with a brief exposition of ideas from co-evolutionary dynamics, particularly around appropriate matching of capabilities of the state to the challenges facing it.

17.2 Definitions of Capacity

The concept of capacity has various definitions depending on practice and there is no broadly accepted definition (Morgan 2006). We develop a definition using work from Honadle (1981) but also build in performance-based and holistic definitions of capacity. Honadle (1981) starts off by refuting the early definitions of capacity as "staying power" of organizations, which involves tracking the ability of organizations to survive. She goes on to argue that capacity is beyond just survival, and includes the ability of organizations to perform their functions effectively. Because of the challenges of stability in Africa, where organizations responsible for delivery of development services have been constituted and reconstituted; government departments have been in place for a longtime or have fallen in short order; the concept of survival of organizations is used by many and is indeed considered an important one (Lenz 1980).

17.2.1 A search for concept and purpose of "capacity"

Honadle (1981) defines "capacity" at the level of organizations and institutions and proposes a framework that encompasses the ability to anticipate and influence change; make informed, intelligent decisions about policy; develop programs to implement policy; attract, absorb, and manage resources; evaluate current activities to guide the future; accumulate experience, learn from it, and apply lessons learned to future activities. This framework is useful for assessing the achievements and challenges of capacity in Africa and also for selecting amongst a suite of policies and actions needed in the future for Africa to successfully achieve development results. However, it suffers from a number of limitations, such as the lack of attention to the role of individuals, which happens to be the critical link in contexts with weak developmental outcomes. Where countries are poor or do not have supporting enabling environments for development, as is the case in fragile and post-conflict countries, the role of the individual is paramount in setting up the enabling environment for other activities to take place, or even in leading change such that results can be achieved.

17.2.2 Performance-based definitions of capacity

We therefore build on Honadle (1981) but also introduce the premise that capacity comprises the ability of people, organizations, and society as whole to manage their affairs successfully; and that it is the process by which people, organizations, and society as a whole unleash, strengthen, create, adapt, and maintain capacity over time (ACBF 2011). Such a definition embeds the concept of a capacity system with different levels including societal and sectoral (McKinsey and Company 2001), as well as geographical or spatial (Figure 17.1).

The African Capacity Building Foundation (ACBF) has been using a definition of capacity that is conceptualized at the level of individuals, organizations, and societies as a whole. Their definition focuses on ability to set goals for development and achieve them;

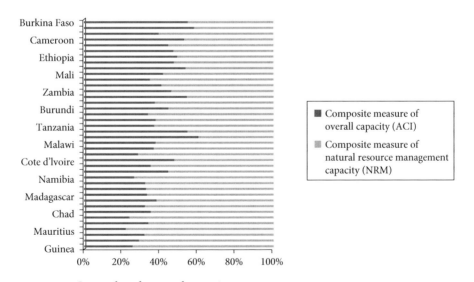

FIGURE 17.1 Sectoral and general capacity.

Source: data from ACBF (2013).

to budget resources and use them for agreed purposes; and to manage the complex purposes and interactions that typify a working political and economic system (ACBF 2011:
30–31). The definition is broad yet specific enough to encompass the variety of contexts in
Africa. A composite index derived from four dimensions is calculated to assess capacity
improvements in Africa. The dimensions include a cluster of indicators around development "policy"; a second cluster around "processes" for implementation; a third cluster on
achieving development "results"; and a final cluster on building "dynamic capabilities."

Such a definition of capacity recognizes that many countries in Africa are starting from
a low base of individual competences and have had to develop a critical mass of people
who can undertake the types of activities that lead to development results. Challenges
such as brain drain also mean that the few competent people who are there are not available for the critical policy and program activities needed for development. Poor incentive
structures in the public sector means at times that competent people may not be contributing effectively or not be committed to achieving results. Policy capacity can be measured by the critical mass of skilled people who can formulate and design effective policies
to secure stable, good sectoral outcomes in service delivery or a stable macroeconomic
environment.

The main challenge is to have skilled people who are competent in a particular sector (education, health, energy, transport, and so on) as well as those who are capable of managing the
processes for implementing policies and programs in the different sectors. High-performing
individuals need to be functioning in a system that can diagnose problems (Spillane and
Coldren 2011), put in place the right strategies, and implement them (Fullan 2010). The kind
of skills needed go beyond academic qualification and relate to the need to be able to manage complex implementation arrangements (de Grauwe 2009). The ability to formulate
and design policy needs to be complemented by management skills that can not only identify the supporters that could enable the policy to be effectively adopted but those advocates
who could help it be recognized, and those analysts who could support the design by doing
the needed analytical work to secure the quality needed for policies to be endorsed broadly.
Credibility of the policymaking process and the dynamism of building coalitions for change
are equally critical, as policymaking is rarely stable and there is a very important role for
entrepreneurial individuals to be effective (Mintrom and Vergari 1996). Such concepts of
entrepreneurship are well placed in the African context, as positioning adequate policies for
implementation require critical knowledge of the local environment to be combined with a
smart strategy for change. Ministerial personnel who are successful at getting policies implemented spend enormous amounts of time trying to get policies adopted once they have been
designed, and also consult with select groups to embed their ideas in the policy design (de
Grauwe 2009).

Characteristics such as the geographic size of the country do also matter for the ability
to achieve capacity for development, in addition to the structure of economies in terms of
dependency on hydrocarbons or minerals for export. Big countries have to have the capacity to deliver services beyond the capital city and to reach the rural and distant areas of the
country. Low capacity to manage the spatial dimension of development affairs can hamper
the achievement of development results, and limit the ability to reduce income and service
inequalities. However, countries rich in natural resources can afford to invest in building

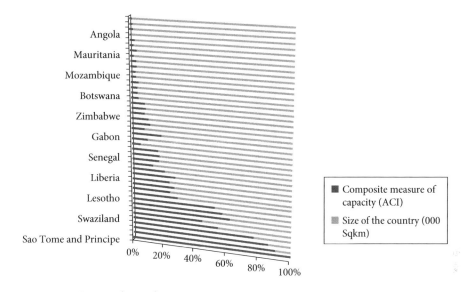

FIGURE 17.2 Geography and capacity.

Source: data from ACBF (2013).

capacity for the future, particularly in terms of investing in improving infrastructure connections and human capabilities (Figure 17.2).

A lot of effort can be expended to build capacity with limited or mixed results if the factors of size, economic structure, and political environment are not taken into consideration. Because Africa has vast territories and countries are geographically spread out with limited access to infrastructure, implementation can be a challenge. Indeed the size of the country has an effect on the achieved level of capacity of the country. Large countries could have more challenges in developing the needed capacity to effectively manage their development results.

Trade-offs are needed to effectively transform physical into human capital. Countries that are small geographically also need to have capacity to manage their development affairs; being not as well endowed in natural resources makes it harder for them to attain the needed resources to be transformed into development results. This is where the question of aid dependency comes in and the ability to effectively manage external aid for development results.

But it is not necessary to have natural resources to succeed (see detailed analysis in the Appendix). Countries that depend on agriculture could also use the knowledge gained in transforming the sector to modernize it and use that capacity as the basis for achieving development results in other areas over time. Mid-sized countries that are not dependent on natural resources can also make progress in capacity achievements, by innovating and extracting value from a diversified economy. Africa's unique combination of a vast geographical territory with high potential for regional integration would thus also require effective institutions for regional integration, for it to achieve the results. The issue of sequencing capacity development is also important. Good performance in one sector can coexist with poor performance across other sectors.

17.2.3 Building capacity in crisis

Because of the variety of countries in Africa that are fragile, post conflict or in conflict, it is important to also bring in the question of building capacity in crisis (Eade 1997). There are three areas that have proven essential to address simultaneously for post-conflict stabilization, recovery, and development, according to Mlambo et al. (2009): (i) rebuilding the state and its key functions; (ii) reviving war-ravaged economies; and (iii) rehabilitating, reconstructing, and reintegrating communities and addressing their urgent needs.

To rebuild the state and its key functions requires capacity to utilize resources effectively, managing skills and knowledge, have effective organizations in place, restructure politics and power arrangements, and put in place the right incentives for development (UNDP 2002: 4, 6). Resources to be managed during periods post conflict include food aid, finances from trust funds and social funds, material and equipment, and budget support. Also needed is capacity to re-skill the population and manage training activities, knowledge and learning, including best use of study tours, technical assistance, and technology transfer. Organizational capacity includes management systems development, effective organizational twinning to learn from peers, restructuring of previous organizations before conflict, and undertaking civil service reform and decentralization. Under politics and power, critical capacities relate to empowering communities, legislative strengthening, and development of alternate politics that can handle ethnic conflicts and the causes of previous conflict. Designing appropriate incentives to undertake sectoral reforms, encourage dialogue and consensus building, strengthen accountability and ensure rule of law are important.

Analysis done in ACBF (2011) shows an important difference in capacities of fragile and non-fragile states. The most critical difference is in organizational capacity to manage the myriad activities needed after conflict. Another important difference is effective use of resources and speeding up of skills building and knowledge transfer. There isn't much difference between fragile and non-fragile states in the sphere of capacity to wage politics and power and to define incentives. What seems to matter is the purpose of the use of politics, power, and incentives, rather than the capacity to do so.

17.2.4 Main considerations for capacity

Building capacity in Africa depends on the strategic use of the unique characteristics and endowments of the continent. Capacity building in Africa has to be people centered, given its youthful and growing population, and success depends on how well "capabilities" have been developed. The continent is rich in natural resources and can transform them into human and institutional capacity, but to do so it has to combine individual capabilities with effective organizational performance. Africa has a vast and diverse geographical territory that is in various stages of connectedness, making it imperative to rely on an effective balance of decentralized approaches and those that rely on collating and coordinating large sources of data from disperse regions. Africa is also at a stage of development where it is competing with other countries in a more globally connected space and can use this level of connectivity to learn from a wide range of geographies and economies and leapfrog into higher performance. Given that capacity development is both a science and an art, and not all approaches succeed at the same level, lessons need to be extracted from within a variety of sources of economic theory and Africa's own achievement.

Holistic definitions of capacity are the most useful, as they allow countries to define the best capacity system that would deliver development results at the overall societal levels, but also at sectoral levels (McKinsey and Company 2001). Explicitly recognizing starting points and endowments at a given position in time is important for building capacity post crisis (Eade 1997).

17.3 CAPABILITY-BASED THEORIES

Because of the tremendous importance of implementation, we shed light in this section on the issue of capability.

Penrose (1959: 85) advanced the idea of a close relationship between various kinds of resources with which a firm works and the development of ideas, experience, and knowledge of its managers and entrepreneurs. Applied to countries, one could see each country as a unique bundle of resources, requiring country-specific managerial experience to get the type of ideas, experience, and knowledge to achieve results. Otherwise put, the country context and historical trajectory traversed by the country will make its policymakers and development actors have a unique experience that cannot be replicated elsewhere. Such experience would be found in the intimate and tacit knowledge of the communities in those countries, in the specificity of the human capital assets at a given point in time, and in the day-to-day operating procedures in the workplace. Compared to people coming from the outside (as in the returning diasporas or external experts), personnel who have been a long time in a ministry or department would have knowledge of the department's capabilities and organizational routines that allows them to envision a "subjective and productive opportunity" set (Penrose 1959: 42) for the country.

Capacity building within a rapidly changing context is a "learning by doing" field, and according to Penrose (1959: 53) in such situations it is experiential knowledge that is being used and such knowledge cannot be transferred as easily as it can rarely be separated from the individuals concerned. As such, it is important to design capacity building programs that take people from their work environment and subject them to learning and exchange with others, exposing them to new material, but with the purpose of having them make micro-improvements in their practices and procedures, if changes or reforms are to be sustainable.

Another key concept from Penrose (1959) is the availability of capable human assets that can be deployed for learning, expanding, and diversifying. A bottleneck to development and sustainable economic growth is the availability of highly skilled and experienced permanent secretaries (partners in the equivalent of the professional services firms studied by Penrose) who can coordinate complex functions, provide oversight over multiple activities and priorities, and leverage the resources of the ministries to deliver on important results. It takes time and effort to accumulate such sector-specific and country-specific knowledge, and hence building an effective civil service is critical for success in transforming societies. There are few shortcuts in learning, growing, and diversifying economies sustainably.

As important as individuals and their tacit knowledge are, so is the importance of how power is exercised in organizations and its impact on organizational performance (Katz and Kahn 1966). Those at the top of public sector organizations responsible for development would not necessarily be aligned to deliver development results. They would be, according to Pfeffer and Salancik (1978), many times engaged in ensuring their own survival and the survival of their department or ministry, seeking to enhance their own autonomy. Thus power would trump development results, and stability of the decision-making system would trump introduction of flexibility and adaptation in strategy and plans for development. Such a tendency is important to understand when developing capacity building strategies so as to better align capacity-building resources towards supporting accountability mechanisms outside of the public sector and to embed incentives for performance within the public sector (Figure 17.3).

Studies show that it is easier to achieve legitimacy of a strategy for development and program for achieving results, then it is to get high levels of flexibility and a good set of incentives that drive high performance behavior in the public sector (ACBF 2011). Effective organizational capacity would include the ability to create value over time (Möller and Törrönen 2003), which in the context of Africa would be to achieve sustainable development results. Effective organizations could seize opportunities and learn from them (Smith et al. 1996). More importantly, organizations responsible for development would have people who are skilled at understanding learning patterns, and learning from existing organizations and practices (Senge 1997). For development organizations in Africa to do so in an effective manner would require not only static capabilities (as in the stock of knowledge that a critical mass of trained professionals in a ministry have), but dynamic capabilities as well, so they can embed concepts of search and learning as they work to get results in a complex development arena (Bar Yam 1997). As such, successful capacity building would be an outcome of an evolution, where countries advance a capability to build organizations from the collective and shared personal experiences of its people.

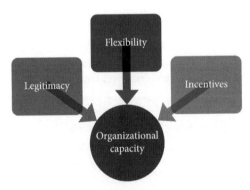

FIGURE 17.3 Legitimacy, flexibility, and incentives in determining organizational capacity.

17.4 ACCUMULATION OF KNOWLEDGE AND CAPABILITIES AT INDIVIDUAL AND ORGANIZATIONAL LEVEL

There are six capacities that are needed for Africa's development (Léautier and Mutahakana 2012): (i) the ability to manage and negotiate conflicts and ensure stability that can attract economic activity and investment; (ii) the policies and programs needed to transform agriculture and guarantee food security within and across country borders; (iii) the skills, competences and decision-making systems and processes to decide on investment priorities; (iv) the skills, competences, and systems for data collection and analysis including those that secure the demand for good data and support the desire for evidence-based policymaking; (v) skills, competences, systems, and processes to manage across sectors, geographies, and generations; and (vi) the mechanisms and practices to engage civil society, the private sector, and the international community on development issues.

The education sector plays a paramount role in building the human capital needed to meet these capacity needs. Universities are at the top of the transformation chain that contributes to generating graduates with skills of defining alternatives, making choices, and implementing programs for development. Success in generating such skilled people relies heavily on how education is viewed, developed, and used, and more importantly on the conception of the capacities needed to move forward (Léautier and Mutahakana 2012).

People, Schultz (1961) famously said, are an important part of the wealth of nations. A strategic capacity building program for Africa would support individuals to acquire knowledge and skills by investing in effective systems of learning and knowledge acquisition. Such systems would develop individuals that can transfer their skills from agriculture into industry and manufacturing. Furthermore, investment in raising the workplace knowledge and functions so as to raise the productive capacity of the workforce is an important role for education. Such investments would be expected to yield results in large populous countries as the labor contribution to output is vastly larger than all other forms of wealth taken together (Schultz 1961).

The education sector is key for capacity development as it draws on the notions of "capabilities" in the sense of "feasibility to achieve" as developed by Sen (1999). The role of universities in innovation and learning systems at individual, societal, and economy levels is important for producing skilled people who can create and use knowledge effectively, thereby raising the quality of administrative decisions at a country level (Hanson and Léautier 2011). Universities have a role to play in generating a culture of social equality, tolerance, and environmental sustainability. Such a culture, coupled with organizations that can source ideas locally, tap into the stock of global knowledge and ideas, and adapt or assimilate practices to local contexts would allow countries to leapfrog into higher levels of performance.

The education sector also plays an important role in research and innovation that could be of significance in a strategy for capacity building in Africa. An effective strategy would rely on leadership of universities to go beyond being good scholars and stewards of accumulation of knowledge, to become executives who are politically astute, economical savvy, business aware, and emotionally intelligent (Higgs 2002; Goleman and Boyatzis 2008).

Universities in Africa need to be flexible and responsive to emerging socioeconomic and knowledge needs, which involves focus on intergenerational learning to carter for life-long learning needs of individuals in economies that are transforming and restructuring (Hanna 2003:25). Cross-disciplinary research and instruction takes on added importance with attention to uncovering the type of discoveries that lead to solving intractable problems in the area of diseases unique to Africa and where countries on the continent face a higher burden to resolve. Education needs to be valuable to society in the short and medium term while generating value and preparing the next generation.

Unique solutions for access to rural information are also important through development of appropriate knowledge sharing systems (Brown and Molla 2005; Boateng 2006; Karamagi-Akiiki 2006). Such innovations have made it possible for scaled-up access to services in rural areas (Boateng 2006; Brown and Molla 2005), all riding on innovations and research into the unique use of information technologies. Scholars have documented similar dynamics in the area of rural information systems, where penetration of information systems from the growth in Internet communication and widespread accessibility to mobile phone technology have combined to alter how knowledge is communicated and disseminated (Karamagi-Akiiki 2006). All these efforts highlight the role of education to ensure shared growth and policies of inclusion by providing individuals with skills that enhance the sense of "control over ones environment" in Nussbaum (2001).

Capacity development is also related to problem solving knowledge embedded in organizations. The concept of animal spirits, which is mostly used to explain the non-rational aspects of economics, can be useful for explaining capacity concepts. Keynes (1936) argued that government should place limits to allow independence to learn and be creative, thereby encouraging innovation and risk taking. As such, the concept of learning and adapting within government structures was very much part of Keynesian thinking.

We take the meaning of animal spirits according to Akerlof and Shiller (2009) to introduce the role of behavior on the performance of public sector agencies and leaders, and to explain the differences across agencies and countries over time. Five key aspects of animal spirits that have implications for the concept of capacity can be distinguished according to Akerlof and Shiller (2009): (i) confidence and its multipliers; (ii) fairness; (iii) corruption and bad faith; (iv) money illusion; and (v) stories.

Confidence has to do with individual expectations of the future, whether rosy future or bleak, and therefore has an impact in the level of trust or belief in a system or an outcome. Confidence would thus drive perception and motivation as well as memory, particularly if relying on gut reactions to make choices or depending on lessons from the past to set priorities. Confidence, when used in the context of capacity development would relate to the adoption of a scenario for the future for strategic choices at the country level for instance (Hanson et al. 2011). If civil servants in a country believe the future of their economies to be rosy, they may make policy decisions that are binding; otherwise they might not. Confidence in the context of capacity to analyze and track trends could also be used to interpret the approach to decision-making in the absence of data or facts, where data paucity makes it challenging to make evidence-based decisions.

Using the definition of confidence can help explain a number of conundrums in capacity development, such as the varied performance in the level of effort of civil servants in countries with roughly the same level of skills. Such diversity could result from the differential level of self-sacrifice people are willing to make or the varying structures of the organizations involved in public service delivery. Confidence could help explain why some public sector personnel are able to make decisions, innovate through risk-taking and act to implement policies and programs within the same bureaucratic setting, while others don't. Understanding how confidence operates in varied settings could help explain the differential performance across countries with similar organizational processes. It could also help understand the dissimilar capacity of organizations with similar functions and processes and why they realize new ways of doing things while others don't.

Fairness relates to social expectations, and has its origins in sociology, being associated in economics to equity and exchange theory (Akerlof and Shiller 2009). When expectations clash in the work place, or across different groups in society, they can lead to lack of coherence. The challenge of building a meritocratic civil service is a case in point. In most African societies, generosity is valued, and hence individuals who follow social norms could practice patronage. Societal pressure for patronage could override organizational pressure of meritocracy in such instances (see Akerlof and Kranton 2005). Fairness can also be used to explain why peer-to-peer learning works; individuals learn better from peers as it is easier to admit not knowing to peers than doing so to others, such as superiors who could judge them on not knowing (Blau 1963).

Money illusion has to do with the lack of awareness on the risk of delaying decisions. A delay in finalizing policy choices, service delivery arrangements, or implementation of projects has a cost that is rarely acknowledged in the discussions on capacity development. Policymakers functioning in an expeditious manner would have better efficiencies as they can spend less to get similar results as policy makers who incur significant delays in decision-making, because of the time value of money. There is generally limited understanding of long-term consequences of borrowing, including the role of inflation on debt, both of which have serious consequences on the efficacy of public spending. The capacity to factor in and explain these issues in order to speed up decisions is a critical gap that needs to be considered as well.

Stories have relevance in the capacity to generate a shared vision and underpin the ideas of learning from success stories and failure. Akerlof and Shiller (2009) depict how human motivation comes from living through a sequence of events, unified by a set of narratives that create a structure for inspiration and action. Stories are important to develop and share a common vision about the future or build confidence about societal expectations and leadership visions. A cohesive story that unites people can allow countries to make great leaps, even when coming out of conflict. Stories can speed up learning and innovation when the recounted experiences include facts that encourage application in other situations. The whole concept of field trips in the area of capacity development can be explained in the context of stories. Storytelling can also be used to motivate higher levels of effort in organizations, or to build confidence and transform entire societies (see Schank and Abelson 1977 for a detailed exposition on the role of stories). At an organizational level one can use storytelling to motivate staff to work harder and achieve greater results. At the societal level storytelling can be used to achieve a flood of change through the contagion rates of good stories (this effect can go in reverse in terms of negative stories as well). The role of the media is particularly relevant in this regard.

Africa's rich cultural assets and historical tradition of learning and sharing positions it well to tap into knowledge and ideas as a source of growth and development. The role of universities and places of learning as well as the concepts of animal spirits applied to capacity building could be valuable.

17.5 CO-EVOLUTIONARY DYNAMICS

Because of Africa's rich natural endowments and its need for capacities to transform them into development results and other forms of capacity, we end this chapter with a brief discussion on the concept of dynamic capabilities. The term refers to "the capacity of an organization to purposefully create, extend, or modify its resource base" according to Helfat et al. (2007). It relates to the competence to co-evolve the capacity to learn, develop or discover new assets and transform existing assets (Teece 2009). It requires ideas from co-evolutionary dynamics, to determine how to appropriately match capabilities of the state to the challenges facing it. Co-evolutionary dynamics can also explain the need to co-evolve the capacity to manage natural endowments while developing capabilities critical for the future.

This theory would be most useful for countries rich in natural resources but with weak capacity to manage their overall development process; exhibiting a sort of "capacity imbalance." Countries have experienced diverse development trajectories and scholars have observed the long-term impact of initial institutional setups, but also of the learning dynamics in a society (Abramovitz 1986). To explain such divergence and investigate the continued capacity to develop policies, make informed decisions, and achieve sustainable development results, we need a concept of "dynamic policy capacity." Having dynamic policy capacity means being able to analyze, design, implement, evaluate, learn, and adapt policies and programs that transform economies (Figure 17.4).

For anticipating and influencing change, one can assess effectiveness of strategies for development and how they are implemented over time; how experience is accumulated; how learning and adaptation takes place; and how lessons are applied to future activities. Such capacities rely on a dynamic concept of ability to transform agriculture, develop human capital, build institutions to convert natural resources into development results, those that can secure fair trade deals, and manage under uncertainty.

These concepts are well needed, as Africa is heavily dependent on exports from natural resources. For a sector such as mining, the needed capacity relates to capacity to develop a strategy for exploiting the mining sector today, ensuring that mining is considered part of a country's National Development Strategy, and managing the externalities from mining activities. This is even more important for hydrocarbon-producing countries because of the need to manage commodity price shocks and other shocks from the external environment. As more countries compete in the market for commodities it becomes important to have the capacity to restructure economies and diversify them, while adding value through processing and industrial transformation of primary commodities. All these capacities are critical for effective development.

Co-evolutionary dynamics allow for inclusion of scientific attitudes and mindsets to device appropriate learning technologies to use for development, improvement, and

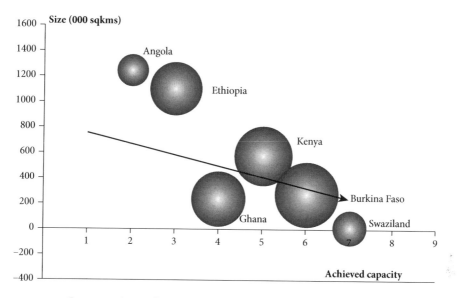

FIGURE 17.4 Country size and capacity.

Source: data from ACBF (2013).

adoption of new ideas and techniques. Co-evolutionary dynamics could also explain why countries exhibit different trajectories and speeds of catching up under different conditions. Such analysis would enable investigation of the stage that Africa has achieved in its path to development and how one can evolve alternative scenarios on the basis of dynamics that can ensue by better matching of capabilities of the state to the challenges by type of country and previous trajectories.

References

Abramovitz, M. (1986) Catching up, forging ahead and falling behind. *Journal of Economic History*, 46(2):385–406.

ACBF (African Capacity Building Foundation) (2011). *Africa Capacity Indicators 2011: Capacity Development in Fragile States*. Harare: ACBF.

ACBF (African Capacity Building Foundation) (2013). *Africa Capacity Indicators 2013—Capacity To Manage Natural Resources*. Harare: ACBF.

Akerlof, G.A., and Kranton, R.E. (2005). Identity and economics of organizations. *Journal of Economic Perspectives*, 19(1):9–32.

Akerlof, G.A., and Shiller, R.S.(2009). *Animal Spirits*. Princeton: Princeton University Press.

Bar-Yam, Y. (1997). *Dynamics of Complex Systems*. Chapter 8: Human Civilization I: Defining Complexity. Reading, Massachusetts: Perseus Books, pp. 699–759.

Blau, P.M. (1963). *The Dynamics of Bureaucracy: A Study of Interpersonal Relations in Two Government Agencies*. Chicago: Chicago University Press.

Boateng, R. (2006). Developing e-banking capabilities in a Ghanaian Bank: preliminary lessons. *Journal of Internet Banking and Commerce*, 11(2), 1–11.

Brown, I., and Molla, A. (2005). Determinants of Internet and cell-phone banking adoption in South Africa. *Journal of Internet Banking and Commerce*, 9(4), pp. 1–9.

De Grauwe, A. (2009). *Without Capacity, There is no Development. Rethinking Capacity Development*. Paris: International Institute for Education Planning, UNESCO.

Eade, D. (1997). *Capacity-Building: An Approach to People-Centred Development*. Oxfam.

Fullan, M. (2010). *All Systems Go: The Change Imperative for Whole System Reform*. Thousand Oaks, CA: Corwin Press.

Goleman, D., and Boyatzis, R. (2008). Social intelligence and the biology of leadership. *Harvard Business Review*, 2008(September):1–9.

Hanna, D.E. (2003). Building a leadership vision: eleven strategic challenges for higher education. *EDUCAUSE Review* 2003(July/August):25–34.

Hanson, K., and Léautier, F.A. (2011). Enhancing institutional leadership in African universities: lessons from ACBF's interventions. *World Journal of Entrepreneurship, Management and Sustainable Development*, 7(2/3/4) 2011. WASD, pp. 386–417.

Hanson, K., Kararach G, Léautier, F.A., and Nantchouang, R. (2011). Capacity development in Africa: new approach motivated by thinking on 'animal spirits'. *World Journal of Entrepreneurship, Management and Sustainable Development*, 7(2/3/4): WASD, pp. 357–384.

Helfat, C.E., Finkelstein, S. Mitchell, W., Peteraf, M.A., Singh, H., Teece, D.J., and Winter, S.G. (2007). *Dynamic Capabilities: Understanding Strategic Change in Organizations*. Oxford: Blackwell.

Higgs, M. (2002). Do leaders need emotional intelligence? A study of the relationship between emotional intelligence and leadership of change. *International Journal of Organizational Behaviour*, 5(6):195–212.

Honadle, B.W. (1981). A capacity-building framework: a search for concept and purpose. *Public Administration Review*, 41(5). http://www.jstor.org/stable/976270 (accessed 04/03/2013).

Karamagi-Akiki, E. (2006). Towards improving farmers livelihoods through exchange of local agricultural content in rural Uganda. *Knowledge Management for Development Journal*, 2(1):66–75.

Katz, D., and Kahn, R.L. (1966). *The Social Psychology of Organizations*. New York: John Wiley and Sons, Inc., p. 111.

Keynes, J.M. (1936): *The General Theory of Employment, Interest and Money*. London: Macmillan in Keynes (1979–1989): Vol. VII, 1973.

Léautier, F.A., and Mutahakana, F. (2012). Capacity development for higher education in Africa: the role of capacity building institutions. ACBF Working Paper No. 23: Harare: ACBF.

Lenz, R.T. (1980). Strategic capability: a concept and framework for analysis. *Academy of Management Review*, 5(2):225–234.

McKinsey & Company (2001). Effective capacity building in nonprofit organizations. Washington DC: Venture Philanthropy Partners, p. 36.

Mintrom, M., and Vergari, S. (1996). Advocacy coalitions, policy entrepreneurs, and policy change. *Policy Studies Journal*, 24(3):420–434.

Mlambo, M.K., Kamarab, A.B., and Nyendeb, M. (2009). Financing post-conflict recovery in Africa: the role of international development assistance. Journal *of African Economies*, 18(1):153–176.

Möller, K.E., and Törrönen, P. (2003). Business suppliers' value creation potential: A capability-based analysis. *Industrial Marketing Management*, 32:109–118.

Morgan, P. (2006). *The Concept of Capacity. Study on Capacity, Change and Performance*. European Centre for Development Policy Management: Brussels.

Nussbaum, M. (2001). *Women and Human Development: The Capabilities Approach.* Cambridge: Cambridge University Press.

Penrose, E.T. (1959). *The Theory of the Growth of the Firm.* London: Blackwell.

Pfeffer, J., and Salancik, G.R. (1978). *The External Control of Organizations: A Resource Dependence Perspective.* New York: Harper & Row Publisher.

Schank, R.C., and Abelson, R.P. (1977). *Scripts, Plans, Goals and Understanding.* New York: Wiley.

Schultz, T.W. (1961). Investment in human capital. *The American Economic Review,* 51(1):1–17.

Sen, A. (1999). *Development as Freedom.* New York: Knopf, p. 291.

Senge, P. (1997). The fifth discipline. *Measuring Business Excellence,* 1(3):46–51.

Smith, K.A., Vasudevan, S.P., and Tanniru, M.R. (1996). Organizational learning and resource-based theory: an integrative model. *Journal of Organizational Change Management,* 9(6):41–53.

Spillane, J.P., and Coldren, A.F. (2011). *Diagnosis and Design for School Improvement.* New York: Teachers College Press.

Teece, D.J. (2009). *Dynamic Capabilities and Strategic Management.* Oxford: Oxford University Press.

UNDP (United Nations Development Programme) (2002). *Human Development Report 2002: Deepening Democracy in a Fragile World.* New York: UNDP.

Appendix

Supporting empirical analysis

Capacity to develop strategy for using Africa's vast natural resources

Indicator	Countries have important natural resources (%)	Have developed strategies for the mining sector (%)	Have embedded mining strategy as part of National Development Strategy
Mineral producers only	43%	21%	37%
Hydrocarbon producers only	5%	50%	50%
Hydrocarbon and mineral producers	36%	19%	56%
Prospecting countries	9%	25%	75%
No mineral or hydrocarbon resources	7%	0%	33%
Total	100%	20%	48%

Source: Data taken from ACBF (2013): Capacity Development for Natural Resource Management. Africa Capacity Indicators 2013. Harare: The African Capacity Building Foundation.

CHAPTER 18

....

GOLD MINING AND ECONOMIC AND SOCIAL CHANGE IN WEST AFRICA

....

MICHAEL KEVANE

18.1 INTRODUCTION

....

THE history of gold mining in West Africa offers an important caveat to the aphorism that "geography is destiny." The aphorism has considerable appeal. Through much of history the economic opportunities available in a geographic region shaped the social infrastructure of people who inhabited the region. The institutions of those who lived by the sea differed from those who roamed the desert. The truism is sometimes validated in empirical analysis: strong correlation across societies of two variables, one geographic and the other social, is interpreted as evidence consistent with a casual story. Alesina, Giuliano, and Nunn (2013), thus, found that regions more adaptable to plow-based agriculture developed social institutions unfavorable to women. Fenske (2012) found that regions exhibiting more ecological diversity were more likely to develop complex proto-state institutions.

Research on historical and contemporary gold mining in West Africa, however, suggests a more nuanced story. The record suggests a variety of outcomes. There is also considerable room for mismeasurement of outcomes. The further back in time economic historians go, the more their stories, woven from sparse facts, become possibilities rather than certainties. Asante and Mali, the two West African empires that were central to political and economic dynamics in West Africa for centuries, may or may not have flourished because of gold. Given the highly unreliable statistics of contemporary West Africa, even in the present there may be much disagreement over basic facts. Mali, Ghana and Burkina Faso, West Africa's leading gold exporters in the 2000–2013 period, may or may not be subject to the "resource curse." Even at the local level, in both past and present, there has been little consensus about how to characterize social institutions in mining regions. The crucible of gold mining has not, apparently, been poured into a standard mold in which economies and societies were cast.

Gold mining in West Africa may be examined by considering two paradoxes. Regions with gold mines may have given rise to stronger and more complex state structures, while gold mining also gave rise to incentives for rent-seeking, conflict, and undermining of state structures. The revenues from taxation of gold mining were likely the primary mechanism for these effects. But another mechanism may have operated. Gold extraction and trade had to be organized through relatively complex social institutions. At the same time, participation in more complex social institutions changed interpersonal relationships and identities. In short, gold mining created manifold local economic and social changes that rippled through the broader economy and society. The nature of these changes and the extent of their impact on broader society, however, remain largely speculative.

The chapter proceeds as follows. Section 2 summarizes relevant research on the magnitudes of the gold mining sectors in West Africa from medieval times to the present. Section 3 discusses the presumption that gold mining was directly implicated in early state formation in medieval times, and strengthened states in subsequent centuries. Section 4 reviews arguments and evidence about how gold mining undermined state functioning. Section 5 briefly reviews work on the social impact of mining. Section 6 concludes by sketching a broad theory of the place of gold mining in West Africa, while noting the severe limitations in the body of evidence available to evaluate the broad theory.

18.2 GOLD MINING IN WEST AFRICA

At various points in the economic history of West Africa, gold mining was quite extensive and valuable, and therefore might have influenced social and economic institutions. Unfortunately, the historical and even contemporary record remains quite unsatisfactory. Historians have pieced together limited time-series of gold production levels for various gold producing areas. Even more uncertain are trends in the value of gold extracted in terms of purchasing power, the population involved in gold production, the forms of organization of production and trade, and the ties of gold-producing regions to state-like political formations. This economic history may be conveniently divided into five periods: (i) the medieval period, when gold from West Africa was a major source of bullion for the growing societies of the Mediterranean and Islamic world; (ii) the period 1700–1850, when bullion exports from the New World, and shifting of commercial interests to the Atlantic slave trade, appear to have discouraged creation of recorded knowledge of gold mining in West Africa, either because all trade in gold became internal to West Africa and hence was a strictly oral affair, or because production levels fell dramatically so there was nothing worth recording; (iii) the late-1800s, when industrial mining techniques were introduced by European entrepreneurs; (iv) the colonial period proper, when colonial administrators organized and regulated gold extraction; and (v) the post-independence period, including especially the mining boom of the 2000s.

Before discussing the magnitude of the gold sector in each period, a digression on production techniques is in order. Gold ore has been excavated in several forms in West Africa. First are alluvial deposits of fairly concentrated gold that is embedded in rock. This gold is extracted by panning the shores of rivers, as the gold-bearing rocks are carried downstream after seasonal rains. Dried up river-beds are also mined for these alluvial deposits. Second are relatively shallow deposits of quartz-bearing rock permeated with gold particles. This gold was extracted through tedious manual digging of pits, crushing of ore, admixture with mercury solutions, panning in water, and heating, concentration, and finally extraction. Since the early 1900s, open-pit mining using explosives, earth-movers, and industrial crushing of ore and industrial-scale leaching has been deployed. Artisanal gold mining persists, however, because of the large capital expenditures involved in industrial mining and consequent risk. Finally, gold may be extracted in deep shaft mines, such as those common in South Africa. West Africa has seen few deep shaft mines. One is the Obuasi Gold Mine in Ghana owned by AngloGold Asante. Given relatively limited mining exploration in the region, there remain possibilities for large strikes deep underground.

Gold in West Africa through the medieval era to the present has come from only a handful of regions, mostly located in a geological zone known as the Birimian greenstone belt. There have been open-pit, alluvial mines in Bambouk (also known as Bambuhu) near the Falamé and Senegal rivers near the town of Kayes, and Bouré, close to the present-day Guinea–Mali border near the town of Siguiri. These are the same regions where industrial and artisanal mining boomed in the 2000s in Mali. The Akan or Asante goldfields became known to early fifteenth-century Portuguese explorers, whose appellation for their first trading post and later castle, Elmina, referred to the mines. The region around the Tarkwa region to the west of Accra in the late 1800s developed large industrial mines. Goldfields in the Lobi area of south-western Burkina Faso near the border with Ghana may also have been significant in the medieval era. Since the rise in gold prices in the early 2000s, new geological exploration techniques have led to the discovery of numerous mining sites scattered throughout Burkina Faso, Cote d'Ivoire, Ghana, Guinea, and Mali.

18.2.1 Medieval period (1300–1700)

The largest sources of gold in West Africa over the 1000–1700 period were Bambouk, Bouré, and Akan (Gautier 1935; Malowist 1970). Estimates of the magnitudes of gold extracted and exported from these three regions in medieval and pre-colonial times are unreliable, given the paucity of documentary records. Moreover, units of measure varied across the different gold-trading posts on the trans-Saharan route.

Bambouk and Bouré were taxed and controlled (to some degree) by the medieval empire of Mali centered, for much of the period, in Nyeni (or Niani). Curtin (1983) suggested that a figure of one ton per year exported across the Sahara was a reasonable educated guess for the magnitude of exports. Numerous anecdotes in the historical record can be triangulated to generate this approximate figure. Bambouk and Bouré were the sources, for example, of Mansa Musa's apparently astonishing pilgrimage to Mecca in 1324, where he transported so much gold that the price on Cairo markets dropped markedly for years afterwards. Numismatic analysis of coins put into circulation in the Mediterranean world suggest that much of the gold currency of North Africa had its origin in African gold rather than central European gold (Messier 1974). Bambouk and Bouré gold transported via trans-Saharan trade was clearly important in the monetization of the Mediterranean basin, and the development of the Arab and Berber dynasties in the Maghreb region.

The Akan or Asante goldfields appear to have been of similar capacity as Bambouk and Bouré. Curtin (1983) proposed that the first 100 years of the Portuguese monopoly over gold trading on the Atlantic side of West Africa, from 1500 to 1600, generated approximately half a ton per year of gold exports.

Several authors have estimated that productivity from both the Mali and Asante gold fields was about one gram of gold per day per worker. There are about 28 grams in an ounce, so a person might have extracted an ounce each month. Thus one person extracted about six ounces during the six-month dry season when the alluvial fields could be worked. In order to have had a production level of approximately 30 000 ounces (one ton), there would have had to have been approximately 5000 people working as active miners. If their households averaged five persons and the wife and children "supported" the miners (by growing food, trading, providing services, and other activities) then about 25 000 persons would have been involved in each of the major gold fields. This would have been quite high population density by medieval standards.

Some more arithmetic offers rough estimates of the value of taxing or controlling the gold extraction sites. Law (1991) reports that on the slave coast of West Africa around 1690 about 1000 cowries traded for an *acky*, a sixteenth of an ounce of gold, and that 50 cowries was roughly consonant with subsistence expenditure (purchasing, for example, one chicken). In other words, an ounce of gold could purchase one more than a year's subsistence. If total extraction was on the order of 30 000 ounces, the entity controlling the gold might then have had purchasing power equivalent to providing subsistence to 30 000 people. Subtracting the subsistence for half a year of the 25 000 people involved in the mining, that would still leave capital to remunerate at basic levels the services of approximately 17 500 persons. That is, control over a major gold site enabled a ruler to fund a well-sized army (with its many retainers), by pre-colonial West African standards.

18.2.2   Rise of the slave trade and New World bullion, 1700–1850

Little is known of gold exports via the trans-Saharan routes for the 1700–1850 period. For the Asante goldfields, Curtin (1983) estimated that during the period from 1700 through 1850 gold production and export was likely on the order of one ton per year. As the slave trade expanded and bullion increasingly was exported from the New World, records on trade in gold become increasingly scarce. Historians have been engaged in a lively controversy over the relative magnitudes of the value of the gold (and commodities more broadly) and slaves (Bean 1974; Eltis and Jennings 1988; Van Den Boogaart 1992). Given the controversy, perhaps the safe conclusion to draw is that slave and gold exports were of the same order of magnitude in value until the early 1800s when the slave trade was gradually abolished.

18.2.3   The late-1800s

Dumett (1998) remains one of the major sources for the Asante goldfields in the 1800s before colonial occupation. He found that relative to investments then taking place in the Americas the investments in Tawku (Tarkwa) in Ghana were quite modest, and that local African entrepreneurs were often major figures in mining activity. Indeed, it appeared likely that African mining entrepreneurs were more successful than European ventures. The European ventures were overwhelming failures, and Dumett suggests that many of the backers of mining ventures were motivated by their ability to float shares in London and then loot the mining company. Despite their financial problems, Dumett argued that local and expatriate mining concessions in Tawku were not merely enclaves, with few ripples on local economic and political landscapes, but were rather quite significant in late nineteenth-century transformations. In particular, he suggested that land tenure formalization and individualization in the region may have been more related to gold mining than cocoa.

Other, apparently smaller, gold fields were known from pre-colonial times, but evidence on production has remained scarce. Kiethega (1983) argued that the gold mines of Poura in what is now south-western Burkina Faso were worked during late 1700s and through the mid-1800s. Output was relatively low: "At its height, the Poura industry may have produced between 5 and 50 kg of gold annually." Perinbam (1988) reviewed gold mining in the Lobi fields near the present-day Burkina Faso–Ghana border. There appears to be little evidence on the magnitudes of gold extracted, since trade was handled by a diaspora of Dioula merchants. Presumably, the lack of evidence indicates that production levels were low.

18.2.4 Colonial gold policy

Military leaders, civilian administrators, and especially commercial interests of France and Britain were optimistic in their early assessments of how much gold there was in West Africa (Macdonald 1902). The British conquest of the Akan empire was accompanied by significant looting of gold wealth and also demands for reparations by the victors in the form of gold. The subsequent transfers were significant.

Commercial gold production was limited in the Bambouk and Bouré areas, while extensive in the Akan region (Brunschwig 1975). A French company, Compagnie des Mines d'Or du Bouré-Siéké et de l'Afrique Occidentale Française, issued shares in France in 1907, only a decade after the full conquest of the region. Yet it became clear even in the very beginning of the colonial period that the security, relative to earlier decades, of colonial rule raised the opportunity cost of labor. Local farmers and migrant labor had better opportunities, and commercial mining enterprises were unprofitable. As Curtin (1973) noted, "By a curious paradox, then, Bambuhu came to have a reputation for great wealth because it produced gold, but it produced gold because it was too poor to do anything else." Once people in the area had other more lucrative opportunities for work, gold mining through artisanal methods was no longer profitable. Moreover, the infrastructure (roads and railroads, skilled technicians, and spare parts resupply) for industrial mining was absent.

Gold production apparently halted in Upper Volta during the colonial period. Moussa (1995) argued that the pre-colonial mining areas of Poura and Gaoua never expanded beyond their production levels of (together) perhaps 100 kg per year. In Gaoua attempts to regulate and improve artisanal mining were eventually abandoned. In Poura an industrial mine was established in mid-1930s. But the mine appears not to have been profitable given the low ratio of gold in the ore, difficulties in obtaining spare parts, and relatively high wages for seasonal labor. In the artisanal sector, the French colonial administration pursued policies that were intended to extend colonial control and manage economic affairs, but had the result of stifling economic activity. The government established a purchasing monopoly on gold. Merchants had to obtain a formal license (*patente*) to purchase gold from miners, and the government fixed the price of gold. The interventions led, apparently, to even lower prices offered to gold miners, who quickly abandoned the arduous work.

In the Gold Coast, the colonial administration eventually undertook significant infrastructure investments to make the Tawku ridge accessible, and industrial mines became well established. Gold production in Ghana in the early 1930s, just before the Depression, was substantial: on the order of 250 000 ounces in 1930 to 700 000 ounces in 1939, which at real price of gold of US$500 per ounce would be $125–$350 million per year (United Kingdom 1936, and other volumes). The gold exported was approximately 20% of the value of all exports from the colony.

18.2.5 Post-independence period

Gold mining policies in post-independence West Africa exemplify generally bad policy choices that undermined economic development across all sectors of post-independence economies. Newly independent authorities that might have used gold revenues to secure political power failed to invest in technology and organizational reform, and so gold mining in West Africa was largely unprofitable and production declined dramatically. Mali and Ghana were both beset by political instability and military coups d'état. Attempts by successive regimes to revive their gold sectors through state-led development ended in repeated failure. The state-owned Poura mine in Upper Volta (and then Burkina Faso) was closed in the mid-1990s.

In the 1980s, influence over economic policymaking shifted to the World Bank, as regimes depended on structural adjustment lending to ensure urban acquiescence to rule (by propping up civil servant hiring and salaries, and subsidizing essential urban commodities such as bread and petrol). The World Bank pushed for liberalization of the mining sector for West Africa. Most countries adopted new mining codes that were favorable to mining companies, with royalty rates around 3% and generous relief from taxation for the initial years of production.

As a result of the reforms, industrial mining was reinvigorated in a number of countries. One country that experienced an early reindustrialization was Guinea in the mid-1990s, particularly in Siguiri (the site of the medieval gold site of Bouré). By the late 2000s, four companies had made significant investments: AngloGold Asante, Societe Miniere de Dinguiraye, Kenon, and Golden Rule Limited. The mines started producing 10–20 tons per year. Mali likewise saw significant mining investment. In Ghana, mines reopened and several new mines were established.

The remarkable quintupling of the world price of gold from US$350 an ounce in 2000 to above $1500 an ounce in 2012 spurred significant exploration and then investment. In Burkina Faso, for example, eight industrial mines opened by the end of the 2000s, and production reached 30 tons per year in 2012. Production in Ghana exceeded 80 tons in 2011. Gold mining became one of the largest single sources of government revenue for Mali, Burkina Faso, and Ghana, surpassing revenue from cotton production and other agricultural activities. Artisanal mining activities in the 2000s boomed and in many countries it has involved hundreds of thousands of people, many of whom had migrated away from their home villages. Young children have been extensively involved (Thorsen 2012).

18.3 GOLD MINING AND STATE FORMATION

A common understanding of state formation in the pre-modern era is to suppose that state structures emerged with social differentiation (Boix 2010). By differentiation is usually meant the process by which specialization and division of labor enable people to pursue different trades, and accumulate greater wealth. Positive and negative implications of differentiation favored state formation. On the positive side, differentiation implied greater returns to specialization and trade. A more complex trading economy benefitted from contract enforcement, a public good. On the negative side, organized looting increasingly became an enduring strategy for some social groups. The attractiveness of looting may have been due to technological innovations: effective offensive raiding may have improved; wealth available to be looted may have increased; stationarity and identification of wealth may have increased as fixed capital became more important in production (Mayshar, Moav, and Neeman 2011). State formation then emerged as an equilibrium from the interaction of offensive groups and defensive groups, and from groups mutually benefitting from contract enforcement. Indeed, encouraging groups to refrain from looting and abstain from cheating may be seen as similar prisoner dilemma-type social problems. Lineage groups presumably evaluated the advantages of a larger and more hierarchical armed force and dispute resolution mechanism. The evaluation presumably was akin to a choice over loyalty or exit. Africanist historians have been clear that in West Africa rulers competed for followers, rather than territory. Members of lineage groups were choosing to be loyal to an established polity. Over time, loyalty was institutionalized into a broader naturalization: the kingdom, sultanate or state came to occupy a legitimate and tolerated position at the top of the social order.

The more homogenous a region, the fewer incentives for raiding and fewer gains from trade, and consequently less need for defense and judiciary, and so the less likely a state would emerge. Early states may have been more like clubs that organized trade or raiding, and the provision of generalized security, justice, and exaltation of the divine—the ideologies of states—were emergent properties of the growing complexity of organized violence.

This common sense theorizing suggests that local potentates who controlled goldfields or gold trade routes may have leveraged resources to expand territory and influence while increasing the complexity and depth of political hierarchy. Thus the early rulers of the Bambouk and Bouré goldfields may have been able to expand and sustain their control over large swathes of West Africa. It is taken as a commonplace that the early kingdoms of Adanse, Denkyira, and Asante arose because of gold (Ofosu-Mensah 2010). Girard (1992) argued, likewise, that trade routes delivering Bambouk gold to seaports in Senegal were a key factor in the rise of the small state of Cantor that eventually became the Mali empire's province of Kaabu and later became an independent kingdom from 1500 to 1800.

There are reasons to doubt the centrality of gold mining in state formation. First, the correlation of gold mining in Bambouk, Bouré, and Akan and early state formation may be entirely spurious. Other forces such as the slave trade and the commercialization of the Atlantic coast were at work. For example, there was considerable potential wealth from exporting commodities through the Saharan trade routes (salt and slaves) and the new Atlantic trade routes opened by the Portuguese in the early 1500s. The concomitant urbanization around new Atlantic ports may have induced more centralized polities (Daaku 1970). In Sahelian West Africa Islamic-oriented jihads were emblematic of patterns of offensive and defensive warfare that may have eventually and indirectly given rise to state formations as in Europe (Tilly 1992). Finally, especially for Asante, the flood of technological innovations from the Atlantic trade (including new currencies, guns, new ships, and crops) was likely to have influenced incentives for state centralization.

For the medieval period, gold extraction may have contributed to state formation indirectly, through a mechanism quite different from state control of revenues and economic differentiation from growing wealth. Gold extraction during the medieval period enabled larger-scale trade with Europe, the Middle East, and India. One perhaps unanticipated byproduct of gold exports was the ability to import cowries on a much larger scale. The subsequent spread of cowrie as low denomination currency possibly enabled the inland areas of the Niger bend to develop much more than they would have in the absence of widespread currency. Currency permitted specialization. Monetization of economies through large-scale circulation of coinage may have been an important component of economic growth. Monetization enabled longer-distance trade, greater specialization (as craftsmen were less constrained by the double-coincidence of wants problem), and development of credit instruments that facilitated investment (because a standard unit of value was available). Currency fostered growth that eventually led to a state, rather than the state fostering growth and eventually establishing a currency.

Second, there is little evidence about how the apparent decline of gold extraction and exports in West Africa, and decline in the relative value of gold after the expansion of bullion production in the New World, affected state formation and dissolution. In the sense, it is not clear how well the theory works "out of sample" as it were. Historical narratives that rely on causality going from the growth of gold to state formation eschew due consideration of the flip side. The gold sector experienced rapid and enduring declines. The discovery of bullion resources in the Americas, especially silver, made the extraction of gold in West Africa practically unprofitable, and gold mining apparently declined precipitously in Mali after the 1600s. If growth led to state formation, did decline not lead to state dissolution? The question has been relatively unexplored. Indeed, an unfortunate trend in recent economic history has been to compress the pre-colonial past of Africa into a single snapshot used to explain the present, with little attention to variation in the past (Austin 2008).

Examination of the local-level issues of gold mining casts further doubt on the commonsense notion that mining may have given rise to robust states. Historical and anthropological accounts suggest that different ethnic groups located in the regions of gold mines had very different responses to the new opportunity. Werthmann (2003), for example, reviewed how in southwestern Burkina Dagara and some other ethnic groups viewed the earnings form gold as "bitter money." Indeed, the appellation has broad echoes to other societies, not just in Africa. Some ethnic groups have shared powerful aversions to certain forms of wealth creation (Luning 2009). Gold mining, associated by Dagara with the earth and ancestors, was viewed as uncontrollably polluting of self and society. Other ethnic groups came, then, to occupy the space of opportunity created. The path from ethnic appropriation of wealth to strengthening of ethnic institutions, to eventually negotiating and challenging state structures, was conditioned importantly by initial cultural understanding. The geography of gold, it turned out, may have mattered more for certain ethnic groups than for others.

18.4 GOLD MINING AND STATE FUNCTIONING

The "resource curse" literature argues that rapid mineral extraction opportunities in weak states would make more difficult the inclination to solidify state legitimacy and hence effective projection of power. The literature appeared to be confirmed by robust negative correlations between the share of natural resources in exports and levels and growth of GDP per capita. The hypotheses were numerous, ranging from political economy to the macroeconomics of the Dutch Disease (Mehlum, Moene, and Torvik 2006; Robinson, Torvik, and Verdier 2006; Ross 1999). Mineral rents were supposed to have induced violent contestation over control of the state. Rents may have perversely affected incentives in the broader economy, leading to longer-term stagnation. Rents may have undermined processes leading to inclusive governance. Moreover, a negative feedback mechanism may have operated, so that rent-dependent polities structured incentives towards more extraction and away from investment, especially investment in public goods. Skeptics have argued that there is no general resource curse and that models tend to assume their conclusion (Brunnschweiler and Bulte 2008). Thus if resources are assumed to induce corruption rather than enable control of corruption, it is not surprising that models generate the result that more resources cause more corruption.

While gold may have been at the origin of state formation in West Africa, it may also have been responsible for the persistence of ineffective provision of the public goods critical for development. There is little evidence on how gold revenues may have undermined governance in pre-colonial states. The argument is sometimes made, though, that the "curse" of gold was what weakened Denkyira, initially the more powerful protostate of the region, enabling the eventual Asante conquest of 1701 (McCaskie 2007).

There is also little consensus on whether the explosion of gold mining in West Africa over the 1995–2013 period has been associated with a resource curse. West Africa in general has been since independence characterized by weak states and weak modern civil society institutions. The weak national state emerged from colonial rule, mutated into the one-party state of the 1960s, and has evolved into myriad semi-authoritarian democracies with opaque and contestable political "rules of the game." Comparatively strong traditional and religious institutions, on the other hand, have largely accommodated themselves to remain outside or interact informally with state structures. With the exception of Casamance, and more recently of the Tuareg rebellion in northern Mali, there have been no significant separatist movements, despite the multi-ethnic character of most countries.

In this environment, gold mining revenues might generate considerable instability. Actors prompted by a voracity effect to reopen foundational bargaining over allocation of power risk an extended interregnum. It is tempting to think, for example, that the resurgence of gold mining in Mali during the 2000s may have played an important role in the disintegration of the central Malian state. Mining revenues had become the single largest source of revenue for the Malian state (on the order of US$500 million per year). In March 2012, President Amadou Toumani Touré and much of the political class abandoned the political "field" when a small unit in the military took control of the Presidential Palace in Koulouba. The interregnum that followed only ended through international intervention, creating a de facto protectorate. While this is a tempting story to tell, there is little evidentiary basis for it given the scarcity of in-depth research on nexus of gold mining and governance in West Africa in the 2000s. It does appear, however, that Guinea has had a similar prolonged interregnum as foundational constitutional bargains are renegotiated. Both countries' central states have less legitimacy and less capacity than in the late 1990s. Ghana and Burkina Faso, on the other hand, appear to have had state legitimacy and capacity strengthened by the boom.

Why has gold mining not strengthened modern civil society and thus generated a reinforcement of counterweight to the state? In all four gold-mining states, the challenge from and response by organized modern civil society has been minimal. The experience of transparency initiatives supported by the World Bank and other donors has been similar in all countries. The discourses civil society organizations evoke and advocate for are heavily conditioned by the semi-authoritarian regimes. Civil society organizations emphasize prostitution, environmental damage, and mine labor relations, and devote little effort to tracking the hundreds of millions of US dollars of revenue generated by mining operations. Organizations such as Revenue Watch and Publish What You Pay have had little impact, and when Extractive Industries Transparency Initiative (EITI) reports are published there are brief mentions in the press but otherwise little genuine public debate emerges. During the interregnums there is relatively little evidence that organized civil society regards the mining sector as a central lever for political transformation.

18.5 LOCAL SOCIAL CHANGE

There have been more hopeful analysts suggesting that the mining sector might engender a more vibrant civil society at the local level. Bryceson and Fisher (2014) noted the "democratizing tendencies" of artisanal mining. Their analysis, based on extensive fieldwork and surveys of Tanzanian artisanal miners, is likely generalizable to West Africa. They argued that the sharp rise in incomes from mining had enabled hundreds of thousands of relatively young men and women to become more civically engaged than they would have had they remained in their villages. Migration to mining areas likewise removed this same population from the gerontocratic and authoritarian structures of village life, into a more complex, and often more free and participatory, social structure of the mining camp. Finally, mining camps often celebrated individuality and responsibility in ways that contrasted sharply with traditional social norms. Perhaps democratic participation would benefit from a greater sense of identity as an individual in society. Artisanal mining centers have become complex communities of young people, loosely subject to existing local social institutions, but more often creating idiosyncratic new social institutions.

Not all social change has to wait for the young generation of mining workers to become civically engaged. Dell (2013) and Arnaldi di Balme and Lanzano (2013) offered detailed studies of the actual institutions of local governance that have emerged in artisanal mining areas in Mali and Burkina Faso, respectively. The weak national state had left the field of local politics open to political entrepreneurs, who proffered a range of state-like functions (from dispute resolution, to security, to insurance). The democratizing tendency of greater local governance may, however, turn into a tendency to place loyalty to local authority above loyalty to the national state; with concomitant danger of rapid descent into warlordism should the central state collapse (Reno 1997; Vinci 2007).

Certainly gold mining is shaping social relations in ways that must be of similar magnitude to the transformations brought about by extensive service in the colonial military. The retired *tirailleurs* and other servicemen brought transformed local politics, according to many accounts (Lawler 1990).

There has been relatively little research, however, on these significant social changes. Anthropologists have noted other changes in, among other things, gender relations, social norms regarding wealth and consumption, aspirations for the future, participation in local and national civic life, and the willingness to undertake risks and invest for the future (Grätz 2009; Werthmann 2008). Quantitative evidence on broad social change is scarcer. In a significant first approach, Kotsadam and Tolonen (2013) examined the incidence of female wage work in communities located near mining areas. Using a comprehensive listing of all mining sites in Africa, they mapped the locations of mines opened or closed since 1975 onto communities surveyed in Demographic and Health Surveys. They used a difference-in-difference estimation strategy to show that changes in mines affected proximate communities, compared with communities further away, before and after the opening or closing of the mine. Women were more likely to report wage employment and less likely to be working in the household.

Whether, and how, these community changes will have systemic effects on broader social trends remains difficult to discern. Moreover, there is a tendency to use representations of social change in discourses concerning mining. An old trope, for example, is that artisanal (and even industrial) mining communities are places where promiscuous sexuality and prostitution are prevalent (Werthmann 2009). This moralizing characterization appears to have been deployed when national elites sense that their control over mining might be jeopardized by nascent local involvement in mining jurisdictions. Thus, the social change itself becomes part of discursive strategies that undermine nascent movement to challenge established orders.

18.6 CONCLUSION

A comprehensive, empirically grounded history of gold mining in West Africa would trace how the economic and social ripples emanating from the local level affect the complex, state-level tension between the impetus and possibility of greater state efficacy as mining revenues grow, with the weakening of central institutions as opportunities for rent-seeking and rebellion improve. Such a narrative would go beyond a simply theory of oscillation, where gold discoveries, high gold prices, and improvements in extraction technology lead to rents, and the rents enable temporary accumulation, but that accumulation leads to a voracity effects that undermines prosperity and institutional stability (Tornell and Lane 1999).

A more micro-sociological account would emphasize how highly contingent initial conditions shape the effects of gold mining. It would trace through the effects of gold mining on nascent social movements and transformations. Then these local emergent changes would be integrated into a larger-scale national and international model of political and economic outcomes.

Such a narrative remains to be written. As scholars continue to uncover new sources and especially new methods of analysis, it is worth recalling that good unifying narratives of economic change (or lack thereof) should not see the historical process in straightforward terms. Instead, historical understanding is of contingent hesitations, with much variation and nuance, characterized by modesty given difficulties in falsifying grand narratives. Moreover, it is worth recalling that a standard critique of statistical confirmation of grand narratives is that they often are influenced by a version of positive significance bias (Austin 2008). That is, contingent patterns that have emerged from data are elevated to status of grand narrative, despite a lack of true statistical significance (because the data have been "mined"), robustness (because checks on alternative specifications and data stop after a handful confirm the initial result), and external validity (because in history the problem addressed is often unique to a region or epoch). These appeals to virtue are an indirect way of concluding: perhaps social scientists and historian will never know the contours of the mold into which gold was cast.

References

Alesina, A., Giuliano, P., and Nunn, N. (2013). On the origins of gender roles: Women and the plough. *The Quarterly Journal of Economics*, 128(2):469–530.

Arnaldi di Balme, L., and Lanzano, C. (2013). «Entrepreneurs de la frontière»: le rôle des comptoirs privés dans les sites d'extraction artisanale de l'or au Burkina Faso. *Politique africaine*, 3:27–49.

Austin, G. (2008). The "reversal of fortune" thesis and the compression of history: perspectives from African and comparative economic history. *Journal of international development*, 20(8):996–1027.

Bean, R. (1974). A note on the relative importance of slaves and gold in West African exports. *Journal of African History*, 15(3):351–356.

Boix, C. (2010). A Theory of State Formation and the Origins of Inequality: Unpublished manuscript, Princeton University.

Brunnschweiler, C.N., and Bulte, E.H. (2008). The resource curse revisited and revised: A tale of paradoxes and red herrings. *Journal of Environmental Economics and Management*, 55(3):248–264.

Brunschwig, H. (1975). Le docteur Colin, l'or du Bambouk et la "colonisation moderne." *Cahiers D'Etudes Africaines*, 15(48):166–188.

Bryceson, D.F., and Fisher, E. (2014). Artisanal mining's democratizing directions and devia-tions, in D.F. Bryceson, E. Fisher, J.B. Jønsson, and R. Mwaipopo (eds), *Mining and Social Transformation in Africa: Mineralizing and Democratizing Trends in Artisanal* London: Routledge, p. 179.

Curtin, P.D. (1973). The lure of Bambuk gold. *Journal of African History*, 14(4):623–631.

Curtin, P.D. (1983). Africa and the wider monetary world, 1250–1850, in J.F. Richards (ed.), *Precious Metals in the Later Medieval and Early Modern Worlds*. Durham, N.C: Carolina Academic Press, pp. 231–268.

Daaku, K.Y. (1970). *Trade and Politics on the Gold Coast, 1600-1720: A Study of the African Reaction to European Trade*. London: Clarendon Press.

Dell, M. (2013). Undermining the "local": migration, development and gold in Southern Kayes. *Journal of Intercultural Studies*, 34(5):584–603.

Dumett, R.E. (1998). *El Dorado in West Africa: the gold-mining frontier, African labor, and colonial capitalism in the Gold Coast, 1875-1900*. Ohio: Ohio University Press.

Eltis, D., and Jennings, L.C. (1988). Trade between Western Africa and the Atlantic world in the pre-colonial era. *The American Historical Review*, 93(4):936–959.

Fenske, J. (2012). *Ecology, Trade and States in Pre-colonial Africa*. Munich: University Library of Munich.

Gautier, É-F. (1935). *L'or du Soudan dans l'histoire*. Paper presented at the Annales d'histoire économique et sociale.

Girard, J. (1992). *L'or du Bambouk: une dynamique de civilisation ouest-africaine: du royaume de Gabou a la Casamance*. Geneva: Georg.

Grätz, T. (2009). Moralities, risk and rules in West African artisanal gold mining communi-ties: a case study of Northern Benin. *Resources Policy*, 34(1):12–17.

Kiethega, J.-B. (1983). *L'Or de la Volta Noire: archêologie et histoire de l'exploitation tradition-nelle (Râegion de Poura, Haute-Volta)*, Vol. 1. Paris: Karthala Editions.

Kotsadam, A., and Tolonen, A. (2013). *African Mining, Gender, and Local Employmen, Mimeo, Department of Economics, University of Gothenburg*.

Law, R. (1991). *The Slave Coast of West Africa, 1550-1750: the impact of the Atlantic slave trade on an African society*. Oxford: Clarendon Press.

Lawler, N. (1990). Reform and repression under the Free French: economic and political trans-formation in the Côte d'Ivoire, 1942–45. *Africa*, 60(1):88–110.

Luning, S. (2009). Gold in Burkina Faso: A wealth of poison and promise, in J. Jansen, S. Luning, E. de Maaker (eds), *Traditions on the Move. Essays in honour of Jarich Oosten*. Amsterdam: Rozenberg Publishers, pp. 117–136.

Macdonald, G. (1902). Gold in West Africa. *Journal of the Royal African Society*, 2: 416–430.

Malowist, M. (1970). *Quelques observations sur le commerce de l'or dans le Soudan occidental au moyen âge*. Paper presented at the Annales. Histoire, Sciences Sociales.

Mayshar, J., Moav, O., and Neeman, Z. (2011). *Transparency, Appropriability and the Early State*. Washington, DC: Center for Economic Policy Research.

McCaskie, T.C. (2007). Denkyira in the making of Asante c. 1660-1720. *The Journal of African History*, 48:1–25.

Mehlum, H., Moene, K., and Torvik, R. (2006). Institutions and the resource curse. *Economic Journal*, 116(508):1–20.

Messier, R.A. (1974). The Almoravids: West African gold and the gold currency of the Mediterranean basin. *Journal of the Economic and Social History of the Orient/Journal de l'histoire economique et sociale de l'Orient*, 17: 31–47.

Moussa, B. (1995). L'or des régions de Poura et de Gaoua: Les vicissitudes de l'exploitation colo-niale, 1925-1960. *International Journal of African Historical Studies*, 28(3):563–576.

Ofosu-Mensah, E.A. (2010). Traditional gold mining in Adanse. *Nordic Journal of African Studies*, 19(2):124–147.

Perinbam, M. (1988). The political organization of traditional gold mining: the western lobby, c. 1850 to c. 1910. *The Journal of African History*, 29(03): 437–462.

Reno, W. (1997). African weak states and commercial alliances. *African Affairs*, 96(383):165–186.

Robinson, J.A., Torvik, R., and Verdier, T. (2006). Political foundations of the resource curse. *Journal of Development Economics*, 79(2):447–468.

Ross, M.L. (1999). The political economy of the resource curse. *World politics*, 51:297–322.

Thorsen, D. (2012). Children working in mines and quarries: evidence from West and Central Africa. Briefing paper No. 4. West and Central Africa Regional Office: UNICEF.

Tilly, C. (1992). *Coercion, capital, and European states, AD 990-1992*. Oxford: Blackwell.

Tornell, A, and Lane, P.R. (1999). The voracity effect. *American Economic Review*, 89(1):22–46.

United Kingdom (1936). Annual Report on the Social and Economic Progress of the People of the Gold Coast, 1934–35. London: His Majesty's Stationary Office.

Van Den Boogaart, E. (1992). The trade between Western Africa and the Atlantic world, 1600–90: estimates of trends in composition and value. *Journal of African History*, 33(3):369–385.

Vinci, A. (2007). "Like Worms in the Entrails of a Natural Man": a conceptual analysis of war-lords. *Review of African Political Economy*, 34(112):313–331.

Werthmann, K. (2003). Cowries, gold and "bitter money": gold-mining and notions of ill-gotten wealth in Burkina Faso. *Paideuma*, 49:105–124.

Werthmann, K. (2008). "Frivolous squandering": consumption and redistribution in mining camps. *Dilemmas of development*, pp. 60–76.

Werthmann, K. (2009). Working in a boom-town: Female perspectives on gold-mining in Burkina Faso. *Resources Policy*, 34(1):18–23.

CHAPTER 19

THE ECONOMIC IMPACTS OF NEW TECHNOLOGIES IN AFRICA

JENNY C. AKER AND JOSHUA E. BLUMENSTOCK

19.1 INTRODUCTION

SINCE the 1960s, a variety of welfare-enhancing technologies have been introduced into developing countries, in sectors ranging from agriculture and health to medicine and energy. Few technologies, however, have spread as quickly as the mobile phone. Over the past decade, mobile phone coverage has expanded rapidly in Africa, Asia, and Latin America; from largely non-existent networks at the turn of the century to a point where over 70 percent of the population of sub-Saharan Africa is covered by the mobile network (GSMA 2013). Coinciding with this increase in mobile network coverage has been an increase in mobile phone adoption and usage: it is estimated that one-third of the population of sub-Saharan Africa has an active mobile phone subscription (GSMA 2013). Roughly 55 percent of the world's 2.3 billion mobile-broadband subscriptions are also based in developing countries, with coverage rates in Africa reaching close to 20 percent in 2014, as compared with 2 percent in 2010 (ITU 2014).

The rapid spread of the mobile phone in developing countries, and sub-Saharan Africa in particular, offers a unique opportunity for economic development. Mobile phones have significantly reduced communication and transfer costs for the rural and urban poor as compared with traditional technologies. This cost reduction may not only improve households' access to public and private information, but can also reduce the transaction costs associated with private and public transfers (Aker and Mbiti 2010). While the potential for these technologies to impact economic development is considerable, the empirical evidence of this impact is relatively recent. Existing studies have demonstrated that the magnitude and extent of impact depends critically on the context, the type of technology and the presence of other market failures.

The rest of this chapter proceeds as follows. Section 2 provides an overview of the growth in mobile phone coverage and adoption in sub-Saharan Africa and discusses some of the determinants of technology adoption. Building upon the work of Aker and Mbiti (2010), section 3 provides a simple framework for understanding how mobile phones might affect economic development, both as a communications device and as a platform for other phone-based services. Section 4 surveys existing empirical evidence of the impact of mobile phones on economic development in sub-Saharan Africa, and section 5 describes several promising areas of ongoing and future research. Section 6 concludes.

19.2 INFORMATION TECHNOLOGY: COVERAGE, ADOPTION AND USAGE IN AFRICA: 1998–2013

19.2.1 Mobile phone coverage and adoption

Despite limited infrastructure investments in sub-Saharan Africa for much of the twentieth century, investment in information technology—and mobile phones in particular—has grown quite substantially. Between 1999 and 2014, the percentage of the population with access to mobile phone coverage grew from 10% to 90% (ITU 2014; GSMA 2013). An estimated 800 million mobile subscriptions have been sold in Africa (Ericsson, 2013; GSMA 2013), reaching roughly 400 million unique subscribers, or approximately one-third of the population in sub-Saharan Africa (GSMA 2013). Growth of the worldwide subscriber base is fastest in these regions, with four out of five new connections being made in the developing world, and 880 million unique developing-market subscribers estimated to register new accounts by 2020 (GSMA 2013).

One of the more remarkable features of this rapid growth of mobile telephony is that it has been driven largely by the private sector. Whereas other technologies have required significant investment and coordination from the public sector, the expansion of mobile networks has been fueled by intense competition between operators for new subscribers. This growth has not been uniformly accessible to all segments of society, and indeed the adoption base has been more traditionally skewed toward a wealthier, educated, urban and predominantly male population (Aker and Mbiti 2010; Blumenstock and Eagle 2012). However, "last mile" regulatory policies designed to connect marginalized individuals are now commonly included in the licenses granted to mobile operators, and current adopters come from all segments of society (Aker and Mbiti 2010).

For urban and rural consumers in sub-Saharan Africa, the mobile phone presents a compelling technology. As originally outlined in Aker (2010b), several factors have helped to enable phones to quickly reach a "critical mass" of adoption (cf. Rogers 1962), even in relatively impoverished areas: First, unlike many "single-use" technologies (such as seeds, fertilizer, or chlorination), the mobile phone serves as a multi-use platform for other services. Beyond simple person-to-person communication via voice and SMS, mobile phones can provide access to the internet, financial services, and other services that can translate into diverse economic and social benefits. Second, many of these benefits are tangible and immediate, thereby allowing people to quickly determine the magnitude of those benefits. For example, unlike an improved seed variety, it is not necessary to wait for the harvest to see the benefits of the yield; in many cases the benefit is delivered instantaneously to the adopter. Third, the costs of using mobile phones are relatively low and largely incremental. Most mobile phone subscriptions in sub-Saharan Africa are pre-paid and billed per-second, thereby allowing credit-constrained users to buy mobile phone airtime as they need it, and for increasingly small amounts. Fourth, basic feature phones are easy to use, even for individuals with little formal education. The interface and software can be adapted, but more commonly the basic features are simply repurposed to fit the needs of the local population and context. And finally, there are spillovers to mobile phone adoption: since multiple individuals can use a mobile phone, its cost can be shared among multiple users, and multiple individuals can benefit from one person's use.

19.2.2 Mobile money and value-added services

Historically, the primary function of the mobile phone has been as a communications device over voice and Short Message Service (SMS) protocols. More recent innovations, however, have utilized the mobile phone network as a platform for other services that facilitate innovation in several sectors, from healthcare and education to finance and governance. More recently, a set of phone-based financial services has been developed, called "mobile money" (or m-money). First introduced in 2005, basic m-money applications allow clients to store value in an account accessible by a handset, convert cash in and out of that account, and make transfers between individual users, as well as between individuals and firms (Aker and Mbiti 2010). As of 2013, over 140 mobile phone operators in over 80 countries worldwide had m-money platforms, with over half in sub-Saharan Africa (GSMA 2013).

While basic mobile telephony was rapidly adopted across sub-Saharan Africa, uptake of m-money has been much less pronounced, with some notable exceptions (e.g. M-Pesa in Kenya and Tanzania). The reasons for these differential trends in adoption are not well understood, and a nascent body of empirical research seeks to identify the binding constraints to m-money adoption (Aker and Wilson 2013; Batista and Vicente 2013). Yet qualitative evidence and much of the policy discourse focuses on a handful of factors that are thought to limit the uptake of m-money (cf. Dzokoto et al. 2011; Aker and Wilson 2013), including:[1]

- *Understanding of benefits:* Unlike simple mobile phone operations, with which many households might have been familiar, electronic person-to-person transfers are a relatively new technology.[2] As a result, households might not know what the technology is or its potential uses and benefits.
- *User knowledge*: Effective use of the mobile money network requires that users register a PIN code and navigate a series of text-based menus, which may be difficult for individuals with limited literacy skills.

[1] Among these factors, access to m-money agents, high cost and limited trust in formal financial systems are frequently cited as the most common reasons for limited initial usage.

[2] There are a variety of electronic and non-electronic transfer systems within sub-Saharan Africa, such as Western Union, MoneyGram, the post office, and via bus. Nevertheless, these systems are not necessarily person-to-person—they usually require some intermediary to enact the transfer.

- *Physical access:* While mobile network coverage is generally widespread, m-money operations (cash-in and cash-out) require access to a secure and reliable mobile agent network.
- *Regulation and registration requirements*: While growth of early m-money networks was largely unregulated, many deployments are now subject to regulations such as Know-Your-Customer (KYC) requirements, which require that individual SIM cards be registered to national identity cards (Davidson 2011).
- *Trust*: To effectively use the m-money system, the user must convert cash to m-money, which requires trust and confidence in the m-money ecosystem.
- *Network effects:* For interpersonal transfers and point-of-sale payments, individuals benefit little from adopting if their network of contacts have not yet adopted, suggesting that a critical mass of users is needed.

19.3 INFORMATION TECHNOLOGY AND DEVELOPMENT: CHANNELS OF IMPACT

This widespread growth of mobile phone coverage and adoption in sub-Saharan Africa has spurred significant interest in the potential of this technology to affect development outcomes. Building upon work by Aker and Mbiti (2010) and Aker (2011), we outline the primary channels through which information and communications technologies—and mobile phones in particular—are likely to affect economic development in Africa. We focus on the four primary ways in which mobile phones are being used in Africa: as a communication device to share (public and private) information; as a transfer device to exchange (public and private) transfers; as a savings device; and as an educational tool for school-aged children and adults.

19.3.1 Information asymmetries and communication

19.3.1.1 *Private information and market efficiency*[3]

A central tenet of economic theory is that for markets to function efficiently, different market agents – producers, consumers, and traders – must have access to perfect information. However, in many real-world markets, and particularly in countries with limited infrastructure, it can be costly for such actors to obtain information (Stigler 1961; Jensen 2007). Traditionally, information is obtained through personal travel, local social networks, radio, and, to a much lesser extent, landlines, letters, newspapers, and television (Aker and Mbiti 2010). However, these mechanisms are often costly, sporadic, and at times unreliable. As a result, imperfect information - on input prices, output prices, weather patterns, jobs, potential buyers and sellers, natural disasters, new technologies, politics, and so on – distort

---

[3] This section draws heavily from Aker and Mbiti (2010).

markets, creating waste, price and wage dispersion (cf. Fafchamps 1992; Jensen 2007; Aker 2010).

Compared to traditional methods for searching for information, mobile phones offer several distinct advantages. Relative to personal travel, the transport and opportunity costs of using a mobile phone are quite low. Information transmission is on-demand and immediate, and is not dependent on the timing of radio broadcasts, newspapers or letters (Aker and Mbiti, 2010).[4] This reduction in search costs should, in theory, allow market actors to search more quickly and over a greater geographic area (Baye et al. 2004; Reinganum 1979; Stahl 1989; Aker 2008; Aker and Mbiti 2010). In theory, this reduction in search costs should decrease equilibrium price dispersion and improve market efficiency, although these predictions depend upon a certain set of assumptions (Reinganum 1979; Stahl 1989).[5]

An example might help to fix ideas (Jensen 2007; Aker and Mbiti 2010). If search costs are prohibitively high, then market agents (e.g. grain traders) will not engage in spatial arbitrage. With the introduction of mobile phones, search costs should decrease, thereby reducing the informational barriers to learning about prices. In theory, this should facilitate the movement of agricultural goods from surplus to deficit markets and reduce inter-market price dispersion for the same good. While this should result in net welfare gains under standard assumptions, the extent of that impact depends upon whether asymmetric information is a market failure and whether other market failures are at play (Burrell and Oreglia 2012).[6] In addition, how these gains are distributed among consumers, producers and firms is theoretically ambiguous (Jensen 2007, Aker and Mbiti 2010). A similar model has also been applied to labor markets (Autor 2001).

19.3.1.2 *(Quasi-) public information*

Beyond the reduction in search costs associated with transmitting private information, mobile phones offer a promising and cost-effective method for the dissemination of public

---

[4] Aker and Mbiti (2010) outline the relative costs of other search mechanisms, such as radios, newspapers and Internet. While radios can be used across all segments of the population, they provide a more limited range of information. Newspapers are primarily concentrated in urban areas, are expensive, and are inaccessible to illiterate populations. Landline coverage is also limited, with less than one landline subscriber per 1000 people in 2008 (ITU 2009). Access to other search mechanisms, such as fax machines, e-mail and internet, is similarly low, primarily due to their dependence upon landline infrastructure.

[5] Reinganum (1979) develops a model of sequential search and firm cost heterogeneity, whereas MacMinn (1980) develops a model of fixed sample search and firm cost heterogeneity. MacMinn (1980) shows that a reduction in search costs can increase price dispersion.

[6] The reduction in search costs could not only affect market efficiency, but also farmers' and consumers' adoption of other potentially welfare-enhancing technologies. For example, the traditional model of "learning from others" model assumes that the farmer can without cost observe the experiments from his or her neighbors, but with error (Foster and Rosenzweig 1995). As a result, the variance is inversely related to the number of persons in the social network who use the technology and the farmer observes. With mobile phones, this could speed up or increase farmers' contact with other adopters in a social network, thereby allowing farmers to learn from more "neighbors'" trials of a new technology or observe those trials more frequently. While this could potentially increase the rate of technology adoption, it could also reduce the rate of adoption in the presence of learning externalities (Aker 2011; Foster and Rosenzweig 1995; Foster and Rosenzweig 2010).

or quasi-public information, such as that provided by the public sector or a private sector "clearinghouse" (Aker 2011).[7] In the past decade, there has been a proliferation of such services, with Nigeria, Ethiopia, and Rwanda leading the pack in sub-Saharan Africa (Rotberg and Aker 2013). About one-third of these have been in the area of mobile health (m-health), followed by agricultural and market information systems (22%), governance (11%), emergency response (6%), and education (5%).

The model for predicting the potential impacts of mobile-based "public" information platforms – especially in the area of agricultural market prices or wages - is similar in spirit to that of the reduction in search costs for private information. For instance, Aker (2011) shows that the mobile phone is far cheaper than traditional agricultural extension visits for disseminating agricultural information, and is as cost-effective as providing the same information via radio. Such innovations, which reduce the cost and difficulty of disseminating technical information, have the potential to increase the scope, scale and quality of agricultural extension (Aker 2011). This could also improve the quality and value of the information provided by ensuring that technical advice or market prices are provided in a more timely manner. In theory, price or labor market information provided via the mobile phone should reduce the costs associated with obtaining that information for a subset of the population, thereby increasing market efficiency (Varian 1980; Baye and Morgan 2002).[8]

In other areas – such as weather or health – the impacts of publicly-provided information are more difficult to predict. If information on droughts, natural disasters or epidemics is provided via public information services, this could enable farmers to better predict the risks associated with particular crops and allocate their resources accordingly, or allow households to make more optimal investments in preventative health measures. Furthermore, the provision of civic education information might enable households to participate more fully in the political system by choosing a candidate that best meets their political preferences or monitoring the performance of those candidates (Callen and Long 2013; Aker, Collier, and Vicente 2013). Finally, providing information on agricultural input use could allow farmers to learn from others more quickly, which could increase or reduce the rate of adoption, depending upon the presence and extent of learning externalities (Foster and Rosenzweig 1995, 2010; Aker 2011).

19.3.1.3 Information, demand uncertainty, and coordination

By reducing communication costs, mobile phones could assist farmers, traders, and firms in identifying potential buyers (suppliers) for their products over larger geographic areas and at crucial moments (Aker and Mbiti 2010; Aker 2011). For example, by improving communication between firms and their suppliers, mobile phones can enable firms to manage their supply chains more effectively and streamline their production processes (Hardy 1980; Röller and Waverman 2001; Aker and Mbiti 2010). Similarly, improved communication

---

[7] A clearinghouse is a either a private or public institution that provides information (or financial services) publicly, at least to a subset of the population. Thus, rather than rely upon members of a social network, an individual can consult the clearinghouse.

[8] With any of these models, a Diamond Paradox could result, which results in monopoly pricing. This would lower price dispersion across markets but would increase (decrease) consumer (producer) prices than the competitive market equilibrium.

between farmers and traders could reduce the uncertainty associated with the demand of certain goods and facilitate the provision of inputs to rural areas, thereby avoiding costly stock-outs (Aker and Mbiti 2010; Debo and Van Ryzin 2013).[9]

19.3.1.4 *Monitoring and moral hazard in risk sharing*

Households in sub-Saharan Africa are prone to a variety of covariate and idiosyncratic shocks. In the absence of formal insurance arrangements, informal risk sharing practices have arisen to mitigate the adverse consequences of these shocks (Townsend 1995; Udry 1994; Rosenzweig and Stark 1989). Such informal contracts, however, are fraught with moral hazard, as commitment is limited by one party's ability to monitor and enforce state-contingent transfers (Thomas and Worrall 1990; Coate and Ravallion 1993). More pragmatically, efficient risk-sharing requires that one household is able to observe when another has suffered an idiosyncratic shock. As a result, traditional risk-sharing networks do not typically function over long distances (Udry 1994; Fafchamps and Gubert 2007). By improving communication among members of a social network, as well as increasing the possibility of monitoring and enforcement, mobile phones can potentially increase geographic scope of risk-sharing networks (Blumenstock et al. 2014). More generally, mobile phones can lead to improved information transmission within social networks, which can in turn increase the likelihood of social learning. Social learning has been linked to higher rates of technology adoption, especially of cash crops (Bandiera and Rasul 2006; Conley and Udry 2010).

19.3.2 Transfers[10]

By providing a platform for electronic transfers, mobile phones can dramatically reduce the costs of sending and receiving money relative to traditional mechanisms such as Western Union, MoneyGram, and the bus. This reduction in transaction costs can, in turn, allow individuals to transfer money when and where they need it (Jack and Suri 2014; Aker et al 2013; Blumenstock et al. 2014), potentially increasing the frequency and amount of transfers received and allowing households to smooth consumption in the face of shocks.

Beyond the potential impact of m-money on private transfers, m-money could also reduce the costs associated with implementing public transfer programs or paying. In addition to potential mechanisms cited above, if the m-transfer mechanism reduces program recipients' costs involved in obtaining the transfer or reduces uncertainty with respect to these costs, this could reduce the opportunity costs associated with obtaining the transfer (Aker et al 2013). Alternatively, if m-money makes it more difficult for program recipients to access their cash due to the limited geographic scope of m-money agents, this could increase costs for program recipients (Aker et al. 2013).[11]

---

[9] The impact of information on stock-outs depends upon the quality of information provided and whether there is consumer heterogeneity.

[10] This section draws from Aker et al. (2013).

[11] If m-money allows households to "cash out" from any m-transfer agent, this may affect the way in which households spent the cash transfer. For example, if program recipients obtain their cash from an agent and kiosk-owner within the village, program recipients might start to change the timing and location of their expenditures (Aker et al. 2013; Blumenstock, Callen, and Ghani 2013).

In addition, since m-transfers reduce the observability of the cash transfer, this could affect inter-household sharing, thereby leaving income available for the household (Aker et al 2013). This could affect the intra-household allocation of resources, especially if these transfers are primarily provided to women (Lundberg et al. 1997; Duflo and Udry 2004; Doepke and Tertilt 2014; Aker et al. 2013).

19.3.3 Savings and financial services

In the rural areas of sub-Saharan Africa, less than 20% of the population has access to any type of formal financial institution (Aker and Wilson 2013). Households in such contexts typically share risk by self-insurance, including at home savings (under the mattress), saving with deposit collectors (*susus* and money guards), or rotating savings clubs (Aker and Wilson 2013). While these strategies are important mechanisms for rural households, they are not without cost, including theft, restricted access, fees, high transaction costs, or societal pressures for sharing.

Beyond money transfers, m-money could be used to create a secure place to save, where individuals can deposit smaller savings amounts for more immediate needs (Mas and Mayer 2012; Aker and Wilson 2013). As the "account" is password-protected, m-money might offer greater security while increasing access. In addition, m-money could encourage individuals to save for particular objectives, thereby serving as a form of mental accounting. Finally, combined with m-money, mobile phones could be potentially used to transfer individual or group-based savings to more formal financial institutions or serve as a gateway through which unbanked households could access financial services (Mbiti and Weil 2013).

19.3.4 Education

In addition to the provision of educational content via the mobile phone, mobile phones have the potential to facilitate the acquisition of educational skills by adults or school-aged children (Aker, Ksoll and Lybbert 2012). For example, individuals may be able to practice their reading and writing skills by using SMS or m-money applications, both of which require familiarity with numbers and letters (Aker, Ksoll, and Lybbert 2012). In addition, mobile phone technology could also affect current and future returns to education (Aker, Ksoll and Lybbert 2012). Finally, the development of mobile phone-based educational applications, even for simple mobile phones, could be used as a teaching device in classrooms, or, in some cases, substitute for teachers.

19.3.5 Data collection

Simple mobile phones can be used as a means of collecting both farmer and agent-level data, thereby improving the accountability of extension services (Dillon 2011; Aker 2011). Voice and SMS can be used to collect data on farmers' adoption, costs, and yields on a more frequent basis, rather than waiting for annual agricultural surveys, when recall data on costs and production are often subject to measurement error (Dillon 2011). In addition, mobile phones can be used to verify agents' visits, similar to what has been done with cameras in Indian schools (Duflo et al. 2012). Both of these applications could improve the monitoring of extension systems, an oft-noted constraint.

19.4 INFORMATION TECHNOLOGY AND DEVELOPMENT: WHAT DO AND DON'T WE KNOW?

The macro-evidence on the links between information technology and development is quite limited, though Roller and Waverman (2001) and Waverman, Meschi, and Fuss (2005) point to a causal link between telecommunications infrastructure and economic growth. There is, however, a growing body of micro literature investigating the impact of information technologies on economic development, which we describe below. While the sum total of empirical evidence generally indicates that mobile phones are having a positive economic effect on the targeted individuals and households in Africa, it is important to note that these benefits do not appear to be uniformly distributed across the population. In fact, economic theory predicts that even if phones can help make markets more efficient, the distribution of these gains across different actors is unclear. In fact, striking disparities exist between the population of mobile phone owners and non-owners, with one study showing that phone owners in Rwanda had roughly twice the per-capita income of non-owners (Blumenstock and Eagle 2012). A further cause for concern is that significant heterogeneity exists *within* the population of mobile phone owners, such that the privileged members of society appear best poised to capitalize on the welfare improvements brought by mobile telephony and other ICTs. For instance, Blumenstock et al. (2014) showed that it is the wealthiest individuals who are most likely to receive interpersonal m-money transfers after idiosyncratic negative shocks.

19.4.1 Agricultural markets and prices

Overall, existing evidence suggests that mobile phone coverage is associated with greater efficiency of agricultural markets, as defined as a reduction in price dispersion (Jensen 2007; Aker 2010; Aker and Mbiti 2010; Aker and Fafchamps 2014). Jensen (2007) found that mobile phones are associated with a reduction in fish price dispersion in India, whereas Aker (2010) and Aker and Fafchamps (2014) found that mobile phones are associated with a reduction in consumer and producer price dispersion for agricultural crops in Niger.

While welfare should improve with more efficient markets, the distribution of welfare gains among consumers, producers and traders is ambiguous. Some studies have found an increase in farm-gate prices (Goyal 2010; Nakasone 2013), whereas others have found little to no effect on farm-gate prices (Aker and Fafchamps 2014; Fafchamps and Minten 2012; Mitra et al. 2013). These seemingly contradictory findings can be explained, at least in part, by differences in the type of information or service provided via the information technology, the degree of information asymmetry and the presence of other market failures.

Beyond the impact of improved access to information on market efficiency and prices, there is a substantial body of literature measuring the empirical effect of mobile phone technology on agents' behavior. For example, Muto and Yamano (2009) found that mobile phone coverage increases the likelihood that farmers sell their commodity, primarily for a perishable crop. Fafchamps and Minten (2012) found that Indian farmers who participated in a private sector mobile information service were more knowledgeable about crop prices, but did not change their crop choice. Yet Cole and Fernando (2012) found that the provision of mobile phone-based agricultural extension information in India encouraged farmers to switch to more optimal inputs and to adopt higher value cash crops. Similarly, Aker and Ksoll (2013) found that farmers who participate in a mobile phone-based adult education program in Niger were more likely to increase the diversity of their crops planted, primarily marginal cash crops grown by women. Finally, Casaburi et al (2014) found that sending SMS messages containing agricultural advice increased sugar cane yields by 11.5%, with relatively larger effects for farmers with no agronomic training.

19.4.2 Interpersonal transfers

By allowing for more efficient transfers within social networks, m-money has been linked with improvements in households' ability to share risk. Jack and Suri (2014) showed that households with access to the m-money network are able to smooth consumption completely in the face of idiosyncratic shocks, whereas households without access to m-money face a 7% reduction in consumption. Consistent with the theory that these efficiencies result from reductions in transfer costs for remittances, they further show that households with access to m-money are more likely to receive remittances, and that these remittances are larger and come from a more diverse set of senders.

Blumenstock, Eagle, and Fafchamps (2014) provided further empirical evidence that m-money facilitates person-to-person transfers in response to negative shocks, and that such m-money transfers often flow over vast geographic distances. By analyzing the records of millions of interpersonal exchanges of m-money in Rwanda, they showed that a small but significant amount of money is sent to individuals affected by earthquakes and other natural disasters. Consistent with a model of risk-sharing under dynamic limited commitment, the transfers are most common in relationships with a history of reciprocity.

19.4.3 Payments and salaries

With the potential reduction in transaction costs associated with m-money, there has been growing interest in using m-money for social protection programs and salary payments. In the area of social protection programs, Aker et al. (2014) found that using m-money in the context of an unconditional cash transfer program in Niger reduced the implementing agency's variable costs of distributing those transfers and reduced program recipients' costs of obtaining those transfers. Those program recipients who received the transfer via m-money also used the transfer to purchase more diverse types of food items, and had higher diet diversity, in part due to cost reduction associated with obtaining the transfer (Aker et al. 2014).

In the context of salaries, Blumenstock, Callen, and Ghani (2013) similarly find that m-money can provide significant cost-savings to firms in contexts where the costs of cash transactions are large. Through a field experiment in Afghanistan in which a random subset of employees of a large firm were transitioned from cash payments onto a m-money salary payment system, they found that the firm was able to reduce costs by approximately 50%, but only in areas where adequate coverage existed for both the mobile network and m-money agents. The disbursement costs were largely reduced by transferring the costs of managing cash liquidity from the firm to the mobile operator, who already operated a network of m-money agents.

19.4.4 Savings

While considerable optimism exists surrounding the potential for the mobile phone to serve as an effective savings device, these features of m-money accounts have not yet gained widespread popularity. In a field experiment in which employees were encouraged to use a phone-based savings account, Blumenstock, Callen, and Ghani (2013) found that employees who received salaries via m-money were slightly more likely to save money on their phone, but that such effects depended on an individual's access to m-money agents. The authors also find that demand for m-money balances decreased (and demand for cash balances increased) when employees reported higher subjective beliefs for future violence, but that this effect was concentrated in areas with few m-money cash-out agents. However, they find no effect on other measures of employee welfare.[12]

19.4.5 Education

Traditionally, the use of ICT as an educational device has primarily focused on computers and laptops, with more limited use of mobile phone-based learning. Aker et al. (2012) conducted a randomized adult education program in Niger, where a mobile phone-based component ("ABC") was added to an otherwise standard adult education program.[13] Overall, the mobile phone technology substantially improved learning outcomes: adults' writing and math test scores were 0.19–0.26 standard deviations higher in the mobile phone education villages immediately after the program, with a statistically significant effect. While these skills depreciated in both groups after the end of the program, the relative educational improvements in ABC villages seem to persist over time, particularly for math.

---

[12] A set of recent studies has shown that although the mobile phone may not yet be commonly used as a savings device *per se*, it can be used to alleviate other savings constraints (cf. Karlan et al. 2012). Karlan et al. (2012) and Karlan and Zinman (2013) study the extent to which SMS reminders to save can increase rates of savings in several countries, and find that such reminders can increase the likelihood of saving and savings balances.

[13] The experiment provided simple mobile phones—which primarily have voice and SMS capability—as opposed to smart or multimedia phones—which often have internet or video capability. In both developed and developing countries, a number of authors have found that computers either have

19.4.6 Accountability and governance

By providing more frequent and transmission of information between citizens and the state, mobile phones can impact the political economy of developing countries. While much of the evidence for such impact is qualitative (Howard and Hussain 2013) several studies have begun to document the quantitative effects of mobile phone technology on governance. For example, a simple camera phone-based intervention that photographed election return forms at polling centers in Afghanistan substantially reduced fraud and improved electoral integrity (Callen and Long 2013). In the 2012 elections in Uganda, a similar experiment decreased the vote share for the incumbent, the candidate most likely to benefit from rigging, and decreased other measures of fraud (Callen et al. 2013). In the 2009 elections in Mozambique. Aker, Collier and Vicente (2013) found that the provision of civic education via SMS, as well as a mobile phone hotline to report electoral fraud, increased individuals' knowledge about the electoral process and increased voter turnout.[14]

19.5 CHALLENGES TO MEASURING IMPACT

While the body of empirical evidence described above provides preliminary evidence of the impact of mobile phone technology in sub-Saharan Africa and elsewhere, there are considerable gaps in our understanding. These gaps are important, and offer a cautionary tale in terms of using existing empirical findings to develop mobile phone-based development policy. The fact that the rollout or adoption of ICTs is generally non-random poses a significant obstacle to identifying the causal effect of mobile phone technology—and ICT more broadly—on development outcomes. Usage of ICTs is highly correlated with other socio-economic and demographic factors (Blumenstock and Eagle 2012), and decisions regarding expansion of ICT infrastructure and ICT-based programs are typically driven by private sector or policy criteria. As a result, the majority of empirical studies have relied on randomized evaluations, instrumental variables, or quasi experiments with a difference-in-differences estimation strategy (cf. Jensen 2007; Aker 2010; Aker and Fafchamps 2014; Jack and Suri 2014).

A second challenge associated with measuring the impact of mobile phone technology on development outcomes is disentangling the effects of the mobile phone from impact of the content or services provided (Aker 2011). If a mobile phone-based intervention seeking to promote agricultural technology adoption also facilitates participants' access to a mobile phone, then mobile phone ownership or usage might have a wealth effect, thereby decreasing

---

no or mixed effects on learning outcomes (Osario and Linden 2009; Fairlie and Robinson 2013; Banerjee et al. 2007).

[14] These effects are not limited to electoral accountability in democratic regimes. Shapiro and Weidmann (2014) provide evidence that mobile communications reduced insurgent violence in Iraq, both at the district level and for specific local coverage areas. By lowering the transaction cost of cooperating with the government, the authors argue that mobile phones made it easier for non-combatants to cooperate with counter-insurgent forces, and that the information provided by non-combatants had a strong negative effect on conflict.

the relative costs of an agricultural technology or increasing the benefits associated with it (Aker 2011). Several experimental studies attempt to address this by providing phones to the control group (Aker et al. 2013; Blumenstock, Callen, and Ghani 2013; Nakasone 2013), thereby allowing them to disentangle the impact of the handset from the content or service provided.

A third challenge associated with measuring the impact of mobile phone technology is associated with the multiple uses of information technology. If participants are participating in a SMS-based agricultural extension or price information program, in theory, they can use the mobile phone handset for a variety of other (non-SMS and non-price) uses. While it is possible to empirically identify the impact of this program on economic outcomes, it can be challenging to measure the mechanisms behind this effect. Some studies have attempted to overcome this constraint by limiting the mobile phone to only provide specific services (Mitra et al. 2013; Nakasone 2013).

A fourth challenge associated with this line of research is understanding the type of information or service being provided (Aker 2011). In most mobile phone-based agricultural extension or health programs, there can be multiple types of services provided, depending upon the mechanism used for disseminating the information (e.g. SMS or voice). The primary challenge is how to interpret the treatment effect; for example, each intervention may not only differ in how it is disseminated, but also the *type of information provided* (Aker 2011). While SMS can provide timely technical reminders or simple content, voice-based services permit farmers or health workers to ask open-ended questions and receive more detailed information; the quality of the technical advice provided by voice services can vary considerably by the type of person providing the service. This implies that the empirical impact of the program will capture the impact of both the information transmission mechanism (SMS, voice) and the information conveyed (Aker 2011).

A final challenge in measuring the impact of mobile phone technology on economic outcomes is the presence of spillovers. With mobile phones, farmers are able to contact members of their social networks more easily, thereby increasing the likelihood of inter-village spillovers (Aker 2011) or encouraging farmers or traders to start selling in different markets. Similarly, health workers with access to disease information could start funneling potential patients to different clinics that are better suited to care for those patients. All of these factors could also lead to broader general equilibrium effects, thus making it more difficult to identify the impact of the mobile phone-based policy or intervention on individual, household and market-level outcomes.

19.6 What Does the Future Hold?

How will mobile phone coverage, adoption and services change over the course of the next ten years in sub-Saharan Africa? And how will this affect economic development? Will mobile phone coverage reach the last mile via the private sector, or will particular policy interventions be required? Will information technology go beyond mobile phone technology to Internet, computers, and smart phones? And how will the development of mobile phone applications reach the continent?

One area of particular promise for development researchers and policymakers is the fact that the rapid proliferation of mobile phones and other ICTs has enabled new forms of empirical research on economic development. Namely, the "digital trace" data generated in the everyday use of technology can provide a powerful instrument for observing the behavior of individuals and households (cf. Lazer et al. 2009). For instance, the data generated by mobile phone users and automatically collected by mobile phone operators can be used to produce high-resolution estimates of poverty and wealth, track patterns of mobility and migration, and predict the transmission and spread of diseases (Blumenstock et al. 2010; Blumenstock 2013; Eagle et al. 2010; Frias-Martinez and Virseda 2012; Wesolowski et al. 2012). In addition, a growing number of mobile applications are being deployed to track respondents and monitor programs. Such applications allow for high-frequency data collection, custom data validation, and low-latency feedback to respondents (Hartung et al. 2010).

Yet there are some important issues about the potential of mobile phones and ICTs as a poverty-reduction device in developing countries. First, while evidence on the impact of mobile phone technology and development has grown considerably over the past few years, these studies are for particular countries, products and markets, and still represent a small percentage of what we should know about their impact for policy decisions (Aker and Mbiti 2010).

Second, while reduced communication and transfer costs can make markets more efficient, this does not necessarily imply that all agents are better off. Having a more efficient agricultural market does not immediately imply that poor farmers will receive higher prices, as existing empirical evidence suggests. In addition, while social networks can certainly expand with mobile phones, they can also weaken existing ones or potentially lead to social exclusion (Burrell 2010).

Third, mobile phones will primarily address market failures that are associated with asymmetric information and high transactions costs. In the presence of other market failures, mobile phones might not have the intended effects (Aker and Mbiti 2010; Aker 2011). For example, even if a farmer is able to obtain price information more quickly and cheaply, if there is an uncompetitive market structure, improved information will not translate into higher farm-gate prices. This therefore suggests that any mobile phone or ICT-based development policy must ensure that public goods are provided or address complementary market failures.

Fourth, using mobile phones for economic development not only requires "hardware"— for example, the handset, application or service—but also an enabling environment that fosters the adoption and use of that technology. Among the 140 m-money programs worldwide, adoption of m-money services remains surprisingly low, except in a few high-profile countries. What this implies for mobile phone operators, as well as public and private mobile phone for development programs, is that the "hardware" must be developed from the end-users' perspective: In other words, the product or service addresses the individuals' needs, for a phone that is locally available, and can be easily learned or used.

And finally, even if mobile phones improve certain development outcomes, it is not clear that this will translate into improved economic growth or higher per capita incomes in sub-Saharan Africa (Aker and Mbiti 2010). Whether there exists a causal relationship between mobile phone coverage and economic growth is an area of active debate, and one that cannot easily be answered.

REFERENCES

Aker, J.C. (2008). Does digital divide or provide? The impact of cell phones on grain markets in Niger. Center for Global Development Working Paper (154). http://papers.ssrn.com/abstract=1093374 (accessed 11 November 2013).

Aker, J.C. (2010a). Information from markets near and far: Mobile phones and agricultural markets in Niger. *American Economic Journal: Applied Economics*, 2(July 2010):46–59.

Aker, J.C. (2010b). "Why Have Mobile phones Succeeded Where Other Technologies have not?" Center for Global Development. http://www.cgdev.org/blog/why-have-mobile-phones-succeeded-where-other-technologies-have-not.

Aker, J.C. (2011). Dial "A" for agriculture: a review of information and communication technologies for agricultural extension in developing countries. *Agricultural Economics*, 42(6):631–647.

Aker, J.C., Boumnijel, R., McClelland, A. et al. (2013). How do electronic transfers compare? Evidence from a mobile money cash transfer experiment in Niger. CGD Working Paper 268. Washington, DC.

Aker, J.C., Collier, P., and Vicente, P. (2013). "Is Information Power? Using Mobile Phones and Free Newspapers during an Election in Mozambique." CGD Working Paper 328.

Aker, J.C., and Fafchamps, M. (2014). Mobile phone coverage and producer markets: Evidence from West Africa. *World Bank Policy Research Working Paper*. Washington, DC: World Bank.

Aker, J.C., and Ksoll, C.J. (2013). "Can Mobile Phones Improve Agricultural Outcomes? Evidence from a Randomized Experiment in Niger." Unpublished working paper. Tufts University.

Aker, J.C., Ksoll, C., and Lybbert, T.J. (2012). Can mobile phones improve learning? Evidence from a field experiment in Niger. *American Economic Journal: Applied Economics*, 4(4):94–120.

Aker, J.C., and Mbiti, I.M. (2010). Mobile phones and economic development in Africa. *The Journal of Economic Perspectives*, 24(3):207–232.

Aker, J.C., and Wilson, K. (2013). Can mobile money be used to promote savings? Evidence from preliminary research in Northern Ghana. Working Paper.

Autor, D. (2001). Wiring the Labor Market. *Journal of Economic Perspectives*. 15(1):25–40.

Bandiera, O., and Rasul, I. (2006). Social networks and technology adoption in Northern Mozambique. *Economic Journal*, 116(514):869–902.

Batista, C., and Vicente, P.C. Vicente (June 2013). Introducing Mobile Money in Rural Mozambique: Evidence from a Field Experiment. Unpublished working paper, Universidade Nova de Lisboa.

Baye, M.R., and Morgan, J. (2002). Information gatekeepers and price discrimination on the internet. *Economics Letters*, 76(1):47–51.

Baye, M.R., Morgan, J., and Scholten, P. (2004). Price dispersion in the small and in the large: Evidence from an internet price comparison site. *Journal of Industrial Economics*, 52(4):463–496.

Bjorkegren, D. (2014). The Adoption of Network Goods: Evidence from the Spread of Mobile Phones in Rwanda. Working Paper.

Blumenstock, J.E. (2012). Inferring patterns of internal migration from mobile phone call records: evidence from Rwanda. *Information Technology for Development*, 18(2):107–125.

Blumenstock, J.E., Callen, M., and Ghani, T. (2013). Violence and precautionary savings: Experimental evidence from mobile phone-based salaries in Afghanistan. *Working Paper*. University of Washington DataLab.

Blumenstock, J.E., and Eagle, N. (2012). Divided we call: Disparities in access and use of mobile phones in Rwanda. *Information Technologies & International Development*, 8(2):1–16.

Blumenstock, J.E., Eagle, N., and Fafchamps, M. (2014). Risk Sharing and Mobile Phones: Evidence in the aftermath of natural disasters. Working Paper. University of Washington DataLab.

Blumenstock, J.E., Gillick, D., and Eagle, N. (2010). *Who's calling? Demographics of mobile phone use in Rwanda.* 2010 AAAI Spring Symposium Series. Palo Alto: AAAI Publications, pp. 116–117.

Burrell, J. (2010). Evaluating shared access: social equality and the circulation of mobile phones in rural Uganda. *Journal of Computer-Mediated Communication*, 15(2):230–250.

Burrell, J., and Oreglia, E. (2012). The Myth of Market Price Information: Mobile Phones and Epistemology in ICT4D. Unpublished mimeo, University of California-Berkeley.

Callen, M., Gibson, C., Jung, D. et al. (2013). Reducing electoral fraud with information and communications technology in Uganda. Working Paper.

Callen, M., and Long, J.D. (2013). Institutional corruption and election fraud: Evidence from a field experiment in Afghanistan. Forthcoming, *American Economic Review*.

Casaburi, L, Kremer, M., Mullainathan, S. and Ramrattan, R. (2014). Harnessing ICT to Increase Agricultural Production: Evidence from Kenya. Unpublished working paper.

Coate, S., and Ravallion, M. (1993). Reciprocity without commitment: Characterization and performance of informal insurance arrangements. *Journal of Development Economics*, 40(1):1–24.

Cole, S. and Fernando, A.N. (2012). The Value of Advice: Evidence from Mobile Phone-Based Agricultural Extension. *Harvard Business School Working Paper 13-047.*

Conley, T.G., and Udry, C.R. (2010). Learning about a new technology: Pineapple in Ghana. *American Economic Review*, 100(1):35–69.

Davidson, N. (2011). Mapping and effectively structuring operator-bank relationships to offer mobile money for the unbanked. Working Paper. GSMA. http://www.gsma.com/mobile-fordevelopment/wpcontent/uploads/2012/03/mappingandeffectivestructuringfinal2643.pdf.

Debo, L., and Van Ryzin, G. (2013). Leveraging quality information in stock-outs. *Chicago Booth Research Paper*, pp. 13–58.

Dillon, A. (2011). Do differences in the scale of irrigation projects generate different impacts on poverty and production? *Journal of Agricultural Economics*, 62(2):474–492.

Dillon, Brian. (2012). Using mobile phones to collect panel data in developing countries. *Journal of International Development*, 24(4):518–527.

Doepke, M., and Tertilt, M. (2014). Does female empowerment promote economic development? *NBER Working Paper No. 19888*, February 2014.

Duflo, E., Hanna, R., and Ryan, S.P. (2012). Incentives work: getting teachers to come to school. *The American Economic Review*, 102(4):1241–1278.

Duflo, E., and Udry, C. (2004). *Intrahousehold resource allocation in Cote d'Ivoire: Social norms, separate accounts and consumption choices.* Cambridge, MA: National Bureau of Economic Research.

Dzokoto, V.A.A., Mensah, E.C., and Opare-Henaku, A. (2011). A bird, a crocodile, and the 21st century cowrie shell: Analyzing Ghana's currency change. *Journal of Black Studies*, 42(5):715–736.

Eagle, N., Macy, M., and Claxton, R. (2010). Network diversity and economic development. *Science*, 328(5981):1029–1031.

Ericsson (2013). *Ericsson mobility report: On the pulse of the networked society.* http://www.ericsson.com/res/docs/2013/ericsson-mobility-report-november-2013.pdf.

Fafchamps, M. (1992). "Cash crop production, food price volatility, and rural market integration in the third world." *American Journal of Agricultural Economics,* 74(1):90–99.

Fafchamps, M., and Gubert, F. (2007). The formation of risk sharing networks. *Journal of Development Economics,* 83(2): 326–350.

Fafchamps, M., and Minten, B. (2012). Impact of SMS-based agricultural information on Indian farmers. *World Bank Economic Review,* 26(3):383–414.

Foster, A.D., and Rosenzweig, M.R. (1995). Learning by doing and learning from others: Human capital and technical change in agriculture. *Journal of Political Economy,* 1176–1209.

Foster, A.D., and Rosenzweig, M.R. (2010). Microeconomics of technology adoption. *Annual Review of Economics,* 2(1):395–424.

Frias-Martinez, V., and Virseda, J. (2012). On the relationship between socio-economic factors and cell phone usage. In: *Proceedings of the Fifth International Conference on Information and Communication Technologies and Development, ACM,* 76–84.

Goyal, A. (2010). Information, direct access to farmers, and rural market performance in Central India. *American Economic Journal: Applied Economics,* 2(3):22–45.

GSMA (2013). *Mobile money for the unbanked: Annual Report 2012.* http://www.gsma.com/mobilefordevelopment/wp-content/uploads/2012/10/2012_MMU_Annual-Report.pdf.

Hardy, A.P. (1980). The role of the telephone in economic development. *Telecommunications Policy,* 4(4):278–286.

Hartung, C., Lerer, A., Anokwa, Y. et al. (2010). Open data kit: Tools to build information services for developing regions. In: *Proceedings of the 4th ACM/IEEE International Conference on Information and Communication Technologies and Development, ACM,* 18.

Howard, P.N., and Hussain, M.M. (2013). *Democracy's fourth wave? Digital media and the Arab Spring.* Oxford: Oxford University Press.

International Telecommunications Union (2014). The World in 2014: ICT Facts and Figures. Technical Report. http://www.itu.int/en/ITU-D/Statistics/Documents/facts/ICTFactsFigures2014-e.pdf.

Jack, W., and Suri, T. (2014). Risk sharing and transactions costs: Evidence from Kenya's mobile money revolution. *American Economic Review,* 104(1): 183–223.

Jakiela, P., and Ozier, O. (2012). Does Africa need a rotten kin theorem? Experimental evidence from village economies. *World Bank Policy Research Working Paper #6085.* Washington, DC: World Bank.

Jensen, R. (2007). The digital provide: information (technology), market performance, and welfare in the South Indian fisheries sector. *Quarterly Journal of Economics,* 122(3):879–924.

Karlan, D., Osei, R.D., Osei-Akoto, I. et al. (2012). *Agricultural decisions after relaxing credit and risk constraints.* Cambridge, MA: National Bureau of Economic Research.

Karlan, D., and Zinman, J. (2013). Price and Control Elasticities of Demand for Savings. Working Paper.

Lazer, D. Lazer, Pentland, A., Adamic, A., Aral, S., Barabasi, A.L., Brewer, D., Christakis, D., Contractor, N., Fowler, J., Gutmann, M., Jebara, T., King, G., Macy, M., Roy, D. and Van Alstyne, M. (2009). Life in the network: the coming age of computational social science. *Science,* 323(5915):721–723.

Lundberg, S.J., Pollak, R.A., and Wales, T.J. (1997). Do husbands and wives pool their resources? Evidence from the United Kingdom child benefit. *Journal of Human Resources,* 32(3):463–480.

MacMinn, R.D. (1980). Search and market equilibrium. *Journal of Political Economy,* 88(2):308–327.

Mas, I. and Mayer, C. (2012). Savings as forward payments: innovations on mobile money platforms. *GSMA*.

Mbiti, I., and Weil, D.N. (2013). The home economics of e-money: velocity, cash management, and discount rates of M-Pesa users. *American Economic Review*, 103(3):369–374.

Mitra, S., Dilip M., Maximo T., and Sujata V. (2013). Asymmetric Information and Middleman Margins: An Experiment with West Bengal Potato Farmers. Unpublished mimeo.

Muto, M., and Yamano, T. (2009). The impact of mobile phone coverage expansion on market participation: panel data evidence from Uganda. *World Development*, 37(12):1887–1896.

Nakasone, E. (2013). The role of price information in agricultural markets: Experimental evidence from rural Peru. *In: 2013 Annual Meeting, August 4-6, 2013*. Washington, DC: Agricultural and Applied Economics Association.

Reinganum, J.F. (1979). A simple model of equilibrium price dispersion. *Journal of Political Economy*, 87(4):851–858.

Rogers, E.M. (2003). *Diffusion of Innovations*, 5th edn. New York: Free Press.

Röller, L.H., and Waverman, L. (2001). Telecommunications infrastructure and economic development: A simultaneous approach. *American Economic Review*, 91(4):909–923.

Rosenzweig, M.R., and Stark, O. (1989). Consumption smoothing, migration, and marriage: Evidence from rural India. *The Journal of Political Economy*, 97(4):905–926.

Rotberg R.I., and Aker, J.C. (2013). Mobile phones: uplifting weak and failed states. *Washington Quarterly*, 36(1):111–125.

Shapiro, J.N., and Weidmann, N.B. (2014). Is the phone mightier than the sword? Cell phones and insurgent violence in Iraq. *International Organization*.

Stahl, D.O. (1989). Oligopolistic pricing with sequential consumer search. *American Economic Review*, 79(4):700–712.

Stigler, G.J. (1961). "The economics of information." *The Journal of Political Economy*, 69(3):213.

Thomas, J., and Worrall, T. (1990). Income fluctuation and asymmetric information: An example of a repeated principal-agent problem. *Journal of Economic Theory*, 51(2):367–390.

Townsend, R.M. (1995). Consumption insurance: An evaluation of risk-bearing systems in low-income economies. *Journal of Economic Perspectives*, 9(3):83–102.

Udry, C. (1994). Risk and insurance in a rural credit market: An empirical investigation in Northern Nigeria. *Review of Economic Studies*, 61(3):495–526.

UNESCO (2013). Turning on Mobile Learning in Africa and the Middle East. UNESCO Working Paper Series on Mobile Learning.

Varian, H.R. (1980). A model of sales. *American Economic Review*, 70(4):651–659.

Waverman, L., Meschi, M., and Fuss, M. (2005). The impact of telecoms on economic growth in developing countries. *Vodafone Policy Paper Series*, 2(3):10–24.

Wesolowski, A., Eagle, N., Tatem, A.J. et al. (2012). Quantifying the impact of human mobility on malaria. *Science*, 338(6104):267–270.

CHAPTER 20

....

INFRASTRUCTURE
IN AFRICA

....

JEAN-JACQUES DETHIER

INFRASTRUCTURE is essential to increase economic productivity and achieve economic growth, therefore its great importance for the African continent. It has an impact on growth through direct and indirect channels. Directly, it increases total factor productivity (TFP) because infrastructure services enter production as an input and have an immediate impact on the productivity of enterprises. Indirectly, it raises TFP by reducing transaction and other costs, thus allowing a more efficient use of conventional productive inputs. In addition, it can affect investment adjustment costs, the durability of private capital and demand for as well as supply of health and education services. If transport, electricity, or telecom services are absent or unreliable, firms face additional costs (e.g. having to purchase power generators) and are prevented from adopting new technologies. Better transportation increases the effective size of labor markets. A majority of economic studies conclude that the impact of infrastructure on growth in developing countries is generally very significant. It is important to point out that infrastructure services are almost always provided through networks—a fact that implies a divergence between marginal and average productivity of investments and a nonlinear relation with output—and that the impact of new investments on economic growth will depend on the extent of the network. The highest marginal productivity of investments is usually found when a network is sufficiently developed but not completely achieved. For instance, telecommunications exhibit pure network externalities (i.e. returns to users increase with the number of users). The same is true of water and sewer networks where the public health value of safe water and sanitation systems is likely to increase the more individuals are served. Roads, rail, and electricity are also networked services. Africa's infrastructure networks lag behind those of other developing countries and are characterized by missing regional links and low household access.

There has been progress in improving infrastructure in Africa but this progress has been slow. At the beginning of the twenty-first century, 70% of the population was unconnected; millions of people had no access to an improved water source and lacked access to improved sanitation; and 33% of the population had access to an all-weather road. Delays of 30 days or more are the norm for connections to electricity, telephone, and water. Slow progress reflects a combination of insufficient and inefficient spending both in capital expenditures and in operations and maintenance. Many African countries are poor and cannot mobilize resources for the purpose of improving infrastructure. When resources are mobilized, they are often spent in a very inefficient way. Many governments, faced with competing priorities or difficult fiscal situations, simply do not or cannot allocate the resources needed to reach desirable levels of access or quality. In addition, infrastructure services often are public goods or natural monopolies (or both) and, as such, are either run or regulated by public entities and suffer from the inefficiencies that are common to public services.

This chapter discusses the role of infrastructure—meaning energy, roads and transport, water and sanitation, and information and communication technology—in the process of economic growth and human development on the African continent.[1]

20.1 THE CHALLENGES FACING THE DEVELOPMENT OF INFRASTRUCTURE IN AFRICA

Infrastructure has been responsible for more than half of Africa's recent improved growth performance. Across the continent, infrastructure contributed 99 basis points to per capita economic growth from 1990 to 2005, compared with 68 basis points for other structural policies (Calderón and Serven 2008). That contribution is almost entirely attributable to advances in the penetration of telecom services. The deterioration in the quantity and quality of power infrastructure over the same period retarded growth, shaving 11 basis points from per capita growth. The growth effects of further improving Africa's infrastructure would be even greater. Simulations suggest that if all African countries were to catch up with Mauritius (the regional leader in infrastructure) per capita growth in the region could increase by 2.2 percentage points.

The economic geography of the continent presents a challenge for infrastructure development. Sub-Saharan Africa comprises 48 nation-states. Most have small populations (more than 20 countries have a population of less than 5 million) and their economies are also small (these countries have a GDP of less than US$5 billion). The small scale means governments have difficulty funding the large fixed costs associated with investment in infrastructure. In addition, 15 African countries are landlocked, meaning that they depend on their neighbors for access to global markets and they suffer from the lack of regional connectivity.

The fragmentation of sub-Saharan Africa has implications for its infrastructure networks. Intraregional connectivity is low whether measured in transcontinental highway links, power interconnectors, or fiber-optic backbones. Most transport corridors are concerned with providing access to seaports; the intraregional road network is characterized by major discontinuities; and cities do not have easily accessible trading channels. Few cross-border

---

[1] This piece draws on recent studies financed by international donors, including *Africa's Infrastructure. A Time for Transformation*, financed by the World Bank and the Agence française de développement (Foster and Briceño-Garmendia 2010); the *Sustainable Energy for All* project (2013) coordinated by the World Bank and the International Energy Agency; and the Programme for Infrastructure Development in Africa (PIDA 2012) led by the African Union Commission (AUC), NEPAD Secretariat, and the African Development Bank.

interconnectors exist to support regional power exchange, even though many countries are too small to produce power economically on their own. Until recently, all of East Africa lacked access to a global submarine cable to provide low-cost international communications and Internet access. The intraregional fiber-optic network is also incomplete, but growing rapidly.

The spatial distribution of Africa's population creates major challenges for reaching universal access to infrastructure services. Africa has low overall population density (36 people per square kilometer), low rates of urbanization (35%), but relatively rapid rates of urban growth (3.6% a year). In rural areas, over 20% of the population lives in dispersed settlements where typical population densities are less than 15 people per square kilometer; hence, the costs of providing infrastructure are comparatively high. In urban areas, population growth rates averaging 3.6% a year are leaving infrastructure service providers severely stretched. As a result, urban service coverage has actually declined over the 2000–2010 decade, and lower-cost alternatives are filling the resulting gap. Low population density in cities means that in general large economies of agglomeration in the provision of infrastructure services cannot be achieved. As a result, the costs of providing a basic infrastructure package can be twice as much as in other developing cities.

A further complication is that the continent experiences particularly high rainfall variability (with huge swings across areas and seasons) which climate change is likely to exacerbate. Africa's water resources are abundant, but because of an absence of water storage and distribution infrastructure, they are grossly underused. Therefore, water security—reliable water supplies and acceptable risks from floods and other unpredictable events, including those from climate change—will require a significant expansion of water storage capacity from the current 200 cubic meters per capita. In other parts of the world, such capacity is in the thousands of cubic meters. The cost of expanding water storage is extremely high in relation to the size of Africa's economies, suggesting the phasing of investments, with initial focus on achieving water security for key growth poles. Water also needs to be distributed for agricultural use. In a handful of countries, only 7 million hectares are equipped for irrigation. Although the irrigation-equipped area is less than 5% of Africa's cultivated area, it produces 20% of the value of agricultural production. An additional 12 million hectares could be economically viable for irrigation as long as costs are contained.

Thus Africa's infrastructure development faces major *geographic and physical challenges*—low population density; low urbanization; large number of landlocked countries; large number of small countries not permitting economics of scale; and ethnolinguistic fragmentation make regional integration a huge challenge. Africa's infrastructure services are twice as expensive as elsewhere in the world, reflecting both diseconomies of scale in production and high profit margins caused by lack of competition. By far the largest challenge for Africa is in energy, with 30 countries out of 54 facing regular power shortages and many paying high premiums for emergency power.

Regional integration of infrastructure is the only way to overcome these challenges. It would allow Africa to increase trade and its participation in the world economy. For example, continental fiber optic submarine cables could reduce Internet and international call charges by one-half. But integration *poses institutional challenges*: building a political consensus; establishing effective regional institutions; setting priorities for regional investments; developing regional regulatory frameworks; and facilitating project preparation and cross-border finance (Kessides and Benjamin 2012).

20.2 ACCESS TO INFRASTRUCTURE SERVICES, POVERTY, AND INEQUALITY

Coverage of modern infrastructure services in Africa is very low by international standards.[2] In part this reflects its relatively low urbanization rates. But household gains in access to those services over 1990–2005 have been very small: in rural areas, service coverage improved only modestly while in urban areas, it has actually declined. For example, urban coverage of piped water fell from 50% in the early 1990s to 39% in the early 2000s, and urban coverage of flush toilets from 32% to 27%. Although many new connections are being made in urban areas, declining urban coverage largely reflects the inability of service providers to keep pace with urban population growth. Some 1.5% of the population gains access to infrastructure services each year to electricity and cellular telephone services but less than 0.5% to the network of piped water and flush toilets. The rate of expansion of alternative services such as latrines, standposts, and boreholes is significantly faster than that of piped water and flush toilets. These regional averages mask huge differences by individual countries. Most households with coverage belong to the more affluent 40% of the population but, even among those households, coverage is far from universal—well under 50% in most cases. Electricity coverage is somewhat higher across all income levels.

For most of Africa, universal access to modern infrastructure services lies 50 years in the future. Projecting current rates of service expansion forward and taking into account expected population growth, less than 20% of sub-Saharan African countries will reach universal access for piped water by 2050, and less than 45% will reach universal access to electricity under "business as usual" assumptions. In one-third of countries, universal access to piped water and flush toilets will not be reached in the twenty-first century.

Low coverage rates reflect both lack of supply and lack of effective demand factors: the customer may be physically distant from a network (and thus have no *access* to the service) or may decide not to connect to a nearby network. The power grid for electricity is physically close to 93% of the urban population but only 75% of those with access actually hook up to the service. Slums (informal settlements) along major road corridors lack power service even though distribution lines run overhead. Piped water networks reach only 73% of the urban population but hook-up rates for those in proximity are only 48%. Households do not connect to newly available infrastructure networks because cheaper substitutes, such as boreholes, exist or because connection charges are too expensive for low-income households.[3] The average African household of five persons has a monthly budget of US$180, ranging from about US$60 in the poorest quintile to US$340 in the richest quintile. Charges for utilities, energy, and transport account for 7% of a household's budget on average but can

---

[2] For instance, coverage of electricity is 20% compared with 33% in South Asia; piped water 12% in Africa vs. 21% in South Asia; flush toilets 6% vs. 34% in South Asia, etc. Only Africa's telecommunications coverage compares favorably with South Asia.

[3] The average connection charge across the region is 28% of gross national income (GNI) per capita. Charges range from about $6 in the Upper Nile in Sudan to more than $240 in Côte d'Ivoire, Mozambique, Niger, and South Africa. For Niger, the charge is more than 100% of GNI per capita. Similarly, the five water utilities in Mozambique charge more than 75% of GNI per capita.

reach 15–25% in some countries. Moreover, about 40% of people connected to infrastructure services do not pay for them. Non-payment rates range from about 20% in the more affluent quintile to about 60% in the poorest quintile. A significant non-payment rate, even among the more affluent, suggests that a culture of payment problems exists in addition to any affordability issues.

Foster and Briceño-Garmendia (2010) consider that an affordability threshold of 5% of household budgets to be a gauge for measuring which utility bills might be affordable for African households. Monthly bills of US$2 are affordable for almost the entire African population. Monthly bills of US$8 would remain affordable for the entire population of the middle-income African countries, so that cost recovery should not be a major problem for these countries. Cost-recovery tariffs would also be affordable for those in low-income countries who have access but not for the remaining population. In low-income countries, monthly bills of US$8 would remain affordable for the richest 20–40% of the population, the only portion enjoying access, but not for the poorest 60–80% that currently lack access even if services were extended to them. Affordability would be a major issue associated with a universal access policy especially in low-income countries like Burundi, the Democratic Republic of Congo (DRC), Ethiopia, Guinea-Bissau, Malawi, Niger, Tanzania, and Uganda where as much as 80% of the population could not afford a monthly bill of US$8.

In the case of transport, affordability refers to the extent to which the financial cost of journeys put an individual or household in the position of having to make sacrifices to travel when they need to. While a family on a low income might be able to afford the necessary journeys to work for the income owners of the family, they might not be able to afford trips to school for their teenage children. For such a family, urban transport would, by most standards, be considered unaffordable. So affordability can be considered as the ability to make necessary journeys to work, school, health and other social services, and visit family or make urgent journeys without having to curtail other essential activities (Carruthers, Dick, and Saurkar 2005). The cost of trips by public transport varies enormously. For instance, a study for South Africa, using household survey data, indicates that in rural arid farming areas, households spend 13% of their income on public transport and that 13% of households have an affordability issue; households in rural commercial areas 19% and 18%; in rural homelands 14% and 31%; metropolitan 18% and 12%; urban periphery 27% and 16%; and urban hinterland 21% and 19% respectively (Venter 2011).

Most African countries heavily subsidize tariffs for power and water services for households and industrial enterprises (Karekezi 2002; Karekezi, Teferra, and Mapako 2002). On average, power tariffs recover only 75% of full costs, and water tariffs only 64%. The resulting implicit service subsidies amount to as much as US$4.1 billion a year (0.7% of Africa's GDP), divided evenly between power and water.

Manufacturing enterprises in Africa often opt for self-generation of electricity, even though it is widely considered a second-best solution. Of the 25 sub-Saharan countries reviewed by Foster and Steinbucks (2009), in-house generation accounts for more than 25% of the installed generating capacity in three countries and for more than 10% in nine others. In Nigeria, where 40% of the electricity consumed is produced with generators, firms spend up to 20–30% of their initial investment enhancing the reliability of their electricity supply. Moreover, in Africa, self-generated electricity is 300% more expensive on average than electricity from the grid. The main victims are likely to be informal firms (Alby, Dethier, and Straub 2013).

20.3 Institutions, Regulation, and the "Infrastructure Gap"

Institutional competence and capacity are important determinants of the performance of infrastructure providers in every sector, market restructuring, private involvement and privatization, establishment of independent regulators, and enhancement of competition, introduced gradually since the 1990s, have started to yield positive results in Africa—with the greatest progress achieved in telecommunications and the least in transport. But institutional and regulatory reforms on the continent still have a long way to go. There have been numerous failures to implement policies; renegotiations or cancellations of contracts with private providers; outcomes below expectations; and a high degree of official skepticism about whether reforms can produce results. In large part this is due to the weakness of African policies and institutions that guide and oversee public and private African infrastructure enterprises.

Regarding private participation in infrastructure, it is only in mobile telephones, power plants, and container terminals that the private sector has been willing to invest. The number of mobile subscribers and the share of the population receiving mobile signals increased by a factor of 10 in 5 years because of competition among private operators. Significant private finance has also gone into thermal power generation (3000 megawatts) and container terminals in ports, though volumes fall substantially short of requirements. Toll-road concessions are confined to South Africa because traffic volumes elsewhere are not enough to make such projects financially self-sustaining. In other sectors relying on concessions and related contracts such as power transmission and distribution, water and railways, there has not been new private finance. None of these businesses delivers cash flows high enough to finance investment because of a combination of low tariffs and low volumes. However, these arrangements have often seen improved operational performance, even if characterized by renegotiation and early cancellation. For road maintenance, there has been an increasing use of the multiyear performance-based contract with the private sector, which shows promise in safeguarding maintenance activities and keeping costs down. Some state-owned enterprises introduced some forms of governance reform, such as incentive-based performance contracts and independent external audits, which seem to be paying off. Corporate governance reforms, including the establishment of a somewhat independent board of directors, have also been introduced but few enterprises have full corporatization that includes limited liability, rate of return, and dividend policies.

Regulatory reforms are only beginning. Some critics argue that regulatory agencies have simply created additional risks because of unpredictable decisions, resulting from excessive discretion and overly broad objectives. Regulatory autonomy remains elusive: in some countries, turnover among commissioners has been high, and the gap between law (or rule) and practice has been wide. For water, where the vast majority of service providers are state-owned enterprises, no evidence exists of any benefit from regulation. For power and telecommunications, some effect is discernible, but it is far from unambiguous. Weak regulatory autonomy and capacity constraints undermine the credibility of independent regulators. Most African regulatory agencies are embryonic, lacking funding and in many cases qualified personnel.

Overall, although all African countries have embarked on institutional reforms, on average they have adopted no more than 50% of good institutional practices. What has lagged are regulatory and governance reforms. The variation in performance across countries is roughly 2 to 1, with the most advanced countries (Kenya) scoring about 70% and those furthest behind scoring 30% (Benin). Also, institutional development in infrastructure is very uneven depending on the sector. Countries that perform fairly well in one aspect do not necessarily do so in another. Sector-specific constraints are as important as country-specific constraints.

Why are institutional and regulatory reforms so important? Because, in general, utilities that are privately owned/operated offer more efficient and better quality services, as shown by a recent study examining the impact of those two factors on the performance of utilities in Latin America during 1995–2007 (Andres, Schwartz, and Guasch 2013). Losses and service interruptions decline, labor efficiency increases, and the duration of outages shrink. There are exceptions: one in ten public utilities performs better than the average private utility. Private utilities have expanded access on average but their access penetration has not grown faster than that of publicly owned utilities. Tariffs of private utilities are not on average lower than the rates of public utilities, particularly for water and power. Efficiency improves but consumer prices remain the same under private provision, suggesting that fewer subsidies cover the cost recovery gap and/or that service providers are capturing a larger part of the benefits of efficiency. This highlights the need for regulatory capacity. Generally, in power, water, and sanitation services and fixed-line telephony, natural monopoly traits still dominate and consumers are not able to rely on competition to regulate prices and service quality. In some markets, generators compete for dispatch, suppliers may compete to sell power or water through existing wires and pipes but generally the most efficient way to build the infrastructure is a network servicing individual households and businesses. Regulation is meant to protect the relationship between the consumer and the utility, and the stronger the regulator's capacity, the better off consumers are—fewer losses, fewer outages, more efficiency gains, quicker corrections of problems. This is true for both private and state-owned enterprises (SOEs).

For Africa, we have a sense of the importance of institutional factors for performance at both sector and enterprise levels, based on a standardized survey on the nature and intensity of institutional reforms (Vagliasindi 2008). This methodology yields a "scorecard" for close to 50 institutional variables in three groups: (i) sectoral policy reforms, defined as implementing sectoral legislation, restructuring enterprises, and introducing policy oversight and private sector participation; (ii) quality of regulation, which entails progress in establishing autonomous, transparent, and accountable regulatory agencies and regulatory tools (such as quality standards and tariff methodology); (iii) corporate governance inside the enterprise (such as strengthening shareholder voice and supervision, board and management autonomy, and mechanisms for accounting and disclosure) and measures aimed at improving the external environment in which the enterprise operates (including outsourcing to the private sector and introducing discipline from a competitive labor and capital market). The scorecards have been collected for the 24 telecommunication providers, 21 railway providers, 30 utilities in the electricity sector, and 52 utilities in the water sector. The extent of institutional reforms differs across these groups. For example, middle-income countries are significantly further ahead with power sector reform, whereas aid-dependent low-income countries are significantly further ahead with water reform, perhaps reflecting the strong role of donors in this sector. For telecommunications reform, the resource-rich low-income countries have higher scores. There is a strong correlation between the quality of infrastructure institutions and the overall level of governance and control of corruption, as well as the quality of public administration.

20.4 INVESTMENT NEEDS AND FINANCE

Meeting Africa's infrastructure needs calls for a very substantial program of infrastructure investment and maintenance. This would include:

- developing new power generation capacity (experts estimate that 7000 megawatts per year are required)
- enabling regional power trade through cross-border transmission lines
- completing the intraregional fiber-optic backbone network and continental submarine cable loop
- interconnecting capitals, ports, border crossings, and secondary cities with a good quality road network
- providing all-season road access to Africa's high-value agricultural land
- more than doubling Africa's irrigated area
- sharply decreasing the proportion of the population without sustainable access to safe drinking water and basic sanitation
- increasing household electrification
- providing global systems mobile voice signal and public access broadband to the entire population.

(See Foster and Briceño-Garmendia 2010.)

Implementing such an ambitious program to address Africa's infrastructure needs would cost US$93 billion a year (about 15% of the region's GDP). Some two-thirds of this total relates to capital expenditure, and the remaining one-third to operation and maintenance requirements. The report of the Commission for Africa chaired by Tony Blair came up with estimates based on a cross-country model in the range of US$80–$90 billion, close to those reported in Foster and Briceño-Garmendia (2010). About 40% of the total spending needs are associated with power, reflecting Africa's particularly large deficits. About one-third of the power investment needs (some US$9 billion a year) are associated with multipurpose water storage for hydropower and water resource management. After power, water supply, and sanitation, transport is the most significant item.

Multilateral banks and donor agencies are reporting significant cost escalations on projects under implementation. For road projects, these escalations have averaged 35% but in some cases have been as high as 50–100%. Planning and social targets rather than economic growth drive a large share of the spending needs, for example, the transport spending needs (which are largely based on connectivity objectives) and the water and sanitation spending needs (based on the Millennium Development Goals). The spending needs with the strongest direct link to economic growth are those for the power sector.

In addition to this, there will be significant financing required for adaptation to and mitigation of climate change. Worldwide, a functioning carbon market, with carbon prices in the range of US$ 20–25 per ton, as well as judicious use of public funds, could generate around US$100-200 billion of gross private capital flows for mitigation—or net flows between US$ 10–20 billion. The potential for private investment is substantial but, to unlock these flows, a range of existing country and project specific barriers will need to be overcome. This in turn will require appropriate domestic and international public interventions. Domestic public policies and programs, international public technical assistance and financial instruments, and carbon markets all represent the tools or levers that can be used to overcome market failures. International private investment flows are essential for the transition to a low-carbon, climate-resilient future. These investments can be stimulated through the targeted application of concessional and non-concessional public financing. Careful and wise use of public funds in combination with private funds can generate truly transformational investments (Patel 2011).

Financing needs for infrastructure differ markedly across country groups. The financing needs on infrastructure of fragile states (Côte d'Ivoire, DRC) are especially large when measured against the size of their economies. In the DRC, for instance, half of infrastructure assets need rehabilitation. Such countries would need to devote 37% of their GDPs to infrastructure to build a solid infrastructure platform—which is impossible. With their difficult environments, they attract relatively little external financing, capturing only 10% of overseas development assistance and 6% of private capital flows allocated to infrastructure. In addition to their huge financing needs, these countries do not use their resource envelope well; they underspend on maintenance and have inefficient service providers. Low-income countries (Senegal, Uganda) need to allocate about a quarter of their GDPs to build and sustain a basic infrastructure platform, a level difficult to envisage in practice. Therefore, these countries will have to make difficult choices to prioritize their investments, and most of them have a long way to go in improving the operational efficiency of existing infrastructure. Resource-rich countries (Nigeria, Zambia) would only need to spend 12% of their GDP on infrastructure and since they received large royalty payments during the commodity boom of the 2005–2012 they have a ready source of finance. Yet they actually lag being low-income countries in terms of infrastructure stock and spend less on infrastructure as they have been devoting their wealth to paying off debts. Finally, middle-income countries (Cape Verde, South Africa) would need only 10% of GDP to finance their infrastructure and they are much stronger in asset maintenance and institutional efficiency.

There are three ways to finance infrastructure projects: public financing (on- or off-budget), private financing, and public–private partnerships (PPPs). Each method has associated costs and benefits. Whilst direct public provision is the most traditional form of financing, a number of countries do not have the fiscal space required to fund necessary infrastructure improvements. Existing spending on infrastructure in Africa amounts to US$45 billion a year all sources included. As much as two-thirds of this overall spending is domestically sourced: US$30 billion of annual spending is financed by the African taxpayer and by user fees, and a further US$15 billion is from external sources. The public sector remains the dominant source of finance for water, energy, and transport in all countries except the fragile states. Public investment is largely tax financed and executed through central government budgets, whereas the operating and maintenance costs often rely on user fees and are executed by state-owned enterprises.

Current levels of public finance are higher as a share of GDP in low-income countries (typically 5–6% of GDP) but absolute amounts are very low (no more than US$20–$30 per capita per year).

Official development assistance (i.e. aid from OECD countries) makes an important contribution to investment in water and transport, particularly in poor countries which cannot access capital markets. The European Commission has increased the size of the EU–Africa Infrastructure Trust Fund, contributing €200 million for 2009–2010, calling on all member states to join the effort. Financing to infrastructure in Africa increased tenfold between 2002 and 2007 and the Infrastructure Consortium for Africa, launched at the G8 Gleneagles Summit in 2005, received US$12 billion in 2007 alone. In addition to grants and loans from these donors, a growing share of the region's infrastructure finance now comes from non-traditional donors such as China, India, and a number of Arab nations. In 2007 the contributions of these donors were estimated at US$5.2 billion, US$0.7 billion, and US$2.6 billion respectively (Commission for Africa 2010). Their investments are concentrated in energy and rail, especially in resource-rich countries. From 2009 to 2012, China increased direct investment in Africa from US$1.4 billion to US$2.5 billion when over 2000 Chinese enterprises were investing and developing in more than 50 African countries and regions in all economic sectors and not only infrastructure. By 2013, China had signed bilateral investment treaties with 32 countries, and established joint economic commission mechanisms with 45 African countries. The China–Africa Development Fund, established at the Beijing Summit, had already invested US$1.8 billion for 53 projects by 2013 (Information Office of the State Council 2013). A good source to monitor Chinese infrastructure projects in Africa is Brautigam (n.d).

Private investment in infrastructure projects in sub-Saharan Africa increased from US$8.7 billion in 2005 to US$13.5 billion in 2008. Private participation, heavily concentrated in ICT, depends on the potential for cost recovery and the regulatory framework. Since expectations of private sector participation did not materialize, this has led to calls for "fiscal space" in public accounts (i.e. less stringent fiscal rules) to finance needed infrastructure. There is evidence that standard fiscal rules adopted to ensure debt sustainability resulted in a reduction in infrastructure spending and that the political and ideological climate in Africa encourages policymakers to postpone large and costly infrastructure investments.

One central question is whether living standards and enterprise productivity would improve more with public or private ownership and operation of infrastructure. On the service delivery side, low-income consumers facing public monopolies have little choice or voice in seeking improvements in access or quality. When prices are kept low by government subsidies before privatization, the benefits often accrue to the middle-class and the rich rather than poor people. Similarly, evidence shows that traditional cross-subsidies associated with monopoly state-owned firms (where some consumers are charged a price much further below marginal cost than others) often benefit the better off more than poor people. It is reasonable to argue that, in many cases, it is cheaper for the government to raise infrastructure funds itself rather than rely on private finance. This is true when the government has greater access to concessional finance, and when private investors make excess profits. This last point highlights the fact that what is important from a value-for-money perspective is not the cost of private capital per se but the price the government pays for it, captured by the internal rate of return (Dethier and Moore 2012). If the cost of private capital *is* greater than public capital, properly adjusted for risk, the case for seeking private investment *for a given project* rests on efficiency gains. Private investment may be a way of ensuring that the best projects are selected and that access is expanded. A large volume of work has compared the efficiency of private and public infrastructure providers, with the general consensus being that private investment has typically brought efficiency gains, but a more important determinant of performance than private ownership is the degree of competition and the incentives created by the market structure. Value-for-money analysis is a means of comparing the cost of various approaches to delivering a given project (though it is not concerned with other important issues such as the selection of projects and the expansion of access). Raising prices to cost covering levels is a useful way to ensure that the best investments are undertaken.

Private participation can also help in expanding access if there is a potential for a return on new investments. Even with cost covering prices, private providers may exert more effort in opening up new markets. *Physical* access to water, telephone, sanitation, and electricity services has indeed improved after privatization around the world, simply through renewed investment in physical networks by the new private owners. *Economic* access—through affordable prices for poor people—is a more complicated issue because it involves the more difficult institutional and design issues associated with regulating prices or designing directed subsidies for poor people. In any case, the scope for improved access will depend on the success in achieving efficiency gains—some increased surplus—that can be passed on to poor people. Thus, in theory, with appropriate regulatory institutions, privatization and concession contracts can deliver both improved access to goods and services for poor people and better financial performance for the company. But many practical difficulties can arise with privatization. First, with limited government finances, direct subsidies for low-cost services for poor people may be difficult to finance. So there is a risk in terms of whether government will be able to sustain transparent subsidies after privatization. These subsidies will compete with other budget demands, while the indirect subsidy of underpricing (and accompanying losses in government owned utilities prior to privatization) often could be hidden for years. There is also a risk that the transfer of assets at the time of privatization could enrich well-connected high-income people rather than the poor. Poorly designed auctions can lead to one-off transfers of wealth from the public sector (taxpayers) to the new investors (domestic elite or foreign investors). If privatized firms are purchased by foreigners, foreign ownership can provoke a political backlash. Governments sometimes exacerbate consumers' frustration with private providers, as when they postpone needed price increases until after privatization—so that private firms, often foreign, get the blame.

20.5 FACING THE CHALLENGES AND OVERCOMING THE CONSTRAINTS

Africa is likely to have a large infrastructure-funding gap each year for many years to come, mostly in the power sector. Addressing a range of inefficiencies could make the existing resource envelope go much further—to the tune of US$17 billion a year. Foster and Briceño-Garmendia (2010) have calculated that the funding gap each year is in the order of

US$31 billion and that it could be reduced to US$17 billion a year if five types of inefficiencies were addressed.

Some countries are spending too much on some types of infrastructure and not enough on others. The largest share of this kind of expenditure relates to public spending on ICT infrastructure that the private sector could provide, particularly in middle-income countries. Although some of this spending may be justified by phasing or sequencing, at least part of these resources could possibly be reallocated to underfunded sectors. Infrastructure expenditure would have to be monitored more closely against identified needs and priorities and considering expected economic returns.

There are substantial delays in budget execution. African countries typically execute only about two-thirds of the budget allocated to public investment in infrastructure. Public investment could in theory increase by 30% without any increase in spending, simply by addressing the institutional bottlenecks that inhibit capital budget execution. This includes better planning of investment projects, earlier completion of feasibility studies, more efficient procurement processes, and a move to medium-term multiyear budgeting.

In a typical African country, about 30% of infrastructure assets need rehabilitation. This share is even higher for rural infrastructure and in conflict countries. Underfunding maintenance represents a major waste since rehabilitating infrastructure is several times more costly than doing preventive maintenance each year. For example, spending US$1 on road maintenance provides a savings of US$4 to the economy. So reallocating resources from investment to maintenance, particularly in low-income countries that spend little on maintenance spending, would save a lot on public spending.

Power and water utilities display high inefficiency in distribution losses, under-collection of revenues, and overstaffing in Africa. Utilities typically collect only 70–90% of billed revenues, and distribution losses can easily be twice the technical best practice. According to household surveys, about 40% of those connected to utility services do not appear to be paying for them, a share that rises to 65% in some countries. Under-collection is also a problem for many road funds. In developing countries state-owned telecommunications companies employ six times the number of employees per connection than do privately operated enterprises, leading to significant losses from overstaffing. Excess employment in power and water utilities ranges from 20% to 80% over benchmarks in other developing areas. The revenues lost through these inefficiencies can easily exceed the current turnover of the utilities by several multiples. For power and water, these losses absorb 0.5% and 0.2% of GDP, respectively, on average in sub-Saharan Africa.

Lastly, infrastructure services are substantially underpriced. Even though infrastructure charges are high by international standards, they often fail to cover operating costs. This represents an implicit subsidy for consumers and industrial customers and a major loss of revenues (see e.g. Kojima 2013). Since access to infrastructure services in Africa is very regressive (with 90% of those who have access to piped water or electricity services belong to the richest 60% of the population), these rich consumers capture almost all the subsidies to residential services.

Dealing with these inefficiencies would go a long way toward reducing the "infrastructure gap." (This gap is the difference between estimated infrastructure spending needs and potential resources including actual spending and potential efficiency gains). This gap can be addressed by raising more finance, by adopting lower-cost technologies or by using less ambitious targets for infrastructure development. Most of the funding gap (60%) is in the power sector. The remainder relates to water and irrigation. The largest gap relates to capital investment but there are also huge shortfalls for operation and maintenance, particularly in fragile states. Since the latter countries would require large amounts of finance to meet basic investment targets in any reasonable time frame, *even* if all the efficiencies mentioned above were fully captured, the latter countries will need to follow other routes. One possibility is to adopt lower-cost technologies to lessen investment needs, for instance to adopt lower-cost road designs or lower-end solutions for water and sanitation (such as standposts and improved latrines). Fragile countries face a stark trade-off between the level of service provided and the speed with which they can serve their entire population.

Some economists (Lin and Monga 2011; Lin 2012; Dinh, Palmade, Chandra, and Cossar 2012) consider that well-designed and well-run industrial parks and clusters could help overcome the curse of the infrastructure gap. This is, after all, what many latecomers into the industrialization process including Ireland, Mauritius or China have done with great success. However, this would imply that long-term finance is available. For infrastructure development, it is necessary to have a reasonably developed local financial system making sustainable and affordable long-term finance available. This implies macroeconomic stability (which now exists in most African countries, except fragile countries) and a basic level of financial intermediation. However, the level of financial depth (i.e. the ratio of total financial intermediaries' assets to GDP) of most African countries is very low. Some countries have ratios exceeding 100% (Cape Verde, Namibia, and South Africa) but the next highest ratio is around 50% (Kenya). Ratios of private credit by banks to GDP also point to a low level of financial intermediation in most African countries. Bank credit to the private sector in those countries has been constrained by various structural impediments to lending that can include poor credit discipline, deficiencies in legal and judicial frameworks, administrative controls on lending rates, and high transaction costs. The ability of commercial banks to finance infrastructure projects is thus limited (except in South Africa). In addition to structural constraints, there would be a significant asset-liability maturity mismatch in the case of most banks in the region, given that deposits and other liabilities in African banks currently tend to have largely short-term maturities, while infrastructure projects require long-term financing. Longer-term deposits are needed to finance longer-term credit commitments. In financial markets where banks make credit available at long terms, they often concentrate their lending on a few large corporate blue-chip borrowers. Even for the few countries where long-term loans with maturities greater than 20 years are available (South Africa, Ghana, Lesotho, Namibia, Uganda, and Zambia), average interest rates sometimes (but not always) exceed 20%, thus rendering them unaffordable for infrastructure lending. This is because it is difficult to find infrastructure projects that generate sufficient returns to cover a cost of debt that is greater than 20% (Irving and Manroth 2009).

It is undeniable that the share of bank loans used to finance infrastructure has increased in Africa—which is a good sign. Transport and communications has been the destination of the largest amount of local bank loans. Yet there is a very limited amount of long-term financing from local banks and only a small amount of outstanding bank loans are for infrastructure purposes. For most of the continent, however, the capacity of local banking systems would be too small to adequately finance infrastructure development needs. For many countries, corporate bonds, followed by equity issues, are more likely to be used for infrastructure purposes than are other sources. Telecommunications companies had the highest number of bond issues, followed by transport companies. Corporate bond financing is increasingly seen as a viable source of finance by infrastructure firms because long-term bank financing is costly and scarce, and macroeconomic conditions have improved. However, further progress is needed in most countries in developing a benchmark for pricing in the form of a well-established yield curve, maintaining low and stable inflation rates and interest rates, improving corporate governance and transparency, developing a larger and well-regulated institutional investor base, putting in place credible rating agencies, and increasing awareness of prospective issuers and investors. With the exception of the Johannesburg Stock Exchange, the stock exchanges of African countries have a small number of equity listings (particularly by local companies), very low ratios of market capitalization to GDP, and low turnover ratios. Many national and regional stock exchanges that operate in Africa (those of Cameroon, Cape Verde, Ghana, Malawi, Mozambique, Namibia, and Zambia) had no equity listings by companies operating in infrastructure at the end of the twentieth century. By contrast, bond listings by companies operating in infrastructure sectors comprised more than half of total outstanding bonds listed on the exchanges of Mozambique and Namibia. Cross-border listings (of corporate bonds and equity issues) and cross-border investment fell short of regional integration of national exchanges, even though such cross-border activity could help overcome national capital markets' impediments of small size, illiquidity, and inadequate market infrastructure and, in so doing, facilitate the ability of companies and governments in these countries to raise financing for infrastructure development. This regional approach to raising infrastructure financing remains untapped. Aside from Kenya Airways, there have not yet been cross-border equity listings by companies in infrastructure sectors on the national and regional exchanges of Africa. The first bond raising finance for an infrastructure sector to be listed on two exchanges (South Africa and Namibia) was a US$62.2 million, 13-year, rand-denominated corporate bond issued in August 2007 by Namibia's electricity utility (Irving and Manroth 2009). Since then several initiatives to integrate capital markets within and across sub-regions have achieved some progress toward harmonizing rules, technology, and systems. Building further on these initiatives could pave the way for more cross-border listings from infrastructure providers and other companies based in the region, potentially offering issuers access to much wider markets, boosting the supply of listed securities, and increasing market capitalization and liquidity.

It is possible to think of an African scenario in which improvements in the development of markets and reductions in inefficiencies, spurred by increases in domestic demand and exports, lead to a virtuous circle, increases in economic growth and better living standards for the majority. To an extent, this has already happened in the most advanced African countries (Mauritius, Namibia, Cape Verde). This can contribute to a change in the "animal spirits" of investors both inside and outside Africa and would lead to a shrinking of the gap between spending needs and available resources for infrastructure.

References

African Development Bank (2012). Programme for Infrastructure Development in Africa (PIDA). http://www.afdb.org/en/topics-and-sectors/initiatives-partnerships/programme-for-infrastructure-development-in-africa-pida/.
Alby, P., Dethier, J.J., and Straub, S. (2013). Firms operating under electricity constraints in developing countries. *World Bank Economic Review*, 27(1):109–132.

Andrès, L., Schwartz, J., and Guasch, J.L. (2013). *Uncovering the Drivers of Utility Performance: Lessons from Latin America and the Caribbean*. Washington DC: World Bank.

Brautigam, D. (n.d.) China in Africa: The Real Story. http://www.chinaafricarealstory.com.

Briceño-Garmendia, C., and Shkaratan, M. (2011). Power Tariffs. Caught between Cost Recovery and Affordability. Policy Research Working Paper No. 5904. Washington, DC: World Bank.

Calderón, C., and Serven, L. (2008). Infrastructure and economic development in Sub-Saharan Africa, Policy Research Working Paper No. 4712. Washington, DC: World Bank.

Carruthers, R., Dick, M., and Saurkar, A. (2005). Affordability of Public Transport in Developing Countries. Transport Paper TP-3. Washington DC: World Bank.

Commission for Africa (2010). *Still Our Common Interest*. London: Commission for Africa http://www.commissionforafrica.info/.

Dethier, J.J., and Moore, A. (2012). Infrastructure in Developing Countries: An Overview of Some Economic Issues, Discussion Paper on Development Policy No. 165. Center for Development Research, University of Bonn, http://www.zef.de/discussionpapers.html.

Dinh, H., Palmade, V., Chandra, V., and Cossar, F. (2012). *Light Manufacturing in Africa. Targeted Policies to Enhance Private Investment and Create Jobs*. Washington, DC: The World Bank.

Economic Commission For Africa (2009). Africa: Review Report on Transport. Sixth Session of the Committee on Food Security and Sustainable Development Regional Implementation Meeting for the 18th Session of the Conference on Sustainable Development, 27–30 October 2009, Addis Ababa, Ethiopia.

Foster, V., and Briceño-Garmendia, C. (2010). *Africa's Infrastructure. A Time for Transformation*. A copublication of the Agence Française de Développement and the World Bank.

Foster, V., and Steinbuks, J. (2009). Paying the Price for Unreliable Power Supplies: In-House Generation of Electricity by Firms in Africa. Policy Research Working Paper No. 4913. Washington, DC: World Bank.

Information Office of the State Council, People's Republic of China (2013). China-Africa Economic and Trade Cooperation. Beijing. http://www.scio.gov.cn/zxbd/wz/Document/1344818/1344818.htm.

Irving, J., and Manroth, A. (2009). Local Sources of Financing for Infrastructure in Africa: A Cross-Country Analysis, Policy Research Working Paper No. 4878. Washington, DC: World Bank.

Karekezi, S. (2002). Poverty and energy in Africa—a brief review. *Energy Policy*, 30(11–12):915–919.

Karekezi, S., Teferra, M., and Mapako, M. (eds) (2002). Africa: improving modern energy services for the poor. *Energy Policy*, 30:11–12.

Kessides, I., and Benjamin, N. (2012). Regionalizing infrastructure for deepening market integration: the case of East Africa, Policy Research Working Paper No. 6113. Washington, DC: World Bank.

Kojima, M. (2013). Petroleum product pricing and complementary policies: experience of 65 developing countries since 2009. Policy Research Working Paper No. 6396. Washington, DC: World Bank.

Lin, J.Y. (2012). *The Quest for Prosperity: How Developing Countries Can Take Off*. Princeton: Princeton University Press.

Lin, J.Y., and Monga, C. (2011). Growth identification and facilitation: the role of the state in the dynamics of structural change. *Development Policy Review,* 29(3):259–310.

Patel, S. (2011). Climate Finance: Engaging the Private Sector. Background paper for Mobilizing Climate Finance, report prepared at the request of G20 Finance Ministers. Washington, DC: International Finance Corporation.

PIDA (2012). Closing the Infrastructure Gap Vital for Africa's Transformation. http://www.afdb.org/fileadmin/uploads/afdb/Documents/Generic-Documents/PIDA%20brief%20closing%20gap.pdf.

PIDA (2012). Interconnecting, Integrating and Transforming a Continent. http://www.afdb.org/fileadmin/uploads/afdb/Documents/Project-and-Operations/PIDA%20note%20English%20for%20web%200208.pdf.

Sub-Saharan Africa Transport Policy Program (2007). Second Development Plan 2008-2011: Fostering Sound Policies and Strategies for the Provision of Reliable, Safe, Efficient, and Affordable Transport. SSATP.

Vagliasindi, M. (2008). *Institutional Infrastructure Indicators: An Application to Reforms, Regulation and Governance in Sub-Saharan Africa, Background Paper for Africa's Infrastructure. A Time for Transformation.* Washington, DC: World Bank.

Vagliasindi, M. (2012). The role of regulatory governance in driving PPPs in electricity transmission and distribution in developing countries: a cross-country analysis. Policy Research Working Paper No. 6121. Washington, DC: World Bank.

Venter, C. (2011). Transport expenditure and affordability: the cost of being mobile. *Development Southern Africa*, 28(1):121–140.

World Bank (2013). *Africa Development Indicators 2012/13.* Washington DC: World Bank.

World Bank and International Energy Agency (2013). *Global tracking framework. Sustainable energy for all.* Washington DC: World Bank. www.worldbank.org/se4all.

World Energy Council (2003). The Potential for Regionally Integrated Energy Development in Africa. A Discussion Document. London: World Energy Council.

CHAPTER 21

FINANCIAL INCLUSION
IN AFRICA
Obstacles and Opportunities

ASLI DEMIRGÜÇ-KUNT, LEORA KLAPPER,
AND PETER VAN OUDHEUSDEN

21.1 INTRODUCTION

FINANCIAL inclusion–defined here as access to and use of formal financial services by individuals and firms–has been recognized by policymakers, researchers, and other financial stakeholders as a key element in reaching inclusive economic development and fighting poverty. In the absence of an inclusive financial system, individuals and firms are forced to rely on their own resources to meet their financial needs. Having access to credit or a formal account facilitates users to better manage cash flows, build assets, and mitigate risks. However, financial penetration in Africa was well below the global average at the end of the 1990s (Honohan 2008), and, although it improved, remained so even a decade later (Demirgüç-Kunt and Klapper 2013).

On the macro-level, financial deepening, and the expansion of individual and firm access to financial services in Africa, may contribute to lower income inequality and faster economic growth. Rajan and Zingales (1998), for example, showed that sectors in which firms are relatively more in need of external finance grow disproportionally faster in countries with better-developed financial systems. Burgess and Pande (2005) showed that branch expansion into rural unbanked locations significantly reduced rural poverty through increased deposit mobilization and credit disbursement by banks. Beck et al. (2007) found that financial development reduces poverty, income inequality, and boosts the growth rate of the income share of the poorest quintile, helping the poor above and beyond the impact of financial development on aggregate growth.[1]

---

[1] See also for example King and Levine (1993), Beck et al. (2000), Clarke et al. (2006), Klapper et al. (2006), and Demirgüç-Kunt and Levine (2009).

Across the African continent, an estimated 24% of adults have a bank account (Demirgüç-Kunt and Klapper 2013). It is important to note that not using an account does not necessarily mean a lack of "access" to financial services, that is, some people might have affordable access, but have no need for financial services and choose not to use them. However, many African adults without a formal account lack access in the sense that costs are prohibitively high, or banks and other financial institutions are located too far away, or financial services are not available because of legal barriers, regulatory constraints, information impediments, or cultural deterrents. The poor, youth, and rural residents are more likely to report greater barriers to access to financial services (Allen et al. 2012).

The focus of government interventions should be to correct these market failures. For instance, a function of the government is to improve the legal and regulatory framework, promote financial education, and expand consumer protection. Policies to expand account penetration—such as permitting bank agents, relaxing documentation requirements, requiring basic/low-fee accounts, and allowing the evolvement of new technologies, such as mobile banking—have proven to be especially effective among those most excluded (Allen et al. 2012). Other direct government interventions—such as direct credit, debt relief, and lending through state-owned banks—tend to be politicized and less successful, particularly in countries with weaker governance (World Bank 2013).

Well-designed efforts to expand financial inclusion might also have social welfare benefits. For instance, if savings constraints impede the ability of the poor to meet lumpy expenses like buying business inventory or paying kids' school fees, intervention could improve social welfare by adding to the economy's stock of physical and human capital.

As an example, savings constraints cause poor households and small businesses to make suboptimal choices. For instance, Dupas and Robinson (2013) showed that the provision of non-interest bearing bank accounts to micro-entrepreneurs in Kenya led to high take-up. This happened despite the accounts being very expensive (high withdrawal fees), pointing to a huge unmet demand for savings products. More importantly, they showed that these accounts led to increases in both investment and consumption, suggesting that there is inefficient allocation in the absence of formal savings mechanisms.

Furthermore, Aportela (1999) and Prina (2012) found that the exogenous provision of accounts to poor households in Mexico and Nepal, respectively, led to high take-up rates and a significant increase in household savings. Burgess and Pande (2005), and Bruhn and Love (2009) found significant increases in income, output and employment as a consequence of bank branch expansion in India and Mexico, respectively. Having a formal account also facilitates the transfer of funds, receipt of wages, remittances or government payments such as welfare benefits. Studies have also found that a lack of access to finance can lead to poverty traps and increase levels of income inequality (Beck et al. 2007).

Inability to smooth consumption during shocks also causes poor households in financially underdeveloped economies to make suboptimal choices. Jacoby and Skoufias (1992), Funkhouser (1999) and Jensen (2000) provided evidence from India, Costa Rica, and Côte d'Ivoire respectively, showing that kids drop out of school in the face of adverse income shocks. Behrman (1988) found that the inability of South Indian households to smooth consumption adversely impacts the health of children, especially girls, just before major harvests. Robinson and Yeh (2011) found evidence that sex workers in Kenya respond to health shocks in the family by engaging in risky behavior that tends to be better remunerated. Rosenzweig and Wolpin (1993) showed that farmers in India sell productive livestock in order to smooth consumption during shocks. In addition, Morduch (1995) made an extremely important observation that households and enterprises might be making inefficient employment and production choices ex ante, simply because they entail a smaller risk (income smoothing, as against the more commonly reported consumption smoothing).

Other studies have also documented a large unmet demand in savings among the poor in developing countries (see Banerjee and Duflo 2007). For example, Collins et al. (2009) documented the household balance sheets of several very poor families that turn to either informal institutions or the space below the mattress to save, due to the absence of formal financial institutions. Besley (1995) wrote of the popular use of moneylenders in Western Africa who charge significant withdrawal fees (effectively, a negative rate of interest) on deposits.

Access to formal savings channels will help these households and enterprises to increase investment and smooth consumption. This could potentially also be addressed through insurance or credit. While these are important aspects of financial inclusion in their own right, they are fraught with questions on financing, potential indebtedness, and agency problems. Another aspect that adds to the appeal of savings is that many barriers to access can be lowered simply by altering the regulatory environment, without resorting to distortionary subsidies.

This chapter is organized as follows. The second section presents new evidence on the scope and gaps in financial inclusion in Africa to better understand the landscape and make comparisons with other developing regions. The third section discusses the obstacles to financial inclusion in Africa, and the fourth section discusses opportunities to broaden financial penetration. Section 5 concludes.

21.2 EXPLAINING FINANCIAL INCLUSION IN AFRICA

Financial inclusion differs enormously between Africa and other parts of the world (Appendix 1). While worldwide 50% of adults have an account at a formal financial institution, barely 23% of adults in Africa do so (Demirgüç-Kunt and Klapper 2013).[2] Even within Africa there are quite some differences. In Southern Africa, for example, account penetration is 51%, comparable with other developing regions such as East Asia and the Pacific, and even exceeding the rates of Latin America and the Caribbean, South Asia, and Europe and Central Asia.[3] In Central Africa, however, this number is barely 12%. In Africa, the country with the highest account penetration is Mauritius with 80%. Niger has the highest share of unbanked, and less than 2% of adults in this country have an account at a formal financial institution.

---

[2] All data is from the Global Financial Inclusion (Findex) database, available at: www.worldbank.org/globalfindex.

[3] The sub-regional classifications are based on those of the World Bank for the regions and the United Nations Statistical Division for Africa. Algeria, Central African Republic, Madagascar, and Somalia are omitted from the analysis since Gallup excludes more than 20% of the population in the sampling, either because of security risks or inaccessibility.

The share of adults in Africa that saved formally in 2011 is around 12%. Although this is lower than the worldwide average of 22%, it is higher than in all of the other developing regions, with the exception of East Asia and the Pacific. There are quite large differences within Africa. The North and Central Africa regions have the lowest share of adults that save at a formal financial institution, while formal savings are particularly common in Kenya, Nigeria, and South Africa. Saving in general is widespread in Africa though. Around 36% of adults report having saved or set aside money, which is on par with the global average and exceeds the 30% found for developing countries. That only 12% of adults, which here is 35% of adults that save, report having saved at a formal financial institution indicates that a disproportionally large share of savings is managed through informal channels.[4]

The pattern of differences in the percentage of adults that borrowed from a formal financial institution, both between regions and within Africa, is similar to that of formal account ownership. In Africa around 4.5% of adults had formal credit in 2011. Use of formal credit is almost twice as high in all other developing regions, and the worldwide average is 9%.

Among formally registered small and medium enterprises (SMEs), account penetration is high, while the use of formal credit is relatively low (Enterprise Surveys, various years).[5] Over 85% of SMEs in Africa use a formal bank account, in line with other regional averages. However, while almost 30% of formal SMEs worldwide have an outstanding loan or line of credit, in Africa only 15% report outstanding debt.

A deeper look at country-level data on bank penetration suggests that while access to financial services is necessary for financial inclusion, it alone may not be sufficient. For example, Morocco and Tunisia both have around 20 commercial bank branches per 100 000 adults, which is comparable to the world average. However, account penetration, formal savings, and formal credit in these countries are well below the world average suggesting that affordability or other reasons may prevent individuals from using financial services. Indeed, more than 25% of the unbanked adults in Morocco and Tunisia mention religious reasons when asked why they do not have an account at a formal financial institution, compared to a global average of 5% that mention this reason.[6]

Country-level measures of financial inclusion also point to relatively low levels of financial development. For example, Allen et al. (2013) showed that across sub-Saharan Africa on average, liquid liabilities and credit to the private sector, both as a share of output, are respectively two-thirds and half of what is expected based on the predicted countries' values of the determinants of financial development as described by Beck et al. (2008). The authors showed that this gap in financial development can be explained by access related measures such as low population density and bank penetration.

The development and market structure of the banking sector in Africa can also help explain the relatively low levels of financial inclusion. Beck and Cull (2014) characterized sub-Saharan Africa's banks as less efficient, more profitable, and operating in less

---

[4] The reliance on informal ways to manage financial needs is discussed in more detail in section 3.

[5] Complete data for the Enterprise Data Surveys is available at: www.enterprisesurveys.org.

[6] In general, the most often mentioned reasons for not having an account are related to affordability. More specifically, these reasons are 'you don't have enough money to use them' and 'they are too expensive' (Demirgüç-Kunt and Klapper 2013). These findings underline that expanding access alone does not necessarily leads to more financial inclusion when the right products, affordable and in line with religious beliefs, are not provided.

competitive environments than their counterparts in other developing regions.[7] The lack of efficiency makes banking services more expensive, as for example reflected in the high interest rate spread between lending and deposit rates, raising concerns about their affordability. Decomposing this interest rate spread, the authors showed that the two main components of the spread are relatively large overhead costs—primarily related to non-interest income—and profit margins. The latter reflect greater concentration of banks, higher risk premiums, and limited competition.

21.3 THE LIMITATIONS OF INFORMAL FINANCIAL SERVICES

The gap in the use of formal financial products might reflect a lack of need or desire for financial services more generally. Yet Figure 21.1 suggests that this is not the case. The share of adults in Africa that used credit or saved is on par (or exceeds) the global average. Given the low use of formal financial services in Africa, this finding suggests that people rely predominantly on informal means, such as family, friends, or semi-formal savings clubs, to service their financial needs. In Africa, around 80% of all credit is obtained from family or friends, compared to only 60% and 30% for other developing and high-income countries, respectively. A third of savers, representing close to 100 million adults in sub-Saharan Africa, use only informal methods, such as Rotating Savings and Credit Associations (ROSCAs) or a person outside the family, while the average for all other developing countries is only 7% of savers. That is, compared to the rest of the world, the financial needs of African people are disproportionally managed through informal channels.

Many savers use formal, informal, and other methods of savings alongside each other, and these methods differ across Africa. For example, in Western Africa, the use of informal savings clubs—where a *susu* is a common form of savings club—is relatively prevalent. In Southern Africa on the other hand, saving by formal means is the dominant method and 21% of adults, almost 70% of adults that save, save at a formal financial institution. In North Africa and Central Africa approximately half of adults who saved did not report having done so using a formal financial institution, informal savings club, or a person outside the family. This means that in these regions alternative methods, which might include saving "under the mattress" or saving through asset accumulation such as gold or livestock, are primarily used to save.[8]

Yet the consequences of having to rely primarily on informal means to manage day-to-day financial needs are well documented by Collins et al. (2009). Using detailed information from financial diaries of individuals, the authors provide insight into the challenges faced by the unbanked. For instance, the financial diaries list the time and effort spent by poor individuals to compensate for the lack of access to services such as savings accounts, credit and insurance.

---

[7] See Beck and Cull (2014) and references within for a detailed discussion of the banking sector in sub-Saharan Africa.

[8] Financial diaries confirm that saving "under the mattress" is commonly used in Africa. In the sample of 166 households, more than 70% of the households had savings at home (www.financialdiaries.com).

It is important to note that some financial transactions might be a form of income redistribution. Redistributive norms in Africa, which are primarily restricted to and relevant within the kinship network, are strong. Moreover, these social norms are enforced by strong witch-beliefs and fear of being accused of witchcraft (Platteau 2009, and references within.) Social pressure to share resources are more likely to be relevant for borrowing, given that the dominant source of credit in Africa is family and friends. Indeed, "borrowers do not feel morally obliged to repay debts incurred from a prosperous relative ... because they tend to view non-compliance as a legitimate manner or redistributing income from lucky to unlucky individuals tied to solidarity obligations" (Platteau 2009: 682).

These issues related to redistribution may be less relevant when looking at savings since these are likely to take place outside the kinship network. However, Jakiela and Ozier (2012) found in Kenya, that women (rather than men) in their experiment that had relatives present were willing to reduce their expected income in order to keep their returns on investment

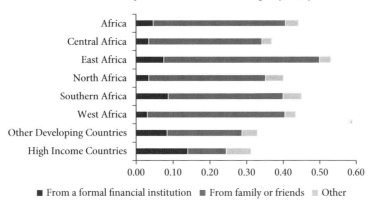

Panel A: share of adults that borrowed in the past year, by source

■ From a formal financial institution   ■ From family or friends   ▒ Other

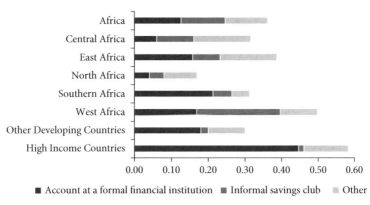

Panel B: share of adults that saved in the past year, by method

■ Account at a formal financial institution   ■ Informal savings club   ▒ Other

FIGURE 21.1 Sources of credit and savings methods.

Notes: All data are from 2011 and taken from the Global Findex database (Demirgüç-Kunt and Klapper 2013). All regional averages are population weighted.

hidden. This finding lends support to the challenge of dealing with the social pressure to share resources, which may lead to underinvestment in business activities.

Evidence from randomized control trials suggests an important role for commitment savings accounts in Africa to address the challenges of redistribution. For example, a field experiment in Malawi randomly assigned smallholder cash crop farmers ordinary savings accounts or commitment savings accounts (Brune et al. 2011). The commitment savings account offered was identical to an ordinary savings account, but allowed customers to restrict access to their funds until a future date of their choosing. The authors find that commitment accounts increased savings, expenditures on productive input, and household expenditures—but found no effect of offering ordinary saving accounts. These findings suggest that self-control problems seem less relevant than problems of social pressure to share resources.

In related research, Dupas and Robinson (2013) examined the impact of ownership of a formal savings account using a field experiment in Kenya. Randomly assigning formal savings accounts to predominantly female market vendors and male bicycle taxi drivers, they find that the treatment group of women entrepreneurs used their accounts and increased their savings, while the male entrepreneurs did not. Given both the lack of interest payments on deposits and the existence of substantial withdrawal fees, the active account use of the female market vendors' treatment group implies that the women entrepreneurs faced substantial negative returns on saving informally. In addition to higher account usage and savings, female markets vendors also increased their productive investment and private expenditures, suggesting positive spillover effects of formal savings and account ownership.

There is less of a consensus regarding the impact of formal credit on firm performance. For example, using a randomized experiment in rural Morocco, Crépon et al. (2011) found that access to credit has on average no effects on consumption, health, or education. Although the effect of opening branches and increasing access to credit was to expand the scale of self-employment activities, this was only found for households with pre-existing self-employment activities. In comparison, Karlan and Zinman (2010) used evidence from a randomized experiment in South Africa to show that access to consumer credit has beneficial effects such as higher economic self-sufficiency, food consumption, subjective well-being, and long term impact on credit scores. Winter-Nelson and Temu (2005) found evidence that supports the beneficial effects of access to finance for credit constrained coffee growers in Northern Tanzania.

The evidence on the heterogeneous effect of gender on the impact of access to credit is also mixed. For instance, Akpalu et al. (2012) studied female-managed enterprises in the Upper East Region of Ghana and found that access to microfinance is positively associated with greater efficiency. However, de Mel et al. (2008) showed that the returns to capital tend to be lower for female- than male-run micro-enterprises.

There is also some evidence that investment in entrepreneurial activities or agricultural inputs only increase when liquidity constrained producers are provided with formal credit as well as insurance against risks such as rainfall or drought. This may be especially relevant when there are no possibilities for producers to insure themselves against these risks. Karlan et al. (2012), for example, examined the relative importance of these two market failures using several experiments in Northern Ghana. Given that the farmers in their study were able to find resources to spend on their business once they were provided with insurance, the authors argued that the binding constraint for farmers is the uninsured risk they face. Combined with the farmers' lack of response to the liquidity constraint relieving elements of the experiment, the evidence found in this study suggests that policies focusing solely on credit market imperfections might not be enough to increase entrepreneurial activities. In related research, Hill and Viceisza (2012), using evidence from a framed field experiment in rural Ethiopia, found that insurance has positive effects on fertilizer purchases.

Despite the benefits that insurance offer, other literature finds that the demand for risk management products is low—consistent with the actual reported usage of agricultural insurance products (Figure 21.2). For example, using evidence from a field experiment in Malawi, Gine and Yang (2009) found that take-up of credit offers that include weather insurance (at actuarially fair rates) is lower than take-up of the same credit offers without insurance. As way of explanation, the authors suggest that farmers prefer the implicit insurance embedded by the limited liability clause in the loan contract. Another explanation for the low demand for insurance is offered by Karlan et al. (2012), who found that demand for insurance becomes lower when farmers previously insured were not confronted by bad weather conditions and no pay-out was made.

The underdevelopment of the financial sector in Africa, both in absolute terms and relative to other developing regions, does not seem to reflect a lack of demand for financial services. Rather, the evidence in previous literature suggests that individuals and entrepreneurs use informal channels on a daily basis to manage their personal finances, run businesses, and minimize their financial risks. Policies to expand financial inclusion should take into consideration social pressures to share resources, while encouraging affordable and accessible financial services.

21.4 OPPORTUNITIES FOR FINANCIAL INCLUSION IN AFRICA

Compared to other developing regions, Africa has lower account penetration and fewer financial providers, and its population relies disproportionally on informal methods and sources to save or borrow. When it comes to mobile banking though, Africa outperforms the rest of the developing world by a wide margin. In Africa, on average, 14% of adults in

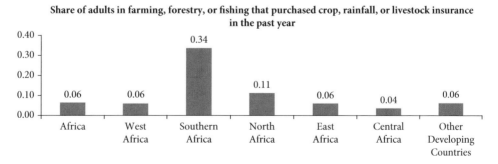

FIGURE 21.2 Purchases of agricultural insurance.

Notes: All data are from 2011 and taken from the Global Findex database (Demirgüç-Kunt and Klapper 2013). All regional averages are population weighted.

2011 used a mobile phone to pay bills, send money, or receive money. In other developing countries, only 3% of adults, less than a quarter of that in Africa, used mobile banking. The use of mobile banking is not uniform within Africa. In approximately half of the countries, mobile banking is less than 7%, and there are quite a few countries that see a higher use, such as Kenya, with over 70% mobile banking penetration.

The high rate of mobile banking in Kenya represents the success of M-Pesa, a financial payment service introduced in March 2007 by Safaricom, Kenya's largest telecom provider. M-Pesa allows mobile phone users deposit money at their agents in exchange for "e-float," which can be transferred to other phone users and exchanged for money at any M-Pesa's agent (for more information see Jack and Suri 2011; Mbiti and Weil 2011). Mbiti and Weil (2011) showed that by 2009 M-Pesa virtually replaced other means of sending and receiving remittances such as checks, busses, post offices, and companies that provided these services (e.g. Western Union).

Besides its success as a financial transaction service, the system is also used as a means of saving. Almost 80% of users say that they use M-Pesa to save, although other savings methods such as merry-go-rounds, bank accounts, and "under the mattress" are still used as well (Jack and Suri 2011). Mobile money service providers have also started offering new products in addition to payments, such as interest earning savings instruments. For instance, the introduction of M-Shwari savings accounts in Kenya, which can be accessed from any mobile phone. Or the "Electronic Dollar a Day" saving scheme in Uganda, which encourages adults to save at least one dollar a day using their mobile money accounts. These products offer the potential for mobile phones to provide accessible and affordable accounts to the unbanked rural poor.

A good example of the potential benefits of mobile money is given by Aker et al. (2013). They draw evidence from a randomized evaluation of the use of mobile money to make government cash-transfer payments in Niger. The authors found that relative to adults that received payments in cash, the group that received electronic payments via their mobile phones reported a significant decrease in costs, due to shorter travel distances and less time waiting on-line. The mobile money transfer group also used a larger proportion of the cash transfer for food-related consumption and on more diverse types of goods.

New technology can also be used to reduce the risks to lenders, which in turn should increase the price and amount of available credit. For example, in a field experiment in Uganda, Cadena, and Schoar (2011) found that sending a monthly text message (SMS) before the loan payment is due has as large an impact on repayment as paying a cash reward upon completion of repayment of the loan. In related research, Gine et al. (2012) analyzed the effects of the use of biometric identification, more specifically fingerprinting, on credit market related outcomes such as debt repayments and loan size. Using a field experiment in Malawi where potential borrowers are randomly assigned into a control group and a group of which fingerprints are taken, they found that fingerprinting led to a substantially higher repayment rate for those borrowers that had an ex ante higher risk of default.[9]

---

[9] Note that in both the control and treatment group, potential borrowers were informed about the importance of credit history in ensuring access to credit in the future.

21.5 CONCLUSION

This chapter summarizes the gaps in financial inclusion in Africa, the obstacles faced in expanding formal financial services, and the opportunities offered by new delivery channels and technology. Despite financial sector growth in Africa over the past decades, many individuals and firms are still excluded from using formal financial services. Ownership of accounts and the use of formal savings and credit are low in Africa, both in absolute terms and relative to other developing regions. However, the low use of formal financial products does not reflect a lack of demand for financial services. Instead, African individuals and firms predominantly rely on informal channels, such as savings with community savings groups and borrowing from family and friends, to manage their financial needs.

Yet new innovations have the potential to bring about dramatic changes—the most evident example being the recent success of mobile money in East Africa—which has encouraged people to make formal payments by lowering entry barriers, reducing costs, and expanding access. By embracing technological progress in mobile technology, establishing an enabling regulatory environment for new financial inclusion initiatives, and increasing public-private partnerships, Africa has taken steps to expanding financial inclusion. New technologies offer the potential to provide affordable and accessible financial services, particularly to the rural poor.

ACKNOWLEDGMENTS

We thank Gallup, Inc. for the excellent survey execution and related support. We are grateful to the Bill & Melinda Gates Foundation for providing financial support making the collection and dissemination of the data possible. This chapter's findings, interpretations, and conclusions are entirely those of the authors and do not necessarily represent the views of the World Bank, their Executive Directors, or the countries they represent.

REFERENCES

Aker, J.C., Boumnijel, R., McClelland, A., and Tierney, N. (2013). How Do Electronic Transfers Compare? Evidence from a Mobile Cash Transfer Experiment in Niger, mimeo, Tufts University.

Akpalu, W., Alnaa, S.E., and Aglobitse, P.B. (2012). Access to microfinance and intra household business decision making: Implication for efficiency of female owned enterprises in Ghana. *Journal of Socio-Economics*, 4(5):513–518.

Allen, F., Carletti, E., Cull, R. et al. (2013). Resolving the African Financial Development Gap: Cross-Country Comparisons and a Within-Country Study of Kenya, Policy Research Paper 6592. Washington, DC: World Bank.

Allen, F., Demirgüc-Kunt, A., Klapper, Leora, and Soledad Martinez Peria, M. (2012). The Foundations of Financial Inclusion: Understanding Ownership and Use of Formal Accounts, Policy Research Paper 6290. Washington, DC: World Bank.

Aportela, F. (1999). Effects of Financial Access on Savings by Low-Income People, mimeo, Banco de Mexico.

Banerjee, A., and Duflo E. (2007). The economic lives of the poor. *Journal of Economic Perspectives*, 21(1):141–167.

Beck, T., and Cull, R. (2014). Banking in Africa, in A. Berger, P. Molyneux, and J. Wilson (eds), *The Oxford Handbook of Banking*, 2nd edn. Oxford: Oxford University Press.

Beck, T., Demirgüç-Kunt, A., and Levine, R. (2007). Finance, inequality and the poor. *Journal of Economic Growth*, 12(1):27–49.

Beck, T., Feyen, E., Ize, A., and Moizeszowicz, F. (2008). Benchmarking Financial Development, Policy Research Working Paper 4638. Washington, DC: World Bank.

Beck, T., Levine, R., and Loayza, N. (2000). Finance and the sources of growth. *Journal of Financial Economics*, 58(1–2):261–300.

Behrman, J. R. (1988). Intrahousehold Allocation of Nutrients in Rural India: Are Boys Favored? Do Parents Exhibit Inequality Aversion? *Oxford Economic Papers*, 40(1):32–54.

Besley, T. (1995). Savings, Credit and Insurance, in J. Behrman and T.N. Srinivasan (eds), *Handbook of Development Economics*, Volume III. Elsevier, pp. 2123–2207.

Bruhn, M., and Love, I. (2009). The economic impact of banking the unbanked: Evidence from Mexico. Policy Research Working Paper No. 4981. Washington, DC: World Bank.

Brune, L., Gine, X., Goldberg, J., and Yang, D. (2011). Commitments to save: a field experiment in rural Malawi, Policy Research Paper 5748. Washington, DC: World Bank.

Burgess, R., and Pande, R. (2005). Do rural banks matter? Evidence from the Indian social banking experiment. *American Economic Review*, 95(3):780–795.

Cadena, X., and Schoar, A. (2011). Remembering to Pay? Reminders vs. Financial Incentives for Loan Payments, NBER Working Papers 17020, National Bureau of Economic Research, Inc.

Clarke, G.R.G., Xu, L.C., and Zou, H.-f. (2006). Finance and income inequality: what do the data tell us? *Southern Economic Journal*, 72(3):578–596.

Collins, D., Morduch, J., Rutherford, S., and Ruthven, O. (2009). *Portfolios of the Poor*. Princeton, NJ: Princeton University Press.

Crépon, B., Devoto, F., Duflo, E., and Parienté, W. (2011). Impact of Microcredit in Rural Areas of Morocco: Evidence from a Randomized Evaluation. MIT, mimeo.

de Mel, S., McKenzie, D., and Woodruff, C. (2008). Returns to capital: results from a randomized experiment. *Quarterly Journal of Economics*, 123(4):1329–1372.

Demirgüç-Kunt, A., and Klapper, L. (2013). Measuring Financial Inclusion: The Global Findex Database. Brookings Papers on Economic Activity.

Demirgüç-Kunt, A., and Levine, R. (2009). Finance and inequality: theory and evidence. *Annual Review of Financial Economics*, 1(1):287–318.

Dupas, P., and Robinson, J. (2013). Savings constraints and microenterprise development: evidence from a field experiment in Kenya. *American Economic Journal: Applied Economics*, 5(1):33–44.

Funkhouser, E. (1999). Cyclical economic conditions and school attendance in Costa Rica. *Economics of Education Review*, 18(1):31–50.

Gine, X., Goldberg, J., and Yang, D. (2012). Credit market consequences of improved personal identification: field experimental evidence from Malawi. *American Economic Review*, 102(6):2923–2954.

Gine, X., and Yang, D. (2009). Insurance, credit, and technology adoption: field experimental evidence from Malawi. *Journal of Development Economics*, 89(1):1–11.

Hill, R., and Viceisza, A. (2012). A field experiment on the impact of weather shocks and insurance on risky investment. *Experimental Economics*, 15(2):341–371.

Honohan, P. (2008). Cross-country variation in household access to financial services. *Journal of Banking & Finance*, 32(11):2493–2500.

Jacoby, H., and Skoufias, E. (1992). Risk, Seasonality and School Attendance: Evidence from Rural India, RCER Working Papers 328, University of Rochester, Center for Economic Research (RCER).

Jack, W., and Suri, T. (2011). Mobile Money: The Economics of M-PESA, NBER Working Papers 16721, National Bureau of Economic Research, Inc.

Jakiela, P., and Ozier, O. (2012). Does Africa need a rotten kin theorem? Experimental evidence from village economies, Policy Research Working Paper Series 6085. Washington, DC: World Bank.

Jensen, R. (2000). Agricultural volatility and investments in children. *American Economic Review*, 90(2):399–404.

Karlan, D., Darko Osei, R., Osei-Akoto, I., and Udry, C. (2012). Agricultural Decisions after Relaxing Credit and Risk Constraints, NBER Working Papers 18463, National Bureau of Economic Research, Inc.

Karlan, D., and Zinman, J. (2010). Expanding credit access: using randomized supply decisions to estimate the impacts. *Review of Financial Studies*, 23(1):433–464.

King, R.G., and Levine, R. (1993). Finance and growth: Schumpeter might be right. *Quarterly Journal of Economics*, 108(3):717–737.

Klapper, L., Laeven, L., and Rajan, R. (2006). Entry regulation as a barrier to entrepreneurship. *Journal of Financial Economics*, 82(3):591–629.

Mbiti, I., and Weil, D.N. (2011). Mobile banking: the impact of M-Pesa in Kenya. NBER Working Papers 17129, National Bureau of Economic Research, Inc.

Morduch, J. (1995). Income smoothing and consumption smoothing. *Journal of Economic Perspectives*, 9(3):103–114.

Platteau, J.-P. (2009). Institutional obstacles to African economic development: state, ethnicity, and custom. *Journal of Economic Behavior & Organization*, 71(3):669–689.

Prina, S. (2012). Do Basic Savings Accounts Help the Poor to Save? Evidence from a Field Experiment in Nepal, mimeo, Case Western Reserve.

Rajan, R.G., and Zingales, L. (1998). Financial dependence and growth. *American Economic Review*, 88(3):559–586.

Robinson, J, and Yeh, E. (2011). Transactional sex as a response to risk in Western Kenya. *American Economic Journal: Applied Economics*, 3(1):35–64.

Rosenzweig, M., and Wolpin, K. (1993). Credit market constraints, consumption smoothing, and the accumulation of durable production assets in low-income countries: investments in bullocks in India. *Journal of Political Economy*, 101(2):223–244.

Winter-Nelson, A., and Temu, A.A. (2005). Liquidity constraints, access to credit and pro-poor growth in rural Tanzania. *Journal of International Development*, 17(7):867–882.

World Bank (2013). *Global Financial Development Report 2014: Financial Inclusion*. Washington, DC: World Bank.

APPENDIX 1

Financial Inclusion in Africa and the Rest of the World

Region	% of adults with formal account (2011)	% of adults with formal savings in the past year (2011)	% of adults with formal credit in the past year (2011)	% of SMEs with a formal account (2011*)	% of SMEs with a loan or credit line (2011*)	commercial bank branches per 100,000 adults (2011*)
Africa	23.44	12.56	4.62	85.23	15.34	5.86
Central Africa	11.95	5.90	3.50	78.76	13.45	2.50
Eastern Africa	28.02	15.65	7.47	85.87	18.05	3.52
North Africa	17.17	4.00	3.40			8.94
Southern Africa	51.14	21.30	8.59	97.39	29.48	10.31
Western Africa	22.58	16.74	2.92	83.86	10.93	5.84
East Asia and Pacific	54.94	28.45	8.59	68.73	26.14	8.24
Europe and Central Asia	44.88	6.97	7.68	90.64	32.23	25.47
High income	89.51	44.67	13.91	91.33	48.55	34.84
Latin America and Caribbean	39.33	9.72	7.94	88.34	48.78	28.79
Middle East	14.83	5.14	7.23	37.10	5.32	6.88
South Asia	32.96	11.09	8.69	77.23	11.05	10.07
World	50.39	22.36	9.06	82.00	29.25	18.73

Notes: The asterisk (*) means data are from the year 2011 or the most recent year available. The variables % of adults with formal (i) account, (ii) savings in the past year, and (iii) credit in the past year are all from the Global Findex database (Demirgüç-Kunt and Klapper 2013). The variables related to the small and medium enterprises (SMEs) are taken from the Enterprise Surveys of the World Bank, and commercial bank branches per 100,000 adults are taken from the Financial Access Surveys of the International Monetary Fund. All regional averages are population weighted.

CHAPTER 22

....

FINANCIAL MARKETS DEVELOPMENT IN AFRICA
Reflections and the Way Forward

....

KALU OJAH AND ODONGO KODONGO

22.1 INTRODUCTION

....

WHAT is the state of Africa's financial markets development and what should it be? The answers to these questions reside within the context of the finance—growth nexus. The decades-long debate about financial development and economic growth has been less about whether or not a nexus exists between them but more about the nature of that association. In other words, does financial development lead economic growth or the other way around? Starting from Schumpeter (1911) to date, several scholars have argued that finance leads economic growth (e.g. Patrick 1966; King and Levine 1993a, b; Levine and Zervos 1998; Odedokun 1996; Rajan and Zingales 1998; Beck et al. 2000; and others) while others have argued that financial development actually follows economic development to supply its expanding financing needs (e.g. Robinson 1952; Lucas 1988; Romer 1990; and others). However, since the influential works of King and Levine (1993a, b), the preponderance of evidence appears to suggest that finance does indeed lead economic growth.

Interestingly designed empirical studies that provide convincing evidence on this dominant viewpoint include Demirguc-Kunt and Maksimovic (1996), Levine and Zervos (1998), Rajan and Zingales (1998), and Beck et al. (2000). Another group of studies nuance further the "how" of the finance-leading-growth phenomenon: Patrick (1966), Rousseau and Watchel (1998, 2000), Luintel and Khan 1999; Beck et al. (2000), Beck and Demirguc-Kunt (2006), and others, found that the level, or stage, of economic development of a country particularly determines the direction of the relation between financial development and economic growth. In fact, these studies show that economies at the take-off and/or fast-growth stages of development generally tend to get the most lift from financial development.[1] This

[1] Most of the noted findings have been registered in developed economies. These economies are usually characterized by various fast evolving production technologies that require equally fast evolving financing models that are responsive to attendant new and special funding needs (Patrick 1966; Chandler 1977; Stern 1989; Boyd and Smith 1996, 1998; Luintel and Khan 1999; Shan et al. 2001).

evidence became so widely accepted that influential international development organizations, such as the IMF and World Bank, bought into it and started pushing for financial system reform, liberalization and development among its member states—especially the developing and emerging economies.

In the light of the pervasive stagnant and retrogressive growth effects of Africa's lost decade (the 1980s), countries in the developing world, particularly in Africa and Latin America, were evidently persuaded to embrace the financial system liberalization and reform agenda (Henry 2000a, b; Kim and Singal 2000; Bekaert et al. 2005; and de la Torre et al. 2007). These reforms took the following forms: establishment of new stock exchanges, privatization of state owned enterprises as a way of deepening the stock exchanges, liberalization of interest rates and foreign exchange regimes; divestment of governments' ownership of banks, opening of bank ownership to foreigners, restructuring of regulations to encourage product innovation and credit provision to the private sector, among other forms.

Expectedly, the reform and development programs African countries embarked upon have yielded some fruits (e.g. Allen et al. 2011, 2012). However, all the reviews, some quite in-depth, unanimously lament how much Africa's financial development lags those of other developing countries, despite acknowledged northward trajectory of Africa's financial markets' growth indicators (Andrianaivo and Yartey 2010; Allen et al. 2011, 2012). Yet, analyses of the finance–growth nexus in Africa (Adjasi and Biekpe 2006; Enisan and Olufisayo 2009; Andrianaivo and Yartey 2010) register results supportive of the beneficial growth lift that can result from financial development.

In other words, these findings hold out an encouraging, if not, great promise from finance for Africa. However, as Allen et al. (2012) incisively point out, that promise could best be realized by unearthing or devising financial markets development methods that are essentially outside of our current standard formulae. Thus, the key questions we explore in this chapter are: (i) Are Africa's financial markets sufficiently developed to lead sustainable and inclusive economic growth?[2] (ii) If the answer to the preceding question is not in the affirmative, as available reviews appear to indicate, what steps should be taken to get the African region there?

We commence our analysis by first recapping, in a broad sense, the state of financial markets development in Africa, with a particular focus on the extent to which they are enabling (or not enabling) meaningful economic activity. A seemingly difficult task is the issue of ascertaining what constitutes "economic relevance" of a financial market. We attempt to resolve this definitional difficulty by gauging the extent of architectural defects of specific financial markets, level of adequate requisite infrastructure underpinning these markets, extent to which suppliers span these markets, and general benchmarking of these markets to their peer groups.

Importantly, the objects of this analysis of economic relevance are the key traditional financial markets of public equity market, private equity (venture capital) market, private debt (banking industry) and public debt (bond) markets. Following the assessment of each market's economic relevance are reasoned ideas that we believe will take the markets to

---

[2] When financial development has a long-term relation with economic growth, it connotes *sustainable* growth. However, when such growth pulls an incremental portion of the formerly unemployed into the employed category, causes a significant number of people to earn incomes that are above the poverty level, or reduces income inequality gap, we deem the growth to be *inclusive*.

where they should be—i.e. to the state where they enable sustainable and/or inclusive economic growth.

Though African countries' macroeconomic and financial landscapes are not homogenous, we focus on major financial markets from regionally representative African countries, which permit a reasonable level of generalization of our analysis. This selection is made up of Kenya, Tanzania, and Uganda (East Africa); Algeria, Egypt, Morocco, and Tunisia (North Africa); Botswana, Mauritius, Namibia, South Africa, Zambia, and Zimbabwe (Southern Africa); and Ghana, Ivory Coast, and Nigeria (West Africa).

The remainder of the study proceeds as follows. Section 2 introduces the economic importance of the public equity market, assesses its current economic relevance within Africa, and presents possible ways by which this market type can be improved to fulfill its potential as a lever for economic growth. Sections 3, 4 and 5, repeat the same set of systematic analyses for private equity, private debt, and public debt markets, respectively. Section 6 summarizes and concludes.

22.2 THE PUBLIC EQUITY MARKET

Public equity markets, generally understood in the context of organized stock exchanges, are the most prominent face of financial markets worldwide. They provide a platform for corporations (or companies) to access external capital funds (primary market), and for holders of these issued ownership certificates to trade them in a secondary market (liquidity provision). The corporation legal form of business separates ownership from the actual operation of the business and permits firms to access funds with contracts of relative "indefinite" maturity.

This separation of ownership from operation raises agency problems which require effective corporate governance to manage; effective governance, in turn, enhances efficiency of firms' operations, normally reflected in their profitability. Further, the attendant widespread following of corporations by investors and other stakeholders makes it easier to ascertain the ownership value of production entities (price discovery). And this price discovery facility essentially turns stock price indices into useful leading economic indicators. In that same vein, Henry (2013) has amply demonstrated its further macroeconomic usefulness as an effective gauge of policy initiatives' likely success or otherwise[3]. Given these flagged important features, it is straight forward to see that a well-functioning stock market can enable increased economic activity. What is the current state of stock markets in Africa?

22.2.1 Current state of public equity markets in Africa

Perhaps an interesting entry point into issues of this sub-section is the debate that is implicit in juxtaposing Singh's (1999) analysis and conclusion to those of both Henry (2013) and other

---

[3] Given that extant stock pricing models rest on discounting of expected future cash flows of companies, Henry (2013) shows that in the aggregate, as reflected in the stock price index, the public equity market provides a useful tool for gauging the likely success or failure of a future-oriented macroeconomic policy. The assumption here is that the national stock market functions reasonably well most of the time (i.e. relatively efficient).

empirical studies mentioned earlier. Firstly, upon comparing economic growth of "stock market-based versus bank-based capitalism" and a broad-brush review of Africa's stock markets, Singh (1999) made his famous statement about "African countries' promotion of stock market capitalism being a costly irrelevance which they can ill-afford."[4] Consequently, he recommends focus on the banking industry as priority for Africa. Yet he notes, in the same breadth, that Africa's banking systems are bedeviled by state ownership which is characterized by inept, corrupt and "political" management; and foreign ownership which, more or less, caters to their home-countries' multinational firms which these foreign banks follow off-shore.

Secondly, the above diagnosis, on its own, seems to us not a strong enough basis upon which to recommend bank- or stock market-based capitalism for Africa. Stacking the above diagnosis against Henry's (2013) observation of the vital role a sufficiently functioning stock market plays in ascertaining likely successful growth policies, and the strong empirical evidence affirming that stock markets and banks are complementary, as mechanisms for enabling economic growth (Demirguc-Kunt and Levine 1996; Levine and Zervos 1998; Garcia and Liu 1999; Naceur et al. 2007; Andrianaivo and Yartey 2010), yields two seemingly obvious takeaways in support of the wisdom of stock market development by African countries. One, stock markets serve an additional development-enabling purpose besides the usual refrain of savings mobilization, resource allocation, liquidity provisioning, risk sharing, etc.

Two, the empirical evidence from analyses of finance—growth nexus appears not to suggest the necessity of sequencing the development of financial market types. In fact, Levine (2002), in a detailed cross-country investigation of differential growth effects of financial market types (structures), concluded that there exists no such differential. Rather, he documents that it is the quality of the financial services provided by either the bank- or stock market-based financial market that enables economic growth. Yet another important complementarity of stock markets and banks which finance—growth nexus models do not usually reflect is the fact that stock market listing plays signaling and bonding roles for the listed firm and, thus, enhance the firm's access to debt funds at a relatively affordable price (Smith 1986). In fact, Singh's (1999) observation that bank-based capital markets such as Germany's and Japan's are superior to stock market-based ones ignores the fact that these countries also have public equity markets. Therefore, given these often ignored reinforcing roles of stock markets coupled with the tax deductibility of debt capital, it is no surprise that firms across the globe universally fill the majority of their external financing need via debt capital, including firms in countries with "stock market-based" capital markets such as the USA and UK (Rajan and Zingales 1995; Gwatidzo and Ojah 2014).

Germane to our analysis is the issue of the "economic relevance" of Africa's national stock markets, which can be assessed by looking at their (i) size, proxied by stock market capitalization scaled by GDP, (ii) efficiency (liquidity), represented by value of traded shares scaled by the stock market capitalization or by GDP, (iii) supply of equity capital, represented by the number of firms listed on the stock exchanges; and (iv) architectural (or infrastructural)

[4] An interesting but often ignored point to note about Singh's (1999) exposition, is his pointing out the fact that the "exemplary" bank-based capitalism which he said yielded superior economic growth relative to market-based capitalism, actually had governments (i.e. of Germany, Japan, Taiwan, and South Korea) use state-owned banks to fund long-life industrial development projects. Not that banks, by construction and of their own volition, embarked upon funding these long-term national industrial projects.

adequacy of the market, represented by trading system, clearing/settlement facility, regulation and legal environment, and/or ICT penetration. These indicators are presented in Tables 22.1 and 22.2, for major African countries.

As Table 22.1 shows Africa's national stock markets are small in size relative to the overall economies they are meant to support and compared to those in representative emerging economies (India, Indonesia, and Korea). Stock market capitalization scaled by GDP of

Table 22.1 Stock market indicators of economic relevance by country and over time

Country	Market capitalization 2000 and 2010		Traded value 2000 and 2010		Turnover ratio 2000 and 2010		Listed firms 2000 and 2010	
East Africa								
Kenya	13.4	46	0.4	3.5	3.6	8.6	57	53
Tanzania	6	10	0.4	0.06	3	-	6	7
Uganda	0.025*	10.4	0.006*	0.058	0.23*	0.36	2*	8
Regional average	**6.5**	**22**	**0.3**	**1.21**	**2.3**	**4.5**	**21.7**	**22.7**
North Africa								
Algeria	-	-	0.04	5.58	-	-	-	6
Egypt	25	13.4	11.1	1.1	34.7	11	876	746
Morocco	29.3	75.8	3.0	11.8	9.2	16.3	-	44
Tunisia	15.2	24.1	3.2	3.8	23.3	17.2	37	54
Regional average	**23.2**	**42.2**	**5.8**	**5.6**	**22.4**	**14.8**	**321.3**	**213**
Southern Africa								
Botswana	13.9	27.4	0.8	0.9	4.8	3.5	14	21
Mauritius	35	66.9	-	3.7	-	6.4	38	86
Namibia	11.8	9.7	0.6	0.2	4.5	1.8	13	7
South Africa	158	278	58.3	93.5	33.9	39.6	469	360
Zambia	8.2	17.4	0.2	0.8	-	4	7	19
Zimbabwe	43	153.6	3.8	15.3	10.8	-	67	76
Regional average	**45**	**92.2**	**12.7**	**19.1**	**13.5**	**11.1**	**101.3**	**95**
West Africa								
Ghana	16.3	11.3	0.2	0.3	1.5	3.4	21	35
Ivory Coast	10.7	31.2	0.3	0.6	2.6	2	36	38
Nigeria	10.1	26.3	0.6	2.7	7.3	12.5	188	215
Regional average	**12.4**	**22.9**	**0.4**	**1.2**	**3.8**	**6**	**81.7**	**96**
Emerging countries	**26.7**	**84**	**66**	**80.7**	**197**	**120.7**	**2504**	**2396**
Developed countries	135	118	284	209	201	189	6355	4279

Sources: World Development Indices.

* As of June 2001. Data obtained from the Uganda Securities Exchange website.

Table 22.2 Infrastructure support indicators of stock markets

Country	Trading system	Clearing and settlement system	Legal environment[1]	ICT facility[2]
East Africa				
Kenya	Electronic	Manual	−0.69	0.904
Tanzania	Electronic	Electronic	−0.46	0.404
Uganda	Electronic	Manual	−0.48	0.586
Regional average	N/A	N/A	**−0.54**	**0.63**
North Africa				
Algeria	Electronic	Electronic	−0.86	8.897
Egypt	Electronic	Electronic	−0.27	14.873
Morocco	Electronic	Manual	−0.13	7.666
Tunisia	Electronic	Electronic	−0.02	12.449
Regional average	N/A	N/A	**−0.32**	**10.97**
Southern Africa				
Botswana	Manual	Manual	0.70	7.349
Mauritius	Electronic	Electronic	0.80	28.659
Namibia	Electronic	Manual	0.22	6.557
South Africa	Electronic	Electronic	0.19	9.657
Zambia	Electronic	Electronic	−0.51	0.770
Zimbabwe	Manual	Manual	−1.92	2.581
Regional average	N/A	N/A	**0.09**	**9.26**
West Africa				
Ghana	Manual	Manual	0.04	1.604
Ivory Coast	Electronic	Electronic	−1.10	1.285
Nigeria	Electronic	Electronic	−0.96	1.046
Regional average	N/A	N/A	**−0.67**	**1.31**
Emerging Countries	Electronic	Electronic	–	–
Developed Countries	Electronic	Electronic	1.39	44.87

[1] Average of regulatory quality, rule of law and control of corruption, as of 2010. Data obtained from World Governance Indices.
[2] Number of main telephone lines per 100 inhabitants (latest available for the period 2000–2008. Data obtained from World Development Indices).
Trading and clearing/settlement systems data are adopted from Allen et al. (2011). N/A denotes not applicable.

representative emerging economies was 84 as at 2010, compared to 28, 42, 92, and 23 for East and Central Africa, North Africa, Southern Africa, and West Africa, respectively. The more telling comparison has to do with the efficiency/liquidity of the markets (turnover ratio) and the extent of equity capital supply (listed firms). None of Africa's regional indicators reaches one tenth of these efficiency and supply indicators of the representative emerging economies. The importance of these indicators can be seen in their sensitivities to business cycle—most African regions, the emerging economies and the developed ones showed a decline in these indicators from 2000 to 2010 (which bears beginning effects of the slow recovery from the global financial crisis of 2007/8).

In terms of what Ladekarl and Zervos (2004) term "plumbing" matters of financial markets (such as trading and clearing systems, regulatory and legal framework, infrastructure, etc.), African countries appear to have made some progress. As at 2010 (Table 22.2), most of Africa's stock exchanges have adopted electronic trading and clearing/settlement systems, and there has been an increased awareness of the importance of effective legal environment needed for well-functioning financial markets. Unsurprisingly, the above summary of African countries' stock market inadequacies supports the detailed analyses by Singh (1999), Andrianaivo and Yartey (2010), Allen et al. (2011), and Allen et al. (2012). However, the focus of this article is both to reinforce the importance of specific financial markets and how they can possibly be improved to reflect effectively that importance in eliciting sustainable growth.

22.2.2 Possible ways of improving Africa's stock markets

As pointed out in section 2.1, the case of African countries establishing stock markets has been made by juxtaposing the insights from Singh (1999) and Henry (2013). Additional to those insights, two further observations are germane. We argue that the cost of embarking upon potentially irrelevant country-wide policies would dwarf the cost of establishing stock markets, mainly because policy decisions are often made without proper sensitivity analysis of the sort highlighted by Henry, and with tax payers' money at risk should these policies fail. Conversely, stock markets are usually managed and sometimes initiated by the private sector. Thus, the cost of stock markets' teething problems will most directly be borne by the private sector while their negative spill-overs (Singh 1999: 352–353) can be addressed partly by the improvement that comes by growth and partly by government oversight.

Furthermore, Singh advises against African countries establishing stock market capitalism, "at this stage in their development," without indicating which stage of development would be more appropriate. We believe that stage or moment could not be any more appropriate than the stage of development where financial constraint has been variously and consistently found to be an important obstacle to growth in Africa (Collier and Gunning 1999; Bigsten et al. 2003; Beck and Demirguc-Kunt 2006; Ojah et al. 2010). With potential growth benefit of stock markets in Africa having been established (Adjasi and Biekpe 2006; Enisan and Olufisayo 2009; Andrianaivo and Yartey 2010), we suggest possible solutions to the problems currently bedeviling Africa's stock markets.

One possible way of addressing the problem of size and illiquidity is mandating investment of ring-fenced portion of public pension funds in domestic stock markets (say a minimum of 30% of such funds). Not only would this increase trading activity of national stock markets, but it can also motivate private companies to go public as a way of accessing the potentially huge savings pool provided by such an important institutional investor. In Africa, Swaziland has enacted a law mandating key institutional investors to channel a significant portion of their long-term assets into the equity market (see Impavido et al. 2003; Swaziland 2005, 2010). This approach has also been used to expand the size of debt and equity markets in some developing economies (Chan-Lau 2004). The timing of this recommendation could not be more appropriate, as Kaniki and Ntuli (2011) have shown the promising commencement and growth of pension funds in Africa.

To complement this size expansion and liquidity enhancement effort, guided-privatization of government-owned or significantly controlled enterprises can augment the effects of legislated investment of pension funds' cash in fledgling public equity markets. As Chan-Lau (2004) observed, the sheer size of pension funds may not find commensurate scale of equity shares supply; thus, making its uptake untenable. The supply of additional equity shares through privatization will go some ways in addressing this problem. Further, the prefix "guided" attached to privatization is meant to stress the need that the suggested government intervention must be aimed at dispersed households directly or by way of institutional investors that represent households (e.g. mutual fund companies). Institutional investors will, in turn, bring additional liquidity to these stock markets.

The chiefs of West African stock exchanges just signed a memorandum of agreement committing them to a virtual tying-up that allows stocks of Ghanaian companies, for instance, to list in Nigerian and Sierra Leonean bourses (Guardian Newspaper 2014). This will increase firms' access to finance across West Africa, increase the liquidity of such cross-listed stocks, and force respective national bourses to upgrade to the standard institutional and physical infrastructures that support well-functioning stock markets. This kind of virtual integration of bourses across sub-regions of Africa should foster the efficiency and supply capacity of Africa's markets, without any of them losing their national identity. These qualities (subsumed broadly under liquidity) are the ingredients that enable stock markets to elicit sustainable economic growth (Levine and Zervos 1998).

The recommended integration of bourses across regions of Africa would also require institutional infrastructures. This is an area of financial markets improvement that is readily amenable to legislative intervention. As Ojah and Mokoaleli-Mokoteli (2012) observe, financial reporting and disclosure are important, often government mandated, mechanism for mitigating information asymmetry between managers of firms and parties contracting with their firms; this in turn enhances liquidity of stock markets and particularly reduces cost of funds. Therefore, government effort at ensuring that quality accounting process and efficient mode of dissemination are followed in reporting listed firms' activities will enhance the efficiency of Africa's stock markets.

A final thought on how to further increase their size and liquidity: establishing and enabling private equity markets could serve as a potentially powerful tool for providing bridge equity finance that invariably deepens public equity markets in Africa. We turn to the analysis of this market type next.

22.3 THE PRIVATE EQUITY MARKET

The private equity market encompasses all equity funding provisioning that are effected outside the public equity market; that is, all platforms that provide equity (ownership) capital to firms that are privately owned and operated. Though the word equity/ownership connotes longevity, it is not necessarily so in the context of the private equity market; rather its use here would be best understood in the context of our more aptly descriptive coinage of "bridge equity capital." It provides long-term funds for a determinate period of typically five to ten years[5] for the purpose of starting a business; shepherding a fledgling business to a viable, going-concern state; and/or aiding the restructuring of an inefficient formerly publicly held business back to the path of efficiency. Private equity markets can be of enterprise-creating or efficiency-enhancing forms. The first form finds expression in venture capital/angel finance-type private equity markets; the second finds expression in the "market for corporate control," usually effected through going private transactions. It is worth noting the necessity that an effective secondary equity market must exist for there to exist a market for corporate control (Smith 1986; Cumming et al. 2007).

As Ojah (2009) points out, there is a private equity market type that is right for Africa's financial landscape and there is a wrong type. Ojah makes a case for the venture capital/angel finance: "it is largely a private equity fund provided to privately-held firms that possess attractive product concept(s) that are yet to attain sustainable consumers' acceptance" (Ojah 2011). Start-ups or fledgling firms characteristically lack track records (transparency) or substantial assets (collateral), which can individually or jointly facilitate access to term loans at attractive prices; and often, they are widespread in legal environments that ordinarily support non-complex financial contracts that avail reasonable capital funds to businesses. Venture capital markets, by construction, internalize the shortcomings of such a less than adequate legal environment by entitling: funds providers' ownership of the venture business, a role in management of the business, and the prerogative of how best to disburse provided funds in ways that foster performance (Sahlman 1990; Black and Gilson 1998).

According to Ojah (2009), the economic importance of the right kind of private equity markets for developing economies, especially those in Africa is one that provides:

- entrepreneurs sorely needed capital funds which more conventional financial institutions, particularly banks, would not provide
- equity capital which, unlike debt capital, is not subject to frequent debt servicing and principal renegotiation obligation
- managerial support that plays the important role of shepherding entrepreneurship to a sustainable, and often, publicly held enterprise, and
- effective exit mechanisms for investors that, in turn, foster efficient allocation of scarce enterprise-creating resources.

22.3.1 Current state of private equity markets in Africa

Apart from South Africa, which has a private equity market as developed and/or sophisticated as private equity markets found in developed national financial markets, private equity markets are fortunately taking root in African countries in largely the form which Ojah (2009) deems the right form for Africa—the venture capital/angel finance form. Private equity markets largely take this form in Kenya, Egypt, Tunisia and Morocco, Mauritius,

---

[5] At the end of the typical holding period, the private equity market provides several exit options to its investors: share buy-back by managers of the venture firm, merger and acquisition with established firms, sell-off of the now viable business to established firms, or initial public offering, whereby the now viable firm transfers its ownership to publicly distributed new owners. Clearly, the last two exit options feed viable enterprises into the pool of listed firms of the public equity market.

Namibia and Zambia, and Ghana, Ivory Coast, and Nigeria. South Africa has a reasonable combination of both forms of the private equity market, with more of the absolute dollar amount in the efficiency-enhancing form of the market (Andrianaivo and Yartey 2010; and Allen et al. 2011).

The collective presence of the private equity markets in Africa is competitive with those in Latin America and Mid East regions, but quite small, in general, by international standards (with the exception of South Africa where its size is about 2.8% of GDP). According to Andrianaivo and Yartey (2010), South Africa and Nigeria account for 90% of the private equity market in Africa, with a share of 80 and 10%, respectively. The bulk of the funds supply to these African markets comes from the US and Europe (about 70%), largely through development finance institutions; the next important source of supply is South Africa's pension and endowment funds.

22.3.2 Possible ways forward for Africa's private equity markets

Interestingly, the bulk of the relatively more advanced public equity markets in Africa have some presence of private equity market activity. This correlation points to a "low hanging-fruit" type solution to an often cited obstacle to venture capital market growth—the lack of effective IPO markets, which obviously depend on the effectiveness of national organized exchanges. Therefore, targeted efforts at improving "plumbing" matters of public equity markets in African countries will attract more private equity funds for enterprise creation.

Though IPOs have been shown to yield the highest investors' return at the point of exiting venture capital investments (Sahlman 1990; Amit et al. 1998; Shepherd and Zacharakis 2001; and Ojah 2011), the Israeli experience provide an alternative effective source of eventual liquidity for Africa's venture capital market—sell-off to firms in "relevant" industries. The majority of venture capital fund-grown enterprises have been divested readily through sell-off to corporations in the US and Europe; importantly, these venture capital-backed firms have largely been in the defense and ICT industries. African countries can leverage this exit alternative by guiding their venture capital funds to growing businesses for which there will be ready markets domestically and/or internationally, for example in: agro-business, biogenetic, renewable energy production, and ICT.

Given that the bulk of the funds supply of this market comes largely from overseas development financial institutions, these suppliers should be encouraged to channel their funds to supporting start-ups and fledgling businesses in the areas that would most readily impact economic activity in African economies and eventually attract ready buyers. To have this foreign intervention be more effective than aids/grants, it must be devoid of direct local political association, except perhaps in jointly creating network of potential ventures needing venture capital (Ojah 2009).

In support of the creative approach of rallying community development funds and deep-pocket individuals for venture capital funds creation, suggested by Ojah (2009), a concerted effort to sell a similar idea to funds in the diasporas would further swell the pool of venture capital funds to support more enterprise creation. Going by the contribution that remittances now make to Africa's GDPs, Diaspora's funds hold promise for Africa's private equity markets if cleverly explored.

22.4 Private Debt Markets

Private debt markets, are financial services firms which pool unconsumed incomes from economic agents (i.e. surplus saving units) with the express intent of, in turn, repackaging the pooled funds into various denominations of credits, via private contracting and for a fee, to finance activities of economic agents in need of funds in excess of that in their possession (i.e., deficit saving units). One can reasonably assert that this intermediation function is performed most effectively by banks: empirical evidence shows that the majority of external finance used by firms across the world is private debt funds provided by banks (Rajan and Zingales 1995, 1998; Mishkin 2004; Gwatidzo and Ojah 2014).

A combination of factors can be adduced as to why banks emerge the dominant financial intermediary for firms' external funds provisioning. The seemingly obvious reason could be their superior expertise around intermediation which has been built up since the inception of fractional reserve banking. This historical fact suggests that, among financial intermediaries, banks are likely best able to reduce transaction costs. As Mishkin (2004) details, banks are able to use private contracts of various degrees of complexity to internalize ramifications of information asymmetry[6] between lenders and borrowers. Consequently, banks are able to provide personal loans, diverse money market- and term-loans to businesses, and even provide frequently rolled-over debt to government by perennially holding in their assets portfolio sizeable amounts of Treasury bills and bonds. They are equally able and versed in pooling funds by raising diverse kinds of IOUs against themselves in addition to using debentures and ordinary and preferred shares for capital structure purposes.

In other words, banks are relatively more adept at sharing and trading risks that are inherent in financial intermediation than are other financial intermediaries, almost all of which are specialized in both their pooling of funds and their provisioning of credits. Therefore, the private contracting flexibility of banks, their versatility at using diverse products for funds pooling and credit provisioning, and their experiential superiority in information gathering and credit risk assessment, highlight their importance as a veritable mechanism for mobilizing investable funds for production in a widespread manner. Essentially, banks are quite effective at intermediating both denominations and maturities of investable funds, and ultimately redistributing risks inherent in the intermediation process in ways that enable production affordably.

Finally, an important and often underappreciated function of the banking industry is that it provides the vital payment and settlement mechanisms within and across nation states. As a result, banks serve as a critical conduit for effecting monetary policy. This, in turn, makes

---

[6] Ramifications of information asymmetry are the costs from "hidden material facts" (adverse selection) and "hidden action" (moral hazard) incurred in the context of financial intermediation (see Stiglitz and Weiss 1981; Diamond 1984; and Mishkin 2004 for details).

their stability a jealously guarded national and international treasure. Any outcome to the contrary portends system-wide risks that can easily become internationally contagious.

22.4.1 The current state of Africa's private debt markets

During the late 1990s when Singh (1999) asserted that African countries ought not to be promoting stock market capitalism, but should instead focus on banks as the financial development vehicle to deliver sustainable economic growth. What was the state of the banking industries in Africa? At that time, Singh noted the following as the prevailing state of Africa's banking industries:

> Most African banks are state or foreign owned. The latter tend to be conservative and generally serve only the needs of large firms and multinational enterprises. The state-owned banks, on the other hand, are inefficiently managed and lend a large part of their resources to government parastatals and neglect the credit needs of domestic small enterprises...
>
> World Bank (1994) rightly notes for African countries the general scarcity of skilled and qualified managers and regulators in this area. Moreover, many countries still need to devise a regulatory and legal framework for the adequate operation of a modern banking system.

A decade after Singh (1999) enumerated these ills while at the same time advising that financial development tonic for economic growth for Africa can only be found in the banking form of financial services and not in the stock market financial services form, a pertinent and sensible question is, what has subsequently happened to Africa's banking industries? We provide answer(s) to this question by drawing largely from a relatively recent and comprehensive survey on Africa's financial markets by Allen et al. (2011), in addition to a few others. We recap the summary of Allen et al.'s survey of Africa's banking industries below.

> Foreign banks have played an important role in banking development in Africa; their share of total African banking has increased significantly... The increase can be attributed to the financial sector reforms that these countries have embarked upon... The banking sector in most of the countries is either dominated by state-owned banks or by a few large, sometimes foreign, banks.
>
> One common feature of the banking system in Africa is that a large number of them invest in government securities, primarily Treasury bills. This is troublesome since it is reflective of a highly dysfunctional banking intermediation that shuns provision of private credit in favour of safer government securities. The observed low level financial development, in terms of private credit, is attributable to this phenomenon.

Allen et al.'s (2011) summation of the state of banking in Africa and Singh's (1999) analysis, have uncanny similarities. These similarities provoke one to wonder how African states would have fared in their pursuit of economic growth had they entirely taken the path pointed out by Singh as the most superior of other options he evaluated. We shall return to this ponder later on in our discussion. Meanwhile, we turn next to indicators that reflect the degree of economic relevance of Africa's banking industries, particularly in eliciting sustainable growth. As is the case with financial development reflected in Africa's public equity markets, the level of financial development reflective of Africa's private debt markets (banks) provides some data which permits us to glean further insights into their current state.

Typically, two main issues are relevant for ascertaining the economic relevance of a banking industry: one is the extent to which the industry provides needed funds to parties most responsible for economic activities that yield incremental output and jobs, and two is the level of infrastructural support that enables the industry to intermediate effectively. Under the first issue, the following questions, among others, pertain:

- What is the relative supply of credit from all financial services firms to non-government economic agents in the country? This would normally be measured by total credit supply to the private sector of the economy scaled by GDP.
- What proportion of available bank credit is channeled to non-government economic agents? This is computed as the amount of bank credit to the private sector scaled by GDP.
- How affordable are the various forms of bank-provided credits? Credits or debt funds prices are usually computed, in the aggregate, as the difference between lending rate (interest income) and deposit rate (interest expense) of financial services firms—interest rate spread.
- What is the relative level of competition in this industry domestically? Under inferences permissible from market structure models, this can be reflected in the level of concentration in the industry (computed as the size of top three or four banks scaled by the size of the banking industry).
- How sufficiently is the industry meeting the economy's demand for debt finance? We proxy this measure by the ratio of external debt to total debt or GDP. (In fact, one minus the ratio of external to total debt should be targeted).

We report, in Table 22.3, these economic relevance indicators for our representative African economies over time, as to gain a sense of their trend as well as benchmark them accordingly.

As is evident in the table and in agreement with Andrianaivo and Yartey (2010), Allen et al. (2011) and others, credit provision from banks as a percent of GDP is quite low in most African countries. Besides banks in North Africa and Southern African regions, with ratios of 46–48% as at 2010 (which are comparable to emerging market countries), banks in East and West Africa have ratios as low as 17–19%, though these two regions show a trend that is a bit more dynamic for the period 2001–2010 than in the other two regions. Though the cost of credits in Africa is generally higher than it is in emerging market countries (interest rate spread of 5–13% versus 4%); again, apart from banks in North Africa where interest rate spread increased from 5 to 6%, the other three regions experienced a decline from as high as 13% to 8% between 2001 and 2010.

In terms of relative competitiveness of the banking industry, which we attempt to gauge by way of industry concentration ratio, all regions except West Africa showed increases over the 2001–2010 period (55–68% in North Africa, 78–81% in Southern Africa, and 60–100% in East Africa); this, in turn, suggests that the competitiveness of these industries may not have improved. However, in a study of banking competition of African countries for the period 2002–2009, Fosu (2013) finds that banking industries in all regions of Africa recorded significant increases in their population and, perhaps as a result, their banking markets have essentially monopolistic competition behavior, as the average emerging market economies. Fosu attributes this improvement to the many banking reforms African countries embarked upon in previous decade.

Table 22.3 Banking industry indicators of economic relevance by country and over time

Country	Total credit to the private sector 2001–2010		Bank credit to the private sector 2001–2010		Interest rate spread 2001–2010		Relative industry competitiveness 2001–2010		Relative debt capacity 2001–2008	
East Africa										
Kenya	25	30	24	26	13	9	60	100	42	25
Tanzania	7	12	5	15	–	–	–	–	69	29
Uganda	6	8	5	10	–	–	–	–	64	16
Regional average	**13**	**17**	**11**	**17**	**13**	**9**	**60**	**100**	**58**	**23**
North Africa										
Algeria	–	–	–	–	3	6	–	–	45	5
Egypt	55	37	49	34	4	6	58	53	25	15
Morocco	45	62	36	50	8	–	62	91	47	28
Tunisia	68	67	54	54	–	–	45	60	67	52
Regional average	**56**	**55**	**46**	**46**	**5**	**6**	**55**	**68**	**46**	**25**
Southern Africa										
Botswana	15	25	14	22	6	6	93	70	–	–
Mauritius	58	86	55	75	11	11	90	74	–	–
Namibia	41	46	–		8	5	–	100	–	–
South Africa	143	148	70	81	4	4	87	84	7	4
Zambia	8	15	6	14	23	15	62	74	168	21
Zimbabwe	35	–	12	–	24	–	60	–	35	120
Regional average	**50**	**64**	**31**	**48**	**13**	**8**	**78**	**81**	**70**	**48**
West Africa										
Ghana	12	18	11	16	–	–	88	60	119	30
Ivory Coast	16	17	15	18	–	–	77	100	110	54
Nigeria	15	36	15	23	8	5	39	39	65	6
Regional average	**14**	**24**	**14**	**19**	**8**	**5**	**68**	**66**	**98**	**30**
Emerging countries	**44**	**61**	**36**	**45**	**3**	**4**	**61**	**65**	**40**	**18**
Developed countries	177	202	124	151	2	1.5	71	74	–	–

Sources: World Bank Database on Financial Development and Structure, Financial Structure Dataset (Fitch's BankScope), World Development Indicators and authors calculations.

In respect of the extent to which banking industries meet the debt financing need of their domestic constituencies, we examine the incidence of seeking such debt financing externally (using the ratio of external debt to GDP) (Muhanji and Ojah 2011). Though, arguably, this measure reflects the external debt capacity of a nation more than the ratio of external debt to total debt, all regions in Africa show a downward trend in this ratio, an indication of improved debt capacity and/or greater provisioning of debt finance by domestic banking industries.

The second main issue regarding ascertaining the economic relevance of the banking market has to do with the infrastructure necessary for effective intermediation (e.g. legal environment supporting property rights, relevant regulation and creditor protection; credible secondary markets for collateralizable assets; physical infrastructure such as ICT and high skill labor). In section 2, we showed that Africa's level of physical infrastructure support for financial services activity has improved, but still lags behind that of the average emerging market economy. However, one relatively affordable and promising infrastructure is mobile telephony, whose enormous effect on banking has been documented by Allen et al. (2012). We also showed in section 2 how much more African countries need to go before their legal environment and/or governance infrastructure becomes competitive and more readily supportive of the financial intermediation business. Yet again, Melecky and Podpiera (2013) listed a significant number of African countries among those with meaningful supervisory structures supportive of financial sectors. We turn next to some possible ways forward for this market.

22.4.2 Ways of further unlocking the economic growth potential of the banking industry

Outside few main cities or towns that dot African countries, these countries are largely rural, with sparse population distribution. Allen et al. (2012) documented how Kenyan banks, especially Equity Bank, has shown the way on using mobile phone banking to form a virtual high population density that is capable of supporting affordable and yet profitable banking services. Other banking industries in Africa can explore this model, especially in countries where mobile telephony has taken significant hold. Where shortage of requisite high-skill managerial input may pose a problem, low-skill labor such as the motorcycle vendor system in Nigeria or ingenious healthcare delivery models used in several corners of the developing world can be imported into banking to increase financial inclusion.

Elsewhere, Ojah (2013) has argued that the ultimate end of financial inclusion is effective and widespread financial intermediation. For the earlier proposed creation of "foot-soldiers driven" virtual high population densities to be effective, significant holding periods of several months must be placed on the savings gathered from dispersed rural dwellers. And to avoid significant mismatch of asset-liability maturities, the pooled savings should be repackaged into loans of similar maturities as the savings' lock-up periods, with possibility of rollover that is predicated on exemplary debt servicing. A relatively safe set of loan recipients of this proposed model can be the same sources of the pooled loanable funds—rural depositors.

Both Singh (1999) and Allen et al. (2011) flag the "political" managerial approach of state-owned banks as a reason why state-owned banks in Africa have been largely inefficient. Yet Singh points out how Japan, Germany and similarly bank-centered financial system countries used banks to prosecute growth-spurring long-live industrial development agendas. The African government-associated bank financing model should therefore use fiscal incentive to (i) channel investable funds to most attractive production activities and (ii) diversify the banking industry's asset holdings, and (iii) ultimately up the level of credit provision to the economy. A tried and tested fiscal incentive is the use of tax holidays or reduction for banks that fund such designated activities and/or industries.

Another means by which government can assist banks to be more effective, without necessarily owning and running them, is to provide liquidity facility; for example, via guaranteed "pass-throughs." Among babies that must not be thrown out with the bath water, in respect of activities surrounding the global financial crisis of 2007/2008, is the importance of securitization. It is a tool governments have used successfully in partnership with the banking industry to increase housing production in countries such as Canada, Denmark, Finland, the USA, and Mexico. In fact, an important way to encourage banking intermediation for high production in an environment of weak legal environment is to support thrift institutions with mutual status—that is, where customers of the organization are equally owners of the organization. This model mitigates information asymmetry as well as reduces transaction cost while providing a much safer credit to borrowers.

A big issue that further militates against loans provision in an environment of weak contract enforcement is the lack of credible secondary market for collateralizable assets. If there are no ready markets for such assets that are put up as collaterals in support of loan demand, then the bank has no real recourse in the case of default even if the courts enforce the underlying contract. It is therefore clear to see a role for being innovative around collateral substitutes akin to the kinds found in the operations of microfinance institutions. This issue also brings up the need for assorted competing debt funds suppliers that could force banks to engage efficiently in financial intermediation to the fullest extent possible (Houston and James 1996; Denis and Mihov 2003; Ojah and Mokoaleli-Mokoteli 2010; and Gwatidzo and Ojah 2014).[7] We turn to this set of remedies in the next section.

22.5 THE PUBLIC DEBT MARKET

The public debt market (the bond market), is the most recognizable non-intermediated debt market across the world. It is a financial market platform that links sets of well-heeled borrowers (i.e., central governments, parastatals, municipalities, and companies) directly to sets of lenders (i.e., households, financial and non-financial services firms, and governments; all of which constitute the *public*) distributed across a nation and/or across national borders. It is designed to provide non-intermediated long-term debt financing to qualified borrowers in ways that particularly avoids the periodic renegotiation and attendant rollovers which are typical of private debt market type financing.

Though money market type debt contracts are also issued via public debt markets, mostly in the form of Treasury bills, the standard capital market contracts that populate public debt markets, in order of risk, liquidity and yield, are Treasury bonds issued by central governments, agency bonds issued by parastatals, municipal bonds issued by

---

[7] Gwatidzo and Ojah (2014) document the importance of nontraditional non-bank debt funds of trade credits and leases in the supply of debt finance in African countries.

municipalities, and corporate bonds issued by companies. They are so ordered to reflect their degree of liquidity and relative costs. That is, Treasury bills/bonds are the least risky of contracts issued in bond markets, primarily because central governments have power of taxation and thus unlikely to default on their obligation, and also have zero liquidity risk. Owing to such a safe profile, yields on treasuries serve as base-rates for pricing several other debt contracts.

Though this market can have its own separate organized securities exchange, as was the case in Bond Exchange of South Africa (BESA) until quite recently, the majority of public debt markets operate through the platform of their national stock (securities) exchanges (Ojah and Pillay 2009). They thus rely on similar listing, registry, clearing and settlement infrastructure, which must be at reasonable levels of efficiency for the bond market to function effectively. Their activities do not all occur physically on the sites of the exchanges; rather, they are mostly conducted over-the-counter by few key market makers (dealers). Public debt markets can indeed provide both complementary financing and, in some specific respects, substitute services, relative to those provided by private debt markets and public equity markets. Consequently, the presence of bond markets has huge implications for overall cost of capital. In fact, costs of public debt market contracts are generally lower than costs of corresponding private debt market contracts. How well-placed are Africa's public debt markets in playing these competition and complementary roles?

22.5.1 Current state of Africa's public debt markets

As Andrianaivo and Yartey (2010) observe, "the market for long-term debt is the least developed segment of Africa's capital market, attracting only a small proportion of total financial system assets. Much of the momentum for growth… has come from the government sector. Corporate debt markets have generally lagged the government bond market." This trend is almost universal except for the part which notes that public debt market contributes the least to external financing of production among the key segments of financial markets that provide capital funds in Africa. There is therefore the issue of not providing competition in supply of funds in a way that can drive down both cost of capital and overall (and systematic) risks of firms, as Ojah and Pillay (2009) documented in the case of South Africa upon the effective commencement of South Africa's organized bond market.

Among the representative countries in our sample, almost all have some kind of government debt market activity, but only South Africa, Nigeria, Mauritius, Egypt, Morocco, Tunisia, Botswana, Ghana, Kenya, Tanzania, Uganda, and Zambia have some corporate bond activity, which in turn reflects some presence of secondary market activity in these markets. Besides governments' dominance of issues in these African public debt markets, another worrying feature is the general low maturity structure of their issues, especially for the corporate bonds where typical average term ranges from three to five years. The persistence of this kind of maturity structure particularly defeats the purpose of providing firms alternative, if not, cheaper source of financing capital projects. Outside of using these markets to raise largely short-term debt funds to finance government deficits, not many of the African countries muster the kind of sizeable borrowing that can fund important infrastructural provision or attract international investors' patronage (Ladekarl and Zervos 2004; and Andrianaivo and Yartey 2010).

22.5.2 Ways to harness the potential of Africa's public debt markets

The public debt market, in so many ways, shares similar degree of importance for enabling and/or fostering sustainable economic growth as does the public equity market. As Ojah and Pillay (2009) found in the case of South Africa, the availability of public debt market reduces cost of capital, which in turn leads to many prospective capital projects becoming positive net present value projects and, thereby, increasing output of the economy (Rajan and Zingales 1998). This evidence is compelling enough to motivate initiation of public debt markets in other African countries, particularly in those countries that already have requisite support infrastructure by way of existing stock exchanges. At the very least, using such available requisite platform to initiate and regularize a reasonably functional government bond market, will help the country reduce or maintain low external indebtedness and begin to provide meaningful vital base interest rates used for benchmarking rates of other non-Treasury debt contracts in the country. To particularly attract and cater for public debt market activity, relevant institutional infrastructure such as creditor protection and effective contract enforcement must complement available physical infrastructure.

Depth is required for public debt markets to deliver their economic development enabling potential. As Ojah and Pillay (2009) also documented, government and financial services firms are important earlier supporters of initiating public debt markets. Infrastructure and municipal bonds are strategically targeted ways of deepening these markets, particularly for productive purposes. The enormous infrastructural deficits of African countries is now commonplace. Therefore, issuance of infrastructure bond via government agencies (e.g. electricity and water/utility companies), with implicit guarantees from the central government will (i) inject a great deal of sizeable issues into these markets in ways that will attract both institutional and foreign investors, (ii) expand investor base, and (iii) importantly, shift government use of this market away from funding budget deficits—which are mainly for recurrent expenditure—to production of economic infrastructure; this would, in effect, expand the production base of the economy. Similarly, increased use of municipal bonds of the "revenue" type would contribute to expanding investor base as well as tie debt servicing to identifiable cash flow sources; this latter point would discourage unproductive use of borrowed funds as well as shield funds from corrupt and kleptomaniac hands of government officials.

The government can further assist in deepening this market not just by providing diverse and especially longer maturity Treasury bonds, but also by providing targeted subsidization of the market by guaranteeing securitized mortgages. So this securitization intervention will provide liquidity to the banking industry as well as to the bond market by increasing investor base, as debt derivatives of CMOs for example enable hedging of debt contracts traded in the bond market. Liquidity enhancement of this market can be pursued further by demanding specific periodic disclosures from issuing companies which regulators can, in turn, relay to potential investors in ways that permit investors to assess the investability of bonds. This approach would most inspire investor confidence in the information they have about the bond because it mitigates the self-serving rating that is often suspected to be given by rating agencies paid by issuing firms.

Another recent research finding-guided solution pertains. Given that Adelegan and Radzewicz-Bak (2008) found that high national savings and stable macroeconomic environments are important determents of bond market development in Africa, African countries must therefore not relent their macroeconomic reform and stabilization effort. They must especially support policies that encourage high savings. Once more recalling Gwatidzo and Ojah's (2014) recent finding about the importance of non-traditional debt funds supply sources of leases and trade credits for many African countries, creative ways of using the bond market to exploit these avenues for credit provisioning seems sensible. For instance, manufacturing firms that use trade credit to drum up sales can issue "equipment sales bond" to raise relatively cheaper than loans debt funds to finance their trade credits.

22.6 Concluding Remarks

In our effort to explore possible ways African countries can best use the levers of financial development to enable sustainable economic growth, we have followed a simple systematic approach. First, we defined the economic importance of four key financial markets that exist in Africa. Next, we assessed the current state of each of these markets, relying largely on data from current surveys of representative countries from East Africa, North Africa, Southern Africa, and West Africa.

Importantly, we offer what we believe are sensible ways of getting these markets to live up to their economic importance. First, governments can improve liquidity of public stock markets by mandating, by way of legislation, institutional investors (pension funds, and, possibly, insurance firms) to invest specified minimum portions of their funds in the stock market; however, because of limited absorption capacity in Africa's fledgling stock markets, a guided privatization of state-controlled enterprises can be undertaken to boost the uptake of funds supplied by institutional investors. Another possible way of improving liquidity, and size, is to enhance turnover—in this regard, we recommend virtual integration of African securities exchanges to ease the listing (and cross-listing) of stocks of companies domiciled in one country in other countries' markets with minimal, enabling, regulations. Fourth, measures should be taken to mitigate information asymmetry and to build confidence of investors in equity markets—for instance, ICT infrastructure should be improved to shorten the processing time of transactions as well as achieve world-class financial reporting and entrench institutional infrastructure practices.

To grow the private equity markets, the success rates of venture capital financing need to be enhanced. A possible way of doing this is to encourage channeling of venture capital funds to growing businesses for which there will be ready markets domestically and/or internationally—e.g. in agribusiness and renewable energy. Secondly, multilateral development finance institutions, who provide the bulk of venture capital funds in Africa, should be encouraged to channel their funds to supporting start-ups and fledgling businesses in the areas that would most readily impact domestic economic activity and such non-local intervention should, as much as possible, be devoid of direct political association. Third, the African diaspora should be urged to join in the effort to further swell the pool of venture capital funds to support more enterprise creation.

In our final set of recommendations, we speak to the least developed financial markets segment in Africa—the debt markets in general. First, we propose the creation of *virtual* high population densities across sparsely populated, and largely rural, Africa, that are capable of supporting affordable but profitable banking services. Such can be achieved via, the increasingly penetrating, mobile telephony and around small business ventures that cater for the needs of unskilled labor cadres that dot all corners of the continent. Second, the virtual high population density model can be actualized by encouraging thrift among the lower-income segments, then packaging for them their savings into loans of maturities matching the savings lock-up periods, that might be rolled over on a needs basis predicated on exemplary debt servicing. Third, to up the reach of financial services and credit provision in the economy, African governments can borrow a leaf from bank-based financial models that have been so effective in such countries as Japan and Germany.

Fourth, governments can step-in, by way of partnerships, to provide a "liquidity facility," say via guaranteed securitization innovations, aimed at easing the provision of credit facilities to targeted strategic sectors such as housing, agriculture, and primary products processing. Fifth, to encourage investor participation in debt markets, deliberate effort should be directed at the provisioning of relevant institutional infrastructure, such as creditors' protection, and effective contract enforcement to complement the existing and, hopefully, to be improved, physical infrastructure. Finally, governments should foster the issuance of infrastructure bonds and municipal bonds to help deepen the debt markets, and longer-term Treasury bonds to lengthen the yield curve. All of these instruments have yet to gain widespread usage in Africa.

These recommendations on ways forward are based largely on sound economic thinking; lessons learned from successful models from elsewhere, with appropriate adaptation to African environment; and particularly guided by an understanding of basic functions of these key markets. Our hope is that this exercise would be successful in stirring up a solution-oriented mindset among African scholars and policy officials. We also hope that reflections and attendant recommendations would also spur researchers to ask more relevant questions whose solutions would be value-adding to Africa's development effort.

References

Adelegan, O., and Radzewicz-Bak, B. (2008). What determines bond market development in sub-Saharan Africa? IMF Working Paper, WP/09/213. Washington, DC: IMF.

Adjasi, C., and Biekpe, N. (2006). Stock market development and economic growth: The case of selected African countries. *African Development Review*, 18:144–161.

Allen, F., Otchere, I., and Senbet, L. (2011). African financial system: A review. *Review of Development Finance*, 1:79–113.

Allen, F., Carletti, E., Cull, R. et al. (2012). Resolving the African financial development gap: Cross-country comparisons and a within-country study of Kenya. NBER Working Paper, no. 18013. Cambridge, MA.

Amit, R., Brander, J., and Zott, C. (1998). Why do venture capital firms exist? Theory and Canadian evidence. *Journal of Business Venturing*, 13:441–466.

Andrianaivo, M., and Yartey, C. (2010). Understanding the growth of African financial markets. *African Development Review*, 22:394–418.

Beck, T., and Demirguc-Kunt, A. (2006). Small and medium-sized enterprises: access to finance as a growth constraint. *Journal of Banking and Finance*, 30:2931–2943.

Beck, T., Demirguc-Kunt, A., and Levine, R. (2000). A new database on the structure and development of the financial sector. *World Bank Economic Review*, 14:597–605.

Bekaert, G., Harvey, C., and Lundblad, C. (2005). Does financial liberalization spur growth? *Journal of Financial Economics*, 77:3–55.

Bigsten, A., Collier, P., Dercon, S., et al. (2003). Credit constraints in manufacturing enterprises in Africa. *Journal of African Economies*, 12:104–125.

Black, B., and Gilson, R. (1998). Venture capital and the structure of capital markets: Bank versus stock markets. *Journal of Financial Economics*, 47:243–277.

Boyd, J., and Smith, B. (1996). The co-evolution of the real and financial sectors in the growth process. *World Bank Economic Review*, 10:371–396.

Boyd, J., and Smith, B. (1998). The evolution of debt and equity markets in economic development. *Economic Theory*, 12:519–560.

Chan-Lau, J. (2004). Pension funds and emerging markets. IMF Working Paper, WP/04/181. Washington, DC: IMF.

Chandler, A. (1977). *The Visible hand: The Managerial Revolution in American Business*. Cambridge, MA Harvard: University Press.

Collier, P., and Gunning, J. (1999). Explaining African economic performance. *Journal of Economic Literature*, 37: 64–111.

Cumming, D., Siegel, D., and Wringht, M. (2007). Private equity, leverage buyouts and governance. *Journal of Corporate Finance*, 13:439–460.

de la Torre, A., Gozzi, J., and Schmukler, S. (2007). Stock market development under globalization: Wither the gains from reforms? *Journal of Banking and Finance*, 31:1731–1754.

Demirguc-Kunt, A., and Levine, R. (1996). Stock market development and financial intermediaries: Stylized facts. *World Bank Economic Review*, 10:291–321.

Demirguc-Kunt, A., and Maksimovic, V. (1996). Financial constraints, uses of funds and firm growth: An international comparison. Working Paper, Washington, DC: World Bank.

Denis, D., and Mihov, V. (2003). The choice among banked debt, non-bank, and public debt: Evidence from new corporate borrowings. *Journal of Financial Economics*, 70:3–28.

Diamond, D. (1984). Financial intermediation and delegated monitoring. *Review of Economic Studies*, 51:393–414.

Enisan, A., and Olufisayo, A. (2009). Stock market development and economic growth: Evidence from seven sub-Saharan African countries. *Journal of Economics and Business*, 61:162–171.

Fosu, S. (2013). Banking competition in Africa: Subregional comparative studies. *Emerging Markets Review*. http://dx.doi.org/10.1016/j.ememar.2013.02.001.

Garcia, V., and Liu, L. (1999). Macroeconomic determinants of stock market development. *Journal of Applied Economics*, 2:29–59.

Guardian Newspaper (2014). Sub-regional stock exchanges' integration enters new phase. *Guardian*, Capital Market Section, February 10.

Gwatidzo, T., and Ojah, K. (2014). Firms' debt choice in Africa: Are institutional infrastructure and non-traditional determinants important? *International Review of Financial Analysis*, 31:152–166.

Henry, P. (2000a). Stock market liberalization, economic reform, and emerging market equity prices. *Journal of Finance*, 55:529–564.

Henry, P. (2000b). Do stock market liberalizations cause investment booms? *Journal of Financial Economics*, 58:301–334.

Henry, P. (2013). *Turnaround: Third world lessons for first world growth*. New York: Basic Books, Perseus Books Group.

Houston, J., and James, C. (1996). Bank information monopolies and the mix of private and public debt claims. *Journal of Finance*, 51:1863–1889.

Impavido, G., Musalem, A., and Tressel, T. (2003). The impact of contractual savings institutions on securities markets. World Bank Policy Research Working Paper 2948, Washington, DC.

Kaniki, S., and Ntuli, M. (2011). Determinants of participation in occupational pension funds by private sector workers in South Africa. *African Finance Journal*, 13:54–73.

Kim, E., and Singal, V. (2000). Stock market openings: experience of emerging economies. *Journal of Business*, 73:25–66.

King, R., and Levine, R. (1993a). Finance and growth: Schumpeter might be right. *Quarterly Journal of Economics*, 108:713–737.

King, R., and Levine, R. (1993b). Finance, entrepreneurship and growth. *Journal of Monetary Economics*, 32:513–542.

Ladekarl, J., and Zervos, S. (2004). Housekeeping and plumbing: the investability of emerging markets. *Emerging Markets Review*, 5:267–294.

Levine, R. (2002). Bank-based or market-based financial system: which is better? *Journal of Financial Intermediation*, 11:398–428.

Levine, R., and Zervos, S. (1998). Stock markets, banks and economic growth. *American Economic Review*, 88:537–558.

Lucas, R. (1988). On the mechanics of economic development. *Journal of Monetary Economics*, 22:3–42.

Luintel, K., and Khan, M. (1999). A quantitative reassessment of the finance—growth nexus: evidence from a multivariate VAR. *Journal of Development Economics*, 60:381–405.

Melecky, M., and Podpiera, A. (2013). Institutional structures of financial sector supervision, their drivers and historical benchmarks. *Journal of Financial Stability*, 9:424–444.

Mishkin, F. (2004). *The Economics of Money, Banking and Financial Markets*, 7th edn. Boston: Pearson Addison-Wesley.

Muhanji, S., and Ojah, K. (2011). Management and sustainability of external debt: A focus on the Emerging economies of Africa. *Review of Development Finance*, 1:184–206.

Naceur, S., Ghazouani, S., and Omran, M. (2007). The determinants of stock market development in the Middle-East and North African region. *Managerial Finance*, 33:477–489.

Odedokun, M. (1996). Alternative econometric approaches for analyzing the role of the financial sector in economic growth: Time-series evidence from LDCs. *Journal of Development Economics*, 50:119–135.

Ojah, K. (2009). The right private equity market for African economies. *Africa Growth Agenda*, July–September, 6:6–9.

Ojah, K. (2011). Is the enterprise creation importance of venture capital in emerging markets real? Answers from JSE's IPOs. *African Finance Journal*, 13:1–24.

Ojah, K. (2013). Financial inclusion in South Africa: An unfinished conversation. *Wits Business School Journal*, October, 34:64–65.

Ojah, K., Gwatidzo, T., and Sheshangai, K. (2010). Legal environment, finance channels and investment: The East African example. *Journal of Development Studies*, 46:724–744.

Ojah, K., and Mokoaleli-Mokoteli, T. (2010). Possible effective financing models for entrepreneurship in South Africa: Guides from microfinance and venture capital finance. *African Finance Journal*, 12:1–26.

Ojah, K., and Mokoaleli-Mokoteli, T. (2012). Internet financial reporting, infrastructures and corporate Governance: An international analysis. *Review of Development Finance*, 2:69–83.

Ojah, K., and Pillay, K. (2009). Debt markets and corporate debt structure in an emerging market: The South African example. *Economic Modelling*, 26:1215–1227.

Patrick, H. (1966). Financial development and economic growth in underdeveloped countries. *Economic Development and Cultural Change*, 14:174–189.

Rajan, R., and Zingales, L. (1995). What do we know about capital structure? Some evidence from international data. *Journal of Finance*, 50:1421–1460.

Rajan, R., and Zingales, L. (1998). Financial development and growth. *American Economic Review*, 88:559–586.

Robinson, J. (1952). The generalization of the great theory, in *The Rate of Interest and Other Essays*. Macmillan: London, pp. 67–142.

Romer, P. (1990). Endogenous technological change. *Journal of Political Economy*, 98:71–102.

Rousseau, P., and Watchell, P. (1998). Financial intermediation and economic performance: Historical evidence from five industrialized countries. *Journal of Money, Credit and Banking*, 30:657–678.

Rousseau, P., and Watchell, P. (2000). Equity markets and growth: cross-country evidence on timing and outcomes, 1980-1995. *Journal of Business and Finance*, 24:1933–1957.

Sahlman, W. (1990). The structure and governance of venture capital organizations. *Journal of Financial Economics*, 27:473–521.

Schumpeter, J. (1911). *A Theory of Economic Development*. Cambridge, MA: Harvard University Press.

Shan, J., Morris, A., and Sun, F. (2001). Financial development and economic growth: An egg and chicken problem. *Review of International Economics*, 9:443–454.

Shepherd, D., and Zacharakis, A. (2001). Speed to initial public offering of VC-backed companies. *Entrepreneurship: Theory and Practice*, 25:59–71.

Singh, A. (1999). Should Africa promote stock market capitalism? *Journal of International Development*, 11:343–365.

Smith, C. (1986). Investment banking and the capital acquisition process. *Journal of Financial Economics*, 15:3–29.

Stern, N. (1989). The economics of development: A survey. *Economic Journal*, 100:597–685.

Stiglitz J., and Weiss, A. (1981). Credit rationing in markets with imperfect information. *American Economic Review*, 71:393–410.

Swaziland (2005). *The Retirement Fund Act*. Mbabane, Swaziland: The Government Printer.

Swaziland (2010). *The Financial Services Regulatory Authority Act*. Mbabane, Swaziland: The Government Printer.

CHAPTER 23

....

ISLAMIC FINANCE IN NORTH AFRICA

....

WAFIK GRAIS

23.1 INTRODUCTION

....

NORTH Africa holds a special place in the development of economic thought and Islamic finance.[1] In the fourteenth century, Ibn Khaldun, born in Tunisia in 1332, became a precursor for modern economic thinking with his Muqqadimah.[2] He held prominent positions, lived throughout the region, and died in Cairo. In the 1960s, in Egypt, Ahmed El Naggar, a precursor in the twentieth century, launched the Mit Ghamr initiative; his experiment was a landmark in the revival of Islamic finance.[3] With these prominent figures, North Africa marked the history of economic thought and the founding and revival of modern Islamic finance.

However, the early moves were not followed up in the region by either a strong tradition in economic thinking or by a flourishing Islamic finance industry. Away from North Africa, Europe carried the flame of the development of economic thought centuries later. Similarly, most Islamic finance's late twentieth- and early twenty-first-century developments occurred in the Gulf Cooperation Council (GCC) countries, Iran and Malaysia.[4] Initial developments of Islamic finance were driven by sponsors setting up financial institutions to conduct financial transactions according to *Shari'a* teachings with an expectation of a strong demand for those services.[5] Capital availability, especially in the aftermath of the first oil crisis in 1973,

---

[1] There are numerous writings on Islamic finance covering its core principles and modes of operation. Also an emerging body of information deals with Islamic finance markets, size, structures and operations (e.g. "Islamic Finance Gateway" from Reuters and Zawya). At its core, Islamic finance is a financial intermediation industry where charging or receiving interests is prohibited; risk sharing is promoted; a clear connection between the financial and underlying real transaction (materiality) required; contracts should be fair; and financing "haram" or sinful activities forbidden. Section 2 below elaborates on these principles from a regulatory perspective. See also Iqbal and Mirakhor (2011).

[2] See Ibrahim Oweiss http://www9.georgetown.edu/faculty/imo3/ibn.htm.

[3] See Hanan I. El Naggar (2011) for a nice overview of the industry's history.

[4] GCC countries include Bahrain, Kuwait, Oman, Saudi Arabia and the United Arab Emirates.

[5] *Shari'a* is the body of religious "legislations" and pronouncements embodying Islamic teachings. Initial providers were Islamic banks such as the Dubai Islamic Bank (1975), or the Kuwait Finance House (1977).

provided an opportunity to multiply these initiatives and expand the presence of Islamic financial services' providers. Motivations of identity assertion and political choices drove also these market developments.

Over the late twentieth century, the authorities in countries put a brake on the industry's development in North Africa. Over that period, political leaders adopted non-religiously based economic governance. In addition, the authorities' perceptions of security requirements led them to view financial flows channeled through Islamic financial institutions with suspicion.[6] As a result, the share of Islamic financial assets remained at less than 5% of each North African country's total financial assets.[7]

The downfall of regional autocratic leaders in 2011 presented an opportunity for political Islam movements to openly voice their agenda.[8] Except in Algeria, Islamic parties were swept to power and seemed to be intent on fostering the development of Islamic finance in the region and ushering a new historical episode for the industry in North Africa. A new political leadership affiliated with those parties promoted a system of governance that it wanted anchored in Islamic teachings as reflected notably in Egypt's short-lived 2012 constitution or Tunisia's dominance by the Islamist EnNahda party.[9] But as emerged in mid-2013, the transitions were not yet settled. Non-Islamist political forces vied for power with determining developments in both Egypt and Tunisia. Islamist political movements were left weakened in both countries, leaving uncertain the nature of political support Islamic finance would receive.

The foregoing political events revealed deep divisions in North Africa's societies. On one side, significant cosmopolitan segments, an emerging middle class, and exposure to international cultural and economic developments notably through information technology instilled aspirations to temporal democratic civil governance, keeping religion outside of politics.[10] On the other side, identity aspirations, unmet welfare expectations, and a religious promise of a better world filled the sails of Islamist movements and those who see religion as an integral part of a state's temporal governance.

These sharp differences in visions of North Africa's future carried through to policies towards Islamic finance, enabling or discouraging it. Politics, market, and policy initiatives were closely intertwined. As a result, Islamic finance got caught in the broader political debates. The industry's fate became tied to rivalries of political visions rather than assessments of benefits and costs.

---

[6] The political establishment perceived Islamic financial institutions as instruments for financing political opposition as well as financing terrorism.

[7] Ernst and Young (2012). The Islamic Republic of Mauritania has a number of Islamic finance institutions and is gradually moving to develop an enabling regulatory environment. Islamic finance assets are reckoned to exceed $1.5 trillion in 2014. Broadly they are distributed in three with a third domiciled in Iran, another third in the GCC and the last third in the rest of the world, with Malaysia having a leading role within the latter. See Grais (2012b).

[8] In 2011, Tunisians toppled Ben Ali's regime, followed by Egyptians toppling Mubarak and Libyans ousting their own leader Qaddafi as well as Moroccans electing an Islamic party. EnNahda party in Tunisia, Justice and development Party in Morocco and the Freedom and Justice Party in Egypt affiliated with the Muslim Brotherhood organization were among those representing political Islam.

[9] For example, by providing a prominent role to Islamic principles as a source of legislation and providing a role to a religious institution in vetting legislation, less so in Tunisia than in Egypt.

[10] See Grais (2012a) for a view on Egypt's transition.

However, it is essential not to let assessments of any economic activity be made on the basis of political positions or religious preferences. Assessments need to be made on the merits and drawbacks of those activities in advancing economic welfare. Such a perspective would apply to Islamic finance as well. First and foremost, Islamic finance has to be viewed as a way of conducting the business of financial intermediation. It is ethical finance, where the ethics happen to be derived from Islamic teachings. It mobilizes financial resources and allocates them to various economic activities like conventional finance, though with restrictions reflecting a code of conduct.[11] As a financial intermediation business, it needs to meet its various stakeholders' expectations. Investors in Islamic finance businesses will expect returns like any other investor. Depositors will look for returns and the safety of deposits. Clients seeking finance will be sensitive to the costs they incur. Regulators and supervisors will need to ensure that financial stability is maintained and fiduciary responsibility is fulfilled. But because it is Islamic finance, stakeholders will be interested in knowing that the Islamic finance industry actually complies with *Sharia* principles. Accordingly, public policy in the region and beyond needs to approach Islamic finance professionally as it would deal with any industry, with rigorous assessments without falling in the trap of easy advocacy or fruitless bashing based on political or religious preferences. Whether Islamic or conventional, financial intermediation is there to fulfill an economic function.

If one accepts this perspective, two considerations become relevant:

1. What *roots and features* facilitate or hinder the industry's development in the region such as: a cultural and religious background that represent a natural connection to Islamic finance; a legacy of economic thinking such as that embodied in Ibn Khaldun's work; precedents to modern Islamic finance; or a dire need to achieve inclusive economic development that needs to harness all modes of financing.
2. What should *public policy's role* be in dealing with the Islamic finance industry; what weight should it give to market outcomes versus voluntary promotion; should public policy's role be to provide a transparent regulatory framework that ensures financial stability, encourages entrepreneurship, but let markets determine the industry's ultimate performance.

Recognizing these two aspects would permit an understanding of the opportunities and challenges of Islamic finance development in the region and enable public policy to design and implement an effective "industrial policy" towards the industry. With this perspective, the following deals in section 2 with North Africa's features, roots and challenges that connect it to Islamic finance. Section 3 suggests a public policy approach that would provide a framework for Islamic finance to develop in compliance with conventional financial regulation and its own tenets while letting market developments determine its future.

23.2 NORTH AFRICA: ROOTS AND FEATURES

One can identify four sets of factors that connect the region to Islamic finance. First, North Africa has a natural religious and cultural connection to Islamic finance. Second, the region

---

[11] See footnote 1 and section 3 for highlights of Islamic finance.

has seen the early development of modern economic thought. Third, Islamic finance has re-emerged in its modern shape in North Africa. Finally, the region is in dire need for inclusive economic development that Islamic finance claims to promote.

23.2.1 Religious and cultural connection to Islamic finance

In 2012, North Africa was home to 176 million people with an overwhelming majority professing the Muslim faith, and in principle following its teachings.[12] In 639, Arab armies coming out of the Arabian Peninsula entered Egypt and North Africa bringing the Arabic language and Islamic faith to the region. They reached the shores of the Atlantic 43 years later. In less than a century, they had subdued the whole of North Africa, instituting a new order. This conquest, from the Nile to the Atlantic, was more complete than anything achieved by previous historical territorial expansions and the changes it wrought proved permanent. The permanence of these changes, the cultural developments they fostered, anchored in the Islamic faith and Arabic language can make one presume that large segments of the population of the region would welcome conducting their financial business according to their religious beliefs. [13]

23.2.2 Ibn Khaldun: economic thought and policy guidance

Ibn Khaldun believed in the role of markets in resource allocation and that of an enabling regulation to foster their development.[14] He argues for providing an enabling public policy framework and letting markets determine the fate of industries. In essence, Ibn Khaldun's message is that policymakers' role is to provide a level playing field to economic activities.

Ibn Khaldun's work is considered the peak of a medieval Arab–Muslim philosophical system about government, society, and economics.[15] Contrary to other scholars of the time, he adopted a positive-rational approach rather than a normative one. He believed strongly in the role of economics in explaining history without it being its exclusive driver. Ibn Khaldun was a pioneer of classical economics who contributed significant insights in what later became theories of production, consumption, trade, taxation, and money. He "elaborates a theory of production, a theory of value, a theory of distribution, and a theory of cycles."[16] He puts forward a rationale for income disparity between richer and poorer areas based on the stronger demand notably for professional labor in urban environment.

---

[12] Here, North Africa includes Algeria, Egypt, Libya, Mauritania, Morocco, and Tunisia. Source: World Bank at http://data.worldbank.org/indicator/SP.POP.TOTL.

[13] North Africa is also home to leading schools of Islamic thinking such as El Azhar in Cairo that have a prominent international role. See also Gearon (2011).

[14] Hakim (undated).

[15] Baloglou (2012): "This tradition of the Arab-Islamic economic thought found its peak in Ibn Khaldun's work. He was both a distinguished jurist trained in traditional Islamic beliefs and a man of action closely involved with the powerful men of that time."

[16] Baloglou (2012).

A strong believer in markets, he argues for free trade and highlights the economic and social benefits and costs of government intervention. He puts forward his concept of social solidarity that provides a foundation for the practice of group lending that contributed so much to microfinance.[17] The same concept can also be seen as a precursor of the major tenet of risk and profit sharing at the core of Islamic finance. His positive-rational approach and his strong belief in the role of markets for resource allocation within an enabling regulatory framework provide guidance to conduct public policy, including the challenges of mainstreaming Islamic finance.

23.2.3 Pioneering modern Islamic finance

The implementation of Islamic finance in Egypt with the Mit Ghamr financial institution provided a concrete test of the conduct of financial intermediation according to the ethics of Islamic teachings. Mit Ghamr carried the message of the feasibility of Islamic finance.

The Mit Ghamr initiative is a leading experiment that conveyed the practicality of Islamic finance.[18] It is the outcome of the exposure of regional intellectuals to Arab–Islamic and international thought. Mit Ghamr brought together European experience and Islamic teachings to bear on the conduct of finance. The experiment reflects the nature of North Africa as fertile land for seeds for adaptation if not innovation, notably because of its geographical location.[19] While Mit Ghamr may be known for being the center of aluminum production in Egypt in the early twenty-first century, it is famous worldwide as the place where the first Islamic bank was established in 1963. Then and there, Dr. Ahmad El Naggar established the Mit Ghamr savings bank that combined the idea of German savings banks with *Shari'a* principles. Though it did not carry the label of Islamic financial institution, the bank was the first *Shari'a*-compliant one in modern times.[20] At the crossroad of East and West, Europe and Africa, Egypt holds, with the Mit Ghamr experiment, a special place in the modern history of Islamic finance as the place of its rebirth.

23.2.4 Aspirations for inclusive economic development

From one perspective, Islamic finance's principles of contract fairness, risk sharing, and required linkage of the financial and underlying real transactions can be perceived to be conducive to inclusive economic development. Furthermore, sizable financial resources channeled through Islamic finance can support economic activity where they can be deployed. From another perspective, North Africa has the utmost need to achieve rapid

[17] Ibrahim Oweiss http://www9.georgetown.edu/faculty/imo3/ibn.htm and Dusuki (2006).
[18] "Dr. El Naggar achievement was to raise the consciousness among Muslim opinion leaders and businessmen that modern alternatives to *riba* were feasible and realistic" in Thomas Abdel Kader et al. (2005).
[19] Stretching from the Red Sea to the Atlantic Ocean on the Southern Shores of the Mediterranean, North Africa is a bridge between Europe and the rest of Africa.
[20] IFIS Analytics (2008).

and inclusive development.[21] Accordingly, it would not be strange to see public authorities pursue the Islamic finance opportunity to garner resources it can make available to their jurisdictions and possibly help fulfill the objective of inclusive development. Naturally, there are those who believe that the constraints *Sharia* compliance puts on the financial industry may limit its overall contribution to economic activity. In particular, Islamic financial intermediation may entail higher transaction costs and require higher shares of liquid reserves.

23.2.4.1 *Financial development and economic growth*

In a 1993 seminal paper, King and Levine provided evidence that financial development is a good predictor of economic growth. They pointed out that "financial depth is positively and significantly related to real per capita GDP growth." Levine and others revisited the issue in a 2000 paper using a better set of dates. Their results confirm the initial work and support elements of causality from finance to growth. They also observe the critical role of broader financial infrastructure in explaining variations of performance.[22] The link between finance and growth has received much attention that generally has confirmed the positive link. A more recent study provides evidence of the link but observes heterogeneity in results attributable notably to regulatory variations as well as the ability of financial systems to reach out and be inclusive. In this respect the study observes smaller beneficial impacts of financial deepening in the Middle East and North Africa (MENA) region than elsewhere.[23] Also, evidence suggests that inclusive financial systems that permit access to financial services to more people and companies promote social inclusion and equity.[24] Ultimately, countries with deeper financial systems appear more likely to achieve higher and more inclusive economic growth.

23.2.4.2 *Financial development in North Africa*

North Africa appears to be lagging behind in terms of depth of its financial institutions and the access they provide. Around 2010, Morocco had the highest share of adults with an account at a financial institution at about 39%, with Tunisia not far behind at 32%. In Egypt the share was just close to 10%. Similarly bank private credit was around 68% of gross domestic product (GDP) in Tunisia and Morocco but less than 31% in Egypt.[25] Other financial indicators point also to lagging financial development. The penetration of the insurance sector is low with life insurance premiums at 1% of GDP in Morocco and 0.3% in Egypt and Tunisia. Furthermore small and medium-sized enterprises (SMEs) have difficulty accessing external finance from the banking system.[26]

---

[21] Without social peace, economic development is bound to be elusive and improved equitable welfare even more so.

[22] King and Levine (2003) and Levine et al. (2000). The broader institutional infrastructure refers to the quality of the legal and regulatory framework, accounting rules and reliability, contract enforcement notably.

[23] Barajas et al. (2013).

[24] See e.g. Honohan (2004).

[25] World Bank (2013).

[26] Rocha et al. (2011).

23.2.4.3 Islamic finance and financial development

In North Africa's circumstances of lagging financial development and the perception that Islamic finance principles may well contribute to inclusive economic growth, it is legitimate to ask whether the development of Islamic finance may increase financial depth and access to financial services.[27] If it does the industry could contribute to a better positioning of the region for more inclusive economic growth.

23.2.4.4 Demand for Islamic financial services

There is not yet a definitive answer to the question. Neither is there a convincing body of research on the existing or potential demand for Islamic financial services that could help address the relationship between Islamic finance and inclusive growth. A big challenge in dealing with such issues is the availability of adequate data that could be used for system-atic assessment of relationships between Islamic finance and growth indicators.[28] Some initial market surveys and analysis seem to point to a positive response to the question with survey participants indicating a preference for *Sharia*-compliant products.[29] However, another study provides mixed results.[30] It finds "no evidence that Muslims are less likely than non-Muslims to report formal borrowing" but also it finds that "Muslims are significantly less likely than non-Muslims to have an account and save at a formal financial institution." Interestingly this study reveals that "self-identification as a Muslim is associated with a 6% decrease in the prob-ability of having a formal account."[31] In a sample focused on North Africa, the same study reports "evidence of a strong hypothetical preference for *Sharia*-compliant products despite higher costs." The foregoing results do not seem to depart drastically with a common view of three-way market segmentation. According to this view, a third of Muslim population would exclusively deal with *Sharia*-compliant finance, another third has no problem dealing with conventional finance, with a third group in the middle having no definite view and would consider switching between the two types of finance according to cost and quality of service.

23.2.4.5 Islamic finance market challenges

Two prominent issues may constrain the potential contribution of Islamic finance: trans-action costs and liquidity requirements. Additional Islamic finance transaction costs

---

[27] True there are challengers to Islamic finance and economics. For challengers, see for example page 303 of Kuran (1997): "the doctrine (Islamic Economics) emerged in late-colonial India as an instrument of identity creation and protection; at least initially, the economics of Islamic economics was merely incidental to its Islamic character."

[28] See World Bank (2014).

[29] See Pearce (2011) that reports that an IFC-commissioned market studies in the MENA region found that "between 20 and 60% of those interviewed (microenterprises, low-income individuals) indicated a preference for *Sharia* compliant products. For some the lack of *Sharia* compliant products is an absolute constraint to financial access, while for others this is a preference and they continue to use conventional financial services in the absence of competitive Islamic ones."

[30] Demirguc-Kunt et al. (2013).

[31] The author has come across cases where devout Muslims may bank with a conventional financial institution using most financial services needed for their transactions but transferring any interest received to charity.

occur at the levels of structuring the transaction and that of vetting its *Shari'a* compliance. In the first case, time and financial costs arise in developing a *Shari'a*-compliant design of a transaction. The financial engineering and associated legal documentation as well as allaying the fears of associated degree of legal uncertainty can generate costs additional to the ones incurred in more standard conventional transactions. For example, the requirement of the link of a *Sukuk* to a material underpinning as well as that of ownership rights of *Sukuk* certificate holders can entail costs that are additional to those incurred with a conventional bonds issue.[32] Similarly Islamic finance liquidity management entails the development of *Shari'a*-compliant instruments that are not interest bearing like those used in conventional finance.[33] As a result, Islamic financial institutions may find themselves having to hold excess liquidity, constraining business expansion. The foregoing limitations can also be reflected in markets having fewer instruments to exchange and accordingly shallower markets entailing costs of financial discovery and wider spreads. However, the increasing number of issues of Islamic finance instruments and the expansion in market size can be expected to lead to standardized structures and costs reduction.

In summary, available elements on the Islamic finance industry point to (i) mixed evidence on the potential demand for Islamic financial services; (ii) potential positive role of Islamic finance on financial access and development; (iii) lagging financial development in North Africa, (iv) presence of Islamic finance private service providers, and (v) higher transaction costs and liquidity management challenges. Under the circumstances, one may want to consider letting public policy follow Ibn Khaldun's guidance of having markets determine outcomes within a transparent regulatory framework that offers a level playing field. Accordingly, it would be reasonable for public authorities to deal with Islamic finance as a financial innovation that can be present on markets within a clear and transparent regulatory framework. If it succeeds, it could enhance access to finance and the region's development prospects.[34]

23.3 PUBLIC POLICY LESSONS: FRAMEWORK FOR DUAL FINANCIAL SYSTEMS

If one accepts the view that Islamic finance is part of the continuous process of financial innovation, one needs to accept that markets would determine its success or failure. The question

---

[32] In an *Ijara sukuk* the issuer may need to "sell" a real estate asset to an SPV and rented back from the SPV to make the SPV an owner of an income-earning asset that can raise money through issuing of *sukuks*. The *sukuk* certificate holder needs to have "ownership" rights in the asset during the time s/he holds the *sukuk* certificate.

[33] For example, conventional banks place excess liquidity by purchasing interest bearing money markets instruments and access liquidity by borrowing on those markets. Similarly central banks conduct monetary policy using interest-bearing instruments. Accordingly, Islamic finance institutions cannot access these facilities and are in need of non-interest bearing instruments that are not yet fully mainstreamed except in a few jurisdictions such as Malaysia. See also section 3.1.

[34] A core aspect of conventional financial finance is the presence of money markets that allow financial institutions to place and access money on short terms and enable them to have smooth operations without continuously maintaining idle excess liquidity in case it is needed. Money markets use generally interest based financial instruments that are not accessible to Islamic finance. Though progress is being made to

is then how to integrate these innovations in the broad development of financial systems from the perspective of markets and regulation. This is a challenge for countries with significant Muslim populations as well as others that simply see Islamic finance as a business opportunity.[35] North Africa's Islamic finance historical record and the way it addresses current market calls for a larger role of Islamic finance can provide useful international benchmarks.

Banking in compliance with *Shari'a* principles has led to the design and implementation of specific financial instruments.[36] For example, in line with the principle of risk sharing, Islamic banks offer investment account deposits to their depositors. The instrument is essentially a middle ground between a conventional deposit and a share in a mutual fund. Accordingly, the integration challenge is to square the regulatory treatment of Islamic investment deposits with that of conventional bank deposits. This particular investment account issue goes to a core feature of banking as the business of intermediation between depositors and the rest of the economy.

One approach to integrate Islamic finance is to extend to it conventional finance laws, regulations, and supervision arrangements. Admittedly, such extension would come along with adaptations and additions as would be the case with conventional financial innovations.[37] Another approach is to consider Islamic finance intrinsically different from conventional finance. Accordingly, it would be difficult to extend the conventional finance framework to Islamic finance; Islamic finance would require specific laws, regulations and supervision arrangements to allow Islamic banks to operate. Malaysia and Bahrain have chosen the latter approach of establishing separate arrangements for Islamic and conventional finance.[38] Other countries have adopted the first approach; they opted for extending the prevailing conventional finance arrangements to Islamic finance, introducing specific regulation and procedures where those of conventional finance do not apply or are lacking.[39]

develop money markets compliant with Islamic finance principles they remain limited, constraining the expansion of Islamic finance and its ability to finance economic activity and growth.

[35] For example, the United Kingdom whose financial authorities see the potential for London to be a center of Islamic Finance. See United Kingdom Islamic Finance Secretariat—UKIFS (2012).

[36] Conventional financial innovations respond to a specific market demand or a perceived opportunity for profit; the innovations of Islamic finance respond to the need to structure products and follow processes complying with *Shari'a* principles to meet a perceived general demand for Islamic financial services.

[37] According to the Central Bank of Nigeria: "Islamic banking as one of the models of non-interest banking, serves the same purpose of providing financial services as do conventional financial institutions save that it operates in accordance with principles and rules of Islamic commercial jurisprudence that generally recognizes profit and loss sharing and the prohibition of interest, as a model."

[38] North African countries seem to have extended regulatory provisions to address Islamic finance issues. Among other countries, for example, the Central Bank of Kuwait has prepared a comprehensive manual encompassing the rules and regulations for the supervision and oversight of Islamic banks. This manual is the counterpart of the Central Bank of Kuwait's supervisory manual for conventional bank supervision.

[39] International standard setting bodies such as AAIOFI and the IFSB seem to have implicitly adopted the first point of view, introducing rules and standards where they think conventional rules and standards are lacking. Of course this is not the case where it concerns AAIOFI's *Shari'a* standards. Similarly, Nigerian regulators require Islamic finance institutions to comply with the Generally Accepted Accounting Principles (GAAP) codified in local standards issued by the NASB and the International Financial Reporting Standards (IFRS)/International Accounting Standards (IAS). For transactions, products and activities not covered by these standards, Nigeria requires to apply the relevant provisions of the financial accounting and auditing standards issued by AAOIFI.

Up to the early 2010s years, North African countries have rather followed the "extension" route. However, the question of the approach to follow has reemerged since then. It has become an issue in the region's financial systems' development strategies.

The following deals with the issue. First, it addresses the degree of consistency of Islamic finance principles with conventional banking regulation. It then offers an organizational framework that can provide space to market based Islamic finance innovations to develop in harmony with conventional finance. The point is to identify inconsistencies between conventional regulation and *Shari'a* compliance. This is then used to design a financial industry organizational framework that maintains a level playing field between Islamic and conventional finance and enables markets to determine the fate of Islamic or conventional financial innovation. This approach and organizational framework can provide guidance to current challenges North African countries face in putting in place an institutional basis for the development of Islamic finance activities.

23.3.1 Consistency of Islamic finance principles with conventional banking regulation

While conventional banking regulation can easily accommodate some Islamic finance principles, others are inconsistent with it. This poses a challenge to the licensing and operation of Islamic banks in an environment where conventional banking prevails. In essence, the practice of Islamic financial intermediation entails complying with the following five principles:[40]

1. "risk—sharing"—reflecting a symmetrical risk/return distribution to each participant to a transaction;
2. "materiality" entailing that a financial transaction needs to have a "material finality" being directly or indirectly linked to a real economic transaction;
3. "no exploitation"—a financial transaction should not lead to the exploitation of any party to the transaction;[41]
4. "no Riba," generally understood as no interest and sometimes as no usury gain;[42] and
5. "no involvement in sinful activities" such as alcoholic beverages or gambling.

The principles of risk-sharing, materiality, and no-Riba (1, 2, and 4 above respectively) pose challenges to the implementation of Islamic banking in a context of a dual conventional—Islamic banking system.[43]

---

[40] See El Hawary, Grais, and Iqbal (2007) and El Tiby and Grais (2014).

[41] No exploitation entails no information asymmetry between the parties to the contract and requires full disclosure of information.

[42] The term *Riba* literally means increase or addition and is recognized in Islamic jurisprudence to encompass notions of usury and interest. Any risk-free or "guaranteed" rate of return on a loan is considered as *Riba* and therefore prohibited.

[43] The two other principles are not inconsistent with prevailing conventional banking regulations. The no-exploitation principle is dealt with in both conventional and Islamic finance by codes of transparency and disclosure. It does not entail the potential of regulatory conflict between both modes of financing.

23.3.1.1 *Risk sharing*

From a conventional banking regulation perspective, the risk-sharing principle raises issues as to the nature of a deposit, depositors' rights as creditors, depositor's voice in governance, and capital adequacy. Risk sharing entails that the value of revenue-earning deposits tracks the performance of the investments they finance. Generally, these deposits are called investment deposits.[44] Their face value is not certain. In contrast, a conventional deposit is a "contractual loan arrangement between a financial institution and a client where the client places funds with the institution for later withdrawal or use for making payments."[45] Thus a deposit in a conventional bank is retrievable by the depositor at its face value. Accordingly, in principle, a revenue earning "deposit" in an Islamic financial institution does not fit the prevailing definition of a deposit in a conventional bank.

Another implication of the risk-sharing principle is that the depositor is not a priority senior creditor of the financial institution in case of its liquidation. Indeed the depositor is assumed to share the risk and bear the loss. This is inconsistent with the prevailing conventional banking practice where depositors normally have priority over secured and unsecured creditors in case of liquidation of a licensed banking institution.

A holder of an investment account in an Islamic finance institution has no voice in the governing bodies of the institution, very much like her/his counterpart depositor in a conventional bank. However, the former bears a risk similar to that borne by shareholders, unlike the conventional bank depositor that enters a contract with the bank with comfort on the face value of the deposit. Accordingly, when carried through to the investment deposit design, the risk sharing principle entails a mismatch between responsibility and accountability of the depositor and the financial institution.

Conventional banking regulation stipulates that a bank needs to have a sufficient *capital cushion* to face unanticipated risks that can adversely affect its revenue performance and asset quality and its ability to honor its liabilities when due. The point is to provide some comfort that a bank can sustain shocks and remain solvent, thus mitigating risks to its creditors, foremost among them depositors. The latter are not supposed to see a loss of value in their deposits. With this rationale in mind, it can be argued that Islamic finance institutions do not face similar obligations in principle as the investment account holders are supposed to share in the upside benefit and in the downside loss. Accordingly, it has been suggested that Islamic investment deposit taking institutions should not be subject to the same capital requirements as conventional banks.[46]

Similarly, the absence of involvement in sinful activities can naturally be accommodated in conventional banking regulation.

[44] Investment deposits are generally based on a *mudaraba* contract where the depositor is *Rab El Mal* (owner of asset) and the financial institution is a *mudarib* (asset manager for the account of the asset owner). In principle the asset manager receives a management fee and shares in the upside gains of the investments undertaken, but does not bear any loss that should be borne by the asset owner, unless there is misconduct on the part of the *mudarib*.

[45] Bollen (2006).

[46] Islamic Financial Services Board (IFSB) has issued a capital standard for Islamic banks that tries to deal with the issue. See IFSB (2005).

23.3.1.2 *Materiality*

The materiality principle entails that a financial transaction need to have a "material finality." Accordingly, it has to be directly or indirectly linked to a real economic transaction.[47] In practice, materiality entails that the financial contract will cover a financial transaction and the real transaction underlying the financial deal.[48] It entails that a bank will need to hold real assets and equity participation in the conduct of its business.

The materiality principle would conflict with the prevailing prohibition for conventional commercial banks to enter into partnerships, joint ventures or the ownership of real estate and common stock. Here, the rationale for unbundling real and financial transactions is to clearly separate real and financial sector activity and avoid risks of conflicts of interests. Financial intermediaries are entrusted with a fiduciary responsibility of management of others' financial resources. Accordingly, it is essential to avoid providing them opportunities to pursue private gains with their clients' resources.

23.3.1.3 *No Riba*

The prohibition of earning or charging interest is the prevailing view among Islamic scholars. It is a central tenet of Islamic finance.[49] Basically it reflects the view that it is unethical to earn from the simple ownership and placement of financial resources without it being the outcome of a value adding economic effort. The remuneration resulting from a placement should not be pre-set and linked to the value placed. It should rather be the result of the efforts made in the economical use of the resources and accordingly should not be set a priori.

However, interest is a core feature of conventional banking. It captures the time value of money, that is, the opportunity cost of not consuming today for the opportunity to consume tomorrow. Conventional banking, central banking, monetary policy, and liquidity management have been built on the premise of the possibility of holding and exchanging interest rate bearing assets.

The prohibition to engage in interest bearing transactions limits the ability of (i) deposit-taking institutions to compete in attracting deposits; (ii) deposit-taking institutions to manage liquidity placing their own excess resources or accessing resources when needed, notably on money markets, or (iii) monetary authorities to conduct monetary policy injecting or withdrawing resources from the financial system.[50]

Competition in attracting deposits has led Islamic banks to adopt return-smoothing practices. The practice of smoothing obscures the actual performance of the investments made. It makes it more difficult for account holders to assess the bank's investment performance.

---

[47] El Hewary et al. (2007).

[48] For example, an Islamic financier would not provide finance to a client desiring to purchase a house, but would enter into a contract that has provisions related to the sale and purchase of the house and its use by the client. See Usmani (2005) for an overview of Islamic contracts and modes of financing.

[49] There are different types of *Riba*, generally understood as interest. The prohibition of *Riba* has generally carried over to the prohibition of charging or receiving interest. A minority interpretation is that *Riba* refers to usury rates and not to "reasonable" rates charged. See Mahmoud El Gamal (2003). See also http://www.islamic-finance.com/item5_f.htm.

[50] Davies (2011).

In addition the use of a profit equalization reserve and an investment risk reserve to manage the smoothing raises issues as to who is entitled to these funds. These reserves are generally funded out of business results, shifting returns distribution across years. Accordingly contributors to those funds and those who may benefit from them may not be the same.[51]

Islamic financial institutions non-access to interest-bearing paper constrains the conduct of monetary policy. Monetary authorities generally do not have at their disposal *Sharia*-compliant instruments to mop up liquidity and raise the cost of funds. The use of central bank certificates or treasury bills bearing interest can only deal with liquidity in the conventional segment. They present an opportunity for conventional banks to hold normally risk-free government paper, an opportunity that escapes Islamic finance institutions, notwithstanding the progress achieved. On the other side, *Sharia*-compliant instruments may lead to market segmentation, limit liquidity, and compound the efficient transmission of monetary policy.[52]

23.3.2 Integrated financial system development: organizational framework

From the foregoing, integrating Islamic banking in mainstream finance faces the challenge of simultaneously (i) be *Sharia* compliant, and (ii) comply with the regulatory framework of conventional banking. Most notably, this challenge is in the choice of regulatory arrangements, licensing and operation, and conduct of monetary policy.[53] As pointed out, designing separate regulation allows for its calibration to Islamic banks. However, it entails loss of transparency of transactions across segments of the financial system and may result in maintaining Islamic finance as a niche activity. Simply extending conventional regulation to Islamic finance remains awkward as it essentially seeks to have Islamic banking formally comply with conventional regulation. In practice, the latter approach entails either loose regulation of Islamic banking or the stifling of its development entailing a non-level playing field across the financial system.[54]

An alternative organizational framework can allow Islamic finance to meet the challenge and provide it with the opportunity to flourish with minimal constraints from existing regulations. Such an organizational framework can be built on two pillars: (i) focus on the *substance of the services Islamic finance offers* and assess the degree of their similarity with services found across conventional finance, especially beyond banking, and (ii) assign the *responsibility of Sharia compliance* with individual Islamic finance institutions. It would end up requiring minor regulatory adaptations while avoiding the hurdles of adopting separate

[51] See Cunningham (2010).
[52] See Sundarajan (2006) and Grais (2008).
[53] Significant efforts have been made in tackling these issues and progress achieved in the regulation and operation of Islamic banks as well as conduct monetary policy.
[54] It is interesting to note Mr. Bernanke's, former US Federal Reserve Chairman, view: "I will argue that central banks and other regulators should resist the temptation to devise ad hoc rules for each new type of financial instrument or institution. Rather, we should strive to develop common, principles-based policy responses that can be applied consistently across the financial sector to meet clearly defined objectives." See Bernanke (2007).

regulations or awkwardly extending ill-suited ones to the industry. [55] However, the envisaged organizational arrangement would require still further progress in developing an effective framework and performing instruments, for systemic liquidity management and the conduct of monetary policy.[56]

In the proposed organizational framework, Islamic financial intermediation could be conducted by a *Holding Group* and its subsidiaries. The subsidiaries would conduct businesses such as (i) "*Amana banking*"; (ii) Private banking; (iii) Leasing-*Ijara*; (iv) Project financing, or (v) Private equity. Other subsidiaries may be established in line with the Holding Group business plans. In particular, the Holding Group may choose to set up an investment banking subsidiary or integrate the activity within the core of the management of the Holding. Investment banking can help structure and place funding instruments such as *Sukuks* for some of the subsidiaries (project financing or leasing).

The Holding Group would seek the licensing of each subsidiary within its overall business strategy. In a natural way, each subsidiary's business would be consistent with existing regulations and the essence of Islamic finance. Internal policies would help achieve full compliance with Islamic finance principles. A *Sharia* board at the level of the Holding Group would perform the roles existing *Sharia* Advisory Boards play. The regulatory challenges of launching new Islamic financial services would be much diminished.

The following highlights the features of subsidiaries and how the framework of the Holding Group permits simultaneous compliance with prevailing regulation and Islamic finance principles.

Amana banking would take Amana deposits that would be guaranteed and non-remunerated thus complying with banking regulations and Islamic finance. It would offer deposit, payments, and transfer services needed in the conduct of current business transactions. It could finance short-term trade transactions according to *murabaha* contracts. If it is established as a cooperative or credit union with Amana depositors being member shareholders, they would share returns realized within each period.[57] It would in essence be a "narrow bank."

Private banking would offer retail financial advisory services and wealth management. It would care for Unrestricted and Restricted Investment Account holders. It would identify and offer them investment opportunities in mutual funds and other *Sharia*-compliant investments. Investment account holders would own certificates in special vehicles or funds with the clear awareness that the certificates' value and returns are not guaranteed. Unlike in the current structure of Islamic banks, unrestricted investment account holders would be certificate holders in special investment vehicles with recognized rights. The Private banking subsidiary

[55] See also El Gamal (2005): "I propose mutuality as a solution to the corporate governance and regulatory problems currently unresolved due to the peculiar investment account structure. I show that mutual banking would be closer to the religious tenets enshrined in the prohibition of *riba*, and thus would strengthen the brand-name of Islamic banking by re-focusing it on the nature of finance and its objectives, and away from formal-legalistic contract mechanics."

[56] The efforts of the International Islamic Liquidity Management (IILM) Corporation go in that direction: "The IILM seeks to foster regional and international co-operation to build a robust liquidity management infrastructure at national, regional and international levels." See http://www.iilm.com/.

[57] These returns are not known ex ante and accordingly their distribution to members–shareholders–depositors would be compliant with the risk-sharing and no guaranteed returns principles.

would not need a deposit taking commercial bank license. It would not be pressed to engage in smoothing of returns as it would be competing with similar service suppliers. There would be clear disclosure of the risk and returns prospects and no need for banking capital requirement. Competition in attracting funds would be based on performance track record across all investment vehicles in the market. This Private banking subsidiary can be licensed within the framework of prevailing regulation and operate in compliance with it. Its internal policies and recourse to a *Shari'a* advisory board would ensure its full compliance with Islamic finance.

The Holding Group would have a *Leasing-Ijara* subsidiary. It would also be regulated and licensed according to the rules in place. It would compete with other leasing companies in the market offering equipment for lease to business entities.[58] The Holding Group's investment banking services can support the *Leasing-Ijara* subsidiary in securing funding for its activities.

A *Project Finance* Company can be a subsidiary of the Holding Group. This subsidiary would be expected to have recourse to various types of contracts as required. One would expect it to rely to a large extent on *bai salam* and *istisna'a*.[59]

The Holding Group can have a *Private equity* management company subsidiary. Private equity fund management is intrinsically consistent with Islamic finance. It uses *mudaraba* contracts on the funding side, extends financing with *musharaka* contracts and complies with the materiality principle. It can naturally be established within the framework of existing regulation. It can be made fully consistent with Islamic finance when the established private equity fund's policy excludes funding of sinful activities. A management fee and a *mudarib's* profit share are earned by the management company. The *Rabul Mal* or Limited Partner gets his share of return. She/he is like a restricted account holder that elects to invest in a particular private equity fund. Clear regulations and practices followed by private equity management ventures can easily be drawn upon.

Whatever the organizational framework adopted, it is essential that stakeholders have confidence that the business complies with the code of conduct it pledges to follow. Confidence can enhance financial performance, mitigate financial risks, and encourage financial inclusion hence social equity. It is important that all Islamic financial institutions develop within a governance framework that promotes stakeholders' confidence that pledges of *Shari'a* compliance are being fulfilled. From an implementation perspective, a pledge to comply with *Shari'a* principles is similar to a pledge to abide by a code of corporate governance. Significant efforts have been made by AAIOFI, the IFSB, and others to set up principles of sound corporate governance for Islamic financial institutions.[60]

23.4 Conclusion

The overarching point in the foregoing is that Islamic finance is the conduct of the business of financial intermediation according to an ethical code derived from Islamic teachings. Accordingly as a business of financial intermediation, it is part of the general continuous

---

[58] Some *Shari'a* pronouncements may restrict the activity to operating leases.
[59] See Zarqa (1997) for how *istisna'a* can be used for project financing.
[60] See IFSB (2006), IFSB (2009), Grais (2009), and Grais and Pellegrini (2006).

process of financial innovation. As such it needs to meet the requirements of fiduciary responsibility, financial stability, and returns. In addition, as financial intermediation pledging to comply with Islamic teachings, it needs to meet the requirement of actually conducting business according to *Sharia* principles and provide assurances to that effect.

North African populations' cultural and religious background and their aspirations for inclusive economic growth were conducive to the modern revival of Islamic finance. The region saw the creation of one of the first financial institutions to conduct business in compliance with *Sharia* in the 1960s. The Mit Ghamr experiment brought together concepts of cooperative financial institutions developed in Europe, the Islamic principles of returns to risk sharing without preset interest rates. It conveyed the sense of practical feasibility of conducting finance according to *Sharia* principles. The Mit Gham experiment finds also roots in the concept of social solidarity advanced by the prominent regional scholar of the fourteenth century, Ibn Khaldun, as well as in his views on the need for public policy to enable private initiative.

The worldwide increase in Islamic finance assets to more than $1.5 trillion faced numerous challenges. They include public policy towards the development of the industry, the uncertain demand for the industry's services and ability to compete with conventional finance, and the institutional set up for its operations such as its regulatory framework.

In North Africa, public policy has been hesitant in endorsing Islamic finance in contrast to other regions. Some policy advice discouraged policy support notably on the grounds of perceived expected inefficiencies due to the constraints *Sharia* compliance imposes on the business of financial intermediation and possible drag on overall productivity growth. Other policy views point out the ability of the industry to mobilize resources to support economic growth and its potential of inclusiveness.[61]

Financial inclusion is a potential major contribution of Islamic finance. It could remove the hurdle of the fear of breaching religious beliefs that access to conventional finance entails. Evidence, from a North African survey, points out to a strong hypothetical preference for *Sharia*-compliant products among Muslims despite higher costs. However, a broader set of data finds no evidence that Muslims are less likely than non-Muslims to report formal borrowing, though it also finds that "Muslims are significantly less likely than non-Muslims to have an account and save at a formal financial institution."[62] There is not yet a definitive assessment of the potential demand for Islamic financial services and contribution to inclusive growth. Data limitations remain a hurdle in trying to assess indicators such as an elasticity of substitution in the demands of conventional and Islamic financial services. Research on the demand for Islamic financial services and their impact on financial inclusion and inclusive growth is needed.

A major challenge has been the development of regulatory arrangements to govern the industry's operations in the presence of existing extensive regulation of conventional finance. This challenge presents the options of either basically extending conventional

[61] Given the large amount of resources channeled through Islamic finance, their potential impact on economic growth and social inclusion as well as their potential damaging effects if managed in an unregulated and unsupervised way, public policy cannot afford to ignore the presence and expansion of Islamic finance. It needs to develop objectives and frameworks for the conduct of Islamic finance activities, in line with views on industrial policy presented in Stiglitz, J., Lin, J., Monga, C., and Patel, E. (2013).

[62] See section 2.4 and Demirguc-Kunt et al. (2013).

finance regulation to Islamic finance with minor adaptation, or designing a separate regulatory framework for Islamic finance. The challenge is particularly relevant for the licensing and operations of Islamic banks. Heretofore, North African countries adopted the former option with consequences on the regulatory set up and the industry's market performance. A particular daunting challenge remains to be the organization of efficient systemic liquidity management arrangements adapted to the requirements of *Shari'a* compliance though progress is being made. This latter challenge bears on the extent of reserve liquidity Islamic financial institutions need to maintain as well as on the ability to conduct monetary policy. Systemic liquidity management and the conduct of monetary policy in the conduct of a dual, Islamic, and conventional financial system deserve research attention.

In the current context of renewed interest for Islamic finance in North Africa, the choice between the foregoing two approaches to regulation gains relevance. The chapter argues that the choice can be resolved by focusing on the nature of Islamic financial services and adapting the industry's corporate arrangements accordingly. Finding the appropriate regulation for Islamic banks requires overcoming the difficult reconciliation of conventional banking regulation with Islamic finance principles of risk sharing, materiality, and no interest. However, a corporate organizational framework that recognizes the banking and non-banking nature of Islamic financial services can comply with *Shari'a* and conventional finance principles. It can avoid the challenges of an Islamic bank guaranteeing earning deposits, dealing with the constraint banks face to holding real assets or finding alternative ways of liquidity management. Such an alternate organization design can be to establish an Islamic finance Holding group to own a combination of "narrow" bank, mutual funds, leasing company, investment bank, or private equity management. These would correspond respectively to the following Islamic finance services: "Amana" banking, unrestricted and restricted "Mudaraba" investment accounts, "Ijara" leasing, *Shari'a*-compliant investment banking, and "Musharak" participation in business ventures. The foregoing arrangement can easily accommodate the requirements of conventional and Islamic finance, alleviate regulatory and compliance costs, and provide transparency.

Ibn Khaldun believed in the role of markets' in resource allocation and the role of enabling regulation to foster their development. He argues for letting markets determine the fate of industries within a clear public policy framework. Policymakers in North Africa and beyond can heed his guidance by providing a clear and transparent framework for Islamic finance activities and letting markets hold the industry to its pledges and determine its performance.

References

Baloglou, C.P. (2012). The tradition of economic thought in the Mediterranean world from the ancient classical times through the Hellenistic times until the Byzantine times and Arab-Islamic world, in P. Backhaus (ed.), *Handbook of the History of Economic Thought: Insights on the Founders of Modern Economics*. London: Springer. http://digamo.free.fr/backhaus122.pdf.

Barajas, A., Chami, R., Yousefi, S.R. (2013). The Finance and Growth Nexus Re-Examined: Do All Countries Benefit Equally? IMF working paper 13/130, May, IMF, Washington.

Bernanke, B.S. (2007). Remarks by Chairman to the Federal Reserve Bank of Atlanta's 2007 Financial Markets Conference, See Island Georgia, May 15; http://www.federalreserve.gov/newsevents/speech/bernanke20070515a.htm.

Bollen, R. (2006). What is a deposit and (why does it matter)? *Journal of Banking and Finance Law and Practice*, 17:283. https://elaw.murdoch.edu.au/archives/issues/2006/2/elaw_definition_deposit_product_191006.pdf.

Cunningham, A. (2010). New guidance on how Islamic banks may smooth return to investors. http://www.darienmiddleeast.com/hidden/new-guidance-on-how-islamic-banks-may-smooth-returns-to-investors-2/.

Davies, B. (2011). "Applying Liquidity Rules to Sharia Banking". Central Banking Journal, February.www.centralbanking.com/static/central-banking.

Demirguc-Kunt, A., Klapper, L., Randall, D. (2013). Islamic Finance and Financial Inclusion: Measuring Use of and Demand for Formal Financial Services among Muslim Adults, October, World Bank, Policy Research Working Paper 6642. http://papers.ssrn.com/sol3/papers.cfm?abstract_id=2341370##.

Dusuki A.W. (2006). Ibn Khaldun's Concept Of Social Solidarity And Its Implication To Group-Based Lending Scheme, Monash University 4th International Islamic Banking and Finance Conference, Kuala Lumpur 13–14 November, http://www.iefpedia.com/english/wp-content/uploads/2010/03/Ibn-Khaldun's-Concept-Of-Social-Solidarity-And-Its-mplication-To-Group-Based-Lending-Scheme-Dr.-Asyraf-Wajdi-Dusuki.pdf.

El-Gamal, M.A. (2003) Interest and the Paradox of Contemporary Islamic Law and Finance, Rice University; http://www.ruf.rice.edu/~elgamal/files/interest.pdf.

El-Gamal, M.A. (2005). Islamic Bank Corporate Governance and Regulation: A Call for Mutualization, Rice University, September, www.ruf.rice.edu/~elgamal/files/IBCGR.pdf.

El Hawary, D., Grais, W., Iqbal, Z. (2007). Diversity in the regulation of Islamic financial institutions. *Quarterly Review of Economics and Finance*, 46:778–800.

El Naggar, H. (2011). Developing Dual Banking System Regulation in Egypt. http://www.regulacao.gov.br/publicacoes/artigos/developing-dual-banking-system-regulations-in-egypt.

El Tiby, A., and Grais. W. (2014). *Islamic Finance and Economic Development. Risk Management, Regulation and Corporate Governance*. New York: Wiley Finance.

Ernst and Young (2012). World Islamic Banking Competitiveness Report 2011-12. A Brave New World of Sustainable Growth. http://emergingmarkets.ey.com/wp-content/uploads/downloads/2012/03/The-World-Islamic-Banking-Competitiveness-Report.pdf.

Gearon, E. (2011). Arab Invasions: The First Islamic Empire. *History Today*, 61(6). http://www.historytoday.com/eamonn-gearon/arab-invasions-first-islamic-empire.

Grais, W. (2008). Islamic banking: policy and institutional challenges. *Journal of Islamic Economics, Banking and Finance*, 4(1)(January–April).

Grais, W. (2009). Issues in the Corporate Governance of Islamic Financial Services, presentation at the Fordham Law School Islamic Law and Finance Symposium, February 26, New York.

Grais, W. and Pellegrini, M. (2006). Corporate Governance in Institutions Offering Islamic Financial Services: Issues and Options, World Bank Policy Research Working Paper 4052, November.

Grais, W. (2012a). Egypt's Transition towards a New Governance for Sustainable Development, The German Marshall Fund for the United States, Mediterranean Policy Program—Series on the Region and the Economic Crisis, June. http://www.gmfus.org/archives/egypts-transition-towards-a-new-governance-for-sustainable-development/.

Grais, W. (2012b). Islamic Finance: A Development Opportunity for Egypt. The American University in Cairo, October. http://www.aucegypt.edu/GAPP/casar/Pages/Research.aspx.

Hakim, C.M. (undated). Ibn Khaldun's Thought In Microeconomics: Dynamic Of Labor, Demand-Supply And Prices, Bank Indonesia. http://www.uned.es/congreso-ibn-khaldun/pdf/03%20Cecep%20Hakim.pdf.

Honohan, P. (2004). Financial Development, Growth and Poverty: How Close Are the Links? World Bank Policy Research Working Paper 3203, February.

Iqbal, Z., and Mirakhor, A. (2011). *An Introduction to Islamic Finance: Theory and Practice*, 2nd edn. New York: Wiley Finance.

IFIS Analytics (2008). *Shariah* Compliant Finance in Egypt, April 21. www.securities.com/IFIS/.

IFSB (2005). Capital Adequacy Standard for Institutions (Other than Insurance Institutions) Offering Only Islamic Financial Services, December. www.ifsb.org.

IFSB (2006). "Guiding Principles On Corporate Governance For Institutions Offering Only Islamic Financial Services (Excluding Islamic Insurance (*Takaful*) Institutions And Islamic Mutual Funds)," December, http://www.ifsb.org/standard/ifsb3.pdf.

IFSB (2009). "Guiding Principles On Governance For Islamic Collective Investment Schemes." January, http://www.ifsb.org/standard/ifsb6.pdf.

King, R.G., and Levine, R. (1993). Finance, entrepreneurship, and growth: theory and evidence. *Journal of Monetary Economics*, 32:513–542.

Levine, R., Loayza, N., and Beck, T. (2000). Financial intermediation and growth: causality and causes. *Journal of Monetary Economics*, 46:31–77.

Kuran, T. (1997). The genesis of Islamic economics: a chapter in the politics of Muslim identity. *Social Research*, 64(2)Summer:301–338.

Pearce, D. (2011). Financial Inclusion in the Middle East and North Africa. Analysis and Roadmap Recommendations, World Bank Staff Policy Research Working Paper 5610, March.

Rocha, R., Farazi, S., Khouri, R, and Pearce, D. (2011). The Status of Bank Lending to SMEs in the Middle East and North Africa Region Results of a Joint Survey of the Union of Arab Bank and the World Bank, March, World Bank Policy Research Working Paper 5607.

Stiglitz, J., Lin, J., Monga, C., and Patel, E. (2013). Industrial Policy in the African Context, World Bank Policy Research Working Paper 6633, September. http://www-wds.worldbank.org/external/default/WDSContentServer/IW3P/IB/2013/10/02/000158349_20131002151707/Rendered/PDF/WPS6633.pdf.

Sundarajan, V. (2006). Systemic Liquidity Infrastructure and Monetary Policy with Islamic Finance, 3rd Islamic Financial Services Board Summit, Beirut, May 17–18, 2006.

Thomas, S., Abdel, K. et al. (2005). *Structuring Islamic Finance Transactions*. Euromoney books.

UKIFS (2012) Islamic Finance, March, Financial Markets Series. http://www.londonstockexchange.com/specialist-issuers/islamic/downloads/city-uk-if-2012.pdf.

Usmani, M.T. (2005). *An Introduction to Islamic Finance*. Karachi: Maktaba Ma'ariful Qur'an.

Zarqa, M.A. (1997). Istisna' financing of infrastructure projects. *Islamic Economic Studies*, 4(2) May. http://www.isdb.org/irj/go/km/docs/documents/IDBDevelopments/Internet/English/IRTI/CM/downloads/IES_Articles/Vol%204-2..Anas%20Zarqa..ISTISNA%20FINANCING...dp.pdf.

World Bank (2013). Global Development Finance Data Base. http://econ.worldbank.org/WBSITE/EXTERNAL/EXTDEC/EXTGLOBALFINREPORT/0,,contentMDK:23269602~pagePK:64168182~piPK:64168060~theSitePK:8816097,00.html.

World Bank (2014). Islamic finance: a quest for publically available bank-level data blog submitted by Amin Mohseni-cheraghlou, 02/10/2014. http://Blogs.Worldbank.Org/Allaboutfinance/Islamic-Finance-Quest-Publically-Available-Bank-Level-Data.

CHAPTER 24

··

REGULATORY REFORM FOR CLOSING AFRICA'S COMPETITIVENESS GAP

··

IOANNIS N. KESSIDES

24.1 INTRODUCTION

OVER the past decade, Africa has been experiencing an economic resurgence. Despite the global economic crisis, Africa's GDP has been growing rapidly, on average almost five percent a year since 2000—second only to developing Asia. Medium-term growth is expected to remain robust, on the heels of a global economic recovery, the prospect of continuing high commodity prices, and investment in productive capacity (Devarajan and Fengler 2013).

Although this period of impressive growth has given rise to increased optimism about Africa's economic prospects, some serious challenges remain. Many African economies continue to figure among the least competitive in the Global Competitiveness Index (GCI)—14 out of the 20 lowest-ranked economies are African. And, overall, the continent's high growth rates have not yet translated into the rapidly improving living standards that have been seen in other regions with a similar growth performance. Low and falling productivity figures are at the core of these differences in living standards (World Bank 2013a).

Africa must make significant progress in many areas in order to enhance its productivity and set itself on a sustainable high-growth trajectory. The continent's gap with comparable regions—such as Southeast Asia and Latin America and the Caribbean—is particularly large in two of the basic building blocks of a competitive economy: governance and institutions, and infrastructure. Beyond these gaps, many of the countries in the region also suffer from small market sizes.

International experience provides a clear measure of the huge upside potential in net economic benefits that competition, liberated from unnecessary regulatory interference, can produce in an increasing number of circumstances. Estimates of these benefits can serve as useful guideposts for the countries in Africa that are contemplating regulatory reform policies. Indeed, by unleashing market forces of competition, regulatory reform and deregulation can make a substantive contribution towards resolving the continent's productivity and competitiveness dilemmas. However, in individual countries regulatory reform, especially when debated one issue at a time, is often blocked by well-organized interest groups that are trying to preserve their status quo benefits.

Network utilities provide crucial services for manufacturing and commerce, and so significantly influence the growth in national production. Thus economic development depends on such infrastructure—and failure to reform and modernize it undermines national competitiveness and risks economic stagnation. By some estimates, infrastructural shortcomings may be depressing firm-level productivity by 40% in some parts of Africa, and investment in infrastructure can potentially boost growth rates in the region by 2 percentage points (Deutsche Bank 2013).

Continued investment in infrastructure will be critical to maintaining and strengthening growth over the medium term. Given the public sector's constrained fiscal space in Africa, the private sector will have to play an increasingly important complementary role in providing the substantial resources needed for improving national and cross-border infrastructure. However, owing to their long histories of arbitrary administrative intervention and political instability, the region's governments continue to have limited capacity to make credible commitments that they will not engage in political expropriation of the sunk investments made by private utilities and investors. Consequently, investors will demand high-risk premia and underinvest.

Thus, Africa's business environment remains challenging in terms of infrastructure and institutions. Increased regionalization could potentially address both of these challenges. In addition to being an important stepping-stone for building economies of scale and fostering economic diversification, regionalization can effectively elevate the domestic political debate about regulatory reform from narrow domestic issues to matters of regional economic cooperation. From a political perspective, making regulatory reform a regional issue is highly desirable. If the regulatory reform debate is elevated to a matter of regional policy that encompasses numerous reform issues, broader attention and participation from all regional interests is more likely, thereby reducing the ability of a single domestic group to block reform. Thus, regionalization of regulatory policy could mitigate the problem of regulatory capture, facilitate regulatory reform, enhance the capacity of national governments to make credible policy commitment and through the pooling of resources, help them overcome technical capacity constraints and establish more effective and credible regional institutions (Kessides et al. 2010).

For these reasons, the framework for regional economic integration in several parts of the African continent includes coordination of policies in core infrastructure industries such as transport, telecommunications, and electricity. Infrastructure development is included in many regional treaties to provide the framework for aligning sector policies, designing regional master plans, developing a portfolio of synergistic projects, harmonizing regulatory regimes and investment codes, and mobilizing investment resources. Increasingly, the African nations have been moving away from integration strategies that are based solely on formal trade agreements and towards strategies that include at least some integration of infrastructure policies.

24.2 Africa's Competitiveness Gap and Regulatory Burden

Many African countries continue to be among the least competitive economies in the world. In the Global Competitiveness Index (GCI), 14 out of the 20 lowest-ranked economies are

African. The region's competitiveness as a whole trails Southeast Asia and Latin America and the Caribbean. However, Africa has not remained stagnant. The region has been improving its competitiveness, although the change has been gradual and modest. Some of Africa's biggest and stubbornly persisting gaps are seen in the quality of institutions/regulatory governance and infrastructure (World Bank 2013a).

In view of the important reciprocal relationships between infrastructure (soft institutional and hard physical) and regional economic integration, and their potential impacts on productivity and growth, the continent's persistent institutional and infrastructure deficiencies, are worrisome—especially at a time of rising global economic uncertainty. Thus, despite the acceleration in the continent's growth during the past decade, serious concerns remain as to how sustainable this African renaissance will be over the longer term. Reducing the competitiveness divide between African economies and other, more advanced regions will be critical for placing the region on a firmly sustainable growth and development path. The pertinent question is whether policymakers are putting into place the fundamental microeconomic reforms that are indispensable preconditions for boosting productivity and competitiveness. One of the key priorities is to maintain the momentum for regulatory reform. Specific priority areas include cutting administrative delays, removing the regulatory impediments to entrepreneurial activity, harmonizing regulations across regional markets, and improving the effectiveness of infrastructure's regulatory governance.

In terms of ease of doing business, regulations have improved in Africa in recent years. Indeed, the continent continues to record a large number of reforms aimed at easing the regulatory burden on local entrepreneurs and building stronger institutions—the majority (29 out of 33) of sub-indicators that are used by the World Bank to estimate the ease of doing business have improved between 2005 and 2012. In 2005 only a third of countries in the region were reforming; now over two-thirds are (*The Economist* 2012). During 2012–2013, over 73 regulatory reforms were adopted (Figure 24.1). Progress in some countries has been truly impressive, with four countries in sub-Saharan Africa having been among the ten top global reformers over the last five years.[1] And out of the 20 economies that have most improved business regulation since 2009, nine are in the region: Benin, Burundi, Côte d'Ivoire, Guinea, Guinea-Bissau, Liberia, Rwanda, Sierra Leone, and Togo (World Bank 2013b).[2]

Over the past five years sub-Saharan Africa reduced the gap with the frontier in regulatory practice by three times as much as OECD high-income economies. All this progress notwithstanding, Africa remains the region with the lowest comparative ranking on the quality of its regulatory environment (Figure 24.2). The region's economies are furthest from the frontier than those of any other region in six of the ten areas measured by *Doing Business*.

---

[1] In the past five years, for example, sub-Saharan Africa accounted for 22 out of the 66 reforms recorded by Doing Business that made it easier to enforce contracts. Some economies in the region overhauled the organization of their courts or systems of judicial case management for commercial dispute resolution. However, the main trend has been to introduce specialized commercial courts that led to greater specialization of judges—resulting in faster resolution times, cheaper contract enforcement, shorter court backlogs and increased efficiency (World Bank 2013b).

[2] Of these, Rwanda has made the most progress overall. The country has embarked on an ambitious program of regulatory and administrative reform explicitly designed to improve the climate for business. In just over five years, Rwanda climbed from the 150th position to 32nd in the ease of doing business ranking of the World Bank's Doing Business (Ernst & Young 2013).

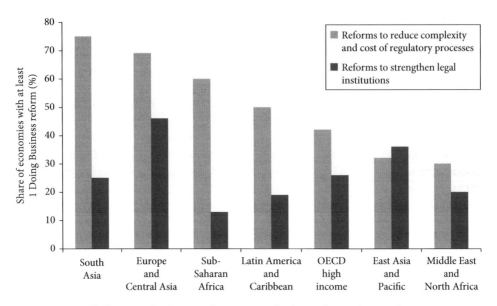

FIGURE 24.1 Reforms reducing regulatory complexity and cost in 2012/13.

Source: World Bank (2013b).

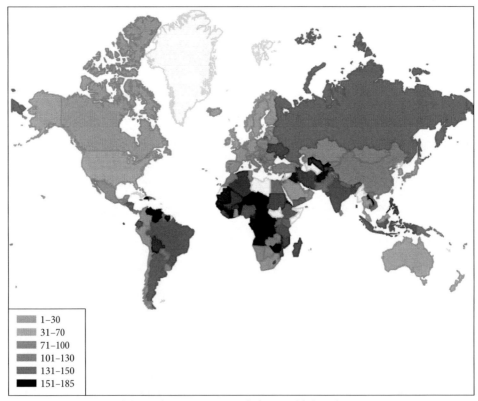

FIGURE 24.2 Ease of doing business, around the world (2013).

Source: Global Finance (2013).

Clearly more needs to be done because entrepreneurs in Africa still face a burdensome regulatory environment.

Business regulatory reform is of particular significance in the low-income economies of the African continent. A variety of studies have detected a negative correlation between economic growth and regulatory intensity—countries with less regulation tend to exhibit higher growth in output per person (Guasch and Spiller 1999). There is also a link between better business regulations and economic growth. Thus both the intensity and quality of regulation have important implications for economic growth. Moreover, recent research shows that economic growth remains the most important factor in determining the pace of income growth for poor people (Dollar et al. 2013). Together, this evidence seems to indicate that an effective program of regulatory reform and deregulation has the potential to make a significant contribution towards reducing poverty and boosting shared economic prosperity in the African continent.

24.3 THE GLOBAL REGULATORY REFORM MOVEMENT

Over the past two decades, substantive steps towards total deregulation of some markets and less comprehensive regulation of others have been taken in many countries around the world. While the most dramatic manifestations of this deregulation revolution have been in industries with competitive market structures, a major reassessment of regulatory policy in industries with natural monopoly (or tightly oligopolistic) characteristics has also taken place. The main impetus for regulatory decontrol was provided by the increasing recognition that government intrusion into pricing, investment, and other such business decisions imposes substantial economic costs—it can discourage investment in innovation, shelter inefficiency, promote misallocation of resources, cause incentive breakdowns, and reduce the price and quality options that the public would be offered under unfettered market allocation. In addition, technological change and regulatory experience facilitated the formulation of policy which permits a much greater toleration of factors that make for natural monopoly while at the same time lessening the need for public intervention.

Regulatory experience and new bodies of economic analysis underpinned the view that: where public measures are called for, the types of market intervention that ought to be undertaken are, in many cases, significantly different from those that have been traditionally employed; and that there are some cases in which public intervention is inappropriate even though it was previously thought to be necessary. Indeed, recent policy developments call for a major reorientation of the traditional regulatory rules and procedures, and offer two types of guidance to regulators. First, they provide an improved set of criteria distinguishing between those cases in which intervention by the public sector is warranted and those in which it is not. Second, they establish an improved set of guidelines for appropriate government intervention in the structure and conduct of firms in those cases in which intervention is called for, that is, they offer more effective tools to the regulators that increase the public welfare effects of intervention. In several countries, innovative methods of regulation have already been introduced and major sectors of their economies have undergone far reaching regulatory reform.

The experience from the economies that have implemented substantive regulatory reforms confirms what theory predicts: decentralized market-oriented decision-making that is freed from unnecessary regulatory control and that is energized by market incentives is the surest means of finding and implementing innovative solutions to problems posed in several sectors of the economy. As a consequence of deregulation, there have been fundamental changes in the way in which firms in these countries are conducting business. By and large, these changes reflect efficiency-enhancing structural reorganization and increasing diversity in price–service options, and greater responsiveness to consumer demands as well as to marketplace opportunities for innovation. The removal of significant impediments to entry and market access has resulted in new opportunities for small entrepreneurial firms and start-ups, more innovation by larger entrepreneurial corporations, and the consequent introduction of new products and services more responsive to consumer demands.

While most firms were quite successful in absorbing the shock of deregulation and operating in a competitive environment, others experienced difficulties of adjustment and major restructuring of their respective industries occurred. Indeed, one of the necessary consequences of regulatory reform is that there must be a possibility that relatively inefficient firms will lose profitability and go into liquidation. Moreover, the post-deregulation period has been characterized by pressures to reduce pay scales toward those in the unregulated economic sectors and to increase productivity through more efficient use of labor. Inevitably, these changes led to some labor displacement. These dangers, of course, are the natural concomitant of a freer competitive environment. Still, the available evidence indicates that, on average, regulatory reform and deregulation have yielded very positive results for both producers and consumers (Kahn 2004; Rose 2014).

24.4 REGULATORY REFORM FOR ENHANCING AFRICA'S COMPETITIVENESS

Regulatory reform improves the efficiency of a nation's economy, enhances its ability to adapt to change, and strengthens its international competitiveness.[3] It unleashes market forces of competition thereby providing powerful incentives for firms to become cost-effective and innovative, to realign prices with resource costs, and to improve the quality of their products and services. Yet, in many African countries there appears to be a strong countervailing reluctance to spin activities out of direct public control and to deregulate economic activity.

---

[3] As Noll (1997) pointed out, as trade barriers fell, regulation became a more significant factor in affecting the relative prices of exports, imports, and domestic production. And regulatory reform began to be perceived as a means by which a nation could capture greater benefits from trade liberalization. This is because inefficient domestic regulations can cause otherwise efficient firms lose sales to less efficient sources of supply from countries with better/less burdensome regulatory systems. For example, inefficient border administration reduces the price competitiveness of African exports in global markets and adds to the cost of imports. The transport and communications infrastructure is far less developed than in other regions, which also significantly raises the cost of trading, particularly for landlocked economies.

This reluctance can be linked to both protection of status quo benefits and to concerns over the transitional problems of deregulation, especially those related to labor entrenchment, tariff rebalancing (and the consequent price increases for certain formerly subsidized services), business liquidation and universal service. Governments do not easily and willingly forgo using the instruments they have in hand for the collection and disbursement of political benefits.

The African continent has a potential for substantial gains from microeconomic and regulatory reform as key sectors of the region's economies remain heavily regulated. However, there are adverse conditions that render the process of such reform somewhat delicate. In view of the delicate macroeconomic condition of some of the continent's economies, their imperfectly developed capital markets, and their generally weak economic institutions, caution is appropriate with respect to regulatory decontrol. For example, major price revisions are likely to be disruptive and, in some instances, are greatly complicated by high rates of inflation.

Determining the full consequences of any regulatory reform is virtually an impossible task. The relaxation of the present constraints upon the operations of national firms will generate opportunities for improvements in the region's economies. But, it will also engender risks and uncertainties which could adversely affect the general welfare. There are also substantial dangers involved in failing to move in the direction of greater reliance on competitive market forces that are freed from unnecessary regulatory controls. The cross-country experience reveals that well-intentioned regulatory controls caused enormous distortions in productivity and in service. Indeed, there is strong evidence from Africa that governmental intrusion into pricing, investment, and other such business decisions has induced substantial inefficiencies and imposed heavy social costs.

All of the above considerations—the difficulties of continuing under the present regulatory regime and the potential, mainly transitional hardships under a more competitive system—lead to policy recommendations that envision an orderly transition to a goal of substantial deregulation of the African economies. The purpose is to implement policy changes that achieve the benefits of deregulation—more efficient industries that are better attuned to the needs of consumers and other users of their services—without threatening the immediate extinction of individual firms or the rapid destabilization of key sectors of the economy.

24.5 REGIONALIZATION FOR MORE EFFECTIVE REGULATORY GOVERNANCE

Africa is facing a significant challenge in accelerating and broadening "enabling environment" reforms to stimulate economic growth, generate employment, and enhance economic prosperity. Outdated, duplicative and unnecessary administrative procedures and other regulations impose substantial efficiency costs on the region's economies, promote corruption, and are needlessly stifling job creation and undermining sustained economic growth. Yet reviewing, assessing, and repealing thousands of rules, administrative procedures, and regulations across many ministries, government agencies, regulatory bodies, and levels of government, is a hugely challenging task. It can also entail significant political costs and can be strenuously resisted by well-organized interest groups whose status quo benefits are threatened by such reforms. Indeed, regulatory and administrative reforms when debated one issue at a time can be effectively blocked by special interest groups.

A broad, systemic and regionally coordinated approach is needed to significantly reduce the administrative burdens that regulation imposes on productive business activity in Africa. Moreover, in view of the enormous pressures and great sense of urgency generated by the continent's continuing competitiveness challenges, there is a need for more rapid and comprehensive microeconomic reforms that will produce faster and sustained benefits for the region's economies. In designing such regulatory reform strategies, Africa can benefit from the implementation experience of other countries that have successfully streamlined regulations constraining investment and employment growth.

The guillotine strategy (pioneered by Sweden in the 1980s), for example, entails a systematic and transparent approach to rapidly reviewing a large number of regulations and eliminating those that are outdated without the need for lengthy and cumbersome legal action on each specific rule. It facilitates a rapid and effective response to fixing unneeded and inefficient regulation. It can also contribute to establishing a sustainable framework for quality control of new business regulations to avoid recurrence of the same problems (so-called creeping re-regulation). It can substantially reduce the costs of reform within political and legislative systems that are already overburdened with difficult reform challenges (Jacobs and Astrakhan 2006).

24.6 REGIONALIZING REGULATION TO MITIGATE REPRESENTATION BIAS AND FACILITATE COMMITMENT

An important advantage of regionalizing regulatory reform is that it can be used to elevate the domestic political debate about regulation from narrow particularistic issues to matters of national economic performance and regional economic cooperation or integration. From a political perspective, making regulatory reform a regional issue is highly desirable. A common political barrier to domestic regulatory reform is that if reform is perceived as a domestic matter and debated one issue at a time, well-organized special interests are more likely to have the political power to block it. For most specific regulatory issues, the beneficiaries of reform are numerous, but their per capita benefits are frequently too low or indirect to generate significant political pressure for reform. If the reform debate is elevated to a matter of regional policy that encompasses numerous reform issues, broader attention and participation from all interests is more likely, thereby reducing the ability of a single group to block reform.

A useful analogy is to the process of setting tariffs. When each nation independently sets each tariff, the outcome is likely to be tariffs that are higher than the tariffs that would be negotiated bilaterally as part of a comprehensive regional trade agreement. The reason is that debating tariffs one product at a time maximizes the opportunity for organized interests with a direct stake in a policy to be unduly influential. If a tariff on a specific product is under review, the domestic industry that produces the product is likely to be intensely interested to exercise whatever political influence it has to obtain a policy decision favorable to itself. However, because the final price of the product is less important to each buyer than to each producer, the former are less likely to participate in the debate. Consequently, each important domestic industry may receive and preserve a tariff or a favorable regulation when policy is debated in a purely domestic context one industry at a time, but receive neither protective tariffs nor protective regulation when policy is developed regionally and covers many industries.

When each regulation is considered separately as a matter of domestic concern within a specialized agency, the government is likely to be under less pressure to adopt an efficient policy. If a regulation imposes unnecessary costs uniformly on firms in a domestic industry, sales of the industry's product may be suppressed somewhat by higher prices, but the individual firms are unlikely to suffer very much because none is being disadvantaged relative to a competitor. If regional/international trade threatens the industry, however, the industry will energetically seek relief. The politically expedient response may be to inhibit trade competition, either by using regulation as an indirect trade barrier or by banning trade while invoking a rhetorical attack on the lax standards of a trading partner. This approach placates the regulated industry and the other interests that place high value on the regulatory policy. The primary organized interest that is harmed, that of foreign producers, is more easily ignored because they do not participate in domestic politics.

Just as simultaneous negotiations over tariffs on all products facilitate reaching agreements that provide freer trade, so too simultaneous negotiations of numerous areas of regulation facilitate eliminating indirect trade barriers. As with tariffs, the inclusion of multiple regulatory policies within the same negotiation creates more opportunities and more mutually beneficial bargains to reduce distortions simultaneously on all fronts. Thus, the incorporation of regulation into regional trade agreements should follow the same principles that have been generally followed with respect to tariffs and quotas. Specifically, if regulatory policy is part of a regional/international agreement, it must reduce, not increase, distortions in the regional/international economy and extend, not contract, the extent of liberalization. Introducing regulation into single-product negotiations is prone to lead to increased trade distortions (by using regulation to inhibit trade). In particular, negotiations about a single product or area of regulation run the risk of creating an alliance between protectionists and the most ardent advocates of a particular regulatory policy who seek regulations that go far beyond those that maximize net social benefits.

The same argument applies to the enforcement of agreements not to adopt anticompetitive regulations. If enforcement powers reside solely in domestic agencies, a case in which a regulation disadvantages foreign producers rests on unbalanced underlying politics. Domestic producers are likely to be more effectively represented than foreigners in the agency and the background political system in which the agency must operate. And domestic regulatory agencies are frequently willing to sacrifice competition as well as some of the effectiveness of regulatory policies in order to advantage domestic producers. Regional institutions for resolving regulatory issues, on the other hand, operate in a more balanced political environment. These institutions can be a means through which nations mutually can commit to maintain pro-competitive regulatory reforms.

For these reasons, regionalization/internationalization of regulatory reform can succeed by enfranchising foreign producers in domestic regulatory policy across a spectrum of industries. In the context of a dispute about the trade effects of a particular regulation, intervention by an international organization frequently is met with cries of outrage—an intervention by foreigners into domestic policy. All international agreements entail some loss of the ability to act independently in order to achieve something else of value, which in this case is a worldwide regulatory system that is more efficient and freer of trade distortions. Such an institution generates net economic benefits to each country, even if some cases create domestic losers. The creation of institutions for enforcing agreements to eliminate indirect trade barriers is a means to balance the political influence of these domestic losers.

24.7 REGIONALIZING REGULATION TO ENHANCE POLICY CREDIBILITY AND COMMITMENT

Services delivered by infrastructure industries are economically and politically important. Because of their importance and ubiquitous consumption, the prices of infrastructure services typically are scrutinized by interest groups and even the general public, and so receive considerable political attention. These characteristics can motivate governments to behave opportunistically vis-à-vis privatized utilities. A large portion of infrastructure costs are fixed and sunk—that is, once the investment is made the assets cannot be redeployed elsewhere. Thus, utilities are vulnerable to administrative expropriation of their sunk investments.

Given the public sector's constrained fiscal space in most African countries, the private sector will have to play an increasingly important complementary role in providing the substantial resources needed for improving regional connectivity through national and cross-border infrastructure investment. However, private utilities and investors that are vulnerable to administrative intervention in Africa can be expected to demand high risk premia and to underinvest in infrastructure unless the region's governments are able to make a credible commitment not to expropriate sunk investments. Owing to their long histories of arbitrary administrative intervention and political instability, these governments have a very limited capacity to make such credible commitments.

Regionalization of regulation creates institutions whose policies and decisions can be changed only by mutual agreement among several nations. Consequently, political change or government opportunism in one country is insufficient to cause a radical change in regulatory governance unless the government is willing to sacrifice all of the other benefits that arise from regional economic cooperation. Thus, regionalization of regulation could enhance the ability of the governments in Africa to credibly commit to a stable regulatory process.

24.8 REGIONALIZATION TO OVERCOME TECHNICAL CAPACITY CONSTRAINTS

Effective regulation, especially in key infrastructure sectors of the economy, requires professional staffs that are expert in the relevant economic, accounting, engineering, and legal principles and familiar with good regulatory practice elsewhere. These types of specialized skills are also needed in the regulated firms. Therefore, the question arises whether some of the poor and especially small African countries would have a sufficient supply of specialists to staff their regulatory agencies, run their utilities, and provide for policy capacity within the relevant sectoral ministries.

The principal difficulty is not in finding a few competent regulatory commissioners. All that is required of an agency's commissioners is to be at least somewhat familiar with the broad regulatory issues and to have some relevant expertise. Commissioners do not need to be up-to-date economic or technical experts. Instead, the more challenging task is to find the necessary expertise for the agency's staff, which performs economic and technical policy analysis and provides institutional continuity for the development and responsiveness of the regulatory system (Stern 2000). The number of technical staff that is necessary to regulate infrastructure industries is very large, and in small, poor nations the number of people with the requisite expertise can be quite small. By pooling resources among nations, regional regulatory authorities alleviate some of the problems that arise from the scarcity of technical and economic expertise at the national level. Moreover, even in middle-income nations, national regulatory agencies can have a high fixed cost relative to market size (Noll 2000; Stern et al. 2002). The creation of regional regulatory authorities can spread the fixed costs of regulation among the larger population of a regional economic community.

24.9 Effective Regulation for Seamless Infrastructure and Greater Connectivity

Africa has substantial human and natural resources. The forces of globalization could potentially have a major transformational impact on the region's role in the world economy. Modern and sophisticated production networks would allow the continent to energetically exploit the opportunities offered by globalization and in consequence to experience sustained economic growth and prosperity. And yet Africa's potential remains largely untapped and it still plays a relatively minor role in global economic activity in part due to insufficient region-wide connectivity. Many parts of Africa with vast resources and a huge number of communities remain economically as well as geographically isolated.

One of Africa's greatest assets is its enormous cultural and physical diversity. However, without good connectivity diversity can lead to conflict and disparity rather than to economic prosperity. Efficient, fast, reliable, reasonably priced, and seamless infrastructure connections are indispensable for the effective exploitation of natural resource and production complementarities and the free flow of goods and services across the entire region. Thus they are crucial for improving the region's productivity and trade competitiveness. Unfortunately, most African countries have inadequate infrastructure characterized by low service quality, high prices (twice as expensive as elsewhere), and missing regional links. Africa's road density—an indicator of connectivity within countries—is substantially lower than in other developing regions: 204 kilometers of road per 1000 square kilometers with only one-quarter paved, compared to a global average of 944 kilometers per 1000 square kilometers, with more than one-half paved. Similarly, the spatial density of the continent's rail networks is low and 13 countries have no operating railway at all. Moreover, most of Africa's major ports suffer from significant capacity constraints and low operating efficiencies. And only one-fifth of the continent's population has access to electricity as compared to one-half in South Asia and more than four-fifths in Latin America. More than 30 African countries are experiencing power shortages and regular interruptions in service, and the cost of generating electricity is exceptionally high and rising (Foster and Briceno-Garmendia 2010).

The resumption of economic growth in recent years has exerted significant pressure on Africa's existing infrastructure networks and is rapidly unmasking a long list of supply-side infrastructure constraints and bottlenecks: poor road and rail networks with important missing links and significant operational capacity problems; congested and inefficient regional ports; inadequate electricity supply; and poor access to information and telecommunications technology. The elimination of these supply-side constraints will require significant amounts of infrastructure investment. The countries in the region do not have the resources to provide the necessary financing from general revenues. Moreover, an investment plan of this magnitude cannot be undertaken by the private sector alone. It will require creative partnerships between the public and private sectors. It will also require effective regulatory governance that is presently lacking.

An important reciprocal relationship exists between infrastructure and economic integration. Cross-border infrastructure facilitates physical connectivity which is essential for enhanced regional cooperation and economic integration. Indeed, the key driving forces behind the recent wave of globalization are lower barriers to trade and investment, and lower transportation and communication costs. Major efficiency improvements in transportation and the application of modern information and communication technologies have facilitated the geographic division of production processes. A much larger number of geographically dispersed production units can participate, contributing to the value added chain according to their comparative advantage. Thus the opportunities of individual economies to participate in international production networks have been broadened considerably (Kuroda 2006; ESCAP 2007).

The development of regional markets, in turn, creates interdependencies that increase the demand for infrastructure. After all, infrastructure networks are the conduits for these flows. Transportation infrastructure is at the heart of regional integration. Traded goods flow through roads, railways, inland waterways, ports, and airports, as do people seeking to take advantage of attractive services or job opportunities in other nations. Therefore, an efficient and integrated transport system facilitates trade and factor mobility. An integrated communications system also can spur the growth of trade as well as reduce costs by enhancing the accessibility and affordability of information, facilitating long-distance transactions, and linking the region with the rest of the world. Not surprisingly, limited development of transport, communications, and energy networks is one of the most frequently cited obstacles to cross-border trade and investment and ultimately to connectivity in many regions of the world (AfDB 2006).

Whereas infrastructure has long been recognized as having a crucial role in facilitating economic integration, some ancillary propositions are not widely recognized. First, greater welfare gains can be realized through deeper forms of regional integration that entail harmonization of legal, regulatory, and institutional frameworks. Second, reforms that reduce cross-border transaction costs and improve the performance of backbone infrastructure services are arguably more important for the creation of an open, unified regional economic space than trade policy reforms narrowly defined. Third, all economies benefit from the more rational use of resources that arises from coordination of regional infrastructure development.

For these reasons, the framework for regional economic integration in several parts of the world includes coordination of policies in core infrastructure industries such as transport, telecommunications, and electricity. Infrastructure development is included in many regional treaties to provide the framework for aligning sector policies, designing regional master plans, developing a portfolio of synergistic projects, harmonizing regulatory regimes and investment codes, and mobilizing investment resources. Increasingly, nations are moving away from integration strategies that are based solely on formal trade agreements and towards strategies that include at least some integration of infrastructure policies (Moreira 2007).

The creation of a seamless infrastructure to enhance connectivity has two components: "hard" or physical infrastructure (i.e. long-term technical structures, equipment, and facilities—roads, water supply, power grids, telecommunications networks, railroads, ports, airports and so forth); and "soft" infrastructure (i.e. regulatory mechanisms and other institutional frameworks, and substantive policies that must be put in place to facilitate the efficient operation and functioning of the hard component). Even greater connectivity and associated welfare gains could be realized with deeper forms of regional cooperation in infrastructure which are not limited to just linking physical networks but also include the harmonization of legal, regulatory, and institutional frameworks. Disparities of regulatory treatment across borders in the region can introduce distortions that hinder trade, the aggregate flows of investment on a regional basis, and ultimately connectivity. Similarly, market opening and restructuring in the backbone infrastructure sectors must have a parallel development (reciprocity) across countries. Otherwise, significant differences in market structures could hinder cross-border trade and connectivity. Regulatory and market structure harmonization, the elimination of trade-distorting inefficient national regulations, and regulatory cooperation to overcome domestic constraints on regulatory capacity and thus achieve regulatory effectiveness, are essential components of regional economic cooperation and connectivity.

24.10 SUMMARY

After a decade of robust growth in the face of a very challenging global economic environment, Africa is at a crossroads. Policy decisions and actions taken today will have profound implications for the sustainability of the continent's economic renaissance and a strong bearing on whether it will succeed in making the transition from resource-driven to higher-value-added growth and thus place itself on a path similar to that of other successful regions such as developing Asia. Although this period of growth has given rise to increased optimism about Africa's economic prospects, the continent is facing several difficult challenges.

Many African countries continue to feature among the least competitive economies in the world. The emerging international experience indicates that regulatory reform and deregulation can make a substantive contribution towards resolving the continent's productivity and competitiveness dilemmas. Indeed, decentralized market-oriented decision-making that is freed from unnecessary regulatory control and that is energized by market incentives is the surest means of finding and implementing innovative solutions to problems posed in several sectors of Africa's economies.

Africa's business environment and competitiveness are adversely affected by (i) inadequate and poor regional infrastructure networks that raise cross-border transaction costs; and (ii) weak institutional capacity. Increased regionalization could potentially address both of these challenges. Regional integration of regulation, combined with regionalization of regulated firms, could assist the countries of Africa in overcoming national limits in technical expertise, enhance national capacity to make credible commitments to stable regulatory policy, facilitate the introduction of competition into historically monopolized markets, improve the efficiency of infrastructure industries by allowing them to grow without respecting economically artificial national boundaries, and ultimately increase infrastructure investment.

ACKNOWLEDGMENT

Section 24.6 "Regionalizing regulation to mitigate representation bias and facilitate commitment" is based on Roger Noll's numerous contributions in this area.

REFERENCES

AfDB (African Development Bank) (2006). Infrastructure Development and Regional Integration: Issues, Opportunities and Challenges. Ministerial Round Table & High Level Seminars Jointly Organized with the UN Economic Commission for Africa. Ouagadougou Conference Centre, 16 May 2006.

Deutsche Bank (2013). Sub-Saharan Africa: A Bright Spot in Spite of Key Challenges. https://www.dbresearch.com/PROD/DBR_INTERNET_EN-PROD/PROD0000000000317226/Sub-Saharan+Africa%3A+A+bright+spot+in+spite+of+key+challenges.PDF.

Devarajan, S., and Fengler, W. (2013). Africa's economic boom: why the pessimists and the optimists are both right. *Foreign Affairs*, May/June Issue, pp. 68–81.

Dollar, D., Kleineberg, T., and Kraay, A. (2013). Growth Still Is Good for the Poor. Policy Research Working Paper 6568. Washington, DC: World Bank.

Ernst & Young (2013). Ernst & Young's Attractiveness Survey: Africa 2013. http://www.ey.com/Publication/vwLUAssets/The_Africa_Attractiveness_Survey_2013/$FILE/Africa_Attractiveness_Survey_2013_AU1582.pdf.

ESCAP (United Nations Economic and Social Commission for Asia and the Pacific) (2007). Toward an Asian Integrated Transport Network. ST/ESCAP/2399.

Foster, V., and Briceno-Garmendia, C. (2010). *Africa's Infrastructure—A Time for Transformation*. A copublication of the Agence Française de Développement and the World Bank.

Global Finance (2013). Best Countries for Doing Business 2013. http://www.gfmag.com/component/content/article/119-economic-data/12525-best-countries-for-doing-business-2013.html#axzz2jiteBkth.

Guasch, L.J., and Spiller, P. (1999). *Managing the Regulatory Process: Design, Concepts, Issues, and the Latin America and Caribbean Story*. Washington, DC: World Bank.

Jacobs, S., and Astrakhan, J. (2006). Bold and Sustainable Regulatory Reform: The Regulatory Guillotine in Three Transition and Developing Countries. World Bank Conference Reforming the Business Environment: From Assessing Problems to Measuring Results, Nov. 29 to Dec. 1, 2005, Cairo.

Kahn, A. (2004). *Lessons from Deregulation*. Washington, DC: AEI-Brooking Joint Center for Regulatory Studies.

Kessides, I., Noll, R., and Benjamin, N. (2010). Regionalising regulatory reform in developing countries. *World Economics*, 11(3):79–108.

Kuroda, H. (2006). Infrastructure and Regional Cooperation. Paper presented at the Annual Bank Conference on Development Economies, Tokyo, Japan. May 29–30.

Moreira, M. (2007). Trade Costs and the Economic Fundamentals of the Initiative for Integration of Regional Infrastructure in South America (IIRSA). INTAL-ITD Working Paper 30.

Noll, R. (1997). International regulatory reform, in P. Nivola (ed.), *Comparative Disadvantage? Social Regulations and the Global Economy*. Washington, DC: Brookings Institution.

Noll, R. (2000). Regulatory reform and international trade policy, in T. Ito and A. Krueger (eds), *Deregulation and Interdependence in the Asia-Pacific Region*. Chicago: University of Chicago Press.

Rose, N.L. (2014). Learning from the Past: Insights for the Regulation of Economic Activity, in N.L. Rose (ed.), *Economic Regulation and Its Reform: What Have We Learned?* Chicago: University of Chicago Press, pp. 1–23.

Stern, J. (2000). Electricity and telecommunications regulatory institutions in small and developing countries. *Utilities Policy*, 9(3):131–157.

Stern, J., Domah, P., and Pollitt, M. (2002). Modelling the Costs of Energy Regulation: Evidence of Human Resource Constraints in Developing Countries. London Business School, Regulation Initiative Working Paper No. 49.

The Economist. (2012). Doing Business 2012: Getting Better. October 27. http://www.economist.com/news/business/21565250-bad-rules-breed-corruption-cutting-them-costs-nothing-getting-better.

World Bank (2013a). *The Africa Competitiveness Report 2013*. Washington, DC: World Bank.

World Bank (2013b). *Doing Business 2014*. Washington DC, Word Bank.

PART III

INSTITUTIONAL/ SOCIAL ECONOMICS

CHAPTER 25

....

SCHOOL ENROLLMENT, ATTAINMENT, AND RETURNS TO EDUCATION IN AFRICA

....

RUTH UWAIFO OYELERE

25.1 INTRODUCTION

....

GROWTH is a necessary condition for development and past research suggests that human capital, accumulated through investments in education, play a significant role in explaining growth differences across countries (Mankiw et al.,1992). Though this relationship between education and economic growth was questioned in the past literature when enrollment was used as a proxy for education (see Pritchett 2001), there is ample evidence of significant positive association between quantitative measures of education and economic growth in recent cross-country growth regression studies.[1]

Education in Africa has different dimensions that are of interest to researchers and policymakers; this chapter focuses on returns to education (RTE), enrollment, and attainment. The chapter is structured as follows. Section 2 examines how returns have been measured and why new estimates of returns are needed for African countries. Section 3 analyzes enrollment trends in sub-Saharan Africa (SSA) and benchmarks these trends against those worldwide. Also in section 3 factors affecting enrollment and attainment in Africa are discussed and the recent literature on this topic is surveyed. Section 4 summarizes finding from a meta-analysis on past estimates of returns for African countries. A summary and conclusion are in the last section.

---

[1] See Pritchett (2006) for a review of this literature and Hanushek and Woessmann (2008) for further explanation on the differences in findings.

25.2 Measuring Returns to Education

25.2.1 Methods used to estimate returns to education

The benefits of education have been estimated using two main approaches in the past literature: the rate of return approach and the wage equation approach. The first approach to estimating economic benefits of education also known as the full method was popularized by Psacharopoulos (1981). He suggested that to estimate the private rate of return (PROR) to a given level of education, one needs to compare the discounted benefits over the lifetime of an educational investment project to the cost of the project. His proposed method for calculation of social rate of return to a level of education is almost identical to his method for calculating PROR. The major difference between the two is the use of pretax income in the computation versus post-tax income. Schultz (1988) and Bennell (1996) highlight some of the problems with deriving estimates using this methodology, and some of these limitations are especially relevant for Africa. For example, the computation of costs in PROR does not include both opportunity costs and direct costs. Although both these costs are hard to estimate and could exhibit significant heterogeneity at each level of education, given both private and public provision of education, both need to be accounted for. Another flaw in this methodology that upwardly biases PROR estimates is assuming the opportunity cost of primary education is 0 in computing the rate of returns to primary education. This assumption highlights the limited applicability of this methodology for many rural societies within Africa. In these setting, children make significant contribution to farm and nonfarm production and assuming the opportunity cost of primary education is zero is incorrect.[2]

The second methodology is the wage equation approach. This approach makes use of the Mincer's (1974) human capital earning function commonly referred to as the Mincer wage equation (MWE). This approach has been commonly used to estimate the private average returns to education (PARTE). The foundation of this equation is the human capital model of household decision-making, which focuses on the notion that education is an investment of current time and money in anticipation of increased earnings (Becker 1964). The link between this equation and Becker's model was expounded in Card (1999).

Equation (1) is a standard Mincer wage equation. Here y is earnings of individual I, α is the constant term, S is years of schooling, X is years of experience, D is a vector capturing possible exogenous variables affecting earning and ϵ is the error term.

$$Log\ y_i = \alpha + \beta S_i + \phi X_i + \lambda X_i^2 + \rho_i D + \varepsilon_i \tag{1}$$

β, which is our estimate of interest, captures the PARTE, which represents the percentage change in earnings for an extra year of schooling. Before the 1990s this equation was estimated solely using the ordinary least square (OLS) estimator. However Griliches (1977) and Card (1995) highlight some potential problems with estimating β using OLS, including selection bias, endogeneity, omitted variable bias, and measurement error. These problems lead

---

[2] See Psacharopoulos and Patrinos (2004) and Oyelere (2009) for a summary of estimates for select countries.

to estimates that are biased and inconsistent. As deriving consistent estimates is necessary for causal interpretation of the impact of schooling on earning, past research has focused on ways to attenuate these biases and address issues of selectivity. In particular, more detailed surveys were conducted that include variables that affect earnings and are correlated with schooling but were not available in prior surveys. While controlling for more factors that affect earnings can attenuate omitted variable bias, the endogeneity problem can persist if there is still an unobserved variable like ability correlated with schooling and earnings.

The instrumental variable (IV) and control function approaches are two of the main techniques used to derive consistent estimates of β in the recent literature. However, the use of the IV approach does not guarantee that consistent estimates will be derived. When the validity of the instrument is questioned with respect to exogeneity and (or) relevance, IV estimates of β could potentially be more biased than OLS estimates.[3]

Another way RTE has been measured is to alter equation (1) and allow for differences in slopes over given years of schooling. This specification is implemented by introducing into the Mincer equation multiple years of schooling variables versus just total years of schooling. For example, equation (1) could include variables capturing years of primary, secondary and tertiary education instead of S. This change to the Mincer equation is relevant as the estimation of β in equation (1) assumes that average and marginal returns are identical. As significant non-linearities in the age earning profile are noted in survey data, a non-linear relationship between schooling and earnings is likely and assuming a linear specification is restrictive. Hence, estimates of PARTE at different levels of education may be more useful than estimates of β in equation (1). Similar to the standard Mincer equation, the OLS estimation technique is frequently used to estimate the returns to an extra year of schooling at each level of education. These estimates could be biased for the same reasons highlighted for the standard Mincer equation. Akin to the discussions above, an IV approach can also be used to derive consistent estimates of returns to an extra year of schooling at each level. However, this analysis is only possible if multiple valid instruments exist, and exceed or are equal to the number of endogenous education variables.

Potential challenges with the aforementioned approach include the structural form of the equation, interpretation of returns at each level of education and finding instruments for three or more potentially endogenous variables versus one. In addition, there is the question of if average return at a particular level is useful given the importance of finishing a level of education in other to experience any significant income change.

Another way the wage equation approach is implemented is to estimate the income gains from different level of education. This approach is typically implemented by including in equation (1) dummy variables for different education levels instead of variable S, and estimating the model using OLS. While estimates of these dummy variables are not returns per se, this specification is common in the past literature and is implemented in two ways. First, dummy variables are included such that estimates capture average difference in earnings at each level of education compared to individuals with no education. Second, estimates capture differences in average earnings at each level compared to the immediate lower level of education. OLS estimates on earnings differences across education levels is informative

---

[3] The problem of invalid, irrelevant and weak instruments has been highlighted in the past literature (see Staiger and Stock 1997).

but cannot be interpreted casually. Hence this approach faces similar challenges as those highlighted above.

25.2.2 Why measure returns to education in Africa?

First, there is substantial evidence that education has significant benefits, yet the demand for education varies across African countries. Heterogeneity in demand is explainable because expected benefits and private costs of education differ across the continent. If individuals choose years of schooling to maximize their returns, the difference between benefits and costs, then measuring RTE is important in understanding variation in education demand across and within African countries.

Second, the private market tends to undersupply education necessitating government supplementary provision given educations' perceived social benefits and positive externalities. In addition, governments invest more in education aimed at reducing private costs when demand for education is low.[4] However, education provision by government is not costless and efficient use of resource is especially critical for small resource-constrained African economies. Moreover, as social costs of education rise with years of schooling, there is a need for reliable estimates of the net social benefit and social rate of return to education. The availability of such estimates for African countries increases the likelihood governments make optimal education investments.[5]

Third, there is need to derive consistent estimates of the private RTE for a wide set of African countries given the ambiguity in the past literature on returns in Africa. In particular, the early empirical literature (Psacharopoulos 1981, 1994) suggest high returns in Africa but anecdotal evidence and some recent literature argue that returns are not as high as earlier estimates indicated (see Bennell 1996; Schultz 1988; Glewwe 1996 critique of the earlier literature).[6] Measuring returns in multiple African countries can elucidate this contention in the past literature.

Over the last decade there has been an increase in consistent estimates of RTE partly due to the significant increase in better quality data and estimation techniques. However, consistent estimates of RTE for African countries are still limited. Moreover there are still several countries in Africa for which no estimates exist. For those countries the need for estimates is not contestable. Even countries for which estimates were derived 10–20 years ago, as those estimates are potentially biased and unreliable, deriving more recent estimates that provide better information and reflect current conditions is useful.

---

[4] Low demand has been linked to high private costs compared to perceived benefits of education and is a challenge in some part of Africa.

[5] See Devarajan et al. (2011) for a good exposition on the problem of university and college education financing in Africa.

[6] They argue that several earlier papers on Africa are flawed. Moreover, Bennell states that Psacharopoulos' (1994) conclusion on African countries relies heavily on dated studies and unreliable data, and that a more careful Mincer type estimation of RTE for similar countries reveals modest effects.

25.3. School Enrollment and Attainment in Africa

25.3.1 Trends in school enrollment

Despite making significant progress over the last four decades, Africa is lagging behind worldwide trends in education-related outcomes. For example, according to the most recent World Development Indicators (WDI), primary completion rate is 69.3% in SSA, which is significantly less than the worldwide rate of 90.6%. Also, literacy rates for youth aged 15–24 years is 72% compared to 90% worldwide. Though the gap in education outcomes for SSA is undeniable, whether or not trends in education indicators are converging over time to worldwide trends is unknown. We investigate this question using WDI data. Figure 25.1(A) highlights the aggregate trend in primary adjusted net enrollment rates (PANER) for SSA between 1970 and 2011. World trends are also included in Figure 25.1(A) and trends by gender are presented in Figure 25.1(B).[7] We highlight PANER versus primary gross enrollment rates at the primary level as the former allows us to focus on the extent to which schooling is accessible to children currently at school entry age.

The worldwide trend in Figure 25.1(A) suggests steady increases in enrollment over time with only a slight decline in the late 1970s. In contrast, the trend for SSA has exhibited some variation, which may suggest education demand responses to short-term shocks. Notice that for SSA, PANER rose steeply from 1970 to 1982 and then declined for the rest of the 1980s. In the 1990s enrollment increased slowly but increased steadily from 2000.

This period of faster increase in PANER in SSA coincides with a period of significant economic growth in several African countries, as well as the adoption of the Millennium Development Goals (MDGs).[8] Hence economic growth and the MDGs initiative launched in 2000 may have created an increased demand for primary education and an incentive to boost enrollment. Although the gap in enrollment between SSA and world aggregates has been declining, the analysis shows that over the last five years, there has been a fall in the rate of decline or what might be referred to as a decline in the rate of convergence of SSA rates to world rates. Understanding what could be driving this trend is useful and involves highlighting countries whose rates are declining or have stagnated over the last few years.

Figure 25.1(B) highlights primary enrollment trends by gender in SSA. Worldwide trends by gender are also included as a benchmark for comparison. One noticeable trend is the decline in the gender gap over time. The adoption of the MDGs may have played a role, as reducing gender inequality is one of its goals. Our evaluation of enrollment trends by gender suggests that male and female rates are converging faster worldwide than in SSA. We also find that in the last few years, the gender gap in enrollment in SSA has not shown significant reduction. What explains the slower convergence in SSA than worldwide trends? What policies can be put in place to close this gap more quickly in SSA? These are important questions

---

[7] See Uwaifo Oyelere (2014) for more detailed coverage on enrollment trends in Africa.

[8] The MDG had as one of its time bounded targets, ensuring that all children complete a full course of primary schooling by 2015.

FIGURE 25.1 Adjusted net enrollment rates (1970–2011).

which can only be answered by looking more careful at individual country trends in Africa. The analyses of country trends suggest that the slowdown in convergence for SSA is driven in part by trends in countries were the gender gap in enrollment rates has stagnated or in some cases increased.[9]

Secondary enrollment trends also provide information on human capital accumulation in SSA. Figure 25.2 highlights trends in secondary gross enrollment rates (SGERs) from 1970 to 2011. These trends are similar to those at the primary level in SSA but the increase in SGER over the last four decades is significantly less than the increase at the primary level. A significant difference however between primary and secondary trends overtime in SSA is changes across gender. In SSA, the gender gap in SGER has increased over the last four decades. Specifically, while the gap was about 4.6% in 1970, the gap is about 7.7% in 2011. The lack of convergence in this rate across gender in SSA is also in contrast to the general convergence worldwide (from a gap of 10.73% in 1970 to 2.27% in 2011).

The SSA trend is unique as convergence across gender in this indicator is noted in developing countries in other regions like the Middle East and North Africa (MENA), South Asia, Europe, and Central Asia. Although the past literature has highlighted factors affecting education enrollment for several African countries, the existence of this growing gender gap at the secondary level highlights a need to isolate factors driving this trend. Analysis of the data suggests heterogeneity in this trend across SSA countries. Specifically, the gender gap grew in many SSA countries over the last four decades and in a few countries the growth in the gap

---

[9] Eretria and Nigeria are example of such countries.

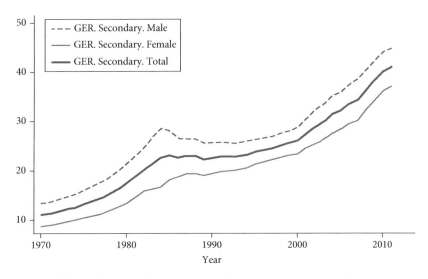

FIGURE 25.2 Trends in secondary gross enrollment rates (1970–2011).

is substantial (over 10 percentage points) and needs further investigation.[10] In contrast, there are countries within Africa that have consistently had higher female secondary enrollment than males. Lesotho for example had a 16.3 percentage point higher rate for girls in 2011. In South Africa also, girls SGER has consistently been higher than boys and in 2011, the gap was 14.3%. The big difference between the trend in Lesotho and South Africa is that in the latter, the gap across gender is converging while diverging in the former. One explanation for the reversed gap in both countries is the higher opportunity cost of secondary education for males given the abundance of relatively good paying jobs in the male dominated mining industry.

An evaluation of trends in tertiary gross enrollment rates from 1970 to 2011 suggests similar findings as those noted for secondary enrollment. In particular, the gender gap in tertiary enrollment just like secondary enrollment is growing in SSA. Also, developing countries in most other regions tend to mirror worldwide trends while trends in SSA tend to be different.

Analyzing aggregate enrollment trends over time has limitations especially for Africa. First, aggregate education indicators in earlier decades might not be directly comparable with estimates in later periods given paucity of reliable data for many countries in the 1970s. Even in recent years, reliable enrollment data for many SSA countries is still not available. Moreover, the countries included in early estimated aggregates may not be identical to those in the latter period. Despite these limitations, the trends at different levels of education over the last four decades suggest that SSA is making progress in education enrollment. However, gender disparities are a significant and growing issue at the secondary and tertiary levels of education.

[10] Examples include Angola, Benin, Chad, Central African Republic, and Congo Democratic Republic.

25.3.2 Countries within SSA with education challenges

Another limitation to broad enrollment trend analysis is that it can hide significant hetero-geneity across countries. The evaluation of enrollment trends for individual SSA countries suggests this is the case. Given this heterogeneity, it is useful to highlight countries where significant challenges exist. These countries are identified based on low primary completion rates, low mean years of schooling, stagnating or declining enrollment, or having enrollment rates significantly below the average in Africa.[11] Liberia and Eritrea are examples of countries with low PANER of 41% and 36% respectively in 2011. Côte d'Ivoire, Mali, Djibouti, Nigeria, Niger, and Equatorial Guinea's also have low primary enrollment rates suggesting primary education challenges. What appear to be more troubling for Nigeria and Côte d'Ivoire are rates that seem to have stagnated or declined recently. Low secondary enrollment rates also suggest future human capital accumulation challenges. Examples of countries that fit this criterion based on 2011 data are Angola (13.46%), Central African Republic (14.13%), and Mauritania (15.71%). For tertiary enrollment, countries that exhibit significant challenges include Malawi at 0.82% in 2011, Niger at 1.51% in 2011, Eritrea at 2.35% in 2010, and Chad at 2.32% in 2010.

Countries with mean years of schooling that are lower than the average in Africa are not always identical to countries with low enrollment rates. Low mean years of schooling sug-gests education challenges in the past and can also signal that such challenges will persist in future if a country presently has low enrollment rates. Burkina Faso, Niger, Gambia, and Mali fall into this categorization while Burundi and Guinea though currently at low mean years of schooling, show prospects of human capital growth in the future as primary enroll-ment rates are over 80% and survival rates to last grade of primary is above 50%.[12]

In the next section key factors affecting enrollment and attainment within Africa are con-sidered. Identifying these factors can improve our understanding as to why SSA lags behind in the education outcomes highlighted above.

25.3.3 Factors affecting school enrollment and attainment

A household/family's decision to enroll a child in school and keep them in school has eco-nomic foundations. Building on the seminal work of Becker (1964), there is a wide literature that examines what affects school enrollment across and intra households, both theoretically and empirically.[13] Similarly, there is also a wide literature investigating what affects school attainment empirically and (or) theoretically assuming basic neoclassical theory of human capital.[14] In developing countries, the economic significance of schooling decisions is more apparent as a parent's decision to enroll a child in school or the choice of who to enroll in

---

[11] Quality of education is also an education challenge in Africa but comparable data on quality across countries is scant.

[12] See Uwaifo Oyelere (2014) for detailed discussions and further examples of SSA countries with education challenge.

[13] See Strauss and Duncan (1995) for a review of empirical modeling of household and family decisions.

[14] See Glewwe and Kremer (2006) for a review of the literature for developing countries in general.

school highlights tradeoffs within the household. Specifically, parents compare the future benefits of investing in a child's human capital with the opportunity costs of schooling. In general, studies investigating factors affecting enrollment or attainment can be classified as either retrospective estimates from cross-sectional data, retrospective estimates from panel data or randomized evaluations. The factors affecting enrollment and attainment considered in these studies can be classified as either demand-sided, supply-sided, or factors that affect both the demand and supply of education. In this section a summary of some important factors that affect or are correlated with school enrollment and attainment in Africa is presented. This summary does not exhaustively cover all past studies considering these associations but instead focuses on highlighting those that may provide more relevant insight on the African experience and also those for which causal inferences are more likely inferable.

One of the biggest challenges in Africa is poverty and at the foundation of many demand-sided factors that explain enrollment, dropout, and attainment in Africa is poverty. When families are poor or have income levels close to the poverty line as is common in many rural agricultural settings in Africa, they are income constrained and vulnerable. This implies that shocks to income, agricultural volatility, or significant food price increases, which affect real income and reduce purchasing power, can force these families not to enroll children or pull kids out of school. In some cases, parents may choose not to enroll children in school or make them dropout of school as part of a strategy to build a buffer stock to insure against unexpected negative income shocks. Cogneau and Jedwab (2012), Dillon (2013) and Kazianga (2012) provide evidence of the aforementioned factors in Côte d'Ivoire, Mali, and Burkina Faso respectively. These papers illustrate that in poor liquidity constrained households, human capital investments tend to be procyclical, which suggests these environments are characterized by missing markets for insurance and limited credit. Hence theoretical models that assume unconstrained households school investment decisions based on permanent income may not be appropriate in understanding school participation choices in rural African economies.

More evidence school enrollment in Africa is linked in part to poverty or significant income constraints is noted in studies that find increased enrollment when the direct and implicit costs of education are reduced. Food for education (FFE) programs, free lunch programs (FLPs), take-home ration (THR), and in-school feeding program (SFP) all lead to increased enrollment (see Vermeersch and Kremer (2005) for evidence in Kenya and Alderman et al. (2012) for Northern Uganda). Similarly past research has shown that programs that provide scholarships and eliminate basic school fees in environments where school is already tuition free, increase enrollment and attainment. These studies again confirm that the decision not to enroll children in school is driven in part by poverty. See Kremer, Miguel, and Thornton (2009), Hoogeveen and Rossi (2013), Borkum (2012), and Linconve (2012) for evidence from rural Kenya, Tanzania, South Africa, and Uganda respectively.

It is useful to mention given the focus on Africa, that while the relationship between income and enrollment is positive, the effect of wealth on enrollment can be ambiguous in poor rural settings. This ambiguity exists because although increases in wealth should lead to higher enrollment in school, the unique nature of wealth in rural agricultural settings can lead to both income and substitution effects. Specifically, land and livestock form a significant part of wealth and while the income effect of wealth is always positive as wealthier parents can afford to send children to school, the substitution effect of this kind of wealth can be ambiguous as sending children to school has an opportunity cost of loss of child's labor on the farm. These costs could be higher the larger the amount of land owned by the family and (or) the higher the selling price for cash crops. If the substitution effect outweighs the income effect, school enrollment would be lower, which can happen below certain levels of income. Ayalew (2005) provides suggestive evidence that the substitution effect is dominated by the income effect in the context of rural Ethiopia.

Other demand-sided factors that recent literature highlights as important for enrollment are a child's health and ability. A household factoring in a child's ability and (or) health in the decisions to enroll children in school again reflects income constraints. However, once a child is enrolled in school, their innate ability, early health, and nutritional status can affect their performance and attainment regardless of their family's current level of income.[15] For example, Alderman et al. (2006) and Alderman et al. (2009) provide evidence of the long-term attainment consequences of early malnutrition in Zimbabwe and Tanzania respectively. Field et al. (2009) also provide evidence from Tanzania that children who were treated with an intensive iodine supplementation that reduced the likelihood of mental retardation had increased attainment in comparison to untreated sibling and peers. Similarly, Miguel and Kremer (2004) provide evidence from Kenya that deworming children, which improves their health status, increases school participation.

Gender is yet another factor that has effects on enrollment and attainment. The main explanation for the gender gap in enrollment and attainment in Africa highlights the opportunity cost of educating girls in the presence of significant income constraints and missing markets. In particular, if parents maximize their lifetime welfare by choosing different quantities of goods subject to a budget constraint, then in cases where families are significantly income constrained and have to choose which children to send to school, male children typically get chosen. The rational for choosing boys in this setting is largely economic and reflects missing institutions like social security, and missing markets for savings and insurance. When pension and retirement plans are not available, parents need to maximize the probability that at least one child would take care of them during old age. In this scenario if families are income constrained and cannot afford to send all children to school, boys get chosen given the perceived higher long-term income benefit accrued to males versus female children in many parts of Africa. In addition, there is a lower likelihood of receiving support from female children when they get married even when educated. This is because women typically have lower bargaining power in the household and may not be allowed to send significant amounts of money to their parents while households-heads who are typically males can. Caring for younger siblings is an additional explanation for why female children may drop out of school or not be enrolled in school in income-constrained households. If a mother has to work on the farm or outside the household (e.g. selling wares in the market or domestic help), having an older child to watch younger siblings becomes important and typically the burden falls on older female children. Hence the opportunity costs of sending female children to school is high when younger children or the old need to be cared for, especially given the perceived lower long-term benefits of educating girls noted above.

[15] See Akresh et al. (2012) and Glick and Sahn (2010) for recent evidence on ability and enrollment in Burkina Faso and Senegal respectively.

There are also cultural factors that may reduce female enrollment and attainment. In many villages, early marriage is common and demanded and leads to high dropout rates from school for girls and low attainment.[16]

Parents' education and attitudes also matters in child enrollment and attainment in Africa. For example, Weir (2011) provides evidence from Ethiopia that parental attitude towards education conditional on income may determine child's enrollment and years of schooling.

Supply-sided factors are also important for enrollment and attainment. This is especially relevant in SSA where most countries are low income or lower middle income according to World Bank classification and infrastructure development has been relatively limited compared to developed countries. The access to educational facilities close to a child's home affects enrollment sometimes through the income pathway but in some cases schools are simply not available within any feasible travel distance to a child's home. The farther schools are from students, the increased cost of attending both time and transportation costs. If households are poor and income constrained, their demand for education is elastic and transportation costs can deter enrollment. Tansel (1997) provides evidence of the negative impact of distance in both Ghana and Côte d'Ivoire on school enrollment. Similarly, distance to school has been negatively associated with education attainment in Ghana (Glewwe and Jacoby 1994; Lavy, 1996) and Tanzania (Bommier and Lambert 2000). Apart from increasing school resources or access, improving school resources have also been shown to increase school attainment for certain groups. If the quality of school resources affects human capital accumulation, earnings and RTE, then demand for schooling should be higher with better school resources. For example, Glewwe and Jacoby (1994) provide evidence of the impact of school quality on attainment in Ghana.

Two factors that affect attainment and enrollment and reflect both supply-sided and demand-sided factors are conflict and disease epidemic. Conflict reduces demand for schooling because of safety concerns of parents. It also reduces supply of schooling resources, which affects future enrollment negatively as school resources and infrastructures get destroyed during periods of conflict. The HIV epidemic in many countries in Africa also created demand and supply sided enrollment problems. On the demand side, children who lost one or both parents (orphans) usually become significantly income constrained and may demand less schooling. On the supply side, the HIV epidemic led to a loss of a lot of human capital including teachers, which also implies a decline in school resources which can have negative effects on attainment.[17]

The studies highlighted above identify factors affecting enrollment and attainment in Africa. The review focused more on recent studies with methodologies like randomized control trials (RCTs) that are likely to lead to casual interpretation (internal validity). However, as most past RCTs focused on identifying causal explanations for school enrollment and attainment in Africa are clustered in a few countries mostly in East Africa, external validity is a legitimate concern. Moreover, policymakers and practitioners looking for solutions to enrollment problems in other African countries should worry about the relevance

---

[16] See Uwaifo Oyelere (2014) for a literature review of papers highlighting some of the gender channels highlighted above.

[17] Uwaifo Oyelere (2014) highlights papers that provide evidence of the effects of conflict/disease on attainment.

of the factors noted in these studies to other-country context given significant heterogeneity across African countries in levels of development, growth, culture, endowment, government, and institutions. As understanding what factors affects enrollment and attainment within a country is important for effective policy, the need for RCTs aimed at isolating relevant factors in other African countries is imperative, especially where current data suggest significant enrollment and attainment challenges.

25.4 Returns to Education in Africa

25.4.1 Findings on returns to education in Africa

In section 2.2 the reasons for measuring returns in Africa were outlined. In this section a brief summary of the main findings from a review of the literature measuring RTE in African countries over the last 15 years is provided. The focus on recent years is useful for reasons including the higher likelihood of estimates being consistent given improvement in methodology over this period. The papers reviewed estimate PARTE using OLS and IV primarily. While the OLS estimates could be biased for reasons highlighted in section 2.1, recent studies like Uwaifo Oyelere (2010) using methodologies that could lead to consistent estimates of returns suggest only minor differences between the OLS and consistent IV estimates of PARTE. Card (1999) also notes from his survey of PARTE estimates that bias in OLS is minimal. Hence, although most past estimates of return for African countries may not be consistent, estimates can still be relevant as bias may be minimal. Moreover, if the bias in the estimated returns is time and country invariant, then a meta-analysis of estimates across time and country could be informative.

Table 25.1 presents RTE estimates from select studies on African countries. The methodologies used in these studies are OLS and IV. However, there is significant variation in how OLS is implemented across these papers with some studies correcting for measurement error, selection bias, and omitted variable bias while others do not. A range of estimates is provided for some studies in Table 25.1 highlighting estimates for different years, groups, and across different methods in the paper. The OLS estimates summarized in Table 25.1 highlight significant heterogeneity in returns across countries. Estimates varied a lot from as high as 43% to as low as 0% for every extra year of schooling. Even within countries overtime, differences in estimates were noted. For countries with multiple studies or studies over multiple years, in some cases returns increased over time while in others returns declined.[18]

It is important to highlight that for several African countries, no estimates of return exist. The lack of estimates for several countries suggests that past estimates of PARTE for

---

[18] Moreover some studies in Table 25.1 noted heterogeneity in returns across gender, age cohort and region. See Uwaifo Oyelere (2014) for a list of countries were no estimate exist and for more details on changes in returns. Also note that changes in PARTE within countries across time only represent actual changes assuming that the potential bias in the OLS estimate is time invariant.

Table 25.1 PARTE estimates for select African countries

Country	Time	PARTE	Methodology	Reference
Botswana	1993/94	3.3–14	OLS	Siphambe (2000)
Eritrea	2001–2002	11	OLS	Kifle (2007)
Ethiopia	1994	15	OLS	Temesgen (2006).
Ethiopia	2002	5.4–6.9	OLS	Temesgen (2006).
Ghana	1989	0–6	IV	Glewwe (1996)
Ghana	1992–1994	7.1	OLS	Jones (2001)
Gambia	1992/98/2003	8–43	IV	Foltz and Gajigo (2012)
Kenya	1986	15	IV	Dabalen (1998)
Kenya	1993/2000–01	11–16	OLS	Söderbom et al. (2006)
Libya	1994/95	6.85	OLS	Arabsheibani and Manfor (2001)
Nigeria	1996–1999	2.8–5.3	OLS	Aromolaran (2006)
Nigeria	1997–2005	2.8–6.4	IV	Uwaifo Oyelere (2011)
Rwanda	1999/2001	17.5	OLS	Lassibille and Tan (2005)
South Africa	1994	19.1–28.1	IV	Dabalen (1998)
South Africa	1993/1998	5–11.4	OLS	Hertz (2003)
Tanzania	1993	6–8	OLS	Söderbom et al. (2006)
Tanzania	2000/01	9–13	OLS	Söderbom et al. (2006)

Africa or SSA are based on estimates for select countries and may not reflect the true average estimates.

A review of the literature that estimates PARTE using the IV approach in African countries was conducted and similar trends as those noted using OLS are observed (see Table 25.1 for select estimates). Specifically, IV estimates exhibits heterogeneity across countries and within countries time differences are noted.

Past studies on African countries for which estimates of PARTE at different levels have been derived and studies estimating returns to different levels of education both provide findings consistent with those noted above.[19] First, heterogeneity across countries in estimates at each level of education is noted. Second for most countries, an upward trend in estimated returns is noted the higher the level of education. For example, Uwaifo Oyelere (2011) finds increasing PARTE the higher the education level. Similarly, Schultz (2004) notes increasing income gains the higher the education level in Ghana, Côte d'Ivoire, Kenya, Nigeria, Burkina Faso, and South Africa. These patterns contradict the thesis of falling returns as education level increases, suggested by Psacharopoulos (1994). Third, time differences in returns are also noted for countries when more than one study exists. In these studies, returns appear to be increasing over the available time periods but the changes in returns overtime at each level differ significantly.

[19] See Uwaifo Oyelere (2014) for tables summarizing PARTE estimates at different levels and estimate of difference in income at different levels of education in select African countries.

25.4.2 Explaining heterogeneity in returns to education

The main finding from the review of the past literature is that significant heterogeneity exists in RTE across countries. Moreover within countries, time differences are present. There is a growing interest in trying to identify the factors that affect RTE and explain changes in returns over time. Isolating such factors is not only relevant for gaining a better conceptual understanding of what affects returns but is useful for policymakers and practitioners interested in keeping demand for education high given its significant social benefits. While several authors provide possible explanations for low or changing RTE, the challenge is identifying causally factors that affect RTE in individual country level context.

One common factor suggested for low returns is quality of education. There is ample evidence that low education quality is a significant challenge for developing countries including countries in Africa (see Gove and Cvelich 2011) but the role of education quality on earning/RTE in the past literature is mixed.[20] This lack of consensus is linked partly with the way education quality is measured. While per student expenditure or school resources and teacher pupil ratios are noisy indicators of quality, learning and cognitive skills are more precise indicators. Recent studies using the latter indicators suggest significant association between quality of schooling and earnings. In addition, recent literature suggests that years of schooling adjusted for quality explains growths differences across countries (Schoellman 2012).

Another explanation suggested is bottlenecks to education. For example Schultz (2004) suggests high returns to secondary or tertiary education in six African countries are linked to bottlenecks to education at those levels, which makes demand for secondary and tertiary graduates much higher than supply. However, this explanation for the noted return is not derived empirically. Moreover, though the explanation above might be relevant for some countries in Africa, high levels of unemployment at the tertiary and secondary levels of education in several SSA countries point to higher supply of graduates at these levels than demand (see World Bank, 2008).

Another explanation for low returns is the scarcity of complementary inputs also referred to as coordination failures. In this scenario, returns are low if there is low stock of physical capital and technology to combine with human capital needed to generate output and increase income. Adam (2001) provides this explanation for low RTE in Tanzania.

Government policy has also been linked with low and changing RTE For example Uwaifo Oyelere (2011) provides evidence that policy reforms following democratization in Nigeria led to about a 3% point increase in returns. Similarly, Said and El-Hamidi (2011) provide evidence suggesting that falling RTE over time in Egypt and Morocco are linked with specific government policy and a reduction in the role of the public sector.

While the aforementioned factors are relevant in explaining low and changing returns in the countries studied, the noted heterogeneity in institutions and labor market conditions across Africa could increase the likelihood that such explanations are not relevant for other countries. Hence, more long-term data collection efforts in several countries in Africa cannot be over emphasized. Gaining a better understanding of what affects RTE;

---

[20] See Moll (1992) and Case and Yogo (1999) for evidence of a positive link between quality of education and returns to education in South Africa.

what contributes to its heterogeneity within and across countries; and what causes returns to change over time is needed.

25.4.3 Limitations of the wage equation approach in Africa

Despite the benefit of having estimates of RTE for different African countries, the general methodologies used to derive these estimates have limitations. Some of these limitations have already been highlighted above but drawing attention to the criticisms of the methodology especially as it related to Africa is useful. Bennell (1996) points out some of these limitations. Specifically, many early studies estimated returns focused solely on individuals in the wage sector. Given the wage sector is a minor employer of labor in most African countries, and the agricultural sector and informal sector are the major employers of labor, then estimates based on the wage sector, which individuals' select into, cannot provide unbiased estimates of RTE in these countries.[21] Even within the wage sector in most African countries, deriving an unbiased estimate of RTE is unlikely because estimates are derived assuming competitive labor markets. However competitive labor markets are only relevant for private formal employment, which is a small share of the wage sector, in most African economies. The lion's share of employment is the public sector where wages tend to be rigid and not directly linked with labor productivity.

25.5. SUMMARY AND CONCLUSION

This chapter has focused on three important aspects of education in Africa: enrollment, attainment, and RTE. Although a number of policy initiatives in Africa over the last few decades have focused on increasing school enrollment and attainment, the need to meet the enrollment MDG may have led countries to focus more on increasing enrollment. This bias inadvertently leads to less attention on issues related to education quality, school retention, and participation which affect attainment, RTE, and ultimately human capital accumulation. The links between attainment, enrollment and RTE suggest that a theoretical framework attempting to explain any needs to consider the other indicators. For example, current enrollment is a function of the perceived RTE, which is linked with levels of attainment.

What are the main highlights from this study? First, the gender gap in secondary and tertiary enrollment is growing in SSA. Second, significant heterogeneity exists across countries in Africa in enrollment, attainment and returns to schooling. In the past, there has been a tendency to make statements about Africa and (or) SSA using education data or findings for a few African countries. Given the heterogeneity across countries in these indicators, such broad statements are not informative. Third, income constraints are at the center of many

---

[21] Some recent estimates have included the informal and agricultural sectors and used an estimate for income in household surveys to estimate returns. The problem here is that the Mincer wage equation is based on a model that presumes individuals earn a wage based on their marginal productivity which is not consistent with these sectors.

of the factors that affect enrollment and attainment in Africa suggesting poverty allevia-tion and addressing missing markets may be effective in increasing attainment and enroll-ment. Fourth, there is evidence of changing RTE overtime in Africa but much less is known about what leads to this change. Although recent studies suggest quality of education and government policy plays a role, there is need for more research to isolate other factors that are important. Finally in a number of African countries, there is need to derive estimates of returns as none is currently available.[22] In such countries especially those with significant education challenges, the benefit of more information could potentially be high. In contrast, there are a few countries in Africa where a significant part of the research in enrollment, attainment and RTE is currently clustered.[23] As the generalizability of the finding from these select countries to other African country's context may be limited, the return to more educa-tion research in these select set of countries may be limited while the benefits from studies on other African countries where little is known could be high.

References

Adam S.I. (2001). *The Industrial Experience of Tanzania*, P. Lapperre, S.I. Adam (eds). Palgrave Press.

Alderman, H., Daniel, G.O., and Lehrer, K. (2012.). The impact of alternative food for educa-tion programs on learning achievement and cognitive development in Northern Uganda. *Economic Development and Cultural Change*, 61(1):187–218.

Alderman, H., Hoogeveen, H., and Rossi, M. (2009). Preschool nutrition and subsequent schooling attainment: longitudinal evidence from Tanzania. *Economic Development and Cultural Change*, 57(2):239–260.

Akresh, R., Bagby, E., De Walque, D., and Kazianga, H. (2012). Child ability and household human capital investment decisions in Burkina Faso. *Economic Development and Cultural Change*, 61(1):157–186.

Arabsheibani, G.R., and Manfor L. (2001) Non-linearities in returns to education in Libya. *Education Economics*, 9(2):139–144.

Aromolaran, A. (2006). Estimates of Mincerian returns to schooling in Nigeria. *Oxford Development Studies*, 34 (2):265–292.

Ayalew, T. (2005). Parental preference, heterogeneity, and human capital inequality. *Economic Development and Cultural Change*, 53(2):381–407.

Becker, G.S. (1964). *Human Capital: A Theoretical and Empirical Analysis, with Special Reference to Education*. New York: National Bureau of Economic Research; distributed by Columbia University Press.

Bennell, P. (1996). Rates of return to education: does the conventional pattern prevail in sub-Saharan Africa? *World Development*, 24(1):183–99.

Bommier, A., and Lambert, S. (2000). Education demand and age at school enrollment in Tanzania. *Journal of Human Resources*, 35(1):177–203.

Borkum, Evan (2012). Can eliminating school fees in poor districts boost enrollment? Evidence from South Africa. *Economic Development and Cultural Change*, 60(2):359–398.

[22] This sample includes Angola, Namibia, Algeria, Burundi, and Swaziland.
[23] This sample includes Kenya, South Africa, Tanzania, Ethiopia, Burkina Faso, and Ghana.

Case, A., and Yogo, M. (1999). Does school quality matter? Returns to education and the characteristics of schools in South Africa (No. w7399). National Bureau of Economic Research.

Card, D. (1995). Earnings, schooling and ability revisited, in Solomon Polachek (ed.), Research in Labor Economics, Volume 14. Greenwich, CT: JAI Press, pp. 23–48.

Card, D. (1999). The causal effect of education on earnings. *Handbook of Labor Economics*, 3:1801–1863.

Cogneau, D., and Jedwab, R. (2012). Commodity price shocks and child outcomes: the 1990 cocoa crisis in Côte d'Ivoire. *Economic Development and Cultural Change*, 60(3):507–534.

Dabalen, A. (1998). Returns to Education in Kenya and South Africa: Instrumental Variable Estimates. University of California, Berkeley Dissertation.

Devarajan, S., Monga, C., and Zongo, T. (2011). Making higher education finance work for Africa. *Journal of African Economies*, 20(Suppl 3):iii133–iii154.

Dillon, A. (2013). Child Labour and Schooling Responses to Production and Health Shocks in Northern Mali. *Journal of African Economies*, 22(2):276–299.

Field, E., Robles, O., and Torero, M. (2009). Iodine deficiency and schooling attainment in Tanzania. *American Economic Journal: Applied Economics*, 1(4):140–169.

Foltz, J.D., and Gajigo, O. (2012). Assessing the returns to education in the Gambia. *Journal of African Economies*, 21(4):580–608.

Glick, P., and Sahn, D.E. (2010). Early academic performance, grade repetition, and school attainment in Senegal: A panel data analysis. *The World Bank Economic Review*, 24(1):93–120.

Glewwe, P., and Jacoby, H. (1994). Student achievement and schooling choice in low-income countries: Evidence from Ghana. *Journal of Human Resources*, 29(3):843–864.

Glewwe, P. (1996). The relevance of standard estimates of rates of return to schooling for education policy: A critical assessment. *Journal of Development Economics*, 51(2):267–290.

Glewwe, P., and Kremer, M. (2006). Schools, teachers, and education out- comes in developing countries. *Handbook of the Economics of Education*, 2:945–1017.

Griliches, Z. (1977). Estimating the returns to schooling: Some econometric problems. *Econometrica Journal of the Econometric Society*, 45:1–22.

Gove, A., and Cvelich, P. (2011). Early Reading: Igniting Education for All. A report by the Early Learning Community of Practice. Revised Edition. Research Triangle Park, NC.

Hanushek, Eric A., and Woessmann, L. (2008). The role of cognitive skills in economic development. *Journal of Economic Literature*, 46(3):607–668.

Hertz, T. (2003). Upward bias in the estimated returns to education: evidence from South Africa. *American Economic Review*, 93(4):1354–1368.

Hoogeveen, J., and Rossi, M. (2013). Enrolment and grade attainment following the introduction of free primary education in Tanzania. *Journal of African Economies*, 22(3):375–393.

Jones, P. (2001). Are educated workers really more productive? *Journal of Development Economics*, 64:67–79.

Kazianga, H. (2012). Income risk and household schooling decisions in Burkina Faso. *World Development*, 40(8):1647–1662.

Kifle, T. (2007) The private rate of return to schooling: evidence from Eritrea. *Essays in Education*, 21:77–99.

Kremer, M., Miguel, E., and Thornton, R. (2009). Incentives to learn. *The Review of Economics and Statistics* 91(3):437–456.

Lassibille, G., and Tan, J. (2005). The returns to education in Rwanda. *Journal of African Economics*, 14(1): 92–116.

Lavy, V. (1996) School supply constraints and children's educational outcomes in rural Ghana. *Journal of Development Economics*, 51(2):291–314.

Mankiw, G., Romer, D., and Weil, D. (1992). A contribution to the empirics of economic growth. *Quarterly Journal of Economics*, 107 (2):407–437.

Miguel, E., and Kremer, M. (2004) Worms: identifying impacts on education and health in the presence of treatment externalities. *Econometrica*, 72(1):159–217.

Mincer, J.A. (1974). Schooling and earnings, in Schooling, experience, and earnings. New York: Columbia University Press, pp. 41–63.

Moll, P.G. (1992). Quality of education and the rise in returns to schooling in South Africa, 1975–1985. *Economics of Education Review*, 11(1):1–10.

Oyelere, R.U. (2009) *Economic and econometric evidence for and against private income and employment benefits of education in Africa*, in V.U. James and J. Etim (eds), Educational Reform in Africa: Essays on Curriculum, Libraries, Counseling and Grade Levels. New York: Edwin Mellen Press, pp. 25–49.

Pritchett, L. (2001). Where has all the education gone? *The World Bank Economic Review*, 15(3):367–391.

Pritchett, L. (2006). Does learning to add up add up? The returns to schooling in aggregate data, in E.A. Hanushek and F. Welch (eds), *Handbook of the Economics of Education*. Amsterdam: North Holland, pp. 635–695.

Psacharopoulos, G. (1981). Returns to education: an updated international comparison. *Comparative Education*, 17(3):321–341.

Psacharopoulos, G. (1994). Returns to investment in education: a global update. *World Development*, 22(9):1325–1343.

Psacharopoulos, G., and Patrinos, H.A. (2004). Returns to investment in education: a further update. *Education Economics*, 12(2):111–134.

Schultz, T.P. (1988). Education investment and returns, in H. Chenery and T.N. Srinivasan (eds), *Handbook of Development Economics*, Volume 1. New York: North-Holland.

Schultz, T.P. (2004). Evidence of returns to schooling in Africa from household surveys: monitoring and restructuring the market for education. *Journal of African Economies*, 13(Suppl 2):ii95–ii148.

Schoellman, T. (2012) Education quality and development accounting. *The Review of Economic Studies*, 79(1):388–417.

Siphambe, H.K. (2000). Rates of return to education in Botswana. *Economics of Education Review*, 19(3):291–300.

Söderbom, M., Teal, F., Wambugu, A., and Kahyarara, G. (2006). The dynamics of returns to education in Kenyan and Tanzanian manufacturing. *Oxford Bulletin of Economics and Statistics*, 68(3):261–288.

Strauss, J., and Duncan, T. (1995). Human resources: empirical modeling of household and family decisions, in J. Behrman and T.N. Srinivasan (eds) *Handbook of Development Economics*, Volume 3A. Amsterdam: Elsevier/North Holland.

Staiger, D., and Stock, J.H. (1997). Instrumental variables regression with weak instruments. *Econometrica*, 65:557–586.

Said, M., and El-Hamidi, F. (2011). Returns to schooling and labor market stratification in the Middle East and North Africa: evidence from Egypt and Morocco. *Middle Eastern Finance and Economics*, 14:83–98.

Tansel, A. (1997). Schooling attainment, parental education, and gender in Cote d'Ivoire and Ghana. *Economic Development and Cultural Change*, 45.4:825–856.

Temesgen, T. (2006). Decomposing gender wage differentials in urban Ethiopia: evidence from linked employer-employee (LEE) manufacturing survey data. *Global Economic Review*, 35(1):43–66.

Uwaifo Oyelere, R. (2010). Africa's education enigma? The Nigerian story. *Journal of Development Economics*, 91(1):128–139.

Uwaifo Oyelere, R. (2011). Have returns to education changed in Nigeria? Uncovering the role of democratic reforms. *Journal of African Economies*, 20(5):737–780.

Uwaifo Oyelere, R. (2014). Education in Africa: recent Findings and Challenges for the Future. Unpublished Working Paper.

Vermeersch, C., and Kremer, M. (2005). *School Meals, Educational Achievement, and School Competition: Evidence from a Randomized Evaluation*, Volume 3523. Washington, DC: World Bank.

World Bank (2008). *Youth in Africa's labor market*. Marito Garcia and Jean Fares (eds). World Bank publication.

Weir, S. (2011). Parental attitudes and demand for schooling in Ethiopia. *Journal of African Economies*, 20(1):90–110.

....

CHAPTER 26

MOBILITY, HUMAN CAPITAL, REMITTANCES, AND ECONOMIC TRANSFORMATION

....

YAW NYARKO

26.1 INTRODUCTION

....

FROM the beginning of time, humans have moved from one place to another to better themselves. Today the movement of people from one country to another is very large in terms of both the total number of people moving and the flows of remittances from the destination back to the source countries. The mother of all migrations is probably that which is thought to have resulted in the movement of people from the birthplace in Africa, through the great East African Rift Valley, and the initial population of the world outside of Africa by people several hundred thousand years ago.

There are two broad sides of the debates and academic analyses of migration: the viewpoints and issues in the destination countries and those in the source countries. In the destination countries the debate is often the tradeoff between the need to allow immigration to boost the local economy against concerns about jobs, cultural change, etc., among those who are "incumbents" in the economy. On the source country there is debate about the tradeoffs between losing the talented and entrepreneurial skills of those leaving on the one hand, versus the return of remittances and the acquisition of the skills of those who leave.

For many destination countries, migrant labor is one of the key policy instruments for economic transformation. The Arab Gulf Countries—UAE, Qatar, Saudi Arabia, etc.—today have large numbers of their populations coming from foreign, and primarily Asian, nations. The migrant labor population in the UAE is around two or three times the size of the local population. European nations are increasingly discussing immigration of particularly skilled workers as their own populations face decreasing fertility rates and aging demographics. At the same time, there is concern that the new migrants are changing the culture or taking jobs away from the locals. Particularly following the Arab Spring, but even before, this has been a concern and there has been legislation in the Arab Gulf nations restricting the inflow of foreigners into the country to preserve jobs for the locals. The UAE has adopted various "Emiratization" laws, and Saudi Arabia has a number of new labor codes, most recently the Nitaqat laws. Europe has had extreme right political parties complaining about immigrants in their countries for some years now.

In the source countries, although the emigrants leaving their countries are often relatively small fractions of their population, they often represent large percentages of their skilled and educated workforce. There is often passionate debate about what is termed the "brain drain," with sensational language which, for example, accuses the West of stealing doctors and nurses from African nations. On the other hand, there is now the realization that remittances are an important source of revenue for home countries.

What is often not understood or appreciated is the enormous potential for migration to increase the skill levels of those who leave, and that since many of those who leave return after a few years, this is an important channel for skills improvement for the country. Indeed, via an initially counterintuitive process, the possibility of skilled migration increases the total number of skilled people remaining in the home country due to the larger numbers who are given the incentive to acquire the human capital needed to leave the country but may not have been able to leave because of, for example, too few opportunities available.

This chapter will argue that there are many benefits of mobility, particularly, as already mentioned, in the area of skills acquisition and remittances. These debates and issues will probably get stronger over time because of two reinforcing demographic trends. On the one hand, Africa is rapidly increasing its population, and that population is relatively young and therefore in need of jobs. It is unlikely that the growth in employment in Africa will be able to adequately absorb all the new young people looking for employment. On the other hand, Europe's population is declining and getting old. The European countries will therefore see the need to get more foreign workers for their domestic economies to make up for the smaller numbers of workers locally. Africa's supply of workers and Europe's need mean that these debates on migration will go on for quite a while.

The ideas on migration, remittances, and human capital acquisition have a number of very important policy implications. As will be discussed in this chapter, these results imply that for human capital development within a nation, one should actively look at the migration process and use the "brain circulation" to aid the development of training programs and institutions which enable source country workers to emigrate, but also enable a lot of locals to get the training that they need.

The other policy implication discussed is the tradeoff between direct spending on cash transfers to the poor relative to spending on education, which increases long-term wages and, through remittances, have secondary effects on the poor.

Finally, the question of skills acquisition among migrants is important in the design of migrant contracts. It will be argued that this is an important consideration in the current debates in the Arab Gulf nations on immigration policy.

The chapter is organized as follows. After this introduction, we first talk about what should be obvious but is often left unstated—which is that there are direct benefits to the migrant that leaves and these should be recorded in the equation on the pluses and minuses of migration.

Following that, we dive immediately into the questions of the brain drain, particularly in Africa. We first present the case for why there is discussion of the problem, and then we point out prior research explaining that when remittances are taken into account, on a purely economic internal rate of return argument, the pluses dominate the minuses in the brain circulation equations. We then very quickly touch on the rates-of-return to education literature and note that the paradox of low returns to education can be resolved if we take into account emigration out of the country.

Finally we point out the possibly counterintuitive result that the incentives to acquire human capital for possible emigration often leads to there being more human capital in the source nation. The section after that will discuss remittances and social security. Some remarks will then be made about unskilled migration in general and unskilled labor in particular, and this will be related to recent work in the Arab Gulf nations. Just before concluding we have a section on the policy implications of the research findings presented in this chapter.

26.2 SOME IMMEDIATE BENEFITS OF THE BRAIN DRAIN: WAGES AND REMITTANCES

As mentioned in the introduction, it is the basic instinct of human beings to better themselves. Migration is a major tool by which we improve our lot. By migrating we can benefit from higher salaries, or learning and training opportunities abroad. We can gain a higher wage to help family back home. We can also escape oppressive governments and harsh economic circumstances at home.

We witness sub-Saharan Africans traversing the Sahara desert to look for better outcomes abroad. We witness families being torn apart so one member—a mother with children at home say—can go abroad for months or years at a time to get money to send those at home to school or to provide them a basic income.

Despite this incredible display of the human spirit, in a lot of the literature on economic development and migration, the migrant, who should be at the center of the story, is often missing. Too often the focus is on those who are left behind and the implications on their welfare. So, we begin our discussion by pointing out the gains to the individual and their families.

First on own wages. Al Awad (2010) and Tong (2010) put the annual average wage of workers in the UAE from India, Pakistan, Bangladesh, and the Philippines, in a sample of 10 954 people, at 25 200 AED (around US$7000 at today's exchange rate). World Bank GDP per capita measures of annual income of those countries at US$3650, US$2745, US$1777, and US$4119 for India, Pakistan, Bangladesh, and the Philippines respectively (see Nyarko 2013). Presumably the mainly construction workers coming from these Asian countries into the UAE are on the very bottom of the wage income distribution, and are possibly unemployed, so we would expect from this data that at the minimum wages are doubled when workers leave the their home countries to go to the UAE. In particular, we have an economic development instrument involving several million workers doubling their wages. It is hard to think of other development strategies which can so quickly and immediate boost salaries.

For Ghana, Nyarko (2011) looked at those at the higher end of the source country income distribution—the tertiary educated. The data there showed conservatively an increase in wages upon migration of 20 times. In particular, there is a very large and immediate benefit to the migrant from migration.

Immediately after the discussion of the benefits to the individual, one needs to discuss the benefits to the family. This usually is in the form of remittances by the migrant from the destination country back home to the source country. These remittances are large, and a big portion of these are sent to the family. From the UAE alone, the remittance firm UAEx alone handles remittances in excess of US$ 17bn per year from the primarily Indian migrants in the country. This data is from current research of the author, which suggests that the remittances going out from the UAE is around US$40bn and, around US$ 410bn is the value of remittances worldwide (as reported by various Worldbank sources, and in particular its KNOMAD group, at www.knomad.org/).

So we have a benefit to both migrant and to the family of the migrant through remittances. The flows of remittances are also large, as just argued. They form a large percentage of the GDP of many nations. In Nyarko (2013) tables were presented showing remittances of the order of 10% of GDP for countries like Nigeria, Sierra Leone and Senegal. Although a smaller part of the GDP of Nigeria, it is a large part of the GDP of some individual states in India like Kerala.

26.3 THE AFRICAN BRAIN DRAIN

As is well known, education levels in sub-Saharan Africa are low, as measured by the average level of schooling of each relevant age cohort in the population. This is particularly so at the tertiary level—there have been low levels of tertiary educated people, and this has been the situation since the times of independence. Indeed, African independence leaders stressed education in their development plans. Kwame Nkrumah of Ghana was emphatic in the need for education in the development plans of Ghana. Teachers were a constraint in the education process, and Kwame Nkrumah was very interested in the Peace Corps program for this reason—Ghana was the first country to receive Peace Corps volunteers.

In the 70s and 80s, under attack from both structural adjustment programs and also the "rates-of-return" literature, many countries backed away from rapid expansions in the tertiary education system. In the rates-of-return literature, it was argued through statistical computations that the return to primary education was much higher than that going to tertiary education so investments in the latter should be scaled down in favor of the former. Although the literature itself was much more nuanced than that description, policymakers took this as a signal that they should not invest too much in tertiary education.

This was an initial blow to human capital formation, particularly at the tertiary education level, in African nations. A second has been the recent concern about the "brain drain" in Africa.

More recently concerns about the "brain drain" have slowed down the desire for flows of Africans to the West for further education, and often also the construction of educational

institutions in African nations. As will be indicated in this chapter, this is probably not justified by the economics.

This chapter will pay a lot of attention to the skills acquisition benefits of the migration, as
well as the remittances, both of which benefit the source countries.

Over the past decade, the other issue that has been getting attention and has the potential
for holding back the growth of the tertiary educated, is the fear of the brain drain. Many
argue that it is wrong to spend on tertiary education when so many of the tertiary educated
in turn leave the country.

On the face of it, there is a case for the brain drain pessimists. Figures presented in Nyarko
(2011) indicate that there are very high rates of emigration of skilled personnel. Around the
year 2000 the data showed that about half of all Ghanaians with tertiary education were
outside the country. Similarly, high figures were obtained for Cape Verde, Sierra Leone,
Gambia, while the figure drops to a lower but still apparently shocking figure of 38% and 36%
for Kenya and Uganda respectively.

One immediate point stressed in the earlier papers mentioned is that these figures do not
tell the full picture. First, the aggregate numbers of the education is very small. My home
university, New York University has about 50 000 students. The data suggest that in 2000
Ghana had resident in the country and outside the country around three or four times that
number of tertiary educated people, in total. So although the percentages are large, the totals
are really small.

There is currently a 2010 Ghana census and the author is updating the figures in new
research. In the next section, we summarize existing research, and primarily that of Nyarko
(2011), which indicates another reason why the concern about the brain drain as defined
above is possibly misplaced.

26.4 THE SIMPLE COST–BENEFIT ANALYSIS AND POSITIVE INTERNAL RATE OF RETURN TO THE BRAIN DRAIN

Nyarko (2011) presented an explicit model of brain circulation. In that paper, an economy
was presented where individuals decide how much schooling to attain. The emphasis there
was on the decision to acquire tertiary schooling. In that paper there is a probability that
after getting schooling one obtains the opportunity to emigrate and receive a much higher
wage abroad.

There are a number of benefits to the acquisition of tertiary education: (i) the increased
wages over and above the secondary level; (ii) the increased salary that one obtains if one emi-
grates out of the country. On the cost side to the central planner (or society) and individual is
the cost of the education and the loss in output while the individual is acquiring the education.

The model allows for migration of the individual. Again there are costs and benefits. The
costs are primarily the foregone earnings. The benefits include remittances back home and
the higher income that the individual enjoys. There is also the possibility that the individual
returns home with the higher skill level.

Costs of education can be obtained from standard measures from UN organizations like UNDP. Various World Bank researchers have computed the brain drain probabilities (see Docquier and Marfouk 2005). Survey data show the rate of return of migrants back to home countries. Early estimates are that 50% of Africa PhDs in the sciences return after five years (see Pires et al. 1999). Various household surveys provide information on the wage level of representative individuals of different education levels. Finally, remittance data is obtained from a variety of sources: IMF data, source country central banks, and various surveys of migrants. Bollard et al. (2010) and Chami et al. (2008) also have data remittances, and provide insights into the patterns of remittances, as do Irving et al. (2010), Kapur, (2004), Ratha et al. (2010).

In the Nyarko (2011) paper all the different pluses and minuses of migration where empirically estimated and put in a model where the internal rates of return could be computed. These rates of return are of course the standard methods used in the economics of education to determine the long-term value of increasing education levels, and it is has a long history in labor economics.

Loosely speaking, the internal rates of return (IRRs) are a measure of how much return on an investment one would get if the money were put in the project in question. (Of course formally the IRRs are a bit more complicated than that, measuring the interest rate at which the net present value is equal to zero. However in many cases it does provide a proxy measure for the importance of different projects.) An alternate measure is the Net Present Value (NPV) of investments in different types of education assuming a fixed (usually 5%) payment to the capital used in the investment.

The chapter first looked at the central planner problem. In particular suppose that a government is spending money on providing tertiary education to one representative person. The government cares about the cost of education, employment of this person only when in the country, and the remittances the individual brings back into the economy, and of course employment within the economy if the person comes back home (usually with higher skills). One can then compute the IRR and NPV, as described earlier, and use this as a measure of how valuable the tertiary investment is. Again, it should be recalled that the computation considers as a cost the lost employment of the individual in the home or source country when that person migrates. The Nyarko (2011) showed that for the Central Planner problem the internal rates of return could be as high as 29%. The net present value of tertiary education assuming a 5% cost of capital is conservatively US$ 24K. Those computations show that there is an extremely high return to tertiary education by the central planner who only cares about employment in the home country and remittances into the country.

One could look at the individual as opposed to the central planner problem. In the individual problem the worker considers his own wages while abroad as a plus, unlike the central planner. The individual is concerned about income he or she makes wherever he or she happens to be (home or abroad) unlike the central planner who only cares about income while at home or which is being sent home.

For the individual problem, Nyarko (2011) showed that for the central planner problem the internal rates of return could be as high as 49%. The net present value of tertiary education assuming a 5% cost of capital is conservatively US$ 126K. These figures are actually the conservative values making a number of assumptions on data.

In particular, when one takes into account the full costs and benefits of skilled migration, one obtains a net benefit to the economy when measured in terms of wages and incomes, as is standard in the labor economics literature. (Similar high rates have been obtained by Gibson and McKenzie 2010).

For clarity, we briefly describe the Nyarko (2011) model here. Suppose that there is a discount factor of $\delta = 1/(1+r)$ in $(0,1)$ with which future incomes are discounted. Let C be the sum of discounted costs of tertiary education. Let $W^{(i)}$ denote the total discounted flow for wages when at education level i, with i=1,2,3 representing primary, secondary and tertiary education. Let R denote the sum of discounted remittances. The model thinks of there being a probability d of being part of the brain drain. Conditional on leaving the country, there is a probability χ of return. Hence one can think of there being three states of the world—stay in the home country; drain and never return; drain and eventually return. These occur with probabilities $(1-d)$, $d(1-\chi)$ and $d\chi$ In these three states, there are different streams of wages and different streams of remittances. The expected return to higher education (secondary over tertiary) is therefore the expected benefit less the cost of education (which equals C):

$$(1-d)z_1 + d(1-\chi)z_2 \text{ and } d\chi z_3 - C$$

where $Z_1 = W^{(3)} - W^{(2)}$ is the sum of discounted incremental wages from acquiring tertiary education for those who stay in the country; Z_2 is the sum of discounted remittances (for the central planner problem) or overseas wages (for the individual problem) less secondary education wages for those who leave the country; and Z_2 is the sum of discounted remittances followed by returnee wages for those who leave the country for a while and then eventually return.

26.5 A QUICK REVIEW OF THE RATES-OF-RETURN LITERATURE

At this stage it may be useful to provide a quick review of the much older rates of return to education literature. The basic model looked at wages w as a function of education levels e as measured by years of schooling, S, and the number of years on a job (measuring experience levels), X. This is put in the standard Mincer regression equation

$$\text{Log wage} = \text{constant} + a_0.S + b_0.X + b_1.X^2 + \epsilon$$

The parameter a_0 is the return to one additional year of schooling. A lot of the early literature found relatively low rates of return to higher education while primary education seemed to have higher returns. Many have argued that this literature resulted in a full-scale onslaught on tertiary education institutions resulting in decline which is only now being slowly addressed.

This has led to what I have called the rate of return paradox: even though rates of return to tertiary education have been shown to be low in Africa, a lot of people are clamoring for that education. Families are saving the meager incomes to enable their children to ultimately make it to the university.

The results of the earlier section resolve this seeming paradox. The principal difference between the computation in the earlier section and that in this section on the rates of return is the inclusion in the former of one thing: migration.

The older rates of return to education literature concerned itself only with the incremental salary within the home country obtained from additional years of schooling. That literature did not account for the possibility that workers would migrate out of the local economy, go abroad and earn a high income. Given the relatively large migration of the educated out of countries like Ghana mentioned above, it is reasonable to think that the possibility of leaving loomed large in the minds of those deciding on whether to embark upon tertiary education.

When the possibility of migration is included in the rates of return analyses, as we did in the earlier section, we see that the low rates of return in the older literature now become very large rates of return for the individual when migration possibilities are allowed. This is a resolution of an old paradox as to why the rates of return to higher education were found in the early literature to be so low, yet almost all in Africa were clamoring for more tertiary education. The missing link is migration and the higher salary it brings to those lucky enough to have left.

Even apart from the problem mentioned above, and its resolution through the brain drain, there is another problem that older rates of return to education literature faces. It is important to remark that those papers did not, and could not, talk about the externalities caused by having large highly educated people—something economists understand much better now. The benefit of having an educated person is not only the private return to that individual (the higher salaries they will earn). There are externalities caused by the ideas and opportunities made possible to others by the educated person's presence—which causes benefits to others not captured in the first person's salary. The general pessimist mood for Africa in those years, the 70s and 80s, meant that nobody was studying these externalities and how important a trained and skilled class is to economic development.

Stated alternatively, the Mincer regressions are wage equations in a fairly static environment. To make the regressions work you need to keep fixed the coefficients. But these cannot remain fixed in the situation of a developing nation where education levels are changing so rapidly and the structure of the economy is undergoing profound changes. The parameters may be endogenously determined by the quantity of skilled in the nation. In other words, the Mincer regressions were taken from the environment of the mature nations to that of developing nations without checking whether the underlying premises of that model hold.

26.6 Education, Remittances, and Social Security

There is an almost immediate corollary to the results above, which provide another very important boost to the importance of migration. The argument involves two steps. First, a lot of countries particularly in sub-Saharan Africa either have or are considering social safety net policies which amount to provision of income to individuals who fall below a given poverty line.

We have argued above that remittances are large. An inspection of many household surveys indicates that many of the poor receive important support from remittances of relatives. Further, the higher is the education level the higher is the wage rate. Also, the more highly educated you are, the easier it is to emigrate. This then brings up a tantalizing question. Suppose one compared direct cash grants to the poor with a policy of first educating the poor so they receive higher incomes, with the possibility of remitting money to poorer relatives, whether or not they emigrate. Is the second policy superior to the first?

All this will depend upon the discount factors used. If all that is important is the cash transfer for today with the future completely unimportant then of course the immediate cash transfer to alleviate poverty today will trump anything else. However, where there are more realistic discount factors, the comparison becomes much more interesting.

This question was taken up by Gyimah and Nyarko (2011a,b). There it is shown indeed that education (secondary in the case) and remittances nexus may dominate cash transfers when the discount factors are at the standard levels used in a lot of development economics.

The Nyarko (2011) paper mentioned the role of return migration but it was constrained by the lack of data ongoing into fuller detail on this. As more data are obtained a better picture will emerge of the importance of the returned migrants who return with new ideas and better skills. Indeed, it is the conjecture of this author that those flows may be eventually of similar orders of magnitude in value as the remittance flows. This research will however have to await much better datasets.

26.7   The Brain Drain the Incentive to Acquire Human Capital

The basic message of this section is that since the brain drain gives an incentive to people to acquire human capital (as it aids migration) and since only a fraction of those who acquire this human capital actually leave (there is a visa or simply that not all are chosen or able to get a foreign job), it is possible that the brain drain causes more higher skilled people to remain in the country after the brain drain than if there was no brain drain.

How does this work? Well, the explanation is somewhat simple. The possibility of migration, if correlated with education, means that a lot of people will acquire that education. From research on Ghanaian emigration, it seems likely that many believe it is university education, which enables one to emigrate the easiest. This will result in many putting in the investment to get that education. The political economy in the country will move in the direction of provision of tertiary education for a large number of people.

On the other hand, because of visa restrictions and the general difficulty in going abroad, although a lot of people have invested in education so as to be able to migrate abroad, only a small fraction of these people will actually make it abroad. A large number of them will fail to make it. It is in their interest to try the migration lottery by acquiring the education because of the high wages obtained if successful. Since a lot of people fail in going abroad the number of people who are skilled and are in the home country then could be a large number—larger than if the incentive to migrate were absent.

This basic intuition has been studied in many papers. In the theoretical literature there are papers by Stark et al. (1998), Stark and Zakharenko (2011), Chand and Clemens (2008), and empirically in Easterly and Nyarko (2009).

It is instructive to note the similarities with soccer in Sub-Saharan Africa, and countries like Ghana in particular. There are now a significant and highly visible number of soccer players of West African origin playing in elite European teams. There is, in effect, a "foot drain" of players leaving their homes in Africa to destinations in the premier leagues in Europe. African soccer players in the home countries spend a lot of resources investing in their skills (time taken to practice, entry into training academies, etc.), so that they could take part in the lottery where they may be called to a European team and hit the jackpot with salaries in the millions.

A lot of Africans train hard and dream of being called to the European leagues. Only a small number of them make it. The total number of trained soccer players in a country like Ghana is probably higher because of the migration of a few to Europe. The "foot drain" has paradoxically resulted in many more skilled feet in Ghana than would have been the case if there was not a drain. The Ghanaian soccer leagues are probably much better than they would have been if some of the players did not emigrate.

The same is true for tertiary education as a whole. The data suggest that the possibility of the brain drain actually results, via the incentive effect, in more brains (skilled people) in the home country than would have been if there was no drain and so no incentive effect.

26.8 MIGRATION TO THE ARAB GULF AND WITHIN AFRICA

One area, which is very interesting in current economic research, is the migration into the Arab Gulf countries. Countries like the UAE and Qatar have enabled the migration of millions of workers, a number, which exceeds their own by a factor of 2, 3, or 4. Saudi Arabia brings in workers, which although a smaller fraction of its population, is still a large number in aggregate.

Just as in the earlier analyses, migration is of enormous benefit to the workers who arrive in these countries. The remittances are extremely large. There are a number of trends in the migration policies of these countries, which are only now being studied. On the one hand, as in the UAE, restrictive practices on workers have been relaxed. In January 2011 the Kafala system was ended—this system bonded a worker to one firm and required that firm to issue a No Objection card before a worker could leave for another job within the UAE. This has led to increased wages and within country mobility for migrant workers (see Naidu, Nyarko and Wang 2014).

In both Saudi Arabia and the UAE, on the other hand, there are attempts to use local native populations to replace the migrant workers. The Nitaquat system in Saudi Arabia is an interesting system of incentives to firms to replace migrant workers with foreign workers. The Emiratization system in the UAE is designed to replace foreign workers with the native Emirati people. The effects of these moves are yet to be studied. The work of this chapter suggests that such schemes should be approached with care as they will have impacts on the migrant workers.

A lot of the research in this chapter has used as examples migration from one continent to another. Within continent movements are important—and in particular there are significant movements of people across nations in Africa. Most of the analyses of this chapter apply in equal force to within Africa migrations. There has been skilled migration from Ghana and Nigeria into East and Southern African legal and civil service sectors. There are large movements of people among nations in West Africa, particularly from the Northern parts of West Africa to the coastal and southern parts. Adepoju (2002, 2006) and many others have done great work on documenting and analyzing these flows.

26.9 Policy Implications

Migration, mobility, and questions of the brain drain will become even more important over time. Africa's population is rising and it is youthful. Europe and many other parts of the world's population is stagnating and/or becoming older. The pressures for migration from Africa to the rest of the world, and Europe in particular, will become greater.

There are a number of policy implications from this work, many of them going counter to many of the proclamations in the media and in policy circles. First, of course, the brain drain should be thought of as something which can help and not always hurt local source economies.

Countries need to think of the brain drain as a source of getting people who will invest in the education. Many will acquire the education and not leave, becoming of benefit locally. Those who leave will enjoy better lives, and this should be thought of as a good thing. Others will leave and then return to the home countries with higher skills and greater motivation.

In particular, this calls for investment in training schools, which has at its core the possibility of people leaving the country. The strategy for getting more doctors and nurses in Africa would be to first build more of such schools with the goal of having some of them leave. The financing of such programs could be from either up front fees or else from the future payments of those who leave the country. The primary purpose of nursing schools in The Philippines is to train nurses to staff hospitals outside the country. The state of Kerala in India has training programs for elevator instructors, firefighters, and air conditioning unit technicians. More of these should be contemplated. In particular, these are institutions which aim at helping prepare those who are planning to leave.

Too often the economic and policy debates stop at the statement that migrants are hurting their home countries by leaving their home countries with their skills. As has been argued above, these arguments are not necessarily valid. The choice between having a doctor in the home country versus that doctor being outside the country is a false choice for many reasons. That doctor may not be there but for the incentive to invest in the medical training spurred by the possibility of migration. There could be other doctors in the pool in the economy because of that possibility. Further, the doctor who leaves may be the one who returns to open a new hospital or cardiac wing of an existing government hospital.

In particular, the policy recommendation is to find a way to creatively construct more institutions which train people in the skills which may be of benefit abroad. The medical profession, doctors and nurses in particular, are obvious candidates. As was mentioned earlier, the change in population numbers between Europe and Africa provide for opportunities for skills development in Africa, as explained by the earlier parts of this chapter. The numbers for the internal rates of return quantify the magnitude of the gain from these investments. In particular, at a policy level, higher education and skills development should be perceived as an industry which has a net positive benefit to the local source economy. Nyarko (2010a,b) go into further details on these policy recommendations.

26.10 CONCLUSION

Migration is an important facet of human economic development. It is one of the oldest methods by which humans have tried to better their economic lot. People go through great lengths and make huge sacrifices in order to migrate and get the opportunity to improve their living conditions. In some ways, migration is the very epitome of the human drive for economic development. In this chapter we have reviewed a bit of the literature on migration, especially as it relates to skills development. In the examples chosen, the emphasis has been on Africa and the Arab Gulf nations.

Education is important for economic development, and indeed can be transformative for economies. The migration of people, the brain drain and the remittances and skills accumulation it results in can be a big, important and positive part of the economic development equation. In particular, we indicate that the "brain drain" (the migration of skilled people), rather than being a problem may also be a source of economic development, helping create higher levels of education in the source countries themselves—it should be "brain circulation." as many of those skilled do return eventually to their home countries, particularly in Africa. We argue that economic policy should be directed at increasing skilled education possibilities even in the face of the brain drain, indeed also precisely because of the incentive effects inherent in the brain drain. Further, we believe that the principal conclusions of this chapter apply more extensively to many countries of the world, developing and developed. Migration could be used as an important driver for the transformation of nations.

We have also argued that remittances are very important. They help sustain family members in home countries. They provide resources for schooling of children and housing of families. In many countries they are the source of a lot of vibrancy in the economies, with new remittance income fueling housing booms in capitals of nations with large migrant populations.

Although hard to measure, the returned migrants with increased skills and drive exert a big influence on their home countries. New activities like laundromats, private universities, Internet cafes, private schools are often brought in by returned migrants.

Because of all the potential benefits to migrants, many who come from very poor nations, destination nations should be congratulated any time they make the lives of these migrants a bit more comfortable. Clearly defined skill requirements in the destination country, with higher salaries obtainable by those able to get the higher skills will encourage skill formation in the home nations. International organizations like the United Nations and the International Organization for Migration (IOM) have been working hard on this and should be encouraged to do more. The European Union and the United States have increasingly been working on new visas (the EU green or blue card) and other special visas for skilled nationals of other nations.

Finally though, we should remember the individual migrant at the heart of our research. The individual migrant to better his or her lot. For the vast majority of those who migrate, the migration results in better standards of living for themselves. This in itself is a huge plus. This chapter has studied this and also, as a bonus to the individual's migration, benefits to the home or source country.

Acknowledgments

I am grateful for funding from the Center for Technology and Economic Development at New York University in Abu Dhabi for research support while this work was undertaken, as well as the CV Starr Center in the Economics department of NYU. I thank participants at numerous conferences, particularly those at the African Development Bank on March 7, 2013. A lot of this work has benefited from affiliates at the CTED Global Labor Markets program (http://www.nyucted.org/).

References

Adepoju, A. (2002). Issues and recent trends in international migration in sub-Saharan Africa. *International Social Science Journal*, 52(165):383–394.

Adepoju, A. (2006). Leading issues in international migration in sub-Saharan Africa, in C. Cross, D. Gelderblom, N. Roux, and J. Mafukidze (eds), *Views on Migration in Sub-Saharan Africa*. Proceedings of an African Migration Alliance Workshop. Human Science Research Council (HSRC) and Department of Social Development, HSRC Press, Cape Town, 25–47.

Al Awad, M. (2010). The Cost of Foreign Labor in the United Arab Emirates. Institute for Social & Economic Research (ISER) Working Paper No. 3. UAE: Zayed University.

Bollard, A., McKenzie, D., and Morten, M. (2010). The Remitting Patterns of African Migrants in the OECD. World Bank Working Paper No. 5260. New York: World Bank.

Chami, R., Fullenkamp, C., and Gapen, M. (2008). Measuring Workers' Remittances: What Should Be Kept In and What Should Be Left Out? International Monetary Fund Working Paper, July. Washington, DC: IMF.

Chand, S., and Clemens, M. (2008). Skilled Emigration and Skill Creation: A Quasi-Experiment. Center for Global Development Working Paper No. 152. Washington, DC: CGD.

Docquier, F., and Marfouk, K. (2005). International Migration by Educational Attainment (1990-2000)—Release 1.1. World Bank Policy Research Working Paper 3381. Washington, DC: World Bank.

Easterly, W., and Nyarko, Y. (2009). Is the brain drain good for Africa? In J. Bhagwati and G. Hanson (eds), *Skilled Migration Today: Prospect, Problems and Policies*. New York: Oxford University Press, pp. 27–33.

Gibson, J., and McKenzie, D. (2010). The economic consequences of brain drain of the best and brightest: microeconomic evidence from five countries. *Economic Journal*, 122(560):339–375.

Gyimah-Brempong, K., Hellwig, K., and Nyarko, Y. (2011a). Social safety nets: the role of education, remittances and migration. European Report on Development. Brussels: European Union, pp. 4–13.

Gyimah-Brempong, K., and Nyarko, Y. (2011b). Social safety nets: the role of education, remittances and migration part 1. *Center for Technology and Economic Development Manuscript*. New York: New York University, pp. 1–36.

Irving, J., Mohapatra, S., and Ratha, D. (2010). Migrant Remittance Flows: Findings from a Global Survey of Central Banks. World Bank Working Paper No. 194. Washington, DC: World Bank.

Kapur, D. (2004). Remittances: The New Development Mantra? United Nations Conference on Trade and Development (UNCTAD), G-24 Discussion Paper Series, No. 29. Washington, DC: UNCTAD.

Naidu, S., Nyarko, Y, and Wang, S. (2014). Worker Mobility in a Global Labor Market: Evidence from the United Arab Emirates. Manuscript Columbia University. New York: Columbia University, pp. 1–58.

Nyarko, Y. (2010a). EU Policies and African Human Capital Development. Prepared for the Conference on Financial markets, adverse shocks and policy in fragile countries, organized by the European Report on Development in Accra, Ghana, 21–23, May, 2009.

Nyarko, Y. (2010b). The United Arab Emirates: Some Lessons in Economic Development. UN University World Institute for Development Economics Research (UNU–WIDER) Working Paper No. 2010/11. New York: UN University.

Nyarko, Y. (2011). The Returns to the Brain Drain and Brain Circulation in Sub-Saharan Africa: Some Computations Using Data from Ghana. National Bureau of Economic Research (NBER), Working Paper 16813. Boston: NBER.

Nyarko, Y. (2013). The Economic Development Benefits of Human Mobility to Source Countries. Conference Paper prepared for the Labour Mobility—Enabler for Sustainable Development, The Emirates Centre for Strategic Studies and Research (ECSSR).

Pires, M., Kassimir, R., and Brhane, M. (1999). *Investing in Return. Rates of Return of African Ph.D.'s Trained in North America.* New York: Social Science Research Council.

Ratha, D., Mohapatra, S., and Silwal, A. (2010). *Outlook for Remittance Flows 2010–11.* World Bank Development Prospects Group. Washington, DC: World Bank.

Stark, O., Helmenstein, C., and Prskawetz, A. (1998). Human capital depletion, human capital formation, and migration: a blessing or a curse? *Economics Letters*, 60(3):363–367.

Stark, O., and Zakharenko, R. (2011). Differential Migration Prospects, Skill Formation, and Welfare. Manuscript, Warsaw School of Economics. Warsaw: Warsaw University, pp. 14–20.

Tong, Q. (2010). Wages Structure in the in the United Arab Emirates. Institute for Social & Economic Research (ISER) Working Paper No. 2. UAE: Zayed University.

CHAPTER 27

··

HEALTH, GROWTH, AND DEVELOPMENT IN AFRICA

··

GERMANO MWABU

27.1 INTRODUCTION

THE chapter documents co-movements in health status and economic growth in Africa for the period 1960–2000. During this period, a large improvement in population health occurred in many African countries but did not last, as it was followed by an even larger decline. This phenomenon—a rapid health gain that was quickly lost—is unique to the first 40 years of independence in the recent history of the African continent. The decline in health status during this period must have entailed substantial human suffering that could have been avoided or mitigated with appropriate policies. Similarly, the economic loss occasioned by the erosion of human capital was not inevitable. The period 1960–2000 provides an opportunity to examine what can be done in the future to improve population health in African countries emerging from economic stagnation or from social and political turmoil and how the progress made can be sustained.

In the synthesis of the evidence reviewed, effort is made to assign causality from health to income and vice versa. Although the evidence has gaps, it is possible to conclude that there is a two-way relationship between health and income in Africa. The two-way relationship suggests existence of a third factor that affects both health and income. Depending on channels through which the third factor affects health and income, it is possible to observe (simultaneously) different patterns of health and income in the population. A potential third factor in the health–income relationship is education. An improvement in education increases both income and health. To the extent that education has an independent impact on health, its health effects are understated or neglected in health-improving models in which health is conditioned on income.

The linkages between health, education, growth, and general welfare are particularly noticeable in sub-Saharan Africa, when the region is viewed vis-à-vis other world regions. Sub-Saharan Africa ranked last among world regions in indicators of health, education, and development over the period 1960–2000 (Schultz 1994, 1995, 1999; World Bank 1993, 2000). In some welfare literatures (e.g. World Bank 2000; Ali and Thorbecke 2000), income poverty is an important summary measure of development. A poverty index reflects effects of growth and distribution on the well-being of the population. It also reflects, albeit imperfectly, the quality of the population as measured by stocks of human capital. Unlike physical capital, which improves the standard of life by increasing consumption opportunities, human capital improves the quality of life directly. The headcount index (the percentage of population below the poverty line) is the statistic commonly used to compare social welfare across regions. In 1998, sub-Saharan Africa had the highest poverty rate in the world (Table 27.1).

Table 27.1 is presented to stress the point that the disadvantaged position of Africa on a welfare scale relative to other regions may not be a coincidence but could be linked to its low health stocks. Even though welfare metrics such as the poverty rates are being continuously updated, Africa ranks last over the period analyzed irrespective of the welfare measure used.

Table 27.1 shows that in 1990s, sub-Saharan Africa had the highest poverty rate in the developing world, with nearly 50% of its population being below the poverty line. In some African countries (Ali and Thorbecke 2000), poverty rates exceeded 70% in the 1990s. Since poverty incidence at a particular date reflects previous economic growth rates and patterns of income distribution—which in turn are outcomes of factor accumulation and productivity, the poverty situation in Africa can partially be accounted for by growth and by the disparity in health human capital in previous decades. There is evidence from the industrialized world that up to 30% of economic growth can be accounted for by human capital accumulation, particularly improvements in nutrition and health (Mayer 2001).

Table 27.2 shows the evolution of health capital in Africa (as measured by life expectancy) vis-à-vis other regions over the period 1970–2000.

The asterisks in Table 27.2 show countries in which life expectancy over the period 1995–2000 was lower than the level in 1970–1975. Over 40% of the African countries at the end of 1990s had life expectancy levels lower than in the early 1970s. Table 27.3 indicates declines in life expectancy in selected African countries over the period 1977–1999.

In Botswana, one of the African countries most hit by the HIV/AIDS pandemic (Ainsworth and Over, 1994; Greener, Jeffris and Siphambe, 2000), life expectancy fell by 21 years between 1977 and 1999. Birdsall and Hamoudi (2001) showed that the decline in life expectation at birth in a given time period is positively associated with a reduction in education attainment in subsequent periods. The reduction in educational attainment associated

Table 27.1 Population living on less than US$1 a day, 1998

Region	Headcount ratio (%)
East Asia and Pacific, including China	11.3
Europe and Central Asia	5.1
Latin America and the Caribbean	15.6
Middle East and North Africa	1.9
South Asia	40.0
Sub-Saharan Africa	46.3

Source: Derived from World Bank (2000), p. 23.

Table 27.2 Life expectancy in Africa relative to other world regions, 1970–2000

Country	1970–1975	1995–2000
South Africa	53.7	56.7
Swaziland	47.3	50.8
Botswana	53.2	44.4*
Zimbabwe	56.0	42.9*
Ghana	49.9	56.3
Kenya	51.0	52.2
Nigeria	44.0	51.3
Sudan	43.7	55.0
Tanzania	46.5	51.1
Uganda	46.4	41.9*
Democratic Republic of Congo	46.0	50.5
Zambia	47.2	40.5*
Malawi	41.0	40.7*
Rwanda	44.6	39.4*
Burundi	44.0	40.6*
Developing countries	55.5	64.1
Sub-Saharan Africa	45.3	48.8
World	59.9	66.4

* Refer to text for explanation.
Source: UNDP 2001.

Table 27.3 Reversals in life expectancy in selected African countries, 1977–1999

Country	Fall in life expectancy, years (1977–1999)
Botswana	−21
Zimbabwe	−16
Zambia	−13
South Africa	−10
Lesotho	−9
Kenya	−8
Uganda	−6
Period mean	−11.9

Source: Derived from Birdsall and Hamoudi (2001), Table 3.

with foreshortening of life expectancy occurs due to one or more of the following (Birdsall and Hamoudi 2001):

- the death of skilled personnel, especially teachers, which negatively affects the training of next generations;
- premature deaths which decrease expected return to schooling, thus reducing demand for education;

- erosion of positive externalities to education through loss of educated people, which reduces growth, and depletes fiscal resources of government, weakening its ability to finance public education systems;
- loss of educated labor, which negatively affects production of school equipment and the machinery needed to train specialized categories of personnel, such as doctors, engineers, and other scientists.

Since the co-movement of health and education is quite strong (Fuchs 1996), it is interesting to discuss these two forms of human capital together. Table 27.4 shows education attainment in Africa relative to other regions over the period 1960–1990. As in previous tables, Table 27.4 is presented to suggest that the relatively low education stocks in Africa might have acted as a constraint on development.

From Table 27.4, it can be seen that although education levels in Africa lagged behind other world regions between 1960 and 1990, the education gaps remained relatively constant, except between Africa and East Asia, where by 1990 the gap had widened considerably. However, the difference between industrialized countries and East Asia narrowed significantly, with East Asia nearly catching up with the industrialized countries. In the case of East Asia and Africa, the African region had fallen further behind by 1990. The gap between Africa and East Asia in terms of economic growth and health status had increased accordingly (World Bank 2000). However, Table 27.4 does not show a true reflection of educational attainment in world regions, especially in Africa, where actual years of schooling in a given period can differ considerably from eventual education outcomes due to repetition or non-completion of grades. Moreover, even ignoring these problems, actual years of schooling are not a good measure of education stocks because they represent a snapshot of an ongoing process of education capital formation by families and governments. A better measure of educational investment is the expected years of schooling (Schultz 1995).

The link between education and health in Africa in the 1970s is suggested by a relationship between fertility and schooling of women (Table 27.5). An added year of schooling, for example, is associated with a 5–10% reduction in child mortality (Schultz 1995). Women's capacity to avoid unwanted pregnancy is one indicator of women's health. Women's ability to

Table 27.4 Average years of schooling in Africa relative to other world regions, 1960–1990

	Average years of schooling among population aged 24 years or more						
Region	1960	1965	1970	1975	1980	1985	1990
Sub-Saharan Africa	1.0	1.2	1.5	1.8	2.0	2.2	2.5
Latin America and Caribbean	3.3	3.2	3.8	4.0	4.2	4.3	4.5
East Asia	4.0	4.3	4.8	5.5	5.8	6.3	7.2
Industrialized countries	6.5	6.8	7.2	7.6	8.2	8.5	8.8

Source: Constructed from Birdsall and Hamoudi (2001), Figure 1.

control fertility is a further measure of population health because it is positively associated with reduction in infant mortality. Table 27.5 shows the relationship between total fertility rates in the 1970s in Africa vis-à-vis other regions by level of schooling of women.

Levels of human capital in 1970s are highlighted because we assume that they are linked to economic and health indicators in subsequent periods, particularly the 1980s and 1990s. Table 27.5 shows that in 1970s, Africa and Asia had the same health status, as measured by the total fertility rate. In both regions, the total fertility rate was around seven children. However, in Africa education of women reduced fertility rate more slowly than in Asia, which suggests that even with the same level of educational investments in the two regions, Africa would, other things being equal, have a lower level of health status than Asia. The table suggests existence of factors unique to Africa (the Africa dummy puzzle in some studies on Africa, for example, Bloom and Sachs 1998), which affects the way women's education influences fertility in the region. These unobservable factors probably include cultural norms and other institutional determinants of demographic changes.

In summary, patterns and levels of human capital investments in Africa over the period 1960–1990 appear to be responsible for both the health and welfare outcomes observed on

Table 27.5 Total fertility rates in Africa relative to other regions by education of women, 1970s

Region	Total fertility rate
Africa	
0 years of schooling	7.0
1–3 years	7.2
4–6 years	6.2
7 or more years	5.0
Difference in fertility rates between least and highly educated mothers (fertility at 0 years minus fertility at 7 or more years)	−2.0
Latin America	
0 years of schooling	6.8
1–3 years	6.2
4–6 years	4.8
7 or more years	3.2
Difference in fertility rates between least and highly educated mothers (fertility at 0 years minus fertility at 7 or more years)	−3.6
Asia and Oceania	
0 years of schooling	7.0
1–3 years	6.4
4–6 years	5.8
7 or more years	3.9
Difference in fertility rates between least and highly educated mothers (fertility at 0 years minus fertility at 7 or more years)	−3.1

Source: Extracted from Schultz (1995).

the continent at the close of the 1990s. That is, health investments over the period 1960–1990 could account for much of the growth rates and poverty levels experienced in Africa over the period 1990–2000. Mayer (2001) documents similar long-term, delayed effects of health on income in South America for the period 1950–1990. Furthermore, to the extent that health and income are linked, economic policies of the 1960–1990 period can explain (at least partially) the downward trend in health status observed in Africa during the last decade of the twentieth century. However, existing data on health and income for all African countries do not permit computations of such long-term impacts. Sections 2 and 3 below draw heavily from Mwabu (2004).

27.2 Effects of Income on Health

In this section, we attempt to answer two questions. First, through what channels does income affect health? Second, what does the available evidence reveal about effects of income on health in Africa? We address measurement issues first. Health is part and parcel of human beings (Schultz 1961). Thus, its measurement must necessarily be undertaken at the individual level. Indeed, aggregate indicators of health status such as life expectancy and mortality rates are proxies for aggregate measures of health stocks of individuals.

Measures of health status at the individual level include nutritional status (Fogel 1997; Schultz 1997), fertility rate (Schultz 1976), physical functioning of individuals as indicated by performance in activities of daily living (ADL) (Strauss et al. 1993) and age- and gender-specific survival probabilities (Mayer 2001). All the individual-level measures have the advantage, over the mortality rates for example, in that they provide information about health status of the living (Strauss et al. 1993). All these measures are correlated with aggregate proxies for health status. For example, life expectancy (mortality rate) increases (decreases) with nutritional status, as measured by body mass index, height-for-age, or weight-for-age. As a further example, life expectancy or mortality rate increases (decreases) with improvements in ADL measures.

The ADL measures derive from questions or direct observations that seek to determine whether one's health limits specific activities such as bending, walking uphill, bathing, among others (Strauss et al. 1993). The ADL are designed to measure adult health, and typically show proportions of the (elderly) population (by age, education, residence location) with limitations in performing specific activities.

Having looked at measurement of health we now turn to conceptual issues associated with health production at the individual level. A unique characteristic of health (WHO 1974) is that it cannot be produced or enhanced by one person on behalf of another. Thus, equity in the use of health inputs is key to equity in health outcomes. In accordance with (Anand and Chen 1996) and the household economics literature (Becker 1991; Strauss and Thomas 1995), we assume that an individual's health is self-produced using market and non-market inputs, the distribution of which determines health equity in the population. The market inputs include medical and non-medical goods (e.g. professional medical care, drugs, housing, clothing, etc.) and non-market goods (own time, genetic endowment, and non-tradable environmental goods, such as climate or social infrastructure).

Absent from the above simple health production model is a description of an incentive system that guides health production decisions of individuals. Schultz (1999) proposes a framework that addresses this issue, and examines the determinants and consequences of accumulating health human capital by households and individuals, including feedback relationships. In Schultz's framework, GDP per capita (a proxy for household income) plays several roles in influencing health. First, it increases demand for purchased inputs that individuals use to produce health, so that other things being equal, health status increases with GDP per capita. The second role of income is to relax household credit constraint in the financing of healthcare because "high-income" is a signal of the ability to repay debt. Thus, low-income imposes a double burden on the poor because they are not only unable to use their income to purchase sufficient quantities of healthcare but also cannot finance this care through borrowing because their low-income is a signal of their inability to meet a debt obligation. The third role of GDP per capita in health production is that it is a proxy for unmeasured health inputs such as micronutrients and environmental ambience.

Furthermore, the Schultz framework provides examples of instrumental variables (commodity prices, health system access factors, terms-of-trade) that can be used to address identification problems in the estimation of health effects of income.

The framework contains two additional novelties. First, aggregate health measures are based on health status of individuals. Second, the framework facilitates the testing of implications of household economics models at micro and macro levels. Since the ideal measures of health indicators can roughly be approximated by standard health indicators, such as mortality and life expectancy, we report effects of income on these indicators based on previous econometric studies that have estimated the effects for Africa.

Table 27.6 shows effects of income on infant mortality, crude death rate, crude birth rate, total fertility rate, and life expectancies of men and women in Africa for the period 1980–1995. The results were obtained by estimating a random effects model for all the 53 African countries. Needless to say, the effects are estimated taking into account other determinants of health.

From column 2 of Table 27.6, it can be seen that health status in Africa improved over the period 1980–1995. This is a notable trend because it coincided with the first phase of the HIV/AIDS pandemic on the continent, during which time little was known about the disease. Moreover, at that time, African economies were under great stress (World Bank 1997). In virtually all African countries, economic growth declined with notable exceptions of Botswana and some island economies. The estimated negative health effects of income shown in Table 27.6 suggest that health status was kept below its potential by the decline in income. The delayed negative effects of HIV/AIDS are also omitted from the estimates.

Table 27.7 reports effects of income on health from a similar study (Cornia and Mwabu 2000) that used a longer time series data.

Taken together, the results in Tables 27.6 and 27.7 suggest that income and health are strongly positively correlated and are generally consistent with the Pritchett and Summers (1996) hypothesis that wealthier populations are healthier populations.

Table 27.6 Effects of income on health in Africa, 1980–1995

Health status indicators in log form	Coefficient of log income (1)	Sample means (2)		
		1980	1990	1995
Infant mortality rate	−0.218	120.35	93.37	85.92
Crude death rate	−0.175	45.21	42.91	39.79
Crude birth rate	−0.059	17.33	14.41	13.36
Total fertility rate	−0.058	6.29	6.04	5.59
Female life expectancy	0.078	50.36	55.06	55.18
Male life expectancy	0.083	47.84	51.72	52.10
Number of countries	42	50-52	53-53	51-52

Source: Mwabu (2001), Table 1; p. 326, and Table 4, p. 331.

Table 27.7 Effects of income on health in Africa, 1960–1995

Health status (log)	Coefficient on log income
Infant mortality	−0.117
Under-five mortality	−0.144
Maternal mortality	−0.256
Female life expectancy	0.005
Sample size	133

Source: Cornia and Mwabu (2000), Table 2.3, p. 33.

27.3 EFFECTS OF HEALTH ON INCOME

This section looks at the evidence on the causal relationship from health to income in the African context. At the micro-level, the issue at hand concerns the effect of individual's health on household income, and at the macro-level, the impact of population health on economic growth. The key issue relates to one of the feedback arms in Schultz's (1999) model of determinants and consequences of health.

As in section 27.2, we first clarify analytical concepts before turning to evidence. The analytic concept remains the production function, or its proxy—the wage function. In section 27.2, the production function details the use of market and non-market inputs by households to produce health. In this section, the production function describes use of health capital by households to increase labor productivity in market and non-market settings. At the macro-level, an aggregate production function describes, *ceteris paribus*, how national income is determined by the stock of population health.

The macroeconomic literature of the effects of human capital on growth is voluminous, and no attempt is made to survey it here (see e.g. Barro and Sala-i-Martin 1995). The macro-economic literature focuses primarily on effects of education on growth. Notable exceptions include papers by Bloom and Sachs (1998), Gallup and Sachs (2000), and McCarthy et al. (2000).

Since education human capital and health human capital are closely related (Fuchs 1996), by focusing on growth effects of education, the growth literature is also indirectly analyzing the health effects. However, there is tension in the literature as to whether effects of health on income are better analyzed at the macro- or micro-level (Bloom and Sachs 1998; Schultz 1999; and Malaney 2000). There are at least two reasons for focusing the analysis at the micro-level in Africa.

First, aggregate data on health and growth in Africa is of questionable quality in many countries so that the estimated growth effects of health likely suffer from biases arising from measurement errors. Indeed, Schultz (1999) has pointed out that the estimated effects of education on growth are too high vis-à-vis the returns to schooling obtained using micro-data. Similarly, the effect of malaria on aggregate growth in Africa reported by Gallup and Sachs (2000) is unbelievably large. Gallup and Sachs (2000) conclude from aggregate evidence of the effects of malaria on economic performance that African incomes are one-third of the countries' that have not had malaria over the previous four to five decades, a finding that attributes nearly 70% of the loss of African wealth to malaria over that period. Much lower economic burdens of malaria in Africa are reported from microeconomic evidence (Shepard et al. 1991; Malaney 2000). The second reason in favor of micro-economic analysis of the effects of health on income is that macroeconomic analysis of these effects necessarily leads to broad, often unwarranted generalizations as to health interventions that should be implemented at the household- and community levels to promote growth.

In view of noise in aggregate data in Africa, it appears prudent to focus on evidence from high-quality micro-data. We start by presenting evidence from Schultz's (1999) work on wage returns to health human capital in Ghana and Cote d'Ivoire. The estimates were obtained from large, nationally representative data sets (Living Standard Measurement Surveys) collected by the World Bank in the 1980s (Grosh and Glewwe 1998). The effects of body mass index (BMI) on wages were estimated, controlling for education of the individual, migration from birthplace, and height. Also included in the estimated equations were ten regions of birth, eight to ten ethnic groups, five age dummies, and the season in which data were collected to capture seasonal cycles in agricultural wages. Table 27.8 shows effects of health (proxied by BMI) on income (proxied by market wage) in Ghana and Cote d'Ivoire in the 1980s, estimated with instrumental variable methods (all the coefficients are statistically significant).

Table 27.8 shows that on average, the effect of health on income in Cote d'Ivoire (in the period indicated) was larger than in Ghana. However, Ghanaian women received higher wage returns from health than their counterparts in Cote d'Ivoire. These wage returns were also higher than those for males in Ghana. In contrast, wage returns to men's health in Ghana are only a half of the returns in Cote d'Ivoire. In particular, a unit increase in BMI is associated with 15.9% increase in wages in Cote d'Ivoire, compared with 7.93% in Ghana. However, results on returns to height (not shown in the table) indicate that both men and women in Ghana benefit more from height improvements than in Cote d'Ivoire. These differences in health returns are due to the fact that height is a measure of long-term investments in health, whereas BMI is a proxy for short-term nutritional status.

Table 27.8 Effects of health on income in Ghana and Cote d'Ivoire, 1985–1989

Log of hourly wage (by country, gender and sample dates (sample sizes in parentheses)	Coefficient on BMI (weight in kilograms divided by height in meters squared)
Cote d'Ivoire (LSMS: 1985–1987)	
Log male wages (1692)	0.159
Log female wages (1180)	0.095
Mean	0.127
Ghana (LSMS: 1987–1989)	
Log male wages (3414)	0.0793
Log female wages (3400)	0.0981
Mean	0.0887

Source: Extracted from Schultz (1999), Table 1, p. 75 (means are author's own calculations).

The results in Table 27.8 have several policy implications. First, they indicate that investments in health would improve household incomes in the two countries. Second, such investments would affect growth rates and income distribution differently. For example, investments in programs aimed at increasing weights of workers would yield a higher growth rate in Cote d'Ivoire than in Ghana, and benefit male workers in Cote d'Ivoire relatively more than other workers. Further, Ghanaian women would benefit from such programs more than their male counterparts in Ghana. Therefore, although the qualitative growth effects of better health are generalizable even to countries outside the West Africa region, size and distributional effects cannot be extended even across the two countries studied.

There are two other studies in Africa on income effects of health that need to be considered, namely Strauss's (1986) study in Sierra Leone and Audibert's (1986) work in Cameroon. Strauss (1986) estimated the effects of nutrition (proxied by calorie consumption) on labor productivity in Sierra Leone and found that the effects were largest among the lowest income households. Again, as in Cote d'Ivoire and Ghana, this study suggests that investment in nutrition would affect household incomes differently. In particular, the finding of the study suggests that investments in nutrition programs would likely be pro-poor. Audibert (1986) estimated effects of health status on rice production in Cameroon, and found that families without schistosomiasis infections were more productive that families that were infected. The author found that a 10% increase in the prevalence of schistosomiasis resulted in a 4.9% reduction in rice production.

The two studies provide evidence that better health and nutrition can improve incomes in non-market settings in Cameroon and Sierra Leone and are to be contrasted with Schultz's study that demonstrates the same effects in market contexts in Cote d'Ivoire and Ghana. The analysis of household data collected in the 1980s in selected African countries shows that investment in health and nutrition increases household income and enhances performance of economies. However, long-term growth effects of health investments cannot be assessed with the available data. To undertake such analysis, panel household data collected over many decades are needed.

27.4 Health, Development, and Lessons Learned

In sections 27.1–27.3, we have treated health, income, and education as both ends and means of development—a sustained improvement in people's living standards. These are standards as to the quantity and quality of things that people value, such as healthcare, nutrition, education, housing, environment, basic freedoms, culture, among others. Development involves much more than economic progress, which, as we have seen, is both a cause and a consequence of health capital.

However, health has two attributes that make it the key to achieving other ends of development. First, by preventing premature death, good health expands the horizon over which other ends of development, such as adequate housing, political freedom, peace, family, and education can be realized and enjoyed. The second fundamental attribute of health (shared with education) is that it is part and parcel of human beings (Schultz 1961). This attribute makes health capital both an end and a means of development. Few other economic goods can claim this status.

As an end, health human capital is part and parcel of human beings, an attribute that is sufficient to justify health expenditures by individuals and governments without regard to its productivity-enhancing role. The strong justification for government spending on health is the need to address social externalities associated with the control of certain diseases through measures that can treat or prevent the diseases. For example, since healthy people are at risk of being infected by individuals with contagious diseases, governments are justified to spend resources to eradicate or control such diseases. As a means, health human capital creates wealth that can be used to achieve other ends of development, such as having the capability to engage in non-economic activities, such as the pursuit of cultural and religious objectives. Good health facilitates acquisition of skills essential for development of new technologies or organizations. Technical change is one of the key processes underlying the development process (Boserup 1995). Thus, good health is essential for transformation of a country from a low- to a high-productivity economy. Such transformation is a prerequisite for raising current and future standards of living.

The health shocks in Africa over the 1960–2000 provide valuable lessons to policy makers on the continent when responding to emergencies that threaten population health or economic prosperity of the region. The first lesson is that an emergence of a new disease need not lead to panic or fear, as there is evidence that severe diseases can be controlled through concerted efforts of national policymakers, development partners, and researchers. The gloomy health and economic effects of HIV/AIDS predicted for Africa over the first decades of the twenty-first century did not materialize. Instead, annual growth in Africa exceeded 5% over the period 2000–2013, with some economies exceeding 10% for nearly a decade (Ndulu et al. 2013). The poverty rate in Africa is declining on a large scale, and life expectancy is on the increase. Thus, despite dire predictions for Africa, particularly in the 1980s, Africa's prospects for strong growth and better health are improving.

The health crisis (Baize et al. 2014) in West Africa (Guinea, Sierra Leone, and Liberia) associated with the outbreak of Ebola virus disease (Ebola) led to panic and fear because it was not viewed from a long-term perspective (World Bank 2014). Panic can hinder careful analysis of a problem and pre-empt design of effective interventions. A long-term perspective on Ebola would have shown that Ebola is not new in Africa. Ebola was discovered in Africa in 1976 (WHO 1978) following its outbreak in South Sudan and the Democratic Republic of Congo. A long-term perspective on Ebola would have shown that it was quickly contained after modes of its infection and transmission were identified (WHO 1978), and that its control is not beyond the reach of science and the concerted efforts of policymakers. The economic losses from the disease in the most affected countries in West Africa (Guinea, Liberia and Sierra Leone) were estimated at 2.1–3.3% of GDP for the first year of the crisis, and projected to rise to 12% in the second year in some of the countries (World Bank 2014). Although these estimates are speculative, they provide rough measures of the economic losses that Africa can suffer from disease epidemics in the absence of effective health policies.

27.5 Conclusion

The chapter has examined the relationship among economic growth, health status, and development in Africa over the period 1960–2000. Between 1960 and the 1970s, health status in Africa expanded rapidly before entering a slow growth phase, from 1980s to the early 1990s. After 1995, health human capital in Africa began to fall, and by the end of 1990s health indicators for many African countries were approaching or already below the indicators for the 1970s. The HIV/AIDS epidemic was the main factor responsible for the sharp decline in health status in Africa (Bonnel 2000).

Based on a review of previous studies on Africa, the chapter shows that health, growth, and development are highly interdependent. In particular, accumulation of health capital in Africa is positively associated with the continent's economic performance. We are able to conclude that one reason why Africa lags behind other world regions in welfare indicators is that its stock of health capital is low. Implementation of interventions to enhance this stock would contribute significantly to poverty reduction on the continent. The chapter points to the need for comparative and long-term perspectives in response to health crises in Africa and elsewhere to avoid panic, fear, inaction, or mistakes.

Acknowledgment

I am very grateful to Célestin Monga and T.P. Schultz for advice and encouragement. However, I am solely responsible for any errors in this chapter.

References

Ainsworth, M., and Over, M. (1994). AIDS and the African development. *World Bank Research Observer*, 9(2):203–240.

Ali, A.G.A., and Thorbecke, E. (2000). The state and path of poverty in sub-Saharan Africa: Some Preliminary Results. *Journal of African Economies*, 9(1):9–40.

Anand, S., and Chen, L. (1996). *Health Implications of Economic Policies: A Framework of Analysis*. Discussion Paper Series. New York: UNDP.

Audibert, M. (1986). Agricultural non-wage production and health status: a case study in a tropical environment. *Journal of Development Economics*, 24:275–291.

Baize, S. et al. (2014). Emergence Zaire Ebola virus disease in Guinea. *New England Journal of Medicine*, 371(15):1418–1425.

Barro, R., and Sala-i-Martin, X. (1995). *Economic Growth*. New York: McGraw-Hill.

Becker, G. (1991). *A Treatise on the Family*. Cambridge, MA: Harvard University Press.

Birdsall, N., and Hamoudi, A. (2001). AIDS and the Accumulation of Human Capital in Africa. AERC Plenary Paper, December, Nairobi, Mimeo.

Bloom, D.E., and Sachs, J.D. (1998). Geography, demography and economic growth in Africa. *Brookings Papers on Economic Activity*, 2:207–295.

Bonnel, R. (2000). HIV/AIDS and Economic Growth: A Global Perspective. *South African Journal of Economics*, 68(5):820–855.

Boserup, E. (1995). Obstacles to the advancement of women during development, in T. Paul Schultz (ed.), *Investment in Women's Human Capital*. Chicago: University of Chicago Press.

Cornia, G.A., and Mwabu, G. (2000). Health status and policy in sub-Saharan Africa: a long-term perspective, in D. Ghai (ed.), *Renewing Social and Economic Progress in Africa*. London: Macmillan Press.

Fogel, R.W. (1997). New findings on secular trends in nutrition and mortality: some implications for population theory, in M.R. Rosenzweig and O. Stark (eds), *Handbook of Population and Family Economics*, Vol. 1A. Amsterdam: North-Holland.

Fuchs, V.R. (1996). Economics, values, and health care reform. *American Economic Review*, March:1–24.

Gallup, J.L., and Sachs, J.D. (2000). The economic burden of malaria. CID Working Paper No. 52, Center for International Development. Cambridge, MA: Harvard University.

Greener, R., Jeffris, K., and Siphambe, H. (2000). The impact of HIV/AIDS on poverty and inequality in Botswana. *South African Journal of Economics*, 68(5):888–915.

Grosh, M., and Glewwe, P. (1998). The World Bank's living standards measurement surveys. *Journal of Economic Perspectives*, 12(1):187–196.

Malaney, P. (2000). The microeconomic burden of Malaria. Center for International Development, Harvard University, Cambridge, MA, Mimeo.

McCarthy, F.D., Wolf, H., and Wu, Y. (2000). Malaria and Growth, Georgetown University, Georgetown, Mimeo.

Mayer, D. (2001). The long-term impact of health on economic growth in Latin America. *World Development*, 29(6):1025–1033.

Mwabu, G. (2001). Health status in Africa: a regional profile. *South African Journal of Economics*, 69(2):319–335.

Mwabu, G. (2004). Health and Growth in Africa, KIPPRA Discussion Paper No. 43.

Ndulu, B. et al. (2013), Growth and employment, in JICA Report to TICAD V, *Research on Policies for African Youth Employment*, Chapter 23, Kobe University. Kobe: Research Institute for Economics and Business Administration.

Pritchett, L., and Summers, L.H. (1996). Wealthier is healthier. *Journal of Human Resources*, 30(4):841–868.

Schultz, T.W. (1961). Investment in human capital. *American Economic Review*, 51(1):1–17.

Schultz, T.P. (1976). Interrelationships between mortality and fertility, in R.G. Ridker (ed.), *Population and development: The Search for Selective Interventions*. Baltimore: Johns Hopkins University Press.

Schultz, T.P. (1994). Human capital, family planning and their effect on population growth. *American Economic Review*, 84(2):255–260.

Schultz, T.P. (ed.) (1995). *Investment in Women's Human Capital*. Chicago: University of Chicago Press.

Schultz, T.P. (1997). Demand for children in low-income countries, in M.R. Rosenzweig and O. Stark (eds), *Handbook of Population and Family economics*, Vol. 1A, Amsterdam: North-Holland.

Schultz, T.P. (1999). Health and schooling investments in Africa. *Journal of Economic Perspectives*, 13(3):67–88.

Shepard, D.S., Ettling, M.B., Brinkman, U., and Sauerborn, R. (1991). The economic cost of malaria in Africa. *Tropical Medicine and Parasitology*, 42:197–223.

Strauss, J. (1986). Does better nutrition raise farm productivity? *Journal of Political Economy*, 94(2):297–320.

Strauss, J., and Thomas, D. (1995). Human resources: empirical modeling of household family decisions, in J.R. Behrman and T.N. Srinivasan (eds), *Handbook of Development Economics*, Vol. IIIA. Amsterdam: North-Holland.

Strauss, J., Gertler, P., Rahman, O., and Fox, K. (1993): Gender and life-cycle differentials in the patterns and determinants of adult health. *Journal of Human Resources*, 28(4):791–837.

UNDP (1995, 2001). *Human Development Report*. Oxford: Oxford University Press.

WHO (1974). *Basic Documents*, 36th edn. Geneva: WHO.

WHO (1978). Ebola haemorrhagic fever in Zaire. *Bulletin of the World Health Organization*, 56(2):271–293.

World Bank (1993). *World Development Report*. Oxford: Oxford University Press.

World Bank (1997). *Confronting AIDS: Public Priorities in a Global Epidemic*. Washington, DC: World Bank.

World Bank (2000). *World Development Report: Attacking Poverty*. New York: Oxford University Press.

World Bank (2014). *The Economic Impact of 2014 Ebola Epidemic: Short and Medium Term Estimates for West Africa*. World Bank, Washington, DC, Mimeo.

CHAPTER 28

....

THE ECONOMICS OF MALARIA IN AFRICA

....

JEAN-CLAUDE BERTHÉLEMY AND
JOSSELIN THUILLIEZ

28.1 INTRODUCTION

....

MALARIA is prevalent throughout most of the tropical world, producing a situation in which an estimated 2.57 billion people living in regions of the world were at risk of *Plasmodium falciparum* transmission in 2010 (798.42 million in Africa; Gething et al. 2011) and 2.85 billion people were exposed to some risk of *Plasmodium vivax* transmission in 2009 (98 million in Africa; Guerra et al. 2010). There were an estimated 1 238 000 million malaria deaths worldwide in 2010 (1 133 000 in Africa; Murray et al. 2012). Malaria is considered one of the most common infectious diseases and the most important of the parasitic diseases.[1] Furthermore, there is currently no vaccine against the parasite.

Malaria is also more than merely a tropical disease that claims a heavy toll on lives in sub-Saharan Africa and is economically costly. In recent debates among development economists, malaria has been at the center of a controversy about the causality between health and economic performances. This relation is probably bidirectional but economic analyses on the cost of malaria in Africa have contributed to this important debate.

In the context of Millenium Development Goals (MDGs), major efforts have been devoted to the fight against malaria. A variety of prevention and treatment measures have

---

[1] Most of infections in humans are caused by four different species of the genus *Plasmodium*. *Plasmodium falciparum*, *Plasmodium malariae*, *Plasmodium vivax*, and *Plasmodium ovale* are associated with different clinical presentations, progression, prevalence, and antimalarial resistance patterns. Recently human malaria cases due to *P. knowlesi* have been detected (Singh and Daneshvar 2013). *P. falciparum* infection results in the highest morbidity and mortality, accounting for almost all of the over 1 million deaths caused by malaria annually, most of them in young children in Africa. The *incidence of malaria* is defined as the number of new cases of malaria for a given population during a specific time period (given in person-time). The *prevalence of malaria* is defined as the total number of malaria cases in a given population at a specific time.

been put in place. The cost-effectiveness of malaria prevention and treatment tools that have been used in malaria control strategies is in principle very high in experimental contexts. However, large-scale results of impact evaluations of antimalaria campaigns are not always as positive as they might be. Malaria continues to be a significant cause of global mortality and morbidity. Indeed, despite the recent decreasing trend in malaria mortality and morbidity in Africa and a renewed optimism, it is still difficult to disentangle the complementary causal effects of existing strategies: net distribution, distribution of new antimalarial drugs (ACTs (artemisinin combination therapies)), and insecticide spraying.

Numerous examples could be given and are illustrative. First, in spite of massive efforts to generalize efficient prevention, such as insecticide-treated mosquito nets (ITNs) or long-lasting insecticidal nets (LLINs), ITN coverage remains low in large populations at risk despite rapid increase, and ITNs are still only used to a limited extent (Flaxman et al. 2010). A second example resides in the controverted results of the Affordable Medicines Facility—malaria (AMFm) program, a sustained global subsidy of ACTs (Arrow 2004). A last example is related to national malaria control programs' official policies and results. Van Eijk et al. (2011) synthesized data from national surveys and concluded that coverage of ITNs and intermittent preventive treatment in pregnant African women is inadequate despite the fact that 45 of the 47 countries surveyed had a policy for distribution of ITNs for pregnant women and 39 had an intermittent preventive treatment policy. These results suggest the need for a deeper economic analysis combined with epidemiological tools that recognize the complex character of malaria. This is all the more feasible in 2013, contrary to 10 years ago, because part of the information gap on malaria morbidity could be filled with the growing number of large-scale malaria indicator surveys.

In addition, the analysis of Arrow (2004) suggested that "insecticide-treated bednets and other, broad environmental strategies offer great potential for synergy when effective drug therapies are available". Indeed, it would be necessary to identify the optimal combination of strategies for action in an integrated way, given the risk of development of ACT-resistant *P. falciparum* malaria parasites.

This chapter is organized as follows. The next section provides a description of malaria control strategies that have been implemented in Africa. Section 3 gives an overview of economic methods used for estimating the economic impact of malaria in Africa and estimating malaria costs, taking into account the endogenous relationship between malaria and economic development. Section 4 presents a malaria economic epidemiology model, aiming at explaining why under some circumstances, policies of dissemination of protection devices cannot eradicate malaria; such circumstances are in particular related to situations where the poverty incidence is high, and section 5 concludes.

28.2 Malaria Control Strategies in Africa: An Overview

28.2.1 Recent history of malaria control in Africa

Figure 28.1 provides a very schematic history of malaria control since 1900. There is evidence that the WHO global initiative to fight malaria launched in the 1950s has been much more effective in Asia than in Africa. The emergence and spread of chloroquine-resistant *P. falci-parum* malaria parasites has been a disaster for world health. This figure is obviously schematic and Murray et al. (2012) have shown that past estimates provided for malaria cases and deaths were probably underestimated, but it is however informative.

The first worldwide eradication program was launched by the WHO in 1955. The program was based on house spraying with residual insecticides, antimalarial drug treatment, and surveillance. However, the most malarious areas such as tropical Africa were excluded due to overwhelming difficulties (Alilio et al. 2004).[2] Newly independent states in tropical Africa were thus relying on marginal sponsored actions (residual insecticide spraying in a few urban centers, or larviciding in limited areas), national health systems and national malaria control programs already operational by the 1950s, hospitals and dispensaries-based antimalarial activities, mass drug administration, and availability of antimalarial drugs in the open market. The extensive use of residual insecticide dichloro-diphenyl-trichloroethane (DDT) and chloroquine (CQ)[3] did benefit Africa, as overall malaria-related deaths in Africa showed evidence of a decline from the 1950s to the 1980s. However, these activities may have promoted the development of both drug and insecticide resistance.

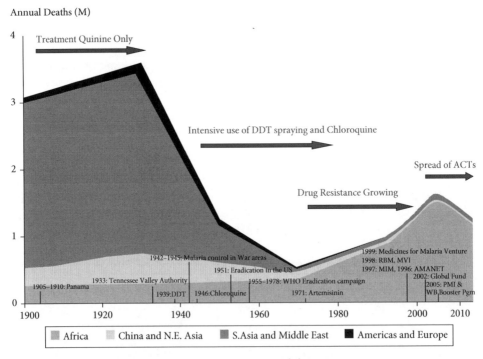

FIGURE 28.1 Schematic overview of malaria control from 1900 to 2010.

Source: authors from Carter and Mendis, (2002)., Alilio et al. (2004), Murray et al. (2012), and RBM (2013).

[2] A full history of malaria control programs in Africa can be found in Carter and Mendis (2002) and Alilio et al. (2004).

[3] A drug used for the treatment and prevention of malaria, discovered in 1934 and established as an effective and safe antimalarial in 1946.

Indeed, the downward trend in malaria-related mortality appears to have reversed in the 1970s due to chloroquine resistance and the small effect of residual insecticide DDT in sub-Saharan Africa. Conversely, Asian malaria transmission was much more sensible to vector control measures using DDT because of the lower intensity of this transmission, a relative organizational and political stability after the Second World War and the massive investment made by the WHO and bilateral assistance. CQ was the main malaria therapy worldwide from the 1940s until the 1990s and Africa is highly vulnerable to the continuing availability of effective antimalarial drugs. That is why preserving drugs' effectiveness is essential. Following the emergence of CQ-resistant *P. falciparum*, most African countries discontinued the use of CQ, and now promote ACT as the first-line treatment (Flegg et al. 2013). This change was generally initiated during the last decade in West and Central Africa (Gharbi et al. 2013). Indeed, in the late 90s, the Chinese drug artemisinin has been hailed as one of the greatest advances in fighting malaria since the discovery of quinine centuries ago. Artemisinin was first extracted by the Chinese in 1971 from *Artemisia annua*. This treatment was not new (Klayman, 1985) but the first ACTs were provided at reduced prices to the WHO only in 2001. Approximately at the same time, in 1998, the WHO launched a second campaign aiming to halve malaria deaths worldwide by 2010 (Nabarro and Tayler, 1998). The Global Fund to Fight AIDS, Tuberculosis and Malaria (GF) was created in 2002 and, soon after its founding became the main multilateral funder in the global health arena.

Nowadays, the primary objective of these new malaria control campaigns is to reduce deaths and illness from the disease. Elimination of infection is far more difficult. The policies and strategies for malaria control are based on LLINs and ACT, plus a revival of support for indoor residual spraying of insecticide (IRS). The combination of these actions has several advantages. First, ITNs are comparable to measles vaccination in their cost-effectiveness in preventing malaria deaths and morbidity and can be used for mosquitoes control and as a preventive measure. Second, the demise of chloroquine and sulfadoxine pyrimethamine leaves ACTs as the best treatment option. The advantages of ACTs (easy to administer, few side-effects, rapid action against the parasite, increase in the efficacy of both drugs) are widely recognized. In addition, patients given two or more effective drugs are less likely to encounter drug resistance and failed treatment, because parasite mutations to both components with different mechanisms of action are less probable. Currently there are six ACTs approved by regulatory authorities (Lin et al. 2010).[4] Third, IRS is the application of insecticides to the inner surfaces of dwellings, where endophilic *Anopheline* mosquitoes often rest after taking a blood meal. According to the WHO, several years of consecutive rounds of IRS are effective in reducing malaria parasite prevalence and incidence in areas of high transmission and can be used in combination with ITNs[5]. Last, Seasonal Malaria Chemoprevention (SMC) is recommended by the WHO in parts of the world where malaria is seasonal such as the Sahel sub-region of Africa. Most childhood malaria mortality and morbidity occurs during the rainy season in these regions. The provision of effective

---

[4] Artemether lumefantrine, artesunate amodiaquine, artesunate mefloquine, artesunate sulfadoxine pyrimethamine, dihydroartemisinin piperaquine, and artesunate pyronaridine.

[5] See Mabaso et al. (2004) for a historical review of malarial control in southern African with emphasis on the use of IRS.

malaria treatment at intervals during this period has been shown to prevent illness and death from malaria among children.[6]

28.2.2 The "value for money" of malaria control programs

Growing "value for money" agenda aims to reduce costs, increase impact per dollar spent and focus investments on the highest impact interventions among the most affected populations (Fan et al. 2013; Glassman et al. 2013).

This agenda is all the more relevant that, according to the 2012 Malaria Report (WHO 2012), the past decade has witnessed tremendous expansion in the financing and implementation of malaria control programs. International disbursements for malaria control rose steeply from less than US$100 million in 2000 to US$1.71 billion in 2010 and were estimated to be US$1.66 billion in 2011 and US$1.84 billion in 2012. Analysis indicates that as funding has risen, international disbursements have been increasingly targeted to the African Region (contrary to the first WHO campaign), to countries with the lowest gross national income (GNI) per capita, and to countries with the highest malaria mortality rates. Domestic government funding for malaria control programs also increased through 2005–2011 and was estimated at US$625 million in 2011.

The paradigm shift from malaria control to malaria eradication following declarations at the Gates Malaria Forum in October 2007 and subsequent support voiced by the WHO, the Board of the Roll Back Malaria (RBM) Partnership, the UN Secretary-General in 2011, and many other institutions has renewed inspiration for innovation and public health action. The GF remains the largest source of funding for malaria control globally, accounting for 39% of estimated disbursed funds in 2011 and 40% in 2012 (WHO 2012). The second and third largest funders are the President's Malaria Initiative and the World Bank's Booster program. However, while there have been substantial increases in funding for malaria control, they continue to fall short of the amount needed to achieve the global goals. The Global Malaria Action Plan (RBM) estimates that US$2.196 billion will be needed annually in 2015 to scale up preventive and curative interventions to reach universal coverage in Africa.

In the past decade a trend has appeared in malaria-induced mortality, with decreasing mortality around 2005 (Figure 28.1, and Murray et al. 2012). It is however difficult to assert a direct causal relationship of all malaria control policies because limited rigorous evaluations have been undertaken. It is possible that this favorable trend is mainly due to the spread of ACTs alone.[7] However, attribution of this recent favorable trend to any of the policies that have been implemented is impossible due to the lack of measurement instruments and formal external large-scale impact evaluations for interventions and service delivery strategies

---

[6] WHO recommends SMC with sulfadoxine pyrimethamine and amodiaquine in areas with highly seasonal malaria transmission in the Sahel sub-region of sub-Saharan Africa, where *P. falciparum* is sensitive to both antimalarial medicines.

[7] Unfortunately, until now, the Global Price Reporting Mechanism (GPRM) hosted by the WHO website (a database recording international transactions of HIV, tuberculosis and malaria commodities purchased by national programmes in low- and middle-income countries) does not provide free access to the data on anti-malaria medicines accessed in January 2014.

(Fan et al. 2013). Randomized studies are needed to assess the efficiency of such programs and optimal combinations of actions from a supply side perspective.

Moreover, we have factual indications that a number of specific initiatives have had moderate positive or negative impact. First, subsidizing treatment may increase their usage among people who do not actually have malaria. Dupas (2014) and Cohen et al. (2011) showed that only 25 % of adults (over age 18) who purchased subsidized ACTs at drug shops were tested malaria positive. Second, as shown by Laxminarayan et al. (2010), at extremely high infection transmission rates (in excess of about 70 infectious bites per year), treatment subsidies may be inefficient because recovering individuals quickly become re-infected so that there is little impact on reducing the size of the infected population. Third, surveillance systems and research studies supported by WHO to monitor antimalarial drugs efficacy in countries do provide evidence that parasites resistant to artemisinin have emerged along the border between Cambodia and Thailand.

In addition, proliferation of insecticide resistance suggests that the spread of insecticide resistance is a major threat for vector control programs, especially pyrethroid resistance in Africa (Santolamazza et al. 2008). Currently, insecticides used for IRS come from only four classes: pyrethroids (the most commonly used class), organochlorines (of which DDT is the only compound in use), organophosphates, and carbamates; all WHO recommended. ITNs and LLINs use pyrethroids. As malaria vector control, and consequently the success of global malaria control, is heavily reliant on a single class of insecticide, the pyrethroids, increasing resistance of malaria vectors to pyrethroids and to other insecticides jeopardizes global malaria control efforts.

Apart from technical considerations, the analysis of demand and supply chain of malaria control tools suggests a number of difficulties that may affect the effectiveness of policies that are currently implemented.

28.2.3 Demand and supply chain

Amongst potential explanations of a relatively limited effect of malaria control, a number of different demand and supply side factors can influence malaria prevention and treatment. On the demand side, financial constraints are the main reasons given by households for not acquiring health products (Guyatt et al. 2002; Bates et al. 2004; Wiseman et al. 2007; Eisele et al. 2009; Afolabi et al. 2009; Krezanoski et al. 2010). Indeed, demand for these products appears quite price elastic. In Kenya, Cohen and Dupas (2010) found that pregnant women universally take up an antimalarial bed net when it is given for free during a prenatal visit, but only 40% buy one at the still highly subsidized price of US$0.60. Understanding this peculiar behavior and its consequences for malaria control requires building an economic-epidemiological model (see Section 4). In addition, bed net coverage remains inequitable among different socioeconomic groups: higher income household are much more likely to possess a bed net (Matovu et al. 2009; Ye et al. 2012; Garcia-Basteiro et al. 2011). However Onwujekwe et al (2004) showed that demand for bed nets increases with income but less than proportionally. Lastly, Tarozzi et al. (2014) highlighted the role of liquidity constraints in explaining low adoption rates (although this study has been undertaken in India).

On the supply side, health centers, dispensaries, and hospitals deliver different types of medical activities: curative and preventive healthcare services, in addition to daily health education, which are characterized by different production processes. The literature on the efficiency of health care systems in developing countries generally focuses on hospital-level data or other aggregated data (health center, health district, regional or national levels). Patient-level data or household data are generally less used for this specific purpose. Nevertheless, the choices people make vary considerably across Africa, depending on the type of delivery strategies that operate in that area. For instance, lack of availability and failure in ITN distribution systems have been identified by Roll Back Malaria as the main limitations (other than cost) of large-scale implementation of ITN use. Cumulative attrition across the different steps of distribution programs, or small failures in the distribution process, result in people dropping out of the system (Marchant et al. 2010). In a literature review of 127 reports and studies, Kilian et al. (2010) found that community-based distribution campaigns achieve rapid increases in bed net coverage, but this coverage fluctuates after a few years. Continuous distribution mechanisms (routine services, retail outlets, assisted or unassisted commercial markets) avoid these fluctuations but are much slower in building-up high coverage levels.[8] Continuous promotion of effective maintenance and routine healthcare education is also needed and efforts to replace damaged nets must be implemented (Githinji et al. 2010). However, many of these strategies have not been assessed to date and only some of the existing cost-estimates have been derived using appropriate methods (Kolaczinski and Hanson 2006). Seban et al. (2013) use a household survey conducted in 2009 in Haut Katanga, DRC. They combine these data with estimates on malaria prevalence from the Malaria Atlas project. Results show that households behave rationally with respect to the disease. They also show that health centers are not the most effective in promoting possession of bed nets, in areas where they are most needed for malaria control. The governments of malaria-endemic countries often lack financial resources. As a consequence, health workers in the public sector are often underpaid and overworked. They lack equipment, drugs, training, and supervision. The local populations are aware of such situations when they occur, and cease relying on the public sector health facilities. Conversely, the private sector suffers from its own problems. Regulatory measures often do not exist or are not enforced. This encourages private consultations by unlicensed, costly health providers, and the anarchic prescription and sale of drugs (some of which are counterfeit products). Correcting this situation is a tremendous challenge that must be addressed if malaria control is to be successful.

28.3 ECONOMIC IMPACT OF MALARIA IN AFRICA

If it is possible to analyze the causal effect of a program, it is probably more difficult to analyze the causal effect of poor health on economic outcomes. This is also true for malaria. In

---

[8]   Other reviews can be found in Stevens (2005); Hill et al. (2006); and Lengeler et al. (2007). Other studies analyse different delivery strategies and the cost-effectiveness of ITN/LLINs (Thomson et al. 1995; Goodman et al. 1999; Chima et al. 2003; Morel et al. 2005, Worrall et al., 2005, Chuma et al., 2006). For a literature survey of studies assessing the economic burden of malaria since 1909, see Packard (2009).

economic terms, the total household cost burden of malaria is estimated to be high in Africa. Early estimates of total costs (Shepard et al. 1991) reported that the total cost of malaria for sub-Saharan Africa was 0.6% of total SSA GDP in 1987 and 1% in 1995. At the household level, Worral et al. (2005) provide an exhaustive literature survey and find mixed evidence on the effects of socioeconomic status (probably due to endogeneity bias) on malaria incidence but find strong evidence that malaria prevention and treatment is related to socioeconomic status.

28.3.1 Malaria, poverty and growth: a circular relationship?

In a neoclassical context, the impact of malaria on income per capita at the steady state will be theoretically undetermined: lower population growth rate leading to higher income per capita by reducing demographic pressure on savings (positive Malthusian effect), lower savings rate (because of a high healthcare expenditure and because the increase in the risk of dying reinforces the preference for the present) and therefore lower per capita product (negative effect), lower labor productivity (absenteeism, fatigue) entailing in a reduction in per capita output (negative effect).

Barlow (1967) examined the economic effects of malaria taking into account the multiplicity of these effects and integrating general equilibrium effects in a macroeconomic demographic model. He identified four effects of malaria eradication on per capita income: effects on population size (increase in population resulting from both declining mortality and rising fertility), effects on labor inputs (increase in labor supply and efficiency), effects on capital inputs (limited and unproductive private saving due to population growth and public investments), effects on output (exploitation of new territories). In his calibrated model, Barlow found a positive impact of malaria eradication in the short run and a negative impact in the long run in Ceylon between 1947 and 1965. Eradication led to immediate increase in labor quality and quantity (through reductions in morbidity and debility and decreased mortality). This increases income per equivalent consumer. After a while (1953–1955), the negative effects of malaria eradication became prominent (increased population, decreased savings, higher demand on the public sector). In his model, the main economic disadvantage of a malaria-eradication program is the rapid increase in the population of children. He suggested that these effects could be contained by birth control. However, Barlow's model is not without limits. Following Newman's (1970) findings, Barlow supposes that malaria eradication will raise fertility, but the demographic effects of malaria are theoretically undetermined. Malaria can have three short-term effects on fertility (Lucas 2013): (i) a negative biological effect on fecundity; (ii) economic theories predict that increased income and the decreased price of a surviving child will increase fertility (positive effect); (iii) the demographic transition theories suggest that increased survival certainty and preferences for quality over quantity will decrease fertility (negative effect). There are two long-term demographic effects of malaria eradication on fertility: (i) women born after eradication will be healthier, leading to higher fertility; (ii) if malaria has a negative effect on education, their additional education increases their opportunity cost of time, potentially lowering total fertility. For instance, Lucas (2013) found that the initial effect of malaria eradication in Sri Lanka (from 1937 to 1953) was actually an increase in fertility (because of the biological effect) but the next generation might have lower fertility and higher education. Therefore, while the initial population growth might be detrimental to GDP per capita, increased education and lower subsequent fertility can mitigate this initial negative growth effect. This seems contradictory to Barlow's findings. It is possible that Barlow's long run was insufficiently long. In Africa, however, there is no clear evidence of the relationship between fertility and malaria and the timing and relative size of population and education increase has not been documented so far. Another controversial aspect of Barlow's hypotheses is that he considers that the malaria eradication will "impose burdens on the educational sector" due to the massive enrolment of new cohorts of children as time progresses. Investments in health are not supposed to improve the quality of the workforce through children human capital accumulation in his model, while the influence of malaria on cognitive capacity of the children is now relatively well documented (see section 3.3.1).

28.3.2   Empirical studies on the macroeconomic effects of malaria

A series of papers have explored the link between economic development and malaria.[9] Contrary to other tropical diseases and since the failure of eradication efforts in the 1980s, malaria has been described as an unavoidable effect of tropical location and natural forces (i.e. heavy rains, floods).

Gallup and Sachs (2001), using a malaria exposure index defined as the fraction of population at risk of contracting *falciparum* malaria in a country, show that poverty is not a leading cause of malaria, *ceteris paribus*. In a cross-country regression framework, the authors find that countries with intensive malaria are poorer and have grown 1.3% less per person per year. These results point to malaria's causing poverty, not vice versa.

In another article, McCarthy et al. (2000), using estimates of malaria morbidity from the WHO, suggested that economic development may influence malaria control. They confirm the dominant role of climate in determining malaria intensity and the negative correlation between malaria and growth but they find that access to rural healthcare and income equality also influence malaria morbidity once one controls for climate. This finding raises the problem of the endogeneity of malaria with respect to growth and the robustness of the results in this field of research.

In contrast, in Acemoglu et al. (2003), malaria "is unlikely to be the reason why many countries in Africa and Asia are very poor today". More generally, Acemoglu and Johnson (2007) also cast doubt on the causal relationship between bad health conditions and poverty.

It is now clear that the Gallup and Sachs (2001) or McCarthy et al. (2000) studies did not prove that malaria is a *cause* of low incomes and poor economic growth. Many other changes occurred simultaneously in the economies where malaria has been eliminated. Malaria eradication can be correlated with many other factors that influence economic growth including governance and the quality of public policies that have been omitted from econometric models. Packard (2009) notes that "given the multiple difficulties associated with past efforts to demonstrate the impact of malaria on economic development and the economic

---

[9]   See for instance McDonald (1950), Barlow (1967), Newman (1968), Gomes (1993), Audibert et al. (1999), and Bowden et al. (2008).

benefits of malaria control, it is surprising that Gallup and Sachs stated their conclusions with such confidence and that their conclusions have been accepted with so little question."

However, the terrible toll on the health and well-being of people living in malaria-endemic or epidemic areas and the convergence between different studies[10] prove at least that the disease could be considered a potential legitimate contributor of poor economic performance (Arrow 2004). The macroeconomic literature is relatively poor compared to the microeconomic literature on malaria. Although macroeconomic effects are not the mere aggregate of microeconomic results, it seems legitimate that, in the absence of reliable aggregate data on malaria and of relevant macroeconomic instruments, that would help to solve the endogeneity issue, most of the recent research on this topic takes a microeconomic orientation.

28.3.3 Cost analysis of malaria in Africa: direct, indirect, and opportunity costs

28.3.3.1 The human capital approach

To disentangle the relationship between malaria and poverty we need first an accurate account of the costs of malaria. Microeconomic studies on malaria mostly use the human capital approach. This approach leads one to estimate the costs of malaria on various levels: those incurred by individuals and households, public health services and governments, and other private agents (firms, NGOs for instance). Direct or immediate costs are distinguished from indirect costs.

Direct costs on household and individual level are expenditures related to prevention and treatment. Seeking treatments at health centers, buying drugs and arranging funerals entail obvious financial costs. For the private business sector, the cost of private healthcare provided by employers may rise. For public health services, public expenditures for malaria prevention and treatment may be substantial even if they are not easily quantified. This lack of quantification can result in a reduction in the standard of care for all patients.

Indirect costs include, among others, lost time due to illness (such as time spent seeking care), long-term losses in household productivity and income, absenteeism from work or school, a decline in activity in various sectors, and excessive use of government resources on related expenditures. Studies on the indirect cost vary widely in their methods and in what they try to assess. Opportunity costs are the costs of spending time and effort to avoid or cure the disease rather than using these resources for an economically productive activity, or the cost equal to what an individual must give up in order to avoid or cure malaria.

28.3.3.2 Specific channels through education and productivity

One area where malaria may have a detrimental effect on economic growth is its impact on the health and mental development of children. For instance, Thuilliez (2010a,b) showed that the relationship between school results (measured by class repeat and completion rates) and *P. falciparum* malaria is strong at the macroeconomic and community levels. There are

---

[10] See for instance Shepard et al. (1991) and Chima et al. (2003).

a number of ways through which malaria can impact children's educational achievement, even if the precise medical mechanisms for the effects of malaria on education and learning remain unknown.[11]

First, because of depressed acquired immunity during pregnancy, malaria is a real treat for both pregnant women and the fetus. Indeed, malaria can lead to anemia, increased risk of premature delivery, low birth weight and fetal growth retardation, which may translate into cognitive, physical or development impairments. Barreca (2010) analyses the long-term economic impact of *in utero* and postnatal exposure to malaria and finds substantial effects on educational attainment in adulthood.

Second, among children under the age of five, complicated forms of malaria may develop rapidly. The effects of severe malaria, better known as cerebral malaria (CM), have been quantified by numerous studies.[12] For instance, Ngoungou et al. (2007) provide a quantification of the burden in Mali. 101 subjects (mean age was 5.6 ± 3.6 years) who had had cerebral malaria in Mali were followed from 1999 to 2001. The authors find that twenty-eight children presented persistent neurological sequelae (26.7%). Among them, eight (7.9%) children had developed these sequelae just after CM and 20 (19.8%) a few months later. These included headaches, mental retardation, speech delay, bucco-facial dyspraxia, diplegia and frontal syndrome (one case each), dystonia (two cases), epilepsy (five cases) and behavior and attention disorders (15 cases). This study shows that neurological signs due to cerebral malaria can persist in the long run (or at least a few months after). Many other studies have analyzed the relationship between severe *falciparum* malaria and developmental and long-term cognitive impairment (Carter and Mendis 2002; Boivin et al. 2007; John et al. 2008).

Third, even during late childhood (which usually extends from 6 to 16 years of age), the protection conferred by acquired immunity is only partial. If cerebral malaria is rare at this stage, uncomplicated malaria, repeated illness, or chronic malaria infections are not. They can have a non-cognitive impact on educational achievement through school absenteeism, general health conditions, and investment in curative strategies (coping strategies against the disease detrimental to educational investments). For instance in a Kenyan case study, Brooker et al. (2000) attributed 13–50% of medically related school absences to malaria. In Kenya, primary school students were determined to miss 11% of the school year (20 school days missed per child-year). In Nigeria, school days missed varied between 2% to 6% of the school year (3–12 days per year per student). In Mali, malaria was the primary cause of absenteeism during a full school year (Thuilliez et al. 2010). Moreover, although the age distribution of uncomplicated malaria and asymptomatic malaria depends on transmission intensity, the total burden of disease may be similar or even higher in settings of low transmission due to patterns of acquired immunity. Malaria morbidity among school-age children increases as transmission intensity decreases, but asymptomatic infections are more frequent in high transmission settings (Clarke et al. 2004; Dicko et al 2007). Fernando et al. (2003) showed a significant negative correlation between the total number of malarial attacks experienced by children and test scores during a six-year follow-up. Fernando et al. (2006) and Jukes et al. (2006) also showed a substantial effect of preventive treatment in two

---

[11] Thuilliez et al. (2010) provides a detailed discussion on potential mechanisms involved in this relationship.

[12] A literature review (from 1960 to 2002) can be found in Mung'Ala-Odera et al. (2004).

randomized studies. Yet, asymptomatic malaria has proven to have detrimental effects on children's cognitive and educational skills in three studies, one being a cluster randomized control trial which suggests either a direct causal effect of the disease or an antimalarial treatment effect (Clarke et al. 2008; Thuilliez et al. 2010; Nankabirwa et al. 2013), although confirmatory studies are needed. The mechanism could include a "toxicity effect, leading to biochemical changes in the central nervous system (CNS); excitation of the immune system, leading to changes in behaviours related to appetite and reaction time; and physiological effects such as discomfort and disturbed sleep, leading to reductions in activity levels or causing behavioural change" (Holding and Snow 2001).

Another area where malaria may have a detrimental effect on economic growth is its impact on productivity. The effect of malaria on farmers' productivity and efficiency has been the subject of careful research (Conly 1975; Audibert et al. 1990, 1999, 2003, 2009; Leighton and Foster 1993). The results from Audibert et al. (2009) suggest that the effect depends on the type of agricultural activity. Indeed malaria has no effect on coffee and cocoa productions but reduces technical efficiency in the cultivation of cotton. One difficulty tackled in later articles on efficiency relates to coping or anticipatory coping strategies adopted by the families (particularly wealthy families) that bias the estimated effects of the disease on production and productivity. The size and direction of this bias depends on the conditions of the labor market and on epidemiologic conditions. Other difficulties come from measurement errors related to health variables, omitted variables or reverse causality leading to endogeneity problems (Strauss 1986). This difficulty suggests the necessity to measure malaria on a very thin scale as the morbidity effects on productivity are often measured imperfectly. Notably asymptomatic malaria in intense transmission area probably has little effects on agricultural productivity as individuals are not strongly invalidated physically.

28.3.3.3 *Natural and quasi-experiments*

Natural experiments do not analyze the direct effect of the disease but provide estimates of the effects of interventions in real world context, in complement to randomized trials used for evaluation in experimental context (already mentioned in Section 2). In a recent paper with a historical perspective, Bleakley (2010) considers the malaria-eradication campaigns in the United States (1920), Brazil, Colombia, and Mexico (1950) to assess the impact of childhood exposure to malaria on labor productivity. Using a cohort-level dataset based on microeconomic data, Bleakley found that cohorts born after eradication enjoyed higher levels of income and literacy as adult than the preceding generation. In India, Cutler et al. (2010), using a similar quasi-experimental framework, find modest increases in income levels for men but not for women and no evidence of increased educational attainment for men but mixed evidence for women. Lastly, one limitation of these studies is that they use data from the "malaria periphery", defined by Lucas (2010, 2013) as areas in which malaria transmission was primarily seasonal or epidemic before eradication. These countries have particular epidemiological settings and were classified as *P. vivax*-dominant areas before eradication campaigns. Thus, they are generally unaffected by the most severe *P. falciparum* malaria, and the external validity is limited to these areas. In Africa, Kuecken et al. (2013) examined the medium-term effects of the Global Fund's malaria control programs on the educational attainment of primary schoolchildren in Sub-Saharan Africa using a quasi-experimental approach. In 14 countries, they found that the program led to substantial increases in years of schooling and grade level as well as reductions in schooling delay.

Mosquito vectors have often been seen as promise to solve malaria endogeneity problem in economic studies. For instance, this line of arguments has first been used for cross-country analysis by Sachs (2003) or recently by Bleakley (2010). The latter uses a malaria ecology index as an instrumental variable for malaria prevalence at a county level. Biological properties of regionally dominant malaria vectors (longevity and human-biting habit) and thus the force of infection, is said to be exogenous to public interventions and economic conditions (Kiszewski et al. 2004). Even if many authors doubted the exogeneity of malaria ecology at the macroeconomic level (Rodrik et al. 2004; Acemoglu 2003), Bhattacharyya (2009) or Carstensen and Gundlach (2006) claimed that these doubts may not be justified because the region-specific dominant malaria vector reflects only the forces of biological evolution.

28.4 Malaria Economic Epidemiology

28.4.1 Fees and behavioral factors

Bates et al. (2012) provide a literature review of randomized experiments on price elasticity of health products, including malaria specific measures. The results show that charging small fees in an attempt to balance access and "sustainability" may not be a good solution, as relative to free distribution, charging even very small user fees substantially reduces adoption and fees do not substantially promote use i.e. charging doesn't encourage use. Behavioral obstacles to efficient control and/or eradication of malaria also appear to have been underestimated. Insecticide-treated bed nets have reduced malaria transmission and child morbidity in short-term trials. However, as shown by various papers (Rhee et al. 2005; Toé et al. 2009), even in experimental contexts in small communities where education on malaria and use of nets was given before net distribution, the proportion of households that used the nets remained low. Use also tended to decrease a few months after the program. Studies in Burkina Faso (Toé et al. 2009) and Madagascar (Krezanoski et al. 2010) revealed that there was a high rate of ITN use for the first few months but that the rate of use subsequently fell for apparently non-objective reasons. This could be due to motivation (Toé et al. 2009), seasonal factors because people stopped using nets when mosquitoes were less noticeable (Baume and Marin 2007), individual perception and room organization (Toé et al. 2009). Toé et al. (2009) also stressed that there had been very few evaluations of the short and long-term impact of motivation campaigns. Their study showed that "LLINs were not used when the perceived benefits of reduction in mosquito nuisance and of malaria were considered not to be worth the inconvenience of daily use." Marchant et al. (2010) also suggested that there might be additional barriers to using an insecticide-treated net, especially among the poor. "Providing incentives for behaviour change is a promising tool that can complement traditional ITN distribution programmes and improve the effectiveness of ITN programmes in protecting vulnerable populations" (Krezanoski et al. 2010).

Berthélemy et al. (2013) provide a theoretical argument to explain such results by economically rational behaviors. When integrated into a dynamical framework this analysis allows for an explanation of the probable endogenous relationship between malaria and poverty, leading to a malaria-related poverty trap, and an integration of possible externalities.

28.4.2 Is there a malaria-related poverty trap?

This section proposes a model for malaria economic analysis by combining economic epidemiology tools with the literature on poverty traps (the full model being provided in Berthélemy et al. 2013). A theoretical model of rational protective behavior in response to malaria is designed, which includes endogenous externalities and disease characteristics.

A standard epidemiological model of malaria was built, with transmission of malaria between a population of humans and a population of mosquitoes (Smith and McKenzie 2004). Simplifying assumptions have been assumed: constant population sizes (human and mosquito) over time, uniform contacts between human and mosquitoes, ignorance of superinfection and immunity. Within the life-time period of humans, malaria prevalence among humans and mosquitoes reaches a steady state. This leads, in absence of protection, to equations based on the McDonald and Ross malaria transmission model (Smith and McKenzie 2004).

The time variation of malaria prevalence among humans can be defined in a simplified way as:

$$\dot{X} = mabZ(1-X) - rX \tag{1}$$

where m is the vector density (ratio of mosquitoes per human), a is the number of bits per unit of time and per mosquito, b is the proportion of infected bites that produce infection among humans, Z is the proportion of infectious mosquitoes, and r is the clearance rate of malaria in humans.

Similarly, the variation of the proportion of infectious mosquitoes, can be written as:

$$\dot{Z} = acX(e^{-gn} - Z) - gZ \tag{2}$$

where c is the proportion of bites on infectious humans that produce infection among mosquitoes, g is the death rate of mosquitoes, and n is the length of sporogonic cycle.

Assuming that the time period of life is long enough, malaria prevalence reaches a steady state equilibrium defined by a function $Q(X, m)$, which depends on all parameters defined in equations (1) and (2) (see Berthélemy et al. 2013).

This function is concave, and characterized by the following properties:

$$\begin{cases} Q(0,m) = 0 \\ Q(1,m) < 1 \end{cases}$$

And its slope at origin, is equal to a number, R_0, that is classically called in the MacDonald (1950, 1957) and Ross tradition the 'basic reproduction rate'. If R_0 is below or equal to 1, then $Q(X,m)$ converges towards the trivial disease free stable steady state. This case is not considered in what follows, as it does not coincide with the persistence of malaria in large regions of the developing world. Conversely, if R_0 is higher than 1, then $Q(X,m)$ converges towards a stable steady state characterized by a strictly positive prevalence of malaria.

28.4.3 Economic epidemiological model with protection

When the basic reproduction number R_0 is higher than 1, using protection tools could nevertheless reduce malaria transmission, and then, the trivial disease free stable steady state could be reached. This is the rationale of ITN/LLINs dissemination policies. In order to assess this possibility, a model of protection behavior has been added to the previous epidemiological model. This behavioral model, as described below, is based on economic mechanisms. Peoples adopt a certain behavior: use of an insecticide-treated net ($h = 1$) or exposure to malaria risk ($h = 0$). It is supposed that the only means by which a person can prevent himself from parasitic infection is to sleep under an ITN/LLIN (even if a person can be infected during the first part of the night). As a first assumption, the use of an ITN/LLIN was supposed to provide complete protection from malaria infection. This assumption can be relaxed without affecting the main findings of the model (Berthélemy et al. 2013). At any time, depending on the use of ITN before, the health status of the individual, $\sigma(h)$ can take one of two values: susceptible, $\sigma(h) = S$, or infected, $\sigma(h) = I$. The probability of being infected at any time, conditionally to the absence of protection before, can then be written as:

$$\pi_I = P(\sigma(h) = I | h = 0) \tag{3}$$

and this probability π_I is equal to the value of the $Q(X,m)$ function defined in the epidemiological model in absence of protection.

If H is the proportion of population using ITN/LLIN, among the $(1–X)$ uninfected persons, the proportion of infected persons can be simply written as:

$$X = (1 - H)\pi_I \tag{4}$$

Furthermore the density of mosquitoes in contact to humans, m, is affected by the presence of ITN/LLIN used by a proportion H of the population. First, as the contact between mosquito and human is more difficult, the denominator of the mosquito density decreases, being now the proportion $1–H$ of non-protected population. Second, as ITN/LLINs do not only protect humans, from anopheles bites, but also kill mosquitoes (knock down effect), the numerator (the number of mosquitoes) decreases with H. Hence m, which was a parameter in the pure epidemiological model, can be now written as a function of H as follows:

$$m(H) = \frac{m(0)}{1 - H}(1 - \gamma(H)) \tag{5}$$

Where $\gamma(H)$ is the proportion of mosquitoes killed by the use of ITN/LLINs, an increasing function of H.

It follows that, at the steady state:

$$\pi_I = Q(X, m(H)) \tag{6}$$

In order to complete the model, the determinants of H were specified in a next step. At the microeconomic level, the choice of protection is determined by maximizing the expected utility of each individual. The decision h of protection ($h=1$ for protection, $h=0$ for non-protection) affects individuals' utility through two channels: (i) an expected positive impact on his/her health status in case of protection and (ii) a private cost, called κ. Hence protection decision is described through the following maximization program:

$$\max_h E[\mu(\sigma(h))] - \kappa W(\omega)h \tag{7}$$

Where $\mu(S)$ or $\mu(I)$ are the utility levels attached to the health status (susceptible, $\sigma(h) = S$, or infected, $\sigma(h) = I$, thus depending on h, the use of a protection), with $0 < \mu(I) < \mu(S)$; ω is the individual income; $W(\omega)$ is the marginal utility of the income ω, supposed as usual to decrease with income.

The expected utility (the expected positive impact of using ITN/LLIN on the health status) can be estimated using the following probabilities of being susceptible or infected, conditionally to the use of protection:

$$\begin{cases} P(\sigma(h) = S | h = 1) = 1 \\ P(\sigma(h) = S | h = 0) = 1 - \pi_I \\ P(\sigma(h) = I | h = 0) = \pi_I \end{cases} \tag{8}$$

In addition, it is assumed that there exists a minimum subsistence level such as in the case a Stone-Geary utility function. This implies that the marginal utility of income $W\omega)$ goes to infinity for all individuals at (or below) the minimum subsistence level, which is classically called the extreme poverty line Ω (*i.e.* the minimum level of income deemed adequate in a given country for an individual or a household). In other words, the extreme poverty line is an income level below which nobody can afford an ITN/LLIN, *i.e.* $h = 0$.

As in standard economic epidemiological models, the individual will use protective tools when $W(\omega)$ is lower than the expected utility loss associated with the risk of infection that occurs in the absence of protection:

$$E[\mu(\sigma(1)) - \mu(\sigma(0))] \geq \kappa W(\omega) \tag{9}$$

According to equation (9) and the three probabilities of equation (10) it follows that:

$$h = 1 \quad \text{if and only if} \quad \mu(S) - (1 - \pi_I)\mu(S) - \pi_I\mu(I) \geq \kappa W(\omega) \tag{10}$$

A person will use ITN/LLIN if the utility of being non-infected is greater than the utility of paying for a protective tool, according to the income and the probability of being infected without using any protection. Hence, protection occurs if and only if:

$$\pi_I \geq \frac{\kappa W(\omega)}{\mu(S) - \mu(I)} \tag{11}$$

This equation shows that there is a threshold probability of infection above which a person engages in protection. The key point in this approach is that the threshold probability of infection depends on the marginal income utility loss associated with using the ITN/ LLIN, $\kappa W(\omega)$, with respect to the net value attached to susceptible health status, $\mu(S) - \mu(I)$. This threshold depends on the individual income ω. The threshold function, linking π_1 to ω, termed $C(\omega)$, is monotonic and $C(\omega) < 0$, as the function $W(O)$ is monotonic and $W'(\omega) < 0$. In addition, the function $C(O)$ is increasing with κ. Consequently:

$$\begin{cases} h = 1 \; if \; \omega \geq C^{-1}(\pi_I) \\ h = 0 \; else \end{cases} \tag{12}$$

and the income threshold conditioning protection, $C^{-1}(\pi_I)$, decreases with κ. Knowing individual protection behaviors, the aggregated level of protection H (the percentage of protected persons) can be computed by integration as follows:

$$H = \int_{C^{-1}(\pi_I)}^{+\infty} f(\omega)d\omega = 1 - F(C^{-1}(\pi_I)) \tag{13}$$

Where f is the probability density function of ω (and F the associated cumulative density function), describing the income distribution of the population. Equations (6), (8) and (13) fully describes the dynamics of H and π_1 as a function of X.

28.4.4 Prevalence-elastic behavior at the steady-state vicinity

Nearby the steady state, the dynamics corresponds to a standard prevalence-elastic behavior of protection (positive malaria prevalence elasticity), where H is an increasing function of X, because it is increasing with π_I (equations (8) and (13)). Note that as a consequence, nearby the steady state, X is not necessarily monotonic in π_I: protection behaviors and epidemiological dynamics go in opposite directions. This is consistent with standard results in economic epidemiology.

More precisely, combining equations (6) and (13) it follows that:

$$X = F(C^{-1}(\pi_I))\pi_I \tag{14}$$

This equation provides us with some economic determinants of protection at individual and aggregated levels that could be possibly tested (see Berthélemy et al. 2013, for tests on Ugandan data). For a given probability of infection in absence of protection, protection decreases with the unit costs of ITN/LLIN, κ (through the function C^{-1}). It also decreases with poverty, as the poorer the individuals, the higher their marginal utility of income.

28.4.5 Long-term properties: conditions of persistence of a malaria trap

The main question to be solved, concerning the long-term properties of this model at the steady-state, is whether malaria can persist in the long run, in spite of the availability of

ITN/LLINs as protection tools since the higher the unit cost κ of ITN/LLINs, the lower the protection. This is why ITN/LLINs programs are usually based on subsidized ITN/LLINs prices. Let us then consider the best case of almost full subsidization, when $\kappa \to o$ (*i.e.* the extreme case being free distribution). Conditions under which, for any positive unit cost κ, the malaria trap persists are given below.

Proposition: For any $\kappa > o$, when $\kappa \to o$ the long-term equilibrium corresponds to a persistence of malaria, if and only if

$$R_0 > \frac{1}{F(\Omega)(1 - m(F(\Omega)))} \tag{15}$$

where $F(\Omega)$ is the proportion of persons under the extreme poverty line in a population, also called the extreme poverty incidence. Note that m depends on H, the proportion of protected persons (equation (7)), which depends itself on income (equation (15)), and, thus, on the extreme poverty incidence.

Given $\kappa \to o$ and $H \to 1 - F(\Omega)$, as the vector density m is a decreasing function of H, the higher the incidence of extreme poverty $F(\Omega)$, the higher the risk of persistence of malaria. Hence, malaria will persist for high enough values of the basic reproduction number R_0 and of the extreme poverty incidence $F(\Omega)$, even when ITN/LLINs are highly subsidized. In the extreme case where all the population is at or below the extreme poverty line, the condition above corresponds exactly to the basic reproduction number, and hence this policy is certainly ineffective as long as $R_0 > 1$.

One could argue that if ITN/LLINs were provided at no cost to individuals ($\kappa=o$), then all individuals, including the extreme poor, would use them. Distribution of ITN/LLINs for free would then possibly be a much more efficient policy to reduce malaria, compared to selling ITN/LLINs at a subsidized price. This is in line with randomized experiments that found that free distribution dramatically increases use of ITN/LLINs (as well as other important products for the poor), compared to charging even very small user fees (Bates et al. 2012).

However, the assumption $\kappa = o$ is merely theoretical, even though it can be possibly obtained in controlled experiments, as in practice κ is not only the price of ITN/LLINs: it involves also all opportunity costs attached to using them for other productive activities. Selling, exchanging, discarding, or re-using the material from ITN/LLINs is not uncommon. For instance, misuse of ITN/LLINs for profit (drying fish and fishing) has been observed by Lake Victoria (Minakawa et al. 2008) and in Zambia (Hopkin 2008). In some cases, nets have even been turned into wedding dresses and water filters.

Two important conclusions emerge from the model. First, agents increase their protective behavior when malaria is more prevalent in a society. This is consistent with the literature on "prevalence-elastic behavior". Second, a malaria-related poverty trap defined as the result of malaria reinforcing poverty while poverty reduces the ability to deal with malaria can theoretically exist and the conditions of existence of this trap are identified. Typically it can be observed when the incidence of extreme poverty is initially very high.

Survey data available for Uganda provides empirical support to the theory of prevalence-elastic protection behaviors, once endogeneity issues related to epidemiology and poverty are solved (Berthélemy et al. 2013), and to the possibility of a malaria-related poverty trap.

28.5 Conclusion

Malaria is a major disease in sub-Saharan Africa, which imposes a heavy human and economic toll on this region. Some of the first analyses on the cost of malaria, which attributed to this disease a very large economic cost, went probably too far in attributing to malaria a significant part of the African economic difficulties. Careful considerations on the bi-directional causality between malaria and poverty or aggregate underdevelopment suggest that the cost of malaria have been initially overestimated.

Nevertheless, such cost cannot be neglected, and policies to control malaria have received more and more attention in the past decade from the development aid community, notably through initiatives funded by the Global Fund to Fight AIDS, Tuberculosis and Malaria (GFATM).

These policies, combining subsidization of new ACT treatments and the dissemination of protection/eradication tools such as ITN/LLINs and IRS, have been coincidental with a recent trend of reduction of malaria mortality in Africa. These policies are however to without difficulties and attributing the small successes observed recently to such policies, or identifying the right mix of policy instruments, are extremely difficult.

As for ACTs, the risk of fast-developing drug-resistance cannot be averted. From a policy point of view, Laxminarayan et al. (2010) have shown in this context the limits of policy of subsidization of ACTs.

As for ITN/LLINs and IRS dissemination, there are also risks of development of resistance to insecticides. Nevertheless, ITN/LLINs are still considered as technically efficient protection tools. In spite of this, the dissemination of ITN/LLINs is very far from satisfactory across the African continent. Beyond possible shortcomings in the supply chain, we point here to another possible difficulty, on the demand side. We have developed an epidemiologic-economic model in which the demand for ITN/LLINs is prevalent-elastic, which in turn leads to situations where the objective of malaria eradication may be out of reach. In particular, we show that in a context of a large extreme poverty incidence, the demand for ITN/LLINS may be too low to allow for complete malaria eradication. In addition, Berthélemy et al. (2015) have also shown that a relatively low price of treatment reduces prevention.

Given these difficulties, the optimal strategy is probably a combination of the different tools. However, more analytical work, combining epidemiological and economic models, and more large-scale impact evaluations of the policies that have been actually implemented, are needed to make progresses in the identification of the right strategy. Given the heavy toll of malaria in Africa, this agenda of research should be given a high priority by economists and epidemiologists.

References

Acemoglu, D., and Johnson, S. (2007). Disease and development: the effect of life expectancy on economic growth. *Journal of Political Economy*, 115:925–985.

Acemoglu, D., Johnson, S., and Robinson, J. (2003). Disease and development in historical perspective. *Journal of the European Economic Association*, 1:397–405.

Acemoglu, D., Johnson, S., Robinson, J., and Thaicharoen, Y. (2003). Institutional causes, macro-economic symptoms: volatility, crises and growth. *Journal of Monetary Economics*, 50:49–123.

Afolabi, B.M. et al. (2009). Household possession, use and non-use of treated or untreated mosquito nets in two ecologically diverse regions of Nigeria-Niger Delta and Sahel Savannah. *Malaria Journal*, 8:30.

Alilio, M.S., Bygbjerg, I.C., and Breman, J.G. (2004). Are Multilateral Malaria Research and Control Programs the Most Successful? Lessons from the Past 100 Years in Africa. *American Journal of Tropical Medicine and Hygiene*, 71(Suppl 2):268–278.

Arrow, K.J., Panosian, C., and Gelband, H. (2004). *Saving lives, buying time: Economics of malaria drugs in an age of resistance*. Washington, DC: National Academy Press.

Audibert, M., Josseran, R., Josse, R., and Adjidji, A. (1990). Irrigation, schistosomiasis, and malaria in the Logone Valley, Cameroon. *American Journal of Tropical Medicine and Hygiene* 42:550–560.

Audibert, M., Mathonnat, J., and Henry, M.C. (2003). Malaria and property accumulation in rice production systems in the savannah zone of Cote d'Ivoire. *Tropical Medicine and International Health*, 8:471–483.

Audibert, M., Mathonnat, J., and Henry, M.C. (2003). Malaria and property accumulation in rice production systems in the savannah zone of Cote d'Ivoire. *Tropical Medicine and International Health* 8:471–483.

Audibert, M., Brun, J.-F., and Mathonnat, J. (2009). Effets économiques du paludisme sur les cultures de rente: l'exemple du café et du cacao en Côte d'Ivoire. *Revue d'économie du développement*, 23:145–166.

Audibert, M., Mathonnat, J., Nzeyimana, I., and Henry, M.C. (1999). Rôle du paludisme dans l'efficience technique des producteurs de coton dans le nord de la Côte d'Ivoire. *Revue d'Economie du Développement, volume spécial Santé et Développement*, 4:121–148.

Audibert, M., Mathonnat, J., and Henry, M.-C. (2003). Social and health determinants of the efficiency of cotton farmers in northern Cote d'Ivoire. *Social Science and Medicine*, 56:1705–1717.

Barlow, R. (1967). The economic effects of malaria eradication. *American Economic Review*, 57:130–148.

Barreca, A.I. (2010). The long-term economic impact of in utero and postnatal exposure to malaria. *Journal of Human Resources*, 45:865–892.

Bates, I. et al. (2004). Vulnerability to malaria, tuberculosis, and HIV/AIDS infection and disease. Part 1: determinants operating at individual and household level. *Lancet Infectious Diseases*, 4:267–277.

Bates, M.A., Glennerster, R., Gumede, K., and Duflo, E. (2012). The Price is Wrong. *Field Actions Science Reports. Special Issue* 4: *Fighting Poverty, Between Market and Gift*. http://factsreports.revues.org/1554.

Baume, C.A., and Marin, M.C. (2007). Intra-household mosquito net use in Ethiopia, Ghana, Mali, Nigeria, Senegal, and Zambia: are nets being used? Who in the household uses them? *American Journal of Tropical Medicine and Hygiene*, 77:963–971.

Berthélemy, J.-C., Thuilliez, J., Doumbo, O., and Gaudart, J. (2013). Malaria and protective behaviours: is there a malaria trap? *Malaria Journal*, 12:200.

Berthélemy, Jean-Claude, Jean Gaudart, and Josselin Thuilliez. (2015). "Prevention or Treatment? The Case of Malaria." *Economics Letters* 131 (June): 16–19.

Bhattacharyya, S. (2009). Root causes of African underdevelopment. *Journal of African Economies*, 18:745–780.

Bleakley, H. (2010). Malaria Eradication in the Americas: A Retrospective Analysis of Childhood Exposure. *American Economic Journal: Applied Economics*, 1–45.

Bleakley, H. (2003). Disease and development: Evidence from the American South. *Journal of the European Economic Association*, 1:376–386.

Boivin, M.J. et al. (2007). Cognitive impairment after cerebral malaria in children: a prospective study. *Pediatrics*, 119:e360–e366.

Bowden, S., Michailidou, D.M., and Pereira, A. (2008). Chasing mosquitoes: An exploration of the relationship between economic growth, poverty and the elimination of malaria in Southern Europe in the 20th century. *Journal of International Development*, 20:1080–1106.

Hopkin, P.A. (2008). Malaria: the big push. *Nature*, 451:1047–1049.

Brooker, S. et al. (2000). Situation analysis of malaria in school-aged children in Kenya–what can be done? *Parasitology Today*, 16:183–186.

Carstensen, K., and Gundlach, E. (2006). The primacy of institutions reconsidered: Direct income effects of malaria prevalence. *World Bank Economic Review*, 20:309–339.

Carter, R., and Mendis, K.N. (2002). Evolutionary and historical aspects of the burden of malaria. *Clinical Microbiology Reviews*, 15:564–594.

Chima, R.I., Goodman, C.A., and Mills, A. (2003). The economic impact of malaria in Africa: a critical review of the evidence. *Health Policy*, 63:17–36.

Chuma, J.M., Thiede, M., and Molyneux, C.S. (2006). Rethinking the economic costs of malaria at the household level: evidence from applying a new analytical framework in rural Kenya. *Malaria Journal*, 5:76.

Clarke, S.E., Brooker, S., Njagi, J.K., Njau, E., Estambale, B., Muchiri, E., and Magnussen, P. (2004). Malaria Morbidity Among School Children Living in Two Areas of Contrasting Transmission in Western Kenya. *American Journal of Tropical Medicine and Hygiene*, 71(6):732–738.

Clarke, S.E. et al. (2008). Effect of intermittent preventive treatment of malaria on health and education in schoolchildren: a cluster-randomised, double-blind, placebo-controlled trial. *Lancet*, 372:127–138.

Cohen, J., and Dupas, P. (2010). Free Distribution or Cost-Sharing? Evidence from a Randomized Malaria Prevention Experiment. *Quarterly Journal of Economics*, 125(1):1–45.

Cohen, J., Dupas, P., and Schaner, S. (2011). Price Subsidies, Diagnostic Tests, and Targeting of Malaria Treatment: Evidence from a Randomized Controlled Trial. Working Paper: Abdul Latif Jameel Poverty Action Lab. Available at povertyactionlab.org.

Conly, G.N. (1975). The impact of malaria on economic development: A case study. *OPS Publicación Científica*. <http://bases.bireme.br/cgi-bin/wxislind.exe/iah/online/?IsisScript= iah/iah.xisandsrc=googleandbase=REPIDISCAandlang=pandnextAction=lnkandexpr Search=183732andindexSearch=ID>.

Cutler, D., Fung, W., Kremer, M. et al. (2010). Early-life malaria exposure and adult outcomes: Evidence from malaria eradication in India. *American Economic Journal: Applied Economics*, 72–94.

Dicko, A. et al. (2007). Year-to-year variation in the age-specific incidence of clinical malaria in two potential vaccine testing sites in Mali with different levels of malaria transmission intensity. *American Journal of Tropical Medicine and Hygiene*, 77:1028–1033.

Eisele, T.P., Keating, J., Littrell, M. et al. (2009). Assessment of insecticide-treated bednet use among children and pregnant women across 15 countries using standardized national surveys. *American Journal of Tropical Medicine and Hygiene*, 80:209–214.

Fan, V.Y., Duran, D., Silverman, R., and Glassman, A. (2013). Performance-based financing at the Global Fund to Fight AIDS, Tuberculosis and Malaria: an analysis of grant ratings and funding, 2003–12. *Lancet Global Health*, 1:e161–e168.

Fernando, D., De Silva, D., Carter, R. et al. (2006). A randomized, double-blind, placebo-controlled, clinical trial of the impact of malaria prevention on the educational attainment of school children. *American Journal of Tropical Medicine and Hygiene*, 74:386–393.

Fernando, S.D. et al. (2003). The impact of repeated malaria attacks on the school performance of children. *American Journal of Tropical Medicine and Hygiene* 69:582–588.

Flaxman, A.D. et al. (2010). Rapid scaling up of insecticide-treated bed net coverage in Africa and its relationship with development assistance for health: a systematic synthesis of supply, distribution, and household survey data. *PLoS Medicine*, 7:e1000328.

Flegg, J.A., Metcalf, C.J., Gharbi, M., Venkatesan, M., Shewchuk, T., Hopkins Sibley, C., and Guerin, P.J. (2013). Trends in Antimalarial Drug Use in Africa. *American Journal of Tropical Medicine and Hygiene*, 89:857–865. Published online September 9, 2013. doi:10.4269/ajtmh.13-0129.

Gallup, J.L., and J.D. Sachs. (2001). The Economic Burden of Malaria. *The American Journal of Tropical Medicine and Hygiene*, 64(1)suppl:85–96.

García-Basteiro, A.L. et al. (2011). Determinants of bed net use in children under five and household bed net ownership on Bioko Island, Equatorial Guinea. *Malaria Journal*, 10:179.

Gething, P.W. et al. (2011). A new world malaria map: Plasmodium falciparum endemicity in 2010. *Malaria Journal*, 10:1475–2875.

Gharbi, M. et al. (2013). Longitudinal study assessing the return of chloroquine susceptibility of Plasmodium falciparum in isolates from travellers returning from West and Central Africa, 2000–2011. *Malaria Journal*, 12:35.

Githinji, S., Herbst, S., Kistemann, T., and Noor, A.M. (2010). Mosquito nets in a rural area of Western Kenya: ownership, use and quality. *Malaria Journal*, 9:250.

Glassman, A., Fan, V., Over, M., Silverman, R., McQueston, K., and Duran, D. (2013). More health for the money. Putting incentives to work for the Global Fund and its partners. http://www.popline.org/node/579250#sthash.SZhaxGWf.dpuf.

Gomes, M. (1993). Economic and demographic research on malaria: a review of the evidence. *Social Science and Medicine*, 37:1093–1108.

Goodman, C.A., Coleman, P.G., and Mills, A.J. (1999) Cost-effectiveness of malaria control in sub-Saharan Africa. *Lancet*, 354:378–385.

Guerra, C.A. et al. (2010). The international limits and population at risk of Plasmodium vivax transmission in 2009. *PLoS Neglected Tropical Diseases* 4:e774.

Guyatt, H.L., Corlett, S.K., Robinson, T.P. et al. (2002). Malaria prevention in highland Kenya: indoor residual house-spraying vs. insecticide-treated bednets. *Tropical Medicine and International Health*, 7:298–303.

Hill, J., Lines, J., and Rowland, M. (2006). Insecticide-treated nets. *Advances in parasitology* 61, 77–128.

Holding, P.A., and Snow R.W. (2001). Impact of Plasmodium Falciparum Malaria on Performance and Learning: Review of the Evidence. In J.G. Breman, A. Egan, G.T. Keusch (eds), *The Intolerable Burden Of Malaria: A New Look At The Numbers: Supplement To Volume 64(1) Of The American Journal Of Tropical Medicine And Hygiene*. Northbrook, IL: American Society of Tropical Medicine and Hygiene. http://www.ncbi.nlm.nih.gov/books/NBK2614/.

John, C.C. et al. (2008). Cerebral malaria in children is associated with long-term cognitive impairment. *Pediatrics*, 122:e92–e99.

Jukes, M.C., Pinder, M., Grigorenko, E.L, Baños Smith, H., Walraven, G. Meier Bariau, E. Sternberg, R.J., Drake, L.J., Milligan, P., Bun Cheung, Y., Greenwood, B.M., and Bundy

D.A.P. (2006). Long-term Impact of Malaria Chemoprophylaxis on Cognitive Abilities and Educational Attainment: Follow-up of a Controlled Trial. *PLOS Hub for Clinical Trials*, 1(4):e19.

Kilian, A., Wijayanandana, N., and Ssekitoleeko, J. (2010). Review of delivery strategies for insecticide treated mosquito nets: are we ready for the next phase of malaria control efforts? TropIKA.*net* 1, 28pp.

Kiszewski, A. et al. (2004). A global index representing the stability of malaria transmission. *American Journal of Tropical Medicine and Hygiene*, 70:486–498.

Klayman, D.L. (1985). Qinghaosu (artemisinin): an antimalarial drug from China. *Science*, 228:1049–1055.

Kolaczinski, J., and Hanson, K. (2006). Costing the distribution of insecticide-treated nets: a review of cost and cost-effectiveness studies to provide guidance on standardization of costing methodology. *Malaria Journal*, 5:37.

Krezanoski, P.J., Comfort, A.B., and Hamer, D.H. (2010). Effect of incentives on insecticide-treated bed net use in sub-Saharan Africa: a cluster randomized trial in Madagascar. *Malaria Journal*, 9:187.

Kuecken, M., Thuilliez, J., Valfort, M-A. (2013). Does malaria control impact education? A study of the Global Fund in Africa. Document de travail du centre d'économie de la Sorbonne no. 13075.

Laxminarayan, R., Parry, I.W., Smith, D.L., and Klein, E.Y. (2010). Should new antimalarial drugs be subsidized? *Journal of Health Economics*, 29:445–456.

Leighton, C., and Foster, R. (1993). Economic impacts of malaria in Kenya and Nigeria. Major Applied Research Paper 6. Bethesda, MA: Abt Associates inc. http://pdf.usaid.gov/pdf_docs/pnabs294.pdf.

Lengeler C. (2004). Insecticide-treated bed nets and curtains for preventing malaria. Cochrane Database of Systematic Reviews 2004, Issue 2. Art. No.: CD000363. doi:10.1002/14651858. CD000363.pub2. 2.

Lin, J.T., Juliano, J.J., and Wongsrichanalai, C. (2010). Drug-resistant malaria: the era of ACT. *Current Infectious Disease Reports*, 12:165–173.

Lucas, A.M. (2010). Malaria eradication and educational attainment: evidence from Paraguay and Sri Lanka. *American Economic Journal: Applied Economics*, 2:46–71.

Lucas, A.M. (2013). The impact of malaria eradication on fertility. *Economic Development and Cultural Change*, 61:607–631.

Mabaso, M.L.H., Sharp, B., and Lengeler, C. (2004). Historical review of malarial control in southern African with emphasis on the use of indoor residual house-spraying. *Tropical Medicine and International Health*, 9:846–856.

Macdonald, G. (1950). The Economic Importance of Malaria in Africa. Unpublished WHO Document.

Macdonald, G. (1957). *The Epidemiology and Control of Malaria*. Oxford: Oxford University Press.

Marchant, T. et al. (2010). Assessment of a national voucher scheme to deliver insecticide-treated mosquito nets to pregnant women. *Canadian Medical Association Journal*, 182:152–156.

Matovu, F., Goodman, C., Wiseman, V., and Mwengee, W. (2009). How equitable is bed net ownership and utilisation in Tanzania? A practical application of the principles of horizontal and vertical equity. *Malaria Journal*, 8:109.

McCarthy, F.D., Wolf, H.C., and Wu, Y. (2000). Malaria and growth. *World Bank Policy Research Working Paper*. http://papers.ssrn.com/sol3/papers.cfm?abstract_id=629153.

Minakawa, N., Dida, G.O., Sonye, G.O. et al. (2008). Unforeseen misuses of bed nets in fishing villages along Lake Victoria. *Malaria Journal*, 7:58.

Morel, C.M., Lauer, J.A., and Evans, D.B. (2005). Cost effectiveness analysis of strategies to combat malaria in developing countries. *British Medical Journal*, 331:1299.

Mung'ala-Odera, V., Snow, R.W., and Newton, C.R. (2004). The Burden of the Neurocognitive Impairment Associated with Plasmodium Falciparum Malaria in Sub-Saharan Africa. *American Journal of Tropical Medicine and Hygiene*, 71:64–70.

Murray, C.J. et al. (2012). Global malaria mortality between 1980 and 2010: a systematic analysis. *Lancet*, 379:413–431.

Nabarro, D.N., and Tayler, E.M. (1998). The' roll back malaria' campaign. *Science*, 280:2067–2068.

Nankabirwa, J. et al. (2013). Asymptomatic Plasmodium Infection and Cognition among Primary Schoolchildren in a High Malaria Transmission Setting in Uganda. *American Journal of Tropical Medicine and Hygiene*, 88:1102–1108.

Newman, P. (1970). Malaria control and population growth. *Journal of Development Studies*, 6:133–158.

Ngoungou, E.B. et al. (2007). Séquelles neurologiques persistantes dues au paludisme cérébral dans une ancohorte d'enfants au Mali. *Revue Neurologique*, 163:583–588.

Onwujekwe, O., Hanson, K., and Fox-Rushby, J. (2004). Inequalities in purchase of mosquito nets and willingness to pay for insecticide-treated nets in Nigeria: challenges for malaria control interventions. *Malaria Journal*, 3:6.

Packard, R.M. (2009). "Roll Back Malaria, Roll in Development"? Reassessing the Economic Burden of Malaria. *Population and Development Review*, 35:53–87.

Rhee, M. et al. (2005). Use of insecticide-treated nets (ITNs) following a malaria education intervention in Piron, Mali: a control trial with systematic allocation of households. *Malaria Journal*, 4:35.

Rodrik, D., Subramanian, A., and Trebbi, F. (2004). Institutions rule: the primacy of institutions over geography and integration in economic development. *Journal of Economic Growth*, 9:131–165.

Roll back Malaria. http://www.rollbackmalaria.org/gmap/fr/1-3.html. Accessed October 2013.

Sachs, J.D. (2003). Institutions don't rule: direct effects of geography on per capita income. National Bureau of Economic Research. http://www.nber.org/papers/w9490.

Santolamazza, F. et al. (2008). Distribution of knock-down resistance mutations in Anopheles gambiae molecular forms in west and west-central Africa. *Malaria Journal*, 7:74.

Seban, J., Thuilliez, J., and Herbreteau, V. (2013). Possession of bed nets in Haut-Katanga (DRC): Prevalence-elastic behaviour or performance of health care system delivery? *Health and Place*. http://www.sciencedirect.com/science/article/pii/S1353829213001172.

Shepard, D.S., Ettling, M.B., Brinkmann, U., and Sauerborn, R. (1991). The economic cost of malaria in Africa. *Tropical Medicine and Parasitology (GTZ)*, 42:199.

Smith, D.L., and McKenzie, F.E. (2004). Statics and dynamics of malaria infection in Anopheles mosquitoes. *Malaria Journal*, 3:13.

Stevens, W., Wiseman, V., Ortiz, J., and Chavasse, D. (2005). The costs and effects of a nation-wide insecticide-treated net programme: the case of Malawi. *Malaria Journal*, 4:22.

Strauss, J. (1986). Does Better Nutrition Raise Farm Productivity? *The Journal of Political Economy*, 297–320.

Tarozzi, A., Mahajan, A., Blackburn, B., Kopf, D., Krishnan, L., and Yoong, J. (2014). Micro-loans, bednets and malaria: Evidence from a randomized controlled trial in Orissa (India). *American Economic Review*, 104(7):1909–1941.

Thomson, M. C. et al. (1995). Entomological evaluation of the Gambia's national impregnated bednet programme. *Annals of Tropical Medicine and Parasitology*, 89:229–241.

Thuilliez, J. (2010a). Fever, malaria and primary repetition rates amongst school children in Mali: Combining demographic and health surveys (DHS) with spatial malariological measures. *Social Science and Medicine*, 71:314–323.

Thuilliez, J. (2010b). Malaria and primary education: a cross-country analysis on repetition and completion rates. *Revue d'économie du développement*, 23:127–157.

Thuilliez, J. et al. (2010). Malaria and primary education in Mali: A longitudinal study in the village of Donéguébougou. *Social Science and Medicine*, 71:324–334.

Toé, L.P. et al. (2009). Decreased motivation in the use of insecticide-treated nets in a malaria endemic area in Burkina Faso. *Malaria Journal*, 8:175.

Van Eijk, A.M. et al. (2011). Coverage of malaria protection in pregnant women in sub-Saharan Africa: a synthesis and analysis of national survey data. *Lancet Infectious Diseases*, 11:190–207.

Wiseman, V., Scott, A., McElroy, B., Conteh, L., and Stevens, W. (2007). Determinants of bed net use in the Gambia: implications for malaria control. *American Journal of Tropical Medicine and Hygiene*, 76:830–836.

World Health Organization (2012). World malaria report 2012. *World Health Organization Geneva*. Available http://www.who.int/malaria/publications/world_malaria_report_2012/en/.

Worrall, E., Basu, S., and Hanson, K. (2005). Is malaria a disease of poverty? A review of the literature. *Tropical Medicine and International Health*, 10:1047–1059.

Ye, Y., Patton, E., Kilian, A. et al. (2012). Can universal insecticide-treated net campaigns achieve equity in coverage and use? The case of northern Nigeria. *Malaria Journal*, 11:32.

CHAPTER 29

AN EMPIRICAL ANALYSIS OF THE ECONOMICS OF MARRIAGE IN EGYPT, MOROCCO, AND TUNISIA

RAGUI ASSAAD AND CAROLINE KRAFFT

29.1 INTRODUCTION

MARRIAGE is the single most important contractual arrangement youth in North Africa undertake as they navigate their transition to adulthood. Despite its importance in shaping subsequent socioeconomic trajectories, there has been limited empirical research on the economics of marriage in much of the developing world. The shortage of research is particularly acute in North Africa, where the up-front cost of marriage is also particularly high. We calculate that in Egypt, the up-front cost of marriage exceeds, on average, eight years of a groom's wages. Because of asymmetric rights within marriage in North Africa, the bride side's bargaining power is greatest up front, during detailed marriage contract negotiations. Drawing on the unifying theoretical framework of Assaad and Krafft (2015), we examine the relationships between marriage outcomes, individual and family characteristics and ability to pay in this context. Marriage outcomes are the result of a game-theoretic bargaining process within the social norms that govern marriage and the economics of the broader marriage market. This chapter presents important new empirical evidence on the determinants of marriage outcomes in North Africa and the linkages and tradeoffs between these different outcomes. We examine a number of marriage outcomes using household survey data from Egypt, Morocco, and Tunisia, including age at marriage, age difference between marriage partners, marriage costs, the bride's side share in these costs, consanguinity, and nuclear residence at marriage.

Besides providing descriptive analyses of the prevalence and patterns of these different marriage outcomes, we examine how individuals' characteristics and ability to pay shape bargaining power and, hence, marriage outcomes, and the various tradeoffs between marriage outcomes. We use multivariate regression models to estimate the relationship between different individual and parental characteristics and marriage outcomes and to test a number of hypotheses raised in the theoretical framework developed in Assaad and Krafft (2015). For instance, one explanation for consanguineous marriage was the economic rationale that these marriages are likely to require less up-front bargaining and therefore be of lower cost (Casterline and El-Zeini 2003; Singerman 2007), a contention that descriptive evidence supports. We demonstrate that, after accounting for other characteristics, consanguineous marriages do not cost less in general, but do allow for earlier marriages and are associated with a higher likelihood of extended household living arrangements upon marriage. Throughout this chapter, we illustrate the potential for empirically assessing the economics of marriage in North Africa within the theoretical framework developed in Assaad and Krafft (2015), contributing to a fuller understanding of this important economic and social transaction.

29.2 DATA

Household surveys from Egypt, Morocco, and Tunisia are used to illustrate patterns and trends in the economics of marriage in North Africa. In Egypt, we use the Egypt Labor Market Panel Survey (ELMPS), which was fielded in 1998, 2006, and 2012.[1] In Morocco, we use the 2009–2010 Morocco Household and Youth Survey (MHYS) (World Bank 2010).[2] In Tunisia, we use the National Survey on Household and Youth in Municipal Centers in Tunisia 2012 (NSHY). All of the surveys are representative of the area covered after the application of sample weights (nationally in Egypt and Morocco, urban and peri-urban areas in Tunisia). Some of the outcome variables we examine, such as the cost of marriage, the bride's side share in the cost, and consanguinity are only available from the ELMPS for Egypt.

29.3 PREVALENCE AND TIMING OF MARRIAGE

The age at which individuals marry and even whether they get married at all impacts their economic and social opportunities. There is substantial variation in both the timing and universality of marriage in Egypt, Morocco, and Tunisia, but there are also a number of similarities. In all three countries, a substantial share of women married earlier than men, often in their teens. Around a quarter of women had married by age 20 in all three countries, but very few men had married by the same age. Men do begin marrying around age 20 and thereafter. In terms of men and women marrying at relatively younger ages, Egypt and Morocco are quite similar, while individuals tend to marry later in Tunisia. At the median and thereafter, both women and men in Egypt are marrying earlier than in other countries, and almost universally. In contrast, while Tunisia is relatively near universal marriage, more than a quarter of women and almost half of men marry after age 30. In Morocco, marriage is not universal. Almost a quarter of men and women never marry. While half of women are married by 25, it

---

[1] See Assaad and Krafft (2013) for additional information on the ELMPS 2012.
[2] See http://microdata.worldbank.org/index.php/catalog/1546 for additional information.

is not until almost 40 that 75% of women are married. In Egypt, the median age of marriage for men is 27 and for women it is 21. Rural males and females marry earlier in Morocco and Egypt, with the gap widening over the distribution in Egypt. Educated individuals marry later, but the gap narrows somewhat over the distribution.

The timing and prevalence of marriage has been changing substantially over time in North Africa, as Figure 29.1 demonstrates. In Egypt, the proportion married by various ages was declining over time, but has reversed course among more recent cohorts, with the median age of marriage decreasing. In Morocco, the proportion of individuals married by different ages has been falling steadily over time, although it may have stabilized for more recent cohorts. Additionally, it is clear that the universality of marriage has been steadily decreasing over time in Morocco. Tunisia has also experienced a falling proportion of individuals married by different ages, and some decreases in the universality of marriage, although it too may be stabilizing.

Figure 29.1 also allows comparisons of various percentiles, including the median age of marriage, over time. In Egypt, the distribution rose gradually over time, with the median for women peaking at age 22 for the birth cohorts of the late 1970s and the median for men peaking at age 28 for the 1970 birth cohort. The distribution has since been shifting downward, with median age of marriage decreasing. Additionally, there appears to be some slight convergence of the 25th and 75th percentiles towards the median. In Morocco, the distribution has shifted towards older ages of marriage, and also widened in variance, with marriage becoming less universal. For both men and women, the median has leveled off and may be decreasing for the most recent cohorts. Tunisia has followed a fairly similar pattern to Morocco, with the 75th percentile for age of marriage for women approaching 36 years. For men it reached 38 years, but the 75th percentile has since fallen and the median flattened.

In North Africa, women marry at earlier ages than men and husbands are often substantially older than their wives. These age differences both reproduce and justify gender inequality within marriage (Hoodfar 1997). We examine the mean age difference between husband and wife for married women ages 30–59 by year of birth. In Egypt, this has increased slowly over time from a six-year to a seven-year difference. In Morocco, the gap has widened from seven to eight years. In Tunisia, the gap has fluctuated around six years. These age differences will have a substantial effect on bargaining within the household, and also affect whether or not the marriage markets will "clear." While there are relatively similar numbers of males and females born in the same year, the population structure in many countries is such that the number of males is not equal to females who are six or seven years younger.

Figure 29.2 demonstrates the population structure of the three countries, and the mismatch between the number of males and females five years younger. Egypt had a youth bulge that was, as of 2012, centered around age 25–29, and additionally has an "echo" of the bulge beginning to form among young children. While 20–24-year-old males in Egypt face a shortage of 15–19-year-old females to marry (because of the narrowing in the population pyramid at that age), otherwise there are consistently relatively more females than males. One factor contributing to this mismatch is the number of men working abroad, which can be seen in terms of the different size of the male and female 25–29 populations. Morocco has a youth bulge whose peak in 2010 was at age 15–19. Thus the Moroccan youth bulge is

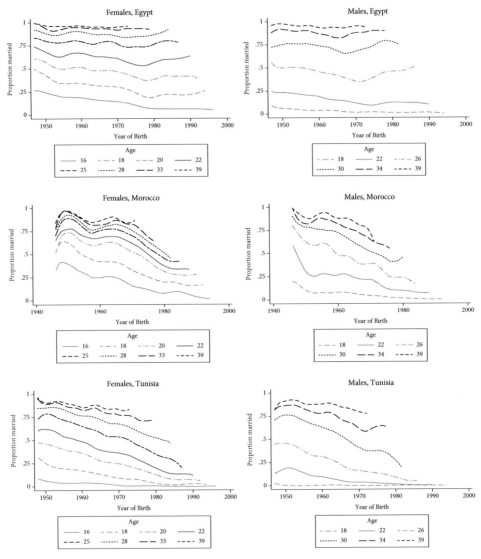

FIGURE 29.1 Proportion married by selected ages and year of birth.

Source: ELMPS 2012, MHYS, NSHY.

approaching marriageable age. Prior to the youth bulge, there had been a relative excess of younger females relative to five-year-older males. This relative oversupply of women is one of the drivers of the unequal prevalence of marriage among males and females seen in Figure 29.1. After the peak of the youth bulge marries, there will be a relative excess of males in Morocco. Tunisia experienced a much more moderate youth bulge. Tunisia as of 2012 has a relative excess of females in their 30s, and will experience a shortage of potential wives for the generation of males that is 5–14 because of the smaller size of recent generations.

These different population structures have and will continue to shape the economics of marriage in North Africa. In Morocco, while men may have trouble marrying early for economic reasons, they face an excess supply of younger women. When the excess of females flips to an excess of males, we expect to see the age gap between males and females decrease in Morocco, as in Tunisia. We also expect a rise in the number of spinsters in Tunisia as the youth bulge of females does not universally marry.

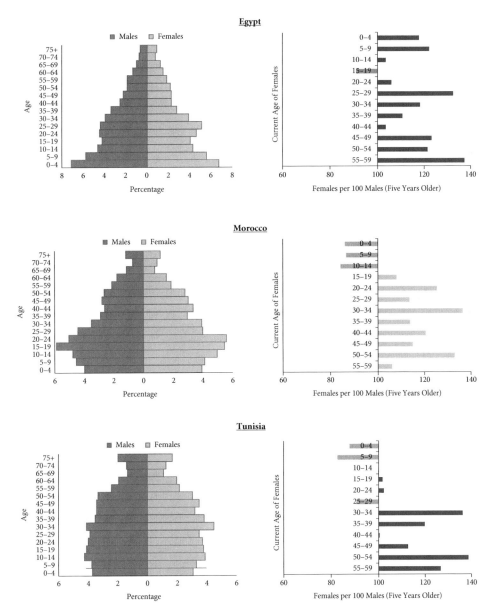

FIGURE 29.2 Population pyramid and ratio of females to males (five years older) by age group, Egypt, Morocco, and Tunisia (urban).

Source: ELMPS 2012, MHYS, NSHY.

29.4 MARRIAGE OUTCOMES

29.4.1 Consanguinity

Consanguinity, marriage with a relative, usually a cousin, is common practice in North Africa. Modernization theories suggest there should be substantial declines in consanguinity over time, but the practice has persisted (Casterline and El-Zeini 2003; Singerman 2007). We analyze the pattern of consanguinity in Egypt from the female perspective. Overall, 28.6% of married women 18–39 are in a consanguineous marriage. Most common are marriages to the son of a father's brother (6.4% of all marriages), but marriages with other first cousins are each around 3–4%, and marriages to other blood relatives total around 11%. Consistent with consanguinity being a "traditional" phenomenon, consanguinity is higher in rural areas and among women with lower education. Consanguinity is around 30% for women with secondary or lower levels of education and drops to around 15% for women with university education. The prevalence of consanguinity has been falling in both urban and rural areas over the past decade. Additionally, comparing marriages in 2000–2005 to 2006–2012, consanguinity rates have gone down for more educated women, but increased for women who have less than a secondary education. This may be because, as education levels increase, women achieving lower levels of education have poorer marriage prospects outside their family. In our multivariate models for consanguinity in Egypt (Appendix Table 29.2), consanguinity does not show a substantial or significant relationship with education, only decreasing for women with university or higher education, and this effect disappears when other marriage outcomes are included as covariates. There are large regional effects, consistent with consanguinity having a substantial cultural component. Overall, there is mixed support for modernization hypotheses related to consanguinity.

29.4.2 Nuclear residence

Whether or not a couple starts their married lives as a separate, nuclear household or living with (the husband's) extended family has substantial implications for individuals' social and economic prospects, particularly for the bride and her decision-making power and status within the household. The prevalence of nuclear household living arrangements varies substantially across North Africa. While 86% of recently married women in Tunisia are in nuclear households, only 41% are in nuclear households in Morocco. Egypt falls in the middle, with 63% of ever-married women 18–39 years living in nuclear households when they married.

Nuclear household living arrangements in Egypt vary with urban/rural location, with individuals married in urban areas more likely to live in a nuclear household after marriage than individuals in rural areas. There is, however, a converging trend, with nuclear household arrangements after marriage increasing more rapidly in rural areas than in urban areas. For women who married in 2011,[3] 88% of urban women took up residence in a nuclear

---

[3] And were 18–39 in 2012.

household after marriage, while 63% of rural women did so. Additionally, housing patterns are shifting in rural and poor urban areas and may be making it difficult to clearly identify households' living arrangements. Extended families living under one roof increasingly have residences in buildings with multiple stories, each containing separate apartments with their own kitchen. As a result families may live in close proximity with their parents or in-laws, sharing some meals but not necessarily all meals, thus blurring the traditional definition of a household.[4]

Nuclear residence is closely linked with education in Morocco and Egypt, but the prevalence of nuclear households is around 85% in Tunisia regardless of a woman's education level. The prevalence of nuclear households only reaches these levels in Egypt and Morocco for women educated at the university level. Additionally, in Egypt, comparing women married in 2000–2005 and 2006–2011, the prevalence of nuclear households rose more quickly at lower levels of education than at higher levels.

In the multivariate models for nuclear residence (Appendix Table 29.A1 and Table 29.2), more educated women are more likely to have nuclear arrangements at marriage, but only significantly so in Egypt. Also, in Egypt, where there is data on parents' education, daughters of men with higher education have a greater chance of nuclear living arrangements upon marriage, an indication of her family's greater bargaining power at marriage.

29.4.3 Costs of marriage

The costs of marriage are the most substantial investment young North Africans make. These costs have been identified as a substantial contributor to delay in age of marriage, and a barrier to adult life (Amin and Al-Bassusi 2004; Assaad, Binzel, and Gadallah 2010; Assaad and Ramadan 2008; Dhillon, Dyer, and Yousef 2009; Rashad, Osman, and Roudi-Fahimi 2005; Singerman 2007). One way to quantify the costs of marriage is in terms of how many months of earnings it would take a groom to cover the entire up-front costs of the marriage. Although costs are generally shared between the bride's side and both the groom and the groom's family, this provides a helpful metric. In Egypt, men who were wage-workers in 1998 and had married in the three years prior to 2006 would have had to save 104 months' worth of salary (8.6 years) in order to pay the total costs of the marriage.[5] Men who were wage-workers in 2006 and had married in the three years prior to 2012 would have had to save 99 months' worth of salary (8.3 years) in order to pay the total costs of the marriage. Although there has been a very slight decline from 2006 to 2012, it is clear that the costs of marriage remain an enormous investment for young people in Egypt.

One measure of whether or not young people struggle to get married is the length of the engagement. Long engagements are often considered a sign of high costs and of difficulty in gathering the necessary economic resources to marry (Amin and Al-Bassusi 2004; Singerman 2007). However, since engagements can be broken off without

---

[4] See Assaad and Krafft (2013) for additional information on changing shelter patterns and identifying households over time in the ELMPS.

[5] Costs in 2006 were collected for the first marriage, while costs in 2012 were collected for the last marriage. For the population (18–39) that we focus on here, the vast majority of first marriages are also the last marriage, and we treat the 2006 and 2012 data as comparable.

substantial social consequences (Hoodfar 1997), further research is needed on the nature of long engagements—they may also represent information issues and uncertainty, and provide a window in which to check a potential spouse's qualities (Hoodfar 1997). Examining the trends in different stages of engagement in Egypt over 2003–2011 for Muslim women, overall, the total length of the time leading up to marriage—from informal engagement to actual wedding—has been relatively flat or decreasing over time. Decreases in the time from formal engagement to legal marriage (*katb kitab*) and legal marriage to actual marriage (*dukhla*) appear to be driving this trend.

There are a number of different components to marriage costs in North Africa. In Egypt, costs consist of the bride price (*mahr*), the jewelry gift given to the bride (*shabka*), the cost of acquiring housing, the cost of furniture and appliances, the cost of the trousseau and home furnishings (*gihaz*), and the cost of the wedding celebration itself. As of 2012, the total costs of marriages (based on marriages that occurred in the preceding three years) were around 62 000 LE (approximately US$ 10 164 at a 2012 exchange rate of 6.1 LE to the US$). The largest components of cost are furniture and housing, followed by the *gihaz*. Jewelry is around 10%, celebrations are around 7% and brideprice is less than 5% of total costs.

We hypothesize that costs of marriage at least in part reflect the bargaining power of women and their families, who try to lock in as much as possible of the groom's economic contribution to the marriage up front. As a result, the costs of marriage will correlate with variables associated with greater bride side bargaining power. For instance, costs of marriage increase and then decrease with age at marriage for women. Costs are high for women who marry between the ages of 20 and 30 (within the optimal window) and highest at age 25. Costs are lower for women who marry before 20 or after 30.

Comparing marriages that occurred in 2003–2005 to those in 2009–2011 (in terms of constant 2012 LE), costs have increased in rural areas from 54 000 LE to 60 000 LE but have actually fallen in urban areas from 78 000 LE to 65 000 LE. Over time, in rural areas, housing costs have become a greater share of what is a higher cost overall. The drop in overall costs in urban areas has been mostly across-the-board, although the cost of celebrations and the *gihaz* have dropped less than other components.

Because of the panel nature of the ELMPS, it is in fact possible to look at the characteristics of married individuals' natal households. We compared the costs of marriage by parental wealth in 2006 for women 18–39 who were married between 2009 and 2011 and were in the panel in 2006 and 2012. Total costs increase substantially—but not proportionately—with wealth level, indicating that the costs of marriage are likely to be particularly burdensome for poorer families. The structure of cost across components is quite similar across wealth levels. Parental resources play an important role in the resources available to a new couple. Marriage thus represents an enormous intergenerational wealth transfer.

In our multivariate models (Appendix Table 29.A2), we estimate models for log total costs, so that the influence of outliers is reduced and coefficients can be interpreted as percentage changes. Costs increase with women's own education, and with highly educated parents, reflecting the bride's side's increased bargaining power. A more educated spouse also increases costs, reflecting his greater ability to pay. Nuclear residence also increases costs by 9.4%, and the pattern of costs and optimal age noted earlier continues to hold in the multivariate model. Models estimated adding parental wealth (not shown) also indicate that women coming from wealthier households have higher marriage costs.

29.4.4 Cost sharing

The cost-sharing structure, meaning the division of costs among the bride, her family, and the groom and his family, is relatively fixed regardless of individuals' characteristics. There is only minor variation between urban and rural areas in terms of the cost burden each party bears. Regardless of education level, brides themselves incur a very limited share (1%) of the total costs. For illiterate or less than primary educated brides, their families pay 31% of the costs, while for brides educated at the primary through the secondary level, their family's share is 34%. Only if the bride has a university education does her family's share of the costs increase to 38%. When the bride is either illiterate or has less than primary education, the groom pays a relatively higher share (42%), and his family a somewhat lower share (26%). For brides with primary and preparatory education, the groom himself covers around a third of the costs of marriage and his family also a third of total costs. Secondary educated brides are associated with a higher groom share and smaller groom's family share. Using data on costs by groom's education, we find fairly similar patterns. Looking at the percentage of costs paid by different parties by parental wealth, the bride side share generally increases when the bride's parents are wealthier. The groom pays the largest share if the bride is from the poorest quintile of households, and otherwise pays about a third of total costs. In the multivariate models (Appendix Table 29.A2),[6] more educated women had a larger bride-side share, as did women with educated mothers.

29.4.5 Costs and consanguinity

It has been argued—although previously without strong empirical evidence—that consanguineous marriages are less costly (Casterline and El-Zeini 2003; Singerman 2007). If an individual is marrying a cousin, there may be more trust between the two families and less of a need to capitalize all the costs up front. The empirical evidence in Egypt suggests that there is not a substantial reduction in costs in consanguineous marriages. The average cost of a consanguineous marriage is around 82% of the average cost of a non-consanguineous marriage. The cost structure is also fairly similar. Housing is a slightly greater share of consanguineous marriage costs, which may represent a larger wealth transfer since resources will remain in the family. There are also only minor variations in the shares paid by different parties. In the multivariate models that included marriage outcomes, there was, in fact, no significant total cost difference for consanguineous and non-consanguineous marriages, after accounting for other characteristics (Appendix Table 29.A2). Cost savings are not the primary driver of this practice, and other explanations for consanguinity should be investigated, such as decreased uncertainty about spouse qualities, spouse and family compatibility, better treatment of wives, and greater marital stability (Casterline and El-Zeini 2003; Hoodfar 1997).

---

[6] We present OLS models but also tried logit transformations for the share and robust GLM; results were similar.

29.5 HOW CHARACTERISTICS SHAPE OUTCOMES

In order to properly test the relationship between individual characteristics and marriage outcomes (as hypothesized in Assaad and Krafft 2015)—the outcomes of a bargaining process where ability to pay and characteristics create bargaining power—we turn to multivariate regression models (Appendix Tables 29.A1 and 29.A2; Tables 29.1 and 29.2). We had previously referred to some of the findings of these models in terms of individual outcomes. In this section we synthesize the effects of various characteristics across different outcomes and, where possible, countries.

5.1 Cohorts and age at marriage

In Egypt (Appendix Table 29.A1), the observed trend of a rise, and more recently a decline in the median age at marriage for both males and females is borne out in the multivariate hazard model. After accounting for other characteristics, the hazard[7] of marriage was lowest for males born around 1965 and females born around 1970, and has risen for recent cohorts, meaning, that all else remaining equal, the age at marriage peaked for men born around 1965 and women born around 1970. In contrast, in Morocco and Tunisia (Table 29.1), the hazard of marriage is consistently lower for later cohorts, pointing towards consistently later ages at marriage.

29.5.2 Place of residence

Differences by region and by urban/rural location are common across different outcomes. In all three countries, certain regions are generally associated with poorer marriage outcomes for women, which may represent different bases for women's status and bargaining power due to regional cultural variations. For instance, in Egypt, Upper Egypt, which tends to be the most culturally conservative and poorest region, has higher rates of consanguinity, lower rates of nuclear residence, lower costs, lower bride's side share, and earlier marriages.

29.5.3 Own education, spouse education, and parents' education

Women's (and men's) own education substantially decreased the hazard of marriage in Egypt, leading to later ages at marriage, even at low levels of education for men, and starting at the secondary level for women (Appendix Table 29.A1). In Morocco (Table 29.1), males and females with at least a primary education had substantially reduced hazards of marriage, and even females with less than a primary education (but who were not illiterate) had lower hazards than illiterate females. The effects were stronger for females, and increased

---

[7] Cox proportional hazard models were used to estimate age at marriage, since this is a potentially right censored outcome if individuals never married, and is most appropriately modeled by survival analysis methods. Hazard ratios greater than 1 (higher hazards) indicate faster, earlier marriage, while hazard ratios less than 1 (lower hazards) indicate slower, later marriage.

Table 29.1 Cox proportional hazard models for time to marriage, Morocco and Tunisia (urban)

	Morocco				Tunisia			
	Females	Males	Females	Males	Females	Males	Females	Males
	Basic spec.	Basic spec.	Basic spec. w/marr. outcomes	Basic spec. w/marr. outcomes	Basic spec.	Basic spec.	Basic spec. w/marr. outcomes	Basic spec. w/marr. outcomes
Own education (illit. omitted)								
Less than primary	0.714***	0.887	0.819**	0.845*	1.011	1.113	0.954	0.900
	(0.055)	(0.063)	(0.060)	(0.065)	(0.084)	(0.114)	(0.083)	(0.094)
Primary	0.692***	0.645***	0.724***	0.641***	1.193**	1.108	1.109	0.890
	(0.065)	(0.057)	(0.058)	(0.059)	(0.074)	(0.088)	(0.070)	(0.077)
Lower secondary	0.535***	0.643***	0.588***	0.680***	1.131	0.997	0.969	0.725***
	(0.051)	(0.066)	(0.054)	(0.070)	(0.073)	(0.083)	(0.064)	(0.070)
Upper secondary	0.488***	0.622**	0.517***	0.676**	1.019	1.108	0.949	0.721***
	(0.063)	(0.091)	(0.050)	(0.080)	(0.080)	(0.092)	(0.065)	(0.063)
Higher education	0.423***	0.638**	0.433***	0.575***	0.793***	0.952	0.734***	0.668***
	(0.068)	(0.097)	(0.076)	(0.085)	(0.046)	(0.078)	(0.044)	(0.062)
Rural	1.165*	1.645***	1.216***	1.238***				
	(0.071)	(0.104)	(0.072)	(0.078)				
64 minus age	1.004	0.984	0.976*	0.940***	0.975**	0.989	0.948***	0.941***
	(0.011)	(0.011)	(0.012)	(0.012)	(0.008)	(0.011)	(0.008)	(0.013)
Square of 64 minus age/100	0.913***	0.937*	1.054*	1.199***	0.974	0.907***	1.124***	1.194***
	(0.024)	(0.026)	(0.028)	(0.035)	(0.018)	(0.025)	(0.022)	(0.043)
Spouse ed. (same omitted)								
Spouse less educ.			1.124	1.221**			0.939	1.185**
			(0.097)	(0.086)			(0.048)	(0.065)
Spouse more educ.			1.002	0.789**			1.082	0.810***
			(0.059)	(0.064)			(0.053)	(0.051)
Spouse educ. miss.			0.944	0.951			0.884	0.771**
			(0.072)	(0.108)			(0.069)	(0.073)
Regions included	No	No	No	No	Yes	Yes	Yes	Yes
N (observations)	2026	2043	1487	1323	4150	3925	3297	2720

Source: Authors' calculations based on NSHY and MHYS.
Notes:
*** $p < 0.001$,
** $p < 0.01$,
* $p < 0.05$.
Coefficients are hazard ratios.
Standard errors in parentheses.
Marriage outcome models are necessarily limited to those who have married.

Table 29.2 Marriage outcomes for females, Morocco and Tunisia (urban)

	Morocco				Tunisia (urban)			
	Age difference OLS		Nuclear residence Probit		Age difference OLS		Nuclear residence Probit	
	Basic spec.	Basic spec. w/marr. outcomes	Basic spec.	Basic spec. w/marr. outcomes	Basic spec.	Basic spec. w/marr. outcomes	Basic spec.	Basic spec. w/marr. outcomes
Own education (illit. omitted)								
Less than primary	0.791	0.499	−0.100	−0.152	−0.909*	−0.824*	0.566	1.119
	(0.494)	(0.516)	(0.191)	(0.208)	(0.371)	(0.373)	(0.405)	(0.653)
Primary	1.842**	1.383*	−0.031	−0.267	−0.241	−0.355	0.108	0.545
	(0.622)	(0.659)	(0.214)	(0.247)	(0.275)	(0.280)	(0.267)	(0.339)
Lower secondary	0.696	0.038	−0.445	−0.810**	−0.179	−0.374	0.012	0.014
	(0.710)	(0.769)	(0.254)	(0.305)	(0.299)	(0.312)	(0.258)	(0.306)
Upper secondary	−1.047	−1.691	0.173	0.007	0.578	0.389	−0.003	0.216
	(1.095)	(1.136)	(0.352)	(0.386)	(0.387)	(0.396)	(0.301)	(0.374)
Higher education	−1.354	−2.277	0.306	0.448	−0.160	−0.671	−0.053	0.208
	(1.483)	(1.529)	(0.596)	(0.646)	(0.319)	(0.344)	(0.243)	(0.316)
Rural	−0.868*	−1.009**	−0.326*	−0.460**				
	(0.379)	(0.382)	(0.163)	(0.177)				
Age at marriage	−0.531**	−0.508**	−0.063	−0.005	−1.421***	−1.419***	0.126	0.114
	(0.188)	(0.188)	(0.082)	(0.090)	(0.112)	(0.111)	(0.075)	(0.093)
Age at marriage sq./100	0.516	0.476	0.159	0.051	2.190***	2.180***	−0.204	−0.153
	(0.379)	(0.379)	(0.155)	(0.170)	(0.205)	(0.205)	(0.118)	(0.149)
Spouse ed. (same omitted)								
Spouse less educ.		0.831		−0.042		−0.038		−0.404*
		(0.632)		(0.249)		(0.264)		(0.204)
Spouse more educ.		−0.851*		−0.689***		−0.945***		0.064
		(0.382)		(0.191)		(0.231)		(0.251)
Spouse educ. miss.		N/A		−1.760***		−1.744		−3.125***
				(0.265)		(1.384)		(0.343)
Constant	26.926***	27.501***	−0.405	−0.057	16.885***	17.190***	0.887	0.999
	(1.472)	(1.475)	(1.164)	(1.447)	(2.276)	(2.274)	(1.115)	(1.221)
Regions included	No	No	No	No	Yes	Yes	Yes	Yes
Pseudo R2			0.032	0.178			0.037	0.378
R2	0.054	0.060			0.109	0.115		
N (observations)	1411	1411	316	316	2926	2926	526	526

Source: Authors' calculations based on NSHY and MHYS.

Notes: *** $p < 0.001$,

** $p < 0.01$,

* $p < 0.05$.

Standard errors in parentheses.

Nuclear marriage based on current residence for marriages in the past five years.

with education for both genders. In Tunisia, higher education levels were generally associated with a decreased hazard of marriage, and therefore later marriages for men and women. In Egypt, a woman's own education decreases consanguinity, increases the probability of nuclear residence, increases total costs and bride's side share of costs, and reduces the spousal age difference (Appendix Table 29.A2). A primary education for women increased the age difference between spouses, but did not significantly affect the probability of nuclear family living. In Tunisia, women who could read and write had smaller spousal age differences than illiterate women.

More educated parents also tended to increase the age at marriage in Egypt. While having a less than intermediate educated mother compared to an illiterate one decreased the chances of nuclear residence, having a highly educated father increased the chances. More educated mothers and fathers were associated with higher total costs. Moderately educated mothers were associated with a greater bride side share, but there was no relationship with father's education. More educated mothers were actually associated with larger age differences between spouses.

In Egypt, having a relatively less educated spouse increased the hazard of marriage for men and decreased it for women; this may mean that men can marry less educated spouses more rapidly and with less investment, while for women less educated spouses are more of a last resort. Only for men did relatively more educated spouses decrease the hazard of marriage, which may be because they need to save more to marry up. In both Morocco and Tunisia, having a less educated spouse increased the hazard of marriage for men but not for women, and for men, relatively more educated spouses were associated with lower hazards of marriage (later marriages). This may be related to bargaining for higher standards of living, which take time to accumulate. There is a clear pattern of tradeoffs in terms of spouse quality (more education) being associated with later marriages for men. If men are willing to settle for a less educated spouse, they can get married sooner.

In terms of other marriage outcomes, having a relatively less educated spouse was associated with consanguinity in Egypt. A relatively more educated spouse increased total costs by 16.2%. In both Egypt and Morocco, if spouse education was missing (because the spouse is not present), there was a lower chance of nuclear living (which may mean that wives are left with in-laws if the husband is working elsewhere). In Morocco a more educated spouse was associated with a smaller age difference, a pattern also observed in Tunisia. In Tunisia, a spouse with less education was associated with a lower probability of nuclear living. In Morocco, the opposite occurred; a more educated spouse was associated with a lower probability of nuclear living.

29.5.4 Father's employment

Only in Egypt was information available about fathers' characteristics. Compared to men with fathers engaged in public sector work, men with fathers in private sector wage work had a significantly lower hazard of marriage (i.e., later marriage), which may be due to a lower ability to pay on the part of the groom's family (Appendix Table 29.A1). In different models, having a father who is an employer or own account worker increased the changes of consanguinity, which may represent a desire to keep business enterprises within the family. Compared to women whose father was in a professional or managerial occupation, women whose father was an agricultural worker have a smaller bride's side share in the costs of marriage, which may be related to ability to pay (Appendix Table 29.A2). Women with fathers in clerical/sales occupations had a significantly higher spousal age difference relative to those with fathers in professional or managerial occupations. This suggests that families may be accepting older husbands as a tradeoff for socioeconomic status of the family and ability to pay.

29.5.5 Natal families: wealth and the supply of cousins

In Egypt, because the ELMPS was the third round of a labor market panel survey, it was possible to determine the characteristics of the natal household (in the previous round, 2006) for individuals who were married in the interim. We focus on natal household assets, which include household wealth (an asset index derived using factor analysis from ownership of durable goods and housing characteristics), the value of livestock, and the amount of agricultural land controlled by the household, all of which we expect will affect bargaining power and ability to pay. We do this for all the regressions for Egypt (results not shown). We find that the natal household wealth index, livestock, and land have no significant effect on the timing of marriage, but that wealthier families are less likely to arrange consanguineous marriages. Wealth also significantly raises the costs of marriage by increasing the ability to pay. Thus, the hypothesis that consanguineous marriages cost less, which we discounted earlier after correcting for other characteristics, may have arisen from the negative association between wealth and consanguinity and the positive association between costs and wealth. No other marriage outcomes are affected by wealth, and none are affected by the value of livestock or land.

Casterline and El-Zeini (2003) had used micro-simulations to examine whether decreasing family size, which affects the supply of kin, would, in turn, affect consanguinity. They find evidence that it is unlikely to do so. Using the same panel data as for the analysis of the impact of assets above, we calculate the number of maternal or paternal aunts or uncles, as a proxy measure for the supply of cousins, and added this to the regression for consanguinity (not shown). We find that a greater number of maternal aunts slightly increases the probability of a consanguineous marriage, but that the other proxies for relatives are not significant. In line with previous findings, the supply of cousins is at most a minor factor in the likelihood of consanguinity.

29.5.6 Housing markets, employment, and migration

Previous research has suggested that, at least in Egypt, one of the factors that has affected marriage outcomes is the housing market (Assaad et al. 2010; Assaad and Ramadan 2008). Since marriage often involves setting up an independent household, the costs of which can be substantial, the availability of housing, especially rental housing, can be of paramount importance. In 1996 in Egypt, a "new rent" law was passed that was designed to liberalize new rental contracts and thus increase the supply of rental housing. To examine the impact of this reform on marriage outcomes, we interacted the proportion of new-rent contracts in an individual's district of birth with a dummy indicating exposure to the new rent law. Males born after 1972 and females born after 1977 were likely to be facing a different rental market at marriage since they are likely to be entering the marriage market after the "new rent" law was passed in 1996. Specifically, we include the percent of rent in all housing in the district of birth, and the percent of "new rent" units in rental housing and the interactions that we expect to show the effect of the law. While new rent and rent overall tend not to be significant, the interactions after the policy change generally are; both the percentage of rent in all housing and the percentage of new rent in rental housing interactions significantly increase the hazard of marriage, decreasing the age at marriage. The interaction of new rent in rental housing also significantly increases the chances of residing in a nuclear household. Thus rental law reforms allowed youth to marry earlier and made it easier for them to form independent households.

Because the Cox proportional hazards model allows for time-varying covariates, we can look at how a number of characteristics that change over time affect the timing of marriage, including prior migration and employment. When men become employed, this significantly increases their hazard of marriage, but employment has no similar effect for women. However, being employed in a formal job increases the hazard for both men and women. The fact that formal employment, but not any employment, increases the hazard of marriage for women suggests that it does so because of the appeal it presents to prospective spouses rather than simply because of her greater ability to pay. When unmarried individuals migrate (which is an almost exclusively male phenomenon in Egypt), their hazard of marrying is lower simply because they spend time away from home. However, work as a migrant may increase their accumulated savings and thus their marriage prospects in the long run.

29.5.7 How outcomes interrelate

There are potential tradeoffs and other relationships between different marriage outcomes. For instance, in Egypt the hazard of marriage is lower for both men and women who have nuclear marriages, meaning that they have to wait longer to secure independent living arrangements. Likewise, higher costs are related to later marriages. In contrast, consanguineous marriages tend to occur at earlier ages, everything else held constant. Nuclear family living is associated with a lower chance of consanguinity, higher total costs, a greater spousal age difference, but not with an increase in the bride's side share. In fact, bride's side share is not significantly associated with any of the other marriage outcomes and seems to be set by convention rather than as a function of ability to pay. Log total costs are significantly associated with nuclear family living, but not with consanguinity, age differences, or the bride's side share. Consanguinity is related to a smaller spousal age difference as well as a lower chance of nuclear living. These associations suggest that given individual characteristics, tradeoffs are made during the bargaining process between different marriage outcomes.

29.6 Conclusions

Marriage is the single most important economic and social transaction undertaken by young North Africans as they negotiate their transition to adulthood. Yet, the transition to marriage has garnered relatively little attention from social and economic researchers. Drawing on Assaad and Krafft's (2015) unifying conceptual framework for understanding the economics of marriage in North Africa, in this chapter we provided an empirical overview of a number of marriage outcomes and tested hypotheses about how they related to individuals' and parents' characteristics and to each other. We presented new evidence on trends in the prevalence and timing of marriage in Egypt, Morocco, and Tunisia, and the characteristics that affect the timing and patterns of marriage—including such important determinants as own education, parental education, employment status and wealth, own employment, migration, and housing markets.

The primary hypothesis of our conceptual framework was that in the context of a legal framework that assigns asymmetric rights within marriage and a social convention that men bear a disproportionate share of the costs of marriage, the bride's side will bargain for as much as possible up front. Greater bargaining power on the bride's side will therefore tend to raise the up-front costs of marriage. Moreover, a more educated bride and one from a more privileged background will have a greater likelihood to marry at an optimal age, to live in a nuclear family arrangement at marriage, not to marry a cousin, and to marry someone who is closer to her in age. We find support for most of these hypotheses in our empirical analysis, with bargaining power based on individual and family characteristics and ability to pay shaping marriage outcomes, along with potential tradeoffs among outcomes.

We hope that this work will advance the embryonic literature on the economics of marriage in North Africa and provide examples of what we can learn, even with existing data. There is a great deal more research that can be done on the marriage market, bargaining, and marriage outcomes. The relationships between the marriage market and other markets, such as labor and housing markets, merit further research, as well as how bargaining and initial marriage outcomes shape bargaining power and other outcomes over the course of individuals' married lives.

References

Amin, S., and Al-Bassusi, N.H. (2004). Education, wage work, and marriage: perspectives of Egyptian working women. *Journal of Marriage and Family*, 66(5):1287–1299.

Assaad, R., Binzel, C., and Gadallah, M. (2010). Transitions to employment and marriage among young men in Egypt. *Middle East Development Journal*, 2(1):39–88.

Assaad, R., and Krafft, C. (2013). The Egypt Labor Market Panel Survey: introducing the 2012 round. *IZA Journal of Labor and Development*, 2(8):1–30.

Assaad, R., and Krafft, C. (2015). The economics of marriage in North Africa: a unifying theoretical framework, in C. Monga and J.Y. Lin (eds), *The Oxford Handbook of Africa and Economics*, Volume 1. Oxford: Oxford University Press.

Assaad, R., and Ramadan, M. (2008). Did housing policy reforms curb the delay in marriage among young men in Egypt? Middle East Youth Initiative Policy Outlook No. 1. Washington, DC.

Casterline, J.B., and El-Zeini, L.O. (2003). Consanguinity in the Arab Region: Current Patterns and Prospects for Change. Conference *Institutions, Ideologies, and Agency: Changing Family Life in the Arab Middle East and Diaspora.* September 2003, University of North Carolina.

Dhillon, N., Dyer, P., and Yousef, T. (2009). Generation in waiting: an overview of school to work and family formation transitions, in Navtej Dhillon and Tarik Yousef (eds), *Generation in Waiting: The Unfulfilled Promise of Young People in the Middle East.* Washington, DC: The Brookings Institution, pp. 11–38.

Hoodfar, H. (1997). *Between Marriage and the Market: Intimate Politics and Survival in Cairo.* Berkeley, CA: University of California Press.

Rashad, H., Osman, M., and Roudi-Fahimi, F. (2005). *Marriage In The Arab World.* Washington, DC: Population Reference Bureau.

Singerman, D. (2007). The Economic Imperatives of Marriage: Emerging Practices and Identities Among Youth in the Middle East. Middle East Youth Initiative Working Paper No. 6.

World Bank (2010). Morocco Household and Youth Survey (MHYS) 2009–2010. Ref. MAR_2009_MHYS_v01_M_PUF. http://microdata.worldbank.org/index.php/catalog/1546 (accessed June 7, 2013).

APPENDIX

....

Appendix Table 29.A1 Cox proportional hazards models for time to marriage, Egypt

	Females	Males	Females	Males	Females Ext. spec. w/marr.	Males Ext. spec. w/marr.
	Basic spec.	Basic spec.	Ext. spec.	Ext. spec.	outcomes	outcomes
Own education (Illit. omitted)						
Read and write	0.872	0.917	0.902	0.895	0.990	0.999
	(0.075)	(0.061)	(0.071)	(0.057)	(0.088)	(0.098)
Primary	1.006	0.885*	1.026	0.825***	1.012	0.915
	(0.052)	(0.044)	(0.048)	(0.040)	(0.059)	(0.060)
Preparatory	0.978	0.742***	1.116	0.713***	1.222**	0.822*
	(0.064)	(0.053)	(0.074)	(0.047)	(0.083)	(0.079)
Secondary	0.773***	0.712***	1.049	0.689***	0.959	0.721***
	(0.025)	(0.028)	(0.037)	(0.026)	(0.044)	(0.044)
Post. sec. inst.	0.604***	0.694***	0.852*	0.684***	0.711***	0.745**
	(0.033)	(0.045)	(0.059)	(0.046)	(0.063)	(0.074)
Univ. and above.	0.504***	0.571***	0.769***	0.606***	0.624***	0.608***
	(0.020)	(0.025)	(0.035)	(0.028)	(0.035)	(0.046)
No. sisters	0.997	1.017*	0.997	1.017*	1.001	1.005
	(0.007)	(0.008)	(0.007)	(0.008)	(0.008)	(0.010)
No. brothers	1.015	0.991	1.014	0.990	1.003	1.006
	(0.008)	(0.008)	(0.008)	(0.008)	(0.010)	(0.011)
Mother's ed. (illit. omitted)						
Read and write	1.101*	0.938	1.130**	0.928	1.071	1.004
	(0.044)	(0.045)	(0.048)	(0.045)	(0.060)	(0.055)
Less than intermediate	0.947	0.806***	0.966	0.818***	0.964	0.984
	(0.048)	(0.046)	(0.052)	(0.046)	(0.052)	(0.063)
Intermediate and above.	1.042	0.962	1.020	0.973	1.049	1.129
	(0.057)	(0.065)	(0.062)	(0.068)	(0.054)	(0.079)
Father's ed. (illit. omitted)						
Read and write	0.960	0.965	0.967	0.960	0.979	0.973
	(0.033)	(0.035)	(0.033)	(0.034)	(0.045)	(0.044)
Less than intermediate	0.909*	0.838***	0.915*	0.837***	0.963	0.894
	(0.040)	(0.038)	(0.041)	(0.038)	(0.049)	(0.058)
Intermediate	0.970	0.922	0.958	0.913	0.944	0.864
	(0.052)	(0.055)	(0.054)	(0.055)	(0.059)	(0.068)
Higher ed.	0.902	0.791**	0.904	0.792**	0.959	0.890
	(0.061)	(0.059)	(0.065)	(0.060)	(0.075)	(0.081)
Father's work (public wage omitted)						
Private wage	0.988	0.913*	0.997	0.929	0.931	0.986
	(0.036)	(0.036)	(0.036)	(0.037)	(0.038)	(0.048)
Self-emp./employer	1.047	0.996	1.042	1.000	0.990	1.050
	(0.037)	(0.039)	(0.037)	(0.039)	(0.040)	(0.048)

(continued)

Appendix Table 29.A1 Continued

	Females	Males	Females	Males	Females Ext. spec. w/marr. outcomes	Males Ext. spec. w/marr. outcomes
	Basic spec.	Basic spec.	Ext. spec.	Ext. spec.		
Unpaid family worker/no job	1.473 (0.346)	1.112 (0.193)	1.445 (0.306)	1.257 (0.163)	0.940 (0.246)	1.118 (0.161)
Father's occupation (manager omitted)						
Clerical/sales	0.950 (0.049)	0.983 (0.051)	0.939 (0.048)	0.961 (0.050)	0.915 (0.057)	1.057 (0.062)
Production non-agricultural	1.012 (0.037)	0.961 (0.039)	0.990 (0.037)	0.945 (0.038)	0.979 (0.044)	1.001 (0.049)
Agricultural	0.998 (0.040)	1.069 (0.044)	0.982 (0.039)	1.039 (0.042)	1.028 (0.051)	0.914 (0.049)
64 minus age	0.979*** (0.005)	0.972*** (0.005)	0.980*** (0.005)	0.976*** (0.005)	0.837*** (0.030)	0.645*** (0.030)
Square of 64 minus age/100	1.054*** (0.011)	1.088*** (0.013)	1.045*** (0.011)	1.078*** (0.013)	1.453*** (0.071)	2.446*** (0.172)
Females per 100 males (5 yrs older)	0.999 (0.001)	0.997* (0.001)	0.998 (0.001)	0.996** (0.001)	0.998 (0.001)	0.996* (0.001)
Rental housing						
Percentage of rent in all housing and M born 1972+ F born 1977+ (SD)			1.074* (0.038)	1.111* (0.046)	1.148 (0.088)	1.107** (0.042)
Percentage of new in rent and M born 1972+ F born 1977+ (SD)			1.108** (0.036)	1.094* (0.041)	1.180* (0.083)	1.102*** (0.028)
Percentage of new in rent (SD)			1.046 (0.025)	1.044 (0.030)	0.901 (0.062)	
Percentage of rent in all housing (SD)			0.979 (0.030)	0.930* (0.034)	0.887 (0.067)	
Employed			1.073 (0.043)	3.131*** (0.259)	1.017 (0.046)	3.016*** (0.381)
Employed in a good job			1.158** (0.061)	1.281*** (0.039)	1.245*** (0.077)	1.145*** (0.042)
In school			0.250*** (0.015)	0.766*** (0.054)	0.416*** (0.025)	0.853 (0.083)
Duration of migration (months)				1.003 (0.006)		1.011 (0.015)

(continued)

Appendix Table 29.A1 Continued

	Females	Males	Females	Males	Females	Males
					Ext. spec. w/marr. outcomes	Ext. spec. w/marr. outcomes
	Basic spec.	Basic spec.	Ext. spec.	Ext. spec.		
Returned migrant				0.705***		0.641***
				(0.045)		(0.072)
Spouse ed. (same omitted)						
Spouse less educ.					0.903**	1.101*
					(0.031)	(0.044)
Spouse more educ.					0.966	0.732***
					(0.037)	(0.033)
Spouse ed. miss.					0.991	0.771
					(0.048)	(0.168)
Father's rel. ed. (same omitted)						
Own father less educ.					0.978	0.962
					(0.035)	(0.035)
Own father more educ.					1.060	1.017
					(0.043)	(0.049)
Marriage outcomes						
Nuclear residence					0.861***	0.817***
					(0.026)	(0.029)
Consanguineous					1.202***	1.151***
					(0.037)	(0.042)
Bride's side share					0.999	0.997*
					(0.001)	(0.001)
Christian					0.904	1.024
					(0.053)	(0.078)
Log of total costs					0.875***	0.819***
					(0.014)	(0.016)
Regions included	Yes	Yes	Yes	Yes	Yes	Yes
N (observations)	10272	10206	10271	10204	6175	4434

Source: Authors' calculations based on ELMPS 2012.
Notes: *** $p < 0.001$,
** $p < 0.01$,
* $p < 0.05$.
Coefficients are hazard ratios.
Standard errors in parentheses.
Marriage outcome models are necessarily limited to those who have married.

Appendix Table 29.A2 Marriage outcomes for females, Egypt

	Consanguinity (Probit)		Nuclear residence (Probit)		Log total costs (OLS)		Bride's side share (OLS)		Female age difference (OLS)	
	Basic spec.	Ext. spec. w/marr. outcomes	Basic spec.	Ext. spec. w/marr. outcomes	Basic spec.	Ext. spec. w/marr. outcomes	Basic spec.	Ext. spec. w/marr. outcomes	Basic spec.	Ext. spec. w/marr. outcomes
Christian	-0.029 (0.133)	0.090 (0.138)	0.261 (0.136)	0.299* (0.141)	-0.097 (0.097)	-0.104 (0.093)	-0.609 (2.018)	-1.289 (1.974)	0.017 (0.549)	0.534 (0.520)
Own education (illit. omitted)										
Read and write	-0.126 (0.191)	-0.157 (0.212)	-0.128 (0.188)	-0.220 (0.206)	0.076 (0.128)	0.094 (0.129)	1.961 (2.335)	1.882 (2.560)	-0.155 (1.076)	0.735 (1.141)
Primary	0.173 (0.131)	0.126 (0.135)	0.147 (0.131)	0.200 (0.140)	0.225* (0.097)	0.263** (0.098)	0.931 (1.447)	0.937 (1.582)	-0.617 (0.677)	-0.518 (0.610)
Preparatory	0.126 (0.135)	0.064 (0.143)	0.274* (0.119)	0.263* (0.134)	0.362*** (0.092)	0.391*** (0.095)	3.267* (1.441)	3.176* (1.577)	0.384 (0.566)	-0.009 (0.493)
Secondary	0.073 (0.089)	0.088 (0.113)	0.303*** (0.089)	0.330** (0.108)	0.478*** (0.066)	0.524*** (0.074)	1.505 (1.050)	2.102 (1.254)	-0.651 (0.496)	0.081 (0.457)
Post. sec. inst.	0.039 (0.160)	-0.077 (0.191)	0.229 (0.156)	0.082 (0.185)	0.580*** (0.110)	0.645*** (0.120)	3.878* (1.685)	3.591* (1.789)	-2.123*** (0.621)	-1.067 (0.644)
Univ. and above	-0.237* (0.114)	-0.138 (0.153)	0.515*** (0.112)	0.424** (0.143)	0.659*** (0.072)	0.713*** (0.086)	1.857 (1.270)	2.402 (1.625)	-1.445** (0.535)	-0.188 (0.557)
No. sisters	-0.013 (0.018)	0.001 (0.019)	0.003 (0.019)	-0.009 (0.020)	-0.011 (0.012)	-0.013 (0.012)	-0.070 (0.217)	-0.050 (0.221)	-0.034 (0.084)	0.034 (0.064)
No. brothers	0.021 (0.021)	0.029 (0.023)	0.010 (0.020)	0.017 (0.022)	0.016 (0.013)	0.014 (0.012)	0.037 (0.242)	0.230 (0.247)	-0.018 (0.089)	-0.019 (0.081)
Mother's ed. (illit. omitted)										
Read and write	0.087 (0.113)	0.104 (0.121)	-0.015 (0.113)	0.042 (0.118)	0.050 (0.078)	0.023 (0.074)	2.232* (1.086)	2.835* (1.135)	-0.100 (0.357)	-0.048 (0.380)
Less than intermediate	-0.036 (0.123)	-0.025 (0.135)	-0.334** (0.126)	-0.306* (0.135)	0.145* (0.069)	0.124 (0.069)	2.254 (1.190)	2.589* (1.269)	0.554 (0.365)	0.814* (0.396)
Intermediate and above	-0.082 (0.130)	-0.093 (0.135)	0.132 (0.121)	0.191 (0.131)	0.155* (0.071)	0.129 (0.069)	1.502 (1.361)	1.767 (1.424)	0.895* (0.446)	0.592 (0.418)

(continued)

Appendix Table 29.A2 Continued

	Consanguinity (Probit)		Nuclear residence (Probit)		Log total costs (OLS)		Bride's side share (OLS)		Female age difference (OLS)	
	Basic spec.	Ext. spec. w/marr. outcomes	Basic spec.	Ext. spec. w/marr. outcomes	Basic spec.	Ext. spec. w/marr. outcomes	Basic spec.	Ext. spec. w/marr. outcomes	Basic spec.	Ext. spec. w/marr. outcomes
Father's ed. (illit. omitted)										
Read and write	0.059 (0.084)	0.129 (0.098)	0.032 (0.083)	0.071 (0.098)	−0.002 (0.063)	0.020 (0.062)	−0.163 (0.894)	−0.749 (1.016)	0.176 (0.330)	0.038 (0.353)
Less than intermediate	0.053 (0.114)	0.133 (0.137)	0.157 (0.099)	0.201 (0.122)	0.041 (0.069)	0.092 (0.079)	0.201 (1.129)	0.520 (1.343)	−0.450 (0.345)	−0.485 (0.411)
Intermediate	0.123 (0.121)	0.146 (0.145)	0.193 (0.122)	0.209 (0.143)	0.054 (0.077)	0.093 (0.086)	−1.144 (1.367)	−0.434 (1.600)	−0.259 (0.399)	−0.443 (0.469)
Higher ed.	0.072 (0.164)	0.127 (0.192)	0.552** (0.170)	0.540** (0.196)	0.249* (0.102)	0.306** (0.104)	1.138 (1.914)	1.313 (1.875)	−0.098 (0.706)	−1.214* (0.564)
Father's work (public wage omitted)										
Private wage	0.149 (0.088)	0.183* (0.093)	0.077 (0.088)	0.095 (0.095)	−0.035 (0.055)	−0.035 (0.053)	−0.642 (0.982)	−1.193 (0.950)	−0.088 (0.328)	−0.018 (0.318)
Self-emp./employer	0.173* (0.085)	0.159 (0.091)	0.153 (0.089)	0.143 (0.097)	0.044 (0.055)	0.039 (0.054)	0.605 (1.138)	−0.185 (0.960)	0.024 (0.324)	−0.100 (0.333)
Unpaid family worker/ no job	0.320 (0.495)	0.384 (0.549)	−0.134 (0.519)	−0.274 (0.584)	0.093 (0.272)	0.125 (0.291)	0.746 (6.559)	−3.486 (6.202)	0.448 (1.172)	1.359 (0.795)
Father's occupation (manager omitted)										
Clerical/sales	0.047 (0.120)	0.068 (0.127)	0.022 (0.129)	−0.000 (0.138)	0.042 (0.068)	0.036 (0.067)	−0.406 (1.234)	−0.236 (1.292)	1.851* (0.885)	1.149* (0.560)
Production non-agricultural	−0.063 (0.095)	−0.132 (0.102)	0.051 (0.101)	0.038 (0.109)	−0.046 (0.059)	−0.049 (0.057)	−1.155 (1.072)	−0.636 (1.114)	0.446 (0.432)	0.103 (0.347)
Agricultural	0.067 (0.103)	−0.008 (0.110)	−0.153 (0.106)	−0.099 (0.114)	−0.057 (0.065)	−0.064 (0.063)	−2.326* (1.158)	−1.959 (1.187)	0.072 (0.519)	−0.276 (0.389)
Females per 100 males (5 yrs older)	0.009*** (0.002)	0.005 (0.003)	−0.004 (0.002)	−0.002 (0.003)	0.002 (0.002)	0.002 (0.002)	−0.065 (0.035)	−0.052 (0.033)	0.012 (0.011)	0.001 (0.009)

	(1)	(2)	(3)	(4)	(5)
Nuclear	−0.280***		0.094*	0.288	0.960***
	(0.069)		(0.043)	(0.761)	(0.244)
Bride's side share	−0.001	0.001	−0.001		0.000
	(0.002)	(0.002)	(0.001)		(0.008)
Log total costs	0.030	0.091*		−0.491	0.033
	(0.041)	(0.040)		(0.439)	(0.143)
Age at marriage	−0.167*	−0.025	0.160**	−0.845	−2.299***
	(0.071)	(0.078)	(0.049)	(0.834)	(0.403)
Age at marr. sq./100	0.267	0.102	−0.345***	1.688	4.457***
	(0.149)	(0.165)	(0.104)	(1.781)	(0.911)
Percentage of rent in all housing and M born 1972+ F born 1977+ (SD)	−0.761	0.280	0.126	−3.621	−0.843
	(0.395)	(0.287)	(0.278)	(4.242)	(2.151)
Percentage of new in rent and M born 1972+ F born 1977+ (SD)	−0.289	0.684*	0.211	−3.195	−0.135
	(0.373)	(0.311)	(0.311)	(5.043)	(2.552)
Percentage of new in rent (SD)	0.328	−0.644*	−0.249	2.618	−0.183
	(0.372)	(0.309)	(0.310)	(5.035)	(2.545)
Percentage of rent in all housing (SD)	0.592	−0.194	−0.209	5.273	0.467
	(0.395)	(0.289)	(0.279)	(4.195)	(2.133)
Spouse ed. (same omitted)					
Spouse less educ.	0.202*	0.100	−0.065	0.266	0.168
	(0.080)	(0.078)	(0.050)	(0.901)	(0.270)
Spouse more educ.	0.035	0.132	0.162**	0.949	0.295
	(0.091)	(0.089)	(0.055)	(0.946)	(0.328)
Spouse ed. miss.	0.018	−0.248*	0.097	−0.557	6.160***
	(0.110)	(0.114)	(0.072)	(1.112)	(1.835)

(continued)

Appendix Table 29.A2 Continued

	Consanguinity		Nuclear residence		Log total costs		Bride's side share		Female age difference	
	Probit		Probit		OLS		OLS		OLS	
	Basic spec.	Ext. spec. w/marr. outcomes	Basic spec.	Ext. spec. w/marr. outcomes	Basic spec.	Ext. spec. w/marr. outcomes	Basic spec.	Ext. spec. w/marr. outcomes	Basic spec.	Ext. spec. w/marr. outcomes
Fathers' rel. ed. (same omitted)										
Own father less educ.		−0.022		−0.009		0.074		−0.940		−0.479
		(0.086)		(0.085)		(0.050)		(0.889)		(0.283)
Own father more educ.		−0.032		−0.003		−0.084		−0.799		0.091
		(0.099)		(0.097)		(0.060)		(1.042)		(0.302)
Consanguinity				−0.298***		0.029		−0.567		−0.632**
				(0.069)		(0.044)		(0.748)		(0.229)
Constant	−2.188***	0.690	1.096***	−0.119	9.983***	8.174***	45.481***	55.249***	4.547**	32.652***
	(0.316)	(0.971)	(0.323)	(0.561)	(0.219)	(0.604)	(4.541)	(11.419)	(1.750)	(4.316)
Regions included	Yes	Yes	Yes	Yes	Yes	Yes	Yes	Yes	Yes	Yes
N (observations)	3396	2985	3396	2985	2985	2985	3396	2985	3098	3098
Pseudo R2	0.081	0.114	0.120	0.145						
R2					0.216	0.238	0.082	0.086	0.036	0.089

Source: Authors' calculations based on ELMPS 2012.
Notes: *** p < 0.001,
** p < 0.01,
* p < 0.05.
Standard errors in parentheses.

CHAPTER 30

....

ECONOMICS, WOMEN, AND GENDER
The African Story

....

SOPHIE BESSIS

Women of Africa toil all their lives on land that they do not own,
to produce what they do not control and
at the end of the marriage through divorce or death,
they can be sent away empty handed.

Julius Kambarage Nyerere

30.1 INTRODUCTION

....

THERE is a student textbook of African economics, both pedagogical and scholarly, that has seen almost ten editions[1] since its first appearance in 1993, certainly useful for generations of francophones, except that the fledgling economists or policymakers who read it could have found nothing there indicating that the economy is first and foremost produced by the activities of men and women. Or rather, they would have found mention there of asexual companies in which there are neither hierarchies nor power relationships, nor distribution of roles and assignments between the sexes. The book states that "The domestic unit or "household" is a center for collective decisions"[2], which is to say that it is a sexually neutral economic unit; we do not know by what means and by whom the decision is made. However, in 1992, one year before the first appearance of this work, a joint report of the United Nations, CEPED (Center for Population and Development), UNFPA (United Nations Population Fund and the URD (Urgency, Rehabilitation, Development)) of the University of Lomé stated, with regard to sub-Saharan Africa that "a significant dimension of shared household responsibilities concerns the relationship, often adversary, between the man and the woman. Each of them usually has different economic and financial strategies. Polygamy, familial pressures,

---

[1] Hugon (2009).   [2] Hugon (2009: 58).

instances of non-coresidence, inheritance problems, and mistrust are often grounds for separate strategies. Within one household, the man and the woman make separate plans." (Ceped 1992: 45). In this chapter it is argued that the family unit is the space where power relationships are concentrated and exacerbated.

Other notable studies of Africa in the 2000s totally or almost totally ignore the question of gender in their analyses and/or scenarios. Thus, in the study entitled *Prospective Africaine* (African Prospective), written by Hugon (2000), there is no mention of women in the analysis of changes that could determine several future scenarios. A single variable relating to them is mentioned—fertility, as always, but without any connection to their status. In the work *Afrique 2025, quels futurs possibles pour l'Afrique au sud du Sahara* (What possible futures for Africa south of the Sahara),[3] prepared by a team of researchers from several countries, the gender aspect of development is also absent, even in the chapters devoted to the question of the peasantry. There are many such examples but it must be said that they are more often found in the work of French education researchers than in publications from the Anglo-Saxon academic world.

In spite of all the advances noted in the past 40 years, in many respects women remain the blind spot in economic discourse, whereas other disciplines, especially anthropology, which cannot be imagined outside of the study of social relations between the sexes, and also the disciplines of demographics and sociology, have long taken into account the centrality of the gendered character of all human activity. Certainly many economists have been trying for several years not to hide the "gendered" dimension, since forgetting this nowadays constitutes "political incorrectness." But with few exceptions, this dimension in their studies is simply added to analysis rather than being used to modify the content and point of view of their investigations. Moreover, the factor is most often included only in microeconomics, whereas the broader sphere of macroeconomics remains almost completely asexual. And finally, up to the present, real attention has been devoted to gender and its implications only by female economists who are usually also classified as feminists. There has been some reorientation of research, but this is still far from being the general case. In fact, it can be said that we had to wait until women began to enter the field before the discipline of economics, long an exclusively masculine domain, noticed that the public and private spheres were indeed gendered.

In the field of development economics that, since the end of the 1950s, has become an almost independent branch of the discipline, women have been, until the 1970s, even more invisible, if we dare to risk the negative comparative. In the old industrialized nations, the two World Wars of the twentieth century in fact accelerated the inclusion of women in the ranks of wage earners, which is the source of their economic and social visibility. But in the "developing" countries, an expression used up to the 1980s, although access to independence often gave women political rights ranging from the right to vote to the possibility of being elected, economic literature does not recognize them and development literature considers them only from the point of view of their reproductive function. No development theory in effect at the time—from the Rostovians to the Dependentists and Marxists—questions the impact on the economy, labor, production, of the traditional sexual roles and their eventual evolution. This is not a topic. During this period, the schools considered progressive

[3] Futurs africains collective (2003).

or heterodox are in no way less deficient in this respect than their counterparts located on the conservative side of the discipline. The review *Development Dialogue*, published by the Dag Hammarskjöld Foundation of Uppsala, Sweden, and until the 1980s considered to be a research Bible for "another development," only deals with women in an anecdotal and marginal fashion.[4] The question begins to be asked timidly in the 1970s, when the topic of poverty intrudes into the debates, the theory of *trickle down* having been contradicted by the facts.

As noted by the UNDP in 1995, "the definitions of productive activity remain strongly connected to the existence of monetary revenue, while women often carry out activities that are truly productive but outside the monetary circuit" (UNDP 1995). Yet, according to the analysis of the Belgian researcher Eliane Vogel-Polsky, the exclusively monetary approaches "hide what women researchers call the division between productive and reproductive work. This work of social reproduction taken on by women in all parts of the world, is not considered to be work; it is not included in the national statistics. However, it does correspond to an activity essential to the reproduction of life in society and corresponds to 'care' [...]. At the heart of all domestic responsibilities is 'care', assuring the reproduction of the male labor force, the socially recognized workers." (Vogel-Polsky 2004). "We must take seriously the thinking of the economists who are proposing to renew the criteria for productive activity and the creation of wealth," added the authors of the UNDP report.[5] The least one can say is that this has not yet happened.

From independence until the 1970s, the economic role of women in sub-Saharan Africa was neglected, despite the fact that they traditionally participate in agricultural food production more than in any other region in the world. Especially in the agricultural sector this has caused tragic errors in orientation to the world of work. Almost all training and popularization programs targeted men, even in policy areas where their involvement was non-existent, while women were provided with no training, or almost none, until the 1990s. The same neglect has been observed in North Africa, that is to say, in Arabized Africa, from Morocco to Egypt. This is surprising because the second half of the nineteenth century and since before colonization, all the intellectual and political debates dealing with modernity in Tunisia and in Egypt especially, have made evolution in the condition of women an inescapable prerequisite for global social change.

Even worse, the preeminence of the Western androcentric economic model has, in many cases, made African women lose prerogatives or economic activities, particularly in the commercial sphere, which were theirs before standards were imposed on them by international donors. Adoption of the Western division of gender roles led to further marginalization of African women: to the exclusions considered traditional, characteristic of African societies, were added exclusions brought in by the androcentric strategies of the donors. Esther Boserup (1970) broadened this observation by suggesting that gender inequalities remained negligible in places where the market economy had not penetrated. With the expansion of the Western model, discrimination against women worsened, thanks to the specialization of

---

[4] For example, the 1978/2 issue devotes a paper to the question of education, "Another development in education," centered on Mozambique, Guinea Bissau, and Zimbabwe, without mentioning the inequalities of school access between boys and girls. The same silence is found in the 1981/1 issue, in a paper entitled "Another development and the local space," that is to say, the special place where feminine economic activities are carried out. There are countless examples, just for this progressive journal, of the invisibility of women in academic or "militant" economic research.

[5] UNDP, World Report 1995.

genders to specific tasks, and the fact that women were confined to "care" while men gained monopoly over lucrative activities.

Economics still finds it hard to accept itself as a social science and always aspires to be seen as an exact science, that is, free of human contingencies. It is not our intention to analyze the intellectual failures from such an obsession, which explains why the study of the importance of women and gender relations in the continent's economy has been a late and slow process and still is not completed. In fact, the level of interest in women's issues and to the problematique of gender has evolved with the meaning of the word "development" itself. Depending on whether the definition of development was primarily determined by economics, by social concerns, or by the need to respect human rights, the importance granted to women in the strategies promoted by experts and other stakeholders has fluctuated on the list of priorities. This chapter discusses the main waves of economic development thinking about women's issues in Africa, and identifies the main intellectual players. It also discusses the impediments to a more complete recognition of gender relations in economic analyses of Africa and how they affect the evolution of knowledge.

30.2 A SLOW EVOLUTION SINCE THE INDEPENDENCE YEARS

Starting at the beginning of the 1970s a series of social dynamics forced first the politicians and then the economists to move toward progressive integration of women's condition into their deliberations and actions.

30.2.1 Change from within

The accession of all the African countries to independence between 1956 (Morocco and Tunisia) and 1974 (sub-Saharan Portuguese colonies) led at varying rates and with different intensities to societal changes with a direct effect on the condition of women.

In addition to granting political rights, as already mentioned, the independence movements were the starting point for a true revolution in education. Several states made universal education a policy priority and devoted a considerable portion of their budgets to it. In this new context, education for girls, up to that time limited to the urban well-to-do, made a trail-blazing leap. Countries north of the Sahara, like Tunisia and Algeria and in the south, a number of nations of Central and Eastern Africa, saw an explosion in the number of educated girls over a period of twenty years. In barely one generation, between the end of the 1950s and the end of the 1970s, women with diplomas, ranging from completion of primary or basic school to the university, held positions in numerous sectors of the world of paid work, chiefly at the lower levels of public functions caught up in expansion and in the fields of health and education.

In the countries that, after a first phase of industrialization by substitution for imports—a system dominant in the 1960s but that rapidly revealed its deficiencies and roadblocks—turned toward the southeast Asian model of development by export of manufactured goods, the feminine workforce increased exponentially. In fact, women made up the great battalions of the manufacturing, food, and textile industries, and later of assembling industrial consumer goods, as was the case in Tunisia, Morocco, Mauritius, and Kenya. In certain countries like Tunisia, a voluntary family planning policy was combined with education to limit fertility and delay the age of the first marriage, increasing women's possibilities of access to paid employment. With a delay of 10–20 years, other states like Algeria, Morocco, Kenya, or Zimbabwe came to almost the same results.

30.2.2 The new feminism and the thinking of international institutions

Coming from the United States in the 1960s, a new moment in the world feminist movement permeated the fields of social science well beyond its activist side. Combined with the first disappointments in post-independence economic development, that forced the actors to ask themselves new questions and to approach problems from other angles, and with slow and uneven but real progress in women's public visibility, feminist research from the early 1970s had a determining influence on the concerns and the discourse of the United Nations.

In Mexico in 1975, by organizing the first international conference devoted to the "second sex," that had been completely ignored up to then by development agencies, the UN opened a cycle that has never been closed since then. The next 30 years were punctuated by a series of world conferences that would attract the attention of the planet's decision makers to the fate of the dominated half of humanity and would forge the instruments of a progressive but radical reform of the traditional relations between the sexes. After the Mexico conference, the three conferences of Copenhagen in 1980, Nairobi in 1985, and Beijing in 1995 presented three occasions for the United Nations to try to mobilize the "international community" behind a topic that had become highly sensitive in the course of the decades and to consolidate the presence of the feminine question on the development agenda. In 2000 and 2005, special sessions of the General Assembly, entitled Beijing + 5 and Beijing + 10, provided an update of progress achieved and evaluated the distance still to be covered before arriving at the equality that has been an official priority of the UN since Mexico. Regular updates have since then been provided by all agencies of the UN system.

The regular organization of international conferences in which the associations of civil society have extensively taken part (in 1995, more than 30 000 women attended the NGO Forum at the Fourth World Conference on Women in Beijing) has, moreover, contributed to the emergence of a global female galaxy playing an increasingly visible part on national and regional scenes. Although the Western feminist movement has been sufficiently massive and organized to exist without the support of the United Nations, women's movements of the developing countries have used the discourse and the normative texts of the United Nations as powerful instruments for the legitimation of their existence and activities. In this dynamic march forward, the creation of *l'Association des femmes africaines pour la recherché et le développement* (Association of African Women for Research and Development) (AFARD) in 1977, introduced in Africa a school of feminist research that has had quite an important impact.

This persistence of UN engagement on this issue since 1975 is also evident in the evolution of the approach to the feminine question by the international organization, as more refined attention has been given to the mechanisms of sexual domination and the number of studies on this subject has been increased. It can be said that the Beijing conference brought a conclusion to two decades of engagement of the UN system in favor of "inclusion of women in development," opening a new cycle of international deliberation, more focused on the problem of gender, that is to say on all the economic, social, and cultural side effects of the sexual division of reproduction and production. In fact, it became clear in a series of reports that policies aimed exclusively at women could not achieve satisfactory results, just as political actions that do not take into account the respective roles of men and women in society could not reduce inequalities. In this domain, the United Nations echoed the deep conceptual evolution experienced by "feminology" during the last decades of the twentieth century.

The World Bank, for its part, started to pay attention to women's issues in the mid-1970s in response to the United Nations' request for participation in the Mexico conference of 1975.[6] The United Nations having proclaimed the years 1975–1985 "International Decade of the Woman," the second half of the 70s saw the flourishing among donor agencies of many ideas on the topic of integrating women into development. The World Bank took part in this in 1977 by naming a woman to be advisor on "women and development" and by publishing in 1979 a major policy document on this topic. In the first half of the 1980s, its interest in this topic grew: 35 case studies and evaluations were published between 1979 and 1985. But the financial commitment necessary to strengthen the position of women in the economy of developing countries was almost nil. Although the Washington institution was willing to encourage thinking about them it was not sufficiently interested to devote financing to them.

The two groups of international organizations (the UN institutions on the one hand and the Bretton Woods institutions—World Bank and International Monetary Fund—on the other hand) based the design of their strategies and feminine policies on different theoretical approaches to the notion of gender. The UN drew on the theories of critical feminist economists. The Bank, on the other hand, used the arguments of the feminist economic school working within neo-classical paradigms, which postulates that the market is sexually neutral.[7] Eliane Vogel-Polsky translates this dichotomy in the following terms: "In the orientation of international financial institutions, we find…neither a questioning of the exclusion of women from all effective participation in political, economic, and social decision making nor the will to reconstruct the problematics of government in terms of gender. On the other hand, it must be noted that for a decade, the orientation of the United Nations (Economic and Social Council, UNDP, etc.) is characterized by a recognition of the integration of the gender dimension in the definition of all the policies within their competence."[8]

In fact, until the 1980s, the only concern was their "integration" into the development process and very few studies emphasized the fact that this integration is as old as economics itself, but has always been a part of a logic of domination and/or exploitation. Gender-specific statistics started to come out, but the economic literature about women remained rudimentary and did not offer any structured analyses. NGOs began tackling the issue in the beginning of the 1970s (Mitchnik 1972).[9] An important study was released at the end of the 1970s,

---

[6] For the history of the recognition of the women's question by the World Bank, see Gender issues in World Bank lending, World Bank (1995).

[7] In this connection, see Miller and Razavi (1998).

[8] Miller and Razavi (1998).

[9] Note that the period is still defining the essence of the subject in the singular.

conducted by the United Nations and the NGO Enda Third World, based in Dakar, opening with a diagnosis of sexual and inegalitarian division of economic tasks in the village environment. "One often tends to exclude the search for causality between gender relations and the economic relations internal to each society. Not identifying real problems is also a way to avoid thinking about the need for structural change" (Langley and Ngom 1978: 17).

On the other hand, the "Berg Report" famous in its day, published in 1981 by the World Bank to discuss the "measures to be taken…in order to remediate the current African economic difficulties" and which favored a liberal shock treatment, only made one mention of women's issues in its diagnosis of the continental situation and this concerns education: "Educated women, even if they do not participate in the labor force, can have a significant impact on the country's economy through lower fertility rates, health information, and more "household production" (Berg 1981: 81). Unarguably, this is less than the minimum.

It was not until the second half of the 1980s that the first consequences of the structural adjustment programs became obvious: that women became the object of an almost completely separate analysis. In sub-Saharan Africa, where development organizations worked to mitigate the particularly brutal effects of the SAPs (Structural Adjustment Programs) and where the international financial institutions were trying to create a liberal[10] *Homo economicus tropicalis*, it becomes obvious that this man may very well be a woman.

30.3 A TURNING POINT IN THE 1980S

30.3.1 Adjustment and women

We will not go back to the content and overall results of the adjustment policies that opened a new era in the history of development and its theories. As far as our subject is concerned, it is only necessary to remember that for workers at the same social level, adjustment policies did hurt women more than men, as they systematically increased the "invisible" part of their work to the detriment of its remunerated part. In the remunerated sector, casual, informal female activities often became the substitute for formal employment. In general, it is the women who are responsible for the reproduction of the labor force and all of what is being called human resources. The cut in social investment imposed by the SAP programs and the obsession for making social enterprises (such as hospitals) profitable led to the shifting of some of the public sector burden toward the domestic sphere, that is, toward women. The reduction of public spending on infrastructure has had similar consequences: in Tanzania and Ghana; it has been observed that the deterioration of roads and the increase in "modern" transportation costs led to an increase of recourse to portage, largely provided by women. As noted by Unicef (1987), the cuts in social investment were "financed" by an increased effort by the poorest women.

Likewise, policies aiming at reducing aggregate demand by increasing the price of available goods transferred some of the burden of the formal sector work toward the family. Thus, the observed decline in the standard of living in Africa led, among other things, to

---

[10] "Liberal" is used in its French sense here to refer to conservative, neo-classical policies.

reduced consumption of manufactured products (domestic or imported), especially in the food sector, as people tried to take advantage of cheaper, non-manufactured goods. As a result, women saw their tasks of artisanal food processing increase. This burdening of their workload was not perceived by the proponents of adjustment, to the extent that it is part of women's unaccounted-for work. In sum, the savings resulting from adjustment in public sector wages have thus largely involved a transfer of public social responsibilities to the unpaid work of women (Bessis 1996).

This radical change of context has given women a more than anecdotal importance in the eyes of experts, and especially those in international development organizations, starting with the World Bank. During the painful years when the poor, indebted countries saw the imposition of drastic austerity programs, where the states stopped recruiting, where unemployment increased, where the only available funds were devoted to repaying the external debt, during these years where the mere word "adjustment" scared the people's neighborhoods from Casablanca to Abidjan, women stopped being invisible. Present on all fronts—from cultivation of food to commerce or to managing community life—everywhere devising survival strategies for the extremely hard times, creating a social bond where families split up because of the crisis and because of the weakening of the status of the men, who were the first to suffer from the slump of the formal economy, they provided enormous efforts and probably made it possible to avoid social explosions. Certainly at an exorbitant price, the decade of the 1980s gave African women the visibility that they had not had before. Although it was obvious in all the developing countries undergoing adjustment, the phenomenon was actually spectacular in sub-Saharan Africa where, because of a certain number of changes undergone by many countries (wars, male migrations, either seasonal or long-term, increased mortality due to AIDS, increase in the number of refugees and displaced persons), more and more women became heads of families: toward the mid-1980s, they led 60% of rural households in Mozambique, 50% in Congo Brazzaville, 45% in Zambia. The totality of rural and urban households led by women south of the Sahara was at that time about 20% (FAO 1987).

30.3.2 Economic "feminism"

There is now wide consensus that women played a major role in the great change imposed on developing economies. This begs the questions: what if, instead of accompanying the changes, they were able to speed them up? What if, by intensifying their involvement in economic life and accumulating more means, precious time was in fact gained by the proponents of a global plan for liberal economic modernization? These hypotheses, based on the discovery of women's ability to manage the crisis, have undeniably changed the perception of women held by international development institutions. With nothing much to lose by the weakening of socio-cultural rigidities that had previously impeded their emancipation, women could actually become ideal agents to spread a pure form of popular capitalism, already visible in their informal sector activities. Incidentally, it is not surprising that the success stories publicized by the World Band in justification of its policies on gender typically refer to entrepreneurial women who have made it through their hard work, with some external help.

The Bank's "feminism" is thus instrumental or, if one prefers, functional. The reason for changing the condition of women is not because it is inconsistent with the modernization model designed for developing countries. Capture by the merchant sphere of the dynamism displayed by the women under all circumstances, including the most difficult, is a significant step toward the imposition of market logic. The question of the law is thus secondary for an organization that perceives women primarily as economic actors of a new type and possible guarantors of a social stability that is more and more difficult to ensure under current global market conditions. Thus, women are instrumentalized as their promotion is not an aim in itself but as a tactic for the implementation of the Bank's policies for growth and the containment of poverty. It is in sub-Saharan Africa that the Bank's gender projects are the most numerous and institution prides itself for having given gender its rightful place in the discussions on poverty since the 1993 Special Program of Assistance for Africa (SPA) launched under the aegis of the United Nations with other donors (Oostendorp 2004).

Given the influence of the World Bank and the spirit of the times, this type of analysis enjoyed a great success starting in the late 1980s and was endorsed by a large number of bilateral and multilateral development agencies. Because it was no longer possible to hide question of male domination and gender relations, they repeated the argumentation of the Bank to justify their interest in women's fate. Accordingly the OECD announced a ministerial conference on the theme of "Competitiveness and Growth: Integration of questions of equality of men and women" in November 2000, insisting on the "economic arguments in favor of integration of equality between men and women in public and private sectors and examples of best practices," and on "the reasons for which integration of equality between men and women contribute to strengthening the performance of economies, competitiveness and growth." The European Commission, for its part, introduced the gender problem in the context of the eighth European Development Fund (EDF), whereas it had not been included in the seventh (1989–1994).

Among the tools developed to concretize the emergence of populist feminine capitalism in Africa, micro-credit took a privileged place. Inspired by the experience of the Grameen Bank, created by Mohammed Yunus in the early 1970s in Bangladesh, and with a majority of the bank's borrowers being women, it spread to the whole developing world during the decades of the1990s and the 2000s to such an extent that the United Nations proclaimed 2005 the "International Year of Microcredit." Institutions granting it mushroomed on the African continent. Until the surge of market finance in a sector whose profitability becomes apparent and the resulting crises starting in 2009, microcredit was advertised by all donors as the ideal instrument to promote the economic emancipation of women. After the setbacks experienced by a number of women's associations because of debt overload, the praise of this type of credit scheme has become more discreet. The hazards of microcredit and its relatively limited effects on the general condition of poor African women in fact show that a technical solution, no matter how ingenious and innovative, can only make marginal corrections of problems that are principally societal and political.

In reality, until recently, whether riddled with contradictions that seemed insurmountable or whether they revealed cynicism, the gender policies of international organizations were marked by a series of paradoxes. While references to the right to equality have become widespread and redefinition of gender roles are now considered necessary, UN actions in the field have often reproduced in almost caricatural fashion the dominant sexual division of labor. Certainly, UN functionaries have learned to master the vocabulary of gender. The integrated approach ("mainstreaming") has no more secrets for them. But who has not seen in sub-Saharan Africa the so-called "income-generating activities" reserved to women and still limited to embroidery—a traditionally masculine trade in Africa but which has become feminized under the effect of dominant models spread by the experts—as well as dyeing, soap-making, and other activities that perpetuate the ghettoization of women in the least rewarding economic work? In fact, there is a continued willingness to "integrate" them in the monetary economy without making the effort to overturn the logic that produces the inequality. Although the discourse on gender has gained recognition, neither the agencies of the UN or those of the World Bank have changed the androcentric logic of their macro-economic programs, their policy tools, their actions in the client countries and their infra-structure plans. Martha Nussbaum has taken these contradictions into account, observing that "economics as now very often practiced cannot deal adequately with the central issues at stake in the lives of women, and with their urgent claims" and in criticizing "a single-minded focus on utility" both in theory and in development practices (Nussbaum and Glover 1995).

30.4 ECONOMICS OVERWHELMED BY LAW

30.4.1 The limits of economism

Since the 2000s, it has become increasingly difficult to address sexual inequalities and to allow women to give their full measure in the economic sphere without examining their legal status in most African countries. The exhaustion of economistic rhetoric of institu-tional gender discourse is more and more obvious, and many of its proponents acknowl-edge that the law must now be taken into account. But the challenge is the following: how to convert women's energies into market-related activities when in most African familial and land-related legislation, women are, among other things, deprived of the right to practice a professional activity without their husband's permission, when land ownership is prohibited to them and when they are intensely discriminated against in matters of inheritance?

This question reveals how law enters the economic sphere. In a way, thinking about the feminine condition—and about labor issues more generally, though in a different way—forces economics to give up its eternal monologue with itself and to acknowledge the many facets of a complex phenomenon. Such a recognition is of major importance as it slowly brings out of the shadows issues that were previously unthinkable. It is increasingly being recognized that denial of a number of rights to women also affects the economy and demographics. The topics of women's access to land or of inequality of the sexes as regards inheritance are shaking up analyses that until now were considered conventional wisdom. If one considered the slow pace of demographic transition in sub-Saharan Africa, in its central and Soudano-Sahelian parts in particular, a factor that drastically limits the rate and the very nature of development, then the issue of legal inequality cannot be underestimated. A few trailblazers, mostly women, economists in the Association of Tunisian Women for Research and Development (ATWRD) and the Collectif Maghreb Egalité[11] (Maghrebian Collective

[11] Among others: Collectif Maghreb-égalité (2006).

for Equality), have conducted path-breaking research on these topics, which the entire discipline of economics must now confront.

In 2004 an OECD study[12] challenged the opinion according to which increased access for women to education, health, credit, and the possibility of employment, in association with economic growth, is sufficient to improve significantly their role in the economy of developing countries. The study argued that these measures may not be effective as long as the institutional leadership limits the participation of women in economic affairs. They estimated that social institutions, that is, the laws, the standards, the traditions, and the codes of behavior of a society, represent the most important factor determining women's freedom of choice in matters of economic activity. These norms not only affect the economic role of women directly, they also determine their access to education and health care. Following this study, the Development Center of the OECD in 2009 developed an index to measure the discrimination restricting women's access to resources. Its "Social Institutions and Gender Index (SIGI)" was introduced as a measure of the inclusion of women in economic and social life. Twelve variables, ranging from institutional norms to domestic behaviors, premature and forced marriages, genital mutilation, restrictions of freedom of movement and inheritance inequality make up this index. In studies conducted in Sudan and Mali, countries where the family codes are among the most discriminatory on the continent, the use of the SIGI has shown that construction of schools for girls or the granting of microcredit do not have much effect if the women do not have freedom of movement and if they are deprived of access to land, technology, and information. It has also been estimated that African women have only received approximately 10% of the total assistance provided for the agricultural sector[13] despite being producers of food. Family laws are far from identical among countries across the continent but everywhere, with the exception of Cape Verde, enshrine the primacy of the male.

In the 1990s the UNDP broke new ground with its index of human development (IHD), which includes a gender-specific index of human development that takes into account gender discrimination in assessing the degree of a society's development. Still, the OCDE studies are interesting for our purposes as they integrate and examine legal issues through an economic lens, showing that it is impossible to dissociate the economy from its political, social, and cultural environment. Culture has always been a framework of analysis used by many development economists who argued that the primacy of the acquisition of social capital against the accumulation of real capital—thought to be an important feature of African societies—has seriously impeded the development of local forms of capitalism.[14] Yet surprisingly, the cultural analysis of African societies has devoted little attention to gender relations. Thus all these new studies are forcing economists to deal with factors they did not think worth considering up to now.

30.4.2 A high-stakes exercise

This brings us to the key question: what is the state of family law in Africa? Few countries have radically modified the law to make it more egalitarian. Tunisia did it from the time of

[12] Morrisson and Jütting (2004).

[13] Source: NGO International, Women's Learning Partnership for Rights, Development, and Peace (WLP). http://www.learningpartnership.org/facts/human.phtml.

[14] Cf. Futurs africains collective (2003). More recently, one of the latest works in French on the African economy, Jacquemot (2013), devoted two chapters to the rationality of traditional and hybrid social systems.

independence in 1956. And whether this is a coincidence or a causal relationship, Tunisia is one of the African, and in particular Arabo-African countries, where women have a high rate of participation in the modern economic sector and where the highest percentage of women CEOs is found.

In the 2000s, several African countries decided to liberalize their family law but did not go as far as ensuring equal rights between genders. Moreover, several conflicting legal regimes exist within the same country: civil legislation called "modern;" religious law, generally Muslim law; and traditional customary law. In several countries, such as South Africa, civil legislation is egalitarian but coexists with profoundly conservative customary law. In countries with this multiplicity of legal regimes, citizens are free to choose the judicial system under which they would like their family matters to be decided. Taking into account the state of submission in which the majority of women are held, it goes without saying that, outside of modestly modernized urban minorities, this choice is made by men.

Throughout Africa, the quest for reforms has led to either new legal frameworks or the resistance from resolutely conservative political classes and religious or traditional elites. These two outcomes are obvious in the following three examples.

In Benin, a new "Code of Persons and of the Family" was adopted in August 2004 after vigorous lobbying by the national organizations defending the rights of women. This text put an end to the dualism between traditional law expressed in legal terms by the French colonists in the 1930s (the "*Coutumier du Dahomey*" [Customary of Dahomey]), and the so-called modern law. In principle, customary law became obsolete after a 1996 decision of the Constitutional Court. A new code provides for equality between men and women concerning the legal age for marriage, set at 18 years, parental authority and inheritance, and prohibits the levirate and polygamy. The promulgation of a 2007 law on rural land, which provides for equal access to natural resources in general and to agricultural land in particular, completed this disposition. The same year, Morocco implemented profound reforms to its family code, the *Muduwana,* which grants to women a series of rights they had been deprived of but does not prohibit polygamy. In both cases, the new legislation permitted undeniable advances without entirely doing away with the privilege of masculinity. However, the new legislation was not actually implemented in either of the two countries; it remains practically ignored in rural areas and the discriminations are far from gone. Mali is a completely different case. At the end of several years of intense debate, a new code of persons and of family was adopted by the National Assembly in 2009. But strong resistance and large demonstrations by conservative and religious forces convinced the Head of State not to promulgate it. Under the pressure of religious organizations, a new code was finally promulgated in 2011, but it reinstated almost all the discriminatory provisions of the former legislation and did not lead to any true progress. These examples show the intensity of resistance to legal equality of the sexes in the great majority of African countries. They also show that dealing with such subjects is politically very sensitive, since in all societies, the status and condition of women is the last refuge for the identities that are considered to be endangered. While most African elites do not see any threat in the profound socioeconomic changes that have occurred in the last half-century and in particular since the 1980s, for some of them, any change in gender relations favorable to women is seen as a danger.

In a context marked by perpetuation of legal discrimination, it seems difficult to achieve true equality among women and men in economic matters. Economists are already insensitive to the importance of gender relations. It is unlikely that they will take on the legal challenges that underline the economic disparities between men and women. Yet these disparities must be addressed before gender issues can be included in economic analysis.

30.5 Conclusion

This chapter has argued that the discipline of economics, by failing to take into account the question of women and gender deprives itself of an excellent analytical tool for the understanding of the changes and resistances to change in African economies. The advances in the last decades have been real, to the extent that these questions are no longer completely ignored, but much remains to be done to strengthen the dominant mode of macroeconomic thinking. Still, given the importance of female labor and the role that women play as shock absorbers in time of crisis, Africa has contributed significantly to bringing gender analysis of economics out of the atmosphere of secrecy to which dominant thought had confined it. One must hope that the pressure of reality will force economics to continue integrating gender analysis into its field and pursue an evolution that it has barely begun.

References

Berg, E. (1981). *Le développement accéléré en Afrique au sud du Sahara, programme indicatif d'action* [Accelerated Development in Sub-Saharan Africa]. Washington, DC: World Bank.

Bessis, S. (1996). La féminisation de la pauvreté [Feminization of poverty], in J. Bisillat (ed.), *Femmes du Sud chefs de famille* [Women of the South, heads of families]. Paris: Karthala.

Boserup, E. (1970). *Woman's Role in Economic Development.* London, George Allen and Unwin Ltd.

Ceped (1992). *Condition de la femme et population, le cas de l'Afrique francophone* [Condition of women and population, the case of francophone Africa]. Office of the United Nations in Vienna and Ceped, with the collaboration of UNFPA and the Unit for demographic research, University of Benin, Lomé, Togo. Ceped, Paris.

Collectif Maghreb-égalité (2006). *Le travail des Maghrébines, l'autre enjeu.* [The work of Maghrebian women, the other stakes]. Rabat: Marsam-GTZ.

Futurs africains collective (2003). Afrique 2025, quels futurs possibles pour l'Afrique au sud du Sahara. Paris: Editions Karthala.

Hugon, P. (2009). *L'économie de l'Afrique.* Paris: Editions la Découverte, collection Repères.

Hugon, P. (ed.) (2000). *Prospective africaine.* Study presented at the Cered-Forum/Cernea Colloquium. May 25.

Jacquemot, P. (2013). *Economie politique de l'Afrique contemporaine* [Political economy of contemporary Africa]. Paris: Armand Colin, collection U.

Langley, P., and Ngom, M. (1978). *Technologies villageoises en Afrique de l'Ouest et du Centre en faveur de la femme et de l'enfant* [*Cameroun, Centrafrique, Guinée, Haute Volta, Sénégal, Zaïre*]. Unicef Publication.

Miller, C., and Razavi, S. (1998). *Gender Analysis, Alternative Paradigms.* Gender in development alternative series. New York: UNDP.

Mitchnik, D.A. (1972). *Le rôle de la femme dans le développement rural au Zaïre* [The role of women in rural development in Zaïre]. Kinshasa: Oxfam.

Morrisson, C., and Jütting, J. (2004). *The impact of social institutions on the economic role of women in developing countries.* Development Center of the OCDE, Working Paper No. 234, May.

Nussbaum, M., and Glover, J. (1995). "Introduction," in M.C. Nussbaum and J. Glover (eds.), *Women, Culture, and Development: A Study of Human Capabilities* Oxford: Oxford University Press.

Oostendorp, R.H. (2004). *Globalization and the Gender Wage Gap.* World Bank Policy Research Working Paper No. 3256, Washington, DC.

UNDP (1995). *Rapport mondial sur le développement humain* [World report on human development]. Paris: éditions Economica.

Unicef (1987). *L'ajustement à visage humain* [Adjustment with a human face]. New York: Unicef.

Vogel-Polsky, E. (2004). *La gouvernance et les femmes* [Governance and women]. Brussels: Free University of Brussels.

CHAPTER 31

GENDER, ECONOMIC GROWTH, AND DEVELOPMENT IN SUB-SAHARAN AFRICA

STEPHANIE SEGUINO AND MAUREEN WERE

31.1. INTRODUCTION

AFTER years of stagnation, African economies are exhibiting promising growth and development prospects. Enhancing, sustaining, and ensuring an all-inclusive growth trajectory remains a challenge, given evidence of wide and persistent economic disparities on the continent. Recent research suggests that intergroup equality, and in particular, gender equality can be a stimulus to growth and development. The research that identifies the macroeconomic role of gender has yet to be integrated into the growth and development research on Africa, however.[1] In an effort to address this lacuna and to forge a link between these two literatures, this chapter explores theories on the role of gender equality in economic growth and development, as well as the implications of macroeconomic policies on gender outcomes, focusing on the sub-Saharan Africa (SSA) region.

31.2 ENGENDERING MACROECONOMIC GROWTH AND DEVELOPMENT THEORIES

In recent decades, observers have linked SSA's poor growth performance to several factors—geography, institutions, and, more recently, ethnic diversity. In many ways, these

---

[1] Two special issues of *World Development* (November 1995 and July 2000), as well as the July 2009 special issue of *Feminist Economics* showcase this body of work.

analyses have been backward looking, attempting to explain why Africa failed to grow as rapidly as other developing regions. A newer approach has been the strategy of growth diagnostics, a tool for identifying country- and region-specific constraints to improving living standards (Rodrik 2007) and policy priorities. Using this approach, Ndulu et al. (2007) identify low returns to physical and capital investment, a demographic burden that results in a high dependency ratio, limited diffusion of technology, and weak institutions as the most important constraints on SSA growth.

Starkly absent in this literature (and, in particular, from growth diagnostics) is the role of gender in influencing macroeconomic well-being. Failure to account for the role of gender can impede efforts to stimulate and sustain growth in SSA, given the growing body of evidence demonstrating the significance of micro-level gender relations as a macroeconomic variable.

A major intellectual project that offers insights for macroeconomic growth and development theory is feminist economic analysis. This has contributed to an understanding of the gendered nature of the economy and of institutions beyond the household to include governments, firms, and markets. The integration of the role of gender—and gender inequality—offers a more complete portrait of the factors influencing economic growth and development, balance-of-payments, and fiscal sustainability of public spending. Armed with this knowledge, scholars have "engendered" traditional macroeconomic theory in order to trace the feedback loops between gender relations at the micro-level and macroeconomic outcomes. The lessons from this research caution us that failure to attend to gender effects can lead to weak, ineffectual, and indeed harmful macro-policy decisions. Moreover, to the extent that policy makers desire to improve broadly shared well-being, intergroup inequality by gender remains a central target of concern.

A major finding of this body of work is that gender inequality affects development and growth, and is itself endogenous—that is, macroeconomic policies and the pace of growth influence the degree of gender equality. Structural adjustment programs in Africa provided the initial impetus for this research. Economic reforms in the 1980s had called for cutbacks in state services such as health care, food subsidies, and education. Feminist economists noted the failure to consider how such changes affected the relationship between the "productive" economy and the "reproductive" economy (Gladwin 1994; Elson 1995). Public sector spending cuts in health and other services transferred the burden of providing care to households where mostly women undertake unpaid work. Already time poor, women then were the unacknowledged shock absorbers that helped households adjust to cuts to state level spending (Blackden and Wodon 2006). Perhaps because unpaid work is invisible in national income accounts, these dynamics that severely strained women's well-being went unnoticed. As we will see later in this chapter, increased time burdens for women can contribute to reduced economy-wide human capacity development, with significant and long-lasting effects on children's future productivity.

A second gendered policy prescription in structural adjustment programs was to shift production from non-tradables to tradable goods to address balance-of-payments constraints. Assumptions about the human resources needed for this shift failed to account for the barriers to labor reallocation due to rigid gender rules on the division of labor and control over resources, with implications for food security. For example, in SSA, men tend to control income from cash crops. As a result, they were largely the beneficiaries of the realignment of incentives to promote cash crop exports. This increased male bargaining power within the household, diminishing women's ability to direct resources to their own and their children's well-being. This outcome is due in part to the fact that household income is frequently not pooled, and men's and women's spending priorities differ (Haddad, Hoddinott, and Alderman 1997).

These are just two examples of the differential gender effects of macroeconomic policy, intended or not. These effects stem from a variety of factors, including a persistent (although varying) gender division of labor within and outside the household and systematic gender inequality in access to and control over resources. Mainstream macroeconomic analysis, which overwhelmingly focuses on the paid economy, has until recently ignored unpaid or non-market work. This stands in contrast to microeconomic analyses of intra-household resource allocation, reproductive labor, and non-market production. And yet, a significant proportion of total economic activity of the developing world takes place within families and households. Care work, reproductive labor, and subsistence production are integral to the well-being of the household and the formation of human capacities used in market production (Folbre 2014).

31.3 The Role of Gender Inequality in Influencing Economic Growth and Development

How would an expanded theoretical framework that incorporates the role of gender in explaining growth and development theory differ from current approaches? A starting point for understanding the role of gender, and in particular gender (in)equality in influencing growth and development is to clearly identify the salient forms of inequality to better understand the transmission mechanisms. Gender inequality occurs in three key domains: *capabilities, livelihoods*, and *empowerment/agency. Capabilities* refers to the functionings required to engage in productive work (paid or unpaid). Literacy rates, educational attainment, and indicators of health and nutrition are commonly used measures with gender inequality accounted for by male-female gaps or female/male ratios. *Livelihoods* indicators assess the extent to which genders are able to apply their functionings to productive activities. Examples of indicators include access to credit, employment, wages, and ownership of assets. Finally, *agency* refers to the ability to participate in decision-making at the household, community and national level, and in the workplace. Measures include female shares of political representation and of supervisory and managerial positions. In this chapter, we focus on the research that links capabilities and livelihoods inequality to macro-level outcomes.

A major contribution of macroeconomics research incorporating the role of gender is the finding that the impact of micro-level gender relations on the macroeconomy will differ, depending on the structure of the economy (e.g., agricultural, labor-intensive manufacturing, or knowledge-intensive economies). Gender is an important marker of job access, due to norms and stereotypes, which implicitly or explicitly define jobs or tasks as "male" or "female." We observe that women tend to be concentrated in certain occupations or sectors such as labor-intensive manufacturing industries, subsistence agriculture, and service sector jobs in health care and education. This holds for both SSA and also for other regions of the world. Men in SSA tend to predominate in cash crop production and in jobs in extractive industries as well as "blue collar" jobs—electricians, plumbers, and truck drivers.

Job segregation is in part due to gendered patterns in job choice, often due to social pressure based on norms that identify tasks with a particular gender.[2] It may also result from employer bias, with women concentrated in occupations and sectors that are lower paid and on the bottom rungs of the job hierarchy while men are offered positions with a job ladder, more secure hours of employment, and benefits. Contrary to neoclassical assumptions, even if women and men are equally qualified, female and male labor are not seen as perfect substitutes as a result of the rigidity of social norms. Because jobs are gendered, the structure of the economy plays a role in determining the relative demand for female and male labor.

Gender effects on the macroeconomy may vary in the short run versus long run. Wages and credit, for example, will have more immediate macroeconomic effects while capabilities variables are slower to produce discernible macroeconomic effects. An example of the latter is gender gaps in education, which are transmitted to the macroeconomy with a lag via effects on fertility and investments in children. Indeed, it is the distinction between the short and long run that contributes to a heated debate amongst theorists and empiricists on the macro-level effects of changes in the degree of gender inequality.

The complexities of economic structure, measures of inequality, and the gender division of labor make it impossible to arrive at universal, time-invariant generalizations with regard to gender effects on macroeconomic outcomes; such effects instead are context-specific. Generalizations are further complicated by the different approaches to macro-modeling. Neoclassical theoretical and empirical approaches almost exclusively emphasize the long-run effects of capabilities inequality on economic growth (Klasen and Lamanna 2009). Few neoclassical economists focus on the implications of wage inequality in the short run. As a group, neoclassical models that incorporate gender are one-size-fits-all. That is, they do not incorporate specific features of economies that interact with gender relations (such as job segregation and trade and investment policies) and macroeconomic performance.

In contrast, heterodox macroeconomic models address underlying power relations and the interconnection of gender relations with other social and economic relationships, including intra-household resource allocation. Further, structuralist macroeconomists and feminist economists (the two groups overlap) account for short- and long-run effects, and the role of inequality in livelihoods, measured as access to employment, gender wage inequality, and asset inequality. By virtue of the focus on income, wages, and assets, this second strand of literature sheds light on the role of bargaining power within households and in labor markets in contributing to inequality (Doss 2006; Berik et al. 2009). We briefly discuss each of these bodies of work and highlight their contradictory findings.

31.3.1 The short run

Short-run stabilization remains a key area of inquiry of macroeconomists. In its own right, macroeconomic instability is cause for concern, particularly in poor countries where the

---

[2] "Male" and "female" tasks differ by country or region. In addition, tasks defined as "female" tend to be of systematically lower status and less remunerative than "male" tasks, regardless of the patterns of job segregation.

possibilities to smooth income are constrained. Secondly, short-run fluctuations in the macroeconomy can lead to hysteresis on the supply side, thus dampening long-run growth prospects (Dutt and Ros 2007). As a result, short-run demand-side effects of efforts to promote gender equality are of great interest and reveal information about the sustainability of efforts to narrow gender gaps in well-being.

Theorists identify short-run effects of gender on the macroeconomy as operating through the *livelihoods* domain where the indicators, such as wages or access to credit, are fast-moving variables with notable short-run effects. This contrasts with gender equality in capabilities (say, in educational attainment or health), which is likely to be transmitted to the macroeconomy, as noted, with a substantial lag.

A straightforward framework for identifying the net effect of greater gender equality in the short run is to evaluate its impact on each of the components of the macroeconomic equilibrium condition in an open economy

$$I + G + X = S + T + M \tag{1}$$

where I is business spending, G is government spending, X is exports, S is savings, T is taxes and M is imports. The balance of payments constraint in the short run is simply net exports

$$NX = X - M \tag{2}$$

where NX is net exports.[3]

A key question regards the macroeconomic effect of a redistribution or improvement in women's relative access to key resources such as wages or credit. Would greater equality have a differential effect on injections versus leakages, thus leading to an economic expansion or contraction? And would the balance of payments be affected? If the net demand-side effect is

$$I + G + X > S + T + M$$

the impact would be expansionary and thus gender cooperative. That is, in this case, gender wage equality is consistent with an expansion of aggregate demand and job growth, thereby benefiting both women and men absolutely (though women gain more, relatively). Conversely, if an increase in female wages (or greater relative access to credit) results in leakages exceeding injections or $I + G + X < S + T + M$, then output and employment fall. This is potentially a gender conflictive outcome if men's employment is negatively affected by economic contraction. Similarly, a narrowing of the gender wage gap that reduces X more than M worsens the current account and thus balance of payments.

The research to date suggests that shifts in wages and other livelihood variables such as access to credit do have discernible impacts on the macroeconomic equilibrium condition and balance of payments constraint. Although much more empirical work is needed to clarify the effects on individual components of the equilibrium condition, we can make a few generalizations, based on inferences about the structure of the economy. To facilitate this, we group developing countries into semi-industrialized export economies (SIEs)

---

[3] For fully developed engendered macro models of this genre, see Blecker and Seguino (2002) and Braunstein, van Staveren, and Tavani (2011).

and low-income agricultural economies (LIAEs). Examples of SIEs are South Africa and Mauritius, as well as Thailand, China, Brazil, and Mexico. LIAEs include many sub-Saharan African economies, and countries such as Pakistan, Paraguay, and Nicaragua, to name a few.

In SIEs, women workers tend to be concentrated in labor-intensive export industries—the kind of firms that can easily relocate if local resource costs rise. Product demand is price elastic since the goods SIE firms produce tend to be relatively homogenous, resulting in ample substitutes, globally. Given the gendered pattern of job segregation in SIEs, higher female wages will very probably have relatively large negative effects on both exports and investment (Seguino 1997, 2000; Busse and Spielmann 2006). Higher female wages that reduce gender wage gaps are thus likely to be contractionary. As a result, we can anticipate that in countries where female wages are relatively lower than those of (equally qualified) men, export growth rates will be higher. Mauritius is an African example of such an economy in which low relative female wages have fuelled exports and growth. There, female wages are half of those of men, a gap only partially explained by productivity differentials (Nordman and Wolff 2010). Mauritius thus owes part of its growth and balance of payments success to gender wage discrimination.

The negative effect of higher female relative wages on demand might be counteracted on the leakages side if gender differences in savings and import propensities are large enough to stimulate domestic consumption. Although it is theoretically plausible that male and female saving and import propensities differ, there is as yet a dearth of empirical evidence to identify the size and direction of those differences. For example, only a few studies examine the relationship between gender equality and aggregate savings[4] and none yet explore effects on import demand. If higher female wages did reduce aggregate saving and imports, the effects would have to be quite large to offset the contractionary effects of declines in I and X, an unlikely scenario in SIEs. As such, research suggests that greater gender wage equality is contractionary and gender conflictive in such economies (Blecker and Seguino 2002; Seguino 2000, 2010).

Most SSA countries, however, fall into the category of LIAEs, where gender effects differ from those in SIEs. In LIAEs, women are concentrated in (unpaid) subsistence food production (for example, food crops such as indigenous fruit, vegetable, and staple food crops), and some off-farm waged labor. Despite their active role in the agricultural sector, women are disadvantaged due to cultural, socioeconomic, and sociological factors, as exemplified by gender biases in asset ownership, land tenure systems, access to credit, education, and extension services (Oduro et al. 2011; World Bank 2011).

In LIAEs, it is men who are likely to be employed in export sector, in particular cash crop production (Were and Kiringai 2003) and mineral extraction. Doss (2002) noted that a strict division of labor in agriculture no longer exists. Women increasingly engage in commercial production as waged workers in non-traditional agricultural exports (NTAEs). And more women workers are entering the mining industry. That said, food security in large part continues to depend on female labor while women comprise only a small share of workers in the export sector of most SSA countries.

Given this division of labor, what would be the effect of greater gender equality in SSA, measured through wages? Although data is limited, we can make inferences, based on what

---

[4] See, for example, Floro and Seguino (2002).

we know about the structure of such economies. The net effect of higher female wages on investment and exports in SSA is likely to be weak, even if negative. That is because, on the investment side, the bulk of large-scale firms are in export-oriented extractive industries and infrastructure. These are male-dominated in employment. Moreover, given the structure of production in SSA, higher female wages in off-farm employment and greater access to credit might very well stimulate investment in on-farm production due to the effect on access to technologies and production inputs (Doss 2001).

With regard to the right-hand side of equation (1), in LIAEs, women in the labor force are more likely to be older and married with children than females in SIEs. Kiringai (2004) found evidence for Kenya that women's consumption propensities exceed men's although detailed empirical work is needed to draw any firm conclusions that could inform theoretical models. Insofar as we do find evidence of higher female marginal propensities to consume, a resource redistribution to women could have positive demand-side effects. Based on the empirical evidence available thus far, combined with what we know about gender segregation in employment and the structure of LIAEs, higher female wages will have a negligible contractionary effect on the macroeconomy in the short run and potentially an expansionary one.

Other measures of gender equality that have short-run effects may be more salient than wages in LIAEs. A significant body of evidence suggests that gender equality in access to inputs (credit, fertilizer, extension services, land title) could raise on-farm productivity in a number of SSA economies (FAO 2011). For example, a study on Burkina Faso notes that fertilizer is more heavily applied to male plots, resulting in their greater productivity relative to female plots, controlling for weather conditions and types and characteristics of plots (Udry 1996). The implication is that equalization of inputs and land rights could raise yields on women's plots. The FAO (2011) estimates that closing gender gaps in input use could feasibly increase production on land controlled by women by 20–30%. This would lead to a 2.4–4.0 percentage point increase in agricultural output, with the potential to reduce the number of under-nourished by 12.0–17.0%.

To the extent that gender equality in inputs, credit, and land title expands food production, the balance of payments may benefit due to reduced reliance on food imports. The data to assess both female and male access to resources (especially agricultural credit) are simply not yet widely available, however. The data challenges of empirically testing theoretical models, then, have been a constraint on research in this area. This is especially so in SSA where time-series data on female and male wages, assets, and credit are severely lacking.

31.3.2 The long run

Gendered macro-models treat all gender well-being indicators as flexible in the long run. This implies that along with livelihood measures of gender inequality, capabilities variables are also incorporated into long-run growth models. The pathways by which livelihoods and capabilities indicators are hypothesized to affect the rate of economic growth vary by theoretical framework.[5] A number of long-run growth analyses have adopted a neoclassical

---

[5] Seguino (2010) develops a framework for comparing the implications of the main distinctions between theoretical approaches.

framework based on the Solow model. Assuming Say's Law (that is, that economies do not face demand-side constraints and thus problems of excess capacity and unemployment), the supply side determines the rate of economic growth in these models. In contrast, Keynesian/Kaleckian models allow for imbalances between potential output and demand.

Gendered neoclassical accounts emphasize the positive effects of gender equality in capabilities, such as education and health (but not wages or credit). The primary pathway is via effects on human capacities, although some consider the effect on investment. Heterodox models differ in that, in addition to human capacities, they pay attention to effects on physical capital accumulation, assessing the impact of livelihoods measures such as wages on long-run growth.

31.3.2.1 *The effect of greater capabilities equality*

There are several pathways by which capabilities equality can raise economy-wide productivity. The first is a direct effect on labor productivity. If innate abilities are similarly distributed across the genders, unequal educational investments in favor of boys lead to inefficiencies due to a selection distortion problem: overinvestment in less qualified males and under-investment in more qualified females. This can lower economy-wide efficiency, implying that gender equality in educational investments can stimulate productivity and economic growth (Baliamoune-Lutz and McGillivray 2009). Klasen and Lamanna (2009) estimated that the cost of education gaps in terms of foregone GDP in SSA amounts to 3.48 percentage points annually relative to East Asia over the period 1960–2000. The effects are both direct (on economy-wide productivity) and indirect (lower female relative productivity dampens business investment).

A second pathway by which greater educational equality can stimulate development and growth is via the impact on children's well-being. Whether due to greater female bargaining power within the household or the enhanced ability to provide better care for children, women's increased educational attainment (relative to men's and absolutely) has been found to produce a positive effect on children's survival, health, and education (Doss 2013). One (indirect) pathway by which children's well-being may be enhanced is through the effect on fertility. As the opportunity cost of having children rises with more education, women's fertility rates decline, reducing the dependency ratio. This permits larger investments in children.

There is broad consensus in the literature that educational equality is growth- and development-enhancing. Although other measures of capabilities such as women's absolute health status have also been linked to children's well-being and cognitive development in micro-level studies (Agénor, et al 2010), there is little macro-level research that explores the impact of relative health inequalities.

31.3.2.2 *The effect of gender equality in labor force participation and wages*

Similar to selection distortion in educational investments, gender differences in labor force participation rates may reduce the economy-wide quality of the labor force. Two studies have empirically assessed the effect of gender gaps in labor force participation. Bandara (2012) using a Solow growth accounting framework to estimate the effect of gender equality in effective labor (the combined effect of gender gaps in labor force participation rates and education), found it could raise output per worker in SSA between 0.3–0.5 percentage points annually for the period 1970–2010. Existing gender gaps in effective labor imply an annual cost of $60 billion in lost output for SSA, or roughly 10% of total SSA GDP (in constant 2010 international dollars). Klasen and Lamanna (2009) also found that higher female/male labor force participation rates stimulate growth in developing countries. In addition to the effect on labor productivity, this effect may operate indirectly by raising women's bargaining power within the household and increasing the share of household spending on children's well-being.

A critical barrier to greater gender equality in labor force participation rates is the burden of unpaid labor, predominantly born by women. Unpaid work includes activities such care of children, subsistence crop production for household consumption, home maintenance, and home-based nursing care for the ill and elderly. A ubiquitous finding is that women perform substantially more unpaid labor than men, although the gender gap in performance of this work varies across SSA (Blackden and Wodon 2006). Holding constant men's performance of unpaid labor, the reduction in time required for such tasks frees up time for women to spend in remunerative activities that can increase their bargaining power within the household, and can reduce child labor. In some cases, this can directly impact girls' education if they are differentially relied on to assist in unpaid labor, as is the case in many SSA countries. Such improvements can be induced via public investments in infrastructure that reduce the time women must allocate to unpaid care work (Fontana and Natali 2008). To the extent that women's relative capabilities, incomes, and assets improve, their bargaining power within the household gives them greater control over their fertility.

Long-run heterodox growth models evaluate the direct role of wages in influencing labor productivity growth via its effect on investment in physical capital. Taking the case of SIEs, the ability to hire women at low wages relative to their productivity can be a stimulus to investment and technological advancement, as noted, via the effect on unit labor costs and profits. This implies that higher female wages have a negative effect on the growth of output, dampening productivity growth. But this is offset, at least in part, by the positive effect of higher female wages on human capital. The chain of causality is that higher relative wages improve women's bargaining power in the household with positive effects on investments in children's well-being and thus long-run economy-wide productivity growth. The net effect on productivity growth in SIEs is thus an empirical question to be determined on a country-by-country basis.

The finding that gender educational equality is a stimulus to growth while wage equality is not may at first glance appear contradictory. Upon further examination, it is not. Greater educational equality contributes to higher relative female labor productivity. But because women tend to occupy the types of jobs where workers have weak bargaining power, their ability to translate their higher productivity into higher wages is constrained. As a result, the gender gap in education will tend to narrow more than the gender wage gap. To see this more clearly, consider the equation for unit labor costs

$$ULC = w_F b$$

where ULC is unit labor costs, w_F is nominal female wages, and b is the labor coefficient (the inverse of labor productivity). Improvement in female education relative to men's lowers the labor coefficient. If women lack the bargaining power to negotiate for a commensurate increase in wages, unit labor costs fall. Gender discrimination (the gender gap between wages and productivity) can raise profits, lower prices, or both, with positive demand-side effects. Thus gender inequality can have a positive effect on growth so long as it does not alter the overall *quality* of the labor force (Berik, et al 2009; Braunstein 2012). This is not an argument in favor of gender wage inequality. Rather, it highlights an underlying tension in the sources of growth in some countries. Reliance on gender wage discrimination to raise economy-wide living standards is contradictory in the sense that it is not compatible with intergroup equality. Further, as noted above, it may not be a sustainable strategy in the long run, even if it does produce a short-run stimulus to growth.

The long-run growth effects of greater gender equality differ in LIAEs such as those in SSA. The dissimilarity turns on the effect of greater wage equality (and other opportunities such as credit, land, and inputs) in stimulating on-farm investment and thus raising productivity and agricultural yields. Here the effect of greater gender equality is likely to be positive, suggesting that the benefits of gender equality in livelihoods for growth are more unambiguously positive in these countries.

This brief summary demonstrates advances in our knowledge of the effect of micro-level gender relations on macro-level outcomes, and in particular, the pathways by which equality may stimulate economic growth and potentially development, defined as broadly shared improvements in well-being. That said, this research agenda is far from complete and its boundaries have not been definitively drawn. The plethora of microeconomic analyses that investigate the impact of gender inequality at the household level and in specific labor market contexts help to identify important potential macroeconomic relationships, but are not generalizable. Macroeconomic studies remain sparse due to limited availability of data except for a few widely used indicators such as education, life expectancy, literacy, and labor force participation. We will be able to say more about how gender affects macroeconomic outcomes and to more accurately quantify those effects with the expansion of gender-disaggregated data.

31.4 Macro-level Policies and Gender Equality

One of the critical findings in the gender and macroeconomics literature is that of a two-way causality between gender and macro-level outcomes. Just as efforts to promote gender equality may have an effect on economic growth, macro-level policies in turn influence the distribution of resources and well-being between women and men. That is, macroeconomic policies are rarely distributionally neutral. Apart from the distributional effects, the importance of understanding the gender impact of macro-level policies lies in the feedback effects to economic growth. Policies meant to stimulate growth or stabilization may fail to achieve their goals if they inadvertently undermine gender equality. This is particularly relevant to SSA where gender equality shows strong evidence of stimulating long-run growth and development.

A number of studies explore the effects of economic growth on measures of gender equality.[6] It is, however, the specific policies implemented by governments that are gendered in their impact, not growth per se. More recently, studies have begun to evaluate the effects of

---

[6] For a review of this literature, see Kabeer and Natali (2013).

specific policies. These include the effect of fiscal and monetary policies, as well as trade and investment liberalization. We review the major findings here, emphasizing results that are of particular relevance for SSA.

31.4.1 Fiscal policy

The public sector has a key role to play in creating the conditions for gender equality. Through its budget allocations, the state has the potential to redress inequalities and discrimination in the household in asset ownership, and in labor and credit markets. Various measures including spending on education and training can narrow gender gaps in access to health care, while targeted physical infrastructure expenditures can reduce women's care burden. To the extent that gender equality is a stimulus to growth, especially as it appears to be in SSA, it is "affordable." That is, by raising incomes, expenditures to promote gender equality can generate the revenue to cover the cost of the initial public expenditures.

Improved water and sanitation facilities, for example, decrease illness and time spent fetching water. Because caring for the ill and fetching water are considered "female" tasks, public expenditures on these could substantially reduce women's unpaid labor burden in SSA. Transportation improvements reduce the time women spend in marketing goods and expand access medical care. Decreases in unpaid labor burdens expand women's opportunities to perform remunerative work. This has benefits for children's well-being. A large body of evidence indicates that improvement in women's access to income results in more resources invested in children's health, education, and development. This is due in part to women's propensity to spend a larger share of their income on children than men (Doss 2013). Improvements in mothers' health have been found to affect children's health *in utero*, with long-term positive effects on children's cognitive skills and thus productivity (Agénor et al. 2010).

Some studies estimate the effect of public sector investments on gender equality. Using data from Tanzanian time-use surveys, Fontana and Natali (2008) simulated the benefits of targeted public sector infrastructure investments that reduce time spent on unpaid care activities. They demonstrated that such investments, by reducing the time spent on fetching water, fuel, and other unpaid household maintenance activities, reduce the care burden, disproportionately raising the earnings potential of women relative to men. Seguino and Were (2014) provided empirical evidence of a positive effect of infrastructure investments on gender equality in employment rates, using a sample of 38 SSA economies for the period 1991–2010.

These linkages imply that physical infrastructure investments to reduce women's care burden and improve their health have long-term economic benefits in the form of a healthier, more educated and productive workforce, and can thereby stimulate economic growth. An added advantage is they contribute to greater gender equality.

Public investment in agriculture (such as credit and extension services) could also reduce gender inequality by improving yields on plots farmed by women, simultaneously decreasing the reliance on imported food. Women's limited access to agricultural inputs is in part due to restrictions on the right to own land (Kevane 2004). As a result, women lack the collateral to access credit needed to purchase inputs. Women's share of small farmer credit in SSA, for example, is estimated to be 10% and for all agriculture, 1% (FAO 2011). Targeting public sector spending to equalization of access to credit and agricultural inputs could have a profoundly positive effect on women's and children's well-being, and on overall agricultural output.

The challenge in SSA and elsewhere is to reframe thinking on public spending that could contribute to greater gender equality by recognizing the investment character of this type of expenditure. Such spending has a public goods quality because it produces spillover benefits to society as a whole, with the stream of returns accruing over many years. By raising labor productivity, such expenditures also raise incomes and thereby generate tax revenues with which to pay down the debt incurred to finance the original investment. In the past, we have merely considered such expenditures as consumption spending, without any feedback effects on labor productivity and thus economic growth.[7]

31.4.2 Monetary policy

A very new area of research is the impact of central bank policies on gender equality. These policies include inflation targeting, exchange rate policies, capital controls, and asset reserve requirements. Properly targeted, these policy tools have the potential to promote gender equality. We discuss gender implications in the context of a changing monetary policy landscape.

The traditional focus of monetary policy had been stabilization of output (employment) and prices. With global financial liberalization, however, the emphasis has shifted to a concern with price stability. Consequently, inflation targeting (IT) became the dominant policy stance and the number of IT countries has been rising. Notwithstanding this trend, IT has many skeptics (Ball and Sheridan 2005). The suitability and effectiveness of the IT framework have been questioned for SSA, owing to the structural supply-side origins of inflation and imperfect monetary policy transmission mechanisms (Heintz and Ndikumana 2011). Additionally, although the economic growth record for Africa improved in the last decade, employment creation remains a pertinent developmental priority for the foreseeable future.

In addition to the development objectives of expanded output and employment that require strategies beyond the narrow focus on inflation, there is an embedded gender dimension. This should not be misconstrued to imply that price stability is not unimportant. If anything, high inflation is bound to disproportionately hurt women, especially with respect to the purchase of basic commodities such as foodstuffs on which women spend a significant portion of their income. Overall inflation in SSA economies tends to be largely driven by food inflation. As noted, women play an important role in ensuring food security and thus price stability. Given the sources of inflationary pressures, targeted fiscal policy expenditures to relax supply-side bottlenecks are more precise tools than contractionary monetary policy, which addresses the inflation problem by reducing demand (Seguino and Were 2014).

Apart from the failure of IT to address the root causes of inflation in SSA, recent research demonstrates that contractionary monetary policy has gendered effects. The effects are hypothesized to work through interest rate and credit channels, resulting in the contraction

---

[7] Although fiscal expenditures tend to receive more attention, taxation policies likewise have gender implications (Grown and Valodia 2010).

of output and employment, both of which have disproportionate gender implications (Braunstein and Heintz 2008; Seguino and Heintz 2012).

Monetary policy also produces gender effects through the exchange rate channel, although here too, much more research is needed. Most African countries liberalized exchange rates as part of trade liberalization reforms although central banks still play a fundamental role in managing exchange rate movements. The exchange rate influences import and export dynamics, and as a result, can have far-reaching consequences at the household level. While depreciation promotes export demand, gender disparities in the ability to export may result, with negative consequences for gender equality in control of resources and bargaining power at the household level. Moreover, SSA economies rely heavily on imported intermediate and essential goods. Unfavorable exchange rates can raise the burden on consumers in the form of higher prices, or by creating unnecessary scarcity. Higher costs of essential goods like pharmaceuticals and medical equipment are likely to increase the care burden of women.

An alternative monetary policy framework that promotes gender equality is one in which the central bank would identify "real" targets such as employment and output of strategic groups, sectors, or regions. One tool that could be used is for central banks to offer loan guarantees to private banks that extend loans in these areas. In agricultural economies in SSA, where women are subsistence farmers, small-scale agriculture is an obvious choice. Loan guarantees are a good way to overcome the credit constraints women face, given restrictions on their ownership of land and thus lack of collateral. In this framework, the private sector would still provide the bulk of credit, but it would be characterized by low interest rates leveraged with government loan guarantees. The feedback effects of such a policy could be substantial, since higher agricultural yields can reduce the demand for food imports, relieving pressure on the balance of payments and exchange rate. Although research in this area is still in its early stages, we can conclude that monetary policy can usefully be conducted through a gender lens—that is, with an eye to understanding its differential effects on women and men.

31.4.3 Trade and investment policies

The impact of trade and investment liberalization policies on gender equality depends on the structure of the economy and, of course, the magnitude of the employment, price, and public sector revenue effects. With regard to structure, as we have noted, in SSA, trade continues to be dominated by minerals and agricultural commodity exports. That said, SSA's participation in global value chains has expanded, mainly at lower ends of supply chain in the areas of textile and apparels, horticulture, and agribusiness. Similar to SIEs, these export-oriented sectors thrive on the availability of cheap labor, notably provided by women. Poor working conditions and low pay persist (Tallontire et al 2005; Chan 2013), with challenges ranging from poor health and safety standards, inadequate leave entitlements, to sexual harassment and wage discrimination.

Much of trade and investment gender research has focused on the impact on female employment and wages (Papyrakis et al. 2012; Wamboye and Seguino 2014). In general, evidence suggests a positive relationship between trade and investment liberalization, on the one hand, and female employment in export-oriented sectors, on the other. In the case of SSA, however, the record is more mixed. Trade liberalization has contributed to deindustrialization in female labor-intensive industries in some cases, as SSA goods have been forced to compete with lower cost Asian goods. The rise in Chinese investment in Africa has not substantially changed the manufacturing landscape as of yet (Carmody 2008). Other measures of gender equality underscore the potential negative effects of trade and investment liberalization in SSA as well. Of particular note, Baliamoune-Lutz (2007) found that greater integration in world markets and growth lead to wider gender gaps in literacy rates is SSA.

A more generalized finding across developing countries is that trade and investment liberalization are also associated with increased downward pressure on wages, increased inequality, and widening discriminatory gender wage gaps (Berik et al. 2009; Menon and Rodgers 2009). The cumulative evidence to date then suggests that trade and investment liberalization have had contradictory effects on gender equality. Although in some cases increasing women's relative access to employment, this shift in macro-level policies results in problematic conditions of work, and does appear to provide a path to gender equality in livelihoods.

Two inferences can be drawn from the discussion on the effect of trade and investment policies on gender equality. First, the degree of gender inequality is a function not only of individual differences in human capital, but also of macro-level policies that interact with gender norms and stereotypes to produce unequal outcomes. Second, this underscores the importance of managing trade and investment in ways that are compatible with gender equality (Tallontire et al. 2005; Seguino and Grown 2006).

31.5 CONCLUSION

A large body of research produced in the last two decades makes a strong theoretical and empirical case that gender is a macroeconomic variable. That is, gender relations at the microeconomic level produce macroeconomic effects that vary by country, structure of production, as well as the macroeconomic policy environment. As of yet, mainstream analyses attempting to identify the policies that will stimulate growth in SSA have yet to integrate the role of gender. This is problematic on several counts. Some empirical accounts suggest gender effects on growth, development, and the balance of payments can be quite large. This suggests a missed growth opportunity and underscores the fact that there is adequate fiscal space to fund gender equality initiatives. Second, a failure to integrate gender into macroeconomic models and policy frameworks misses important economic dynamics taking place in African economies. Failure to account for them can lead to policies that are ineffective, or even harmful for the macroeconomy.

Having argued that gender matters in the macroeconomic world of theory and policy, the effects of gender equality can be contradictory, depending on whether initiatives raise labor productivity or the cost of labor. Further, there is much to learn about the size of the short- and long-run effects of gender equality. A significant issue for SSA is the role of gender equality in expanding agricultural output, and the effects of this on price stability, the import bill, and the balance of payments. During the last decade (2000–2010), net food imports into SSA rose 60% (FAO 2011). This is a drain on foreign exchange that could otherwise be used to import capital- and skill-intensive goods that would raise productivity. Increasing food production and reducing food imports also has beneficial effects for monetary policy and exchange rate management.

It is not enough to "engender" growth models. Account also has to be taken of the feedback loops from macro-level policies to gender equality. Macroeconomic policies that worsen gender equality can undermine growth objectives if in fact gender equality is itself a stimulus to growth. The growing body of work that analyzes the impact of fiscal, monetary and trade and investment policies provides some guidance on the pathways by which gender relations are affected. Although more research is needed in this area, one clear area of focus is the beneficial gender effect of targeted public investments that can be sustainable, in light of the investment quality of such spending. Monetary policy tools, too, can be utilized in innovative ways, to overcome gender inequalities in asset ownership. A more challenging problem is how to ensure trade and investment policies are gender equitable. In view of the changing global landscape, trade policies that ignore the gender-specific constraints in capabilities and competencies to trade are bound to be sub-optimal.

References

Agénor, P.-R., Canuto, O., and da Silva, L.P. (2010). *On Gender and Growth: The Role of Intergenerational Health Externalities and Women's Occupational Constraints.* World Bank Policy Research Working Paper, No. 5492.

Baliamoune-Lutz, M. (2007). Globalisation and gender inequality: Is Africa different? *Journal of African Economies*, 16(2):301–348.

Baliamoune-Lutz, M., and McGillivray, M. (2009). Does gender inequality reduce growth in sub-Saharan Africa and Arab countries? *African Development Review*, 21:224–242.

Ball, L., and Sheridan, N. (2005). Does inflation targeting matter? in Ben Bernanke and Michael Wood (eds), *The Inflation-Targeting Debate*, pp. 249–276. Chicago: University of Chicago Press.

Bandara, A. (2012). Economic Cost of Gender Gaps in Effective Labor: Africa's Missing Growth Reserve. Mimeo. UNDP Tanzania, Dar-es-Salaam.

Berik, G., van der Meulen Rodgers, Y., and Seguino, S. (2009). Feminist economics of inequality, development, and growth. *Feminist Economics*, 15(3):1–33.

Blackden, M., and Wodon, Q. (2006). *Gender, Time Use and Poverty in Sub-Saharan Africa.* World Bank Working Paper 73. Washington, DC: World Bank.

Blecker, R., and Seguino, S. (2002). Macroeconomic effects of reducing gender wage inequality in an export-oriented, semi-industrialized economy. *Review of Development Economics*, 6(1):103–119.

Braunstein, E. (2012). *Neoliberal Macroeconomics: A Consideration of Its Gendered Employment Effects.* UNRISD Research Paper 2012-1. Geneva: UNRISD.

Braunstein, E., and Heintz, J. (2008). Gender bias and central bank policy: Employment and inflation reduction. *International Review of Applied Economics*, 22(2):173–186.

Braunstein, E., van Staveren, I., and Tavani, D. (2011). Embedding care and unpaid work in macroeconomic modeling: A structuralist approach. *Feminist Economics*, 17(4):5–31.

Busse, M., and Spielmann, C. (2006). Gender inequality and trade. *Review of International Economics*, 14(3):362–370.

Carmody, P. (2008). Exploring Africa's economic recovery. *Geography Compass*, 2(1):79–107.

Chan, M.-K. (2013). Informal workers in global horticulture and commodities value Chains: A review of literature. WIEGO Working paper No. 26. Cambridge, MA: Women in Informal Employment: Globalizing and Organizing (WIEGO).

Doss, C. (2001). How does gender affect the adoption of agricultural innovations? The case of improved maize technology in Ghana. *Agricultural Economics*, 25(1):27–39.

Doss, C. (2002). Men's crops? Women's crops? The gender patterns of cropping in Ghana. *World Development*, 30(11):1987–2000.

Doss, C. (2006). The gender asset gap: What do we know and why does it matter? *Feminist Economics*, 12(1–2):1–50.

Doss, C. (2013). Intrahousehold Bargaining and Resource Allocation in Developing Countries. World Bank Policy Research Working Paper No. 6337.

Dutt, A., and Ros, J. (2007). Aggregate demand shocks and economic growth. *Structural Change and Economic Dynamics*, 18:75–99.

Elson, D. (1995). Gender awareness in modeling structural adjustment. *World Development*, 23(11):1851–1868.

Folbre, N. (2014). The care economy in Africa: Subsistence production and unpaid care. *Journal of African Economies*, 23(AERC supplement 1):i128–i156.

Floro, M., and Seguino, S. (2002). *Gender Effects on Aggregate Savings: A Theoretical and Empirical Analysis*. World Bank Policy Research Paper on Gender and Development, No. 23.

Fontana, M., and Natali, L. (2008). Gendered patterns of time use in Tanzania: Public investment in infrastructure xan help. Paper prepared for the IFPRI Project on *Evaluating the Long-Term Impact of Gender-focused Policy Interventions*.

Food and Agriculture Organization (FAO) (2011). *The State of Food and Agriculture 2010-11. Women in Agriculture Closing the Gender Gap for Development*. Rome: FAO.

Gladwin, C. (1994). *Structural Adjustment and African Women Farmers*. Gainesville, FL: University Press of Florida.

Grown, C., and Valodia, I. (eds) (2010). *Taxation and Gender Equity: A Comparative Analysis of Direct and Indirect Taxes in Developing and Developed Countries*. Routledge for the IDRC.

Haddad, L., Hoddinott, J., and Alderman, H. (eds) (1997). *Intrahousehold Resource Allocation in Developing Countries*. Johns Hopkins University Press for International Food Policy Research Institute (IFPRI).

Heintz, J., and Ndikumana, L. (2011). Is there a case for formal inflation targeting in sub-Saharan Africa? *Journal of African Economies*, 20(AERC Supplement 2):ii67–ii103.

Kabeer, N., and Natali, L. (2013). Gender equality and economic growth: Is there a win-win? IDS Working Paper Volume 2013, No. 417.

Kevane, M. (2004). *Women and Development in Africa: How Gender Works*. Boulder, CO and London: Lynne Rienner.

Kiringai, J. (2004). Understanding the Kenyan economy: An accounting multiplier approach. Mimeo. Kenya Institute for Public Policy Research and Analysis.

Klasen, S., and Lamanna, F. (2009). The impact of gender inequality in education and employment on economic growth: New evidence for a panel of countries. *Feminist Economics*, 15(3):91–132.

Menon, N., and van der Meulen Rodgers, Y. (2009). International trade and the gender wage gap: New evidence from India's manufacturing sector. *World Development*, 37(5):965–981.

Ndulu, B., Chakraborti, L., Lijane, L. et al. (2007). *Challenges to African Growth: Opportunities, Strategies, and Strategic Directions*. Washington, DC: World Bank.

Nordman, C., and Wolff, F.-C. (2010). Gender differences in pay in African manufacturing firms, in J. Arbache, A. Kolev, and E. Filipiak (eds), *Gender Disparities in Africa's Labor Market*, pp. 155–192. Washington, DC: Agence Française de Développement and the World Bank.

Oduro, A., Baah-Boateng, W., and Boakye-Yiadom, L. 2011. *Measuring the Gender Asset Gap in Ghana*. Department of Economics, University of Ghana.

Papyrakis, E., Covarrubias, A., and Verschoor, A. (2012). Gender and trade aspects of labour markets. *Journal of Development Studies*, 48(1):81–98.

Rodrik, D. (2007). *One Economics, Many Recipes.* Princeton, NJ: Princeton University Press.

Seguino, S. (1997). Gender wage inequality and export-led growth in South Korea. *Journal of Development Studies*, 34(2):102–132.

Seguino, S. (2000). Gender inequality and economic growth: A cross-country analysis. *World Development*, 28(7):1211–1230.

Seguino, S. (2010). Gender, distribution, and balance of payments constrained growth in developing countries. *Review of Political Economy*, 22(3):373–404.

Seguino, S., and Grown, C. (2006). Gender equity and globalization: Macroeconomic policy for developing countries. *Journal of International Development*, 18(8):1091–1104.

Seguino, S., and Heintz, J. (2012). Monetary tightening and the dynamics of race and gender stratification in the US. *American Journal of Economics and Sociology*, 71(3):603–638.

Seguino, S., and Were. M. (2014). Gender, development, and growth in sub-Saharan Africa. *Journal of African Economies.* 23 (AERC supplement 1):i18-i61.

Tallontire, A., Dolan, C., Smith, S., and Barrientos, S. (2005). Reaching the marginalised? Gender value chains and ethical trade in African horticulture. *Development in Practice*, 15(3–4):559–571.

Udry, C. (1996). Gender, agricultural production, and theory of the household. *Journal of Political Economy*, 104(5):1010–1046.

Wamboye, E., and Seguino, S. (2014). Economic structure, trade openness, and gendered employment in sub-Saharan Africa. *Feminist Economics*. doi: 10.1080/13545701.2014.927583.

Were, M., and Kiringai, J. (2003). *Gender Mainstreaming in Macroeconomic Policies and Poverty Reduction Strategy in Kenya*. Nairobi: African Women's Development and Communication Network (FEMNET).

World Bank (2011). *World Development Report 2012: Gender Equality and Development.* Washington, DC: World Bank.

CHAPTER 32

....

GENDER ECONOMICS IN NORTH AFRICA

....

MINA BALIAMOUNE-LUTZ

32.1 INTRODUCTION

....

NORTH African countries are part of the Middle East and North Africa (MENA) region. They share important historical and contemporary economic, political, cultural, and religious features with other MENA countries. North Africa also shares important historical and geographical features with other African countries. Yet, women in North Africa, and Tunisia in particular, have enjoyed for decades rights that women in some other parts of the Arab world (e.g. in Saudi Arabia) do not yet exercise, such as the right to vote.[1] Asset ownership (including ownership of land) by women in North Africa is much more predominant than women's asset ownership in other African countries and is protected by national laws. However, women's empowerment remains weak in at least two areas: economic and political participation. In addition, there are large disparities in gender equality between Tunisia and the other North African countries.

In this chapter, I primarily discuss major issues and developments related to gender economics in four North African countries, Algeria, Egypt, Morocco, and Tunisia. I analyze historical trajectories of widely used gender inequality indicators and explore how the differential treatment of women and men in North Africa's patriarchal societies has influenced the status of women, focusing in particular on the behavior of fertility.

Analysis of historical data shows that the long-term behavior of fertility and mortality in Tunisia was significantly different from that in Algeria, Egypt, and Morocco, and that the difference was primarily due to major differences in the governments' approaches to population policy and family planning. Moreover, the diverse experiences of North African countries suggest that Tunisia's outperformance of the other countries in gender equality is due to a large extent to the "legal empowerment" of women which resulted from the 1956 *Code of Personal Status* and was strengthened by important policies and programs implemented during the Bourguiba regime (1957–1987).

---

[1] Saudi women will be able to vote starting in 2015.

On the other hand, female active participation in politics and labor markets (non-agricultural paid work) in North Africa, including Tunisia, has been markedly low, which points to the critical importance of understanding how *gendered* labor markets and political institutions come about and how they hinder women's empowerment. The historical trajectories of the four North African countries are, for the most part, inconsistent with the classical demographic transition theory, as well as with Becker's micro economic theory of fertility (Becker 1960).

The remainder of the chapter is organized as follows. Section 2 briefly reviews the literature on the role of women in development. Section 3 analyzes the trends in gender equality indicators, focusing on fertility, female health and education, as well as country progress towards achieving millennium development goal (MDG) 3. In particular, I discuss the so called "gender equality paradox" in North Africa, referring to the fact that the significant progress in closing gender gaps in education and health was not accompanied by a commensurate increase in female economic and political participation. In section 4, I comment on the contributions made by family planning programs and pro-women legal institutions to gender equality in Tunisia and the major disparities with other North African countries. I discuss how Tunisia's *Code of Personal Status* (CPS) of the 1950s has influenced the promotion of gender equality and enabled Tunisian women to have significantly greater freedom and exercise rights women in other countries in the region were not allowed to have. The last section provides a discussion and conclusions.

32.2 THE ROLE OF WOMEN IN DEVELOPMENT

United Nations MDG 3, which focuses specifically on promoting gender equality and empowering women, is possibly the most important of all eight Millennium Development Goals (MDGs) (Baliamoune-Lutz and McGillivray 2009) as it has major implications for the other MDGs. Numerous studies and reports have focused on the state of women's welfare, the constraints they face, the legal, economic, and social settings that shape such constraints, and the significant positive gains that would accrue to society from empowering women (Dollar and Gatti, 1999; Klasen 1999 and 2002; Duflo 2012; World Bank 2011). A key message in the World Bank's World Development Report 2012 (*Gender Equality and Development*, World Bank 2011) is that besides the fact that gender equality has an intrinsic value, it is also smart economics, as "greater gender equality can enhance productivity, improve development outcomes for the next generation, and make institutions more representative."

There are various areas where women may face gender-based discrimination and thus could be restricted from making positive contributions to growth and development. Among these areas, education, health, access to paid work, and legal rights—especially rights pertaining to asset ownership, inheritance, and participation in political processes—have been widely identified as key to understanding gender inequities and their effects on women's various contributions to development.

32.2.1 Female education

The positive link between gender equality in education and economic growth and development has been extensively documented in the literature (Hill and King 1995; Klasen 2002;

Schultz 2002; Knowles et al. 2002; Baliamoune-Lutz and McGillivray 2009; Klasen and Lamanna 2009). Knowles et al. (2002: 119) noted that "there is evidence that female education, especially in developing countries, also produces social gains by reducing fertility and infant mortality, improving family and child health, increasing life expectancy, and increasing the quantity and quality of children's educational attainment." Klasen (2002) finds that gender inequality in education has direct and indirect effects on growth. Lower female education lowers the average level of human capital and thus, has a negative (direct) impact on growth, while gender inequality has an influence on investment and population growth, producing an indirect effect on growth. Schultz (2002: 208) contended that "regions that have lagged behind in their growth—notably South and West Asia, the Middle East and North Africa, and sub-Saharan Africa—have lagged badly in their relative investments in women's schooling, thus limiting women's contributions to economic and social progress." Baliamoune-Lutz and McGillivray (2009) performed generalized method of moments (GMM) estimations on data from sub-Saharan Africa and Arab countries and find a significant negative growth effect of gender inequality in literacy rates, with the effect being stronger in Arab countries. Several other studies also documented that the positive effects of female access to education on growth and development tend to significantly operate through an impact on fertility and child mortality, i.e. improvements in human (Becker et al. 1990; Schultz 1993; Hill and King 1995; Klasen 1999).

32.2.2 Female reproductive health

In general, health can be used as an indicator of (male and female) human capital. Reproductive health, and in particular fertility, maternal mortality, and contraception use, are of particular relevance to gender equality. While low fertility rates are a major concern in many developed countries, in developing countries high fertility rates are generally considered a serious constraint to development. In developing economies, high fertility rates are generally correlated with greater gender inequality. This is because in the absence of gender equality—which tends to be the norm in patriarchal societies that are often predominant in developing regions—gender systems where men tend to make decisions about the use of contraceptives, desired number of children, and son preference are dominant. Mason (2001: 164) notes that "gender systems that maintain high levels of economic and social inequality between women and men seem likely to retard the onset of fertility decline." Moreover, some studies have found that in patriarchal societies more children can represent more security (against divorce) and status for mothers (Morgan and Niraula 1995; Izugbara and Eze 2010), which underscores the role played by gender inequities as reflected in women's unequal access to productive assets, education, and legal rights.

While it is observed that more developed economies have much lower fertility rates, it is not always clear whether causality runs from development to fertility or in the reverse direction (Ashraf et al. 2013).[2] This is because transition from high to low fertility rates, as argued by McDonald (2000a 2000b),[3] has been associated primarily with greater gender

---

[2] Bryant (2007) provides and interesting discussion on various propositions on the relationship between development and fertility. See also Das Gupta, et al. (2011).

[3] See also Mason (1997).

equity which occurred "almost exclusively within family-oriented institutions." McDonald (2000a: 437) further notes:

> The fall in fertility is associated with women acquiring rights within the family that enable them to reduce the number of their births to more desirable levels. However, change in the institution of the family proceeds slowly because the family system is strongly linked to conservative institutions such as religion.

In general, the literature identifies various pathways through which fertility affects growth and development in developing countries. Lower fertility was shown to have a positive effect on human capital, as reflected in women's and children's education, health, and women's greater participation in the labor force (Bloom et al. 2009; Rosenzweig and Zhang 2009; Miller 2010).

32.2.3 Gender equality and child health

Gender equality, especially through greater access to education for women, can have significant positive effects on child health and survival (Das Gupta 1990; Thomas 1990; Murthi et al. 1995; Klasen 1999). For example, Thomas (1990) found that the effects of the mother's unearned income on child health is much more significant compared with the effects of the father's unearned income. The author notes that "unearned income in the hands of the mother is estimated to have a bigger impact on her family's health than income attributed to the father. For child survival probabilities, the effect is almost 20 times bigger" (Thomas 1990:660). Similarly, Klasen (1999) found that reducing the gender bias in education greatly lowers child mortality rates.

Fielding and Torres (2009) documented the existence of a vicious circle between high child mortality and high fertility. The authors note that "[a] higher level of child mortality leads to higher fertility rates as households struggle to replace dying children, but the higher fertility in itself is bad for health."

32.2.4 Women's participation in the labor force

Women's access to paid work is key to their economic participation and economic empowerment, and has been shown to have a strong positive correlation with growth and development (Cuberes and Teignier 2012; Duflo 2012; World Bank 2011; Blackden and Hallward-Driemeier 2013). However, as emphasized by Elson (1999) and Baliamoune-Lutz (2007), women's participation in labor markets does not automatically empower them, as labor market institutions may remain gender-biased.

Galor and Weil (1996) showed that raising women's relative wages lowers fertility and lower fertility in turn increases capital per worker. In the presence of gender inequality, women face unequal access to jobs, especially high-paying jobs and thus end up over-represented in low-pay low-productivity jobs (Boserup 1970; Seguino 2000; Baliamoune-Lutz 2007). Consequently, women's economic independence, as well as their potential contributions to development, can be severely restricted and this in turn leads to persistence of gender inequities, thus creating a vicious circle.

32.3 TRENDS IN GENDER EQUALITY IN NORTH AFRICA

32.3.1 Historical trajectories of relevant indicators

32.3.1.1 *Fertility and health*

There are significant cross-country differences in the long-run trend of fertility rates. As Figure 32.1 shows, in the first two decades (1960–1979), Egypt had the lowest total fertility rates (births per woman). This trend was reversed so that since 1994 Egypt has had the highest fertility rates among the four countries. On the other hand, Algeria had the highest fertility rates from 1960 to 1993 and then reduced the rates significantly, at an average exceeding 5% per year, until 2000. Since 2001, however, the decline has slowed down, with Algeria's fertility rates in the late 2000s (and 2011) higher than those registered in the late 1990s. Fertility behavior in Morocco was quite similar to that in Tunisia for most of the 1960s. However, the two countries started to diverge towards the late 1960s, and especially in the 1980s and 1990s, with Tunisia significantly lowering fertility rates, while the pace of the decline in Morocco's fertility was much slower. Thus, Tunisia is the only country in the region that has consistently and significantly reduced fertility rates over at least 4 decades, and then stabilized them

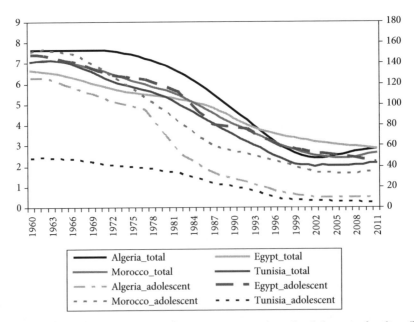

FIGURE 32.1 Fertility rates: Total (births per woman) and adolescent fertility (births per 1000 women ages 15–19, right scale).

Source: World Development Indicators database online (accessed on September 19, 2013)

around 2.1% in the last decade. In 2011, fertility rates in Tunisia were at least 0.5 births points lower than those in Morocco, and 0.7 births lower than the rates in Algeria and Egypt.

Similarly, there are stark differences in adolescent fertility rates (Figure 32.1). Tunisia started with significantly lower rates in 1960 and remained the country with the lowest rates until now. Algeria achieved significant progress in lowering adolescent fertility rates. On the other hand, adolescent fertility rates in Egypt and Morocco, although much lower than in the 1960s and 1970s, remain relatively high. In fact, adolescent fertility in Egypt in 2011 is at levels similar to those registered in Tunisia in the late 1960s and early 1970s, while the rates in Morocco in 2011 are almost the same as those registered in Tunisia in the early 1980s. However, in 2011 the rates in all four countries were lower than the world average (46 live births per 1000 woman, ages 15–19), with the rates Algeria and Tunisia being significantly lower.

High adolescent fertility rates can have significant impact both on gender inequality and development through adverse effects on girls' ability to stay in school, maternal and child heath, young women's access to labor markets, and by contributing to high population growth that is not supported by output growth. At the same time, both greater development and greater gender equality, at least in theory, can lead to lower adolescent fertility rates.

Figure 32.2a shows that Tunisia maintained the highest rate of adult mortality throughout the 1960s. However, mortality declined rapidly so that by the early 1970s, Tunisia began to outperform Algeria (which had the second highest rates in the 1960s) and shortly after that it started to outperform Morocco. By the early 1990s, Tunisia managed to achieve the lowest adult mortality rates for both men and women, registering one of the best performances in the world, within three decades. The remarkable success of Tunisia in this area contrasts with the slow progress of Egypt. Interestingly, female mortality rates in Algeria, Egypt, and Morocco seem to converge to similar levels (between 120 and 124 per 1000 female adult in 2011). To put the numbers into perspective, in 2011 the world average female mortality rate was 140, while the rate for male mortality was 196.5. All four North African countries had lower adult female mortality rates (with the rate in Tunisia being exactly half the world average) and all but Egypt had male mortality rates lower than the world average in 2011.

The convergence of female mortality rates in Algeria, Morocco, and Egypt is consistent with data on female life expectancy at birth. In 2011, female life expectancy in Tunisia was 76.7 years, while in Algeria, Egypt, and Morocco, it was 72.4, 73.1, and 72.2 years, respectively. Male life expectancy (in 2011) was 72.9 years in Tunisia versus 69.2, 68.4, and 68.7, in Algeria, Egypt, and Morocco, respectively.

Similarly, according to data available since 1990, Tunisia performed remarkably well, having the lowest maternal mortality rates for at least two decades (Figure 32.2b), while Morocco shows the highest, and Egypt the second highest, maternal mortality rates. Morocco and Egypt, however, registered the greatest decline in mortality rates; reducing maternal mortality by about two-thirds, from 300 to 100 in Morocco, and from 230 to 66 in Egypt, in 2010 relative to 1990.

As noted earlier, many studies have documented a strong link between child health and gender equality indicators, especially as measured by the mother's education (Caldwell and McDonald 1982; Klasen 1999; Bhandari et al. 2005). The four North African countries had different levels of child mortality rates (Figure 32.2c) over the period 1990–2012, although they all have achieved notable progress in reducing child mortality. Algeria and Tunisia maintained

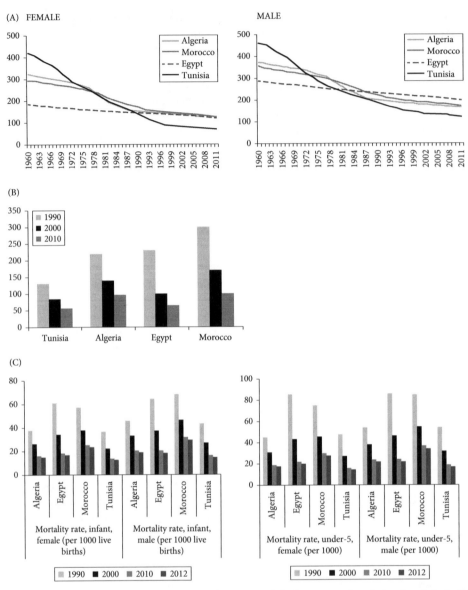

FIGURE 32.2 Mortality rates. (A) Mortality rate, adult (per 1000 female/male adults). (B) Maternal mortality ratio (modeled estimate per 100,000 live births). (C) Child mortality.

Source: World Development Indicators database online (accessed on September 19, 2013).

lower rates throughout this period, with Tunisia, again, being the best performer in the region. On the other hand, Morocco and Egypt started the period with much higher child mortality rates and achieved very substantial improvement in the course of a decade. Egypt and Morocco reduced child mortality rates by 44% and 34% in the first decade, and by 72% and almost 60% over the entire period, respectively. In 2012, the four countries all had child mortality rates lower than the averages for the Arab World and middle-income countries. In fact,

Tunisia's rates are comparable to those of some of the best performing emerging economies such as Turkey, Argentina, Brazil and Mexico, and Algeria is not far behind.

32.3.1.2 Labor force participation

Labor force participation for women (ages 15–64) in Algeria, Egypt and Tunisia has been low (Figure 32.3a) for over two decades, remaining below 30%, which is significantly lower than the world average. On the other hand, in Morocco, female labor force participation rates have consistently and significantly exceeded those in the other North African countries and have been only slightly below the world average (although female employment in the non-agricultural sector remains low). Young (ages 15–24) women's labor force participation rates are quite low in all four countries.[4] It is rather surprising that Tunisia, which

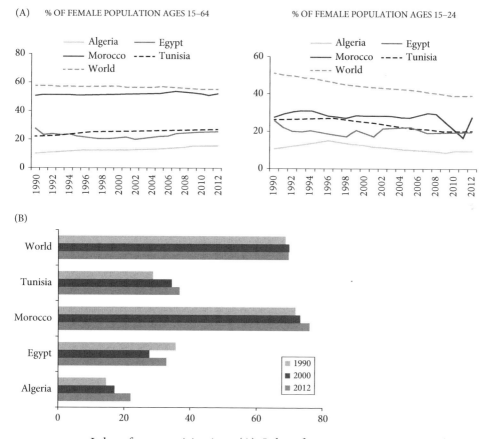

FIGURE 32.3 Labor force participation. (A) Labor force participation rates, female. (B) Ratio of female to male labor participation rate, 15+ (%).

Source: World Development Indicators database online (accessed on September 20, 2013).

---

[4] It is worth noting that the world average for young female labor participation rates has fallen dramatically over this period, from about 50% in 1990 to 39% in 2012.

outperforms North African countries and most Arab and African countries in gender equality in education and in fertility and other health indicators, still performs poorly in women's participation in labor markets.

32.3.1.3 Education: literacy and school enrolments

Female adult literacy rates are relatively low, generally less than 72%, in all four countries and are lower than male literacy rates. Morocco has the lowest rates of adult literacy for both male and female and also has the highest gender gap in literacy, with a 25 percentage point difference. Tunisia has the lowest gender inequality in adult literacy, while the difference in Algeria and Egypt (with a gap of 17 points) is also significantly lower than in Morocco. With 87% for men and 72% for women, Morocco also has the lowest male and female youth literacy rates, while both Algeria and Tunisia have rates exceeding 90%. Again, Tunisia shows the lowest levels of gender inequality.

All four countries have increased primary enrolments for both males and females to 100% or higher (Tunisia had 100% or higher already in 1991), except for Egypt which was slightly below the target (but in 2011 it had increased female primary enrolment rates to over 99%). Morocco had a significant decline in male and female primary enrolment rates in 1991, which might have been caused by the adverse effects of the early 1990s Gulf war on the tourist industry in the country and several years of drought in the late 1980s. Oddly, both female and male secondary enrolment ratios (Figure 32.4) in Egypt declined in the late 2000s, while Morocco registered the greatest progress in the 2000s, increasing secondary enrolment rates from 44% to about 72% in 2011 for males and from 35% to about 62% for females over the same period, but the country still has the highest gender inequality in secondary enrolments in North Africa.

Egypt had the best performance for both female and male enrolments in tertiary education until the start of the 2000s. However, in 2003 Tunisia took the lead in female tertiary

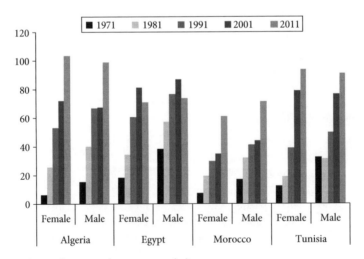

FIGURE 32.4 Secondary enrolment rates (%).

Source: World Development Indicators database online (accessed on September 20, 2013).

Egypt: 2010 instead of 2011.

enrolments and has remained since then the country with the highest female tertiary enrolment rates in North Africa. Tunisia also has the highest female-to-male ratio in tertiary education (1.52), followed by Algeria at a ratio of 1.46. On the other hand, Egypt and Morocco still have some gender inequality in female-male tertiary education levels, with Morocco also having the lowest tertiary enrolment rates for both women and men (less than 15% which is about half the rate in the other countries).

32.3.2 Assessing progress towards achieving MDG 3

MDG 3 is about promoting gender equality and empowering women. The target associated with this goal is to "eliminate gender disparity in primary and secondary education, preferably by 2005, and in all levels of education no later than 2015." To assess progress toward achieving this target, the world community, represented by the United Nations, has identified three indicators: (i) ratios of girls to boys in primary, secondary and tertiary education (Table 32.1); (ii) share of women in wage employment in the non-agricultural sector; and (iii) proportion of seats held by women in national parliaments.

Data related to these indicators suggest that Tunisia and Algeria achieved the target for gender parity in primary and secondary education in 2005, and Egypt, at a ratio of 95%, was near the target. On the other hand, Morocco was at least 11 percentage points away from complete gender parity in primary and secondary education. Similarly, Morocco and Egypt are about 10 percentage points away from gender parity in tertiary education. Interestingly, Algeria and Tunisia currently seem to be experiencing a reversal of gender inequality in tertiary education, with the ratio of women to men in higher education around 1.5 or greater.

The proportion of seats held by women in national parliaments is low, especially in Egypt. Until recently, Tunisia was the only country in the region with a share higher than 26%. Only recently—primarily as part of reforms motivated by the Arab spring in the region—did Algeria change from low proportion (8% or less until 2011) of parliamentarian women to 32%, making Algeria the first and only Arab country to exceed 30%.

Progress on the third indicator in MDG 3 has been rather slow in all four countries. The share of women employed in the nonagricultural sector remains low, at 21% or less in the late

Table 32.1 Ratio of girls to boys in primary, secondary, and tertiary education (2011 or as noted)

	Primary			Secondary			Tertiary		
	Female	Male	Ratio	Female	Male	Ratio	Female	Male	Ratio
Algeria	105.70	112.14	0.94	103.81	99.50	1.04	38.28	26.14	1.46
Egypt	99.24	105.27	0.94	71.05[a]	73.86[a]	0.96	26.27	29.20	0.90
Morocco	111.76[b]	117.86[b]	0.95	63.95[b]	75.46[b]	0.85	13.28[a]	14.99[a]	0.89
Tunisia	107.80	111.81	0.96	94.14	91.11	1.03	44.88	29.49	1.52

Source: World Development Indicators database online (accessed on September 20, 2013).
[a] 2010
[b] 2012.

2000s. This is significantly lower than Latin America's average of 43% or the world's average of 36%. North Africa shares this feature with other countries in the MENA region. Indeed, the share of women employed in the nonagricultural sector in the MENA region in 2010 was 19.3% and remains below 25% as of 2013. This phenomenon of important progress in reducing gender inequality in health and education that has not been accompanied by a significant increase in female participation in labor markets and politics has been dubbed the "gender-equality paradox" in the MENA region (Klasen and Lamanna 2009; World Bank 2013). Indeed, World Bank (2013:3) noted that "[a]lthough most MENA countries have made admirable progress in closing their gender gaps in education and health outcomes, these investments in human development have not yet translated into commensurately higher rates of female participation in economic and political life."

32.4 THE CONTRIBUTION OF FAMILY PLANNING TO GENDER EQUALITY: THE IMPORTANCE OF FAMILY LAW

For many years, women in Tunisia enjoyed a higher level of political empowerment compared to women in other North African countries, primarily due to having a higher level of "legal" empowerment. In 1956, the year the country gained its independence from France, Prime Minister Habib Bourguiba (who would become president in 1957) signed the Decree of 13 August 1956, which defined the laws governing personal status, known collectively as *Code du Statut Personnel* (the Code of Personal Status or CPS). [5] The CPS "reformed Marriage, divorce, custody, and to some extent inheritance. On all these dimensions, it expanded women's rights by eradicating some of the most patriarchal arrangements of the Shari'a. It abolished polygamy, eliminated the husband's right to repudiate his wife, allowed women to file for divorce, and increased women's custody rights" Charrad (1997: 294–295). The CPS also raised the minimum age at which men and women can get married to 20 and 17, respectively (prior to the CPS, the minimum age commonly used was the age of puberty). This has been generally credited for contributing to more boys and girls staying in school longer and improving heath for mothers and children (Baliamoune-Lutz 2011). Tunisia also revoked the law prohibiting the importation and sale of contraceptives, and restricted welfare support to the first four children. In 1962, the Tunisian government began discussions with the Ford Foundation on family planning, and in 1965 the country legalized abortion for women with five or more living children (Povey and Brown 1968).

A number of authors have studied Tunisia's great success and the much weaker performances of other North African countries in controlling population, some using data from as early as the 1960s (Lapham 1970; Lecomte and Marcoux 1976; Lee et al. 1998; Vignoli 2006; Eltigani 2000 and 2009). Many studies of the differences in family planning programs in North Africa have focused on investigating the use of contraceptives and their effectiveness in limiting birth rates. For example, Lapham (1970) estimated 1967–1968 birth rates that were

---

[5] This section draws on the discussion in Baliamoune-Lutz (2011).

avoided by contraceptive use in Tunisia and concluded that contraceptives were one of three main explanations of the significant drop in birth rates. He found that only about one-third of the fall in birth rates can be attributed to the family planning program (contraceptive use). The other two factors were changes in the age structure and the social status of women, with fewer women in the peak reproductive ages and the marriage age becoming higher. Lecomte and Marcoux (1976) used survey data to compare the experiences of Morocco and Tunisia and find that the two countries exhibited different approaches to population policy and family planning programs, and these different approaches were a result of their differing attitudes towards demographic problems.

Several studies have examined fertility behavior in Egypt and have demonstrated that the country lagged behind Tunisia (Eltigani 2000 and 2009; Rashad and Eltigani 2005; Robinson and El-Zanaty 2006). For example, Eltigani (2009) noted that although Egypt and Tunisia began their fertility transition around the same time, Tunisia reached replacement fertility levels (2.1 children per woman) by 2001, while Egypt is still significantly above replacement levels. The author put forward two potential explanations for this divergence. First, Tunisian women in all regions and at all educational levels "experienced a rapid and sustained decline of fertility during the course of the transition" whereas in Egypt, the sustained reduction in fertility rates was predominantly among rural and illiterate women. Second, the performance of national family planning programs "was greatly influenced by the commitment of political leaders, the integration of the programs within the wider framework of planning for socioeconomic development, and the passage of legislation concerning the family and the social, economic, and health aspects of the program" (Eltigani 2009: 225).

Similarly, studies that compared Algeria's family planning programs and fertility behavior to those in Tunisia concluded that Algeria was much slower in reducing fertility rates, and reaching replacement levels around the time Tunisia did, mainly because of weaknesses in its family planning programs and policies. For example, Lee et al. (1998) noted that Tunisia's institutional mobility seems to have been balanced by a policy risk sharing (or spread) among government agencies, which gave family planning a "firmer institutional support base" compared with family planning in Algeria. The authors note:

> During the 1970s, the ONFP [Tunisia's Office National de Famille et Population] was located within the MOPH [Ministry of Public Health] and managed by a Board of Directors representing eight ministries and three national organisations (Gueddana 1994). In 1982 the ONFP became affiliated with the Ministry of Women and Family Affairs, and in 1986 it moved back again to the MOPH. Throughout this period, the rationale of improving the status of women was consistently given for the FP [family planning] programme. In Algeria FP remained defined and institutionally fixed as a component of maternal and child health (MCH) within the MOH.
>
> Lee et al. (1998: 955)

32.5 DISCUSSION AND CONCLUSIONS

The literature contains numerous studies that have demonstrated the important role of gender systems in the demographic transition (Dyson and Moore 1983; Kabeer 1985; Mason 2001; Malhotra et al. 1995; Ergöçmen 1997; Abbasi-Chavazi et al. 2009). A useful approach to assessing women's status is to examine historical trajectories of fertility. This is because fertility seems to be a particularly strong chain linking women's status and their ability to make decisions in the household, societal views of women-men relations, prevalent legal and political institutions that shape family laws, and population control policies. In this chapter, I followed this approach as it seems highly appropriate in the context of gender economics in North Africa.

The analysis of country-level data reveals important differences in fertility and mortality levels and trends, especially between Tunisia and the other countries, underscoring differences in the pace and timing of the demographic transition, as well as significant differences in gender equality. Indeed, compared with the other countries, Tunisia experienced a more rapid, sustained, and earlier demographic transition.

The behaviors of fertility and mortality in Morocco, Algeria and Egypt, and the weak participation of North African women in labor markets in spite of declining fertility, especially in the case of Tunisia, seem at odd not only with the classical demographic transition theory put forward by demographers, but also with the neoclassical microeconomic theory of fertility (Becker 1960).[6]

At least four important lessons can be drawn from the diverse experiences of these four North African countries. First, the legal empowerment of women is a necessary but not sufficient condition for women's economic and political empowerment and de facto gender equity. It is necessary because, as the experience of Tunisia shows, it can lead to greater access to education and health for women. In Algeria, Egypt, and Morocco (at least prior to 2004),[7] family laws for over half a century were clearly biased against women and so most women in these countries could not achieve the status Tunisian women reached decades ago. Women's legal empowerment is however not sufficient because gender systems can be very complex, especially in patriarchal societies such as those in North Africa and the Middle East (but also in other parts of the world). As the experience of Tunisia shows, the importance of a nondiscriminatory family law is crucial to gender equality, but the so-called "gender-equality paradox" in North Africa demonstrates that a nondiscriminatory family law does not automatically lead to more economic and political empowerment.

Second, labor markets, as noted in Elson (1999), "are gendered institutions operating at the intersection of the productive and reproductive economies. Participation in labor markets does not automatically empower women." Labor market regulations that protect women against discriminatory practices are crucial to women's economic empowerment.

Third, gender inequality in labor markets can also be caused by societal views of women (culture, religion, kinship system). Youth unemployment, especially for young women, in North Africa is quite high. It is believed that this is what triggered the Arab Spring in Tunisia.

While women in North Africa played an important role in the Arab Spring, the level and nature of their active participation was different across countries. Women were more vocal and

---

[6] The demographers' classical demographic transition theory and the neoclassical microeconomic theory of fertility have been widely criticized in the literature (Knodel and van de Walle 1979; Cleland and Wilson 1987; Cleland 1985; McDonald 1993; Mason 1997).

[7] Morocco introduced a new Moudawana (Moroccan family code) with the view to eliminate a number of discriminatory practices and advance women's rights. However, women's organizations are critical of the new Moudawana and argue it still contains several discriminatory (against women) articles. An unofficial English translation is available online at: http://www.hrea.org/moudawana.html).

active in Tunisia compared with the other countries, allegedly due to greater gender equality in Tunisia. An important question that arises in Tunisia and Egypt, in particular, concerns the implications the Arab Spring has (or will have) for women empowerment and gender equality. As noted in Baliamoune-Lutz (2013), "[t]he rise of Islamist parties that have secured de jure (and possibly also de facto) political power in some countries seems to create new concerns about the fate of gender equality." Given that Egyptian women currently have weaker political and legal empowerment (relative to Tunisian women), it is likely that gender inequality will not be significantly reduced, regardless of whether the regime is Islamist or military.

Finally, given that fertility decline is vital to capturing the demographic dividend in SSA, there are important lessons related to the relationship between urbanization and demographic transition (classical demographic theory). Algeria has the highest urbanization rate in North Africa, (74% in 2012), yet there is no convincing evidence that urbanization has caused sustained demographic transition in the country. Many sub-Saharan African countries experienced significant increase in urbanization but still have fertility rates above 4%. For example, Gabon, which has the highest urbanization rate in Africa (86% in 2011, which is similar to the level in France), has a fertility rate of 4.2% (2011). Thus, in the absence of gender equality and economic transformation (based primarily on industrialization and agriculture transformation), African countries may end up with high urbanization and high fertility with potentially disastrous consequences on the quality of infrastructure, employment, and human wellbeing.

REFERENCES

Abbasi-Shavazi, M.J. McDonald, P., and Hosseini-Chavoshi, M. (2009). Women Autonomy and Fertility Behavior, in *The Fertility Transition in Iran: Revolution and Reproduction*. Dordrecht: Springer.

Ashraf, Q.H., Weil, D.N., and Wilde, J. (2013). The effect of fertility reduction on economic growth. *Population and Development Review*, 39(1):97–130.

Baliamoune-Lutz, M. (2007). Globalisation and gender inequality: Is Africa different? *Journal of African Economies*, 16(2):301–348.

Baliamoune-Lutz, M. (2011). The making of gender equality in Tunisia and implications for development. *World Bank Development Report 2012*. Background Paper. Washington, DC: available (under country case studies) at http://econ.worldbank.org/WBSITE/EXTERNAL/EXTDEC/EXTRESEARCH/EXTWDRS/EXTWDR2012/0,,contentMDK:22850830~menuPK:8155094~pagePK:64167689~piPK:64167673~theSitePK:7778063,00.html.

Baliamoune-Lutz. M. (2013). Tunisia's Development Experience: A Success Story? in A. Fosu (ed.), *Achieving Development Success: Strategies and Lessons from the Developing World*. Oxford: Oxford University Press, pp. 457–480.

Baliamoune-Lutz, M., and McGillivray, M. (2009). Does gender inequality reduce growth in sub-Saharan African and Arab countries? *African Development Review*, 21(2):224–242.

Becker, G. (1960). An economic analysis of fertility, in *Demographic and Economic Change in Developed Countries*. Princeton, NJ: NBER, Princeton University Press, pp. 209–331.

Becker, G., Murphy, K.N., and Tamura, R. (1990). Human capital, fertility, and economic Growth. *Journal of Political Economy* 98:S12–S37.

Bhandari, N., Bhan, G., Taneja, S. et al. (2005). The effect of maternal education on gender bias in care-seeking for common childhood illnesses. *Social Science & Medicine*, 60(4):715–724.

Bloom, D.E., Canning, D., Fink, G., and Finlay, J. E. (2009). Fertility, female labor force partici-pation, and the demographic dividend. *Journal of Economic Growth*, 14(2):79–101.

Boserup, E. (1970). *Women's Role in Economic Development*. New York: St. Martin's Press.

Bryant, J. (2007). Theories of fertility decline and the evidence from development indicators. *Population and Development Review*, 33(1):101–127.

Caldwell, J., and McDonald, P. (1982). Influence of maternal education on infant and child mortality: levels and causes. *Health Policy and Education*, 2(3–4):251–267.

Charrad, M.M. (1997). Policy shifts: sate, Islam, and gender in Tunisia, 1930s-1990s. *Social Politics*, 4(2):284–319.

Cleland, J. (1985). Marital fertility decline in developing countries: theories and the evidence, in J. Cleland and J. Hobcraft (eds), *Reproductive Change in Developing Countries: Insights from the World Fertility Survey*. Oxford: Oxford University Press, pp. 23–52.

Cleland, J., and Wilson, C. (1987). Demand theories of the fertility transition: an iconoclastic view. *Population Studies*, 41(1):5–30.

Cuberes, D., and Teignier, M. (2012). Gender Gaps in the Labor Market and Aggregate Productivity. Sheffield Economic Research Paper SERP 2012017.

Das Gupta, M., Bongaarts, J., and Cleland, J. (2011). Population, Poverty, and Sustainable Development: A Review of the Evidence. World Bank Policy Research Working Paper 5719. Washington, DC: World Bank.

Das Gupta, M. (1990). Death clustering, mother's education, and the determinants of child mortality in rural Punjab, India. *Journal of Population Studies*, 44:489–505.

Dollar, D., and Gatti, R. (1999). Gender Inequality, Income, and Growth. Are Good Times Good for Women? World Bank Gender and Development Working Paper No. 1. Washington, DC: World Bank.

Duflo, E. (2012). Women empowerment and economic development. *Journal of Economic Literature*, 50(4):1051–1079.

Dyson, T., and Moore, M. (1983). On kinship structure, female autonomy and demographic behaviour in India. *Population and Development Review*, 9(March):35–60.

Elson, D. (1999). Labor markets as gendered institutions: equality, efficiency and empower-ment issues. *World Development*, 27(3):611–627.

Eltigani, E.E. (2000). Changes in family-building patterns in Egypt and Morocco: A compara-tive analysis. *International Family Planning Perspectives*, 26(2):73–78.

Eltigani, E.E. (2009). Toward replacement fertility in Egypt and Tunisia. *Studies in Family Planning*, 40(3):215–226.

Ergöçmen, B.A. (1997). Women's status and fertility in Turkey, in A. Hancıoğlu, B.A. Ergöçmen, and T. Ünalan (eds), *Fertility Trends, Women's Status, and Reproductive Expectations in Turkey*. Calverton, MD: Hacettepe Institute of Population Studies and Macro International Inc, pp. 79–102.

Fielding, D., and Torres, S. (2009). Health, wealth, fertility, education, and inequality. *Review of Development Economics*, 13(1):39–55.

Galor, O., and Weil, D.N. (1996). The gender gap, fertility, and growth. *American Economic Review*, 86(3):374–387.

Gueddana, N. (1994). Population Policies and Programs: Determinants and Consequences in Tunisia (1956–1992). Unpublished case study.

Hill, M.A., and King, E.M. (1995). Women's education and economic well-being. *Feminist Economics*, 1(2):21–46.

Izugbara, C.O., and Ezeh, A.C. (2010). Women and high fertility in Islamic northern Nigeria. *Studies in Family Planning*, 41(3):193–204.

Kabeer, N. (1985). Do women gain from high fertility? in H. Afsar (ed.), *Women, Work and Ideology in the Third World*. London: Tavistock Publications.

Klasen, S. (1999). Does Gender Inequality Reduce Growth and Development? World Bank Policy Research Report Working Paper No. 7. Washington, DC: World Bank.

Klasen, S. (2002). Low schooling for girls, slower growth for all? Cross-country evidence on the effect of gender inequality in education on economic development. *World Bank Economic Review*, 16(3):345–373.

Klasen, S., and Lamanna, F. (2009). The impact of gender inequality in education and employment on economic growth: new evidence for a panel of countries. *Feminist Economics*, 15(3):91–132.

Knodel, J., and van de Walle, E. (1979). Lessons from the past: policy implications of historical fertility studies. *Population and Development Review*, 5(June):217–245.

Knowles, S., Lorgelly, P.K., and Owen, P.D. (2002). Are educational gender gaps a brake on economic development? Some cross-country empirical evidence. *Oxford Economic Papers*, 54(1):118–149.

Lapham, R.J. (1970). Family planning and fertility in Tunisia. *Demography*, 7(2):241–253.

Lecomte, J., and Marcoux, A. (1976). Contraception and fertility in Morocco and Tunisia. *Studies in Family Planning*, 7(7):182–187.

Lee, K., Lush L., Walt G., and Cleland, J. (1998). Family planning policies and program in eight low-income countries: a comparative policy analysis. *Social Science & Medicine*, 47(7):949–959.

Malhotra, A., Vanneman, R., and Kishor, S. (1995). Fertility, dimensions of patriarchy, and development in India. *Population and Development Review*, 21:281–305.

Mason, K.O. (1997). Explaining fertility transitions. *Demography*, 34(4):443–454.

Mason, K.O. (2001). Gender and family systems in fertility transition. *Population and Development Review*, 27(Supplement):160–176.

McDonald, P. (1993). Fertility transition hypotheses, in R. Leete and I. Alam (eds), *The Revolution in Asian Fertility: Dimensions, Causes, and Implications*. Oxford: Clarendon Press, pp. 3–14.

McDonald, P. (2000a). Gender equity in theories of fertility transition. *Population and Development Review*, 26(3):427–439.

McDonald, P. (2000b). Gender equity, social institutions and the future of fertility. *Journal of Population Research*, 17(1):1–16.

Miller, G. (2010). Contraception as development? New evidence from family planning in Colombia. *Economic Journal*, 120(545):709–736.

Morgan, S.P. and Niraula, B.B. (1995). Gender inequality and fertility in two Nepali villages. *Population and Development Review*, 21(3):541–561.

Murthi, M., Guio, A-C., and Drèze, J. (1995). Mortality, fertility, and gender bias in India: a district-level analysis. *Population and Development Review*, 21:745–782.

Povey, W.G., and Brown, G.F. (1968). Tunisia's experience in family planning. *Demography*, 5(2):620–626.

Rashad, H., and Eltigani, E.E. (2005). Explaining fertility decline in Egypt, in G.W. Jones and M.S. Karim (eds), *Islam, the State and Population*. London: C. Hurst & Co, pp. 174–198.

Robinson, W.C., and El-Zanaty, F.H. (2006). *The Demographic Revolution in Modern Egypt*. Lanham, MD: Lexington Books.

Rosenzweig, M.R., and Zhang, J. (2009). Do population control policies induce more human capital investment? Twins, birth weight and china's 'one-child' policy. *Review of Economic Studies*, 76(3):1149–1174.

Schultz, T.P. (1993). Investments in the schooling and health of women and men: quantities and returns. *Journal of Human Resources*, 28(4):694–734.

Schultz, T.P. (2002). Why governments should invest more to educate girls. *World Development*, 30(2):207–225.

Seguino, S. (2000). "Gender inequality and economic growth: A cross-country analysis." *World Development*, 28 (7): 1211-1230.

Thomas, D. (1990). Intrahousehold resource allocation: an inferential approach. *Journal of Human Resources*, 25:634–664.

Vignoli, D. (2006). Fertility change in Egypt: from second to third birth. *Demographic Research*, 15(18):499–516.

World Bank (2011). *World Development Report 2012. Gender Equality and Development.* Washington, DC: World Bank.

World Bank (2013). *Opening Doors: Gender Equality and Development in the Middle East and North Africa.* Washington, DC: World Bank.

CHAPTER 33

....

THE ECONOMICS OF THE AFRICAN MEDIA

....

JULIA CAGÉ

33.1 INTRODUCTION

....

BUILDING state capacity. Making governments more accountable. Fighting corruption. Improving the provision of public goods. These challenges are central for achieving long-term sustainable and inclusive growth in developing countries, especially in sub-Saharan Africa.[1] A common denominator and a necessary condition for these countries to succeed and to develop democratically[2]—condition that one tends to forget from today's developed countries' perspective—is the power of information. An informative press is indeed a potent check on corruption; it enhances effective and active monitoring of public goods delivery (e.g. health and education) and is an instrument of public accountability.[3]

---

[1] The geographical coverage of this chapter is partial. Because North African and sub-Saharan African newspapers developed differently at different time periods, and because the current state of the media market differs from one region to the other, analyzing both cases is beyond the goal of this work. The focus of this chapter is on sub-Saharan Africa; this geographical choice is driven both by the need to increase our knowledge of the sub-Saharan African media market—I will come back to this point below but nearly no research in economics has been done on this topic—and by the lessons that can be learned from this special case for other developing and developed countries.

[2] Of course many countries—China is but one example—have developed, i.e. grow economically, without a free media. But in these countries corruption is still very high and economic growth tends not to be inclusive.

[3] Using the example of Sierra Leone, Casey (2010) shows that the quality of information available to voters influences the choices they make in the polling booth and in turn affects the strategies of political parties competing for their support in developing countries. Cagé (2009) finds that increasing the information available to citizens increases the efficiency of official development aid in developing countries. Exploiting a newspaper campaign in Uganda aimed at reducing the capture of public funds by providing schools with systematic information to monitor local officials' handling of a large education grand program, Reinikka and Svensson (2005) show that public access to information can be a powerful deterrent to the capture of funds at the local level and that the reduction in the capture of funds that resulted had a positive effect on school enrollment and learning outcomes.

Moreover, not only a free and informative press is crucial to good governance and democratic development, but it also affects economic development—through its impact on social capital (Olken 2009) or women empowerment (Jensen and Oster 2009)—as well as the effective functioning of markets.[4]

Despite this central importance of an informative press for the future of Africa, the literature has overlooked the issue of what makes it viable.[5] The media are businesses and are shaped by many economic factors. The focus of this chapter is on the economics of the sub-Saharan African media.[6] Using the history of sub-Saharan African newspapers as well as historical evidence from Europe and the United States, I study the rise—and sometimes the failure—of market-oriented journalism and of an independent and informative press in sub-Saharan Africa. Do sub-Saharan African newspapers have followed the same "steps" of development than newspapers in other countries, moving from living off patronage and government favors to moving more towards mass sales and advertising revenues? And is the story of the sub-Saharan African media a simple story of catching up and convergence?

One may argue that it would be absurd to make too many broad generalizations about media in sub-Saharan Africa. But when it comes to the economics of the media, sub-Saharan African countries share certain features in common. Importantly, through the study of the economics of the sub-Saharan African media, this chapter challenges two traditional views of the media. First, the study of Africa shows that there exist multiple possible long-term paths in media development. In particular, this chapter questions the long-term sustainability of advertising-dependent media systems; it discusses a new framework to improve the financial sustainability of mass media while preserving the independence of media outlets. Second, this chapter questions the view that more media competition is always socially efficient and necessary to ensure diversity. Press freedom and diversity are naturally desirable; but we learn from the history of sub-Saharan Africa media that chaotic proliferation of low-quality media outlets may be bad. In order to analyze the optimal industrial organization of the media sector, it is critical to better understand the economic incentives of the media to deliver news (see e.g. Cagé 2014).

One may think that an analysis of the economics of the media with a focus on newspapers in developing countries, especially in sub-Saharan Africa, is a misplaced emphasis. Not only radio has the widest population reach in sub-Saharan Africa[7] but, as we will see, newspaper penetration is still very low in a number of African countries compared to developed

---

[4] Using the Market Information Service project in Uganda—that collected data on prices for the main agricultural commodities in major market centers and disseminated the information through local FM radio stations in various districts—Svensson and Yanagizawa (2009) show that market information improves farmers' relative bargaining position vis-à-vis local traders.

[5] More generally, the focus of the media economics literature until now has been on developed countries, especially the United States. In my view, one of the main challenges today is to study the media—and how it affects the political process—in developing countries.

[6] The main focus of this chapter is on print media (newspapers) rather than on television or radio. I come back to this point below.

[7] Television is less widely available, although it is seen as a growing force.

countries where the newspaper market is of much more importance. The point, however, is that countries in Africa are among the only countries in the world where the reading of newspapers will continue its expansion during the coming decades. While newspaper sales are generally said to be falling, as traditional print media struggle to compete with broadcasting and online media, newspaper circulations are growing in many countries across sub-Saharan Africa: the newspaper market expands as literacy steadily increases, whereas other media like television or the internet require capital that most sub-Saharan Africans do not have. More importantly, newspapers tend to be relatively independent, while in most sub-Saharan African countries, State-controlled radio and television services still command the biggest audiences.[8] On the whole, private newspapers tend to be more outspoken than radio and television stations.

Before turning to the analysis, let me finally underline that there is a dearth of publicly available data on the media sector in sub-Saharan Africa, both for historical and current data; future research should aim at filling this knowledge gap. In this chapter, I use data that I collected for previous research I did on sub-Saharan African media, as well as a number of different datasets.[9]

The rest of the chapter is organized as follows. Section 2 provides a very simple conceptual framework to rationalize the relationship between the quality of the media and political well-being. Section 3 discusses the historical development of the African Media. Section 4 provides evidence on the current state of the African media and highlights that the traditional media system models need to be enhanced to understand the complexity of the sub-Saharan African situation and to draw lessons for the future and for the rest of the world. Section 5 presents alternative economic models for the press. Section 6 concludes.

---

[8] In Angola, the government has a monopoly on all TV and national radio. All terrestrial channels are owned by the state. The state owns and runs the two major radio stations and has a monopoly on television in Botswana. In Cameroon, the state-run Cameroon Radio Television (CRTV) is the only station with a national footprint. Similarly, in Chad, the only radio station with nationwide reach is the government-run Radiodiffusion Nationale du Tchad and the only TV station is the state-run TéléTchad. State-run Radio Television Ivoirienne has an official monopoly on free-to-air television broadcasting in Cote d'Ivoire and is tightly controlled by the government. In Ethiopia, nearly all radio and TV stations are owned by the government. While state-owned Ethiopian Radio is the dominant radio player, the state-owned Ethiopian Television retains its monopoly on domestic-free-to-air TV. In Ghana, the only nationwide radio broadcaster is the state-owned Ghana Broadcasting Corporation and state-owned Ghana TV is the only station that has a national broadcast footprint. Similarly in Guinea, Guinea's state broadcaster Radiodiffusion-Television Guinéenne is the country's only nationwide radio and television services. These are but a few examples.

[9] Angola (AMDI), Benin (Afrobarometer), Botswana (AMDI, Afrobarometer); Cameroon (AMDI); Chad (Infoasaid); Côte d'Ivoire (Infoasaid); Democratic Republic of Congo (AMDI, Infoasaid); Ethiopia (AMDI, Infoasaid); Ghana (AMDI, Afrobarometer); Guinea (Infoasaid); Kenya (AMDI, Afrobarometer, Infoasaid); Lesotho (Afrobarometer); Madagascar (Afrobarometer); Malawi (Afrobarometer); Mali (Afrobarometer); Mozambique (AMDI, Afrobarometer, Infoasaid); Namibia (Afrobarometer); Niger (Infoasaid); Nigeria (AMDI, Afrobarometer, mediaReach OMD); Senegal (AMDI, Afrobarometer); Sierra Leone (AMDI); Somalia (AMDI, Infoasaid); South Africa (AMDI, Afrobarometer, mediaReach OMD); South Sudan (Infoasaid); Tanzania (AMDI, Afrobarometer, Ipsos); Uganda (AMDI, Afrobarometer; Ipsos); Zambia (Afrobarometer, AMDI); Zimbabwe (AMDI, Afrobarometer, Infoasaid). AMDI stands for American Media Development Initiative.

33.2 A VERY SIMPLE CONCEPTUAL
FRAMEWORK

What is the relationship between the quality of the media and political well-being? We know at least since Condorcet (1785) that political institutions have a constructive role to play in order to allow for an efficient aggregation of all the socially useful information that is dispersed among individuals (see e.g. Piketty 1999, who discusses this information-aggregation approach to political institutions). While information pertinent to individual decisions never exists in aggregated form but solely as the dispersed bits of incomplete information, efficient political institutions should allow for an efficient use of these dispersed bits of information.

The so-called "Condorcet Jury Theorem" can be—in its simplest form—stated as follows. First, assume that a population of size N has to choose between two possible policies $P = A$ or B and that all agents have the same state-dependent utility function $U(P/s)$; in other words, if the state of the world s is equal to s_A, they all prefer policy A to policy B: $U(A/s_A) > U(B/s_A)$. Second, assume that all agents have the same initial prior beliefs about the unobservable state of the world $\mu(s_A) = \mu(s_B) = \frac{1}{2}$. Finally, assume that all agents receive a signal $\sigma = \sigma_A$ or σ_B drawn from the same conditional distribution, such that $Prob(\sigma=\sigma_A/s=s_A) = Prob(\sigma=\sigma_B/s=s_B) = p > \frac{1}{2}$. The Condorcet Jury Theorem states that if majority-rule voting elections are held, the probability that the efficient policy (A in state s_A, B in state s_B) wins a majority of the vote tends to 1 as N goes to $+\infty$. In other words, majority-rule voting allows efficient information aggregation.

The role of the media in this framework is key: the quality of the information framework, i.e. of the signals received by the agents, is indeed central for the efficiency of the political process. To understand why, one has to relax some assumptions of the very simple Condorcet framework. While Condorcet (1785) assumes exogenous signal acquisition, central is to explain why some agents choose to acquire information while others do not. Assume that only a fraction q of the agents acquired a signal and that among the informed agents, the fraction which observes the message $\sigma \in \{\sigma_A, \sigma_B\}$ in state σ is $\rho \in (0.5,1]$ (see e.g. Feddersen and Pesendorfer 1996; Feddersen and Sandroni 2006a, b). When ρ is close to 0.5 the message is a very noisy signal of the true state, while when ρ is close to 1, the message almost perfectly conveys the true state. The media enters this simple conceptual framework in two important ways: first, the share of informed agents q that decide to acquire a signal depends on the cost of information acquisition, that is, on the cost (through their price or accessibility) of newspapers (if one focuses on print media); second, the quality of the signal ρ is an increasing function of the quality of the newspapers (see e.g. Cagé 2014). In such a framework, one can show that the information aggregation property of large elections improves as the quality of information increases and also depends on the cost of information acquisition.

The rest of the chapter presents the evolution of the sub-Saharan print media and discusses different business models for an informative press—an accessible high-quality press—such an informative press being key for the information aggregation property of elections, that is, for democracy.

33.3 THE HISTORICAL DEVELOPMENT OF THE AFRICAN MEDIA[10]

....

Do sub-Saharan African newspapers follow the same "steps" of development than other newspapers? For instance, will a "social history" of American newspapers such as the one of Schudson (1981) be of any help to understand the history of newspapers in other countries in the world? While we tend to think that newspapers in the West historically developed as a product either of the political world or the market economy,[11] the study of the historical development of sub-Saharan African newspapers sheds a new light on the development of media markets. The sub-Saharan African case indeed highlights important aspects of what makes the media industry viable that have been overlooked in the existing literature.

The press in sub-Saharan Africa is relatively young when compared to the rest of the world. While the first newspapers in the West appeared in the seventeenth century[12]—in France for example, the first newspaper was created in 1631 and the first daily in 1777 (Daubert 2009); and the first "corantos," the forerunners of the modern newspaper, came out in the urban centers as early as 1607 in Amsterdam (Hallin and Mancini 2004)—the first newspapers in sub-Saharan Africa did not appear before the beginning of the nineteenth century. The *Cape Town Gazette* appeared in South Africa in 1800 and the *Royal Gazette* in Sierra Leone a year later. The first truly indigenous press—the black Africa's press—was founded in Liberia in 1826 with the monthly *Liberia Herald* of Charles Force (Mytton 1983), in Ghana in 1857 (the *West African Herald*—the first newspaper of an African from Africa) and in Nigeria in 1859 (*Iwe Irohin—"The Newspaper"*).

Why is the press in sub-Saharan Africa so young? First and foremost because in order to produce newspapers, one needs economic and technological development, and in particular the printing press technology. In sub-Saharan Africa, Protestant missionaries—because they needed to print Bibles and educational material in order to spread their religious beliefs[13]—were the first both to import the printing press technology and to allow the indigenous population to use it (Woodberry 2012; Cagé and Rueda 2013). This early availability of the printing technology enabled the local development of a culture of writing and information diffusion. Thanks to early access to the printing press, local newspapers developed first in certain African regions and not in others.

---

[10] Part of this section relies on my work with Valeria Rueda on "The Long-Term Effects of the Printing Press in sub-Saharan Africa" (Cagé and Rueda 2013).

[11] According to Hallin and Mancini (2004: 90), "the media developed in Southern Europe as an institution of the political and literary worlds more than of the market. In Northern Europe and North America, the commercial bourgeoisie, whose success in a market economy depended on a steady flow of reliable information about trade, navigation, technology, and politics, played a key role in the development of the first newspapers."

[12] There is an open debate in the literature on whether newspapers appeared in the non-Western world in the first place. While some researchers point out that in China for example, the *Pekin Gazette* dates back to the eighth century, others argue that such a publication cannot be considered as a newspaper and that newspapers did not exist in East Asian countries before they opened to the West.

[13] According to the principle of the *Sola Scriptura* central to the Protestant doctrine, every Protestant should be able to read the Bible.

Because Protestant missionaries made printing presses available to the native population, most of the first indigenous newspapers were printed and sponsored by mission centers.[14] The first newspaper intended for black readers, the *Umshumayeli Wendaba ("Publishers of the News")*, written in Xhosa, was published as an irregular quarterly in 1837 and printed at the Wesleyan Missionary Society in Cape Colony. The London Missionary Society and Methodist missions also produced the earliest journals aimed at the Tswana Christian community from their stations at Kuruman and Thaba'Nchu. *Mokaeri Oa Becuana, Le Muleri Oa Mahuku ("The Teacher of the Bechuana, the Announcer of the News")*, which started in 1857, is regarded as the oldest newspaper in the Tswana language (Switzer 1984). *Isigidimi samaXhosa ("The Xhosa Messenger")*, the first African newspaper edited by Africans, was first released in 1876 and printed at the Lovedale Mission Press. Eight years later, in 1884, the English/Xhosa weekly *Imvo Zabantsundu ("The African Opinion")* was published. It was the first black-owned and controlled newspaper in South Africa (Switzer and Switzer 1979).

The role played by Protestant missions in the introduction of the first newspapers is thereby key; strikingly, in regions where Protestant missions were less active, the first newspapers appeared only at the beginning of the twentieth century and no indigenous newspapers were created before World War I. While by the end of the nineteenth century, about 34 newspapers had appeared in Sierra Leone, nineteen in the Gold Coast, nine in Nigeria[15] and one in the Gambia (Mytton 1983), before the war, the printing presses were still mostly owned by the colonial powers in former French colonies. In these colonies, the only publications were religious or official publications; newspapers were made by and intended for Europeans (Daubert 2009).[16] The first paper in Cote d'Ivoire to be owned and edited by an African, the *Eclaireur de la Cote d'Ivoire*, only appeared in 1935 (Mytton 1983).[17] More importantly, this lag of more than one century in the timing of creation of the first indigenous newspapers appears as one the determinants of the differences in the current state of the newspaper industry in different sub-Saharan African countries. Newspapers take time to consolidate. At the time of independence, 88% of the former English colonies had a private press, against only 27% of the former French colonies (including Madagascar and Maurice) (Daubert 2009).[18] Moreover, in most sub-Saharan African countries, the newly established government tried to take control of the press after independence. These nationalizations did not succeed in countries where newspapers were well established, stable and independent before colonization (see e.g. Faye 2008). In Nigeria, for instance, despite the coup d'état, the ensuing military regime and the development of a state-owned press, independent newspapers managed to survive. Similarly, even during Apartheid in South Africa, the black press and anti-Apartheid white-owned

---

[14] The study of a possible agenda of these newspapers is well beyond the scope of this chapter. However, it is important to highlight that these newspapers often provided spaces for intellectuals to discuss reform ideas; criticisms of colonization and statements in favor of slavery abolitions were part of these newspapers that may be viewed as the seeds for nationalist movements (see e.g. Woodberry 2004).

[15] Between 1859 and 1937, a little more than four dozen newspapers were established in Nigeria (Omu 1957).

[16] The situation is similar in former Portuguese colonies. In these colonies, the printing press was introduced only in 1854. In May 1854, the *Boletin do governo de Provincia de Moçambique* was published, an official newspaper. The first private newspaper, *O Progresso*, appeared in 1868 but was banned after the first issue, and one has to wait until 1870 to see published a new newspaper, *A Impresa* (Tudesq 1995).

[17] The French discouraged the establishment of indigenous African publishing. All the early newspapers—such as *Le Réveil du Sénégalais* launched in 1886 and *L'Union Africaine* in 1896—were published by Frenchmen (Mytton 1983).

[18] In French West Africa (*Afrique Occidentale Française*—AOF) at the time of the independences, among the 132 "newspapers" registered in 1958, nearly half is made of handouts (trade-union, political, or

presses continued to exist. The *Daily Dispatch*, the *SASO Newsletter* or *The World* regularly dif-
fused their anti-Apartheid stances. This was not the case in former French colonies.

Figure 33.1 (from Cagé and Rueda 2013) shows the cross-country correlation between the
number of newspapers that have existed and the average distance to the closest historical
mission settlement with a printing press. The figure displays a negative correlation between
the average distance to the printing press and the total number of newspapers recorded.
Figure 33.2 shows the correlation between the date of publication of the first newspaper and
the average distance to the closest historical Protestant mission station with a printing press.
There is a positive correlation between the distance to the printing press and the publication
date of the first newspaper: the closer a location is to a historically attested printing press, the
sooner the first newspaper is recorded. In other words, thanks to early access to the printing press, newspapers emerged earlier around mission stations and this concentration pattern persists over time. In a very careful analysis of the historical determinants of newspaper
readership in sub-Saharan Africa, Cagé and Rueda (2013) find that proximity to a historical missionary settlement endowed with a printing press significantly increases newspaper
readership today within regions located close to historical mission settlements.

What lessons can we draw from this brief overview of the history of sub-Saharan African newspapers? First, that there is a lot of persistence in reading habits. In the sub-Saharan African case,

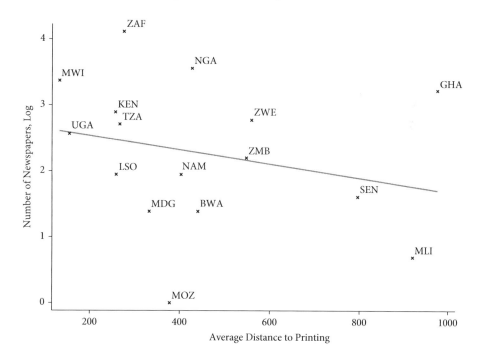

FIGURE 33.1 Distance to the printing press and cumulated number of newspapers
(1800–2000).

Source: Cagé and Rueda (2013). BWA: Botswana; GHA: Ghana; KEN: Kenya; LSO: Lesotho; MLI: Mali;
MDG: Madagascar; MOZ: Mozambique; MWI: Malawi; NAM: Namibia; NGA: Nigeria; SEN: Senegal; TZA: Tanzania;
UGA: Uganda; ZAF: South Africa; ZMB: Zambia; ZWE: Zimbabwe.

confessional bulletins) of random existence. Only a dozen can be considered as real newspapers sold on a
regular basis and written by a permanent team (Perret 2005).

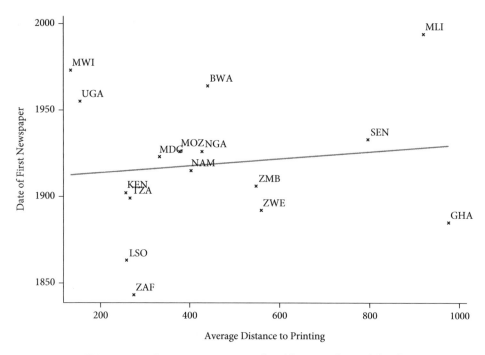

FIGURE 33.2 Distance to the printing press and publication date of the first newspaper.

high circulation newspapers[19] may have developed in some countries while in other they do not because in some countries individuals became used to read newspapers before getting access to the radio, while in others—in which a private newspaper industry appeared after the radio—they do not. In the last, one may say that sub-Saharan African media have skipped the print newspapers phase of media development, the countries having gone straight from "nothing" to radio.

33.4 THE CURRENT STATE OF THE AFRICAN MEDIA

The economics of a newspaper may be studied from different perspectives. In order to discuss the sub-Saharan African situation, this chapter relies on—and challenges—the different media system models developed by Hallin and Mancini (2004) in their path-breaking comparative study of news systems.[20]

Hallin and Mancini (2004), focusing on the Western world, distinguish three media system models:

---

[19] I cannot use the terminology "mass circulation newspapers" in the sub-Saharan African case; I come back to this point below.

[20] Nor in Hallin and Mancini (2004) which consider 18 advanced capitalist democracies in Western Europe and North America neither in their follow-up book focusing of the non-Western world (Hallin and Mancini 2012)—to the exception of a chapter on South Africa, the sub-Saharan African case is used to build insights on the economics of the media all around the world.

1. The "Liberal Model," which prevails across Britain, Ireland, and North America and is characterized by a relative dominance of market mechanisms and of commercial media.
2. The "Democratic Corporatist Model," which prevails across northern continental Europe (Austria, Belgium, Denmark, Finland, Germany, the Netherlands, Norway, Sweden, and Switzerland), is characterized by a historical coexistence of commercial media and media tied to organized social and political groups, and by a relatively active but legally limited role of the state.
3. The "Polarized Pluralist Model," which prevails in the Mediterranean countries of southern Europe (France, Greece, Italy, Portugal, and Spain), is characterized by integration of the media into party politics, weaker historical development of commercial media, and a strong role of the state.

Their classification relies on four dimensions according to which media systems can usefully be compared in their view:

1. The development of media markets, with particular emphasis on the strong or weak development of a mass circulation press.
2. Political parallelism, that is, the degree and nature of the links between the media and political parties or, more broadly, the extent to which the media system reflects the major political divisions in society.
3. The development of journalistic professionalism.
4. The degree and nature of state intervention in the media system.

This chapter highlights that these dimensions—despite their general relevance—are not enough to understand the complexity of the sub-Saharan African situation as well as of other countries. In particular, one has also to take into account (i) the business model of the newspapers, and in particular their reliance on advertising revenues versus revenues from sales or from other sources; and (ii) the issue of the access to the media—that one tends to forget in developed countries but that is still a key issue in developing countries, as will appear clearly below.

33.4.1 A mass circulation press?

As it appeared clearly above, the state of the press varies from countries to countries in sub-Saharan Africa—and some of these differences come from differences in the historical development of the media in these countries. Nonetheless, it is hard to argue that any of the sub-Saharan African countries have ever had a mass circulation press. There are two ways to approach this question. First, by looking at the aggregate newspaper readership at the country level. Second, by analyzing the number of newspapers and studying the readership of each newspaper.

Before moving further, it is important to have some basic orders of magnitude in mind about what mass newspaper readership means historically in Western democracies. Both in Europe and in Northern America, the rise of modern democracy and universal suffrage has come together with a state of affairs where at least half of the electorate—and usually as much as two thirds or three quarters—reads a newspaper on a daily basis. For instance, in France, the circulation—that is, the number of daily copies sold—of local daily newspapers has been of the order of 20–25% of the electorate throughout the 1950–2010 period (and even more if one also takes into account national daily newspapers). The average number of readers per copy seems to have been relatively stable around 3, so this corresponds to a readership rate around 60–75% (Cagé 2014). In the United States, existing historical evidence suggests similar magnitudes, and newspaper penetration tends to be even higher in Northern Europe.[21]

As compared to this standard, African newspaper readership at the aggregate country level varies from country to country but is everywhere very far from mass circulation.[22] According to the 2005 Afrobarometer surveys[23], on average only 33% of the individuals surveyed read a newspaper at least once a month (while 86% listen news on radio and 45% watch news on TV) in sub-Saharan Africa. A recent survey made by the Lumina Foundation in southern and middle-belt Nigeria finds that 13% of the individuals read a national newspaper every day (Fraser 2008). The order of magnitude is the same for Ethiopia: 13% of the respondents to the ERIS Audience Survey Ethiopia 2011 said that they receive information from newspapers. In the sub-Saharan African country with the highest newspaper penetration, South Africa, 40% of the population read a newspaper at least once a week.[24] In Nigeria, depending on the surveys, newspapers achieved 20–40% penetration among the adult population.

The number of newspapers also varies widely from country to country, but a high number of newspapers does not always reflect a good state of the industry. In the Democratic Republic of Congo for instance, while there were close to 700 registered publications in 2012, fewer than 250 appeared on a regular basis. And all these publications tend to have a very low circulation. The largest circulation newspaper—the private weekly newspaper *Le Soft*—has a circulation of only 2500 copies. Even the largest dailies in Kinshasa such as *Le Phare*, *L'Avenir*, and *Le Potentiel*, only print about 2000 copies. In the same order of magnitude, Chad's only daily newspaper, *Le Progrès*, print 3000 copies a day, and Chad's weekly and twice-weekly newspapers never sell more than 4000 copies per edition. In Côte d'Ivoire, the government daily *Fraternité Matin* has the largest circulation with 13 000–16 000 copies sold per day in 2010, but most newspapers sell only between 2000 and 10 000 copies per day. Ethiopia's biggest daily newspaper, the government daily *AddisZemen* has a print run of fewer than 13 000 copies. The privately owned weekly *Addis Admas* has an average print run of 21 000–25 000 copies; however, most titles in Ethiopia have small print runs of only about 3000 copies. On

[21] According to the World Association of Newspapers (*World Press Trends*), newspaper reach as a percentage of all adults is 76% in Sweden, 73% in Finland, and 68% in Norway in 2012.

[22] This low readership level may be due in part to low literacy rates. If more than half of the population is illiterate (which is the case for example in Ethiopia), then one can hardly expect to observe a readership rate above 50%. I come back below to the issue of the access to the media.

[23] There are 17 sub-Saharan countries in these surveys: Benin, Botswana, Ghana, Kenya, Lesotho, Madagascar, Malawi, Mali, Mozambique, Namibia, Nigeria, Senegal, South Africa, Tanzania, Uganda, Zambia, and Zimbabwe. Surveys are based on interviews conducted in the local languages from a random sample of either 1200 or 2400 individuals of voting age in each country. Overall, they cover approximately 21 000 individuals sampled to constitute representative groups at the national level.

[24] According to AMPS 2013 BA (July 2012—July 2013), 29.4% of all adults aged 15 and over were reached by the average issue of all 22 daily newspapers monitored by the survey, 31.8% by the weeklies, and 47.7% when considering all the AMPS newspapers. When also taking into account the magazines, this share increases to 63.6%.

the contrary, South Africa has "only" 43 daily, weekly, and bi-weekly commercial newspapers but the *Daily Sun*, the South African daily newspaper with the largest circulation, has a circulation of nearly 300 000 copies a day and an estimated readership of 5 500 000 individuals.

It is hard to determine the minimum number of copies sold necessary for a newspaper to be profitable, in particular because it depends on the reliance of the newspaper on revenues from sales (versus revenues from advertising—which themselves are a function of the number and types of readers—or other sources), as well as on the production and distribution costs of the newspaper. Key for the analysis is the understanding of the business model of the newspaper industry.

33.4.2 The business model of newspapers

Newspapers are businesses and are shaped by many economic factors. From the developed countries' perspective, newspapers rely mainly on revenues from sales and revenues from advertising, sometimes also on government subsidies. As it will appear clearly below, this has not always been the case—papers were not run as businesses in the United States before the end of the nineteenth century and relied strongly at that time on political parties and corruption—and everywhere in the world, including in developed countries, we still observe strong ties between newspapers and political parties or the government. This section highlights the extent of newspaper reliance on corruption in sub-Saharan Africa, which does not mean that this is an African characteristic; but the lack of advertising resources make corruption—in the broader sense—central for the survival of many sub-Saharan African newspapers. In the majority of the sub-Saharan African countries, the advertising market is indeed very tight and newspapers are thus unable to rely on advertising revenues. In Angola, for example, advertising is scarce and there are few advertising agencies. Moreover, only long-established newspapers with a high-enough circulation and a constant identifiable readership can capture the few advertising resources.

Only in a few countries, the advertising market is growing. This is the case for example in Nigeria. According to mediaReach OMD Nigeria, the total money spent on advertising (for all media sectors combined) rose by more than 50% between 2000 and 2004 (from US$63.076 million to US$117.537 million). In Senegal, even if more slowly, the advertising market is also expanding rapidly because of the development of the private sector, with the creation of small businesses and bigger brands which need visibility. Similarly with South Africa's consumer boom, advertising has increased and newspapers have been able to charge higher advertising rates. Total advertising spending on newspapers increased by 44% between 2002 and 2005 (Nielsen Media Research cited in OMD 2005). And the main newspapers are profitable in South Africa.

In the vast majority of the other sub-Saharan African countries, newspapers however tend not to be profitable, or at least not profitable in a *classic* way, when looking at revenues from sales and from advertising. The Vietnamese example is particularly relevant and may apply to a number of countries in sub-Saharan Africa: "A thriving local newspaper sector in such countries might seem to reflect strong communities and emerging democracy—but not necessarily. [...] Extortion business, digging the dirt on local politicians and businesspeople, and asking to be paid not to publish it"

(Hallin and Mancini 2012: 201). In other words, many newspapers do not operate as conventional businesses. First, many newspapers—this is the case for example in Chad and in the Democratic Republic of Congo—survive on the generosity of politicians who dictate the publication schedule. Newspaper owners use their publications to gain social and political influence and tend to subsidize their newspapers from other sources of income. Second, many newspapers survive thanks to extortion and *coupage*: "in the Democratic Republic of Congo, coupage journalism (literally, "taking a cut") is so institutionalized that there are standard rates. For example, $20–30 will buy a story from a radio journalist" (Susman-Pena 2012: 20-21). Evidence of *coupage* exists in many other countries, for instance in Côte d'Ivoire (Waliyu 2007). This practice is institutionalized not only from the point of view of the *coupage* rates, but also from the one of media owners. A large number of owners hire journalists without a contract, do not pay them a regular salary and expect them to earn a living by publishing news reports—journalists receiving cash payments for writing promotional pieces—or not (*coupage*) in exchange for money.

Paid journalism is also used in some countries by governments as a more subtle way than censorship to limit criticism. On the one hand, governments tend to withdraw public sector advertising from critical newspapers and inversely to reward publications which support the official line with advertising.[25] On the other hand, governments—this is the case for example in Mozambique—invite journalists to accompany officials on trips. Not only in these cases the government pays for the journalists' travel costs and accommodation but it also provides them with a per diem that is sometimes more than their monthly salary.

Hence many papers are not run as businesses. With low circulation figures and little advertising to support them, they do not make money. Or more precisely they make money with very little by way of conventional sales or advertising revenue. Again, reliance on "corruption," e.g. through disguised forms of advertisement, is not a sub-Saharan African specificity and sub-Saharan African newspapers do not intrinsically lack ethical standards and make the voluntary choice of corruption; but the extent of this phenomena is particularly important in sub-Saharan Africa because of the lack of other sources of revenues. The exchange in "My Fair Lady" among Henry Higgins, Colonel Pickering, and Alfie Doolittle, a Cockney dustman, quoted in Jones (2010: 104), provides an interesting light on this issue:

"Have you no morals, man?" says Pickering.
Doolittle shakes his head self-pityingly and replies, "Can't afford them, governor. Neither could you if you was as poor as me."

With low sales levels and a tight advertising market, newspapers have in a way no other choice that to rely on corruption to survive. Moreover, another key obstacle to the development of viable newspapers is the size of the operating costs: in nearly all sub-Saharan African countries, paper is expensive, operating budgets are high, there are scarce printing facilities and there is nearly no official government subsidies to newspapers. A necessary condition for newspapers to avoid extraction is thus economic growth and increase in consumption, which will lead to an

---

[25] This is far from being specific to sub-Saharan African countries. In the case of Argentina between 1998 and 2007, Di Tella and Fransceschelli (2011) find for example that the more monthly government advertising, the less coverage of the government's corruption scandals in the four main newspapers.

increase in advertising revenues.[26] A second necessary condition is an increase in the access to newspapers.

33.4.3 Access to the media

While the literature tends to focus on media freedom, access to the media is also of key importance. A free press that it is not accessible to citizens cannot be of great help in making governments more accountable. Yet in many sub-Saharan African countries the press is very urban because distribution outside the capital and the big cities is too costly for newspapers and there is a flagrant lack of transport facilities.[27]

In Benin and in Togo for instance, there is no modern newspaper distribution corporation. According to Faye (2008), Beninese and Togolese journalists, in order to sell their newspapers in rural areas, have to go early in the morning to bus stations and request from the so-called "bush taxi drivers" to deliver the copies to rural resellers. The risk born by newspapers in this improvised system is too high and tends to deter them to sell outside the big cities. On the contrary in Senegal, where there is a newspaper distribution corporation—l'Agence de Distribution de la Presse (ADP)—newspaper penetration in rural areas is higher, but the distribution network is still very sparse.

The weakness of the distribution system may be viewed as an inheritance of the colonial area. In many Francophone countries, a French company—Presstalis, the French media distribution company—has had for years a monopoly on the distribution network. Analyzing the extent to which the distribution network aims at protecting French interests is far beyond the goal of this chapter, but it is important to stress that many have argued that this network is often used as a form of censorship—not distributing a newspaper amounts to be the same thing that censoring its content.

Another important impediment to media access is linguistic diversity—this chapter abstracts from the literacy question which has already been considered extensively in the existing literature. People do not have access to newspapers because newspapers are written in a language they do not spoke. In Côte d'Ivoire, nearly all newspapers are written in French while more than 60 African languages are spoken. In Chad, the official languages are French and Standard Arabic, but very few people speak either of these as a first language. Nevertheless, French is the language of most of the print media. Similarly in Mozambique, while only 40% of the population speaks Portuguese, the main newspapers are published in this language.

---

[26] "Ethics codes began when commercial success made them, as Doolittle would say, affordable. In the 19th and early 20th centuries, journalists typically took money to write favorable stories, and the concept of a conflict of interest was laughable. Reporters were usually paid badly, had little education, and were looked on as a raffish and unscrupulous brotherhood. Journalists worked in an atmosphere of dog-eat-dog competition, and bribing sources to get the jump on sensational scoops was a part of the game. But as newspapers became more prosperous, they also became more respectable" (Jones 2010).

[27] The question of media access is also relevant when considering radio and television. In many countries, people do not have access to television because they do not have electricity.

Moreover, access to the media is limited by the prohibitively high price of the newspapers. In Côte d'Ivoire for instance, given the relatively high cover price of the main newspapers (around US$0.44, that has to be compared to an average daily per capita GDP lower than US$3), only affluent Ivoirians can afford to buy one on a regular basis, especially in the interior where purchasing power is lower. Similarly, in Chad or in the Democratic Republic of Congo—where newspapers cost at least US$1 each, i.e. half of the average daily per capita income—most people cannot afford to buy a newspaper. *Le Soft* in the Democratic Republic of Congo, the private weekly newspaper with the largest circulation, costs US$7 and thus only prints 2500 copies a day. On the contrary, the success of the people press in Senegal may be due to its low price (US$0.20), which makes it more affordable. Moreover, this prohibitively high price of newspapers may explain why according to sub-Saharan African surveys the ratio between newspaper readership and circulation varies between 10 and 20, while in other countries like France or the United States, the average number of readers per newspaper issue is lower than three.

These limits to media access have to be taken into account in an analysis of a viable model for the press.

33.5 TOWARD A NEW MODEL OF THE ECONOMICS OF THE MEDIA

It appears clearly from the previous section that with high levels of illiteracy, underdeveloped consumer markets—low sales and advertising revenues—an inadequate technology infrastructure, and high input prices, newspapers have no choice but to rely on corruption and extraction. The problem is that corruption prevents newspapers to play their role of potent check on corruption and to increase government accountability. Hence one has to think of different economic foundations of the media. In this section, I first discuss what I call the "advertising illusion," the idea that given that advertising has been the way out of corruption in the United States it should be the case in any other countries of the world. I then present alternative economic models for the press.

33.5.1 The advertising illusion

It has been widely documented—for example by Hamilton (2004)—that non-partisan reporting and an independent press emerged as a commercial product in the 1870s in the United States. At that time, advertising became an important way for companies with nationally and locally distributed brands to raise awareness of their products. Papers with larger audiences attracted more attention from advertisers. This incentivized newspapers to increase readership, drop overt political bias and proclaim their independence in uncovering news. In other words, advertising revenues created an independent press (see e.g. Gentzkow, Glaeser, and Goldin 2006; Petrova 2011).

One may argue that the fact that the commercial advertising market is reportedly underdeveloped in most sub-Saharan African countries demonstrates that sub-Saharan African newspapers are still in their infancy, and that with the future growth of consumption and the advertising market, sub-Saharan African newspapers will follow the path of their North American predecessors. However this might not be the case, for at least two reasons. First because advertising funding sources for newspapers are shrinking all around the world. And second because this decline is not new. It is often improperly associated to the introduction of the Internet or the recent financial crisis, but advertising revenues in newspapers have decreased since the 1950s both for instance in the United States (Schiffrin 2010) and in France (Martin 1992). Advertisers opted for television well before the apparition of the Internet. In the United States, the share of advertising in newspapers in total media advertising has decreased from 26% in 1990 to 10% in 2009. In other words, as highlighted by McChesney and Nichols (2010: 88), "the economic downturn did not cause the crisis in journalism; nor did the Internet."

Moreover, print advertising does not longer account for the lion's share of newspaper revenues, even in the United States where it now represents less than half of the total revenues (Newspaper Association of America). The share of advertising in the total revenues of national daily newspapers in France has similarly been decreasing since 2000, from nearly 60% of the total revenues to less than 40% today (Cagé 2014).[28] Even in the few sub-Saharan African countries which have a growing advertising market and where advertising revenues are important today for the profitability of newspapers—Nigeria and South Africa—we observe a decreasing trend. In South Africa, there has been a dramatic decline in print revenues between 1997 and 2012, from 40% to 29% of the total advertising expenditures, in favor of both television and the Internet. Similarly, despite the increase in advertising expenditures in Nigeria, advertising expenditures in the press began to decrease in 2011; both the share of the press in total advertising expenditures and the amount of print advertising decreased.

In addition, note that the very large growth in advertising at the end of the 19th century in the United States was not only due to a growth in consumer spending, but to the development of what has been called "monopoly capital" (Baran and Sweezy 1966). This type of capitalism, typified by large corporations competing in oligopolistic markets, is best exemplified by the United States. On average in the United States, advertising have accounted for over 2% of GDP in the twentieth century. But there is no evidence pointing in the direction of a similar increase in sub-Saharan African in the forthcoming decades. Moreover, even in the United States, advertising is becoming a smaller portion of the sales effort while non-advertising marketing expenses—in particular direct marketing—are growing (McChesney et al. 2010). Hence not only the share of the press in total advertising is declining, but explicit media advertising may decline in the future.

This is a key point: in the long run, one needs to find a new business model for newspapers that does not depend so much on advertising revenues.[29] While one century and a half of American newspapers relying mainly on advertising leads us to think that it may be the Grail of the freedom of the press, not only it is no longer the case, but it might never be the

---

[28] Advertising revenues similarly represent less than 40% of the total revenues of French local daily newspapers.

[29] Another potential advantage—that I won't discuss here—of having media system relying less on advertising revenues would be that it may lead media to favor news over entertainment. A number of studies have indeed found—both theoretically and empirically—that media tends to produce more entertainment when they rely more on advertising.

case for newspapers in sub-Saharan African. If and when the growth of mass consumption and hence of advertising expenses finally takes place in Africa, it is very likely that it will only be to the benefit of television and the Internet. From this point of view, sub-Saharan African newspapers have skipped the reliance on advertising revenues business model period of newspapers.

33.5.2 Perspectives for a new business model

In this last section, using the evidence from the economics of the sub-Saharan African media, I discuss perspectives for a new business model. This includes the following issues: (i) the pros and cons of ownership concentration; (ii) the development of synergies between national and local newspapers; and finally (iii) the development of non-profit media organization.

33.5.2.1 *Ownership concentration*

Advocating for higher ownership concentration in the media sector may seem to be highly controversial. Media competition is indeed often viewed—with good reasons—as a guarantee for press freedom and diversity and de facto media monopoly is never a solution and raises the issue of media capture. However, chaotic proliferation of low-quality media outlets—as it has often happened in sub-Saharan African countries in the last decades, with very short-lived outlets—may be bad. Under certain conditions, an increase in media competition can lead to a decrease in both the quantity and quality of news provided—and so a decrease in government accountability (Cagé 2014). With tight advertising markets and low consumer purchasing power as in many sub-Saharan African countries, a market can only support a limited number of media outlets, due to both the endogenous and exogenous fixed costs of news production.

If we further examine the example of South Africa, one of the reasons of the recent success—and growth—of the print media sector may come from concentration in ownership. Publishers have indeed been able to keep their costs down by sharing resources and editorial copy. The majority of South African newspapers are indeed owned by only four companies (Naspers Ltd, Johnnic Communications Ltd, Caxton and CTP Publishers and Printers Ltd, and Independent News & Media South Africa). Similarly in Guinea, though in a very different media environment with low circulation and few advertising revenues, the oldest and most respected independent weeklies, *Le Lynx* (7000 copies a week) and *La Lance* (6000 copies per week) are owned by the same publishing house. The Lynx-Lance group owns its own printing press and employs 54 people. The only large privately owned multi-media group in Mozambique, the Sociedade Independente de Comunicacões (SOICO), runs a TV station, a radio station, Mozambique's largest independent daily newspaper, *O País*,[30] and a monthly magazine, *Fama*. A team of about 20 journalists provides news for SOICO's media outlets. This may seem a small newsroom from the point of view of Western newspapers, but in fact it is a large one compared to the average number of journalists working in sub-Saharan African newspapers. *O País* can rely on such a newsroom—and provides

---

[30] Which prints 30 000 copies per day.

relatively high-quality news—thanks to the economies of scale enabled by several media outlets owned by the same media company and thus sharing the same newsroom. Moreover the group has provincial offices with correspondents who provide news coverage for both the television and *O País* from cities in the interior.

33.5.2.2 *Developing synergies between national and local newspapers*

Another way to take advantage of the increasing returns to scale that characterize the newspaper industry and moreover at the same time to increase media access, will be to develop synergies between national and local newspapers, between mass and small-scale media. As of today in sub-Saharan African countries, only community-based radio stations communicate in local languages in order to reach marginalized groups.[31] Newspapers also have to develop local content and languages. By doing so they will facilitate media access of an important share of the population which is, as I underlined above, de facto excluded from newspapers because of a language barrier, and increase their readership. But given the economies of scale involved in news production, local content should be developed by national newspapers publishing several local editions in local languages—editions distributed in rural areas—rather than by a variety of very small local newspapers which cannot be viable from an economic view point (except of course if they chose to rely on extraction and corruption, which cannot be considered as a good business model for newspapers).

This business model of newspapers sharing their newsroom—whether they are owned by the same media company or not—may moreover be an interesting model for the future of the news industry beyond sub-Saharan Africa. In the United States for instance, the American Newspaper Preservation Act (NPA) (1970)—a broad antitrust exemption—permits qualifying newspaper competitors to enter into a joint operating agreement and to combine business operations (printing, delivery and advertising employees and expenses), thereby reducing costs and boosting profits (Greenberg 2012). Ohio's eight largest newspapers[32], forming the "Ohio News Organization," share that way state, business, sports, arts, and entertainment news reporting, as well as various kinds of features, editorials, photographs, and graphics (Downie and Schudson 2009). Similarly in France, daily local newspapers from the news company "EBRA" decided in 2013 to pool their national and international information pages through an agency based in Paris (Cagé 2014).

33.5.2.3 *Non-profit media organizations*

Finally, there is an ongoing debate—in particular in Western countries—on the efficiency of direct government subsidies for the press, in particular because there is always a risk that subsidies may jeopardize newspapers' independence.[33] Given the weakness of many governments

---

[31] Television stations also tend increasingly to do so.

[32] *The Plain Dealer* in Cleveland, *The Akron Beacon Journal*, *The* (Canton) *Repository*, *The Columbus Dispatch*, *The* (Cincinnati) *Enquirer*, the *Dayton Daily News, The* (Toledo) *Blade*, and *The* (Youngstown) *Vindicator*.

[33] Even if there are various direct government subsidies in many European countries, these subsidies do not seem to have a noticeably chilling effect on newspapers' willingness to print criticism of those governments.

in sub-Saharan African countries, the issue of corruption and government accountability and the low level of public good provision, such subsidies may in any case not be relevant. However, an alternative to subsidies could be "philanthropy." Schizer (2011) proposes to provide a subsidy through the charitable deduction. Greenberg (2012) similarly defends the idea of indirect support via tax benefits by facilitating newspaper conversion to non-profit status. Making independent non-profit media as the centerpiece of the press system—possibly in some sub-Saharan African countries with the support of the international community—may indeed be an important step toward a viable business model of independent newspapers which will fully play their role of watchdogs.[34] Given the decline of advertising revenues and the high cost of producing high-quality news, profit margins will never be high again in the newspaper industry, neither in the Western world nor in sub-Saharan Africa. A non-profit model—with a commitment to journalism—has this advantage that a reduction of the editorial budgets won't be used as a systematic answer—as it is unfortunately too often the case today—to a decrease in profit margins. In my view, countries should also develop non-profit news agencies that should be subsidized by the government.[35] Subsidizing non-profit news agencies would be a way for government funding to apply uniformly across the newspaper industry.[36]

33.6 CONCLUSION

"[Newspapers] may have a mission, but they are also business, with all that implies."

(Jones 2010)

Newspapers are businesses and are shaped by many economic factors. These factors have to be taken into account when analyzing the economics of the newspapers.

But newspapers are particular businesses. They cannot be considered just as any firms. Information is a public good, but one that cannot be delivered by the government, an informative press being a check on government accountability. Hence a good business model for newspapers is one that guarantees both newspaper viability and independence, as well as access to newspapers.[37] One of the crucial lessons of this chapter is that

[34] There is a long tradition of non-profit journalism in the United States, from the creation of the Associated Press—which is cooperatively owned by the thousands of newspapers and broadcasting stations it serves—to newspapers such as the *Christian Science Monitor*, the *St. Peterburg Times* or the *Delaware State News*.

[35] The three largest news agencies in the world are Associated Press, Reuters and "Agence France-Presse" (AFP). In France, government subscriptions to AFP are a way to subsidize news production by the agency.

[36] An important caveat that one has to keep in mind is nevertheless that such a non-profit model of the media may not work in those sub-Saharan African countries that are "weak states." As stressed by Monga (2009), it is far from easy in weak states to *"disentangle pro-democratic activities by civil society groups from routine power struggle by political entrepreneurs who hide behind civic or charitable organizations to pursue an often unethical agenda."* In such weak states, the move towards a non-profit model of the media would perhaps have to be done more progressively, beginning first by a decrease in the tax barriers to media entry that exist today.

[37] The solution cannot be to have very costly newspapers reserved to an elite. Because an informative press useful to monitor public good delivery must be a mass-circulation one.

advertising-dependent media systems may not be sustainable in the long run; and may never be a solution for many sub-Saharan African countries. Advertising revenues have historically been the principal source of income for daily newspapers, but they are declining everywhere.

It is thus necessary to think about a new business model. This chapter presents some perspectives for such a new model. It discusses the pros and cons of ownership concentration and argues in favor of the development of synergies between national and local newspapers as well as of the development of non-profit media organizations. I hope it will provide food for thought for future research. There is an increasing demand for news content but the economic base of the newspapers—particularly so in sub-Saharan Africa but also all around the world—are fragile; we have to find a sustainable way to satisfy this demand.

African media did not follow the same development pattern as other parts of the world and is not in a satisfactory state—to say the least. At the present time, this is a liability for African democratic and economic development. But this can become an asset if Africa—probably the only continent with sustained population growth in the century under way—uses this opportunity to invent a novel model for offering information to new generations of readers, viewers, and citizens.

References

Baran, P.A., and P.M. Sweezy (1966). *Monopoly Capital: An Essay on the American Economic and Social Order*. New York: Monthly Review Press.

Cagé, J. (2009). Asymmetric Information, Rent Extraction and Aid Efficiency, Discussion paper, PSE Ecole normale supérieure.

Cagé, J. (2014). Media Competition, Information Provision and Political Participation. Harvard Working Paper. http://scholar.harvard.edu/cage/publications/media-competition-and-provision-information.

Cagé, J., and V. Rueda (2013). The long-Term Effects of the Printing Press in Sub-Saharan Africa. Harvard Working Paper.

Casey, K. (2010). Crossing Party Lines: The Effects of Information on Redistributive Politics. Working Paper.

Condorcet, N. (1785). Essai sur l'application de l'analyse à la probabilité des décisions rendues à la pluralité des voix, Landmarks of science. De l'Imprimerie royale.

Daubert, P. (2009). La presse écrite d'Afrique francophone en question: essai nourri par l'essor de la presse française, Etudes Africaines. Paris: L'Harmattan.

Di Tella, R., and Franceschelli, I. (2011). Government Advertising and Media Coverage of Corruption Scandals. *American Economic Journal: Applied Economics*, 3(4):119–151.

Downie, L., and Schudson, M. (2009). The reconstruction of American journalism. *Columbia journalism Review*, published online on October 19. http://www.cjr.org/reconstruction/the_reconstruction_of_american.php?page=all.

Faye, M. (2008). *Presse privée écrite en Afrique francophone: enjeux démocratiques*. Études africaines. Paris: L'Harmattan.

Feddersen, T., and Pesendorfer, W. (1996). The swing voter's curse. *American Economic Review*, 86(3):408–424.

Feddersen, T., and Sandroni, A. (2006a). A theory of participation in elections. *American Economic Review*, 96(4):1271–1282.

Feddersen, T., and A. Sandroni (2006b). Ethical voters and costly information acquisition. *Quarterly Journal of Political Science*, 1(3):187–311.

Fraser, R. (2008). *Book History through Postcolonial Eyes: Rewriting the Script*. Abingdon: Routledge.

Gentzkow, M., Glaeser, E., and Goldin, C. (2006). The rise of the fourth estate: how newspapers became informative and why it mattered, in *Corruption and Reform: Lessons from America's Economic History*. Cambridge, MA: National Bureau of Economic Research.

Greenberg, B.A. (2012). A public press? Evaluating the viability of government subsidies for the newspaper industry. *UCLA Entertainment Law Review*, 19:189–244.

Hallin, D. C., and Mancini, P. (2004). *Comparing Media Systems: Three Models of Media and Politics, Communication, Society and Politics*. Cambridge: Cambridge University Press.

Hallin, D. C., and Mancini, P. (2012). *Comparing Media Systems Beyond the Western World, Communication, Society and Politics*. Cambridge: Cambridge University Press.

Hamilton, J. (2004). *All the News That's Fit to Sell: How the Market Transforms Information Into News*. Princeton, NJ: Princeton University Press.

Jensen, R., and Oster, E. (2009). The power of TV: cable television and women's status in India. *Quarterly Journal of Economics*, 124(3):1057–1094.

Jones, A.S. (2010). *Losing the News. The Uncertain Future of the News that Feeds Democracy*. Oxford: Oxford University Press.

McChesney, R., and Nichols, J. (2010). *The Death and Life of American Journalism: The Media Revolution that Will Begin the World Again*. Philadelphia: Nation Book.

Monga, C. (2009). Uncivil Societies: A Theory of Sociopolitical Change. World Bank Policy Research Working Paper no. 4942.

Mytton, G. (1983). *Mass Communication in Africa*. Edward Arnold.

Olken, B. A., and Singhal, M. (2009). Informal Taxation. NBER Working Papers 15221. National Bureau of Economic Research, Inc.

Omu, F.I.A. (1978). *Press and Politics in Nigeria, 1880–1937*. Ibadan History Series. London: Longman.

Perret, T. (2005). *Le temps des journalistes: l'invention de la presse en Afrique francophone*. Collection Tropiques. Paris: Karthala.

Petrova, M. (2011). Newspapers and parties: how advertising revenues created an independent press. *American Political Science Review*, 105(4):790–808.

Piketty, T. (1999). The information-aggregation approach to political institutions. *European Economic Review*, 43(4–6):791–800.

Reinikka, R., and Svensson, J. (2005). Fighting corruption to improve schooling: evidence from a newspaper campaign in Uganda. *Journal of the European Economic Association*, 3:259–267.

Schiffrin, A. (2010). *L'argent et les mots*. Paris: La Fabrique.

Schizer, D.M. (2011). Subsidizing the press. *Journal of Legal Analysis*, 3(1):1–64.

Schudson, M. (1981). *Discovering the News: A Social History of American Newspapers*. New York: Basic Books.

Susman-Pena, T. (2012). Making Media Development More Effective. A special report to the center for international media assistance.

Svensson, J., and Yanagizawa, D. (2009). Getting prices right: the impact of the market information service in Uganda. *Journal of the European Economic Association*, 7(2–3): 435–445.

Switzer, L., and Switzer, D. (1979). *The Black Press in South Africa and Lesotho: a Descriptive Bibliographic Guide to African.* Coloured, and Indian Newspapers, Newsletters, and Magazines, 1836–1976, Bibliographies and guides in African studies. Hall.

Tudesq, A.-J. (1995). *Feuilles d'Afrique: étude de la presse de l'Afrique sub-saharienne*, Editions de la maison des sciences de l'homme d'Aquitaine.

Woodberry, R.D. (2004). The Shadow of Empire: Christian Missions, Colonial Policy, and Democracy in Postcolonial Societies, Ph.D. thesis, University of North Carolina at Chapel Hill.

Woodberry, R.D. (2012). The Missionary Roots of Liberal Democracy. *American Political Science Review*, 106(02):244–274.

PART IV

OLD AND NEW DEVELOPMENT PLAYERS

CHAPTER 34

....

WHAT DO DEVELOPMENT NGOs ACHIEVE?

....

CHRIS ELBERS AND JAN WILLEM GUNNING[1]

34.1 INTRODUCTION

....

How do we know that a development non-governmental organization (NGO) is effective? Evaluation reports written by commercial consultants typically describe what an NGO has done and how outcomes have changed over time, *implying* that these changes can be attributed to the NGO's actions. This was never convincing but only recently has the disenchantment with such before-after comparisons in most evaluation reports become widespread.

There now is a surge of interest in using rigorous impact evaluation methods such as randomized control trials (RCTs) to assess what works in development.[2] These experimental methods are now commonly applied to evaluate NGOs in Africa. Indeed one of the most famous papers in the RCT literature, the "deworming paper" of Miguel and Kremer (2004), describes an RCT evaluation of an NGO in Kenya.

While these methods are now widely used, they are sometimes resisted, particularly by development NGOs. Often this reflects no more than an irrational aversion to rigor and quantitative methods. But NGOs can also object on the grounds that some NGO activities do not lend themselves to impact evaluation methodologies such as RCTs. This position deserves to be taken seriously. It is the main focus of this chapter.

NGOs active in development are engaged in capacity building, advocacy, service delivery or some combination. The objections raised to the use of RCTs differ between these three types of activities. In the case of capacity building, for example, a training program for the staff of a partner organization, the objection is that the treatment group is typically very small and in any case not randomly selected. In the case of advocacy the objection is that there is obviously little scope for RCTs when other NGOs target the same policies or when the policies the NGO is trying to get changed cover large geographical areas. In the

....

[1] This chapter draws on Elbers and Gunning (2014) and Gunning (2012, 2012a).
[2] Duflo et al. (2008) and Banerjee and Duflo (2011) describe such methods; Ravallion (2009, 2012) and Deaton (2010) are well-known critiques of this approach.

extreme case of *national* policies there clearly is no scope at all for RCTs: since everybody is affected the impact of the policy cannot be identified. The third type of activity, service delivery, would seem to be best suited to RCTs. However, we will suggest that even in this context RCTs may not be appropriate. The reason is that in many NGOs local staff can use their discretion in selecting communities or individuals for participation in, say, a sanitation program. A standard RCT will then be misleading since it cannot mimic the use of private knowledge of local circumstances in such targeting.

We consider these three cases in turn in sections 2, 3, and 4. Section 5 concludes the chapter.

34.2 Capacity Building

Many international NGOs are engaged in capacity building for partner organizations, e.g. African NGOs. Such activities are usually evaluated with qualitative methods.[3] Often two reasons are invoked for not using formal methods (e.g. Barrett et al. 2012). First, capacity building usually involves only a very small number of partner organizations (perhaps only a single one) so that the treatment group is too small for statistical analysis. Secondly, many NGOs are *sui generis* so that no meaningful control group can be identified. (Where in many African countries there are dozens of NGOs focusing on issues such as maternal health, enrolment of girls, or microfinance this objection seems to be exaggerated.)

However, there is some scope for going beyond informal, qualitative methods provided one is willing to judge the capacity that is being built in terms of *actual* rather than *potential* change in the way the partner organization functions. In other words, instead of assessing informally what the organization was previously unable to do but now can do, one assesses whether the organization actually functions better than a similar organization which was not subjected to capacity building. That assessment is based on how the intended beneficiaries are affected by the NGO. Hence one would compare the beneficiaries (say a group of women targeted by a women empowerment program) of the partner organization with the beneficiaries of other NGOs (in this case also aiming at women empowerment).

This does not, of course, address the second objection but it does address the first one. By focusing not on organizations but on their beneficiaries one may well be able to

[3] The Netherlands government supports Dutch development NGOs through a co-financing program. The current phase of that program (called MFS II) is currently being assessed in a massive evaluation of a large sample of projects, stratified by country, NGO and type of activity. The sample covers six countries, including four in Africa: the DRC, Ethiopia, Liberia and Uganda. Barrett et al. (2012) describe the evaluation methodology used by most country teams for the capacity building projects. Essentially this involves an informal assessment of success along various dimensions where the assessment is done by the staff of the NGO involved, external stakeholders and the evaluators themselves. There is no comparison with other organizations (e.g. a control group of comparable NGOs which were not involved in the capacity building by the Dutch NGO). In effect this shifts the attribution problem to the respondents: they have to decide informally to what extent changes over time can be attributed to the capacity building. Such evaluation approaches are quite common.

reach a reasonable sample size and in fact follow a difference-in-differences (diff-in-diff) approach.

34.3 ADVOCACY: ACHIEVING CHANGE INDIRECTLY

As already noted in the Introduction evaluating the advocacy activities of an NGO is inherently difficult, for two reasons. First, usually there are other institutions, including other NGOs, aiming at the same policy change. This makes attribution difficult: if the intended policy change occurs, this need not be the result of the NGO's efforts. Secondly, when the policy in question is a national one, a convincing counterfactual cannot be constructed. In particular, one cannot assess the effect of the policy change by comparing randomly selected locations with and without the policy since *all* locations are affected, although not necessarily to the same extent. Hence either the evaluator cannot say how much difference the policy change made or he cannot attribute that change to the NGO in question. Perhaps all he can say is that if the policy was *not* changed there is a prima facie case for concluding that the NGO was not effective.

But often one can go further. We illustrate this with the example of an East African NGO, Twaweza.[4] Twaweza, based in Dar es Salaam, is active in three countries: Tanzania, Kenya, and Uganda. The organization is involved in numerous activities. It is particularly active in national debates on the quality of public services and lobbies for policy changes in the health and education sectors. Clearly, the two limitations on the evaluation of advocacy apply to this part of Twaweza's work.

But another part of Twaweza's work is aimed at *indirect* policy change. The idea is to change, through advocacy, the information available at the local level, to trigger through that information local collective action and thereby to improve development outcomes. This can be seen as a theory of change with three steps:

1. Advocacy changes the information available at the local level. For example, people in rural areas learn through a radio program that children learn very little in schools.
2. This information leads to collective action. For example parents complain to the school principal or to their MP about the quality of education.
3. This action leads to better outcomes. For example, the principal reacts by reducing teacher absenteeism and this results in better learning.

Note that this implies three different tests and that the theory must be rejected if it fails any of them. In that sense there is no need to test steps 2 and 3 if the evaluator has already found that the theory does not pass the first test. However, increasingly evaluations are seen as inputs into a learning process rather than as one-off assessments. A learning organization would definitely want the evaluator in this example to proceed with testing steps 2 and 3 after a negative finding in step 1. For if the theory passes those tests then the NGO would have learned that it needs to change the way it gets information to villages and that it is worth

---

[4] See http://www.twaweza.org.

doing so since if information reaches the villages it does lead, as intended, to collective action and better outcomes.

Any test of the first step is clearly asymmetric: if no such information reaches the village then the theory obviously fails the test, but if it does arrive then one cannot confidently attribute this to the NGO, notably because many other organizations may be active in a similar way.

How can one test the first step? RCTs are of no use here, even if the NGO uses locationally specific channels, for example, radio programs which can be heard only in certain parts of the country. The reason is that such a geographic limitation does not involve randomization so that it cannot be used as the basis for defining treatment and control groups. In general villages where the program can be heard will differ in many other respects from other villages.

The alternative is to use a team of respondents in a representative sample of villages and to ask them frequently what people talk about, in particular if it is related to health and education, and what the source of their information is.[5] An ongoing (2012–2014) evaluation of Twaweza, in which we are involved together with colleagues at the Institute of Rural Development planning (IRDP) at the University of Dodoma, uses this approach. Respondents in a sample of 250 locations throughout Tanzania are interviewed by mobile phone at high frequency (every three weeks) over the two-year period. The interviewers, who are IRDP staff members, guide the respondents through a semi-structured interview. Respondents are asked whether there is any news (since the previous conversation) regarding health and education. If this is the case, the interviewer asks a series of questions to establish the source of that information: a visitor from another village, a politician who gave a speech, a religious leader who came to the village, a radio or TV program, and so on. At a later stage the interviewer asks more leading questions, for example, whether the respondent knows of a particular radio program (e.g. one sponsored by Twaweza, although the respondent need not know that).

This procedure can generate three types of evidence:

1. information which Twaweza promotes does not reach the village, or does so only rarely;
2. this information does reach the village, but this cannot be attributed to Twaweza's efforts, for example, because there are other organizations who also provide information about the poor quality of teaching in primary schools;
3. such information does reach the village and it is clear that this can be attributed to Twaweza, for example, because the respondent identifies a Twaweza-supported radio program as his source.[6]

The phone panel also collects data on collective action, for example, parents challenging teachers, holding politicians to account or engaging in self-help schemes. In this case too, the

[5] This can be seen as a mix of the approach of the traditional anthropologist (who finds out what people talk about in the village he lives in) and the economist (who wants to generalize and therefore collects data in a representative sample of villages). The anthropologist's information is typically richer (but limited to quite a small sample), that of the economist superficial (but suitable for generalization).

[6] At the time of writing much of the evidence is of the first type, but this is a very preliminary finding.

respondent is first given an opportunity to volunteer such information without any prompting from the interviewer. If he does not do so, the interviewer follows up with more "leading" questions in order to establish whether actions not yet mentioned by the respondent have in fact taken place.

Now consider the second step in the theory of change. Here the question is whether information about, say, health and education (irrespective of whether it comes from Twaweza) leads to collective action. There is no particular reason why this should be so. The theory of change implies that there is only one reason that people do not act collectively: they do not know how bad the situation is. In that case the provision of credible information about that situation will indeed trigger collective action. But there are many reasons why this need not be the case. The information may contain no news for the parents: they may already know very well how badly their children are taught but have decided they cannot do anything about it. Collective action is notoriously difficult to organize since there are strong incentives for free riding behavior, people may be afraid of retaliation by people in power, they may be convinced that action cannot succeed and so on.[7]

There is some scope for using RCTs to test whether information leads to collective action and in the case of Twaweza there have been several such studies. Closest to the spirit of Twaweza's theory of change is the study by Lieberman et al. (2013). This study used an RCT to investigate the effect of providing information to 20 households in each of 30 randomly selected villages in Kenya. Children in the treatment households were tested and parents were informed about the literacy and numeracy skills of each child. They were also provided with a list of actions they could take to improve their child's skills. This included helping at school, attending a parents-teacher meeting or discussing their child's performance with its teacher. The RCT evidence in this study is very clear: one cannot reject the hypothesis that information triggers neither such public action, nor any private action (such as helping a child with its homework). Essentially the provision of information has *no* effect.

The alternative to such an RCT is to use observational data. In the case of the Twaweza evaluation the high frequency cell phone interviews provide data on both information received and any collective action undertaken. These data can be used in a regression analysis to assess whether information (of all types, i.e. not necessarily information provided by Twaweza) leads to action. The obvious objection is that in such a regression "information" is endogenous: there may be something special about villages that pick up (or report) information and that "something" might also make them more likely to engage in action. However, such omitted variables are likely to be time-invariant so that a diff-in-diff approach (which is feasible since the data are panel data) can deal with the resulting omitted variable bias.

Clearly, the communication strategy adopted by an NGO such as Twaweza may imply that information is more likely to arrive in those villages where it can trigger effective collective action. This non-random allocation is part of the program's effectiveness and it would therefore be wrong to eliminate it, as would an RCT.[8] However, this case is also problematic for a standard diff-in-diff regression approach: it is plausible that there are differences between

---

[7] See Lieberman et al. (2013), Figure 1.

[8] We do not wish to suggest that this invalidates the Lieberman et al. (2013) study. Whether treatment heterogeneity (and the correlation with assignment) is important in the case of Twaweza remains to be seen. This question can be answered once the regression analysis can be performed. Clearly, the two approaches may reach the same conclusion that information does not induce collective action.

locations in the effect of information on collective action (treatment heterogeneity) and that these differences are correlated with the "assignment" (the information picked up in the village). This introduces a type of endogeneity that cannot be dealt with by double differencing. However, the method of Elbers and Gunning (2014) can be used in this case to obtain a consistent estimate of the impact of the program, taking into account this correlation.[9]

For the evaluation of the second step in the theory of change one can therefore choose between two quite different approaches, relying on experimental data in the one case and on observational data in the other. The RCT approach has the advantage that it is far easier to implement: setting up a large phone panel of rural respondents and maintaining it for a long period is quite difficult. The RCT approach also has a disadvantage: an RCT will focus on a very specific form of information provision whereas an NGO may use various channels (as does Twaweza) and change their use over time. A narrowly designed RCT may therefore raise external validity concerns which need not arise in the regression approach.

The effect of collective action, the third step in the theory of change can also be addressed with regression analysis. In the Twaweza evaluation there was a baseline household survey conducted in 2012 in the same 250 villages which are used as the sample for the phone panel. This survey collected data on household and community characteristics and also data on outcomes, notably quality indicators for health and education services and on collective action. The survey will be repeated, probably in 2014. Changes in outcomes (the differences between the endline and baseline surveys) can then be regressed on various explanatory variables from the phone panel, including measures of public action in the intervening years. As before, omitted variables will introduce endogeneity which can be eliminated by differencing. In this case too treatment effects are likely to be correlated with the extent of collective action. Again, this type of endogeneity can be dealt with by using the approach of Elbers and Gunning (forthcoming), which will be explained at length in the next section.

It is often suggested that advocacy activities of NGOs do not lend themselves to rigorous evaluation. This position is defensible if those activities are to be evaluated as an integrated whole so that the entire chain, from the advocacy itself, though the responses of citizens end the resulting changes in outcomes, must be evaluated as an integrated whole. In this case finding a credible counterfactual will rarely be feasible. However, the perfect should not be the enemy of the good: a substantial part of the theory of change *does* lend itself to rigorous analysis in the example. This involves "opening the black box" by testing the various components of the theory of change separately. Both the effect of information on collective action and the effect of the latter on development outcomes can be investigated rigorously. We have indicated that in some cases RCTs are not suitable for this purpose and that instead regression methods should be applied to observational data (as opposed to the experimental data generated by an RCT).

We expect that the type of endogeneity we have focused on (arising from correlation between program assignment and heterogeneous treatment effects as a result of the discretionary powers of the program officer) will come to be seen as a central problem in evaluations, certainly those of NGOs. In this situation RCTs are less suitable than is commonly assumed but a regression-based alternative approach exists. The issue is not specific

---

[9] This method is explained in section 4.

to advocacy. We will see in the next session that it also very much affects the evaluation of NGOs involved in service delivery.

34.4 IMPERFECT CONTROL IN SERVICE DELIVERY

Of the three types of NGPO activities we have distinguished service delivery lends itself best to an RCT evaluation. However an ex ante evaluation is sometimes not feasible: donors often set up an evaluation when project activities have already started so that there is no longer scope for randomization. Since the treatment group has already been selected the evaluation is of the ex post type. In this case the evaluator can construct a control group, using matching techniques to ensure its comparability with the given group of beneficiaries. Instead of RCTs the evaluation then applies diff-in-diff techniques to baseline and endline data for the two groups of beneficiaries.[10] This is a sensible approach but may produce biased estimates when the NGO's control over program participation is imperfect. In this section we focus on that case.

In many NGOs policy makers at headquarters set policies only in quite general terms. They may, for example, decide that a particular educational program is to be implemented in villages which are poor according to some criterion. Specific decisions on program participation are often left to staff in the field ("program officers") who can exercise considerable discretion within the wide guidelines of the HQ policy. In particular, program officers can use private information on where the program is likely to be most effective.

Such delegation of decision-making power is, of course, entirely sensible. However, it presents a problem for an evaluation since it creates a correlation between treatment effects and assignment and this implies endogeneity.[11] The problem arises if two conditions are both satisfied: the effect of the program differs between individuals or locations (treatment heterogeneity) and the program officer bases his decisions on what communities or individuals can participate in the program at least in part on those differences. Since this conjunction is quite common in NGOs the issue needs to be taken seriously.

To see the problem it is helpful to write the evaluation in regression form. Denote the outcome variable (e.g. a measure of learning in an education intervention) as y, a vector of intervention variables (e.g. the number of school books and the number of trained teachers in a particular school) as P, a vector of control variables as X and the error term as ε. We eliminate the effect of (time-invariant) unobservables by taking differences.[12] This gives the regression equation as:

---

[10]   In the evaluation of the Netherlands government's support for Dutch development NGOs (cf. footnote 3) this approach has been adopted by all country teams to assess the impact of the program in terms of the Millennium Development goals.

[11]   This is an example of what Heckman et al. (2006) termed essential heterogeneity. See also Ravallion (2011). Note that the correlation can arise in two ways, depending on whether the behavioral response to the treatment heterogeneity comes from the program officer or the beneficiary. We focus on the former case, Ravallion (2011) on the latter, i.e. the case of selective take up.

[12]   This implies the assumption of parallel trends.

$$\Delta y_i = \alpha \Delta X_i + \beta_i \Delta P_i + \gamma + \Delta \varepsilon_i = \alpha \Delta X_i + \bar{\beta} \Delta P_i + \gamma + [(\beta_i - \bar{\beta})\Delta P_i + \Delta \varepsilon_i] \qquad (1)$$

where i denotes the unit of observation (e.g. a school or a child) and α, β_i, γ parameters.[13] The effect of the treatment is measured by β and the notation β_i indicates that we allow for treatment heterogeneity: the treatment effect can differ across i.

We assume that in (1) the controls X are exogenous. There is, however, another source of endogeneity. Who can participate in the NGO program (or is offered the opportunity to participate) is decided by local staff and these program officers base their decisions on their estimates of β_i, the effectiveness of the program at the individual level. This private information need not be correct: we only assume that the program officer's estimates, and hence his decisions, are correlated with the individual treatment effects.

Since β_i and ΔP_i are correlated it is clear from the second part of equation (1) that OLS estimation would be inappropriate: ΔP_i is correlated with the error term in square brackets. In the terminology of Heckman et al. (2006) this is the case of essential heterogeneity which we already encountered in the previous section. The usual remedy of instrumental variable estimation now necessarily fails: as can be seen from (1) any variable which is correlated with ΔP_i must also be correlated with the error term in square brackets. Therefore a variable which satisfies both requirements for a valid instrument does not exist. It follows that an evaluation using standard regression methods on observational data runs into an insurmountable endogeneity problem.

In general an RCT will fare no better. In non-technical terms: an RCT would be invalid in this context since it would choose participants (e.g. schools in the treatment group) randomly whereas in actual practice they would be chosen non-randomly by the program officers. The RCT is misleading since it does not mimic how "treatment" (or at least the offer of treatment) is assigned in practice. It could produce a "false negative," concluding that the intervention is not effective when in fact it is.

In this situation the objection of an NGO that an RCT misses a key aspect of the way the NGO functions, its reliance on the private information of program officers, would be correct. This is a situation where indeed standard evaluation methods are not appropriate for an NGO.[14]

The solution might seem to apply an RCT at a higher level, by randomizing at the level of program officers rather than beneficiaries (schools in this example). A drawback is that this method involves loss of statistical power.[15] The method is inefficient since the program will, obviously, not be offered to any of the schools in the control group, but since program officers can exercise their discretion it will also not be offered to some of the members of the treatment group. As a result the proportion of actually treated cases in the trial is too small.

A much more serious problem is that randomization over program officers may destroy internal validity of the RCT. This would arise if program officers were stationed in particular areas of the country on the basis of, say, their membership of an ethnic group or their

---

[13] Note that γ picks up the effect of a linear time trend.

[14] We are not suggesting that this problem is specific to NGO evaluations, only that in that context it is quite likely to occur.

[15] This is analyzed in detail in the supplemental material of Elbers and Gunning (2014) but the key point is straightforward.

knowledge of relevant farming methods. This would lead to a correlation between characteristics of the program officer and X and thereby between P and X at the individual level. In this case randomization in a small sample of program officers would result in systematic differences between the treatment and control groups: it is unlikely that randomization over P will also achieve randomization over X. Hence internal validity is no longer guaranteed: differences between the group may reflect the differences in X rather than the treatment.

If neither RCTs nor standard regressions can be used then evaluation would appear to be impossible. In Elbers and Gunning (forthcoming) we propose a solution to this fundamental problem. This involves collecting observational data[16] on the variables in equation (1), for example, in the case of a sanitation program changes in outcomes such as health, participation and other determinants of the outcomes such as household income. These data can be used in a regression to estimate the effect of the program in a way which avoids the endogeneity problem. We are interested in an estimate of the total program effect $E\beta_i\Delta P_i$, the expected value (in the population) of the intervention and its individual effect, taking into account the correlation between the two.[17]

The trick is to allow explicitly for a dependence of the assignment on the individual treatment effects (which we cannot observe) and the control variables (which are observed):

$$\Delta P_i = f(\beta_i, \Delta X_i)$$

If this function can be inverted we have:

$$\beta_i = g(\Delta P_i, \Delta X_i) \tag{2}$$

We can therefore rewrite the regression equation as

$$\Delta y_i = \alpha\Delta X_i + E(\beta_i \mid \Delta X_i, \Delta P_i)\Delta P_i + \gamma + \omega_i \tag{3}$$

where $\omega_i = \Delta\varepsilon_i + \left(\beta_i - E\left(\beta_i \mid \Delta X_i, \Delta P_i\right)\right)\Delta P_i$ and this is uncorrelated with ΔX_i and ΔP_i.

Using a polynomial approximation we can write the term $E(\beta_i \mid \Delta X_i, \Delta P_i)$ as a series of terms in ΔX_i and ΔP_i. For example, for a linear approximation:

$$E(\beta_i \mid \Delta X_i, \Delta P_i) \approx \delta_0 + \delta_1\Delta X_i + \delta_2\Delta P_i$$

Substituting this in (3) gives

$$\Delta y_i = \gamma + \theta_1\Delta X_i + \theta_2\Delta P_i + \theta_3\Delta X_i \otimes \Delta P_i + \theta_4\Delta P_i \otimes \Delta P_i + \omega_i \tag{4}$$

Using observational data this equation can be estimated using OLS.

The effect of the program, which we call the total program effect (TPE), can now be estimated by multiplying the regression coefficients of all terms involving ΔP with the sample means of the regressors:

---

[16] That is administrative or survey data rather than experimental data.
[17] Note that we cannot estimate a selection equation: we observe ΔP_i but not β_i.

$$T\hat{P}E = \hat{\theta}_2 \overline{\Delta P_i} + \hat{\theta}_3 \overline{\Delta X_i \otimes \Delta P_i} + \hat{\theta}_4 \overline{\Delta P_i \otimes \Delta P_i} \tag{5}$$

where bars denote the sample means.[18] This gives a consistent estimate of the total program effect provided the observational data are from a representative sample (or can be reweighted).

In practice this means that one regresses ΔY_i on ΔX_i, ΔP_i and their interactions with ΔP_i and collects all terms involving ΔP_i to calculate the total program effect. Since the estimated TPE is linear in the $\hat{\theta}$ parameters its standard error can be obtained straightforwardly from the covariance matrix of the OLS coefficients.

It is useful to stress why this approach provides a solution. The expected value of the treatment effect $E\beta_i$ is a parameter that can be obtained in an RCT (with randomization over beneficiaries) but not in a regression (because of essential heterogeneity). However, irrespective of whether it can be estimated or not, it is of no use in an evaluation since in practice program assignment is not random.

The total program effect is the expected value of the product $\beta_i \Delta P_i$. Clearly, this is equal to the product of the expected value of the two components only if these are independent, but in this case they are correlated (because the assignment decision has been delegated to the program officers). Our approach cuts this Gordian knot by focusing directly on the product, the total program effect itself, rather than on its components.

It is instructive to consider the special case where $D_i = \Delta P_i$ is a binary variable taking the value 1 for the treatment group and 0 for the control group. Equation (4) now reduces to

$$\Delta y_i = \gamma + \theta_1 \Delta X_i + \theta_2 D_i + \theta_3 D_i \Delta X_i + \omega_i$$

since in the binary case $D_i^2 = D_i$. The total program effect will then be estimated as

$$T\hat{P}E = \hat{\theta}_2 \overline{D_i} + \hat{\theta}_3 \overline{D_i \Delta X_i} \tag{6}$$

As before, this shows that when the sample is representative sample means can be used to construct the total program effect. The interaction term in (6) avoids the bias resulting from correlations between treatment effects and either program participation or controls.

Standard diff-in-diff regressions usually omit this interaction term (e.g. Khandker et al. 2009; Almeida and Galasso 2010). In addition our method can also be used in the general case when the intervention is multidimensional and at least some of its components are multi-valued rather than binary.

How can this method be applied in practice? The evaluator should first ascertain how the NGO works. If program officers have discretion to determine whether someone receives "treatment" (and how much) and they base that decision in part on the differences they see between beneficiaries in the effect of the treatment then RCTs are inappropriate. The evaluation should then use observational data and employ the method we have described to estimate the effectiveness of the NGO.[19]

---

[18] Obviously, to identify θ_4 a restriction on parameters like $\theta_{4,k\ell} = \theta_{4,\ell k}$ is required.

[19] One can test whether the variables which would normally not be included in the regression: the interactions of treatment variables with themselves and with the controls, are jointly significant. When this test indicates that treatment heterogeneity cannot be rejected it is advisable to calculate the TPE. This

NGOs, in Africa and elsewhere, have often reacted in extreme ways to the recent enthusiasm for RCTs. Some have embraced the methodology uncritically in the hope that the "rigor" of RCT evaluations will give their work greater credibility. Other NGOs have rejected the methodology without fully understanding it, often arguing that quantitative methods miss the essence of their work. Neither reaction is appropriate. Much of the work of NGOs involved in service delivery (e.g. programs in health and education) is likely to be of the type which we have characterized as that of program officer discretion. In that case RCTs indeed miss the essence of the NGOs work and their results can be misleading.[20] Fortunately, the problem can be addressed with the method we have proposed. As data availability continues to improve this will become easier to apply.

We do not wish to suggest that there is no role for RCTs in this case. However, their role is to produce a convincing "proof of principle." Beyond that they reach a natural limit: if treatment heterogeneity is important then an RCT cannot predict the effect of a program which in practice will be assigned in a way different from the assignment in the RCT.

34.5 CONCLUSION

NGOs are a major presence in African economies. In many ways they attempt to do what governments are not able or willing to do. Their effectiveness has only recently begun to be assessed rigorously, for example, by using RCTs to evaluate their activities.

In this chapter we have argued that when deciding what can and cannot be evaluated it is important to distinguish between three types of activity of development NGOs: capacity building, advocacy, and service delivery. (Of course, many NGOs are involved in some combination of these three types of activity.) That service delivery activities can be evaluated rigorously is generally accepted. On the other hand it is commonly suggested that there is very little scope for rigorous evaluation of capacity building and advocacy activities of NGOs. We have suggested that this position is exaggerated.

We have also argued that the case for RCT evaluations is overstated. The very nature of NGOs with their non-hierarchical organization, leaving considerable scope for discretion to staff in the field, makes it unlikely that RCTs will produce useful estimates, at least in situations where treatment heterogeneity is important. While the issue of essential heterogeneity may sound as an esoteric concern of econometricians, the problem is likely to be pervasive, certainly in the case of NGOs. We therefore very much agree with Ravallion's statement that "Essential heterogeneity is such an intuitively plausible idea that the onus on analysts should be to establish *a priori* grounds why it does *not* exist."[21] This suggests greater reliance on

---

simple test should in our view always be performed. Allowing for treatment heterogeneity may turn out to be an unnecessary precaution but this is small price to pay for avoiding a biased estimate of the effect of the NGO's activities.

[20] Clearly, the problem is not the quantitative nature of an RCT. Indeed, any qualitative method faces the same issues.

[21] Ravallion (2011: 9); italics and underlining in the original. Recall, however, that Ravallion is concerned about self-selection into treatment rather than the case we have focused on where assignment is decided by the program officer who uses private information on treatment effects.

observational instead of experimental data. (As data availability improves this will become easier to implement.) We have indicated how observational data can be used to evaluate NGO programs when standard RCT methods would fail because of essential heterogeneity.

REFERENCES

Almeida, R.K., and Galasso, E. (2010). Jump-starting Self-employment? Evidence for Welfare Participants in Argentina. *World Development*, 38:742–755.

Banerjee, A., and Duflo, E. (2011). *Poor Economics: A Radical Rethinking of the Way to Fight Global Poverty*. New York: Public Affairs.

Barrett, J., Bilinsky, P., Desalos, C. et al. (2012). *Evaluation Methodology MFS II Country Evaluations; Capacity of Southern Partner Organisations (5 Cs) Component; Evaluation Methodology for DRC, Ethiopia, India, Indonesia, Liberia and Uganda*. Wageningen: Center for Development Innovation.

Deaton, A. (2010) Instruments, randomization, and learning about development. *Journal of Economic Literature*, 48:424–455.

Duflo, E., Glennerster, R., and Kremer, M. (2008). Using randomization in development economics research: a toolkit, in T.P. Schultz and J. Strauss (eds), *Handbook of Development Economics*. Amsterdam: North-Holland, pp. 3895–3962.

Elbers, C., and Gunning, J.W. (2014). Evaluation of Development Programs: Randomized Controlled Trials or regressions? *World Bank Economic Review*, 28:432–445. doi: 10.1093/wber/lht025.

Gunning, J.W. (2012). How Can Development NGOs Be Evaluated? FERDI Working Paper 51, Clermont-Ferrand: FERDI.

Gunning, J.W. (2012a). Evaluating Development NGOs, Policy Brief 56. Clermont-Ferrand: FERDI.

Heckman, J.J., Urzua, S., and Vytlacil, E. (2006). Understanding instrumental variables in models with essential heterogeneity. *Review of Economics and Statistics*, 88:389–432.

Khandker, S.R., Bakht, Z., and Koolwal, G.B. (2009). The poverty impact of rural roads: evidence from Bangladesh. *Economic Development and Cultural Change*, 57:685–722.

Lieberman, E.S., Posner, D.N., and Tsai, L.L. (2013). Does information lead to more active citizenship? Evidence from an education intervention in rural Kenya, September, MIT Political Science Department Research paper No. 2013-2. Cambridge, Mass: Masschusetts Institute of Technology.

Miguel, E., and Kremer, M. (2004). Worms: identifying impacts on education and health in the presence of treatment externalities. *Econometrica*, 72:159–217.

Ravallion, M. (2009). Evaluation in the practice of development. *World Bank Research Observer*, 24:29–53.

Ravallion, M. (2011). On the Implications of Essential Heterogeneity for Estimating Causal Impacts Using Social Experiments, World Bank Staff Working Paper 5804. Washington, DC: World Bank.

Ravallion, M. (2012). Fighting Poverty One Experiment at a Time: a Review of Abhijit Banerjee and Esther Duflo's *Poor Economics: A Radical Rethinking of the Way to Fight Global Poverty*. *Journal of Economic Literature*, 50:103–114.

CHAPTER 35

TRADE UNIONS IN SOUTH AFRICA

HAROON BHORAT, KARMEN NAIDOO, AND DEREK YU

35.1 INTRODUCTION

As an upper middle-income country within Africa and the continent's largest economy, South Africa often attracts specific interest in terms of its economic growth and development dynamics. This is of course also in part a function of the country's unique history, based on the notorious system of apartheid. Often under-appreciated is the extent to which this history of racial segregation and discrimination has generated so many of the outlier features of this economy. From high levels of spatial segregation and a very small informal economy, to extraordinary economic and social inequalities amongst the citizens of the country and a surprisingly deep inherited social assistance scheme—South Africa remains a country of unusual and unexpected statistics. Nowhere is this feature more evident than in the labor market of this economy.

Perhaps the most relevant outlier statistics lie in the areas of unemployment and income inequality. In the case of the former, South Africa has had an average unemployment rate, since 1994, of about 25%. This unemployment rate remains one of the highest in the world. The figure has a low standard deviation over the sample period and for the immediate future is unlikely to change significantly. In terms of income inequality, the latest estimate for 2010, places the Gini coefficient at 0.69, ranking South Africa as one of the most unequal societies in the world today. Underlying this high inequality is the notion that the moderate economic growth rate since 1994, averaging at 3.3% per annum, has yielded a modest poverty reduction, but sharp rises in household inequality (Bhorat and van der Westhuizen 2013b). At the heart of the debate around the country's "twin peaks" of unemployment and inequality is the role played by the labor market in generating unequal returns as well as large quantity-based disequilibria. The role then, played by wages and institutions in the labor market, in generating these outcomes has been a focus of research in these areas in South Africa (Armstrong and Steenkamp 2008; Bhorat, van der Westhuizen and Goga 2009b; Bhorat, Goga and van der Westhuizen 2012a; Bhorat, Kanbur, and Mayet 2012b). In this chapter, we attempt to consider the role played by institutions in the South African economy with a focus on the trade union movement and the labor-regulating architecture of the country.

The chapter thus first provides a historical overview of the South African trade union movement before and after the end of apartheid, followed by a brief discussion of the labor market legislation and institutions formed since 1994. Thereafter, there is a detailed evaluation of the impact of trade unions and wage legislation on labor market outcomes in South Africa. Lastly, the chapter culminates in a discussion on the political economy effects shaping South Africa's employment relations in light of the tripartite structure of the ruling governmental party, before concluding.

35.2 THE SOUTH AFRICAN TRADE UNION MOVEMENT: A BRIEF HISTORY

The Union of South Africa, formed in 1910, was characterized by a political partnership between English-speaking and Afrikaans-speaking Whites, representing their mining and agricultural interests respectively. The Union formally excluded the African majority from any formal political expression[1]. A series of laws was passed that would deleteriously impact on the smooth functioning of the labor market. For instance, the 1911 Mines and Works Act reserved skilled mining jobs for Whites, while the 1913 Land Act forbade Africans from owning land in designated "White" areas and resigned Africans to "reserves" accounting for only 7% (increasing to 13% later) of the total land area of the country. Also, the pass laws curtailed the free flow of African labor, thereby forcing many African workers into low-wage sectors and occupations (Van der Berg and Bhorat 1999; Woolard 2001). As a result, the labor market was characterized by a strong racial division of labor that would persist for decades to come.

The core foundation of collective bargaining legislation in South Africa was the Industrial Conciliation Act of 1924, which provided for the voluntary establishment of permanent collective bargaining institutions, namely Industrial Councils (ICs), by employers' organizations and registered non-African trade unions (Godfrey, Maree, Du Toit, and Theron 2010). Within its legal ambit, for the first five decades after being established, the ICs denied African workers access to centralized collective bargaining and despite the lack of racial representation within the bargaining structures, could set minimum wages for the sectors concerned. Since only non-African trade unions were recognized and allowed to negotiate, they were in a favorable position to protect the wage interests of their non-African members. Needless to say, this reinforced discrimination against Africans, as they were placed outside the ambit of IC agreements (Nattrass and Seekings 1997; Butcher and Rouse 2001; Rospabé 2001; Woolard 2001).

The Industrial Conciliation Act was amended in 1930 by stipulating that the agreements reached at the IC could be extended by the Minister of Labour to all workers (including Africans) in the industry concerned, regardless of whether the workers belonged to the trade union(s) participating in the negotiation. Although this amendment did improve wages of

[1] There are four population groups in South Africa, namely African, Coloured, Indian and White. African, Coloured and Indian individuals are collectively referred to as Black.

African workers, the real aim was to protect the jobs and living conditions of White workers, given that the 1924 act unintentionally incentivized employers to dismiss White employees and replace them with the African employees at lower wages (Godfrey et al. 2010). In addition, influx control was implemented in the 1940s to limit the geographic mobility of African workers, so that White workers would face less competition in the labor market from African workers, who were prepared to accept lower wages and inferior working conditions (Rospabé 2001).

After the National Party came into power in 1948, various new acts (e.g. 1950 Groups Area Act, 1953 Bantu Education Act, 1959 Extension of Universities Education Act) were implemented to limit the education prospects of Africans and deny them the right of residence in urban areas with more profitable work opportunities. In addition, job reservation was tightened in the mining industry and even extended to the manufacturing and commerce industries, favoring the employment of White workers (Van der Berg and Bhorat 1999; Woolard 2001). The Industrial Conciliation Act was amended again in 1956, with the primary aim of extending and refining racial segregation within the industrial relations system. In particular, no new "racially mixed" unions[2] could be registered, unless the number of members who were not White was too small to make a separate trade union viable. For the existing "racially mixed" unions, they were required to establish two separate branches (one for Whites and one for Coloureds and Indians) and hold separate branch meetings, but only White members could sit on such union's executive committee (Godfrey et al. 2010).

In the 1960s, the South African economy experienced a decade of rapid growth exceeding 5% per annum. In order to meet the increasing demand for skilled labor without undermining apartheid, the government created a "floating" job bar: a White skilled job was fragmented, with African employees being allowed to perform the less skilled part of a job. However, no White worker could be replaced by a Black worker and no White worker could work under a Black worker. Conditional labor market mobility then was provided to an African workforce desperately required for a fast-growing economy (Van der Berg and Bhorat 1999; Woolard 2001).

With rising inflation but persistently low remuneration, more frequent strikes by African workers founded on wage demands took place in the early 1970s. As a result, the Settlement of Disputes Act in 1973 provided for joint liaison committees of employers and African workers, along with the existing racially divided committees (Godfrey et al. 2010). The remainder of the 1970s saw mounting pressure on the government from various sources such as the slow-down of economic growth, the 1974 imposition of international trade sanctions, and the defining 1976 Soweto uprising of Black youths. Hence, there was an increasing realization that the job reservation policy, trade union registration and collective bargaining systems, which favored the White workers, were generating significant social and economic instability in the South African economy at the time (Van der Berg and Bhorat 1999).

In the labor market specifically, the 1973 wildcat strikes—both spontaneous and widespread—were a watershed event in the country's labor movement history and forced government and employers to rethink their approach to industrial relations. The Wiehahn and Riekert Commissions of 1979 represented their response to the increasing labor unrest. The former commission recommended the legalization of Black trade unions and eradicated

---

[2] A "racially mixed" union consists of Coloured, Indian and White workers.

job reservation through the Industrial Conciliation Amendment Act of 1979, which widened the definition of an employee to include African workers. Only two years later was the ban also lifted on non-racial trade unions (Rospabé 2001; Godfrey et al 2010). The result of the Wiehahn Commission then was an increasingly empowered Black workforce with greater bargaining power and rising participation in the regulated labor market, where they would be covered by legislation on minimum employment conditions. The latter commission focused on issues of labor mobility and argued for the relaxation of controls on workers who held rights of urban residence or employment. Pressure from both the mining and manufacturing sectors for a stable workforce finally led to the eradication of influx control in 1986 (Van der Berg and Bhorat 1999).

This crucial moment in 1979 represents a turning point in the Black trade union movement, as it signaled the formal legal recognition of this burgeoning movement representing the aspirations and demands of Black workers. As a result of their new legal status and recognition by employers, these trade unions grew rapidly in size and strength—from a membership of 70 150 in 1979 to almost 300 000 in 1983 (Maree 1987). Trade unions, it must be noted, became a crucial economic and political force against the apartheid regime from the mid-1980s onward. The Black trade unions effectively became the voice of the marginalized majority of working-class South Africans and by extension, the voice of the country's politically marginalized majority. In this sense—and it is a point we allude to later in the chapter—the Black trade union movement was historically at the center of the political struggle against apartheid in South Africa. In industries in which Black trade unions were already established, the unions pressurized employers' associations to agree to their amalgamation into a national bargaining council and in industries with no bargaining councils, large Black trade unions successfully managed to lobby for the creation of a national bargaining council (Godfrey et al. 2010). This led the way toward more centralized collective bargaining from the 1990s onward.

The brief history of South Africa's trade union movement highlights the extent to which the trade union movement has been inextricably linked to the anti-apartheid movement and clearly positions it as a central agent in the struggle for democracy. The late 1970s legalization of Black trade unions provided further impetus to the already strong labor movement that then eventually achieved the abolition influx control in 1986. In this sense, the goals of the broader anti-apartheid movement, that of a non-racial and democratic society, underpinned the goals of the trade union movement along with the more specific aims to improve employment conditions for all members.

These developments, along with post-apartheid amendments to labor legislation that promoted the registration of trade unions in all sectors of the economy, paved the way for considerable growth in the number of unions and unionized workers since 1994. Currently, there are 22 trade union federations in the country (South African Labour Guide 2013a), with four of them being organized on a national basis, namely the Congress of South African Trade Unions (COSATU), the Federation of Unions of South Africa (FEDUSA), the National Council of Trade Unions (NACTU), and the Confederation of South African Workers' Union (CONSAWU).

COSATU was established in November 1985 and is arguably the largest federation, with a membership of 20 trade union affiliates, representing more than 2 million members (COSATU 2013). COSATU plays an influential role in the direction of transformation and economic restructuring of South Africa, and it is argued that its power resides in the size of its affiliated

Table 35.1 Trade union membership of public and private sector employees in formal sector, selected years

	Private sector		Public sector	
Year	Number of union members	Union members as % of workers	Number of union members	Union members as % of workers
1997	1 813 217	35.6%	835 795	55.2%
2001	1 748 807	30.6%	1 070 248	70.1%
2005	1 925 248	30.1%	1 087 772	68.4%
2010	1 888 293	26.3%	1 324 964	74.6%
2013	1 868 711	24.4%	1 393 189	69.2%

Source: Authors' calculations, using 1997 October Household Survey, 2001 and 2005 Labour Force Surveys, 2010 and 2013 Quarterly Labour Force Surveys.

unions' membership; capacity to mobilize employees; strong links with the government; as well as regional and international credibility (Finnemore 2009). How COSATU functions as part of South Africa's ruling party's tripartite alliance will be discussed in more detail in section 5.

At present, there are 189 registered unions in South Africa (South African Labour Guide 2013a). Table 35.1 shows that the proportion of the public sector's formal workforce who are union members—or the public sector's union density—rose from 55% in 1997 (834 thousand workers) to almost 70% in 2013 (1.4 million workers). Interestingly, the 2013 figure is 5 percentage points lower than at the peak of unionization in 2010. The private sector union density displays the opposite overall trend, declining from 36% in 1997 to 24% in 2013, while the absolute number of private sector unionized workers has remained fairly constant. Notably then, the growth of the private sector workforce has outstripped the rate of unionization.

The downward trend of union density since 2010 has been driven at a sectoral level primarily by declining membership numbers in the manufacturing, construction, finance, and agricultural[3] sectors. However, the mining sector, historically South Africa's most highly unionized sector, continues to show increasing union density rates over time, increasing from 71% in 1997 to 80% in 2013. The dominant union in this sector has been the National Union of Mineworkers (NUM), founded in 1982 and with a current membership of more than 300 000 workers, equating to almost all formal mining sector employees.[4]

Set against South Africa's history of racial segregation and marginalization of the African workforce, amendments to the legislation that aimed to empower the majority of the country's workers can be expected to have increased union density. The public sector unionization rates are evidence of this. However, when comparing South Africa to a range of OECD countries, as in Figure 35.1, it is clear that on these estimates South Africa's union density figures are not an outlier in this sample.

---

[3] According to our own calculations using the 1997 October Household Surveys, 2001 and 2005 Labour Force Surveys, 2010 and 2013 Quarterly Labour Force Surveys; disaggregated at a sectoral level. The data is not tabulated here.

[4] More recently, the Association of Mineworkers and Construction Union (AMCU) has been formed and it is estimated to currently have approximately 50,000 members from both sectors in total.

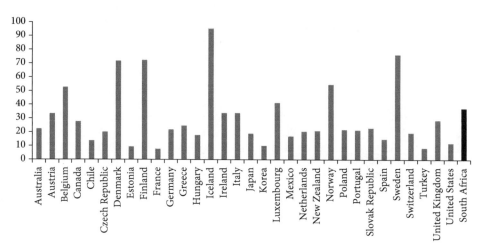

FIGURE 35.1 2005 Union Density Estimates for OECD Countries and South Africa.

Source: OECD Stat (2013) and LFS 2005:2 (Statistics South Africa).

The average union density for the counties represented in the figure was 30% and South Africa was to some extent above this mean at 37.5%. Statistics reported by the International Labour Organisation suggest that in 2001, Brazil had a union density of as high as 71% (Lawrence and Ishikawa 2005). Thus, the combined evidence at least initially suggests that the level of union membership in South Africa does not reflect an unusually highly union-ized labor market. Hence, whilst unions may not have relatively large membership figures, it is entirely possible that the relevant regulatory environment has ensured that their wage and non-wage demands are more easily attained. We turn then in the next section to assessing the post-1994 labor regulatory environment in South Africa.

35.3 THE POST-1994 ENVIRONMENT: FROM LEGISLATION TO LABOR MARKET INSTITUTIONS

The two most relevant acts in the post-apartheid period to understanding South Africa's labor regulatory regime are the Labour Relations Act (LRA) and the Basic Conditions of Employment Act (BCEA).[5]

The LRA 66 of 1995 aims at the promotion of economic development, social justice, labor peace and democracy in the workplace. This is achieved by regulating the organizational rights of trade unions, as well as promoting and facilitating collective bargaining at the workplace

---

[5] Other legislations (i.e. Employment Equity Act, Occupational Health and Safety Act, Compensation for Occupational Injuries and Diseases Act, Skills Development Act, Skills Development Levies Act, Unemployment Insurance Act, and Unemployment Insurance Contributions Act) fall beyond the scope of this chapter and will not be discussed.

and at a sectoral level. Bargaining councils (BCs)—formerly known as ICs as mentioned in section 2—are voluntary bodies established by registered trade unions in collaboration with employer-organizations within a specific sector and area. Collective agreement on various issues, ranging from minimum wage to conditions of employment, is reached during the collective bargaining process. Furthermore, the LRA promotes the dispute resolution and labor peace with the establishment of the Commission for Conciliation, Mediation and Arbitration (CCMA), Labour Court and Labour Appeal Court (Republic of South Africa 1995 and 2002a).

As far as the BCEA 75 of 1997 is concerned, it provides for minimum working conditions regarding issues such as work hours, overtime payment, annual leave and sick leave (Republic of South Africa 1997). The Act was revised in 2002 to provide for the establishment of the Employment Conditions Commission (ECC), which makes recommendations to the Minister of Labour in respect of minimum wages and other conditions of employment in vulnerable sectors (Republic of South Africa 2002b). Currently, 11 areas of economic activity have such sectoral determinations in place.[6]

It is argued that in an overly regulated labor market, labor laws, while protecting worker rights, create a disincentive to fire workers even if they might not be productive. This is because when firms dismiss workers, they need to follow a complex set of procedures that in South Africa's case can include activities such as time-consuming hearings with the CCMA. This argument is supported by the results of a few recent studies (Benjamin and Gruen 2006; Bhorat, Pauw, and Mncube 2009a) which found that the turnaround time for dispute resolution is relatively longer in some CCMA regional offices (e.g. those in the Eastern Cape and North West provinces) and industries (e.g. agriculture and mining). For instance, in 2006, the average time taken to complete the conciliation cases was the longest in the mining industry (37.3 days, which is above the stipulated duration of 30 days). Furthermore, Bhorat, Jacobs and van der Westhuizen (2013a) found that, ceteris paribus, regions characterized by lower number of industrial disputes but greater efficiency of the regional offices to handle the disputes (i.e. those offices with shorter conciliation, arbitration, and con-arb mean time) are associated with higher levels of employment.

To gauge whether these findings, on a basis of a comparative ranking of labor laws, are indicative of an overly regulated or rigid labor market, the World Bank's Doing Business (DB) survey provides a set of normalized Employment Protection Legislation measures. Using the 2013 DB results, Table 35.2 presents five key measures of the "employing workers" indices by country income level. First, the "difficulty of hiring" index measures restrictions on part-time and temporary contracts, together with the wages of trainees relative to worker value-added. Second, the "difficulty of firing" index assesses and ranks specific legislative provisions on dismissals. Third, the "rigidity of hours" index measures the various restrictions around weekend, Sunday and public holiday work, limits on overtime, etc. Fourth, "non-wage labour costs" encompass social protection costs and measure all social security and health costs associated with hiring a worker. Lastly, the "firing cost" measures the cost of terminating the employment of an individual in terms of legislated prior notice requirements, severance pay, and so on.

---

[6] These sectors include children in the performance of advertising, artistic and cultural activities; civil engineering; contract cleaning; domestic workers; farm workers; forestry sector; hospitality workers; learnerships; private security sector; taxi sector; wholesale and retail sector (Department of Labour 2013b).

The aggregate cross-country data in Table 35.2 shows that the countries at the two ends of the spectrum—low-income and high-income OECD countries—display the highest average scores of labor market rigidity, non-wage labor costs and firing costs. Countries falling in between these two categories show on average declining rigidity and firing costs as national income levels rise, however, non-wage labor costs increase with income level, as expected.

South Africa then, falling into the upper middle income range, exhibits rankings of the indices for firing costs and non-wage labor costs that are all below the means for its income-level category and well as the world means. However, the measures for the difficulty of hiring and firing and rigidity of hours are above the respective means, more remarkably for the difficulty of hiring index. Thus, South Africa's higher than global average measure of aggregate labor market rigidity is primarily driven by the difficulty in hiring. These results suggest that South Africa's labor legislation translates into a labor market that is relatively flexible in terms of hiring and firing costs—that is, not overly-regulated. In these respects, however, the greater legislative requirements regarding the procedures to hire workers, in particular, introduces a degree of inflexibility.

The World Economic Forum (2013) also had similar findings with regard to rigidity of the South African labor market. Despite the fact that South Africa was ranked 53rd out of 148 countries in the overall global competitiveness index, the country was only ranked 116th in in terms of its labor market efficiency, one of the 11 pillars that comprise the overall index.

Table 35.2 Mean measures of labor regulation, by income level

Area of regulation	Low income	Lower-middle income	Upper-middle income	High-income: non-OECD	High-income: OECD	South Africa	All countries
Difficulty of hiring	50.89	35.28	30.40	17.79	27.72	55.67	33.13
Difficulty of firing	36.88	33.96	25.60	16.25	22.26	30.00	27.95
Rigidity of hours	19.38	18.33	14.00	16.67	24.52	20.00	18.16
Aggregate rigidity of employment index	35.71	29.19	23.33	16.90	24.83	35.22	26.41
Non-wage labor costs*	12.40	16.01	17.31	21.43	10.17	2.40	15.62
Firing costs*	65.32	50.91	44.63	31.32	54.64	24.00	51.34

Source: Authors' own calculations using World Bank (2013b) data; Benjamin, Bhorat and Cheadle (2010).
* Results from the 2006 Doing Business Report, which focused on the jobs challenge and thus provided more detailed labor market indicators.
Regarding the consistency of South Africa's ranking over time, the 2013 results show no change in South Africa's relative position (compared to each country income-category and the global averages) in the aggregate rigidity of employment index from 2006 to 2013.

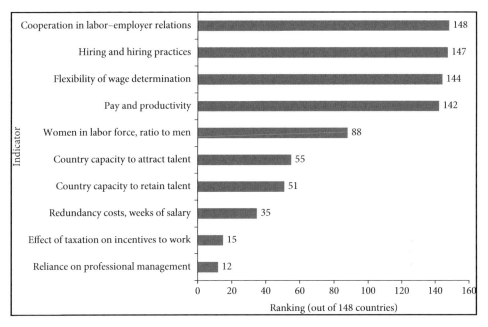

FIGURE 35.2 South Africa's labor market efficiency.

Source: World Economic Forum (2013: 347).

Looking at the labor market efficiency in greater detail (Figure 35.2), although South Africa performs well in half of the indicators,[7] including on the firing costs (35th); it was almost the worst ranked country in terms of hiring and firing procedures (147th). These findings support our conclusions on the World Bank's DB results.

The previous two sections have illustrated that within an international context, South Africa has neither an unusually highly unionized nor an overly-regulated labor market. An element of rigidity, however, does exist specifically around the difficulty of hiring workers. This notion of rigidity in hiring procedures has been supported quite widely in the local labor literature (Benjamin et al. 2010; Cheadle 2006; CDE 2013). Despite these features, the discourse around South Africa's labor markets often serves to perpetuate the perception of a more broadly overly regulated or rigid market, partly based on seemingly politically influential trade unions. To address this issue, the next section assesses in more empirical detail, the impact that trade unions and labor legislation have on employment and earnings.

35.4 THE IMPACT OF TRADE UNIONS AND LABOR LEGISLATION ON LABOR MARKET OUTCOMES IN SOUTH AFRICA

Given South Africa's persistent high unemployment levels, sclerotic competitiveness and the perceived political power of the union movement, the impact that trade unions may have on

---

[7] Five of South Africa's labor market indices ranking above the median.

raising average wage levels has long dominated the debates around trade union power and job creation. This section then first aims to assess the legal rights afforded by the country's legislation specifically to trade unions. In turn then, we present a more considered set of trade union wage premia based on recent econometric evidence for South Africa.

To measure South Africa's relative union power and protection of workers during collective disputes, Bhorat (2008) draws on a dataset compiled by Botero, Djankov, La Porta, Lopez-De-Silanes, and Schleifer (2004),[8] whose seminal study on the impact of labor regulation around the world makes use of data from 85 countries for the late 1990s. The results are presented in Table 35.3 and highlight most remarkably that South Africa's labor union power index, encompassing employees' right to unionize and to collective bargaining, is much higher than the mean value for all other countries, even when comparing South Africa to the upper-middle income category into which it falls. In contrast, South Africa's measure relating to collective disputes—a more appropriate measure of the protection offered to workers during collective disputes, such as large-scale dismissals—is both below the global average and also all income-classified country categories. Therefore, the relatively higher aggregate collective relations index is driven disproportionately by the labor union power index, otherwise understood as the basic rights to organize and form a trade union, rather than the protection of workers during collective disputes. Importantly, while this initially seems incompatible with the union density figures discussed earlier, it is actually more reflective of a highly protective labor legislation and constitution regarding the *right to unionize* and not necessarily that that South Africa's workforce is overly unionized to give labor unions disproportionate power in the arena of employment relations.

To further this discussion, we assess the wage premia associated with trade union membership as measure of their associated power. Although there is extensive literature on the union wage gap in South Africa, the studies on the bargaining council premium are fewer. In addition, there is little consensus on the appropriate method to correct for the endogeneity of union membership or on the magnitude of the institutional wage premium. Taking account of this, Bhorat et al. (2012a) used the 2005 South African Labour Force Survey data to investigate the union and bargaining council wage premiums and correct for the endogeneity of union status through a two-stage selection model, controlling for firm-level and job characteristics. In their most richly specified estimation[9] it is found that union members outside of the bargaining council system earned a premium of 7.04% and that members of private and public bargaining councils not belonging to unions earned a 8.97% and 10.5% premium over non-union workers outside of the bargaining council system, respectively.[10] The total estimated premium to union workers within the public bargaining council stands at 22%.

Therefore, there is evidence that belonging to either unions or bargaining councils are associated with statistically significant wage premia, and furthermore that unions may negotiate at the plant level for additional gains for their members within the bargaining council system. Most importantly, however, although this paper confirms the clear wage benefit

---

[8] The World Bank's "Employing Workers" indices are derived using the methodology developed in Botero et al. (2004) and was only introduced into the overall "Ease of Doing Business" index in 2006.

[9] Including dummy variables for union status, private and public bargaining council status, type of work, firm characteristics, and non-wage benefits.

[10] With significance at the 5% level.

Table 35.3 Average measures of trade union power in the late 1990s, by country income level

Area of regulation/ income level	Low income	LMI	UMI	HI–non-OECD	HI–OECD	South Africa	Total
Labor union power	0.348	0.422	0.489	0.463	0.305	0.714	0.425
Collective disputes	0.431	0.504	0.465	0.456	0.458	0.333	0.465
Aggregate collective relations Index	0.389	0.463	0.477	0.460	0.382	0.524	0.445

Source: Dataset compiled by Botero et al 2004 (http://www.andrei-shleifer.com/data.html), and authors' own calculations.

LMI refers to lower middle income countries; UMI to upper middle income countries and HI to high income economies either within the OECD or not. These are standard classification drawn from the World Bank's World Development Report (2005).

Labor union power measures the statutory protection and power of unions as the average of the following seven dummy variables which equal 1: (1) if employees have the right to unionize, (2) if employees have the right to collective bargaining, (3) if employees have the legal duty to bargain with unions, (4) if collective contracts are extended to third parties by law, (5) if the law allows closed shops, (6) if workers, or unions, or both have a right to appoint members to the Boards of Directors, and (7) if workers' councils are mandated by law.

Collective disputes measures the protection of workers during collective disputes as the average of the following eight dummy variables which equal one: (1) if employer lockouts are illegal, (2) if workers have the right to industrial action, (3) if wildcat, political, and sympathy/solidarity/secondary strikes are legal, (4) if there is no mandatory waiting period or notification requirement before strikes can occur, (5) if striking is legal even if there is a collective agreement in force, (6) if laws do not mandate conciliation procedures before a strike, (7) if third-party arbitration during a labor dispute is mandated by law, and (8) if it is illegal to fire or replace striking workers.

The Collective Relations Index measures the protection of collective relations laws as the average of (1) labor union power and (2) collective disputes.

of union membership, particularly within the bargaining council system, it also uncovers that institutional wage premiums in South Africa may be much smaller than previously estimated, with most of the previous studies reporting a premium in excess of 20%, possibly overstated through not accounting for BC coverage (Butcher and Rouse 2001; Armstrong and Steenkamp 2008; Miliea, Rezek, and Pitts 2013). Internationally, estimates of conditional union wage premiums range from 5% in Japan and the Republic of Korea, up to 15% in countries such as Brazil, Ghana, Mexico, Canada, Germany, and Malaysia (World Bank 2013a; Freeman 2009; see Table 35.4). Falling broadly within this range, the results for South Africa therefore suggest that union power is not evidently resulting in excessive wage premia for its members.

An alternative argument for South Africa's high levels of unemployment being driven by higher than optimal wages would be that wage legislation, particularly minimum wage

Table 35.4 Estimates of union effects on wages in developing countries

Country	Union wage premium
Brazil	5–12%
Ghana	6–16%
Mexico	10–15%
Malaysia	15–20%
Republic of Korea	3–7%
South Africa*	7%

Source: Freeman (2009);
* Bhorat et al. (2012a).

laws, has led to rising wage levels in the targeted sectors. Since the introduction of minimum wages in 1999, South Africa has instituted about 11 different sectoral minimum wage laws through a process of union, business, and government negotiation. Reliable economic research on the effects of minimum wages on labor market outcomes or household poverty in South Africa is limited and the few studies that exist mostly focus on a single sector.

As one of the most comprehensive studies on the impact of sectoral wage laws in South Africa, Bhorat et al. (2012b), investigate the impact of minimum wage laws applied to the Retail, Domestic work, Forestry, Security, and Taxi sectors, on employment, wages and hours of work. They use the biannual South African Labour Force Survey (LFS) data for the 2000–2007 period. These sectors were specifically chosen as representative of low wage sectors. Using different specifications of a difference-in-differences model, they were able to control for sector-specific factors that may be impacting the outcome variables. The authors report three important results. Firstly, there is no significant negative effect of the minimum wage on the probability of employment for all focus sectors, except the Taxi sector and in fact, for three of the remaining four sectors, there is a significantly positive relationship. Secondly, there is evidence of a significant increase in real hourly wages in the post-law period as a result of the minimum wage law (between 5% and 20%), where the increase is proportionately higher in district councils where pre-law wages were further below the introduced minimum. Lastly, the results show that employers in some sectors have responded to the introduction of a minimum wage by reducing the number of weekly hours worked, however, three of the five sectors show that the increase in real hourly wages was sufficient to outweigh any adjustments to working hours, resulting in these workers experiencing an improvement in their real monthly income.

Therefore, where there are real wage increases, they are not of a magnitude higher than 20% and in most cases can be interpreted to be a wage catch-up as these sectors, particularly Domestic work, have been historically low paying sectors. This is supported by the outcome that the probability of employment after the minimum wage law implementation in the sectors that experienced real wage increases was not negative. This result is particularly important in shaping our understanding of South Africa's labor market dynamics. Indeed, the result of a benign impact at the extensive or intensive margin from minimum wage laws is not an unusual result, with the "new minimum wage" literature being sparked of course by the work of Card and Krueger (1994) on the US labor market.

A key caveat to this conclusion, however, is that labor outcomes may respond quite differently to minimum wage legislation across different sectors. Bhorat, Kanbur, and Stanwix (2012c) estimate the impact of the 2003 introduction of the minimum wage law in South Africa's agricultural sector, using the same data and approach as Bhorat et al. (2012b). Their results show a significant increase in farmworker wages (at a magnitude of 17%) along with a significant fall in employment in response to the law, rather than any adjustments at the intensive margin—that is in the number of hours worked on average.[11] In this instance, further contextual detail is needed to understand the apparent employment loses during a time of fairly stable agricultural output. The primary reasons argued by Bhorat et al. (2012c) are that agriculture was employing excess labor in the pre-law period thus the higher wage encouraged farmers to shed excess unskilled labor in favor of fewer more skilled workers; the possibility that many permanent workers were converted to casual or seasonal employees; and that the minimum wage law was implemented amidst fears of land redistribution in South Africa (with land reforms in full-swing in neighboring Zimbabwe). Arguably, job-shedding served as a defensive response to White farm-owners' insecurities about possible increased state interference in their industry.[12]

Therefore, using both the standard "trade union" impact measure, namely the OLS earnings functions estimates, together with the canonical model on the impact of minimum wages, there is no convincing evidence that South Africa's trade union movement is unusually strong or powerful in its ability to realize significant returns for its members. Perhaps then, their impact is at the margin through high-impact strike action, which leads to another relevant consideration when assessing trade union power—organizational capacity. Unions which prioritize collective bargaining require higher levels of membership density and financial resources to sustain prolonged disputes. However, if organizational resources are modest, mobilization on the streets may be easier to conduct than sustained strike action, which is "certainly an important component of bargaining power, even if not its only source" (Hyman and Gumbrell-McCormick 2010: 318). Put differently, relatively weak trade unions can gain huge "multiplier effects" through public displays of strike action, hence raising their perceived bargaining power during the dispute process. Through an international comparison of South Africa's strike intensity, we aim then to assess whether the perceived power of the country's trade unions stems from their relatively greater ability to organize members into prolonged strike action.

In the year from August 2012, South Africa experienced a period of relatively more frequent strike action, particularly in the mining sector, which has garnered the perception within the media and foreign investor community that the country's strong labor movement actions have the potential to lead to wider social unrest. In some quarters, it has been argued that this strike action may be an indicator of greater challenges to South Africa's macroeconomic policy framework and broader institutions. This was reflected in two major

---

[11] These results are consistent with Conradie (2004), which focused on South African grape farmers; however, in contrast to Murray and Van Walbeek (2007), who report no large disemployment effect for sugarcane farmers as a result of the law. The latter study, however, does show a decrease in the average number of hours worked as a result of the minimum wage and that farmers moved toward more capital-intensive farming methods where possible.

[12] Furthermore, prior to the agricultural minimum wage implementation, there was a 1997 Extension of Security of Tenure Act (ESTA), which served to increase the tenure rights of agricultural workers.

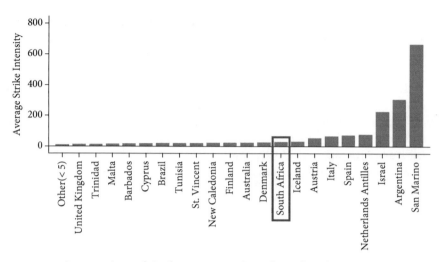

FIGURE 35.3 Average Annual Strikes Intensity (Number of Strikers per 1000 workers).
Source: LABORSTA Labour Statistics Database; International Labour Organisation (2013) and Own calculation.
Note: Average Annual Strike Intensity is the mean of annual strike intensity over the period from 1999 to 2008.
See Footnote 13 for details on deriving Annual Strikes Intensity.

international credit rating agencies, Fitch Rating Agency and Standard and Poor's Rating Services, downgrade of both South Africa's long-term foreign and local currency credit ratings between October 2012 and March 2013.[13]

A more measured view of South African workers' propensity to strike is obtained by calculating the country's strike intensity,[14] using data from the South African Department of Labour's (DoL) Annual Report on Industrial Action (2003, 2007, 2012) on the number of striking workers per year, which is then normalized to the number of formal sector employees. On average, striking workers represented 1.1% of all workers in 2003, 7% in 2007, and only 2% in 2011—all fairly low proportions. To place South Africa's strike intensity in an international context, Figure 35.3 illustrates the average annual strike intensity for a range of different countries during the 1998–2008 period. On average, only 2.8% of South African workers were involved in strike action over the period, a similar intensity to countries such as Australia, Denmark and Iceland.

---

[13] In October 2012, Standard and Poor's lowered its long-term foreign currency sovereign credit ratings on South Africa and maintained an overall negative investment outlook. The downgrading was based on a number of factors, including an expected increase in fiscal spending pressures due to the country's social challenges and upward pressure on public sector wages (Stanlib, 2013). On 10 January 2013, Fitch downgraded all three of South Africa's credit ratings (for long-term foreign currency and local currency credit, and short-term credit), and placed the country on a stable outlook. Regarding the reasons cited, along with a deteriorated growth performance, a secular decline in competitiveness reflecting wage settlements above productivity and the increase of social and political tensions were cited (National Treasury 2013). Furthermore, in light of potential further downgrades in October 2013, South Africa's Finance Minister stated to a joint committee that credit ratings depend not only on good governance but also on perceptions of the country, therefore "news flows" often contributed towards negative perceptions of the country (Mittner 2013).

[14] The proportion of formal sector workers involved in strike actions.

Put differently, South Africa is less strike intense than economies such as Italy (6.6% of workers), Spain (7.3% of workers), and Argentina (30.7% of workers). Thus, the evidence would seem to contradict the notion that South Africa is a high strike intensity economy.

Despite the above, it is possible that although relatively fewer workers are on average involved in strike action in South Africa, the strike length may be above global averages, hence generating significantly greater costs to the economy. Calculations using data from South Africa's DoL (2012) to derive the proportionate number of working days lost over the last decade show that 0.05%, 0.45%, and 0.13% of working days were lost due to strike action in the three years of 2003, 2007, and 2011[15], respectively. These proportions correspond to an underlying total number of strike days lost at 920 000 in 2003, 952 000 in 2007, and a more rapid increase to 2.8 million in 2011. The increasing trend in the number of strike days lost may be misleading however, as the number of strike days lost has grown more slowly than the number of individuals working, so lowering the overall proportion of working days lost due to strikes.[16]

Another perspective on strike action would be to consider strike depth. That is the percentage of strikers' work days lost per year, which provides insights into the duration of strike activity.[17] Comparing South Africa to relevant comparator countries including the BRICS[18] nations over the 1999–2008 period (Table 35.5), we see that South Africa—at 3.77%—ranks below both Brazil and India in terms of the average proportion of strikers' workdays lost per year due to strikes. Furthermore, other middle-income emerging economies of Nigeria and Turkey display a proportion of strike-related lost workdays that are respectively three and five times the estimate for South Africa's.

In essence, our data above would seem to suggest that strike action in South Africa is not remarkably different from similar activity in other similar emerging economies. In particular, it has been shown that South Africa's strike intensity and the cost to the economy in terms of the proportion of strikers' workdays lost due to strikes is not an international outlier and do not present themselves to be defining characteristics of South African labor market relations.

The evidence reviewed in this section suggests that the impact of trade unions in generating a segmented labor market through high wage demands are not so clear, given the lower than previously estimated wage premia. Similarly, wage legislation was shown to have little impact on labor market outcomes in many sectors, barring the agricultural sector. In that

---

[15] Percentage of working days lost is calculated as the total number of working days lost per year (the product of number of strikers and the number of striking days per year), divided by the total number of working days (product of employees and the actual working days per year). Actual working days per worker, per year, is equal to 21.67 working days per month, multiplied by 12 months, which is equal to 260.04 working days per year; less 15 days of leave and less 12 sick leave days per year; is equal to 233 actual working days per worker, per year.

[16] It is important to note that the number of working strike days lost per year is normalised to the total number of working days, which is the product of employees and the actual working days per year. Since the actual working days per year are kept constant over time, it follows then that the 2007–2011 increase in the number of strike days lost is more than overcome by a proportionately faster increase in the number of employees, therefore lowering the overall proportion of working days lost due to strikes.

[17] Percentage of strikers' working days lost is calculated as the total number of working days lost per year (the product of number of strikers and the number of striking days per year), divided by the total number of striker working days (product of number of strikers and the actual working days per year).

[18] BRICS is a grouping of the emerging markets of Brazil, the Russian Federation, India, China, and South Africa. China is excluded for lack of data.

Table 35.5 Average percent of strikers' workdays lost per year and relative average strikers' workdays lost, 1999–2008

Country	Average percentage of strikers' workdays lost per year	Relative average workdays lost to SA
Brazil	46.40	12.30
Russia	2.51	0.67
India	8.02	2.13
South Africa	3.77	1.00
Nigeria	10.94	2.90
United States	9.51	2.52
Turkey	19.77	5.24

Source: LABORSTA Labour Statistics Database, International Labour Organisation (2013) and Own Calculation.
Note: Average percentage strikers' workdays lost per year is the mean of percentage strikers' workdays lost per year from 1999–2008. Relative average workdays lost to SA is calculated as the ratio of each country's average percentage workdays lost per year over South Africa's average percentage workdays lost per year.

case, the political economy aspects of the South African agricultural sector were thought to be important in understanding of the apparent employment loses at the time. Therefore, strong political economy effects may have the potential to impact labor market outcomes in a way that estimates on direct union or regulatory intervention may not fully capture, which is the focus of the section that follows.

35.5 The Political Economy of High Unemployment

Perhaps the most important component to understanding trade unions and trade-unionism in South Africa is their role in the very fabric of the political economy of the society. This section aims to provide a political economy overview of the ruling party's tripartite alliance and how COSATU functions as part of South Africa's ruling party alliance. We interrogate the view that an implicit growth contract is struck between big business, big labor and often times, big government. Many have argued that rent seeking with this "second" alliance may exclude the unemployed and the non-unionized from the growth process. This political economy model of a middle-income country growth trap then, is closed as it were, by foreign investor sentiment, which is very sensitive to the political muscle of the trade union movement.

Employers' organizations and trade unions are not merely economic agents, they are necessarily key actors in the political arena. These organizations influence the laws that regulate labor markets and may even influence policies beyond the sphere of labor relations. Furthermore, unions which represent public sector employees—and it was shown in South Africa, union density is significantly higher in the public sector than the private sector—must inevitably address the policies of the state (Hyman and Gumbrell-McCormick 2010). The nature of trade union involvement in the political arena depends on the norms and institutional framework of the society in which they exist. Historically, labor unions have contributed to the establishment of social and labor rights, as well as to political change in many countries (World Bank 2013a), of which South Africa is no exception. In effect, the historically radical nature of South Africa's labor movement against the backdrop of apartheid has no doubt become an entrenched part of the country's trade union movement today. In some countries, perhaps like South Africa, the political involvement of unions can overshadow their activities at the workplace and because their membership is strong in the civil service and in protected sectors, unions have often opposed reforms involving fiscal consolidation, privatization, or liberalization (World Bank 2013a). As such, the dual economic and political role is both complex and often times contradictory.

In South Africa, COSATU is in a strategic political alliance with the African National Congress (ANC) and the South African Communist Party (SACP). When political organizations were unbanned, in early 1990, the ANC, SACP and COSATU agreed to work together as an alliance—formally known as the tripartite alliance. This implicit and explicit political contract has held its political position since the ANC was democratically elected into power in 1994. The ANC's 1994 election manifesto was defined by the Reconstruction and Development Programme (RDP), initially outlined by COSATU. Not only was COSATU central to the drawing up of the RDP, but the federation released 20 of its leaders to stand as candidates for Parliament on the ANC's national list in 1994, and numerous others to stand for the party for election to provincial legislatures and, in 1995, to stand in the local government elections (Southall and Webster 2010). This flow of union leaders into senior positions in government has continued steadily over the last 20 years of South African democracy.

Despite its discontentment with government policy over time, COSATU's membership has been a significant net beneficiary of ANC rule and has thus unsurprisingly remained consistently loyal to the ruling party and the tripartite alliance since 1994. Expectations of a split in the tripartite alliance were heightened in 2002 when President Thabo Mbeki criticized ultra-leftists in COSATU and the SACP, suggesting they should comply or leave the alliance (Pillay 2006). Yet by early 2004, COSATU and SACP were campaigning for an overwhelming ANC victory in national elections. Revealingly, in parts of the country where the local-level ANC lacks coherent structures and faces budgetary constraints, the ANC has been known to rely on COSATU's networks, organizational structures, and capacity, members and active involvement in electioneering, such as precisely during the 2004 election campaign (Coetzee, Daniel and Woolfrey 2012). This provides COSATU with significant leverage within the tripartite alliance.

The more recent tension between COSATU and the ANC originating from disagreements on economic and social policy eventually led to the 2007 "coup" at Polokwane, resulting in the ousting of then president, Thabo Mbeki (Bendix 2010). This push from COSATU to end Mbeki's presidential term was as a result of mounting pressure arising from ideological differences between government policy and the union movement. Government's continued attempts to create an investor-friendly economy; COSATU's giving priority to the RDP; the adoption of GEAR; and the privatization of public enterprises have all been strong points of disagreement between these two arms of the alliance (Bendix 2010).

It is clear that COSATU engages with the government in a number of areas. An important part of this engagement is their participation in the National Economic Development and Labour Council (NEDLAC) with business and a community chamber, which was established in 1995 to provide an institutional forum for policy negotiation between organized business, government and organized labor. Importantly then, the association between trade unions and economic rent-seeking is critical in understanding how the political economy effect of trade unions in South Africa can potentially influence the country's development trajectory.

Economic theorists have long agreed that the poor protection of property rights is bad for economic growth (North 1981). The theory tells us that economic rents may have either static or dynamic effects on the economy where static effects lower welfare and dynamic effects lower the growth rate. These two effects are associated with different types of rent-seeking, with private rent-seeking attacking the productive sector of the economy whereas public rent-seeking attacks innovation, since innovators need government-supplied goods such as permits and licenses (Murphy, Shleifer, and Vishny 1993). Not only are new innovators reliant on license issuance, but even established producers in sectors characterized by higher levels of government involvement are subject to the threat of revoked licenses, such as those in South Africa's mining sector in particular. The dynamic effects of rent-seeking then are particularly attributed to public rent-seeking, which takes the form of lobbying, corruption and so on.[19] In particular, these rents impact on the savings and investment channels within a country, which has the potential to severely hamper longer-term growth and development.

In South Africa there are clear signs that business acknowledges the political economy strength of the trade union movement and hence are participants in this social contract as they pursue short-term business needs. An example of this was the delay by Anglo American Platinum (Amplats) to act upon its January 2013 announcement that it would retrench nearly 14 000 workers, after a memorandum of demands by COSATU and NUM to stop the retrenchment action immediately were handed over to the mining company (South African Labour News 2013). By September 2013, Amplats revised its proposed retrenchment plans so that it would only affect 3300 workers but after an 11-day strike by AMCU members, these members were granted voluntary separation packages and so no employees were effectively retrenched (Greve 2013). The September strike action cost Amplats 44 000 platinum ounces and their medium-term outlook report has downwardly revised its targeted production capacity due to both lower platinum demand growth and a number of "structural challenges" that has eroded profitability in recent years (Anglo American 2013). Of course, mining is perhaps the sector associated with one of highest costs of non-compliance with government and labor since government has the ability to revoke mining licenses.

Therefore, in sectors where the cost of not complying with big government and big labor is high, big business' growth and development trajectory is invariably shaped by the implicit contract between these three actors. The perceived balance of power amongst these agents is a key determinant of foreign investor sentiment toward South Africa and is most exposed in the downgrading of the country's credit ratings and investment outlook by major

[19] In contrast, private rent-seeking takes the form of theft, piracy, litigation and other forms of transfer between private parties where rent-seekers attack existing stocks of wealth (Murphy et al. 1993).

international ratings agencies at times of peaked social tensions, more recently related to labor market disputes.

35.6 Conclusion

This chapter has attempted to locate and understand the role played by trade unions in particular and the labor regulatory environment in general in South Africa, in shaping labor market outcomes. In particular, we have attempted to ascribe the relevance of these factors to understanding the economy's high unemployment rates and severe labor market disequilibria. We find that despite a long history in South Africa, trade union membership levels, their impact on average wage levels, and indeed their pursuit of strike action has resulted in a relatively benign economic impact either within-country or when compared with other economies around the world. In the case of labor regulation, whilst there is strong evidence of a negative employment effect from the minimum wage, in the case of other sectoral minimum wage laws, there are no sufficiently compelling reasons here which explain the economy's labor market disequilibria.

Ultimately then, we seek analytical refuge in the political economy make-up of the South African economy. We argue that standard economic and econometric evidence of the power of trade unions and labor legislation, measuring their impact on labor market outcomes in South Africa, merely exposes the limitation of these tools. These powerful, yet limiting tools then, cannot uncover or appreciate the centrality of the social contract within the tripartite alliance and its dominance in shaping the country's economic development trajectory. The political economy of wage formation and economic activity in South Africa, we argue, are central to appreciating the economy's current domestic labor market disequilibria. Unlocking the kind of inclusive growth necessary to overcome the country's large structural unemployment challenge means, therefore, that a space at the negotiation table must be found for the informal sector and the unemployed—key groups which continue to be underrepresented in the current growth and development discourse of South Africa.

References

Anglo American (2013). Quarterly Review and Production Report for the Period 01 July 2013 to 30 September 2013. Available: http://www.angloplatinum.com/pdf/2013/3Q13_production_review_report.pdf.

Armstrong, P., and Steenkamp, J. (2008). South African trade unions: an overview for 1995 to 2005. Stellenbosch Economic Working Papers: 10/08. Stellenbosch: Stellenbosch University.

Bendix, S. (2010). *Industrial Relations in South Africa*, 5th edn. Claremont: Juta and Co. Ltd.

Benjamin, P., Bhorat, H., and Cheadle, H. (2010). The cost of "doing business" and labour regulation: the case of South Africa. *International Labour Review*, 149(1):73–91.

Benjamin, P., and Gruen, C. (2006). The regulatory efficiency of the CCMA: A statistical analysis of the CCMA's CMA database. DPRU Working Paper 06/110. Cape Town: Development Policy Research Unit, University of Cape Town.

Bhorat, H. (2008). Unemployment in South Africa: Descriptors and Determinants. Development Policy Research Unit, University of Cape Town, South Africa.

Bhorat, H., Goga, S., and Van der Westhuizen, C. (2012a). Institutional wage effects: revisiting union and bargaining council wage premia in South Africa. *South African Journal of Economics*, 80(3):400–414.

Bhorat, H., Jacobs, E., and Van der Westhuizen, C. (2013a). Do industrial disputes reduce employment? Evidence from South Africa. Africa Growth Initiative Working Paper No. 6. Washington, DC: Brookings Institution Press.

Bhorat, H., Kanbur, R., and Mayet, N. (2012b). The impact of sectoral minimum wage laws on employment, wages and hours of work in South Africa. DPRU Working Paper 12/155. Cape Town: Development Policy Research Unit, University of Cape Town.

Bhorat, H., Kanbur, R., and Stanwix, B. (2012c). Estimating the impact of minimum wages on employment, wages and non-wage benefits: The case of agriculture in South Africa. DPRU Working Paper 12/149. Cape Town: Development Policy Research Unit, University of Cape Town.

Bhorat, H., Pauw, K., and Mncube, L. (2009a). Understanding the efficiency and effectiveness of the dispute resolution system in South Africa: An analysis of CCMA data. DPRU Working Paper 09/137. Cape Town: Development Policy Research Unit, University of Cape Town.

Bhorat, H., Van der Westhuizen, C., and Goga, S. (2009b). Analysing wage formation in the South African labour markets: The role of bargaining councils. DPRU Working Paper 09/135. Cape Town: Development Policy Research Unit, University of Cape Town.

Bhorat, H., and Van der Westhuizen, C. (2013b). Non-monetary dimensions of well-being in South Africa, 1993–2004: A post-apartheid dividend? *Development Southern Africa*, 30(3):295–314.

Botero, J.C., Djankov, S., La Porta, R., Lopez-De-Silanes, F., and Shleifer, A. (2004). The regulation of labor. *Quarterly Journal of Economics*, 119(4):1339–1382.

Butcher, K.F., and Rouse, C.E. (2001). Wage effects of unions and industrial councils in South Africa. Policy Research Working Paper No. 2520. Washington, DC: World Bank.

Card, D., and Kreuger, A.B. (1994). Minimum wages and employment: a case study of the fast-food industry in New Jersey and Pennsylvania. *American Economic Review*, 84(4):772–793.

Centre for Development and Enterprise (CDE) (2013). Rethinking South Africa's Labour Market: Lessons from Brazil, India and Malaysia. CDE Round Table No. 22. Available: http://www.cde.org.za/83-jobs-and-growth/409-rethinking-south-africa-s-labour-market-lessons-from-brazil-india-and-malaysia.

Cheadle, H. (2006). Regulated Flexibility and Small Business: Revisiting the LRA and the BCEA. DPRU Working Paper 06/109. Cape Town: Development Policy Research Unit, University of Cape Town.

Coetzee, K., Daniel, R., and Woolfrey, S. (2012). An overview of the political economy of South Africa. Workshop proceedings, Grenoble Ecole de Management. Grenoble, March 5–6.

Conradie, B. (2004). Wages and Wage Elasticisties for Wine and Table Grapes in South Africa. Centre for Social Science Research, Working Paper 90, University of Cape Town.

COSATU (2013). Brief History of COSATU. Available: http://www.cosatu.org.za/show.php?ID=925.

Department of Labour (2012). *Annual Industrial Action Report 2012*. Pretoria: Department of Labour.

Finnemore, M. (2009). *Introduction to Labour Relations in South Africa*, 10th edn. Durban: LexisNexis Butterworths.

Freeman, R.B. (2009). Labour Regulations, Unions, and Social Protection in Developing Countries: Market Distortions of Efficient Institutions? *Handbook of Development Economics*. Cambridge, MA: Harvard and NBER.

Godfrey, S., Maree, J., Du Toit, D., and Theron, J. (2010). *Collective Bargaining in South Africa: Past, Present and Future?* 1st edn. Claremont: Juta & Co, Ltd.

Greve, N. (2013). Amplats Modifies Retrenchment Plans, Strike Costs 44,000 oz of Output. Mining Weekly. Available: http://www.miningweekly.com/article/amplats-modifies-retrenchment-plans-strike-cost-44-000-oz-of-output-2013-10-11.

Hyman, R., and Gumbrell-McCormick, R. (2010). Trade unions, politics and parties: is a new configuration possible? Transfer. *European Review of Labour and Research*, 16(3):315–331.

International Labour Organization (2013). LABORSTA Labour Statistics. Available: http://laborsta.ilo.org/.

Lawrence, S., and Ishikawa, J. (2005). Trade union membership and collective bargaining coverage: Statistical concepts, methods and findings. INTEGRATION Paper No. 59. Geneva: International Labour Organization.

Maree, J. (1987). *The Independent Trade Unions, 1974–1984: Ten Years of the South African Labour Bulletin*. Ravan Press: Johannesburg.

Millea, M.J., Rezek, J.P., and Pitts, J. (2013). Minimum wages in a segmented labour market: evidence from South Africa. Conference proceedings, Economic Society of South Africa, Bloemfontein, 25–27 September.

Mittner, M. (2013). Gordhan warns of consequences of negative news on credit ratings. Business Day Live. Available: http://www.bdlive.co.za/economy/2013/10/27/gordhan-warns-of-consequences-of-negative-news-on-credit-ratings.

Murphy, K.M., Shleifer, A., and Vishny, R.W. (1993). Why is rent-seeking so costing to growth? *American Economic Review*, 83(2):409–414.

Murray, J.J., and Van Walbeek, C.P. (2007). Impact of the sectoral determination for farm workers in the South African sugar industry: Case study of the KwaZulu-Natal North and South Coasts. *Agrekon*, 46(1):116–134.

National Economic Development and Labour Council (NEDLAC) (2013). NEDLAC: Introduction. Available: http://www.nedlac.org.za/about-us/introduction.aspx.

National Treasury (2013). National Treasury Statement on Fitch Ratings Downgrade. Available: http://www.treasury.gov.za/comm_media/press/2013/2013011101.pdf.

Nattrass, N., and Seekings, J. (1997). Citizenship and welfare in South Africa: deracialisation and inequality in a labour-surplus economy. *Canadian Journal of African Studies*, 31(3):452–481.

North, D. (1981). *Structure and change in Economic History*. New York: Norton.

Pillay, D. (2006). COSATU, alliances and working-class politics, in Buhlungu, S. (ed.), *Trade unions and democracy: COSATU workers' political attitudes in South Africa*. Cape Town: Human Sciences Research Council Press, pp. 167–198.

Republic of South Africa (1995). Labour Relations Act No. 66 of 1995. Available: http://www.labour.gov.za/DOL/legislation/acts/labour-relations/labour-relations-act-1/.

Republic of South Africa (1997). Basic Conditions of Employment Act 75 of 1997. Available: http://www.labour.gov.za/DOL/downloads/legislation/acts/basic-conditions-of-employment/Act%20%20Basic%20Conditions%20of%20Employment.pdf.

Republic of South Africa (2002a). Labour Relations Amended Act 12 of 2002. Available: http://www.labour.gov.za/DOL/downloads/legislation/acts/labour-relations/amendments/Amendment%20%20Labour%20Relations%20Act%202002.Pdf.

Republic of South Africa (2002b). Basic Conditions of Employment Amended Act 11 of 2002. Available:http://www.labour.gov.za/DOL/legislation/acts/basic-conditions-of-employment/read-online/amended-basic-conditions-of-employment-act.

Rospabé, S. (2001). Making racial wage relations fair in South Africa: a focus on the role of trade unions. DPRU Working Paper 01/48. Cape Town: Development Policy Research Unit, University of Cape Town.

Southall, R., and Webster, E. (2010). Unions and parties in South Africa: COSATU and the ANC in the wake of Polokwane, in Beckman, B., Buhlungu, S., and Sachikonye, L. (eds), *Trade unions and Party Politics: Labour Movements in Africa*. Cape Town: Human Sciences Research Council Press, pp. 131–166.

South African Labour News (2013). Unions Get Tough with Amplats and Impala Platinum. Available: http://www.salabournews.co.za/index.php/component/content/article/70-labour-news/9097- unions-get-tough-with-anglo-platinum-and-impala.html.

Stanlib. (2013). S&P affirmed South Africa's credit rating as BBB, with a negative outlook. Available: http://www.stanlib.com/EconomicFocus/Pages/SPaffirmedSouthAfrica'screditratingMar2013.aspx.

The South African Labour Guide (2013a). Registered trade unions in South Africa for October 2013. Available: www.labourguide.co.za/general/trade-unions-78.

Van der Berg, S., and Bhorat, H. (1999). The present as a legacy of the past: the labour market, inequality and poverty in South Africa. DPRU Working Paper 01/29. Cape Town: Development Policy Research Unit, University of Cape Town.

Woolard, I. (2001). Income Inequality and Poverty: Methods of Estimation and Some Policy Applications for South Africa. Unpublished Doctorate Dissertation. Cape Town: University of Cape Town.

World Bank (2006). *Doing Business in 2006: Creating Jobs*. Washington, DC: World Bank.

World Bank (2013a). *World Development Report 2013: Jobs*. Washington, DC: World Bank.

World Bank (2013b). Employing Workers database. Available: http://www.doingbusiness.org/data/exploretopics/employing-workers.

World Economic Forum (2013). *The Global Competitiveness Report 2013–2014*. Geneva: World Economic Forum.

CHAPTER 36

AFRICAN
DEVELOPMENT BANKS
Lessons for Development Economics

ERNEST ARYEETEY

36.1 INTRODUCTION

SUB-SAHARAN Africa's financial sector remains the least developed, even by developing country standards, in spite of the implementation of various financial sector reforms over the last two decades (Allen et al. 2012). A substantial body of literature has documented the important role a well-developed and robust financial sector plays in promoting growth and development (e.g. World Bank 2001). Among the important functions such institutions provide are the mobilization of savings, the allocation of capital and risk reduction through aggregation and risk transfer to the relatively less risk averse. The big question remains how this can be achieved in sub-Saharan Africa.

In terms of development finance, probably one of the most critical challenges is the mobilization of medium- to long-term capital for financing the existing large development needs of sub-Saharan Africa and bridging the gap between it and the rest of the world. Investing in areas such as infrastructure, both "soft" and "hard," is an important requirement for accelerating poverty reducing growth. While the majority of the poor in sub-Saharan Africa are engaged in agriculture, they rely on poor technologies and infrastructure. As a result of poor road networks, about half of all output is lost even before it reaches the market. Providing affordable housing is an important challenge in most sub-Saharan Africa countries with only 1–2% of GDP accounting for available housing finance compared with up to 21% in other developing countries. This is what has made Development Banks (DBs) relevant in the discussion of long-term finance in Africa.

DBs have had a longish history in post-colonial Africa, even if that history has not always been positive, as will be seen in section 3. The justification for their existence has often been obvious to proponents while others have generally failed to see that in many instances. Recent calls for new DBs (cf. Luna-Martinez and Vicente 2012) in developing economies need to be seen as continuing an inconclusive debate that has been around for several decades, but needs to be concluded in order to generate meaningful ways of financing the future growth and transformation of African economies.

The transformation of African economies into high productivity economies is generally understood as an essential step in the campaign to lift over 400 million people out of poverty. This requires major new capital investments in most of the economies, but there have always been considerable challenges facing financial institutions as they attempt to provide the needed finance. Incomplete and missing markets in the region increase significantly the risk associated with financing investments beyond levels that financial institutions, such as banks, generally can carry. It is the search for alternative sources of long-term finance that has often made DBs attractive.

At the beginning of development banking, the banks were defined as: "An institution to promote and finance enterprise in the private sector" (Diamond 1957). Kane (1975) described them as "A financial intermediary supplying long-term funds to bankable economic development projects and providing related services." Boskey (1959) referred to them as "Institutions, public or private, which have as one of their principal functions the making of medium or long term industrial projects." Other definitions have tended to focus more on the nature of their products. Thus, DBs have sometimes been seen to be financial institutions with a primary mandate of making available long-term borrowing facilities for projects that are public utility increasing. The positive externalities generated by such projects and their non-rivalry and non-excludability nature make for under-financing, if at all, by the private sector. Many DBs have core mandates towards sectors such as agriculture and infrastructure and may work through other financial institutions. The developmental goal is the main rationale for DBs, as the name suggests.

In this chapter, DBs refer mainly to national and regional financial institutions that are so established for the purpose of providing medium- to long-term capital for investment in sectors of an economy that private commercial capital is unwilling/unable to reach. The fact that governments have been forced to step in to make DBs functional is noteworthy. As a consequence, DBs are generally associated with state interventions and state ownership, even if this needs not be the case at all times. The term Development Bank is sometimes used almost synonymously with Development Finance Institution (DFI) here.

The involvement of the state in development banking has often been central to how such institutions have been seen by economists. There has been some aversion to governments' active participation and ownership of financial institutions (or firms in general), just as there has been advocacy for such participation (Hawtrey 1926; Lewis 1950). As noted by Shleifer (1998: 134) "even many of the laissez-faire economists focused overwhelmingly on the goal of achieving competitive prices, even at the cost of accepting government ownership in non-competitive industries." The role of the state will be a main theme in our proposal for making DBs more effective.

This chapter examines the case for and the historical roles of DBs in providing the leverage required for financing Africa's economic development. The chapter first presents the generic case made for DBs and then documents the story of DBs in Africa, covering the extant empirical research literature. It presents policies and practices across the region since the post-independence era. There appears to be a growing view, as other existing pieces of literature have documented, that DBs can play a more positive role in stimulating economic development, even in developed economies. Although Luna-Martínez and Vicente (2012) have shed some light on DBs, they also concede that there still exist gaps in our understanding of these institutions, particularly due to their heterogeneity.

The chapter also examines conditions under which, and why the economic rationale for DBs appears not to have followed as successful a trajectory as one might have expected in the presence of such bottlenecks as political patronage and rent-seeking. The chapter looks at some current questions and debates on the issue of African DBs and alternative sources of development financing. Finally, Africa-specific lessons on DBs for economics as a discipline are provided.

A discussion of development banking is relevant for the *Handbook of Africa and Economics* for a number of reasons. First, in many African countries, the initial necessary conditions for profitable investments are less attractive compared with many other developing countries. There are obvious significant structural and policy issues to explain the situation. The question of which explanations are more credible remains a relevant question for development economics. Related to this is the role of DBs in providing the required initial conditions for Africa's economic development. It is important to document existing knowledge in the African context which could help answer the question of why there appears to be some divergence between the theoretical economic position and observed practices in many African countries in respect of the rationale for DBs. Second, in documenting existing stock of knowledge on DBs in Africa it is possible to highlight areas that economics alone as a discipline fails to provide insight into why DBs may not achieve their objectives in specific African country contexts.

36.2 THE CASE FOR DEVELOPMENT BANKING

What has been the case put forward in support of DBs? La Porta et al. (2002) provide a summary of the two main arguments for the state's active participation in financial markets which support the creation of DBs. First, citing the case of Russia in Gerschenkron (1962), where the scarcity of capital resulting from corruption and bankruptcy made it almost impossible for the private banking system to finance industrialization of the time, it has been argued that under such circumstances, only state participation in financial markets can help raise the requisite capital for development. This is a part of the "development" argument in support of DBs. The advocacy for government ownership, or at least active participation, in so called strategic sectors of the economy, including banks, led to the "take-over" (and in some cases the creation) in the 1960s and 1970s of private firms, including banks and other financial institutions. This "development" view for the creation of DBs can be seen as one of meeting a social and economic welfare objective.

Embedded in the development view is the infant industry argument for state ownership or direct participation in the banking sector. This was the basis for the establishment of national banks. Another "development view" argument for DBs is to help finance national development plans and accelerate economic growth. This argument is based on the supposition that the state is in a better position to identify and finance investments that are of a wider social benefit. An argument that has come up more strongly in recent times is that state involvement is necessary for averting and/or responding to financial crisis. In this case

DBs play "a counter cyclical role" by bailing out private banks during crisis periods, as the recent financial meltdown has demonstrated.

Second, governments participate in financial markets for "political" reasons. That is, control over otherwise private firms, including banks, gives government control over resources which it can then distribute to political followers in the form of jobs and subsidies, for example, in exchange for votes (Kornai, 1979; Shleifer and Vishny 1994). This motive for instituting DBs has been most pronounced in countries with poor financial systems and the lack of strong institutions that protect private property rights (La Porta et al. 2002).

State participation in financial markets need not take the form of outright ownership. It could be in the form of providing incentives to private commercial banks to provide lending facilities to "strategic" sectors of the economy, for example. However, outright ownership by the state appears to be the most common, accounting for about 74% of DBs surveyed in 2011 by the World Bank and the World Federation of Development Financial Institutions (WFDFI) in low- and middle-income countries (Luna-Martínez and Vicente 2012). In Africa, only four out of the 14 DBs or DFIs covered in the survey were not wholly state owned (Table 36.1). This might be seen as consistent with the finding that state ownership of banks is larger in low-income countries with underdeveloped financial markets and poor enforcement of private property rights. Outright state ownership, "allows the government extensive control over the choice of projects being financed while leaving the implementation of these projects to the private sector" (La Porta et al. 2002: 266). This could help achieve both

Table 36.1 Development financial institutions in Africa and extent of state ownership

Name of Institution	Country	Year established	% State owned
Uganda Development Bank Limited	Uganda	1972	100
Banco De Poupança E Crédito S.A.R.L	Angola	1991	100
Nigerian Export-Import Bank (NEXIM)	Nigeria	1991	100
Industrial Development and Workers Bank of Egypt	Egypt	1976	87.7
Banque de l'Habitat de Côte d'Ivoire (BHCI)	Côte d'Ivoire	1994	69.8
The Agricultural Bank of Sudan	Sudan	1959	100
Rwanda Development Bank BRD)	Rwanda	1967	38.8
FPI—Industrial Promotion Fund	DRC	1989	100
Tanzania Investment Bank Limited	Tanzania	1970	100
Development Bank of Southern Africa	South Africa	1983	100
Industrial and Commercial Development Corporation (ICDC)	Kenya	1954	100
Kenya Tourist Development Corporation (KTDC)	Kenya	1965	100
IDB Capital Ltd	Kenya	1973	100
National Investment Bank Limited	Ghana	1963	23.5

Source: World Bank and WFDFI survey on Development Banks, 2011.

the "development" and "political" objective. Do these views provide enough justification for having DBs? This question is addressed later in this chapter.

Contrary to what one might expect as a result of the massive privatization drives over the past two to three decades, a large proportion of DBs established since the 1970s were still operating during a recent survey of DBs in 2011. Indeed, while privatization of state owned enterprises thrived, several new DBs were being established in African and other developing countries. State ownership of banks is still pervasive across the globe (La Porta et al. 2002). Indeed, in emerging market economies, DBs constitute a major source of long-term capital for sectors such as agriculture, housing, and infrastructure (Luna-Martínez and Vicente 2012).

36.3 A History of Development Banking in Sub-Saharan Africa

Soon after African countries began the move towards becoming independent, beginning in the mid-1950s, there was a new attention to how long-term finance could be made available to new African entrepreneurs. Governments were concerned that the focus of their banking systems had been largely the mining businesses and commercial entities involved with import–export trade, without providing for the needs of a new middle class that wanted to produce goods and services for both domestic consumption and for export.

In Ghana the National Investment Bank was established in 1963 to support the industrial sector while the Agricultural Development Bank (ADB) was set up in 1965 through an Act of Parliament. The ADB began as the Agricultural Credit and Co-operative Bank and was directed to support the agricultural sector, initially using public resources. In 1970 Parliament granted the bank full commercial banking powers and it began to take deposits from the public. Other similar development or specialized banks set up in Ghana include the Bank for Housing and Construction and the Co-operative Bank.

The first industrial development bank in Nigeria began operation in 1964 under the first National Development Plan. It was created for the purpose of providing medium- and long-term finance to Nigerian enterprises. Similar banks were set up by the state in most African countries throughout the 1960s and 70s with the objective of providing credit for agricultural or industrial development under conditions that that would not satisfy the requirements of largely foreign-owned commercial banks. They were established when the supply-leading approach to financing was dominant (Nissanke 1994). The main motivation of governments was to ensure that medium-long term credit flowed to priority sectors of the economies and that there was increased concessionary lending to rural areas. Established by the state, they were funded either wholly by the state or with external finance guaranteed by the state and engineered by the central bank. Essentially they were borrowing from either the state or from outside in order to lend.

By the middle of the 1980s, the financial systems of most African countries were assessed to be in extremely poor shape (Aryeetey and Nissanke 1998). Most affected were the fairly large state-owned banks, most of which were DBs. Operating in a very risky environment, their situation had been made more acute by a very poor regulatory regime that allowed governments and their functionaries to use banks for financing politically motivated initiatives (World Bank 2001). There were two characteristic features of these institutions, namely they suffered from an "excess liquidity syndrome" and a high prevalence of non-performing loans (Aryeetey and Nissanke 1998). By the first feature, banks held cash and other liquid assets far in excess of what they were required to hold by central banks, thus generating no returns on these. The World Bank (2001) estimated that 20% of total loans in developing countries were non-performing. Aryeetey and Nissanke (1998) estimated that loan repayment rates throughout sub-Saharan Africa were as low as 20–40%.

Nissanke (1994) wrote that "Most DFIs or special schemes have not been involved in mobilization of local savings to any significant extent and loan recovery was not given any high priority, with the inevitable consequence on their funds. Their portfolio position is further weakened by taking on large financial risks by specializing in long-term lending to high-risk areas such as agricultural and industrial finance. Their excessive exposure in high risk sectors is compounded by generally poor risk analysis, excessive political pressures on lending decisions and limited opportunities for assets divestiture" (113). She observed further that frequent recapitalization of banks in difficulty had not helped much.

In the 1990s era of financial sector liberalization, many governments came under pressure to close down or restructure many of these institutions. An example was the liquidation of Co-operative Bank and also Bank for Housing and Construction in Ghana in 1994. But, despite the fact that these specialized banks were clearly out of favor in the 1980s there remain a number of such institutions running in many countries (Table 36.1). Aryeetey (2009) argues that they continue to operate because governments find that there are no new institutions to provide the type of finance that they were intended to provide. No new post-reform institutions provide term finance for industrial development, agriculture and for housing at reasonable interest rates. Governments cannot easily support them financially as they pursue market-based reforms. Confronted with the need to find new finance many of them have moved into universal banking. Thus, there are very few institutions that still describe themselves as DBs, even if the demand for their services remains hugely significant. Governments clearly need to determine the future path to development finance.

36.4 Africa and Long-term Finance

It is estimated that about US$93 billion is required annually for financing infrastructure (power, water and sanitation, transport, ICT) in Africa (ICA 2012) over the next decade or more. Less than half of this amount is being raised annually through foreign and domestic resource mobilization, leaving an infrastructure-financing gap of about US$48 billion per year. This is only in respect of hard infrastructure. The important question that remains is where to raise the shortfall.

According to available data from the Infrastructure Consortium for Africa (ICA), less than 15% of infrastructure financing comes from private financial institutions (only 11.5% in 2011).[1] The rest are from traditional donors, China, and domestic resources. China's

---

[1] Most of the infrastructure investment by the private sector is in the ICT sector (CEPA 2012).

contribution has been growing; about 15% of infrastructure financing in African for the year 2011 came from China.

Given the enormity of the development finance gap (not just infrastructure finance), there is clearly the need to mobilize all available sources: private, public, bilateral, and multilateral. Development assistance to sub-Saharan Africa has followed a generally increasing trend although there have been contractions during periods of severe financial crisis in donor countries (Figure 36.1). Neither private nor public financing alone is adequate for meeting the development finance gap in Africa. But many of the investments needed in key areas may not, given initial conditions, be attractive to the private sector. With globalization the provision of financial services go beyond the boundaries of any country. The liberalization of capital accounts to, among others, attract private capital inflows has been found to lead to increased volatility (United Nations Conference on Trade and Development 2000) although such liberalization has been seen to be generally positive (Henry 2006).

The need for leverage and coordination of all existing sources of finance is crucial for raising the needed capital for development finance in Africa, and this does not exclude the role of DBs. Indeed, regional DBs such as the African Development Bank (AfDB) have financed infrastructure development to the tune of over US$5.4 billion through collaboration with both the public and private sector over the past half-decade. Of cause, such amounts are not large relative to the existing financing gap but it does contribute significantly to reducing it. Historically, the state has financed the economic fundamentals that create greater incentive for private sector investments that spur growth. Even under current globalized conditions,

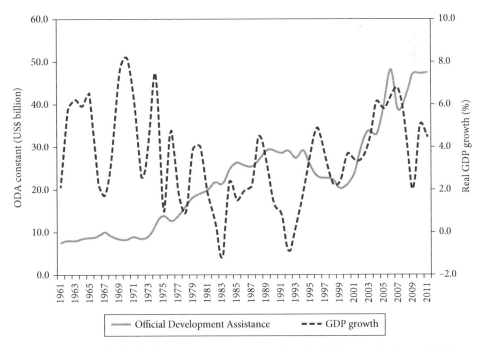

FIGURE 36.1 Official development assistance and real GDP growth in sub-Saharan Africa.

Source: World Development Indicators, World Bank.

the burden of proof should lie with those who suppose that the fundamental investments required for raising private sector investments incentives can be achieved without the need for DBs.

36.4.1 Capital markets and capital mobilization

In the aftermath of the collapse of development banking in the 1990s a lot of effort went into developing capital markets to become the main source of term finance. In Aryeetey and Senbet (2004) they provide a discussion of the early performance of new African capital markets. They describe the markets as thin and illiquid after a decade of their introduction. Only the stock markets in Nigeria and South Africa had more than 100 firms listed. More recent assessments of capital market performance in the region indicate clearly that the situation is changing, but slowly (Allen, Otchere, and Senbet 2011). Market capitalization has improved considerably in a number of West African stock markets, but the improvements have not reflected a significant transformation of the financial markets.

In recent times a number of innovative capital market strategies have been used to finance specific development projects across Africa. These include long-term sovereign infrastructure bonds which can be issued on both international and domestic markets. Kenya issued a 12-year bond in 2009 raising US$232.6 million (PWC 2010). But African sovereign bonds have often been considered risky by investors in part because of speculative credit ratings on the bonds. This situation has improved over the past few years as indicated by the over subscription of bonds issued by countries such as Ghana and Zambia in 2012.

The diaspora bond has been cited as another capital market instrument that holds great potential for raising substantial funds for development in Africa. Ethiopia was one of the first countries in Africa to issue such a bond. The first one was issued in 2011 but faced several drawbacks due to the perception risks resulting from macroeconomic instability and questions on country governance. Despite the potential these innovative capital market instruments may hold, to date, the extent to which African governments have been able to use them to raise the requisite capital for investments in the relevant sectors remains to be seen.

36.4.2 Universal banking

Universal banking without significant preferential treatment for strategic sectors of an economy makes sectors such as agriculture unable to compete in such credit markets because of incomplete insurance markets, among other factor. Long-term financing for development hinges on core principles including the availability of capital with long maturities that meet the investment needs of the real sector. Such instruments should cover a broad spectrum of financial instruments tailored to meet the needs of different groups (Group of Thirty 2013).

Over the past decade, there has been an increase in the number of banks providing universal banking services but most of such banks (most of which are private) have been concentrated in areas with high population density and have not reached some of the most critical sectors of African economies responsible for most of the pro-poor growth required (see, for example, Allen et al. 2012). Increasing availability and access to long-term funds calls for, aside from the above innovative ideas, expanding the capacity of the banking sector as a whole. This need not be restricted to private or domestic financial institutions but also international and SFIs.

36.5 Explaining the Performance of Development Banks

As seen earlier, assessments of the performance of DBs have generally been poor, and this may have been on account of the conventional assessment tools used, including returns on equity or assets and the extent of non-performing loans (Caprio et al. 2004). But such measures of success may not be entirely justified. This may be particularly so if benefits to an economy as a whole of the activities of DBs exceed private gains. Some analysts have only counted the costs associated with direct lending, subsidies to "special sectors" of an economy, and fiscal constraints that may arise from the activities of DBs without comparing these costs to the benefits that may arise or the cost of doing nothing under circumstances where private financial institutions would not offer any respite although critical.

La Porta et al. (2002) used data on government ownership of banks in 92 countries (including ten from Africa) to answer questions which include those bordering on the performance of SFIs, particularly, as per the main arguments advanced for having them. The important finding from their analysis was that state ownership of banks in the 1970s was associated with slower per capita income and productivity growth. In effect, state ownership of banks led to politicization of resource allocation, which then had negative implications for resource use efficiency. Given the relatively small number of African countries in their sample, it is not clear the extent to which this finding is relevant to Africa.

To a large extent, the findings in La Porta et al. (2002) have been used by the World Bank to push for the privatization of SFIs as demonstrated in World Bank (2001). The suggestion is that "whatever its original objectives, state ownership tends to stunt financial sector development, thereby contributing to slower growth" (World Bank 2001: 123). But this statement, it appears, is contradicted by the concession that "stable and efficient provision of financial services—regardless of who owns the financial firms providing them—is a realistic goal for all countries" (World Bank 2001). Acemoglu et al. (2008) have shown analytically that market based allocation of resources is not necessarily superior to government allocations, and that although political economy distortions do dissipate the potential gains of risk sharing and consumption smoothing by government as opposed to markets, there are circumstances under which such distortions may be countenanced in order to achieve generally more positive outcomes. Stricter controls on politicians, for example, could make governments more attractive relative to markets. Besides, Andrianova et al. (2008) has demonstrated that institutional factors are more important than political factors in determining the role of government in banks and financial institutions. At low levels of institutional development, their findings are averse to the privatization of state-owned banks because private banks are hesitant in entering the market due to depositor mistrust. The strengthening of institutions must go hand in hand with encouraging privatization of previously state-owned banks.

Indeed, more recently, Andrianova et al. (2012) have provided contrary evidence to the findings of La Porta et al. (2002). Using cross-country data (including 21 African countries) covering the period 1995–2007, they show that state ownership of banks precipitated higher average rates of growth. They show that "conditioning on other determinants of growth, countries with government-owned banks have, on average, grown faster than countries with no or little government ownership of banks" (463). In fact, evidence elsewhere suggests that the efficiency argument against DBs does not always hold; they are not inherently less efficient than privately owned banks (Altunbas et al. 2001; Rousseau and Xiao 2007). Most of the evidence of inefficiency of DBs in the case of Africa is anecdotal.

Andrianova et al. (2012) argued that the results provided by La Porta et al. (2002) and other researchers indicating a negative relationship between state bank ownership and economic growth is not robust. This may be justified because of the difficulty in detangling the effect of the "development view" from the "political view" since, as noted by Yeyati et al. (2004), "both financial development and institutional quality are closely related to economic growth" and this makes identification of the effects in an econometric model difficult because of the endogeneity effect. A statement of causality in such a case is a thorny one. Clearly, to identify a "true" effect one must address the issue of identification and causality, which Andrianova et al. (2012) do a better job at.

36.6 CORPORATE GOVERNANCE AND POLITICAL INTERFERENCE

It has been noted that politicians can use government-owned banks as a means of distributing rents to political supporters. Indeed the findings of Micco et al. (2007) that the difference in performance between state-owned and private banks in developing countries increase during election years lends support to the view that state banks are utilized for political reasons, and is consistent with the political view for establishing SFIs. The lending behavior of state-owned banks has been found to be influenced by election outcomes of affiliated parties. Indeed, areas with strong political party presence of the government in power have been found to be associated with lower bank interest rates (Sapienza 2004). Dinç (2005) arrived at similar conclusions but the data used in these analyses are heavily skewed towards immerging market economies and although there is no reason to believe that the political view argument may not be even more important in sub-Saharan Africa there is no empirical research evidence that this holds. But, as the authors emphasize, there is no evidence to suggest that the political and developmental view are mutually exclusive and that these SFIs might well perform roles that hitherto may be allusive under wholesale privatization. Indeed, the developmental benefit, at some point in the process of development, might outweigh the political cost.

The empirical research literature on such political views for establishing SFIs or DBs in particular is very thin. This is more so in the case of Africa. But one would expect the political view to be more entrenched in Africa than many other developing countries given that it brothers largely on corruption which has been found to be prevalent in Africa (de Sardan 1999; Gyimah-Brempong 2002). The argument against SFIs in general and DBs in particular bother largely on issues of bad corporate governance, of which political interference is a major one (Scott 2007; Luna-Martínez and Vicente 2012; Calice 2013).

The main issues related to corporate governance and political interference include: politicians' direct intervention in routine decisions of SFIs, including selection of beneficiaries of bank facilities and loan indebtedness forgiveness; executive heads of such institutions (having normally been appointed by the government in power) acting autonomously so long as they pursue the political ambitions of their political parties; lack of competence and independence of board members to undertake their duties in a professional manner; incomplete and inaccurate reporting on the business of SFIs (both internal and external, financial and non-financial) which provides inadequate grounds for decision-making, and thereby misleading even political heads, the government as a whole, and the entire public. Scott (2007) notes that ensuring that SFIs have the right corporate governance structures to avoid the consequences of the lack thereof are both difficult and expensive.

Where institutions are strong there is a much weaker relationship between bank ownership and performance even when assessed using only profitability criteria (Micco et al. 2007). But wholesale liberalization does not solve institutional challenges in the financial sector. Financial liberalization, widely considered critical in delivering a more efficient and competitive banking system, has frequently been followed by financial instability, especially where rule-of-law and regulation were weak (Arestis and Demetriades 1999; Kaminsky and Reinhart 1999). Some have maintained that at very low levels of institutional quality, the creation of SFIs and DBs is still important for jump starting financial and economic development in many countries in Africa (Andrianova et al. 2008). As institutions improve SFIs are likely to disappear because they may not be needed as market failures, including insurance market failures, are reduced to the minimum.

Andrianova et al. (2008) notes that the inefficiency of SFIs, as suggested by the political view, means that once institutional quality improves, market failures minimized and subsidies to inefficient SFIs withdrawn, they would be unable to compete with their private counterparts and thereby lead to their collapse. Thus, quality institutions will discourage exploitative and rent-seeking activities. If institutions are not well developed as is the case in most of Africa, then "privatizing state banks would be detrimental" (Andrianova et al. 2008: 248). Instead, there is the need for a concerted effort at building quality institutions rather than privatizing DBs.

Drawing from the recent DBs survey data, Table 36.2 compares some of the broad indicators of corporate governance for the African countries included in the data with the averages

Table 36.2 Comparing the transparency of African development banks with others

Information disclosure	Percent of all DFIs	Percent of African DFIs
Annual report	96	93
Audited financial statements	93	78
Off-balance sheet items	71	57
Governance and risk management framework	63	57
Regulated capital and capital adequacy ratio	64	50

Source: World Bank and WFDFI survey on Development Banks, 2011.

from the entire sample published in Luna-Martínez and Vicente (2012). It is observed that on all the indicators the percentages are lower for African countries than the rest of the world. For example, while 93% of DBs in general publish their audited financial statements, only 78% do so among the African DBs included in the survey. There is only a 6 percentage point difference in the proportion of DBs that publish their governance and risk management framework between all other DBs and those from Africa. But the percentage point difference is larger (14 percentage points) for the disclosure of regulatory capital and capital adequacy ratio.

As noted by Luna-Martínez and Vicente (2012) it is important that DBs have in place a framework for managing risk and that this is an important governance issue. While 88% of all DBs in the survey had a risk management unit, only 50% of the African DBs had the same. As noted by Scott (2007) having in place such a governance structure is necessary but not sufficient for addressing some of the corporate governance challenges faced by DBs. Such structures must operate effectively. It is commonplace in Africa that such institutions and structures exist on paper but are not as effective as required.

36.7 MOVING FORWARD: SHOULD DEVELOPMENT BANKS BE STATE OWNED?

The argument that has generally been made for supporting the operations of DBs through state intervention is that they perform the following functions:

- they ensure the security of the banking system;
- they provide a solution to the problem of capital and financial market imperfections due to costly transactions and asymmetric information;
- they provide finance for projects that may not pass the financial viability test of private banks but which are of the social good;
- they provide financial services in isolated areas that would not otherwise be covered by the private banking system (Yeyati et al. 2004).

The important question in this regard becomes: to what extent should the state intervene, if at all, and what form should such interventions take?

First, it is important to point out that even if all the arguments for intervention were valid, it might not necessarily warrant a state take-over. For example, unless large negative consequences may result from the vulnerability of the banking system, government intervention may be unnecessary. The mitigation of market failures is probably one of the strongest arguments for state involvement in the banking sector. For example, credit rationing resulting from asymmetric information may lead to underfinancing or lack of finance for important projects. Related to this is the limited incentive for private banks to finance projects whose benefits cannot be internalized, warranting government intervention. In the absence of developed credit markets for alternative financing, which is absent in most African countries, one may justify government intervention.

As earlier seen, governments interested in the mobilization of domestic resources to finance development have often used DBs as an important source in Africa (Aryeetey 2009). But, among the many problems responsible for low domestic resource mobilization in the region is the low savings rates exacerbated by the absence of financial institutions in isolated regions, calling for state intervention to reach the unbanked and marginal clients. The risks associated with banking in the region are often too large for the private sector to tackle. Besides, it has been shown that access to banking services helps increase financial development, which has a positive effect on economic growth and poverty reduction (Burgess and Pande 2005). The presence of banks, irrespective of who owns them, could lead to more competitive behavior, further accelerating financial sector development. But does this warrant state ownership of banks? Yeyati et al. (2004) argued this may be warranted only where the capacity of regulatory authorities is weak, which may be a result of weak institutions in general.

Given the prevalence of all the above factors in most African countries, some degree of state intervention is clearly possible. The issue that needs addressing is the specific form of state intervention. Possible options are effective regulation, engagement of independent entities, or direct government ownership. Note that the latter is the case in 71% of the African DBs included in the survey published by Luna-Martínez and Vicente (2012).

In theory, so long as the state has a clearly articulated objective of delivering goods and services that are of a public good nature, and which otherwise cannot be provided by a private entity, it could either hire the services of a private bank to provide the goods and services or provide these directly. Both options have pros and cons as argued by Hart et al. (1997) and Yeyati et al. (2004). Take, for example, the objective of an African government to promote agricultural modernization through the establishment of an agricultural development bank to make available subsidized credit facilities to the agriculture sector. This could, in essence, be done by either establishing a development bank that is publicly owned or by contracting an existing private financial institution. According to Hart et al. (1997), although the private entity may have an incentive to reduce cost this may conflict with the social utility and the agriculture modernization objective, warranting a direct state ownership, at least theoretically.

But this argument has not taken into account the political view for establishing DBs discussed earlier, which should be an important consideration in the African context. This view is the key argument against government intervention. But, as has been argued earlier, with the conditions persisting in Africa, particularly with regard to weak institutions, it is not clear that a laissez faire situation, or contracting a private entity to help ensure that the social utility function is maximized necessarily eliminates corruption and patronage. At least, it has not worked so far after several years of privatization. Yeyati et al. (2004) noted that "while state ownership may increase the opportunities for corruption and patronage, a "weak" state makes contracting and regulation more difficult and may thus increase the benefits of state ownership" (10). Although it will seem that regulation and supervision in the presence of deposit insurance can reduce the cons of contracting a private entity to meet the developmental agenda, as the case has been in the developed world, weak institutions do not allow regulation and deposit insurance to work effectively in Africa. This is a challenge.

A government intervention in financial markets through "well-targeted" provision of subsidies and credit guarantees and the "imposition of co-financing restrictions" are instruments for maximizing the inherent positive effects of development institutions such as DBs (de Aghion 1999). DBs operating in such a way will likely result in more effective credit allocation, limiting the likelihood of politically motivated misallocations due to the independent co-financing element.

Some guiding principles for maximizing the potential benefit of DBs in Africa while minimizing the potential negative consequences include: granting operational independence to development bank executives; making the appointment of bank executives non-coterminous with the government that may have appointed them, as in the case of the appointment of supreme court judges in some countries; and including people from different cross-sections of society, including civil society organization, on the board of DBs. Although the state can set specific objectives, as through a national development plan, the development bank should be given a free hand to operate through a non-partisan board.

36.8 CONCLUSION

There is no doubt that various recent institutional developments in the financial sectors of most African countries have not led to a solution to the dearth of long-term finance for many development projects. Reforming the institutions and introducing new players and rules over two decades did not necessarily solve the problem. This is largely attributable to the peculiar risk configuration that financial institutions face, driven by the structural and governance characteristics of many African states, and these are changing only very slowly.

But the need to finance development projects, including large infrastructure, agriculture and industry remains significant. The justification for introducing DBs in the 1960s and 1970s appears to be still relevant as the new capital markets have not had the expected impact on providing term finance.

The challenge for many states is how to have DBs that will not suffer from the same constraints that the first generation of DBs faced. Considering that the private sector is not likely to go into development banking without significant support from the state, the argument made in this chapter is that the state does not have much of a choice but to take the lead in the setting up or strengthening of DBs, and develop for these such institutional arrangements as will insulate them from political interference, as happened three decades ago.

One can make the argument that the African state today is a whole lot different from what it was three decades ago, even if change has been slow in coming and uneven. Constitutionalism prevails in a number of countries and this has been used to shield important state institutions from political interference. Central banks have greater independence than they did in the past. Other regulatory bodies have been set up in many countries to augment the work of central banks. The significant improvement in the regulatory environment offers some hope that new institutions can be better regulated to ensure improved performance. Lessons from the more recent governance experiences could be drawn in fashioning a new generation of DBs.

This chapter supports the idea of putting in place governance arrangements that will make DBs efficient and effective in the delivery of financial services. These might include the state partnering with private sector firms to manage DBs under clearly articulated and enforced guidelines for operations. While many might see the state's participation in the financial sector as *déjà vu*, the case for the state's involvement appears strong using infant industry arguments. A new generation of DBs can and should take advantage of the new opportunities offered by a globalized monitoring of institutions and a more competitive environment.

References

Acemoglu, D., Golosov, M., and Tsyvinski, A. (2008). Markets versus governments. *Journal of Monetary Economics*, 55(1):159–189.

Allen, F Otchere, I., and Senbet, L.W. (2011). African Financial Systems: A Review, *Review of Development Finance*, 1(2, April–June):79–113.

Allen, F., Carletti, E., Cull, R. et al. (2012). Resolving the African Financial Development Gap: Cross-Country Comparisons and a Within-Country Study of Kenya. NBER Working Paper No. 18013. http://www.nber.org/papers/w18013, Last accessed: 20/11/2013.

Altunbas, Y., Evans, L., and Molyneux, P. (2001). Bank ownership and efficiency. *Journal of Money, Credit and Banking*, 33(4):926–954.

Andrianova, S., Demetriades, P., and Shortland, A. (2008). Government ownership of banks, institutions, and financial development. *Journal of Development Economics*, 85(1–2):218–252.

Andrianova, S., Demetriades, P., and Shortland, A. (2012). Government Ownership of Banks, Institutions and Economic Growth. *Economica*, 79(315):449–469.

Arestis, P., and Demetriades, P.O. (1999). Financial liberalization: The experience of developing economies. *Eastern Economic Journal*, 25(4):441–457.

Aryeetey, E., and Senbet, L. (2004). "Essential Financial Market Reforms in Africa", Technical Publication No. 63, Legon, Institute of Statistical, Social and Economic Research, University of Ghana.

Aryeetey, E. (2009). The global financial crisis and domestic resource mobilization in Africa. Working paper series No. 101. African Development Bank, Tunis, Tunisia. http:www.afdb. org/. Last accessed: 10/10/2013.

Aryeetey, E., and Nissanke, M. (1998). *Financial Integration and Development: Liberalization and Reform in Sub-Saharan Africa*. London: Routledge and ODI.

Boskey, S. (1959). *Problems and Practices of Development Banks*. Baltimore: Johns Hopkins University Press.

Burgess, R., and Pande, R. (2005). Do rural banks matter? Evidence from the Indian social banking experiment. *American Economic Review*, 95(3):780–795.

Calice, P. (2013). African Development Finance Institutions: Unlocking the Potential. Working Paper No. 174. African Development Bank Group. http://www.afdb.org/. Last accessed: 12/11/2013.

Caprio, G., Fiechter, J., Pomerleano, M., and Litan, R.E. (2004). The future of state-owned financial institutions. Brookings Institution. www.brookings.edu/research/papers/. Last accessed: 02/11/2013.

CEPA (2012). Assessment of project preparation facilities for Africa Volume A: Diagnostic and recommendations. Cambridge Economic Policy Associates Ltd. Available: http://www.icafrica. org/. Last accessed: 19/11/2013.

de Aghion, B.A. (1999). Development banking. *Journal of Development Economics*, 58(1):83–100.

de Sardan, O.J.P. (1999). A moral economy of corruption in Africa? *Journal of Modern African Studies*, 37(1):25–52.

Diamond, W. (1957). *Development Banks*. Baltimore: Johns Hopkins University Press.

Dinç, I.S. (2005). Politicians and banks: Political influences on government-owned banks in emerging markets. *Journal of Financial Economics*, 77(2):453–479.

Gerschenkron, A. (1962). *Economic Backwardness in Historical Perspective*. Cambridge, MA: Harvard University Press.

Group of Thirty (2013). *Long-term finance and economic growth*. Washington, DC: Group of Thirty.

Gyimah-Brempong, K. (2002). Corruption, economic growth, and income inequality in Africa. *Economics of Governance*, 3(3):183–209.

Hart, O., Shleifer, A., and Vishny, R.W. (1997). The proper scope of government: theory and an application to prisons. *Quarterly Journal of Economics*, 112(4):1127–1161.

Hawtrey, R.G. (1926). *The Economic Problem*. London: Longmans, Green and Co.

Henry, P.B. (2006). Capital account liberalization: Theory, evidence, and speculation. Working Paper 12698. National Bureau Of Economic Research, Cambridge, Massachusetts. http://www.nber.org/, Last accessed: 10/11/2013.

ICA (2012). Financial commitments and disbursements for infrastructure in Africa: Annual report 2011. The Infrastructure Consortium for Africa. http://www.icafrica.org/. Last accessed: 20/11/2013.

Kaminsky, G.L., and Reinhart, C.M. (1999). The twin crises: the causes of banking and balance of-payments problems. *American Economic Review*, 89(3):473–500.

Kane, J. (1975). *Development Banking*. Lexington: Lexington Books.

Kornai, J. (1979). Resource-constrained versus demand-constrained systems. *Econometrica*, 47(4):801–819.

La Porta, R., Lopez-De-Silanes, F., and Shleifer, A. (2002). Government ownership of banks. *Journal of Finance*, 57(1):265–301.

Lewis, W.A. (1950). *The Principles of Economic Planning*. London: G. Allen & Unwin.

Luna-Martínez, J.D., and Vicente, C.L. (2012). Global Survey of Development Banks. Policy Research Working Paper 5969. World Bank, Washington, DC. http://acf.eabr.org/. Last accessed: 10/08/2013.

Micco, A., Panizza, U., and Yañez, M. (2007). Bank ownership and performance. Does politics matter? *Journal of Banking and Finance*, 31(1):219–241.

Nissanke, M. (1994). Financial Linkage Development in Sub-Saharan Africa, in *Economic Policy Experience in Africa: What Have we Learned?* Nairobi: African Economic Research Consortium, pp. 105–125.

PWC (2010). Infrastructure finance: Uncertainty and change in Sub-Saharan Africa. PricewaterhouseCoopers. http://www.pwc.com/ke. Last accessed: 20/10/2013.

Rousseau, P.L., and Xiao, S. (2007). Banks, stock markets, and China's "great leap forward." *Emerging Markets Review*, 8(3):206–217.

Sapienza, P. (2004). The effects of government ownership on bank lending. *Journal of Financial Economics*, 72(2):357–384.

Scott, D. H. (2007). Strengthening the governance and performance of state-owned financial institutions. Policy Research Working paper 4321. World Bank, Washington, DC. http://elibrary.worldbank.org/. Last accessed: 18/11/2013.

Shleifer, A. (1998). State versus private ownership. *Journal of Economic Perspectives*, 12(4):133–150.

Shleifer, A., and Vishny, R.W. (1994). Politicians and firms. *Quarterly Journal of Economics*, 109(4):995–1025.

United Nations Conference on Trade and Development (2000). Capital flows and growth in Africa.

World Bank (2001). *Finance for Growth: Policy Choices in a Volatile World*. Oxford: Oxford University Press.

Yeyati, E.L., Micco, A., and Panizza, U. (2004). Should the government be in the banking business? The role of state-owned and development banks. Research Department Working Papers 517. Inter-American Development Bank. http://idbdocs.iadb.org/. Last accessed: 10/11/2013.

CHAPTER 37

....

THE POLITICAL ECONOMY OF AID IN NORTH AFRICA

....

HAMED EL-SAID

37.1 INTRODUCTION

....

Two related questions have occupied the attention of most of the literature on aid over the past five decades or so:[1] Is aid awarded according to recipient need—the needier the recipient the more aid received—or is aid awarded on the basis of the commercial and geopolitical interests of the donor? And, what factors most affect aid effectiveness?

Regarding the former, the general belief is that "both recipient need and donor interest variables determine the amount of foreign aid" to developing countries (Feeny 2003: 1; Feeny and McGillivray 2004). With regard to the second question, the consensus is that aid is more effective in environments characterized by good policies and strong state institutions and "has little effect in the presence of poor policies" (Burnside and Dollar 2004: 1). Although related, these questions are often studied "independently" and in isolation of each other (Feeny and McGillivray 2004: 2).

This chapter addresses an important gap in the literature by simultaneously analyzing the impact and determinants of foreign aid in North Africa (NA), defined by the United Nations to include Algeria, Egypt, Libya, Morocco, Sudan, and Tunisia. It starts by providing a historical overview of foreign flows into NA since 1960, and identifies the main donors and sources of flow. It is an interesting region to study from a number of perspectives. Firstly, since the 1960s, it has been a constant recipient of relatively large amounts of aid from different donors. Secondly, with the exception of Libya, all the countries have reformed their economies in collaboration with multilateral, International Financial Institutions (IFIs), particularly the International Monetary Fund (IMF) and the World Bank. This means that past and continuing flows to NA include both bilateral aid, which is

---

[1] Feeny and McGillivray (2004) summarize the literature on the first question; Mosley (1987) and Pack and Pack (1993) summarize the literature on the second question. Maizels and Nissanke (1984) and McKinlay and Little (1977) have also made important contributions to both questions.

often viewed as particularly donor interest-influenced, and multilateral aid, which is often conditional upon economic reforms and viewed as more recipient need-sensitive. Third, the IMF and World Bank have generally praised North African Countries (NACs) as good pupils and "top reformers" (IMF 2010, 24), and as a model for the IMF and World Bank policy lending reforms. This also suggests that the region has followed the "good policies" that the literature associates with improved aid effectiveness. NA therefore provides important lessons for the donor community with regard to aid allocation, aid effectiveness, and economic reforms.

37.2 THE EVOLUTION OF AID TO NORTH AFRICA

NA is wrongly perceived by observers of the Arab World to be, "for many decades ... the world's largest recipient of foreign aid in per capita terms" and "the third largest global recipient of aid in absolute terms" (Harrigan 2011: 1). Figure 37.1 shows that this has not really been the case, and that, in relative terms, NA has historically been a low recipient of Overseas Development Assistance (ODA). In fact, NA has been the lowest recipient of ODA among all developing regions of the world since 1960. Between 1960 and 2011, NA received only US$64.1 billion in current prices (US$83.1 billion if Sudan is included) from DAC countries. This figure represents less than 2% of total aid given to all developing regions of the world. Even in terms of per capita income, Table 37.1 also shows that, since the early 1980s, NA has lost its historic position (as the world's largest recipient of foreign aid per capita) to Sub-Saharan Africa (SSA) and Eastern Europe and Central Asia (ECA).

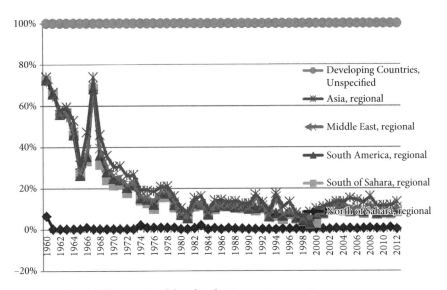

FIGURE 37.1 Total ODA received by developing regions, 1960–2012.

Source: OECD DAC Database.

Table 37.1 Net total bilateral aid received per capita by region and countries, 1960–2011 (current US$)

Region	Average 1960–79	1980–99	2000–11
EAP	1.2	4.03	4.4
ECA	1.23	6.64	23.59
LAC	5.59	10.2	13.6
South Asia	2.7	4.79	6.5
SSA	6.47	26.36	40.5
NA	16.18	22.44	21.3
MENA	15.66	28.36	43.6
NA Countries			
Algeria	13.81	8.27	6.7
Egypt	19.0	*41.12*	14.29
Libya	11.89	3.02	22.8 (2005–11)
Morocco	10.4	*30.57*	25.16
Tunisia	25.08	*29.23*	37.57

Source: Calculated by the author from OECD DAC data.

1960–2011

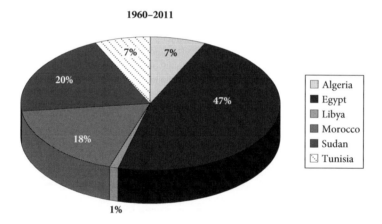

FIGURE 37.2 ODA distribution in NA.

Source: OECD DAC database.

ODA across NA is highly uneven. Figure 37.2 shows that one country alone, Egypt, received almost half (47%) of all ODA sent to the region between 1960 and 2011 (38% of the total ODA received by NA between 2000 and 2011). Sudan emerges as the second largest recipient, followed by Morocco and Tunisia, receiving 20%, 18%, and 7% of total ODA respectively between 1960 and 2011 (Figure 37.2).

As for the main donors, the US has been and still is the largest provider of foreign aid to NA, followed by the EU. Between 1960 and 2011, the US provided 57.1% (or US$47.5 billion) of total ODA, while the EU provided 42.6% (or 35.4 billion) (OECD DAC Data).

37.3 DETERMINANTS OF AID: THE SPECIFICITY OF THE MENA REGION

The literature on foreign aid is voluminous and contentious. The debate revolves around two issues, which are not mutually exclusive. The first issue is the question of whether aid to a country is allocated according to the needs of the recipient country or the interests of the donor country or institution. The second issue focuses on aid effectiveness and the conditions under which aid can deliver and realize its developmental objectives, particularly the reduction of poverty and the achievement of sustainable growth. These questions are addressed here in the same order.

The donor self-interest argument "asserts that development assistance promotes the economic or political interest of the donor country" (Ruttan 1987: 2). More recently, Feeny and McGillivray (2004: 192) defined those interests as derived from "donor policy statements, especially those of the larger donors ... to emphasize humanitarian, commercial and political, and diplomatic and strategic objectives." Such interests are reflected in the promotion of commercial ties, exports, and employment in the donor's economy, through such mechanisms as technical assistance, food aid, tied aid, and opening new markets for, as well as providing protection to the donor's multinational corporations. On the other hand, the primary rationale of the strategic and political self-interest argument focuses on the need to "strengthen the political commitment of the aid recipient to the donor country or to the West" (Ruttan 1987: 5). This includes defending the stability and enhancing the political appeal of a regime perceived by the donor to be a close ally in its fight against hostile ideologies or doctrines (communism, for example) and resisting aggression against countries considered to be politically committed to the West. Such donor self-interest factors played a key role in motivating bilateral aid during the Cold War. As Ruttan (1987: 5) wrote: "Strategic concerns, particularly during the Cold War, included fighting communism and resisting external aggression and the enhancement of political appeal of centrist political forces."

However, although the end of the Cold War in the late 1980s and early 1990s might appear to undermine the strategic and political factors behind the aid-for-self-interest argument, the Cold War's ending did in fact strengthen the case: "Even before the collapse of communism in the late 1980s and early 1990s, a new theory was emerging to the effect that Islam [is] the new communism and that it therefore represents a grave threat to Western civilization." (El-Said and Harrigan 2006: 449.) While "The Cold War years saw a high amount of aid ... as each super power and their allies aided regimes friendly to their interests" (Shah 2012: 4), the end of the Cold War saw the main donors allocating aid to "good or bad regimes," or to those perceived to be "with us" and depriving those perceived to be "against us" (El-Said and Harrigan 2006: 450). This doctrine was constitutionalized in America's foreign policy after 9/11 and was popularized by President George W. Bush's famous statement that "All nations, if they want to fight terror, must do something ... You're either with us or you're against us" (BBC News 2001). This marked the beginning of a polarizing war, the first worldwide "War on Terror."

Terror, especially the so-called "Islamic terror," has replaced communism as the main threat to the West. Since 9/11 in particular, "the war on terror ... beg[an] to look increasingly like the Cold War," with the main donors (the USA and EU) directing their aid to regions and countries where they have concerns related to national security, but also commercial ties, economic benefits, and strategic interests (Lobel 2004), and in particular the MENA region. After the 2004 Madrid terror attacks, the EU went as far as the "rush[ing] of new EU proposals" that sought "to link aid to the fight against terrorism" (Bianchi 2004). EU officials also announced that, "aid and trade could be affected if the fight against terrorism was considered insufficient" (Bianchi 2004). On the subject of US bilateral aid, Lobel (2004) argued "the recent US aid has taken on militaristic angles ... following similar patterns to aid during the Cold War. The war on terrorism is also having an effect as to what aid goes where and how much is spent." (See also Shah 2012: 40.)

For example, Israel's massive ODA receipts could never be justified by purely economic needs. Israel is a high-income country with low poverty rates, yet since its peace treaty with Egypt in the late 1970s it has been receiving US$5 billion annually in bilateral aid from the US alone. Egypt has also seen its bilateral aid from the USA, EU, and other DAC donors increase dramatically following its Camp David Accord with Israel. Before the Camp David Accord (between 1975 and 1977 for example), Egypt received an annual average of US$431 million in foreign aid. In return for abandoning the Soviet Union and reorienting its foreign policy towards the West and Israel, Egypt has been receiving an annual average of US$1.5 billion between 1980 and 2008 from the US alone. Also, for facilitating and ensuring Arab support for the American-led war against Iraq in 1991, "Egypt received a large increase in aid flows as well as massive debt forgiveness of US$15 billion from the West, the highest debt forgiveness package in the history of MENA" (Harrigan 2011: 2).

Egypt, Afghanistan, Iraq, and Pakistan (the last three countries suddenly became the largest recipients of ODA in the World after 9/11) all require foreign aid to rebuild infrastructure, develop human and physical capital, reduce poverty, and increase prosperity. However, aid to those countries is motivated more by the political and strategic interests of donors than recipient need. The problem with aid-for-self-interest is that it is ineffective in achieving developmental goals. Hirvonen (2005) agrees: "Aid systems based on the interests of donors instead of the needs of recipients make development assistance inefficient." Feeny and McGillivray (2004: 115) also express support: a "country's lingering donor interests could potentially hamper the effectiveness of its aid." In their work on "past aid flows to the region" (flows before 2006 and mainly to four MENA countries: Egypt, Jordan, Morocco, and Tunisia), Harrigan, Wang and El-Said (2006) noticed that past flows "have been heavily influenced by the political interests of donors and this has reduced the effectiveness of the aid donated to the region" (also quoted in Harrigan 2011: i).

Even with regard to multilateral aid—with most studies "suggest[ing] that donor self-interest plays a relatively large role in bilateral assistance while recipient needs play a larger role in multilateral assistance" (Ruttan 1987: 2)—MENA also provides an exception to this norm. Harrigan, Wang and El-Said (2006), while analyzing the economic and political determinants of IMF and World Bank lending to five MENA countries (four of which are in NA: Algeria, Egypt, Morocco, and Tunisia), found that these two important IFIs were also subject to pressure and influence from Western powers, particularly the USA, in their policy advice to the region. The USA's voting power in both institutions puts the USA in a strong position of influence over the flow of funds from the Washington-based multilateral institutions that represent the core pillars of the so-called "Washington Consensus." Using both qualitative and quantitative analysis, these authors showed that both recipient need and donor interest influences IMF and World Bank policy on lending to the MENA region. However, the qualitative analysis produced little evidence of economic need as aid-determinative when the first phase of the IMF loans program commenced (based on macroeconomic performance and indicators that involve the IMF in each country). Only in the case of Egypt in NA in the mid-1970s was there clear evidence of recipient economic and social needs determining aid granting, in terms of deterioration of macroeconomic and social indicators.

This leads to the second question that preoccupies much of the aid literature: aid effectiveness. The World Bank has made significant headway in achieving better understanding of the factors that determine aid effectiveness. According to the World Bank, the effectiveness of foreign aid on economic growth, poverty, and development outcomes may depend heavily on the kind of policies implemented by, and the policy environment prevailing in, the recipient countries (Burnside and Dollar 1997, 2000). Repeating their earlier (1997) study, Burnside and Dollar in 2000 used "a new data-set focusing on the 1990s," and concluded that, "The evidence supports the view that the impact of aid depends on the quality of state institution and policies" implemented in the recipient country (Burnside and Dollar 2004: 1). The World Bank's research into aid effectiveness has major implications for aid allocation process. "Specifically, the World Bank research suggests that aid only really works when government policies are good, and that a more selective allocation of aid to poor countries pursuing sound policies will lead to larger reductions in poverty" (Beynon 2003: 1). Feeny and McGillivary (2004) and Burnside and Dollar (2004: 1) showed that the World Bank recommendations have been taken seriously by the donor community and that "in the 1990s the allocation of aid to low income countries favoured ones with better institutional quality" and policies.

However "good government policies" are defined in terms of the type of policies promoted by the IMF and World Bank. Divergence from such policies indicates a "bad policy environment." The broadest criticism of this approach has perhaps been most clearly articulated by Van Waeyenberge (2009) and is focused on "the close relationship between the implicit conceptualization of the policy environment as being almost coterminous with the liberalization principles of the Washington Consensus" (in Tribe 2013: 8). Joseph Stiglitz (2002) showed that alternative development paradigms exist, and might be more successful in achieving developmental objectives in emerging economies than the standard recipe of the Washington Consensus. While the political and strategic interests of donors have motivated most aid to MENA after 2001, have MENA countries been at least rewarded for achieving a good policy environment? How did the neoliberal reforms by IFIS, not totally immune from western pressure, affect the economic and social performance of the NA countries? That question is addressed in the next section.

37.4 AID EFFECTIVENESS IN NORTH AFRICA

The aid literature is generally pessimistic about its effectiveness, particularly with regard to the main objectives of ODA, namely, "the promotion of economic development and welfare of development countries," in which "reduc[ing] poverty and achiev[ing] sustainable development" are key objectives (Feeny and McGillivray 2004: 102). Aid literature that discusses recipient need suggests that "The humanitarian objective of reducing poverty and achieving sustainable development involves allocating aid either favoring those countries in greatest need or," following the World Bank work, to "those which can best achieve development outcomes" (Feeny and McGillivray 2004: 102). The previous section showed that most ODA to MENA has been largely based on the geo-strategic (and commercial) interests of the donors, and less on the needs of the recipients. Indeed, MENA is geostrategically and commercially significant to the West. The region's geostrategic location on the main trade routes, its containment of the world's largest oil reserves (the principal fuel upon which most industrialized countries' economies continue to rely), the presence of the Israeli state in the heart of the Arab World (with its political and strategic significance as well as its powerful lobby and pro-Israeli forces in the West), and "Islamism which largely originates in the Middle East," and which is perceived by some to "present a civilizational danger" all reinforce the geo-strategic significance of MENA which the West cannot afford to ignore (National Review Online 2012).

By the late 1970s and early 1980s, all North African countries were facing economic and financial crises. These were brought about by a powerful version of state-led development and inherent contradictions of import substitution industrialization strategies (ISI), which all North African Countries (NACs) subscribed to after independence. In each country, the state controlled, expropriated, and reserved for itself all resources, and then sought to redistribute them as a form of New Social Contract (NSC), a kind of New Deal, in which the state sought to incorporate all societal elements in return for fealty and political autonomy (Pfeifer 1999a and 2000). The pillars of the NSC were based on three key elements (Iqbal 2006; Harrigan and El-Said 2009a,b): subsidies to basic food staples and energy that benefited the poor and the middle class; free education and healthcare that were equally undiscriminating in their reach; jobs in the public sector that provided stable employment for labor unions, and professional careers for the middle class.

State-led development made important strides with regard to reduction of poverty and inequality, and improvement of human development indicators. Statism was associated with rapid economic growth, large improvements in per capita income, massive reductions in poverty and inequities, and remarkable improvement in human development indicators (Iqbal 2006: xviii).

By the late 1970s, the NA social contract was no longer esteemed. Inefficiencies were associated with state-led development and internal contradictions of ISI widened trade and balance of payments deficits. Also, the welfare state proved fiscally unsustainable, particularly in the face of declining oil prices and other rents (remittances, transit fees, and aid). By the early 1980s, all the NA countries had accumulated large amounts of foreign debt and developed large fiscal and trade deficits, experienced double-digit inflation, and suffered from low or zero growth rates (Harrigan and El-Said 2009a, b).

Since the early 1980s, all NA countries, except Libya, received frequent and continuous assistance from the IMF and World Bank in the form of Standby-Agreements (SBAs) and Structural Adjustment Lending Programs (SALs), all of which have been comprehensively listed by Harrigan and El-Said (2009a, b, SBAs and SALs are financial and technical programs extended to countries suffering from economic and financial crisis in return for policy reform. It is this conditionality element which makes multilateral aid generally less vulnerable to influence by Western governments.

SBAs and SALs often seek to stabilize the main macroeconomic indicators, stimulate growth, productivity and bring about a structural change. They typically include stabilization measures (devaluation or floating of the currency, large reductions in government spending as well as expenditure raising measures to rein in inflation and reduce fiscal deficit as quickly as possible), and higher interest rates to increase domestic savings and improve the efficiency of investments. SALs, on the other hand, often include institutional reforms such as privatization, trade liberalization, price, and financial deregulation, all of which aim at boosting competition and efficiency in the economy through creating a competitive market and promoting the role of the private sector in the economy (Pfeifer 1999a, b, 2000).

Put differently, the kind of policies that the IMF and World Bank recommended to NA were similar, if not identical, to the kind of policies that parts of the aid literature, led mainly by the World Bank itself, describe as the "good policies" necessary to improve aid effectiveness. Furthermore, and as mentioned earlier, NA has generally been commended and praised by the IMF and World Bank for their low slippage rate and for being good pupils and models of reform in the region.

The outcome of reforms, or what the World Bank called "the transition" to a market economy in MENA in general and in NA in particular, excluding Tunisia, has been disappointing. The World Bank itself recognized this disappointing outcome when it stated that:

> By 2000, the region's average per capita output had ... not fully recovered to its 1985 level ... Very little progress was made on the poverty front. The region's average poverty rate fluctuated between 20 and 25% during the entire decade of the 1990s. By 2001, approximately 52 million people were poor, an increase in absolute numbers of approximately 11.5 million people, compared with the situation in 1987.
>
> (Iqbal 2006: xix)

More recently, Kadri (2012) has given an even more pessimistic view of the outcome of reform during the transition phase in NA.

Between 2000 and 2010, NA achieved more respectable GDP growth rate of 4.6% (UNDP 2012: 143). Although this is still the lowest regional GDP growth rate achieved in the world, the World Bank attributed it to two main factors, one "driven to a large degree by high oil prices and a favourable global environment," and, secondly, "by reform policies that ... are generally on the right track" (quoted in Harrigan 2011: 9). There are also other factors, however, some have less to do with the IMF and World Bank reforms while others are more directly associated with them, that still affected the social and economic performance of North African countries over the past three decades, since the transition to neoliberal, market-oriented policies started in the early 1980s.

First, and as Lal (2011: 18) argued, even a small amount of aid can boost growth, and "A little growth is better than no or negative growth." Foreign inflow of funds played a key role in boosting MENA growth, particularly inflow in the form of foreign assistance. As discussed earlier, IMF and World Bank policy reforms in MENA have been supported by large infusions of capital, on both concessional and grant terms. Pfeifer (1999a: 446) noted, "steady access to regular infusions of international capital on concessional terms have been 'essential to the success of this strategy'" and have enabled NA reformers "to survive this long period of repeated austerity and structural adjustment with less pain and more growth than other severely indebted countries." Within the region, Morocco was one of the countries earmarked for special debt relief treatment under the Brady Plan. Rabat received seven mul-tilateral debt relief agreements between January 1980 and September 1991. The frequency and highly concessional elements of these loans played a key role in Morocco's, and other NA reformers' laudable performance (1999a: 446).

One of the major deficits of the neoliberal reforms across MENA in general and NA in particular is the neglect of social safety nets. When the old social contract came under severe fiscal pressure in the late 1970s and early 1980s, neoliberal economic reforms undermined it further, instead of replacing it by a new, more acceptable and sustainable social contract. As the UNDP 2012 (9, 90) Report on the Arab World stated, the "greatest deficits [of neoliberal reforms] are in the areas of social protection and social dialogue ... transition to market economies [was] driven by uncritical reductions in public social spending and privatiza-tion without accompanying social protection mechanisms." Even the Fund's new Managing Director, Christine Lagarde, acknowledged recently that equity and social safety nets have been ignored and neglected by the economics profession, of which the Fund and the Bank form an integral part:

> I believe that the economics profession and the policy community have downplayed inequal-ity for too long ... Now all of us have a better understanding that a more equal distribution of income allows for more economic stability, more sustained economic growth, and healthier societies with stronger bonds of cohesion and trust.

(cited in Tribe 2013: 8)

The 2009 UN Arab Human Development Report (pp. 9 and 18) concurs. It concluded that growth in the region during the transition period lacked "social justice" and "continued to benefit a few ... mainly benefit[ted] establishment elites and excluded the majority of ordi-nary citizens." According to the same source (242), the richest 20% in North Africa today control more than 45% of income or expenditure, while the poorest 20% control only 7% of income or expenditure.

In their extensive work on the social and economic impact of the IMF and World Bank-policy lending in MENA, Harrigan and El-Said (2009a,b, 2010) showed that, as a result of reforms' neglect of social aspects, a gap in the social sector appeared in MENA reforming countries, caused by the state's withdrawal from social provision and the increasing assump-tion of social welfare provision by faith-based organizations. This included in particular the Muslim Brotherhood and its offspring organizations across the Arab World. The most popular of these in NA have been the Muslim Brotherhood (in Egypt), Islamic Salvation Front (Algeria), *Jama'a al Adl wal Ihsan*—Justice and Spirituality Organization (Morocco), and the Sudanese Islamic Movement and National Islamic Front (NIF) (El-Said 2014a, b). These movements, through their social provisions, created a state within a state situation, by extending their influence into almost every social area: education, health, charity, direct transfers, food distribution, emergency aid, clothing, even stationery and school books for poor children. In countries like Sudan, Egypt, and Morocco, Islamist movements provided better quality and fairer access for the general public to social services than their respective states. Even the World Bank acknowledges that any improvement in human development in MENA since the mid-1980s "can not be explained by ... income growth and public spend-ing profile" alone, and that "other areas," including "private spending" and deliveries might have had a role too (Iqbal 2006: 34). The rise of faith-based organizations as social welfare providers contributed to further "erod[ing] the legitimacy of the regime[s]" in MENA and their reforms, as well as simultaneously shoring up the legitimacy and credibility of Islamist movements (Amin 2012: 7). Not surprisingly therefore, the rise of "political Islam," has been one of the most significant outcomes of the Arab Spring (Deutsche Bank 2013: 1).

Adams and Page (2003: 2027) while analyzing economic growth and human development in MENA in the 1980s and 1990s also did not credit the neoliberal policies for not having an even higher level of poverty in MENA at the beginning of the twenty first century. "Two factors," they argued, "account for this situation: international migration/remittances and public sector (government) employment."

Traditionally, immigration and migration have been important features of labor markets in MENA (UNDP 2012: 27, 42). Remittances from workers abroad have also traditionally played a key role in reducing poverty in MENA. "Relative to the size of their economies (GDP), the MENA [countries] … receive large inflows in the form of remittances," with Egypt and Morocco among "the ten countries receiving most remittances" in terms of GDP (Gammeltoft 2002: 181; see also UNDP 2012: 42; UN 2009).

Despite nearly three decades of reforms in MENA, the size of the public sector has remained large. Privatization generally proved an arduous and very gradual process. Its scale also remained trivial when compared to, for instance, privatization programs implemented in Eastern Europe following the end of the Cold War in the late 1980s and early 1990s. Political economy issues, particularly political and bureaucratic opposition to reform, prevented the emergence of a productive and "affordable … public sector work force," as the World Bank noted (World Bank and Dubai School of Government 2011: 4).

In other words, neoliberal reforms in MENA did not usher in "a full-blown commitment to a market economy" (Knowles 2011: 106). MENA regimes were reluctant to surrender their control and power over economic affairs. This led Richards and Waterbury (1996: 223) to argue that "the wisdom in the Middle East is that economic reform programs are the result of leaders' survival strategies," through which those leaders hoped to improve economic performance and hence enhance their legitimacy but without giving up their economic powers. Knowles (2011: 101) concurs, adding that reforms were used by the state for "self-preservation," to reposition the state in a place where it can safeguard the interests of its main elites and interest groups.

Neoliberal reforms, moreover, have failed to create a level playing field that is so necessary to facilitate private investment and improve the business environment. The upshot has been the prevention of genuine private markets from emerging, which often occurs when reforms are independent of political influences of the elites.

These developments have had far reaching consequences for the outcome of reform. Regime survival trumped everything else, including efficiency and productivity concerns. As a result, the main pillar of the World Bank reforms that is "the desire to increase the involvement of the private sector in the economy at the expense of the state" failed to materialize (Knowles 2011: 89). The new state "capitalist class" not only resisted its own shedding rather successfully, but also created a predatory relationship with the private sector (Amin 2012: 7; and El-Said and Becker 2001), and began living of the activities of the private sector by striking deals with its elites (Luciani 2005). Both the UN Arab Human Development Report (2009) and the UNDP 2012 Report on the Arab World showed that the MENA business environment remains hamstrung by a high degree of bureaucracy, red tape, and rent seeking activity.

According to the World Bank Ease of Doing Business Survey, MENA is one of the worse performing regions in the world, where operating a business requires more procedures than in any region except sub-Saharan Africa (SSA), where starting a business is slower than in most other developing regions, and where operating a businesses is more costly (as a percentage of GNI) than in any region except from SSA (http://doingbusiness.org). A more recent survey on the investment environment of most Arab states concluded, "enterprises identify macro-economic instability, corruption, anti-competitive practices and high taxes (to support a large public sector) as principal constraints (UNDP 2012: 35).

Even in terms of Foreign Direct Investment (FDI), a good indicator of the degree to which a country or region has become integrated into the global economy, MENA fares less than most other regions of the world. In 2009, even before the Arab Spring erupted, the Arab World's share of global FDI was around 2%. Only SSA receives less FDI than MENA. Other indicators, such as the levels of protection in the economy, point to similar directions. The rates of both tariff and non-tariff protections in NA are still today much higher than the average for developing regions. They have also certainly stayed at levels much higher than what the IMF and the World Bank would have liked (El-Said and Harrigan 2014).

Given the way neoliberal reforms proceeded, most observers do not associate reforms in MENA with efficiency and productivity gains, the primary objectives of SALs. As Harrigan, Wang, and El-Said (2006: 263) argued, MENA growth has been modest and:

> not the type of export-led intensive growth normally expected of a successful stabilization and structural reform program guided by the IMF and World Bank. Instead, growth has been extensive rather than intensive i.e., based upon increased factor inputs rather that productivity gains and focused on the non-tradable sector.

To be sure, growth over the past decade or so in MENA, although insufficient, was not without job creation. However, the jobs created were not in high value activities, taking place mostly in mining, construction and services. They therefore did not provide decent and stable incomes to protect and improve the living standards of the majority of job seekers (UNDP 2012: 30).

Today, informal economic activity represents a significant source of income for large sections of North African populations. Amin (2012: 36) argues that informal sector activities represent the most important source of income for the majority of people in Egypt, "statistics say 60%." Consequently, "unemployment in the [MENA] region remains the highest of any region" in the world, with male unemployment in Tunisia, the country where the Arab Spring began, standing at 13.5%, which is the "highest in the world" (UNDP 2012: 23). In NA particularly, the youth unemployment rate is one of the world's highest (24.8% in 2012), ranging from 17.6% in Morocco, 20% in Sudan, 21.5% in Algeria, 25.4% in Egypt, 29.4% in Tunisia, and 35.1% in Libya (UNDP 2012: 134). NA unemployment rates are exceeded only by SSA at 46.9%.

The preceding analysis does not suggest that reforms in NA took the form of quick, therapy-shock approach often preferred by the IFIs. Nor does it imply that NA has been the good pupil that the Fund and the Bank portrayed them to be. Reforms in NA proceeded more gradually and at a much slower pace than hoped for by the IMF and World Bank. It is also true that the IMF and the World Bank complained, on several occasions, about both the quality and pace of reform in the region (Harrigan and El-Said 2009a,b).

It is important to note here that the World Bank, driven mainly by concerns over aid effectiveness, attempted to push its policy frontiers significantly "by endorsing good governance as a core element of its development strategy" (Santiso 2001: 2). However, the World Bank pushed its policy frontier without acknowledging the link between democracy and good governance, overlooking Santiso's observations (2001: 2) that "quality of governance is ultimately attributable to its democratic content," and "neither democracy nor good governance is sustainable without the other." The inability of the Fund and the Bank, as well as the donor community, to adopt a more radical approach towards democracy has undermined their ability to promote good governance, a fact that failed to promote a level playing field and eventually undermined the outcome of reforms.

37.5 OTHER FACTORS AFFECTING AID EFFECTIVENESS IN NORTH AFRICA

37.5.1 Alternative sources of finance

The pace and quality of reform in MENA have also been influenced by, in addition to domestic political economy issues, the presence of alternative sources of funding. The latter has come mostly from the rich Arab oil Gulf states, who accumulated windfall of more than US$1.3 trillion since 9/11 as a result of increased oil prices during the roaring 2000s. In recent years, the oil-rich Arab Gulf States have emerged as the largest donor to NA, providing grants, concessional loans, and investment (mostly in real estate and services). For countries like Egypt, the oil-rich oil Arab states continue to represent the largest source of remittances from emigrant Egyptian workers, thus providing another, important source of foreign exchange (Pfeifer 2011).

"Arab–Arab," aid has become increasingly prominent since the beginning of the Arab Spring in late 2010. In 2011, for example, during a period of perceived increase in threat from a nuclear Iran, the six GCC Oil Arab States announced, the establishment of "a five-year Development Aid Programme for Morocco and Jordan," in which they pledged "$ 2.5 billion for each country" (Albawaba Business 2011). Following the removal of Hosni Mubarak from power in 2011 and the election of President Mohammed Morsi to power one year later, Qatar alone provided Cairo in 2012 with about US$8 billion in aid, while Turkey provided another a US$2 billion concessional loan. When Mohammed Morsi was removed from power by the Egyptian Army in July 2013, Saudi Arabia and the United Arab Emirates, traditionally hostile to the Brotherhood's Islamist agenda, pledged another US$8 billion in cash and concessional loans to Cairo (Worth 2013).

The presence of large aid inflows from alternative sources has undermined the leverage of the IMF and World Bank in NA, as well as American aid, in the region. Arab–Arab aid has allowed, for example, higher slippage rates than permitted by the IMF or the World Bank. More importantly, alternative high-volume inflows, which now dwarf American aid to NA, have enabled Cairo "to avert painful economic reforms being urged by the … Fund as the price for its own U$ 4.8 billion aid package" (Worth 2013). As Harrigan and El-Said (2009b) argued, the World Bank, as a result of the large inflow of funds during the past decade, has been content to take a back seat and play the role of advisor to NA governments, instead of dictator of economic policies.

37.5.2 Quality of aid

So far, this chapter has focused on the policy environment of the recipient country and geo-strategic interests of donors to gauge the impact of aid on poverty reduction and human development indicators in MENA. But the quality of aid itself, which relates to outputs or forms of aid given, is also important. Aid today takes different forms, including food aid, emergency aid, debt relief, debt forgiveness, and military aid, all of which "bear little relationship to the needs of the developing countries for long term development capital" (Shah 2012: 32). A great deal of aid to MENA takes the form of debt relief and debt forgiveness, as occurred with, for example, Egypt between 1990 and 1991, Jordan in 1993, and Iraq since 2003. Aid relief and aid forgiveness are reflected in the ODA figures to MENA as large, sudden spikes (Figure 37.1).

Stork and Pfeifer (1987) have shown that food aid "represents an important currency in US relations with the [MENA] region, second perhaps only to weapons," and is an "important point of leverage for Washington on Egypt's political options." More than 50% of all aid received by Egypt, Jordan, and Israel also takes the form of military assistance. To reflect their generosity, donors today include all these forms of aid in the statistics of their bilateral assistance. However, these same forms are excluded from the *official definition* of ODA, which recognizes only development aid as crucial to helping poor developing nations grow out of poverty.

Other forms of aid, such as tied aid that seeks to support the economy of the donor country, technical assistance, or technical cooperation grants that pay for the services of donor country nationals, and export credits that seek to subsidize donors' exports, also undermine aid effectiveness, but still create a generous picture of the donor. Again, many such forms of aid have acted as an important currency in the relationship between donors and the MENA region (Stork and Pfeifer 1987). This led Shah (2012: 1), in his general assessment of aid effectiveness in developing countries, to state that "In reality, both the quantity and quality of aid have been poor and donor nations have not been held to account."

Reflecting the perceived importance of both the quality of aid and "good policies" for aid effectiveness, most of the literature on aid effectiveness in MENA in general and in NA in particular has painted a pessimistic picture of the impact of aid in the region. Harrigan (2011: 14) recently reflected this pessimistic strand when she concluded that "Aid to North Africa has clearly done little to help solve the region's pressing socioeconomic problems such as poverty, inequality and unemployment."

Further reductions in poverty and improvements in income inequities in some NA states have been undermined by exogenous factors that, although unrelated to actual aid, have nevertheless weakened aid effectiveness. Wars and civil wars, for example, are known to stifle economic growth, undermine entrepreneurship, lead to capital flight, destroy livelihood, displace populations, and bring misery to millions. In his work on the question of why some countries remain poor, Collier (2008) ranked war and civil war as the number one reason for his four-poverty trap model, arguing that "73% of those in the poorest billion of the world's population are either involved in or recovering from civil war."

Indeed, and despite having one of the highest real GDP growth rates in the world between 2000 and 2008 (over 7%), almost half of the total Sudanese population today is living under the international poverty line (US$2 per day). The UNDP (2013) recently noted, " … overall economic growth [in Sudan] has not been translated into equivalent human development improvements and poverty reduction realities." Not surprisingly, Sudan, one of the largest aid recipients and dependents in the area, has not only failed to reduce poverty, but also has the largest number of poor in NA today (UNDP 2013).

Algeria is another case in point. The country suffered tremendously from civil war between 1990 and 1997 and is still recovering from its aftermath. More than 200,000 Algerians were killed during that decade and hundreds of thousands were uprooted in what came to be known as the "Dirty War" (El-Said and Harrigan 2013). Despite the country's large oil rents, which have had a similar impact to aid, today Algeria has the lowest rate of poverty reduction and the second highest incidence of poverty after Sudan.

Aid has limits. Not only the policy environment of the recipients and political and economic interests of the donors affect aid effectiveness. The quality as much as the quantity of aid and the presence/lack of peace are other important factors.

37.6 CONCLUSION

This chapter had several objectives and examined several issues simultaneously. It started with a historical overview of aid flow to NA. It then discussed two related key questions that have dominated the aid literature over the past five decades or so. These were, first, whether aid is allocated according to recipient need or donor self-interest; second, whether or not aid is more effective in environments characterized by "good policies" and strong state institutions.

This chapter demonstrated that compared to other developing regions, NA is historically a low aid recipient: this finding contradicts the general perception that it is highly debt dependent. The bulk of NA's aid, before the eruption of Arab Spring in late 2010, came from two sources: the USA primarily and the EU secondarily. Also, NA has been receiving aid over a long period—at least since independence—during which the region experienced severe and recurrent economic crises.

Over the past decade or so, it has reduced its reliance on aid from Western countries noticeably. This partly relates to changes in the region's economic landscape, resulting from countries graduating from low to higher income countries. It is also caused by a shift in the sources of aid from Western to Arab donors, with the latter imposing less economic conditions than the former. However, distribution of aid to NA remains highly uneven.

Finally, aid effectiveness in NA has been subject to several pressures. These include economic and geostrategic interests of donors, policy environment and institutions prevailing in recipient countries, the quantity and quality of aid itself, and other environmental factors prevailing in the recipients (war, civil war, etc.). Space and time limitations, unfortunately, have not permitted a more thorough investigation of each country's economic performance under Aid. Harrigan and El-Said (2009a, b) have shown that NA's economic performance was not uniform and that Tunisia performed much better than other countries in the region. This cautions against sweeping generalizations and suggests that policy environment, institutional capacity, leadership, history, and bargaining power of recipient countries' bureaucracy are significant determinants of aid effectiveness in NA. Aid, in other words, need not go down the drain, and this chapter has not been able to demonstrate that North Africa, despite its economic and social plights, would have been better off without Aid altogether.

References

Adams, R., and Page, J. (2003). Poverty, inequality and growth in selected Middle East and North Africa countries, 1980–2000. *World Development*, 31(12):2027–2048.

Amin, S. (2012). *The People's Spring: The Future of the Arab Revolution*. Dakar: Pambazuka Press.

Albawaba (2011). Business. http://www.albawaba.com/business.

BBC News (2001). Bush urges anti-terror allies to act. November 6. http://news.bbc.co.uk/1/hi/world/americas/1642130.stm.

Beynon, J. (2003). Poverty Efficient Aid Allocations—Collier/Dollar Revisited, *ESAU Working Paper 2*, Overseas Development Institute, Economic and Statistics Analysis Unit: London. http://www.odi.org.uk/sites/odi.org.uk/files/odi-assets/publication.

Bianchi, S. (2004). POLITICS-EU: War on Terror Threatens Aid, *International Press Service*, March 25. http://www.ipsnews.net/2004/03/politics-eu-war-on-terror-threatens-aid/.

Burnside, C., and Dollar, D. (1997). Aid, Policies, and Growth. Policy Research. Working Paper 1777. Washington, DC: World Bank Development Research Group.

Burnside, C., and Dollar, D. (2000). Aid, policies, and growth. *American Economic Review*, 90(4):847–868.

Burnside, C., and Dollar, D. (2004). Aid, policies and growth. *American Economic Review*, September.

Collier, P. (2008). Why Some Countries Remain Poor: Poverty Traps, August 8. http://makewealth-history.org/2008/12/08/why-some-countries-remain-poor-paulcolliers-four-poverty-traps/.

Deutsche Bank (2013). Two years of Arab Spring: Where are we now? What's next? *Current Issues Emerging Markets*. January 25. https://www.dws-investments.com/EN/docs/research/Two_yrs_arab_spring_article.pdf.

Feeny, S. (2003). What determines foreign aid to Papua New Guinea? An inter-temporal model of aid allocation. Discussion Paper No. 2003/05. Helsinki: UNU–WIDER.

Feeny, S., and McGillivray, M. (2004). Modeling inter-temporal aid allocation: a new application with an emphasis on Papua New Guinea. *Oxford Development Studies*, 32(1):100–118.

El-Said, H., and Becker, K. (eds) (2001). *Management and International Business Issues in Jordan*. London: The Haworth Press.

El-Said, H., and Harrigan, J. (2006). Globalisation, International finance and political Islam in the Middle East and North Africa. *Middle East Journal*, 60(3):236–251.

El-Said, H., and Harrigan, J. (2013). *Deradicalising Violent Extremists: Counter Radicalisation and Deradicalisation Programmes in Muslim Majority States*. London: Routledge.

El-Said, H., and Harrigan, J. (2014). Economic reform, social welfare and political instability in the Arab world: The Case of Jordan, Egypt, Morocco, and Tunisia 1983–2004. *Middle East Journal*.

El-Said, H. (2014a). The evolution of economic thinking in North Africa, in V. Barnet (ed.), *The Handbook of the History of Global Economic Thought*. London: Routledge.

El-Said, H. (2014b). *Radicalisation, Counter Radicalisation and Deradicalisation Programs: Evaluating the Impact in Muslim Majority and Western Democracies.* London: Palgrave McMillan.

Gammeltoft, P. (2002). Remittances and other financial flows to developing countries. *International Migration,* 40(5):180–211.

Harrigan, J., and El-Said, H. (2006). The IMF and World Bank in Jordan: elusive growth and social instability. *Review of International Organisations,* 1(September):236–251.

Harrigan, J. (2011). *The Political Economy of Aid Flows to North Africa.* United Nations University, World Institute for Development Economics. Working Paper No. 2011/72, November.

Harrigan, J., Wang, C., and El-Said, H. (2006). The economic and political determinants of IMF and World Bank Lending in the Middle East and North Africa. *World Development,* 34(2):247–270.

Harrigan, J., and El-Said, H. (2009a). *Aid and Power: the IMF and World Bank Policy Lending in the Middle East and North Africa.* London: Palgrave McMillan.

Harrigan, J., and El-Said, H. (2009b). *Economic Liberalization, Social Capital, and Islamic Welfare Provision.* London: Palgrave McMillan.

Harrigan, J., and El-Said, H. (2010). The economic impact of IMF and World Bank Programs in the Middle East and North Africa: a case study of Jordan, Egypt, Morocco and Tunisia, 1983–2004. *Review of Middle East Economics and Finance,* 6(2):1–25.

Hirvonen, P. (2005). Why Recent Increases in Development Aid Fail to Help the Poor *Global Policy Forum,* August.http://www.globalpolicy.org/component/content/article/240-international-aid/45056-stingy-samaritans.

Iqbal, F. (2006). *Sustaining Gains in Poverty Reduction and Human Development in the Middle East and North Africa.* Washington, DC: World Bank. http://books.google.de/books?id=g5snppnf9IcC&printsec=frontcover&hl=de&source=gbs_ge_summary_r&cad=0#v=onepage&q&f=false.

Lal, E. (2011). A Hurting Hand: Why Foreign Aid Does Not Work, GLBL 496 Azusa Pacific University, April 26. http://www.academia.edu/1315470/A_Hurting_Hand_Why_Foreign_Aid_Does_not_Work.

IMF (2010). Arab Republic of Egypt: 2010 Article IV Consultation—Staff Report; Public Information Notice on the Executive Board Discussion; and Statement by the Executive Director for the Arab Republic of Egypt, Washington, DC: IMF www.imf.org/external/pubs/ft/scr/2010/cr1094.pdf.

Kadri, Ali (2012). Revisiting Arab Socialism, in World Economics Association. *World Economic Review,* 1(1), Jan 11. MEI/NUS. http://werdiscussion.worldeconomicsassociation.org/wp-content/uploads/Arab_socialism_version_one_.pdf.

Knowles, W. (2011). *Jordan since 1989: A Study in Political Economy.* London: Tauris.

Lobel, J. (2004). U.S: Foreign Aid Budget Takes on Cold War Cast. *International Press Service,* Feb. 3, 2004. http://www.ipsnews.net/2004/02/us-foreign-aid-budget-takes-on-cold-war-cast/.

Luciani, G. (2005). Oil and political economy in the international relations of the Middle East, in L. Fawcette (ed.), *International Relations of the Middle East.* Oxford: Oxford University Press, pp. 79–102.

McKinlay, R., and Little, R. (1977). *A Foreign Policy Model of U.S. Bilateral Aid Allocation. World Politics,* 30(1):58–86.

Maizels, A., and Nissanke, M. (1984). *Motivations for Aid to Developing Countries. World Development,* 12(9):879–900.

Mosley, P. (1987). *Foreign Aid: Its Defense and Reform*. Lexington, KY: The University Press of Kentucky.

National Review Online (2012). *Will the Middle East Lose its Importance?* July 2. http://www.nationalreview.com/corner/304530/will-middle-east-lose-its-importance-daniel-pipes#.

Pack, H., and Pack, R. (1993). Foreign aid and the question of fungibility. *Review of Economic and Statistics*, 75(2):258–265.

Pfeifer, K. (1999a). Parameters of economic reform in NA. *Review of African Political Economy*, 82:441–554.

Pfeifer, K. (1999b). How Tunisia, Morocco, Jordan and even Egypt became IMF success stories in the 1990s. *Middle East Research and Information Project*, 210:23–27.

Pfeifer, K. (2000). Does SA spell relief from unemployment? A comparison of four IMF success stories in the MENA, in W. Shagin and G. Dibeh (eds), *Earnings Inequality, Unemployment, and Poverty in the Middle East and North Africa*. Westport: Greenwood Press, pp. 111–128. http://books.google.co.uk/books?hl=en&lr=&id=21FarAOLIQwC&oi=fnd&pg=PA111&dq=elated:uzSjFYUCdXPpUM:scholar.google.com/&ots=QwtFFWWuLA&sig=xTbdKM DECWCcqvFHInAoM4FdNMw#v=onepage&q&f=false.

Pfeifer, K. (2011). September 11 decade. *Middle Eastern Research and Information Project*, 260 (41). http://www.merip.org/mer/mer260/petrodollars-work-play- post-september-11-decade.

Richards, A., and Waterbury, J. (1996). *A Political Economy of the Middle East*. London: WestPress.

Ruttan, Vernon (1987). *Why Foreign Economic Assistance? Economic Development Centre*. Minneapolis: University of Minnesota.

Shah, A. (2012). Foreign Aid for Development Assistance, Global Issues, http://www.globalissues.org/article/35/foreign-aid-development-assistance.

Santiso, C. (2001). Good governance and aid effectiveness: the World Bank and conditionality. *George Town Public Review*, 7(1):1–22.

Stiglitz, J. (2002). *Globalisation and its Discontents*. New York: Penguin Books.

Stork, J., and Pfeifer, K. (1987) Bullets, Banks and Bushels: The Struggle for Food in the Middle East. *Middle East Report*, 145(17), March/April. http://www.merip.org/mer/mer145/bullets-banks-bushels.

Tribe, M. (2013). Aid and Development: Issues and Reflections. Department of Economics, University of Strathclyde, Glasgow (13-09). http://www.strath.ac.uk/media/departments/economics/researchdiscussionpapers/2013/13-09FINAL.pdf.

UN (2009). *Private Capital Flows, Foreign Direct Investment and Portfolio Investment*. New York: UN. http://www.undp.org/content/dam/undp/library/Poverty%20Reduction/Inclusive%20development/Towards%20Human%20Resilience/Towards_Sustaining MDGProgress_Ch3.pdf.

UNDP (2012). Rethinking Economic Growth: Towards Productive and Inclusive Arab Societies, International Labour Organization. http://www.ilo.org/wcmsp5/groups/public/---arabstates/---ro-beirut/documents/publication/wcms_208346.pdf.

UNDP (2013). Sudan. http://www.sd.undp.org/sudan%20overview.htm.

Van Waeyenberge, E. (2009). Selectivity at work: country policy and institutional assessments at the World Bank. *European Journal of Development Research*, 21(5):792–810.

World Bank and Dubai School of Government (2011). *Case Studies in Governance and Public Management in the Middle East and North Africa*. Washington, DC and Dubai School of Government, Number 2. http://www.academia.edu/1078022/Downsizing_Moroccos_Public_Sector_Lessons_from_the_Voluntary_Retirement_Program.

Worth, R. (2013). Egypt is Arena for Influence of Arab Rivals. *The New York Times*, July. http://www.nytimes.com/2013/07/10/world/middleeast/aid-to-egypt-from-saudis-and-emiratis-is-part-of-struggle-with-qatar-for-influence.html.

CHAPTER 38

AID TO AFRICA
The Changing Context

TONY ADDISON, SAURABH SINGHAL, AND
FINN TARP

38.1 INTRODUCTION

To continue its economic growth and create new and better livelihoods, Africa must transform the productive side of its economy. Ongoing globalization—in trade, finance, and technology—opens up new possibilities for structural transformation, but also new risks as Africa's integration with the global economy evolves. Climate change is impacting productive sectors and the livelihoods linked to them. Consolidating war-to-peace transition remains imperative for Democratic Republic of Congo (DRC), Somalia and others, as they need inclusive growth to reinforce the politics of peace. This is the context within which official development assistance (ODA) must operate and evolve if it is to remain useful.

In a nutshell, the argument of this chapter is as follows. While aid has been successful in helping countries achieve growth, this rests on too narrow a base, and Africa remains vulnerable to shocks. Growth also needs to reach more of Africa's half a billion poor people if rising inequality is to be avoided.[1] By investing in more infrastructure, especially for regional economic integration, aid can help improve both growth and equity; and infrastructure is also central to building climate change resilience. Aid has demonstrated success in the social sectors, which receive the largest share of aid, driven by the Millennium Development Goals (MDGs) with their human development focus.

The 2013 UN High-Level Panel report on the post-2015 development agenda emphasizes economic (i.e. structural) transformation to create better livelihoods. While improving education and health do contribute to this, donors must rethink their engagement with the productive side of African economies if they are to contribute meaningfully to inclusive growth, especially job creation and employment. This implies reversing the neglect of agriculture

[1] Some 413.7 million people in SSA were poor at US$1.25 day (Purchasing Power Parity (PPP)) and 667 million people at US$2.5 a day (PPP) in 2010, on World Bank estimates (http://povertydata.worldbank.org/poverty/region/SSA).

that has characterized aid over the last 25 years, and addressing the growth and equity dilemmas in smallholder versus larger-scale farming. Donors must also become more open to new forms of industrial policy that help countries "learn to compete" in the global manufacturing and service economies.

Our chapter has a focus on growth, but we are cognizant of the key importance of issues associated with equity and sustainability; an increased economic pie can, if shared well, provide better lives for the many, not just the few, and the environmental capital on which Africa's prosperity rests must be preserved.[2] This chapter does not attempt coverage of the institutional issues around bilateral and multilateral aid, nor does it address the division of labor between traditional (OECD-DAC) donors and emerging ("new") donors, nor the large subject of humanitarian aid. Peter Quartey (*Handbook*, this volume, Chapter 43) analyses the trend, volume, and composition of aid, and issues around those data. Accordingly, we do not discuss these topics here.

The structure of this chapter is as follows: Aid and Growth: What Does Research Tell Us? (section 2); Africa in the Global Economy: How Can Aid Help? (section 3); Development Strategy Post 2015: What Role for Aid? (section 4); Conclusions: What Might the Future Hold for Aid to Africa? (section 5).

38.2 AID AND GROWTH: WHAT DOES RESEARCH TELL US?

Growth itself has many determinants and it is important to start with the research literature on the aid-growth relationship; as much of the popular debate on aid is bedeviled by the notion that aid has consistently failed to help achieve growth in the developing world. That literature until 2008 can usefully be divided into four generations, reflecting changes in both economic methodology and paradigms of development.

First, in the early years (roughly until around 1980) aid was seen as filling the gap between low domestic savings and high investment need, and financing the gap between imports and exports. Development was typically seen as a stable and linear relationship between investment and growth, and the consensus held that aid increased investment and thereby growth.

A *second* generation of studies was stimulated by the "micro–macro paradox" identified by Mosley (1987), whereby good returns at the project level did not seem to show up in macroeconomic cross-country studies. The expectations that all capital investment translates into economic output, and that all aid is used as investment were questioned. It also pointed out that countries tend to receive aid because they are poor and because their economic performance is poor. This endogeneity problem must be accounted for if empirical studies are to be accurate. Concerns were also raised about the misuse of aid by dictatorial regimes.

Doubts about the assumptions at the core of previous research, as well as the new availability of panel data, which allowed researches to look into the impact of aid both across and within countries over time, motivated a *third* generation of studies beginning in the early

---

[2] For comprehensive analysis of the many issues around aid, refer to UNU-WIDER's programme: Research and Communication (ReCom) on Foreign Aid (http://wider.unu.edu/recom).

1990s. Boone (1996), famously reviewed by *The Economist* under the heading: "Aid Down the Rat hole," found that aid had no impact on investment, infant mortality, and other indicators of human development. His work did not stand unchallenged for long. Burnside and Dollar (2000) argued that aid works, but only when "good" policies are in place. The third generation ended up being cautiously optimistic, but with disagreement over the circumstances under which aid works and has a positive impact.

This optimism is not reflected in the *fourth* generation that became influential around 2005. Rajan and Subramanian (2008) found that at the macro-level it is difficult to identify "any systematic effect of aid and growth." The study is widely used by aid's critics, and for researchers it seemed to resurrect the micro-macro paradox. A variety of explanations have been offered ranging from "Dutch Disease" (when a capital inflow appreciates the currency, potentially reducing exports) to the potential for aid to keep rent-seeking governments and poor institutions in place. However, aid could have the opposite effects: it can stimulate exports by improving infrastructure for example, and it can encourage institutional reform. Interesting theories and stories can be developed that both criticize and support aid, but few have actually tried to test them systematically with the available data.

Why have widely different conclusions been drawn in the aid–growth debate, given that many studies use the same publically available data? One major analytical difficulty is the question of causation. Aid is given to countries that are poor and are in difficulty. When they grow and do better donors tend to give less aid. So, it may look to the uninformed eye as if less aid is a good thing. It is of course a good thing to do better, but this by no means implies that aid did not support the growth to begin with. This analytical challenge is clearly not unique to the aid-growth debate and must be properly accounted for in any meaningful analysis.

Moreover, it is often said that since econometric models do not find a statistically significant effect of aid on growth then such a relationship does not exist. Yet, absence of evidence about impact is by no means equivalent to evidence of absence of impact. The fact that the relationship does not always seem to be statistically significant may have many causes, including problems with the length of time the dataset covers or the care with which the econometric analysis is done.

To move ahead, we need to disentangle the mechanisms through which aid may affect growth, and vice versa. Recent research since 2008 (a *fifth* generation maybe) has made important strides in this direction, including three main findings (UNU-WIDER 2013a).[3] First, an inflow of aid at the level of 10% of GDP spurs a more than 1 percentage point increase in annual per capita growth rate on average (Arndt et al. 2011). Thus foreign aid has facilitated economic growth at the aggregate level over the long term (i.e. the period 1970–2007). Investment in physical capital and health are two clearly identifiable channels through which aid promotes growth; education is another important area (see section 4 for further discussion) (Arndt et al. 2013a). Second, views that posit a non-existent or negative impact of development aid on growth have typically been based on misspecified models and errors in data interpretation (Juselius et al. 2011). Third, when foreign aid is evaluated as an investment, it has had very respectable internal rates of return since the mid-1970s (Arndt et al. 2013b).

---

[3] See also Brückner (2013), Clemens et al. (2012), and Minoiu and Reddy (2010).

Thus, the overall conclusion is that aid has, on balance and based on the latest up-to-date research since 2008, had a respectable effect on growth. This effect is in fact equivalent to what economists would generally expect based on current growth theory. So, there is no micro–macro paradox to be explained. In sum, aid has worked in promoting growth, and has worked well. At the same time, no informed individual would argue that aid has worked with equal effectiveness everywhere and that failures have not occurred Success is not assured; private investment also has its failures. Development is a risky business, especially in Africa.

38.3 Africa in The Global Economy: How Can Aid Help?

The organization and delivery of aid is characterized by complexity, high transactions costs, and insufficient coordination. Bigsten and Tengstam (2012) calculated that annual savings ranging from US$915 million to US$2 billion and beyond could be achieved if donors switch more of their aid from projects to programs, reduce the number of partner countries each works in, and generally coordinate more with each other and with recipient governments. The weaknesses are well known, and there are many ideas for improving the efficiency of aid, but political action has been slow (see Kharas and Rogerson 2012; Manning 2012). Consequently, rather than focusing on aid efficiency, we focus here on some of the bigger *strategic* questions for aid policy with respect to growth, equity, sustainability, and peace (a demanding set of objectives).

A number of African countries have graduated, or are near graduation, from LIC to MIC status.[4] The region's resource boom is one reason, and the dangers of "Dutch Disease" are much discussed. Some observers see it as a foregone conclusion that this story will end badly (Diamond and Mosbacher 2013). Yet, Dutch Disease is not inevitable if the resource rents are invested to diversify economies and reduce structural constraints; transactions costs then fall, and productivity rises. This amounts to shifting the export–supply curve rightwards to offset the impact on overall national competitiveness of the real exchange rate appreciation induced by the resource boom.

Aid is already doing this when it finances infrastructure investments serving the tradable sectors. This is one reason why aid itself has less of a Dutch Disease effect than the critics allege (see previous section). If aid helps facilitate the deepening of domestic financial markets, then it will make monetary policy instruments more effective in sterilizing the real-economy impact of resource revenues. More ambitiously, aid could engage closely with national strategies for structural transformation. There is a link here to the post-2015 development agenda which is discussed in the next section.

Terms of trade shocks are a concern, as most economies are small and open, and over-dependent on commodity exports, which provide nearly 80% of the region's total export earnings—with oil accounting for 57% of export earnings (AfDB et al. 2013: 66). Some 12 countries are net oil exporters, 44 are net importers.[5] Some 12 countries are net food

[4] Success in moving up from LIC to MIC status implies that countries will also graduate from concessional assistance from the International Development Association (IDA).
[5] US Energy Information Administration (http://www.eia.gov/).

importers, making them potentially vulnerable to global food price spikes (Ng and Aksoy 2008: 12). Africa's reliance on trade finance makes it especially vulnerable to banking crises in its trade partners (Berman and Martin 2012).

Africa's foreign exchange reserves are historically high; these cushioned the 2008–09 shocks from the financial crisis in the high-income countries. This is fortunate since bilateral aid is pro-cyclical with respect to the business cycle in high-income countries: recessions reduce aid by around 11% on average (Dabla-Norris et al. forthcoming). DAC aid is expected to show slower growth as the denominator in the ODA/GNI commitments is now below its pre-crisis trend (Addison et al. 2011).

Aid is more volatile than other sources of government revenue (Bulíř and Hamann 2008), imparting uncertainty to recipient budgets, which hinders public investment and macro-economic management. This is despite repeated pledges to make aid flows more predictable; see for example the "Paris Declaration" and the "Accra Agenda for Action" (OECD 2008). Aid for industrial development is the most volatile among the sectors that aid supports (Hudson forthcoming). This must change if donors want to engage with industrial policy (see next section).

The emerging economies now account for nearly a quarter of the market for Africa's commodity exports.[6] This partly offset the demand shock to commodity exports from the financial crisis in the high-income countries. But Africa is still vulnerable to any *synchronized* slowdown in both the high-income and emerging economies.

In summary, Africa's commodity exports are simultaneously a source of strength *and* weakness. Moving Africa up the global value-chain and diversifying reduces the risk of being over-dependent on unprocessed commodity exports; aid's role in agricultural and industrial development is discussed in section 4. Moreover, development cooperation has a continuing role to play in helping construct systems of public finance that transparently use resource rents and other revenues to expand public spending on services and infrastructure of benefit to the poor.

Stimulating internal demand as a driver of economic growth can also reduce the risks from global economic shocks. This is already happening as Africa's middle class is expanding with the growth of the last decade. But the opportunities existing at the "bottom of the pyramid" remain latent as income growth amongst the poor is still too slow.

To do this, donors can provide more support to smallholder agriculture (especially women farmers) and the rural non-farm economy (discussed in section 4). Emerging economies, notably the Latin Americans, can bring their expertise and innovation in social protection to Africa. Social protection raises (and stabilizes) consumption amongst the poor and can be a driver of local economy activity, especially in regions stuck in spatial poverty traps (still only weakly connected to national and international markets).[7]

---

[6] Emerging economies accounted for 22 per cent of Africa's exports in 2011, up from 8 per cent in 2000 (AfDB et al. 2013: 66).

[7] The Northern Uganda Social Action Fund provides one example of this linkage between consumption, livelihood and growth. A cash transfer programme to young people has the express objective of promoting local structural change, and this is working; those who receive the cash transfers are more likely to report non-agricultural work as their main occupation than those who did not (Blattman et al. 2013).

This approach is not new: Arthur Lewis emphasized rural demand as a promoter of industry in the Gold Coast (Lewis 1953). It also featured in early analysis of East Asia's take off (Ranis and Fei 1961), where the very first aid programs supported rural transformation. Altering the pattern of domestic demand in this way can help resolve the "iron triangle" of growth, inequality, and poverty (Bourguignon 2004) in favor of the poor—in addition to reducing growth's present dependence on global demand.

However, there is a catch: poor economies acting alone won't get very far; few local producers will prosper serving only a small home market—even a buoyant one. Regional market integration is imperative for domestic consumption growth to spread itself across borders and stimulate investment by producers. Inter-country trade is only 11% of Africa's total trade flow (in Asia it is 52%) and it has fallen in half over the last decade as commodity exports surged (AfDB et al. 2013: 67). Linkages to the continent's big growth poles (Nigeria and South Africa, especially) and between sub-Saharan Africa (SSA) and North Africa remain weak.

This is one reason to invest in cross-border transport and communications infrastructure (in addition to national infrastructure that shrinks spatial poverty traps). Another reason is to connect landlocked countries to coastal ports and global trade. Coastal countries do not internalize the positive externalities accruing to landlocked neighbors from transport infrastructure; under-investment is the result. Aid could be catalytic but it must leverage in private capital given the huge investment gap (and it needs to invest in both LICs *and* MICs to link lagging economies with those advancing). High tariffs and non-tariff barriers reduce the return on infrastructure investments that facilitate cross-border trade (UNCTAD 2013; World Bank 2012). If aid is to finance more infrastructure then it must do so within a policy framework for regional economic integration, including reduced trade barriers.

Infrastructure is also central to another big challenge for Africa and for aid: climate change, and environmental sustainability more broadly. Long-term planning and investment in road infrastructure must account for the increased maintenance and construction costs caused by increases in temperature, precipitation and flooding, (see Arndt et al. 2012 on the case of Mozambique, for example). Energy is also at a crunch point. Donors are pulling away from financing power generation from coal, a resource in which southern Africa is abundant. They are committed to renewables, which feature in the doubling of aid to the SSA energy sector over 2005–2011.[8] Yet, this amounts to only US$1 billion per annum, a drop in the ocean when compared to Africa's energy investment needs. Private sector investment in renewables is small, mainly due to the high cost of financing the capital for green energy. This leaves a vast financing gap that is presently unfilled.

Of course, action on climate change entails much more than infrastructure investment; societies must build resilience to cope with an increased frequency of natural disasters. At present, much more aid goes into emergency responses and reconstruction than disaster prevention (World Bank 2013). Climate change is an issue in which aid can only work well if a solid and comprehensive policy framework is created at the global level; this is not yet in place (UNU-WIDER 2013b). Africa's progress in growth could slide back with climate change, taking domestic revenues with it, thereby reversing the recent decline in aid dependence. Climate change is destabilizing and could reverse the progress achieved over the last decade in reducing conflict and state fragility in Africa.

---

[8] OECD-DAC data (http://stats.oecd.org/).

The ability of Africa's existing fragile states to absorb more aid (which often constitutes their largest financial inflow) is limited until their budgetary institutions show further improvement. This will slow the concentration of aid allocations on fragile states, which is occurring as LICs graduate to MICs, and as resource revenues rise. While the strategies of bilateral donors give more priority to fragile states, political criticism of any failure tends to raise their risk aversion. This intensifies their bias towards implementation via projects, which can be more tightly monitored and controlled than programme support to state-building. Fundamentally, the objective must be to help fragile states reduce their integration in the global economy via bad ways (piracy, human trafficking, narcotics, etc.) and increase the control of their states over resource revenues (which are often now in private hands) and invest these in inclusive growth via a transparent fiscal process (Addison 2012).

While growth reduces the probability of internal conflict, it is not a universal remedy. Conflict and political instability in Kenya (2008), Madagascar (2009), and Northern Uganda all occurred in periods of robust growth (and large aid inflows). Indeed, highly unequal growth can be destabilizing when the poor, having weak property rights, lose their access to assets, and when resource revenues are distributed unequally by the state. The risk of exclusive growth as an outcome of the iron triangle can be reduced if aid assists in diversifying economies, promotes domestic consumption as a growth driver, and helps regional economic integration. We now place these strategic considerations in the context of recent debate around the post-2015 development agenda.

38.4 DEVELOPMENT STRATEGY POST 2015: WHAT ROLE FOR AID?

The social sectors are at the core of OECD-DAC donor support to the Millennium Development Goals (MDGs), accounting for 42.6% of their aid commitments in 2011.[9] This aid has helped reduce under-five mortality, increase school enrolment, and combat HIV/AIDs, although social sector aid, along with aid in general, is still too fragmented to be fully effective (UNU-WIDER 2013c).

Will aid continue with its social sector focus after 2015? This would seem likely given the scale of education, health etc. in aid allocations, and the political support within donor countries for a human development approach. Yet the UN High-Level Panel report on the post-2015 development agenda calls for: "… A quantum leap forward in economic opportunities and a profound economic transformation to end extreme poverty and improve livelihoods" (UN 2013: 8). The report makes frequent reference to employment and inclusive growth. What does this imply?

Aid to the social sectors might be interpreted as broadly helping make this "quantum leap," through human capital formation, and the economic growth that results. There is evidence for this: Arndt et al. (2013a) found that an average annual inflow of US$25 aid per capita over the period of 1970-2007 augmented average schooling by 0.4 years, boosted life expectancy

---

[9] OECD-DAC data (http://stats.oecd.org/).

by 1.3 years, and reduced infant mortality by seven in every 1000 births. Improved human capital is one channel from aid to growth, livelihoods, and poverty (Arndt et al. (2013a) find a reduction in poverty of around 6.5 percentage points).

Nevertheless, the high-level panel report could be read as implying that in future donors should engage more *directly* with transformation and livelihoods.[10] This could lead to a change in aid policy, although aid is a slow-moving ship, and we should not expect any rapid reallocations.

There are many ways that donors could recalibrate their aid effort towards structural transformation and livelihoods if they decide to do so. Here we focus on agriculture, which remains central, and actions around the "new industrial policy," which has promise. Both need to take place within a framework of green growth, including adaption to climate change, and both entail large-scale infrastructure investment, as discussed in the previous section.

Moving their agriculture up the global value chain is one way that small open economies with good natural capital become richer. But what blend of large and small farms will achieve this for Africa? Will the poor participate as smallholders or, increasingly, as wage-laborers? How will Africa's women farmers fare? The closing of Africa's land frontier is already pushing many people towards wage-labor, and communal tenure is giving way to individual tenure (see Chapter 31, *Handbook*, this volume). In shrinking the area of cultivable land, climate change adds to the pressure.

Following the perceived failure of aid to large farms in the 1970s, agricultural aid now focuses on smallholders, encouraged by the "small but efficient" research literature. Investment in smallholder agriculture can help turn the iron triangle in favor of the poor, and there is some success.[11] But could large farms, interacting with small farms in ways that encourage scale economies in processing and marketing, deliver more of the productivity surge that Africa needs? Collier and Dercon (2013) argue this case, while rejecting "super-farms" of Latin American size.

Whether to expand donor support beyond small landholders is a key strategic issue for the future of aid to African agriculture. A well-designed strategy that does raise productivity through a blend of small and large farms, integrated with each other, could accelerate structural transformation. Yet, if large farms fail, then it is difficult to reverse back towards a small-holder path, and historically, large farm investment has led to land "grabbing" when property rights are weak (Deininger and Byerlee 2012). If large farms deliver growth, but higher inequality, then the poverty side of the iron triangle could actually worsen. India's Naxalite/Maoist conflict illustrates what happens when growth dispossesses the rural poor. An efficiency case for more large-scale farms may evolve, but when social stability is factored in, the large-farm case could still be second best to a smallholder focus. There are a series of dilemmas here that donors need to consider, as any deep engagement with Africa's structural transformation must put agriculture at its center—the question is how.

---

[10] The High Level report itself is quite light on discussion of aid, mostly reaffirming the need to keep to commitments, and to using aid to leverage more private capital (UN 2013: 3, for instance).

[11] In Malawi, the EU's Farmers Income Diversification Programme (FIDP) has successfully raised smallholder productivity and diversified crop income (Zant 2012). And in Mozambique, an integrated rural development project has improved food security (Nyyssölä et al. 2012).

Whichever pathway donors do support, their influence on the eventual outcome will be marginal if aid to African agriculture remains at today's very low level.[12] Agriculture's share fell to 2.7% of OECD-DAC aid in 2005.[13] It was 6% in 2011, but US$1.7 billion is tiny given that two-thirds of Africans make a living in agriculture. A refocusing of aid on agriculture is required if the "quantum leap" desired by the UN High Level Panel is to be a realistic aspiration. And this aid will be more effective if combined with less protectionism against agricultural exports in which Africa competes with high-income countries (the situation for aid-dependent Malawi, for example).

Structural transformation entails a movement out of agriculture (accelerating as its productivity rises) and into non-farm employment, ideally into manufacturing and services, with rising value-added (often with an urban location to reap the externalities that clustering offers). If achieved, this would secure a "quantum leap." But Africa is still far from this ideal; agriculture's employment share is falling, but informal services, mainly in petty commerce, account for most of the non-farm employment.[14] They provide a livelihood for the poor (women, especially) but typically a meager one.

Ideally, donors would back national strategies that have a realistic prospect of moving Africa decisively into today's global economy characterized by advanced manufacturing processes and high-value services, all connected by information technology. This is a global economy in which countries compete on quality, not just on price—often characterized by the sale of intermediate goods from one firm to another—and one which builds national capabilities by the interaction of domestic capital with foreign capital and knowledge, often via foreign direct investment (FDI) (Sutton 2012).[15] Aid-financed infrastructure investments in energy, transport and communications can help attract this FDI (Page 2012).

For development cooperation to move in this way, donors would need to absorb the knowledge on industrial policy and structural transformation now emerging from research. For the moment they have barely begun to engage with the idea of industrial policy as it is now debated. Instead, most of their attention is confined to small and medium-sized enterprises (SMEs) (Page and Söderbom 2012). Their virtue is labor intensity, so they offer the prospect of employment growth. But SMEs must overcome multiple constraints, not least in their access to credit (especially evident for female-owned firms: see Asiedu et al. 2013). The policy framework also over-regulates and over-taxes SMEs, and training is limited by a weak post-primary education system that leaves much of Africa's demographic "youth bulge" unskilled. Aid might help overcome such constraints, but spreading itself too thinly across a myriad of small-scale projects (as at present) will not work. Indeed, it could reinforce one of the weaknesses of Africa's SME manufacturing sector, which is that the average firm size is very small, and small firms find it hard to grow and export.[16]

---

[12] Chimhowu (2013) discusses the decline in agricultural aid.

[13] OECD-DAC data (http://stats.oecd.org/).

[14] See UNU-WIDER (2013a), and Jones and Tarp (2013) on Mozambique, for instance.

[15] This is important as well for improving macroeconomic stability, as noted earlier. The share of manufactures in the value of African exports fell from 21% in 2000 to 16% in 2011 (AfDB et al. 2013: 66).

[16] A comparison using World Bank enterprise surveys finds that in SSA the average size is about 47 employees; this contrasts with 171 employees in Malaysia, 195 in Vietnam, 393 in Thailand, and 977 in China (Clarke and Dinh 2012: 6).

SMEs will prosper if they have a chance of participating in well-defined strategies for industrial and service-sector development that build national capabilities and reduce national constraints; donors need to thoroughly understand how these can be built, drawing especially on the knowledge around Asia's successes.[17]

38.5 Conclusions: What Might the Future Hold for Aid to Africa?

The slogans "trade not aid," "foreign investment not aid", and so on are regularly trotted out as if these were substitute pathways for development that African governments must choose between. This chapter has emphasized how aid might stimulate trade in ways that accelerate development, crowd-in private investment by providing public goods, and integrate Africa in the global economy in ways that promote inclusive growth, and thereby peace.

The context within which ODA operates has shifted dramatically since the heady optimism of the post-independence 1960s, the disillusion of the 1970s, the trauma of the 1980s, and the strife of the 1990s which gave way to the optimism of today. The very success of many African countries in achieving growth reduces old risks, but opens them to new risks for policymakers to grapple with. Development strategy is never finalized, it must be adjusted over time to take new opportunities, deal with new risks—and cope with the unexpected. Donors must bring good *ideas* to the table, not just finance, for aid is now a declining part of a growing and more diverse system of development finance, as the other chapters in this *Handbook* show.

The resolution of Africa's "iron triangle" in favor of inclusive growth requires attention to the productive sectors, a priority highlighted by the UN high-level panel on the post-2015 development agenda. But the volume of aid is now growing at a slower rate than before the financial crisis. It seems therefore that any meaningful rise in agricultural and industrial aid must come from the social sectors, which is undesirable, given aid's high returns in education and health. Yet if aid for the productive sectors does not rise from its currently low level, then donors could find themselves irrelevant to the "quantum leap" demanded by the UN high level panel. This is a dilemma that the donor community must address over the coming years.

References

AfDB/OECD/UNDP/UN-ECA (2013). *African Economic Outlook 2013: Structural Transformation and Natural Resources*. African Development Bank, Organisation for Economic Co-operation and Development, United Nations Development Programme, Economic Commission for Africa.

Addison, T. (2012). The political economy of fragile states, in G.K. Brown and A. Langer (eds), *Elgar Handbook of Civil War and Fragile States*. Cheltenham: Edward Elgar, pp. 363–378.

[17] See Lin (2011) and Page (2012) for instance.

Addison, T., Arndt, C., and Tarp, F. (2011). The triple crisis and the global aid architecture. *African Development Review*, 23(4):461–478.

Arndt, C., Chinowsky, P., Strzepek, K., and Thurlow, J. (2012). Climate change, growth and infra-structure investment: the case of Mozambique. *Review of Development Economics*, 16(3):463–475.

Arndt, C., Jones, S., and Tarp, F. (2011). Aid Effectiveness: Opening the Black Box. WIDER Working Paper 2011/44, Helsinki: UNU-WIDER.

Arndt C., Jones S., and Tarp, F. (2013a). Assessing foreign aid's long-run contribution to growth in development, WIDER Working Paper 2013/072. Helsinki: UNU-WIDER.

Arndt, C., Jones, S., and Tarp, F. (2013b). What is the Aggregate Economic Return to Foreign Aid? WIDER Working Paper. Helsinki: UNU-WIDER.

Asiedu, E., Kalonda-Kanyama, I., Ndikumana, L., and Nti-Addae, A. (2013). Access to credit by firms in sub-Saharan Africa: how relevant is gender? *American Economic Review*, 103(3):293–297.

Berman, N., and Martin, P. (2012). The vulnerability of sub-Saharan Africa to financial crises: the case of trade. *IMF Economic Review*, 60(3):330–364.

Bigsten, A., and Tengstam, S. (2012). International Coordination and the Effectiveness of Aid, WIDER Working Paper 2012/32, Helsinki: UNU-WIDER.

Blattman, C., Fiala, N., and Martinez, S. (2013). Generating skilled self-employment in devel-oping countries: Experimental evidence from Uganda. *Quarterly Journal of Economics*.

Boone, P. (1996). Politics and the effectiveness of foreign aid. *European Economic Review*, 40(2):289–329.

Bourguignon, F. (2004). The Poverty-Growth-Inequality Triangle. Paper presented at the Indian Council for Research on International Economic Relations, New Delhi, February 4.

Brückner, M. (2013). On the simultaneity problem in the aid and growth debate. *Journal of Applied Econometrics*, 28(1):126–150.

Bulíř, A., and Hamann, J. (2008). Volatility of development aid: From the frying pan into the fire? *World Development*, 36(10):2048–2066.

Burnside, C., and Dollar, D. (2000). Aid, policies, and growth. *American Economic Review*, 90(4):847–868.

Chimhowu, A. (2013). Aid for Agriculture and Rural Development: A Changing Landscape with New Players and Challenges, WIDER Working Paper 2013/014. Helsinki: UNU-WIDER.

Clarke, G.R.G., and Dinh, Hinh T., (2012). Overview, in H.T. Dinh and G.R.G. Clarke (eds), *Performance of Manufacturing Firms in Africa: An Empirical Analysis*. Washington, DC: World Bank, pp. 1–26.

Clemens, M., Radelet, S., and Bhavnanni, R. (2012). Counting chickens when they hatch: tim-ing and the effects of aid on growth. *Economic Journal*, 122(558):1–28.

Collier, P., and Dercon, S. (2013). African agriculture in 50 years: Smallholders in a rapidly changing world? *World Development*.

Dabla-Norris, E., Minoiu, C., and Zanna, L-P. (forthcoming). Business cycle fluctuations, large macroeconomic shocks, and development aid. *World Development*. UNU-WIDER Special Issue on Aid Policy and the Macroeconomic Management of Aid.

Deininger, K., and Byerlee, D. (2012). The rise of large farms in land abundant countries: do they have a future? *World Development*, 40(4):701–714.

Diamond, L., and Mosbacher, J. (2013). Petroleum to the people: Africa's coming resource curse—and how to avoid it. *Foreign Affairs*, September/October.

Hudson, J. (forthcoming). Consequences of Aid Volatility for Macroeconomic Management and Aid Effectiveness, *World Development*. UNU-WIDER Special Issue on Aid Policy and the Macroeconomic Management of Aid.

Jones, S., and Tarp, F. (2013). Jobs and Welfare in Mozambique: Country Case Study for 2013 World Development Report, WIDER Working Paper 2013/45. Helsinki: UNU-WIDER.

Juselius, K., Møller, N.F., and Tarp, F. (2011). The Long-Run Impact of Foreign Aid in 36 African Countries: Insights from Multivariate Time Series Analysis. WIDER Working Paper 2011/51. Helsinki: UNU-WIDER.

Kharas, H., and Rogerson, A. (2012). *Horizon 2025: Creative Destruction in the Aid Industry.* London: Overseas Development Institute.

Lewis, A.W. (1953). *Report on the Industrialisation of the Gold Coast.* Accra: Government Printer of the Gold Coast.

Lin, J.Y. (2011). From Flying Geese to Leading Dragons: New Opportunities and Strategies for Structural Transformation in Developing Countries. WIDER Annual Lecture 15. Helsinki: UNU-WIDER.

Manning, R. (2012). Aid as a Second-Best Solution: Seven Problems of Effectiveness and How to Tackle Them. WIDER Working Paper 2012/32. Helsinki: UNU-WIDER.

Minoiu, C., and Reddy, S.G. (2010). Development aid and economic growth: A positive long-run relation. *Quarterly Review of Economics and Finance,* 50(1):27–39.

Mosley, P. (1987). *Overseas Aid: Its Defence and Reform.* Brighton: Wheatshead Books.

Ng, F., and Aksoy, M.A. (2008). Who Are the Net Food Importing Countries? World Bank Policy Research Working Paper 4457.

Nyyssölä, M., Pirttilä J., and Sandström, S. (2012). Helping Poor Farmers to Help Themselves: Evidence from a Group-Based Aid Project in Mozambique. WIDER Working Paper 2012/88. Helsinki: UNU-WIDER.

OECD (2008). *The Paris Declaration on Aid Effectiveness and the Accra Agenda for Action.* Paris: OECD.

Page, J. (2012). Aid, Structural Change and the Private Sector in Africa. WIDER Working Paper 2012/21. Helsinki: UNU-WIDER.

Page, J., and Söderbom, M. (2012). Is Small Beautiful? Small Enterprise, Aid and Employment in Africa. WIDER Working Paper 2012/94. Helsinki: UNU-WIDER.

Rajan, R.G., and Subramanian, A. (2008). Aid and growth: What does the cross-country evidence really show? *Review of Economics and Statistics,* 90(4):643–665.

Ranis, G., and Fei, J.C.H. (1961). A theory of economic development. *American Economic Review,* LI(4):533–565.

Sutton, J. (2012). *Competing in Capabilities: The Globalization Process.* Oxford: Oxford University Press (Clarendon Lectures).

UN (2013). *A New Global Partnership: Eradicate Poverty and Transform Economies Through Sustainable Development.* New York: United Nations.

UNCTAD (2013). *Economic Development in Africa Report 2013: Intra-African Trade: Unlocking Private Sector Dynamism,* Geneva: UNCTAD.

UNU-WIDER (2013a). *Aid, Growth and Employment.* Helsinki: UNU-WIDER (ReCom Position Paper).

UNU-WIDER (2013b). *Aid, Environment, and Climate Change.* Helsinki: UNU-WIDER (ReCom Position Paper).

UNU-WIDER (2013c). *Aid, Poverty and the Social Sectors.* Helsinki: UNU-WIDER (ReCom Position Paper).

World Bank (2012). *De-Fragmenting Africa: Deepening Regional Trade integration in Goods and Services.* Washington, DC: World Bank.

World Bank (2013). *World Development Report 2014: Risk and Opportunity—Managing Risk for Development*, Washington DC: World Bank.

Zant, W. (2012). Is EU Support to Malawi Agriculture Effective? Tinbergen Institute Discussion Paper TI 2012-090/V, Faculty of Economics and Business Economics, VU University Amsterdam, and Tinbergen Institute.

CHAPTER 39

......

REMITTANCES TO AFRICA AND ECONOMICS

......

CHRISTIAN NSIAH AND BICHAKA FAYISSA

39.1 INTRODUCTION

ACCORDING to the World Bank (Ratha et al. 2011), remittances to Africa since 1990 have quadrupled to about US$40 billion representing about 2.6% of GDP in 2010, making it the continent's largest inflow of foreign capital after foreign direct investment (FDI). The large increase in remittances can serve as a boon to recipient countries because remittances are more stable and countercyclical in nature, thus helping to smooth domestic consumption, investment, and foreign exchange reserves. Remittances can also help reduce poverty and income inequality, increase educational attainment, and spur domestic investment. However, large inflows of remittances may cause an appreciation of domestic currencies and thereby cause domestically produced tradables to be less competitive globally.

The contribution of remittances as a proactive development strategy has been controversial in the literature. Many empirical studies have shown a positive effect of remittances on economic growth and development (e.g. Stark and Lucas 1988; Bansak and Chezum 2009; Fayissa and Nsiah 2010). The proponents of the positive impact of remittances argue for its consumption smoothing, investment in physical and human capital, and reduction of poverty contribution. On the other hand, opponents argue that the negative effects of remittances on economic growth outweigh their positive effects if the inflow of remittances cause exchange rate volatility, inflation, or overheating of the economy by increasing consumption and displacing savings (e.g. Chami et al. 2003; IMF 2005), resulting in a phenomenon known as the "Dutch disease."

This chapter presents both sides of this debate, drawing from the existing literature and applying them to the role that remittances play in African economies. The chapter provides some hints towards future policy directions for leveraging remittances as a supplemental growth initiative. Efforts will be made to evaluate the uniqueness, long-run reliability, and resilience of remittances made by African migrants who are typically younger and relatively more educated than their cohorts from other regions of the world.

The main goal of economic growth and development is to improve the well-being of people by reducing poverty and income inequality. For the majority of African countries, which heavily rely on the external sources for financing their development projects, any financial injection which bolsters the domestic financial sources is crucial in providing critical services including health, education, transportation, etc. Even though many African countries possess vast raw material endowments, for myriad of reasons the domestic resource base has not yet been fully harnessed to address major development challenges of the continent.

The chapter is organized as follows. Section 2 presents the theoretical underpinnings of the motives of remittances. This section also examines the determinants of remittances in order to understand the causal factors enhancing or impeding the propensity of migrants to remit. In section 3, we present the impact of remittances on key growth and development indicators. Section 4 provides summary and conclusion and also hints at future policy directions.

39.2 REMITTANCE MOTIVES

39.2.1 Microeconomic theory

Given the growing importance of remittances as a source of foreign capital, it is imperative to discuss how international remittances arise. Previous studies (UNCTAD 2011) have shown that international remittances have been rising, globally reaching US$300 billion over the past two decades and surpassing development assistance (ODA) and FDI. Therefore, analyses of the determinants and the channels through which remittances impact economic growth in Africa is essential. The unique features of remittances to Africa are that they are less volatile in comparison to the ODA or FDI (Gupta et al. 2007) and that most African migrants have relatively higher level of educational attainment than their cohorts. An OECD database (OECD 2006) reveals that more than half of educated African workforce migrates to OECD Countries. Such substantial "brain drain" begs the question of whether there is a net gain from migration considering the balance between the loss of skilled workers and the remittance inflows which are expected to be invested in health and education beyond what is used for consumption smoothing, resulting in "brain gain." It may be reasonable to presume a net gain from the stock of African migrants considering the widespread instability and internal strife which tend to limit productive employment opportunities of the educated workforce which is better equipped to flow to the poles of opportunities.

In spite of the sustained growth of remittances to Africa, its determinants, impact, reliability, and sustainability are all controversial topics of discussion. This section discusses the overarching theoretical motives of remittances to Africa.

Demographically, African migrants are more educated than their cohorts from other countries. The stringent nature of acquiring visas to travel from African countries to the major host countries may have resulted in the selection bias toward more educated and skilled African migrants to reduce the probability of dependency of migrants once they are allowed to enter host countries, especially when the economy of host countries are experiencing downturns. According to data from the Immigration Policy Center of the American Immigration Council (2012), for example, almost 40% of African migrants in the USA worked in professional fields including positions in management, business, science, and arts in 2010.

The literature on migration and remittances indicates that there are many theories of why migrants remit to their home countries, but we focus on the two main reasons[1] to remit, which include pure altruism on one hand and self-interest to secure some type of inheritance and/or to invest in home country assets with the expectation of a return on this investment (Lucas and Stark 1985). The widely cited motive of remittances is altruism or the unselfish concern for the welfare of others (Carling 2008; Lartey, 2013). For purely altruistic motive, migrants remit solely for the upkeep of family members in the home countries, increasing with migrants' income and decreasing with rising of recipients' income (countercyclical). Remittances may be used to finance consumption of both durable and non-durable goods, health, and education expenditures, with a small portion going to savings and long-term investments.

The self-interest motive indicates that migrants remit in order to invest in real estate, land, financial markets, or in a business at home. This type of remittances may increase with migrant's proximity to family at home, migrant's intention to return, or higher expected return which depends on the economic conditions at home, financial services development, and transaction costs (procyclical).

The literature for the altruistic motives has been expanded to reveal other possible reasons why people may remit including: repayment of prior loans, insurance, diversifying risk, and exchange for a variety of services including parent and child care, and protection of property. Lucas and Stark (1985) call these motives "enlightened selfishness," whereas Adreoni (1989) identifies them as "impure altruism." These motives which lie between pure altruism and pure self-interest in the continuum of motives to remit have given rise to two new theories of remittances including social network (SN) and New Economics of Labor Migration (NELM) theories.

Under the SN theory, remittances are regarded as an exchange between members of a social network linked by some commonalities (mostly family ties). The transfers between the members of network are based on explicit or implicit arrangements between the migrants and the members of the network in the home country where migrants remit in exchange for past, current, or future exchanges including child and parent care, protection of investment (such as real estate) at home. According to Englama (2009), such remittance types may be lower when the home economies are not doing well and higher during good economic times because labor compensations may rise in the home country.

The NELM theory states that migration occurs as a risk sharing strategy of families, where individual families try to diversify their resources including labor in order to minimize their risk exposure (Lucas and Stark 1985; Quinn 2006). Here, family members subscribe to implicit co-insurance agreements to finance the migration of a family member who will reimburse them through regular remittances, or assist them in times of need. This allows the migrant's family to smoothen their consumption pattern at home. There is no conclusive empirical evidence on the overall motive of remittances in the African case. While some find altruism as the main reason, others find self-interest as the main motive to remit.

---

[1] Lucas and Stark (1985) pioneered the theoretical research on the motives for remittances which can span the continuum between pure altruism and self-interest (investment) purposes.

Fonchamnyo (2012) found a positive and significant relationship between remittances and the per capita income (PCI) differential between host and home countries and the age dependency ratio, and a negative relationship between the level of PCI of the home country and remittances received when altruism is an important motive. Lartey (2013) concurred with Fonchamnyo's (2012) assertion that altruism is the main driving motive for Africans to remit based on close ties between migrants and family members at home. Kemegue et al. (2011) found that remittances from South Africa to the South African Development Cooperation (SADC) region are primarily driven by: the quality of financial service delivery, investment opportunities in the home country, and migrant expectations of home country exchange rates. These discussions on the motives to remit suggest that a variety of non-mutually exclusive motives may determine the propensity and magnitude of remittances by African migrants.

39.2.1.1 Remittance and time

Ghosh (2006) argued that remittances may decay over time primarily due to deterioration of the bonds between the migrants and their family at home over time, caused in part by the assimilation of migrants into the host country's society. In particular, he argues that the propensity and size of remittances are comparatively larger for low-skilled migrants because high-skilled migrants integrate to the host's society faster and are more likely to invest in host countries. If this finding holds for all developing countries, then the future growth prospects of remittances for African countries is not encouraging, especially considering the fact that African migrants tend to be more educated and as such assimilate faster. Remittance decay may also be due to reverse migration caused by either migrants returning home to take advantage of lucrative positions provided by improved home country economic conditions, or just to start their own businesses with accrued wealth.

De Hass and Plug (2006), however, indicated that remittance decay is yet to be observed at least at the rate predicted by the decay hypothesis because of the sustained family bonds and sustained migration. The extended family system is the utmost system in Africa, making people raised in such environment naturally bonded to their extended family for ages. The current improvement in reliability, access, and cost of international communication including innovations and the wide spread use of tools such as mobile phones, Skype, Facebook, etc., makes it easier, convenient, and cheaper for migrants to stay in touch with their families back at home, thus lessening the possibility of significant family bond and remittances decay overtime. Further, the wealth acquired by returning migrants serves as a catalyst for many others to migrate.

It's argued that the educated migrants are less likely to remit home because they are likely to invest in host countries. Since high-skilled migrants are more likely to settle in the host country, they have a choice between investing in the host country or at home, and as such are less likely. Rational theory predicts that they will always choose to invest in a market with the highest expected return on their investment. Thus, to sustain the propensity and magnitude of remittances of the skilled workers, it will be imperative for the home country governments to implement policies which increase the expected return on investment including land and property rights protection, financial sector development, political and economic stability, and an increased voice for its members in diaspora.

39.2.2 Macroeconomic determinants of remittances

39.2.2.1 *Migrant stock*

At the macroeconomic level, one of the main determinants of remittances is the size of stock of migrants. It is plausible to posit that higher levels of remittance inflows to the home country would occur when there are a large number of migrants in a host country (Freund and Spatafora 2005).

One may, however, argue that it is not the size of migrants that determines the volume of remittances, but rather the quality of the migrant population. Migrants who hold better paying jobs based on their skillset and experience are likely meet their own immediate needs and be able to remit home to support their family in paying for better education and health. Most studies on remittances to sub-Sahara African countries exhibit a positive relationship between remittances and migrant stock. For example, Fayissa and Nsiah (2010) and Singh et al. (2011) argue that countries with large migrants in the diaspora attract more remittances. Using data from *World Development Indicators* for 1980 to 2011, we plot average remittances to migrant stock for each African country in Figure 39.1. The trend line shows a slight positive relationship between remittances and migrant stock. The migrant stock, however, does not explain much of the variation in remittances for the period under consideration (R^2=0.0018). This indicates that other variables and migrant characteristics may explain most of the variation in remittances.

Other reasons why migrant stock may not determine remittances may include issues relating to opportunities for integration and settlement, and the exclusion of Africans in the diaspora from the politics and society of their home countries. If these migrants feel as integral members of their countries with a voice in the affairs of their country, and the protection and preservation of their rights and privileges as citizens of their home country, they may be inclined to remit more, however, many African countries have rules that may alienate some of their migrants which may lead to lower remittances.

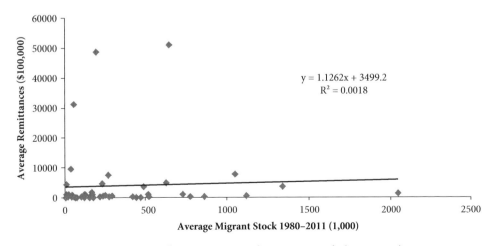

FIGURE 39.1 Average annual remittances and migrant stock (1980–2011).

Since the era of independence of many African countries in the 1950s and 1960s, migrants were denied dual citizenship primarily in an effort to ensure loyalty. For example, only 11 African countries allow for unrestricted dual citizenship after naturalization as of 2012.[2] Currently, there are 23 African countries that allow for some level of dual citizenship. Ghana is an interesting example because it allows for dual citizenship, but bans dual citizens from holding public positions. All else equal, migrants from African countries that allow for dual citizenship will have more home affinity and as such have "home return" desire at heart and, hence, may remit more for both altruistic and self-interest reasons.

Given their immense contributions via remittances, it is justified that members of the diaspora have the right to participate in the electoral process, making voting rights for Africans in the diaspora in their home countries an important issue. Allowing migrants to feel part of the decision-making process at home may result in less decrease in remittances regardless of the motives to remit. Some African countries have started including provisions in their constitution to extend this right to their citizens in the diaspora; however, the main issue holding back this process is the logistics of implementing these policies and the lack of trust in the electoral process in most African nations. African governments may also develop creative financial instruments like the Indian government's diaspora bonds, floated to entice Indians in the diaspora to invest in India. Well-developed financial markets may provide dispersed Africans more options for portfolio investments at home.

39.2.2.2 *Home country's economic and political situation*

Previous research on the impact of the home country economic and political situation on remittances has been inconclusive. If remittances are sent for purely altruistic purposes, then they will increase during bad economic conditions and fall during good economic conditions (Bouhga-Hagbe 2006). According to Cox et al. (1998), the relationship between home country income and remittances may not be linear (i.e. varying according to different income quantiles).

The economic condition in the home country may impact remittances via other channels. From the self-interest theory of remittances, one can argue that depending on the expected returns, migrants may remit for investment purposes. Purely monetary expected returns will mean that improved economic and political conditions at home may lead to increased remittances, indicating a pro-cyclical relationship (Higgins et al. 2004).

If remittances are for investment purposes, then the level of remittances may be inversely related to the general risks of the home country, including political instability, rule of law, and property rights. Political instability or low levels of law and order may deter remittances since such an environment is not conducive for investment purposes (IMF 2005). Macroeconomic instability such as high inflation or real exchange rate hyperinflation may cause a reduction in remittances (Glytsos 1988; Elbadawi and Rocha 1992). Other general conditions in the home country such as exchange rate policy and interest rate differentials between home and host country may have an impact on the levels of remittances.

---

[2] The African countries that allow for general dual citizenship are: Benin, Burkina Faso, Cape Verde, Central African Republic, Cote d'Ivoire, Ghana, Morocco, Namibia, Nigeria, Togo, and Tunisia.

From the self-interest theory perspective, one can infer that a high interest rate differential between the home country and the host country will push rent-seeking African migrants to remit more money home to take advantage of the high interest rates. However, general empirical studies on remittances including El-Sakka and McNabb (1999), Elbadawi and Rocha (1992), Chami et al. (2003, 2009) found remittances are either negatively associated with high interest rate differentials, or don't find any significant relationship at all. In the case of sub-Sahara African countries, Singh et al. (2011) found a significantly negative association between remittances and interest rate differentials because high interest rates in the African countries are likely to be indicative of instability in sub-Saharan African countries; however, they found a positive relationship between institutions and remittances. Kemegue et al. (2011) on the other hand found that interest rate differentials between home and host countries significantly and positively impact remittances, given that exchange rate expectations are predictable. Other domestic conditions found to positively impact remittances include institutions (Singh et al. 2011) and economic performance (Adenutsi et al. 2011).

39.2.2.3 Host country economic condition

The well-being of migrants in the host nation is an important determinant of remittances flows. The IMF (2005) argued that improved economic conditions in host nations increase migrant's earnings prospects, which increases their disposable income, thus increasing remittances.

Contrarily, migrants may see investment in home country as a substitute for investment in the host country and as such may channel more of their income to investment opportunities at home by remitting more during bad economic conditions in the host country and vice versa if the two economies are not positively correlated.

From the altruistic motive for remittances, one would have expected a wholesale and continuous reduction to the propensity and magnitude of remittances to this region and all other developing countries during the recent global crisis; however, disregarding a slight dip in 2009, remittances to Africa have experienced continuous growth. Specifically, Ratha and Sirkeci (2010) found that remittances to developing countries only fell by 5.2% in 2009, thus proving to be the most resilient source of foreign capital flows.

In their analysis of remittances to Africa, Singh et al. (2011) and Kemegue et al. (2011) found that host country economic conditions have a positive impact on remittances to sub-Saharan Africa indicating that African migrants remit more when economic conditions in host countries positively impact their income. Generally, they find that both host and home country conditions impact remittances, however, host country conditions trumps that of home countries in determining remittances to sub-Saharan Africa.

39.2.3 Channels, costs, and speed of remittance transfers

39.2.3.1 Transaction costs

According to the World Bank, about 50% of all remittances go through informal channels (Niimi and Özden 2006). The figure for the informal channel may even be higher for African countries due to the high transaction costs of remittances. Based on the World Bank's Send

Money to Africa database, the cost is very high, with the most expensive remittance corridors found in Africa. The average international remittances to Africa in December 2012 costs about 12% of the remittance amount, whereas inter-African regional remittances cost about 20% of the remittances in comparison to the global average of about 9% (Kamgnia and Murinde 2012).

In dollar terms, of the US$51 billion formal remittances sent by African migrants to their home countries, about US$8 billion is paid as transaction fees to the banks and money transfer institutions (MTIs), resulting in a decrease in the propensity and magnitude of remittances, and the use of informal means of remitting by African migrants (i.e. friends and acquaintances). According to the World Bank report, the cost has been increasing rather than decreasing over time. Freund and Spatafora (2008) found that remittance fees are negatively related with total remittance flows. The high transaction costs also leads to a leakage from the potential multiplier effect of remittances on economic growth and poverty reduction, resulting in their real impact unknown.

Remittances transaction costs are normally comprised of a fee charged by remittance services providers and currency conversion fees for the delivery of the domestic currency to recipients in the home countries. The reasons why transaction costs for remittances to African countries are so high include lack of transparency, competition, regulatory framework, exclusive contracts, and financial sector underdevelopment.

Competition in the money transfer business, just like any other market leads to high efficiency levels which can be passed on to customers in the form of lower transaction costs. The competitiveness of a country's money transfer industry is determined by the number and types of market players, their operation efficiency, and the range of services they provide. Several African countries have a legal and regulatory framework set up to deal with large cross-border transactions between corporations rather than the flow of small denomination transfers. These regulatory set-ups hinder the entry of other financial intermediaries into the remittances transfer business thus establishing a market with few players having a significant market power, impacting the transaction costs, the speed and ease with which these transactions are completed. Whereas only a few countries allow other institutions such as Forex exchange centers, microfinance institutions, post offices, etc., to serve as payout centers, most of the payments occur in banks.

Generally, advanced financial sectors are expected to increase competition, reduce costs, and also in many cases offer potential portfolio investment options for African migrants seeking rents on their remittances. The creation and implementation of innovative financial products such as microfinance institutions will positively impact recipients' and remitters' marginal propensity to save and invest for every amount remitted is essential. Thus all else equal, we expect remittances to increase with improvements in the financial sector. However, remittances may serve as "vacuum filler" for imperfect financial markets and credit systems with very poor financial infrastructure. Because of the very primitive nature of African financial systems, remittances are used to loosen liquidity constraints, serve as collateral, and finance small-scale investment projects. This argument leads to the remittances-led financial services sector growth (RLG) hypothesis, where remittances lead to financial deepening in the recipient countries. Kemegue et al. (2011) found that African countries with well-developed and technologically advanced financial services industry and institutions attract more formal remittances.

Freund and Spatafora (2008) also showed that remittances are transmitted through formal channels in countries with well-developed financial systems, whereas the patronage of the informal sector is larger for countries with less financial sector development. For example, in a dynamic panel study of African and Latin American countries, Fayissa and Nsiah (2012) found that financial sector development has a positive and statistically significant effect on remittances.

A new development likely to help resolve the problems of accessibility, capacity, speed, flexibility, and high transaction cost of remittance transfer to Africa is telecommunication companies implementing mobile phone remittance payment services. The most successful African mobile remittances payout network is the M-Pesa in Kenya which has experienced astronomical growth in use since its inception in 2007. All else equal, countries with advanced mobile pay systems in place will experience lower transaction costs for remittances due to increased competition and easy access to market. In particular, Mbiti and Weil (2011) found that the wide use of M-Pesa will likely cause decreases in the prices of competing MTI's including Western Union and MoneyGram.

Another reason why the transaction cost is high for the African continent as a whole is because most of the countries have exclusivity contracts with one or both of the major players in the continent's money transfer business (Western Union and MoneyGram), thus restricting entry of other firms. Some countries including Ghana and Nigeria have recently moved to ban such exclusive contracts between their banks and the two money transfer giants.

Further, lack of transparency associated with the industry may contribute to the high transaction costs. The inability to compare prices of MTIs makes intentional selection of lowest cost alternative impossible. The World Bank and some of its development partners have collaborated to facilitate the African Union Commission in establishing the African Institute for Remittances (AIR) project whose main objective is to develop the capacity of the member states of the African Union, remitters and recipients, and other stakeholders to implement concrete strategies and operational instruments to use remittances as a development tool for poverty reduction. The AIR project and the World Bank recently launched the "Send Money Africa" remittance price database, which is designed to allow users to compare costs charged by remittance service providers to Africa.

39.3 REMITTANCES AND ECONOMIC DEVELOPMENT

There are two opposing viewpoints when it comes to the impact of remittances on economic growth and development. The optimistic view argues that remittances represent a positive inflow of funds to receiving households and could be used to alleviate poverty, promote economic growth through savings and investments in both physical and human capital, and also ease pressures on governments due to external deficits. The pessimists treat remittances as a detriment to the growth and development of the receiving countries causing the "Dutch disease."

It is in the contexts of the above viewpoints we explore the role of remittances on the economic growth and development of African countries. More specifically, we address the role that remittances by African migrants play in providing the much-needed funds from external sources, not only for consumption smoothing, but also for investment in human capital in the form of education, health, and nutrition. Specifically, this section will address the link between remittances and economic growth and development in terms of: human capital development, poverty reduction, health, inequality, domestic investments/savings, and the Dutch Disease.

39.3.1 Remittances and household consumption smoothing

The effect of household consumption shocks due to recurrent draught periods and crop failures, unemployment, and under-employment can be partially mitigated by remittance inflows by a household member who sends money to avoid the instability of consumption spending during hard economic conditions (Azam and Gubert 2005). In a recent study, Combes and Ebeke (2011) find that remittances significantly reduce household consumption instability because they serve as insurance by dampening the effect of consumption fluctuations in less financially developed countries precipitated by natural disasters, agricultural shocks (crop failure), and austere discretionary fiscal policy. This stabilizing effect of remittances may in itself generate sustained levels of investments that will lead to more economic growth. Note that even if the largest portion of remittances is geared toward consumption, they may still have a growth effect through the multiplier effect and since remittances are more stable than other foreign sources of income, the growth associated with remittances may actually be sustainable in the long run.

39.3.2 Remittances and human capital formation

Remittance receiving households experience a loosening of their budget constraints, thereby increasing consumption of durable and non-durable goods and investment in human capital. From previous research, one can argue that remittances generally tend to have a positive impact on human capital formation and economic growth. Increasing income through remittances may increase investment in children's education by relaxing household budget and capital constraints (Bansk and Chezum 2009). According to Ratha et al. (2011), remittance receiving households spent more on education than non-remittance receiving households. Thus, remittances may be the catalyst of higher human capital attainment in the continent.

Bansak and Chezum (2009) suggested that observable progress toward gender parity has been made in Africa in primary and secondary education over past two decades through remittances. While a conclusive direct link may be difficult to establish, there is no question that remittances have played a role toward gender parity of girls and boys. Women are gaining ground in the labor market and are assuming powerful leadership roles in parliaments.

The other avenue through which remittances can impact human capital is through health. With the increase in funds through remittances, households are able to consume ample amount of nutrients, increased access to healthcare, and improvement in the overall health of the workforce, which may all improve economic growth and development of recipient countries. While the positive impact of remittances on economic growth and development is empirically supported (Stark and Lucas 1988; Ahortor and Adenutsi 2009)

39.3.3 Remittances, poverty, and inequality

According to the 2012 World Bank's Regional Highlights of the *World Development Indicators*, a third of the world's poorest people live in sub-Saharan Africa. The report also indicates that for the first time, in 2005 the number of people living in extreme poverty (under US$1.25 a day) started to decline in Africa, but the number of people living on US$2 a day is increasing. Without an injection of foreign capital, this scenario may perpetuate a long-term vicious cycle of poverty.

With remittances overtaking all other sources of foreign capital inflows to Africa, except FDI, its impact on poverty has become more important. Theoretically, one can assume that increases in remittances can lead to the loosening up of recipient households' budget constraints thus leading to an increase in the consumption of both durable and non-durable goods, increased savings through innovative financial mechanism like microfinance ventures which may allow marginalized people access to required credit for business and human capital investments. Anyanwu and Erhijakpor (2010) and Gyimah-Brempong and Asiedu (2011) found that international remittances decrease the probability of a family being poor, or chronically poor. Contrarily, Louise and Clovis (2012) argued that migrant remittances do not significantly lead to a reduction in poverty.

39.3.4 Remittances and physical capital investment

One of the most damming criticisms leveled against remittances is that it doesn't lead to development because the households receiving the remittances used it for non-productive consumption which ends up having small, if any, long-term multiplier effects on the general economy of the recipient countries (de Haas 2007). Recently, a study by Rapoport and Docquier (2006) provided evidence that the propensity to invest is comparatively higher for remittance recipient households, thus leading to increased self-employment and investments in small-scale businesses, which are the engines of growth. Most African nations have a primitive financial system, thus the poor do not have access to credit and consequently constraining their investment opportunities. In an analysis of sub-Saharan African countries, Lartey (2011) found evidence for the existence of an investment channel through which remittances impact the growth of recipient African nations. The marginal propensity to invest may be dependent on institutions, government policies, and the overall expected return on these investment ventures

39.3.5 Remittances and Dutch disease

For the remittance receiving countries, it can be argued that the increase in remittances may cause an appreciation of the real exchange rate for the recipient countries, therefore, resulting in reduced global competitiveness of these economies and dampening their economic growth and development (Lartey et al. 2012). According to Bourdet and Falck (2006), however, remittances do not seem to have had a negative impact on the global competitiveness of most remittance recipient African countries, apart from smaller economies such as Lesotho and Cape Verde for which remittances make up more than 10% of the their GDP. Furthermore, unlike other forms of foreign capital inflows and financial windfalls from natural resources, remittances tend to be stable, as indicated by the relative resilience of remittances during the recent global financial crisis and its associated economic slowdown in migrant host countries. However, the risk of remittances causing "Dutch disease" in the recipient African nations is low compared to that posed by windfalls from reliance on natural resources and/or all other types of foreign inflows of capital (Ratha et al. 2011).

39.4 Conclusions

In this chapter, we have explored the determinants and impacts of remittances on the African economies. Our analysis of the extant literature reveals that remittances are surpassing ODA and are catching up to FDI, not only in volume, but also in terms of their relative stability of their response to international financial shocks. We have examined whether remittances are a reliable hedge against shocks and are sustainable long-run sources of finance for economic growth and development.

In an effort to put in context the contributions of remittances to economic growth and development, we have presented and discussed the dual motives of remittances, i.e. the altruistic vs. the profit motive of remittances both from the microeconomic and macroeconomic perspectives. Overall, the profit (investment) motive of remittances seems to outplay the altruistic motive of remittances (Ruiz-Arranz 2007), although both motives are in play. Since most empirical studies suggest that remittances play a crucial role in the development effort, we survey the key determinants of remittances including: the size of migrant stock, economic, political situation in home country, economic condition in host country, channels, transaction costs, and speed of remittance transfers.

Our analysis shows that the size and quality of the migrant stock do matter in terms of the remittance flows from the host to the home country of migrants. In general, African migrants have a relatively higher education attainment which gives them the edge for getting high paying jobs which allow them to send money home. This potential earning and remitting to their home countries is, however, conditioned by a number delicate issues. On the one hand, African migrants are more likely to integrate with and invest in the host countries than their cohorts, dampening the amount remitted. The incentive to remit of African migrants may also be limited by the fact many African countries are opposed to the notion of dual citizenship, and diaspora voting. Migrants may also be skeptical of the general political climate to send money home for fear of the limited or no protection of their rights, property, or other privileges.

With respect to the future prospect of remittances of as an engine of growth and economic development, there is little doubt that the burden of the high transaction costs presents a thorny issue which needs to be resolved. The development of financial services sector in the home countries of migrants is critical. African countries may encourage an orderly and secure use of mobile money transfer services in addition to promoting competition of the currently monopolistic market in the delivery of money from the senders to the receivers. The advancement of technology has made major strides toward the provision of the delivery of such services a reality. All it takes is the will and determination of African countries to harness the technological promise for cost effective transfers of money which bolsters the anemic development budgets of African economies.

Our survey and analysis of the literature on the macroeconomic impact of remittances on economic growth and development efforts of African countries through various transmission mechanisms lead us to make a number of conclusions. By and large, remittances serve as an important factor in consumption smoothing, especially during episodic draught and crop failures (Perakis 2011). Remittances also tend to enhance the ability of a country in achieving gender parity and empowerment of women through human capital formation (Bansak and Chezum 2009). Although the overriding evidence reveals a positive impact of remittances on consumption expenditures, physical and human capital formation, one must not totally neglect the possible negative effect of remittances on African economies experiencing inflationary pressures, otherwise known as the Dutch disease.

Another unrelated issue that may negatively impact remittances is the alleged link between remittances and terrorism activities. Few studies, including Mascarenhas and Sandler (2013), have argued that remittances may be used to support domestic and international terrorist activities. Consequently, the heightened scrutiny of remittances may result in the slowing down and reduction of money transferred by migrants to their home countries over time. Since the enduring motives of remittances are for consumption smoothing, human capital formation (education, health, and nutrition), and investment in high return business ventures on the home front, their role as an important external source of capital for economic growth and development is sustainable.

Finally, the main threads which tie the issues discussed in this chapter are the following. The transfer of remittances for economic growth and development will continue to be potentially reliable and resilient external funding source. The unique feature of remittances to Africa is that African migrants tend to have relatively higher educational attainment than their cohorts from other regions. To harness the full potential of remittances as one source of resources for African economies, the following critical issues have to be addressed. First, African governments may consider a policy of dual citizenship for migrants to encourage them to invest in the home country and to enlarge the size of remittances. Second, it is imperative for African governments to promote a competitive environment in the money transfer services by negotiating with providers in major host countries to bring the exorbitant transaction costs for the benefit of the recipient households and the home countries. Third, African countries may consider to create a competitive environment for the formation of private money transfer services institutions to contain the high transaction cost of remittances.

References

Adenutsi, D.E., Aziakponu, M.J., and Ocran, M.K. (2011). The Changing Nature of Macroeconomic Environment on Remittances Inflows in sub-Saharan Africa. MPRA working paper no. 37067. http://mpra.ub.uni-muenchen.de/370671.

Adreoni, J. (1989). Giving with impure altruism: applications to charity and Ricardian equivalence. *Journal of Political Economy*, 97(6):1447–1458.

Ahortor, C.R.K., and Adenutsi, D.E. (2009). The impact of remittances on economic growth in small-open developing economies. *Journal of Applied Sciences*, 9: 3275–986.

American Immigration Council (2012). African Immigrants in America: A Demographic Overview. http://www.immigrationpolicy.org/just-facts/african-immigrants-america-demographic-overview

Anyanwu, J.C., and Erhijakpor, A.E.D. (2010). Do international remittances affect poverty in Africa? *African Development Review*, 22(1):51–91.

Azam, J., and Gubert, F. (2005). Those in Kayes. The impact of remittances on their recipients in Africa. *Revue économique, Presses de Sciences-Po*, 56(6):1331–1358.

Bansak, C., and Chezum, B. (2009). How do remittances affect human capital formation of school age boys and girls? *American Economic Review*, 99:145–148.

Bouhga-Hagbe, J. (2006). Altruism and workers' remittances: evidence from selected countries in the Middle East and central Asia. IMF Working Paper WP/06/130. https://www.imf.org/external/pubs/ft/wp/2006/wp06130.pdf.

Bourdet, Y., and Falck, H. (2006). Emigrants' remittances and the Dutch disease in Cape Verde. *International Economic Journal*, 20(3):267–284.

Carling, J. (2008). The determinants of migrant remittances. *Oxford Review of Economic Policy*, 24:581–598.

Chami, R., Fullenkamp, C., and Gapen, M. (2009). Measuring workers' remittances: What should be kept in and what should be left out. Mimeo. Washington, DC: International Monetary Fund.

Chami, R., Fullenkamp, C., and Jahjah, S. (2003). Are Immigrant Remittances Flows a Source of Capital for Development? IMF Working Paper 03/189. Washington, DC: International Monetary Fund.

Louise, T.D., and Clovis, M.W. (2012). Workers remittances and economic development in Sub-Saharan African Countries. *International Research Journal of Finance and Economics*, 88:24–38.

Cox, D., Eser, Z., and Jimenez, E. (1998). Motives for private transfers over the life-cycle: an analytical framework and evidence from Peru. *Journal of Development Economics*, 55(1):57–80.

Combes, J-L., and C. Ebeke (2011). The Short and Long Run Effects of Migration and Remittances: Some Evidence from Northern Mali. http://www.csae.ox.ac.uk/conferences/2010-EDiA/papers/368-Ebeke.pdf.

de Haas, H. (2007). Remittances, Migration, and Social Development. A Conceptual Review of the Literature. UNRISD Social Policy and Development Program Paper no. 34, 1–38. http://www.unrisd.org/80256B3C005BCCF9/(httpAuxPages)/8B7D005E37FFC77EC12573A600439846/$file/deHaaspaper.pdf.

de Haas, H., and Plug, R. (2006). Cherishing the goose with the golden eggs: trends in migrant remittances from Europe to Morocco 1970–2004. *International Migration Review*, 40(3):603–634.

Elbadawi, I.A., and Rocha, R.R. (1992), Determinants of Expatriate Workers' Remittances in North Africa and Europe. World Bank Working Paper Series, No. 1038. http://www.wds.worldbank.org/external/default/WDSContentServer/IW3P/IB/1992/11/01/000009265_3961003170048/Rendered/PDF/multi_page.pdf.

El-Sakka, M.I.T., and McNabb, R. (1999). The macroeconomic determinants of emigrant remittances. *World Development*, 27(8):1493–1502.

Englama, A. (2009). *The Economics of Remittances, Theories and Issues*. West African Institute of Financial and Economic Management.

Fayissa, B., and Nsiah, C. (2010). The impact remittances on economic growth and development in Africa. *American Economist*, 55(Fall):92–104.

Fayissa, B., and Nsiah, C. (2012). Financial Development and Remittances in Africa and the Americas: A Panel Unit-Root Tests and Panel Cointegration Analysis. Working Paper 201201, Middle Tennessee State University, Department of Economics and Finance.

Fonchamnyo, D.C. (2012). The altruistic motive of remittances: a panel data analysis of economies in sub-Saharan Africa. *International Journal of Economics and Finance*, 4(10):192-200. doi: 10.5539/ijef.v4n10p192.

Freund, C., and Spatafora, N. (2008). Remittances, transaction costs, and informality. *Journal of Development Economics*, 86:356–366.

Freund, C., and Spatafora, N. (2005). Remittances, Transaction Costs, Determinants, and Informal Flows. World Bank Policy Research Working Paper, 3704. http://elibrary.worldbank.org/doi/pdf/10.1596/1813-9450-3704.

Ghosh, B. (2006). *Migrants' Remittances and Development: Myths, Rhetoric and Realities*. The Hague: International Organization for Migration, Geneva, and The Hague Process on Refugees and Migration.

Glytsos, N.P. (1988). Remittances in temporary migration: a theoretical model and its testing with the Greek-German experience. *Weltwirtschafliches Archiv (Review of World Economics)*, 124:524–549.

Gyimah-Brempong, K., and Asiedu, E. (2011). Remittances and poverty in Ghana. Paper presented at the 8th IZA Annual Migration Meeting, Washington, DC, May 12–15 20. http://www.iza.org/conference_files/amm2011/gyimah-brempong_k6955.pdf.

Higgins, M.L., Hysenbegasi, A., and Pozo, S. (2004). Exchange-Rate Uncertainty and Worker's Remittances. *Applied Financial Economics*, 14(6):403–411.

IMF (2005). *World Economic Outlook*. Washington, DC: International Monetary Fund.

Kamgnia B.D., and Murinde, V. (2012). High remittance costs in Africa: is building regulatory capacity for microfinance institutions the answer? *ADB Africa Capacity Development Brief, Chief Economist Complex*, 3(1):1–12.

Kemegue F.M., Owusu-Sekyere, E., and Eyden, R.V. (2011). What drives remittance inflows to Sub-Saharan Africa: A dynamic panel approach. Working Paper 262. http://www.econrsa.org/publications/working-papers/what-drives-remittance-inflows-sub-saharan-africa-dynamic-panel-approach.

Lartey, E.K.K. (2013). Remittances to Sub-Saharan Africa: Altruistic or Self-Interest? California State University, Fullerton Working Paper. http://business.fullerton.edu/economics/elartey/rem_exvol.pdf.

Lartey, E.K.K., Mandelman, F.S., and Acosta, P.A. (2012). Remittances, exchange rate regimes and the Dutch disease: a panel data analysis. *Review of International Economics*, 20(2):377–395.

Lartey, E.K.K. (2011). Remittances, investment and growth in sub-Saharan Africa. *Journal of International Trade & Economic Development: An International and Comparative Review*, 22(7):1038–1058.

Lazare, S. (2013). World Bank Admits: "Economic Growth" in Africa = Resource Extraction, Inequality, Poverty. New report shows so-called growth is "bleeding Africa dry." Common Dreams. https://www.commondreams.org/headline/2013/10/08-7.

Lucas, R., and Stark, O. (1985). Motivations to remit: evidence from Botswana. *Journal of Political Economy*, 93:901–918.

Mbiti, I., and Weil, D.N. (2011). Mobile Banking: The Impact of M-PESA in Kenya. NBER Working Paper Series 17129. http://www.nber.org/papers/w17129.

Mascarenhas, R., and Sandler, T. (2013). Remittances and terrorism: A global analysis. *Defense and Peace Economics*, 25(4):331–347. doi: 10.1080/10242694.2013.824676

Niimi, Y., and Özden, C. (2006). Migration and Remittances: Causes and Linkages. World Bank Policy Research Working Paper No. 4087. http://ssrn.com/abstract=951134.

Perakis, S.M. (2011). The Short and Long Run Effects of Migration and Remittances: Some Evidence from Northern Mali, Selected Paper prepared for presentation at the Agricultural & Applied Economics Association's 2011 AAEA & NAREA Joint Annual Meeting, Pittsburgh, Pennsylvania, July 24–26. http://ageconsearch.umn.edu/bitstream/103704/2/PERAKIS_AAEA_05_03_11.pdf.

OECD (2006). Migration and the brain drain phenomenon. Migration and the brain drain phenomenon. http://www.oecd.org/social/poverty/migrationandthebraindrainphenomenon.htm

Quinn, M.A. (2006). Relative deprivation, wage differentials and Mexican migration. *Review of Development Economics*, 10(1):135–153.

Ratha, D., Mohapatra, S., Ozden, C., Plaza, S., Shaw, W., and Shimeles, A. (2011). *Leveraging Migration for Africa: Remittances, Skills, and Investments*. Washington, DC: World Bank.

Ratha, D., and Sirkeci, I. (2010). Remittances and the global financial crisis. *Migration Letters*, 7(2):125–131.

Rapoport, H., and Docquier, F. (2006). The economics of migrants' remittances, in S.-C. Kolm and J.M. Ythier (eds), *Handbook of the Economics of Giving Altruism and Reciprocity*. New York: Elsevier, pp. 1135–1198.

Ruiz-Arranz, M. (2007). Macroeconomic Determinants of Workers' Remittances, paper presented at the conference: Policy Options and Challenges for Developing Asia. Perspectives from the IMF and Asia. http://www.imf.org/External/NP/seminars/eng/2007/jbic/pdf/s4/04_8%20present.pdf.

Singh, R.J., Haacker, M., Lee, K-W., and Goff, M.L. (2011). Determinants and macroeconomic impact of remittances in sub-Saharan Africa. *Journal of African Economies*, 20(2):312–340.

Stark, O., and Lucas, R. (1988). Migration, remittances, and the family. *Economic Development and Cultural Change*, 36:465–481.

UNCTAD (2011). Report of the Expert Meeting on Maximizing the Development Impact of Remittances. http://unctad.org/en/docs/ciem4d3_en.pdf.

CHAPTER 40

FOREIGN DIRECT INVESTMENT IN AFRICA
Lessons for Economics

JOHN C. ANYANWU

40.1 INTRODUCTION

FOREIGN direct investment (FDI) is investment that is made to acquire a lasting management interest (usually a minimum of 10% of voting stock) in an enterprise operating in a country other than that of the investor, one of the investor's purposes being an effective voice in the management of the enterprise. Thus, FDI occurs when a firm invests directly in production or other facilities in a foreign country over which it has effective control. It is the sum of equity capital, reinvestment of earnings, intra-company loans, other long-term capital, and short-term capital as shown in the balance of payments accounts/statements of the reporting country (OECD 2008). FDI modes of entry include international franchising, branches, contractual alliances, equity joint ventures, and wholly foreign-owned subsidiaries. FDI could take the form of Greenfield investment, cross-border mergers, cross-border acquisitions, and sharing or utilizing existing facilities (see Shenkar and Luo 2008).

40.2 FDI: THEORETICAL PERSPECTIVES

For more comprehensiveness and practicality, we classify the various theories based on whether they are static, dynamic as well as assuming perfect/near perfect and imperfect markets (Table 40.1).

Table 40.1 Summary of key theories of FDI

	Static theories/models		
Theoretical tradition	Major theory	Variants/examples	Original lead author(s)
Neoclassical theories— Assuming Perfect Markets	1. Capital Theory Tradition	1. Differential Rate of Return 2. Portfolio Approach 3. Risk Diversification Hypothesis	Mundell, 1957. Tobin, 1958; Markowitz, 1959.
	2. The International Trade Tradition/Factor Endowments Tradition	1. Mundell & the Hecksher-Ohlin Model 2. Kojima's Macroeconomic Approach 3. The Product Life Cycle Model - Mark I Product Cycle - Mark II Product Cycle	Mundell, 1957; Rugman, 1975; Lessard, 1976. Kojima, 1973. Vernon, 1966
Market imperfections and industrial organization theories— assuming imperfect markets	1. Hymer-Kindleberger Hypothesis/Monopolistic Advantage Theory		Hymer, 1960; Kindleberger, 1969; Caves, 1971.
	2. Internalization Theory/ Approach	1. The original Internalization Theory 2. Differential Currency Areas 3. Industry Technology Cycle 4. Oligopolistc Behavior Theory 5. Behavioral Theory of the Firm	Buckley and Casson, 1976; Hennart (1982) based on Coase, 1937. Aliber, 1970 Johnson, 1968 Knickerbocker, 1973. Aharoni, 1960.
	3. The Eclectic Paradigm (OLI Framework)		Dunning, 1979.
	Dynamic approaches to FDI flows and international production		
Market imperfections	1. Scandinavian/Uppsala School or the Internationalization Theory—Network Approach or Evolutionary Approach	1. Three-Stage Internationalization Process Model 2. Extension to Five-Stage Internationalization process	Johanson and Wiedersheim-Paul, 1975; Johanson and Vahlne, 1977; Nelson and Winter, 1982; Kogut and Zander, 1993; Teece et al., 1997. Ohmae, 1991.
	2. The Investment Development Path/Cycle or the Dynamic Approach to the OLI Paradigm		Dunning, 1981a,b; Tolentino, 1992; Dunning and Narula, 1996.
	3. The Dynamic Capability Perspective		Luo, 2000.
	4. The Integration-Responsiveness (I-R) Perspective/Paradigm		Prahalad and Doz, 1987.

Source: Author, based on the literature.

40.2.1 Static theories

40.2.1.1 Neo-classical theories—assuming perfect markets

40.2.1.1.1 The capital theory tradition

The differential rate of return theory sees FDI as a response to the differences in the rate of return on capital between countries. Apart from not standing empirical testing, the differential rate of return hypothesis was not consistent with several observed characteristics of international investment.

The portfolio theory assumes that part of the excess profits that should be earned in foreign markets is simply rents for higher risk associated with this alternative use of capital. The shortcomings of the differential rate of return hypothesis fully apply to the portfolio theory while the theory cannot explain the differences between industries' propensities to invest abroad.

The risk diversification theory argues that the international diversification of portfolios is a way of reducing the firm's risk hence making the multinational enterprise (MNE) a vehicle for geographical diversification of investments. However, in practice, the diversification of MNEs is more likely to result from investments that were propelled by other motives.

40.2.1.1.2 The international trade tradition

There are three key variants of the international trade tradition, namely, the Mundell and Hecksher-Ohlin model, the Kojima theory, and the product cycle model.

The Mundell and Hecksher-Ohlin Model argues that the introduction of trade tariffs would induce a flow of FDI towards the protected countries. However, the model cannot explain network FDI while evidence suggests that trade and FDI are complements.

The Kojima "Macroeconomic Approach" groups motives of FDI into four categories: (i) to seek natural resources, (ii) to take advantage of cheap labor cost in the host country, (iii) to avoid tariff and non-tariff barriers, and (iv) to take advantage of oligopolistic power owing to technology and knowledge advantage. Owing to its narrow assumptions, Kojima's approach is not applicable even to most Japanese direct investment.

The product cycle model argues that each product has a life cycle and will go through three phases: innovation, maturity and standardization. In the Mark I version of the theory, FDI takes place as the cost of production becomes an important consideration, which is the case when the product reaches maturity and standardization. However, the product cycle is not, in itself, a complete theory of FDI as it does not explain the ownership of production. The successive revision of the model—Product Cycle Mark II ("new" product life cycle theory)—indicates that import-substituting FDI was expected as the product and technology matured. While this theory adequately describes how a new MNE develops a new product and then engages in FDI; it fails to describe the actions of existing MNEs with substantial FDI that may skip steps in the model or even reverse the process.

40.2.1.2 *Market imperfections and industrial organization theories—assuming imperfect markets*

40.2.1.2.1 *Hymer–Kindleberger hypothesis*

This theory, alternatively referred to as the "monopolistic advantage theory," is based on the "market power school" and sees FDI as a means of transferring knowledge and other firm assets, both tangible and tacit, in order to organize production abroad. The existence of FDI is exclusively results from international market imperfection for these assets hence the firm "internalizes or supersedes" these market failures through direct investment. According to Kindleberger's (1969) modification, instead of MNE behavior determining the market structure, it is the market structure—monopolistic competition—that will determine the conduct of the firm, by internalizing its production. Comparative advantage has to be firm specific and must be transferable to foreign subsidiaries, in addition to being large enough to overcome its disadvantages.

40.2.1.2.2 *Internalization theory*

The original internalization theory posits that transnational companies are organizing their internal activities so as to develop specific advantages, which can then be exploited. It also claims that some transactions are more cost saving if they are performed inside the firm than in the market and internalization will happen as far as the benefits are not outweighed by the cost of communication, coordination, and control. FDI occurs to capture those kinds of benefits.

This Differential Currency Areas and the Effect of Exchange Rates Theory is based on capital market relationships, foreign exchange risk, and the market's preference for holding assets denominated in strong currencies. It postulates that countries with strong currencies tend to be sources of FDI, while countries with weak currencies tend to be host countries or recipients of FDI. The theory suggests that firms internalize imperfections in the capital and exchange rate markets, as they do with any other market failure.

The industry technology cycle theory argues that the incentive for firms to internalize the market for technology varies over time. New technologies are more subject to "appropriability" or more likely to be internalized, but as the technology matures licensing becomes increasingly attractive since the licensing of a mature technology is easier to price and cheaper to monitor, thus reducing the risks and costs associated with the non-internalization of the firm's ownership advantage.

With respect to the Oligopolistic Behavior Theory, it is argued that due to oligopolistic behavior foreign subsidiaries tend to be clustered hence firms tend to follow competitors in their internalization decisions as a strategic response to locational variables and to the anticipated behavior of their competitors.

Another extension of the internalization theory is the behavioral theory of the firm that introduces the role of management and decision-making process in the explanations of the internationalization of the firm.

40.2.1.2.3 *The eclectic paradigm*

The paradigm's original formulation in 1979 provides an ownership (O-), location (L-), and internalization (I-) (OLI) advantages-based framework to analyze why, and where,

MNEs would invest abroad. In 1983, Dunning reformulated the ownership advantages as arising from asset (Oa) ownership advantages and transaction (Ot) ownership advantages. Dunning (1993a,b) added a fourth, long-term management strategy. While offering the most comprehensive explanation of FDI than previous theories, the OLI framework does not adequately address how MNEs' ownership-specific advantages such as distinctive resources and capabilities should be deployed and exploited in international production. Also, it does not explicitly delineate the ongoing, evolving process of international production while it is inadequate in illuminating how geographically dispersed international production should be appropriately coordinated and integrated.

40.2.2 Dynamic approaches to FDI flows and international production

To redress the deficiencies of the earlier theories, a number of dynamic theoretical perspectives have emerged in recent years. Their major thrust is that a firm's knowledge and skills constitute tacit ownership advantages that take time to evolve. MNEs, with their ability to devise and manage complex organizational structures, sustain such advantages by leveraging them through worldwide investments (Shenkar and Luo 2008).

40.2.2.1 Scandinavian/Uppsala School or the internationalization theory network approach or evolutionary approach

The Uppsala model comprises the three-stage internationalization process model and its extension to a five-stage model. It proposes that MNEs engage in FDI incrementally with commitment or "international experiential knowledge" and with respect to the firms' "psychic distance" to each potential host country, organizational capabilities, strategic objectives, and environmental dynamics. The development of FDI strategy is a product of learning, experience, and adaptation to the complexities of global markets.

Three stages were proposed in the internationalization process. During the first stage, internationalization starts with exports through independent representatives or agents/ trading companies, while during the second stage, the firm establishes sales subsidiaries in the foreign markets, specializing in marketing and promotion. During the third stage, manufacturing facilities or productive subsidiaries are established overseas. Network of relationships permits the creation of a capital of trust that reduces transaction costs and increases cooperation in the development of new products and technology.

Ohmae (1991) extended the above three-stage process of internationalization by including a fourth stage ("insiderization") and fifth stage (complete globalization). During the insiderization stage, MNEs replicate all the main activities of their home base business system within their major foreign markets, allowing these operations to fully tailor their strategies to the needs of local customers. At the fifth stage, MNEs integrate some activities on a global basis to prevent fragmentation of the business as a whole, whilst still meeting the needs of local customers.

40.2.2.2 *The investment development path*

The investment development path (IDP) approach was introduced as a dynamic and macroeconomic approach to the OLI paradigm. The approach posits an association between a country's level of development (proxied by GDP per capita) and its international investment position (net outward FDI stock per capita). As the country develops, the conditions facing domestic and foreign companies change, thus affecting the flows of inward and outward FDI though inward and outward FDI also affect the economic structure.

The approach proposes that countries evolve through five stages of development. The first stage is associated with pre-industrialization and a country at this stage is presumed to have no inflows of FDI or no outflows of FDI. It may be important to note that most African countries are currently at this stage. At the second stage, inward FDI starts to rise but at slower rate than outward FDI. At the fourth stage, countries have outward FDI still growing faster than inward FDI, signifying that domestic firms are now growing in size and diversified both geographically and in terms of industries, possess the ownership advantages to compete in any domestic or foreign market. The fifth stage sees a fluctuating balance between outward and inward FDI according to the short-term evolution of exchange rates and economic cycles. Most advanced industrial economies are at this last stage.

40.2.2.3 *The dynamic capability perspective*

The dynamic capability perspective posits that the critical element in FDI strategy is the ability to continuously develop the right dynamic capabilities to fully exploit the organization's global potential in relation to the real opportunities that exist in the business environment. The dynamic capabilities require capability exploitation as well as capability building.

40.2.2.4 *The integration–responsiveness perspective (I-R paradigm)*

The global integration-local responsiveness paradigm aims at maximizing the advantages to be gained from global integration while at the same time developing the ability to respond flexibly to variations in demand from specific markets. But the strategic flexibility view of the I-R framework was incorporated into the I-R framework to enrich it by Kogut (1984, 1985) and this is composed of two related, complementary concepts: operational flexibility and strategic options. Five opportunities arising from strategic flexibility include production movement, tax avoidance, financial arbitrage, information transfer, and competitive power.

Do we have convergence in theories as a lesson for economics? The answer is a clear, no. From the foregoing, it can be argued that there is no "unique" or unified established theory of FDI and it seems at this point very unlikely that such a unified theory will emerge. Rather, what we have are various hypotheses emphasizing different macroeconomic and microeconomic factors that are likely to have an effect on foreign direct investment. Though prior studies have identified several factors that impact on the FDI decision of an international business, those factors are generally applicable only to the specific context considered, or else affect just the initial market entry. A comprehensive theoretical formulation that helps to analyze patterns of FDI across different geographical regions has proved elusive. In addition, FDI patterns need to be examined over time, because factors favoring an international business' initial investment into a country could change, prompting it to move new investments elsewhere. Several strategic considerations could motivate such shifts, such as increased competitive intensity at the original location, cost-cutting requirements which prompt the search for new low-cost production locations, or pressure to enter new markets in response to similar moves by rivals. Measures undertaken by various governments in liberalizing investment regimes also deeply affect FDI decisions. FDI trends are a complex, multidimensional phenomenon, which need to be examined from macroeconomic as well as firm strategy perspectives for a more realistic analysis. However, shifts in FDI destinations over time should be analyzed at a country or within-country level because the determinants under investigation affect all international investors uniformly. Most of the theories were developed on the basis of FDI from developed countries to developing countries hence do not adequately explain FDI from Africa to developed countries or intra-African FDI and FDI from emerging economies to Africa, which have become significant and important in recent years.

40.3 FDI Flows: Taxonomy of Approaches, Benefits, and Costs

40.3.1 Taxonomy of approaches

The approaches to FDI can be broadly classified into pro- and anti-FDI. The pro-foreign investment approaches are the business-school approach, the traditional economic approach, and the neo-traditional approach. On the other hand, the anti-foreign investment approaches are the nationalist approach, the dependence approach, and the Marxist approach.

The business school approach believes in the moral and practical virtues of the free enterprise system. The traditional economic approach argues that FDI is a net addition to investible resources in host countries, and as such raises their rates of growth as well leading to ancillary advantages to the recipient economy. The protagonists of the neo-traditionist approach believe in the virtues of early capitalism but are worried by the giantism and power of the present multinational enterprises (see Anyanwu 1998).

The nationalist approach argues that FDI damages host economies through the suppression of domestic entrepreneurship, importation of unsuitable technology and unsuitable products, the extension of oligopolistic practices such as unnecessary product differentiation, heavy advertising, or excessive profit-taking, and the worsening of income distribution by a self-perpetuating process which simultaneously reinforces high-income élites and provides them with expensive consumer goods. This approach also argues that FDI has the potential of introducing unsuitable products or technology or the misuse of transfer pricing and other tools to remit hidden profits, while seeing free (freer) trade more damaging than beneficial to economic growth.

The dependence approach posits that the inherent dependent status which FDI brings can never permit real development in host countries. Thus, FDI is seen as a link between the centers of the world economy and its exploited periphery. According to the radical, Marxist approach (social anti-capitalistic), FDI brings about neo-imperialism and exploitation, class conflict, and economic surplus. FDI is therefore seen as Trojan horses of western colonialism and imperialism against the Third World hence the effect of such investments is irrelevant as it is ultimately equated with exploitation.

However, by the end of the 1980s, the radical stance was in retreat almost everywhere in favor of pragmatic nationalism and mixed economic system. This development is agreement with the "modernization school," which views FDI as a prerequisite and catalyst for sustainable growth and development. To them, for FDI to fulfill its crucial role, economies have to be freed from distorting state interventions and opened to foreign investment and trade. This stance is reflected in the big bang theories that favor all-encompassing privatization and structural adjustment norms for the transformation of economic and political structures to overcome poverty in developing areas like Africa.

40.3.2 Benefits and costs

It has been argued that FDI is a driver of employment, technological progress, productivity improvements, and ultimately economic growth. It plays the critical roles of filling the development, foreign exchange, investment, and tax revenue gaps in developing countries. In particular, FDI can play an important role in Africa's development efforts, including: supplementing domestic savings; employment generation and growth; integration into the global economy; transfer of modern technologies; enhancement of efficiency; and raising skills of local manpower (Dupasquier and Osakwe 2003; Anyanwu 2006).

However, FDI may be a source of conflict in destination countries, lower or replace domestic savings and investment, transfer technologies that are low level or inappropriate for the host country's factor proportions, target primarily the host country's domestic market and thus not increase exports, inhibit the expansion of indigenous firms that might become exporters, and not help developing the host country's dynamic comparative advantages by focusing solely on local cheap labor and raw materials.

40.4 AFRICA'S FDI FLOWS AND STOCKS: TRENDS, PATTERNS/CHARACTERISTICS

As Figure 40.1 shows, Africa has never been a major recipient of FDI flows and lags behind other regions of the world. However, Africa was the only region that saw FDI inflows rise in 2012, up 5% to US$50 billion. By 1990, Africa's share was a mere 1.37% compared to Asia's 10.9% and by 2012 while Africa's share was just 3.7%, Asia received a whopping 30% (Figure 40.2). Just as FDI inflows to Africa represent a low percentage of the global total, they also represent a low percentage of its GDP—just 2.3% in 2012 against 4.3% in developing Americas.

FDI inflows to Africa vary across sub-regions. North Africa dominated between 2004 and 2010 before West Africa took over from 2011. However, these mask country differences and major recipients. Between 2003 and 2012, the top ten country recipients are Nigeria, Egypt, South Africa, Morocco, Sudan, Congo, Algeria, Tunisia, Libya, and Ghana, most of which are fossil fuel producers and exporters and their collective inflows representing almost 70%

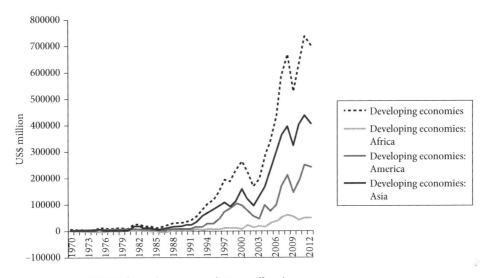

FIGURE 40.1 FDI Inflows by Region (US$ million).

Source: Author, using UNCTADStat online data.

FIGURE 40.2 FDI Inflows (Percentage of total world), by region.

Source: Author, using UNCTADStat online data.

of the total inflows. Though, FDI is still concentrated in natural resources (especially mineral resources, coal, oil and natural gas), since 2005, investment has been diversifying away from natural resources as well as an associated increase of the share of investment in manufacturing and for services and other sectors, including financial services.

FDI outflows mirror the inflows in terms of size and percentage of global total in comparison with other regions. For example, between 1970 and 2012, FDI outflows from Africa averaged US$2.221 billion against US$22.1 billion from developing America and US$58.5 billion from developing Asia, representing 0.5%, 2.4%, and 6.7%, respectively, of total global outflows. The picture is changing gradually. For example in 2012, outward FDI flows from Africa increased from US$5 billion to US$14 billion (almost a triple) but mainly due to large flows from South Africa in mining, the wholesale sector and health-care products.

In terms of FDI stock, Africa's averaged US$178.9 billion between 1970 and 2012 against US$546 billion in developing America and US$1.2 trillion in developing Asia. These represent 3%, 7%, and 19%, respectively, of the total global stock. Interestingly, Malaysia, South Africa, China and India (in that order) are the largest developing-country investors in Africa in terms of FDI stock.

There are other interesting and changing characteristics of FDI in Africa. One of them is the growing FDI inflows from emerging markets. For example, FDI activity in Africa by emerging economies grew by 13% per annum between 2003 and 2010, compared to 7% growth for developed economies. Secondly, related to the above is the fact that BRICS countries (especially China) are becoming significant investors in Africa. The third is that there has been significant growth in intra-African investment into new FDI projects—a 21% compound annual growth rate between 2003 and 2010. However, while intra-African investment has grown considerably in terms of number of new projects, it tends to be far less capital-intensive than investment by other emerging economies. Consequently, even at its peak between 2003 and 2010, intra-African FDI was only 27% of the total investments by emerging economies (Ernst & Young 2013).

The question of the prospects for FDI in Africa then arises. Africa's attraction of less than 5% of global FDI does not reflect the increasing attractiveness of the continent as having one of the fastest economic growth rates (over 5% on average since 2000) and highest returns on investment in the world (UNCTAD 2013; Mckinsey & Company, 2010). For example, while the global average rate of return on FDI for 2006–2011 was 7%, the average inward rate for developed economies was 5.1%. In contrast, the average rate for Africa was 11.4% during the same period. Indeed, in Africa, natural resources, extractive and processing industries consistently contribute to higher rates of return. Therefore, Africa continues to offer numerous opportunities for foreign investors not only due to high rate of returns but also due to projected sustainability of relatively high growth rate both in the medium and long term, among other factors. Also, Africa has the fastest-expanding labor force in the world. Today, there are more than 500 million people of working age (15–64) in Africa, and that number is expected to pass 1.1 billion by 2040—to be larger than China and India—providing the needed human capital and skills for successful and profitable FDI. In addition, African countries have taken measures to improve the business environment as a strategy to attract more FDI. Increasing number of African countries are among the top reformers in the world and they have been making changes in domestic policy to improve the process of dealing with construction permits, protecting investors and paying taxes, among other areas. There is also the increasing prevalence of peace, democratic elections and improved governance across the continent. Furthermore, through the phenomenal rate of urbanization, Africa has a growing population of very young, ambitious, often well-educated, globally minded people who are increasingly moving into middle-income brackets thus offering the needed market and consumer demand for market-seekers. Also, the continent's resources—extractives and fertile land for commercial agriculture, among others—are in high demand and remain very profitable. The huge infrastructure gap (about US$90 billion to US$100 billion a year is needed) in the continent presents further opportunities for increased and sustained FDI inflows just as African countries believe that FDI can play a critical role in helping to accelerate and sustain inclusive growth and development across the continent just as emerging market investors are positive about Africa's attractiveness.

40.5 CONSTRAINTS AND INCENTIVES

40.5.1 Constraints

A number of reasons have been adduced for low level of FDI flows to Africa, ranging from political and macroeconomic instability to inhospitable regulatory frameworks and weaknesses in infrastructure provision, governance, and institutions in general. The major factors emerging from the literature include: high degree of uncertainty; general poor governance, corruption, and low human capital development; unfavorable regulatory environment and poor infrastructure; small individual country market sizes; high dependence on primary commodities exports and increased competition; and continued negative perception of the continent in spite of great positive changes in recent years (Anyanwu 2006).

40.5.2 Incentives

African governments have increasingly adopted measures to facilitate the entry of FDI. Examples include liberalizing investment regimes and the laws and regulations for the admission and establishment of foreign investment projects; reducing market distortions, simplifying procedures and dissemination of information about investment opportunities through investment promotion agencies, providing guarantees for repatriation of investment and profits; capital repatriation rights and establishing mechanisms for the settlement of investment disputes. Other incentives include either one or a combination of: fiscal incentives, direct and indirect financial subsidies, training support, infrastructure improvement, bilateral investment treaties, simplified border procedures, and establishment of export processing zones.

Countries like Egypt, Kenya, Mauritius, Madagascar, Mozambique, Namibia, and Tunisia have established export-processing zones, where various incentive packages are offered to companies operating within those zones. With the exception of Port St. Louis in Mauritius and perhaps Madagascar, most of these zones have failed to attract significant inflows. Other countries like Ghana offer low tax rates and free zones while those like Botswana offer depreciation on a straight line. Others like South Africa and Kenya offer accelerated depreciation in addition to several industry-specific incentives and activities. Since the 1980s, all SADC governments have relaxed regulations for foreign investors.

The FDI incentive framework in Africa is characterized by continuing entry barriers, low impact of FDI promotion, and costly investment incentives. In particular, the incentive structure has not been favorable in attracting "efficiency-seeking," "export-oriented," and "high-quality" FDI.

James (2009) concludes that FDI incentives have limited effects on investments hence countries must also improve their investment climates. If used, investment incentives should be used minimally (mainly to address market failures and generate multiplier effects); incentives should be awarded with as little discretion and as much transparency as possible, using automatic legal criteria; to the extent possible, incentives should be linked to investment growth, and tax holidays should be avoided; only the tax administration should administer tax incentives; regional cooperation should be encouraged to prevent harmful tax competition between countries; and governments should regularly prepare tax expenditure statements to measure and monitor the costs of tax incentives. In addition, incentive policies should be reviewed periodically to assess their effectiveness in helping meet desired goals. According to James (2009), whatever incentives a government decides to offer and however it structures them, every effort should be made to ensure that they are affordable, targeted, simple, and periodically reviewed.

40.6 DETERMINANTS/MOTIVATING FACTORS— IS AFRICA DIFFERENT?

The literature on the forces driving FDI has also identified both policy and non-policy factors as drivers of FDI and whether they are "pull" or "push" factors, "demand side" or "supply side," or institutional factors, among others. These are alternatively viewed as basic economic factors, trade and the exchange market policies, and other aspects of the investment climate. Does the African case conform to these theoretical propositions or are there things Africa is teaching Economics with respect to the drivers of FDI?

40.6.1 Basic macroeconomic and other factors

Nnadozie and Osili (2004) find less robust evidence on the role of GDP per capita on FDI inflow but GDP growth is found to have significant impact. Market size is found to play an important role in FDI inflows (Anyanwu 1998, 2012a) though the results of Kyereboah-Coleman and Agyire-Tettey (2008) indicate that most foreign investors do not consider this factor in making a decision to invest or otherwise in Ghana. Lederman et al. (2010) found some differences between SADC and the rest of the world in FDI behavior: in SADC, the income level is less important and openness more so. However, relative to other regions of the world, SADC's low FDI inflows are explained by economic fundamentals.

Inflation has been found to negatively affect FDI inflows (Nnadozie and Osili 2004) though the findings of Brahmasrene and Jiranyakul (2001) indicate otherwise. Trade openness has also been found to be positively associated with FDI inflows (Asiedu 2002). Oladipo (2008) examines the determinants of Nigeria's FDI inflow for the period 1970–2005 and finds that the nation's potential market size, the degree of export orientation, human capital, providing enabling environment through the provision of infrastructural facilities, and macroeconomic stability are important determinants of FDI flows. A case study on Ghana by Kyereboah-Coleman and Agyire-Tettey (2008) showed that the volatility of the real exchange rate has a negative influence on FDI inflow. However, Brahmasrene and Jiranyakul (2001) found no statistically significant relationship between the level of the exchange rate and FDI inflows.

40.6.2 Foreign aid

The literature has identified five possible multiple channels through which foreign aid affects FDI, positively and negatively. These channels include (i) a positive "vanguard effect; (ii) a positive "financing effect"; and (iii) a negative "Dutch-disease effect"; (iv) a negative "rent-seeking effect"; and (v) a positive "infrastructure effect" (Kimura and Todo 2010; Harms and Lutz 2006; Arellano et al. 2009) and hence raises the marginal product of capital in a country. Kimura and Todo (2010) found robust evidence that foreign aid from Japan in particular has a vanguard effect (that is, Japanese aid promotes FDI from Japan but does not attract FDI from other countries. Their finding is consistent with Blaise (2005), who used province-level data and found that Japanese aid in China has a positive and significant impact on the locational choice of Japanese private investors in China. On the other hand, Harms and Lutz (2006) found that the effect of aid on FDI is generally insignificant but significantly positive for countries in which private agents face heavy regulatory burdens.

Yasin (2005) showed that bilateral official development assistance to selected SSA countries has a significant and positive influence on foreign direct investment flows while multilateral development assistance does not have a statistically significant effect on foreign direct investment flows. Also, Anyanwu (2012a), using cross-country time series data of African countries for the period, 1996–2008, found that higher FDI goes where foreign aid also goes in Africa.

40.6.3 Infrastructure development

Dupasquier and Osakwe (2006) show that FDI in Africa is dependent on the development of infrastructure. The results of a study on US FDI flow to Africa by Nnadozie and Osili (2004) found less robust evidence on the role of infrastructure on foreign direct investment. Results from Anyanwu and Erhijakpor (2004) indicated that telecommunications infrastructures significantly increase FDI inflows to Africa. Sekkat and Veganzones-Varoudakis (2007) indicated that infrastructure availability is important for South Asia, Africa, and the Middle East in attracting FDI.

40.6.4 Institutional factors and investment climate

Results from Baniak et al. (2005) showed that high volatility of fiscal and business regulations makes the inflow of FDI smaller, macroeconomic and legal instability leads to adverse selection of the investors, and higher variability of basic macroeconomic fundamentals reduce the inflow of FDI. Asiedu (2004) found that the impact of capital controls on FDI inflows varies by region and has changed over time: in the 1970s and 1980s, none of the policies had a significant impact on FDI inflows but in the 1990s, all three were significant. However, capital controls have no effect on FDI to SSA and the Middle East, but adversely affect FDI to Latin America and East Asia.

40.6.5 Attraction of natural resources

Dupasquier and Osakwe (2006), Asiedu (2002), and Anyanwu (2012a) found that the availability of natural resources has a positive and significant effect on FDI inflows. Also, Asiedu (2006), Hailu (2010), and Mohamed and Sidiropoulos (2010) found that countries that are endowed with natural resources attract more FDI.

40.6.6 Human resources development, productivity, and cost

Reiter et al. (2010) show that FDI inflows are more strongly positively related to improvement in human development when FDI policy restricts foreign investors from entering some economic sectors and when it discriminates against foreign investors relative to domestic investors. In addition, it finds that the relationship between FDI and improvement in human development is also more strongly positive when corruption is low. Rodríguez and Pallas (2008) found that human capital is the most important determinants of inward FDI. Alsan et al. (2006) found that gross inflows of FDI are strongly and positively influenced by population health (life expectancy) in low- and middle-income countries.

40.7 EFFECTS OF FDI ON AFRICAN ECONOMIES

Enhancing sustainable inclusive economic growth and poverty reduction have become the most important development challenges for Africa, and an important driver for achieving these is through productive FDI. Empirical results about FDI and growth, as well as poverty reduction, are ambiguous. Sander and Macdonald (2009) found that while FDI has a positive growth impact in lower and upper middle-income countries (mostly Latin American, Northern African, Eastern European, and South East Asian countries), in low-income countries (mostly sub-Saharan Africa) there is no positive relationship between FDI and growth. The authors suggest that this is due to a lack of absorptive capacity in these low-income countries. Brambila-Macias and Massa (2010) found that both FDI and cross-border bank lending have significant, positive impacts on growth. Also, Esso's (2010) results showed a positive long-run relationship between FDI and economic growth in Angola, Cote d'Ivoire, Kenya, Liberia, Senegal, and South Africa. Anyanwu and Erhijakpor (2009), using the Nigerian data from 1970–2004, found a very high positive and significant effect of foreign direct investment on economic growth. Also Ncube and

Anyanwu (2012) found that while FDI reduces income inequality in the MENA region, it increases poverty.

Estimates indicate that in the last eight years, FDI has helped create 1.6 million new jobs in Africa (Ernst & Young 2013). But Anyanwu (2012b) found that FDI has a positive but insignificant effect on female employment in both overall African and SSA results. It, in fact, reduces male employment in North Africa without any significant effect on those for sub-Saharan Africa (Anyanwu 2013a). Also Anyanwu (2013b) found that FDI has positive significant on youth employment in sub-Saharan Africa and not in the overall African and North African samples. The result does not support the proposition that the inflow of FDI enhances youth employment in Africa as a whole. This is not surprising given that most FDI inflows to Africa go to the natural resources sectors such as minerals, which are enclave and capital-intensive sectors, creating little local employment. In addition, Anyanwu and Augustine (2013) found that FDI has a negative and statistically significant effect on gender equality in employment in sub-Saharan Africa but has statistically significant positive effect on gender equality in North Africa.

Te and Morrissey (2001) found that foreign ownership is associated with a 20–40% increase in individual wages (conditional on age, tenure and education) on average but this is halved to 8–23% if account is taken of the fact that foreign-owned firms are larger and locate in high-wage sectors and regions. They also find that there is a tendency in some countries for more skilled workers to benefit more from foreign ownership than less skilled workers, and this conclusion holds after accounting for the size distribution of foreign firms. From a microeconomic perspective, Lederman et al. (2010) show that FDI appears to have facilitated local development in the SADC region.

In sum, the evidence so far indicates that the effect of FDI on African economies has been mixed. However, we believe that FDI can play a critical role in helping to accelerate and sustain growth and development across Africa. Besides being a critical source of long-term capital for investment in infrastructure and other developmental initiatives, FDI also provides a positive ripple effect, including: job creation; development of local suppliers (local sourcing policies help to create extended supply chains of domestic providers); skills, technology, and knowledge transfer; and a catalyst for economic diversification (helping African economies move beyond overdependence on natural resources).

40.8 SUMMARY OF LESSONS FOR ECONOMICS, POLICY IMPLICATIONS, AND OUTLOOK/PROSPECTS

Following Casson (1990), it is safe to conclude that existing FDI theories are a "logical intersection" of theories from trade theories (explaining location of production and markets for sales of products), the theory of international capital markets (explaining financing and risk-sharing), the theory of the firm (explaining location of headquarters, management, and material utilization). These theories, originating from different philosophical perspectives seem fragmented, offering little converging and unified theory. Questions relating to risk-sharing, business cycle transmission and behavior, exchange rate behavior, industry-specific considerations, and the structures and sources of FDI financing could have non-trivial implications for a reformulation of FDI theories and towards a unified one. Existing theories suffer from the fact that they were not conceptualized with FDI in developing countries such as those in Africa in mind. In addition, the theories of FDI are centered on the explanation of responses by MNEs to imperfect markets. They generally tend to explain the phenomenon of international production and the existence of growth of MNEs.

Rising intra-African FDI points to a "proximity motive" in global FDI theorizing that compels a firm to establish a plant abroad, allowing it to serve the foreign market while circumventing trade costs. The African experience also points to the role of "industrial structure" as an issue of central importance in measuring the determinants and welfare effects of FDI flows.

An important lesson is that MNEs entering African economies through FDI face unique host country institutional (formal and informal) environments and market economy values, which influence their choices and strategies substantially. Therefore, it will be important to further develop theories that incorporate the effect of "institutional distance" (i.e. differences in institutional environments of home and host countries of MNEs) and strength of "market-conforming values" on FDI choices. In a polycentric and globalizing world facing Africa, a new FDI theory that encompasses the following new and important factors is imperative: (i) SMEs not only playing active roles in local markets, but also globally, exploiting new global opportunities; (ii) nation-states as major players with specific interests at local and global levels; and (iii) the process of SME-MNE involvement in global value chains.

The FDI inflow outlook in Africa is bright because the continent continues to offer numerous opportunities, though the options are as varied as the countries themselves. The results of recent Africa attractiveness surveys and Doing Business reports attest to this as they paint a reasonably positive picture reflecting, at a high level at least, growing confidence in Africa's prospects. Certainly, Africa has all the makings of a compelling FDI case—abundant and varied natural resources, rapid economic and population growth, maturing political/governance systems, investment returns that are second to none, and a rapidly improving investment and business environment.

A key challenge for African policymakers is to turn around lingering negative perceptions in the international community of Africa. Thus Africa and its friends need to better articulate and "sell" the story of growth and investment opportunity in the continent. In addition, African countries need to accelerate regional integration and eliminate the infrastructure deficit, while further improving business and investment climate. Going forward, efforts must be made to enhancing the investment climate while focusing on attracting substantial amount of export-oriented, efficiency-seeking, and high-quality FDI. This will entail upgrading national laws and offering of some feasible investment incentives (those adaptable with development objectives), implementing strong international best practices, rationalizing tax rates, reducing transaction costs related to export–import, dealing with bureaucracy besetting setting up of businesses in the continent, privatizing and fully liberalizing entry into key services such as telecommunications, transport and power sectors, and promoting more regional arrangements that increase the regional market size as well as the predictability, stability and transparency of the environment for investment in Africa while coordination and limiting excessive competition when providing incentives for FDI.

References

Aharoni, Y. (1960). *The Foreign Investment Decision Process*. Cambridge, MA: Harvard University Business School.

Aliber, R.Z. (1970). A theory of direct foreign investment, in C. Kindleberger (ed.), *The International Corporation: A Symposium*. Cambridge, MA: The MIT Press.

Alsan, M., Bloom, D.E., and Canning, D. (2006). The effect of population health on foreign direct investment inflows to low- and middle-income countries. *World Development*, 34(4):613–630.

Anyanwu, J.C. (1998). An econometric investigation of the determinants of foreign investment in Nigeria, in Nigerian economic society (ed.), *Rekindling Investment for Economic Development in Nigeria*. Ibadan: NES, pp. 219–241.

Anyanwu, J.C. (2006). Promoting of investment in Africa. *African Development Review*, 18(1):42–71.

Anyanwu, J.C. (2012a). Why does foreign direct investment go where it goes? New evidence from African countries. *Annals of Economics and Finance* 13(2):433–470.

Anyanwu, J.C. (2012b). Accounting for female employment in Africa. *European Economics Letters*, 1(1):14–26.

Anyanwu, J.C. (2013a). Driving factors of male employment in African countries. *African Statistical Journal*, 16 (May):12–46.

Anyanwu, J.C. (2013b). Characteristics and macroeconomic determinants of youth employment in Africa. *African Development Review*, 25(2):107–129.

Anyanwu, J.C., and Augustine, D. (2013). Gender equality in employment in Africa: empirical analysis and policy implications. *African Development Review*, 25(4):400–420.

Anyanwu, J.C., and Erhijakpor, A.E.O. (2004). Trends and determinants of foreign direct investment in Africa. *West African Journal of Monetary and Economic Integration*, Second Half:21–44.

Anyanwu, J.C., and Erhijakpor, A.E.O. (2009). Managing oil revenues in Africa: the Nigerian case. *Nigerian Journal of Securities and Finance*, 14(2):61–92.

Arellano, C., Bulir, A., Lane, T., and Lipschitz, L. (2009). The dynamic implications of foreign aid and its variability. *Journal of Development Economics*, 88(1):87–102.

Asiedu, E. (2002). On the determinants of foreign direct investment to developing countries: is Africa different? *World Development*, 30(1):107–119.

Asiedu, E. (2004). Capital controls and foreign direct investment. *World Development*, 32(3):479–490.

Asiedu, E. (2006). Foreign direct investment in Africa: the role of natural resources, market size, government policy, institutions and political instability. *World Economy*, 29(1):63–77.

Baniak, A., Cukrowski A.J., and Herczynski, J. (2005). On the determinants of foreign direct investment in transition economies. *Problems of Economic Transition*, 48(2):6–28.

Blaise, S. (2005). On the link between Japanese ODA and FDI in China: A micro economic evaluation using conditional logit analysis. *Applied Economics*, 37(1):51–5.

Buckley, P.J., and Casson, M. (1976). *The Future of the Multinational Enterprise*. London: Macmillan.

Brahmasrene T., and Jiranyakul K. (2001). Thailand inward foreign direct investment: what factors matter? *Academy for Studies in International Business Proceedings*, 1(2):13.

Brambila-Macias, J., and Massa, I. (2010). The global financial crisis and sub-Saharan Africa: the effects of slowing private capital inflows on growth. *African Development Review*, 22(3):366–377.

Casson, M. (1990). The theory of foreign direct investment, in P.J. Buckley (ed.), *International Investment*. Aldershot: Edward Elgar.

Caves, R.E. (1971). International corporations: the industrial economics of foreign investment. *Economica*, 38(149):1–27.

Dunning, J.H. (1979). Explaining changing patterns of international production: in defence of the eclectic theory. *Oxford Bulletin of Economics and Statistics*, 41(4):269–295.

Dunning, J.H. (1981a). Explaining the international direct investment position of countries: towards a dynamic or development approach. *Weltwirtschaftliches Archiv*, 117(1):30–64.

Dunning J.H. (1981b). *International Production and Multinational Enterprises*. London: George Allen and Unwin.

Dunning J.H. (1993a). *The Globalization of Business*. London: Routledge.

Dunning J.H. (1993b). *Multinational Enterprises and the Global Economy*. Reading, MA: Addison-Wesley.

Dunning, J.H., and Narula, R. (1996). The investment development path revisited: some emerging issues, in J.H. Dunning and R. Narula (eds), *Foreign Direct Investment and Governments: Catalysts for Economic Restructuring*. London: Routledge, pp. 1–41.

Dupasquier, C., and Osakwe, P.N. (2003). Performance, Promotion, and Prospects for Foreign Investment in Africa: National, Regional, and International Responsibilities, Paper Prepared for the Eminent Persons' Meeting on Promotion of Investment in Africa, Tokyo, February.

Dupasquier, C., and Osakwe P.N. (2006). Foreign direct investment in Africa: performance, challenges, and responsibilities. *Journal of Asian Economics*, 17(2):241–260.

Ernst & Young (2013). *Ernst & Young's 2012 attractiveness survey Africa 2013: Getting Down to Business*. London: EYGM Limited.

Esso, L. (2010). Long-run relationship and causality between foreign direct investment and growth: evidence from ten African countries. *International Journal of Economics and Finance*, 2(2):168–177.

Hailu, Z.A. (2010). Demand side factors affecting the inflow of foreign direct investment to African countries: does capital market matter? *International Journal of Business and Management*, 5(5):104–116.

Harms, P., and Lutz, M. (2006). Aid, governance, and private foreign investment. *Economic Journal*, 116(513):773–790.

Hennart, J.F. (1982). *A Theory of Multinational Enterprise*. Ann Arbor, MI: University of Michigan Press.

Hymer, S.H. (1960). The international operations of national firms: a study of direct investment. Ph.D. thesis. Cambridge, MA: MIT Press.

James, S. (2009). *Incentives and Investments: Evidence and Policy Implications, Investment Climate Advisory Services of the World Bank Group*. Washington, DC: The World Bank Group.

Johnson, H.G. (1968). *Comparative Cost and Commercial Policy Theory for a Developing World Economy*. Stockholm: Almquist and Wiksell.

Johanson, J., and Vahlne, J.E. (1977). The internationalization process of the firm—a model of knowledge development and increasing market commitments. *Journal of International Business Studies*, 8(1):23–32.

Johanson, J., and Wiedersheim-P.F. (1975). The internationalisation of the firm—four Swedish cases. *Journal of Management Studies*, 12(3):305–322.

Kimura, H., and Todo, Y. (2010). Is foreign aid a vanguard of foreign direct investment? A gravity-equation approach. *World Development*, 38(4):482–497.

Kindleberger, C.P. (1969). *American Business Abroad*. New Haven: Yale University Press.

Knickerbocker, F.T. (1973). *Oligopolistic Reaction and the Multinational Enterprise*. Cambridge, MA: Harvard University Press.

Kogut, B. (1984). Normative observations on the value added chain and strategic groups. *Journal of International Business Studies*, 15(2):151–168.

Kogut, B. (1985). Designing global strategies: Profiting from operational flexibility. *Sloan Management Review*, 27(1):27–38.

Kogut, B., and Zander, U. (1993). Knowledge of the firm and the evolutionary theory of the multinational corporation. *Journal of International Business Studies*, 24(4):625–645.

Kojima, K. (1973). A macroeconomic approach to foreign direct investment. *Hitotsubashi Journal of Economics*, 14(1):1–24.

Kyereboah-Coleman, A., and Agyire-Tettey K.F. (2008). Effect of exchange-rate volatility on foreign direct investment in sub-Saharan Africa: the case of Ghana (case study). *Journal of Risk Finance*, 9(1):52–70.

Lederman, D., Mengistae, T., and Xu, L.C. (2010). *Microeconomic Consequences and Macroeconomic Causes of Foreign Direct Investment in Southern African Economies*. World Bank Policy Research Working Paper 5416. Washington, DC: World Bank.

Lessard, D.R. (1976). World, country and industry factors in equity returns: implications for risk reductions through international diversification. *Financial Analysts Journal*, 32(1):32–8.

Luo, Y. (2000). Dynamic capabilities in international expansion. *Journal of Word Business*, 35(4):355–378.

Markowitz, H.M. (1959). *Portfolio Selection: Efficient Diversification of Investment*. New York: John Wiley & Sons.

McKinsey & Company (2010). *Lions on the Move: The Progress and Potential of African Economies*. London: McKinsey Global Institute.

Mohamed, S.E., and Sidiropoulos, M.G. (2010). Another look at the determinants of foreign direct investment in MENA countries: an empirical investigation. *Journal of Economic Development*, 35(2):75–96.

Mundell, R.A. (1957). International trade and factor mobility. *American Economic Review*, 47(3):321–335.

Ncube, M., and Anyanwu, J.C. (2012). *Inequality and the Arab Spring Revolutions in North Africa and the Middle East*. AfDB Africa Economic Brief. 3(7):July.

Nelson, R., and Winter, S. (1982). *An Evolutionary Theory of Economic Change*. Cambridge, MA: Belknap Press of Harvard University Press.

Nnadozie, E., and Osili, U.O. (2004). U.S. Foreign Direct Investment in Africa and its Determinants, UNECA Workshop of Financial Systems and Mobilization in Africa, November 2, 2004.

OECD (2008). *OECD Benchmark Definition of Foreign Direct Investment*, 4th edition. Paris: OECD.

Ohmae, K. (1991). *The Borderless World: Power and Strategy in the Interlinked Economy*. New York: HarperCollins Publishers Inc.

Oladipo, O.S. (2008). Foreign Direct Investment Flow: Determinants and Growth Effects in a Small Open Economy. Proceedings of the Northeast Business & Economics Association, Northeast Business & Economics Association 35th Annual Conference, Long Island, New York, November 6th–8th.

Prahalad, C.K., and Doz, Y. (1987). *The Multinational Mission*. New York: Free Press.

Reiter, S.L. et al. (2010). Human development and foreign direct investment in developing countries: the influence of FDI policy and corruption. *World Development*, 38(12):1678–1691.

Rodríguez, X., and Pallas, J. (2008). Determinants of foreign direct investment in Spain. *Applied Economics*, 40(19):2443–2450.

Rugman, A.M. (1975). Motives of foreign investment: the market imperfections and risk diversification. *Journal of World Trade Law*, 9(5):567–574.

Sander, K.K., and MacDonald, R. (2009). Capital flows and growth in developing countries: a dynamic panel data analysis. *Oxford Development Studies*, 37(2):101–122.

Sekkat, K., and Veganzones-Varoudakis, M.-A. (2007). Openness, investment climate, and FDI in developing countries. *Review of Development Economics*, 11(4):607–620.

Shenkar, O., and Luo, Y. (2008). *International Business*, 2nd edition. Thousand Oaks: Sage Publications Inc.

Te Velde, D.W., and Morrissey, O. (2001). Foreign Ownership and Wages: Evidence from Five African Countries. Centre for Research in Economic Development and International Trade (CREDIT) Research Papers 01/19, November.

Teece, D.J., Pisano, G., and Shuen, A. (1997). Dynamic capabilities and strategic management. *Strategic Management Journal*, 18(7):509–533.

Tobin, J. (1958). Liquidity preferences as behavior toward risk. *Review of Economic Studies*, 25(1):65–86.

Tolentino, P.E. (1992). *Technology, Innovation and Third World Multinationals*. London: Routledge.

UNCTAD (2013). *World Investment Report 2013*. New York & Geneva: UNCTAD.

UNCTADStat Database. http://unctadstat.unctad.org/ReportFolders/reportFolders.aspx?s RF_ActivePath=p,5&sRF_Expanded=,p,5

Vernon, R. (1966). International investment and international trade in the product cycle. *Quarterly Journal of Economics*, 80(2):190–207.

Yasin, M. (2005). Official development assistance and foreign direct investment flows to sub-Saharan Africa. *African Development Review*, 17(1):23–40.

CHAPTER 41

......

INTERNATIONAL CAPITAL FLOWS TO AFRICA

......

MWANZA NKUSU AND MALOKELE NANIVAZO[1]

41.1 INTRODUCTION

......

THE importance of capital flows for Africa takes its cue from the Harrod-Domar/ financing-gap model further developed by Chenery and Strout (1966). This model postulates that economic development in poor countries is constrained by inadequate domestic savings relative to the level of investment needed to bring economic growth to a certain level. In essence, the model suggests that one could estimate the level of investment associated with a desired rate of economic growth and derive the amount of foreign capital necessary to fill the gap between domestic savings and the required level of investment. In the same vein, some economists argue that inadequacy or lack of capital keeps countries trapped in poverty in the developing world (Nelson 1956; Sachs 2005). In the spirit of the financing gap model, the African Union's 2001 framework of the New Partnership for Africa's Development (NEPAD) stipulates in its Article 144 that to achieve the estimated 7% annual growth rate needed to meet the Millennium Development Goals (MDGs), particularly, the goal of reducing by half the proportion of Africans living in poverty by the year 2015, Africa needs to fill an annual resource gap of 12% of its gross domestic product (GDP), or US$64 billion (African Union 2001). While recognizing the need to increase domestic savings, the framework indicates that the bulk of the needed funds will have to come from outside the continent.

The expectation that capital should come from outside the continent is in line with the neoclassical model's prediction that capital should flow from richer countries to poorer ones. This implies that the poorest countries that open up to cross-border finance would run current account deficits covered by foreign capital. As Sub-Saharan Africa (SSA) generally has limited or no access to international capital markets, the two most relevant forms of capital flows are foreign aid and foreign direct investment (FDI). Remittances complement domestic savings to ease the financing constraint and are assimilated to foreign capital. Their

[1] Mwanza Nkusu: International Monetary Fund; Malokele Nanivazo: UNU-WIDER.

growing importance in financing domestic demand in developing countries somewhat blurs the notion that foreign capital is the financing side of the current account. From an accounting perspective, remittances are not part of capital flows per se. They are recorded as private current transfers and, as such, are an integral part of the current account. From a pure financing perspective, remittances, along with current official grants, are assimilated to various components of cross-border capital flows whose determinants, trends, relevance, and implications for the socioeconomic development are the subject of this chapter and others in this handbook. However, they will not be the focus of our analysis.

This chapter focuses on foreign aid and FDI and examines their role in the socio-economic development of Africa from different angles. The struggle of most African countries—especially those in the Sub-Saharan region—to break out of poverty despite decades of aid disbursement and FDI inflows to exploit the region's vast natural resources remains one of the most debated issues among researchers and international development stakeholders. Views on various aspects of these flows sometimes get polarized. With regard to aid's effectiveness in promoting growth and reducing poverty, many researchers argue that aid works while others see it as not working or even "dead" (Moyo 2009). For FDI, to the extent that the bulk of FDI flows to Africa are directed to the extractive industry, these flows are seen as not promoting development because of the so-called natural resource curse. Our objective is to show that there is a way to advance the debate on the role of capital flows for Africa's development without extreme generalizations that can be misleading. Considering that chapters specific to the different types of capital flows provide more elaborate literature reviews, we focus on insights from the literature on the complex relationships between poor institutions in recipient countries and both aid and FDI flows to draw attention to the question of why these flows have had a limited impact on the continent's development. Against this background, we hope to refocus the debate on how to make aid and FDI work better for Africa.

The chapter is structured as follows. The next section discusses Africa's need for foreign capital, elaborating on the financing gap identified in the NEPAD's 2001 framework. Sections 3–5 are structured around the following three questions: (i) What drives aid and FDI? (ii) What are the macroeconomic effects of aid and FDI? and (iii) How can capital flows help Africa in its quest for growth and poverty reduction? Section 6 concludes.

41.2 AFRICA'S NEED FOR FOREIGN CAPITAL

Africa's need for capital is less a subject of controversy than the appropriateness of the Harrod–Domar model as a development framework for the continent. The poor state of Africa's infrastructure and human capital and the pervasive poverty suggest that Africa can benefit from foreign finance that could be used to boost its capital stock. The NEPAD framework highlights the need to attract private capital as a long-term endeavor, while stressing the importance of additional foreign aid in the short to medium term, in particular for the least-developed countries. However, attracting capital flows does not guarantee that output will grow at some determined rate. A number of factors, including institutions, macroeconomic policies, and income distribution, contribute to shaping the relationship between investment and output, as well as that between foreign capital and economic development.

The annual financing gap put forth in the 2001 NEPAD framework begs attention simply because it is part of a development agenda adopted by African leaders. To put this gap into a historical perspective, we document SSA's experience with capital flows so as to gauge the severity of possible financial "shortfalls," as well as the potential growth benefits that additional finance could provide. We compare the purported financing gap to actual flows recorded during 1980–2010, with no intention of discussing trends in capital flows, to which a different chapter in this volume is devoted. As regards the financing gap, in the absence of details on both its derivation and breakdown among countries or country groups, we assume that it pertains to SSA.

The analysis supports the view that the financing gap model may not be an appropriate framework within which to discuss Africa's need for foreign capital. The US$64 billion and the 12% of GDP, referred to as representing "the annual financing gap," cannot be one and the same measure over time. The dollar amount of 64 billion turns out to represent 12% of the 2001 GDP of SSA expressed in 2005 dollars but it corresponds to a declining share of the region's GDP at current dollars, reaching almost 5½% by 2010. The data suggest that recorded net annual inflows—including official development assistance (ODA), FDI, private portfolio flows, and remittances—have, by far, exceeded US$64 billion since 2005 (Figure 41.1, left). From this perspective, there is apparently no financing shortfall and, the question of whether the targeted 7% GDP growth would be guaranteed no matter what can be asked. In contrast, under the yardstick of 12% of GDP annual financing needed, shortfalls emerge. By 2010, the dollar figure corresponding to 12% of GDP balloons to nearly 100 billion and 137 billion at constant 2005 dollars and current dollars, respectively (Figure 41.1, right). Thus, it is clear that US$64 billion and 12% of GDP cannot be equivalent over time. Further, the fact that US$64 billion represents a declining share of GDP theoretically undermines the achievement of the growth target under the financing gap model: assuming foreign finance goes to

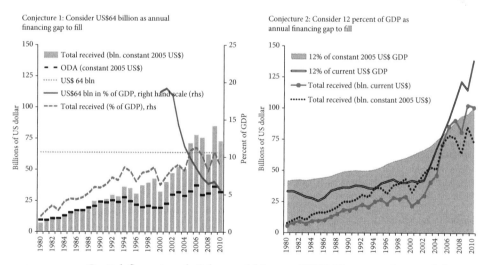

FIGURE 41.1 Capital flows to sub-Saharan Africa vs. NEPAD's reported annual financing gap (1980–2010).

Source: IMF, World Economic Outlook (WEO); World Bank, World Development Indicators (WDI)—October 2013.

Note: Total received comprises the following flows: net FDI, net portfolio, net ODA, and net remittances.

investment, if it drops while domestic savings remain constrained, the investment rate drops and, growth cannot accelerate to the desired level.

Aid and FDI flows to SSA are the focus of our analysis. Though international bank lending and portfolio flows have become an increasingly important part of private capital flows to Africa, for most African countries, the nature of private capital flows has not changed much. Except for South Africa, and North Africa that have more developed financial systems, most African countries attract relatively little portfolio flows.[2] In a few countries, improved institutional quality and deepening of local financial markets have attracted portfolio flows. In the majority of countries, FDI, remittances, and foreign aid—encompassing official grants and concessional loans—are the most relevant forms of cross-border financial flows. Remittances have become an important source of foreign capital and contribute to building human capital as transfers from migrants help recipient families cover education and heath expenses. They can also ease the foreign exchange constraint on development. However, to the extent that they do not accrue to government, they can hardly be integrated into a government-led development strategy, except if they can be clearly linked to productive investments or boosting tax revenue. FDI has been the main source of non-remittances private flows to SSA and has a potential to promote the region's development by allowing for the expansion of its productive capacity. Aid, on which many low-income countries (LICs) have depended for decades, is unique in that it can be channeled directly into development projects in areas such as health, education, and physical infrastructure.

41.3 DETERMINANTS OF AID AND FDI: SHAPING OUTCOMES IN AFRICA?

There is a wealth of studies suggesting that the factors explaining aid allocation or a country's attractiveness to FDI may have a bearing on the effectiveness of these two types of capital flows. We review in turn insights from the literature on various factors driving aid and FDI inflows.

41.3.1 Foreign aid: for donors' self-interests, recipients' needs, or both?

The debate on the factors behind aid allocation has been active for decades and can be traced back to the early 70s (McGillivray 2003).[3] A very interesting study that best summarizes different views on the determinants of aid allocation is Schraeder et al. (1998). The study suggests that the factors driving the provision of foreign aid fall within three competing paradigms of international relations. First, the realist paradigm, according to which aid policies are driven primarily by the strategic interests of donor countries such as self-preservation

[2] Hou et al. (2013) provide more information on private capital flows to SSA countries.
[3] See Mckinlay and Little (1977) and Maizels and Nissanke (1984).

and national security. As a result, aid is only marginally related to recipient countries' humanitarian and economic development needs. Second, the idealist paradigm, which purports that the humanitarian needs in recipient countries form the cornerstone of many foreign aid programs. Accordingly, scholars adhering to this paradigm are particularly optimistic about the potential impact of foreign aid in promoting development in poorer countries and promoting broadly shared prosperity across nations. Finally, there is a more broadly defined neo-Marxist paradigm, which relates to the first insofar as the centrality of the economic interests of the donor countries is concerned. Under the assumption that capitalist exploitation enhances the power of elites in both industrialized and developing countries, neo-Marxist scholars argue that foreign aid constitutes an extension of highly exploitative North–South relationships that perpetuate economic disparities between the two.

Several empirical studies support the realist paradigm of aid being driven primarily by donors' interests. They suggest that, in providing aid, bilateral donors generally follow purely political, economic, and strategic agenda. Schraeder et al. (1998) provides insights on aid allocation to Africa during the last decade of the cold war, but the ideas they develop retain their pertinence in analyses of aid allocation in general. They investigate the role played by six groups of variables—humanitarian need, strategic importance, economic potential, cultural similarity, ideological stance, and region—in explaining aid allocated by the United States, Japan, France, and Sweden. Their findings suggest that while the foreign aid policies of these four donors are complex and varied, the realist paradigm of aid allocation prevails. On this basis, they reject the suggestion that aid is an altruistic tool of foreign policy. The thrust of their findings was confirmed later by Alesina and Dollar (2000) and Hoeffler and Outram (2011). Specific aid allocation criteria include colonial past, trade partnership, or voting with a particular donor in the United Nations. Another aspect of donors' own interest that affects aid allocation is their desire to be more influential in recipient countries' policies by positioning themselves as major aid providers. In this context, the probability of securing the position of primary donor in a particular recipient country exerts a positive and significant effect on aid provided to that country (Lebovic 2005).

Several studies that focus on the role recipient countries' socioeconomic and institutional characteristics play in aid allocation find that these characteristics matter to various degrees among donor countries though they are sometimes on the back burner. Characteristics whose influence on aid has been examined include corruption, democracy, human rights, income level, and infant mortality. Findings suggest, with a few exceptions, that these characteristics matter little or not at all in aid allocation. For instance, Alesina and Weder (2002) find no evidence that less corrupt governments receive more aid. Neumayer (2003) finds that few donor countries give preference to good record on personal integrity rights or human rights in their allocation of aid. In the same vein Nunnenkamp and Thiele (2006) find that donors are not sensitive to changing policy and institutional conditions in the recipient countries, including the rule of law, corruption, and openness to trade. On a positive note, according to Trumbull and Wall (1994) infant mortality rates and the respect of political/civil rights positively affect aid allocation. Also, Nordic countries are found to be more sensitive to recipient countries' income levels and seem to reward good policies and institutions (Alesina and Dollar 2000; Alesina and Weder 2002). Furthermore, Berthélemy (2006) finds that on average, aid allocated to a particular recipient is positively correlated with poverty level (poorer), democracy level (more democratic), and bilateral export intensity.

41.3.2   Foreign direct investment: in which sectors, which countries, and why?

In SSA, FDI flows have, unsurprisingly, been predominantly directed to the oil- and minerals sectors in resource-rich countries for a couple of reasons. First, compared with developing countries in other regions, SSA countries are likely to be less attractive to foreign investment in non-resource sectors as such investment is more sensitive to country characteristics on which SSA fares poorly such as the stock of human capital, market size, democracy, and the rule of law. Second, SSA is rich in natural resources and, as several studies suggests, the abundance of natural resources is positively associated with FDI (Asiedu 2002). Also, there is a complex relationship between FDI and democracy that could explain the attractiveness of natural resource-rich countries to FDI, particularly those with corrupt and/or undemocratic government systems.

Corruption and lack of democracy can be pull factors for FDI in extractive sectors in resource-rich countries. Kolstad and Wiig (2013) investigate whether corruption attracts or deters FDI in the extractive sectors using a sample of 81 countries covering the period 1996–2009. They find that increased corruption within a country is associated with increased extractive industry FDI, but at a diminishing rate after corruption worsens beyond a certain level. Asiedu and Lien (2011) investigate the determinants of FDI in more than 100 developing countries during 1982–2007 and find that democracy promotes FDI if and only if the share of mineral and oil exports is below a certain threshold. Beyond that threshold, democratization may deter FDI. They suggest that all else being equal, foreign direct investors prefer less democratic governments in over 20 countries included in the sample. Several African countries make the list including Algeria, Angola, Congo Republic, Gabon, Niger, Nigeria, Oman, Seychelles, and Zambia.

The corruption–FDI and democracy–FDI relationships are independent of the origin of the foreign investor. In the past several years, the investment and trade relations between the Africa region and dynamic emerging markets (EMs)—Brazil, China, India, and to some extent Russia—have expanded significantly. These EMs have become big players in the extractive sectors of many African countries, attracted probably by the same factors that have attracted traditional investors for decades. Flows from China have particularly attracted the attention of researchers, policymakers, and various international institutions. In a study focused on China's FDI in 29 African countries during the period 2003–2006, Kolstad and Wiig (2011) find that Chinese FDI is attracted to countries with large natural resources, and more so the worse the institutional environment of host countries. They conclude that China is not different from other investors in this respect and indicate that exploiting resources and weak institutions appears to be the name of the investment game in Africa.

41.4   THE MACROECONOMIC EFFECTS OF AID AND FDI TO AFRICA

With insights from the literature on the factors behind aid allocation and FDI, we now turn to the literature on the effectiveness of both aid and FDI, which are widely disputed. The evidence on the impact of these two types of flows is abundant and covers a variety of aspects. For aid, three of its most covered impacts are the impact on the real exchange rate, on growth, and on socioeconomic indicators. For FDI, the impacts on domestic investment, employment, and growth have been widely discussed. However, findings on the effectiveness of both aid and FDI in promoting socioeconomic development are mixed.

The role of corruption and poor institutions in constraining the effectiveness of aid and FDI is a recurrent and less disputed finding. Corruption and poor bureaucratic quality make Africa a net exporter of capital, in line with the Lucas Paradox discussed in Lucas (1990). Some studies suggest that aid and FDI flows to Africa may not have contributed to growth because of offsetting illicit outflows, some related to corruption. In many African countries, in particular oil and mineral exporters, illicit capital outflows are very significant and can even exceed aid and FDI combined (Asiedu et al. 2012; Boyce and Ndikumana 2011). Alfaro, Kalemli-Ozcan, and Volosovych (2008) also link the Lucas Paradox to corruption in developing countries. Their findings suggest that institutional quality is the variable that explains the Lucas Paradox over the period 1970–2000. Accordingly, they indicate that policies aimed at strengthening the protection of property rights, reducing corruption, and increasing government stability, bureaucratic quality, and law and order should be a priority for policymakers seeking to increase capital inflows to poor countries. For Africa, these recommendations are not new. They resonate with what the NEPAD framework envisages.

41.4.1 Aid effectiveness: mixed findings

The effectiveness of aid hinges on various factors. Several studies suggest that aid is more beneficial to growth under certain conditions such as good policies (Burnside and Dollar 2000) or a minimum level of financial development (Nkusu and Sayek 2004). Though the beneficial impact of good policies on aid effectiveness has been challenged, common sense suggests that improving the policy environment is relevant not only for aid effectiveness but also socioeconomic development in general. Factors that limit aid effectiveness include its allocation to wasteful spending (Boone 1994, 1996), flaws in the aid bureaucracy, including high overhead costs, lack of transparency, fragmentation, and lack of donors' accountability to beneficiary communities in recipient countries are also considered as undermining aid effectiveness (Easterly and Pfutze 2008). Several studies suggest that aid fails to promote development because it weakens the revenue effort, encourages corruption, and hampers exports' diversification through Dutch disease effects associated with large aid flows (Gupta et al. 2008; Knack, 2000; Rajan and Subramanian, 2011).

For almost every claim, there is a counter-claim. The evidence of the limited effectiveness of aid in promoting growth can be attributed to the fact that economic growth and development are so complex that establishing a one-to-one relationship linking them to aid may not be appropriate as they depend on a host of factors. Studies that adopt a narrower approach focusing on the impact of sectoral aid on social indicators such as health and education outcomes find that aid is effective whereas in studies focusing on growth findings on the effectiveness of aid are inconclusive. This is known as the micro–macro paradox (Mosley 1985). As for the impact of aid on revenue, weaknesses in the revenue effort of aid-recipient countries is not necessarily because of aid. Where there is a strong commitment to promote self-reliance, there would be reforms aimed at boosting revenue performance. With regard to real exchange rate (RER) appreciations that could be considered as symptoms of the Dutch disease, the evidence is weak even though the mainstream view has been that large aid flows tend to appreciate the RER. Failure of the increase in spending induced by large aid flows or other sectoral booms to give rise to the Dutch disease is documented for several countries, including Botswana (Harvey 1992) and Uganda (Nkusu 2004; Berg et al. 2007). Moreover, as noted in Nkusu (2004), even if aid-induced spending were to be associated with a RER appreciation, such appreciation need not necessarily be a sign of the Dutch disease.

The mixed results on the effectiveness of aid can be attributed to technical and statistical issues, or to deficiencies in the mechanisms through which aid affects outcomes. The technical or statistical issues include the time horizon over which the impact of aid is assessed; endogeneity of the aid–growth relationship; and the difficulty of determining the direction of causality. As regards the mechanisms through which aid affects growth and development, Bourguignon and Sundberg (2007) identify three causality chains that evolve around policy design and implementation. The causality links run as follows: from donors to policymakers in recipient countries through policy advice and conditionality, from policymakers to policies through governance systems, and from policies to outcomes.

41.4.2 FDI and economic growth in host economies

FDI flows, which are generally more stable than portfolio flows for instance, can contribute to development on a lasting basis, especially if they relate to greenfield projects or sectors with positive externalities. The sectors to which FDI is attracted matter a great deal when it comes to spillovers in the host economy and the impact on growth itself and its inclusiveness. For instance, greenfield FDI in labor-intensive manufacturing and services sectors can contribute to creating jobs and promoting inclusive growth. This is generally not the case for FDI in capital-intensive resource sectors that lack forward and backward linkages with the host economy. However, to the extent that foreign capital invested in the exploitation of natural resources can contribute to fiscal revenue through royalties and other taxes, it may help finance socioeconomic development.

The theoretical arguments that FDI promotes growth are not controversial, but evidence from empirical analyses does not always point in the same direction. Several studies lend support to the theoretical literature suggesting that FDI promotes growth (Hansen and Rand 2006). Others suggest that the impact can be negative (Moran 1999) while several others find that FDI does not exert a robust positive impact on growth (Carkovic and Levine 2005; Herzer et al. 2008). Another strand of the empirical literature suggests that FDI is beneficial to growth only under certain conditions in the recipient country as discussed below, finding for which Herzer et al. (2008) find no support.

Could it be the case that SSA has not benefitted much from FDI because local conditions are not favorable? Some studies find that LICs do not enjoy substantial growth benefits from FDI as do more-developed countries (Blomström et al. 1994). A certain threshold level of development is necessary to absorb new technology from investment of foreign firms. In the same vein, Wu and Chih-Chiang (2008) find, in a study including African countries, that FDI alone has an ambiguous impact on growth as such impact depends on absorptive capacity of the host country. Some of the absorptive capacity indicators identified in the literature include a minimum level of human capital (Borensztein et al. 1998) or financial sector development (Alfaro et al. 2004; Hermes and Lensink 2003), or institutions (Olofsdotter 1998). In some studies of the impact of FDI on growth that include a dummy for Africa, this dummy emerges with a negative sign even after controlling for the absorptive capacity indicators (Borensztein et al. 1998; Li and Liu 2005), suggesting that FDI does not benefit growth in African countries as much as it does elsewhere.

41.4.3 Can the effectiveness of aid and FDI on growth in SSA be enhanced?

The concerns about the limited effects of aid on poverty reduction are legitimate, but they should not be used to cast doubt on the usefulness of aid. It is true that aid has been misused by some recipient countries' governments, but also delivered through aid agencies whose practices have been called into question. Some of the deplored practices include lack of transparency, fragmentation, and no accountability to populations in recipient countries. These practices notwithstanding, it could be argued that where aid has been used to support a clear development policy, it has worked as discussed next.

The resounding success of Botswana and South Korea in developing their respective economies is sometimes discussed without giving due consideration to the role foreign aid played. Botswana, which has reached middle-income status, was aid-dependent for decades and used aid in its development process. Korea's example also suggests that aid can be used to enhance the socioeconomic infrastructure needed for development. Foreign assistance was used to overcome various hurdles to development and to support a government-led development strategy encompassing also an industrial policy component. Korea moved from being one of the poorest nations in the world and a major recipient of aid for about 50 years to becoming the thirteenth largest economy in the world, an aid provider, and a member of the Development Assistance Committee of the Organization for Economic Co-operation and Development (OECD) since 2009 (Kim 2011). Strong government ownership and commitment are credited with enabling the country to be one of the very few cases in which foreign aid contributed to promoting self-supporting economic development of the recipient country. This suggests that it is not aid that is bad, but rather what drives it and how it is used. Therefore, though development is complex and multifaceted, the Korean experience can offer some useful insights on current issues, inform the debate on financial integration and international cooperation, and help devise constructive responses to development challenges facing many SSA countries.

The different development pathways that resource-rich countries around the world have had speak to the role of institutions. In South Africa, natural resources contributed to building an enclave relatively prosperous economy though the prosperity was not shared for a long time owing to segregation. Botswana has moved from the poor, aid-dependent country it was prior to the discovery of diamonds to middle-income status. Outside Africa, Norway, and Australia are examples of countries that have succeeded in benefiting from investment in their oil and mineral sectors. This diversity enriches the analysis and provides insights into the menu of policy options available to some of the lagging countries.

Undoubtedly, the socioeconomic benefits of FDI in the extractive sectors are likely to be subdued or even negative in countries with corrupt officials and undemocratic systems of government. For foreign investors, countries with poor institutions where people have no voice offer an opportunity to maximize profits by exploiting cheap labor and overlooking environmental standards. The framework could be characterized as one of "bribe, invest, extract, pollute, and export (BI-EPE)."[4] As the cycle of extract, pollute, export (EPE) continues over the years, host countries' endowments in natural resources end up being used to provide personal gains to individual politicians or connected officials and huge profits to foreign investors while contributing little or nothing to socioeconomic development. Considering also that extractive industries such as oil are not labor intensive and generally lack backward and forward linkages to host economies, externalities for host countries can even be negative if oil rents are embezzled, supporting the so-called natural resource curse and even fuelling communities' resentment towards multinational enterprises (MNEs).[5]

A number of multilateral global initiatives can help make FDI in the oil and mining sectors benefit host countries, but these countries' own responsibility is critical. The OECD has guidelines for mining companies aimed at promoting "the positive contributions that MNEs can make to economic, environmental, and social progress." The guidelines of corporate social responsibility cover a variety of areas including employment, human rights, environment and information disclosure. The Extractive Industries Transparency Initiative (EITI) aims at improving openness and accountable management of revenues from natural resources. These initiatives will only contribute to helping Africa harness its natural resources to create wealth for the well-being of its people if African governments work for their people. It is only then that natural resources would be a blessing, which is the way they should be perceived.

41.5 Using Capital Flows to Advance Africa's Quest for Growth and Poverty Reduction

Just as economic development is a complex process, both the attractiveness to- and the growth-effects of capital flows hinge on various factors. These include endowment in natural resources, the level of development of infrastructure and institutions, the level of development of human capital, and the macroeconomic policy framework. Against the background of African countries' different circumstances, their experiences with aid and FDI vary. However, there is ample evidence that for many countries, the development benefits of aid

---

[4] Non-Government Organizations (NGOs) such as Global Witness expose cases of corruption on natural resource-related transactions that suggest the problem is serious and unfortunately quite frequent. (http://www.globalwitness.org).

[5] A 2013 Deloitte and Touch report on the challenges facing mining companies in South Africa—titled Tough Choices Facing the South Africa Mining Industry—indicates that the government increasingly expects mining companies to fulfill social needs such as the provision of basic services, education and healthcare. The report indicates also that communities often perceive companies as generating wealth and repatriating dividends, leaving behind a damaged environment with little lasting benefit for the community. The reported perception South African communities have of mining companies will resonate in several other countries across Africa.

and FDI have been limited at best. Nonetheless, there is no reason why aid and FDI should not promote growth and reduce poverty.

Our review of the literature suggests that categorical extreme views on the development effects of capital flows are not warranted. Peeling away ideologies and dissecting the evidence can shed light on why aid or FDI have generally not lifted numerous African countries out of poverty though some have made strides to middle income status. In some countries, aid flows helped fund initiatives that catalyze private sector development, contributing to making them move up the development ladder. Likewise, some countries have used revenues from mineral resources for socioeconomic development. This begs the question of what is the role of aid and FDI in the socioeconomic development of SSA countries. We argue that they have primarily a supportive role.

As the examples of formerly aid-dependent countries and successful resource-rich countries discussed above suggest, both aid and FDI in the extractive sectors can be used to promote development. The greatest responsibility for Africa's development lies first and foremost in the hands of Africa's leaders and people themselves. With clear visions about what they want to achieve for their countries, governments can use aid for infrastructure and human capital development. They can continue strengthening institutions and policies to attract FDI and, in resource-rich countries, ensure that mineral revenues contribute to funding various development initiatives. The importance of internalizing the fact that aid is not necessarily altruistic cannot be overemphasized. Bilateral aid will almost always be driven to an extent by the interests of the donor countries. Also, transformational development of host countries is not and cannot be an objective of profit-seeking foreign investors. Therefore, whether investors are from western countries or from dynamic EMCs such as the BRICS, FDI is foremost for profit. It is up to African governments to have people-centered partnerships with foreign capital providers based on shared responsibility and mutual interest. These people-centered arrangements should go hand in hand with the implementation of the stipulations of NEPAD's Democracy and Political Governance Initiative as well as the Economic Governance Initiative.

Finding ways to address weaknesses that have undermined aid and FDI's contribution to Africa's development on several fronts is a challenge worth taking for African Leaders. First, the commitment to improve economic and political governance, if followed through with consistent actions across countries, would improve the use of scarce resources—domestic or foreign—for development. In resource-rich countries, such improvement will enable harnessing natural resource wealth to finance productive investment, raise living standards, and avoid the so-called natural resource curse. As Collier and Venables (2011) suggest, the potential financial flows from resource exports dwarf aid, remittances, and FDI, providing a big opportunity for development. Second, in the context of NEPAD's long-term vision of an African-led and African-owned development strategy, governments are expected to proactively seek foreign capital to invest in well-designed and potentially high impact projects such as the ones discussed next.

The presence of new players in the provision of capital to Africa and the existence of NEPAD offer an opportunity to forge development partnerships aimed at decisively easing the most pressing infrastructure challenges as infrastructure has been one of the major constraints to Africa's development. The BRIC's revealed interest in Africa as a source of natural resources and a market for their exports can be used to encourage them to contribute to financing flagship infrastructure projects to advance Africa's regional and continental economic integration through, for instance, a framework in which each BRIC country specializes in a specific domain of infrastructure such as roads, rail, electricity, or several BRICS collaborate in infrastructure joint ventures joining finances and technical expertise. If African policymakers and their foreign partners can devise mechanisms for implementing such a framework, there will be a break with the ongoing fragmentation and an opportunity to boost the effectiveness of foreign capital, including through economies of scale in integrated regional markets and attractiveness to FDI in the non-resource sectors in which SSA has not been very competitive.

Besides African leaders, foreign providers of capital and all interested in international development and the fate of Africa in particular have an important role to play to give the continent a chance to benefit more meaningfully from capital flows. Stepping up ongoing efforts to increase transparency in mining contracts and in the use of proceeds from natural resources would be important as even more African countries join the group of resource-rich. As regards official assistance, efforts in addressing weaknesses identified in the provision of aid will make it more effective. Last, but not least, cooperation to end the documented phenomenon of capital inflows being offset by illegal outflows from corrupt leaders would also be important.

41.6 Concluding Remarks

This chapter discusses capital flows to Africa, highlighting various factors that drive these flows and contribute to shaping their socioeconomic impacts on Africa. It suggests that the focus on a financing gap can distract from the more important issue of proactively seeking foreign capital that can advance a well-defined development strategy and making such capital work. Further, the documented large size of illicit capital flowing out of Africa obviates the rhetoric on financing gaps. Focusing on aid and FDI to SSA, we argue that these flows have a role to play in Africa's development even though they are generally seen as having had mixed or limited effects on the development of many SSA countries. Examples of countries whose use of aid or FDI in the resource sector contributed to socioeconomic development under relatively good economic and political governance suggest that extreme rhetorical statements as to whether aid or FDI work or do not work are not warranted. The documented evidence on the factors that tend to undermine the effectiveness of aid and FDI provides insights on how to move the discussion to what can be done to make these flows work for SSA. We highlight possible policy implications relevant for African leaders as well as their development partners. For African leaders, the criticality of having clear people-centered development strategies and establishing institutions that facilitate the implementation of such strategies cannot be overemphasized. Also, finding the right balance between the interests of providers of foreign capital and the contribution of such capital to the implementation of national development strategies should be of paramount importance.

REFERENCES

African Union (2001). The New Partnership for Africa's Development. Framework Document. http://www.nepad.org/nepad/knowledge/doc/1767/nepad-framework-document.

Alesina, A., and Dollar, D. (2000). Who gives foreign aid to whom and why? *Journal of Economic Growth*, 5(1):33–63.

Alesina, A., and Weder, B. (2002). Do corrupt governments receive less foreign aid? *American Economic Review*, 92(4):1126–1237.

Alfaro, L., Chanda, A., Kalemli-Ozcan, S., and Sayek, S. (2004). FDI and economic growth: the role of local financial markets. *Journal of International Economics*, 64(1):89–112.

Alfaro, L., Kalemli-Ozcan, S., and Volosovych, V. (2008). Why doesn't capital flow from rich to poor countries? An empirical investigation. *Review of economics and Statistics*, 90(2):347–368.

Asiedu, E. (2002). On the Determinants of foreign direct investment to developing countries: is Africa different? *World Development*, 30(1):107–119.

Asiedu, E., and Lien, D. (2011). Democracy, foreign direct investment and natural resources. *Journal of International Economics*, 84(1):99–111.

Asiedu, E., Nana, F., and Nti-Addae, A. (2012). The paradox of capital flight from a capital-starved continent. *Association of Concerned Africa Scholars, Bulletin*, 87(Fall):22–64.

Berg, A. et al. (2007). The Macroeconomics of Scaling Up Aid: Lessons from Recent Experience. IMF Occasional Papers 253, International Monetary Fund.

Berthélemy, J.C. (2006). Bilateral donors' interest vs. recipients' development motives in aid allocation: do all donors behave the same? *Review of Development Economics*, 10(2):179–194.

Blomström, M., Kokko, A., and Zejan, M. (1994). Host country competition and technology transfer by multinationals. *Weltwirtschaftliches Archiv*, 130:521–533.

Boone, P. (1994). *The Impact of Foreign Aid on Savings and Growth*. London School of Economics, Mimeo.

Boone, P. (1996). Politics and the effectiveness of foreign aid. *European Economic Review*, 40(2):289–329.

Borensztein, E., De Gregorio, J., and Lee, J.W. (1998). How does foreign direct investment affect economic growth? *Journal of International Economics*, 45(1):115–135.

Bourguignon, F., and Sundberg, M. (2007). Aid effectiveness: opening the black box. *American Economic Review*, 97(2):316–321.

Boyce, J., and Ndikumana, L. (2011). *Africa's Odious Debts: How Foreign Loans and Capital Flight Bled a Continent*: London: Zed Books.

Burnside, C., and Dollar, D. (2000). Aid, policies, and growth. *American Economic Review*, 90(4):847–868.

Carkovic, M., and Levine, R. (2005). Does foreign direct investment accelerate economic growth? in Theodore H. Moran, Edward D. Graham, and Magnus Blomström (eds), *Does Foreign Direct Investment Promote Development?* Washington: Institute for International Economics, 2005, pp. 195–220.

Chenery, H.B., and Strout, A.M. (1966). Foreign assistance and economic development. *American Economic Review*, 56(4):679–733.

Collier, P., and Venables, A. (2011). Harnessing windfall revenues: optimal policies for resource-rich developing economies. *Economic Journal*, 121:1–30.

Easterly, W., and Pfutze, T. (2008). Where does the money go: best and worst practices in foreign aid. *Journal of Economic Perspectives*, 22(2):29–52.

Gupta, S. et al. (2008). Foreign aid and revenue response: does the composition of aid matter? Chapter 14 in S. Gupta, B. Clements, and G. Inchauste (eds), Helping Countries Develop: The Role of Fiscal Policy (Washington: International Monetary Fund).

Hansen, H., and Rand, J. (2006). On the causal links between FDI and growth in developing countries. *The World Economy*, 29(1): 21–41.

Harvey, C. (1992). Botswana: is the economic miracle over? *Journal of African Economies*, 1:335–368.

Hermes, N., and Lensink, R. (2003). Foreign direct investment, financial development and economic growth. *Journal of Development Studies*, 40(1):142–163.

Herzer, D., Klasen, S., and Nowak Lehmann, F.D. (2008). In search of FDI-led growth in developing. *Economic Modelling*, 25:793–810.

Hoeffler, A., and Outram, V. (2011). Need, merit, or self interest—what determines the allocation of aid? *Review of Development Economics*, 15(2):237–250.

Hou, Z. et al. (2013). The Changing Nature of Private Capital Flows to Sub-Saharan Africa. Shockwatch Bulletin Working Paper, 376.

Hou, Z., et al. (2013). Shockwatch Bulletin: The Changing Nature of Private Capital Flows to Sub-Saharan Africa. *ODI Working Paper*, 376. London: Overseas Development Institute.

Kim, J. (2011). Foreign aid and economic development: the success story of South Korea. *Pacific Focus*, 26(2):260–286.

Knack, S. (2000). Aid dependency and the quality of governance: a cross-country empirical analysis. World Bank Policy Research Paper 2396. Washington, DC: World Bank.

Kolstad, I., and Wiig, A. (2011). Better the devil you know? Chinese foreign direct investment in Africa. *Journal of African Business*, 12(1):31–50.

Kolstad, I., and Wiig, A. (2013). Digging in the dirt: extractive industries' FDI and corruption. *Economic Governance*, 14:369–383.

Lebovic, J. (2005). Donor positioning: development assistance from the U.S., Japan, France, Germany, and Britain. *Political Research Quarterly*, 58(1):119–126.

Li, X., and Liu, X. (2005). Foreign direct investment and economic growth: An increasingly endogenous relationship. *World Development*, 33(3):393–407.

Lucas, R. Jr. (1990), Why doesn't capital flow from rich to poor countries. *American Economic Review*, 80(2):92–96.

Maizels, A., and Nissanke, M.K. (1984). Motivations for aid to developing countries. *World Development*, 12(9):879–890.

McKinlay, R.D., and Little, R. (1977). A foreign policy model of US bilateral aid allocation. *World Politics*, 30(1):58–86.

McGillivray, M. (2003). *Modelling Aid Allocation: Issues, Approaches and Results. WIDER Discussion Papers*. Helsinki: World Institute for Development Economics (UNU-WIDER).

Mosley, P. (1985). The political economy of foreign aid: a model of the market for a public good. *Economic Development and Cultural Change*, 33:373–394.

Moran, T. (1999). Foreign direct investment and development: a reassessment of the evidence and policy implications. OECD Conference on the Role of International Investment in Development. Paris: Organization for Economic Cooperation and Development.

Moyo, D. (2009). *Dead Aid: Why Aid Is Not Working and How There Is Another Way For Africa*. New York: Farrar, Straus and Giroux.

Nelson, R.R. (1956). A theory of the low-level equilibrium trap in underdeveloped economies. *American Economic Review*, 46:894–908.

Neumayer, E. (2003). Do human rights matter in bilateral aid allocation? A quantitative analysis of 21 donor countries. *Social Science Quarterly*, 84(3):650–666.

Nkusu, M. (2004). Aid and the Dutch disease in low-income countries: informed diagnoses for prudent prognoses. IMF Working Papers. Washington, DC: International Monetary Fund.

Nkusu, M., and Sayek, S. (2004). Local financial development and aid-growth relationship. IMF Working Papers. Washington, DC: International Monetary Fund.

Nunnenkamp, P., and Thiele, R. (2006). Targeting aid to the needy and deserving: nothing but promises? *World Economy*, 29(9):1177–1201.

Olofsdotter, K. (1998). Foreign direct investment, country capabilities and economic growth. *Weltwitschaftliches Archive*, 134(3):534–547.

Rajan, R.G., and Subramanian, A. (2011). Aid, Dutch disease, and manufacturing growth. *Journal of Development Economics*, 94(1):106–118.

Sachs, J. (2005). *The End of Poverty: Economic Possibilities for our Time*. New York: Penguin Books.

Schraeder, P.J., Hook, S.W., and Taylor, B. (1998). Clarifying the foreign aid puzzle: A comparison of American, Japanese, French, and Swedish aid flows. *World Politics*, (50):294–323.

Trumbull, W.N., and Wall, H.J. (1994). Estimating aid-allocation criteria with panel data. *Economic Journal*, 104(425):876–882.

Wu, J., and Chih-Chiang, H. (2008). Does foreign direct investment promote economic growth? Evidence from a threshold regression analysis. *Economics Bulletin*, 15(12):1–10.

CHAPTER 42

THE THREE PHASES/ FACES OF CHINA IN INDEPENDENT AFRICA
Reconceptualizing China–Africa Engagement

EMMANUEL AKYEAMPONG AND LIANG XU

CHINA's presence in independent Africa itself has evolved historically, and one can distinguish three qualitative phases. The first two or three decades of independence in the 1960s and 1970s comprise the first phase, when China as a Third World country expressed solidarity with the non-aligned movement and built significant projects like the TAZARA railway to link Zambia's Copperbelt with Tanzania, though China was then not a major global economic player. The "return" of China to Africa in late 1980s and 1990s through selective investment and more vigorous diplomatic outreach represents the second phase. The current engagement since about the late 1990s and early 2000 constitutes a third, and has witnessed the emergence of China as the second largest economy in the world after the United States. Throughout this post-colonial engagement between China and Africa, China has represented an alternative option to the West where Africa is concerned. It is important to keep this in mind, and to review how African countries have sought to use China, as individual countries, trade regions and the African Union all forge their "China policies." And in the meantime, it has become increasingly important for African countries to realize the complications of China's presence in Africa by recognizing the different "faces" of China. They are the Chinese state/state-owned enterprises, Chinese industrialists, and Chinese private immigrant adventurists.[1] Understanding the phenomenon that is "China," and making sense of the differing agendas and interests of these three "faces" would be extremely crucial as African countries begin to frame their China policy.

---

[1] Our "three faces" concept refers to Chinese economic actors in Africa and not forms of economic engagement. Hence the focus in this chapter is not a detailed examination of the different forms of Chinese engagement—aid, trade, and investment.

This chapter uses three country case studies to illustrate both the temporal and multifaceted dynamics of China's engagement with Africa: Zambia, South Africa, and Ghana. Key or unique insights from other countries in Africa are not ignored. China built the TAZARA Railway between 1967 and 1976 when all western countries and agencies had turned down this important Zambian need as economically unfeasible. It is noteworthy that China then had a per capita income that was less than a third of the average of Sub-Saharan African countries.[2] South Africa turned to Taiwan and Hong Kong (now part of the People's Republic of China) during the apartheid era in the mid-1980s, seeking investment that would make the "African Homelands" or "Bantustans" more economically viable and promote elite African endorsement of this apartheid policy of separate development. China was represented at Ghana's independence celebrations in 1957 and sent a Chinese acrobatic troupe as part of the first anniversary festivities. Ghana was the second sub-Saharan African country to officially recognize the Beijing government after the expulsion of Taiwan. The socialist-leaning Nkrumah visited Beijing in 1961, 1964, and 1966, the last coinciding with the military coup that overthrew his government. For Ghana, China has been a big player where aid, investment, and trade are concerned. However, Ghana's recent ambiguous response to Chinese illegal gold mining is a good case in point to show the complications of its current engagement with China. Generally speaking, China's engagement with Africa over the past six decades as a non-imperial power, at least in the high modern sense, with no "moral" demands has had value for African governments after the condescension of colonial and post-colonial European and western relations. This explains the paradox of the eagerness of African leaders to engage China despite the West's criticisms of "Beijing's perceived amoralism."[3]

42.1 TAZARA RAILWAY AND STATE-LED DEVELOPMENT

In April 1955, 29 African, Asian and Arab countries gathered in Bandung, Indonesia, to hammer out the framework of what became the non-aligned movement. While many were liberated from European colonialism, others like Ghana and the Central African Federation were going through the twilight of colonial rule. China attended at the invitation of Jawaharlal Nehru of India, who saw China's presence as instrumental to the building of productive regional relations. Lee points out that the "common ground and frequently cited at the conference was the history of western imperialism in Asia, Africa, and the Middle East since the sixteenth century."[4] This was in the words of key organizers like Nehru an "Afro-Asian Conference," and it is intriguing how the rhetoric of this era has resurfaced in China's official

---

[2] See *Handbook*, this volume, Chapters 49 and 53.

[3] Ian Taylor, "Governance in Africa and Sino-African Relations: Contradictions or Confluence," *Politics*, Vol. 27, No. 3 (2007), p. 139.

[4] Christopher J. Lee, "Between a Moment and an Era: The Origins and Afterlives of Bandung," in Christopher J. Lee (ed.), *Making a World after Empire: the Bandung Moment and its Afterlives,* Athens, OH: Ohio University Press, 2010, p. 10.

statements of its engagement with the developing world today. Bandung was hugely significant for China.

> Given its exclusion from the U.N., Zhou Enlai, China's foreign minister … perceived Bandung as a moment of legitimating China in the purview of its regional neighbors. Despite the tensions with the US over Taiwan and North Korea and its concurrent alliance with the USSR, the Bandung meeting presented a forum through which China could state its peaceful intentions and overcome a sense of isolation within the international community.[5]

The strong anti-imperial, and anti-colonial spirit at Bandung was infectious, causing China's foreign minister to declare that China had no plans for dominating its neighbors. The retreat of empire, the Cold War politics of this era, Western reaction to the Cultural Revolution in China in the 1960s, and the developmental challenges of African countries that were becoming increasing skeptical about western-articulated modernization theory's ability to deliver development all came together to create a unique moment in the TAZARA Railway linking Zambia to Dar es Salaam in coastal Tanzania. A project intended to break Zambian dependence on white-ruled Southern Rhodesia (Zimbabwe), South Africa, and Angola in exporting its copper, the TAZARA project was portrayed as anti-apartheid and anti-imperialist. It was an opportunity to showcase what Afro-Asian solidarity could do for the African quest for development at a time when Western commitment to African modernization had come into question. Funded at the cost of US$400 million through a long term interest-free loan, when Western countries and agencies had declared it economically unfeasible, and built with Chinese technical expertise with African capacity building as a major goal, the TAZARA Railway gave China political and moral capital in Africa that has not yet dissipated.

During the transition to independence in the early 1960s, Zambian President Kenneth Kaunda and Tanzanian President Julius Nyerere began to discuss the possibility of constructing a railway that would link the Zambian Copperbelt with the Indian Ocean, a project that Germany and Britain had long envisioned but failed to deliver during their colonial rule. Imagined as a grand "Freedom Railway" by Nyerere and Kaunda, the project would "liberate the two countries from the colonial division of transport infrastructures into southern and eastern African railway networks, networks that operated on different-sized gauges."[6] However, the two initial railway surveys that were carried out in 1963–1964, one by the World Bank and the other by the United Nations, concluded that the imagined Freedom Railway "would be neither economically feasible nor sustainable," and that the vision of building this infrastructure was simply an "ideological" rather than an "economic" proposition.[7]

China received the first request to finance the railway in early February 1965, when a Tanzanian trade delegation visited China as a preparatory mission for President Nyerere's arrival several days later. Abdulrahman Babu, then Minister of Trade and head of the trade delegation, mentioned to his Chinese counterparts that his government faced "difficulties" in trying to "secure financing for the rail link."[8] Nyerere raised this request himself during

---

[5] Christopher J. Lee, "Between a Moment and an Era: The Origins and Afterlives of Bandung," p. 12.

[6] Jamie Monson, *Africa's Freedom Railway: How a Chinese Development Project Changed Lives and Livelihoods in Tanzania*, Bloomington: Indiana University Press, 2009, p. 15.

[7] Jamie Monson, *Africa's Freedom Railway*, p. 15.

[8] Alicia Altorfer-Ong, "Tanzanian 'Freedom' and Chinese 'Friendship' in 1965: Laying the Tracks for the TanZam Rail Link," LSE Ideas-Cold War Studies Working Paper Series, 2009, p. 9.

his meeting with Chinese Chairman Mao Zedong, President Liu Shaoqi and Premier Zhou Enlai on February 18, 1965. Liu assured Nyerere by promising that "if the railway is important to you and Zambia, we will build it for you."[9] According to some Chinese sources, Zhou Enlai was in fact informed beforehand by then Chinese Ambassador in Tanzania, Ying He, of the possibility that Nyerere might make such a request. He immediately consulted the Minister of Railways and other experts about the material, financial and technological feasibility of the project, after which he submitted before Nyerere's visit a report to Chairman Mao, stating that "in order to help the newly independent African countries and support their national liberation effort, if President Nyerere raises the railway financing request, I would suggest we agree."[10]

However, recent scholarship has suggested that both Nyerere and Kaunda showed certain degrees of reluctance to formally accept Chinese offer. For Nyerere, although he had a firm offer from the Chinese government both during his visit in Beijing, which was further confirmed by Zhou Enlai during his reciprocal visit to Tanzania in June 1965, he "decided to keep his options open for other donors."[11] This is due to several factors. One possibility is pressure from Kaunda, who in the initial stages was strongly opposed to Chinese funding. A second explanation would be that Nyerere was concerned about "the political pressure from the major Western countries once China entered East Africa "on such a large scale." Another plausible reason is that Nyerere "believed a Western donor … would do a better job" in terms of technology and material resources.[12] Compared to Nyerere, Kaunda's opposition to Chinese aid was much more rigid. Kaunda on several occasions expressed his strong "unwillingness," and attempted to persuade Nyerere from unilaterally accepting China's assistance. In June 1965, for instance, on a Commonwealth conference occasion in London, Kaunda directly criticized the government of Tanzania for approaching China on the TAZARA project. Even during his official visit to Beijing in June 1967, when asked by his Chinese hosts about the railway project, Kaunda responded by expressing his preference of having the project funded by four private companies from the USA, Japan, UK and France.[13]

This "reluctance" can only be fully understood in a broader context of Cold War as well as Africa's post-colonial politics. Ghana under Nkrumah, Senegal under Senghor, and Tanzania under Nyerere had all experimented with socialism or "African Socialism." By 1967, suspected Western interference had toppled two socialist-inspired leaders: Patrice Lumumba of Congo and Nkrumah of Ghana. Kaunda and Nyerere's caution was against these developments. Also, it is understandable that accepting economic aid from a communist China would potentially jeopardize their non-alignment position in the international arena, not to mention the fear of a possible revenge attack from neighboring countries like Angola and Mozambique where China was actively supporting "revolutionary" rebels. In addition, it is safe to argue that British moral pressure in "Northern Rhodesia" remained strong after its independence, and there were still many British "settlers" in Zambia who were active in the

---

[9]   Alicia Altorfer-Ong, "Tanzanian 'Freedom' and Chinese 'Friendship' in 1965," p. 9.
[10]   Shen Xipeng, "Zhou Enlai's Role in Contribution of Tanzania-Zambia Railway," *Journal of Anhui Normal University*, Vol. 37, No. 2 (2009), p. 227.
[11]   Alicia Altorfer-Ong, "Tanzanian 'Freedom' and Chinese 'Friendship' in 1965," p. 11.
[12]   Alicia Altorfer-Ong, "Tanzanian 'Freedom' and Chinese 'Friendship' in 1965," pp. 11–12.
[13]   Shen Xipeng, "Zhou Enlai's Role in Contribution of Tanzania-Zambia Railway," pp. 227–28.

local economy. Given the fact that British and American companies controlled almost the entire copper industry, there was little room for Zambia to maneuver diplomatically.[14]

What really crystallized the decision-making processes were two developments. One was the unilateral declaration of independence by Southern Rhodesia in November 1965 and the international economic boycott of Rhodesia that ensued in the following year, which created a transportation emergency for Zambia. As Julius Nyerere reminded us in a 1970 speech, during the colonial period, Zambia only dealt with Southern African countries. Although Tanganyika was also under the British rule, there were no railways connecting the two countries. And the overland roads could only serve light traffic during the dry season.[15] Therefore, international sanctions imposed on Southern Rhodesia also forced Zambia to limit its economic relations with Southern Rhodesia, which posed tremendous difficulties for the newfound Zambia's national economy. Since Zambia could no longer rely on Rhodesia Railways for her traffic as it did in the past, the need for an alternative exit to the Tanzanian seaport became urgent.

The other was the relatively negative response from major Western donors. It is clear that in September 1965, letters were sent out by Tanzania and Zambia to the governments of Japan, Canada, France, and West Germany, "inviting them to consider participating in the provision of finance for the project."[16] Not surprisingly, the UK, the United Nations, and the USA were also approached. Contrary to China's swift and positive reaction, no serious offer was made by any of these major donors. For instance, British Minister for Overseas Development, Barbara Castle, during her visit in Tanzania in April 1965, declined the financial assistance for the project by emphasizing Britain's own financial difficulties. Instead, she offered a £75,000 sterling contribution "towards a joint British-Canadian feasibility study for the railway."[17] Around that time, the USA was preoccupied with developments in Vietnam and tended to perceive East and Southern Africa as "a British responsibility." Also, the US State Department and the US Agency for International Development (USAID) at that time were in favor of a road improvement project and against the railway one.[18] As one memorandum from the Zambian Foreign Affairs Ministry summarized very well, "the West has nobody else to blame but themselves, since offers to build the Tan–Zam railway were made to all potential candidates and only China has responded positively with a definite and unmistakable commitment."[19]

---

[14] Shen Xipeng, "Causes of Zambia's Refusal to Accept China's Aid of Tanzam Railway," *Journal of Anhui Normal University*, Vol. 38, No. 6 (2010), pp. 726–27.

[15] Julius Nyerere's speech at TAZARA Railway inauguration ceremony, Kapiri Mposhi, Zambia, October 28th, 1970. See Julius Nyerere, "Tanzania-Zambia Railway," in Anshan Li and Haifang Liu eds., *Annual Review of African Studies in China (2012)*, Beijing, China: Social Sciences Academic Press, 2013, p. 294.

[16] Jamie Monson, *Africa's Freedom Railway*, p. 24.

[17] It later became the Maxwell Stamp Report, completed in 1966, the only one that concluded the project as economically feasible. See Alicia Altorfer-Ong, "Tanzanian 'Freedom' and Chinese 'Friendship' in 1965," pp. 15, 28; see also Kasuka S. Mutukwa, *Politics of the Tanzania-Zambia Railway Project: A Study of Tanzania-China-Zambia Relations*, Washington, DC: University Press of America, 1977.

[18] Alicia Altorfer-Ong, "Tanzanian 'Freedom' and Chinese 'Friendship' in 1965," p. 20, The American road improvement project, the Tanzania-Zambia highway, was later completed in the early 1970s.

[19] Permanent Secretary Foreign Affairs to Minister Foreign Affairs, September 19, 1967, NAZ MFA 1/103/115, quoted from Jamie Monson, *Africa's Freedom Railway*, pp. 25–26.

In September 1967, China, Tanzania, and Zambia signed the first tripartite agreement for the construction of the TAZARA railway. It is probably safe to argue that by the late 1960s, both Tanzania and Zambia had become convinced that a "Freedom Railway" funded by Western capital was not going to be possible any more. They opted for an alternative investment from China. The final agreement between the three countries was signed in Beijing on July 12 in 1970, after the survey and design work had all been completed and the financial and technical specifics had been negotiated and agreed on. By its completion in 1976, China had provided over US$400 million in a long-term interest-free loan and dispatched over 50 000 experts and workers for the construction of the "Freedom Railway."

Apart from various rhetorical propagandas, it is true that when China offered to fund the TAZARA line, China did have its own agendas. Part of the motivation was Sino–Soviet rivalry. China wanted to limit Soviet influence in East Africa and to label herself as a great "fighter" against both imperialist powers: USA and USSR. China, while having no intention to control the local economy or to profit directly from TAZARA's construction in any significant economic terms, did expect through investing in TAZARA to establish itself as a regional strategic player in competition with USSR, US and European interests. It is also evident that China wanted to gain support through funding the project from African countries over its efforts to replace Taiwan in the United Nations.

With no doubt, "Freedom Railway" is a potent symbol for Africa's liberation and solidarity. But at the same time, it has also become a milestone project in China's historical engagement with Africa. What can this unique history teach us about China–Africa cooperation? First, it showcases an earlier period of "state-led development cooperation" when resources were scarce both in China and in Africa.[20] Indeed, China was using development assistance in Africa to achieve strategic goals, largely diplomatic at the time. Monson argues, however, that "economic factors remained important to the way China articulated its development vision, affecting the way the project was funded and the legacy it left behind in rural areas."[21] The project demonstrated an alternative model by which development can be obtained through collaborations among "the poor." In the early 1970s, when China was committed to the construction of the railway, the income per capita in China was "much lower than in Tanzania and Zambia,"[22] not to mention China's domestic political turmoil due to the Cultural Revolution. Even in 1980, China's income per capita remained at US$250, much lower than Zambia's US$680 income per capita.[23] Thus, given China's monetary constraints at the time, especially a severe shortage of foreign exchange as China was trying to repay her own debt to the Soviet Union, the railway was constructed by using African and Chinese labor and limited industrial equipment. It was more of a labor-intensive than a capital-intensive project, and it had to be conducted by resorting to an "in-kind" assistance. It is not surprising that local expenses were supported through the sale of Chinese commodities in Tanzania and Zambia.[24]

[20] Jamie Monson, *Africa's Freedom Railway*, p. 154.

[21] Jamie Monson, *Africa's Freedom Railway*, p. 33.

[22] Célestin Monga, "The Political Economy of Dignity: On the New Asia-Africa Dynamics," keynote lecture given at Goethe University, Frankfurt, Germany, February 7, 2013, p. 6.

[23] World Bank data on GNI per capita (current international $) based on purchasing power parity (PPP), see http://data.worldbank.org/indicator/NY.GNP.PCAP.PP.CD.

[24] Jamie Monson, *Africa's Freedom Railway*, pp. 30, 34.

Second, it demonstrates that Chinese aid was not imposed upon a vulnerable Africa. As shown in this case, Tanzania and Zambia managed to attract, and if necessary, use Chinese assistance to serve their own political and economic agendas. China, to a certain extent, becomes a "card" that African countries can play when dealing with the West. Last but not the least, it also showcases that technology transfer is not only possible but can be sustainable. Recent scholarship, based on intensive life histories of experts and workers who contributed to the construction and management of the TAZARA Railway, has defied the old argument that tends to treat the TAZARA Railway as a political calculation and hence "economically irrational" and that Chinese railway experts and engineers were only "political tools" and "secretive participants" of the railway project.[25] In 1976, there were 986 Chinese experts helping maintain and manage the railway. The number of Chinese experts has been declining since the 1980s, and was reduced to ten in 2004/2005 when Chinese team delegated the technological supervising and managerial roles to their African peers, and lowered themselves only as coordinators.[26] It is now clear that Chinese technological support for the railway and capacity building on the Africa part has been consistent in the past 37 years. At the end of the day, TAZARA is an African "Freedom Railway." And, this is precisely what President Nyerere emphasized in 1970:

> We are extremely grateful to the Chinese People's Republic for their help in the railway project … A railway is a railway, that is what we want, and that is what we are being helped to build. But there is something more, this railway will be our railway. It will not be a Chinese railway, because the Chinese are not building a Chinese railway![27]

42.2 CHINESE PRIVATE INVESTMENT AND SOUTH AFRICA'S GARMENT INDUSTRY

In 2010, the South African National Bargaining Council for the Clothing Manufacturing Industry (NBC), dominated mainly by big and high profit margin firms in the Cape region and the trade unions, launched a "compliance drive," the objective of which was to "force all firms in the industry to comply with the minimum wages agreed to in the Council by member employer associations and the Southern African Clothing and Textile Workers Union (SACTWU)."[28] It declared that: "firms that did not pay these minima, as well as various levies to the NBC, would be pursued through the courts, served with compliance orders, and eventually shut down by writs of execution served by the local sheriff."[29] The same year,

---

[25] Haifang Liu and Jamie Monson, "Railway Time: Technology Transfer and the Role of Chinese Experts in the History of TAZARA," in Anshan Li and Haifang Liu, eds, *Annual Review of African Studies in China (2012)*, Beijing, China: Social Sciences Academic Press, 2013, pp. 190–91.

[26] Haifang Liu and Jamie Monson, "Railway Time," pp. 194, 203.

[27] Julius Nyerere, "Tanzania-Zambia Railway," p. 296.

[28] Nicoli Natrass and Jeremy Seekings, "Job Destruction in the South African Clothing Industry," CDE Focus paper, January 2013, p. 7.

[29] Nicoli Natrass and Jeremy Seekings, "Job Destruction in the South African Clothing Industry," p. 7.

NBC planned to close at least 47 factories nationally to show its determination to "recoup wages owed to workers." What was at issue was the Council's wish that employers pay workers a minimum of 324 Rands per week. Among the aforementioned 47 factories, nine were in Newcastle, a small former "border" industrial town in current day KwaZulu-Natal Province.[30] Most of these factories survive on a low-profit cut, make and trim (CMT) operation. What followed was rather unique and dramatic: an employer's strike, which was virtually unheard of in South Africa, a country notorious for its aggressive union actions. In September and October 2010, the rest of Newcastle's Chinese/Taiwanese clothing factories, led by Alex Liu and his Newcastle Chinese Chamber of Commerce, shut down unanimously for several days as a gesture of protest. Similar actions were repeated in 2011. All of a sudden, the Newcastle clothing industry seems to have become a metaphor for the broader debate about jobs and employment in the country. And unsurprisingly, since Chinese factory owners were at the very front in the conflict, it has been also understood in the light of China's engagement with Africa.

But to start with, one has to examine the history of the arrival of these Chinese industrialists to understand the context and dynamics of their protest. After the National Party took power in South Africa in 1948, it applied "apartheid" in a plethora of laws and executive actions.[31] One of the core objectives at the heart of the apartheid system, however, was the governance of the African population. In 1951, the government abolished the only official countrywide African institution, the Natives Representative Council. Then it grouped the reserve lands into eight (eventually ten) territories. Each territory became a "homeland" for a potential African "nation," "administered under white tutelage by a set of Bantu authorities, consisting mainly of compliant hereditary chiefs (the non-compliant were displaced)."[32] The legislative framework, begun by Verwoerd, was eventually completed in 1971, when the Bantu Homelands Constitution Act empowered the government to grant independence to Homelands. The direct consequence of granting independence to the homelands, from a political economy stand-point, was what James Ferguson has rightly summarized as "obscuring regional connections and localizing responsibility for poverty within national borders."[33] Therefore, black Africans in theory were no longer citizens of South Africa, but belonged to individual Bantustans. The secret of such a design could be best captured as "internal outsourcing" of the national economy of "white South Africa," meaning white South Africa could "contain the political implications of the massive poverty of its labor reserve within the ideological borders" of Bantustans.[34] Movement of the massive migrant labor would then be tightly controlled and monitored by a system of passes and curfews.

[30] Edward West, "Wage Blitz Stitches up Clothing Factories," *Business Day*, August 27, 2010.

[31] For discussion on specific laws and regulations, see Leonard Thompson, *A History of South Africa*, New Haven: Yale University Press, 2001 (third edition), pp. 190–95.

[32] Leonard Thompson, *A History of South Africa*, New Haven: Yale University Press, third edition, 2001, p. 191.

[33] James Ferguson, *Global Shadows: Africa in the Neoliberal World Order*, Durham, NC: Duke University Press, 2006, p. 65. For a detailed discussion, see Chapter 2 (Paradoxes of Sovereignty and Independence) of the book.

[34] James Ferguson, *Global Shadows*, p. 64. On this "internal outsourcing," see also Harold Wolpe, *Race, Class and the Apartheid State*, London, UK: Currey, 1988; Heribert Adam, *Modernizing Racial Domination: South Africa's Political Dynamics*, Berkeley, CA: University of California Press, 1971.

The political and economic rationale of the homeland policy is revealed more clearly in its industrial development scheme. On March 21, 1960, the notorious Sharpeville Massacre, which protested this system of "influx" control, shook the entire world. To mitigate international condemnation as well as to better "control" the black population, Prime Minister Verwoerd announced that encouragement would be given to the establishment of industries on sites near the homelands.[35] Since one of the keys to implementing the homeland policy was to "buy" support from chiefly families, the industrial development scheme would help the government waive a "carrot" to win their support.[36] As a result, by industrial decentralization the white government was able to greatly limit the physical movement of the black population, while simultaneously keeping them within reach as a source of cheap industrial labor.

As one of the border growth points, Newcastle's development greatly sped up after 1969, when Iscor, South Africa's parastatal steel company, decided to set up a plant there, followed by a series of infrastructure projects.[37] However, this optimism did not last long. Iscor started to privatize in 1983. Apart from the decline in employment, the most immediate consequence was the underutilization of the newly built infrastructure. The Newcastle government had to search for other investors to fill this gap and to boost the local economy. After several failed missions in Europe, the Newcastle local government decided to look east.[38] They sent out a delegation to Hong Kong and Taiwan to explore new sources of investment, which turned out to be a huge success.

The idea to invite industrialists from Taiwan was the local replication of a national strategy to develop labor-intensive employment for blacks who had been resettled near and in the underdeveloped "homelands." When P.W. Botha took office in September 1978, South Africa was facing more severe economic sanctions from the international community. As a reaction to these mounting sanctions, Botha devised a diplomatic strategy of "forging alliances with other countries which were pariahs within the international community, then notably Israel and Taiwan."[39] During the 1980s, with generous South African government incentives, industrialists from Taiwan and Hong Kong (the majority being the Taiwanese)

[35] The idea of placing a scheme of improvement and development of the Reserves in response to the "overpopulation and overstocking" issue dates back to the 1930s and was treated with heightened urgency in 1956 after the Tomlinson Commission Report. For a detailed discussion on the origins of the border industry scheme, see Trevor Bell, *Industrial Decentralization in South Africa*, Oxford: Oxford University Press, 1973, Chapter 1.

[36] For an excellent discussion on Bantustan authorities, see Harold Wolpe, *Race, Class and the Apartheid State*; Heribert Adam, *Modernizing Racial Domination: South Africa's Political Dynamics*; see also Mahmood Mamdani, *Citizen and Subject: Contemporary Africa and the Legacy of Late Colonialism*, Princeton, NJ: Princeton University Press, 1996. In his book, Mamdani terms this particular mode of rule as "decentralized despotism". For the benefits that Bantustan administrators would receive under industrial decentralization schemes, for instance, control of land, high salaries, shares in development corporations and expensive cars, see The South African Council of Churches and the Southern African Catholic Bishops' Conference, *Relocations: The Churches Report on Forced Removals*, 1984, p. 46.

[37] Anthony Lemon, *Apartheid: A Geography of Separation*, Farnborough: Saxon House, 1976, pp. 183–84.

[38] They conducted an active marketing campaign in Belgium and other European countries. Field interview with former town steward of Newcastle, Mr. Le Roux, July 8, 2013.

[39] Melanie Yap and Dianne Leong Man, *Colour, Confusion and Concessions: The History of the Chinese in South Africa*, Hong Kong, China: Hong Kong University Press, 1996, pp. 410.

began to invest in border industrial areas. Scholars have pointed out that in the changing geography of manufacturing industry in the world economy Taiwanese companies were then also "seeking production locations with cheap labor and access to restricted markets."[40] According to a 1996 census conducted by Taiwanese Embassy in South Africa, Taiwanese businessmen had by 1996 invested an estimated amount of US$1.5 billion (R6.45 billion at the 1996 exchange rate) in South Africa and created over 41 240 jobs. As of 1996, there were 13 176 Taiwanese in the country. In total, there were 620 Taiwanese firms in South Africa, among which 280 were in the industrial sector (mostly clothing factories) employing 36 224 people. It was estimated that "half of all new factory employment created in the homelands under the decentralization policy of the 1980s was in fact from Taiwanese factories."[41]

Starting in 1991, when the De Klerk government slashed industrial decentralization subsidies as a response to mounting pressures from large-scale corporations and the trade unions, Taiwanese industrialists began to retreat. This gradual decrease corresponded to a massive influx of Mainland Chinese into South Africa. At their height, there were a reported 30 000 Taiwanese in South Africa, but now only about 6,000 remain in the country.[42] In the meantime, from late 1980s, South Africa began to witness unprecedented waves of Chinese migration from Mainland China.[43] Now, the estimated Chinese population varies depending on sources, but is believed to be somewhere between 300 000 and 500 000. In Newcastle, Mainland Chinese began to arrive in the mid-1990s, notably after the establishment of formal diplomatic relations between South Africa and China in 1998. With a population of about 50 000 (40% white), Newcastle currently hosts nearly 1000 Mainland Chinese and about 450 Taiwanese.[44] Businessmen from Shanghai, Jiangsu and Shandong provinces are the most visible. The majority of their factories run cut, make and trim (CMT) operations on low profit margins by producing garments from supplied materials. Currently, there are in total about 130 factories in Newcastle, among which 80 are owned and run by Chinese. And Chinese factories currently employ a total of about 13 000 workers. Given the 54% unemployment rate in Newcastle, the stakes for keeping these Chinese factories are fairly high.[45]

In the mid-1980s, the Newcastle delegates in Taiwan relentlessly "extolled the control exercised by Inkatha in Madadeni and Osizweni," and carefully differentiated to the Taiwanese counterparts and industrialists "these peaceful and non-unionized places from the chaos

---

[40] See John Pickles and Jeff Woods, "Taiwanese Investment in South Africa," *African Affairs*, Vol. 88, No. 353 (1989), pp. 514–15; see also Geoffrey Roger Woods, "Taiwanese Investment in the Homelands of South Africa," Ph.D. dissertation, Ohio University, 1991, Chapter 3.

[41] The Taipei Liaison Office Archives Depot (TLO Archives), Pretoria: *1996 Census of ROC Investment in South Africa, Press Release: 620 ROC Business Aid SA Economic Growth*, July 1996, pp. 1–4, cited from Song-Huann (Gary) Lin, "The Relations between the Republic of China and the Republic of South Africa, 1948-1998," Ph.D. dissertation, University of Pretoria, 2001, pp. 153–54.

[42] Yoon Jung Park, "Chinese Migration in Africa," SAIIA Occasional Paper, No. 24, January 2009, p. 14.

[43] Anna Ying Chen and Yoon Jung Park have identified three distinct periods: the first from the late 1980s to the mid-1990s; a second from the mid to late 1990s; and a third wave that began in the early 2000s. For details, see Yoon Jung Park, "Chinese Migration in Africa," pp. 14–15.

[44] Field interview with Ferdie Alberts, head of the Newcastle Municipality's economic development unit, August 10, 2012.

[45] Field interview with Ferdie Alberts, August 10, 2012.

of Soweto."[46] It turned out that their strategy and avid persuasions "succeeded beyond their wildest dreams":

> We concentrated on Taiwan. Sixty-five factories have come in, bringing 10,000-11,000 new jobs and a capital investment of R120 million. They have had a tremendous impact on the town. Property values have soared and there has been a commercial boom. Also, related service industries have been established. The economy of the town has grown by 3% per year, and South African companies have also established themselves in Newcastle.[47]

About 30 years later, these economic gains seem to have faded away. Apartheid has ended, and an African-led ANC government is in power. The strategic considerations that privileged Taiwanese investment in the 1980s no longer hold sway. When facing a possible exodus of Taiwanese and Mainland Chinese factories due to the minimum wage crisis, local officials in Newcastle confessed:

> But we have no input into national legislation. Outsiders [Pretoria, the central government, now interestingly seen as an external power] make the laws, but we have to deal with the effects of these decisions. Upwards of 6500 jobs will be lost in Newcastle if factories are closed down for non-compliance. Then what? What are we going to replace them with? What other industry can you set up so quickly? It's going to have a hell of an effect on the socio-economics of Newcastle.[48]

In June 2011, five small Chinese-owned firms in Newcastle initiated legal proceedings against the NBC and the Minister of Labor over the extension of minimum wages to them. On June 1, 2012, the Department of Labor announced that the current council only represented 27.53% of the employers in the sector hence inappropriate to continue enforcing its agreements.[49] The court case was heard on January 29 in 2013. After two months of diligent efforts and with an expenditure of four to five million Rands in legal costs, on March 13 in 2013, Chinese employers won their case. Judge Piet Koen of the KwaZulu-Natal High Court in Pietermaritzburg ruled that: "small clothing factories owned by families of Chinese and Taiwanese descent in Newcastle are exempt from a 2010 bargaining council agreement on wages."[50]

Many reports have depicted Chinese/Taiwanese owners' non-compliance as a conflict that somehow "substantiates" the notion of a greedy Chinese business style, and malpractice and unfair competition of Chinese companies.[51] It has been argued elsewhere, however, that the real root causes of the ongoing minimum wage crisis in Newcastle are threefold: defects in South African national industrial development strategy, the biased representation in the

---

[46] Gillian Hart, *Disabling Globalization: Places of Power in Post-apartheid South Africa*, Berkeley, CA: University of California Press, 2002, pp. 151–52.

[47] Gillian Hart, *Disabling Globalization: Places of Power in Post-apartheid South Africa*, p. 150.

[48] Stephen Cohen, "Newcastle on a Knife Edge," *The Witness*, June 1, 2011. This quote is in line with my own field interview with Ferdie Alberts, August 10, 2012.

[49] Field interview with Alex Liu, President of the Newcastle Chinese Chamber of Business, August 11, 2012.

[50] Edward West, "Victory for Small firms in Minimum Wages Case," *Business Day*, March 14, 2013.

[51] "The Chinese in Africa: Trying to Pull Together," *The Economist*, April 20, 2011.

bargaining council, and the deadlock in South Africa's land reform processes.[52] In fact, a recent study has proved that potential job destruction in places like Newcastle due to the execution of a minimum wage does not benefit sufficiently compliant firms in places like Cape Town. This is because the "non-compliant firms compete mostly with producers in Lesotho and China," and it is very clear that "allowing low-wage producers to continue to operate in places like Newcastle [would in fact] provide [much needed] employment for less skilled workers in impoverished areas."[53]

This chapter suggests that the South African experience is not entirely unique, for as early as from the 1960s and 1970s private Chinese textile and clothing manufacturing companies also made their entry to other African countries like Lesotho, Mauritius, Ghana, and Nigeria, and have produced rather different but interesting legacies respectively.[54] What this South Africa case has illuminated for us is rather clear: as the number of Chinese private companies increases rapidly in Africa and Chinese manufacturing industry accelerates its relocation to the continent, disputes and debates over labor practices, taxation issues, environmental degradation, and corporate social responsibilities will continue to rise, if not necessarily exacerbate. Therefore, African governments must anticipate these problems and do their best to mitigate the negative impact on development, and eventually to take advantage of Chinese private manufacturing capital to transform their own economies.

42.3 CHINESE ENTREPRENEURS AND GOLD MINING IN GHANA

In July 2012 the youth of the village of Manso-Nsiena in the gold-rich Amansie West District in the Ashanti Region of Ghana clashed with some Chinese suspected to be engaged in illegal mining operations in the district. The cause of the confrontation was the destruction of the local environment in a community with a history of "buruli ulcer," a disease closely associated with environmental changes. National attention was riveted and tempers provoked by images carried in national news media, such as those in the *Daily Graphic* of July 20, 2012, which showed half-dressed Chinese miners swinging shotguns, which they fired in the air to deter the youth of Manso-Nsiena from approaching the mining camp. An armed police detachment rushed in from the nearest large town of Manso-Nkwanta to defuse the situation and detained nine Chinese. Then followed a few days of utter confusion and national

[52] Liang Xu, "Chinese Textile Factories in Newcastle (South Africa) and the Minimum Wage Crisis: An Alternative Perspective," paper presented at the ANR-EsCA Conference on Chinese-African Spaces of Interaction, Paris, April 23, 2013.

[53] Nicoli Nattrass, "Job Destruction in Newcastle: Minimum Wage-setting and Low-Wage Employment in the South African Clothing Industry," paper presented at the Harvard Africa Workshop, Harvard University, November 4, 2013, p. 18.

[54] For a good case study on Chinese clothing industry in Mauritius, see Deborah Brautigam, "Close Encounters: Chinese Business Networks as Industrial Catalysts in Sub-Saharan Africa," *African Affairs*, Vol. 102, No. 408 (2003), pp. 447–467; for an excellent case study on Chinese clothing industry in Lesotho, see Sanjaya Lall, "FDI, AGOA and Manufactured Exports by a Landlocked, Least Developed African Economy: Lesotho," *Journal of Development Studies*, Vol. 41, No. 6 (2005), pp. 998–1022.

debate on radio and in newspapers about who authorized these Chinese miners to engage in mining operations in Manso-Nsiena, their blatant disregard of Ghanaian laws seen not only in their mining without a license but also the bearing of arms, and what disciplinary measures should be enforced against them. Part of this confusion can, perhaps, be traced to what Lloyd Amoah has critiqued as the absence of a coherent Ghana policy on China, and the ambivalence that marks official relations with China and public uneasiness of increasing Chinese presence in retail trade and even illegal mining.[55]

The confused official response to Chinese illegal mining incidents may have two dimensions. First is the ambivalence stemming from Western condemnation of China's lack of support for human rights in Africa. Highly conscious of its much-lauded democratic credentials and its interest to keep donor funds flowing, Ghana, Amoah argues, engages in "self-censorship regarding her dealings with China at the expense of elaborating an independent, pragmatic China policy."[56] Second, and perhaps more importantly, the confused official response reflects the reality of dealing with the three "faces" of China in Africa: the state-owned enterprises that act as multinational corporations; the large private industries that sometimes operate with state backing; and the huge influx of ordinary Chinese who have flooded Africa in the past decade in search of a brighter economic future. So there is, for instance, Ghana's dealing with Sinohydro, which has built the Bui hydroelectric dam on the Volta River at the price tag of US$622 million or the China National Offshore Oil Corporation that has invested in Ghana's oil and gas industry. Then there are the established private industries such as Huawei Technologies that is installing fiber optic cables in Ghana and manufactures the wireless router people now use for Internet service through the mobile phone provider Airtel.[57] Lastly, there are the ordinary Chinese who have entered the retail market in Ghana, flouting rules that limit the retail sector to only Ghanaians.[58]

Historically speaking, there have been three major waves of Chinese migration to Africa. South Africa is a good case in point. The earliest major wave of Chinese migrants came to South Africa in the early twentieth century as indentured labor on the mines. Colonial Ghana similarly experimented with Chinese labor on the mines in the same period.[59] The second wave, mostly Taiwanese and Hong Kong migrants, came under South African government invitation in the 1970s and 1980s. For the third wave, which commenced from the late 1990s, as Chris Alden has suggested, some were part of Chinese government projects in Africa and chose to remain while others follow the time honored process of joining family members in a new country. The most vibrant group consists of those who are "pursuing opportunities and have used migrant brokers, both legal and illegal, to obtain

[55] Lloyd G. A. Amoah, "Ghana-China Relations: From Ambivalence and Fear to Vision and Action," paper presented at a roundtable conference organized by the Development Policy Institute in Accra, November 2007.

[56] Lloyd G. A. Amoah, "Ghana-China Relations: From Ambivalence and Fear to Vision and Action."

[57] Heidi Frontani and Anna McCracken, "China's Development Initiatives in Ghana, 1961-2011," *Journal of Sustainable Development in Africa*, Vol. 14, No. 8 (2012), pp. 275–86.

[58] The Busia government (1969–1972) passed the Ghana Business Promotion Act, which restricted retail trade to Ghanaians.

[59] Kwabena O. Akurang-Parry, "We Cast about for a Remedy: Chinese Labor and African Opposition in the Gold Coast, 1874-1914," *International Journal of African Historical Studies*, Vol. 34, No. 2 (2001), pp. 365–84.

the necessary paperwork to immigrate to Africa."[60] For many Africans, the relatively sudden and large-scale influx of Chinese immigrants, both the transient and long-term ones, is rather "puzzling," especially "in light of their low level skills and their apparently limited financial means and in the face of local lack of employment and prospects."[61] As Alden has warned us, the presence and conduct of these Chinese immigrants have already triggered a variety of local responses, which have gone "beyond the unreserved enthusiasm initially expressed by African governments," and "these changing dynamics, whether Beijing likes it or not, begin to draw China into Africa's politics."[62] It is probably safe to suggest that the response of African governments and publics will be crucial in shaping Beijing's emerging Africa policy.

As Ghanaian officials contemplate the three faces of China, the increasing imprint of China in Ghana is evident even in the Ghanaian landscape through building projects such as the National Theater built by the Chinese government as a gift to Ghana and the four stadia rehabilitated or built from scratch by a Chinese construction company. Senior police officials on the spot in Ashanti Region during the uproar over illegal Chinese mining worried about the possible "international dimension" as to how the illegal Chinese miners were treated, and waited for instructions from higher up.[63] Resolution, ironically, came from Chinese officials. On the front page of the *Daily Graphic* on June 27, 2012 was boldly printed the headline news: "Deal with Chinese 'Galamseyers', says Government of China."

> The Government of the People's Republic of China has given its backing to the Government of Ghana and the rest of Africa to sanction Chinese companies and individuals whose actions go contrary to the laws and welfare of the citizens of their host countries. Prof. Jianbo Luo from the Party School of the CPC Central Committee said it had come to the government's attention that some Chinese investors and private citizens were destroying the image of China by engaging in activities that did not augur well for the welfare of their host countries. He made specific mention of Ghana and Nigeria, where some Chinese companies and individuals had been cited for environmental pollution and human rights abuses....
>
> He hinted that the Ministry of Commerce was drawing up a program to guide the activities of Chinese enterprises in Africa. He, however, indicated that it would be difficult to capture all of them under one umbrella due to the large number of Chinese citizens, adding that several efforts to capture all Chinese investors into a register at the embassies had proved futile because not all of them showed up. "China is not capable of regulating all of its investments in Africa. We can only control the state-owned industries and a few private ones," he said.[64]

In short, Luo conceded the multiple faces of China in Africa, and confessed the Chinese state's inability to regulate any but the state-owned-enterprises and the very large private companies.

---

[60] Chris Alden, *China in Africa*, New York: Zed Books Ltd, 2007, p. 52.

[61] Chris Alden, *China in Africa*, p. 54.

[62] Chris Alden, *China in Africa,* p. 58.

[63] Superintendent S. K. Kwakye, Commander of Amansie West District Police, explained his uncertainty about arresting the illegal Chinese migrants in their confrontation with the villagers of Manso-Nsiena as "the whole matter had an 'international dimension' and that it would not be proper to arrest the Chinese." *Daily Graphic*, July 20, 2012.

[64] *Daily Graphic*, June 27, 2012. "Galamsey" is a Ghanaian term for illegal mining. A "Galamseyer" is an illegal miner.

Chinese presence is unlike historic, foreign trading diasporas in Africa, such as the Indians in East Africa or the Lebanese in West Africa.[65] Neither the Indians nor the Lebanese trading diasporas in Africa had a state-backed component. Indian mercantile activity has a long history in East Africa, and can be documented at least from the 18th century. Lebanese immigrants showed up in West Africa from the 1860s, and continued Lebanese immigration has been fueled by foreign and local dynamics. Colonial governments later came to adopt Indians and Lebanese as auxiliaries, but did not originate nor sustain these dispersions. Nor does China's presence conform to the pattern of non-colonial countries like Canada or Denmark, officially represented in Africa largely by their international development agencies, such as CIDA or DANIDA respectively. There is no western parallel of state-owned-enterprises operating as multinational companies. The former colonial powers, for example, have their official development agencies, official development assistance, and private investment. For the majority of Africans and their governments, the tendency to perceive a Chinese state behind any Chinese person on the ground, as they try to parse the three faces of China, is understandable.

It has only recently been realized that the Chinese state may not align itself with its "people" in Africa. The most recent crackdown on Chinese illegal mining in Ghana further substantiates our argument here. According to a *Guardian* report in 2013, more than 50 000 Chinese gold miners have been to Ghana since 2005, two-thirds of them from Shanglin, an impoverished county in southern Guangxi province where news of the gold rush spread by word of mouth. It is another manifestation of China being both a global power and at the same time a developing country; a country that despite its miraculous economic achievements in the recent decades still struggles with massive domestic poverty.[66] Although the reported number of Chinese gold miners might have been exaggerated, as our interviews suggest that there were about 11 000 Shanglin miners at its peak in mid-2013, and that combined with miners from other parts of China, the total number would probably be around 20 000, the economic and political implications of a crackdown operation at such a scale are far-reaching.[67] It is also interesting to note, according to another report, when these Chinese illegal miners approached Chinese embassy for help, they were told, "You are all illegal; how dare you to call us now?"[68] Our field work in various mining areas in Ghana has revealed a widely shared dissatisfaction and anger amongst the Chinese miners at the relative "inaction" of the Chinese Embassy in Accra.[69]

[65] For some excellent reference on this topic, see Abdul Sheriff, *Dhow Cultures of the Indian Ocean: Cosmopolitanism, Commerce, and Islam*, London: Hurst, 2010; Gijsbert Oonk, *The Karimjee Jivanjee Family: Merchant Princes of East Africa 1800-2000*, Amsterdam: Pallas Publications, 2009; Dana A. Seidenberg, *Mercantile Adventurers: The World of East African Asians 1750-1985*, New Delhi: New Age International, 1996; Emmanuel K. Akyeampong, "Race, Identity and Citizenship in Black Africa: the Case of the Lebanese in Ghana," *Africa*, Vol. 76, No. 3 (2006), pp. 297–323; Albert Hourani and Nadim Shehadi, eds, *The Lebanese in the World: A Century of Emigration*, London: Centre for Lebanese Studies in association with I.B. Tauris, 1992.

[66] Than Kaiman and Afua Hirsch, "Ghana Arrests 168 Chinese Nationals in Illegal Mining Crackdown," *The Guardian*, June 6, 2013

[67] Field interview with Mr. Wu, a gold miner and leader of the Shanglin community in Ghana, August 3, 2013.

[68] Adam Nossiter and Yiting Sun, "Chasing a Golden Dream, Chinese Miners Are on the Run in Ghana," *New York Times*, June 10, 2013.

[69] Field interviews with Chinese gold miners in Tema and Kumasi, July and August 2013.

In the aftermath of the task force operation, both the Ghanaian government and the Chinese Embassy in Ghana have reflected on if they could have better handled this case of illegal Chinese miners. The loss of cash and capital goods to the Chinese, the impact on rural economies that benefitted from their presence and purchases, the injection of small-scale technologies that revolutionized mining for ordinary Ghanaians, all testify that the Chinese presence in small-scale mining was not completely adverse. For instance, in northern areas like Bole, where the Chinese are not directly involved in the mining of gold but supply equipment, service and repair some mining equipment, and purchase processed gold, Ghanaian miners express satisfaction about the presence of the Chinese since they have helped them with inexpensive machines that ease the mining process. The situation in the south ended catastrophically partly because of the lack of a China policy on the part of the Ghanaian government, appreciative of its economic relations with the Chinese government but still treading unfamiliar territory in its larger engagement with China; and partly because of China's interest in the activities of its state-owned enterprises and large private firms who pursue Chinese strategic interests overseas, but a disinterest or an inability to monitor the activities of ordinary Chinese who immigrate to African countries. This chapter suggests that there is significant economical potential in this third level of Chinese investment because of the possible synergies with Ghanaian private capital. The challenge would be to streamline and direct it to where economic investment and activity is much needed and to monitor it.

42.4 Conclusion

As seen in the three cases presented above, the three faces of China's current engagement has begun to generate tensions in Africa–China relations, and contradictions in China's avowed policy towards Africa. How Africans make sense of the reality that China is both a global power and also a developing economy is a crucial question that needs to be addressed and dealt with properly and wisely. However, simultaneously engaging China at its multiple levels is completely new, and African leaders need to wrap their minds around this in their forging of China policies. And this has no easy historical precedent; it represents the new face of deregulated global politicoeconomic extension, which does not conform to prior models of colonialism or imperialism. Needless to say, Zambia, South Africa, Ghana now all have to deal with China at the three levels outlined above.

For Africa, the stakes are high, as seen in China's emergence since 2009 as Africa's largest trade partner. China–Africa trade increased from US$1 billion in 2000 to US$55 billion in 2007 and to an astounding US$198.4 billion in 2012.[70] China reportedly gets a third of its oil and natural resources from Africa. For emerging economic powers such as China and India, Africa is a preferred investment destination, and foreign direct investment in Africa grew even at a time of global financial crisis. By the year 2011, according to UNCTAD, China has accumulated US$16 billion of cumulative FDI stock in Africa, making it the sixth largest investor on the continent preceded by France, USA, UK, Malaysia, and South Africa, the last one being of course part of the continent itself.[71] However, according to David Shinn,

[70] *Xinhua News*, see http://news.xinhuanet.com/english/china/2013-03/25/c_124496973.htm.
[71] UNCTAD, "The Rise of BRICS FDI and Africa," March 25, 2013.

778 OLD AND NEW DEVELOPMENT PLAYERS

FDI that passes through places like Hong Kong, the Cayman Islands and the British Virgin Islands, as well as investment in the financial sector are not included in the UNCTAD report. Therefore, it might be correct to "conclude that as of the end of 2011 China had more cumulative FDI in Africa than either South Africa or Malaysia but not more than the UK, US, or France."[72]

Meanwhile, physical infrastructure that had seen no significant expansion since the end of colonial rule are now been rehabilitated and expanded with Chinese capital and technology, and this is a dimension that other kinds of private foreign investment, often enclaved and closely focused on extraction, does not engage. In the area of development aid, a recent report suggests that between 2000 and 2011, China had funded 1673 projects in 51 African countries with a total of US$75 billion in commitments of official finance, while US had offered US$90 billion official finance during this time.[73] Despite the reliability of numbers, the report does convince the reader that China's actual official aid commitment to Africa may be traceable and very likely is much bigger than people tend to think.[74] A better received recent report by the Rand Corporation suggests that between 2001 and 2011, "49 countries in Africa received approximately US$175 billion dollars in pledged assistance which includes grants, interest-free loans and concessional loans," and that around the same time span the actual "cumulative delivered aid increased from US$52 million in 2001 to US$18.4 billion in 2011."[75] The report also points out that infrastructure remains the most significant portion of China's African bound assistance.[76] In addition, it is estimated that Africa now hosts as many as one million Chinese immigrants, both legal and illegal. It is yet to be seen how the presence of these Chinese men and women would impact Africa–China engagement in both the short and long term.

At first glance, China's presence on the continent seems "overwhelming." Without a proper reconceptualization, the China-in-Africa "elephant" will continue to be rather daunting for "blind men" to fully appreciate. This paper has argued that China has been in history and will continue to be an alternative foreign source of capital to the West as the primary source for Africa's development. Although Chinese investment has been criticized as a new form of colonialism ("neocolonialism"), scholars point out that it does not differ from its Western or any major international counterparts, which have similar commercial objectives in exports, and strategic value (natural resources) for imports. In terms of conduct, studies also show that Chinese capital, particularly in the resource industry, behaves in the same way as capital

---

[72] For instance, China's $5.5 billion purchase of 20 percent of Standard Bank of South Africa is not reflected in the cumulative figures for FDI to Africa. See http://davidshinn.blogspot.com/2013/03/foreign-direct-investment-in-africa.html.

[73] Austin Strange, Bradley Parks, Michael J. Tierney, Andreas Fuchs, Axel Dreher, and Vijaya Ramachandran, "China's Development Finance to Africa: A Media-Based Approach to Data Collection," Working Paper 323, Center for Global Development (Washington D. C), April 2013.

[74] For a good critique of the report, see Deborah Brautigam, "Aid Data: Why it is not Wikipedia," May 2, 2013, accessible at http://www.chinaafricarealstory.com/2013/05/aiddata-why-it-is-not-wikipedia.html.

[75] Charles Wolf, Xiao Wang, and Eric Warner, "China's Foreign Aid and Government-Sponsored Investment Activities: Scale, Content, Destinations, and Implications," the Rand National Defense Research Institute, 2013, p. 29.

[76] Charles Wolf, Xiao Wang, and Eric Warner, "China's Foreign Aid and Government-Sponsored Investment Activities: Scale, Content, Destinations, and Implications," p. 32.

of other nations. Nevertheless, the Chinese have become "the sole target of resource nationalism."[77] Key differences do exist between Chinese and other investment. The most salient one is that Chinese investment provides resource-backed infrastructural loans, which is potentially a prime opportunity for African states to build regional infrastructure and productive capacity. This is of vital interest to African governments, who see in this facility the opportunity to expand their physical infrastructures to support more diversified economies. Indeed, China's presence is an important factor in Africa's impressive growth rates in the past decade.[78]

This chapter has shown that there is no singular "Chinese" interest always capable of imposing itself on a singular and vulnerable Africa. It is simply not the case. As the cases presented above have suggested, the phenomenon that is "China" must be examined on multiple levels, namely, the state and the state-owned enterprises, private companies and the grassroots immigrants. Tensions in Africa–China relations caused by the complications of China in Africa both provide the context for and demonstrate the urgency for a China policy from the African governments at the national, regional and perhaps, continental levels. In the backdrop of a rising China and Africa, how Africa's political economies intersect with the differing agendas and interests of the aforementioned three "faces" of China will be crucial as we enter into a new era of Africa–China engagement.

[77] Ching Kwan Lee, "Raw Encounters: Chinese Managers, African Workers and the Politics of Casualization in Africa's Chinese Enclaves," *The China Quarterly*, Vol. 199 (2009), p. 666.

[78] According to the IMF and *The Economist*, over the past decade (2000-2010), African economies grew at an annual rate over 5%, and six of the world's ten fastest-growing countries were African. In eight of the ten years, Africa has grown faster than East Asia. Even allowing for the knock-on effect of the northern hemisphere's slowdown, Africa grew by about 6% in 2012. See "Africa Rising," *The Economist*, December 3rd, 2011; "Africa's Impressive Growth," *The Economist*, January 11th, 2013; "Africa's Growth Rate Ahead of Other Regions; but Growth Must Lead to Equality," *World Bank News*, April 25, 2013.

CHAPTER 43

AID TO AFRICA

Emerging Trends and Issues

PETER QUARTEY AND GLORIA AFFUL-MENSAH

43.1 INTRODUCTION

THE importance of aid is derived from the Harrod–Domar growth literature that countries should save between 15–20% of their national income to invest in order to grow. In its simplest form, the model assumes that output is a function of capital stock and that the production function exhibits constant returns to scale (that is, the marginal product of capital is constant). One of the major conclusions made by the model is that the output growth (which can be used as a proxy for economic growth) is the savings rate times the marginal product of capital less the rate of depreciation. By implication, the savings rate and marginal product of capital have a positive relationship with the growth rate of output. The interpretation is that increasing savings rate and increasing the marginal product of capital will increase economic growth. Thus, economic growth is dependent on increase investment by increasing savings and using investment efficiently. On the other hand, output will grow if there is a decline in the depreciation rate. Now, in such a model, if the level of investment depends on savings, then, savings is a very critical variable in achieving economic growth.

Relating the conclusion from the Harrod–Domar growth model to most African countries raises doubt about the ability to achieve desirable output or economic growth levels. The fact is, many African countries do not have high-income levels and so have been unable to save adequately to either enhance accumulation of capital stock through investment or to transform their economies. For instance, in 2011, savings as a percentage of GNI in Ghana, Senegal, Sierra Leone, and South Africa were 9.1%, 22.0%, 9.9%, 16.8% compared to the World average of 23.1% (World Bank 2013). In addition, there are inadequate domestic resources to finance investment expenditures and foreign exchange that can enable the importation of goods and technology that are growth enhancing (Gomanee, Girma, and Morrissey 2005). Meanwhile, the literature goes on to suggest that countries that are unable to save enough can resort to foreign direct investment (FDI) or Aid suggesting that foreign aid may be an alternative in boosting savings rate in such economies in order to achieve the targeted economic growth rate. Yet, neither of these countries has been able to attract significant FDI and where they have done so, FDI has gone into the extractive sectors of their economies. Rather, many African countries have relied on aid to finance their budgets but more especially to finance capital expenditures (Gomanee, Girma, and Morrissey 2002a, 2002b). Consequently, significant amounts of aid have been received by African countries to fill in the savings–investment gap and trade gap.

Foreign aid can take several forms and these may include inter alia programme loan, project aid, commodity aid, technical assistance, and emergency relief. It is important to emphasize the point that foreign aid is not necessarily a free resource and in some instances, aid comes with certain economic and political conditionalities. In such cases, recipient countries may not be at liberty to channel the aid resources into what they may consider as "priority areas." From these types of aid, it is also obvious that not all funds are intended to affect growth levels through investment and similarly, not all investment is financed by foreign aid. However, the impact of such aid on economic growth may also vary. While some may not have direct impact, others may rather have either short to medium term impact or long-term impact on growth. For instance, whereas aid in the form of technical assistance is believed to have short- to medium-term impact on growth, those in the form of investment are argued to rather have long-term growth effects on growth (Gomanee, Girma, and Morrissey 2005). Even in the case of aid on consumption, even though it is argued to have almost no effect on growth, the recipient economies benefit greatly since some of them may be used for the social services sector and this may serve as a way of improving human capital. In this case, human capital development can impact on growth positively.

Modeled on the success of the Marshal Plan, developing economies including Africa has received more aid but many people have raised concerns about the development effectiveness of these flows and its sustainability particularly in view of recent downturns in donor countries (Hansen and Tarp 2001; Lensink and White 2001). Overseas Development Assistance (ODA) flows analyzed by largest bilateral donor (USA) since 1970 have increased from US$1.2 billion to US$18.4 billion in 2010. That of France has increased from US$3 billion to US$4.1 billion over the same period. Africa's share of total ODA has been higher than Asia between 1990 and 1998 and between 2006 and 2010 and often ranged between 30–45% of total ODA (OECD 2013). Also, analysis of the top ten donors between 2009 and 2011 shows very revealing information; Africa as a percentage of each donor's aid ranged between 55% (Sweden) to 82% (Ireland). In terms of total amount disbursed over the period 1970–2010/2011, the USA provided the highest share (22%) followed by France (15.4%), Germany (9.5%), UK (7.4%), and Japan (6.4%). The other countries still within the top ten were the Netherlands (4.8%), Canada (4.5%), Italy (4.0%), Sweden (3.6%), and Norway (3.5%) with the rest of the bilateral donors accounting for the rest. Analysis of the 10 multilateral donors to Africa also reveal that the UK accounts for 30% of net disbursements between 2009 and 2011, followed by IDA (27%), AfDB (13%), Global Fund (9%), IMF Concessional Trust Funds (8%), with UNICEF, GAVI, Arab Fund, UNDP, Global Environmental Facility (GEF), and other multilateral donors accounting for the rest. While aid from the EU, IDA and AfDB increased consistently between 1970 and 2010, institutions such as the UNDP and World Food Programme (WFP) showed a downward trend since the 1990s.

It is also important to understand the aid architecture by analyzing the flows in terms of the top ten recipients in Africa. Similarly, within the same period (1970–2010/2011) and in terms of amount disbursed, Egypt tops the list of 10 ODA recipients in Africa with about 9.4%, followed by Congo and Tanzania (each with 5.7%), Ethiopia (5.6%), Mozambique (4.1%) and

Sudan (4.0%). Kenya received 3.7%, followed by Morocco (3.6%), with Nigeria and Ghana receiving 3.5% and 3.1% respectively, and the remaining going to the other African countries. This analysis seems to suggest relatively lower aid flow to West Africa countries than to their eastern and southern counterparts as only Ghana and Nigeria are among the top ten recipients within the period. In terms of sectors, the social sectors received the highest amount of aid ranging from 18% of total ODA to 41% between 1970 and 2010 followed by the economic sector (16–20%) over the same period.

Despite the interesting trends described above, ODA flows have declined in recent times due to the continuing global financial crisis and the challenges within the Eurozone. This has led several governments to tighten their budgets with severe repercussions on development aid. In 2012, development aid declined by 4% in real terms as compared to the 2% decline recorded in the preceding year (OECD 2013). It has also been observed that there has been a shift in aid allocations from poorest countries to middle-income countries despite the largest fall recorded since 1997. It is, however, reassuring to note that despite the decline, Aid for core bilateral projects and programs (excluding debt relief and humanitarian aid) increased by 2% in real terms in 2012. Also, despite the fall in bilateral aid by about 7.9% in 2012, some donors have continued to exceed the UN ODA target of 0.7% of GNI. These largest donors (by volume) include USA, UK, France, Japan, Denmark, Luxemburg, the Netherlands, Norway, and Sweden.

This analysis really shows donors commitment to ensure that the developmental objectives of Aid are achieved and this is premised on the fundamental assumption that aid works in reducing poverty and achieving other human development outcomes (see Collier and Dollar 2001; Collier and Dollar 2004). However, the effectiveness of aid have been critiqued by many scholars with some describing aid as harmful, a failure or counterproductive in achieving its effectiveness goal. Well as such criticisms regarding Aid effectiveness are made, it is important to note that in the midst of the global downturn, the population growth rates in almost all Aid recipient countries have increased rapidly and hence may be a reason why aid in per capita terms has been declining. Even among the recipient economies, the rate of growth of populations varied from one economy to another. This therefore means that the impact of the declining aid trends may also vary from one country to another depending on the internal arrangements, resource endowments, fiscal, and monetary policies, etc., prevailing in the respective countries.

The trends in aid flows described above is also quite revealing and points to Less Developed Countries (LDCs) overdependence on aid which has to be gradually curtailed in view of its volatility and the future uncertainty surrounding such flows. Rather, other forms and sources of debt finance should be ascertained. The trends also raise a number of issues; for instance, should Africa turn to the new sources of development finance such as Brazil, Russia, India, China, and South Africa (BRICS)? Given the new oil and other natural resource discoveries in a number of African countries, should alternative sources of financing such as the floating of bonds or borrowing from the commercial markets be considered? Will such new forms of borrowing revisit the debt crisis of the late 1970s and 1980s? What about enhancing the internal sources of finance in these countries? Should the focus be more aid or better aid? Can African countries rely on their capital markets to finance development projects as is being done in many western countries after the global financial crisis? These issues form the focus of the next sections. The rest of the chapter looks at the aid effectiveness discourse, followed by a section analyzing the changes in the aid architecture and its implications for growth. This is followed by a discussion of the global financial crisis and emerging issues for Africa. The final section provides the concluding remarks.

43.2 THE AID EFFECTIVENESS DEBATE

The role of foreign aid in Africa's growth process cannot be underestimated even though it continues to be a debate particularly in the development economics literature. Empirical research continues to establish the exact relationship between aid and growth and yet, this relationship remains inconclusive. This section of the chapter looks at both the theoretical and the empirical arguments regarding the relationship between foreign aid and economic growth.

On one hand, there are the "optimists" who believe in the positive association between foreign aid and growth and this usually stems from the Harrod–Domar growth model and the overlapping generations model. The fundamental idea behind the Harrod–Domar model is the "supposed" stable linear relationship between growth and investment in physical capital. While the Harrod–Domar growth model does not necessarily consider foreign aid and its repercussions on growth, the model asserts that countries need to save up to a certain level in order to achieve a targeted output growth and this can be used as a proxy for economic growth. In this case, foreign aid can influence savings and subsequently economic growth positively. With this underlying assumption, if all aid is invested, the calculation of the amount of aid required for achieving a targeted growth rate will be very simple and so given this positive relationship between aid and growth; the main focus will be on how to increase savings and investment in recipient economies (Tarp 2009). This condition will therefore depend largely on the management of aid funds which is usually carried out by the public sector or the government.

The overlapping generations' model that was originally proposed by Diamond (1965) is an alternative approach for explaining the aid-growth relationship. Using its augmented form, by including aid in the original model, Dalgaard, Hansen, and Tarp (2004) simulated the relationship between aid and growth. The model assumes competitive markets in a closed economy (except for transfer). The economy involved is therefore made up of two different periods characterized by "young" and "old" people (who represent the two groups of people living in the economy) with a positive growth rate of the population. Given that there are no technological progress and capital depreciation in the overlapping generation framework, transfers are to be shared equally between the "young" and the "old." It is important to note here too that, in reality, transfers or foreign aid funds are to be managed and, in this case, shared by the government, which again emphasizes the role of government in resource management. Now in the event where there is any "expropriation," the summation of the transfers to the two groups of people living (young and old) will be lower than the total transfer (Dalgaard, Hansen, and Tarp 2004). According to the authors, bad policy could be a cause of the disproportional allocation of resources/transfers and the possible returns to foreign aid. Generally, the evidence supporting the positive aid-growth relationship seems to suggest that increases in aid inflow make living standards better in recipient economies in that poverty and inequalities would have been worse in the absence of aid inflow to such countries.

On the other hand, there are the "pessimists" views that assert that aid does not necessarily induce economic growth. Undoubtedly, most of such views emanate from some empirical findings that tested for non-linearity in the aid-growth relationship whereby after a certain level of aid, the relationship becomes negative (e.g. Hansen and Tarp 2000, 2001; Burnside and Dollar 2000; Dalgaard, Hansen and Tarp 2004; Lensink and White 2001; Hudson and Mosley 2001; Moyo 2009). Generally, findings in support of this view assert that there are negative returns when the aid inflow reaches between 15% and 45% of GDP, indicating limited aid absorptive capacities, with recipient governments being limited in terms of the amounts of aid they can use effectively (Clemens and Radelet 2003; cited in McGillivray 2004: 6). Hence, it is not surprising that aid to Africa is believed by some to be ineffective given that the GDP levels in the region are almost stable.

Obviously, the controversies surrounding aid–growth relationship has led to a number of studies in the form of cross-country analysis, specific or individual country studies or broad surveys that employ both qualitative and interdisciplinary approaches. In addition, inferring from the different categories of aid, the issue of aid effectiveness becomes a complex one and therefore raises a number of questions.[1] In Africa, another sensitive aspect of aid analysis emanates from the fact that in some instances, the performance of governments are judged based on how much aid they have been able to attract to their respective countries within their term of office given that aid is viewed as a cultural "commodity."[2] In this regard, using residual generated regressors for a sample of 25 sub-Saharan African (SSA) countries who were major aid recipients (over 1970–1997) by Gomanee, Girma and Morrissey (2005), aid was found to have a positive significant effect on economic growth. Specifically, the study identified investment as the most significant transmission mechanism through which aid affects economic growth. The results revealed that on average, every 1.0 percentage point increase in the aid/GNP ratio leads to about one quarter of 1.0 percentage point to the economic growth. The result from the study emerged consistent with earlier findings by Lensink and Morrissey (2000). In a related study, Tarp (2009) argued that even though there exists positive relationship between aid and economic growth, the extent of benefit may not necessarily be as large as being argued and may also accrue over a considerable period of time; typically at least 30 years.

There are also arguments that foreign aid, particularly aid to SSA countries is growth enhancing if there are good macroeconomic and political conditions. Most empirical findings in this line of argument were inspired by earlier revelations by Burnside and Dollar (2000) and Collier and Dollar (2001). That is, using the budget surplus, inflation and trade openness as index for good policy (fiscal, monetary, and trade policies respectively), the

---

[1] Riddell (2007) raises very interesting questions. For instance; should aid be considered a success if it is only directed to those able to use it effectively ignoring those who need it but are less likely to use it well? Is aid to be judged a success or otherwise if it achieves its immediate objectives but the wider policies which donors promote as part of "aid package" are found to be misguided? Should aid be considered a success if it simply arrives and contributes to meeting the pressing needs of recipients or should be judged with respect to how efficiently and cost-effectively it is provided? (see Riddell 2007 for more).

[2] According to Moyo (2009), Africa lives in a culture of aid whereby the general belief is that the rich must give alms to the poor and hence making aid a cultural commodity in the continent such that millions march for it (http://www.fordham.edu/economics/mcleod/Dambisa_moyo_DeadAidForward.pdf.

authors revealed that aid in developing countries is only effective where there are good policies. From the findings, while the authors do not entirely rule out the possibility of aid's influence on economic growth positively, it also implies that economic growth depends on the "supposed" good macroeconomic indicators. In another study, a slightly modified Overlapping Generations (OLG) model used by Dalgaard, Hansen, and Tarp (2004) revealed that foreign aid inflows generally affect long run productivity positively. However, the extent of the impact on the steady state productivity remained ambiguous such that bad economic management (on government's part) was expected to make aid ineffective.

The study therefore revealed aid to be relatively less effective in the geographic tropics. For example, while climate on one hand may directly affect productivity and subsequently impact on the capital–labor combination in production, climate may in another instance influence the evolution of other slow-moving structural characteristics (such as institutions). The latter reinforces the theoretical model that aid has been relatively more effective in places with stronger slow-moving structural characteristics (Dalgaard, Hansen, and Tarp 2004). Hence, the study concludes that aid effectiveness largely may depend on policies, deep structural characteristics and the size of the inflow. On the contrary, a major criticism on aid particularly to Africa is one presented by Moyo (2009) where a comparison between the 1950s and the present suggest a positive correlation between aid and poverty levels in Africa given that poverty levels have rather worsened. Thus according to the author, many of the woes facing Africa and the inability of the continent to turn things around in order to make the economies function better as happening in most developed countries is as a result of aid to the region[3].

While the controversies surrounding aid effectiveness still exist, in recent times, there seem to be a gradual consensus with respect to the positive impact of aid on economic growth. Thus, regardless of the view on aid effectiveness and the conditions surrounding the transmission mechanism in ensuring the effectiveness, there are enough empirical findings that aid indeed works. That is, on one hand, aid works with "good policies" and on the other hand, it works even without the so-called "good policies." Meanwhile, given that economic growth, economic development and poverty reduction are quite complex processes, issues relating to aid effectiveness are also complex. Aside from these, aid to Africa is faced with "unrealistic" expectations in terms of the numerous objectives set to be achieved based on the fact that it has a positive relationship with economic growth which may subsequently reduce poverty. In other words, in the midst of the countless difficulties faced by the SSA region (high morbidity and mortality levels, high illiteracy rates, inadequate/poor infrastructure, unfavorable macroeconomic policies, etc.), aid inflow is expected to abruptly improve living standards of recipient countries. Yet, if for nothing at all, aid can contribute to accelerating growth and development and reducing poverty by filling some crucial immediate gaps inhibiting growth and development processes by helping to meet some pressing needs in terms of for example providing funds to those adversely affected by structural changes (Riddell 2007).

---

[3] Moyo (2009) admits the improvements in some African countries in terms of *inter alia* favorable commodity prices (for African exports), some social indicators and stock market, yet, more than half of the population continued to live with a per capita income of almost US$ 1 daily with the worst happening in SSA. In addition, in the midst of increasing aid to the continent, life expectancy has either stagnated or declined mainly as a result of HIV/AIDS pandemic, cholera, bilharzia, etc.

43.3 THE CHANGING AID ARCHITECTURE AND IMPLICATIONS ON GROWTH AND DEVELOPMENT

While the debate still exists, the evaluation of aid effectiveness may be affected by the changing architecture of aid to Africa. Aid to the continent has and is still going through significant changes in terms of the number or donors, the strategy or mode of delivery and the composition of the aid funds. Foreign aid is generally given for different purposes and some of them may include inter alia infrastructure construction and/or expansion, expansion of education, health and other social services, agriculture modernization and humanitarian emergencies.

Foreign aid has evolved from generally being grants to hard loans with conditionalities attached probably as a response to the global economic and financial changes. In another sense, it can also be explained by the ongoing arguments for good policies in ensuring aid effectiveness particularly in developing countries and so some donors have restrategized their aid delivery methods by allocating foreign aid to only countries with good economic and political conditions. Thus in some cases aid comes with prescribed policies to ensure effectiveness. Hence as a strategy to increase aid effectiveness, the aid delivery approach by donors particularly majority of the traditional donors is based on the selectivity concept whereby aid agreements are made with countries with acceptable policies (Mosley, Hudson and Verschoor 2004).

While an immediate evaluation of this approach may seem good, such tied aid funds have also raised a number of concerns with respect to their effectiveness. For instance, some agreements made on tied aid may restrict recipients from channeling aid resources into where they consider very important sectors in the economy and may be compelled to embark on policies and government structures considered by donors as effective. In this case, recipient governments are not given the opportunity to own their economic growth and development policies and strategies. This may in the end contribute to ineffectiveness of aid funds since there may be little or no impact on the citizenry.

The aid architecture has also witnessed "new" or "emerging" donors especially China[4] with different aid delivery mechanisms which are mostly characterized by ex-post verification and in some cases, no conditionalities are attached. However, it is argued that on one hand, aid with no or few conditionalities allow the recipient governments to channel resources to growth enhancing areas and such aid funds usually turn out to be relatively more effective and more responsive to a country's needs by improving the living standards of the people. In another instance, it is argued that the "no conditionality approach" of aid delivery may play a significant role in the expropriation of aid funds given that recipient governments may become less transparent in the use of aid funds. In addition, some donors have developed a strategy of rarely disclosing foreign aid and China is usually criticized in this regard (Dreher, Nunnenkamp, and Thiele 2010). Such a strategy is likely to influence corruption and directing of funds into unproductive sectors that may have almost no impact from aid and even in some instances retard economic growth.

---

[4] Between 1995 and 2009, China has provided US$10.8 billion in concessional loans (ODA) to 76 foreign countries including Africa but the proportion to Africa is unknown (http://www.american.edu/sis/faculty/upload/Brautigam-Chinese-Aid-in-Africa.pdf).

Other countries like Brazil, India, Korea and South Africa have developed an aid strategy of non-interfering in recipients' domestic affairs and respect for a country's sovereignty. While this may seem appealing, it fails to ensure good governance. Now, given the various empirical findings that good policy environment (economically and politically) is necessary for aid effectiveness (see Burnside and Dollar 2000; Collier and Dollar 2000; Dalgaard, Hansen, and Tarp 2004), there is no doubt that adopting such a strategy may contribute to aid ineffectiveness.

Furthermore, given that most of the ongoing studies challenging the Harrod-Domar growth model and other aid–growth positive relationship are more empirical, a major argument in assessing aid effectiveness may be raised from the various methodologies adopted in estimating the relationships. Thus the controversies surrounding aid–economic growth relationship can be linked to the evidence and the method of assessment (Riddell 2007). Unfortunately, not much attention is given to these two critical issues when considering the conclusions drawn by the opposing views regarding aid–growth relationship. Firstly, how good a result is in any empirical study is largely dependent on the nature of data (accuracy, reliability, data collection period, measurement techniques, etc.) and the method of analysis. In cases where the data is collected for a number of countries, there is the need to consider internal variations (poverty levels, macroeconomic indicators, the amount and the flow of aid, etc.) within individual country. Also, in conducting such a study especially cross-country studies, some create a dummy for the various continents or sub-regions in the regression analysis. In such analysis, an "African" dummy usually emerges negatively significant suggesting that there is an inverse relationship between aid and growth in Africa. According to Collier and Gunning (1999), this relationship could probably be because there are certain globally growth enhancing variables which may be low in Africa (cited in Gomanee, Girma, and Morrissey 2005: 1). This means that in certain parts of the world, the traditional positive relationship between aid and economic growth may exist and hence not necessarily disprove the general positive relationship between aid and growth.

Since the different categories of aid may take relatively different time period to impact on economic growth and/or development, it may not be entirely wrong to suggest that this can lead to invalid conclusions. Closely related to this is the issue of biased estimates for studies that omit the "investment" variable in their estimations. Although not always the case, we cannot rule out the possibility that some proportions of aid funds are not spent on current consumption but are invested. In such situations, omitting the "investment" variable ignores the effect of aid on growth through investment and hence may produce biased estimates. Although multicollinearity is almost always present in every regression analysis, in some cases, the inclusion of an "investment" and "aid" variables in the analysis may also yield bias results especially if there is a high correlation between aid and investment and hence increasing the degree of multicollinearity.[5] Aside from these, data on growth levels (even in the developed economies) may be inaccurate and may affect the conclusions drawn for

---

[5] Again, it is important to note that in any time series analysis as in the case of aid-growth relationship, the problem of endogeneity may arise due to measurement error (especially given that aid may take several forms either in cash or in kind), autocorrelation in the errors and also from omitted variables and hence make the independent variables correlate with the error terms. Thus, the fact that it is difficult to account for all forms of aid even in a single country analysis, we cannot rule out the possibility of correlation between the error and the regressor in such aid analysis and hence bring in an endogeneity problem which may affect conclusions. Here, it is important to also add that if the correlation is not contemporaneous, then the estimates may still be consistent.

aid-growth relationship. Thus if the assertion by Morgenstern (1963) that data on national accounts in industrialized countries are subject to an error of about at least 10% is true, then Africa (where the countries are either underdeveloped or developing) which is mostly characterized by inadequate information, the error margin may be greater and therefore may contribute to inaccurate conclusions with respect to the relationship between foreign aid and economic growth.

43.4 THE GLOBAL FINANCIAL CRISIS, EMERGING DONORS AND AID FLOWS

The financial crisis of 2007/08 is regarded by many as the worse financial crisis since the Great Depression in the 1930s and has played a significant role in the decline of global economic activities between the period 2008 and 2012 especially in terms of weak demand and challenging environment particularly for exporters and the financial sector. This undoubtedly contributed to the contraction of GDP, increased unemployment and the decline in savings. Being a severe threat to the stability, safety and soundness of the entire financial system in an economy, the financial crisis presents a major challenge to governments and especially for economies without strong fiscal discipline. Even though the crisis mainly emanated from the failure of EU economies in limiting their deficit spending by resorting to securitizing future government revenues in order to cut down their debt and/or deficits, eventually, the crisis spread to non-EU member states given the interconnectedness of the global economy in terms of trade, finance and investments.

However, it is important to also quickly add that the extent of the impact was largely dependent on the degree of a country's integration with the global economy as well as the various internal policies and strategies designed in the respective economies. In response, individual countries initiated several reform processes and this included tightening budgets, reduction in capital subscriptions to international organizations and multilateral institutions and other austerity measures. One major problem associated particularly with the tightening of donor budgets is the flow of assistance in the form of foreign aid to low income countries given that this happened at a time when we were barely five years away from the end date of the Millennium Development Goals (MDGs) set to be achieved by the year 2015. Thus, the global financial crisis and the Euro zone crisis compelled most donor governments/institutions to cut down the amount of ODA to developing countries.

ODA flows to Africa after the global financial crisis continued to increase from $45,173 million in 2008 to US$47 976 million in 2010 and US$51 261 in 2011 (OECD 2013). On the other hand, the periods after the Euro zone crisis generally recorded reductions in ODA in real terms. By the year 2012, ODA from EU member states (who were also Development Assistance Committee - DAC members) had fallen by about 7.4% compared to the preceding year. Specifically, among the DAC-EU countries, between the period 2011 and 2012, Spain recorded the largest decline in her contribution to ODA (−49.7%) followed by Italy (−34.7%), Greece (−17%), Portugal (−13.1%), and Belgium (−13.0%) respectively. It is important to note that Spain's decline in ODA to developing countries was largely attributed to the financial crisis while those of Italy, Portugal and Belgium were mainly due to the overall cuts in their respective budgets (OECD 2013) probably as a result of the global economic down-turns. It is also interesting to note that in the midst of these challenges, even though ODA by DAC-EU member states was US$63.7 billion in 2012 representing a decline of about 7.4% compared to 2011, the total net ODA from all EU member countries was US$64.9 billion representing 0.39% of their GNI (OECD 2013) and also revealing the significant role played by the DAC-EU contributions to foreign aid to the developing nations.

Although most of the austerity measures by donor governments initially seemed harsh (particularly between the late 2010 and 2011), these were gradually relaxed leading to increased government spending and hence gradual recovery of most aid recipient countries. While the economic environment in most EU countries since the late 2012 appears good as a result of successful fiscal consolidation and the implementation of structural reforms suggesting a good sign for investment, a DAC Survey on Donors' Forward Spending Plans suggests a changing trend for aid to developing countries. Thus the Survey suggests a likely increased aid (mostly in the form of soft loans) to middle-income countries but a stagnated amount of Country Programmable Aid (CPA) to the largest MDG gaps and poor countries. This follows a similar pattern in the 1990s whereby the decline in aid amounts to SSA was not entirely as a result of overall contraction in world aid but donors rather allocated away from the region (McGillivray 2004). Now, given the nature of the CPA which represents the component of aid whereby partner countries have significant influence, SSA countries that are mostly aid dependent may be at a great disadvantage and therefore this should send a clear signal to these countries to look for alternative sources of finance to boost growth and development in their respective economies.

Finally, the aid architecture is going through significant changes, especially with entrance of "new," "non-traditional," "emerging" or non-DAC donors. Aside from receiving the tra-ditional foreign assistance from member states of the OECD Development Assistance Committee or DAC donors, SSA have in recent times been receiving substantial amount of foreign aid from non-DAC members in the wake of dwindling aid from the DAC donors. The debate has been how to bring both types of donors to the negotiation table to ensure that processes are harmonized to promote the development effectiveness of aid.

43.5 CONCLUSION

The chapter generally set out to look at the emerging trends and issues regarding Aid to Africa after the global financial crisis. An attention was given to the theoretical and empirical con-troversies surrounding aid and growth. The chapter argues that while aid is good in terms of promoting economic growth and human capital development whether directly or indirectly, there is no doubt that even if the positive relation exists, such benefits may only accrue to a country probably in the medium to long term.[6] This implies that aid cannot be considered as a "solution" to the many challenges experienced in most countries in Africa. This therefore seems to suggest that other sources of finance must be explored in order to avoid making the

[6] Tarp (2009) estimates this to be at least 30 years.

continent aid dependent. Probably African countries may have to consider attracting funds from the capital markets as adopted by many developed nations.

It is interesting to note that a lot of the countries in the continent are very well endowed with natural resources and some are even still discovering new resources. Unfortunately, many of these countries are either suffering from the Dutch disease (e.g. Cameroon, Gabon, and Nigeria) or risk being affected (e.g. Ghana). This obviously affects the growth process even in the presence of large aid inflows. Therefore, Africa must take advantage of these discoveries by saving and investing the proceeds from the sales of natural resources in productive activities in order to reduce her dependence on foreign aid. It is also important to emphasize the need for good and prudent monetary and fiscal discipline in order not to turn the natural resource "blessings" into a "curse."

It is generally accepted that aid works in good policy environments and Africa is no exception. However, the uniqueness of Africa's aid architecture comprising of complex institutions and players makes aid effectiveness a major challenge. There are many donors with complex demands on recipients in terms of triggers and reporting which often makes the transactions costs of aid to the continent huge. Some countries have tried to overcome this by using the multi-donor budgetary arrangement but this forms only 30% of total aid flows to these countries. Thus, this chapter proposes that significant proportions of aid should be channeled through the MDBS arrangements to minimize transactions costs and make reporting simpler.

Another major area of concern is the need to strengthen institutions in Africa to make aid flows more transparent and accountable. Donors are often reluctant to use country systems because they are weak and not until both parties (donors and recipients) build country systems, aid effectiveness challenges will continue to remain.

Finally and also related to the above, while more aid inflow is good, the focus should rather be on better aid or being able to utilize aid funds efficiently and at the same time, allowing for some degree of freedom on the part of the recipient governments as is being practiced by some non-DAC donors. In addition, ensuring "better aid" also requires greater accountability of aid funds as well as allowing aid funds to be channeled into priority and growth enhancing sectors of the economies involved will enhance the development effectiveness of aid greatly.

References

Burnside, C., and Dollar, D. (2000). Aid, policies, and growth, *American Economic Review*, 90:847–868.

Clemens, M., and Radelet, S. (2003). The Millennium Challenge Account: How Much is too Much, How Long is Long Enough? Centre for Global Development Working Paper No. 23. Washington, DC: Centre for Global Development.

Collier, P., and Dollar, D. (2001). Can the world cut poverty in half? How policy reform and effective aid can meet the international development goals? *World Development*, 29(11):1787–1802.

Collier, P., and Gunning, J. (1999). Explaining African economic performance. *Journal of Economic Literature*, 37(1):64–111.

Collier P., and Dollar, D. (2000), "Can the World Cut Poverty in Half? How policy reform and effective aid can meet international development goals", Policy Research Working Paper Series 2403. Washington, DC: World Bank.

Collier, P., and Dollar, D. (2004). Development effectiveness: what have we learnt? *Economic Journal*, 114(496):244–271.

Dalgaard, C.-J., Hansen, H., and Tarp, F. (2004). On the empirics of foreign aid and growth. *Economic Journal*, 114:F191–F216.

Diamond, P. (1965). National debt in a neoclassical growth model. *American Economic Review*, 55:1126–1150.

Dreher, P., Nunnenkamp, P., and Thiele, R. (2010). Are New Donors Different? Comparing the Allocation of Bilateral Aid between Non-DAC Donor Countries, Center for European, Governance and Economic Development Research (CEGE), Discussion Papers vol. 96.

Gomanee, K., Girma, S., and Morrissey, O. (2002a). Aid and Growth in Sub-Saharan Africa: Accounting for Transmission Mechanisms. CREDIT Research Paper 02/05, Centre for Research in Economic Development and International Trade, University of Nottingham, Nottingham.

Gomanee, K., Morrissey, O., Mosley, P., Verschoor, A. (2002b). Aid, Pro-poor Government Expenditure and Welfare. CREDIT Research Paper, Centre for Research in Economic Development and International Trade, University of Nottingham, Nottingham.

Gomanee, K., Girma, S., and Morrissey, O. (2005). Aid and Growth in Sub-Saharan Africa, Accounting for Transmission Mechanisms, UNU—WIDER Research Paper No. 2005/60.

Hansen, H., and Tarp, F. (2000). Aid and performance: a reassessment. *Journal of Development*, 12:375–398.

Hansen, H., and Tarp, F. (2001). Aid and growth regressions. *Journal of Development Economics*, 64(2):547–570.

Hudson, J. and Mosley, P. (2001). "Aid Policies and Growth: in search of the Holy Grail". *Journal of International Development*, 13:1023–1038.

Lensink, R., and Morrissey, O. (2000). Aid instability as a measure of uncertainty and the positive impact of aid on growth. *Journal of Development Studies*, 36(3):31–49.

Lensink, R., and White, H. (2001). Are there negative returns to aid? *Journal of Development Studies*, 37(6):42–64.

Morgenstern, O. (1963). *On the Accuracy of Economic Observations*, 2nd edn. Princeton, NJ: Princeton University Press.

McGillivray, M. (2004). Is Aid Effective? Mimeo, Helsinki, UNU-WIDER.

Mosley, P., Hudson, J., and Verschoor, A. (2004). Aid, poverty reduction and the new conditionality. *Economic Journal*, 114:217–243.

Moyo, D. (2009). Dead Aid, Why Aid is not Working and How there is a Better Way for Africa, http://www.fordham.edu/economics/mcleod/Dambisa_moyo_DeadAidForward.pdf, accessed 29 March 2014.

OECD (2013). *Development Aid at a Glance, Statistics by Region, Africa*. Paris: OECD.

Riddell, R.C. (2007). *Does Aid Really Work?* New York: Oxford University Press.

Tarp, F. (2009). Aid Effectiveness. Available at http://www.un.org/en/ecosoc/newfunct/pdf/aid_effectiveness-finn_tarp.pdf, accessed 25 October 2013.

World Bank (2013). World Development Indicators 2013. Washing, DC: World Bank.

CHAPTER 44

···

CHINA–AFRICA COOPERATION IN STRUCTURAL TRANSFORMATION
Ideas, Opportunities, and Finances

···

JUSTIN YIFU LIN AND YAN WANG

44.1 INTRODUCTION

···

WHY was it possible for China to achieve such a dramatic transformation? Is it possible for the low-income African countries to achieve the same? What is the role of China in Africa's economic transformation? Based on the theoretical foundation of New Structural Economics (NSE) (Lin 2010, 2011, 2012b), this chapter examines China's and Africa's development cooperation from the angle of structural transformation as a major driver of growth and job creation. The objective is to review past experiences of structural transformation in emerging markets, examine how China has been "doing what she knows best" using the tacit knowledge to contribute to Africa's economic transformation. The chapter also presents the future prospect—how a new type of learning partnership can accelerate the transformation in Africa. We go beyond the discussion of Official Development Aid (ODA) to cover South–South development cooperation (SSDC) with a broader definition, and provide a way of thinking "out of the box" of "aid effectiveness."

We consider that Africa and China are partners in climbing the same mountain of structural transformation. All climbers have the freedom to select their partners. On the one hand, China, being a bit ahead in structural transformation, has been attempting to help build "bottleneck-releasing" infrastructure and Special Economic Zones (SEZs) in Africa to facilitate structural transformation, which was based on China's own ideas and experiences. As the labor costs are rising rapidly in China, African countries can benefit from seizing the opportunities to attract labor-intensive enterprises relocating outside of China. On the other hand, African countries should also push China to learn to become a better development partner by "selecting desired partners" and regulating partner behaviors, and thereby forcing partners/companies to abide local laws and regulations as well as international principles for development.

The second section summarizes China's dramatic transformation and the key underlying factors: openness to ideas, trade, and the experimental/incremental approach. The third section examines the relevance of SEZs and cluster development. The fourth section examines the logic or philosophy underlying China's cooperation in Africa, which is largely based on China's own tacit knowledge and intimate experiences in the past 35 years. The issues, challenges, and prospects on development financing are discussed in the last section.

44.2 China's Dramatic Structural Transformation: Ideas

The NSE (Lin 2012b) points out that economic development is a dynamic process, which entails learning, industrial upgrading, and corresponding improvements in "hard" (tangible) and "soft" (intangible) infrastructure, at each level. Such upgrades and improvements require an inherent coordination, with large externalities to firms' transaction costs and returns to capital investment. Thus, the information and knowledge to identify a country's existing and latent comparative advantage are considered public goods and services that government should provide. In addition to an effective market mechanism, the government should play an active role in learning and facilitating structural transformation, diversification, and industrial upgrading (Lin 2012b: 14–15).

The NSE postulates that each country at any specific time possesses given factor endowments consisting of land (natural resources), labor, and capital (both human and physical), which represent the total available budget that the country can allocate to primary, secondary, and tertiary industries to produce goods and services. The relative abundance of endowments in a country are given at any given specific time, but changeable over time. In addition, infrastructure is a fourth endowment which is fixed at any given specific time and changeable over time (Lin 2012b: 21).

This framework implies that at any given point in time, the structure of a country's factor endowments, that is the relative abundance of factors that the country possesses, determines the relative factor prices and thus the optimal industrial structure. Therefore, the optimal industrial structure in a country, which will make the country most competitive, is endogenously determined by its endowment structure at each point in time. It follows that the import/export structures are also largely determined *endogenously* by their different endowments.

Many countries have in the past succeeded in structural transformation,[1] upgrading from resource based or agrarian economies to manufacturing powerhouses. According to Angus Maddison, it took 1400 years to double per capita income before the eighteenth century, but as the industrial revolution spread, it took only 70 years to double per capita income from the eighteenth century to the mid-nineteenth century. Now it took the developed countries 35

---

[1] There is an extensive literature on structural transformation, see for example, Akamatsu 1962, Kuznets 1966, North 1981, Solow 1957, Stiglitz 1996, and Lin 2010 and 2011.

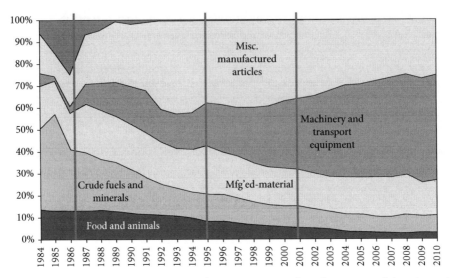

FIGURE 44.1 China's export structure: from raw material in the 1980s to labor intensive manufacturing product in the middle 1990s.

Source: Lin and Wang 2008 and updated by Yan Wang using COMTRAD data.

Note: "Mfg'ed material" stands for manufactured materials.

years to double the per capita income (Maddison 2001, 2007; Spence 2011; and World Bank 2008). This process of economic transformation has been accelerated in the case of 13 rapidly growing emerging economies (mostly East Asian economies), notably Korea, Taiwan (China), and other East Asian newly industrialized economies (NIEs), and, later, China and others, following a pattern that is well characterized by the "flying geese model" (Akamatsu 1962).

For Korea, it took only 35 years to grow from a war-torn agrarian economy in 1953 to a manufacturing leader in 1988. The share of manufactures in gross domestic product (GDP) rose from merely nine per cent in 1953 to 30.1% in 1988, while that of agriculture and mining sector shrunk to single digits in the 1990s. (Chandra, Lin, and Wang 2013).

When China started its economic transformation in 1978, it was an agrarian economy with agriculture as its largest sector, accounting for 71% of total employment. Its per capita income was US$154 in 1978, less than one-third of the average in SSA countries. Like many of them today, China was an exporter of primary product: In as late as 1984, 50% of China's export was concentrated in crude materials including oil, coal, food and animals, and other agricultural products. Since then, China has grown to become one of the largest manufacturing powerhouses in the world (Figure 44.1).

44.3 TRANSFORMATION CAN BE ACHIEVED THROUGH PARTIAL REFORMS VIA SEZs

During the transition process, China adopted a pragmatic, gradual, dual-track approach. The government first improved the incentives and productivity by allowing the workers in the collective farms and state-owned firms to be residual claimants and to set the prices for selling at the market after delivering the quota obligations to the state at fixed prices (Lin 1992). At the same time, the government continued to provide necessary protections to nonviable firms in the priority sectors to avoid their collapse and simultaneously liberalized the entry of private enterprises, joint ventures, and foreign direct investment (FDI) in labor-intensive sectors in which China had a comparative advantage but that were repressed before the transition to promote dynamic growth (Lin 1992, 2009).

With the liberalization of entry to the new sectors, the Chinese government recognized the needs to help firms to overcome all kinds of inherent hurdles in the transition process: The business environment was poor,[2] the infrastructure was very bad, and the investment environment was harsh.[3] The advice based on the Washington Consensus was to improve everything for the whole nation simultaneously without the attempt to pick/focus on specific sectors and regions. Many of those "undesirable" distortions in the business and investment environment, such as the control of import and restriction on foreign ownership, in fact were necessary for protecting the nonviable firms in the old priority sectors. If China removed all those distortions/regulations, many of the nonviable firms might have bankrupted, causing the collapse of the economy as what happened in many Eastern European and former Soviet Union countries during their transition process. Moreover, even if China adopted that approach, it might have taken China decades or generations, due to the government's limited implementation capacity and availability of resources, to achieve the desirable business environment and infrastructure. Instead the Chinese government mobilized its limited resources and capability to build up SEZs and industrial parks (Zeng 2010, 2011). Within the zones and parks, the infrastructure and business environment were made very competitive, but outside the zones and parks, they were improved only gradually. The labor costs were low due to large surplus labor in rural area when China started the transition. But China lacked the knowledge about how to turn that advantage to produce labor-intensive goods with quality acceptable by the international market and international buyers did not have confidence that Chinese firms would be able to deliver the goods in timely manner either. To overcome those difficulties, the Chinese governments at all levels and regions proactively approached prospect foreign investors, especially those manufacturers in developing Asia who were about to relocate their labor-intensive processing to other low-wage economies, and incentivized them to make investments in the SEZs and industrial parks (Wei and Liu 2001). With that approach, China developed labor-intensive light manufacturing and became the world factory quickly.

This experimental transition strategy allowed China to both maintain stability by avoiding the collapse of old priority industries and achieve dynamic growth by simultaneously pursuing its comparative advantage and tapping the advantage of backwardness in the industrial upgrading process. In addition, the dynamic growth in the newly liberalized sectors created the conditions for reforming the old priority sectors. Through this gradual, dual-track

---

[2] In 2013, after more than three decades of market-oriented reform, China still ranked (http://www.doingbusiness.org/rankings).

[3] In the World Bank's Investing Across Borders 2010, China's investment environme worst among the 87 economies covered in the study. See http://iab.worldbank.org/~/me IAB/Documents/IABreport.pdf.

approach China achieved reform without losers' (Lau et al. 2000; Naughton 1995; Lin 2012a) and moved gradually but steadily to a well-functioning market economy.

In sum, China's structural transformation had started before its infrastructure bottle-necks had been relieved, and before business environment and investment climate had been improved. Through experimenting via SEZs and industrial parks, the country and people had been learning, imitating, investing, acquiring tacit knowledge, accumulating factor endowments such as human and physical capital, and expanding its comparative advantages. Now China is utilizing its own ideas and experiences in providing (SSDC), following the thousand-year tradition of not only "offering fish" but also "teaching how to fish" (Lao Tze, 604-531 BCE).

44.4 CHINA AND AFRICA COOPERATION FOR STRUCTURAL TRANSFORMATION: OPPORTUNITIES AND FINANCES

The China–Africa relationship has been the subject of many heated debates, which has escalated in the recent years. Many of the critics seem to have forgotten that China is big but not yet rich—it was a low-income country when it started providing development cooperation to African countries in the 1960s. The past 50 some years have witnessed a joint learning process for economic transformation in China and Africa.

The past literature on aid or aid effectiveness has largely focused on donors' behaviors—who provides aid, for what objective/motivation, and their effects. There is an extensive literature on aid effectiveness, for example, Burnside and Dollar (2000); Easterly (2003); Easterly et al. (2003); Collier and Hoeffler (2004); Rajan and Subramanian (2008); Roodman (2007); Arndt et al. (2010); among others. Only a limited number of authors have focused on the institutional economics of aid (Martens et al. 2002),[4] and recently on the sectoral allocation of foreign aid and growth and employment (Akramov 2012;[5] Van der Hoeven 2012).[6] The issues of imperfect information and agency problem in "aid with conditionality" are under-researched.

---

[4] Based on agency theory and four case studies, Martens el al. (2002) pointed out the "principal-agent" problems in the donor-recipient relationship, and found that "the nature of foreign aid—with a broken information feedback loop—... put a number of inherent constraints on the performance of foreign aid programs. All these constraints are due to imperfect information flows in the aid delivery process" (p. 30).

[5] Akramov (2012), in particular, found that economic aid, including aid to productive sectors and economic infrastructure, contributes to economic growth by increasing domestic investment. Aid to social sectors, however, does not appear to have a significant impact on human capital and economic growth.

[6] Van der Hoeven (2012) took note of China's approach of focusing on economic infrastructure, pointed to the neglect of concern for employment and inequality in Millennium Development Goals (MDGs) in 2000. He called for the "refocusing of development efforts," "combining a greater share of development aid for employment and productivity enhancing activities with a change in national and international economic and financial policies, so as to make employment creation (together with poverty reduction) an overarching goal" (p. 24).

What are the unique features of China's SSDC? As one of the poorest developing countries in the 1980s, China has been utilizing its comparative advantage, working together with African countries to enhance the capacity in self-development. China's approach in SSDC differs from the international aid literature of established donors, focusing on utilizing "what China owns and knows best" by combining trade, investment, and development cooperation. In official language, China follows the principles of equality and mutual respect, reciprocity, mutual benefit, and noninterference of domestic affairs. Aside from adherence to the "One China" principle, no political strings are attached to China's cooperation (State Council Information Office 2011). This is not to say that China's aid or development cooperative activities are "altruistic," they are not. The government "never regards such aid as a kind of unilateral alms but as something mutual." This "mutual (economic) benefit" is based on the simple idea of "exchanging what I have with what you have" (*hutong youwu*, or 互通有无) from which both can gain, as we learned from Adam Smith.

Based on the structure of trade, some criticized China "practicing neocolonialism" (importing resources and exporting manufactures). However the analysis has often ignored two basic factors: first, the import–export patterns of countries are largely *endogenously determined* by their respective natural and factor endowment structures. China-Africa trade pattern is not a result of "deliberate" foreign policy. What China has been doing is following its comparative advantages, and there is nothing wrong with African countries following their respective comparative advantages in each step of their own transformation. As Paul Krugman said, "Comparative advantage still explains much, perhaps most of world trade. However, both traditional location theory and recent work in economic geography generally assume away inherent differences between locations, and instead explain regional specialization in terms of some kind of external economies."

As acknowledged by Krugman, trade between countries with different endowment structures due to different stages of development can be better explained by the Heckscher–Ohlin model. As African countries continue to accumulate factor endowment such as human, physical, and financial capital, their export structures will transform and upgrade.

Second, the size of China's aid and South–South cooperation is small and commensurate with its per capita income level. Many analysts have tried to compare the amount of ODA between China and established donors such as the USA without considering the huge differences in income per capita, which is rather misleading.[7] When China started to provide development assistance to African countries 50 years ago, it was poorer than most of the SSA countries. Even now, China's per capita income, at US$6560 dollars in 2013, is only one-fourth or one-eighth of that for the established Organisation for Economic Co-operation and Development (OECD) donor countries.

China's definition of aid differs from that of the OECD–Development Assistance Committee (DAC),[8] and therefore, direct comparison does not make sense. According to the State Council Information Office White Paper on "China's Foreign Aid" (2011), China

---

[7] Studies include, for example, Wolf et al. (2013) and Strange et al. (2013) from Center for Global Development.

[8] According to the OECD definition, ODA includes grants or loans which are (i) undertaken by the official sector; (ii) with promotion of economic development and welfare as the main objective; and (iii) "is concessional in character and conveys a grant element of at least 25% (calculated at a rate of discount of 10%)." See http://www.oecd.org/dac/stats/officialdevelopmentassistancedefinitionandcoverage.htm.

Table 44.1 China's foreign aid and its composition

Dimensions	Categories
Financial resources for foreign aid	Grant
	Interest-free loans
	Concessional loans
Forms of foreign aid	Complete projects
	Goods and materials
	Technical cooperation
	Human resource development cooperation
	Chinese medical teams working abroad
	Emergency humanitarian aid
	Overseas volunteer programs
	Debt relief
Distribution of foreign aid	Agriculture
	Industry
	Economic infrastructure
	Public facilities
	Education
	Medicine and public health
	Clean energy and coping with climate change

Source: State Council Information Office (2011).

provides grants, interest-free loans, and concessional loans, with eight types of foreign aid: "complete (turn-key) projects,[9] goods and materials, technical co-operation, human resource development co-operation, medical teams sent abroad, emergency humanitarian aid, volunteer programs in foreign countries and debt relief." (State Council Information Office 2011: 8). See Table 44.1 for a classification of China's foreign aid. There are other official flows (OOFs) and OOF-like loans and investments, which are not included in the official definition of foreign aid—see Bräutigam (2011) for a discussion of these definitions.

Based on strong demand from African countries, new types of SSDC have been added in the recent years, including for example, OOFs (large but less concessional loans and export credit provided by the Eximbank of China); resource for infrastructure (RfI) packages; equity investment by China–Africa Development (CAD) fund; infrastructure investment by China Development Bank (CDB) and other commercial banks (which are OOF-like loans and investments with the intention for development, but non-concessional, and suitable for long-term infrastructure investment).

In Figure 44.2, we take into consideration of different stages of development, and compare China's total ODA as a percent of GNI, to those of the OECD countries. We found that

[9] Turnkey projects and in-kind assistance were developed in the 1960s and 1970s, when China itself was in shortage of foreign exchange. These types of projects allowed poor countries to help each other without using US$ or other foreign exchange. The TAZARA railway was completed in 1975 by Chinese and African workers working together using labor-intensive technology. This is also a unique way of avoiding issues of misuse of funds of both partners.

China's aid to developing countries started from a relatively low per capita income level in the 1960s. We use a recent estimate of China's ODA carefully done by Kitano and Harada 2014, which puts China's net ODA at $7.1 billion in 2013. They then estimated the net disbursement of preferential export buyer's credit of $7 billion in 2013. Adding the two elements together, one would reach a total of $14.1 billion as China's development financing (a conservative estimate). We found that China's net ODA accounted for 0.08% of GNI in 2013, while China's DF reached 0.15% of GNI in the same year. The first ratio is lower than some of the OECD Countries. However, if one draws a linear regression line on this scatter chart, China is located well above the regression line, indicating China is contributing a relatively significant proportion of its GNI to aid and development cooperation as compared to its per capita income level of $6,560 in 2013 ($11,850 using GNI at PPP international dollar) (Figure 44.2).

Our proposition 1 is that, a partner who is successful in transformation can utilize its comparative advantage in development cooperation to help diffusing "tacit" knowledge on the "how to" issues of development. China has thousands of years of history on "learning from friends from afar," and believed in "teaching it only if you know it well." Many Chinese officials have said, when interviewed, that "China is successful because she is a good student." It is just natural that a good student, who is fast in learning and industrial upgrading, can help other classmates in the same class in transforming "what they have" to "what they can potentially do well." For example:

- China is financing the construction of 24 agricultural technical demonstration centers in Africa—thereby transferring suitable agricultural and aquatic technologies to

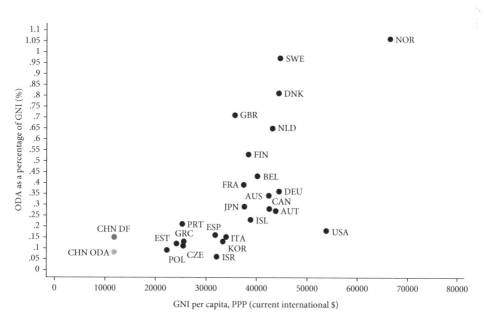

FIGURE 44.2 China's ODA: comparison with OECD countries on two dimensions, 2013.

Source: Wang and Yan 2011: 22. Updated based on the AidFlow 2013 data, accessed on July 31, 2014. See Kitano and Harada 2014 for their estimates of China's ODA and Development Finance.

Africa. One of the earlier agricultural–technological centers has been development into a sugarcane farm and a Sukala Sugar Refinery in Segou, Mali, operating for over 17 years since 1996.
- For 50 years, China has been sending medical teams, teachers, and agricultural experts to African countries, providing scholarships for African students, thereby provide hand-in-hand transmission of "tacit knowledge" and experiences. The feedbacks from Africa on Chinese medical teams are overwhelmingly positive and appreciative.

Our proposition 2 is that learning can happen only by taking tiny steps, "one step at a time," which is commensurate to a country's natural endowment or accumulated factor endowment. Since China has conducted partial reforms via experimental approach, it can help others with partial reforms through SEZs and experimentation. A country can change its endowment structure through saving, investment, and learning to accumulate natural, physical, human and institutional capital. It is impossible for a capital-scarce country to "defy comparative advantages" and become a capital-intensive manufacturer. For example,

- Many of Chinese firms relocating to Africa are producing labor-intensive light manufacturing products. See, for example, Shen (2013); World Bank (2013), including the case of Huajian Shoe Company.
- Chinese technology has been considered inexpensive and more appropriate to low-income countries. One example is the hand-held water pump; another is the herb medicine for malaria (artemisinin, also called Qinghaosu). In other words, China is able to help low-income African countries because they have a similar level of human, physical, and institutional capital. China cannot help others to "leapfrog" because of its own limitations and constraints. For instance, if China itself is not a knowledge economy, it cannot help others to become a knowledge-intensive or service-oriented economy. What Chinese companies know best is labor-intensive light manufacturing, not capital-intensive sector or knowledge-intensive services. As China itself is struggling with challenges of implementing its own labor and environmental standards (with domestic problems), and Chinese firms are still to be educated and trained in those aspects, these firms' overseas projects would bound to have such issues with the labor and environmental standards. Here comes the need for mutual learning.

An analogy is that China and Africa are like teammates in climbing the same mountain of structural transformation (as shown later). And a good climber can help a teammate by pulling them up a step, but the good climber themselves may also need to be "pushed up" in case of need. African people, the media, and non-governmental organizations (NGOs), can help to "pull" or "push" the partners and to be selective and induce the desired partner behavior: to abide by local laws and regulations, and follow international labor and environmental standards (Figure 44.3).

China's development cooperation follows the logic of NSE by helping Africans to take small but realistic steps in agriculture, infrastructure, and labor-intensive light manufacturing sectors. Partial reforms through SEZs can also help in structural transformation, as shown by China's experiences (Zeng 2011). Partner countries need to have more recent intimate "tacit" knowledge and experiences in order to be able to help in such an experimental approach because of similar endowment, similar institutional constraints, and similar human capital structure.

44.4.1 China's development cooperation helps to address Africa's bottlenecks

Non-traditional bilateral development financiers such as China, India, the Arab countries, and Brazil have emerged as major financiers of infrastructure projects in Africa. Overall, infrastructure resources committed to Africa by these countries jumped from US$1 billion per year in the early 2000s to over US$10 billion in 2010. China held a portfolio of some US$20 billion in active infrastructure projects in more than 40 African countries. Chinese financing for African infrastructure structure projects is estimated to have reached a record level of roughly US$5.1 billion in 2009, though it fell to around US$2.3 billion in 2010. A new study found that China alone accounts for 34% of all aid to infrastructure in SSA, higher than other multi- and bilateral donors (Chen 2013).

In particular, China has been working in bottleneck-releasing sectors, such as power generation and transmission. While "Donors have neglected power since the 1990s" (Foster and Briceño-Garmendia 2010: 25), 50% of China's commitment on infrastructure was allocated to electricity. A recent study found that China has contributed, and is contributing, to a total of 9.024 gigawatts of electricity generating capacity, including completed, ongoing, and committed

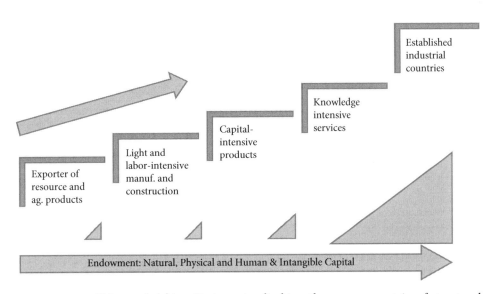

FIGURE 44.3 China and Africa: Partners in climbing the same mountain of structural transformation. Learning and building on the comparative advantage determined by a country's endowment.

power projects.[10] The impact of this investment is likely to be transformative when one considers that the entire installed capacity of the 47 SSA countries excluding South Africa countries is 28 gigawatts.

From 2010 to May 2012, China approved concessional loans worth a total of US$11.3 billion for 92 African projects. For example, the Addis Ababa–Adama Expressway in Ethiopia and the Kribi Deep-water Port in Cameroon were both funded by concessional loans from China. Some of China's main commercial banks have also started buyer's credit businesses in Africa, supporting the power grid in Ghana, hydropower stations in Ethiopia, a west–east expressway in Algeria, and other projects (MOFCOM 2013).

44.4.2 China has been helping to develop clusters-based industrial parks

The idea that industrial clusters can promote structural transformation is not new. Economists have emphasized that clusters take advantage of economies of scale, reduce transaction costs and search and learning costs (Greenwald and Stiglitz 2014; Stiglitz 1996; Lin and Monga 2011). Agglomeration helps firms to benefit from knowledge spillovers, create a market for specialized skills, and backward and forward linkages (good access to large input suppliers, logistics, privileged network with customers, etc.). These agglomeration benefits reduce the individual firm's transaction costs, and increase the competitiveness of a nation's industry, compared with the same industry in other countries at a similar level of development. (Lin 2012b). Deng Xiaoping, once said "the SEZ is a window, a window of technology, a window of management skill, a window of knowledge.... from SEZs we can bring in technology, acquire knowledge and learn management skill" (*People's Daily* 2009). The role of SEZs or industrial parks has been proven by the successful experiences of emerging markets. In particular, investing in SEZs can (i) provide a bundling of public services in a geographically concentrated area; (ii) improve the efficiency of limited government funding/budget for infrastructure; (iii) facilitate cluster development, or agglomeration of certain industries; (iv) propel urban development and conglomeration of services; and thus (v) they are conducive to growth, job creation, and income generation (Lin and Wang 2013: 14).

In particular, China has been supporting several SEZs in Africa aimed to improve investment climate and encourage outward investment into these low-income developing countries if there is a need (World Bank 2011). According to detailed studies by Bräutigam and Tang (2012 and 2013), in total China has jointly established six industrial zones in Africa. Over 80 companies have signed agreements and settled in these industrial zones, creating over 11,000 jobs for African workers.

China's labor cost was rising rapidly from US$150 per month in 2005, to US$500 in 2012, and was over US$600 in coastal regions in 2013 (growing at the rate of 15% annually plus currency appreciation of nearly three per cent). More Chinese enterprises facing the pressure of seeking low-cost locations are moving inland or "going global." China has an estimated 85 million workers in manufacturing, most of them in labor-intensive sectors, as compared to 9.7 million in Japan in

---

[10] The Hoover Dam in Colorado, by comparison, is a two gigawatt facility, producing on average electricity for about 390,000 US homes. See Chen (2013).

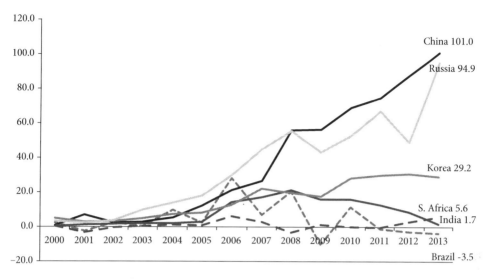

FIGURE 44.4 Outward FDI from China and other BRICKS countries, 2000–2013 (unit: $billions).

Source: Authors based on UNCTAD data, accessed in October, 2014.

1960 and 2.3 million in Korea in 1980. The reallocation of China's manufacturing to more sophisticated, higher value-added products and tasks will open great opportunities for labor abundant, lower-income countries to produce the labor-intensive light-manufacturing goods that China leaves behind. As a result, China will not be a *goose* in the traditional flying-geese model but a leading *dragon*, which opens up a huge opportunity for numerous lower income countries to step into the vacuum left by its industrial upgrading (Lin 2012c; Chandra, Lin, and Wang 2013).

African countries can benefit from seizing the opportunities to attract labor-intensive enterprises relocating out of China. While there is widespread suspicion on China's motivations and criticisms of its record of following international standards, some studies have shown that the investment has generated employment opportunities.[11] One of the high profile examples is the Huajian Shoe Company in Ethiopia's Oriental Industrial Park, which has created more than 3,000 local jobs (World Bank 2012).

In particular, in SSA, the scarcity of local entrepreneurial skills and investment capital are invariably the top two constraints for a competitive manufacturing sector. Evidently, availability of outward FDI enables them to overcome these constraints and take advantage of enterprises relocating from China and other emerging markets. Figure 44.4 shows that China is taking the lead amongst the Brazil, Russia, India, China, Korea, and South Africa (BRICKS) countries in outward FDI, with the amount rising from a few million to over US$84 billion in 2012 and US$101 billion in 2013, with Russia, Korea, India, and Brazil following (UNCTAD Statistics website). Roughly 60% of outward FDI from developing countries went into other developing countries, mostly in the form of greenfield investments that

---

[11] A few studies have found that China's outward FDI has contributed to employment generation in both developing and industrial nations, see for example, Shen (2013); Weisbrod and Whalley (2011); Mlachila and Takebe (2011); Rosen and Hanemann (2011); Scissors (2012); and World Bank (2012) on "China's FDI in Ethiopia."

can typically open the door for South–South relocation of various industries from China and other emerging economies.

According to Chinese MOFCOM statistics, "in January–November 2013, Chinese investors made direct investment overseas in 4522 enterprises in 156 countries and regions. Direct investment overseas amounted to US$80.24 billion, up by 28.3% year-on-year. As of the end of November, China's non-financial direct investment overseas totaled US$515.7 billion" (2013). A small but increasing share of China's outward FDI is flowing to Africa, "From 2009 to 2012, China's direct investment in Africa increased from US$1.44 billion to US$2.52 billion, with an annual growth rate of 20.5%." Ministry of Commerce (2013). "The cumulative direct investment in Africa increased from US$9.33 billion in 2009 to US$21.23 billion in 2012, 2.3 times the amount in 2009. Currently, over 2000 Chinese enterprises are investing and developing in more than 50 African countries" (MOFCOM 2013). Manufacturing is China's key investment field in Africa. From 2009 to 2012, Chinese enterprises' direct investment volume in Africa's manufacturing sector totaled US$1.33 billion. By the end of 2012, China's investment in Africa's manufacturing industry had reached US$3.43 billion. Mali, Ethiopia, and other resource-poor countries have also attracted a large amount of Chinese investment (MOFCOM 2013).

But these statistics may be an underestimation. A recent study (Shen 2013) found that:

- The government statistics have underestimated the size of China's outward FDI.
- The government plays a lesser role in outward FDI: the private sector—usually small to midsized, closed held firms—is responsible for 55% of Chinese FDI in Africa.
- Manufacturing accounts for the bulk of private Chinese investment.
- Chinese investment produces jobs, which African leaders appreciate, while expressing concerns about "technology transfer" and "language and cultural barriers."
- Chinese firms come to Africa because their domestic market is saturated and African labor costs less than Chinese labor.
- Operating in Africa is expensive due to infrastructure gaps and security issues.
- Private Chinese investors do what all international business people do: pursue new markets beyond their home countries for economic gain (Shen 2013).

44.5 FUTURE PROSPECTS OF DEVELOPMENT FINANCE

Based on the projections by the World Bank Global Development Horizon 2013, developing and emerging economies will provide two-thirds of the global growth, and one-third of the global capital flows in the next decade.

As some established donors are constrained by their heavy debt burden and slow growth, development financing will come less from ODA, but more and more from the OOFs, OOF-like loans, and OOF-like investments from development banks in emerging economies. Therefore, the prospect of China–Africa development cooperation is likely to expand, and become more significant in the future. For instance, China will fulfill its commitment to provide US$20 billion loans to Africa, which will be used for infrastructure construction, as well as the development of agriculture, manufacturing, and small- and medium-sized enterprises (MOFCOM 2013). These loans are not necessarily ODA as defined by OECD-DAC, but more likely to be OOF-like loans due to the nature of infrastructure projects.

We propose to start a discussion to broaden the definitions of "development financing." The OECD-DAC definitions of ODA and OOFs are a good starting point, but they are not sufficient to take into account all forms of finances aimed to support development. In monetary policy instruments we have M0, M1, M2, and M3. In development finance, we can define DF1, DF2, DF3, and DF4 similarly, according to (i) the extent of "concessionality"; (ii) the source (the extent of "official" or state involvement); (iii) the destination countries (low income developing countries); and (iv) objectives of the financing (for economic development and welfare). This idea was also eluted in several previous studies including Bräutigam (2011), Center for Global Development (China-aid database 2013), and other studies. A new set of clearer definitions would facilitate transparency, accountability, and selectivity by development partners, encourage Sovereign Wealth Funds (SWFs) to invest in developing countries, as well as facilitate public–private partnerships (PPP) in developing country infrastructure.

In particular, SWFs in the world are managing huge amounts of assets, in excess of US$6 trillion US dollars and many of them are seeking higher risk-adjusted returns. Some of them have traditionally underinvested in the emerging and developing countries with less than ten per cent of assets allocated to these countries. Norway, for example, with the largest SWF in the world, is having a national debate on how best to reallocate some of its huge asset to developing countries. Currently, the Norwegian Government Pension Fund (GPF) is now the world's largest SWF with US$818 billion asset, which is expected to grow to more than US$1100 billion by 2020. But it allocates 90% of assets in "liquid" developed country equities, with a real rate of return of mere 3.17% since 1998, much lower than above (Kapoor 2013). On the other hand, a much smaller fund investing in developing countries, the NorFund, has a higher rate of return than the larger GPF. Redefining development finance, as we proposed, would help sway public opinions toward SWFs investing in developing countries, and expand the sources of development finance.

Concretely, we propose to redefine development finance (DF) in the following ways, for instance,

DF1 = ODA, as defined by OECD-DAC;
DF2= DF1+ OOFs, as defined by OECD-DAC;
DF3= DF2+OOF-like loans (loans from state entities for development but at market interest rate);
DF4=DF3+OOF-like investment (equity investment by SWFs or enterprises/corporations for development with state intervention through the use of guarantees or other instruments.). For example, PPP for public infrastructure, such as electricity, water, sanitation, transportation, and other pressing infrastructure bottlenecks. Other categories may include pure private contributions to development without state involvement. Some element of SSDC cannot be monetized, such as number of volunteers and medical doctors, separate categories can be established for those. Figure 44.5 roughly summarizes our ideas.

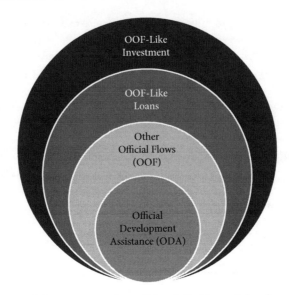

FIGURE 44.5 Proposal for an expansion of the definition of development financing.

Notes: The circles correspond to DF1= ODA; DF2=ODA+OOF; DF3=DF2+OOF-like loans; and DF4=DF3+OOF-like investment. Other categories may be added separately for those forms of SSDC that cannot be monetized.

44.5.1 Global governance matters

The availability of international DFs, however, also depends on the institutional arrangements, the channels of financing and coordination, and ultimately, the global environment and the structure of global governance. In other words, it depends on whether the SSDC or DF are welcomed, whether and how much the voice of emerging market partners are being included, and whether they are invited to the table for shaping the global "rules of the road." Two possible trends are emerging:

Multilateralism: China and southern partners will potentially move toward more multi- and trilateral collaboration with the World Bank and other established regional development banks. This can provide more learning opportunities for emerging partners, enhance triangular knowledge exchange, and hopefully, improve the effectiveness of both the established and emerging donors. For example, recently China Eximbank and CDB have both signed memorandums of understanding (MOUs) with the World Bank (September 2013), to conduct tri-lateral collaboration. Concrete "parallel projects" are being prepared in Africa and moving forward. China has also contributed to the African Development Bank, Development Bank of Southern Africa (DBSA) and Inter-America Development Bank (IDB). In addition, China has long been cooperating with United Nation's Food and Agriculture Organization (UNFAO) on tri-lateral cooperation. There are however obstacles on this path, for instance, the issues related to enhancing the voice of Southern partners in the International Monetary Fund (IMF) and the World Bank have not been resolved.

New groupings: In response to this gridlock in reforming the global governance structure, new groupings have, and will continue to, emerge outside the "established" international development financial organizations. For example, Trans-Pacific Partnership (TPP) negotiations and ASEAN plus 6 negotiations are moving in parallel. BRICS countries have proposed to establish a BRICS Bank, with the concrete steps being taken after the summit meetings of the BRICS leaders. In addition, Chinese leader Xi Jinping has proposed to establish two new banks: The Shanghai Cooperative Organization Bank, and the Asian Infrastructural Investment Bank (AIIB). Premier Li Keqiang has signed some agreements with Eastern European countries to jointly develop High-Speed Rails (HSR) and the New Silk Road Economic Corridor. According to China Development Bank, negotiations with 17 countries on HSR are being conducted. There is also an additional proposal to establish a Global Structural Transformation Fund (GST Fund), which will help funding the transformation process in Africa

(Lin and Wang May 2013 for the United Nations "Post 2015 High Level Panel").

44.5.2 Issues and challenges in China's SSDC

The first challenge is the lack of transparency in China's SSDC—official data at the project level is not readily available, especially related to large RfI deals, or, the Angola model. The publication of the White Paper on "China's Foreign Aid" (State Council Information Office 2011) and *China Africa Economic and Trade Co-operation 2013* (MOFCOM 2013), is a progress in the right direction. Governments should be more open and pro-active in providing more accurate data, making laws and regulations clear on development cooperation. This would help improve accountability to tax payers in China, as well as to the international development community.

The second concern is about "tied aid" and inadequate technological diffusion and spill-over effect. Most of Chinese aid is tied, a practice the members of OECD-DAC agreed to move away from progressively since 1995, since tied aid may increase the cost and reduce efficiency. However, China's own experience indicates that tied aid had some advantage of facilitating "learning by doing" and learning by implementing projects. According to Hausmann, "the tricks of the trade are acquired from experienced senior workers" (Hausmann 2013; Bahar et al. 2014). There is important academic literature on aid and trade that has found mixed results (Wagner 2003; Lloyd et al. 2000; and Morrisey and White 1996). The value of implementing actual projects in learning and development seems to be underappreciated by economists and the donor community. In the 1980s and 1990s, most donor-financed projects located in China were tied aid, and Chinese workers and project managers have learned and benefited from them (Wang 2011). Actually, "learning from aid projects" is one of the reasons why Chinese companies are so competitive in implementing construction projects.

The third concern is that Chinese aid projects seem to have generated few local employment opportunities. Many African officials are concerned that Chinese workers are displacing local workers. Although data and evidence need to be discussed on a case by case basis, clearly, the indirect employment generation from China-financed economic infrastructure has been under-researched.

The IMF (2013) finds that: "In recent years, China has become the largest single trading partner for Africa and a key investor and provider of aid." And "a 1% point increase in China's real domestic fixed asset investment growth has tended to increase SSA's export growth rate on average by 0.6 percentage point" (IMF 2013: 5). Better education and training should be provided to Chinese companies to abide by laws and regulations regard labor, social, and the environmental standards. In addition, better training and capacity development programs should be provided to African workers and managers, in order to fulfill the requirement of timely completion of projects showing tangible results.

No two countries are the same in their economic transformation. China has made some mistakes and paid "high tuition" in the process: for instance, China's strong drive for rapid growth and industrialization is associated with widening rural-urban income disparities and a degrading environment. In March 2007, the former Chinese Premier Wen Jiabao pointed out that China's growth was "imbalanced, inequitable and unsustainable." Since then there has been tremendous effort to "rebalance" the economy—reducing its reliance on export, investment and paying more attention to the quality and efficiency of growth. However, making deep transformations and upgrading industries is proven extremely difficult, as reforms often go against the vested interest groups. In this sense African countries need to be selective, to avoid these mistakes China has made. African governments, NGOs and civil societies can play important roles in providing pressure to "push" or "pull" development partners including China and Chinese companies to the right directions.

44.6 CONCLUSION

The next 50 years will witness a significant structural transformation in most of the African continent, with China and other emerging market economies playing an important role, working together with African partners in providing ideas, tacit knowledge, intimate experiences, financing, as well as investing in the infrastructural, human and other productive assets. Just as China and Vietnam have learned from the faster—growing East Asian NIEs and maintained rapid GDP growth of nearly ten per cent a year in the past decades, African countries can also achieve the same—to reach eight per cent growth rates or higher in the coming decades. In particular, they can seize the opportunities of labor intensive industrial relocating from China and other emerging markets (Lin 2012b; Chandra, Lin, and Wang 2013; and Monga 2013).

We examine China and Africa cooperation as a co-transformation process—not a donor–client relationship. China, being a bit ahead in transformation, can provide ideas, experiences, tacit knowledge, opportunities, and finances in Africa's transformation. We also present preliminary evidence on whether, and to what extent, Chinese infrastructural projects have matched Africa's bottlenecks; and whether China's experience in SEZs can be useful to Africa's transformation. We argue that in a sense, China and African countries are teammates climbing the same mountain of structural transformation (in Figure 44.3), hand in hand, and helping each other in every step of the way. They are each utilizing their own comparative advantages, exchanging tools from time to time, and complementing each other, while each facing own constraints. Working together, they can learn and progress faster.

China needs to continue to learn to become a better development partner, by listening to the voices from Africans and interacting with the partner governments, NGOs, and civil societies. China needs to be more open and transparent in providing accurate data on international development financing and activities. It is our view that "any deals made in the dark are more likely to be revoked or renegotiated by the next government of the client country in the future" (Lin and Wang, in World Bank 2014). The political economy dynamics must be taken into consideration when discussing with the current government of the client country. The established donors among OECD countries also need to see if China's approach provides useful lessons to improve the effectiveness of the conventional North–South aid. A recent study by the World Bank has also reviewed the approach of RfI deals, finding this approach to be more effective in advancing the developmental impact "many years ahead of" the conventional North-South approaches (World Bank 2014). Many African leaders find China's approach (in RfI) more desirable as it has led to "inexpensive and tangible results" within the time span of three to four years, coinciding with the political cycle in a democracy.

The world needs a more active China in the international development arena, not merely a defensive one. China needs to describe its approaches based on solid economic foundation, and takes a leadership role in global development. For example, using the NSE as the theoretical foundation, China could develop its own development cooperation theory and draft a law for international aid and cooperation. China could take a lead in coordinating and setting up a few infrastructural investment banks, and a Global Structural Transformation (GST) fund as proposed by Lin and Wang (2013) for the United Nations Post-2015 High Level Panel. Many SWFs are seeking higher risk-adjusted returns in a low-yield environment, and it is not unrealistic to predict that many SWFs will join this effort.

In the next decades, development financing will come less from ODA, but more and more from the OOFs, OOF-like loans, and OOF-like investment from development banks, SWFs, in emerging economies. Therefore, we propose to expand the definitions of development financing to include them, which could induce more contributions from SWFs and other public or private entities. In a multipolar world, the prospect of South-South and China–Africa development cooperation is likely to expand. However, established development partners need to be more inclusive to enhance the voice of emerging partners, and provide a place "at the table" for these emerging partners. Otherwise, we may see a world with a more disintegrated and fragmented development financing architecture, with new groupings and regional investment banks emerging and competing with each other.

ACKNOWLEDGMENTS

The authors thank Deborah Bräutigam, Chuan Chen, Vivien Foster, Célestin Monga, Finn Tarp, Xiaofang Shen, Xiaoyang Tang, Shuilin Wang, and Douglas Zeng for their comments and input, and Haixiao Wu for excellent research assistance.

REFERENCES

Akamatsu, K. (1962). A historical pattern of economic growth in developing countries. *Developing Economies*, 1(s1):3–25.
Akramov, K.T. (2012). *Foreign Aid Allocation, Governance, and Economic Growth*. Washington, DC: IFPRI.

Arndt, C., Jones, S., and F. Tarp (2010). Aid, Growth and Development: Have we come full circle? WIDER Working Paper 2010/096. Helsinki: UNU-WIDER.

Bahar, D., Hausmann, R., and Hidalgo, C.A. (2014). Neighbors and the Evolution of the Comparative Advantage of Nations: Evidence of International Knowledge Diffusion? *Journal of International Economics*, 92(1):111–123.

Bräutigam, D. (2011). Aid with Chinese Characteristics: Chinese Foreign Aid and Development Finance meet the OECD-DAC Aid Regime. *Journal of International Development*, 23(5): 752–764.

Bräutigam, D., and Tang, X. (2012). Economic statecraft in China's new overseas special economic zones: soft power, business or resource security? *International Affairs*, 88(4):799–816.

Bräutigam, D., and Tang, X. (2013). Going global in groups: structural transformation and China's special economic zones overseas. *World Development*. Available from http://www.sciencedirect.com/science/article/pii/S0305750X13002222 (accessed 12 November 2013).

Burnside, C., and Dollar, D. (2000). Aid, policies, and growth. *American Economic Review*, 90(4):847–868.

Chandra, V., Lin, J.Y., and Wang, W. (2013). Leading dragon phenomenon: new opportunities for catch-up in low-income countries. *Asian Development Review*, 30(1):52–84.

Chen, C. (2013). South-South Co-operation in Infrastructure in Sub-Saharan Africa. Working paper for ECOSOC, United Nations.

Collier, P., and Hoeffler, A. (2004). Aid, policy and growth in post-conflict societies. *European Economic Review*, 48(5):1125–1145.

Easterly, W. (2003). Can foreign aid buy growth? *Journal of Economic Perspectives*, 17(3):23–48.

Easterly, W., Levine, R., and Roodman, D. (2003). New data, New Doubts: A Comment on Burnside and Dollar's Aid, Policies and Growth (2000). NBER Working paper 9846. Cambridge, MA: NBER.

Foster, V., and Briceno-Garmendia, C. (2010). *Africa's Infrastructure: A Time for Transformation*. Washington, DC: World Bank.

Greenwald, B., and Stiglitz, J.E. (2014). Industrial policies, the creation of a learning society, and economic development, in J.E. Stiglitz and J.Y. Lin (eds), *The Industrial Policy Revolution I: the Role of Government Beyond Ideology*. New York: Palgrave Macmillan.

Hausmann, R. (2013). The Tacit Knowledge Economy. Project Syndicate. Available at: http://www.project-syndicate.org/commentary/ricardo-hausmann-on-the-mental-sourcesof-productivity-growth (accessed 30 October 2013).

IMF (2013). Regional Economic Outlook: Sub-Saharan Africa–Keeping the Pace. Washington, DC: IMF.

Kapoor, S. (2013). Investing for the Future: Good for Norway—Good for Development. Re-Define and NCF Discussion Paper 01/2013.

Kitano, N., and Harada, Y. (2014). Estimating China's Foreign Aid 2001-2013, JICA Research Institute Working Paper No. 78. Comparative Study on Development Cooperation Strategies: Focusing on G20 Emerging Economies. June.

Kuznets, S. (1966). *Modern Economic Growth: Rate, Structure and Spread*. New Haven, CT: Yale University Press.

Lau, L.J., Qian, Y., and Roland, G. (2000). Reform without losers: an interpretation of China's dual-track approach to transition. *Journal of Political Economy*, 108(1):120–143.

Lin, J.Y. (1992). Rural reforms and agricultural growth in China. *American Economic Review*, 82(1):34–51.

Lin, J.Y. (2009). *Economic Development and Transition: Thought, Strategy, and Viability*. Cambridge: Cambridge University Press.

Lin, J.Y. (2010). New Structural Economics: A Framework for Rethinking Development. Policy Research Working Paper 5197. Washington, DC: World Bank.

Lin, J.Y. (2011). New structural economics: a framework for rethinking development. *World Bank Research Observer*, 26(2):193–221.

Lin, J.Y. (2012a). *Demystifying the Chinese Economy*. Cambridge: Cambridge University Press.

Lin, J.Y. (2012b). *New Structural Economics: A Framework for Rethinking Development and Policy*. Washington, DC: World Bank.

Lin, J.Y. (2012c). From flying geese to leading dragons: new opportunities and strategies for structural transformation in developing countries. *Global Policy*, 3(4):397–409.

Lin, J.Y., and Monga, C. (2011). Growth identification and facilitation: the role of the state in the dynamics of structural change. *Development Policy Review*, 29(3):264–290.

Lin, J.Y., and Wang, Y. (2008). China's Integration with the World: Development as a Process of Learning and Industrial Upgrading. Policy Research Working Paper 4799. Washington, DC: World Bank.

Lin, J.Y., and Wang, Y. (2013). Beyond the Marshall Plan: A Global Structural Transformation Fund Background research paper for the UN High Level Panel on the Post-2015 Development Agenda. Available at: http://www.post2015hlp.org/wpcontent/uploads/2013/05/Lin-Wang_Beyond-the-Marshall-Plan-A-Global-Structural-Transformation-Fund.pdf.

Lloyd, T., McGillivray, M., Morrissey, O., and Osei, R. (2000). Does Aid Create Trade? An Investigation for European Donors and African Recipients. *European Journal of Development Research*, 12(1):107–123.

Maddison, A. (2001). *The World Economy: A Millennial Perspective*. Paris: OECD Development Centre.

Maddison, A. (2007). *Chinese Economic Performance in the Long Run—Second Edition, Revised and Updated: 960–2030 AD*. Paris: OECD Development Centre.

Martens, B., Mummert, U., Murrell, P., and Seabright, P. (2002). *The Institutional Economics of Foreign Aid*. Cambridge, UK, and New York: Cambridge University Press.

MOFCOM (2013). *China Africa Economic and Trade Co-operation 2013*. Published in August 2013, http://english.mofcom.gov.cn/article/newsrelease/press/201309/20130900285772.shtml.

Monga, C. (2013). The Mechanics of Job Creation: Seizing the New Dividends of Globalization. Policy Research Working Paper 6661. Washington, DC: World Bank.

Morrisey, O., and White, H. (1996). Evaluating the Concessionality of Tied Aid. *Manchester School*, 64(2):208–226.

Naughton, B. (1995). *Growing Out of the Plan: Chinese Economic Reform, 1978–1993*. New York: Cambridge University Press.

North, D. (1981). *Structure and Change in Economic History*. New York: W.W. Norton.

Rajan, R.G., and Subramanian, A. (2008). Aid and growth: what does the cross-country evidence really show? *Review of Economics and Statistics*, 90(4):643–665.

Roodman, D. (2007). The anarchy of numbers: aid, development, and cross-country empirics. *World Bank Economic Review*, 21(2):255–277.

Shen, X. (2013). Private Chinese Investment in Africa: Myths and Realities. World Bank Policy Research Working paper 6311. Washington, DC: World Bank.

Spence, M. (2011). *The Next Convergence: The Future of Economic Growth in a Multispeed World*. New York: Farrar, Straux and Giroux.

Solow, R.M. (1957). Technical change and the aggregate production function. *Review of Economics and Statistics*, 39(3):312–320.

State Council Information Office (2011). China's Foreign Aid. White Paper, April 2011. Beijing: State Council Information Office.

Stiglitz, J.E. (1996). Some Lessons from the East Asian Miracle. *World Bank Research Observer*, 11(2):151–177.

Strange, A., Parks, B., Tierney, M.J. et al. (2013). China's Development Finance to Africa: A Media-Based Approach to Data Collection. Center for Global Development Working Paper 323. Washington, DC: Center for Global Development.

Van der Hoeven, R. (2012). Development Aid and Employment. WIDER Working Paper 2012/107. Helsinki: UNU-WIDER.

Wagner, D. (2003). Aid and trade—an empirical study. *Journal of the Japanese and International Economies*, 17(2):153–173.

Wang, Y. (2011). Development Partnership. In China-OECD/DAC Study Group, Economic Transformation and Poverty Reduction: How it happened in China, helping it happen in Africa. Available at http://www.oecd.org/development/povertyreduction/49528657.pdf

Wei, Y., and Liu, X. (2001). *Foreign Direct Investment: Determinants and Impact*. Northampton, MA: Edward Elgar.

Weisbrod, A., and Whalley, J. (2011). The Contribution of Chinese FDI to Africa's Pre-Crisis Growth Surge. NBER Working Paper 17544. Cambridge, MA: NBER.

Wolf, C. Jr., Wang, X., and Warner, E. (2013). *China's Foreign Aid and Government –Sponsored Investment Activities: Scale, Content, Destinations, and Implications*. RAND National Defense Research Institute.

World Bank (2008). *The Growth Report: Strategies for Sustained Growth and Inclusive Development*. Washington, DC: World Bank.

World Bank (2011). *Chinese investments in Special Economic Zones in Africa: Progress, Challenges and Lessons Learned*. Final Report. Washington, DC: World Bank.

World Bank (2012). *Chinese FDI in Ethiopia*. A World Bank Survey. Washington, DC: World Bank.

World Bank (2013). *World Bank Global Development Horizons*. Washington, DC: World Bank.

World Bank (2014*). Resource financed infrastructure: a discussion on a new form of infrastructure financing*. Washington DC: World Bank. June.

Zeng, D.Z. (2010). *Building Engines for Growth and Competitiveness in China: Experience with Special Economic Zones and Industrial Clusters*. Washington, DC: World Bank.

Zeng, D.Z. (2011). How Do Special Economic Zones and Industrial Clusters Drive China's Rapid Development. Policy Research Working Paper 5583. Washington, DC: World Bank.

PART V

LOOKING FORWARD

....

CHAPTER 45

CHINA'S RISE
AND STRUCTURAL
TRANSFORMATION
IN AFRICA
Ideas and Opportunities

....

JUSTIN YIFU LIN

BEFORE its transition from planned to market economy at the end of the 1970s, China, like countries in Africa, had been trapped in poverty for centuries. Its per capita income was US$154 in 1978, less than one-third the average in sub-Saharan African countries.[1] China was an inward-looking country as well. Its trade dependence (trade-to-GDP (gross domestic product)) ratio was only 9.7% and three-quarters of its exports were agricultural products or processed agricultural products.

China's growth since then has been miraculous. Annual GDP growth averaged 9.8% over the 35-year period from 1978 to 2013 and annual growth in international trade was 16.6%. China is now an upper middle-income country, with per capita GDP of US$6800 in 2013, and more than 680 million people have escaped poverty. Its trade dependence ratio has reached around 50%, the highest among the world's large economies with population exceeding 100 million. In 2009 China overtook Japan as the world's second largest economy and in 2010 replaced Germany as the world's largest merchandise exporter. The spectacular growth over the past three decades has made China not only a driver for world development, but also a stabilizing force in the world economy, as demonstrated by China's role during the East Asian financial crisis in late 1990s and the recent global crisis. This extraordinary performance has far exceeded the expectations of anyone at

---

[1] Unless indicated otherwise, the statistics on the Chinese economy reported in the chapter are from the *China Statistical Abstract 2010, China Compendium of Statistics 1949–2008*, and various editions of the *China Statistical Yearbook*, published by China Statistics Press.

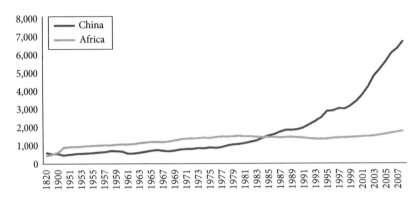

FIGURE 45.1 Per capita income in China and Africa (in 1990 international dollars).

Data source: Angus Maddison, Historical Statistics of the World Economy: 1–2008.

the outset of the transition, including Deng Xiaoping, the architect of China's reform and opening-up strategy.[2]

Africa's economy, measured by per capita income, was higher than China's at the end of 1970s, when China started its spate of dynamic growth, as shown in Figure 45.1. African countries also carried out various reforms to reduce government interventions and liberalize their economies in the 1980s and 1990s for the purpose of improving economic performance. Nevertheless, per capita income in Africa declined in the 1980s and recovered slightly after the mid-1990s. In 2010, per capita income in Africa was only about a quarter of that in China.

In this chapter, I discuss five related questions: Why was it possible for China to achieve such extraordinary performance during its transition? Why was China unable to attain similar success before its transition started? Why did most other transition economies, both socialist and non-socialist, including those in Africa, fail to achieve a similar performance? Can African countries have a similar performance as China had in the past three decades and how to do that? What are the opportunities open for other developing countries from China's rise?

45.1 THE REASON FOR CHINA'S EXTRAORDINARY PERFORMANCE IN TRANSITION

Rapid, sustained increase in per capita income is a modern phenomenon. Studies by economic historians, such as Angus Maddison (2001), show that average annual per capita income growth in the West was only 0.05% before the eighteenth century, jumping to about 1% in the nineteenth century, and reaching about 2% in the twentieth century. That means

---

[2] Deng's goal at that time was to quadruple the size of China's economy in 20 years, which would have meant an average annual growth of 7.2%. Most people in the 1980s, and even as late as the early 1990s, thought that achieving that goal was a mission impossible.

that per capita income in Europe took 1400 years to double before the eighteenth century, about 70 years in the nineteenth century, and 35 years thereafter.

A continuous stream of technological innovation is the basis for continuous improvement of productivity and income and thus sustained growth in any economy. The dramatic surge in growth in modern times is a result of a paradigm shift in technological innovation. Before the industrial revolution in the eighteenth century, technological innovations were generated mostly by the experiences of craftsmen and farmers in their daily production. After the industrial revolution, experience-based innovation was increasingly replaced by field experimentation and, later, by science-based experiments conducted in scientific laboratories (Lin 1995; Landes 1998). This shift accelerated the rate of technological innovation, marking the coming of modern economic growth and contributing to the dramatic acceleration of income growth in the nineteenth and twentieth centuries (Kuznets 1966).

The industrial revolution not only accelerated the rate of technological innovation, but also transformed industrial, economic, and social structures. Before the eighteenth century, every economy was agrarian; 85% or more of the labor force worked in agriculture, mostly in self-sufficient production for the family. The acceleration of growth was accompanied by the movement of labor from agriculture to manufacturing and services. The manufacturing sector gradually moved from very labor-intensive industries at the beginning to more capital-intensive heavy and high-tech industries. Finally, the service sector came to dominate the economy. Accompanying the change in industrial structure was an increase in the scale of production, required capital and skill, market scope, and risks. To exploit the potential unleashed by new technology and industry and to reduce the transaction costs and share risks requires innovations as well as improvements in an economy's hard infrastructure, such as power and road networks, and its soft infrastructure, including elements such as the rules and values, the legal framework, financial institutions, and the education system (Lewis 1954; Kuznets 1966; North 1981; Lin 2011, 2012b).

A developing country like China, which started its modernization drive in 1949 after the socialist revolution, potentially has the advantage of backwardness in its pursuit of technological innovation and structural transformation (Gerschenkron 1962). In advanced, high-income countries, technological innovation and industrial upgrading require costly and risky investments in research and development, because their technologies and industries are located on the global frontier. Moreover, the institutional innovation required for realizing the potential of new technology and industry often proceeds in a costly trial-and-error, path-dependent, evolutionary process (Fei and Ranis 1997). By contrast, a latecomer country in the catching-up process can borrow technology, industry, and institutions from the advanced countries at low risk and costs. So if a developing country knows how to tap the advantage of backwardness in technology, industry, and social and economic institutions, it can grow at an annual rate several times that of high-income countries for decades before closing its income gap with those countries (Lin 2009; Vu 2013).

In the post-World War II period, 13 of the world's economies achieved average annual growth of at least 7% for 25 or more years. The Commission on Growth and Development, headed by Nobel Laureate Michael Spence, finds that the first of five common features of these 13 economies is their ability to tap the potential of the advantage of backwardness.

In the Commission's language, the 13 economies "imported what the rest of the world knew and exported what it wanted" (World Bank 2008: 22).[3]

After the transition from a planning economy to a market economy was initiated by Deng Xiaoping in 1979, China adopted the opening-up strategy and started to tap the potential of importing what the rest of the world knows and exporting what the world wants. This is demonstrated by the rapid growth in its international trade, the dramatic increase in its trade dependence ratio, and the large inflows of foreign direct investment. While in 1979 primary and processed primary goods accounted for more than 75% of China's exports, by 2009 the share of manufactured goods had increased to more than 95%. Moreover, China's manufactured exports upgraded from simple toys, textiles, and other cheap products in the 1980s and 1990s to high-value and technologically sophisticated machinery and information and communication technology products in the 2000s. The exploitation of the advantage of backwardness has allowed China to emerge as the world's workshop and to achieve extraordinary economic growth by reducing the costs of innovation, industrial upgrading, and social and economic transformation.

45.2 WHY CHINA FAILED TO ACHIEVE RAPID GROWTH BEFORE 1979

China possessed the advantage of backwardness long before the transition to a market economy began in 1979. The socialist government won the revolution in 1949 and started modernizing in earnest in 1953. Why did China fail to tap the potential of the advantage of backwardness and achieve dynamic growth before 1979? This failure came about because China adopted a wrong development strategy at that time.

China was the largest economy and among the most advanced, powerful countries in the world in pre-modern times (Maddison 2007). Mao Zedong, Zhou Enlai, and other first-generation revolutionary leaders in China, like many other Chinese social and political elites, were inspired by the dream of achieving rapid modernization for China's renaissance.

The lack of industrialization—especially the lack of large heavy industries that were the basis of military strength and economic power—was perceived as the root cause of the country's backwardness. It was natural for the social and political elites in China to prioritize the development of large, heavy, advanced industries after the Revolution as they started building the nation.[4] In the nineteenth century, the political leaders of France, Germany, the United States, and other Western countries pursued effectively the same strategy, motivated by the contrast between Britain's rising industrial power and the backwardness of their own industry (Gerschenkron 1962; Chang 2003).

---

[3] The remaining features are macroeconomic stability, high rates of saving and investment, a market system, and committed, credible, and capable government. Lin and Monga (2012) show that the first three features are the result of following the economy's comparative advantages in developing industries at each stage of its development and the last two features are the preconditions for the economy to follow its comparative advantages in developing industries.

[4] The desire to develop heavy industries existed before the socialist elites obtained political power. Dr. Sun Yat-sen, the father of modern China, proposed the development of "key and basic industries" as a priority in his plan for China's industrialization in 1919 (Sun 1929).

Starting in 1953, China adopted a series of ambitious Five-Year Plans to accelerate the building of modern advanced industries, with the goal of overtaking Britain in ten years and catching up to the United States in 15 years. But China was a lower-income agrarian economy at that time. In 1953, 83.5% of its labor force was employed in the primary sector, and its per capita income (measured in purchasing power parity terms) was only 4.8% of that of the United States (Maddison 2001). Given China's employment structure and income level, the country did not possess comparative advantage in the modern advanced industries of high-income countries, whether latent or overt, and Chinese firms in those industries were not viable in an open, competitive market.[5]

To achieve its strategic goal, the Chinese government needed to protect the priority industries by giving firms in those sectors a monopoly and subsidizing them through various price distortions, including suppressed interest rates, an overvalued exchange rate, and lower prices for inputs. The price distortions created shortages and the government was obliged to use administrative measures to mobilize and allocate resources directly to nonviable firms (Lin 2009; Lin and Li 2009).

These interventions enabled China to quickly establish modern advanced industries, test nuclear bombs in the 1960s, and launch satellites in the 1970s. But the resources were misallocated, the incentives were distorted, and the labor-intensive sectors in which China held a comparative advantage were repressed. As a result, economic efficiency was low and growth before 1979 was driven mainly by an increase in inputs.[6] Despite a very respectable average annual GDP growth rate of 6.1% in 1952–1978 and the establishment of large modern industries, China was almost a closed economy, with 71.3% of its labor force still in traditional agriculture. In 1952–1978, household consumption grew by only 2.3% a year, in sharp contrast to the 7.1% average growth after 1979.

45.3 WHY OTHER TRANSITION ECONOMIES HAVE NOT PERFORMED EQUALLY WELL

After World War II, all other socialist countries and most developing countries, including those in Africa, adopted a development strategy similar to that of China. The strategy was influenced by the Soviet Union's experience of rapid industrialization before World War II and the import-substitution strategy based on the prevailing structuralist development thinking at that time (Lin 2012b,c). Most colonies gained political independence after the 1950s. Compared with developed countries, these newly independent developing countries had extremely low per capita income, high birth and death rates, low average educational

---

[5] While the policy goal of France, Germany, and the United States in the late nineteenth century was similar to that of China in the mid-1950s, the per capita incomes of the three countries were about 60–75% of Britain's at the time. The small gap in per capita incomes indicated that the industries on the governments' priority lists were the latent comparative advantages of the three countries (Lin and Monga 2011).

[6] Estimates by Perkins and Rawski (2008) suggest that the average annual growth of total factor productivity was 0.5% in 1952–1978 and 3.8% in 1978–2005.

attainment, and very little infrastructure—and were heavily specialized in the production and export of primary commodities while importing most manufactured goods. The development of modern, advanced industries was perceived as the only way to achieve rapid economic takeoff, become an advanced country, and avoid dependence on the Western industrial powers (Prebisch 1950).

It became a fad after the 1950s for developing countries in both the socialist and non-socialist camps to adopt such a heavy industry-oriented development strategy (Lal and Mynt 1996). But the capital-intensive modern industries on their priority lists defied the comparative advantages determined by the endowment structure of their low-income agrarian economies. To implement their development strategy, many socialist and non-socialist developing countries introduced distortions and government interventions like those in China.[7] This strategy made it possible to establish some modern industries and achieve investment-led growth for one or two decades in the 1950s to the 1970s. Nevertheless, the distortions led to pervasive soft budget constraints, rent-seeking, and misallocation of resources. Economic efficiency was unavoidably low. Stagnation and frequent social and economic crises began to beset most socialist and non-socialist developing countries by the 1970s and 1980s. Structuralism was replaced by neoliberalism after the 1970s (Lin 2012b, c). As encapsulated in the Washington Consensus, liberalization from excessive state intervention became a trend in the 1980s and 1990s.

The symptoms of poor economic performance and social and economic crises and their root cause in distortions and government interventions were common to China and other socialist transition economies as well as other developing countries. But the Washington Consensus reforms, advocated by the academic and policy communities in the 1980s, did not realize that those distortions came from second-best institutional arrangements that were endogenous to the needs of providing protections to nonviable firms in the priority sectors. Without such protections or subsidies, those firms could not survive. As a result, policymakers and academics recommended that socialist and other developing countries immediately remove all distortions by implementing simultaneous programs of liberalization, privatization, and marketization, with the aim of quickly achieving efficient, first-best outcomes.

But if those distortions were eliminated immediately, many nonviable firms in the priority sectors would collapse, causing a contraction of GDP, a surge in unemployment, and acute social disorders. To avoid those dreadful consequences while still attempting to possess those advanced, modern industries for national security or pride, many governments continued to subsidize the nonviable firms through other, disguised, less efficient subsidies and protections (Lin and Tan 1999). Transition and developing countries thus had even poorer growth performance and stability in the 1980s and 1990s than in the 1960s and 1970s (Easterly 2001).

---

[7] There are different explanations for the pervasive distortions in developing countries. Acemoglu, Johnson, and Robinson (2005); Engerman and Sokoloff (1997); and Grossman and Helpman (1996) propose that these distortions were caused by the capture of government by powerful vested interests. Lin (2009, 2003) and Lin and Li (2009) propose that the distortions were a result of conflicts between the comparative advantages of the economies and the priority industries that political elites, influenced by the dominant social thinking of the time, targeted for the modernization of their nations.

During the transition process, China adopted a pragmatic, gradual, dual-track approach. The government first improved incentives and productivity by allowing workers in collective farms and state-owned firms to be residual claimants and to set the prices for selling at the market after delivering the quota obligations to the state at fixed prices (Lin 1992). At the same time, the government continued to provide necessary protections to non-viable firms in the priority sectors to avoid their collapse. The government simultaneously liberalized the entry of private enterprises, joint ventures, and foreign direct investment in labor-intensive sectors, in which China had comparative advantages but that were repressed before the transition to promote dynamic growth.

With liberalization of entry into the new sectors, the Chinese government recognized the need to help private firms overcome all kinds of inherent hurdles in the transition process: The overall business environment was poor,[8] the infrastructure in most parts of China was bad,[9] and the nation's investment environment was harsh.[10] The advice based on the Washington Consensus was to improve everything for the whole nation simultaneously without attempting to pick or target specific sectors and regions. Many of those "undesirable" distortions in the business and investment environment, such as controlling imports and charging high tariffs on cars, equipment, and capital-intensive products, in fact were necessary for protecting nonviable firms in the old priority sectors. If China had removed all those distortions and regulations, many of the non-viable firms might have gone bankrupt, causing the collapse of the economy as happened in many Eastern European and Former Soviet Union countries during their transition process. Moreover, if China had adopted the recommended approach, it might have taken the country decades or generations to achieve the desirable business environment and infrastructure for the whole nation and every industry, because of the government's limited implementation capacity and availability of resources.

Instead, the Chinese government mobilized its limited resources and capability to build up special economic zones and industrial parks (Zeng 2010, 2011). Within the zones and parks, the infrastructure and business environment were made very attractive, but outside the zones and parks, they were improved only gradually. The labor costs were low because of the large amount of surplus labor in rural areas when China started the transition. But China lacked the knowledge about how to turn that surplus labor to an advantage by producing labor-intensive goods of acceptable quality for the international market. And international buyers were not confident that Chinese firms would be able to deliver the goods in a timely manner. To overcome those difficulties, the Chinese governments at all levels and in all regions proactively approached prospective foreign

---

[8] In 2013, after more than three decades of market-oriented reform, China still ranked 91 in the World Bank's Doing Business survey (http://www.doingbusiness.org/rankings).

[9] I still remember vividly the experience of my travel by car from Guangzhou, the capital city of Guangdong province, to Shenzhen, the newly established special economic zone, for the first time in 1984. The car had to cross rivers by ferry three times and it took me more than 12 hours to travel the distance of 300 km. The infrastructure at that time in China was worse than any African countries where I travelled extensively as the Chief Economist of the World Bank in 2008–2012.

[10] In the World Bank's *Investing Across Borders 2010*, China's investment environment was ranked the worst among the 87 economies covered in the study. See http://iab.worldbank.org/~/media/FPDKM/IAB/Documents/IAB-report.pdf.

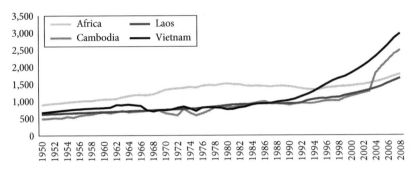

FIGURE 45.2 Per capita income in Africa, Cambodia, Laos, and Vietnam (in 1990 international dollars).

Data source: Angus Maddison, Historical Statistics of the World Economy: 1–2008.

investors, especially those manufacturers in developing Asia that were about to upgrade their operations in the value chain and relocate their labor-intensive processing to other low-wage economies because of rising wages in their own economies. China provided tax holidays to incentivize foreign manufacturers to make investments in the special economic zones and industrial parks (Wei and Liu 2001; Graham and Wada 2001). With that approach, China developed labor-intensive light manufacturing and quickly became the world's factory.

This transition strategy allowed China to maintain stability by avoiding the collapse of old priority industries and to achieve dynamic growth by simultaneously turning its comparative advantages into competitive advantages and tapping the advantage of backwardness in the industrial upgrading process. In addition, the dynamic growth in the newly liberalized sectors created the conditions for reforming the old priority sectors. Through this gradual, dual-track approach, China achieved "reform without losers" (Lau, Qian, and Roland 2000; Lin, Cai, and Li 2003; Naughton 1995; Lin 2012a) and moved gradually but steadily to a well-functioning market economy.

With a similar gradual, dual-track approach, a few other socialist economies—such as Vietnam, Cambodia, and Laos, which share the same colonial legacy as the African countries and have been inflicted by prolonged post-colonial civil wars—were able to achieve outstanding growth performance with very poor infrastructure and business environments during their transitions from a planned economy to a market economy.[11] As shown in Figure 45.2, in 1980, per capita income in Vietnam, Cambodia, and Laos was, respectively, 49.9%, 57.8%, and 54.6% of the average in Africa; in 2008, the ratio jumped to 166.9%, 139.4%, and 93.8%, respectively.

The gradual, dual-track approach also worked in Africa. Mauritius, like many other African countries, adopted an import-substation strategy in the 1960s and followed a gradual, dual-track approach in the 1970s to reduce distortions caused by the country's

[11] The Doing Business ranking in 2013 for Vietnam, Cambodia, and Laos was 99, 133, and 163, respectively, whereas the average annual growth rate of gross national income in 2000–2011 was 7.8%, 7.7%, and 7.1%, respectively.

import-substitution strategy. Its economy has grown dynamically since then and Mauritius became an African success story (Subramanian and Roy 2003).[12]

45.4 AFRICAN COUNTRIES CAN GROW AS DYNAMICALLY AS CHINA

The nature of modern economic growth is a process of structural transformation characterized by continuous technological innovation and industrial upgrading. Every developing country has the opportunity to accelerate its growth if it knows how to facilitate the development of industries according to its comparative advantages under a poor infrastructure and business environment and if it can tap the advantage of backwardness in its technological innovation and industrial upgrading during the process of its structural transformation.

Theoretically, a well-functioning market is a precondition for developing an economy's industries according to its comparative advantages, because only with such a market can relative prices reflect the relative scarcities of factors of production in the economy. Such a well-functioning market naturally propels firms to enter industries consistent with the country's comparative advantages. If a developing country follows its comparative advantages in technological and industrial development, the factor costs of production for the economy's industries will be at the lowest possible level internationally. If the transaction costs for the operation of firms in those industries are also low, those industries will be competitive in domestic and international markets. The economy will grow fast, accumulate capital rapidly, and upgrade its endowment structure quickly.

When the endowment structure is upgraded, the economy's comparative advantages change and its industrial structure as well as hard and soft infrastructure need to be upgraded accordingly so as to reduce firms' transaction costs in their operations. In the process, it is desirable for the state to play a proactive, enabling role to facilitate the upgrading smoothly and quickly. An enabling government should compensate the pioneer firms in industrial upgrading for the information externalities generated by their upgrading; the government should also coordinate the required investments and improvements in soft and hard infrastructure, which individual firms cannot internalize in their decisions. Through the appropriate functions of an effective market for resource allocation and an enabling state to facilitate technological innovation and industrial upgrading according to the changes in its comparative advantages, a developing country can tap the potential of the advantage of backwardness and achieve dynamic growth (Lin 2011, 2012b).

---

[12] In the 1980s, the Former Soviet Union, Hungary, and Poland adopted a gradual reform approach. However, unlike the case of China, their state-owned firms were not allowed to set prices for selling on the market after fulfilling their quota obligations. Private firms' entry into repressed sectors was subject to severe restrictions, but wages were liberalized (while in China wage increases were subject to state regulation). These reforms led to wage inflation and exacerbated shortages. See the discussion about the differences in the gradual approach in China and the Former Soviet Union and Eastern Europe in Lin (2009: 88–89).

Most African countries, as a result of their governments' previous policy failures, have poor business environments and infrastructure.[13] In this respect, China's experience during its transition also provides useful lessons. It is desirable for African governments to use their limited resources and administrative capacity strategically and pragmatically to facilitate the growth of sectors in which they have comparative advantages. They can do this by building up the necessary infrastructure and improving the business environment specifically for those sectors, as Mali has done for its mango exports and Ethiopia has done for its cut-flowers exports[14] (Chuhan-Pole and Angwafo 2011).

For the development of light manufacturing, in which many African countries have comparative advantages but are lacking now, governments can also develop special economic zones and industrial parks. African governments can proactively promote investment to attract foreign firms from other dynamic growing countries, which have the incentives to relocate production to take advantages of low wages in Africa (Monga 2013). The quick success of Huajian Shoe Factory in Ethiopia provides a convincing example of this approach. According to research at the World Bank (Dinh et al. 2012), the wage rate of the footwear industry in Ethiopia in 2010 was one-eighth to one-tenth that in China and about one-half that in Vietnam. Labor productivity in Ethiopia's footware industry is about 70% that in China and almost the same as that in Vietnam. Therefore, Ethiopia is potentially highly competitive in the footwear industry. But in 2010, China had about 19 million workers in its footwear industry and Vietnam had 1.2 million, while Ethiopia had only 8000 workers. Informed by these research findings and the rising wages and pending relocation of many Chinese shoe factories to other low-income countries, in August 2011, Ethiopia's late Prime Minister Meles Zenawi personally went to Shenzhen to invite Chinese shoe manufacturers to invest in Ethiopia. Huajian, a designer shoe manufacturer in China, visited Addis Ababa in October 2011. Convinced of the opportunity, Huajian set up a shoe factory with 550 workers in the Oriental Industrial Park near Addis Ababa in January 2012, expanded to 3,500 workers by December 2013, and projected it would hire 30,000 workers by 2016 (ACET 2013).

The success stories of Huajian in Ethiopia, mangos in Mali, apparel in Lesotho, horticulture in Kenya, and many others show that African countries, in spite of their poor overall infrastructure and business environment, can immediately begin a dynamic structural transformation through the government's active facilitation to remove bottlenecks for the development of sectors in which they have comparative advantages. Targeted government interventions are essential for utilizing limited resources and administrative capacity to reduce transaction costs in specific sectors in an environment where high transaction costs caused by the poor infrastructure and business environment may outweigh the advantages of low factor costs of production. By focusing on the specific sectors that are consistent with the country's comparative advantages and as such have low factor costs of production, such interventions will allow countries to reduce transaction costs and promote the nation's competitive advantages quickly.

---

[13] Among the 44 sub-Saharan African countries in the World Bank's Doing Business ranking in 2013, 36 of them ranked below 120.

[14] Mali's Doing Business ranking was 151 and Ethiopia's was 127 in 2013.

45.5 OPPORTUNITIES FOR AFRICA FROM CHINA'S RISE

After more than three decades of dynamic growth, China has depleted its surplus labor and wages have started to rise rapidly. Manufacturing wages increased from US$150 a month in 2005 to around US$350 a month in 2010 (Lin 2012d). In the 18th Party Congress in October 2012, China set a target to double per capita income by 2020 compared with 2010. Per capita income in 2010 was US$4400. Taking into account appreciation of the Chinese yuan, it is likely that China's per capita income will reach US$12 700, the threshold for a high-income country, by 2020 or soon after that. China will have to follow the path of the earlier success economies in East Asia—Japan in the 1960s and Hong Kong, Korea, Singapore, and Taiwan in the 1980s—and begin relocating its labor-intensive industries to low-income countries.[15] Indeed, this is already happening. A large share of China's outward foreign direct investment in Africa, which reached US$9.3 billion by the end of 2009, has gone to manufacturing (22%), second only to mining (29%). And China is building six economic and trade cooperation zones in the Arab Republic of Egypt, Ethiopia, Mauritius, Nigeria, and Zambia.[16] More such initiatives are likely.

As China moves ahead, there will be a major difference from previous patterns in East Asia: China's economy is substantially larger than the other economies. China has an estimated 85 million workers in manufacturing, most of them in labor-intensive sectors, compared with 9.7 million in Japan in 1960 and 2.3 million in Korea in 1980. The reallocation of China's manufacturing to more sophisticated, higher value-added products and tasks will open great opportunities for labor-abundant, lower-income countries to produce the labor-intensive manufacturing goods that China leaves behind. As a result, China will not be a *goose* in the traditional flying geese model but a leading *dragon*, which opens up a huge opportunity for numerous lower-income countries to step into the vacuum left by its industrial upgrading (Lin 2012d; Chandra, Lin, and Wang 2013).

Africa will be an important destination for China's outward reallocation of labor-intensive manufacturing. Vietnam, Cambodia, and Myanmar are close to China geographically. However, their populations are small compared with China's 1.3 billion: 88 million in Vietnam, 14 million in Cambodia, and 48 million in Myanmar. If a significant portion of the 85 million labor-intensive jobs were relocated to those countries, their wages would increase sharply, reducing the gap with China.[17] Only Africa, with its population of one billion,

[15] Estimates by Maddison (2010) indicate that China's per capita income (measured in purchasing power parity) was $6,725 in 2008, the same level as in Japan in 1966, Korea in 1986, and Taiwan in 1983. These economies started to relocate their labor-intensive manufacturing industries at that income level—Japan to the East Asian Tigers, which in turn relocated labor-intensive manufacturing to mainland China.

[16] State Council of China 2010.

[17] In the World Bank's light manufacturing study (Dinh, et al. 2012) the wage rate for footwear workers in Vietnam was about one-quarter of China's in 2010. In the past few years, because of the increasing relocation of China's footwear firms to Vietnam, wages there have increased to one-half to two-thirds of wages in China.

many of them young, will be large enough to absorb the relocation of China's processing manufacturing.

Total manufacturing employment in Africa is estimated to be around 10 million. This suggests that absorbing even a small share of the relocation of China's 85 million labor-intensive manufacturing jobs would go a long way toward creating opportunities for employment and sustained growth in Africa (Monga 2013).

The relocation of 9.7 million manufacturing jobs from Japan to Korea, Taiwan, Hong Kong, and Singapore helped the four East Asian small dragons as they started their dynamic structural transformation and growth. The relocation of labor-intensive manufacturing jobs from the four East Asian small dragons to China helped China start its export-oriented, light manufacturing development and become the world's factory. Governments in Africa and low-income countries in other parts of the world can play an enabling role in pragmatically addressing their poor infrastructure and business environment and proactively attracting the relocation of China's labor-intensive manufacturing to their countries. If they do so, the rise of China will leave enough space for all low-income countries to start their journey of industrialization and structural transformation through the development of light manufacturing. They may be able to escape the low-income trap and climb to middle-income status or even become high-income countries within one or two generations.

45.6 CONCLUDING REMARKS

Like many other developing countries, China was trapped in poverty for centuries before its miraculous rise after the transition from a planned economy to a market economy in 1979. During the transition process, China did not follow the Washington Consensus recommendation to remove all distortions simultaneously by shock therapy. And China did not refrain from implementing location and sector-specific policies to support targeted industries that were opposed by the neoliberalism. Instead, China adopted a dual-track approach. On the one hand, the government provided transitory protection and subsidies to nonviable firms in old priority industries to maintain stability. On the other hand, it liberalized the entry of private firms into new sectors that were repressed before the transition but consistent with China's comparative advantages. China also built up special economic zones and industrial parks, providing road, power, water and sewerage, and one-stop service to overcome the constraints of the country's overall poor infrastructure and business environment. China proactively attracted labor-intensive firms from newly industrialized economies in East Asia and other higher-income countries as they relocated their manufacturing to the special economic zones and industrial parks. This pragmatic approach has enabled China to maintain stability and achieve miraculous growth even with the overall adverse infrastructure and business environment.

The quick success of the Huajian Shoe Factory in Ethiopia as well as other indigenous success stories, such as mangos in Mali, cut flowers in Ethiopia, horticulture in Kenya, and apparel in Lesotho, demonstrate that a pragmatic approach is equally applicable to Africa. Africa does not have to wait to start its industrialization, structural transformation, and dynamic growth until after it improves its infrastructure, business environment, governance, education, and health, which are stressed by the global academic and development community. Governments must play an enabling role by providing adequate incentives proactively to attract foreign direct investments and assist domestic firms to enter sectors in which they have comparative advantages. Governments should use their limited resources and administrative capacity to build up industrial parks and special economic zones with adequate infrastructure and the regulation required for reducing transaction costs in those sectors. In this way, their products can be competitive in international markets even if the nation's overall infrastructure and business environment are poor. The success of those sectors will generate resources and confidence for further industrial upgrading and gradual improvement of infrastructure and the business environment for the whole nation. This is a virtuous circle. If African countries can adopt such a pragmatic approach, the pending relocation of 85 million manufacturing jobs from China will enable African countries to grow in the coming decades as dynamically as China and other East Asian countries have in the past decades.

References

Acemoglu, D., Johnson, S., and Robinson, J.A. (2005). Institutions as the fundamental cause of long-run growth, in P. Aghion and S.N. Durlauf (eds), *Handbook of Economic Growth*, vol. 1A. Amsterdam: Elsevier, pp. 385–472.

ACET (African Center for Economic Cooperation) (2013). *African Transformation Report*. ACET, Johannesburg.

Chandra, V., Lin, J.Y., and Wang, Y. (2013). Leading dragon phenomenon: new opportunities for catch-up in low-income countries. *Asian Development Review*, 30(1):52–84.

Chang, H. (2003). *Kicking Away the Ladder: Development Strategy in Historical Perspective*. London: Anthem Press.

Chuhan-Pole, P., and Angwafo, M. (2011). *Yes Africa Can: Success Stories from Dynamic Continent*. Washington, DC: World Bank.

Easterly, W. (2001). *The Elusive Quest for Growth: Economists' Adventures and Misadventures in the Tropics*. Cambridge, MA: MIT Press.

Engerman, S.L., and Sokoloff, K.L. (1997). Factor endowments, institutions, and differential paths of growth among new world economies: a view from economic historians of the United States, in S. Haber (ed.), *How Latin America Fell Behind*. Stanford, CA: Stanford University Press, pp. 260–304.

Fei, J., and Ranis, G. (1997). *Growth and Development from an Evolutionary Perspective*. Malden, MA: Blackwell.

Gerschenkron, A. (1962). *Economic Backwardness in Historical Perspective: A Book of Essays*. Cambridge, MA: Belknap Press of Harvard University Press.

Graham, E.M., and Wada, E. (2001). Foreign Direct Investment in China: Effects on Growth and Economic Performance, in P. Drysdale (ed.), *Experience of Transitional Economies in East Asia*. Oxford: Oxford University Press.

Grossman, G. M., and Helpman, E. (1996). Electoral Competition and Special Interest Politics. *Review of Economic Studies*, 63(2):265–286.

Dinh, H.T., Palmade, V., Chandra, V., and Cossar, F. (2012). *Light Manufacturing in Africa*. Washington, DC: World Bank.

Kuznets, S. (1966). *Modern Economic Growth: Rate, Structure and Spread.* New Haven, CT: Yale University Press.

Lal, D., and Mynt, H. (1996). *The Political Economy of Poverty, Equity, and Growth: A Comparative Study.* Oxford: Clarendon Press.

Landes, D. (1998). *The Wealth and Poverty of Nations: Why Some Are So Rich and Some So Poor.* New York and London: Norton.

Lau, L.J., Qian, Y., and Roland, G. (2000). Reform without losers: an interpretation of China's dual-track approach to transition. *Journal of Political Economy*, 108(1):120–143.

Lewis, W.A. (1954). Economic development with unlimited supply of labour. *Manchester School of Economic and Social Studies*, 22(2):139–191.

Lin, J.Y. (1992). Rural reforms and agricultural growth in China. *American Economic Review*, 82(1):34–51.

Lin, J.Y. (1995). The Needham puzzle: why the industrial revolution did not originate in China. *Economic Development and Cultural Change*, 43(2):269–292.

Lin, J.Y. (2003). Development strategy, viability and economic convergence. *Economic Development and Cultural Change*, 53(2):277–308.

Lin, J.Y. (2009). *Economic Development and Transition: Thought, Strategy, and Viability.* Cambridge: Cambridge University Press.

Lin, J.Y. (2011). New structural economics: a framework for rethinking development. *World Bank Research Observer*, 26(2):193–221.

Lin, J.Y. (2012a). *Demystifying the Chinese Economy.* Cambridge: Cambridge University Press.

Lin, J.Y. (2012b). *The Quest for Prosperity: How Developing Economies Can Take Off.* Princeton, NJ: Princeton University Press.

Lin, J.Y. (2012c). *New Structural Economics: A Framework for Rethinking Development and Policy.* Washington, DC: World Bank.

Lin, J.Y. (2012d). From flying geese to leading dragons: new opportunities and strategies for structural transformation in developing countries. *Global Policy*, 3(4):397–409.

Lin, J.Y., and Li, F. (2009). *Development Strategy, Viability, and Economic Distortions in Developing Countries.* Policy Research Working Paper 4906. Washington, DC: World Bank.

Lin, J.Y., and Monga, C. (2011). Growth Identification and facilitation: the role of the state in the dynamics of structural change. *Development Policy Review*, 29(3):264–290.

Lin, J.Y., and Monga, C. (2012). The Growth Report and New Structural Economics, in J.Y. Lin (ed.), *New Structural Economics: A Framework for Rethinking Development and Policy.* Washington, DC: World Bank.

Lin, J.Y., and Tan, G. (1999). Policy burdens, accountability, and soft budget constraints. *American Economic Review*, 89(2):426–431.

Lin, J.Y., Cai, F., and Li, Z. (2003). *The China Miracle: Development Strategy and Economic Reform.* Hong Kong SAR, China: Chinese University Press.

Maddison, A. (2001). *The World Economy: A Millennial Perspective.* Paris: OECD Development Centre.

Maddison, A. (2007). *Chinese Economic Performance in the Long Run—Second Edition, Revised and Updated: 960–2030 AD.* Paris: OECD Development Centre.

Maddison, A. (2010). Historical Statistics of the World Economy: 1-2008 AD. http://www.ggdc.net/maddison/Historical_Statistics/horizontal-file_02-2010.xls.

Monga, C. (2013). *The Mechanics of Job Creation: Seizing the New Dividends of Globalization.* Policy Research Working Paper No. 6661. Washington, DC: World Bank.

Naughton, B. (1995). *Growing Out of the Plan: Chinese Economic Reform, 1978–1993*. New York: Cambridge University Press.

North, D. (1981). *Structure and Change in Economic History*. New York: W.W. Norton.

Perkins, D.H., and Rawski, T.G. (2008). Forecasting China's Economic Growth to 2025, in L. Brandt and T.G. Rawski (eds), *China's Great Economic Transformation*. Cambridge: Cambridge University Press, pp. 829–885.

Prebisch, R. (1950). *The Economic Development of Latin America and Its Principal Problems*. New York: United Nations. Reprinted in 1962 in *Economic Bulletin for Latin America* 7(1):1–22.

Subramanian, A., and Roy, D. (2003). Who can explain the Mauritian miracle? Mede, Romer, Sachs, or Rodrik? in D. Rodrik (ed.), *In Search of Prosperity: Analytic Narratives on Economic Growth*. Princeton: Princeton University Press, 205–243.

Sun, Y.S. (1929). *The International Development of China (Shih yeh chi hua)*, 2nd edn. New York: G.P. Putnam's Sons.

Vu, K.M. (2013). *The Dynamics of Economic Growth: Policy Insights from Comparative Analyses in Asia*. Edward Elgar.

Wei, Y., and Liu, X. (2001). *Foreign Direct Investment: Determinants and Impact*. Northampton, MA: Edward Elgar.

World Bank (on behalf of Commission on Growth and Development) (2008). *The Growth Report: Strategies for Sustained Growth and Inclusive Development*. Washington, DC: World Bank.

Zeng, D.Z. (2010). *Building Engines for Growth and Competitiveness in China: Experience with Special Economic Zones and Industrial Clusters*. Washington, DC: World Bank.

Zeng, D.Z. (2011). How Do Special Economic Zones and Industrial Clusters Drive China's Rapid Development? Policy Research Working Paper 5583. Washington, DC: World Bank.

CHAPTER 46

....

ECONOMICS AND POLICY
Some Lessons from Africa's Experience

....

AKBAR NOMAN AND JOSEPH STIGLITZ

46.1 INTRODUCTION

....

SUB-SAHARAN Africa (which we also refer to in this chapter simply as Africa) has experienced reasonably rapid growth of nearly 5% since the turn of the century. But this followed a "lost quarter century" during which, after a prolonged collapse, per capita income in 2000 was still below its level of 25 years earlier as was the share of manufacturing in GDP. By 2008 per capita income had just about recovered to its previous peak more than three decades earlier, but the share of manufacturing in GDP has yet to do so.[1] Along with the economic meltdown of the former Soviet Union and Eastern Europe in the transition to a market economy, this possibly ranks as one of the biggest economic disasters in history since records of national accounts began. (The current crisis in parts of southern Europe may be on the way to joining this select list.)

The size and diversity of the region means, of course, that averages have much to conceal. There have been many successes in Africa in many dimensions in different periods, including GDP growth and managing the resource curse. There have been substantial periods of considerable successes in natural resource-abundant economies like Cote d'Ivoire, Mozambique and above all Botswana, the fastest growing economy in the world during 1960–2000. Even more impressive are several countries without natural resource wealth—such as Ethiopia, Ghana, Tanzania, Rwanda, and Mauritius—that have achieved reasonably rapid growth exceeding 5% for a decade or more. These countries clearly owe their growth resurgence to rather deeper transformations of economic policies, institutions, and structures. While much of the enhanced growth since the turn of the century is attributable to booming commodity prices and hydrocarbon discoveries,[2] the long history of resource-rich countries

---

[1] Noman and Stiglitz (2012).

[2] There is some controversy on the relative roles of commodity booms and improved policies and on different types of policies, but that the former have been very important is beyond dispute.

that have mismanaged their wealth shows that an abundance of resources and booming prices are no guarantee of success.

While much research has focused on the lessons of success provided by the experiences of East Asia,[3] relatively little attention has been paid to insights to be gleaned from the study of the economic failures and successes of Sub-Saharan Africa. We focus in particular on the question, Why did the region go through such a prolonged period of economic decline during its lost quarter century? What are the lessons for policy, especially for sustaining and accelerating the resurgence of growth there and elsewhere?

In answering those questions, much attention has been focused on institutional issues, especially governance. We argue here that Africa's experience highlights the limitations of ad hoc and over-generalized institutional explanations that confuse cause and effect as well as ends and means. It is clear and obvious that where states have failed or at war there is little that economics has to offer as solutions. But it is too simplistic too blame economic failure on political failure: economic failure contributes to political crises. There is a growing body of research investigating the determinants of conflicts, including, notably, the forms of inequality that are more likely to give rise to conflict. This set of issues about failed states and armed conflict is beyond the scope of this essay.

We focus, in particular, on the following subset of issues raised by Africa's "lost quarter century": (i) prioritization and sequencing of reforms; (ii) institutions both of public governance and of markets; (iii) static efficiency versus dynamic gains; and (iv) finance. We begin our discussion with an overview of the debate over the lost quarter century.

46.2 EXPLAINING AFRICA'S LOST QUARTER CENTURY

The facts of Africa's lost quarter century are well-known—a steady decline of per capita income between 1980 and 1995 and a recovery to the 1980 level as late as 2005; deindustrialization, with the value added of manufacturing toGDP yet to recover (indeed, at 11.0% in 2013, this share was below its 1975 level of 17.7%).[4] Africa's share of world trade shrank even more sharply and its share in global foreign direct investment went down from 5.1% in 1970–79 to 2.5% in 1980–1989 and 1.9% in 1990–1999 before rising to 2.4% in 2000–2006[5]. But the explanation of the lost quarter century remains in dispute. In particular, what was the role of the structural adjustment policies foisted on the sub-continent?

The period of Africa's severest economic decline, 1980–1995, was also one of a plethora of reform programs typically reflecting the advice and conditionalities of external agencies, spearheaded by the IMF and the World Bank. These programs were manifestations of a particular brand of economics that came to be labeled the "Washington Consensus"

[3] For example, the World Bank's study of the East Asia Miracle (World Bank, 1993) and the Growth Commission report, (2008) confirming the insights of that earlier study; Stiglitz (1996), Stiglitz and Uy (1996), Helmann, Murdoch, and Stiglitz (1997), Amsden (1989 and 2001), Wade (1990), Chang (2003).
[4] World Bank World DataBank.
[5] Jomo, K.S. and von Arnim, R, (2012).

(WC).[6] Here and elsewhere (Noman and Stiglitz 2012) we explain how those policies contributed to the lost quarter century (on balance, notwithstanding some positive effects);
how it was anticipated that the policy reforms would lead to the creation of new jobs reflecting the countries' (static) comparative advantage, even as old jobs in protected sectors were
destroyed; and how it was anticipated that the improved policy frameworks would attract foreign direct investment. Jobs were destroyed by the liberalization measures; but the hoped-for
new businesses and FDI did not materialize. Defenders of the Washington Consensus argued
for "doubling down." The problem in their view was not that the policies were wrong, but that
they needed to be accelerated and extended. These responses were reminiscent of those of
medieval bloodletters to the failure of their remedies: what was needed was more bloodlet-
ting. Later in this chapter we will describe how these failures also gave rise to a search for new
explanations for successful development—including a focus on "governance." (It is perhaps
too easy and misleading to blame the Bretton Woods institutions for imposing the conditions
based on this flawed doctrine: it was not just that other institutions, notably the US Treasury,
also supported these policies, but also that these policies reflected what became the dominant
orthodoxy in economics, neo-liberalism. The influence of this doctrine lingers—including in
some of the responses to the global crisis that broke out in 2008—notwithstanding its failures
and empirical and theoretical research showing the inadequacies in the underlying theories,
and presenting mounting evidence against its postulates. Some countries almost seemed to
take pride in formulating "IMF programs without the IMF.")

Just as there is controversy surrounding the causes of the lost quarter century, there is controversy concerning Africa's recent resurgence, both its causes and its sustainability.

Not surprisingly, advocates of the WC policies believe that Africa's recovery is
sustainable—if only the countries persist in the WC policies, to which they give credit for the
revival. Thus Shanta Devarajan, the Chief Economist of the World Bank's Africa Region, was
quoted in a recent interview as saying, "There is no question that one of the major reasons
for Africa's growth over the last 10–15 years is because of [sic] macro-economic policies have
improved. Average inflation is half of what it was in the 1990s. Fiscal deficits are down; current account deficits are down. The reason is that African policymakers followed Structural
Adjustment Programs over the last 10–15 years. It worked, it delivered results. It delivered
economic growth and poverty reduction. You can't dispute that."[7]

That interpretation ascribes little weight to the boom in commodity prices, or to
the success of the countries like Ethiopia, Botswana and Rwanda that, while adopting
some of the WC consensus policies, resisted others. It ignores the deindustrialization
that accompanied the WC policies and the fact that outside of the natural resource sector, FDI has remained anemic. It ignores too the particular failures of some of the critical reforms in some of the countries in areas such as agriculture and finance. More
generally, even if it were true that these countries were successful in increasing GDP

---

[6] John Williamson coined the term Washington Consensus, describing the consensus of policies
surrounding the reforms advocated by the Washington based institutions in Latin America. But the term
has come to refer to a broader set of policies, advocated not only in Latin America but in other developing
countries and today, often referred to as being based on "neo-liberalism." See Williamson (1991, 2008)
and Stiglitz (2008).

[7] "World Bank-'Structural Adjustment Programmes Worked in Africa,'" Think Africa Press (London).
[Interview]. Lambert Mbom 10/05/2013.

because of the structural adjustment policies, this interpretation does not take account of the performance of the economy in terms of broader (and better) measures of success (see the report of the Commission on the Measurement of Economic Performance and Social Progress, published as Stiglitz, Sen, and Fitoussi, 2009), and in particular and more generally to the high cost of such benefits as ensued from the WC policies, including notably the adverse impact on poverty.

That extraordinarily confident assertion in the face of widespread and far-ranging disillusionment with the structural adjustment programs indicates the difficulties of establishing undisputable causal links between economic policies and outcomes. And it illustrates that the slavery to defunct economists to which Keynes famously alluded remains to be abolished.[8]

The disagreements concerning the sustainability of Africa's growth were highlighted by an on-line debate in *The Economist* magazine in March 2013 on the topic, "Is Africa Rising?"[9] The argument for Africa's resurgence emphasized, in particular, the revival of fairly rapid growth for more than a decade, reduction in poverty, improvements in social indicators and considerable increase in foreign investment. The gist of the argument questioning the sustainability of recent growth emphasized the disappointing record judged against the "conventional" definition of development: "the transition of economies based on primary agriculture and extractive industries to economies focused on manufacturing and value-added services."

In an earlier paper (Noman and Stiglitz 2012) we examined the debate over the source and sustainability of Africa's resurgence in some detail. Here we confine ourselves to noting that while there is reason to cheer and be optimistic about Africa's prospects and that policy improvements, especially better macroeconomic management have been important, there are real concerns about the nature of the growth and its sustainability in many (most?) countries. These stem from the lack of economic transformation referred to above.[10] Not only has foreign investment been overwhelmingly concentrated in extractive activities, but a disproportionate share of the growth in employment is in informal activities where jobs may also serve to disguise unemployment. In sum, there has been little or no progress in transforming economies to be based on the learning and associated dynamism that is the ultimate source of sustained growth and development. Noman and Stiglitz (2012) ask "is the improvement in growth rates a result of the elimination of distortions caused by previous policies—implying a one-time gain—or the result of a policy environment which is more conducive to sustained faster growth" (to the kind of learning that we focus on in section 4).

Suffice it to say, much controversy remains regarding these matters. The standard methodology used by economists for quantitatively ascertaining the relative importance

[8] "The ideas of economists and political philosophers, both when they are right and when they are wrong, are more powerful than is commonly understood. Indeed the world is ruled by little else. Practical men, who believe themselves to be quite exempt from any intellectual influence, are usually the slaves of some defunct economist. Madmen in authority, who hear voices in the air, are distilling their frenzy from some academic scribbler of a few years back." Keynes, John Maynard (1936 [2007]) *The General Theory of Employment, Interest and Money* (London: Macmillan), p. 383.

[9] Available on http://www.economist.com/debate/overview/249

[10] This issue is a focus of African Center for Economic Transformation (ACET) (2014) *African Transformation Report:Growth With Depth.*

of different factors has, itself, come under attack. Such studies look at the differences in performance (for instance, as measured by growth rates) in different countries and/or different periods and relate them to different "explanatory" factors.[11] Critics focus on deficiencies in measurement both of the performance variables (GDP) and of the explanatory variables; the problem of causation (does trade cause growth or growth trade); the problem of simultaneity (the oil price shock of the 1970s lowered real income of oil importing countries and resulted in inflation though some have seemed to suggest that the cause of the decline in real income was an increase in inflation[12]); and the problem of "omitted variables." (Some third factor explains why some countries responded to the oil price shock by allowing more inflation; it was not the inflation itself, but this omitted third factor, which is to blame for the poor performance.) Advocates of the methodology say that, notwithstanding these concerns, it is the best or "least-worst" way of sorting out the relative roles played by different factors.[13]

Some defenders of the WC policies, even while conceding that they were not always as successful as hoped—and in some cases may even have had serious adverse effects—assert (i) the problems were not with the policies themselves but with the way they were implemented, and (ii) that the criticisms are the results of hindsight: there was no alternative at the time and without the experience that we have had, those policies represented the best option. But both of these are unpersuasive. There *was* something wrong with the policies: they were based on simplistic and "incorrect" models of how economies perform and what makes for sustainable growth. Moreover, given the prevalence of failure, one must observe that good policies have to be designed to be implementable by those that responsible for the task. If they cannot be, then they are not good policies; at the very least, they have not been adequately adapted to the circumstances at hand (Stiglitz 2002). The second claim, that the criticisms are just a matter of hindsight, is a very curious assertion, given that WC and associated "structural adjustment" policies were always highly controversial, especially in Africa and especially for ignoring the lessons of successful development.

---

[11] Note that the methodology that has become so popular in development of randomized controlled experiments is not really relevant for answering these fundamental questions: there is not a large set of seemingly similar countries among which one can randomly choose some to be exposed to structural adjustment policies and others given some "placebo."

[12] Even studies that attempt to look at the relationship more carefully, by showing that countries exposed to similar shocks that did better in controlling inflation, are not immune to such criticisms; for there may be (and typically are) differences between these countries that account for differences in policies or differences in outcomes from similar policies, and it is difficult, if not impossible, to control for all of these differences.

[13] Noman and Stiglitz (2012), p. 19. The deficiencies in the standard methodology are illustrated by the controversy over whether East Asia's growth was caused by trade liberalization. Advocates of trade liberalization note that trade and growth are correlated. Correlation does not, of course, imply causation. The fact that the increase in trade preceded trade liberalization suggests that trade liberalization had little to do with the success of these countries. See Greenwald and Stiglitz (2014) and Charlton and Stiglitz (2013). So too, the interpretations and policy implications for such analyses conducted in the early years of the transition from Communism to the market (World Bank WDR 1996) have been questioned by subsequent events, and even subsequent studies using similar methodologies. See Godoy and Stiglitz (2006).

46.3 Speed, Sequencing, Selectivity

The first generation of the so-called "structural adjustment programs" in Africa were, in general, such an acute failure with severe economic contraction and growth rates invariably far below those projected at the times they were adopted that the issue of what went wrong shouted out for attention. Reform programs may fail because of their inherent weaknesses (bad policies, or at least policies inappropriate to the circumstances of the country), or because they are not adequately implemented, or because of unanticipated exogenous shocks. The difficulties of parsing these issues are an important source of controversy. Before turning to the inadequacies of the content of the reform programs and the underlying or implicit economic model on which they were based, we turn to lessons from Africa for the speed, sequencing and selectivity of reforms. We noted earlier that even defenders of the WC policies admit that at least in many cases there were failures in implementation.

But part of the explanation of the widespread failure in implementation was that insufficient attention was paid to the pacing and sequencing of reforms. Sequencing is especially important because economic reforms to remove distortions face the second-best dilemma: eliminating only some of the many distortions may make matters worse. While standard economic theory had long emphasized the importance of second best considerations (see Lancaster and Lipsey 1956; Meade 1955)—advocates of WC policies gave these concerns short shrift.[14]

This is clearly demonstrated by Africa's experience with, for example, financial sector, agricultural pricing, and trade policy reforms. One of the reasons that trade liberalization was marked by more job destruction than job creation was that in most of the countries; there was a shortage of entrepreneurs, especially those with capital, and an absence of a financial sector to provide funds to the entrepreneurs that already existed. The elimination of agricultural marketing boards often did not lead to as much, if any, higher prices for the farmers, as a result of lower transactions costs, as had been hoped; rather, it sometimes led to farmers being exploited by monopolistic middle men. The competitive marketplace that the reform advocates hoped would arise spontaneously did not emerge—partly because some of the reforms that would have enabled the emergence had not yet been put into place.

46.3.1 The pacing of reforms

While this argues for comprehensiveness in reforms, limitations in the capacity for implementing reforms mean that not all reforms can be put into place simultaneously; and this points to the vital importance of prioritization and sequencing. The initial explanation for the poor supply response from the purveyors of the reform programs was to say that the mistake was excessive ambition. They attempted to do too much. (Particularly in the aftermath of

---

[14] Indeed, even as the advocates of WC/neo-liberal policies starting urging ("forcing") African countries to liberalize their trade regimes, it was shown that trade liberalization, in the absence of good risk markets, could make *everyone* worse off. It was not just that there were some winners and some losers. Everyone could be a loser. See Newbery and Stiglitz (1984).

the East Asia crisis, it was recognized that far too many conditions had been imposed on the countries; in some cases, the excessive conditionality had even undermined the coherence of the policies by sending out so many signals that they were unintelligible. This led to attempts to streamline conditionality by reducing the number of conditions in the first wave of reforms of the reforms.)[15]

Thus, one lesson of the programs that failed in Africa is that reforms need to be mindful not just of the second-best dilemma, but also of the "absorptive" reform capacity the ability to digest and respond to the myriad of changes. This concern applies to both government—in the political economy sense—and private agents. Moreover, no reform is ever perfect. Any successful implementation process must entail learning, both about what is working and what is not, and adapting policies in response to what is learned. Information about reforms and what they entail is neither costless nor instantaneously and universally available. The "quality" of the reform may decrease as the "quantity" of reforms undertaken increases.

This is not a general argument for always going slow[16]: there may be threshold effects that require decisive, critical minimum efforts. Thus, for example, when Ethiopia launched its reform program in the early 1990s, it moved rapidly to establish macroeconomic stability, dismantle collectivized agriculture, and establish a system of famine prevention. But Ethiopia has been much more measured and gradual in other areas, such as financial liberalization. While it might be argued that, in some areas, Ethiopia could have moved faster (e.g. telecommunications),[17] its mixture of rapidity and gradualism has generally served the country well, with its economy growing at a rate approaching 10% per annum during nearly a decade that culminated in the global crisis of 2008. Further afield, perhaps the most notable case of combining fast and slow reforms is that of China; its success stands in marked contrast with the "shock therapy" of the former Soviet Union.[18] In China the initial focus was predominantly if not exclusively on agriculture and subsequently on two-track price and privatization reforms. The privatization agenda did not really start strongly until after a host of new enterprises (mostly TVEs, Township and Village Enterprises) had been created. In the case of the India, the world's second most populous country, a different sort of gradualism might have worked.[19]

The issue is thus not a simplistic one of how fast or how slow policies should be implemented, but one of priorities and sequencing, given the country's capacities for implementation, given the transactions and opportunity cost of any set of policy measures, and given the country's ability to gather information about the successes and failures of each policy

---

[15] Whether these attempts actually succeeded is another matter: there was a tendency to reduce the number of conditions by simply combining them so that what might otherwise be two or three conditions were often combined into one.

[16] Indeed, in some cases, it may even be easier to move simultaneously on several fronts than to move ahead on one front, especially if that front is not well chosen. If trade liberalization is undertaken before a vibrant financial sector that provides finance to new enterprises is created, the government will be forced to address a host of other economic and social problems: how to deal with the consequences of the mounting unemployment.

[17] Though even here, it was arguably wise to resist the policies of selling off licenses to foreign firms, instead focusing on procuring particular services from foreign providers.

[18] See Stiglitz (1999).

[19] See Ahluwalia, Montek S. (2002).

measures and to adapt the policies in response. An approach that allows for experimentation and flexibility, in which successes can be scaled-up and failures can be abandoned quickly is an important ingredient of success.

46.4 The Inadequacy of the Agenda of "Getting Prices Right"

The economic model underlying the WC postulated that (trade) liberalization would serve to get "prices right" and combined with privatization and deregulation would unleash growth and development in conditions of macroeconomic stability. Africa's lost quarter-century is a particularly vivid testament to how wrong these beliefs were; this postulate was based on a strong set of unfounded assumptions. Take for example the cases of agriculture, manufacturing and the financial sector.

While there was a strong case for liberalization of agricultural markets and ending marketing boards, the first generation of WC reforms assumed that such markets were well functioning (e.g. competitive) or would emerge and become well functioning almost overnight once impediments like pricing regulation and marketing boards were removed. Often this turned out to be mistaken and, as we have already noted, the prices and incentives faced by farmers did not improve as expected. Moreover farmers were constrained by the non-existence or severe imperfections of input and credit markets. Infrastructural shortfalls added to the constraints facing farmers, especially in more remote areas. Cereal yields in Africa pretty much stagnated between 1960 and 2005 at around 1 ton per hectare—in a period during which yields were soaring elsewhere.[20] The reforms, viewed as a package, were a dismal failure.

Similarly, in the case of financial sector reforms, liberalization of interest rates to make them market-determined typically faced the pitfall of a total lack of financial markets, or financial markets that were thin and highly imperfect, e.g. for government securities whose auctions were to determine the rates. The all-too-common result was exceptionally high real interest rates (10–15% was not uncommon) and the absence of long-term credit for investment. No doubt, at least in some countries, this was an important contributor to the limited economic transformation, and indeed the deindustrialization of Africa.

The financial follies that led to the Great Recession of 2008 have highlighted the imperfections of financial markets even in advanced industrial countries and the dangers of unfettered markets. They showed how even in "sophisticated" economies, under-regulated banks developed greater capacities in exploiting unsophisticated borrowers than in ascertaining the risks associated with different firms that might create jobs or even in managing their own risks.

---

[20] There were, of course, a number of contributing factors. The WC policies also underemphasized the importance of public investments in technology, including extension services. Increased intensification of the use of land may have contributed to a decline of land productivity. WC policies proscribed government subsidies for fertilizer. The green revolution never really came to Africa.

Privatization, trade policy and related reforms compounded the difficulties posed by (and confronting[21]) the financial sector that emerged from WC reforms. While there was much to be said for rationalizing the trade regimes and public sector enterprises, the structure, pacing, and sequencing of trade liberalization and privatization led to the deindustrialization of Africa, instead of the emergence of a more competitive and vibrant sector and one that attracted the foreign investment that had been expected and promised.

46.5 INSTITUTIONS

The question of why WC reforms did not work as predicted fed a renewed interest in institutions. As Thandika Mkandawire puts it, the failure of the "good policies" of "getting prices right" prompted those multilateral institutions and aid donors advocating such policies to turn their attention to an institutional agenda.[22]

An earlier literature had recognized the importance of institutions and indeed explained economic success as a result of institutional innovations. Perhaps the best known of this type of analysis is Alexander's Gerschenkron's iconic analysis of how continental European countries narrowed and caught up with England, which led the way the founder of industrialization and modern economic growth.[23] His work showed the importance of the role that the state can play in fostering institutions conducive to growth as it did, especially by filling a void in finance, in the late developing European countries of the 19th century. In particular, Gershenkron argued that the later the start of development and the greater the degree of relative backwardness, the larger should be the state's role in helping channel capital to nascent industries. There is a large literature on the *development state,* emphasizing the role of the state in successful development, not just in the East Asian "miracle" economies but also in many of the now developed countries elsewhere.[24] This literature notes the important role the state played in creating the institutions that were central to development.

Of course, markets can, themselves be viewed as institutions. But in practice, the market is a far cry from what is depicted in standard textbooks, or assumed in the models underlying neo-liberalism and WC policies. We have come to see them as often highly imperfect. (Indeed, in the United States, in the aftermath of the Great Recession, there is a reform agenda called "making markets act like markets," emphasizing that they are often not competitive and transparent—Adam Smith pointed out that there were strong forces to reduce competition, and recent literature in the economics of information has noted corresponding forces to reduce transparency.) It is clear that markets are not (i) self-creating; (ii) self-regulating; or (iii) self-stabilizing. To function in the manner that economic theory

---

[21] Openness, by increasing the risks arising from external shocks, increased the challenges confronting financial institutions in assessing the risks associated with different borrowers and managing those risks.

[22] Mkandawire (2012).

[23] Gerschenkron (1962).

[24] On East Asia, see for example Amsden (1989, 2001), Wade (1990), Stiglitz, World Bank (1993). Ha-Joon Chang (2003) covers both East Asia as well as the developed countries of North America and Europe.

postulates, requires a plethora of other institutions such as laws[25] pertaining to contract enforcement, property rights, corporate governance and competition, as well as institutions for managing the multiple problems arising from externalities and information imperfections and asymmetries (including those associated with "agency" and delegation), and on account of coordination failures.

What good institutions are, how they are created, and how institutional deficiencies are addressed are critical for developmental success, but unfortunately, there are no easy answers. The 2008 crisis exposed fundamental institutional weaknesses in the United States (including in some of its most venerable institutions, e.g. the Federal Reserve). But here too the neo-liberal WC served Africa poorly. Some of the policies weakened (or in the case of development banks and marketing boards, eliminated) state institutions, rather than attempting to reform and strengthen them.

Belatedly, as the failure of the WC policies become evident, blame was shifted to deficiencies in public governance. Privatizations failed, it was argued, because they were not carried out well; too often public assets were turned over to private agents not on the basis of who would manage those assets the best, but on the basis of who would pay the biggest bribes. As Stiglitz (2002) observed, too often privatization was more aptly labeled "briberization."

These concerns led to the emergence of a particular agenda of institutional reforms in Africa under the label of "good governance" (GG). This agenda reflected a particular view of the relative roles of the state and markets. It assigned what Meles Zenawi refers to as a "night-watchman" role for the state, confining it to what is required to make markets work better. (Even then, the agenda was excessively narrow, paying, for instance, too little attention to the importance of financial regulation.) In Mushtaq Khan's words, this so-called "good governance" agenda is more accurately referred to as an agenda of "market-enhancing governance" that emphasizes what Thandika Mkandawire calls "restraining" as opposed to "transformative" institutions in Africa.[26] The focus of GG is on public governance related to bureaucratic hurdles, corruption, feeble enforcement of contracts and other laws, and generally poor implementation of the sort of policy initiatives that were mostly directed at reducing the role of the state.

To be sure, corruption and lack of competence of state institutions can lead to bad economic outcomes. (And this is not only true in developing countries: the failure of central banks in the developed countries to regulate adequately the financial sector were at the center of the Great Recession; and American-style corruption played a big role, as campaign contributions and revolving doors were pivotal in legislative changes that led to and supported the reckless financial sector.[27]) But the GG agenda has been used to promote a particular view of which institutions are important for development and how they should be designed:[28] a view that is embedded in neo-liberalism and its precepts on the roles of the

---

[25] It should be clear that there is not just a single, best "rule of law," and that developing countries in Africa should be wary about adopting wholesale legal frameworks from an advanced industrial country. The appropriate legal framework should be particularly attentive towards promoting development. (See Kennedy and Stiglitz, 2013)

[26] See Meles Zenawi (2012), Mushtaq Khan (2012), and Thandika Mkandawire (2012).

[27] Of course, as in Africa, ideas mattered as well: many of the regulators in the developed countries suffered from cognitive capture just as they did in the developing world.

[28] As a specific example: it was often argued with the GG agenda that there should be independent central banks focusing (exclusively) on inflation. While this particular institutional view was questioned

state and markets, and a view that gives short shrift to other institutional arrangements, such as the role of cooperatives and other not-for-profit institutions.[29]

This view is profoundly ahistorical. It sees flawed public institutions as hindrances to markets performing in the way the neo-liberalism presumes that they perform when they are unencumbered. It fails to pay attention to institutions that can improve on or substitute for markets (e.g. by addressing market failures).

An influential argument for the importance of the standard GG agenda is based on statistical relationship between growth and governance as measured by the standard indicators. But it is highly questionable whether there is in fact a meaningful statistical relationship. More precisely, Khan (2012) shows that developing countries can be divided into high-growth "converging" economies and low-growth "diverging" economies, and that within each group there is no relationship between growth and these measures of governance. And a look at the factors that could explain whether a country is in the high or low performing group suggests that GG is unlikely to be a decisive factor. Indeed, it may well be that causality runs the other way: for instance, when a country is doing poorly, public officials are poorly paid, and that makes them more susceptible to corruption.

The eminently desirable ends that the GG agenda encapsulates may well be good for and in turn be an outcome of development. But the GG reforms are neither necessary nor sufficient for economic success.

The GG agenda exhibited many of the same deficiencies that characterized earlier WC "reforms." Too often, too little attention was paid to how such an agenda might be implemented. It sometimes seemed as if the proponents of the agenda believed in the power of a lecture: simply explain to the country why GG is essential for growth and the country will reform. And if the country do not reform on its own, make it a condition for assistance. But why should we believe that a country without GG would suddenly get GG just because of a lecture? Unless there are more fundamental reforms in the political and economic system, deep and sustained reforms are likely to be resisted.

The previous section argued for the importance of setting priorities and sequencing of institutional reforms. The critical question, typically not addressed by the advocates of the GG agenda, is which of the reforms should be given priority, and how the prioritization and sequencing of these reforms should be meshed with other economic reforms. Arguably, no country has ever implemented the GG agenda first and then developed—neither the now-advanced economies in the past nor the rapidly transforming ones of East Asia today. This may be partly because poverty and stagnation provide a context that is inimical to a GG agenda.[30]

What is needed is not a simplistic market-enhancing, one-size-fits- all GG agenda but growth-enhancing governance. This entails a pragmatic focus on selected measures that are

---

before the 2008 crisis (Stiglitz 1998), the crisis has resulted in more extensive doubts. Countries with less independent central banks performed better than those with more independent central banks. The United States began focusing its monetary policy on *employment,* not inflation; and it was widely recognized that the excessive focus on inflation had detracted attention from a far greater risk, that of financial fragility.

[29] Bangladesh provides what is arguably the most striking example of the important role that such institutions can play as exemplified by BRAC and the Grameen Bank.

[30] See, for example, Mushtaq Khan (2012).

most relevant for the tasks at hand depending on the particular stage of development and the key issues confronting economic management. The so-called developmental states of East Asia as well as those in which development occurred before the Second World War intervened in markets successfully in ways that required governance capacities other than simply those adumbrated under the GG agenda. In saying this we echo Mariana Mazzucato's call for the state to go beyond "simply fixing 'market failures'" to become entrepreneurial and encourage and lead innovation. [31] In the next section, we show that enhancing growth entails facilitating learning and promoting economic transformation. Doing so requires explicit policies, sometimes referred to as industrial policies, though the term has come to be applied to policies that go well beyond promoting *industry*. Accordingly, growth-enhancing governance reforms should prioritize enhancing those capabilities that facilitate *learning* and the implementation of effective industrial policies. Africa has suffered because of the neglect of such considerations.

The GG agenda originated in part, as we noted earlier, as an explanation for the failure of the WC policies. If only countries had had GG, then the WC policies would have succeeded (so claim the proponents of the WC). The countries would have grown rapidly, including by attracting foreign investment in non-extractive activities. But this prediction (like the earlier prediction that the structural adjustment policies would bring growth) has been contradicted by the facts. Quite a few African countries that have made reasonable progress in implementing the GG agenda have had little or no success in attracting foreign investment in activities other than extraction of mineral resources. Domestic investment too has languished in transformational, learning-intensive sectors, especially manufacturing.

To us, this failure is not a surprise. Markets on their own typically do not manage structural transformations well, for reasons related to their inherent limitations.[32] What is needed are industrial and trade policies that promote learning, the subject to which we now turn.

46.6 STATIC EFFICIENCY VS. DYNAMIC GAINS: LEARNING, INDUSTRIAL, AND TECHNOLOGY POLICIES

Allocating a given amount of resources at a point in time in a way that is consistent with *static* efficiency, as desirable as it may seem, may actually impede development and growth. Development and growth, and societal transformation, depend on *learning*, in all of its forms—including closing the knowledge gap that separates developing and developed countries. But there may be a conflict between policies that enhance static efficiency and those that contribute to learning (see Greenwald and Stiglitz 2006, 2014). Striking the right balance is at the core of success in achieving growth and development. The neoliberal WC

---

[31] Mazzucato (2013).

[32] Many of which we have referred to earlier, e.g. imperfections of capital and risk markets. Gaffeo (2012) and Yoshi (2012) explain how these imperfections give rise to labor market frictions, impeding structural transformation.

policies paid no attention to learning, seemingly unaware of the potential conflict, and thus failed to strike the right balance.

Patent laws illustrate the trade-off: they restrict the availability of knowledge, a public good, and confer monopoly power, thus entailing static inefficiency but the rationale for these "distortions" is that the resulting loss in static efficiency will be more than offset by the dynamic gains from investment in new technologies that they encourage.[33] Patents also, of course, give rise to rents—a forceful demonstration that rent seeking can be channeled in ways that promote economic progress.[34] Building governance capabilities to ensure that rent seeking is so directed ought to be a vital aim of reforms that serve to move the economy to a sustained, higher growth path.

Industrial policy in the broad sense in which the term has come to be used refers to any actions that aims to alter the allocation of resources (or the choice of technology) from what the market left to itself would bring about. In this broad sense industrial policy is not confined to industry but refers also to policies aimed at other sectors, notably modern services like finance or information technology and agriculture. Indeed the green revolution in South Asia can be said to be a prime example of successful industrial policy.[35] African agriculture languished, in part because it had no such significant policy support.

In one sense, industrial policies are unavoidable: all countries have industrial policies whether they know it or not. Public expenditure (e.g. the location of highways and the design of the education system) and regulatory and legal regimes (e.g. bankruptcy law) affect the utilization of resources. Our concern here, however, is more narrow: with the deliberate actions intended to promote particular kinds of activities, especially those that have come to be referred to as "Learning, Industrial and Technology" (LIT) policies (we shall use that term interchangeably with the more familiar "industrial policy").

LIT policies are multidimensional and take many different forms across and within countries. The most famous examples are those of the so-called East Asian "developmental state" economies, especially Korea, Taiwan, Singapore, and in an earlier era Japan. Japan is by no means the only rich country today that pursued LIT policies: they were central to almost all countries that caught with the technological frontier and became developed. (Ha-Joon Chang documents this insightfully and comprehensively).[36]

There are, of course, good theoretical reasons why LIT policies are desirable. They focus on learning, especially by infant industries and economies (which are so prototypical in Africa); they address externalities, knowledge spillovers, coordination failures, and deficiencies in risk and capital markets.

They are *not* about picking winners and losers, as the issue is often misleadingly phrased. Properly designed LIT policies aim to minimize the risks of picking "losers," of state capture, and of industrial policies shifting away from their catalytic role in development and

[33] What constitutes a good patent law is another matter. The details of design make some entail more static losses and/or less dynamic gains than others. See e.g. Stiglitz.

[34] Arguably, the East Asian countries did this very successfully. See references cited in previous footnotes.

[35] In both India and Pakistan the green revolution was facilitated by policies of price support setting a floor on output prices as well as input subsidies, including notably for electricity that enhanced the profitability of tube-well irrigation.

[36] Chang, Ha-Joon (2003).

addressing deficiencies in markets. One of the major risks of LIT policies that its critics have emphasized is that such policies are vulnerable to capture and corruption. But such risks are by no means the preserve of LIT policies: as illustrated by the fact that Central banks, in the advanced industrial country were "captured" by the financial sector they were supposed to regulate.

Indeed, the agenda of liberalization and privatization in Africa, as elsewhere, which was argued for on the basis that it would limit the scope for capture and corruption, actually was captured and became the source of enormous corruption in many countries, both in the developed and developing world.[37] Frameworks were created that gave rise to enormous rents and scope for anti-competitive practices, the exploitation of workers and consumers, and market manipulation.

Indeed, in the absence of LIT policies, the emphasis on liberalization and privatization has arguably been a major source of corruption and a major impediment to development and growth. Mineral rights have been sold to foreign firms in processes that have given rise to corruption and have been totally divorced from any benefits of learning, technology acquisition, or spillovers that might have emanated from the development of these resources.[38]

The fact that there have been some "failures" in industrial policies is no more a reason for eschewing such policies than the failures in macro, monetary, and financial policies that were so evident in the run-up to the 2008 crisis is an argument against having macro-, monetary, and financial policies. In the aftermath of the 2008 crisis, we have sought to learn from those failures. So too, we should seek to learn from the failures of industrial policies. While LIT policies have risks, they also have rewards. Indeed, there are few successful economies in which governments have not pursued such policies. Arguably, Africa has paid a high price for foregoing the rewards of LIT policies.

Thus, many of the criticisms of industrial policies are fundamentally flawed. They focus on the risks and failures of industrial policies, which were deemed to be inevitably and inherently exorbitantly costly, and invariably doomed to failure. Indeed "industrial policy" acquired such bad connotations that it could be said to have become unmentionable in polite company. But Africa's experience shows the enormous price of neglecting the pursuit of these policies.[39] Elsewhere, among those that attempted such policies, there were many outstanding successes.

Still, there are many who say such policies, while they may have worked elsewhere, are inappropriate for Africa because of the failure of governance. But at the early stages of development in which the East Asian countries adopted such policies, they too had far greater deficiencies in governance than they have today.

Limitations in state capacity (deficiencies in governance) may, of course, affect the form that industrial policies take. Several African countries—Ethiopia, Kenya, Mauritius, South Africa—have shown that they can manage industrial policies and use them to enhance

[37] Stiglitz (2002) described the process of privatization in many countries as one of "briberization." Much of the inequality in wealth and income that has become such a subject of concern in recent years and which Stiglitz (2010) has argued has had significant adverse effects on growth and economic performance, arose out of these poorly designed privatizations.

[38] See Jourdan (2014) for an excellent discussion how the development of natural resources can be the basis of broader based growth through the design of appropriate industrial policies.

[39] See Lin and Stiglitz (2014).

growth. These success stories show the potential, and they highlight the importance of the growth-enhancing GG agenda that we stressed in the previous section.

46.7 FINANCE AND SELECTED OTHER ISSUES

The availability of finance on appropriate terms is a key element of success with LIT policies and indeed more generally it is necessary to promote growth. The financial crisis of 2008 and the ensuing recession have drawn attention to the issue of making finance serve the economy rather than the other way round. In Africa, the reforms of the financial sector combined with macroeconomic stability served to do away with the highly negative real interest rates that had become somewhat common in Africa.[40]

But in Africa, financial liberalization failed, not just because it led in some cases to instability, but more often than not saddled Africa with very high real interest rates and a dearth of long-term credit. At the same time the banking sector has tended to have excess liquidity, preferring short-term government securities to lending.[41]

In finance especially, the reform programs of Africa's lost quarter century completely ignored the lessons of success in development, especially of East Asia. The analysis of the extraordinary success of East Asian economies has shown the vital role of state interventions in finance. Stiglitz and Uy (1996) and Hellman et al. (1997)[42] brought out the role of financial restraint (or mild financial repression), which held real interest rates low and enhanced access to and confidence in the financial system. They show that the system of financial restraint was highly effective in mobilizing savings—far more so than would have been the case had there been high real interest rates.

Ensuring access to long-term credit at moderate real rates, sometimes through development banks, promoted long term investments that are so essential to sustainable growth. Development banks in East Asia and elsewhere have played an important role in encouraging the kind of economic transformation based on learning and the LIT policies that we discussed above. Development banks have made important contributions in other regions at different stages: South Asia, especially India and Pakistan in the 1950s and 1960s, as well as Latin America, including notably in Brazil, Chile, and Colombia, not just in those earlier decades but also more recently.

In Africa too there is the example of the positive role played by a development bank in recent years in one of the very few economies in the region that still have such a bank: Ethiopia, where financing by the development bank was crucial to the impressive success of industrial policies that promoted the development of horticulture and manufactured leather exports.

---

[40] Note that the real interest rate in the United States and Europe in recent years has been negative. Hellman, Murdock, and Stiglitz (1997) distinguish between the potentially beneficial effects of mild financial restraint (often associated with slightly negative real interest rates) and financial repression, marked by highly negative real interest rates.

[41] Rashid (2011) documents the adverse effects of financial liberalization on the availability of loans to small and medium sized enterprises and growth.

[42] See, for example, Stiglitz and Uy (1993). See also World Bank (1993).

While there have been failures (though nothing to match the scope and breadth of the failures associated with America's banking system), there have been notable successes, and considerable learning by the most successful of such banks on how to increase the odds of success.[43] We now have a much better understanding of these lessons than we did in the era of a naïve faith in state interventions that neglected the risks of government failure. Clearly the answer is not to replace that naïve faith with another in unfettered markets that neglects the reality of market failure and the risks that it imposes on overall economic performance, and that ignores the limitations of markets, for example, in providing long-term credit or credit to SMEs. (Even the United States, with its well-developed financial markets, has found it desirable to have active state provision of credit: the Small Business Administration plays a major role in the provision of small business loans, the Export–Import Bank is a major provider of lending support, especially for exporters like Boeing, and more than 90% of all mortgages are underwritten by the Federal government).[44]

The response of the WC reform program was not to reform development banks but to dismantle them. As with LIT policies more generally, this stance against development banks made Africa pay the price of foregoing the potential rewards of development banks rather than getting the risk-reward ratio right. (This is especially true for those countries that have demonstrated a capacity to implement effective industrial policies. Countries that can do so might be expected to have the capacity to run an effective development bank.)

As with all areas of reforms and good economic management, the issue is not one of abandoning reforms but of learning lessons of successes and failures. Development banking raises governance issues that underline the salience of the "growth-enhancing governance" that we have emphasized.

46.8 CONCLUDING REMARKS

One hopes that, Africa—and the world have learned—or will do so quickly—the lesson of the lost quarter century. We have suggested that many of the policies that were pushed and the manner in which they were pushed contributed to the deindustrialization, low growth, and poor performance of Africa. There was too little attention to the benefits of "learning," too little attention to critical issues of pacing, sequencing, and the development of state capacity, including the capacity to implement growth enhancing policies; and too much faith in markets, too much faith, in particular, that markets on their own, would be efficient and stable and that they could lead to a developmental transformation.

Given the failure of the structural adjustment policies, it was natural that the reform agenda be broadened. Proper governance—both in the public and private sectors—is important for good economic performance; but we have argued that what we referred to

---

[43] In Africa, the failures often stemmed from some combination of poor governance of such banks, with loans often given on the basis of political influence rather than the merit of the project, and an economic environment characterized by macroeconomic instability, and other policy failings, especially of trade and exchange rate policies.

[44] Shahe Emran and Stiglitz provide a theoretical explanation for why, without government intervention, there will be an undersupply of loans to small businesses.

as the "good governance agenda," pushed by the international institutions, is both too narrow and too ambitious: it focuses on restraining the role of government, limiting its role to "enabling" the private sector; rather than developing the state capacities that have marked the Development State and have played such an important role in many of the most successful countries. We have argued, for instance, that industrial policies, including development banks, have played a critical role in many countries, including some in Africa, and could, in the future, play an even more important role.

We have illustrated these ideas looking at several concrete issues, in particular industrial policy and the reform of financial markets. But each area of policy can be viewed from the perspective of a *development transformation*. Consider, for instance, exchange rate policy. In natural resource-rich economies the market left to itself yields exchange rates that result in the Dutch disease—high exchange rates that inhibit both export and import competing industries. In Africa, this common problem is compounded in some heavily aid-dependent economies by aid inflows. But there are notable examples both of countries that are resource rich (Malaysia and Chile) and of those that are not (like China) that have managed their exchange rates in ways that have promoted growth and a developmental transformation.

Today is a particularly opportune time for a change in Africa's development strategy in the direction we have advocated. There are major changes occurring in the global economic landscape. China provides a very large and rapidly growing market for African exports, and not just for its natural resources. Moreover, wages in China are rising. There will be "space" in world markets for labor-intensive, simple manufactures that Africa could easily occupy, and eventually, for less labor-intensive and more complex manufacturers as well. To the extent such a window opens, it might not be for long: other low-income economies could fill the void rapidly. This enhances the urgency of the sort of trade, industrial, and financial reforms that we suggest should be high on the policy agenda of the region. This is the all more urgent given the heavy reliance of Africa's growth revival on a commodity/oil boom and the notable exceptions of Ethiopia and Rwanda, two of the fastest growing economies since 2000, which, instead of relying on natural resources, built transformational policies broadly in line with those we advocate.

Acknowledgment

Justin Lin, Célestin Monga, and other participants at an author's meeting in December 2013 in Beijing provided valuable comments that are gratefully acknowledged.

References

African Center for Economic Transformation (ACET) (2014). *African Transformation Report: Growth with Depth*. Accra and Washington, DC: ACET.

Ahluwalia, M.S. (2002). Economic Reforms in India Since 1991: Has Gradualism Worked? *Journal of Economic Perspectives*, 16(3):67–88.

Amsden, A. (2001). *The Rise of The Rest: Challenges to the West From Late-Industrializing Economies*. Oxford: Oxford University Press.

Amsden, A. (1989) *Asia's Next Giant: South Korea and Late Industrialization*. Oxford: Oxford University Press.

Chang, H.-J. (2003). *Kicking Away the Ladder: Development Strategy in Historical Perspective*. London: Anthem Press.

Charlton, A., and Stiglitz, J.E. (2013). The Right to Trade: A Report for the Commonwealth Secretariat on Aid for Trade. London: Commonwealth Secretariat.

Commission on Growth and Development (2008). *The Growth Report: Strategies for Sustained Growth and Inclusive Development*. Washington, DC: World Bank.

Gaffeo, E., Gallegati, M., and Gostoli, U. (2012). An Agent-Based 'Proof or Principle' for Walrasian Macroeconomic Theory. CEEL Working Papers 1202, Cognitive and Experimental Economics Laboratory, Department of Economics, University of Trento, Italia.

Gerschenkron, A. (1962). *Economic Development in Historical Perspective: A Book of Essays*. Cambridge, MA: Harvard University Press.

Godoy, S., and Stiglitz, J.E. (2006). Growth, Initial Conditions, Law and Speed of Privatization in Transition Countries: 11 years later, NBER working paper no. 11992 (January 2006).

Greenwald, B., and Stiglitz, J.E. (2006). Industrial Policies, the Creation of a Learning Society, and Economic Development, in J.E. Stiglitz and J.Y. Lin (eds), *The Industrial Policy Revolution I: The Role of Government Beyond Ideology*. Houndmills, New York: Palgrave Macmillan.

Greenwald, B., and Stiglitz, J.E. (2014). Learning and industrial policy: implications for Africa, in J.E. Stiglitz, J. Yifu Lin, and E. Patel (eds), *The Industrial Policy Revolution II: Africa in the 21st Century*. Houndmills, New York: Palgrave Macmillan, pp. 25–29.

Hellman, T., Murdock, K., and Stiglitz, J.E. (1997). "Financial Restraint: Toward a New Paradigm," in M. Aoki, H. Kim, and M. Okuna-Fujiwara (eds.), *The Role of Government in East Asian Economic Development*. Oxford: Clarendon Press, 1997, pp. 163–207.

Jomo, K.S., and von Arnim, R. (2012). Economic liberalization and constraints to growth in sub-Saharan Africa, in Noman et al. (eds), *Good Growth and Governance in Africa: Rethinking Development Strategies*. Oxford: Oxford University Press.

Kennedy, D., and Stiglitz, J.E. (2013). Introduction, in D. Kennedy, and J.E. Stiglitz (eds), *Law and Economic Development with Chinese Characteristics: Institutions for the 21st Century*. Oxford: Oxford University Press.

Keynes, J.M. (1936[2007]). *The General Theory of Employment, Interest and Money*. London: Macmillan.

Khan, M. (2012). Governance and growth: challenges for Africa, in A. Noman et al. (eds), *Good Growth and Governance in Africa: Rethinking Development Strategies*. Oxford: Oxford University Press.

Lipsey, R.G., Lancaster, K. (1956). The general theory of second best. *Review of Economic Studies*, 24(1):11–32.

Lin, J.Y., and Stiglitz, J.E. (eds) (2014). *The Industrial Policy Revolution: The Role of Government Beyond Ideology*. Houndmills: Palgrave Macmillan.

Mazzucato, M. (2013). *The Entrepreneurial State: Debunking Public vs. Private Sector Myths*. London: Anthem Press.

Meade, J. (1955) *The Theory of International Economic Policy: II. Trade and Welfare*. Oxford: Oxford University Press.

Mkandawire, T. (2012). Institutional monocropping and monotasking in Africa, in A. Noman et al. (eds), *Good Growth and Governance in Africa: Rethinking Development Strategies*. Oxford: Oxford University Press.

Noman, A. and Stiglitz, J.E. (2012). Strategies for African development, in A. Noman et al. (eds), *Good Growth and Governance in Africa: Rethinking Development Strategies*. Oxford: Oxford University Press.

Rashid, H. (2011). Credit to Private Sector, Interest Spread and Volatility in Credit-Flows: Do Bank Ownership and Deposits Matter? DESA Working Paper No. 105 ST/ESA/2011/DWP/105 May 2011.

Shahe Emran, M., and Stiglitz, J.E. (2009). Financial Liberalization, Financial Restraint, and Entrepreneurial Development. Available at SSRN: http://ssrn.com/abstract=1332399 or http://dx.doi.org/10.2139/ssrn.1332399.

Stiglitz, J. E. (1999). Whither Reform: Ten Years of the Transition, Annual Bank Conference on Development Economics, Washington, DC, April 28–30, 1999.

Stiglitz, J.E. (2002). New perspectives on the role of the state, in H. Lim, Ungsuh K. Park, and G.C. Harcourt (eds), *Editing Economics; Essays in Honour of Mark Perlman*. Routledge-Taylor & Francis Group.

Stiglitz, J.E. (2010). Interpreting the causes of the Great Recession of 2008, in Financial System and Macroeconomic Resilience: Revisited, *BIS Paper No. 53*, Basel, Switzerland: Bank for International Settlements, September, pp. 4–19.

Stiglitz, J.E. (2008). Is there a post-Washington Consensus consensus? in N. Serra and J.E. Stiglitz (eds), *The Washington Consensus Reconsidered: Towards a New Global Governance*. New York: Oxford University Press, 2008, pp. 41–56.

Stiglitz, J.E., Sen., A., and Fitoussi, J.P. (2009). *Mismeasuring Our Lives: Why GDP Doesn't Add Up*. New York: The New Press.

Stiglitz, J.E., Serra, N., and Spiegel, S. (2008). Introduction: from the Washington Consensus towards a new global governance, in N. Serra and J.E. Stiglitz (eds), *The Washington Consensus Reconsidered: Towards a New Global Governance*. New York: Oxford University Press, pp. 3–13.

Stiglitz, J.E., and Uy, M. (1996) Financial markets, public policy and the East Asian miracle. *World Bank Research Observer*, 1(2):249–276.

Think Africa Press (London). Interview of Shanta Devarajan by Lambert Mbom, 10/05/2013.

Wade, R. (1990). *Governing the Market: Economic Theory and the Role of the Government in East Asian Industrialization*. Princeton: Princeton University Press.

Williamson, J. (1991). What Washington means by policy reform, in J. Williamson (ed.), *Latin American Adjustment: How much Has Happened?* Washington, DC: Institute for International Economics.

Williamson, J. (2008). A short history of the Washington Consensus, in N. Serra and J.E. Stiglitz (eds), *The Washington Consensus Reconsidered: Towards a New Global Governance*. Oxford: Oxford University Press.

World Bank (1993). *The East Asian Miracle: Economic Growth and Public Policy*. Oxford: Oxford University Press.

Zenawi, M. (2012). States and markets: neoliberal limitations and the case for developmental state, in A. Noman et al. (eds), *Good Growth and Governance in Africa: Rethinking Development Strategies*. Oxford: Oxford University Press.

CHAPTER 47

THE PROSPECTS FOR AN IMMINENT DEMOGRAPHIC DIVIDEND IN AFRICA

The Case for Cautious Optimism

ALAKA M. BASU AND KAUSHIK BASU

47.1 INTRODUCTION

IN the last two decades, interest in a country's population and its implications for economic growth and development has moved from a concern with the size and distribution of a population to its composition. In particular, various studies of surges in economic development in a number of developing countries have noted the role of the *age* composition of the population during such surges. It seems to be a common theme that, demographically, what pushes a nation onto a high-growth path is not so much the growth (positive or negative) of its population as a palpable change in its age structure. When there is a rise in the proportion of the population of working age, other things being held constant, there is a fall in what is called the "dependency ratio"—the number of dependents supported by the working age population. Such a decline in dependency ratios means that more of the incomes of the working age groups can be diverted to productive investments rather than being used up in the maintenance and upkeep of the non-productive part of the population. The freeing up of these resources in turn fuels further economic growth and improves the standard of living of the general population.

Since such a change in dependency ratios is usually (but not necessarily always and not necessarily only) an outcome of falling fertility, it has also been described as a demographic dividend or a demographic bonus, because it is a gift bestowed upon a population by demographic factors. It is also called a demographic window of opportunity because it cannot last forever—once the relatively small cohort that results from reduced fertility itself reaches working age, dependency ratios will again rise unless the fertility decline is continuous so that each succeeding generation is smaller in relative size than its predecessor; which cannot happen indefinitely. Moreover, as the children from a low-fertility cohort reach working age, dependency ratios also begin to rise because they now have a relatively larger older age (i.e. non-working) population to support.

Studies of the prospects for economic development therefore need to pay attention to demographic factors as much as to economic policies and political capabilities and a host of other environmental and social correlates of development. The contribution of demographic change has been emphasized in the massive growth in gross domestic products (GDPs) that occurred in the 1980s in East Asia and in Ireland as well as many of the Latin American countries during the 1990s (see, for example, the review in Bloom and Canning 2003) and perhaps the Indian sub-continent more recently (Aiyar and Mody 2011). For many of these places, the window of opportunity has already shut, and while it was open policies and background factors have taken more or less advantage of it. Indeed, this question of strong supporting policies, related to education and human capital as well as to increased economic opportunities to absorb the productive labor of the labor force, has occupied much of the recent literature on the demographic dividend. But here we want to do something different.

In this paper, we speculate on the specific nature and possibility of a demographic dividend in Africa, independently of its potential for success once it rears its head. But we also, in the next section, discuss some of the economic implications of a demographic dividend in the specific context of Africa. We do this relatively briefly both because much of what one can say about it is relevant to economic policies in general and not related only to the demographic dividend.

47.2 THE ECONOMICS OF A DEMOGRAPHIC DIVIDEND

In this section, we focus on the nature of the economic dividend and loss possible from changing age structures. In the process we also touch briefly upon the economic determinants of these gains and losses; that is, on the background and policy factors that determine the nature and level of a realized dividend from changes in age structure.

Africa has had a good run as an economy over the last decade. Poverty, as measured by the percentage of the population living on less than US$1.25 (purchasing power parity adjusted) per day, has seen a steady decline, which was not the case earlier. In 2013, when most countries were under economic and financial strain, sub-Saharan Africa grew by a remarkable 4.7%. And according to the World Bank's most recent forecast, it will grow by 5.3% in 2014 (World Bank 2014). Of course, every forecast comes with upside and downside risks. African has in recent times relied increasingly on China in terms of both trade and capital flows. If China has a slowdown as it tries to rein in its large credit and shadow-banking sector, this could have a substantial negative impact on Africa.

On the upside, Africa as we elaborate in later sections, is at a nascent stage of a demographic bulge in the working age population. This can confer a dividend to the region's economy. However, the demographic dividend comes with its own complexities and will need nurture and complementary policies. The potential benefits of a rise in the proportion of working age population are obvious. Since the proportion of breadwinners rises during such a phase, there is a direct increase in per capita income in the economy. Secondly, there is enough evidence that the age group of roughly 20–65 years consists of the high savers in a nation (Basu 2007). Hence, one side effect of demographic dividend is a rise in the savings rate in the economy. In relatively poor nations with surplus labor, as is the case in most African economies, a rise in the savings rate translates into higher growth (Solow 1994). Further, it is possible that during such phases, there is migration of labor from rural to urban areas, which causes a concomitant rise in labor income (Basu 1997).

However, as the introduction to this paper emphasized, the demographic dividend is only a *potential* dividend. Whether these potential gains from changing age structures are realized and how they may be realized depends a lot on labor market conditions. In addition, the shift from a changed age structure brought about by falling fertility to actual gains in welfare can be thought of as being influenced by a number of socioeconomic and political factors as well as resulting in socioeconomic and political changes.

What are some of the potential problems with the rise in the proportion of working age population that a demographic dividend refers to? Two of these bear specific mention here. First, if there is a rise in the proportion of the working age population but without access to the actual work that these working age people need to immerse themselves in and need to generate the incomes and productivity that will now go into supporting the smaller number of dependents that falling fertility results in, what we could have on our hands is what the pessimists call a "youth bulge" or, more darkly, a "demographic disaster." In a situation of high unemployment, mechanical improvements in age-based dependency ratios are not a proxy for improvements in actual economic dependency ratios (Basu 2011). Worse, this surge in the relative size of the working age population, when combined with the economic and political disenfranchisement that high unemployment reflects, can be a source of political and social instability that in turn worsens economic strain.

What do employment levels and trends in Africa tell us about the possibility of such a negative demographic dividend as fertility levels begin to fall more rapidly in many parts of the continent? Unfortunately, unemployment data for developing countries are either not reported or, more alarmingly, reported. The alarm is caused by the fact that work has such varied meanings in developing countries that employment statistics are hard to interpret. The World Bank's (2013) compendium of development indicators leaves the unemployment columns for most African countries blank; this is not surprising. But some hints of the trouble that poor employment prospects coupled with large increases in the youth population can lead to appear in the rises in political instability that some of the poorest parts of the continent have seen in recent years. At the same time, even if there is a relationship, it is not clear whether it is one with rises in the *absolute* numbers of the young or their *relative* numbers. Intuitively both these rises can be expected to contribute to political and social trouble under the right conditions. But it would be unwise to take this thread any further without a more serious analysis of demographic trends and political trouble, so all we do is flag the question here.

At the same time, one needs to avoid the kind of misleading fear mongering about the rise of working age population that is seen emblazoned in headlines like "x million new jobs will need to be created each year," where x is an impressively large number. The reason this is misleading is that it creates the impression that all the new entrants into the working age population will be seekers of jobs, with the responsibility for creating jobs being with the government and international organizations. In reality, many of the new young will be entrepreneurs looking for hands to employ. Indeed, by going to the other extreme and assuming that all the new young will be entrepreneurs, the headline could be made equally alarming (and misleading) in the reverse way by saying that "y million additional workers will be needed each year."

The truth of the matter is that with the demographic dividend, Africa will have both new workers and new employers. Hence the overwhelming odds for Africa are that it will benefit from the demographic structural shift over the coming decades. The governments do not have to take on the primary responsibility for creating jobs. They will have a lot of responsibility nevertheless, but that will be more about providing an enabling ethos and an effective regulatory system, and providing for the basic needs of citizens and keeping a check on excessive inequality. Alongside this, there will be a need for governments to keep a check on the strains on the environment that will inevitably come from larger populations and greater economic activity.

The second possible economic fallout of fertility decline relates to inequality. Unless the changing age structure that frees up resources for productive investment occurs across the board, the groups that are at the forefront of the fertility decline will benefit more than the laggards, thereby worsening inequalities, given that it is usually those that are already better off that usually lead a fertility decline. So, other things remaining the same, the longer the gap in the onset of fertility decline between different groups, the greater the chances of growing socioeconomic inequality (Eloundou-Enyegue 2013). This increase in inequality can occur at regional, national, or subnational levels. For example, the earlier and more rapid falls in fertility in Northern Africa (and to some extent in Southern Africa) documented later in this paper imply that the head start that these regions have in economic conditions could become even more of a handicap to the Central and Western African countries (especially Congo, Niger, Mali, and the Gambia) that are slower to begin their fertility transition.

At the national level, if different socioeconomic groups within a country have radically different rates of fertility change these socioeconomic differentials can become exacerbated as the groups with more fertility declines have more resources to invest into productively gains. For example, Demographic and Health Surveys data suggest that in Liberia and Zambia the total fertility rate of the lowest socioeconomic group is at least 2.5 times that of the highest groups (Eloundou-Enyegue 2013), a difference that has the potential to dramatically widen the socioeconomic gap between groups.

This widening can become even more severe in the long run as countries or groups get ready to benefit from the gains of what has been called the *second* demographic dividend—the stage during which the children of low-fertility cohorts grow up and enter the labor force. The children from these cohorts will be more productive than their peers from high-fertility parents since they should have had more invested in their education and health just because there were fewer of them.

Government policies can mitigate some of this inequality potential in two ways: (i) by investing in health and family planning services that make fertility decline more universal within a country or region rather than confined to the better off; and (ii) by investing in the health and education of *all* children, those from low-fertility as well as high-fertility families, so that at working age there is a reduced gap in potential productivity. That is, if it is a benign state rather than private family resources that provides for child education and health, the gains of reduced fertility can be less lopsidedly invested. In addition, if the fertility decline is large or widespread enough to generate greater savings that can be deployed in higher investment, the changing age structure in some groups of a population can benefit the prospects of an entire population even as it waits for the laggards to begin their own fertility decline.

At the same time, there is a positive caveat to the inequality question. Africa is a large and diverse continent and there is at least one way in which the absence of simultaneous and rapid fertility declines across the continent may be good for the economy. As the forerunners of the fertility decline (in this case the northern and southern regions of Africa) begin to reach the end of their demographic dividend and begin to actually experience a labor shortage, this shortage can conceivably be met by the relatively large working age population of the slow fertility decline countries or regions. Naturally this depends on the ease of migration, the match between the skills demanded by host countries and available in sending countries, and so on; but in principle at least, some of the pressures of continuing high fertility can be absorbed by countries with sustained fertility decline more easily within Africa than they can be when migrants have to cross continents and greater cultural divides for work. Something like this certainly has happened and is happening in India, where the labor shortages of the low-fertility southern part of the country are being increasingly met by migration of labor from the high-fertility central states, to the benefit of both regions.

The logic of differential fertility already explains a part of the contemporary migration from Africa into the industrialized countries. Many of these host countries are experiencing a rise in their older populations at the same time as long declining fertility has reduced the relative size of their labor force, and the still growing youth populations of Africa are stepping in to fill this gap. Given the political, physical, and economic challenges to this kind of intercontinental migration, inequalities in the timing of the demographic dividend within Africa should make things easier for both sending and receiving countries within the region. As it is, intraregional migration accounts for half of all migration from African countries; this figure is even higher—about 65%—for migration from sub-Saharan countries (Ratha et al. 2011). With the right policies this preference for relatively short distance and relatively culturally homogeneous migration can be exploited for the economic development of the continent, at least in the short run when there are labor shortages in some countries and labor surpluses in others.

Of course all of this assumes that the resources freed up by falling dependency ratios at the national or family level do get used productively (for the short, as in through infrastructure or job creation for example, or long, as in through greater investments in human capital, run). If instead the savings are used largely for present consumption by either, or both, families or the state, then the demographic dividend can be at best a very short-term gain.

In sum, the state's responsibility in harnessing a demographic dividend will be for the gamut of what is called development policy to facilitate a society's taking advantage of the natural benefits from a demographic dividend. That is, the demographic dividend merely provides a favorable background for economic development. How this (temporarily) favorable background is exploited depends crucially on the framing and execution of development policy.

However, we will not do much more than flag these questions here as central to any speculation on the relationship between demographic and age structure change and economic development in Africa. Instead, the next sections of this paper focus on the first piece of the process—on our reasons for expecting the demographic and age structure changes that create a demographic dividend to become more easily and quickly visible in Africa in the coming years.

47.3 THE PROSPECTS FOR A DEMOGRAPHIC DIVIDEND IN AFRICA

We ask the following question in the rest of this paper: Is there a demographic dividend already on the scene in some parts of Africa. And where there is not, is there one on the horizon? On both these questions, we challenge the current pessimism about high African population growth using the past experience of demographic change in other parts of the world and the current state of fertility in Africa to make the case for a cautious optimism about the arrival of the demographic dividend on the continent.

Our contingent optimism is based on the recent evidence of fertility decline, on recent changes in some of the determinants of fertility decline, and on some background cultural conditions in many parts of Africa that have the potential to magnify the impact of a demographic dividend once it does occur. We also comment on the fortuitous combination of current national and international policy processes that make fertility decline, and therefore more advantageous population age structures, more possible in Africa today than would have been the case a decade or two ago.

One unsurprising but important finding that emerges from our perusal of the data on all these matters is that the truism that Africa is a continent and not a country is literally true as well as true in the often vast regional and country differentials that exist in all our indicators and therefore predict important continuing differentials in the emergence and speed of emergence of a demographic dividend. At the same time we want to make the case that perhaps this moment in time is one that is most capable of narrowing these differentials if the bull is taken by the horns so to speak.

Thinking about the demographic dividend is also a way of addressing the underlying pessimism in the newly revised population projections from the United Nations, which have received wide public attention. The September 2013 revision of the 2012 projections now expects the global population to reach about 9.6 billion in 2050, compared to its earlier estimate of 9.3 billion (United Nations 2011, 2013). Almost all this extra growth is expected to come from Africa, where, according to the UN Population Division, population growth rates have not subsided as much as had been expected and where, in some cases there has actually been a rise in fertility, so that the projection for Africa for 2050 of 2.19 billion made in 2010 has been revised in 2012 to 2.39 billion. The point we make here is that both these factors—the slower decline in fertility and possible rises in some places (which are related but not completely the same thing) are in fact signals that we could see significant declines in each of these factors in the coming years. Which also means that perhaps we can anticipate the appearance of an important demographic dividend in Africa in the not too distant future.

47.3.1 Trends in the emergence of the demographic dividend in Africa

Before we talk about future prospects, what does the demographic dividend in Africa look like just now? Table 47.1 uses a proxy for dependency ratios—the proportion of the

Table 47.1 Population aged 20–64 years (% of total population)

	1980	1990	2000	2010	Total population, 2010
Eastern Africa	**40.56**	**40.00**	**40.39**	**41.51**	**342 595 134**
Burundi	41.52	40.02	36.32	42.27	9 232 753
Comoros	41.04	41.20	43.60	45.28	683 081
Djibouti	39.65	41.94	45.15	50.69	834 036
Eritrea	41.47	41.19	39.00	44.16	5 741 159
Ethiopia	42.23	40.33	39.53	40.98	87 095 281
Kenya	36.39	37.27	41.09	44.30	40 909 194
Madagascar	39.89	40.91	41.69	42.81	21 079 532
Malawi	40.08	41.34	40.87	39.88	15 013 694
Mauritius	49.39	55.74	59.49	62.89	1 230 659
Mayotte	36.40	39.25	42.13	43.28	204 353
Mozambique	42.95	39.07	42.44	40.98	23 967 265
Réunion	45.11	53.01	56.04	58.16	844 579
Rwanda	39.18	37.64	38.22	43.55	10 836 732
Seychelles	43.44	48.39	54.23	62.00	91 208
Somalia	42.80	41.84	39.93	39.00	9 636 173
South Sudan	42.78	42.59	42.19	42.79	9 940 929
Uganda	39.53	38.85	37.25	37.61	33 987 213
United Republic of Tanzania	40.44	40.64	41.34	41.50	44 973 330
Zambia	39.59	40.20	40.44	39.79	13 216 985
Zimbabwe	37.29	39.95	41.66	42.40	13 076 978
Middle Africa	**41.95**	**40.83**	**40.25**	**40.90**	**124 977 662**
Angola	40.35	39.75	39.35	39.23	19 549 124
Cameroon	41.86	40.01	40.30	42.31	20 624 343
Central African Republic	43.70	42.52	42.81	44.66	4 349 921
Chad	41.65	39.18	37.67	37.73	11 720 781
Congo	41.32	41.86	43.73	44.38	4 111 715
Democratic Republic of the Congo	42.32	41.37	40.40	40.87	62 191 161
Equatorial Guinea	36.70	49.25	45.36	47.47	696 167
Gabon	46.20	43.05	43.15	45.61	1 556 222
Sao Tome and Principe	37.31	36.56	38.78	44.16	178 228
Southern Africa	**44.32**	**46.28**	**51.67**	**54.38**	**58 802 729**
Botswana	40.26	41.76	46.66	50.99	1 969 341
Lesotho	40.70	40.72	42.48	45.98	2 008 921
Namibia	39.68	41.74	45.60	47.22	2 178 967
South Africa	44.92	47.05	52.77	55.36	51 452 352
Swaziland	37.79	38.38	40.13	44.95	1 193 148
Western Africa	**42.61**	**41.45**	**42.38**	**42.94**	**305 088 164**
Benin	40.99	40.29	41.17	42.99	9 509 798
Burkina Faso	40.73	38.84	39.28	40.64	15 540 284
Cape Verde	34.74	39.16	41.15	50.30	487 601
Côte d'Ivoire	42.91	42.74	44.36	44.44	18 976 588
Gambia	43.20	41.27	40.32	40.95	1 680 640
Ghana	41.08	42.51	44.64	46.74	24 262 901

(*continued*)

Table 47.1 Continued

	1980	1990	2000	2010	Total population, 2010
Guinea	45.07	43.02	42.18	43.27	10 876 033
Guinea-Bissau	44.25	39.99	42.46	44.40	1 586 624
Liberia	42.35	41.53	42.76	43.50	3 957 990
Mali	43.09	38.96	39.32	39.89	13 985 961
Mauritania	40.97	41.42	43.30	45.86	3 609 420
Niger	40.88	40.28	39.89	37.74	15 893 746
Nigeria	43.23	41.87	42.79	43.00	159 707 780
Senegal	40.65	39.09	40.35	42.31	12 950 564
Sierra Leone	43.71	41.82	43.30	44.93	5 751 976
Togo	40.55	40.10	41.48	44.39	6 306 014
Northern Africa	**42.08**	**44.30**	**48.13**	**53.65**	**199 619 977**
Algeria	39.48	41.87	49.45	58.21	37 062 820
Egypt	44.45	45.96	48.19	53.37	78 075 705
Libya	40.86	43.94	50.78	56.53	6 040 612
Morocco	40.84	45.01	49.75	56.71	31 642 360
Sudan	39.76	40.67	42.52	44.18	35 652 002
Tunisia	42.80	47.43	53.13	60.46	10 631 830

Source: United Nations, Department of Economic and Social Affairs, Population Division (2013). World Population Prospects: The 2012 Revision, DVD edition.

population of working age, taken to be 20-64—in the different countries of Africa. While most official agencies provide labor force statistics for the 15+ population, one of the features of development is surely to increase the human resources of a population, which in turn means increasing the number of years of education significantly. If that kind of development accompanies the demographic dividend in Africa (or anywhere in the world for that matter), then we may be looking at somewhat lower labor force participation rates if we continue to use the 15+ cut-off. Our labor statistics will have to be focused on the 20+ age group. In addition, with increasing longevity, a cut-off of 59 for labor force participation looks increasingly untenable. That is why Table 47.1 uses this slightly unusual 20–64 grouping.

The most important finding here is that, except for the countries of Northern Africa and a little bit for the countries on Southern Africa, favorable changes in this proportion are incipient at best. In several cases, we even have a *decline* in the proportion of working age population in the 1980s and 1990s. But we do not view this finding with as much disappointment as it might warrant in a casual observer of the data, because we try to look *behind* the figures and conclude that (i) some of the slow pace of change is for positive factors like major falls in child mortality, and (ii) some of it may be due to increases in fertility, but (iii) in both these cases there cannot but be soon enough a compensating fall in fertility. In addition, real dependency ratios will improve further as (i) adult mortality (especially from HIV/AIDS) also falls further, and (ii) as African women, who already have a long history of participation in the labor force, become more productive as their birth rates fall.

In the next few sections, we elaborate on all these hypotheses and try to justify what we call our "cautious optimism."

47.3.2 Africa and the preconditions for fertility decline

In a seminal paper, Ansley Coale (1973) identified three broad "preconditions" for a sustained and significant fertility decline to occur in any society. These are:

1. The idea of fertility control has to enter the calculus of conscious choice. This phrase, the calculus of conscious choice, has acquired iconic status in the field of demography and refers to the change in social conditions from a situation in which reproduction and childbearing and numbers of children are treated as (if they are consciously thought about at all) matters for some higher authority to determine to one in which it becomes something on which in principle at least individuals and couples can exercise some control.
2. The advantages of fewer births should outweigh the disadvantages and/or should be perceived by couples to be so.
3. The means to achieve fewer births than before should be available.

For birth rates to come down, all three conditions need to be met; too often either one or two of them is not. In a slightly different formulation, Lesthaeghe and Vanderhoeft (2001) described this situation as one in which couples were "ready, willing and able" to practice birth control, by whatever means.

Looking at Africa today, on the whole one might say that condition 1 has already been met; indeed the global push towards family planning programs since the middle of the twentieth century means that there is hardly any part of the world any more in which families do not know that it is possible to choose one's numbers of births. As we discuss in a later section, at the present time, with a new international effort to increase access to contraception in the developing world, condition 3 is also coming closer to be met.

So it is condition 2, really, the evolving rationale for fewer births, that will determine the timing and speed of a fertility decline in the African countries and in the following section, we focus on one of the central motivations for such a rationale—significant perceived improvements in child survival.

47.3.2.1 Mortality decline as a precondition for fertility decline

In the large and sometimes contentious literature on the preconditions for fertility decline—Is it the costs of children that matter more, or the benefits? Are children needed for old age security or to satisfy one's ancestors? Do opportunities for women's education lower fertility more or opportunities for women's employment?, and so on—if there is one precondition that no one argues about, it is a decline in mortality. Until parents can feel more confident that their offspring will survive to adulthood, the premise is, they will feel obliged to have larger numbers of births to guard against the few that must inevitably die in childhood.

Indeed, traditional demographic transition theory is built around the idea that as societies modernize, first mortality falls, and then, usually after a lag, fertility decline takes off. Further theorizing talks about the evolutionary reasons for this ordering of demographic change and the micro-compulsions that persuade families to reduce fertility as mortality levels fall. Empirically, too, barring a few small examples from historical Europe, there is no evidence of significant *voluntary* declines in fertility in the face of continuing high mortality, high childhood mortality in particular.

What does this theory and empirical evidence say about the prospects for fertility decline in Africa in the near future? Table 47.2 displays trends in child mortality rates since the 1980s. After very little progress during the 1980s and often even the 1990s, the new century has thus far seen remarkable declines in the probability of a child dying by the age of 5 in country after country. At least partly this is a result of the impetus given to attempts to improve child survival thanks to the Millennium Development Goals (MDG) project.

Of course there is still a long way to go and except for the countries of Northern Africa (barring Sudan) and Mauritius, nowhere has the child mortality rate dropped below 50. The conflict-ridden states do especially poorly and underline once more how important political stability is for the well-being of the vulnerable. What is possible is of course not always (or even usually) what is probable, but the pace of decline in the last decade suggests that the next ten years could conceivably see even faster rates of reduction than the rate shown for the last 20 years in the last column of Table 47.2.

If that happens, there will indeed be a rise in dependency ratios as the child population swells (this time due to fewer child deaths rather than to more child births) but all past experience suggests that this will be a very temporary phenomenon and will soon be more than compensated by the decline in birth rates that tends universally to follow major declines in child mortality rates. Indeed, it is very likely this initial rise in child population due to falling mortality that accounts for at least some of the slow rise in the proportion of the working age population in Table 47.1.

So we are inclined to convert some of the pessimism about dependency ratios falling too slowly into optimism about the future given this particular reason for the slow rise.

Such optimism is also generated by the important changes in adult mortality that are taking place in Africa, thanks mainly to a greater control of the HIV/AIDS epidemic. To the extent that HIV disproportionately affects young adults, reducing this spread means increasing the numbers of working age (and working, since the illness is so often debilitating) individuals; in turn, this should change dependency ratios in a favorable direction more quickly than the fertility decline that will do so after a lag as it compensates for better child survival.

Data on trends in prevalence rates of HIV/AIDs indicate that the rise in prevalence until 2000 has in the last decade actually shown a slow but steady decline. This is a very good sign, even if the prevalence rates are falling more slowly than we like, because one reason for the continued high prevalence is the larger numbers of young adults now living with the infection rather than dying of it. This becomes clearer from incidence rates; incidence measures the presence of new cases of the infection and here the declines in the last decade are much sharper.

To sum, trends in mortality are good news for the demographic dividend in the short run because of falling adult mortality and then become good news in the longer run too as falling child mortality ignites falling fertility.

Table 47.2 Trends in childhood mortality

	1980	Under five mortality rate 1990	2000	2012	Annual rate of reduction 1990-2012
Eastern Africa					
Burundi	199	164	150	104	2.1
Comoros	165	124	99	78	2.1
Djibouti	205	119	108	81	1.8
Eritrea	192	150	89	52	4.8
Ethiopia	212	204	146	68	7.9
Kenya	115	98	110	73	1.4
Madagascar	175	159	109	58	4.6
Malawi	255	244	174	71	5.6
Mauritius	40	23	19	15	1.9
Mozambique	235	233	166	90	4.3
Réunion					
Rwanda	209	151	182	55	4.6
Somalia		177	171	147	0.8
Tanzania					
Uganda	172	178	147	69	4.3
Zambia	155	192	169	89	3.5
Zimbabwe	116				
Middle Africa					
Angola	265	213	203	164	1.2
Cameroon	173	135	150	95	1.6
Central African Republic	188	171	164	129	1.3
Chad	228	209	189	150	1.5
Congo	104	100	118	96	0.2
Democratic Republic of the Congo	213	171	171	146	0.7
Equatorial Guinea		182	143	100	2.7
Gabon	116	92	86	62	1.8
Northern Africa					
Algeria	134	50	35	20	4.1
Egypt	176	86	45	21	6.4
Libya	70	43	28	15	4.7
Morocco	144	80	50	31	4.3
Sudan	136	128	106	73	2.6
Tunisia	100	51	30	16	
Western Sahara					
Southern Africa					
Botswana	82	48	85	53	(-)0.5
Lesotho	132	85	114	100	(-)0.7
Namibia	98	73	73	39	2.9
South Africa	90	61	74	45	1.4
Swaziland	138	71	121	80	(-)0.5

(continued)

Table 47.2 Continued

	1980	Under five mortality rate			Annual rate of reduction 1990-2012
		1990	2000	2012	
Western Africa					
Benin	212	181	147	90	3.2
Burkina Faso	240	202	186	102	3.1
Cabo Verde	80	62	38	22	4.6
Cote d'Ivoire	168	152	145	108	1.6
Gambia	214	170	116	73	3.8
Ghana	150	128	103	72	2.6
Guinea	277	241	171	101	3.9
Guinea-Bissau		206	174	129	2.1
Liberia	240	248	176	75	5.4
Mali	300	253	220	128	3.1
Mauritania	155	128	111	84	1.9
Niger	310	326	227	114	4.8
Nigeria	228	213	188	124	2.5
Senegal	213	142	139	60	3.9
Sierra Leone	318	257	234	182	1.6
Togo	176	143	122	96	1.8

Source: 1980, World Bank; 1990, 2000, 2010, UN Inter-Agency Group for Child Mortality Estimation.

47.3.3 Other reasons for cautious optimism

47.3.3.1 *The African advantage in timing*

In a recent paper, Bongaarts (2013) looks at the timing of the onset of fertility decline in Africa to find three important differences with fertility decline in Asia and Latin America in the twentieth century:

1. Fertility decline began in Africa much later (in the 1980s and 1990s, compared to the 1960s and 1970s in Asia and Latin Africa).
2. Fertility decline in Africa began at lower levels of national development than it did in these other regions.
3. However, once begun, the pace of decline was slower in Africa than it was in these other regions.

The first point above is consistent with the fact that socioeconomic development in Africa took off later than it did in Asia and Latin America. The second finding is consistent with the fact that social change (which is largely what fertility decline exemplifies) in the latecomers is usually helped by learning from the experience of the forerunners. And the third point raises (although Bongaarts does not specifically address this) questions about the role of active voluntary family programs in hastening the speed of decline once it has begun. The 1980s and 1990s were for a variety of reasons a period during which the world lost interest in family planning (compared to the often excessive enthusiasm for it in the 1960s and 1970s) an it is possible that the African fertility decline, beginning as it did during this same period) suffered from the lack of facilitating conditions that such programs might provide.

Fortunately, and perhaps precisely because fertility declines have been slow or stalled in many parts of Africa, after a period of relative hiatus, global and national interest in non-coercive but proactive family planning programs has experienced a major upswing in recent years. While some would say that high fertility in Africa only demonstrates that the supply of family planning cannot create a demand (see, for example, Pritchett 1994), other research suggests that while existing demand is important, family planning programs still have a very important role to play in both hastening and sometimes directing the speed of fertility declines (see, for example, Bongaarts 1994; Tsui 2001; Bongaarts 2011). If one accepts this second view, then being on the cusp of a demographic dividend at this time is in Africa's favor: the easier and more officially committed access to contraceptive advice and services in this decade will at the very least do much to reduce the unmet need for family planning that exists in many parts of the developing world even after more than a half century of official family planning programs.

Table 47.3 demonstrates both the progress (sometimes very slow) that has been made as well as the challenges that remain. Couple Protection Rates (or CPRs: the use of contraception by sexually married couples) have risen uniformly in most countries. Among the larger countries in which it has not risen appreciably is Nigeria and Table 47.3 highlights the need for greater effort in this case.

The figures for unmet need for contraception (the proportion of couples who do not want another child ever or at least at the moment, but is not doing anything to prevent a pregnancy) in the second third of Table 47.3 tell us another part of the story. In all parts of Africa, the unmet need for contraception is high. Even in Nigeria, 13% of non-contracepting couples do not want another child and 6 percent of non-contracepting couples want to delay the next birth. If all these couples could be helped to achieve this wish to not become pregnant, birth rates in this country would fall significantly and perhaps temper the current pessimism of global population projections since expectations for Nigeria contribute significantly to this pessimism.

Using Table 47.3, one way of classifying the countries in Africa in terms of their potential to move quickly towards a demographic dividend (see Table 47.4) might be based on whether they have a high (>30%) level of contraceptive use and whether they have a high (>15%) level of unmet need for contraception, in the following way:

A. High CPR/Low Unmet Need: These countries are already on their way to achieving significant fertility decline and need mainly support to maintain the situation. While all these countries are in Northern Africa (Egypt, Morocco, Tunisia) or in Southern Africa (South Africa, Swaziland), several countries in Eastern Africa (Kenya, Uganda, Rwanda, Zambia, Zimbabwe) are getting close to entering this A category; this movement can also be gauged from the relatively sharp declines they have experienced in the levels of unmet need since the 1990s.

Not only do these countries offer leadership in actualizing a demographic dividend, their experience can also offer lessons to the countries in category B. In particular the

Table 47.3 Trends in fertility and contraceptive use

	Couple Protection Rate (CPR)		Unmet Need for FP		Total Fertility Rate		
	Around 1990	Around 2010	1990s	2000s	1990	2000	2010
Eastern Africa							
Burundi	8	22	25	29	7.54	7.06	6.30
Comoros	21	26	36		5.57	5.32	4.92
Djibouti		18			6.09	4.47	3.60
Eritrea	8	8	30	29	6.49	5.94	4.97
Ethiopia	5	29	37	25	7.25	6.53	4.90
Kenya	33	46	38	26	6.04	5.01	4.62
Madagascar	17	40	32	19	6.26	5.55	4.65
Malawi	13	46	37	26	7.00	6.25	5.64
Mauritius	75	76	6	4	2.32	1.99	1.47
Mozambique	6	12	25	19	6.24	5.78	5.41
Rwanda	21	52	38	19	7.27	5.90	4.84
Somalia	8	15			7.40	7.61	6.87
Tanzania					6.21	5.69	5.43
Uganda	5	30	30	38	7.09	6.87	6.16
Zambia	15	41	30	27	6.47	6.07	5.81
Zimbabwe	43	59	19	16	5.18	4.07	3.72
Southern Africa							
Botswana	33	53	27		4.70	3.41	2.76
Lesotho	23	47		23	4.92	4.09	3.21
Namibia	29	55	22	21	5.23	4.03	3.23
South Africa	50	60	17	14	3.66	2.87	2.47
Swaziland	20	65		13	5.74	4.21	3.56
Central Africa							
Angola	8	6			7.17	6.84	6.22
Cameroon	16	23	22	21	6.43	5.62	5.02
Central African Republic	15	19	19		5.78	5.45	4.63
Chad	4	3	17	21	7.31	7.35	6.60
Congo, Rep.		45		20	5.35	5.13	5.07
Congo, Dem. Rep.	8	18	27	24	7.13	7.09	6.25
Equatorial Guinea	2	9	25	22	5.90	5.77	5.14
Gabon		33		28	5.42	4.60	4.21
Northern Africa							
Algeria	51	61			4.76	2.51	2.82
Egypt, Arab Rep.	48	60	23	12	4.35	3.31	2.88
Libya	45				4.97	3.05	2.53
Morocco	42	63	24	12	4.06	2.70	2.58

Table 47.3 Continued

	Couple Protection Rate (CPR)		Unmet Need for FP		Total Fertility Rate		
	Around 1990	Around 2010	1990s	2000s	1990	2000	2010
Sudan	10	9	29	29	6.15	5.44	4.64
Tunisia	50	60		12	3.54	2.08	2.13
Western Africa							
Benin	16	17	28	27	6.74	5.98	5.10
Burkina Faso	8	16	25	30	7.01	6.59	5.87
Cape Verde	24	61	14	17	5.31	3.70	2.43
Cote d'Ivoire	11	13	30		6.36	5.38	4.91
Gambia	12	18			6.11	5.92	5.80
Ghana	17	24	37	36	5.62	4.67	4.05
Guinea	2	9	25	22	6.58	5.94	5.17
Guinea-Bissau		14			6.65	5.85	5.12
Liberia	6	11	33	36	6.50	5.88	5.02
Mali	5	8	21	20	7.06	6.84	6.84
Mauritania	4	9		32	5.98	5.38	4.84
Niger	4	11	19	16	7.76	7.73	7.58
Nigeria	6	14	22	19	6.49	6.10	6.02
Senegal	7	13	37	29	6.63	5.56	5.05
Sierra Leone	3	8		28	6.53	5.92	4.94
Togo	34	15	28	19	6.33	5.29	4.79

Source: CPR and Unmet Need: United Nations Population Division online; TFR: World Bank, Gender Statistics.

remarkable recent progress in Rwanda in improving access to voluntary family planning shows that policy can make a difference.

B. High CPR/High Unmet Need: All that these countries are waiting for is good family planning programs; obviously a demand for them exists and the high levels of simultaneous contraceptive use even with simultaneously high unmet need suggests that there are few entrenched barriers to contraceptive practice. It is not surprising that many of the countries in this category are in Eastern Africa (Kenya, Madagascar, Malawi), given the lead provided by their neighbors (Rwanda, Zambia and Zimbabwe) as discussed. For the same reason, nor is it surprising that the rest of the countries here are in Southern Africa (Botswana, Lesotho, Namibia).

C. Low CPR/High Unmet Need: These are the countries where a demand for lower fertility exists but where meeting this demand faces important structural or cultural barriers, as reflected in the low overall levels of contraceptive use. Most of these countries are in Middle Africa or Western Africa and most of them are relatively small in overall population size. Among the larger countries in category C, one (Ethiopia) is in Eastern Africa and seems to be rapidly catching up with its neighbors, three (Cameroon, Democratic Republic of the Congo and Sudan) are in Middle Africa and the rest in Western Africa (Burkina Faso, Cote d'Ivoire, Ghana, Mali, Niger, and Nigeria). Except for Nigeria, both contraceptive use rates and unmet needs trends provide some evidence of recent success and the new Gates Foundation inspired Family Planning 20/20 initiative will hopefully come up with the programmatic innovations and communication strategies to accelerate these trends.

Unfortunately, the largest country in Africa, Nigeria with a population of 162 million, bucks all these trends and is likely to pull down averages for the region for a considerable more time. However, even here, the latest projections from the United Nations foresee a gradual rise in the proportion of the population of working age and given the theories of the global diffusion of the motivations for fertility decline, perhaps Nigeria will still turn out to be one of those later-but-faster birth rate decliners.

D. Low CPR/Low Unmet Need: The good news is that no country in Africa today falls in this disappointing category. Perhaps Niger, with a population of 16 million, comes closest to still belonging to this category, but even here the trends are not hopeless. On the whole, where contraceptive use is still to pick up, the unmet need is high and often rising (meaning an increase in demand) and where the unmet need is low, contraceptive use is high (meaning a satisfied demand).

Table 47.4 Countries classified according to potential for fertility decline

A. High CPR (>30%; Low Unmet Need (<15%)
Eastern Africa: Mauritius
Middle Africa: XX
Northern Africa: Egypt, Morocco, Tunisia
Southern Africa: South Africa, Swaziland
Western Africa: XX

B. High CPR (>30%; High Unmet Need (>15%)
Eastern Africa: Kenya, Madagascar, Malwai, Rwanda*, Uganda, Zambia, Zimbabwe*
Middle Africa: Congo, Gabon
Northern Africa: XX
Southern Africa: Botswana*, Lesotho, Namibia
Western Africa: Benin

C. Low CPR (<30%); High Unmet Need (>15%)
Eastern Africa: Burundi, Comoros, Eritrea, Ethiopia*, Mozambique
Middle Africa: Cameroon, Chad, Democratic Republic of the Congo, Equatorial Guinea
Northern Africa: Sudan
Southern Africa: XXZ
Western Africa: Burkina Faso, Cote d'Ivoire, Ghana*, Guinea, Liberia, Mali, Mauritania, Niger**, Nigeria**, Senegal, Sierra Leone, Togo

D. Low CPR (<30%); Low Unmet Need (<15%)
Eastern Africa: XX
Middle Africa: XX
Northern Africa: XX
Southern Africa: XX
Western Africa: XX

Source: Derived from Table 47.3;
* close to entering one category up;
** close to belonging to one category down; XX: none.

This new commitment to good voluntary family planning services is already evident in many countries in Africa and also already showing impressive results in some of them. The two countries repeatedly cited as examples of both today are Ethiopia and Rwanda, where through a mix of innovative interventions (such as using community level family planning workers and/or home visits by family planning workers, as well as guaranteed supplies of contraceptive methods), rapid increases in contraceptive use and rapid declines in fertility no longer appear impossible to achieve.

At the end of this section, one must however return to another important finding in the last third of Table 47.3, which will make one pessimistic or optimistic depending partly on one's disposition. This is the fact that while the trends in fertility displayed in the last three columns of the table are consistent with the sharp increases in contraceptive use seen in the same table for the countries of Southern Africa, in Eastern Africa, on the other hand, the impressive increases in CPRs do not seem to be accompanied by equally impressive declines in fertility. Here even many of the countries that have reached CPR levels of 40–50 percent still have total fertility rates around 5. This inconsistency is not unexpected to the demographer familiar with African social practices. What we may be seeing is the next step from the initial pretransition fertility increases discussed in the next section.

47.3.3.2 *The counter-intuitive fact of pre-decline increases in fertility*

When Coale (1973) and others theorized about the preconditions for fertility decline, they were looking at the kinds of intuitive as well as empirical changes that occurred in people's lives that then made them choose to reduce the number of births and children they wanted and therefore bore. Later research however (see in particular Nag 1980; Dyson and Murphy 1985) found another interesting feature of the situation at the onset of a sustained fertility decline in historical as well as contemporary populations. This was an almost universal, relatively short but still noticeable *rise* in birth rates before the fertility transition actually took off. It is not possible to definitively attribute cause and effect to this phenomenon or to call such rises in fertility a precondition for fertility decline, but it is not inconsistent with such hypotheses either as we expand later in this section.

In the case of Africa, while none of the TFR trends in Table 47.3 show a rise in fertility, the relatively slow pace of decline in overall fertility at the national level is at least partly a result of rises in the fertility of sub-groups of the population. Disaggregated fertility estimates from the demographic and health surveys find such a rise in fertility, sometimes in the recent past, sometimes currently, for such groups, and especially so for rural populations, in several countries for which trend data are available.

The universally observed pre-decline rises in fertility have been attributed to some of the very factors that precede fertility decline. Most of them have to do with modernization and the shedding of traditional practices that put something of a break on what is called *natural* fertility—the fertility levels that result when there is nothing being done to consciously have fewer births. Even when there is no such conscious behavior, social practices ensure that no population reaches birth rates as high as those biologically possible in principle. These social practices include a host of social and cultural behaviors to do with the timing of marriage/sexual activity, the length of infant breastfeeding (which acts as a natural contraceptive up to a point), and norms about the temporary cessation of sexual activity at several life cycle stages (especially important is the norm about post-partum abstinence is many parts of

Africa) as well as at several other culturally defined periods, norms about widow remarriage, and so on. Different norms and practices operate at different times and in different places but they all end up in a situation in which there are hardly any instances of populations with sustained Total Fertility Rates above 7 or so.

Modernization is usually accompanied by a breakdown of many of these norms and practices and therefore a potential rise in natural fertility. Sometimes, even without a change in these behaviors, changes in economic conditions that also accompany modernization can also increase natural fertility. One of the most important such changes is of course the fall in mortality that accompanies development. Falls in adult mortality in particular have the potential to increase marital fertility even in the absence of changes in widow remarriage norms because they increase the length of time that women spend within marriage. Similarly, declines in illnesses that cause sub-fecundity can also, other things remaining unchanged, increase fertility.

As for these rises in fertility actually hastening the fertility transition, it could well be that as the rise is perceived widely enough, at first deliberate efforts are made to return to pre-rise fertility levels, usually by substituting birth control practices for these previously fertility suppressing social practices; once this first step has been taken, it is quite plausible that the *idea* of fertility control that it introduces encourages reflection on the value of and perhaps the need active effort to bring down birth rates even further to get them in tune with the same modern realities that raised them to begin with.

Dyson and Murphy (1985) did not have many African instances of pre-decline fertility rises in their global review in the mid 1990s, but something like this may be happening or on the verge of happening in Africa today. We do know that there have been important changes in breastfeeding and post-partum abstinence behavior (even if lip service continues to be paid to the norms themselves); the last decade has finally seen a waning of adult mortality, especially from HIV/AIDS; the UN tells us that many parts of Africa have seen recent rises in fertility; anthropologists like Bledsoe et al. (1984) have pointed out that the use of modern contraception in sub-Saharan Africa in the recent past has merely been substituting for traditional birth spacing practices, a conclusion now supported by the mismatch between couple protection rates and total fertility rates in Table 47.3 alluded to in the last section.

To the pessimist, this mismatch is disappointing; it shows that contraceptive use cannot be an indicator of a demand for fewer births. This is true, but to the optimist, the big rises in contraceptive use in this region also strongly suggest that at the next step, that is when family size desires fall more rapidly, negative attitudes to or fears of contraception will not be a major hindrance to achieving this lower desired fertility.

But all this also hinges on the success of the new family planning program initiatives. The goal of FP20/20 to provide voluntary contraception to 100 million more women over the next seven years is not ambitious enough to the extent that it does not take into account the rise in women needing contraceptive services as the population of the developing world continues to grow. Still, if the initiative is visible enough and innovative enough, there are bound to be spillover effects that will serve to further lower the unmet need for birth control in Africa.

47.3.3.3 *Magnifying the demographic dividend: Africa's relative advantage*

In practical terms, the demographic dividend is important because it implies that each person of working age (*in principle*, this means each worker) now has fewer non-working age people to support and there is therefore a fall in what is known as the dependency ratio. But the phrase "*in principle*" in the above sentence is important here because of course not all persons of working age are actually productive. In particular, in most parts of the world, many women of working age are not part of the labor force and this means that, strictly speaking, they add to the dependents that each worker has to support.

One of the reasons for this absence from the labor force of many women of working age is the time and energy devoted to pregnancy and childbearing. And so when family planning access allows women to have only the number of births they want to have, some of their time and energy are freed up and can be put to other uses. If these women decide to now join the labor force, in effect they are magnifying the potential effect of a demographic dividend by creating what one may call an additional "female demographic dividend." This female demographic dividend is a result not of a fall in the number of young dependents (i.e. babies, or the numerator in dependency ratio calculations) but of a rise in the number of *productive* adults (i.e. working women, or the denominator in the dependency ratio). We have plenty of evidence of this process. At a general level, in most parts of the world there is a negative relationship between fertility and female labor force participation rates. But two of the most compelling examples of the direct link between fertility control/contraceptive access and women's labor force participation come from the mid-twentieth-century USA and late twentieth-century Ireland.

In the case of the USA, research shows that during the 1960s and 1970s, state-wise differences in the timing of legal access to the contraceptive pill by young unmarried women were mirrored by state-wise differences in rises in women's age at marriage as well as rises in women's entry into more careerist educational streams (Goldin and Katz 2002; Bailey 2006). And in Ireland, the liberalization of contraceptive access in 1980 seems to be associated with a jump in women's labor force participation rates between 1980 and 2000, a factor which lowered the dependency ratio independently of the lowering caused by a drop in fertility rates (Bloom and Canning 2003).

But a relationship between fertility decline and increased participation of women in the labor force as well as the increased productivity of women workers is not inevitable. In many parts of the world historical and cultural factors do not support and may even actively discourage women's participation in the labor force. The best example f such normative disapproval of women in the marketplace is seen in counties in South Asia where the tendency is for women to withdraw from the labor force once household social or economic conditions rise (see, for example, the recent World Bank report on *Gender and Economic Empowerment in India*). In these situations, without active policies to entice women into the labor force, the potential gains from ta demographic dividend can be only partially realized.

But much of Africa has an advantage on this matter. As Table 47.5 shows, some 54 percent of African women aged 15+ are labor force participants, with the number rising to as much as 62 percent for sub-Saharan Africa as a whole and 76 percent in Eastern Africa. Compare this to 40 percent in South Central Asia and 38 percent in Central America and one can see that it should be much easier to fast forward the returns from a demographic dividend in Africa than from most other parts of the world.

One additional factor in its favor is the fact that these historically high levels of female labor force participation in Africa have also been high for participation in activities outside the home, again unlike in other parts of the world where many of the women who are economically productive tend to seek home-based work. Work outside the home has many other advantages—monetary and non-monetary, micro- and macro-level—in its

Table 47.5 Gender differences in labor force participation rates

	% 15+ economically active 2005	
	Female	Male
SSA	61	80
Eastern Africa	78	87
Burundi	91	88
Comoros	74	85
Djibouti	62	79
Eritrea	63	83
Ethiopia	81	90
Kenya	76	88
Madagascar	84	89
Malawi	75	79
Mauritius	41	75
Mozambique	83	91
Réunion	47	67
Rwanda	85	87
Somalia	64	87
Tanzania	87	90
Uganda	81	91
Zambia	66	86
Zimbabwe	65	79
Middle Africa	62	86
Angola	73	90
Cameroon	48	86
Central African Republic	69	87
Chad	67	88
Congo	58	83
Democratic Republic of the Congo	62	85
Equatorial Guinea	45	91
Gabon	63	84
Northern Africa	27	76
Algeria	37	80
Egypt	22	75
Libya	25	79
Morocco	26	80
Sudan	31	74
Tunisia	26	71
Western Sahara		
Southern Africa	48	62
Botswana	46	65
Lesotho	56	69
Namibia	54	81
South Africa	48	61
Swaziland	36	58

(continued)

Table 47.5 Continued

	% 15+ economically active 2005	
	Female	Male
Western Africa	50	76
Benin	67	78
Burkina Faso	78	91
Cabo Verde	54	81
Cote d'Ivoire	51	82
Gambia	71	85
Ghana	74	75
Guinea	79	89
Guinea-Bissau	60	84
Liberia	67	76
Mali	38	67
Mauritania	59	81
Niger	39	88
Nigeria	39	73
Senegal	65	89
Sierra Leone	65	68
Togo	64	86
Central America	38	81
South America	53	79
Western Asia	28	73
South Central Asia	40	84
Southeast Asia	59	84
East Asia	70	84
Northern Europe	58	72
Western Europe	50	65
Eastern Europe		65
Southern Europe		65
Oceana		72
North America	60	75

Source: Population Reference Bureau (2005); 2005 Women of Our World.

favor and here again, well thought out policies to exploit this tendency can get more out of a demographic dividend than they would in societies in which women prefer work opportunities that allow them to operate from home.

One final note of caution: The female demographic dividend rests on the availability of more jobs and better jobs. Otherwise, women will continue to work but work in low-productivity occupations, often unpaid (as is the case today in many parts of the continent) or else they will merely take over some of the jobs currently being done by men; thereby keeping the size of the active labor force more or less unchanged and/or increasing the possibility of social and political tensions as male unemployment manifests itself in male discontent that is destabilizing.

The potential gains from such increased female productivity as fertility falls can be immense. A recent World Bank study on India for instance estimates that GDP in India would be 25 percent higher if female labor force participation rates were to match male rates.

47.4 CONCLUDING REMARKS

This paper examines the changing age structures of populations across Africa and their possible effects on economic development. It reflects on the possibility of imminent fertility declines in the continent by examining not just current trends in fertility but also the underlying conditions that might be favorable for new or further fertility declines in the near future. While many of these background conditions are still nascent, some of them are strongly suggestive of more immediate and rapid fertility declines to come in several parts of Africa.

In turn this means that the shifts in age structure that accompany fertility declines and that make up the idea of a demographic dividend might also be something that the continent is more ready for than is generally assumed. Under the right economic and social conditions, in turn, this means that perhaps we can be even more optimistic about economic development in the region than the recent relatively good economic growth allows us to be. Such optimism could be strengthened even further by the fact that historical and cultural conditions specific to Africa might make the continent more able to exploit the demographic dividend. In particular, we expect the historically high levels of female labor force participation in sub-Saharan Africa to provide a double fillip to making a potential demographic dividend into an actual economic bonus.

How exceptional is the African experience of a demographic dividend? Our paper suggests that Africa is different in two ways that might be called cultural and two ways that may be referred to as temporal, all three of which should have a bearing on the timing and the nature of the demographic dividend. First, the demand for high fertility is probably stronger than predicted by the usual socioeconomic correlates of fertility; this represents a potential bottleneck. But secondly and at the same time, once such a decline occurs, many parts of the continent are probably better poised to convert the resultant change in age structure into a dividend because of the historical and cultural approval of women's participation in the labor force.

The temporal difference is much less *intrinsic* to Africa and has two components. First, because socioeconomic development has come later to the region than to other parts of the developing world, it has the advantage of the rest of the world's hindsight as well as the advantage of being able to absorb social change faster than might be dictated by its economic circumstances. This question of timing probably explains Bongaart's (2013) conclusion that fertility decline in Africa has begun more recently than in other parts of the developing world but has begun at lower levels of socioeconomic development than was the case in these other regions. Temporality also enters the picture in the sense that the African fertility decline is occurring at a time when is much more international attention to women's reproductive needs and rights and ensuring access to safe and effective contraception is an important part of this new commitment.

Finally, one might mention one more positive factor that might make Africa different: this is the more rapid pace of urbanization on the continent; urban growth is currently about 3.5 percent annually and between 2000 and 2050 the urban population is expected to double. While this does present several challenges to development (and there is no shortage of research and writing on these challenges), it is also offers opportunities to increase investments in human capital and in productivity somewhat more easily than in rural areas, both of which considerably brighten the prospects for a demographic dividend.

In spite of all that has been said in the last few paragraphs, one needs to not overdo the idea of African exceptionality. By giving in to the tendency to describe each region as exceptional, as we at times do, we ensure that it is not exceptional to be "exceptional." Most of the African region's problems and potential solutions are very similar to those encountered in different parts of the non-industrialized world at different times; circumstances change or can be made to change and when they do, the responses of the population are unlikely to be very different from those in other parts of the world. In that sense, given that Africa is a latecomer to economic development, perhaps it has more lessons to pick up from the experience of other countries than to offer these countries as they go about trying to meet their own socioeconomic challenges.

Acknowledgments

The authors are grateful to comments and suggestions from participants at the meeting of contributors to the Handbook of Africa and Economics at Peking University, School of Development, in December 2013.

References

Aiyar, S., and Mody, A. (2011). The demographic dividend: Evidence from the Indian states. Washington, DC: International Monetary Fund, Working Paper 11/38.

Bailey, M. (2006). More power to the pill: The impact of contraceptive freedom on women's life cycle labour supply. *Quarterly Journal of Economics*, 121(1):289–320.

Basu, A.M. (2011). The demographic dividend revisited: The mismatch between age and economic-activity based Dependency ratios. *Economic and Political Weekly*, XLVI(39):53–58.

Basu, K. (1997). *Analytical Development Economics: The Less Developed Economy Revisited*. Cambridge, MA: MIT Press.

Basu, K. (2007). India's Demographic Dividend. BBC News, 25 July. http://news.bbc.co.uk/2/hi/6911544.stm.

Bledsoe, C., Hill, A.G., D'Alessandro, U., and Langerock, P. (1984). Constructing Natural Fertility: The use of Western Contraceptive Technologies in Rural Gambia. *Population and Development Review*, 20(1):81–113.

Bloom, D., and Canning, D. (2003). "Contraception and the Celtic Tiger." *The Economic and Social Review*, 34(1):229–247.

Bloom, D., Canning, D., and Sevilla, J. (2003). *The Demographic Dividend: A New Perspective on the Economic Consequences of Population Change*. Santa Monica, CA: Rand Corporation.

Bongaarts, J. (1994). The impact of population policies: Comment. *Population and Development Review*, 20(3):616–620.

Bongaarts, J. (2011). Can family planning programs reduce high desired family size in sub-Saharan Africa? *International Perspectives in Sexual and Reproductive Health*, 3(4):209–216.

Bongaarts, J. (2013). How exceptional is the pattern of fertility decline in sub-Saharan Africa? Paper prepared for the Expert Group Meeting on Fertility, Changing Population Trends and Development: Challenges and Opportunities for the Future. New York: United Nations Population Division.

Coale, A. (1973). The demographic transition. In *Proceedings of the International Population Conference*, Vol. 1. Liege: International Union for the Scientific Study of Population.

Dyson, T., and Murphy, M. (1985). The onset of fertility transition. *Population and Development Review*, 11(3):399–440.

Eloundou-Enyegue, P. (2013). Harnessing a demographic dividend: Challenges and opportunities in high and intermediate fertility countries. Paper prepared for the Expert Group Meeting on Fertility, Changing Population Trends and Development: Challenges and Opportunities for the Future. New York: United Nations Population Division.

Goldin, C., and Katz, L. (2002). The power of the pill: Oral contraceptives and women's career and marriage decisions. *Journal of Political Economy*, 110(4):730–770.

Lesthaeghe, R., and Vanderhoeft, C. (2001). Ready, willing and able—A conceptualization of transitions to new behavioural forms, in J.B. Casterline (ed.), *Diffusion Processes and Fertility Transition: Selected Perspectives*. Washington, DC: National Academy Press, National Research Council.

Nag, M. (1980) How modernization can also increase fertility. *Current Anthropology*, 21(5):571–580.

Pritchett, L. (1994). Desired fertility and the impact of population policies. *Population and Development Review*, 20(1):1–55.

Ratha, D. et al. (2011). *Leveraging Migration for Africa: Remittances, Skills and Investments*. Washington, DC: World Bank.

Solow, R. (1994). Perspectives on Growth Theory. *Journal of Economic Perspectives*, 8:45–54.

Tsui, A.O. (2001). Population policies, family planning programs, and fertility: the record. *Population and Development Review*, 27, Supplement: Global Fertility Transition, pp. 184–204.

United Nations (2011). *World Population Prospects: The 2010 Revision*. New York: United Nations Population Division.

United Nations (2013). *World Population Prospects: The 2012 Revision*. New York: United Nations Population Division.

World Bank (2013). *World Development Indicators 2013*. Washington, DC: World Bank

World Bank (2013). *Gender and Economic Empowerment in India*. New Delhi: World Bank.

World Bank (2014). *Global Economic Prospects, January*. Washington, DC: World Bank.

....

CHAPTER 48

AFRICA'S DEMOGRAPHIC TRANSITION AND ECONOMIC PROSPECTS

....

JEFFREY D. SACHS

THE economic prospects of sub-Saharan Africa (hereafter "Africa" for short) have brightened markedly since the year 2000. Consider the economic changes shown in Table 48.1, comparing the decade 2000–2010 with the preceding decade 1990–2000. Economic growth accelerated; poverty declined; and several health indicators improved markedly. It seems that Africa may finally be breaking free of the poverty trap.

Africa's opportunity to escape from poverty is real and opportune. Yet serious risks continue. As I will describe below, long-term climate change is perhaps the most serious risk of all, especially in view of the threats to Africa's food security. The most important risk under Africa's own control is the delayed demographic transition to low mortality and low fertility. Without a faster demographic transition, Africa is likely to experience an unmanageable surge of population, youth dependency, and other ills.

This paper focuses on the positive role that an accelerated demographic transition would play in Africa's economic development between now and 2050. The demographic transition would combine greatly improved health outcomes with a large, rapid, and voluntary reduction of fertility rates. The argument proceeds in eight sections that follow. First, I summarize Africa's progress and continuing development risks. Second, I describe the multiple channels by which Africa's delayed demographic transition can imperil future economic growth. Third, I present comparative international evidence on Africa's demographic exceptionalism. Fourth, I describe some of the hypotheses that have been offered to account for Africa's delayed demographic transition. Fifth, I introduce a small simulation model of an accelerated African demographic transition. Sixth, I describe the major lessons of the simulation model. Seventh, I outline the principle policy conclusions. Eighth, and finally, I offer some conclusions and suggested extensions of the analysis.

Table 48.1 Accelerated poverty reduction in sub–Saharan Africa

	1990	2000	2010	% Annual rate of improvement 1990–2000	% Annual rate of improvement 2000–2010
Poverty rate (proportion of population living on less than $1.25 a day)	56.5	58.0 (1999)	48.4	−0.3	1.6
Under-5 mortality rate	178	154	109 (2011)	1.4	3.1
Malaria deaths, total (000s)	832	1401	1134	−5.3	2.1
Maternal mortality rate	850	740	500	1.4	3.8
Real GDP (1990=100)	100	126	219	2.3	5.7

Source: Sachs (2013).

48.1 AFRICA'S RECENT ECONOMIC PROGRESS AND CONTINUING RISKS

There are several factors helping to explain Africa's recent economic progress. The Millennium Development Goals (MDGs) launched in 2000 have a played a role, by successfully focusing political attention, financial resources, and effective investments on the fight against extreme poverty and preventable disease. Debt cancellation under the Heavily Indebted Poor Countries (HIPC) program, in part spurred by the MDGs, gave fiscal and financial space to African countries for a restoration of public investment and growth. The information and communications technology (ICT) revolution has enabled Africa to leapfrog in telecommunications, skipping landlines and going directly to mass mobile connectivity, and skipping brick-and-mortar banking and jumping straight to online banking. The end or at least diminution of several regional wars (Liberia, Sierra Leone, Sudan, Somalia, among others) has allowed some recovery in war-torn regions. And last but not least, the rise of China to global economic preeminence has also made a huge difference for Africa. China and Africa are complementary economies: China offers Africa access to low-cost technology and infrastructure, while Africa offers China access to a wide range of primary commodities, including hydrocarbons and agricultural products.

One might be tempted to declare victory, to declare that Africa is now solidly and robustly on a path of rapid "catch-up" growth that will continue to slash poverty and raise living standards. Such a positive trajectory is indeed possible. Yet unfortunately it is far from inevitable. There are two ominous realities that continue to threaten Africa's long-term economic prospects. The first is largely out of Africa's control. The second is almost entirely within Africa's control.

Africa's greatest twenty-first century risk is likely to be human-induced climate change, a phenomenon that deeply threatens Africa's economy, food security, and public health. Ironically, Africa has played almost no role in the rising greenhouse gas concentrations that drive climate change. For this reason alone, social justice dictates that the world assist Africa generously to cope with an ill that is not at all of its own making.

Most of Africa is drylands, ranging from sub-humid to hyper arid. These drylands are particularly vulnerable to the rising temperatures and changing patterns of precipitation that will accompany human-induced climate change this century. In some regions, such as Southern Africa, rainfall is expected to decline markedly. Even where overall rainfall remains the same or even increases, soil moisture is likely to dry as the result of much greater evapo-transpiration. The net result is likely to be a significant decline of food production (especially in rain-fed regions that dominate African agriculture). There are also significant risks of greater disease transmission of various communicable diseases such as malaria where the force of infection tends to rise with the ambient temperature.

The second long-term risk, one that is very much in Africa's control, is long-term demographic change. Africa is the only region of the world that has not yet experienced a demographic transition to low rates of mortality and fertility. Africa remains the world's region with both the highest mortality rates and highest fertility rates. For reasons described later, the high fertility rates drive rapid population growth even in the presence of high mortality rates; in essence, the fertility rates more than compensate for the exceptionally high child mortality rates.

The lack of a full demographic transition in Africa is the most important single internal bottleneck to Africa's successful development in the next generation. As I will describe, the dangers of high fertility and mortality are pervasive. They affect educational attainment, dependency ratios, the adequacy of infrastructure, and many other key determinants of long-term economic development.

The danger and opportunity is illustrated in Figure 48.1, which shows the UN's recent assessment of Africa's population trajectory in the twenty-first century. As usual, the UN has presented four fertility variants. The medium-fertility variant is the UN's judgment of the business-as-usual trajectory, taking into account existing trends and patterns of gradually falling mortality and fertility rates. The low-fertility variant differs from the median variant

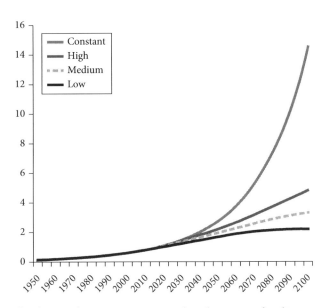

FIGURE 48.1 Africa's population trajectory under alternative fertility assumptions.

Source: UN Population Division, 2012 Revision.

by assuming a total fertility rate (TFR) that is 0.5 children *lower* than in the medium-fertility variant. The high-fertility variant assumes a TFR that is 0.5 children *higher* than in the medium-fertility variant. The constant-fertility variant examines the population path assuming that age-specific fertility rates remain unchanged after 2010 throughout the remainder of the century. This is not meant to be a realistic possibility. Rather, it is meant to illustrate the extent of fertility decline that is already built into the medium, low, and high variants.

The simple message of Figure 48.1 is stark. Africa's population is on a startling rate of increase. Starting in 1950 with a population of 179 million, Africa's population has by now increased to around 950 million in 2015, more than five times the 1950 level. Yet what lies ahead is even more astounding. On the medium-fertility trajectory, Africa's population is slated to increase to 3.8 billion by 2100, a remarkable increase of more than four times this century, and an overall increase of 20 times between 1950 and 2100. The medium scenario already builds in a significant if gradual decline in the TFR, from 5.1 in 2010–2015 to 3.2 in 2045–2050 and 2.1 in 2095–2100.

The medium variant may be compared with the constant-fertility scenario, which reaches 16.3 billion by 2100. With an unchanged fertility pattern, Africa would have an explosion of its twenty-first-century population vastly higher than any ability of the region to cope economically, socially, or environmentally. This constant-fertility scenario illustrates the importance of Africa achieving *at least* the TFR reductions embedded in the medium-fertility variant.

The differences in population pathways among the low-fertility, medium-fertility, and high-fertility variants merit our full attention. These scenarios offer a range of plausible outcomes. With the low-fertility variant, Africa's population would stabilize by the end of the century at around 2.6 billion. With the high-fertility variant, Africa's population would soar to an almost unimaginable 5.4 billion, fully 30 times the 1950 level. All of the three fertility scenarios (low, medium, and high) suppose a significant decline of the TFR during the twenty-first century. The question is the pace and depth of fertility change.

Of course Africa's demographic challenge must be seen in light of the risks to Africa of human-induced climate change. It would be hard enough for Africa to absorb an increase of several billion people even with a stable climate. In the context of long-term climate change, however, the risks to Africa are gravely multiplied, especially in view of the dire forecasts for food production and food security.

48.2 Adverse Implications of Africa's High Fertility Rates

In this section I describe *five channels* by which Africa's high mortality and fertility rates, and their net effect of very rapid population growth, continue to hold back Africa's economic development.

48.2.1 Falling ratio of arable land to population

A region's food security and rural incomes depend on the ratio of arable land to population. When the arable land per person is high, farm sizes are also large, and a relatively

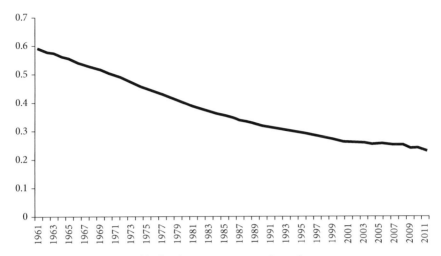

FIGURE 48.2 Declining arable land per capita in Africa, hectares per person.

Source: World Bank.

small share of the population as farmers can meet the food needs of the entire population. When the arable land per person is low, farm sizes will tend to be small, and a larger
proportion of the population will be needed in farming to meet the food needs of the
population.

This tendency is already well advanced in Africa. Since 1950, the ratio of arable land to
population has been declining markedly. Though Africa's arable land has increased, for
example, through deforestation, the rise in arable land area has not kept pace with the five-
fold rise of population. This is shown in Figure 48.2. One result is that a large part of the
African population continues to eke out an existence as subsistence farmers working tiny
land plots. The situation is likely to be gravely exacerbated in the future for several reasons, including the difficulty of finding new arable land to cultivate with adequate productive conditions (e.g. water, soils, slope, and climate); the new difficulties that will arise with
climate change reducing long-term farm yields; and the probable challenges of freshwater
supplies as a result of groundwater depletion, reduced river flows, and changing patterns of
precipitation.

48.2.2 Higher youth-dependency ratio

A high fertility rate and high resulting population increase means a large youth population
as a share of the total population. The result is a high proportion of the population not in the
labor force because they are of school age or younger. The result is to depress the per capita
gross domestic product (GDP). We can think of the GDP per population (P) as being the
product of GDP per worker (W) multiplied by workers per working age population (WAP)
multiplied by WAP per P:

$$GDP / P = (GDP / W) \times (W / WAP) \times (WAP / P)$$

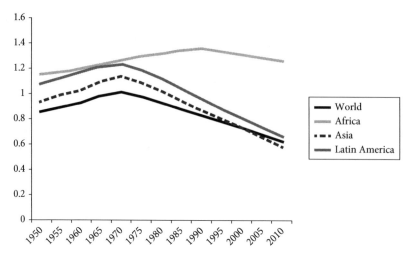

FIGURE 48.3 Youth dependency ratio (population 0–20 relative to population 20–65).

Source: UN Population Division, 2012 Revision.

A high fertility rate reduces the share of the working-age population in the total population (WAP/P), and also tends to reduce the participation rate of women as well, thus lowering W/WAP.

Consider the youth dependency ratio, which I define as the ratio of youth (ages 0–20 years) relative to working age population (ages 20–65 years), shown in Figure 48.3. In all parts of the developing world, the youth dependency ratio was between 0.8 and 1.2 in 1950, the highest ratio being in Africa. Because of relatively high fertility rates in all regions in 1950, the dependency ratio rises in all regions until 1970. After that, it declines in Asia and Latin America, while continuing to rise in Africa. By 2010, the youth dependency ratio in Africa is nearly twice that of the rest of the developing world, 1.2 versus 0.6. The consequence is to lower GDP per capita in Africa relative to the other developing regions.

48.2.3 Lower investment per child in human capital

One of the most important implications of the demographic transition is the transition from investment in the quantity of children to investment in the quality of children, a pattern known as the quantity–quality tradeoff. If the youth cohort is too large, the public sector will be unable to provide a basic education for all children. Let us illustrate this with a simple example.

Suppose that the government spends around 4% of GDP on public education. Suppose, as well, that the cost per student for one year of public education (primary or secondary) costs around 25% of GDP per person. Each year, the public education system can therefore afford to train a student cohort equal to 16% of the total population (= 4%/25%). If the size of the student cohort is larger than 16%, then the budget will be unable to meet the total needs. Either the quality of education will suffer or some students will lack places in school.

In high-income countries in 2010, the size of the student-age cohort, which I take to be ages 5–20 years, averages around 16.9% of the total population in 2010. At a cost per student of 25% of GDP, the education budget comes to 4.2% of GDP. In Africa, by contrast, the size of the student cohort ages 5–20 years comes to an astounding 37% of the total population. This larger cohort is the result of a far higher TFR. The total required education outlays would then come to around 9.3% of GDP, an amount that outstrips the budgetary means of the African governments.

The same squeeze on investments per child arises within the household as well. Parents can allocate only a given proportion of the household food supply, budget, and parental time to the children. As the number of children increases, the ability of the household to invest in each child diminishes. A poor African household with six or more children will be unable to provide each child with the necessary access to healthcare, nutrition, cognitive stimulation, and educational outlays needed to enable the child to reach his or her potential.

48.2.4 Slower growth of infrastructure per person

The productivity of the economy and the quality of life, especially in urban areas, depends heavily on public investments in urban infrastructure, including power, roads, public transport, water and sewerage, waste management, and others. These are generally the responsibility of government, and as such must be financed through a combination of general revenues and tariffs on public services. Faster population growth puts enormous pressure on the capacity of infrastructure, and requires that a significant proportion of the public budget should be set aside simply to keep up with a rising population. Scarce public revenues and saving that would otherwise go towards raising living standards are instead expended merely to keep pace with the rising population.

Suppose that public infrastructure requires a level of public capital K equal to a multiple Θ of national income Y, K = Θ Y. Assuming that the population grows at rate g, K and Y must also grow at the rate g just to maintain living standards. Therefore, $K(t+1)=(1+g)K(t)=(1+g)\Theta Y(t)$. Since public investment I(t) equals $K(t+1)-K(t)+\delta K(t)$ where δ is the rate of depreciation, we can see that for K to keep up with population, public investment must equal $I(t)=(g+\delta)\Theta Y(t)$. Suppose, for example, that the total public infrastructure should equal 125% of national income. A population growth rate g of 3% requires 3.75% of national income in public investment just to keep up with population growth. This might constitute around one-fifth of the total budget.

48.2.5 Slower growth of total factor productivity

Rapid population growth will hinder the rise of total factor productivity (TFP) in many ways. Two channels are most important. First, with a lower average level of education, the population will be less able to promote technological upgrading, whether through domestic innovation or the adoption of technologies from abroad. (This is often known as the Nelson–Phelps channel linking the rate of technological growth to the level of education.) Second, a larger population and therefore a lower ratio of arable land to population will tend to lower the rate of urbanization, and more of the population will remain in subsistence farming. Since the urban economy is more likely to be the font of innovation, even for agricultural production, a lower rate of urbanization is likely to slow the economy-wide rate of TFP improvement.

The combined effect of these five factors is to slow the growth of incomes per capita and the rise in living standards across generations. Africa is held back by its unusual demographic patterns, especially very high fertility rates, high youth dependency, low human capital investments per child, and rapid overall population growth rates. In the next section, we illustrate the combined effect of these factors in a small simulation model that links demography with overall economic development.

48.3 Africa's Demographic Exceptionalism

From the start of the UN population data in 1950, sub-Saharan Africa's demographic patterns stand out from those of the rest of the world. Sub-Saharan Africa has consistently evidenced the highest rates of total fertility, child mortality, and overall population growth. I shall argue shortly that these exceptional demographic patterns are all interconnected, with the prime mover likely to be Africa's extraordinarily high disease burden, itself rooted in Africa's extraordinary physical geography.

Africa's exceptionally high total fertility rates are evident in Figure 48.4(A) for the period 1950–2010, and Figure 48.4(B) for the forecasts for 2010–2050. In 1950, Africa's TFR of 6.5 in 1950 was the highest of any region in the world, yet other developing regions (e.g. Asia and Latin America shown in the figure) also had very higher TFRs, around 6.0. Starting in the 1960s, however, the TFRs in Asia and Latin America (and in the world on average) began to decline rapidly, while in Africa, the TFR actually *rose* gradually to a peak of 6.8 in 1975–1980, and remaining above 6.0 until 1995–2000, when it declined to 5.9. By then, the TFR in Asia had declined to 2.5 and in Latin America to 2.8. As of 2010–2015, the UN Population Division puts Africa's TFR at 5.1, compared with 2.2 in both Asia and Latin America.

The UN Population Division medium-fertility variant projects that Africa's TFR will decline gradually throughout the period to 2050, yet will still be above 3.0 by 2045–2050 (Figure 48.4). Note that in all of the other developing regions, the TFR is close to the replacement ratio. Africa is the only major region with fertility still far above the replacement rate.

Africa's under-5 mortality rates (U5MR) are similarly very high when compared with the rest of the world, as shown in Figure 48.5. As with TFR, all developing regions had very high U5MRs in 1950, but Africa's mortality rate was far above the rest, at 307 per 1000 live births, compared with 237 per 1000 in Asia and 188 per 1000 in Latin America. As with TFR, Africa's U5MR declined only very gradually, staying above 200 until 1980–1985, and above 100 until now. In Asia, by contrast, U5MR fell below 200 in 1965–1970 and below 100 in 1985–1990. During 2010–2015, according to the UN Population Division, Africa's U5MR remains as high as 110/1000, compared with 39/1000 in Asia and 23/1000 in Latin America.

The theory of demographic transition holds that the TFR is a function of the U5MR, as well as other variables. When U5MR is high, the TFR tends to be high as well. As the U5MR declines, so too does the TFR. Eventually, U5MR falls to a very low level (less than 10/1000 in the more developed regions) and TFR then falls to the replacement rate (just slightly above 2.0) or even lower. Figure 48.6 shows the scatter plot of TFR (on the y-axis) versus U5MR (on

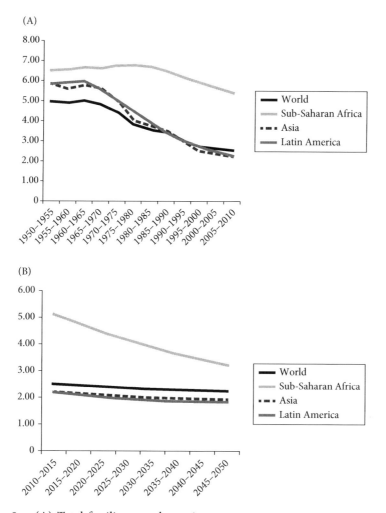

FIGURE 48.4 (A) Total fertility rates by region, 1950–2010.

Source: UN Population Division.

(B) Total fertility rates by region to 2050, medium-fertility variant.

Source: UN Population Division, 2012 Revision.

the x-axis). A mortality rate around 200/1000 is associated with a TFR around 8. The fertility rate of 2.0 is associated with a U5MR around 12.5/1000. The regression line is TFR = 1.6 + .032 * TFR.

The surprising but robust implication is that on a cross-country basis, higher child mortality is strongly associated with higher, not lower, overall population growth, since the higher fertility associated with high child mortality more than offsets the higher mortality of young children. When the mortality rate is 13/1000, 98.7% of children survive their fifth birthday. If each couple has an average of 2.03 children, then on average two survive their early childhood (2.03 × 0.987). On the other hand, if the U5MR is 100, and TFR is 4.8, then on average 4.3 children survive

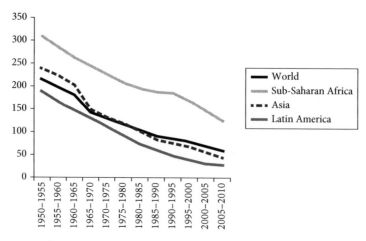

FIGURE 48.5 Under-5 mortality rates by region, 1950–2010.

Source: UN Population Division.

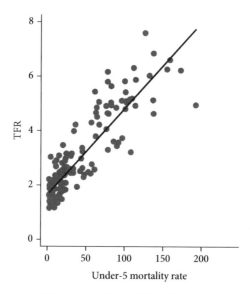

FIGURE 48.6 Under-5 mortality rate and total fertility rate, 2010.

(4.8 × 900/1000). Note that in this case, each mother has on average 2.1 surviving daughters. The children's generation has more than doubled the population of the parent's generation!

This is the pattern that has characterized Africa since the middle of the twentieth century. In 1950, the population stood at around 180 million. By 2013, it stood at 900 million, or five times the level of 1950 (see Figure 48.7). The doubling time of the population was roughly every 27 years, essentially once per generation. Note that sub-Saharan Africa and Latin America had roughly the same population in 1950, 179 million and 168 million respectively. Yet by 2013, Africa's population had reached 900 million, compared with 617 million in Latin America.

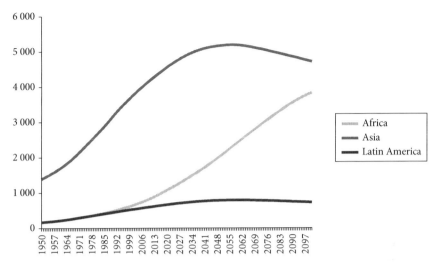

FIGURE 48.7 Population history and projections, medium-fertility scenario, 1950–2100.

Source: UN Population Division, 2012 Revision.

It may seem puzzling that fertility rates would remain so high that population doubles each generation. Why, after all, wouldn't the fertility rate adjust downward to produce a stable population? One possibility is that the observed TFRs are in fact not a true equilibrium, but are still adjusting downward. Another possibility is that actual fertility is significantly above desired fertility because of unwanted pregnancies and lack of access to reliable modern contraceptive services. A third possibility is that risk-averse households compensate for the risk of child mortality by having many more children than would compensate for the risk of child mortality. Let us explore that possibility briefly. I take up the other factors in the next section.

Suppose that households want to ensure *at least two surviving children* with a very high probability, say 98%. How many children should the couple have if they choose the total family size before observing the survival of the individual children? Assume, for purposes of illustration, that each child has the same independent probability of survival as indicated by the U5MR. The probability of mortality of each child is U5MR/1000, and the survival probability is therefore (1–U5MR/1000).

Suppose, for example, that U5MR is 10/1000. Each child has a survival probability of 99%. If the couple has two children, the probability that both survive is therefore 98.01%, just sufficient to reach the 98% target. Suppose, instead, that U5MR is 100/1,000. In that case, the survival probability of each child is just 90%, and the survival probability for two children is 81%, far below the parent's acceptable threshold. If the couple has three children, the probability that all three survive is 72.9%, and that exactly two survive is 24.3%. This still isn't good enough since there would still be an unacceptably high 2.8% chance that fewer than two children survive. Thus, the household would choose to have four children. Each couple would have on average 3.6 surviving children, or each mother would have on average 1.8 surviving daughters. The population would be nearly doubling across generations.

As I described earlier, the UN's medium-fertility scenario envisions a gradually declining TFR and U5MR for Africa throughout the twenty-first century. The TFR reaches 2.14 in 2100, implying that fertility remains above the replacement rate during the entire century. The implication of course is a continuing rapid rise in population, much faster than all other parts of the world. Just to cite one striking comparison, Latin America's medium-fertility scenario puts Latin America's population in 2100 at 736 million, less than one-fifth of Africa's projected population. In 1950, however, Latin America and sub-Saharan Africa had almost the same population (168 million and 179 million, respectively)!

48.4 Hypotheses Regarding Africa's Delayed Demographic Transition

Africa's demographic transition is the most delayed in the world. Many demographers have begun to speak of the "stall" in Africa's demographic transition that began in the mid-1990s (see Bongaarts 2008; Goldstone et al., 2014.) While most of the world has experienced a dramatic decline in both mortality and fertility rates, and therefore in population growth rates, Africa's mortality, fertility, and population growth rates remain very high. The high fertility rates, we have noted, pose several serious challenges to Africa's long-term economic growth. On the other hand, Africa stands ready to achieve an historic growth dividend by encouraging a rapid, voluntary transition to lower fertility rates.

The demographic literature is replete with possible explanations for Africa's demographic exceptionalism. To some extent of course, Africa's demographic exceptionalism is simply part of Africa's overall development exceptionalism, as Africa is the only region of the world with nearly half of the entire population still stuck in extreme poverty. The conditions of poverty—high rural population, high adult illiteracy, low access to the formal health system, high child mortality, and low maternal educational attainment—all predict persistently high fertility rates.

Yet other very poor parts of the world, notably in Asia, have experienced rapid demographic transition even in advance of overall economic development. Perhaps the most striking example is Bangladesh, which has experienced a decline in the TFR from 6.9 in 1970–1975 to 2.2 during 2010–2015. This rapid and voluntary decline in fertility occurred while Bangladesh remained extremely poor and mostly rural. Such examples suggest that Africa has distinguishing characteristics beyond mere rural poverty that help to account for its unusual demographic pattern.

Recent comparative studies have identified some of the following possible factors:

1. *Kinship system.* Many analysts have argued that Africa's kinship system induces a strong incentive to maximize the number of children to strengthen the power and continuity of the lineage (Romaniuk 2011; see also Caldwell and Caldwell 1987; Bongaarts and Casterline 2013).
2. *Polygyny.* It is argued that polygyny leads to "a more complete mobilization of women into marriage and reproduction" (Romaniuk 2011: 9).

3. *Child fosterage.* It is argued that extended family households, with children fostered by relatives, reduces the direct costs of childrearing, and thereby creates strong pronatalist incentives (Goldstone et al., 2014).

4. *Pronatalist politics.* It is argued that Africa's politicians, unlike Asian politicians, have resisted the role of promoting family planning and smaller family sizes. This may be out of deference to the opposition of religious leaders and groups, or perhaps out of the "demographic competitiveness" of one tribe versus another, by attempting to outpace the rival groups in population size (see especially McNicoll 2011, in a comparison of fertility reduction in Indonesia versus persistent high fertility in Nigeria).

5. *Exceptional disease burden.* My co-authors and I (McCord, Conley, and Sachs, 2010) have argued that Africa's uniquely heavy disease burden has been a major factor in explaining Africa's exceptionally high fertility rates.

While all of these factors have played some role, my own hunch is that the heavy disease burden, manifested in part as an extraordinarily high rate of under-5 mortality, has been the most important of all. Africa's exceptionally high child mortality rates are very longstanding, stretching back over many centuries. They in turn have helped to shape Africa's pronatalist culture.

The particular role of malaria in this regard should be noted. Africa's ecology—combining high temperatures, favorable breeding conditions for mosquitos, and particular mosquito species especially adapted to human-to-human transmission of malaria—has led to an especially high burden of malaria mortality through Africa's history, evidenced for example by the high prevalence of hemoglobin anomalies (such as sickle-cell trait) that are associated with high burdens of malaria deaths.

The malaria burden contributed to exceptionally high rates of child mortality not experienced in other parts of the world, sometimes reaching rates of 400–500 per 1000 before the middle of the twentieth century. As child mortality rates have partially declined since then, but still remain the highest in the world, Africa's fertility rates have also declined, but not sufficiently to forestall the surge in Africa's population growth.

The evidence also suggests that *despite* the longstanding cultural tendencies towards high fertility, many African countries would respond to the kinds of programmatic approaches that accelerated the demographic transition in Asia. These programmatic methods include (i) child survival programs, which not only would save children's lives by the millions, but would also encourage households to reduce their desired number of births by encouraging the confidence that almost all children born will survive to adulthood; (ii) girls' secondary education as a way to empower women, raise their earning potential, and delay marriage and the age of first births; (iii) national political and cultural leadership in support of family planning, giving confidence to households that lower fertility rates will be socially (and politically) supported; and (iv) ensured access of poor families to family planning programs and modern long-term contraceptives.

This package is now being implemented in Rwanda. So far the results are encouraging. The TFR has declined from 6.2 during 1995–2000 to 4.6 during 2010–2015, just 15 years later. The expectation in Rwanda is for further rapid reductions in TFR in the coming decade.

48.5 A SIMULATION MODEL OF ACCELERATED DEMOGRAPHY TRANSITION

We now introduce a formal model to examine the benefits to economic growth and development of speeding the demographic transition. The benefits are achieved through several distinct channels already mentioned: (i) lower population growth rates; (ii) higher land-to-population ratios; (iii) greater investments in education per child; (iv) a higher proportion of the population in urban employment; (v) a higher proportion of working age population; and (vi) faster endogenous technological change. Using a simulation approach below, we find that Africa's GDP per capita in 2050 can be raised by as much as 50% above the baseline projection by achieving a more rapid transition to lower fertility.

The model below is meant to be a provisional basis for more detailed modeling in the future. At this point, the parameters are mostly illustrative. They point the way, I believe, to more detailed empirical modeling in the future. The purpose here is to show how a simple structural model can depict and help to measure the main structural pathways linking mortality, fertility, education, and GDP growth.

To examine these questions, we introduce a two-sector model of the African economy. The food sector (also the rural sector) produces food F using arable land A (assumed to be in fixed supply) and labor:

$$F(t) = \pi(t)^\alpha \left[h(t) L_F(t) \right]^\beta A^{(1-\beta)} \tag{1}$$

L is the labor input, and the subscript F signifies labor in the food sector. Note the variable h(t), which is the level of human capital in period t. The product of L and h is the effective labor supply. I will describe the evolution of human capital below. The parameter $\pi(t)$ signifies a TFP shift parameter, described below. It is raised to a power $\alpha < 1$ in food production.

The total population is P(t). I assume a fixed per capita food need Ψ so that the total food needed in the economy in period t is $\Psi^* P(t)$. I assume that food is inelastically demanded to the level $\Psi^* P(t)$. Therefore, we can determine the size of rural employment by equating food needs with food production. We find:

$$L_F(t) = \left[\Psi^* P(t) / \pi^\alpha \right]^{(1/\beta)} A^{-(1-\beta)/\beta} \left[1/h(t) \right] \tag{2}$$

The total labor force L(t) is allocated between the Food sector and the Manufacturing sector, so that:

$$L(t) = L_F(t) + L_M(t) \tag{3}$$

Clearly (2) and (3) determine the size of labor inputs into manufacturing, and also the size of the urban sector, as I assume that all food production is rural and all manufacturing production is urban.

The manufacturing sector has a neo-classical production function of the form:

$$M(t) = \pi(t)\left[h(t)L_M(t)\right]^\gamma K_M(t)^{(1-\gamma)} \tag{4}$$

I assume for simplicity that the manufacturing capital is supplied from abroad at fixed global cost of capital r. Thus, the marginal production of capital MPK(t) is set equal to r. Since $MPK(t) = \partial M(t)/\partial K(t) = (1-\gamma)\pi(t) L_M(t)^\gamma K_M(t)^{-\gamma} = r$, we find that $K_M(t) = [(1-\gamma)\pi(t)/r]^{(1/\gamma)} L_M(t)$. Substituting this expression in (4) yields the following equation for M(t):

$$M(t) = \pi(t)^{(1/\gamma)}[(1-\gamma)/r]^{(1-\gamma)/\gamma} h(t) L_M(t) \tag{5}$$

The two main implications are that manufacturing output is linear in effective labor, h(t) L_M(t), and that TFP π(t) raises manufacturing output more than proportionately, that is, with an exponent greater than 1.

Real GDP in purchasing-power-adjusted terms is found by summing the per capita outputs of the two sectors, using international prices P_F and P_M as weights:

$$GDP(t) = P_F F + P_M M \tag{6}$$

GDP per capita is simply GDP/P, where P is the total population. Note that F/P is simply the parameter Ψ so that GDPpc(t) is given by:

$$GDPpc(t) = P_F \Psi + P_M (M/P) \tag{7}$$

Note that $P_F \Psi$ is the world price of the basic food basket. I put that at US$ 500 in PPP terms. Note also that M/P may be written as $(M/L_M)(L_M/L)(L/W)(W/P)$. I set $\lambda(t) = L_M(t)/L(t)$. The variable λ(t) is both the share of employment in non-agriculture, and also the rate of urbanization. I set $\omega(t) = L/W$, which is the labor-force participation rate, and $\sigma(t) = W/P$, which is the share of the population at working age. Combining terms, and using (5), we can find an equation for GDPpc(t):

$$GDPpc(t) = 500 + \pi(t)^{(1/\gamma)}[(1-\gamma)/r]^{(1-\gamma)/\gamma} h(t)\omega(t)\sigma(t) \tag{8}$$

For simplicity at this stage, I assume that labor force participation is constant (the alternative would be to make labor force participation a function of income and fertility):

$$\omega(t) = 0.70 \tag{9}$$

I next turn to the evolution of the population and human capital. The total population at time t is P(t). We divide the population into five-year age intervals, indexed by i, so that i = 0–4, 5–9, 10–14, ..., 95–100. At any time t, the population of interval i is denoted as P(t,i). I also treat the time period t as a five-year interval, with t = 2005–2010, 2010–2015, 2015–2020, ..., 2045–2050.

I let m(t,i) be the age-specific mortality rate for age i in period t. We then assume that:

$$P(t+1,i+1) = \left[1-m(t,i)\right] * P(t,i) \tag{10}$$

As an illustration, the number of 25–29-year-olds in 2030–2035 equals the number of 20–24-year-olds in 2025–2030 multiplied by the mortality rate of 20–24-year-olds as of 2025–2030. I take these age-specific and period-specific mortality rates from the UN Population Division.

At any period t, the number of births is determined by the female population by age group F(t,i) and the age-specific fertility rate f(t,i), with total births B(t,i) given as:

$$B(t) = \sum_i f(t,i)F(t,i) \tag{11}$$

Of course the sum in (6) is taken over the subset of age groups in the reproductive years, taken to be ages 15–49. Note that the total fertility rate is calculated simply as the sum of f(t,i) taken over all reproductive ages:

$$TFR(t) = \sum_i f(t,i) \tag{12}$$

The simulation model endogenously determines the TFR in each period t. Yet knowing the evolution of TFR(t) is not enough to determine the evolution of the age-specific fertility rates f(t,i). In order to determine the f(t,i), I use the following assumption.

I start with Africa's baseline age-specific fertility profile for the years 2005–2010, denoted as f(2005–2010,i). I assume that Africa's age-specific fertility rates will approach those of the more developed countries as of 2005–2010 as Africa's overall TFR approaches the TFR of the more developed countries. I denote the age-specific fertility rates of the more developed countries as f*(2005–2010,i). Africa's TFR in 2005–2010 is 5.4 compared with 1.7 in the more developed countries. I therefore apply the following formula to determine f(t,i) for Africa as a function of Africa's TFR(t,i):

$$f(t,i) = \mu(t)\, f(2005-2010,i) + \left[1-\mu(t)\right] f*(2005-2010,i)$$
$$\text{where } \mu(t) = \left[TFR(t) - 1.7\right]/(5.4 - 1.7) \tag{13}$$

As Africa's TFR declines from 5.4 to 1.7, the age-specific fertility rates approach those of the more developed countries. It is easy to verify that (12) is satisfied by the assumption in (13).

Once the births B(t) are known, we apply the mortality rates for ages 0–4 to determine P(t,0–4):

$$P(t,0-4) = \left[1 - m(t,0-4)\right] * B(t) \tag{14}$$

I assume that half of the births are boys and half are girls. With these assumptions, it is then possible to apply (6) to calculate the evolution of the population of each sex over time. (In fact, I use a combined age-specific mortality rate that is applied to both males and females.)

To complete the model I must determine the evolution over time of TFR(t), h(t,i) and $\pi(t)$. I assume that TFR(t) evolves as a linear function of U5MR(t), parental education E(t), and GDP per capita (expressed in logarithms):

$$TFR(t) = 5.4 + 0.022 * \left[U5MR(t) - 126\right] - 0.55 * LN\left[GDPpc(t)/800\right] \tag{15}$$

Since U5MR(2005–2010) is 126, and GDPpc(2005–2010) = 800, equation (15) shows that TFR(2005–2010) equals 5.4.

Human capital depends on schooling. I assume that all schooling is finished by age 20–24, so that the schooling of older cohorts is determined by the schooling attained when they are younger. The amount of schooling achieved by 20–24-year-olds as of period t is taken to be a function of three variables: the schooling of their parents 20 years earlier, the GDPpc of the economy during the period 10 years earlier, and the total fertility rate lagged 10 years, reflecting the quality–quantity tradeoff:

$$S(t,20-24) = .45 * S(t-20,20-24) + .55 * LN[GDPpc(t-10)/800] + \qquad (16)$$
$$.55 * LN[GDPpc(t-15)/800] - 0.3[TFR(t-10)-5.4] + 7$$

Notice that a high TFR reduces the schooling achieved one decade later by 20–24-year-olds. For older cohorts, the level of schooling is simply determined by the schooling that they achieved as of age 20–24:

$$S(t+1,i+1) = S(t,i) \text{ for } i > 20-24 \qquad (17)$$

Human capital is determined by the schooling of each age cohort, using the human-capital specification adopted by the Penn World Tables study. Specifically, let h(t,i) be the human capital of cohort i at period t. The human capital is given as follows:

$$h(t,i) = \exp[\varphi(t,i)]$$
$$\text{where } \varphi(t,i) = .134 * S(t,i) \qquad \qquad \text{if } S(t,i) < 4$$
$$.134 * S(t,i) + .101[S(t,i)-4] \qquad \text{if } 4 < S(t,i) < 8 \qquad (18)$$
$$.134 * S(t,i) + .101[S(t,i)-4] + .068[S(t,i)-8] \quad \text{if } 8 < S(t,i)$$

Essentially the first four years of schooling have a return of 13.4% per year; the next four years have a return of 10.1% per year; and schooling beyond eight years has a return of 6.8% per year. The total human capital of the working age population is then given by:

$$h(t) = \sum_i h(t,i) \, P(t,i) / \sum_i P(t,i) \qquad (19)$$

where the summation in (19) is taken over the working ages, 20–65.

The final assumption needed to close the model is the evolution of TFP. We adopt the assumption of learning by doing in the manufacturing sector. In turn, the rise in TFP in manufacturing, which I have denoted as $\pi(t)$, also spills over into the agriculture sector, though with an elasticity $\alpha < 1$. Specifically, I define cumulative per capita production of manufacturing as follows:

$$cuman(t) = cuman(t-1) + [M(t)/P(t)]/700 \qquad (20)$$

The value 700 is to normalize the cumulative productive as equal to multiples of the baseline manufacturing production per capita, assumed equal to US$ 700 in 2005–2010 in PPP terms. Then, TFP exhibits an experience curve, specified as follows:

$$\pi(t) = 1/\{1 + 3 * \exp[-.5 * cuman(t)]\} \qquad (21)$$

As manufacturing experience increases, TFP rises by a factor of 4, from 0.25 in 2005–2010 to a maximum of 1 as cuman(t) becomes large.

It is worthwhile to summarize once again the various ways that U5MR and TFR will affect the dynamics of this economy. As U5MR declines, so too will TFR, at a rate sufficient to decrease the overall rate of population growth. If we compare a high-TFR and a low-TFR trajectory, the low-TFR trajectory will have the following characteristics:

- lower population growth rate
- lower youth dependency ratio
- higher ratio of arable land to population
- higher rate of urbanization
- higher level of schooling
- higher level of human capital
- higher TFP
- higher GDP per capita.

48.6 SIMULATION RESULTS

I study two scenarios. The baseline scenario assumes that U5MR declines gradually from the baseline level of 126/1000, reaching 46/1,000 in 2045–2050. The alternative scenario assumes that U5MR declines far more rapidly, to a value of 20/1000 by 2025–2030. The two scenarios of U5MR are shown in Figure 48.8. The second scenario of rapid decline of U5MR also assumes that TFR declines rapidly in response to the declining mortality rate. This may happen "automatically," as households quickly adjust to the falling

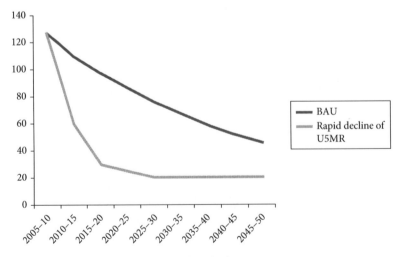

FIGURE 48.8 The BAU and rapid mortality-decline scenarios.

Source: Model calculations, see text.

U5MR. More likely, the decline in U5MR would have be combined with a massive scale up of family planning services to ensure that TFR declines alongside U5MR, with no major lag.

The decline in U5MR triggers a rapid decline in TFR, with the many feedback effects that I have described. These are summarized in Figure 48.9, where we compare the outcomes on TFR, GDP per capita, Population, TFP, and Urbanization. The general results are clear. A faster decline of U5MR, accompanied by a faster decline of TFR, spurs many favorable development trends. The growth of population is much lower, resulting in 1.3 billion people in Africa in 2050 compared with 1.9 billion on the baseline. The growth of GDP per capita is much higher, resulting in a per capita income of US$ 5600 in 2050, compared with just US$ 2700 on the baseline trajectory. Similarly, the pace of urbanization is much higher, as fewer

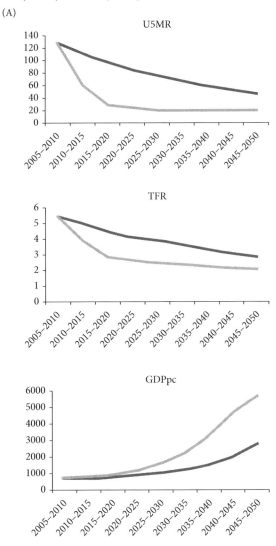

FIGURE 48.9 Comparison of business as usual (black) and rapid mortality decline (grey).

(B)

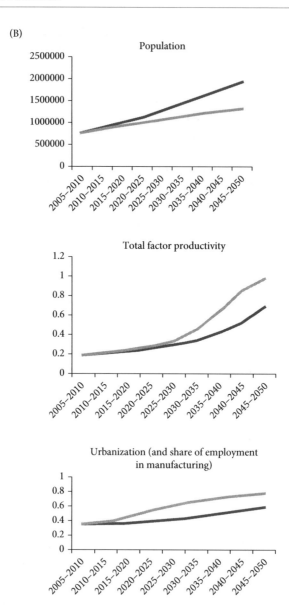

FIGURE 48.9 Continued

farmers are needed to feed the smaller and more productive population. In both scenarios, Africa becomes substantially urbanized by 2050, around 60% in the baseline and nearly 80% in the alternative scenario.

At this stage, the model estimates should be regarded as qualitative rather than truly quantitative. The parameterization of the structural model remains crude, and requires further verification with more sophisticated statistical tests and more examination of ranges of possible parameter values.

48.7 POLICY IMPLICATIONS

The relevance of the alternative scenario is predicated on a basic idea: that targeted interventions in health care, education, and family planning can decisively change Africa's demographic trajectory and thereby raise its development prospects. The key, we have noted, is to reduce child mortality rates significantly, to create the conditions for a sharp decline in fertility rates. Most likely, the decline in fertility rates would be gradual, unless public policy strengthens the provision of health care services and access to contraceptives and family planning. The fertility reduction would also be strengthened markedly by a scaling up of financing for girls' secondary education, as secondary education not only directly reduces fertility rates (by delaying marriage) but also indirectly by raising the economic opportunities available to young women. The reductions in fertility and mortality rates assumed in the alternative simulation are most likely well within reach. They would enable Africa to close the demographic divide that opened with the rest of the developing world during the 1960s and 1970s.

48.8 CONCLUSIONS AND EXTENSIONS

This is an initial modeling exercise into the question of how an alternative demographic trajectory can bolster Africa's economic development. The baseline trajectory, underpinned by the UN Population Division medium-fertility variant, is clear and disturbing. Africa's high total fertility rates and high child mortality rates are assumed to decline only gradually, leading to decades more of very high population growth rates, with the attendant pressures on the land and food security. There is a strong case for accelerating the demographic transition. By doing so, it would be possible to limit the rise in Africa's future population substantially, and thereby accelerate urbanization, schooling, technological advance, and economic growth.

The simulation model is a new and useful tool to model the implications of alternative demographic pathways. It is, as yet, a rather rough and still-unproven tool, with much further work ahead to refine the structure of the model and the parameter choices. Nonetheless, even in its earliest variant, the lessons are clear: Africa's economic future can be greatly enhanced through an accelerated transition to low mortality and fertility.

REFERENCES

Behrman, J., and Kohler, H.-P. (2013). Population quantity, quality, and mobility. Global Citizen Foundation Working Paper 2(June). Geneva: Global Citizen Foundation.

Bloom, D., and Canning, D. (2008). Global demographic change: dimensions and economic significance. *Population and Development Review*, 34:17–51.

Bloom, D., Canning, D., and Malaney, P. (2000). *Population and Development Review*, 26 (Supplement), 257–290.

Bongaarts, J. (2008). Fertility Transitions in Development Countries: Progress or Stagnation? Population Council Working Paper No. 7/2008. New York: Population Council.

Bongaarts, J., and Casterline, J. (2013). Fertility transition: is sub-Saharan Africa different? *Population and Development Review*, 38 (Supplement):153–168.

Bongaarts, J., and Sinding, S. (2009). A response to critics of family planning programs. *International Perspectives on Sexual and Reproductive Health*, 35(1):39–44.

Caldwell, J., and Caldwell, P. (1987). The cultural context of high fertility in sub-Saharan Africa. *Population and Development Review*, 13(3):409–437.

Ezeh, A., Mberu, B., and Emina, J. (2009). Stall in fertility decline in Eastern African countries: regional analysis of patterns, determinants and implications. *Philosophical Transactions of the Royal Society B*, 364:2991–3007.

Goldstone, J., Korotayev, A., and Zinkina, J. (2014). Fertility stall in tropical Africa: its causes, risks, and possible responses. Unpublished.

Gupta, N., and Mahy, M. (2003). Adolescent childbearing in sub-Saharan Africa: Can increased schooling alone raise ages at first birth? *Demographic Research*, 8(4):93–106.

McCord, G., Conley, D., and Sachs, J. (2010). Improving Empirical Estimation of Demographic Drivers: Fertility, Child Mortality & Malaria Ecology. http://papers.ssrn.com/sol3/papers.cfm?abstract_id=1647901.

McNicoll, G. (1994). Institutional analysis of fertility. Population Council Working Paper No. 72/1994. New York: Population Council.

McNicoll, G. (2011). Achievers and laggards in demographic transition: a comparison of Indonesia and Nigeria. *Population and Development Review*, 37:191–214.

Phillips, J., Jones, T., Nyonator, F., and Ravikumar, S. (2003). Evidence-based development of health and family planning programs in Bangladesh and Ghana. Population Council Working Paper No. 175/2003. New York: Population Council.

Romaniuk, A. (2011). Persistence of high fertility in tropical Africa: the case of the Democratic Republic of the Congo. *Population and Development Review*, 37(1):1–28.

Sachs, J. (2013). MDGs and the Accelerated Decline of Poverty and Disease in Sub-Saharan Africa. August. http://jeffsachs.org/2013/08/mdgs-and-the-accelerated-decline-of-poverty-and-disease-in-sub-saharan-africa/.

Samir, K., and Lutz, W. (2014). Demographic Scenarios by Age, Sex, and Education Corresponding to the SSP Narratives. *Population and Environment*, 35:243–260.

USAID (2006). *Achieving the Millennium Development Goals: The Contribution of Fulfilling the Unmet Need for Family Planning*. Washington, DC: USAID.

Verpoorten, M. (2012). Leave none to claim the land: a Malthusian catastrophe in Rwanda? *Journal of Peace Research*, 49:547–563.

Name Index

Abbas, S.M.A. 187–8
Abdih, Y. 124
Acemoglu, D. 516, 671, 820n
Adam, C. 74, 76
Adam, S.I. 474
Adams, R. 689
Adelegan, O. 418–19
Adepoju, A. 490
Adreoni, J. 713
Agenor, P.-R. 76, 77n
Agyire-Tettey, K.F. 738–9
Aker, J.C. 396
Akerlof, G.A. 334–5
Akpalu, W. 394
Akramov, K.T. 796n
Al Awad, M. 482
Alden, C. 774–5
Alderman, H. 470
Alesina, A. 340, 751
Alfaro, L. 753
Alichi, A. 82
Allen, F. 391, 402, 407, 412–13, 4151
Alsan, M. 740
Amin, S. 690
Amoah, L. 774
Andrianaivo, M. 407, 410, 413, 417
Andrianova, S. 671–3
Andrle, M. 82–3
Anyanwu, J.C. 721
Aportela, F. 389
Araujo-Bonjean, C. 242
Aristotle 14
Arnaldi di Balme, L. 350
Arndt, C. 704
Arrow, K.J. 509
Arvis, J.F. 240n
Aryeetey, E. 14
Asiedu, E. 75, 721, 739–40

Audibert, M. 503, 519
Augustine, D. 741
Ayalew, T. 470

Babu, A. 764
Badiane, O. 43
Baier, S. 237
Baldini, A. 77n, 82
Baliamoune-Lutz, M. 584
Baloglou, C.P. 427n
Banaante, C. 298
Bandara, A. 578
Banerjee, A. 629n
Baniak, A. 739
Bansak, C. 720
Barlow, R. 515–16
Barreca, A.I. 518
Barrett, J. 630n
Barro, R.J. 7n, 72n, 95–6
Bates, M.A. 520
Bates, R.H. 59
Beck, T. 162–3, 388, 391–2
Becker, G.S. 462, 468, 589
Behmran, J.R. 389
Ben Ali, Z. 425n
Benes, J. 75
Bennell, P. 462, 464n, 475
Berg, E. 134
Bergstrand, J. 237
Berlin, P. 134
Bernanke, B.S. 436n
Berthélemy, J.C. 751
Besley, T. 1–2, 390
Bhattacharyya, S. 520
Bigsten, A. 701
Birdsall, N. 495
Blair, T. 379
Blaise, S. 739

SUBJECT INDEX

Printed and bound by CPI Group (UK) Ltd, Croydon, CR0 4YY